THE
College Reader

EDITED BY

ROBERT MORSS LOVETT
UNIVERSITY OF CHICAGO

AND

HOWARD MUMFORD JONES
UNIVERSITY OF MICHIGAN

HOUGHTON MIFFLIN COMPANY
BOSTON · NEW YORK · CHICAGO · DALLAS · ATLANTA · SAN FRANCISCO
The Riverside Press Cambridge

THE SELECTIONS REPRINTED IN THIS COLLECTION ARE USED
BY PERMISSION OF AND SPECIAL ARRANGEMENT WITH
THE PROPRIETORS OF THEIR RESPECTIVE COPYRIGHTS

The Riverside Press
CAMBRIDGE · MASSACHUSETTS
PRINTED IN THE U.S.A.

FOREWORD

THE COLLEGE READER is designed to supply college classes with modern material for reading, and class discussion, and to furnish suggestions for writing. In arrangement of the whole, and of the several parts, it proceeds from the simpler to the more complex forms. The first part of the book deals chiefly with Experience, generally recorded in narrative form. There will be noted, however, a tendency to pass from a simple narrative of events into what may be called generalized narrative, and thence into reflection upon the experience presented. The autobiographical passage from Mr. Sherwood Anderson's *Tar*, Mr. Stuart Chase's chapter on a Mexican Village, and Professor W. J. Turner's paper on the Influence of the Frontier in American History are cases in point. In the second part, Reflection is the basic element, recorded in the form of discourse called Exposition, of which the prevailing type is furnished by the essay. The essay in turn looks back to experience for the source of its material. The personal or informal essay, in particular, may include a narrative of experience, hardly to be distinguished from reflective autobiography; the portrait essay or character sketch may involve a brief biographical record. The term essay has, however, in its modern use been widened to include serious, authoritative, scientific articles summing up conditions in some department of human inquiry, and presenting the writer's conclusions thereon. Hence the formal essay. Literary criticism is a special type of reflection. In place of a presentation of formal argument a number of pieces have been grouped together to represent Persuasion in regard to a question of universal interest — War. In the third portion of the book, human experience, and reflection upon it, are enlarged and given an independent life by Imagination, which may be defined as vision permitting the writer to see into or beyond the immediate facts of the material world. This element is present, indeed, in the best writing classified under the earlier headings, but it is especially the distinguishing quality of literary art in fiction, of which the leading forms are the short story, the drama, the novel, and in poetry.

The book is primarily a reading book. The introductions to the several divisions are designed to interest the reader in the formal requirements of various types of literature, to stimulate his appreciation, and give him a basis for sound criticism and guidance in further reading. At the same time, the book should prove an invitation to the student's own efforts in writing. Appreciation of literature, as of any other art, can be promoted by practice, and accordingly certain selections are included which set a standard not too far beyond the possibility of achievement by young writers.

The subject matter of the book is chiefly contemporary, presenting the experience, thought and art of today, but the editors have not hesitated to include material from earlier times when clearness of illustration and stimulation of interest are served by it.

CONTENTS

PART TWO

REFLECTION, ESSAYS

PART THREE

IMAGINATION

PART FOUR

POETRY

CONTENTS

PART ONE

EXPERIENCE

PART ONE
EXPERIENCE

EXPERIENCE

EXPERIENCE is the original material of the writer. It denotes the world of events and persons, the world that is lived, suffered, and enjoyed before it is thought about. In a sense all writing is retrospective, the result of memory; but in Part One of this book, which bears the title Experience, the chief interest is in the happenings, although the writing about them tends to pass over into the mental reaction upon them which we call reflection. Sometimes the experience recorded is immediate and personal, as in the sections devoted to autobiography, letters, travel; sometimes it is that of others, as in biography and history. In any case the natural way of writing about experience is narration, and most of the selections in Part One are examples of that form.

AUTOBIOGRAPHY

IN WRITING there are three factors, the writer, the subject matter, and the audience. Autobiography is theoretically the simplest form of literature because the writer and the subject matter are one, and indeed the writer is his own immediate audience — he writes with a primary pleasure in recalling his own past experience. This is notably the case with one of the most famous autobiographies, the *Diary of Samuel Pepys*. In the reign of Charles II, Pepys made a voluminous record of the events of his life, even the most trivial, in cipher, apparently for his own enjoyment in later years. Autobiography has, however, a wider appeal, as is shown by the popularity of Pepys's deciphered narrative. The experience of a human being has perennial interest for other human beings. Some of the greatest books in world literature are autobiographies, confessions like those of Saint Augustine and Rousseau. Aside from these great names there have been many examples of successful autobiographies written by individuals whose careers had little distinction in the eyes of their contemporaries. As Carlyle said in writing of his friend John Sterling: "A true delineation of the smallest man, and his scene of pilgrimage through life, is capable of interesting the greatest man."

The first requisite of autobiography is that it be sincere. It is hard to tell the truth. Even for the chief actor to give a perfectly accurate account of an event is difficult and the difficulty is increased when a series of events or a period of life is summarized. The line is not sharply drawn between the actual and the ideal, the objective and the subjective, what one did and what one wishes he had done, reality and dream. Stevenson held in "The Lantern-Bearers" that the dream is often truer to the character of the writer than the reality. Nevertheless, the appeal of autobiography lies in the belief that the writer is giving a true picture of himself. Even when we suspect that he has yielded to the temptation of coloring or exaggerating facts to his own advantage, as in the famous autobiography of Benvenuto Cellini, the Florentine craftsman and sculptor of the Renaissance, the fake is recognized as part of the truth to character.

The substance of autobiography is experience. Its immediate form is simple narrative, which, however, often becomes generalized. Miss Addams's chapter upon her girlhood from *Twenty Years at Hull-House* is, moreover, distinguished for its use of significant detail. Instead of a single experience, incidents almost anecdotal in their brevity are introduced, with touches of interpretation which look forward to a later career. In the selection from Sherwood Anderson's *Tar* the working of reflection upon experience is still more pronounced. Both contain character sketches of other persons, especially of the fathers of the writers. It is not difficult to see in these two passages of personal recollection the tendencies which made Jane Addams a worker for the welfare of her fellows, and Sherwood Anderson a writer who reveals such human beings in significant fiction. The Autobiography of Thomas H. Huxley is an example of generalized narrative giving a summary of experience in the straightforward style of a scientist.

Besides the autobiographies already mentioned, the student will be interested in Kropotkin's *Memoirs of a Revolutionist*, J. S. Mill's *Autobiography*, *The Education of Henry Adams*, Mr. Lincoln Steffens's *Autobiography* with its reaction to events and characters in the American scene of the last forty years, and the recent *Experiment in Autobiography* of Mr. H. G. Wells, which presents an equally vivacious survey of experience and characters in England during the same period.

JANE ADDAMS

JANE ADDAMS (1860–1935) so much belonged to the world of international affairs, it is sometimes difficult to remember that most of her life has been spent in Illinois, chiefly in Chicago, where, with the opening of Hull House in 1889, she became the pioneer in the settlement house movement in America. A graduate of Rockford College, she received honorary degrees from many universities in recognition of her labors both at Hull-House and for world peace. Her written work lies mainly in these fields, including such books as *Democracy and Social Ethics, Newer Ideals of Peace, The Spirit of Youth and the City Streets, Twenty Years at Hull-House,* which has been followed by a sequel, *The Second Twenty Years at Hull-House.*

TWENTY YEARS AT HULL–HOUSE *

CHAPTER I: EARLIEST IMPRESSIONS

ON THE theory that our genuine impulses may be connected with our childish experiences, that one's bent may be tracked back to that "No-Man's Land" where character is formless but nevertheless settling into definite lines of future development, I begin this record with some impressions of my childhood. . . .

It must have been from a very early period that I recall "horrid nights" when I tossed about in my bed because I had told a lie. I was held in the grip of a miserable dread of death, a double fear, first, that I myself should die in my sins and go straight to that fiery Hell which was never mentioned at home, but which I had heard all about from other children, and, second, that my father — representing the entire adult world which I had basely deceived — should himself die before I had time to tell him. My only method of obtaining relief was to go downstairs to my father's room and make full confession. The high resolve to do this would push me out of bed and carry me down the stairs without a touch of fear. But at the foot of the stairs I would be faced by the awful necessity of passing the front door — which my father, because of his Quaker tendencies, did not lock — and of crossing the wide and black expanse of the living room in order to reach his door. I would invariably cling to the newel post while I contemplated the perils of the situation, complicated by the fact that the literal first step meant putting my bare foot upon a piece of oilcloth in front of the door, only a few inches wide, but lying straight in my path. I would finally reach my father's bedside perfectly breathless and, having panted out the history of my sin, invariably received the same assurance that if he "had a little girl who told lies," he was very glad that she "felt too bad to go to sleep afterwards." No absolution was asked for nor received, but

* By permission of The Macmillan Company, publishers.

apparently the sense that the knowledge of my wickedness was shared, or an obscure understanding of the affection which underlay the grave statement, was sufficient, for I always went back to bed as bold as a lion, and slept, if not the sleep of the righteous, at least that of the comforted.

I recall an incident which must have occurred before I was seven years old, for the mill in which my father transacted his business that day was closed in 1867. The mill stood in the neighboring town adjacent to its poorest quarter. Before then I had always seen the little city of ten thousand people with the admiring eyes of a country child, and it had never occurred to me that all its streets were not as bewilderingly attractive as the one which contained the glittering toyshop and the confectioner. On that day I had my first sight of the poverty which implies squalor, and felt the curious distinction between the ruddy poverty of the country and that which even a small city presents in its shabbiest streets. I remember launching at my father the pertinent inquiry why people lived in such horrid little houses so close together, and that after receiving his explanation I declared with much firmness when I grew up I should, of course, have a large house, but it would not be built among the other large houses, but right in the midst of horrid little houses like these.

That curious sense of responsibility for carrying on the world's affairs which little children often exhibit because "the old man clogs our earliest years," I remember in myself in a very absurd manifestation. I dreamed night after night that everyone in the world was dead excepting myself, and that upon me rested the responsibility of making a wagon wheel. The village street remained as usual, the village blacksmith shop was "all there," even a glowing fire upon the forge and the anvil in its customary place near the door, but no human being was within sight. They had all gone around the edge of the hill to the village cemetery, and I alone remained alive in the deserted world. I always stood in the same spot in the blacksmith shop, darkly pondering as to how to begin, and never once did I know how, although I fully realized that the affairs of the world could not be resumed until at least one wheel should be made and something started. Every victim of nightmare is, I imagine, overwhelmed by an excessive sense of responsibility and the consciousness of a fearful handicap in the effort to perform what is required; but perhaps never were the odds more heavily against "a warder of the world" than in these reiterated dreams of mine, doubtless compounded in equal parts of a childish version of "Robinson Crusoe" and of the end-of-the-world predictions of the Second Adventists, a few of whom were found in the village. The next morning would often find me, a delicate little girl of six, with the further disability of a curved spine, standing in the doorway of the village blacksmith shop, anxiously watching the burly, red-shirted figure at work. I would store my mind with such details of the process of making wheels as I could observe, and sometimes I plucked up courage to ask for more. "Do you always have to sizzle the iron in water?" I would ask, thinking how horrid it would be to do. "Sure!" the good-natured blacksmith would reply, "that makes the iron hard." I would sigh heavily and walk away, bearing my responsibility as best I could, and this of course I confided to no one, for there is something too mysterious in the burden of "the winds that come from the fields of sleep" to be communicated, although it is at the same time too heavy a burden to be borne alone.

My great veneration and pride in my father manifested itself in curious ways. On several Sundays, doubtless occurring in two or three different years, the Union Sunday School of the village was visited by strangers, some of those "strange people" who live outside a child's realm, yet constantly thrill it by their close approach. My father taught the large Bible class in the left-hand corner of the church next to the pulpit, and to my eyes at least, was a most imposing figure in his Sunday frock coat, his fine head rising high above all the others. I imagined that the strangers were filled with admiration for this dignified person, and I prayed with all my heart that the ugly, pigeon-toed little girl, whose crooked back obliged her to walk with her head held very much upon one side, would never be pointed out to these visitors as the daughter of this fine man. In order to lessen the possibility of a connection being made, on these particular Sundays I did not walk beside my father, although this walk was the great event of the week, but attached myself firmly to the side of my Uncle James Addams, in the hope that I should be mistaken for his child, or at least that I should not remain so conspicuously unattached that troublesome questions might identify an Ugly Duckling with her imposing parent. My uncle, who had many children of his own, must have been mildly surprised at this unwonted attention, but he would look down kindly at me, and say, "So you are going to walk with me today?" "Yes, please, Uncle James," would be my meek reply. He fortunately never explored my motives, nor do I remember that my father ever did, so that in all probability my machinations have been safe from public knowledge until this hour.

It is hard to account for the manifestations of a child's adoring affection, so emotional, so irrational, so tangled with the affairs of the imagination. I simply could not endure the thought that "strange people" should know that my handsome father owned this homely little girl. But even in my chivalric desire to protect him from his fate, I was not quite easy in the sacrifice of my uncle, although I quieted my scruples with the reflection that the contrast was less marked and that, anyway, his own little girl "was not so very pretty." I do not know that I commonly dwelt much upon my personal appearance, save as it thrust itself as an incongruity into my father's life, and in spite of unending evidence to the contrary, there were even black moments when I allowed myself to speculate as to whether he might not share the feeling. Happily, however, this specter was laid before it had time to grow into a morbid familiar by a very trifling incident. One day I met my father coming out of his bank on the main street of the neighboring city which seemed to me a veritable whirlpool of society and commerce. With a playful touch of exaggeration, he lifted his high and shining silk hat and made me an imposing bow. This distinguished public recognition, this totally unnecessary identification among a mass of "strange people" who couldn't possibly know unless he himself made the sign, suddenly filled me with a sense of the absurdity of the entire feeling. It may not even then have seemed as absurd as it really was, but at least it seemed enough so to collapse or to pass into the limbo of forgotten specters.

I made still other almost equally grotesque attempts to express this doglike affection. The house at the end of the village in which I was born, and which was my home until I moved to Hull-House, in my earliest childhood had opposite to it — only across the road and then across a little stretch of greensward — two mills belonging to my father; one flour mill, to which the various grains were brought by the neighboring farmers, and one sawmill, in which the logs of the native timber were sawed into lumber. The latter offered the great excitement of sitting on a log while it slowly approached the buzzing saw which was cutting it into slabs, and of getting off just in time to escape a sudden and gory death. But the flouring mill was much more beloved. It was full of dusky, floury places which we adored, of empty bins in which we might play house; it had a basement, with piles of bran and shorts which were almost as good as sand to play in, whenever the miller let us wet the edges of the pile with water brought in his sprinkling pot from the mill-race.

In addition to these fascinations was the association of the mill with my father's activities, for doubtless at that time I centered upon him all that careful imitation which a little girl ordinarily gives to her mother's ways and habits. My mother had died when I was a baby and my father's second marriage did not occur until my eighth year.

I had a consuming ambition to possess a miller's thumb, and would sit contentedly for a long time rubbing between my thumb and fingers the ground wheat as it fell from between the millstones, before it was taken up on an endless chain of mysterious little buckets to be bolted into flour. I believe I have never since wanted anything more desperately than I wanted my right thumb to be flattened, as my father's had become, during his earlier years of a miller's life. Somewhat discouraged by the slow process of structural modification, I also took measures to secure on the backs of my hands the tiny purple and red spots which are always found on the hands of the miller who dresses millstones. The marks on my father's hands had grown faint, but were quite visible when looked for, and seemed to me so desirable that they must be procured at all costs. Even when playing in our house or yard, I could always tell when the millstones were being dressed, because the rumbling of the mill then stopped, and there were few pleasures I would not instantly forego, rushing at once to the mill, that I might spread out my hands near the millstones in the hope that the little hard flints flying from the miller's chisel would light upon their backs and make the longed-for marks. I used hotly to accuse the German miller, my dear friend Ferdinand, "of trying not to hit my hands," but he scornfully replied that he could not hit them if he did try, and that they were too little to be of use in a mill anyway. Although I hated his teasing, I never had the courage to confess my real purpose.

This sincere tribute of imitation which affection offers to its adored object, had later, I hope, subtler manifestations, but certainly these first ones were altogether genuine.   In this case, too, I doubtless contributed my share to that stream of admiration which our generation so generously poured forth for the self-made man.   I was consumed by a wistful desire to apprehend the hardships of my father's earlier life in that far-away time when he had been a miller's apprentice.   I knew that he still woke up punctually at three o'clock, because for so many years he had taken his turn at the mill in the early morning, and if by chance I awoke at the same hour, as curiously enough I often did, I imagined him in the early dawn in my uncle's old mill reading through the entire village library, book after book, beginning with the lives of the signers of the Declaration of Independence.   Copies of the same books, mostly bound in calfskin, were to be found in the library below, and I courageously resolved that I too would read them all and try to understand life as he did.   I did in fact later begin a course of reading in the early morning hours, but I was caught by some fantastic notion of chronological order and early legendary form.   Pope's translation of the "Iliad," even followed by Dryden's "Virgil," did not leave behind the residuum of wisdom for which I longed, and I finally gave them up for a thick book entitled "The History of the World" as affording a shorter and an easier path.

Although I constantly confided my sins and perplexities to my father, there are only a few occasions on which I remember having received direct advice or admonition; it may easily be true, however, that I have forgotten the latter, in the manner of many seekers after advice who enjoyably set forth their situation but do not really listen to the advice itself.   I can remember an admonition on one occasion, however, when, as a little girl of eight years, arrayed in a new cloak, gorgeous beyond anything I had ever worn before, I stood before my father for his approval.   I was much chagrined by his remark that it was a very pretty cloak — in fact so much prettier than any cloak the other little girls in the Sunday School had, that he would advise me to wear my old cloak, which would keep me quite as warm, with the added advantage of not making the other little girls feel badly.   I complied with the request but I fear without inner consent, and I certainly was quite without the joy of self-sacrifice as I walked soberly through the village street by the side of my counselor.   My mind was busy, however, with the old question eternally suggested by the inequalities of the human lot. Only as we neared the church door did I venture to ask what could be done about it, receiving the reply that it might never be righted so far as clothes went, but that people might be equal in things that mattered much more than clothes, the affairs of education and religion, for instance, which we attended to when we went to school and church, and that it was very stupid to wear the sort of clothes that made it harder to have equality even there.

It must have been a little later when I held a conversation with my father upon the doctrine of foreordination, which at one time very much perplexed my childish mind.   After setting the difficulty before him and complaining that I could not make it out, although my best friend "understood it perfectly," I settled down to hear his argument, having no doubt that he could make it quite clear. To my delighted surprise, for any intimation that our minds were on an equality lifted me high indeed, he said that he feared that he and I did not have the kind of mind that would ever understand fore-ordination very well and advised me not to give too much time to it; but he then proceeded to say other things of which the final impression left upon my mind was, that it did not matter much whether one understood foreordination or not, but that it was very important not to pretend to understand what you didn't understand and that you must always be honest with yourself inside, whatever happened. Perhaps on the whole as valuable a lesson as the Shorter Catechism itself contains.

My memory merges this early conversation on religious doctrine into one which took place years later when I put before my father the situation in which I found myself at boarding school when under great evangelical pressure, and once again I heard his testimony in favor of "mental integrity above everything else."

At the time we were driving through a piece of timber in which the wood choppers had been at work during the winter, and so earnestly were we talking that he suddenly drew up the horses to find that he did not know where he was. We were both entertained by the incident, I that my father had been "lost in his own timber" so that various cords of wood must have escaped his practiced eye, and he on his side that he should have become so absorbed in this maze of youthful speculation. We were in high spirits as we emerged from the tender green of the spring woods into the clear light of day, and as we came back into the main road I categorically asked him: —

"What are you? What do you say when people ask you?"

His eyes twinkled a little as he soberly replied:

"I am a Quaker."

"But that isn't enough to say," I urged.

"Very well," he added, "to people who insist upon details, as someone is doing now, I add that I am a Hicksite Quaker"; and not another word on the weighty subject could I induce him to utter.

These early recollections are set in a scene of rural beauty, unusual at least for Illinois. The prairie round the village was broken into hills, one of them crowned by pine woods, grown up from a bagful of Norway pine seeds sown by my father in 1844, the very year he came to Illinois, a testimony perhaps that the most vigorous pioneers gave at least an occasional thought to beauty. The banks of the mill stream rose into high bluffs too perpendicular to be climbed without skill, and containing caves of which one at least was so black that it could not be explored without the aid of a candle; and there was a deserted limekiln which became associated in my mind with the unpardonable sin of Hawthorne's "Lime-Burner." My stepbrother and I carried on games and crusades which lasted week after week, and even summer after summer, as only free-ranging country children can do. It may be in contrast to this that one of the most piteous aspects in the life of city children, as I have seen it in the neighborhood of Hull-House, is the constant interruption to their play which is inevitable on the streets, so that it can never have any continuity — the most elaborate "plan or chart" or "fragment from their dream of human life" is sure to be rudely destroyed by the passing traffic. Although they start over and over again, even the most vivacious become worn out at last and take to that passive "standing 'round" varied by rude horse-play, which in time becomes so characteristic of city children.

We had of course our favorite places and trees and birds and flowers. It is hard to reproduce the companionship which children establish with nature, but certainly it is much too unconscious and intimate to come under the head of aesthetic appreciation or anything of the sort. When we said that the purple windflowers — the anemone patterns — "looked as if the winds had made them," we thought much more of the fact that they were wind-born than that they were beautiful: we clapped our hands in sudden joy over the soft radiance of the rainbow, but its enchantment lay in our half belief that a pot of gold was to be found at its farther end; we yielded to a soft melancholy when we heard the whippoorwill in the early twilight, but while he aroused in us vague longings of which we spoke solemnly, we felt no beauty in his call.

We erected an altar beside the stream, to which for several years we brought all the snakes we killed during our excursions, no matter how long the toilsome journey which we had to make with a limp snake dangling between two sticks. I remember rather vaguely the ceremonial performed upon this altar one autumn day, when we brought as further tribute one out of every hundred of the black walnuts which we had gathered, and then poured over the whole a pitcherful of cider, fresh from the cider mill on the barn floor. I think we had also burned a favorite book or two upon this pyre of stones. The entire affair carried on with such solemnity was probably the result of one of those imperative impulses under whose compulsion children seek a ceremonial which shall express their sense of identification with man's primitive life and their familiar kinship with the remotest past.

Long before we had begun the study of Latin at the village school, my brother and I had learned the Lord's Prayer in Latin out of an old copy of the Vulgate, and gravely repeated it every night in an execrable pronunciation because it seemed to us more religious than "plain English."

When, however, I really prayed, what I saw before my eyes was a most outrageous picture which adorned a song-book used in Sunday School, portraying the Lord upon His throne surrounded by tiers and tiers of saints and angels all in a blur of yellow. I am ashamed to tell how old I was when that picture ceased to appear before my eyes, especially when moments of terror compelled me to ask protection from the heavenly powers.

I recall with great distinctness my first direct contact with death when I was fifteen years old: Polly was an old nurse who had taken care of my mother and had followed her to frontier Illinois to help rear a second generation of children. She had always lived in our house, but made annual visits to her cousins on a farm a few miles north of the village. During one of these visits, word came to us one Sunday evening that Polly was dying, and for a number of reasons I was the only person able to go to her.

I left the lamp-lit, warm house to be driven four miles through a blinding storm which every minute added more snow to the already high drifts, with a sense of starting upon a fateful errand. An hour after my arrival all of the cousin's family went downstairs to supper, and I was left alone to watch with Polly. The square, old-fashioned chamber in the lonely farmhouse was very cold and still, with nothing to be heard but the storm outside. Suddenly the great change came. I heard a feeble call of "Sarah," my mother's name, as the dying eyes were turned upon me, followed by a curious breathing and in place of the face familiar from my earliest childhood and associated with homely household cares, there lay upon the pillow strange, august features, stern and withdrawn from all the small affairs of life. That sense of solitude, of being unsheltered in a wide world of relentless and elemental forces which is at the basis of childhood's timidity and which is far from outgrown at fifteen, seized me irresistibly before I could reach the narrow stairs and summon the family from below.

As I was driven home in the winter storm, the wind through the trees seemed laden with a passing soul and the riddle of life and death pressed hard; once to be young, to grow old and to die, everything came to that, and then a mysterious journey out into the Unknown. Did she mind faring forth alone? Would the journey perhaps end in something as familiar and natural to the aged and dying as life is to the young and living? Through all the drive and indeed throughout the night these thoughts were pierced by sharp worry, a sense of faithlessness because I had forgotten the text Polly had confided to me long before as the one from which she wished her funeral sermon to be preached. My comfort as usual finally came from my father, who pointed out what was essential and what was of little avail even in such a moment as this, and while he was much too wise to grow dogmatic upon the great theme of death, I felt a new fellowship with him because we had discussed it together.

Perhaps I may record here my protest against the efforts, so often made, to shield children and young people from all that has to do with death and sorrow, to give them a good time at all hazards on the assumption that the ills of life will come soon enough. Young people themselves often resent this attitude on the part of their elders; they feel set aside and belittled as if they were denied the common human experiences. They too wish to climb steep stairs and to eat their bread with tears, and they imagine that the problems of existence which so press upon them in pensive moments would be less insoluble in the light of these great happenings.

An incident which stands out clearly in my mind as an exciting suggestion of the great world of moral enterprise and serious undertakings must have occurred earlier than this, for in 1872, when I was not yet twelve years old, I came into my father's room one morning to find him sitting beside the fire with a newspaper in his hand, looking very solemn; and upon my eager inquiry what had happened, he told me that Joseph Mazzini was dead. I had never even heard Mazzini's name, and after being told about him I was inclined to grow argumentative, asserting that my father did not know him, that he was not an American, and that I could not understand why we should be expected to feel badly about him. It is impossible to recall the conversation with the complete breakdown of my cheap arguments, but in the end I obtained that which I have ever regarded as a valuable possession, a sense of the genuine relationship which may exist between men who share large hopes and like desires, even though they differ in nationality, language, and creed; that those things count for absolutely nothing between groups of men who are trying to abolish slavery in America or to throw off Hapsburg oppression in Italy. At any rate, I was heartily ashamed of my meager notion of patriotism, and I came out of the room exhilarated with the consciousness that impersonal and international relations are actual facts and not mere phrases. I was filled with pride that I knew a man who held converse with great minds and who really sorrowed and rejoiced over happenings across the sea. I never recall those early conversations with my father, nor a score of others like them, but there comes into my mind a line from Mrs. Browning in which a daughter describes her relations with her father: —

> "He wrapt me in his large
> Man's doublet, careless did it fit or no."

SHERWOOD ANDERSON

SHERWOOD ANDERSON (1876–   ) illustrates the almost inseparable relation between the facts of an author's life and the fiction he writes. He has produced two autobiographical books — *A Story Teller's Story* (1924) and *Tar* (1927), both of them works not of fact alone, but of art, for he sees himself and explores himself and his background as he explores the inward lives of his frustrated characters. His genius for heightening the significance of lives outwardly ordinary, by revealing in the simplest language their inner complexities, shows itself not only in the following excerpts from *Tar*, but in such volumes of stories as *Winesburg, Ohio* (1919) and *The Triumph of the Egg* (1921). Anderson was born in Ohio, went to a public school, was a laborer in Chicago, a soldier in the Spanish-American War, and, after a comparatively successful life in business and advertising, one day "walked out" of his office into literary fame.

TAR *

CHAPTER III

MEN live in one world, women in another. People kept coming to the kitchen door to talk to Mary Moorehead when Tar was a small child. There was an old carpenter whose back had been hurt by a fall from a building and who was sometimes drunk. He did not enter the house but sat on the steps by the kitchen door and talked with the woman while she worked at her ironing board. A doctor also came. He was a tall thin man with strange looking hands. The hands were like old grape vines that cling to the trunks of trees. People's hands, rooms in houses, the faces of fields were things the child did not forget. The old carpenter had short stumpy-looking fingers. The nails were black and broken. The fingers on the doctor were like his mother's, rather long. Afterward Tar used the doctor in several of his printed tales. When the boy grew up he did not remember exactly how the old doctor looked but his imagination had by that time invented a figure to take his place. What he got from the doctor, the old carpenter and from several of the women visitors was a sense of gentleness. They were all people defeated by life. Something had gone wrong with them as something had gone wrong with Tar's mother.

Could it have been her marriage? He did not ask himself that question until long afterward. When he grew to be a man Tar found in an old trunk a diary kept by his father during his time in the war and immediately afterward. The notes were short. For several days there would be nothing written and then the soldier had written page after page. He also had an inclination to be a scribbler.

All during the war there was something eating at the soldier's conscience.

* Boni and Liveright. By permission of the author.

Knowing his brothers would be enlisted on the Southern side he was beset
by the notion that some day he might meet one of them in battle. Then,
if nothing worse happened, he would be found out. How could he explain,
"Well, the women were cheering, the flags flying, the bands playing."
When he fired a shot in a battle the bullet, flying across the space between
the Northern and Southern men, might lodge in the breast of a brother or
even in his father's breast. Perhaps his father had also enlisted, on the
Southern side. He had himself gone into the war without convictions,
almost casually, because the men about him were going, for the sake of a
captain's uniform and a sword to hang at his side. If a man thought much
about any war he wouldn't go in — of course. As for the niggers — their
being free men or slaves — he had still the Southern attitude. If walking
in the street with Dick Moorehead you had seen a negro woman who was
in her own way beautiful, who walked with an easy care-free carriage, whose
skin was in color a lovely golden brown, and had mentioned the fact of her
beauty, Dick Moorehead would have looked at you with amazement in his
eyes. "Beautiful! I say! My dear fellow! She is a nigger." Looking at
negroes Dick saw nothing. If a negro served his purpose, if he was amusing
— very well. "I am a white man and a Southerner." "I belong to the
ruling race. We had an old black at home. You should have heard him
play the pipes. Niggers are what they are. Only we Southerners understand them."

The book kept by the soldier, during the war and later, was full of notes
concerning women. Sometimes Dick Moorehead was a religious man, going
regularly to church, and sometimes he was not. In one town, where he had
lived immediately after the war, he was superintendent of a Sunday School
and at another place taught the Bible class.

When he had become a grown man Tar looked at the book, filled with
delight. He had quite forgotten his father was so naïve, so charmingly
human and understandable. "I was at the Baptist Church and succeeded
in taking Gertrude home. We went the long way by the bridge and stopped
almost an hour. I tried to kiss her and at first she would not let me but
later she did. Now I am in love with her." "On Wednesday evening Mable
went past the shop. I closed up at once and followed her to the end of
Main Street. Harry Thompson was after her and had got his boss to let
him off, on some trumped up excuse. We were both sailing down the street
but I got there first. I went home with her but her father and mother were
still awake. They sat up until I had to go so I gained nothing. Her father
is a fearful talker. He has got a new driving horse and talked and bragged
about the horse all evening. For me the evening was a failure."

Note after note of that sort in the diary kept by the young soldier after
he had got home from the war and when he had begun his restless march
from town to town. At last he had found, in one of the towns, the woman
Mary and had married her. Life took on for him a new flavor. Having
a wife and children he now sought the company of men.

In some of the towns into which Dick went after the war life went well
enough but in others he was unhappy. For one thing, and although he had

gone into the war on the Northern side, he would not forget the fact that he was a Southerner and therefore a Democrat. In one of the towns there was a half insane man the small boys used to tease. There he was, Dick Moorehead, the young merchant, the ex-officer in the army who, whatever his inner feeling may have been, had nevertheless fought for the preservation of the Union, who had helped hold together these United States, and there on the same street was that crazy man. The crazy man walked with his mouth hanging open and with a queer vacant look in his eyes. Winter or summer he wore no coat but went about in his shirt sleeves. He lived with a sister in a little house at the edge of the town and when let alone was harmless enough but when small boys, concealed behind trees or in the doorways of stores, shouted, calling him a "Democrat," he became furiously angry. Running into the roadway he picked up stones and threw them recklessly. Once he broke a window in a storefront and his sister had to pay for it.

Was it not an insult to Dick? A Democrat indeed! When he wrote about it in his notebook his hand trembled. Being the only real Democrat in the town the cries of the small boys made him want to run and beat them. He kept his dignity, did not betray himself but as soon as he could he sold his shop and moved on.

Well, the crazy man in his shirt sleeves was not really a Democrat, he wasn't like Dick, a born Southerner. The word, picked up by the boys and repeated over and over, merely touched off his half-hidden insanity but for Dick the effect was something special. It made him feel that, although he had fought in a long and bitter war, he had fought in vain. "Such people," he muttered to himself as he hurried away. When he had sold his shop he had to buy, in the next town, a somewhat smaller one. After the end of the war and his marriage Dick was constantly sliding down the financial hill.

For the child the man of the home, the father, is one thing and the mother quite another. The mother is something warm and safe toward which the child may go, while the father is the one who goes out into the world. Now the house in which Tar lived was something he began to understand a little. Even though you live in many houses in many towns a house is a house. There are walls and rooms. You go through doors into a yard. There is a street with other houses and other children. You can see a long way along the street. On Saturday evenings sometimes a neighbor woman, who had been engaged for the purpose, came to care for the other children and Tar was permitted to go uptown with his mother.

Now Tar was five and his older brother John was ten. There was Robert, now three, and a new babe, always lying in a crib. Although the babe could do nothing but cry it already had a name. It was called Will and, when she was at home, was always in the mother's arms. What a little pest! And to have a name too, a boy's name! There was another Will in the street, a tall freckle-faced boy who sometimes came to the house to play with John. He called John "Jack" and John called him "Bill." He could throw a ball like a shot. There was a trapeze John had hung from a tree and the boy named Will could hang by his toes. He went to school, as John and Margaret did, and had been in a fight with a boy two years older than himself. Tar had heard John speak of it. When John was not about he himself spoke of it to Robert, pretending he had seen the fight. Well, Bill had punched the boy, had knocked him down. He had given the boy a bloody nose. "You should have seen it."

It was something right and proper that such a one should be named Will and be called Bill, but a babe in a crib, a little thing always in its mother's arms —! What nonsense!

On Saturday nights, sometimes, Tar was permitted to go with his mother down into town. They could not start until the lights were lit. First of all the dishes had to be washed, Margaret helping, and then the baby had to be put to sleep.

What a fuss he made, the little wretch. Now, when he might so well have ingratiated himself with his brother by being reasonable, he cried and cried. First Margaret had to hold him and then Tar's mother had to take her turn. It was fun for Margaret. She could pretend she was a woman and girls liked that. When there were no babies around they made them out of rags. They talked and scolded and cooed and held the things in their arms. Tar was already dressed and so was his mother. The best part of going to town was the feeling of being alone with her. Nowadays that so seldom happened. The baby was spoiling everything. Pretty soon it would be too late to go, the stores would be closed. Tar moved restlessly about the front yard wanting to cry. If he did he would have to stay at home. He had to appear at ease, say nothing.

The neighbor woman came and the baby went to sleep. Now his mother had stopped to talk to the woman. They talked and talked. Tar had hold of his mother's hand and kept pulling but she paid no attention. At last, however, they got into the street and into darkness.

Tar walked along holding his mother's hand and took ten steps, twenty, a hundred. He and his mother had got through the gate and were walking on a sidewalk. They passed the Musgrave house, the Wellivers' place. When they had got to the Rogers' house and had turned a corner they would be safe. Then, if the baby cried, Tar's mother could not hear.

He began to feel at ease. What a time for him. Now he was going out into the world, not with his sister — who had her own ways and thought too much of herself and her own desires — or with a neighbor woman in a buggy, a woman who could understand nothing, but with his mother. Mary Moorehead had put on her black Sunday dress. That was fine. When she wore the black dress she wore also a bit of white lace about the neck and other bits about the wrists. The black dress made her look young and slender. The lace was fine and white. It was like cobweb. Tar wanted to touch it with his fingers but did not dare. He might tear it.

They walked past one street lamp and then another. Electric lights had not yet come and the streets of the Ohio town were lighted by kerosene lamps set on posts. They were far apart, at the street corners mostly, and between the lamps was darkness.

What fun to walk in darkness feeling safe. Going anywhere with his mother was to Tar like being at home and at the same time abroad.

When he and his mother had got out of their own street the adventure began. The Mooreheads lived nowadays always in small houses in streets far out at the edges of towns but when they went to Main Street they went through streets lined with tall houses. The houses were set far back in lawns and great trees were growing along the sidewalks. There was a large white house with women and children sitting on a wide front porch and as Tar and his mother passed a carriage with a negro driver came out at a driveway. The woman and child had to stand aside to let it pass.

What a princely place. The white house had at least ten rooms and lamps of its own hanging from the ceiling on the front porch. There was a girl of about Margaret's age dressed all in white. The carriage Tar saw the negro driving, could go right into the house. There was a porte-cochère. His mother told him. What splendor!

The Mooreheads were poor and were getting every year poorer but that Tar did not know. He did not ask himself why his mother he thought so beautiful had but one good dress and walked while another woman rode in a carriage, why the Mooreheads lived in a small house through the cracks of which the snow sifted during the winter, while others were in warm brightly lighted houses.

The world was the world and he was seeing it, his mother's hand in his. They passed other street lamps, went through other dark places and now they had turned a corner and there was Main Street.

Now life had indeed begun. How many lights, how many people! To the town droves of country people had come for the Saturday night and the street was filled with horses, wagons and buggies.

Young fellows with red faces, who all week had been at work in cornfields, had come into town dressed in their best clothes and wearing white collars. Some of them rode alone while others, more fortunate, had girls with them. They hitched their horses to posts along the street and walked on the sidewalk. Grown men went clattering through the street on horseback and women stood talking at the doors of stores.

The Mooreheads were living for the moment in quite a large town. It was a county-seat and there was a square and a courthouse past which the main street ran. Well, there were stores on the side streets, too.

A patent medicine seller had come to town and had set up his stand at a corner. He bawled in a loud voice, inviting people to stop and hear him and for a few minutes Mary Moorehead and Tar stood at the edge of the crowd. There was a sputtering torchlight at the end of a pole and two negro men who sang the songs. Tar remembered one of the verses. What did it mean?

> *"The white man he lives in a big brick house,*
> *The yellow man wants to do the same,*
> *The old black man lives in the county jail,*
> *But he's got a brick house just the same."*

When the black men sang the verses the crowd whooped with delight and Tar also laughed. Well, he laughed because he was so excited. His eyes shone with excitement. When he grew to be a man he would spend all his time in the midst of crowds. He and his mother moved off along the street, the child clinging to the woman's hand. He did not dare wink for fear of missing something. Again the Moorehead house seemed miles away, in another world. Now even the baby could not come between him and his mother. The little wretch might cry but he need not care.

John Moorehead, his brother, was almost grown. On Saturday evenings he sold newspapers on Main Street. He sold a paper called the "Cincinnati Enquirer" and another called the "Chicago Blade." The "Blade" had brightly colored pictures and sold for five cents.

There was a man leaning over a pile of money on a table and another fierce-looking man was creeping upon him with an open knife in his hand.

A wild-looking woman was about to throw a babe off a bridge to the rocks below but a boy rushed forward and saved the babe.

Now a train rushed around a curve in the mountains and four men on horseback and with guns in their hands were waiting. They had piled rocks and trees on the tracks.

Well, they intended to force the train to stop and then rob it. It was Jesse James and his band. Tar had heard his brother John explain the pictures to the boy Bill. Later when no one was about he had looked long and long. Looking at the pictures made him dream bad dreams at night but during the day they were wonderfully exciting.

It was fun, during the daytime, to imagine yourself a part of the adventures that went on in life, in the world of men. The people who bought John's papers sure got a lot for five cents. Why, you could take such a scene and change it all about.

What you did was to sit on the porch of your house and close your eyes. John and Margaret had gone to school, the baby and Robert were both asleep. The baby slept well enough when Tar did not want to go somewhere with his mother.

You sat on the porch of the house and closed your eyes. Your mother was ironing. Damp clean clothes being ironed made a nice smell. That old crippled carpenter, who could not work any more, who had been a soldier and drew what was called a pension, was on the back porch of the house talking. He was telling Tar's mother of buildings on which he had worked when he was young.

He told of how log cabins were built in the forest when the country was new and of how men went out to shoot wild turkey and deer.

It was fun enough to hear the old carpenter talk but more fun to make up your own talk, build your own world.

The colored pictures in the papers John sold on Saturdays had become indeed alive. In fancy Tar had grown to be a man, and what a brave one. He took part in all of the desperate scenes, changed them about, thrust himself into the very midst of the swirl and hurly-burly of life.

A world of grown people moving about and Tar Moorehead among them.

Somewhere in the crowd on the street John was now running about selling his papers. He pushed them under people's noses, showed the colored pictures. Like a grown man John went into saloons, into the stores, into the courthouse.

Soon now, Tar himself would be grown. It could not possibly take very long. How long, though, the days sometimes seemed.

With his mother he threaded his way through the crowd. Men and women spoke to his mother. A tall man did not see Tar and knocked against him. Then another very tall man with a pipe in his mouth gave him a regular bang.

The man wasn't so nice. He apologized and gave Tar a nickel but that did not do any good. It was the way he did it that hurt more than the bang. Some men think a child is only a child.

And now they had got off Main Street and into the one where Dick had his shop. There were plenty of people on Saturday nights. Across the street was a two-storied building in which a dance was being held. It was a square dance and a man's voice was calling off. "Do-se-do. Gentlemen all lead to the right. Balance all." The whining voices of fiddles, laughter, many voices talking.

Dick Moorehead was as yet able to put on some style. He had still the watch with the heavy silver chain and for the Saturday evening's rush had been shaved and had waxed his mustache. A silent old man, much like the carpenter who came to visit Tar's mother, was employed in the shop and was there now at work, seated on his wooden horse. He was sewing a strap.

It seemed to Tar that the life led by his father was something magnificent. When the woman and the child came into the shop Dick ran at once to a drawer and taking out a handful of money offered it to his wife. It may have been all the money he had but that Tar did not know. Money was something with which you bought things. You had it or you did not have it.

As for Tar he had money of his own. He had the nickel the man on the street had given him. When the man had banged him and had given him the nickel his mother had asked sharply, "Well, Edgar, what do you say?" and he had replied by looking at the man and saying rudely, "Give me some more." It had made the man laugh but Tar had not seen the sense of his laughing. The man had been rude and he had been rude too. His mother was hurt. It was very easy to hurt his mother.

In the shop Tar was seated on a chair at the back and his mother was on another chair. She had taken but a few of the coins offered by Dick.

Again there was talk. Grown people are always indulging in talk. A half dozen farmers were in the shop and when Dick had offered the money to his wife he did it with a flourish. Dick did everything with a flourish. That was his nature. He said something about the cost of women and children. He was being rude like the man on the street but Dick's being rude never mattered. He did not mean what he said.

Anyway Dick was a man of affairs.

How he bustled about. Men kept coming into the shop bringing harnesses and throwing them down with a bang on the floor. The men talked and Dick talked. He talked more than all the others. At the back of the shop there was only Tar, his mother and the old man on the horse sewing the strap. The man was like the carpenter and the doctor who came to the house when Tar was at home. He was small and shy and spoke timidly, asking Mary Moorehead about the other children and the baby. Presently he got off the bench and coming to Tar gave him another nickel. How rich Tar was getting. This time he did not wait for his mother to ask but said at once what he knew he should say.

Tar's mother had gone away and left him in the shop. Men came and went. They talked. With some of the men Dick went out into the street. A business man who has taken an order for a new harness is expected to set-em-up. Each time when he came back from such a trip Dick's eyes shone more brightly and the mustache stood out straighter. He came and stroked Tar's hair.

"He's a bright one," he said. Well, Dick was bragging again.

It was better when he talked to the others. He told jokes and the men laughed. When the men were doubled up with laughter, Tar and the old harness maker on the horse looked at each other and also laughed. It was as though the old man had said, "We're out of it, my boy. You are too young and I am too old." As a matter of fact the old man said nothing. It was all imagined. All the best things for a boy are always imagined. You sit in a chair at the back of your father's shop on a Saturday night, while your mother goes to the stores, and such thoughts you have. There is the sound of the fiddle in the dance hall outside in the street and the nice sound of men's voices far away. At the front of the shop there is a hanging lamp and harnesses are hanging on the walls. All is neat and in order. Harnesses have silver buckles, they have buckles of brass. Solomon had a temple and in the temple were shields of brass. There were vessels of silver and gold. Solomon was the wisest man in the world.

In a harness shop on a Saturday evening the oil lamps hanging from the ceiling sway a little. Everywhere bits of brass and silver. The lamps, when they sway, make tiny lights appear and disappear. The lights dance, men's voices are heard, there is laughter, the sound of a fiddle. In the street outside people are walking up and down.

CHAPTER IV

FOR the boy as for the man there is the world of fancy and the world of facts. Sometimes the world of facts is very grim.

Solomon had vessels of silver, he had vessels of gold, but Tar Moorehead's father was not a Solomon. Within a year after the Saturday evening when Tar sat in his father's shop seeing the bright glitter of the buckles in the swaying lights, the shop had been sold to pay Dick's debts and the Mooreheads were living in another town.

All summer Dick had been working as a house-painter but now cold weather had come and he had got a job. He was now but a workman in a harness shop and sat on the harness-maker's horse sewing straps. The silver watch and the watch chain were gone.

The Mooreheads lived in a mean little house and all through the fall Tar had been ill. As the fall advanced there was a time of bitter cold days and then there came a period of soft days.

Tar sat on the porch wrapped in a blanket. Now the corn in distant fields was in shocks and the other crops had been hauled away. In a small field near at hand where the corn crop had not been good a farmer had gone into the field to pick the corn and then had turned cows into the field to nibble at the stalks. In the woods the red and yellow leaves were falling fast. With every gust of wind they flew like brightly colored birds across the field of Tar's vision. In the corn field the cows making their way among the dry standing corn stalks made a low crashing sound.

Dick Moorehead had names Tar had never heard before. One day when he sat on the porch of the house a man with a board balanced across his shoulder came along the road past the house and seeing Dick Moorehead coming out at the front door stopped and spoke to him. He called Dick Moorehead "Major." "Hello, Major," he shouted.

The man's hat was tilted jauntily on the side of his head and he smoked a pipe. After he and Dick had gone off along the road together Tar got up out of his chair. It was one of the days when he felt quite strong. The sun was shining.

Going around the house he found a board fallen out of a fence and tried to carry it as had the man in the road, balancing it on his shoulder as he walked up and down a path in the back yard, but it fell and an end of it hit him on the side of the head, raising a large bump.

Tar went back to sit alone on the front porch. There was to be a new baby in the house. He had heard his father and mother speak of it at night. With three children in the house younger than himself it was time he grew up.

His father was called Captain and Major. Tar's mother sometimes called her husband Richard. How grand to be a man and have so many names.

Tar had begun to wonder if he would ever be a man. How long to wait! How annoying to be sick and not able to go to school.

Nowadays, immediately after he had bolted his food, Dick Moorehead hurried away from the house. At night he did not come home until all had gone to bed. In the new town he had joined a brass band and belonged to several lodges. When he did not have to work in the shop at night there was always a lodge to attend. Although his clothes had grown shabby Dick wore two or three brightly colored badges in the lapel of his coat and on special days gayly colored ribbons.

One Saturday evening when Dick came home from the shop something had happened.

All the house felt it. It was dark in the street outside and the evening meal had been waiting for a long time. When at last the children of the house heard their father's footsteps on the sidewalk that led from the gate to the front door, all became silent.

How very strange. The footsteps came along the hard road outside and then stopped before the house. Now the front gate had opened and Dick was going around the house to the kitchen door where all the rest of the Moorehead family were sitting and waiting. It was one of the days when Tar felt strong and had come to the table. When the footsteps were still in the road outside, his mother stood silently in the middle of the room but as they moved about the house she hurried to the stove. When Dick came to the kitchen door she did not look at him and all through the evening meal, eaten in a strange new kind of silence, she did not speak to her husband or to the children.

Dick had been drinking. Many times when he came home during that fall he had been drinking but the children had never before seen him when he was really off balance. When he had come along the road and the path that led around the house, all of the children had recognized his footsteps that were at the same time not his footsteps. There was something wrong. All in the house felt it. Each step was taken uncertainly. The man had, quite deliberately perhaps, surrendered something of himself to some power outside himself. He had surrendered control over his faculties, his mind, his fancy, his tongue, the muscles of his own body. He was for the time quite helpless in the hands of something his children could not understand. There was a kind of assault upon the spirit of the house. At the kitchen door he lost control over himself a little and had to catch himself quickly, his hand on the door frame.

When he got into the room and had put aside his hat he went at once to where Tar sat. "Well, well, how are you, little monkey?" he cried, standing before Tar's chair and laughing, a little foolishly. No doubt he felt the eyes of all the others upon him, felt the frightened silence of the room.

To pass it off he took Tar up in his arms and tried to go toward his place at the head of the table, to sit at the table. He almost fell. "How big you are getting," he said to Tar. He did not look at his wife.

Being in his father's arms was like being in the top of a tree pitched and tossed by a wind. When Dick had managed to get his balance again he got to the chair and sitting down put his cheek against Tar's. For several days he had not shaved and there was a half-grown beard that hurt Tar's face and his father's long mustache was wet. His breath smelled of something strange and pungent. The smell made Tar a little ill but he did not cry. He was too frightened to cry.

The fright of the child, of all the children in the room, was something special. The feeling of discouragement that had for months brooded over the house had come to a head. Dick's drunkenness was a kind of assertion. "Well, life has proven to be too much of a job. I shall let things go. There is a man in me and there is something else. I have tried being a man but I cannot make it. Look at me. Now I have become what I am. How do you like it?"

Watching his chance Tar crept out of his father's arms and went to sit near his mother. All of the children of the household had instinctively edged their chairs along the floor so that the father was left quite alone, with a wide open space on either side. Tar felt feverishly strong. His brain was making strange pictures, one after the other.

He kept thinking of trees. Now his father was like a tree in the middle of a great open meadow, a tree tossed by a wind, a wind all the others, standing at the edge of the meadow, could not feel.

The strange man who had suddenly come into the house was Tar's father and was at the same time not his father. The man's hands kept making uncertain movements. There were baked potatoes for supper and he tried to begin serving the children by sticking a fork into a potato but missed and the fork struck on the side of the dish. It made a sharp metallic sound. He tried two or three times and then Mary Moorehead, getting up from her place, walked around the table and took the dish away. Having been served, all began eating in silence.

The silence was unbearable to Dick. There was a kind of accusation in it. All of life, now that he was married and the father of children, was a kind of accusation. "There is too much accusation. A man is what he is. You are expected to grow up, be a man, but what if you are not made that way?"

It was true Dick drank, that he did not save money, but other men were that way. "There is a lawyer in this very town who gets drunk two or three times every week but you look at him. He is successful. He makes money and dresses well. With me everything is a muddle. To tell the truth I made a mistake in being a soldier and going back on my father and brothers. I have always been making mistakes. Being a man is not so easy as it seems.

"I made a mistake when I married. I love my wife but I have been able to do nothing for her. Now she shall see me as I am. My children shall see me as I am. What do I care?"

Dick had worked himself into a state. He began to talk, addressing not his children or his wife but the kitchen stove that stood in a corner of the room. The children were eating in silence. All had grown white.

Tar turned to look at the stove. How odd, he thought, that a grown man should be talking to a stove. It was a thing such as a child like himself might have done when alone in a room but a man was a man. As his father talked he saw in fancy and quite distinctly the faces of people appearing and disappearing in the darkness back of the stove. The faces, called into being by the voice of his father, emerged quite distinctly out of the darkness back of the stove and then as rapidly disappeared. They danced in the air, became large and then small.

Dick Moorehead talked as though making a speech. There were certain men who, when he lived in another town and owned a harness shop, when he was a man of business and not, as now, a mere workman, had not paid for harnesses bought in his shop. "How can I get along if they do not pay?" he asked aloud. Now he held a small baked potato balanced on the end of a fork and began waving it about. Tar's mother was looking at her plate but his brother John, his sister Margaret and his younger brother Robert were all looking at their father with staring eyes. As for Tar's mother, when something happened she did not approve she went about the house with a strange lost look in her eyes. The eyes frightened. They frightened Dick Moorehead as well as the children. All became self-conscious, afraid. It was as though she had been struck a blow and when you looked at her you felt at once that your hand had delivered the blow.

The room in which the Mooreheads now sat was lighted only by a small oil lamp on the table and by the glow from the stove. As it was already late in the fall darkness had come. In the kitchen stove were many cracks through which ashes and bits of burning coal sometimes fell. The stove was bound together with wires. The Mooreheads were indeed very hard up just at that time. They had reached the low stage in all the memories Tar afterward kept of his childhood.

Dick Moorehead declared his position in life a terrible one. In the house at the table he kept looking into the darkness back of the kitchen stove and thinking of the men who owed him money. "Look at me, I am in a certain position. Well, I have a wife and children. I have these children to feed and men owe me money they do not pay. I am down and out and they laugh at me. I want to do my part like a man but how can I manage?"

The drunken man began calling out a long list of names of men who he declared owed him money and Tar listened filled with wonder. It was an odd circumstance that when he grew to be a man and became a writer of tales Tar remembered many of the names called out by his father that evening. Many of them were afterwards attached to characters in stories of his.

His father called off names and condemned the men who had not paid for harnesses bought when he was prosperous and owned a shop of his own but Tar did not afterward connect the names with his father or with any injustice done to his father.

Something had happened. Tar sat on a chair near his mother facing the stove in the corner.

Light appeared and disappeared on the wall. As Dick talked he held the small baked potato balanced on the end of a fork. The baked potato made dancing shadows on the face of the wall.

The outline of faces began to appear. As Dick Moorehead talked a movement began in the shadows.

One by one the names were called and then the faces appeared. Where had Tar seen the faces before? They were the faces of men seen passing the Moorehead house, faces seen traveling on trains, faces seen from the seat of the buggy, that time Tar went into the country.

There was a man with a gold tooth and an old man with his hat pulled down over his eyes and these were followed by others. The man who had balanced the board on his shoulder and who had called Tar's father "the Major," came out of the shadows to stand looking at Tar. The illness from which Tar had been suffering and from which he had begun to recover was now coming back. The cracks in the stove made dancing lights on the floor.

The faces Tar saw emerging so suddenly out of darkness and then so quickly disappearing again, he did not connect with his father. Each face as it appeared had for him a life of its own.

His father kept talking in the thick angry voice and the faces kept appearing and disappearing. The meal progressed but Tar did not eat. The faces seen in the shadows did not frighten, they filled the child with wonder.

He sat by the table looking occasionally at his angry father and from him to the men who had so mysteriously come into the room. How glad he was his mother was there. Did the others see what he saw?

The faces now dancing on the walls of the room were the faces of men. Some time he would himself be a man. He watched and waited but as his father talked did not connect the faces with the words of condemnation that were coming from his lips.

Jim Gibson, Curtis Brown, Andrew Hartnett, Jacob Wills — men of an Ohio countryside, who had bought harnesses of a small harness maker and then had not paid. Names were themselves something to think about. Names were like houses, they were like pictures people hang on the walls of a room. When you see a picture you do not see what the man saw who painted the picture. When you go into a house you do not feel what the people feel who live in the house.

Names called out make a certain impression. Sounds also make pictures. There are too many pictures. When you are a child and ill the pictures crowd in upon each other too fast.

Now that he was ill Tar sat too much alone. On rainy days he sat by a window inside the house and on fair days sat on a chair on the porch.

His illness had made him habitually silent. All during his illness Tar's older brother John and his sister Margaret had been kind. John, who nowadays had much business going on, in the yard and in the road, and who was often visited by other boys, came to bring him marbles and Margaret came to sit with him and tell him happenings at school.

Tar sat staring about and saying nothing. How could he tell anyone what was going on inside. There was too much going on inside. With his weak body he could do nothing but inside his body there was intense activity.

Something peculiar there was, down inside, something constantly being torn apart and then joined together again. Tar did not understand and never did understand.

For one thing, everything kept going far away. There was a tree at the side of the road before the Moorehead house that kept coming out of the ground and floating away into the sky. Tar's mother came to sit in the room with him. She was always at work. When she was not bending over the wash tub or over the ironing board, she was sewing. She also, the chair in which she sat, even the walls of the room, seemed to float away. Something inside Tar struggled constantly to bring everything back and put everything in its place. If things would only stay in their places how calm and nice life would be.

Tar knew nothing of death but was afraid. Things that should be small became large, things that should remain large became small. Often Tar's own hands, white and small, seemed to leave his arms and float away. They floated away over the tops of the trees seen through the window, almost disappeared into the sky.

Not to have everything disappear was Tar's problem. It was a problem he could not explain to anyone, and absorbed him completely. Often the tree that had come out of the ground and had floated away became merely a black dot in the sky but it was his problem not to lose sight of it. If it happened that you lost sight of the tree you lost sight of everything. Tar did not know why that was true but it was. Grimly he held on.

If he held on the tree would come back, everything would come back. Some day he would get all adjusted again.

If Tar held on things would at last be all right. Of that he was quite sure.

The faces in the street before the houses in which the Mooreheads had lived had sometimes floated across the fancy of the sick boy as now in the kitchen of the Moorehead house the faces were floating on the wall back of the stove.

Tar's father kept calling new names and new faces kept coming. Tar had grown very white.

The faces on the wall appeared and disappeared faster than ever. Tar's white small hands gripped the edges of his chair.

Had it become a test for him to follow with his fancy all of the faces, must he keep track of them as he did of the trees when they seemed to float into the sky?

The faces had become a whirling mass. His father's voice seemed far away.

Something slipped. Tar's hands that had been gripping so tightly the edges of his chair let go their hold and with a little sigh he slipped from the chair to the floor, into the darkness.

THOMAS HENRY HUXLEY

THOMAS HENRY HUXLEY (1825–1895), though not the most prominent scientist of his time, was probably the most widely influential scientific writer in nineteenth-century England. His career is too well known to require comment; but it will be recalled that, more than anyone else, he made his contemporaries accept the scientific point of view, even when, as in the case of evolution, the theory which Huxley was championing ran counter to their inherited beliefs and prejudices. This astonishing triumph he won by his persuasiveness, his honesty, his argumentative ability, and the clearness, force, and charm of his style, perhaps the most remarkable style for expository purposes written in Victorian England. The fragmentary "Autobiography" which follows illustrates these characteristics, save that there is no occasion in it for argument. Among Huxley's best known essays are: "The Physical Basis of Life," "Man's Place in Nature," and "Evolution and Ethics."

AUTOBIOGRAPHY*

And when I consider, in one view, the many things... which I have upon my hands, I feel the burlesque of being employed in this manner at my time of life. But, in another view, and taking in all circumstances, these things, as trifling as they may appear, no less than things of greater importance, seem to be put upon me to do. — *Bishop Butler to the Duchess of Somerset.*

THE "many things" to which the Duchess's correspondent here refers are the repairs and improvements of the episcopal seat at Auckland. I doubt if the great apologist, greater in nothing than in the simple dignity of his character, would have considered the writing an account of himself as a thing which could be put upon him to do whatever circumstances might be taken in. But the good bishop lived in an age when a man might write books and yet be permitted to keep his private existence to himself; in the pre-Boswellian epoch, when the germ of the photographer lay concealed in the distant future, and the interviewer who pervades our age was an unforeseen, indeed unimaginable, birth of time.

At present, the most convinced believer in the aphorism "Bene qui latuit, bene vixit," is not always able to act up to it. An importunate person informs him that his portrait is about to be published and will be accompanied by a biography which the importunate person proposes to write. The sufferer knows what that means; either he undertakes to revise the "biography" or he does not. In the former case, he makes himself responsible; in the latter, he allows the publication of a mass of more or less fulsome inaccuracies for which he will be held responsible by those who are familiar with the prevalent art of self-advertisement. On the whole, it may be better to get over the "burlesque of being employed in this manner" and do the thing himself.

It was by reflections of this kind that, some years ago, I was led to write and permit the publication of the subjoined sketch.

I was born about eight o'clock in the morning on the 4th of May, 1825, at Ealing, which was, at that time, as quiet a little country village as could be found within a half-a-dozen miles of Hyde Park Corner. Now it is a suburb of London with, I believe, 30,000 inhabitants. My father was one of the masters in a large semi-public school which at one time had a high reputation. I am not aware that any portents preceded my arrival in this world, but, in my childhood, I remember hearing a traditional account of the manner in which I lost the chance of an endowment of great practical value. The windows of my mother's room were open, in consequence of the unusual warmth of the weather. For the same reason, probably, a neighbouring beehive had swarmed, and the new colony, pitching on the window-sill, was making its way into the room when the horrified nurse shut down the sash. If that well-meaning woman had only abstained from her ill-timed interference, the swarm might have settled on my lips, and I should have been endowed with that mellifluous eloquence which, in this country, leads far more surely than worth, capacity, or honest work, to the highest places in Church and State. But the opportunity was lost, and I have been obliged to content myself through life with saying what I mean in the plainest of plain language, than which, I suppose, there is no habit more ruinous to a man's prospects of advancement.

Why I was christened Thomas Henry I do not know; but it is a curious chance that my parents should have fixed for my usual denomination upon the name of that particular Apostle with whom I have always felt most sympathy. Physically and mentally I am the son of my mother so completely — even down to peculiar movements of the hands, which made their appearance in me as I reached the age she had when I noticed them — that I can hardly find any trace of my father in myself, except an inborn faculty for drawing, which unfortunately, in my case, has never been cultivated, a hot temper, and that amount of tenacity of purpose which unfriendly observers sometimes call obstinacy.

My mother was a slender brunette, of an emotional and energetic temperament, and possessed of the most piercing black eyes I ever saw in a woman's head. With no more education than other women of the middle classes in her day, she had an excellent mental capacity. Her most distinguishing characteristic, however, was rapidity of thought. If one ventured to suggest she had not taken much time to arrive at any conclusion, she would say, "I cannot help it, things flash across me." That peculiarity has been passed on to me in full strength; it has often stood me in good stead; it has sometimes played me sad tricks, and it has always been a danger. But, after all, if my time were to come over again, there is nothing I would less willingly part with than my inheritance of mother wit.

I have next to nothing to say about my childhood. In later years my mother, looking at me almost reproachfully, would sometimes say, "Ah! you were such a pretty boy!" whence I had no difficulty in concluding that I had not fulfilled my early promise in the matter of looks. In fact, I have a distinct recollection of certain curls of which I was vain, and of a conviction that I closely resembled that handsome, courtly gentleman,

Sir Herbert Oakley, who was vicar of our parish, and who was as a god to us country folk, because he was occasionally visited by the then Prince George of Cambridge. I remember turning my pinafore wrong side forwards in order to represent a surplice, and preaching to my mother's maids in the kitchen as nearly as possible in Sir Herbert's manner one Sunday morning when the rest of the family were at church. That is the earliest indication I can call to mind of the strong clerical affinities which my friend Mr. Herbert Spencer has always ascribed to me, though I fancy they have for the most part remained in a latent state.

My regular school training was of the briefest, perhaps fortunately, for though my way of life has made me acquainted with all sorts and conditions of men, from the highest to the lowest, I deliberately affirm that the society I fell into at school was the worst I have ever known. We boys were average lads, with much the same inherent capacity for good and evil as any others; but the people who were set over us cared about as much for our intellectual and moral welfare as if they were baby-farmers. We were left to the operation of the struggle for existence among ourselves, and bullying was the least of the ill practices current among us. Almost the only cheerful reminiscence in connection with the place which arises in my mind is that of a battle I had with one of my classmates, who had bullied me until I could stand it no longer. I was a very slight lad, but there was a wild-cat element in me which, when roused, made up for lack of weight, and I licked my adversary effectually. However, one of my first experiences of the extremely rough-and-ready nature of justice, as exhibited by the course of things in general, arose out of the fact that I — the victor — had a black eye, while he — the vanquished — had none, so that I got into disgrace and he did not. We made it up, and thereafter I was unmolested. One of the greatest shocks I ever received in my life was to be told a dozen years afterwards by the groom who brought me my horse in a stable-yard in Sydney that he was my quondam antagonist. He had a long story of family misfortune to account for his position, but at that time it was necessary to deal very cautiously with mysterious strangers in New South Wales, and on inquiry I found that the unfortunate young man had not only been "sent out," but had undergone more than one colonial conviction.

As I grew older, my great desire was to be a mechanical engineer, but the fates were against this and, while very young, I commenced the study of medicine under a medical brother-in-law. But, though the Institute of Mechanical Engineers would certainly not own me, I am not sure that I have not all along been a sort of mechanical engineer *in partibus infidelium*. I am now occasionally horrified to think how very little I ever knew or cared about medicine as the art of healing. The only part of my professional course which really and deeply interested me was physiology, which is the mechanical engineering of living machines; and, notwithstanding that natural science has been my proper business, I am afraid there is very little of the genuine naturalist in me. I never collected anything, and species work was always a burden to me; what I cared for was the architectural and engineering part of the business, the working out of the wonderful unity of plan in the thousands and thousands of diverse living constructions, and the modifications of similar apparatuses to serve diverse ends. The extraordinary attraction I felt towards the study of the intricacies of living structure nearly proved fatal to me at the outset. I was a mere boy — I think between thirteen and fourteen years of age — when I was taken by some older student friends of mine to the first *post-mortem* examination I ever attended. All my life I have been most unfortunately sensitive to the disagreeables which attend anatomical pursuits, but on this occasion my curiosity overpowered all other feelings, and I spent two or three hours in gratifying it. I did not cut myself, and none of the ordinary symptoms of dissection-poison supervened, but poisoned I was somehow, and I remember sinking into a strange state of apathy. By way of a last chance, I was sent to the care of some good, kind people, friends of my father's, who lived in a farmhouse in the heart of Warwickshire. I remember staggering from my bed to the window on the bright spring morning after my arrival, and throwing open the casement. Life seemed to come back on the wings of the breeze, and to this day the faint odor of woodsmoke, like that which floated across the farm-yard in the early morning, is as good to me as the "sweet south upon a bed of violets." I soon recovered, but for years I suffered from occasional paroxysms of internal pain, and from that time my constant friend, hypochondriacal dyspepsia, commenced his half century of co-tenancy of my fleshly tabernacle.

Looking back on my "Lehrjahre," I am sorry to say that I do not think that any account of my doings as a student would tend to edification. In fact, I should distinctly warn ingenuous youth to avoid imitating my example. I worked extremely hard when it pleased me, and when it did not — which was a very frequent case — I was extremely idle (unless making caricatures of one's pastors and masters is to be called a branch of industry), or else wasted my energies in wrong directions. I read everything I could lay hands upon, including novels, and took up all sorts of pursuits to drop them again quite as speedily. No doubt it was very largely my own fault, but the only instruction from which I ever obtained the proper effect of education was that which I received from Mr. Wharton Jones, who was the lecturer on physiology at the Charing Cross School of Medicine. The extent and precision of his knowledge impressed me greatly, and the severe exactness of his method of lecturing was quite to my taste. I do not know that I have ever felt so much respect for anybody as a teacher before or since. I worked hard to obtain his approbation, and he was extremely kind and helpful to the youngster who, I am afraid, took up more of his time than he had any right to do. It was he who suggested the publication of my first scientific paper — a very little one — in the *Medical Gazette* of 1845, and most kindly corrected the literary faults which abounded in it, short as it was; for at that time, and for many years afterwards, I detested the trouble of writing, and would take no pains over it.

It was in the early spring of 1846, that, having finished my obligatory medical studies and passed the first M.D. examination at the London University — though I was still too young to qualify at the College of Surgeons

—I was talking to a fellow-student (the present eminent physician, Sir Joseph Fayrer), and wondering what I should do to meet the imperative necessity for earning my own bread, when my friend suggested that I should write to Sir William Burnett, at that time Director-General for the Medical Service of the Navy, for an appointment. I thought this rather a strong thing to do, as Sir William was personally unknown to me, but my cheery friend would not listen to my scruples, so I went to my lodgings and wrote the best letter I could devise. A few days afterwards I received the usual official circular acknowledgment, but at the bottom there was written an instruction to call at Somerset House on such a day. I thought that looked like business, so at the appointed time I called and sent in my card, while I waited in Sir William's ante-room. He was a tall, shrewd-looking old gentleman, with a broad Scotch accent — and I think I see him now as he entered with my card in his hand. The first thing he did was to return it, with the frugal reminder that I should probably find it useful on some other occasion. The second was to ask whether I was an Irishman. I suppose the air of modesty about my appeal must have struck him. I satisfied the Director-General that I was English to the backbone, and he made some inquiries as to my student career, finally desiring me to hold myself ready for examination. Having passed this, I was in Her Majesty's Service, and entered on the books of Nelson's old ship, the *Victory*, for duty at Haslar Hospital, about a couple of months after I made my application.

My official chief at Haslar was a very remarkable person, the late Sir John Richardson, an excellent naturalist, and far-famed as an indomitable Arctic traveller. He was a silent, reserved man, outside the circle of his family and intimates; and, having a full share of youthful vanity, I was extremely disgusted to find that "Old John," as we irreverent youngsters called him, took not the slightest notice of my worshipful self either the first time I attended him, as it was my duty to do, or for some weeks afterwards. I am afraid to think of the lengths to which my tongue may have run on the subject of the churlishness of the chief, who was, in truth, one of the kindest-hearted and most considerate of men. But one day, as I was crossing the hospital square, Sir John stopped me, and heaped coals of fire on my head by telling me that he had tried to get me one of the resident appointments, much coveted by the assistant surgeons, but that the Admiralty had put in another man. "However," said he, "I mean to keep you here till I can get you something you will like," and turned upon his heel without waiting for the thanks I stammered out. That explained how it was I had not been packed off to the West Coast of Africa like some of my juniors, and why, eventually, I remained altogether seven months at Haslar.

After a long interval, during which "Old John" ignored my existence almost as completely as before, he stopped me again as we met in a casual way, and describing the service on which the *Rattlesnake* was likely to be employed, said that Captain Owen Stanley, who was to command the ship, had asked him to recommend an assistant surgeon who knew something of science; would I like that? Of course I jumped at the offer. "Very well, I give you leave; go to London at once and see Captain Stanley." I went, saw my future commander, who was very civil to me, and promised to ask that I should be appointed to his ship, as in due time I was. It is a singular thing that, during the few months of my stay at Haslar, I had among my messmates two future Directors-General of the Medical Service of the Navy (Sir Alexander Armstrong and Sir John Watt-Reid), with the present President of the College of Physicians and my kindest of doctors, Sir Andrew Clark.

Life on board Her Majesty's ship in those days was a very different affair from what it is now, and ours was exceptionally rough, as we were often many months without receiving letters or seeing any civilised people but ourselves. In exchange, we had the interest of being about the last voyagers, I suppose, to whom it could be possible to meet with people who knew nothing of fire-arms — as we did on the south coasts of New Guinea — and of making acquaintance with a variety of interesting savage and semi-civilised people. But, apart from experience of this kind and the opportunities offered for scientific work, to me, personally, the cruise was extremely valuable. It was good for me to live under sharp discipline; to be down on the realities of existence by living on bare necessaries; to find out how extremely well worth living life seemed to be when one woke up from a night's rest on a soft plank, with the sky for canopy and cocoa and weevilly biscuit the sole prospect for breakfast; and, more especially, to learn to work for the sake of what I got for myself out of it, even if it all went to the bottom and I along with it. My brother officers were as good fellows as sailors ought to be and generally are, but, naturally, they neither knew nor cared anything about my pursuits, nor understood why I should be so zealous in pursuit of the objects which my friends, the middies, christened "Buffons," after the title conspicuous on a volume of the *Suites à Buffon*, which stood on my shelf in the chart room.

During the four years of our absence, I sent home communication after communication to the "Linnean Society," with the same result as that obtained by Noah when he sent the raven out of his ark. Tired at last of hearing nothing about them, I determined to do or die, and in 1849 I drew up a more elaborate paper and forwarded it to the Royal Society. This was my dove, if I had only known it. But owing to the movements of the ship, I heard nothing of that either until my return to England in the latter end of the year 1850, when I found that it was printed and published, and that a huge packet of separate copies awaited me. When I hear some of my young friends complain of want of sympathy and encouragement, I am inclined to think that my naval life was not the least valuable part of my education.

Three years after my return were occupied by a battle between my scientific friends on the one hand and the Admiralty on the other, as to whether the latter ought, or ought not, to act up to the spirit of a pledge they had given to encourage officers who had done scientific work by contributing to the expense of publishing mine. At last the Admiralty, getting tired, I suppose, cut short the discussion by ordering me to join a ship, which thing I declined to do, and as Rastignac, in the *Père Goriot* says to Paris, I said to London "*à nous deux*." I desired to obtain a Professorship of either Physiology or Comparative Anatomy, and as vacancies occurred I applied, but in vain. My friend, Professor Tyndall, and I were candidates at the same time, he for the Chair of Physics and I for that of Natural History in the University of Toronto, which, fortunately, as it turned out, would not look at either of us. I say fortunately, not from any lack of respect for Toronto, but because I soon made up my mind that London was the place for me, and hence I have steadily declined the inducements to leave it, which have at various times been offered. At last, in 1854, on the translation of my warm friend Edward Forbes, to Edinburgh, Sir Henry de la Beche, the Director-General of the Geological Survey, offered me the post Forbes vacated of Paleontologist and Lecturer on Natural History. I refused the former point blank, and accepted the latter only provisionally, telling Sir Henry that I did not care for fossils, and that I should give up Natural History as soon as I could get a physiological post. But I held the office for thirty-one years, and a large part of my work has been paleontological.

At that time I disliked public speaking, and had a firm conviction that I should break down every time I opened my mouth. I believe I had every fault a speaker could have (except talking at random or indulging in rhetoric), when I spoke to the first important audience I ever addressed, on a Friday evening at the Royal Institution, in 1852. Yet, I must confess to having been guilty, *malgré moi*, of as much public speaking as most of my contemporaries, and for the last ten years it ceased to be so much of a bugbear to me. I used to pity myself for having to go through this training, but I am now more disposed to compassionate the unfortunate audiences, especially my ever friendly hearers at the Royal Institution, who were the subjects of my oratorical experiments.

The last thing that it would be proper for me to do would be to speak of the work of my life, or to say at the end of the day whether I think I have earned my wages or not. Men are said to be partial judges of themselves. Young men may be, I doubt if old men are. Life seems terribly foreshortened as they look back and the mountain they set themselves to climb in youth turns out to be a mere spur of immeasurably higher ranges when, by failing breath, they reach the top. But if I may speak of the objects I have had more or less definitely in view since I began the ascent of my hillock, they are briefly these: To promote the increase of natural knowledge and to forward the application of scientific methods of investigation to all the problems of life to the best of my ability, in the conviction which has grown with my growth and strengthened with my strength, that there is no alleviation for the sufferings of mankind except veracity of thought and of action, and the resolute facing of the world as it is when the garment of make-believe by which pious hands have hidden its uglier features is stripped off.

It is with this intent that I have subordinated any reasonable, or unreasonable ambition for scientific fame which I may have permitted myself to entertain to other ends; to the popularization of science; to the development and organisation of scientific education; to the endless series of battles and skirmishes over evolution; and to untiring opposition to that ecclesiastical spirit, that clericalism, which in England, as everywhere else, and to whatever denomination it may belong, is the deadly enemy of science.

In striving for the attainment of these objects, I have been but one among many, and I shall be well content to be remembered, or even not remembered, as such.   Circumstances, among which I am proud to reckon the devoted kindness of many friends, have led to my occupation of various prominent positions, among which the Presidency of the Royal Society is the highest.   It would be mock modesty on my part, with these and other scientific honours which have been bestowed upon me, to pretend that I have not succeeded in the career which I have followed, rather because I was driven into it than of my own free will; but I am afraid I should not count even these things as marks of success if I could not hope that I had somewhat helped that movement of opinion which has been called the New Reformation.

LETTERS

A SPECIAL type of personal writing is correspondence. In its most intimate form it is communication between two persons, and its charm consists in its privacy. In such cases the substance of the letter — personal experience, news of common friends, comment on common interests — will naturally be of immediate concern.

Probably the best letters are those in which the two impelling forces, the subjective and the objective, are most nearly in equilibrium. Such is the case in Jane Austen's letters to her sister Cassandra, who seems to have had the same keen satirical view of the life and characters of the English village that makes *Pride and Prejudice* and *Mansfield Park* such delightful books. It is hard to say exactly what gives their charm to these personal chronicles of simple country life at the end of the eighteenth century. One source of pleasure is the style, which meets the requirement of Dorothy Osborne, a delightful letter writer of a century earlier: "All letters mee thinks should be free and easy as one's discourse." We almost hear the writer's voice from the printed page. Another source is the sense of close relation between two people which recalls the philosopher's dictum that "shared experience is the greatest of human goods." Lamb's letters also have the intimate quality of his essays, and Mrs. Carlyle's suggest a genius which might have flowered into more pretentious literature but for her absorption in the career of her husband.

The seventeenth and eighteenth centuries in France and England were the golden age of letter writing. In France, Madame de Sévigné holds priority in the field; in England the letters of Pope, of Lady Mary Wortley Montagu, of Lord Chesterfield, and of Horace Walpole are pre-eminent. So common and widespread was the habit of communication by letter in the eighteenth century that novelists like Richardson adopted it as a means of conducting a story through several volumes. In the nineteenth century the letters of Byron, of Lamb, and of Carlyle, especially his correspondence with Emerson, are notable. That the art of letter writing has not been lost may be seen in the selections given from William Vaughn Moody. Other examples are included in Mr. E. V. Lucas's volumes, *The Gentle Art*.

The letter writer is not always single-minded in his restriction of his appeal to an audience of one, or a few. A person of distinction, especially in public affairs, knows that his letters will form part of his biography. This sense of writing ultimately for the great reading public tends to limit the freedom of self-revelation, though few writers have been so self-conscious as Pope, who altered his personal letters for publication. Many letters have been written in a conscious effort to influence public opinion, the writer preferring intimacy of approach to the impersonal form of the essay. Such public letters were usual in the eighteenth century, as witness Swift's *Drapier's Letters*, the letters of Junius, and Burke's "Letter to a Noble Lord." Two letters which have achieved historical importance are given, as examples of vigorous style, and hard hitting. The letter of Samuel Johnson to Lord Chesterfield marked the independence of the author from the institution of patronage. The letter of Abraham Lincoln to Horace Greeley stated precisely the great issue of the Civil War. In both cases the letter is a part of experience, an act in itself.

JANE AUSTEN

In reading the letters of Jane Austen (1775–1817), it is not difficult to see the source of such a novel as *Pride and Prejudice*. The daughter of a provincial clergyman, she spent her life, except for occasional visits to Bath or Lyme, the popular English watering places of her time, in a country parish, where, though excitements were few, she nevertheless managed to amuse herself (and the world ever since) by observing and shrewdly describing the foibles of life and society about her.

To Cassandra Austen

Steventon, *Saturday (October* 27), 1798

My dear Cassandra,

Your letter was a most agreeable surprise to me today, and I have taken a long sheet of paper to show my gratitude.

We arrived here yesterday between four and five, but I cannot send you quite so triumphant an account of our last day's journey as of the first and second. Soon after I had finished my letter from Staines, my mother began to suffer from the exercise or fatigue of travelling, and she was a good deal indisposed. She had not a very good night at Staines, but bore her journey better than I had expected, and at Basingstoke, where we stopped more than half an hour, received much comfort from a mess of broth and the sight of Mr. Lyford, who recommended her to take twelve drops of laudanum when she went to bed as a composer, which she accordingly did.

James called on us just as we were going to tea, and my mother was well enough to talk very cheerfully to him before she went to bed. James seems to have taken to his old trick of coming to Steventon in spite of Mary's reproaches, for he was here before breakfast and is now paying us a second visit. They were to have dined here today, but the weather is too bad. I have had the pleasure of hearing that Martha is with them. James fetched her from Ibthorp on Thursday, and she will stay with them till she removes to Kintbury.

We met with no adventures at all in our journey yesterday, except that our trunk had once nearly slipped off, and we were obliged to stop at Hartley to have our wheels greased.

Whilst my mother and Mr. Lyford were together I went to Mrs. Ryder's and bought what I intended to buy, but not in much perfection. There were no narrow braces for children and scarcely any notting silk: but Miss Wood, as usual, is going to town very soon, and will lay in a fresh stock. I gave 2s. 3d. a yard for my flannel, and I fancy it is not very good, but it is so disgraceful and contemptible an article in itself that its being comparatively good or bad is of little importance. I bought some Japan ink likewise, and next week shall begin my operations on my hat, on which you know my principal hopes of happiness depend.

I am very grand indeed; I had the dignity of dropping out my mother's laudanum last night. I carry about the keys of the wine and closet, and twice since I began this letter have had orders to give in the kitchen. Our dinner was very good yesterday, and the chicken boiled perfectly tender; therefore I shall not be obliged to dismiss Nanny on that account.

Almost everything was unpacked and put away last night. Nanny chose to do it, and I was not sorry to be busy. I have unpacked the gloves and placed yours in your drawer. Their colour is light and pretty, and I believe exactly what we fixed on.

Your letter was chaperoned here by one from Mrs. Cooke, in which she says that "Battleridge" is not to come out before January, and she is so little satisfied with Cawthorn's dilatoriness that she never means to employ him again.

Mrs. Hall, of Sherborne, was brought to bed yesterday of a dead child, some weeks before she expected, owing to a fright. I suppose she happened unawares to look at her husband.

There has been a great deal of rain here for this last fortnight, much more than in Kent, and indeed we found the roads all the way from Staines most disgracefully dirty. Steventon lane has its full share of it, and I don't know when I shall be able to get to Deane.

I hear that Martha is in better looks and spirits than she has enjoyed for a long time, and I flatter myself she will now be able to jest openly about Mr. W.

The spectacles which Molly found are my mother's, the scissors my father's. We are very glad to hear such a good account of your patients, little and great. My dear itty Dordy's remembrance of me is very pleasing — foolishly pleasing, because I know it will be over so soon. My attachment to him will be more durable. I shall think with tenderness and delight on his beautiful and smiling countenance and interesting manner until a few years have turned him into an ungovernable, ungracious fellow.

The books from Winton are all unpacked and put away; the binding has compressed them most conveniently, and there is now very good room in the bookcase for all that we wish to have there. I believe the servants were very glad to see us. Nanny was, I am sure. She confesses that it was very dull, and yet she had her child with her till last Sunday. I understand that there are some grapes left, but I believe not many; they must be gathered as soon as possible, or this rain will entirely rot them.

I am quite angry with myself for not writing closer; why is my alphabet so much more sprawly than yours? Dame Tilbury's daughter has lain in. Shall I give her any of your baby clothes? The laceman was here only a few days ago. How unfortunate for both of us that he came so soon! Dame Bushell washes for us only one week more, as Sukey has got a place. John Steevens' wife undertakes our purification. She does not look as if anything she touched would ever be clean, but who knows? We do not seem likely to have any other maidservant at present, but Dame Staples will supply the place of one. Mary has hired a young girl from Ashe who has never been out to service to be her scrub, but James fears her not being strong enough for the place.

Earle Harwood has been to Deane lately, as I think Mary wrote us word, and his family then told him that they would receive his wife, if she continued to behave well for another year. He was very grateful, as well he might; their behaviour throughout the whole affair has been particularly kind. What a prodigious innate love of virtue she must have, to marry under such circumstances!

It is now Saturday evening, but I wrote the chief of this in the morning. My mother has not been down at all today; the laudanum made her sleep a good deal, and upon the whole I think she is better. My father and I dined by ourselves. How strange! He and John Bond are now very happy together, for I have just heard the heavy step of the latter along the passage.

James Digweed called today, and I gave him his brother's deputation. Charles Harwood, too, has just called to ask how we are, in his way from Dummer, whither he has been conveying Miss Garrett, who is going to return to her former residence in Kent. I *will* leave off, or I shall not have room to add a word tomorrow.

Sunday. — My mother has had a very good night, and feels much better today.

I have received my Aunt's letter, and thank you for your scrap. I will write to Charles soon. Pray give Fanny and Edward a kiss from me, and ask George if he has got a new song for me. 'Tis really very kind of my Aunt to ask us to Bath again; a kindness that deserves a better return than to profit by it.

Yours ever,
J. A.

MISS AUSTEN,
    GODMERSHAM PARK, FAVERSHAM, KENT.

To CASSANDRA AUSTEN

STEVENTON, Thursday (November 20), 1800

MY DEAR CASSANDRA,

Your letter took me quite by surprise this morning; you are very welcome, however, and I am very much obliged to you. I believe I drank too much wine last night at Hurstbourne; I know not how else to account for the shaking of my hand today. You will kindly make allowance therefore for any indistinctness of writing, by attributing it to this venial error.

Naughty Charles did not come on Tuesday, but good Charles came yesterday morning. About two o'clock he walked in on a Gosport hack. His feeling equal to such a fatigue is a good sign, and his feeling no fatigue in it a still better. He walked down to Deane to dinner; he danced the whole evening, and today is no more tired than a gentleman ought to be.

Your desiring to hear from me on Sunday will, perhaps, bring you a more particular account of the ball than you care for, because one is prone to think much more on such things the morning after they happen, than when time has entirely driven them out of one's recollection.

It was a pleasant evening; Charles found it remarkably so, but I cannot tell why, unless the absence of Miss Terry, towards whom his conscience reproaches him with being now perfectly indifferent, was a relief to him. There were only twelve dances, of which I danced nine, and was merely prevented from dancing the rest by the want of a partner. We began at ten, supped at one, and were at Deane before five. There were but fifty people in the room; very few families indeed from our side of the county, and not many more from the other. My partners were the two St. Johns, Hooper, Holder, and very prodigious Mr. Mathew, with whom I called the last, and whom I liked the best of my little stock.

There were very few beauties, and such as there were were not very handsome. Miss Iremonger did not look well, and Mrs. Blount was the only one much admired. She appeared exactly as she did in September, with the same broad face, diamond bandeau, white shoes, pink husband, and fat neck. The two Miss Coxes were there: I traced in one the remains of the vulgar, broad-featured girl who danced at Enham eight years ago; the other is refined into a nice, composed-looking girl, like Catherine Bigg. I looked at Sir Thomas Champneys and thought of poor Rosalie; I looked at his daughter, and thought her a queer animal with a white neck. Mrs. Warren, I was constrained to think a very fine young woman, which I much regret. She danced away with great activity. Her husband is ugly enough, uglier even than his cousin John; but he does not look so *very* old. The Miss Maitlands are both prettyish, very like Anne, with brown skins, large dark eyes, and a good deal of nose. The general has got the gout, and Mrs. Maitland the jaundice. Miss Debary, Susan, and Sally, all in black, but without any statues, made their appearance, and I was as civil to them as circumstances would allow me.

They told me nothing new of Martha. I mean to go to her on Thursday, unless Charles should determine on coming over again with his friend Shipley for the Basingstode ball, in which case I shall not go till Friday. I shall write to you again, however, before I set off, and I shall hope to hear from you in the meantime. If I do not stay for the ball I would not on any account do so uncivil a thing by the neighborhood as to set off at that very time for another place, and shall therefore make a point of not being later than Thursday *morning*.

Mary said that I looked very well last night. I wore my aunt's gown and handkerchief, and my hair was at least tidy, which was all my ambition. I will now have done with the ball, and I will moreover go and dress for dinner.

Thursday evening. — Charles leaves us on Saturday, unless Henry should take us in his way to the island, of which we have some hopes, and then they will probably go together on Sunday.

The young lady whom it is expected that Sir Thomas is to marry is Miss Emma Wabshaw; she lives somewhere between Southampton and Winchester, is handsome, accomplished, amiable, and everything but rich. He is certainly finishing his house in a great hurry. Perhaps the report of his being to marry a Miss Fanshawe might originate in his attentions to this very lady — the names are not unlike.

Summers has made my gown very well indeed, and I get more and more pleased with it. Charles does not like it, but my father and Mary do. My mother is very much resigned to it; and as for James, he gives it the preference over everything of the kind he ever saw, in proof of which I am desired to say that if you like to sell yours Mary will buy it.

We had a very pleasant day on Monday at Ashe, we sat down fourteen to dinner in the study, the dining-room being not habitable from the storms having blown down its chimney. Mrs. Bramston talked a good deal of nonsense, which Mr. Bramston and Mr. Clerk seemed almost equally to enjoy. There was a whist and a casino table, and six outsiders. Rice and Lucy made love, Mat. Robinson fell asleep, James and Mrs. Augusta alternately read Dr. Finnis' pamphlet on the cow-pox, and I bestowed my company by turns on all.

On inquiring of Mrs. Clerk, I find that Mrs. Heathcote made a great blunder in her news of the Crooks and Morleys. It is young Mr. Crook who is to marry the second Miss Morley, and it is the Miss Morleys instead of the second Miss Crook who were the beauties at the music meeting. This seems a more likely tale, a better devised imposture.

The three Digweeds all came on Tuesday, and we played a pool at commerce. James Digweed left Hampshire today. I think he must be in love with you, from his anxiety to have you go to the Faversham balls, and likewise from his supposing that the two elms fell from their grief at your absence. Was not it a gallant idea? It never occurred to me before, but I dare say it was so.

Hacker has been here today putting in the fruit trees. A new plan has been suggested concerning the plantation of the new inclosure of the right-hand side of the elm walk: the doubt is whether it would be better to make a little orchard of it by planting apples, pears, and cherries, or whether it should be larch, mountain ash, and acacia. What is your opinion? I say nothing, and am ready to agree with anybody.

You and George walking to Egerton! What a droll party! Do the Ashford people still come to Godmersham church every Sunday in a cart? It is *you* that always disliked Mr. N. Toke so much, not *I*. I do not like his wife, and I do not like Mr. Brett, but as for Mr. Toke, there are few people whom I like better.

Miss Harwood and her friend have taken a house fifteen miles from Bath; she writes very kind letters, but sends no other particulars of the situation. Perhaps it is one of the first houses in Bristol.

Farewell; Charles sends *you* his best love and Edward his worst. If you think the distinction improper, you may take the worst yourself. He will write to you when he gets back to his ship, and in the meantime desires that you will consider me as

Your affectionate sister,

J. A.

JANE WELSH CARLYLE

THE vigorous and racy style of Jane Welsh Carlyle (1801–1866) as expressed in her letters shows that if she had not decided to bask in her husband's glory, she might easily have taken an important place in literature herself. As it is, she enjoys increasing fame as one of the best letter-writers in England, and is read and enjoyed by many who do not care to make their way through the tortured prose of the greater figure. She married Thomas Carlyle in 1826; later they retired to her farm at Craigenputtock in Scotland. In 1834 they moved to London, setting up a household in Cheyne Row, Chelsea, which became a gathering place for the leading literary figures of the day. The performance referred to was that of *Every Man in his Humour* by the amateur company directed by Charles Dickens.

To T. CARLYLE, ESQ. *Scotsbrig*

Tuesday, September 23, 1845

"NOTHINK" for you today in the shape of inclosure, unless I inclose a letter from Mrs. Paulet to myself, which you will find as "entertaining" to the full as any of mine. And *nothink* to be told either, except all about the play; and upon my honour, I do not feel as if I had a penny-a-liner genius enough, this cold morning, to make much entertainment out of that. Enough to clasp one's hands, and exclaim, like Helen before the Virgin and Child, "Oh, how expensive!" But "how did the creatures get through it?" Too well; and not well enough! The public theatre, scenes painted by Stansfield, costumes "rather exquisite," together with the certain amount of proficiency in the amateurs, overlaid all idea of private theatricals; and, considering it as public theatricals, the acting was "most insipid," not one performer among them that could be called good, and none that could be called absolutely bad. Douglas Jerrold seemed to me the best, the oddity of his appearance greatly helping him; he played Stephen the Cull, Forster as Kitely, and Dickens as Captain Bobadil, were much on a par; but Forster preserved his identity, even through his loftiest flights of Macreadyism; while poor little Dickens, all painted in black and red, and affecting the voice of a man of six feet, would have been unrecognisable to the mother that bore him! On the whole, to get up the smallest interest in the thing, one needed to be always reminding oneself: "all these actors were once men!" [1] and will be men again tomorrow morning. The greatest wonder for me was how they had contrived to get together some six or seven hundred ladies and gentlemen (judging from the clothes) at this season of the year: and all utterly unknown to me, except some half-dozen.

So long as I kept my seat in the dress circle I recognised only Mrs. Macready (in one of the four private boxes), and in my nearer neighbourhood

[1] Speech of a very young Wedgwood at a Woolwich review: "Ah, papa, all these soldiers were once men." (Carlyle's note.)

Sir Alexander and Lady Gordon. But in the interval betwixt the play and the farce I took a notion to make my way to Mrs. Macready. John, of course, declared the thing "clearly impossible, no use trying it"; but a servant of the theatre, overhearing our debate, politely offered to escort me where I wished; and then John, having no longer any difficulties to surmount, followed, to have his share in what advantages might accrue from the change. Passing through a long dim passage, I came on a tall man leant to the wall, with his head touching the ceiling like a caryatid, to all appearance asleep, or resolutely trying it under the most unfavourable circumstances. "Alfred Tennyson!" I exclaimed in joyful surprise. "Well!" said he, taking the hand I held out to him, and forgetting to let it go again. "I did not know you were in town," said I. "I should like to know who you are," said he; "I know that I know you, but I cannot tell your name." And I had actually to name myself to him. Then he woke up in good earnest, and said he had been meaning to come to Chelsea. "But Carlyle is in Scotland," I told him with humility. "So I heard from Spedding already, but I asked Spedding, would he go with me to see Mrs. Carlyle? and he said he would." I told him if he really meant to come, he had better not wait for backing, under the present circumstances; and then pursued my way back to the Macreadys' box; where I was received by William (whom I had not divined) with a "Gracious heavens!" and spontaneous dramatic start, which made me all but answer, "Gracious heavens!" and start dramatically in my turn. And then I was kissed all round by his women; and poor Nell Gwyn, Mrs. G—— seemed almost pushed by the general enthusiasm on the distracted idea of kissing me also!

They would not let me return to my stupid place, but put in a third chair for me in front of their box; "and the latter end of that woman was better than the beginning." Macready was in perfect ecstasies over the "Life of Schiller," spoke of it with tears in his eyes. As "a sign of the times," I may mention that in the box opposite sat the Duke of Devonshire, with Payne Collier! Next to us were D'Orsay and "Milady"!

Between eleven and twelve it was all over — and the practical result? Eight-and-sixpence for a fly, and a headache for twenty-fours! I went to bed as wearied as a little woman could be, and dreamt that I was plunging through a quagmire seeking some herbs which were to save the life of Mrs. Maurice; and that Maurice was waiting at home for them in an agony of impatience, while I could not get out of the mud-water.

Craik arrived next evening (Sunday), to make his compliments. Helen had gone to visit numbers,[1] John was smoking in the kitchen. I was lying on the sofa, headachey, leaving Craik to put himself to the chief expenditure of wind, when a cab drove up. Mr. Strachey? No. Alfred Tennyson alone! Actually, by a superhuman effort of volition he had put himself into a cab, nay, brought himself away from a dinner party, and was there to smoke and talk with me! — by myself — me! But no such blessedness was in store for him. Craik prosed, and John babbled for his entertainment; and I, whom he had come to see, got scarcely any speech with him. The exertion, how-

---

[1] No. 5, or the like, denoting maid-servants there. (Carlyle's note.)

ever, of having to provide him with tea, through my own unassisted ingenuity (Helen being gone for the evening) drove away my headache; also perhaps a little feminine vanity at having inspired such a man with the energy to take a cab on his own responsibility, and to throw himself on providence for getting away again! He stayed till eleven, Craik sitting him out, as he sat out Lady H——, and would sit out the Virgin Mary should he find her here.

What with these unfortunate mattresses (a work of necessity) and other processes equally indispensable, I have my hands full, and feel "worried," which is worse. I fancy my earthquake begins to "come it rather strong" for John's comfort and ease, but I cannot help that; if I do not get on with my work, such as it is, what am I here for? — Yours,

                                                                      J. C.

CHARLES LAMB

To PARAPHRASE Isaak Walton's famous remark about God and strawberries, doubtless better letters than Charles Lamb's (1775–1834) could have been written, but doubtless they never were. Like his essays (notably the *Essays of Elia*, first collected in 1823), and much else that he wrote, Lamb's letters are charged with candid revelation of himself and with the gentle humor and irony that dominated his spirit despite his unhappy domestic problems. His friendship with Coleridge began when both were students at Christ's Hospital (see "Recollections of Christ's Hospital" and "Christ's Hospital Five and Thirty Years Ago" in *Elia*) and endured, but for one brief misunderstanding, till the end. The letters to Thomas Manning, a mathematician of Caius College, who went to China in 1806, are among the best. The most complete edition of Lamb's correspondence (first published by Talfourd in 1834) is edited by E. V. Lucas.

LONDON, *September* 24, 1802

MY DEAR MANNING, — Since the date of my last letter I have been a traveller. A strong desire seized me of visiting remote regions. My first impulse was to go and see Paris. It was a trivial objection to my aspiring mind, that I did not understand a word of the language, since I certainly intend some time in my life to see Paris, and equally certainly never intend to learn the language; therefore that could be no objection. However, I am very glad I did not go, because you had left Paris (I see) before I could have set out. I believe, Stoddart promising to go with me another year prevented that plan. My next scheme (for to my restless, ambitious mind London was become a bed of thorns) was to visit the far-famed Peak in Derbyshire, where the Devil sits, they say, without breeches. *This* my purer mind rejected as indelicate. And my final resolve was a tour to the Lakes. I set out with Mary to Keswick, without giving Coleridge any notice; for my time being precious did not admit of it. He received us with all the hospitality in the world, and gave up his time to show us all the wonders of the country. He dwells upon a small hill by the side of Keswick, in a comfortable house, quite enveloped on all sides by a net of mountains: great floundering bears and monsters they seemed, all couchant and asleep. We got in in the evening, travelling in a post-chaise from Penrith, in the midst of a gorgeous sunshine, which transmuted all the mountains into colours, purple, etc. etc. We thought we had got into fairyland. But that went off (as it never came again — while we stayed we had no more fine sunsets); and we entered Coleridge's comfortable study just in the dusk, when the mountains were all dark with clouds upon their heads. Such an impression I never received from objects of sight before, nor do I suppose I can ever again. Glorious creatures, fine old fellows, Skiddaw, etc. I never shall forget ye, how ye lay about that night, like an entrenchment; gone to bed, as it seemed for the night, but promising that ye were to be seen in the morning. Coleridge had got a blazing fire in his study; which is a large, antique, ill-shaped room, with an old-fashioned organ, never played upon, big enough for a church, shelves of scattered folios, an Æolian harp, and an old sofa, half-bed, etc. And all looking out upon the last fading view of Skiddaw and his broad-breasted brethren: what a night! Here we stayed three full weeks, in which time I visited Wordsworth's cottage, where we stayed a day or two with the Clarksons (good people and most hospitable, at whose house we tarried one day and night), and saw Lloyd. The Words-worths were gone to Calais. They have since been in London and passed much time with us; he is now gone into Yorkshire to be married. So we have seen Keswick, Grasmere, Ambleside, Ulswater (where the Clarksons live), and a place at the other end of Ulswater — I forget the name — to which we travelled on a very sultry day, over the middle of Helvellyn. We have clambered up to the top of Skiddaw, and I have waded up the bed of Lodore. In fine, I have satisfied myself, that there is such a thing as that which tour-ists call *romantic*, which I very much suspected before: they make such a spluttering about it, and toss their splendid epithets around them, till they give as dim a light as at four o'clock next morning the lamps do after an illumination. Mary was excessively tired, when she got about half-way up Skiddaw, but we came to a cold rill (than which nothing can be imagined more cold, running over cold stones), and with the reinforcement of a draught of cold water she surmounted it most manfully. Oh, its fine black head, and the bleak air atop of it, with a prospect of mountains all about, and about, making you giddy; famous in song and ballad! It was a day that will stand out, like a mountain, I am sure, in my life. But I am returned (I have now been come home near three weeks — I was a month out), and you cannot conceive the degradation I felt at first, from being accustomed to wander free as air among mountains, and bathe in rivers without being controlled by any one, to come home and *work*. I felt very *little*. I had been dreaming I was a very great man. But that is going off, and I find I shall conform in time to that state of life to which it has pleased God to call me. Besides, after all, Fleet-Street and the Strand are better places to live in for good and all than among Skiddaw. Still, I turn back to those great places where I wandered about, participating in their greatness. After all, I could not *live* in Skiddaw. I could spend a year — two, three years — among them, but I must have a prospect of seeing Fleet-Street at the end of that time, or I should mope and pine away, I know. Still, Skiddaw is a fine creature. My habits are changing, I think: *i.e.* from drunk to sober. Whether I shall be happier or not remains to be proved. I shall certainly be more happy in the morning; but whether I shall not sacrifice the fat, and the marrow, and the kidneys, *i.e.*, the night, the glorious care-drowning night, that heals all our wrongs, pours wine into our mortifications, changes the scene from indiffer-ent and flat to bright and brilliant! — O Manning, if I should have formed a diabolical resolution, by the time you come to England, of not admitting any spirituous liquors into my house, will you be my guest, on such shameworthy terms? Is life, with such limitations, worth trying? The truth is, that my liquors bring a nest of friendly harpies about my house, who consume me.

This is a pitiful tale to be read at St. Gothard; but it is just now nearest my heart. Fenwick is a ruined man. He is hiding himself from his creditors, and has sent his wife and children into the country. Fell, my other drunken companion (that has been: *nam hic caestus artemque repono*), is turned editor of a "Naval Chronicle." Godwin (with a pitiful artificial wife) continues a steady friend, though the same facility does not remain of visiting him often. That Bitch has detached Marshall from his house, Marshall the man who went to sleep when the *Ancient Mariner* was reading: the old, steady, unalterable friend of the Professor. Holcroft is not yet come to town. I expect to see him, and will deliver your message. How I hate *this part* of a letter. Things come crowding in to say, and no room for 'em. Some things are too little to be told, *i.e.* to have a preference; some are too big and circumstantial. Thanks for yours, which was most delicious. Would I had been with you, benighted, etc. I fear my head is turned with wandering. I shall never be the same acquiescent being. Farewell; write again quickly, for I shall not like to hazard a letter, not knowing where the fates have carried you. Farewell, my dear fellow.

C. LAMB

January 2, 1810

Mary sends her love.

DEAR MANNING, — When I last wrote to you, I was in lodgings. I am now in chambers, No. 4, Inner Temple Lane, where I should be happy to see you any evening. Bring any of your friends, the Mandarins, with you. I have two sitting-rooms: I call them so *par excellence*, for you may stand, or loll, or lean, or try any posture in them; but they are best for sitting; not squatting down Japanese fashion, but the more decorous use of the posteriors which European usage has consecrated. I have two of these rooms on the third floor, and five sleeping, cooking, etc., rooms, on the fourth floor. In my best room is a choice collection of the works of Hogarth, an English painter of some humour. In my next best are shelves containing a small but well-chosen library. My best room commands a court, in which there are trees and a pump, the water of which is excellent — cold with brandy, and not very insipid without. Here I hope to set up my rest, and not quit till Mr. Powell, the undertaker, gives me notice that I may have possession of my last lodging. He lets lodgings for single gentlemen. I sent you a parcel of books by my last, to give you some idea of the state of European literature. There comes with this two volumes, done up as letters, of minor poetry, a sequel to *Mrs. Leicester:* the best you may suppose mine; the next best are my coadjutor's; you may amuse yourself in guessing them out; but I must tell you mine are but one-third in quantity of the whole. So much for a very delicate subject. It is hard to speak of one's self, etc. Holcroft had finished his life when I wrote to you, and Hazlitt has since finished his life — I do not mean his own life, but he has finished a life of Holcroft, which is going to press. Tuthill is Dr. Tuthill. I continue Mr. Lamb. I have published a little book for children on titles of honour: and to give them some idea of the difference of rank and gradual rising, I have made a little scale, supposing myself to receive the following various accessions of dignity from the king, who is the fountain of honour — As at first, 1, Mr. C. Lamb; 2, C. Lamb, Esq.; 3, Sir C. Lamb, Bart.; 4, Baron Lamb of Stamford;[1] 5, Viscount Lamb; 6, Earl Lamb; 7, Marquis Lamb; 8, Duke Lamb. It would look like quibbling to carry it on further, and especially as it is not necessary for children to go beyond the ordinary titles of sub-regal dignity in our own country, otherwise I have sometimes in my dreams imagined myself still advancing, as 9th, King Lamb; 10th, Emperor Lamb; 11th, Pope Innocent, higher than which is nothing but the Lamb of God. Puns I have not made many (nor punch much), since the date of my last; one I cannot help relating. A constable in Salisbury Cathedral was telling me that eight people dined at the top of the spire of the cathedral; upon which I remarked, that they must be very sharp-set. But in general I cultivate the reasoning part of my mind more than the imaginative. Do you know Kate*********. I am stuffed out so with eating turkey for dinner, and another turkey for supper yesterday (turkey in Europe and Turkey in Asia), that I can't jog on. It is New-Year here. That is, it was New-Year half a-year back, when I was writing this. Nothing puzzles me more than time and space, and yet nothing puzzles me less, for I never think about them. The Persian ambassador is the principal thing talked of now. I sent some people to see him worship the sun on Primrose Hill at half past six in the morning, 28th November; but he did not come, which makes me think the old fire-worshippers are a sect almost extinct in Persia. Have you trampled on the Cross yet? The Persian ambassador's name is Shaw Ali Mirza. The common people call him Shaw-Nonsense. While I think of it, I have put three letters besides my own three into the Indian post for you, from your brother, sister, and some gentleman whose name I forget. Will they, have they, did they, come safe? The distance you are at, cuts up tenses by the root. I think you said you did not know Kate*********. I express her by nine stars, though she is but one, but if ever one star differed from another in glory ——. You must have seen her at her father's. Try and remember her. Coleridge is bringing out a paper in weekly numbers, called the *Friend*, which I would send, if I could; but the difficulty I had in getting the packets of books out to you before deters me; and you'll want something new to read when you come home. It is chiefly intended to puff off Wordsworth's poetry; but there are some noble things in it by the by. Except Kate, I have had no vision of excellence this year, and she passed by like the queen on her coronation day; you don't know whether you saw her or not. Kate is fifteen; I go about moping, and sing the old pathetic ballad I used to like in my youth —

> "She's sweet Fifteen,
>   I'm one year more."

Mrs. Bland sung it in boy's clothes the first time I heard it. I sometimes think the lower notes in my voice are like Mrs. Bland's. That glorious singer Braham, one of my lights, is fled. He was for a season. He was a

---

[1] Where my family come from. I have chosen that if ever I should have my choice.

rare composition of the Jew, the gentleman, and the angel, yet all these elements mixed up so kindly in him, that you could not tell which predominated; but he is gone, and one Phillips is engaged instead. Kate is vanished, but Miss B****** is always to be met with!

> "Queens drop away, while blue-legg'd Maukin thrives;
> And courtly Mildred dies, while country Madge survives."

That is not my poetry, but Quarles's; but haven't you observed that the rarest things are the least obvious? Don't show anybody the names in this letter. I write confidentially, and wish this letter to be considered *private*. Hazlitt has written a *grammar* for Godwin; Godwin sells it bound up with a treatise of his own on language, but the *grey mare is the better horse*. I don't allude to Mrs. Godwin, but to the word *grammar*, which comes near to *grey mare*, if you observe, in sound. The figure is called paranomasia in Greek. I am sometimes happy in it. An old woman begged of me for charity. "Ah! sir," said she, "I have seen better days"; "So have I, good woman," I replied; but I meant literally, days not so rainy and overcast as that on which she begged! she meant more prosperous days. Dr. Dawe is made associate of the Royal Academy. By what law of association I can't guess. Mrs. Holcroft, Miss Holcroft, Mr. and Mrs. Godwin, Mr. and Mrs. Hazlitt, Mrs. Martin and Louisa, Mrs. Lum, Capt. Burney, Mrs. Burney, Martin Burney, Mr. Rickman, Mrs. Rickman, Dr. Stoddart, William Dollin, Mr. Thompson, Mr. and Mrs. Norris, Mr. Fenwick, Mrs. Fenwick, Miss Fenwick, a man that saw you at our house one day, and a lady that heard me speak of you; Mrs. Buffam that heard Hazlitt mention you, Dr. Tuthill, Mrs. Tuthill, Colonel Harwood, Mrs. Harwood, Mr. Collier, Mrs. Collier, Mr. Sutton, Nurse, Mr. Fell, Mrs. Fell, Mr. Marshall, are very well, and occasionally inquire after you.

WILLIAM VAUGHN MOODY

WILLIAM VAUGHN MOODY (1869–1910) was hailed as the leader of American poetry in the first decade of the present century. His untimely death in his forty-second year left the promise of a greater future unfulfilled. Born in the Middle West, he returned thither after his graduation from Harvard to teach in the newly founded University of Chicago. His letters to friends in Cambridge reveal a certain nostalgia for the established civilization he had left, and at the same time a sense of the inspiration of Chicago's imperfect and struggling culture. They remain a striking revelation of personality in a charmingly intimate form. His poetry and prose dramas are published in two volumes, and a selection from the poetry is included in the Riverside Literature Series. *Some Letters of William Vaughn Moody*, edited by Daniel Gregory Mason, from which the present selections are taken, appeared in 1913; *Letters to Harriet*, edited by Percy MacKaye, appeared in 1936.

To MARY L. MASON *

CHICAGO, *Jan.* 11, 1896

MY DEAR MRS. MASON,

I have postponed writing because I suspected you would rather have a letter written composedly out of a rising desire for talk or its substitute, than a hurried note setting forth with a prim gasp that I had got here with no broken bones. I have not quite got accustomed to the raw bite of things again, after humoring my skin with the delicate eastern impingements. Indeed I have been since getting back as helpless a victim to the blue devils as it is my temperament ever to be. The gross result of the life one can lead in a place like this is satisfactory enough, but the net result, the fine slow-oozing crystal distillation, is tragically small — and I fancy that for such as I the unsublimated mass must always keep a disheartening suggestion. The enervating thing about the place is its shallow kindness. People are so eager to give you credit for virtues that you do not possess that you feel ashamed to put forth those that are yours. Then when you do take heart of grace, and do or say or think a really good thing, and win the facile applause, you have a bad taste in the mouth to think that any jigster's trick would have won you the same magnificent triumph. I sigh, like the ancient worthy, for a stern friend, one who will not be gulled by any thimble-rig sophistry, who will puncture with sweet skepticism my little soap-bubble eloquences, and by so doing give me heart to try and be wise. I recognize of course that the wish is a weak one, that I ought to be my own detective, gendarme, judge, and hangman; and I have made some flabby efforts to execute these functions upon myself, but so far with indifferent success. Do you think a wife would do any good? I have cast appalled glances at that ultimate rigor of self-discipline, but my eyes have been blest by no reassuring light. Some-

* By permission of Daniel Gregory Mason and Houghton Mifflin Company.

thing I must have to key life up, to give it musical pitch and the knit coherence of music. If I were free I could get all that out of my little gift and great passion for the poet's craft, but hampered as I am by intellectual drudgery that is only one burden more, and adds the last note of poignancy to the tedium of the days. I have lately thought with envy amounting to wickedness of D——'s complete service of the thing that seems to him real under the sun: if he were not so dear, I could find it in my heart to hate him cordially for it.

Another thing that afflicts my soul is the delicate strange light that lies over a certain hill called Milton, at the rising of the sun and the going down thereof, and the tentative fluttering talk of a girl who is destined to tread much in the lonely places of life and suffer much. Fortunately, there is there too the talk of a brave woman who sees life clearly and sees it whole, and whose verdict is, I am sure, that in spite of suffering and lonely places it is worth while.

I have not been able to get the edition of Keats's letters that I wanted you to see; I hope you will like the little picture which I send instead.

Faithfully yours,
WILLIAM VAUGHN MOODY

To DANIEL GREGORY MASON

CHICAGO, Feb. 16, 1896

DEAR DAN:

I have just heard from your sister-in-law of your enforced furlough. I am not going to help you curse your luck, knowing your native capabilities in that direction to be perfectly adequate, but my Methodist training urges me to give you an epistolary hand-grasp, the purport of which is "*Keep your sand.*" I could say other things, not utterly pharisaical. I could say what I have often said to myself, with a rather reedy tremolo perhaps, but swelling sometimes into a respectable diapason. "The dark cellar ripens the wine." And meanwhile, after one's eyes get used to the dirty light, and one's feet to the mildew, a cellar has its compensations. I have found beetles of the most interesting proclivities, mice altogether comradely and persuadable; and forgotten potatoes that sprouted toward the crack of sunshine with a wan maiden grace not seen above. I don't want to pose as resourceful, but I have seen what I have seen.

The metaphor is however happily inexact in your case, with Milton to retire to and Cambridge humming melodiously on the horizon. If you can only throttle your Daemon, or make him forego his leonine admonition "Accomplish," and roar you as any sucking dove the sweet vocable "Be," —— you ought to live. I have got mine trained to that, pardee! and his voice grows not untunable. I pick up shreds of comfort out of this or that one of God's ashbarrels. Yesterday I was skating on a patch of ice in the park, under a poverty-stricken sky flying a pitiful rag of sunset. Some little muckers were guying a slim raw-boned Irish girl of fifteen, who circled and darted under their banter with complete unconcern. She was in the fledgling stage, all legs and arms, tall and adorably awkward, with a huge hat full of rusty feathers, thin skirts tucked up above splindling ankles, and a gay aplomb and swing in the body that was ravishing. We caught hands in midflight, and skated for an hour, almost alone and quite silent, while the rag of sunset rotted to pieces. I have had few sensations in life that I would exchange for the warmth of her hand through the ragged glove, and the pathetic curve of the half-formed breast where the back of my wrist touched her body. I came away mystically shaken and elate. It was thus the angels converse. She was something absolutely authentic, new, and inexpressible, something which only nature could mix for the heart's intoxication, a compound of ragamuffin, pal, mistress, nun, sister, harlequin, outcast, and bird of God — with something else bafflingly suffused, something ridiculous and frail and savage and tender. With a world offering such rencontres, such aery strifes and adventures, who would not live a thousand years stone dumb? I would, for one — until my mood changes and I come to think on the shut lid and granite lip of him who has had done with sunsets and skating, and has turned away his face from all manner of Irish. I am supported by a conviction that at an auction on the steps of the great white Throne, I should bring more in the first mood than the second — by several harps and a stray dulcimer.

I thoroughly envy you your stay at Milton — wrist, Daemon, and all. You must send me a lengthy account of the state of things in Cambridge... If the wrist forbids writing, employ a typewriter of the most fashionable tint — I will pay all expenses and stand the breakage. I stipulate that you shall avoid blonds however, they are fragile.

WILLIAM VAUGHN MOODY

To MRS. C. H. TOY

(CHICAGO, *August* 11, 1896)

As FOR Chicago, I find that it gives me days or at least hours of broad-gauge Whitmanesque enthusiasm, meagrely sprinkled over weeks of tedium. The tedium is not of the acid-bath sort, however. Genuinely, I feel mellower, deeper-lunged, more of a lover of life, than I have ever felt before, and the reason is that I have had long somnolent spaces in which to feel the alchemy of rest. I am writing, not much, but with time enough to listen for the fairy echoes, to turn and taste again, to fix and prefer. I shall never have a lordly shelf-full of books to point to ("Paint my two hundred pictures, some good son!") but if I live out the reasonable span, I think I can hope to have one little one at least, or two maybe, which will be in their way *vocal* from cover to cover. Whether the voice will be one that people will care to hear, matters less to me than it did — perhaps less than it should. Safely stowed in my gum-cell, with my globule of amber honey, I find it easy to forget Leviathan and his egregious spoutings. He begins to seem the least bit comical, Leviathan, from the gum-cell outlook. The fact that we and our cell could hang unobserved on one of his eyelashes, doesn't negate our importance in the least...

SAMUEL JOHNSON

WRITING at a time when a rich and influential patron seemed necessary to literary success, Samuel Johnson (1709-1784) in 1747 addressed to Lord Chesterfield the "Plan" of his Dictionary. The noble lord, however, failed to respond until, on the launching of that great work, he wrote two papers praising it in the "World." This belated favor Johnson rejected with characteristic dignity and directness in one of the most famous letters ever penned. The incident is told at length in Boswell's classic *Life of Samuel Johnson*, published in 1791.

TO THE RIGHT HONOURABLE THE EARL OF CHESTERFIELD

February 7, 1755

My Lord,

I have been lately informed, by the proprietor of the World, that two papers, in which my Dictionary is recommended to the publick, were written by your Lordship. To be so distinguished, is an honour, which, being very little accustomed to favours from the great, I know not well how to receive, or in what terms to acknowledge.

When, upon some slight encouragement, I first visited your Lordship, I was overpowered, like the rest of mankind, by the enchantment of your address, and could not forbear to wish that I might boast myself *Le vainqueur du vainqueur de la terre;* — that I might obtain that regard for which I saw the world contending; but I found my attendance so little encouraged, that neither pride nor modesty would suffer me to continue it. When I had once addressed your Lordship in publick, I had exhausted all the art of pleasing which a retired and uncourtly scholar can possess. I had done all that I could; and no man is well pleased to have his all neglected, be it ever so little.

Seven years, my Lord, have now past, since I waited in your outward rooms, or was repulsed from your door; during which time I have been pushing on my work through difficulties, of which it is useless to complain, and have brought it, at last, to the verge of publication, without one act of assistance, one word of encouragement, or one smile of favour. Such treatment I did not expect, for I never had a Patron before.

The shepherd in Virgil grew at last acquainted with Love, and found him a native of the rocks.

Is not a Patron, my Lord, one who looks with unconcern on a man struggling for life in the water, and when he has reached ground, encumbers him with help? The notice which you have been pleased to take of my labours, had it been early, had been kind; but it has been delayed till I am indifferent, and cannot enjoy it; till I am solitary, and cannot impart it; till I am known, and do not want it. I hope it is no very cynical asperity, not to confess obligations where no benefit has been received, or to be unwilling that the

Publick should consider me as owing that to a Patron, which Providence has enabled me to do for myself.

Having carried on my work thus far with so little obligation to any favourer of learning, I shall not be disappointed though I should conclude it, if less be possible, with less; for I have been long wakened from that dream of hope, in which I once boasted myself with so much exultation,

My Lord,
Your Lordship's most humble
Most obedient servant,
SAM. JOHNSON

ABRAHAM LINCOLN

"WHEN I came of age," wrote Lincoln, "I did not know much." Yet the unschooled Kentuckian became not only one of America's greatest political figures, but one of the world's masters of English prose. How he achieved his matchless simplicity, his compression, his clarity, and the forceful movement of his sentences is one of the mysteries of literature. These qualities are nowhere more clearly seen than in his celebrated answer to Horace Greeley, owner and editor of the New York *Tribune*, who in an "Open Letter" under the title of "A Prayer of Twenty Millions" complained that the administration's stand on slavery was indecisive. Lincoln influenced public opinion in the following reply.

EXECUTIVE MANSION
WASHINGTON, *August* 22, 1862

HON. HORACE GREELEY

DEAR SIR: — I have just read yours of the 19th, addressed to myself through the New York *Tribune*. If there be in it any statements of assumptions of fact which I may know to be erroneous, I do not, now and here, controvert them. If there be in it any inferences which I may believe to be falsely drawn, I do not, now here, argue against them. If there be perceptible in it an impatient and dictatorial tone, I waive it in deference to an old friend, whose heart I have always supposed to be right.

As to the policy I "seem to be pursuing," as you say, I have not meant to leave anyone in doubt.

I would save the Union. I would save it the shortest way under the Constitution. The sooner the national authority can be restored, the nearer the Union will be "the Union as it was." If there be those who would not save the Union unless they could at the same time save slavery, I do not agree with them. If there be those who would not save the Union unless they could at the same time destroy slavery, I do not agree with them. My paramount object in this struggle is to save the Union, and is not either to save or to destroy slavery. If I could save the Union without freeing any slave, I would do it; and if I could save it by freeing all the slaves, I would do it; and if I could save it by freeing some and leaving others alone, I would also do that. What I do about slavery and the colored race, I do because I believe it helps to save the Union; and what I forbear, I forbear because I do not believe it would help to save the Union. I shall do less whenever I shall believe what I am doing hurts the cause; and I shall do more whenever I shall believe doing more will help the cause. I shall try to correct errors when shown to be errors, and I shall adopt new views so fast as they shall appear to be true views. I have here stated my purpose according to my view of official duty, and I intend no modification of my oft-expressed personal wish that all men, everywhere, could be free.

Yours,

A. LINCOLN

TRAVEL

Travel is a special type of personal experience which may take the form of simple narrative or be so amplified that it passes over into the essay of interpretation. The earliest accounts of travel were in connection with exploration, or with voyages like Marco Polo's into lands already civilized but hitherto unknown to the traveler's countrymen. Such travel is apt to be prompted by simple romanticism, a hunger for the new and strange, a thirst for adventure. And its literary fruit will satisfy a more passive form of that same hunger and thirst. It may at the same time be highly informative.

Of this type is Major Powell's report to the Smithsonian Institution of the first journey by white men through the Grand Canyon. The same quality which prompts a man to make such an expedition is a great factor in the success with which he describes it; namely, his vivid and undeviating interest in what he encounters. He offers us, not his comments on what he saw and did, but the experience itself as it unfolds before him and his men. The reader's interest is also fixed on the things described and the hazards overcome rather than on the personality which relays them or the manner in which it is done.

A country need not be unexplored, however, in order to provide excellent material to the traveling author. In a sense the author writes always as an explorer, since his chief qualification is the ability to see even the familiar with new eyes. Many simple accounts of travel are written about countries that are slightly, or even well known. A large part of such writing is scenic description. The success of such descriptive writing is peculiarly dependent upon the poetic qualities of the language — the rhythm, the richness of association and expressiveness through sound of the words employed. Scenic description has played a large role in fiction and the essay as well as in the literature of travel, and has varied both in manner and in popularity from time to time. In the Victorian Age, a love of Nature bore an almost moral sanction, and hence the writing of that period abounds in protracted descriptions.

A simple account of travel may deal with new peoples and customs rather than new lands. This is the type of Marco Polo, who describes with such zest the alien ways of life he beholds. But the interest may become more complicated, more sophisticated. It may find in foreign sights a stimulus to reflection, pricked on by comparison with the familiar. It may adopt an evaluative, even a moralistic tone, praising or condemning either the novel or the accustomed in contrast with the other. It may have a historical, a philosophical, a political or sociological tinge, or be chiefly aesthetic.

Obviously the appeal of such writing springs only in part from the material observed, depending largely upon what the author personally can offer in terms of background, of perspective, of intellectual or aesthetic power, and at least in the last instance, of native charm. Mr. Chase's view of Mexico, for example, is determined and enriched by his viewpoint as an economist. Thoroughly sensitive to the glamour of the scene and the exotic culture, he finds in it not only enjoyment of its novelty and beauty, but also material to test and to develop his theories of society.

Among the accounts of travel which communicate the excitement of adventure into unknown or little known places are Kinglake's *Eothen*, Doughty's *Arabia Deserta*, Stanley's *How I Found Livingstone* and *In Darkest Africa*. As the remote places of the earth have become better known, the literature of travel has tended more and more to the reflective rather than the simple narrative type. In the latter manner are Lafcadio Hearn's *Two Years in the French West Indies*, D. H. Lawrence's *Sea and Sardinia* and *Mornings in Mexico*, Aldous Huxley's *Jesting Pilate* and *Along the Road*, Havelock Ellis's *The Soul of Spain*.

JOHN WESLEY POWELL

THE son of English parents, Major Powell (1834–1902) studied at Illinois and Oberlin, and at the outbreak of the Civil War joined the Union Army as a private. He lost his right arm at the battle of Shiloh, but continued in active service to the close of the war. In 1865 he became professor of geology and curator of the museum in Illinois Wesleyan University. In 1867 he went on exploring expeditions to the Rockies and to the canyons of the Green and Colorado rivers. In 1869 he made his daring three months' journey in small boats through the unexplored river channel of the Grand Canyon, perhaps the most famous geological journey in American history. His findings led to the establishment of the United States Geological Survey of the Rocky Mountain region, later a part of the United States Geological Survey, of which Powell became director in 1881. The account from which this excerpt is taken is a classic in geological literature, and was originally published in a government report as *Explorations of the Colorado River of the West*.

CHAPTER VIII

THE GRAND CAÑON OF THE COLORADO

AUGUST 13. — We are now ready to start on our way down the Great Unknown. Our boats, tied to a common stake, are chafing each other, as they are tossed by the fretful river. They ride high and buoyant, for their loads are lighter than we could desire. We have but a month's rations remaining. The flour has been resifted through the mosquito net sieve; the spoiled bacon has been dried, and the worst of it boiled; the few pounds of dried apples have been spread in the sun, and reshrunken to their normal bulk; the sugar has all melted, and gone on its way down the river; but we have a large sack of coffee. The lighting of the boats has this advantage: they will ride the waves better, and we shall have but little to carry when we make a portage.

We are three-quarters of a mile in the depths of the earth, and the great river shrinks into insignificance, as it dashes its angry waves against the walls and cliffs, that rise to the world above; they are but puny ripples, and we but pigmies, running up and down the sands, or lost among the boulders.

We have an unknown distance yet to run; an unknown river yet to explore. What falls there are, we know not; what rocks beset the channel, we know not; what walls rise over the river, we know not. Ah, well! we may conjecture many things. The men talk as cheerfully as ever; jests are bandied about freely this morning; but to me the cheer is somber and the jests are ghastly.

With some eagerness, and some anxiety, and some misgiving, we enter the cañon below, and are carried along by the swift water through walls which rise from its very edge. They have the same structure as we noticed yesterday — tiers of irregular shelves below, and, above these, steep slopes to the foot of marble cliffs. We run six miles in a little more than half an hour, and emerge into a more open portion of the cañon, where high hills and ledges of rock intervene between the river and the distant walls. Just at the head of this open place the river runs across a dike; that is, a fissure in the rocks, open to depths below, has been filled with eruptive matter, and this, on cooling, was harder than the rocks through which the crevice was made, and, when these were washed away, the harder volcanic matter remained as a wall, and the river has cut a gate-way through it several hundred feet high, and as many wide. As it crosses the wall, there is a fall below, and a bad rapid, filled with boulders of trap; so we stop to make a portage. Then on we go, gliding by hills and ledges, with distant walls in view; sweeping past sharp angles of rock; stopping at a few points to examine rapids, which we find can be run, until we have made another five miles, when we land for dinner.

Then we let down with lines, over a long rapid, and start again. Once more the walls close in, and we find ourselves in a narrow gorge, the water again filling the channel, and very swift. With great care, and constant watchfulness, we proceed, making about four miles this afternoon, and camp in a cave.

August 14. — At daybreak we walk down the bank of the river, on a little sandy beach, to take a view of a new feature in the cañon. Heretofore, hard rocks have given us bad river; soft rocks, smooth water; and a series of rocks harder than any we have experienced sets in. The river enters the granite![1]

We can see but a little way into the granite gorge, but it looks threatening.

After breakfast we enter on the waves. At the very introduction, it inspires awe. The cañon is narrower than we have ever before seen it; the water is swifter; there are but few broken rocks in the channel; but the walls are set, on either side, with pinnacles and crags; and sharp, angular buttresses, bristling with wind and wave polished spires, extend far out into the river.

Ledges of rocks jut into the stream, their tops sometimes just below the surface, sometimes rising few or many feet above; and island ledges, and island pinnacles, and island towers break the swift course of the stream into chutes, and eddies, and whirlpools. We soon reach a place where a creek comes in from the left, and just below, the channel is choked with boulders, which have washed down this lateral cañon and formed a dam, over which there is a fall of thirty or forty feet; but on the boulders we can get foothold, and we make a portage.

Three more such dams are found. Over one we make a portage; at the other two we find chutes, through which we can run.

As we proceed, the granite rises higher, until nearly a thousand feet of the lower part of the walls are composed of this rock.

About eleven o'clock we hear a great roar ahead, and approach it very cautiously. The sound grows louder and louder as we run, and at last we

---

[1] Geologists would call these rocks metamorphic crystalline schists, with dikes and beds of granite, but we will use the popular name for the whole series — granite. — [Powell's note.]

find ourselves above a long, broken fall, with ledges and pinnacles of rock obstructing the river. There is a descent of, perhaps, seventy-five or eighty feet in a third of a mile, and the rushing waters break into great waves on the rocks, and lash themselves into a mad, white foam. We can land just above, but there is no foothold on either side by which we can make a port-age. It is nearly a thousand feet to the top of the granite, so it will be impossible to carry our boats around, though we can climb to the summit up a side gulch, and, passing along a mile or two, can descend to the river. This we find on examination; but such a portage would be impracticable for us, and we must run the rapid, or abandon the river. There is no hesitation. We step into our boats, push off and away we go, first on smooth but swift water, then we strike a glassy wave, and ride to its top, down again into the trough, up again on a higher wave, and down and up on waves higher and still higher, until we strike one just as it curls back, and a breaker rolls over our little boat. Still, on we speed, shooting past projecting rocks, till the little boat is caught in a whirlpool, and spun around several times. At last we pull out again into the stream, and now the other boats have passed us. The open compartment of the *Emma Dean* is filled with water, and every breaker rolls over us. Hurled back from a rock, now on this side, now on that, we are carried into an eddy, in which we struggle for a few minutes, and are then out again, the breakers still rolling over us. Our boat is unmanageable, but she cannot sink, and we drift down another hundred yards, through breakers; how, we scarcely know. We find the other boats have turned into an eddy at the foot of the fall, and are waiting to catch us as we come, for the men have seen that our boat is swamped. They push out as we come near, and pull us in against the wall. We bail our boat, and on we go again.

The walls, now, are more than a mile in height — a vertical distance difficult to appreciate. Stand on the south steps of the Treasury building in Washington, and look down Pennsylvania Avenue to the Capitol Park, and measure this distance overhead, and imagine cliffs to extend to that altitude, and you will understand what I mean; or, stand at Canal Street, in New York, and look up Broadway to Grace Church, and you have about the distance; or, stand at Lake Street bridge, in Chicago, and look down to the Central Depot, and you have it again.

A thousand feet of this is up through granite crags, then steep slopes and perpendicular cliffs rise, one above another, to the summit. The gorge is black and narrow below, red and gray and flaring above, with crags and angular projections on the walls, which, cut in many places by side cañons, seem to be a vast wilderness of rocks. Down in these grand, gloomy depths we glide, ever listening, for the mad waters keep up their roar; ever watching, ever peering ahead, for the narrow cañon is winding, and the river is closed in so that we can see but a few hundred yards, and what there may be below we know not; but we listen for falls, and watch for rocks, or stop now and then, in the bay of a recess, to admire the gigantic scenery. And ever, as we go, there is some new pinnacle or tower, some crag or peak, some distant view of the upper plateau, some strange shaped rock, or some deep, narrow side cañon. Then we come to another broken fall, which appears more difficult than the one we ran this morning.

A small creek comes in on the right, and the first fall of the water is over boulders, which have been carried down by this lateral stream. We land at its mouth, and stop for an hour or two to examine the fall. It seems possible to let down with lines, at least a part of the way, from point to point, along the right hand wall. So we make a portage over the first rocks, and find footing on some boulders below. Then we let down one of the boats to the end of her line, when she reaches a corner of the projecting rock, to which one of the men clings, and steadies her, while I examine an eddy below. I think we can pass the other boats down by us, and catch them in the eddy. This is soon done and the men in the boats in the eddy pull us to their side. On the shore of this little eddy there is about two feet of gravel beach above the water. Standing on this beach, some of the men take the line of the little boat and let it drift down against another projecting angle. Here is a little shelf, on which a man from my boat climbs, and a shorter line is passed to him, and he fastens the boat to the side of the cliff. Then the second one is let down, bringing the line of the third. When the second boat is tied up, the two men standing on the beach above spring into the last boat, which is pulled up alongside of ours. Then we let down the boats, for twenty-five or thirty yards, by walking along the shelf, landing them again in the mouth of a side cañon. Just below this there is another pile of boulders, over which we make another portage. From the foot of these rocks we can climb to another shelf, forty or fifty feet above the water.

On this beach we camp for the night. We find a few sticks, which have lodged in the rocks. It is raining hard, and we have no shelter, but kindle a fire and have our supper. We sit on the rocks all night, wrapped in our ponchos, getting what sleep we can.

August 15. — This morning we find we can let down for three or four hundred yards, and it is managed in this way: We pass along the wall, by climbing from projecting point to point, sometimes near the water's edge, at other places fifty or sixty feet above, and hold the boat with a line, while two men remain aboard, and prevent her from being dashed against the rocks, and keep the line from getting caught on the wall. In two hours we have brought them all down, as far as it is possible, in this way. A few yards below, the river strikes with great violence against a projecting rock, and our boats are pulled up in a little bay above. We must now manage to pull out of this, and clear the point below. The little boat is held by the bow obliquely up the stream. We jump in, and pull out only a few strokes, and sweep clear of the dangerous rock. The other boats follow in the same manner, and the rapid is passed.

It is not easy to describe the labor of such navigation. We must prevent the waves from dashing the boats against the cliffs. Sometimes, where the river is swift, we must put a bight of rope about a rock, to prevent her being snatched from us by a wave; but where the plunge is too great, or the chute too swift, we must let her leap, and catch her below, or the undertow will drag her under the falling water, and she sinks. Where we wish to run her out a little way from shore, through a channel between rocks, we first throw in little sticks of drift wood, and watch their course, to see where we must steer, so that she will pass the channel in safety. And so we hold, and let go, and pull, and lift, and ward, among rocks, around rocks, and over rocks.

And now we go on through this solemn, mysterious way. The river is very deep, the cañon very narrow, and still obstructed, so that there is no steady flow of the stream; but the waters wheel, and roll, and boil, and we are scarcely able to determine where we can go. Now, the boat is carried to the right, perhaps close to the wall; again, she is shot into the stream, and perhaps is dragged over to the other side, where, caught in a whirlpool, she spins about. We can neither land nor run as we please. The boats are entirely unmanageable; no order in their running can be preserved; now one, now another, is ahead, each crew laboring for its own preservation. In such a place we come to another rapid. Two of the boats run it perforce. One succeeds in landing, but there is no foothold by which to make a portage, and she is pushed out again into the stream. The next minute a great reflex wave fills the open compartment; she is water-logged, and drifts unmanageable. Breaker after breaker rolls over her, and one capsizes her. The men are thrown out; but they cling to the boat, and she drifts down some distance, alongside of us, and we are able to catch her. She is soon bailed out, and the men are aboard once more; but the oars are lost, so a pair from the *Emma Dean* is spared. Then for two miles we find smooth water.

Clouds are playing in the cañon today. Sometimes they roll down in great masses, filling the gorge with gloom; sometimes they hang above, from wall to wall, and cover the cañon with a roof of impending storm; and we can peer long distances up and down this cañon corridor, with its cloud roof overhead, its walls of black granite, and its river bright with the sheen of broken waters. Then, a gust of wind sweeps down a side gulch, and, making a rift in the clouds, reveals the blue heavens, and a stream of sunlight pours in. Then, the clouds drift away into the distance, and hang around crags, and peaks, and pinnacles, and towers, and walls, and cover them with a mantle, that lifts from time to time, and sets them all in sharp relief. Then, baby clouds creep out of side cañons, glide around points, and creep back again, into more distant gorges. Then, clouds, set in strata, across the cañon, with intervening vista views, to cliffs and rocks beyond. The clouds are children of the heavens, and when they play among the rocks, they lift them to the region above.

It rains! Rapidly little rills are formed above, and these soon grow into brooks, and the brooks grow into creeks, and tumble over the walls in innumerable cascades, adding their wild music to the roar of the river. When the rain ceases, the rills, brooks, and creeks run dry. The waters that fall, during a rain, on these steep rocks, are gathered at once into the river; they could scarcely be poured in more suddenly, if some vast spout ran from the clouds to the stream itself. When a storm bursts over the cañon, a side gulch is dangerous, for a sudden flood may come, and the inpouring waters will raise the river, so as to hide the rocks before your eyes.

Early in the afternoon, we discover a stream, entering from the north, a clear, beautiful creek, coming down through a gorgeous red cañon. We land, and camp on a sand beach, above its mouth, under a great, over-spreading tree, with willow shaped leaves.

August 16. — We must dry our rations again today, and make oars.

The Colorado is never a clear stream, but for the past three or four days it has been raining much of the time, and the floods, which are poured over the walls, have brought down great quantities of mud, making it exceedingly turbid now. The little affluent, which we have discovered here, is a clear, beautiful creek, or river, as it would be termed in this western country, where streams are not abundant. We have named one stream, away above, in honor of the great chief of the "Bad Angels," and, as this is in beautiful contrast to that, we conclude to name it "Bright Angel."

Early in the morning, the whole party starts up to explore the Bright Angel River, with the special purpose of seeking timber, from which to make oars. A couple of miles above, we find a large pine log, which has been floated down from the plateau, probably from an altitude of more than six thousand feet, but not many miles back. On its way, it must have passed over many cataracts and falls, for it bears scars in evidence of the rough usage which it has received. The men roll it on skids, and the work of sawing oars is commenced.

This stream heads away back, under a line of abrupt cliffs, that terminates the plateau, and tumbles down more than four thousand feet in the first mile or two of its course; then runs through a deep, narrow cañon, until it reaches the river.

Late in the afternoon I return, and go up a little gulch, just above this creek, about two hundred yards from camp, and discover the ruins of two or three old houses, which were originally of stone, laid in mortar. Only the foundations are left, but irregular blocks, of which the houses were constructed, lie scattered about. In one room I find an old mealing stone, deeply worn, as if it had been much used. A great deal of pottery is strewn around, and old trails, which in some places are deeply worn into the rocks, are seen.

It is ever a source of wonder to us why these ancient people sought such inaccessible places for their homes. They were, doubtless, an agricultural race, but there are no lands here, of any considerable extent, that they could have cultivated. To the west of Oraiby, one of the towns in the "Province of Tusayan," in Northern Arizona, the inhabitants have actually built little terraces along the face of the cliff, where a spring gushes out, and thus made their sites for gardens. It is possible that the ancient inhabitants of this place made their agricultural lands in the same way. But why should they seek such spots? Surely, the country was not so crowded with population as to demand the utilization of so barren a region. The only solution of the problem suggested is this: We know that, for a century or two after the settlement of Mexico, many expeditions were sent into the country now comprised in Arizona and New Mexico, for the purpose of bringing the town building people under the dominion of the Spanish government. Many of their villages were destroyed, and the inhabitants fled to regions at that time unknown; and there are traditions, among the people who inhabit the *pueblos* that still remain, that the cañons were these unknown lands. Maybe these buildings were erected at that time; sure it is that they have a much more modern appearance than the ruins scattered over Nevada, Utah, Colorado, Arizona, and New Mexico. Those old Spanish conquerors had a monstrous greed for gold, and a wonderful lust for saving souls. Treasures they must have; if not on earth, why, then, in heaven; and when they failed to find heathen temples, bedecked with silver, they propitiated Heaven by seizing the heathen themselves. There is yet extant a copy of a record, made by a heathen artist, to express his conception of the demands of the conquerors. In one part of the picture we have a lake, and near by stands a priest pouring water on the head of a native. On the other side, a poor Indian has a cord about his throat. Lines run from these two groups, to a central figure, a man with beard, and full Spanish panoply. The interpretation of the picture writing is this: "Be baptized, as this saved heathen; or be hanged, as that damned heathen." Doubtless, some of these people preferred a third alternative, and, rather than be baptized or hanged, they chose to be imprisoned within these cañon walls.

August 17. — Our rations are still spoiling; the bacon is so badly injured that we are compelled to throw it away. By an accident, this morning, the saleratus is lost overboard. We have now only musty flour sufficient for ten days, a few dried apples, but plenty of coffee. We must make all haste possible. If we meet with difficulties, as we have done in the cañon above, we may be compelled to give up the expedition, and try to reach the Mormon settlements to the north. Our hopes are that the worst places are passed, but our barometers are all so much injured as to be useless, so we have lost our reckoning in altitude, and know not how much descent the river has yet to make.

The stream is still wild and rapid, and rolls through a narrow channel. We make but slow progress, often landing against a wall, and climbing around some point, where we can see the river below. Although very anxious to advance, we are determined to run with great caution, lest, by another accident, we lose all our supplies. How precious that little flour has become! We divide it among the boats, and carefully store it away, so that it can be lost only by the loss of the boat itself.

We make ten miles and a half, and camp among the rocks, on the right. We have had rain, from time to time, all day, and have been thoroughly drenched and chilled; but between showers the sun shines with great power, and the mercury in our thermometers stands at 115°, so that we have rapid changes from great extremes, which are very disagreeable. It is especially cold in the rain tonight. The little canvas we have is rotten and useless; the rubber ponchos, with which we started from Green River City, have all been lost; more than half the party is without hats, and not one of us has an entire suit of clothes, and we have not a blanket apiece. So we gather drift wood, and build a fire; but after supper the rain, coming down in torrents, extinguishes it, and we sit up all night, on the rocks, shivering, and are more exhausted by the night's discomfort than by the day's toil.

August 18. — The day is employed in making portages, and we advance but two miles on our journey. Still it rains.

While the men are at work making portages, I climb up the granite to its summit, and go away back over the rust colored sandstones and greenish yellow shales, to the foot of the marble wall. I climb so high that the men and boats are lost in the black depths below, and the dashing river is a rippling brook; and still there is more cañon above than below. All about me are interesting geological records. The book is open, and I can read as I run. All about me are grand views, for the clouds are playing again in the gorges. But somehow I think of the nine days' rations, and the bad river, and the lesson of the rocks, and the glory of the scene is but half seen.

I push on to an angle, where I hope to get a view of the country beyond, to see, if possible, what the prospect may be of our soon running through this plateau, or, at least, of meeting with some geological change that will let us out of the granite; but, arriving at the point, I can see below only a labyrinth of deep gorges.

August 19. — Rain again this morning. Still we are in our granite prison, and the time is occupied until noon in making a long, bad portage.

After dinner, in running a rapid, the pioneer boat is upset by a wave. We are some distance in advance of the larger boats, the river is rough and swift, and we are unable to land, but cling to the boat, and are carried down stream, over another rapid. The men in the boats above see our trouble, but they are caught in whirlpools, and are spinning about in eddies, and it seems a long time before they come to our relief. At last they do come; our boat is turned right side up, bailed out; the oars, which fortunately have floated along in company with us, are gathered up, and on we go, without even landing.

Soon after the accident the clouds break away, and we have sunshine again.

Soon we find a little beach, with just room enough to land. Here we camp, but there is no wood. Across the river, and a little way above, we see some drift wood lodged in the rocks. So we bring two boat loads over, build a huge fire, and spread everything to dry. It is the first cheerful night we have had for a week; a warm, drying fire in the midst of the camp, and a few bright stars in our patch of heavens overhead.

August 20. — The characteristics of the cañon change this morning. The river is broader, the walls more sloping, and composed of black slates, that stand on edge. These nearly vertical slates are washed out in places — that is, the softer beds are washed out between the harder, which are left standing. In this way, curious little alcoves are formed, in which are quiet bays of water, but on a much smaller scale than the great bays and buttresses of Marble Cañon.

The river is still rapid, and we stop to let down with lines several times, but make greater progress as we run ten miles. We camp on the right bank. Here, on a terrace of trap, we discover another group of ruins. There was evidently quite a village on this rock. Again we find mealing stones, and much broken pottery, and up in a little natural shelf in the rock, back of the ruins, we find a globular basket, that would hold perhaps a third of a bushel.

It is badly broken, and, as I attempt to take it up, it falls to pieces. There are many beautiful flint chips, as if this had been the home of an old arrow maker.

August 21. — We start early this morning, cheered by the prospect of a fine day, and encouraged, also, by the good run made yesterday. A quarter of a mile below camp the river turns abruptly to the left, and between camp and that point is very swift, running down in a long, broken chute, and piling up against the foot of the cliff, where it turns to the left. We try to pull across, so as to go down on the other side, but the waters are swift, and it seems impossible for us to escape the rock below; but, in pulling across, the bow of the boat is turned to the farther shore, so that we are swept broadside down, and are prevented, by the rebounding waters, from striking against the wall. There we toss about for a few seconds in these billows, and are carried past the danger. Below, the river turns again to the right, the cañon is very narrow, and we see in advance but a short distance. The water, too, is very swift, and there is no landing place. From around this curve there comes a mad roar, and down we are carried, with a dizzying velocity, to the head of another rapid. On either side, high over our heads, there are overhanging granite walls, and the sharp bends cut off our view, so that a few minutes will carry us into unknown waters. Away we go, on one long, winding chute. I stand on deck, supporting myself with a strap, fastened on either side to the gunwale, and the boat glides rapidly, where the water is smooth, or, striking a wave, she leaps and bounds like a thing of life, and we have a wild, exhilarating ride for ten miles, which we make in less than an hour. The excitement is so great that we forget the danger, until we hear the roar of the great fall below; then we back on our oars, and are carried slowly toward its head, and succeed in landing just above, and find that we have to make another portage. At this we are engaged until some time after dinner.

Just here we run out of the granite!

Ten miles in less than half a day, and limestone walls below. Good cheer returns; we forget the storms, and the gloom, and cloud covered cañons, and the black granite, and the raging river, and push our boats from shore in great glee.

Though we are out of the granite, the river is still swift, and we wheel about a point again to the right, and turn, so as to head back in the direction from which we came, and see the granite again, with its narrow gorge and black crags; but we meet with no more great falls, or rapids. Still, we run cautiously, and stop, from time to time, to examine some places which look bad. Yet, we make ten miles this afternoon; twenty miles, in all, today.

August 22.— We come to rapids again, this morning, and are occupied several hours in passing them, letting the boats down, from rock to rock, with lines, for nearly half a mile, and then have to make a long portage. While the men are engaged in this, I climb the wall on the northeast, to a height of about two thousand five hundred feet, where I can obtain a good view of a long stretch of cañon below. Its course is to the southwest. The walls seem to rise very abruptly, for two thousand five hundred or three thousand feet, and then there is a gently sloping terrace, on each side, for two or three miles, and again we find cliffs, one thousand five hundred or two thousand feet high. From the brink of these the plateau stretches back to the north and south, for a long distance. Away down the cañon, on the right wall, I can see a group of mountains, some of which appear to stand on the brink of the cañon. The effect of the terrace is to give the appearance of a narrow winding valley, with high walls on either side, and a deep, dark, meandering gorge down its middle. It is impossible, from this point of view, to determine whether we have granite at the bottom, or not; but, from geological considerations, I conclude that we shall have marble walls below.

After my return to the boats, we run another mile, and camp for the night. We have made but little over seven miles today, and a part of our flour has been soaked in the river again.

August 23.— Our way today is again through marble walls. Now and then we pass, for a short distance, through patches of granite, like hills thrust up into the limestone. At one of these places we have to make another portage, and, taking advantage of the delay, I go up a little stream, to the north, wading it all the way, sometimes having to plunge in to my neck; in other places being compelled to swim across little basins that have been excavated at the foot of the falls. Along its course are many cascades and springs gushing out from the rocks on either side. Sometimes a cottonwood tree grows over the water. I come to one beautiful fall, of more than a hundred and fifty feet, and climb around it to the right, on the broken rocks. Still going up, I find the cañon narrowing very much, being but fifteen or twenty feet wide; yet the walls rise on either side many hundreds of feet, perhaps thousands; I can hardly tell.

In some places the stream has not excavated its channel down vertically through the rocks, but has cut obliquely, so that one wall overhangs the other. In other places it is cut vertically above and obliquely below, or obliquely above and vertically below, so that it is impossible to see out overhead. But I can go no farther. The time which I estimated it would take to make the portage has almost expired, and I start back on a round trot, wading in the creek where I must, and plunging through basins, and find the men waiting for me, and away we go on the river.

Just after dinner we pass a stream on the right, which leaps into the Colorado by a direct fall of more than a hundred feet, forming a beautiful cascade. There is a bed of very hard rock above, thirty or forty feet in thickness, and much softer beds below. The hard beds above project many yards beyond the softer, which are washed out, forming a deep cave behind the fall, and the stream pours through a narrow crevice above into a deep pool below. Around on the rocks, in the cave-like chamber, are set beautiful ferns, with delicate fronds and enameled stalks. The little frondlets have their points turned down, to form spore cases. It has very much the appearance of the Maiden's hair fern, but is much larger. This delicate foliage covers the rocks all about the fountain, and gives the chamber great beauty. But we have little time to spend in admiration, so on we go.

We make fine progress this afternoon, carried along by a swift river, and shoot over the rapids, finding no serious obstructions.

The cañon walls, for two thousand five hundred or three thousand feet, are very regular, rising almost perpendicularly, but here and there set with narrow steps, and occasionally we can see away above the broad terrace, to distant cliffs.

We camp tonight in a marble cave, and find, on looking at our reckoning, we have run twenty-two miles.

August 24.— The cañon is wider today. The walls rise to a vertical height of nearly three thousand feet. In many places the river runs under a cliff, in great curves, forming amphitheaters, half-dome shaped.

Though the river is rapid, we meet with no serious obstructions, and run twenty miles. It is curious how anxious we are to make up our reckoning every time we stop, now that our diet is confined to plenty of coffee, very little spoiled flour, and very few dried apples. It has come to be a race for a dinner. Still, we make such fine progress, all hands are in good cheer, but not a moment of daylight is lost.

August 25.— We make twelve miles this morning, when we come to monuments of lava, standing in the river; low rocks, mostly, but some of them shafts more than a hundred feet high. Going on down, three or four miles, we find them increasing in number. Great quantities of cooled lava and many cinder cones are seen on either side; and then we come to an abrupt cataract. Just over the fall, on the right wall, a cinder cone, or extinct volcano, with a well defined crater, stands on the very brink of the cañon. This, doubtless, is the one we saw two or three days ago. From this volcano vast floods of lava have been poured down into the river, and a stream of the molten rock has run up the cañon, three or four miles, and down, we know not how far. Just where it poured over the cañon wall is the fall. The whole north side, as far as we can see, is lined with the black basalt, and high up on the opposite wall are patches of the same material, resting on the benches, and filling old alcoves and caves, giving to the wall a spotted appearance.

The rocks are broken in two, along a line which here crosses the river, and the beds, which we have seen coming down the cañon for the last thirty miles, have dropped 800 feet, on the lower side of the line, forming what geologists call a fault. The volcanic cone stands directly over the fissure thus formed. On the side of the river opposite, mammoth springs burst out of this crevice, one or two hundred feet above the river, pouring in a stream quite equal in volume to the Colorado Chiquito.

This stream seems to be loaded with carbonate of lime, and the water, evaporating, leaves an incrustation on the rocks; and this process has been continued for a long time, for extensive deposits are noticed, in which are basins, with bubbling springs. The water is salty.

We have to make a portage here, which is completed in about three hours, and on we go.

We have no difficulty as we float along, and I am able to observe the wonderful phenomena connected with this flood of lava. The cañon was doubtless filled to a height of twelve or fifteen hundred feet, perhaps by more than one flood. This would dam the water back; and in cutting through this great lava bed, a new channel has been formed, sometimes on one side, sometimes on the other. The cooled lava, being of firmer texture than the rocks of which the walls are composed, remains in some places; in others a narrow channel has been cut, leaving a line of basalt on either side. It is possible that the lava cooled faster on the sides against the walls, and that the center ran out; but of this we can only conjecture. There are other places, where almost the whole of the lava is gone, patches of it only being seen where it has caught on the walls. As we float down, we can see that it ran out into side cañons. In some places this basalt has a fine, columnar structure, often in concentric prisms, and masses of these concentric columns have coalesced. In some places, when the flow occurred, the cañon was probably at about the same depth as it is now, for we can see where the basalt has rolled out on the sands, and, what seems curious to me, the sands are not melted or metamorphosed to any appreciable extent. In places the bed of the river is of sandstone or limestone, in other places of lava, showing that it has all been cut out again where the sandstones and limestones appear; but there is a little yet left where the bed is of lava.

What a conflict of water and fire there must have been here! Just imagine a river of molten rock, running down into a river of melted snow. What a seething and boiling of the waters; what clouds of steam rolled into the heavens!

Thirty-five miles today. Hurrah!

August 26.— The cañon walls are steadily becoming higher as we advance. They are still bold, and nearly vertical up to the terrace. We still see evidence of the eruption discovered yesterday, but the thickness of the basalt is decreasing, as we go down the stream; yet it has been reinforced at points by streams that have come down from volcanoes standing on the terrace above, but which we cannot see from the river below.

Since we left the Colorado Chiquito, we have seen no evidences that the tribe of Indians inhabiting the plateaus on either side ever come down to the river; but about eleven o'clock today we discover an Indian garden, at the foot of the wall on the right, just where a little stream, with a narrow flood plain, comes down through a side cañon. Along the valley, the Indians have planted corn, using the water which bursts out in springs at the foot of the cliff, for irrigation. The corn is looking quite well, but is not sufficiently advanced to give us roasting ears; but there are some nice, green squashes. We carry ten or a dozen of these on board our boats, and hurriedly leave, not willing to be caught in the robbery, yet excusing ourselves by pleading our great want. We run down a short distance, to where we feel certain no Indians can follow; and what a kettle of squash sauce we make! True, we have no salt with which to season it, but it makes a fine addition to our unleavened bread and coffee. Never was fruit so sweet as these stolen squashes.

After dinner we push on again, making fine time, finding many rapids, but none so bad that we cannot run them with safety, and when we stop, just at dusk, and foot up our reckoning, we find we have run thirty-five miles again.

What a supper we make; unleavened bread, green squash sauce, and strong coffee. We have been for a few days on half rations, but we have no stint of roast squash.

A few days like this, and we shall be out of prison.

August 27.— This morning the river takes a more southerly direction. The dip of the rocks is to the north, and we are rapidly running into lower formations. Unless our course changes, we shall very soon run again into the granite. This gives us some anxiety. Now and then the river turns to the west, and excites hopes that are soon destroyed by another turn to the south. About nine o'clock we come to the dreaded rock. It is with no little misgiving that we see the river enter these black, hard walls. At its very entrance we have to make a portage; then we have to let down with lines past some ugly rocks. Then we run a mile or two farther, and then the rapids below can be seen.

About eleven o'clock we come to a place in the river where it seems much worse than any we have yet met in all its course. A little creek comes down from the left. We land first on the right, and clamber up over the granite pinnacles for a mile or two, but can see no way by which we can let down, and to run it would be sure destruction. After dinner we cross to examine it on the left. High above the river we can walk along on the top of the granite, which is broken off at the edge, and set with crags and pinnacles, so that it is very difficult to get a view of the river at all. In my eagerness to reach a point where I can see the roaring fall below, I go too far on the wall, and can neither advance nor retreat. I stand with one foot on a little projecting rock, and cling with my hand fixed in a little crevice. Finding I am caught here, suspended 400 feet above the river, into which I should fall if my footing fails, I call for help. The men come, and pass me a line, but I cannot let go of the rock long enough to take hold of it. Then they bring two or three of the largest oars. All this takes time which seems very precious to me; but at last they arrive. The blade of one of the oars is pushed into a little crevice in the rock beyond me, in such a manner that they can hold me pressed against the wall. Then another is fixed in such a way that I can step on it, and thus I am extricated.

Still another hour is spent in examining the river from this side, but no good view of it is obtained, so now we return to the side that was first examined, and the afternoon is spent clambering among the crags and pinnacles, and carefully scanning the river again. We find that the lateral streams have washed boulders into the river, so as to form a dam, over which the water makes a broken fall of eighteen or twenty feet; then there is a rapid, beset with rocks, for two or three hundred yards, while, on the other side, points of the wall project into the river. Then there is a second fall below; how great, we cannot tell. Then there is a rapid, filled with huge rocks, for one or two hundred yards. At the bottom of it, from the right wall, a great rock projects quite half way across the river. It has a sloping surface extending up stream, and the water, coming down with all the momentum gained in the falls and rapids above, rolls up this inclined plane many feet, and tumbles over to the left. I decide that it is possible to let down over the first fall, then run near the right cliff to a point just above the second, where we can pull out into a little chute, and, having run over that in safety, we must pull with all our power across the stream, to avoid the great rock below. On my return to the boat, I announce to the men that we are to run it in the morning. Then we cross the river, and go into camp for the night on some rocks, in the mouth of the little cañon.

After supper Captain Howland asks to have a talk with me. We walk up the little creek a short distance, and I soon find that his object is to remonstrate against my determination to proceed. He thinks that we had better abandon the river here. Talking with him, I learn that his brother, William Dunn, and himself have determined to go no farther in the boats. So we return to camp. Nothing is said to the other men.

For the last two days, our course has not been plotted. I sit down and do this now, for the purpose of finding where we are by dead reckoning. It is a clear night, and I take out the sextant to make observation for latitude, and find that the astronomic determination agrees very nearly with that of the plot — quite as closely as might be expected, from a meridian observation on a planet. In a direct line, we must be about forty-five miles from the mouth of the Rio Virgen. If we can reach that point, we know that there are settlements up that river about twenty miles. This forty-five miles, in a direct line, will probably be eighty or ninety in the meandering line of the river. But then we know that there is comparatively open country for many miles above the mouth of the Virgen which is our point of destination.

As soon as I determine all this, I spread my plot on the sand, and wake Howland, who is sleeping down by the river, and show him where I suppose we are, and where several Mormon settlements are situated.

We have another short talk about the morrow, and he lies down again; but for me there is no sleep. All night long, I pace up and down a little path, on a few yards of sand beach, along by the river. Is it wise to go on? I go to the boats again, to look at our rations. I feel satisfied that we can get over the danger immediately before us; what there may be below I know not. From our outlook yesterday, on the cliffs, the cañon seemed to make another great bend to the south, and this, from our experience heretofore, means more and higher granite walls. I am not sure that we can climb out of the cañon here, and, when at the top of the wall, I know enough of the country to be certain that it is a desert of rock and sand, between this and the nearest Mormon town, which, on the most direct line, must be seventy-five miles away. True, the late rains have been favorable to us, should we go out, for the probabilities are that we shall find water still standing in holes, and, at one time, I almost conclude to leave the river. But for years I have been contemplating this trip. To leave the exploration unfinished, to say that there is a part of the cañon which I cannot explore, having already almost accomplished it, is more than I am willing to acknowledge, and I determine to go on.

I wake my brother, and tell him of Howland's determination, and he promises to stay with me; then I call up Hawkins, the cook, and he makes a like promise; then Sumner, and Bradley, and Hall, and they all agree to go on.

August 28.— At last daylight comes, and we have breakfast, without a word being said about the future. The meal is as solemn as a funeral. After breakfast, I ask the three men if they still think it best to leave us. The elder Howland thinks it is, and Dunn agrees with him. The younger Howland tries to persuade them to go on with the party, failing in which, he decides to go with his brother.

Then we cross the river. The small boat is very much disabled, and unseaworthy. With the loss of hands, consequent on the departure of the three men, we shall not be able to run all of the boats, so I decide to leave my *Emma Dean*.

Two rifles and a shot gun are given to the men who are going out. I ask them to help themselves to the rations, and take what they think to be a fair share. This they refuse to do, saying they have no fear but that they can get something to eat; but Billy, the cook, has a pan of biscuits prepared for dinner, and these he leaves on a rock.

Before starting, we take our barometers, fossils, the minerals, and some ammunition from the boat, and leave them on the rocks. We are going over this place as light as possible. The three men help us lift our boats over a rock twenty-five or thirty feet high, and let them down again over the first fall, and now we are all ready to start. The last thing before leaving, I write a letter to my wife, and give it to Howland. Sumner gives him his watch, directing that it be sent to his sister, should he not be heard from again. The records of the expedition have been kept in duplicate. One set of these is given to Howland, and now we are ready. For the last time, they entreat us not to go on, and tell us that it is madness to set out in this place; that we can never get safely through it; and, further, that the river turns again to the south into the granite, and a few miles of such rapids and falls will exhaust our entire stock of rations, and then it will be too late to climb out. Some tears are shed; it is rather a solemn parting; each party thinks the other is taking the dangerous course.

My old boat left, I go on board of the *Maid of the Cañon*. The three men climb a crag, that overhangs the river, to watch us off. The *Maid of the Cañon* pushes out. We glide rapidly along the foot of the wall, just grazing one great rock, then pull out a little into the chute of the second fall, and plunge over it. The open compartment is filled when we strike the first wave below, but we cut through it, and then the men pull with all their power toward the left wall, and swing clear of the dangerous rock below all right. We are scarcely a minute in running it, and find that, although it looked bad from above, we have passed many places that were worse.

The other boat follows without more difficulty. We land at the first practicable point below and fire our guns, as a signal to the men above that we have come over in safety. Here we remain a couple of hours, hoping that they will take the smaller boat and follow us. We are behind a curve in the cañon, and cannot see up to where we left them, and so we wait until their coming seems hopeless, and push on.

And now we have a succession of rapids and falls until noon, all of which we run in safety. Just after dinner we come to another bad place. A little stream comes in from the left, and below there is a fall, and still below another fall. Above, the river tumbles down, over and among the rocks, in whirlpools and great waves, and the waters are lashed into mad, white foam. We run along the left, above this, and soon see that we cannot get down on this side, but it seems possible to let down on the other. We pull up stream again, for two or three hundred yards, and cross. Now there is a bed of basalt on this northern side of the cañon, with a bold escarpment, that seems to be a hundred feet high. We can climb it, and walk along its summit to a point where we are just at the head of the fall. Here the basalt is broken down again, so it seems to us, and I direct the men to take a line to the top of the cliff, and let the boats down along the wall. One man remains in the boat, to keep her clear of the rocks, and prevent her line from being caught on the projecting angles. I climb the cliff, and pass along to a point just over the fall, and descend by broken rocks, and find that the break of the fall is above the break of the wall, so that we cannot land; and that still below the river is very bad, and that there is no possibility of a portage.

Without waiting further to examine and determine what shall be done I hasten back to the top of the cliff, to stop the boats from coming down. When I arrive, I find the men have let one of them down to the head of the fall. She is in swift water, and they are not able to pull her back; nor are they able to go on with the line, as it is not long enough to reach the higher part of the cliff, which is just before them; so they take a bight around a crag. I send two men back for the other line. The boat is in very swift water, and Bradley is standing in the open compartment, holding out his oar to prevent her from striking against the foot of the cliff. Now she shoots out into the stream, and up as far as the line will permit, and then, wheeling, drives headlong against the rock, then out and back again, now straining on the line, now striking against the rock. As soon as the second line is brought, we pass it down to him; but his attention is all taken up with his own situation, and he does not see that we are passing the line to him. I stand on a projecting rock, waving my hat to gain his attention, for my voice is drowned by the roaring of the falls.

Just at this moment, I see him take his knife from its sheath, and step forward to cut the line. He has evidently decided that it is better to go over with the boat as it is, than to wait for her to be broken to pieces. As he leans over, the boat sheers again into the stream, the stem-post breaks away, and she is loose. With perfect composure Bradley seizes the great scull oar, places it in the stern rowlock, and pulls with all his power (and he is an athlete) to turn the bow of the boat down stream, for he wishes to go bow down, rather than to drift broadside on. One, two strokes he makes, and a third just as she goes over, and the boat is fairly turned, and she goes down almost beyond our sight, though we are more than a hundred feet above the river. Then she comes up again, on a great wave, and down and up, then around behind some great rocks, and is lost in the mad, white foam below. We stand frozen with fear, for we see no boat. Bradley is gone, so it seems. But now, away below, we see something coming out of the waves. It is evidently a boat. A moment more, and we see Bradley standing on deck, swinging his hat to show that he is all right. But he is in a whirlpool. We have the stem-post of his boat attached to the line. How badly she may be disabled we know not.

I direct Sumner and Powell to pass along the cliff, and see if they can reach him from below. Rhodes, Hall, and myself run to the other boat, jump aboard, push out, and away we go over the falls. A wave rolls over us, and our boat is unmanageable. Another great wave strikes us, the boat rolls over, and tumbles and tosses, I know not how. All I know is that Bradley is picking us up. We soon have all right again, and row to the cliff, and wait until Sumner and Powell can come. After a difficult climb they reach us. We run two or three miles farther, and turn again to the north-west, continuing until night, when we have run out of the granite once more.

August 29.— We start very early this morning. The river still continues swift, but we have no serious difficulty, and at twelve o'clock emerge from the Grand Cañon of the Colorado.

We are in a valley now, and low mountains are seen in the distance, coming to the river below. We recognize this as the Grand Wash.

A few years ago, a party of Mormons set out from St. George, Utah, taking with them a boat, and came down to·the mouth of the Grand Wash, where they divided, a portion of the party crossing the river to explore the San Francisco Mountains. Three men — Hamblin, Miller, and Crosby — taking the boat, went on down the river, to Callville, landing a few miles below the mouth of the Rio Virgen. We have their manuscript journal with us, and so the stream is comparatively well known.

Tonight we camp on the left bank, in a *mesquite* thicket.

The relief from danger, and the joy of success, are great. When he who has been chained by wounds to a hospital cot, until his canvas tent seems like a dungeon cell, until the groans of those who lie about, tortured with probe and knife, are piled up, a weight of horror on his ears that he cannot throw off, cannot forget, and until the stench of festering wounds and anaesthetic drugs has filled the air with its loathsome burthen, at last goes out into the open fields, what a world he sees! How beautiful the sky; how bright the sunshine; what "floods of delirious music" pour from the throats of birds; how sweet the fragrance of earth, and tree, and blossom! The first hour of convalescent freedom seems rich recompense for all — pain, gloom, terror.

Something like this are the feelings we experience tonight. Ever before us has been an unknown danger, heavier than immediate peril. Every waking hour passed in the Grand Cañon has been one of toil. We have watched with deep solicitude the steady disappearance of our scant supply of rations, and from time to time have seen the river snatch a portion of the little left, while we were ahungered. And danger and toil were endured in those gloomy depths, where ofttimes the clouds hid the sky by day, and but a narrow zone of stars could be seen at night. Only during the few hours of deep sleep, consequent on hard labor, has the roar of the waters been hushed. Now the danger is over; now the toil has ceased; now the gloom has disappeared; now the firmament is bounded only by the horizon; and what a vast expanse of constellations can be seen!

The river rolls by us in silent majesty; the quiet of the camp is sweet; our joy is almost ecstasy. We sit till long after midnight, talking of the Grand Cañon, talking of home, but chiefly talking of the three men who left us. Are they wandering in those depths, unable to find a way out? are they searching over the desert lands above for water? or are they nearing the settlements?*...

* The men who left the party were lost.

STUART CHASE

STUART CHASE (1888–   ) was educated at the Massachusetts Institute of Technology and Harvard University. As a public accountant he participated in exposing the scandalous exploitation of the American people by business interests during the War. He was one of the founders of the Labor Bureau Inc. to obtain economic data for the labor movement. He has been one of the most vigorous critics of the present social order in several books, *The Tragedy of Waste*, *Men and Machines*, *The Economy of Abundance*, etc. *Mexico — A Study of Two Americas*, of which Marian Tyler (Mrs. Chase) is part author, is a contrast between the civilization of handicraft and that of the machine age. The selection given is the first chapter of this book.

MOUNTAIN VILLAGE *

IN TEPOZTLAN one does not say "north" or "south" when giving directions; one says "up" or "down." This holds true for most of Mexico. It is a country set on edge; where straight lines and plane surfaces are virtually homeless. One goes up, in loops and zigzags, and one comes down. Topography is the despair of railroad and mining engineers. Topography, more than any other single factor, has saved Mexico from becoming Hispanized, westernized, mechanized or Americanized; saved it, by and large, from becoming anything but itself.

We loop up from Mexico City to the 10,000-foot pass which divides the central plateau from the valley to the south, the pass over which Mr. Dwight Morrow was wont to drive his car to his charming country seat in Cuernavaca. We loop down the southern wall to a tiny railroad station and disembark. For an hour we see the smoke of our locomotive descending towards Cuernavaca. We take a burro road which also twists downward but at a different angle, and come finally to a place where beetling cliffs wall us on every side. The burro trail proceeds, finding its way somehow between the precipices. We turn left on a foot-path, soon to be lodged, like ants in the crack of a tree, in a perpendicular crevice which splits the eastern rock wall. Ladders help us from time to time. Climbing at 8,000 feet one's breath comes shorter than it should. We wriggle and crawl, and at last emerge on the little *mesa* which crowns one of the lower pinnacles of the cliff. The main mass still towers above us to the north.

We come out upon a tiny field of grass, a thatched hut where somebody has recently slept, a ruined pyramid which seems to grow from the living rock, and one of the fairest views which it has ever been given mortal eyes to see. Before us lie a good many hundred square miles of Mexico; a great section of the land which mothered the Aztecs and taught them to build pyramids, weave cloth of humming birds' feathers, and read the stars with almost Greenwich precision.

* From *Mexico*, by permission of The Macmillan Company, publishers.

In this temple lived a god named Tepoztecatl. He was the presiding deity of *pulque*, a drink made from the milk of the *maguey*, or century plant, to which the Aztecs were much addicted, and which their descendants still drink in enormous quantities. It is about as intoxicating as strong beer. He was also the god of Tepoztlan, the patron and protector of the little town which lies below us, as the stones of Broadway lie under the Woolworth Tower — except that it is 800 feet to Broadway and twice as far to this red-roofed village. Looking down as from an airplane, we see the roofs as red pavements on the ground; the only structure which actually rises is a great white cathedral at the head of the green square which must mark the plaza. Yes, there is the tiny circle of the bandstand.

About the town lie cornfields, with here and there a patch of vivid green which may mean an irrigation ditch and sugar-cane. Near one of these green strips, a puff of smoke rises lazily, and two seconds later, a dull report. Another rises, and another. "A battle!" we cry. "Bandits; a revolution!" "No," says the friend who has brought us here, "rockets. It's probably the beginning of a fiesta. I understand they are always having one in Tepoztlan."

Directly opposite us, perhaps five miles away, the village fields terminate in another sheer rock wall, castellated and carved as though by human hands. Here is a sculptured chasm which looks like a huge fortified gateway, there a turret which would dignify any castle on the Rhine. The whole mass is perhaps four miles long and 2000 to 3000 feet high. It blocks the valley to the south, but above it rise, in waves of blue and lavender, higher and fainter mountain ridges. To the west dreams Cuernavaca, twenty miles away, faint white towers in an opal haze, and beyond them the fields and mountains of the state of Morelos. To the east, the village lands dip to a throat between more of the fantastic cliffs. We catch a glimpse of a long rolling plain below, and then, springing halfway to the zenith, the snowy masses of Popocatepetl and Ixtaccihuatl, the Mountain who Smokes and the White Woman. Hand in hand these great mountains stand, the one in his glittering cone like Fujiyama, the other a broader, serrated peak. Where their hands join in a lofty pass, Cortez caught his first glimpse of the city he had come to conquer.

A fitting place for any god to live. With what an infinity of consecrated labour must men have toiled up these precipices to build a house for Tepoztecatl. Small wonder that their descendants in the village, despite the shifting centuries, the ruined walls, the encroaching forest, the graven image overthrown by the good Dominicans, feel his brooding presence, and in solemn pantomime and dance still celebrate his divinity.

We turn to the pyramid. Like all Mexican pyramids it is terraced rather than straight lined. The great pyramid of the sun at Teotihuacan — with a total mass said to be greater than that of Cheops — has four indented terraces before the broad top is reached, 200 feet above the plain. Tepoztecatl's house is tiny in comparison. It is perhaps 100 feet square at the base, with three low terraces; and in its ruined state rises nowhere more than forty feet. An enclosed altar rests on the flat summit, and here we

From *Mexico*, by permission of The Macmillan Company, Publishers.

find great stones with curious and still beautiful carvings replete with un-ciphered words. There is a date which corresponds, according to the German archeologist Seler, to 1502, about twenty years before the Spanish conquest. The temple covers every foot of the pinnacle upon which it is built (the little field lies somewhat lower to the east), yet carries on the design of nature with flawless rectitude. It seems to have been born with the stony hills, and will remain until they too crumble.

We place a flagon of wine on the altar stone, and eat our lunch in the holy of holies. Tepoztecatl will not care, for Mexican gods are notoriously worldly. It might have been more courteous to have replaced the wine with pulque, but none of us can abide the milky brew with its abominable smell. No more rockets rise from the fields; the village looks infinitely peaceful sleeping in the sun; a green shelf set in the mountain side. "How do you drive in to it?" we asked, perplexed, disclosing the naïveté of the newcomer. "You walk," our guide replies, "or go on horseback. Mostly, if you are an Indian, you walk."

"But how does one get supplies?" As an economist, I cannot repress a base interest in the means by which people eat.

"They carry them on their backs, or on the backs of burros; chiefly on their own."

"And no wheel has ever turned on these streets?"

"Never. There are hundreds of villages in Mexico where no wheel has ever turned."

I toss the empty wine bottle to hear it crash in a gulch 1000 feet below, and ponder this remark. Indeed, questions have been growing ever since we set foot in Mexico, some weeks before. The buried cities with their white pyramids which we saw in the jungles of Yucatan; the spotless Maya Indians with their carved, fine faces; the great calendar stones in the National Museum in Mexico City; Mexico City itself, part Seville, part Atlanta, part indigenous Indian, embroidered with billboards, electric lights, tabloids, Tom Thumb golf courses and taxicabs; the eye-shattering spirals by electric engine from Vera Cruz to the rim of the plateau 7000 feet above (and how did Cortez ever negotiate the ascent without annihilation?); these great churches, monasteries, palaces in the most dramatic and inaccessible places, decaying with such charm; and these massive temples of an earlier age which bid fair to long outlast them....

In the country that I call home, the Atlantic seaboard of the United States, we have dignified and moderate mountains, not these fantastic crags. We have modern buildings, Victorian buildings, and a few colonial buildings which we call old. There the record stops. Here, on the other hand, are a few modern buildings in the cities; a vast architectural wealth of Spanish colonial structures, invariably in stone, not only in cities but on plain, hilltop, mountain side, already older than anything in my country; and underneath it all, solid and eternal, these pyramids and temples built 1000, 2000, unknown thousands of years before.

At home we have Americans, Negroes, and assorted immigrants, more or less naturalized. Here we have Indians, a reasonable number of *mestizos* —

half and quarter breeds, most of them living like Indians — and a few whites in the cities. The Indians built the pyramids, the Indians built the churches and the palaces for their Spanish masters, the Indians do ninety-five per cent of the nation's work today. This is their country; they have always lived in it; and as the traveller looks about him, it is evident that they always propose to. In my nation, the old world has wiped out the Indian and made a totally new culture. Here, despite onslaught after onslaught for 400 years, the Indian has withstood the Old World. It has twisted him, changed him, but it has not broken him. Europe and Africa have taken over the land north of the Rio Grande. South of it the indigenous continent of North America sturdily survives. Suddenly my heart warms to these Indians for the fight that they have made. Mailed chargers and gunpowder, money changers and Christian crosses, prime movers and high-pressure sales talk have not prevailed against them.

How would this village have looked today if Cortez had never come; if his stout lieutenant, Bernal Diaz, had not reported "fine women and much loot" in Tepoztlan? What was Aztec civilization really like, and how much of its culture still persists? When the forbears of these villagers marched out to meet the Spaniards, how were they dressed, how did they deploy, how did they fight? Would that we might see the meeting from this cliff. How did the Spaniards change the country, and how did it change them? What did Tepoztecatl do to the trinity and to the Saints of Rome? There in Cuernavaca, where water tumbles in every street in the driest season, royal viceroy after royal viceroy maintained his palace. Cortez lived there for a time, building the first sugar mill in Mexico; after him, 300 years of grandees and dons. What legacy did they leave, and why were they at last so summarily overthrown?

Among other bequests it is certain that they left a century of revolutions, nor is the end in sight. In a romantic interlude, an emperor and an empress, Maximilian and Carlotta, worshipped in one of these hazy towers across the plain. Why did they come, and why was an emperor murdered who meant so well? This valley knew the peace of Porfirio Diaz, and the march of the grey-clad *rurales*, and anon, of all the valleys in Mexico, it flamed most violently when that peace was ruptured. Through it Zapata stormed, shouting Land for the landless! And Tepoztlan became a town of the dead, its citizens living in caves here in the cliffs, "coming down in the night to rob their own fruit trees." What is the meaning of that wild cry, and what sort of peace was that of Diaz, that ended in such a holocaust?

What do these people want? Only to be left alone? What has a roving American, watching a soaring *zopilote*, to learn from them; aye, what has America itself to learn from them, and what has it to give them? And why, in the face of this timeless pyramid, should we arrogate to ourselves the name "America" at all?

It is pleasant to lie here in the sun, to commune with gods and philosophize at random, but if we would sleep in a bed tonight we must somehow march on our own feet to Cuernavaca, and that is twenty and something miles away. We retreat gingerly down the crevice with its ladders, take the burro trail again, and drop, at say seventy degrees instead of eighty-nine, to the foot of the cliff, a tiresome descent and very hot. We emerge, perspiring and thirsty, in a miniature garden of Eden. A stream of water gushes from the rock face, filling a masonry pool which proves to be the town water supply. Only by the most rigorous concentration on the sublimities of sanitation, can we restrain ourselves from diving in. For a fellow citizen of Colonel Goethals to corrupt an Indian's drinking water would hardly do. So we drink, and wash circumspectly in the overflow. Above us are mulberry trees, *ahuehuetes*, and the great green *machetes* of banana trees. It is divinely cool. Here is a little clearing with a stone bench or two, and a globe of stone, five feet in diameter, surmounted by a cross. It marks the spot, according to hearsay, where the image of Tepoztecatl was shattered when the Dominicans hurled it from the pyramids, thereby proving to the benighted natives that their god was not omnipotent. What the good monks did not quite understand was something the Indians were well aware of — and still know for that matter — that a god does not die when his man-made image is broken. It shows deplorable manners, hardly more.

The fragments were borne away to be incorporated into the walls of the church, and the natives were baptized according to a sort of ecclesiastical mass production, in the fountain which flows from the rock. That was in 1575 or thereabouts. As the conquest of the Mexican plateau was well concluded by 1525, it seems to have taken the church some fifty years to bestow the blessing of baptism upon Tepoztlan. Thousands of villages are more remote (Tepoztlan is only about sixty miles from Mexico City) and presumably took even longer to be baptized. Indeed it is a matter of record that to some the true faith has not yet penetrated, so high on the mountains are they, or so deep in the jungle.

Refreshed, we follow the iron water pipe down to the town, a distance of only a few hundred yards. It has been said, and I think with some truth, that Mexico is sightly in the general, and messy in the particular; that it looks clean and tidy, but does not always survive a closer inspection — say the inquiring nose of a New England housewife. Or to put it another way: in Mexico, the community is always fair, while the individual may be untidy. In the United States, the individual is often clean, while the community — say the average Main Street — is a blistering eyesore. Mexico is easier on the eyes and harder on the nose. Which is worse I do not know.

Tepoztlan, then, is very good to look at. Here are some 700 houses — the total population is 4000 souls — arranged along little shaded streets, many of them bowered in flowers. Flowers are more important to Mexicans than are motor cars, radios, and bathtubs combined, to Americans. The houses are small and very simple. Their walls are of adobe brick, sometimes whitewashed; their roofs are of red tile or of thatch; they have no chimney, frequently no windows, no glass; very little woodwork. In the front yard stands the circular corncrib made of cornstalks, precisely as it stood in the days of Montezuma; behind there is often a vegetable garden. There may be a shed for horse, cow or burro, while turkeys, chickens and pigs wander introspectively over the foreground. Dogs invariably take their siestas in the street. As why should they not? Wheeled vehicles are unknown.

We are beginning to meet people. They are stolid but polite. To each one of our party they give a "*Buenas tardes*" and receive one in return. Our somewhat bizarre tramping costumes excite them not at all; the quiet children stare gravely, a woman looks curiously from a doorway. A little boy asks "What *pueblo* do you come from?" We answer Mexico City, and he is filled with awe. What Spanish blood there is, is admirably concealed; men, women and children look pure Indian, with beautiful bronzed skins, high cheek-bones, black straight hair, and a haunting touch of the Mongolian. Señor Bernal Diaz reported many beautiful women in Tepoztlan in 1521. In 1930, most women are comely, but few are pretty. In all Mexico there are few pretty women judged by northern standards. In the cities one finds a certain number of ravishing *señoritas*, creole or mestizo, but the Indian women are rarely beautiful save in the matchless grace of their carriage. Some of the older women have that carved, serene beauty which one associates with the face of a philosopher. And it is only fair to say that Charlot, the French artist, after seeing the flowing garments of the Indians, compares them with the virgins of the Parthenon, and holds the fitted clothes of western women to be absurd.

The men are mostly in white pyjamas, sandaled and sombreroed. Many carry, almost as an article of dress, a long, murderous-looking machete. This ferocious blade, however, is rarely used on human beings; it is in constant demand for the humbler uses of wood chopping, bush clearing, carpentry, agricultural and household tasks generally. In Tepoztlan, the blade curves at the end. In other parts of Mexico it may be straight. In Acapulco, on the Pacific, it is frequently as long as the boy who carries it. The women are in some such clothes as up-country farm women wore a generation ago in the United States, petticoat, skirt, and blouse — save for the *reboso*, or blue shawl, the vivid colours, the earrings, and save the fact that most of them are barefooted. Everybody looks reasonably well fed, and nobody is hurrying. Unconsciously we moderate our gait. Here are some men and boys making adobe bricks in a back yard. Tall ochre piles of finished brick and tile are drying in the sun. Here a man and a woman are spinning rope of horsehair, employing a curiously whirling wheel. And here through a cottage door we catch a glint of metal, and going nearer find a sewing-machine. Thus the machine age makes its breach in the Aztec wall. The town also boasts, we are told, a phonograph, and a rickety steam flour mill which the housewife, pounding her own cornmeal, is usually too proud to patronize.

We turn a corner, no children following, and advance upon the *zocalo*, or plaza, a little grass-covered park with flowers and shade trees and a small Victorian bandstand (doubtless erected in the days of the Diaz peace). About it are several two-story houses with wrought-iron balconies, belonging to *los correctos*, the quality of the town. Here too is a little general store which puts me in mind somehow of the general stores I used to see in the White Mountains of New Hampshire. It smells the same; but of twenty bins of dried seeds and berries I recognize only three.

Beside the plaza rises the great church, cream coloured and streaked with grey and rose. It is clear that every iota of surplus wealth — labour, materials, artistic ability — of the entire community has gone into its construction; even as in Aztec days it went into the temple 2000 feet above. Like many Mexican churches, it has two towers flanking the entrance doors of old carved wood, and a long nave, terminating in a big dome which rises almost as high as the towers. The dome is tiled, and the towers are full of bells. As everywhere, part of the structure is decomposing — but with what charm and grace! To the right are the ruined arches of a long cloister, where Dominicans once told their beads. In front of the doorway stands a stone cross whose arms end in symbolic Aztec serpents. On the screen inside the door is suspended a sign to the effect that a lottery for dead souls is in progress. The names of departed parishioners are listed, each with a lottery number, and a mass is promised the soul of the winner on a given date. But the loser need not despair; a sort of blanket mass will be celebrated a few days later for all the remaining luckless candidates together.

Two pigs are asleep in the churchyard among the graves. A hen approaches, with some misgiving, the church door. A pony with a resplendent silver-studded saddle waits patiently in front of the store. Men, women, children and animals are sunk in a divine lethargy. It is the siesta hour, which even the northerner on schedule must come to respect. We shall drink our beer here in the shade, watch the sleepy zocalo, admire the old rose and ivory of the crumbling church, try to believe that the cliffs from which we have descended are authentic and not a Hollywood backdrop, and presently, when it is a little cooler, ask an Indian boy to guide us over the *pedregal* — a heaving waste of lava rock — to Cuernavaca.

I stayed in Tepoztlan but a short time in the spring of 1930. Some months later there came into my hands a book by Mr. Robert Redfield, an American ethnologist from the University of Chicago, who had remained there nearly a year, studying every phase of the town's life. With this invaluable document, I was able to check my own impressions, and still better, to draw evidence for a more serious study in comparative civilizations. Robert Redfield's *Tepoztlan*, laid upon Robert and Helen Lynd's *Middletown*, provides as exciting a series of parallel columns as any sociologist could wish. One can compare item by item the work habits, play habits, religious habits; the food, houses, clothing, education, social organization of two communities, one north, the other south of the Rio Grande, but a whole world apart. The one is still following the leisurely pattern of the handicraft age, with many cultural traditions from the greatest indigenous civilization which the Western Hemisphere produced; the other is firmly locked into the culture of the machine age, deriving most of its traditions and *mores* from the Eastern Hemisphere. The machine has entered Tepoztlan, as we have seen, but it is as yet the shyest of visitors. If it and its products were barred tomorrow, the white pyjamas of the men would have to give way to native cloth woven from a local tree fibre (the old looms still survive). Otherwise the village life would proceed largely unimpaired.

Tepoztlan is far more American than Middletown, when all is said and done, but it is alien to everything we regard as typically "American." Nor does the irony end here. Middletown, you will remember, is the pen name for Muncie, Indiana. If there is an Indian in Muncie, Indiana, he belongs in a museum. Of the 40,000 people in the town, ninety-nine per cent are of European or African stock. It has been estimated, on the other hand, that no more than fifty Spaniards ever settled in Tepoztlan. After 400 years this Hispanic strain does not amount to much. The southern community is ninety-nine per cent Indian. Thus in race as well as in culture, Tepoztlan is almost pure American, while the northern community, in the state called Indiana, is an omelette of English, French, Poles, Italians, Czechs, Russians, Negroes, Germans, Irish, and heaven and the Bureau of the Census know how many other nationalities.

The Lynds estimate that of all the great tonnage of factory goods which Middletown produces, only a tiny fraction — perhaps one per cent — is locally consumed. The rest takes rail and moves to the ends of the earth. The city grows a somewhat larger fraction, but still a negligible one, of its food supply. With its railroads and highways cut, Middletown would very shortly starve to death. It exists only as a cell in a vast interdependent industrial structure. About both towns stand fields of corn — that maize which the forbears of the Aztecs learned to domesticate. Middletown does not eat corn in any quantity, and most of its enveloping crop is used to fatten steers. But the cornfields of Tepoztlan take on a sacramental dignity. For centuries these *milpas* have been cultivated from father to son, and their sowing and harvesting are the outstanding ceremonies of the year. It is said that no Mexican revolution can survive the harvest season. The army deserts in a unit to tend its ancestral milpas. From this corn, from the squashes which grow between the furrows, the beans clambering on the cornstalks, and the wild fruits in the hills, Tepoztlan can feed itself if it must. Probably nine tenths of its food comes from within its own boundaries. It trades with the surrounding villages, the storekeeper buys cotton cloth and a few notions from Mexico City, but by and large, in dramatic contrast with Middletown, it is not a cog in the wheel, but an economically independent community. This costs something to be sure in terms of the efficiency of specialization, but it also gives something, as we shall see.

Indeed there is no end to the dramatic contrast. The typical community in the United States is urban and industrialized; the typical community in Mexico is rural and lives from the soil and the forests. The gospel of Middletown is work, and the gospel of Tepoztlan is play — one day in three, the year round, the southern community is celebrating a major or minor fiesta. Yet for all their hard work, a fraction of the men of Middletown is constantly unemployed and bowed down with fear and worry. Unemployment is unheard of in Tepoztlan, and fear stalks only when earthquakes rumble, or a Zapata comes riding over the mountains, federal troops at his heels.

Middletown is essentially practical, Tepoztlan essentially mystical in mental processes. Yet in coming to terms with one's environment, Tepoztlan has exhibited, I think, the superior common sense. Middletown has its due quota of neurotic and mentally unbalanced individuals. In

Tepoztlan a Freudian complex is unthinkable. The men of the south are craftsmen — many students call them artists — they can put their hands to almost anything, fashion it, repair it, recreate it. Their popular arts, their weaving, pottery, glass work, basketry, are as authentic and delightful as any the modern or the ancient world has seen. (Tepoztlan has not a craft specialty, as have many other villages, but every boy is taught to work with stone, wood, metal, clay and thatch.)

I fear I am tipping the scales. In this dreamy haze, amid snow-capped volcanoes, it is all too easy to become sentimental. Let us endeavor to right the balance. There is not a bathtub in Tepoztlan, or a telephone or a radio (to the best of my knowledge), or a movie palace (but the village band boasts one saxophone), or a pair of silk stockings, or a refrigerator, or an electric light, or a spring bed, or a newspaper, or an overstuffed davenport, or a cock-tail shaker, or a decent cup of coffee, or a baseball team, or a dance hall (they dance in the church), or running water from a tap, or a straight eight. Children do not sit on trees and establish records; nobody sends copy to confession magazines; to three districts in the town the postman never delivered a letter in the months of Mr. Redfield's residence. There are only two small schools, and the majority of the population is illiterate. All speak two languages, however, their own Aztec and Spanish.

There are thirteen native herb specialists and ten midwives, but not a doctor in the town. A lawyer would have nothing to do. The people look healthy, but according to Dr. Ernest Gruening, commenting on Mexico generally, the question of public health has been seriously neglected. Particularly appalling is infant mortality. I suspect — Mr. Redfield does not help us here — that despite its neurotics and its industrial and automobile accidents, Middletown has a better health record than Tepoztlan. Certainly in the matter of health and sanitation the pointer swings sharply to the north, and here we touch upon one of the harshest features of Mexican village life. The weak die early. Only the strong survive.

There are other harsh features, as we shall see in due time. Nowhere in Europe, not even in Russia, have I seen a community so alien to the way of life in my own country. Yet we are both members of the same continent, a muddy river between us. It is the purpose of the following chapters to generate a modicum of understanding between — shall we say — old family Americans and their parvenu cousins. Ordinarily I am proud of the nine generations of New England behind me, but I feel like the rawest immigrant compared to the little brown boy up there in the belfry, who, with all the gusto in the world, is tipping one of the great tower bells in full somersault to announce the hour of vespers.

HISTORY

In *Heroes and Hero-worship* Carlyle sets forth his view that "the history of what man has accomplished in this world is at bottom the history of the great men who have worked here." At the time when Carlyle was illustrating his theory in the examples of Cromwell and Frederick the Great, another thinker, Karl Marx, was putting forward a contradictory belief, to the effect that forces which we call historical are not personal, but reside in the depths of mass unconsciousness, in the impulse to survive and to live more abundantly in the material world. This economic interpretation of history is clearly allied to Darwin's theory of evolution as a survival of the fittest in the struggle of life. Both schools of historical writing are dependent for their material on the record of actual fact by eye witnesses or participants. Both appeal to the sense for truth and reality, but while the former emphasizes the detail for its dramatic effectiveness, the latter digests detail into large generalizations concerning the movements of mankind under the impact of social forces. The natural form of the first type of history is narrative; of the second, exposition.

The first element of historical writing is to be found in reporting, which is a form of personal experience. The success of the reporter consists in being on the spot, recording vividly and truly what is seen, and supplementing this record by the evidence of others. Mr. Gunther's report of the assassination of Chancellor Dollfuss in 1934 is an admirable example of this elementary process of historical writing. James Anthony Froude is an exponent of the drama of history. His account of the execution of Mary Queen of Scots deals with an event long past with the attention fixed on the behavior of the chief actor as recorded by eye witnesses, whom the historian has estimated according to their capacity and willingness to tell the truth. Partisanship is frequently a characteristic of the dramatic historian, but although Froude strongly upholds the Protestant side and judges Mary severely it is noteworthy that he draws his evidence concerning this final scene chiefly from "a true report" which was probably written by one of the queen's household. Parkman like Froude writes with a sense of dramatic values. He studied the topography of the scene which determined the outcome of the long struggle between France and England, and he gathered the traditions which recorded the behavior and very words of the two protagonists. Professor Turner has drawn his evidence from a multitude of sources, and has fused it into a single generalization. The frontier has long been the great source of purely American material for fiction and drama. From Cooper's *Leatherstocking Tales* to Mr. Owen Wister's *The Virginian*, there have been innumerable tales of pioneer life and experience. The frontier was the great nursery of individualism and gave birth to a multitude of heroes, but its final importance was not in them. Not until Professor Turner's paper was the social significance of the frontier clearly understood in its moulding of American character, political and economic institutions, and social ideals. As Professor Turner says: "Behind institutions, behind constitutional forms and modifications, lie the vital forces that call these organs into life."

JOHN GUNTHER

AFTER being graduated from the University of Chicago, John Gunther (1901–) joined the staff of the Chicago *Daily News*, became assistant London correspondent in 1924, and since then has written for his paper and for many leading periodicals from almost every country in Europe. He has also written novels. Mr. Gunther has not only the necessary "nose for news," but the less common ear for living, disciplined prose. His style makes his reporting worth reading long after the mere topical interest has passed. The present article was published in *Harper's Magazine* for November, 1934.

POLICY BY MURDER *

THE STORY OF THE DOLLFUSS KILLING

LITTLE Dr. Dollfuss is dead and Europe is still jittery with its worst war scare since 1914. The Nazis murdered the Austrian Chancellor on July 25th, and only because of a couple of miraculous accidents did their plan to seize and sack Austria fail. The story is worth telling both from the human and political points of view. It is the story of an organized conspiracy to murder. I saw some of it, and I should like to set the record down.

The situation is quickly outlined. The Nazis, who are pan-German or nothing, and whose leader, Hitler, is Austrian-born with deep feelings for his motherland, thought that Austria would fall into their lap when Hitler became German chancellor in January, 1933. Indeed, it almost did. The reason it did not was Dollfuss. Therefore the Nazis hated and attacked him. They adopted assassination as a policy when other methods to defeat him had failed.

Dollfuss was a peasant, an illegitimate farmer boy, who became Chancellor in Austria in May, 1932. He was tenacious, nimble, devout, parochial, simple-minded, and sincere. During 1933, David against Goliath, he aroused admiration almost everywhere by his fight to keep Austria independent and to avert the international catastrophe which Nazi *Gleichschaltung* (assimilation) of Austria might have caused. In February, 1934, he gravely weakened himself by ruthlessly and stupidly bombarding the Vienna socialists out of existence. The Nazi onslaught meantime was continuing. The Munich radio station poured out incessant vituperative propaganda; bombs, supplied mostly by Germany, spluttered all over Austria; an "Austrian Legion," thirty thousand strong, composed of refugee Austrian Nazis, was organized within Germany on the Bavarian frontier. By midsummer Austria was virtually in a state of civil war.

This caused serious international tension, because Italy threatened to invade Austria to "protect" it from Germany if the Nazi attack should succeed. Internally it caused a complete dislocation of Austrian life. Austria

* Copyright, 1934, by Harper and Brothers. Reprinted by permission of the author.

is after all German, and thousands upon thousands of Austrians were Nazi even without the stimulus of German aggression. A sort of secret state within a state came to exist in Austria. The Austrian Nazis maintained their ranks and discipline. They held meetings and even secret evening drill; they were rigidly if secretly organized; their influence swayed whole towns and provinces. Naziism penetrated the law courts and high government services; labor and industry; even the army and especially the police. Latent discontent practically passed the borderline to spontaneous conspiracy.

But Dollfuss, largely because of international support, especially that of Mussolini, was winning. Therefore the July 25th plot was hatched.

Its origins are not yet completely clear because the ringleaders died with their lips sealed, but some details are known. All the Putschists seem to have been members of the 89th S.S. regiment, one of the four S.S. (Hitlerite guard) detachments which secretly existed inside Austria. In October, 1933, it is interesting to recall, Dollfuss had been shot by a young Nazi, Dertil, but escaped with a light flesh wound; Dertil is supposed to have been a member of this same regiment. The rank and file of the plotters were former non-commissioned officers or privates of the regular Austrian army who had been dismissed from the service for their Nazi sympathies. Also among them were active police officers whose secret Nazi activities had escaped detection — an extremely important point.

The plotters looked for spiritual sustenance in three directions: (1) In Germany there were Frauenfeld and Habicht, the exiled leaders of the Austrian section of the Nazi party. (2) In Vienna there was a group of high police executives and officials, who have since been arrested or have fled the country. (3) In Rome there was "King Anton" Rintelen. There was another leader, a mysterious civilian whose *nom de complot* was Kunze, of whom more later.

Dr. Anton Rintelen, a white-cropped man of fifty-eight, who looks less like a conspirator than almost anyone I have ever met, was promoted by Dollfuss to be Austrian Minister in Rome in order to get him out of the country. He was too powerful to be overtly sacked, or else Dollfuss was too timid or slipshod to sack him. For ten years Rintelen had been Governor of Styria, the turbulent province south of Vienna. He was clever and cold and ambitious and, though named by the Nazis as their chancellor, he was not a Nazi. He was Rintelen. Years ago he flirted with the socialists hoping to reach power by a socialist coalition. When the socialists faded and the Nazis rose he intrigued with the Nazis. It is not the least of the tragedies of July 25th that this chief actor in it should have been motivated by such unspiritual aims. He ran with the Nazis not because he loved Hitler but because he wanted a job and loved power. The Nazis, on their side, needed him. He was "respectable" and they knew they could most easily gain Austria through the medium of a transitory coalition government. Rintelen was their Austrian Papen.

Various Styrian industrialists were friends of Rintelen. In their factories, like the Alpine Montan Gesellschaft, the largest industrial concern in Austria, the workmen were secretly organized on an S.A. basis.   Here the Styrian rebels hid their arms.

Germany fed the springs of dissatisfaction and treachery with a powerful stream of gold.   I have it on what seems to be indisputable authority that the Germans spent seventy-five million marks in Austria for propaganda in the seventeen months between January, 1933, and July, 1934.   Of German moral responsibility for the Dollfuss murder there can be no doubt.   Munich day in, day out, preached violence.   And there was not only moral responsibility.   No one knows if people in Germany were aware beforehand of the exact manner in which Dollfuss was to be killed.   But they knew beyond doubt that *something* was going to happen in Austria July 25th, and the death of the Chancellor was indissolubly connected with their plans.   There is plenty of indication of German foreknowledge.   As witness:

(1) The Munich headquarters of the Nazi party, according to the official *Wiener Zeitung*, had a special airplane ready at 9 A.M. on the 25th for the victorious flight of Habicht and Frauenfeld to Vienna.

(2) As early as July 21st a Berlin photo agency sent out pictures of Rintelen marked "New Austrian Chancellor — Hold for Release."

(3) A Nazi named Abereger, arrested in Innsbruck and later sentenced to life imprisonment for bomb smuggling, testified that on July 22nd, three days before the murder, he was informed by courier from Munich that an armed rising was scheduled in Austria for the 25th.

(4) Italian secret agents reported movements of the Austrian Legion (Austrian Nazis on German soil) to the frontier on the evening of the 24th. The legion was to take posts two miles behind the border.

(5) Most striking of all, the official German news agency, the Deutsches Nachrichten Buro, issued at 10:45 A.M. on July 25th instructions to all German papers to use only official German accounts of the news anticipated from Austria *that day*.   Later this same agency prepared and distributed a story of the "successful" Austrian revolt although at this time the Putsch had barely started.

We do not yet know the precise interrelations of Germany, Rintelen, and the actual Putschists.   Rintelen came to Vienna on July 20th, ostensibly on a holiday.   The Putschists were in a hurry because Dollfuss planned to go to see Mussolini in Riccioni later that week, and the Nazis feared that some new agreement between Mussolini and Dollfuss would finally beat them. There is a story that Dollfuss planned to go to Riccioni on the 23rd but received a mysterious telephone call from someone in Rome purporting to be an official personage who told him to delay the trip two days.   Another story is that the Putsch was first planned for July 24th, but was postponed a day when inside information came to the plotters, possibly from Rintelen, that Dollfuss's last cabinet session in Austria would take place on the 25th, not on the 24th as first believed.   It was the intention of the conspirators to capture the whole cabinet.

So much for the setting.   The actual events of July 25th began as follows:

At about 11 A.M. the conspirators assembled at various points in the streets of Vienna.   Their organization was excellent and they acted with the utmost smoothness and precision. One group gathered, man by man, on the sidewalk of the Kolowat Ring. They had received weapons from their leaders the night before, and some had found cards in their letter boxes notifying them of the rendez-vous. Not all the plotters knew who the higher-ups were; the password was the number "89." Fourteen started from Kolowat Ring for Ravag, the radio headquarters, where the signal for the Putsch was given. They were not disguised and they went on foot. Loitering on the Johannesgasse, where the Ravag is situated, were two uniformed policemen, members of the gang, who "covered" them and led them to the door.

A larger group meantime assembled at the gymnasium of the German Athletic Club on Siebensterngasse (Seven Stars street). This building, it is interesting to note, directly adjoins an army barracks. The plot had been organized with such care that one of the conspirators confessed later to having been informed by telegram where to come and what to do. The group numbered 144, of whom no fewer than 106 were former army non-coms or privates, and ten were *active* police. The hour of attack was chosen with beautiful precision so that the plotters would reach the chancellery at the moment of the changing of the guard, when it was most vulnerable.

At about 11:15 a spy telephoned Major Wrabel, the aide-de-camp of the Heimwehr [1] leader, and minister of public security, Major Emil Fey, that some sort of action was being prepared at Siebensterngasse. Wrabel sent a trusted detective, Marek, to investigate. On arrival, Marek saw the plotters, but the presence of uniformed police threw him off the track. Nevertheless, his suspicions grew and three times he telephoned to Wrabel between 11:30 and 12:30, once from a public 'phone booth, once from a coffee house, once from a furniture shop. It seems that Wrabel did not transmit the alarm to police headquarters until 12:35. Meantime the loyal police had been misled by clever and daring spies who told headquarters that an attack on Dollfuss was being prepared in a different part of town.

After his third call Marek was spotted by the conspirators and they seized him. He was dragged into the hall, where he saw the men changing into army uniform, the uniform of the crack Vienna "Deutschmeister" regiment. The rebels clambered into three private trucks which they had hired, one marked BUTTER AND EGGS, and started for the chancellery. They did not know what to do with Marek and so (amazing cheek) they took him with them. When they were a block from the chancellery Marek jumped out, and none of the Nazis, for fear of raising the alarm, dared shoot him. The reader may well ask how three trucks full of "soldiers" could traverse a dozen blocks of a crowded city at noon without attracting attention; but troop movements were not uncommon in Vienna at this time, and the uniformed police on the running boards allayed suspicion.

The plotters reached the chancellery at 1:02 P.M. The scene was set for dramatic and terrible events. But first there is the Ravag episode to tell.

[1] The Heimwehr is the auxiliary armed force that supported the Dollfuss government.

II

July 25th was a hot day, though not sunny, and I wanted to go swimming.
I had finished my morning's work and put on my hat to leave for lunch when
at 1:07 the telephone rang. One of my tipsters said in a low voice, "Have
you heard the radio? The Vienna radio has just given this announcement:
'*The government of Dr. Dollfuss has resigned. Dr. Rintelen has assumed
power.*' It may be a joke. I don't know. I'll check it up and call in a
minute."

I put in a call for Paris at once (we send our stories by 'phone) and while
waiting for it I telephoned (a) the American legation, (b) a friend, Fodor of
the *Manchester Guardian*, with whom I work closely, (c) the Bundeskanzleramt or chancellery. The legation had heard the radio announcement and
was investigating. Fodor rushed to meet me downtown. The Bundeskanzleramt — interesting! — did not answer. Then Telegrafen-Compagnie,
a local news service, called with the radio announcement and said that a
Nazi Putsch was in progress. I wrote a brief story and finished it just when
the Paris call came through. It was 1:19. I still had my hat on.

I lost about ten minutes because a police officer stopped me and made me
drive him to his headquarters. A general alarm had been sounded, he said,
but he didn't know about what. I got to the Bundeskanzleramt at about
1:35. The tawny oak doors were shut and a few policemen were outside,
but otherwise nothing seemed wrong. I assumed that the government had
locked itself in, preparing defense.

An armored car passed by and with a couple of the newspaper men I followed it. It turned away from the Bundeskanzleramt and lurched round
the Ring to the Johannesgasse, the Ravag headquarters. The locale is
comparable to 43rd or 44th street in New York. The car got into position
and the police on the turret ducked inside the steel shell. Then I heard
revolver shooting and machine-gun fire. The police were storming Ravag
to blast out the Nazi Putschists there. I had a feeling that it was all mon-
strously unreal. The police pushed us back, but we were eager to see: it
isn't often you get a pitched battle in the heart of downtown Vienna. Then
prprprffbum we heard exploding hand-grenades. A waiter in a white-duck
jacket slid through the crowd with a platter of beers.

What had happened at Ravag was this. At two minutes to one the fourteen plotters from Kolowat Ring entered the building. They shot the loyal
policeman on guard and the chauffeur of the Ravag director who were lounging in the doorway. Four Nazis reached the studio, where a broadcast of
phonograph records was going on. They grabbed the announcer, put a gun
in his ribs, and made him give their message. This was the signal for the
Putsch.

But a courageous telephone girl had had time to sound an alarm, although
all the lines to police headquarters — an interesting point — were "busy."
And an official with great presence of mind cut the wires to Bisamberg, the
sending station, so that the Nazis were unable to give a second message.
Their plan had been to repeat "Dollfuss has resigned; Rintelen is Chancellor," every ten minutes, interspersing this aerial tattoo with instructions to

the country, false news, and so on, which would have paralyzed any defense action of the government. I remember that a British radio man told me years before how marvelously a revolution might be organized by radio.

An unfortunate actor rehearsing a broadcast skit became hysterical with excitement, started to scream, and was shot. The police broke into the building and another policeman was killed, also the Nazi leader. Of the five who died, three bled to death because no doctor was available. Outside we waited till the police, victorious, began to drag out their captives at about 3:20. I proceeded home and wrote my story, longer this time, and put in my Paris call.

I went to the Bundeskanzleramt again at about 3:50. On the way I ran into Gedye of the New York *Times*, who was returning from Ravag, and we stopped a second, both saying, "Well, it seems to be all over." We certainly were wrong, but very few people knew then that anything was amiss except at Ravag. I had passed the Bundeskanzleramt myself before, and it looked entirely normal except for the closed doors. Feeling a flicker of doubt, I said to Gedye, "You know, a government doesn't usually lock itself *in* at a moment of great crisis." He agreed. "Funny." And we remembered that the telephone had not answered. I walked toward the building. A patrol had been flung round the area and I couldn't get in. Then the story burst.

III

The Bundeskanzleramt, or Federal Chancellery, is the old Metternich palace where the Congress of Vienna met in 1815. Certainly from that day to this it can have witnessed no more dramatic and agitated a situation. A stately baroque building, its cream-colored façade opens on the Ballhausplatz. Grilled balconies of graceful iron project twenty feet over the sidewalk. Directly opposite is a post office built into the heavy walls of the Hofburg, the former imperial palace, and on the west side a high gate leads to the green meadow of the Burg garden.

The 144 Nazis from Siebensterngasse, sweeping into the courtyard, had seized those members of the government within, Dollfuss, Fey, and Fey's assistant Karwinsky, and about 150 members of the staff, civil servants, clerks, and so on. The guards in the building, 60 strong, suspected nothing or at least put up no resistance and were disarmed and arrested. The police plotters knew well the corridors and rooms of the complicated building (some of them, indeed, had previously been posted there on duty), and the occupation was quick and thorough. The analogy for America would be the seizure of the White House, since the Bundeskanzleramt is the central ganglion of government in Austria.

Nothing whatever of these events was known to the small group outside the building. Among the newspaper men who, having heard the radio signal, had arrived by 1:15 and stayed till nightfall were Nypels of the Amsterdam *Handelsblatt*, Diez of the New York *Herald-Tribune*, two Hungarians, one Albanian, and one Czech. They did not succumb to the temptation to follow the armored car which led me away to Ravag. They saw the whole story, and from a correlation of their records I have made the following chronology.

The very first arrival on Ballhausplatz after Nypels was a tall, blond, youthful, German photographer, who — remarkable coincidence if coincidence it was — had arrived in Vienna from Berlin the day before. Calmly he set up his tripod. At 1:25 some plain-clothes detectives and four uniformed police wearing steel helmets and carrying rifles arrived. A shout pierced the basement window, "Go away or we shoot." At 1:55 a Heimwehr lieutenant arrived, unarmed and alone, and smashed his fists against the door, shouting with quixotic magnificence, "I give you five minutes to open the door, or I will blow it up." This gesture accomplished, he went away and was not seen again.

(Dollfuss was already bleeding to death by this time, the blood pumping from the hole in his throat, but no one knew....)

Several other officers arrived, looked about, decided that nothing was wrong, and went away again. Traffic was still entirely normal. Then, at 2:05, came Dr. Funder, the venerable editor of the government organ *Reichspost*. A voice from inside was heard, "*Machen Sie keinen Sorgen*. (Don't be alarmed.) Rintelen is Chancellor and a new police chief is coming from Berlin." Funder hurried away. Many Heimwehr men and police had now arrived. At about 2:30 began a series of ultimatums that lasted the whole day. A Heimwehr officer knocked on the door at 2:35 and said, "We give you twenty minutes and then we blow up the building." "Go away or we shoot" a voice, distorted and hollow, answered through the door. The impression was now general that the whole government had been taken prisoner.

At 3 Major Baar, a Heimwehr officer and vice-governor of Lower Austria, arrived. A police officer shouted to him, "I don't know what to do. I am awaiting reinforcements and orders." The Heimwehr was now massed along the garden road to the Burg Theater, but the police pushed them back. "Who is inside?" Baar was asked. He answered, "Dollfuss, Fey, and Karwinsky are inside, prisoners of the Putschists. A new government has been formed and is meeting at the War Ministry on Stubenring." Police reinforcements came and a courteous officer said, "Look here, gentlemen, this is not a good place to stand because here you are in the direct line of fire." At 3:45 traffic was finally stopped and the little group of onlookers were a compact island in the broad empty pond of the square.

At 3:57 Major Fey, who has a face like a battle-axe, appeared for the first time on the balcony. He was pale as paper. He wrung his hands as if to free them from dust on the doorhandle. With him was Holzweber, the leader of the rebels, a meager, bespectacled little man who looked like a clerk on a stool despite his captain's uniform, blazing with decorations. The crowd started to shout, and Fey called in a low voice, "*Ruhe!*" (Quiet.)

Everyone thought at once, "It is a Putsch made by Fey and the regular army."

Fey called, "Where is the commandant?" He could not be found, but a policeman walked up and saluted respectfully. "Who are you?" Fey asked. "I am Captain Eibel awaiting orders," the policeman said. Holzweber whispered to Fey and Fey said, "Come without weapons to the back door." Eibel nodded and Holzweber called after him, "Be sure you are without arms and come alone."

Heimwehr men in the square had recognized Fey and they began to shout: "Fey! Our Fey!"

At 4:08 Eibel returned from the back door on Metastasiogasse. He was running hard, his helmet was off, and his hair was damp and disorderly. He grabbed an open alarm 'phone. Everyone heard what he said, talking to headquarters:

"I've been inside, I've spoken with Fey. The Bundeskanzler (Dollfuss) is apparently badly wounded. He has resigned. There is a new government, and Fey remains vice-chancellor." Headquarters asked something and Eibel replied, "They are disciplined and look like the military. The staff of the chancellery, one hundred and fifty men and women, are under guard in the courtyard."

By this time the commandant, Hofrat Humpel, had turned up and he said to Eibel, "If the Chancellor is wounded he should have a physician. Run to the back door and offer to bring a doctor." Eibel came back and said: "I knocked and the sentry said, 'No need for a physician any more.'" So it was known to this limited group that the Chancellor was dead.

At 4:20 Fey appeared on the balcony again, Holzweber at his elbow. The idea that it was a Putsch with Fey in charge was exploded because obviously Holzweber was in command and giving Fey orders. Fey called "*Ruhe!*" (Quiet.) Then, bending over the balcony, he called, "Where is Rintelen?" The Heimwehr started to shout to the Nazis inside:

"Woe on you if you harm our Fey. Touch our Fey, and we will hang every one of you on these trees."

Fey shouted: "*Nichts unternehmen!* (Take no action.) Nothing may be done until I give the order. I am in command here." He beckoned to Humpel and ordered him round to the back door. A big Heimwehr man, just under the balcony, crossed his hands like a seat and gestured to Fey to jump. Humpel came back in about twenty minutes and shouted, "Rintelen is chancellor, Fey is vice-chancellor. They are waiting for Rintelen, who will come in a few minutes."

IV

But it was not Rintelen who came; it was quite another person, Neustädter-Stürmer, delegate of the rump (loyalist) government in the Ministry of War. He waited a few moments and then Fey appeared on the balcony again and called, "Where is Rintelen?"

Neustädter-Stürmer shouted, "*Rintelen kommt nicht!*" (Rintelen is not coming.)

Astonished, Fey turned to Holzweber at his elbow and a Heimwehr man called, "Shall we storm the building?"

Fey said, "No, nothing is to be done. Take no action without my orders."

Neustädter-Stürmer answered, "A new government has been formed and I represent it. In the name of the government I promise a safe conduct to the rebels. They will be conducted to the German frontier. If you do not surrender in twenty minutes we storm the building."

Fey said, "No. You will not storm the building. I am state secretary of public security, and you are to take no action without my authority."

Neustädter-Stürmer (sharply): "*Sie irren sich*, Herr Fey! (You are mistaken!) The members of the government who are prisoners are under duress and are not competent to give orders. It is now 5:28. At 5:48 the building will be stormed."

When the ultimatum expired everyone took cover but there was no shooting. Neustädter-Stürmer kept pacing up and down and Fey had disappeared. "It was just an Austrian ultimatum," someone joked. But the tension was terrific. At 6:04 Fey came out again and said that the rebels agreed to surrender but asked what guaranty there was of safe conduct. They wanted military protection to the border. "That can be arranged," Neustädter-Stürmer replied, and Fey, speaking for Hudl (another rebel on the balcony), called, "Can we have fifteen minutes more?" A civilian shouted, "They mustn't harm anyone in the building."

At 6:30 Fey came out once more. He tried to talk to General Zehner, the undersecretary of state for war, who had taken charge. There was such a tumult that no one could hear. Police, journalists, Heimwehr, lookers-on were all under the balcony shouting. So Zehner and Neustädter-Stürmer went round to meet Fey at the back door. Then Dr. Rieth, the German Minister, arrived. At about 6:50 Zehner reappeared and announced, "They will get military protection to the frontier under the command of a staff officer."

At about 7:30 Fey came out the back door. He walked up to Neustädter-Stürmer and said, "Give me a cigarette." A journalist called, "*Pfui* on their safe conduct!" Fey, lifting his voice with effort, said, "Quiet!" Neustädter-Stürmer asked him, "Is it true that Dollfuss is dead?" Fey said, "Yes, I spoke to him just before he died. When I came in he was lying on a divan wounded and bleeding." He crushed the cigarette in his hand and said, "Give me another cigarette."

At 7:40 Rieth and Karwinsky came out. Schuschnigg, the new Prime Minister, arrived and led Fey, Zehner, and Neustädter-Stürmer into the Burg garden. The police closed the gates behind them and, standing there on the grass, in the dusk, they held a cabinet meeting. By now twenty military trucks were lined up along the Ballhaus, and police streamed into the building to disarm the rebels and conduct them to the frontier. The rebels came out cocky and confident. Everyone thought their free passage to Germany was assured. They thought so too. But they were wrong.

V

Dollfuss had opened his last cabinet meeting at eleven. Among the items on the agenda were — of all things — regulations governing a famous Vienna theater devoted to comic opera. The warning did not reach the cabinet till about 12:50, although Major Wrabel, Fey's aide, had conveyed the alarm to the police at about 12:30. Vienna *Schlamperei* (slovenliness), as well as treason, is probably responsible for the fact that the chancellery doors were not shut. Once he got the alarm, Dollfuss acted with great energy and coolness. He instantly dismissed the cabinet and ordered the ministers to scatter to their separate offices, only Fey and Karwinsky remaining. This saved Austria, because if Schuschnigg and Neustädter-Stürmer had not been outside the building the Putsch would probably have succeeded.

At 1:02 the rebels were inside the gates, 144 of them. "We arrest you in the name of President Miklas," they falsely shouted.

Officials at the chancellery told me the next day that they first thought a surprise military drill was in progress. The uniforms seemed genuine and the men were disciplined. Then, along each tier of offices, rude voices shouted, "Come out! Hands up!" Doors were battered down and the staff herded into the courtyard. The more prominent officials were imprisoned in a small room and told that they were the first batch of hostages who would be shot if the plot miscarried. A second batch was then chosen to be shot after the first batch. It became clear that the men were Nazis when the first thing they did was to open the telephone switchboard and get in touch with the German legation. And one rebel told a friend of mine, "Curious, are you? In half an hour you'll hear all about it on the Munich radio."

Immediately on entrance one detachment of rebels went up the main staircase, ignoring other objectives, to search the state departments, find Dollfuss, and murder him. There is little doubt but that this group was specifically charged with this duty. It was led by an ex-corporal in the army, Planetta, with a chin like a boxing glove. Dollfuss was given no chance to escape. He might easily, like Fey and the others, have been captured alive. But the rebels had one main aim, to kill him. They entered the building at 1:02 and by 1:10 at latest he was shot.

Having dismissed the cabinet, Dollfuss retired to his private study, a small room bound in yellow silk. His valet, Hedvicek, looked out of the window and saw the rebel trucks unloading in the courtyard. He told Dollfuss to try to escape through a passage that led through the complicated web of archive rooms upstairs. Briskly the Chancellor left the yellow room and started across an oyster-white room toward the famous Congress hall. The oyster-white room has three doors. One gives on the main staircase, and here the rebels entered. The door to the Congress hall was locked and Hedvicek fumbled with the key. Dollfuss, a small man, reached up for the knob and at a range of about twenty inches Planetta shot him in the exposed armpit. Dollfuss reeled and Planetta fired again, this time in the throat, at about a distance of eight inches. The Chancellor fell. ("How his head cracked on the floor!" Hedvicek said.)

"*Hilfe, Hilfe!*" Dollfuss muttered. ("Help, help.")

Planetta said, "Stand up."

"I cannot," Dollfuss whispered.

They picked him up and laid him on the rose-and-cream Louis XV divan. Servants were still sucking up the dust and blood with vacuum cleaners when I saw the room next morning. On the embroidery of the divan were three large blood spots, almost exactly the shape and color of large oak leaves.

Fey, who was detained nearby, had heard the shots but did not know their meaning. At about 2:30 a group of Nazis summoned him and led him to the room where Dollfuss was still dying. The Chancellor recognized him and whispered weakly:

"I charge you to take care of my family if I die."

The rebels had a revolver in Fey's ribs and permitted him to say nothing. Dollfuss went on, very faintly:

"Where is Schuschnigg?"

Fey shook his head and, mustering strength, Dollfuss whispered, "Try to settle this without bloodshed. Tell Rintelen to make peace."

Fey was hustled out of the room. He appealed to the rebels to get a doctor or at least a priest. They refused, although they asked the prisoners if a doctor were among them, and one of them gave the dying Chancellor a glass of water. Dollfuss must have thought he had been betrayed by his own army; not only that the Putsch had succeeded but that his own men had killed him. Later (in delirium?) he apparently believed that loyal troops, not rebels, were surrounding him, staring at his shrunken face, because he whispered, "*Kinder* (children) you are so good to me. Why are the others not as you are? I wanted only peace. May God forgive the others." The last blood was now streaming from his small body. At 3:45 he died.

The rebels thought they had won until about 5 P.M. At 4:30 Hudl, the second in command, told the prisoners in the courtyard that a new government had been formed and that Rintelen, the new chancellor, would arrive in a few minutes. Thereupon about twenty officials gave him the Hitler salute and others called out, "Heil Hitler." Hudl testified at his trial that Wrabel, who was caught inside the building, gave him his card and said, "Call me *du*." (The German familiar form of the second person.)

After five, when Neustädter-Stürmer was outside, the rebels began to crack. Holzweber went to Fey and said frankly, "There has been some hitch. I do not know what do do." Fey shrugged. Then, a characteristically Viennese touch, Holzweber proceeded, "Ah! I shall telephone the Café Eiles and ask if Herr Kunze is there." So with the Chancellor dead, the government disrupted, Austria convulsed, and Europe at the ragged edge of war, the leader of the rebels rang up (of all things) a coffee house, to ask if a man who *might* be there could tell him what to do.

Kunze was a civilian who had been at Siebensterngasse. Holzweber led the first truck and Hudl the second and Kunze was to have been in the third. But he never arrived. No one knows exactly what happened to him or who he is or where. He is one of the central mysteries of the whole story. The Viennese police think he is a Nazi lawyer who fled to Germany.

The Putschists were more light-fingered than disciplined "idealists" have a right to be, according to the Austrian government. They stole gold watches from desks, sixteen schillings from the bureau of President Miklas, and Dollfuss' pocketbook, it is said.

After six the rebels decided to surrender, following the promise of safe conduct. All the one hundred and fifty prisoners would be shot, Holzweber declared, if free passage was not given. Fey said to the government negotiator, "Do not allow considerations of my safety to influence you one way or another." Then Hudl suggested telephoning to Dr. Rieth, the German Minister, as witness for the safe conduct. Fey explained the proposition over the telephone, and Rieth asked him whether or not to come. Fey said, "It is not my business to give you orders or dissuade you. I have only to pass on these men's demand." Rieth came, the negotiations were completed, and the exodus began.

Still the mass of the imprisoned hostages did not know the Chancellor was dead. Leaving the building, one of the rebels called out, "We've left a dead one in the corner room upstairs." An official rushed up and found Dollfuss there. The body had completely shriveled like a raisin and was clammy blue. The face was uncovered and wore an expression of extremest agony. A piece of canvas covered part of the body. There was a terrible wound in the throat. Underneath the divan, spilled beyond the basin, was a lake of blood.

VI

And now about Rintelen. Why did Rintelen not come? Why did the Putsch fail?

He did not come because he was arrested. He was arrested not by the police or government, but by his old friend Dr. Funder, the editor of the *Reichspost*, who, leaving the chancellery at 2:10, went straight to the Hotel Imperial where Rintelen was staying and on his own responsibility persuaded him to give himself up at the War Ministry, in order to avert scandal. Owing to his position as a minister, Rintelen was not searched. It is said that the Ravag had telephoned Rintelen at about 1:50 and asked him to deny the radio report naming him chancellor. "I have no authority to do that," Rintelen answered, and rang off. At midnight that night Rintelen shot himself. The wound was not mortal, though so dangerous that the actual heart had to be stitched up.

When Rintelen left the hotel with Funder he told the hall porter, "I will be back in half an hour." The fact of Rintelen's basic association with Nazis is indisputable, but it is possible, just possible, that the Putschists may have used his name without his knowledge....

About the position of Fey there will probably be dispute as long as the story is told. I do not think he knew anything about the plot. He was not a traitor, but he behaved like a poltroon. No one knows yet exactly what passed between Fey and the rebels when they first arrested him; but the evidence of both police officers who entered the building is that they understood (from the rebels?) that Fey, with Dollfuss dead hardly a minute, was vice-chancellor in the new Rintelen regime. On the other hand, Fey can hardly be blamed for telling the loyalist forces not to bombard the building. He had not only his own life to save but he was responsible for the safety of the one hundred and fifty other hostages. If Fey had shouted early in the afternoon, "They have murdered the Chancellor; storm the building even if we die," it would have been a magnificent gesture but it would have cost much bloodshed. One must remember that Fey knew nothing of what was going on outside. He thought Rintelen *was* chancellor. Even so, if he had greeted Neustädter-Stürmer's appearance with a whisper of pleasure instead of a reiterated demand for Rintelen his reputation for loyalty, if not for courage, would not have suffered such a severe setback.

There is much bad feeling about the withdrawal of the safe conduct. The rebels were shipped, not to the German frontier, but to the Marokanner police barracks hardly a mile away. The government defends what was certainly bad faith by saying (a) Fey was not authorized to give a safe-conduct, and (b) Neustädter-Stürmer gave it unaware that the rump cabinet at 5 o'clock made it conditional on no casualties. I imagine the final decision not to free the Nazis was taken at the cabinet meeting outside the chancellery at 7:30. Here Schuschnigg was informed for the first time of the circumstances of Dollfuss's death and he decided simply not to let the murderers go. Neustädter-Stürmer said at Holzweber's trial, "Yes, I gave my soldier's word of honor. But a soldier's word of honor is given to other soldiers, not to men who deny medical aid and priestly services to a mortally wounded man."

Another reason for the failure of the Putsch is that the country as a whole did not rise. In Styria and Carinthia, where the Nazis had arms, there was severe but brief fighting, but nowhere else. For a year all of us had been deluded into believing that the Nazis were sixty per cent, seventy per cent, eighty per cent of the country. Possibly, even now, this is true, but at the critical moment the Nazis did not take action. The rebel signal had reverberated through the land; for four hours there was no regular government; but nothing happened. The Nazis had not bothered to arm their adherents, feeling sure that the army would mutiny and provide weapons; but the army remained loyal. Thus they lost their supreme chance.

JAMES ANTHONY FROUDE

JAMES ANTHONY FROUDE (1818–1894) met Carlyle in 1849 and became a disciple. Carlyle's view of history as action compounded of innumerable biographical facts undoubtedly influenced Froude. The great work of Froude is his *History of England from the Fall of Wolsey to the Defeat of the Spanish Armada*, which occupied him from 1856 to 1870. History as the drama of action has its limitations; and Froude has been severely criticized for inaccuracy arising from his emphasis upon personalities. The criticism has, however, been over-severe; and the literary form, the unified view of events and characters, the vividness of his "scenes" make him a truer restorer of the past than more meticulous workmen. The present selection is part of the XXXIVth chapter of the *History of England*.

THE EXECUTION OF MARY OF SCOTLAND *

MEANWHILE as the weeks had passed on Mary Stuart's confidence had returned. She had nerved herself for the worst and had dared it. Believre had written, entreating her to make her peace with the queen before it was too late; her fate was still in her own hands. But she feared that she might be betrayed. A confession would disqualify her for the martyr's attitude which, if she was to die, she meant to assume; and though she interpreted a sound of hammers in the hall into the erection of a scaffold, she had remained defiant. Day had followed day, and she had heard no more. She understood Elizabeth as well as Elizabeth understood her. Her almoner had been permitted to resume his duties, and the unwelcome offer of an English minister had not been again obtruded upon her. She had written Elizabeth one of her most pathetic letters, protesting and swearing her innocence, attributing the accusations against her to a conspiracy of the Puritans, hinting in her old way that she had secrets of the gravest moment to impart to her if she could but communicate with her in private, and addressing her in a tone in which affection and tender reproach were melted into resignation.

No answer had been sent, but she had counted justly on the effect it would produce. "There has been a letter," said Leicester, "which hath wrought tears."

The blow when it came at last therefore came suddenly. Beale rode hard — for unless, which is unlikely, he trusted the letter to Kent to a second hand he called at Wrest on his way down — and he arrived at Fotheringay on Sunday evening. The purpose of his coming was not made known in the castle. Early on Monday he went in search of Lord Shrewsbury, while a message was despatched to the Sheriff of Northamptonshire to be in attendance on Wednesday morning. On Monday evening the Earl of Kent came. Shrewsbury appeared on Tuesday before noon, and when the early castle dinner was over, they sent a servant to the Queen of Scots with a request to be admitted to her presence.

Shrewsbury had not seen her since she had passed from under his charge.

* By permission of Charles Scribner's Sons.

He had not been on the commission which tried her; illness had prevented him from attending the last Parliament, and he had taken no public part in the prosecution; and although he had signified privately as his personal opinion that her death was necessary, it could not have been without emotion that he was once more brought into a brief relation with her in so terrible a form. Kent was an austere Puritan, to whom she was merely a wicked woman overtaken at last by the punishment which she had too long deserved and escaped.

Briefly, solemnly, and sternly they delivered their awful message. They informed her that they had received a commission under the great seal to see her executed, and she was told that she must prepare to suffer on the following morning.

She was dreadfully agitated. For a moment she refused to believe them. Then, as the truth forced itself upon her, tossing her head in disdain and struggling to control herself, she called her physician and began to speak to him of money that was owed to her in France. At last it seems that she broke down altogether, and they left her with a fear either that she would destroy herself in the night, or that she would refuse to come to the scaffold, and that it might be necessary to drag her there by violence.

The end had come. She had long professed to expect it, but the clearest expectation is not certainty. The scene for which she had affected to prepare she was to encounter in its dread reality, and all her busy schemes, her dreams of vengeance, her visions of a revolution, with herself ascending out of the convulsion, and seating herself on her rival's throne — all were gone. She had played deep, and the dice had gone against her.

Yet in death, if she encountered it bravely, victory was still possible. Could she but sustain to the last the character of a calumniated suppliant accepting heroically for God's sake and her creed's the concluding stroke of a long series of wrongs, she might stir a tempest of indignation which, if it could not save herself, might at least overwhelm her enemy. Persisting, as she persisted to the last, in denying all knowledge of Babington, it would be affectation to credit her with a genuine feeling of religion; but the imperfection of her motive exalts the greatness of her fortitude. To an impassioned believer death is comparatively easy.

Her chaplain was lodged in a separate part of the castle. The commissioners, who were as anxious that her execution should wear its real character as she was herself determined to convert it into a martyrdom, refused, perhaps unwisely, to allow him access to her, and offered her again the assistance of an Anglican dean. They gave her an advantage over them which she did not fail to use. She would not let the dean come near her. She sent a note to the chaplain telling him that she had meant to receive the sacrament, but as it might not be she must content herself with a general confession. She bade him watch through the night and pray for her. In the morning when she was brought out she might perhaps see him, and receive his blessing on her knees. She supped cheerfully, giving her last meal with her attendants a character of sacred parting; afterwards she drew aside her apothecary M. Gorion, and asked him if she might depend upon his fidelity. When he satisfied her that she might trust him, she said she had a letter and two diamonds which she wished to send to Mendoza. He undertook to melt some drug and conceal them in it where they would never be looked for, and promised to deliver them faithfully. One of the jewels was for Mendoza himself; the other and the largest was for Philip. It was to be a sign that she was dying for the truth, and was meant also to bespeak his care for her friends and servants. Every one of them so far as she was able, without forgetting a name, she commended to his liberality. Arundel, Paget, Morgan, the Archbishop of Glasgow, Westmoreland, Throgmorton, the Bishop of Ross, her two secretaries, the ladies who had shared the trials of her imprisonment, she remembered them all, and specified the sums which she desired Philip to bestow on them. And as Mary Stuart then and throughout her life never lacked gratitude to those who had been true to her, so then as always she remembered her enemies. There was no cant about her, no unreal talk of forgiveness of injuries. She bade Gorion tell Philip it was her last prayer that he should persevere, notwithstanding her death, in the invasion of England. It was God's quarrel, she said, and worthy of his greatness; and as soon as he had conquered it, she desired him not to forget how she had been treated by Cecil, and Leicester, and Walsingham; by Lord Huntingdon, who had ill-used her fifteen years before at Tutbury; by Sir Amyas Paulet, and Secretary Wade.

Her last night was a busy one. As she said herself, there was much to be done and the time was short. A few lines to the King of France were dated two hours after midnight. They were to insist for the last time that she was innocent of the conspiracy, that she was dying for religion, and for having asserted her right to the crown; and to beg that out of the sum which he owed her, her servants' wages might be paid and masses provided for her soul. After this she slept for three or four hours, and then rose and with the most elaborate care prepared to encounter the end.

At eight in the morning the provost-marshal knocked at the outer door which communicated with her suite of apartments. It was locked and no one answered, and he went back in some trepidation lest the fears might prove true which had been entertained the preceding evening. On his returning with the sheriff, however, a few minutes later, the door was open, and they were confronted with the tall majestic figure of Mary Stuart standing before them in splendour. The plain grey dress had been exchanged for a robe of black satin; her jacket was of black satin also, looped and slashed and trimmed with velvet. Her false hair was arranged studiously with a coif, and over her head and falling down over her back was a white veil of delicate lawn. A crucifix of gold hung from her neck. In her hand she held a crucifix of ivory, and a number of jewelled paternosters was attached to her girdle. Led by two of Paulet's gentlemen, the sheriff walking before her, she passed to the chamber of presence in which she had been tried, where Shrewsbury, Kent, Paulet, Drury, and others were waiting to receive her. Andrew Melville, Sir Robert's brother, who had been master of her household, was kneeling in tears. "Melville," she said, "you should rather rejoice than weep that the end of my troubles is come. Tell my friends I die a true

Catholic. Commend me to my son. Tell him I have done nothing to prejudice his kingdom of Scotland, and so, good Melville, farewell." She kissed him, and turning asked for her chaplain du Preau. He was not present. There had been a fear of some religious melodrame which it was thought well to avoid. Her ladies, who had attempted to follow her, had been kept back also. She could not afford to leave the account of her death to be reported by enemies and Puritans, and she required assistance for the scene which she meditated. Missing them she asked the reason of their absence, and said she wished them to see her die. Kent said he feared they might scream or faint, or attempt perhaps to dip their handkerchiefs in her blood. She undertook that they should be quiet and obedient. "The queen," she said, "would never deny her so slight a request"; and when Kent still hesitated, she added with tears, "You know I am cousin to your queen, of the blood of Henry VII, a married Queen of France, and anointed Queen of Scotland."

It was impossible to refuse. She was allowed to take six of her own people with her, and select them herself. She chose her physician Burgoyne, Andrew Melville, the apothecary Gorion, and her surgeon, with two ladies, Elizabeth Kennedy and Curle's young wife Barbara Mowbray, whose child she had baptized.

"Allons donc," she then said — "Let us go," and passing out attended by the earls, and leaning on the arm of an officer of the guard, she descended the great staircase to the hall. The news had spread far through the country. Thousands of people were collected outside the walls. About three hundred knights and gentlemen of the county had been admitted to witness the execution. The tables and forms had been removed, and a great wood fire was blazing in the chimney. At the upper end of the hall, above the fire-place, but near it, stood the scaffold, twelve feet square and two feet and a half high. It was covered with black cloth; a low rail ran round it covered with black cloth also, and the sheriff's guard of halberdiers were ranged on the floor below on the four sides to keep off the crowd. On the scaffold was the block, black like the rest; a square black cushion was placed behind it, and behind the cushion a black chair; on the right were two other chairs for the earls. The axe leant against the rail, and two masked figures stood like mutes on either side at the back. The Queen of Scots as she swept in seemed as if coming to take a part in some solemn pageant. Not a muscle of her face could be seen to quiver; she ascended the scaffold with absolute composure, looked round her smiling, and sat down. Shrewsbury and Kent followed and took their places, the sheriff stood at her left hand, and Beale then mounted a platform and read the warrant aloud.

In all the assembly Mary Stuart appeared the person least interested in the words which were consigning her to death.

"Madam," said Lord Shrewsbury to her, when the reading was ended, "you hear what we are commanded to do."

"You will do your duty," she answered, and rose as if to kneel and pray.

The Dean of Peterborough, Dr. Fletcher, approached the rail. "Madam," he began, with a low obeisance, "the queen's most excellent majesty";

"madam, the queen's most excellent majesty" — thrice he commenced his sentence, wanting words to pursue it. When he repeated the words a fourth time, she cut him short.

"Mr. Dean," she said, "I am a Catholic, and must die a Catholic. It is useless to attempt to move me, and your prayers will avail me but little."

"Change your opinion, madam," he cried, his tongue being loosed at last; "repent of your sins, settle your faith in Christ, by him to be saved."

"Trouble not yourself further, Mr. Dean," she answered; "I am settled in my own faith, for which I mean to shed my blood."

"I am sorry, madam," said Shrewsbury, "to see you so addicted to popery."

"That image of Christ you hold there," said Kent, "will not profit you if he be not engraved in your heart."

She did not reply, and turning her back on Fletcher, knelt for her own devotions.

He had been evidently instructed to impair the Catholic complexion of the scene, and the Queen of Scots was determined that he should not succeed. When she knelt he commenced an extempore prayer in which the assembly joined. As his voice sounded out in the hall she raised her own, reciting with powerful deep-chested tones the penitential psalms in Latin, introducing English sentences at intervals that the audience might know what she was saying, and praying with especial distinctness for her holy father the pope.

From time to time, with conspicuous vehemence, she struck the crucifix against her bosom, and then, as the dean gave up the struggle, leaving her Latin, she prayed in English wholly, still clear and loud. She prayed for the Church which she had been ready to betray, for her son whom she had disinherited, for the queen whom she had endeavoured to murder. She prayed God to avert his wrath from England, that England which she had sent a last message to Philip to beseech him to invade. She forgave her enemies, whom she had invited Philip not to forget, and then, praying to the saints to intercede for her with Christ, and kissing the crucifix and crossing her own breast, "Even as thy arms, O Jesus," she cried, "were spread upon the cross, so receive me into thy mercy and forgive my sins."

With these words she rose; the black mutes stepped forward, and in the usual form begged her forgiveness.

"I forgive you," she said, "for now I hope you shall end all my troubles." They offered their help in arranging her dress. "Truly, my lords," she said with a smile to the earls, "I never had such grooms waiting on me before." Her ladies were allowed to come up upon the scaffold to assist her; for the work to be done was considerable, and had been prepared with no common thought.

She laid her crucifix on her chair. The chief executioner took it as a perquisite, but was ordered instantly to lay it down. The lawn veil was lifted carefully off, not to disturb the hair, and was hung upon the rail. The black robe was next removed. Below it was a petticoat of crimson velvet. The black jacket followed, and under the jacket was a body of crimson satin. One of her ladies handed her a pair of crimson sleeves, with which she hastily covered her arms; and thus she stood on the black scaffold with the black figures all around her, blood-red from head to foot.

Her reasons for adopting so extraordinary a costume must be left to conjecture. It is only certain that it must have been carefully studied, and that the pictorial effect must have been appalling.

The women, whose firmness had hitherto borne the trial, began now to give way, spasmodic sobs bursting from them which they could not check. "Ne criez vous," she said, "j'ay promis pour vous." Struggling bravely, they crossed their breasts again and again, she crossing them in turn and bidding them pray for her. Then she knelt on the cushion. Barbara Mowbray bound her eyes with a handkerchief. "Adieu," she said, smiling for the last time and waving her hand to them, "Adieu, au revoir." They stepped back from off the scaffold and left her alone. On her knees she repeated the psalm, In te, Domine, confido, "In Thee, O Lord, have I put my trust." Her shoulders being exposed, two scars became visible, one on either side, and the earls being now a little behind her, Kent pointed to them with his white wand and looked inquiringly at his companion. Shrewsbury whispered that they were the remains of two abscesses from which she had suffered while living with him at Sheffield.

When the psalm was finished she felt for the block, and laying down her head muttered: "In manus, Domine tuas, commendo animam meam." The hard wood seemed to hurt her, for she placed her hands under her neck. The executioners gently removed them, lest they should deaden the blow, and then one of them holding her slightly, the other raised the axe and struck. The scene had been too trying even for the practised headsman of the Tower. His arm wandered. The blow fell on the knot of the handkerchief, and scarcely broke the skin. She neither spoke nor moved. He struck again, this time effectively. The head hung by a shred of skin, which he divided without withdrawing the axe; and at once a metamorphosis was witnessed, strange as was ever wrought by wand of fabled enchanter. The coif fell off and the false plaits. The laboured illusion vanished. The lady who had knelt before the block was in the maturity of grace and loveliness. The executioner, when he raised the head, as usual, to show it to the crowd, exposed the withered features of a grizzled, wrinkled old woman.

"So perish all enemies of the queen," said the Dean of Peterborough. A loud Amen rose over the hall. "Such end," said the Earl of Kent, rising and standing over the body, "to the queen's and the Gospel's enemies."

Orders had been given that everything which she had worn should be immediately destroyed, that no relics should be carried off to work imaginary miracles. Sentinels stood at the doors who allowed no one to pass out without permission; and after the first pause, the earls still keeping their places, the body was stripped. It then appeared that a favourite lapdog had followed its mistress unperceived, and was concealed under her clothes; when discovered it gave a short cry, and seated itself between the head and the neck, from which the blood was still flowing. It was carried away and carefully washed, and then beads, Paternoster, handkerchief — each particle of dress which the blood had touched, with the cloth on the block and on the scaffold, was burnt in the hall fire in the presence of the crowd. The scaffold itself was next removed: a brief account of the execution was drawn up, with which Henry Talbot, Lord Shrewsbury's son, was sent to London, and then everyone was dismissed. Silence settled down on Fotheringay, and the last scene of the life of Mary Stuart, in which tragedy and melodrama were so strangely intermingled, was over.

FRANCIS PARKMAN

THE career of the American historian Francis Parkman (1823–93) showed marked singleness of purpose. Interested as a young man in Indian life and the New England border wars, he determined, while still an undergraduate at Harvard, to write about them. After two years of post-graduate study in law, followed by excursions into Pennsylvania and neighboring regions, he went west, returning with material for his first book, *The California and Oregon Trail* (1849). But his health broke down, and for the rest of his life he was an invalid. Nevertheless he embarked upon his famous work, *France and England in North America*. He performed this task so ably as to make unnecessary a repetition of it by later historians. Preceding the portion here given of Chapter 27 from *Montcalm and Wolfe*, the climax of the story, Parkman movingly describes the anxieties of both French and English forces, and the preliminary skirmishes leading to the critical attack.

THE HEIGHTS OF ABRAHAM *

...AT LAST the time for action came. On Wednesday, the twelfth, the troops at St. Nicolas were embarked again, and all were told to hold themselves in readiness. Wolfe, from the flagship "Sutherland," issued his last general orders. "The enemy's force is now divided, great scarcity of provisions in their camp, and universal discontent among the Canadians. Our troops below are in readiness to join us; all the light artillery and tools are embarked at the Point of Levi; and the troops will land where the French seem least to expect it. The first body that gets on shore is to march directly to the enemy and drive them from any little post they may occupy; the officers must be careful that the succeeding bodies do not by any mistake fire on those who go before them. The battalions must form on the upper ground with expedition, and be ready to charge whatever presents itself. When the artillery and troops are landed, a corps will be left to secure the landing-place, while the rest march on and endeavor to bring the Canadians and French to a battle. The officers and men will remember what their country expects from them, and what a determined body of soldiers inured to war is capable of doing against five weak French battalions mingled with a disorderly peasantry."

The spirit of the army answered to that of its chief. The troops loved and admired their general, trusted their officers, and were ready for any attempt. "Nay, how could it be otherwise," quaintly asks honest Sergeant John Johnson, of the fifty-eighth regiment, "being at the heels of gentlemen whose whole thirst, equal with their general, was for glory? We had seen them tried, and always found them sterling. We knew that they would stand by us to the last extremity."

Wolfe had thirty-six hundred men and officers with him on board the

* From *Montcalm and Wolfe*, Volume II. By permission of the publishers, Little, Brown and Company.

vessels of Holmes; and he now sent orders to Colonel Burton at Point Levi to bring to his aid all who could be spared from that place and the Point of Orleans. They were to march along the south bank, after nightfall, and wait further orders at a designated spot convenient for embarkation. Their number was about twelve hundred, so that the entire force destined for the enterprise was at the utmost forty-eight hundred. With these, Wolfe meant to climb the heights of Abraham in the teeth of an enemy who, though much reduced, were still twice as numerous as their assailants.

Admiral Saunders lay with the main fleet in the Basin of Quebec. This excellent officer, whatever may have been his views as to the necessity of a speedy departure, aided Wolfe to the last with unfailing energy and zeal. It was agreed between them that while the General made the real attack, the Admiral should engage Montcalm's attention by a pretended one. As night approached, the fleet ranged itself along the Beauport shore; the boats were lowered and filled with sailors, marines, and the few troops that had been left behind; while ship signalled to ship, cannon flashed and thundered, and shot ploughed the beach, as if to clear a way for assailants to land. In the gloom of the evening the effect was imposing. Montcalm, who thought that the movements of the English above the town were only a feint, that their main force was still below it, and that their real attack would be made there, was completely deceived, and massed his troops in front of Beauport to repel the expected landing. But while in the fleet of Saunders all was uproar and ostentatious menace, the danger was ten miles away, where the squadron of Holmes lay tranquil and silent at its anchorage off Cap-Rouge.

It was less tranquil than it seemed. All on board knew that a blow would be struck that night, though only a few high officers knew where. Colonel Howe, of the light infantry, called for volunteers to lead the unknown and desperate venture, promising, in the words of one of them, "that if any of us survived we might depend on being recommended to the General." As many as were wanted — twenty-four in all — soon came forward. Thirty large bateaux and some boats belonging to the squadron lay moored alongside the vessels; and late in the evening the troops were ordered into them, the twenty-four volunteers taking their place in the foremost. They held in all about seventeen hundred men. The rest remained on board.

Bougainville could discern the movement, and misjudged it, thinking that he himself was to be attacked. The tide was still flowing; and, the better to deceive him, the vessels and boats were allowed to drift upward with it for a little distance, as if to land above Cap-Rouge.

The day had been fortunate for Wolfe. Two deserters came from the camp of Bougainville with intelligence that, at ebb tide on the next night, he was to send down a convoy of provisions to Montcalm. The necessities of the camp at Beauport, and the difficulties of transportation by land, had before compelled the French to resort to this perilous means of conveying supplies; and their boats, drifting in darkness under the shadows of the northern shore, had commonly passed in safety. Wolfe saw at once that, if his own boats went down in advance of the convoy, he could turn the intelligence of the deserters to good account.

He was still on board the "Sutherland." Every preparation was made, and every order given; it only remained to wait the turning of the tide. Seated with him in the cabin was the commander of the sloop-of-war "Porcupine," his former schoolfellow, John Jervis, afterwards Earl St. Vincent. Wolfe told him that he expected to die in the battle of the next day; and taking from his bosom a miniature of Miss Lowther, his betrothed, he gave it to him with a request that he would return it to her if the presentiment should prove true.

Towards two o'clock the tide began to ebb, and a fresh wind blew down the river. Two lanterns were raised into the maintop shrouds of the "Sutherland." It was the appointed signal; the boats cast off and fell down with the current, those of the light infantry leading the way. The vessels with the rest of the troops had orders to follow a little later....

For full two hours the procession of boats, borne on the current, steered silently down the St. Lawrence. The stars were visible, but the night was moonless and sufficiently dark. The General was in one of the foremost boats, and near him was a young midshipman, John Robison, afterwards professor of natural philosophy in the University of Edinburgh. He used to tell in his later life how Wolfe, with a low voice, repeated Gray's *Elegy in a Country Churchyard* to the officers about him. Probably it was to relieve the intense strain of his thoughts. Among the rest was the verse which his own fate was soon to illustrate —

"The paths of glory lead but to the grave."

"Gentlemen," he said, as his recital ended, "I would rather have written those lines than take Quebec." None was there to tell him that the hero is greater than the poet.

As they neared their destination, the tide bore them in towards the shore, and the mighty wall of rock and forest towered in darkness on their left. The dead stillness was suddenly broken by the sharp *Qui vive!* of a French sentry, invisible in the thick gloom. *France!* answered a Highland officer of Fraser's regiment from one of the boats of the light infantry. He had served in Holland, and spoke French fluently.

A quel régiment?

De la Reine, replied the Highlander. He knew that a part of that corps was with Bougainville. The sentry, expecting the convoy of provisions, was satisfied, and did not ask for the password.

Soon after, the foremost boats were passing the heights of Samos, when another sentry challenged them, and they could see him through the darkness running down to the edge of the water, within range of a pistol-shot. In answer to his questions, the same officer replied, in French: "Provision-boats. Don't make a noise; the English will hear us." In fact, the sloop-of-war "Hunter" was anchored in the stream not far off. This time, again, the sentry let them pass. In a few moments they rounded the headland above the Anse du Foulon. There was no sentry there. The strong current swept the boats of the light infantry a little below the intended landing-place. They disembarked on a narrow strand at the foot of heights as steep as a hill covered with trees can be. The twenty-four volunteers led the way, climbing with what silence they might, closely followed by a much larger body. When they reached the top they saw in the dim light a cluster of tents at a short distance, and immediately made a dash at them. Vergor leaped from bed and tried to run off, but was shot in the heel and captured. His men, taken by surprise, made little resistance. One or two were caught, and the rest fled.

The main body of troops waited in their boats by the edge of the strand. The heights near by were cleft by a great ravine choked with forest trees; and in its depths ran a little brook called Ruisseau St.-Denis, which, swollen by the late rains, fell plashing in the stillness over a rock. Other than this no sound could reach the strained ear of Wolfe but the gurgle of the tide and the cautious climbing of his advance-parties as they mounted the steeps at some little distance from where he sat listening. At length from the top came a sound of musket-shots, followed by loud huzzas, and he knew that his men were masters of the position. The word was given; the troops leaped from the boats and scaled the heights, some here, some there, clutching at trees and bushes, their muskets slung at their backs. Tradition still points out the place, near the mouth of the ravine, where the foremost reached the top. Wolfe said to an officer near him: "You can try it, but I don't think you'll get up." He himself, however, found strength to drag himself up with the rest. The narrow slanting path on the face of the heights had been made impassable by trenches and abattis; but all obstructions were soon cleared away, and then the ascent was easy. In the gray of the morning the long file of red-coated soldiers moved quickly upward, and formed in order on the plateau above.

Before many of them had reached the top, cannon were heard close on the left. It was the battery at Samos firing on the boats in the rear and the vessels descending from Cap-Rouge. A party was sent to silence it; this was soon effected, and the more distant battery at Sillery was next attacked and taken. As fast as the boats were emptied they returned for the troops left on board the vessels and for those waiting on the southern shore under Colonel Burton.

The day broke in clouds and threatening rain. Wolfe's battalions were drawn up along the crest of the heights. No enemy was in sight, though a body of Canadians had sallied from the town and moved along the strand towards the landing-place, whence they were quickly driven back. He had achieved the most critical part of his enterprise; yet the success that he coveted placed him in imminent danger. On one side was the garrison of Quebec and the army of Beauport, and Bougainville was on the other. Wolfe's alternative was victory or ruin; for if he should be overwhelmed by a combined attack, retreat would be hopeless. His feelings no man can know; but it would be safe to say that hesitation or doubt had no part in them.

He went to reconnoitre the ground, and soon came to the Plains of Abraham, so called from Abraham Martin, a pilot known as Maître Abraham, who had owned a piece of land here in the early times of the colony. The

Plains were a tract of grass, tolerably level in most parts, patched here and there with cornfields, studded with clumps of bushes, and forming a part of the high plateau at the eastern end of which Quebec stood. On the south it was bounded by the declivities along the St. Lawrence; on the north, by those along the St. Charles, or rather along the meadows through which that lazy stream crawled like a writhing snake. At the place that Wolfe chose for his battle-field the plateau was less than a mile wide.

Thither the troops advanced, marched by files till they reached the ground, and then wheeled to form their line of battle, which stretched across the plateau and faced the city. It consisted of six battalions and the detached grenadiers from Louisbourg, all drawn up in ranks three deep. Its right wing was near the brink of the heights along the St. Lawrence; but the left could not reach those along the St. Charles. On this side a wide space was perforce left open, and there was danger of being outflanked. To prevent this, Brigadier Townshend was stationed here with two battalions, drawn up at right angles with the rest, and fronting the St. Charles. The battalion of Webb's regiment, under Colonel Burton, formed the reserve; the third battalion of Royal Americans was left to guard the landing; and Howe's light infantry occupied a wood far in the rear. Wolfe, with Monckton and Murray, commanded the front line, on which the heavy fighting was to fall, and which, when all the troops had arrived, numbered less than thirty-five hundred men.

Quebec was not a mile distant, but they could not see it; for a ridge of broken ground intervened, called Buttes-à-Neveu, about six hundred paces off. The first division of troops had scarcely come up when, about six o'clock, this ridge was suddenly thronged with white uniforms. It was the battalion of Guienne, arrived at the eleventh hour from its camp by the St. Charles. Some time after there was hot firing in the rear. It came from a detachment of Bougainville's command attacking a house where some of the light infantry were posted. The assailants were repulsed, and the firing ceased. Light showers fell at intervals, besprinkling the troops as they stood patiently waiting the event.

Montcalm had passed a troubled night. Through all the evening the cannon bellowed from the ships of Saunders, and the boats of the fleet hovered in the dusk off the Beauport shore, threatening every moment to land. Troops lined the intrenchments till day, while the General walked the field that adjoined the headquarters till one in the morning, accompanied by the Chevalier Johnstone and Colonel Poulariez. Johnstone says that he was in great agitation, and took no rest all night. At daybreak he heard the sound of cannon above the town. It was the battery at Samos firing on the English ships. He had sent an officer to the quarters of Vaudreuil, which were much nearer Quebec, with orders to bring him word at once should anything unusual happen. But no word came, and about six o'clock he mounted and rode thither with Johnstone. As they advanced, the country behind the town opened more and more upon their sight; till at length, when opposite Vaudreuil's house, they saw across the St. Charles, some two miles away, the red ranks of British soldiers on the heights beyond.

"This is a serious business," Montcalm said; and sent off Johnstone at full gallop to bring up the troops from the centre and left of the camp. Those of the right were in motion already, doubtless by the Governor's order. Vaudreuil came out of the house. Montcalm stopped for a few words with him; then set spurs to his horse, and rode over the bridge of the St. Charles to the scene of danger. He rode with a fixed look, uttering not a word.

The army followed in such order as it might, crossed the bridge in hot haste, passed under the northern rampart of Quebec, entered at the Palace Gate, and pressed on in headlong march along the quaint narrow streets of the warlike town: troops of Indians in scalp-locks and war-paint, a savage glitter in their deep-set eyes; bands of Canadians whose all was at stake — faith, country, and home; the colony regulars; the battalions of Old France, a torrent of white uniforms and gleaming bayonets, La Sarre, Languedoc, Roussillon, Béarn — victors of Oswego, William Henry, and Ticonderoga. So they swept on, poured out upon the plain, some by the gate of St. Louis, and some by that of St. John, and hurried, breathless, to where the banners of Guienne still fluttered on the ridge.

Montcalm was amazed at what he saw. He had expected a detachment, and he found an army. Full in sight before him stretched the lines of Wolfe: the close ranks of the English infantry, a silent wall of red, and the wild array of the Highlanders, with their waving tartans, and bagpipes screaming defiance. Vaudreuil had not come; but not the less was felt the evil of a divided authority and the jealousy of the rival chiefs. Montcalm waited long for the forces he had ordered to join him from the left wing of the army. He waited in vain. It is said that the Governor had detained them, lest the English should attack the Beauport shore. Even if they did so, and succeeded, the French might defy them, could they but put Wolfe to rout on the Plains of Abraham. Neither did the garrison of Quebec come to the aid of Montcalm. He sent to Ramesay, its commander, for twenty-five field-pieces which were on the Palace battery. Ramesay would give him only three, saying that he wanted them for his own defence. There were orders and counter-orders; misunderstanding, haste, delay, perplexity.

Montcalm and his chief officers held a council of war. It is said that he and they alike were for immediate attack. His enemies declare that he was afraid less Vaudreuil should arrive and take command; but the Governor was not a man to assume responsibility at such a crisis. Others say that his impetuosity overcame his better judgment; and of this charge it is hard to acquit him. Bougainville was but a few miles distant, and some of his troops were much nearer; a messenger sent by way of Old Lorette could have reached him in an hour and a half at most, and a combined attack in front and rear might have been concerted with him. If, moreover, Montcalm could have come to an understanding with Vaudreuil, his own force might have been strengthened by two or three thousand additional men from the town, and the camp of Beauport; but he felt that there was no time to lose, for he imagined that Wolfe would soon be reinforced, which was impossible, and he believed that the English were fortifying themselves, which was no less an error. He has been blamed not only for fighting too soon, but for fighting at all. In this he could not choose. Fight he must, for Wolfe was now in a position to cut off all his supplies. His men were full of ardor, and he resolved to attack before their ardor cooled. He spoke a few words to them in his keen, vehement way. "I remember very well how he looked," one of the Canadians, then a boy of eighteen, used to say in his old age; "he rode a black or dark bay horse along the front of our lines, brandishing his sword, as if to excite us to do our duty. He wore a coat with wide sleeves, which fell back as he raised his arm, and showed the white linen of the wristband."

The English waited the result with a composure which, if not quite real, was at least well feigned. The three field-pieces sent by Ramesay plied them with canister-shot, and fifteen hundred Canadians and Indians fusilladed them in front and flank. Over all the plain, from behind bushes and knolls and the edge of cornfields, puffs of smoke sprang incessantly from the guns of these hidden marksmen. Skirmishers were thrown out before the lines to hold them in check, and the soldiers were ordered to lie on the grass to avoid the shot. The firing was liveliest on the English left, where bands of sharpshooters got under the edge of the declivity, among thickets, and behind scattered houses, whence they killed and wounded a considerable number of Townshend's men. The light infantry were called up from the rear. The houses were taken and retaken, and one or more of them was burned.

Wolfe was everywhere. How cool he was, and why his followers loved him, is shown by an incident that happened in the course of the morning. One of his captains was shot through the lungs; and on recovering consciousness, he saw the General standing at his side. Wolfe pressed his hand, told him not to despair, praised his services, promised him early promotion, and sent an aide-de-camp to Monckton to beg that officer to keep the promise if he himself should fall.

It was towards ten o'clock when, from the high ground on the right of the line, Wolfe saw that the crisis was near. The French on the ridge had formed themselves into three bodies, regulars in the centre, regulars and Canadians on right and left. Two field-pieces, which had been dragged up the heights at Anse du Foulon, fired on them with grape-shot, and the troops, rising from the ground, prepared to receive them. In a few moments more they were in motion. They came on rapidly, uttering loud shouts, and firing as soon as they were within range. Their ranks, ill ordered at the best, were further confused by a number of Canadians, who had been mixed among the regulars, and who, after hastily firing, threw themselves on the ground to reload. The British advanced a few rods; then halted and stood still. When the French were within forty paces the word of command rang out, and a crash of musketry answered all along the line. The volley was delivered with remarkable precision. In the battalions of the centre, which had suffered least from the enemy's bullets, the simultaneous explosion was afterwards said by the French officers to have sounded like a cannon-shot. Another volley followed, and then a furious clattering fire that lasted but a minute or two. When the smoke rose, a miserable sight was revealed: the ground cumbered with dead and wounded, the advancing masses stopped short and turned into a frantic mob, shouting, cursing, gesticulating. The order was given to charge. Then over the field rose the British cheer, mixed with the fierce yell of the Highland slogan. Some of the corps pushed forward with the bayonet; some advanced firing. The clansmen drew their broadswords and dashed on, keen and swift as bloodhounds. At the English right, though the attacking column was broken to pieces, a fire was still kept up, chiefly, it seems, by sharpshooters from the bushes and cornfields, where they had lain for an hour or more. Here Wolfe himself led the charge, at the head of the Louisbourg grenadiers. A shot shattered his wrist. He wrapped his handkerchief about it and kept on. Another shot struck him, and he still advanced, when a third lodged in his breast. He staggered, and sat on the ground. Lieutenant Brown, of the grenadiers, one Henderson, a volunteer in the same company, and a private soldier, aided by an officer of artillery who ran to join them, carried him in their arms to the rear. He begged them to lay him down. They did so, and asked if he would have a surgeon. "There's no need," he answered; "it's all over with me." A moment after, one of them cried out: "They run; see how they run!" "Who run?" Wolfe demanded, like a man roused from sleep. "The enemy, sir. Egad, they give way everywhere!" "Go, one of you, to Colonel Burton," returned the dying man; "tell him to march Webb's regiment down to Charles River, to cut off their retreat from the bridge." Then, turning on his side, he murmured, "Now, God be praised, I will die in peace!" and in a few moments his gallant soul had fled.

Montcalm, still on horseback, was borne with the tide of fugitives towards the town. As he approached the walls a shot passed through his body. He kept his seat; two soldiers supported him, one on each side, and led his horse through the St. Louis Gate. On the open space within, among the excited crowd, were several women, drawn, no doubt, by eagerness to know the result of the fight. One of them recognized him, saw the streaming blood, and shrieked, "*O mon Dieu! mon Dieu! le Marquis est tué!*" "It's nothing, it's nothing," replied the death-stricken man; "don't be troubled for me, my good friends." ("*Ce n'est rien, ce n'est rien; ne vous affligez pas pour moi, mes bonnes amies.*")

FREDERICK JACKSON TURNER

PERHAPS the single most influential historical essay written in recent times by an American historian is Frederick Jackson Turner's "The Significance of the Frontier in American History," first published in 1893. This essay changed the current of the interpretation of American history by showing that the American element — the frontier — is a primary force in the shaping of the nation. Previous historians had been too content with merely political history, or had become absorbed in tracing the transplantation of European, especially supposedly "Germanic" institutions to America. The author (1861–1932) was born in Portage, Wisconsin, was a student at the University of Wisconsin, and later a professor of history at his Alma Mater and at Harvard University. Just before his death he was attached to the Henry E. Huntington Library, San Marino, California. He was the author of various books and articles, one of which, *The Frontier in American History* (1920), is an expansion and application of the theory of his famous essay.

THE SIGNIFICANCE OF THE FRONTIER IN AMERICAN HISTORY*

IN A recent bulletin of the Superintendent of the Census for 1890 appear these significant words: "Up to and including 1880 the country had a frontier of settlement, but at present the unsettled area has been so broken into by isolated bodies of settlement that there can hardly be said to be a frontier line. In the discussion of its extent, its westward movement, etc., it can not, therefore, any longer have a place in the census reports." This brief official statement marks the closing of a great historic movement. Up to our own day American history has been in a large degree the history of the colonization of the Great West. The existence of an area of free land, its continuous recession, and the advance of American settlement westward, explain American development.

Behind institutions, behind constitutional forms and modifications, lie the vital forces that call these organs into life and shape them to meet changing conditions. The peculiarity of American institutions is, the fact that they have been compelled to adapt themselves to the changes of an expanding people — to the changes involved in crossing a continent, in winning a wilderness, and in developing at each area of this progress out of the primitive economic and political conditions of the frontier into the complexity of city life. Said Calhoun in 1817, "We are great, and rapidly — I was about to say fearfully — growing!" So saying, he touched the distinguishing feature of American life. All peoples show development; the germ theory of politics has been sufficiently emphasized. In the case of most nations, however, the development has occurred in a limited area; and if the nation has expanded, it has met other growing peoples whom it has conquered. But in the case of the United States we have a different phenomenon. Limiting our atten-

* From *The Frontier in American History*, by Frederick Jackson Turner. Copyright 1920, Henry Holt and Company. Reprinted by permission.

tion to the Atlantic coast, we have the familiar phenomenon of the evolution of institutions in a limited area, such as the rise of representative government; the differentiation of simple colonial governments into complex organs; the progress from primitive industrial society, without division of labor, up to manufacturing civilization. But we have in addition to this a recurrence of the process of evolution in each western area reached in the process of expansion. Thus American development has exhibited not merely advance along a single line, but a return to primitive conditions on a continually advancing frontier-line, and a new development for that area. American social development has been continually beginning over again on the frontier. This perennial rebirth, this fluidity of American life, this expansion westward with its new opportunities, its continuous touch with the simplicity of primitive society, furnish the forces dominating American character. The true point of view in the history of this nation, is not the Atlantic coast, it is the great West. Even the slavery struggle, which is made so exclusive an object of attention by writers like Professor von Holst, occupies its important place in American history because of its relation to westward expansion.

In this advance, the frontier is the outer edge of the wave — the meeting point between savagery and civilization. Much has been written about the frontier from the point of view of border warfare and the chase, but as a field for the serious study of the economist and the historian it has been neglected.

The American frontier is sharply distinguished from the European frontier — a fortified boundary running through dense populations. The most significant thing about the American frontier is, that it lies at the hither edge of free land. In the census reports it is treated as the margin of that settlement which has a density of two or more to the square mile. The term is an elastic one, and for our purposes does not need sharp definition. We shall consider the whole frontier belt, including the Indian country and the outer margin of the "settled area" of the census reports. This paper will make no attempt to treat the subject exhaustively; its aim is simply to call attention to the frontier as a fertile field for investigation, and to suggest some of the problems which arise in connection with it.

In the settlement of America we have to observe how European life entered the continent, and how America modified and developed that life and reacted on Europe. Our early history is the study of European germs developing in an American environment. Too exclusive attention has been paid by institutional students to the Germanic origins, too little to the American factors. The frontier is the line of most rapid and effective Americanization. The wilderness masters the colonist. It finds him a European in dress, industries, tools, modes of travel, and thought. It takes him from the railroad car and puts him in the birch canoe. It strips off the garments of civilization and arrays him in the hunting shirt and the moccasin. It puts him in the log cabin of the Cherokee and Iroquois and runs an Indian palisade around him. Before long he has gone to planting Indian corn and plowing with a sharp stick; he shouts the war cry, and takes the scalp in orthodox Indian fashion. In short, at the frontier the environment is at first too strong for the man. He must accept the conditions which it furnishes, or perish, and so he fits himself into the Indian clearings and follows the Indian trails. Little by little he transforms the wilderness, but the outcome is not the old Europe, not simply the development of Germanic germs, any more than the first phenomenon was a case of reversion to the Germanic mark. The fact is, that here is a new product that is American. At first, the frontier was the Atlantic coast. It was the frontier of Europe in a very real sense. Moving westward, the frontier became more and more American. As successive terminal moraines result from successive glaciations, so each frontier leaves its traces behind it, and when it becomes a settled area the region still partakes of the frontier characteristics. Thus the advance of the frontier has meant a steady movement away from the influence of Europe, a steady growth of independence on American lines. And to study this advance, the men who grew up under these conditions, and the political, economic, and social results of it, is to study the really American part of our history.

At the Atlantic frontier one can study the germs of processes repeated at each successive frontier. We have the complex European life sharply precipitated by the wilderness into the simplicity of primitive conditions. The first frontier had to meet its Indian question, its question of the disposition of the public domains, of the means of intercourse with older settlements, of the extension of political organization, of religious and educational activity. And the settlement of these and similar questions for one frontier served as a guide for the next. The American student needs not to go to the "prim little townships of Sleswick" for illustrations of the law of continuity and development. For example, he may study the origin of our land policies in the colonial land policy; he may see how the system grew by adapting the statutes to the customs of the successive frontiers. He may see how the mining experience in the lead regions of Wisconsin, Illinois, and Iowa was applied to the mining laws of the Rockies, and how our Indian policy has been a series of experimentations on successive frontiers. Each tier of new States has found in the older ones material for its constitutions. Each frontier has made similar contributions to American character, as will be discussed farther on.

But with all these similarities there are essential differences, due to the place element and the time element. It is evident that the farming frontier of the Mississippi Valley presents different conditions from the mining frontier of the Rocky Mountains. The frontier reached by the Pacific Railroad, surveyed into rectangles, guarded by the United States Army, and recruited by the daily immigrant ship, moves forward at a swifter pace and in a different way than the frontier reached by the birch canoe or the pack horse. The geologist traces patiently the shores of ancient seas, maps their areas, and compares the older and the newer. It would be a work worth the historian's labors to mark these various frontiers and in detail compare one with another. Not only would there result a more adequate conception of

American development and characteristics, but invaluable additions would be made to the history of society.

Loria, the Italian economist, has urged the study of colonial life as an aid in understanding the stages of European development, affirming that colonial settlement is for economic science what the mountain is for geology, bringing to light primitive stratifications. "America," he says, "has the key to the historical enigma which Europe has sought for centuries in vain, and the land which has no history reveals luminously the course of universal history." There is much truth in this. The United States lies like a huge page in the history of society. Line by line as we read this continental page from west to east we find the record of social evolution. It begins with the Indian and the hunter; it goes on to tell of the disintegration of savagery by the entrance of the trader, the pathfinder of civilization; we read the annals of the pastoral stage in ranch life; the exploitation of the soil by the raising of unrotated crops of corn and wheat in sparsely settled farming communities; the intensive culture of the denser farm settlement; and finally the manufacturing organization with city and factory system. This page is familiar to the student of census statistics, but how little of it has been used by our historians. Particularly in eastern States this page is a palimpsest. What is now a manufacturing State was in an earlier decade an area of intensive farming. Earlier yet it had been a wheat area, and still earlier the "range" had attracted the cattle-herder. Thus Wisconsin, now developing manufacture, is a State with varied agricultural interests. But earlier it was given over to almost exclusive grain-raising, like North Dakota at the present time.

Each of these areas has had an influence in our economic and political history: the evolution of each into a higher stage has worked political transformations. But what constitutional historian has made any adequate attempt to interpret political facts by the light of these social areas and changes? The Atlantic frontier was compounded of fisherman, fur-trader, miner, cattle-raiser, and farmer. Excepting the fisherman, each type of industry was on the march toward the West, impelled by an irresistible attraction. Each passed in successive waves across the continent. Stand at Cumberland Gap and watch the procession of civilization, marching single file — the buffalo following the trail to the salt springs, the Indian, the fur-trader and hunter, the cattle-raiser, the pioneer farmer — and the frontier has passed by. Stand at South Pass in the Rockies a century later and see the same procession with wider intervals between. The unequal rate of advance compels us to distinguish the frontier into the trader's frontier, the rancher's frontier, or the miner's frontier, and the farmer's frontier. When the mines and the cow pens were still near the fall line the traders' pack trains were tinkling across the Alleghanies, and the French on the Great Lakes were fortifying their posts, alarmed by the British trader's birch canoe. When the trappers scaled the Rockies, the farmer was still near the mouth of the Missouri.

Having now roughly outlined the various kinds of frontiers, and their modes of advance, chiefly from the point of view of the frontier itself, we may next inquire what were the influences on the East and on the Old World.

A rapid enumeration of some of the more noteworthy effects is all that I have time for.

First, we note that the frontier promoted the formation of a composite nationality for the American people. The coast was preponderantly English, but the later tides of continental immigration flowed across to the free lands. This was the case from the early colonial days. The Scotch Irish and the Palatine Germans, or "Pennsylvania Dutch," furnished the dominant element in the stock of the colonial frontier. With these peoples were also the freed indented servants, or redemptioners, who at the expiration of their time of service passed to the frontier. Governor Spottswood of Virginia writes in 1717, "the inhabitants of our frontiers are composed generally of such as have been transported hither as servants, and, being out of their time, settle themselves where land is to be taken up and that will produce the necessarys of life with little labour." Very generally these redemptioners were of non-English stock. In the crucible of the frontier the immigrants were Americanized, liberated, and fused into a mixed race, English in neither nationality nor characteristics. The process has gone on from the early days to our own. Burke and other writers in the middle of the eighteenth century believed that Pennsylvania was "threatened with the danger of being wholly foreign in language, manners, and perhaps even inclinations." The Germans and Scotch-Irish elements in the frontier of the South were only less great. In the middle of the present century the German element in Wisconsin was already so considerable that leading publicists looked to the creation of a German state out of the commonwealth by concentrating their colonization. Such examples teach us to beware of misinterpreting the fact that there is a common English speech in America into a belief that the stock is also English.

In another way the advance of the frontier decreased our dependence on England. The coast, particularly of the South, lacked diversified industries, and was dependent on England for the bulk of its supplies. In the South there was even a dependence on the Northern colonies for articles of food. Governor Glenn, of South Carolina, writes in the middle of the eighteenth century: "Our trade with New York and Philadelphia was of this sort, draining us of all the little money and bills we could gather from other places for their bread, flour, beer, hams, bacon, and other things of their produce, all which, except beer, our new townships begin to supply us with, which are settled with very industrious and thriving Germans. This no doubt diminishes the number of shipping and the appearance of our trade, but it is far from being a detriment to us." Before long the frontier created a demand for merchants. As it retreated from the coast it became less and less possible for England to bring her supplies directly to the consumer's wharfs, and carry away staple crops, and staple crops began to give way to diversified agriculture for a time. The effect of this phase of the frontier action upon the northern section is perceived when we realize how the advance of the frontier aroused seaboard cities like Boston, New York, and Baltimore, to engage in rivalry for what Washington called "the extensive and valuable trade of a rising empire."

The legislation which most developed the powers of the National Government, and played the largest part in its activity, was conditioned on the frontier. Writers have discussed the subjects of tariff, land, and internal improvement, as subsidiary to the slavery question. But when American history comes to be rightly viewed it will be seen that the slavery question is an incident. In the period from the end of the first half of the present century to the close of the civil war slavery rose to primary, but far from exclusive, importance. But this does not justify Dr. von Holst (to take an example) in treating our constitutional history in its formative period down to 1828 in a single volume, giving six volumes chiefly to the history of slavery from 1828 to 1861, under the title "Constitutional History of the United States." The growth of nationalism and the evolution of American political institutions were dependent on the advance of the frontier. Even so recent a writer as Rhodes, in his History of the United States since the compromise of 1850, has treated the legislation called out by the western advance as incidental to the slavery struggle.

This is a wrong perspective. The pioneer needed the goods of the coast, and so the grand series of internal improvement and railroad legislation began, with potent nationalizing effects. Over internal improvements occurred great debates, in which grave constitutional questions were discussed. Sectional groupings appear in the votes, profoundly significant for the historian. Loose construction increased as the nation marched westward. But the West was not content with bringing the farm to the factory. Under the lead of Clay — "Harry of the West" — protective tariffs were passed, with the cry of bringing the factory to the farm. The disposition of the public lands was a third important subject of national legislation influenced by the frontier.

It is safe to say that the legislation with regard to land, tariff, and internal improvements — the American system of the nationalizing Whig party — was conditioned on frontier ideas and needs. But it was not merely in legislative action that the frontier worked against the sectionalism of the coast. The economic and social characteristics of the frontier worked against sectionalism. The men of the frontier had closer resemblances to the Middle region than to either of the other sections. Pennsylvania had been the seed-plot of frontier emigration, and although she passed on her settlers along the Great Valley into the west of Virginia and the Carolinas, yet the industrial society of these Southern frontiersmen was always more like that of the Middle region than like that of the tide-water portion of the South, which later came to spread its industrial type throughout the South.

The Middle region, entered by New York harbor, was an open door to all Europe. The tide-water part of the South represented typical Englishmen, modified by a warm climate and servile labor, and living in baronial fashion on great plantations; New England stood for a special English movement — Puritanism. The Middle region was less English than the other sections. It had a wide mixture of nationalities, a varied society, the mixed town and county system of local government, a varied economic life, many religious sects. In short, it was a region mediating between New England and the South, and the East and the West. It represented that composite nationality which the contemporary United States exhibits, that juxtaposition of non-English groups, occupying a valley or a little settlement, and presenting reflections of the map of Europe in their variety. It was democratic and nonsectional, if not national; "easy, tolerant, and contented"; rooted strongly in material prosperity. It was typical of the modern United States. It was least sectional, not only because it lay between North and South, but also because with no barriers to shut out its frontiers from its settled region, and with a system of connecting waterways, the Middle region mediated between East and West as well as between North and South. Thus it became the typically American region. Even the New Englander, who was shut out from the frontier by the Middle region, tarrying in New York or Pennsylvania on his westward march, lost the acuteness of his sectionalism on the way.

The spread of cotton culture into the interior of the South finally broke down the contrast between the "tide-water" region and the rest of the State, and based Southern interests on slavery. Before this process revealed its results the western portion of the South, which was akin to Pennsylvania in stock, society, and industry, showed the tendencies to fall away from the faith of the fathers into internal improvement legislation and nationalism. In the Virginia convention of 1829-'30, called to revise the constitution, Mr. Leigh, of Chesterfield, one of the tide-water counties, declared:

> One of the main causes of discontent which led to this convention, that which had the strongest influence in overcoming our veneration for the work of our fathers, which taught us to contemn the sentiments of Henry and Mason and Pendleton, which weaned us from our reverence for the constituted authorities of the State, was an overweening passion for internal improvement. I say this with perfect knowledge, for it has been avowed to me by gentlemen from the West over and over again. And let me tell the gentleman from Albemarle (Mr. Gordon) that it has been another principal object of those who set this ball of revolution in motion, to overturn the doctrine of State rights, of which Virginia has been the very pillar, and to remove the barrier she has interposed to the interference of the Federal Government in that same work of internal improvement, by so reorganizing the legislature that Virginia, too, may be hitched to the Federal car.

It was this nationalizing tendency of the West that transformed the democracy of Jefferson into the national republicanism of Monroe and the democracy of Andrew Jackson. The West of the war of 1812, the West of Clay, and Benton, and Harrison, and Andrew Jackson, shut off by the Middle States and the mountains from the coast sections, had a solidarity of its own with national tendencies. On the tide of the Father of Waters, North and South met and mingled into a nation. Interstate migration went steadily on — a process of cross-fertilization of ideas and institutions. The fierce struggle of the sections over slavery on the western frontier does not diminish the truth of this statement; it proves the truth of it. Slavery was a sectional trait that would not down, but in the West it could not remain sectional. It was the greatest of frontiersmen who declared: "I believe this Government can not endure permanently half slave and half free. It will become all of one thing or all of the other." Nothing works for nationalism like intercourse within the nation. Mobility of population is death of localism, and the western frontier worked irresistibly in unsettling the population. The effects reached back from the frontier and affected profoundly the Atlantic coast and even the Old World.

But the most important effect of the frontier has been in the promotion of democracy here and in Europe. As has been indicated the frontier is productive of individualism. Complex society is precipitated by the wilderness into a kind of primitive organization based on the family. The tendency is anti-social. It produces antipathy to control, and particularly to any direct control. The tax-gatherer is viewed as a representative of oppression. Professor Osgood, in an able article, has pointed out that the frontier conditions prevalent in the colonies are important factors in the explanation of the American Revolution, where individual liberty was sometimes confused with absence of all effective government. The same conditions aid in explaining the difficulty of instituting a strong government in the period of the confederacy. The frontier individualism has from the beginning promoted democracy.

The frontier State that came into the Union in the first quarter of a century of its existence came in with democratic suffrage provisions, and had reactive effects of the highest importance upon the older States whose peoples were being attracted there. An extension of the franchise became essential. It was *western* New York that forced an extension of suffrage in the constitutional convention of that State in 1821; and it was *western* Virginia that compelled the tide-water region to put a more liberal suffrage provision in the constitution framed in 1830, and to give to the frontier region a more nearly proportionate representation with the tide-water aristocracy. The rise of democracy as an effective force in the nation came in with western preponderance under Jackson and William Henry Harrison, and it meant the triumph of the frontier — with all of its good and with all of its evil elements. An interesting illustration of the tone of frontier democracy in 1830 comes from the same debates in the Virginia convention already referred to. A representative from western Virginia declared:

But, sir, it is not the increase of population in the West which this gentleman ought to fear. It is the energy which the mountain breeze and western habits impart to those emigrants. They are regenerated, politically, I mean, sir. They soon become *working politicians*; and the difference, sir, between a *talking* and a *working* politician is immense. The Old Dominion has long been celebrated for producing great orators; the ablest metaphysicians in policy; men that could split hairs, in all abstruse questions of political economy. But at home, or when they return from Congress, they have negroes to fan them asleep. But a Pennsylvania, a New York, an Ohio, or a western Virginia statesman, though far inferior in logic, metaphysics, and rhetoric to an old Virginia statesman, has this advantage, that when he returns home he takes off his coat and takes hold of the plow. This gives him bone and muscle, sir, and preserves his republican principles pure and uncontaminated.

So long as free land exists, the opportunity for a competency exists, and economic power secures political power. But the democracy born of free land, strong in selfishness and individualism, intolerant of administrative experience and education, and pressing individual liberty beyond its proper bounds, has its dangers as well as its benefits. Individualism in America has allowed a laxity in regard to governmental affairs which has rendered possible the spoils system and all the manifest evils that follow from the lack of a highly developed civic spirit. In this connection may be noted also the influence of frontier conditions in permitting lax business honor, inflated paper currency and wild-cat banking. The colonial and revolutionary frontier was the region whence emanated many of the worst forms of an evil currency. The West in the war of 1812 repeated the phenomenon on the frontier of that day, while the speculation and wild-cat banking of the period of the crisis of 1837 occurred on the new frontier belt of the next tier of States. Thus each one of the periods of lax financial integrity coincides with periods when a new set of frontier communities had arisen, and coincides in area with these successive frontiers, for the most part. The recent Populist agitation is a case in point. Many a State that now declines any connection with the tenets of the Populists, itself adhered to such ideas in an earlier stage of the development of the State. A primitive society can hardly be expected to show the intelligent appreciation of the complexity of business interests in a developed society. The continual recurrence of these areas of paper-money agitation is another evidence that the frontier can be isolated and studied as a factor in American history of the highest importance.

.   .   .   .

From the conditions of frontier life came intellectual traits of profound importance. The works of travelers along each frontier from colonial days onward describe certain common traits, and these traits have, while softening down, still persisted as survivals in the place of their origin, even when a higher social organization succeeded. The result is that to the frontier the American intellect owes its striking characteristics. That coarseness and strength combined with acuteness and inquisitiveness; that practical, inventive turn of mind, quick to find expedients; that masterful grasp of material things, lacking in the artistic but powerful to effect great ends; that restless, nervous energy; that dominant individualism, working for good and for evil, and withal that buoyancy and exuberance which comes with freedom — these are traits of the frontier, or traits called out elsewhere because of the existence of the frontier. Since the days when the fleet of Columbus sailed into the waters of the New World, America has been another name for opportunity, and the people of the United States have taken their tone from the incessant expansion which has not only been open but has even been forced upon them. He would be a rash prophet who should assert that the expansive character of American life has now entirely ceased. Movement has been its dominant fact, and, unless this training has no effect upon a people, the American energy will continually demand a wider field for its exercise. But never again will such gifts of free land offer themselves. For a moment, at the frontier, the bonds of custom are broken and unrestraint is triumphant. There is not *tabula rasa*. The stubborn American environment is there with its imperious summons to accept its conditions; the inherited ways of doing things are also there; and yet, in spite of environment, and in spite of custom, each frontier did indeed furnish a new field of opportunity, a gate of escape from the bondage of the past; and freshness, and confidence, and scorn of older society, impatience of its restraints and its ideas, and indifference to its lessons, have accompanied the frontier. What the Mediterranean Sea was to the Greeks, breaking the bond of custom, offering new experiences, calling out new institutions and activities, that, and more, the ever retreating frontier has been to the United States directly, and to the nations of Europe more remotely. And now, four centuries from the discovery of America, at the end of a hundred years of life under the Constitution, the frontier has gone, and with its going has closed the first period of American history.

BIOGRAPHY

THE most immediate form of biography is that of one's self, already discussed as autobiography. To some extent the same qualities of authorship appear in both. Some writers of autobiography achieve such detachment from their subject that they seem to be able to look at themselves objectively, as at another individual. Undoubtedly Henry Adams had such an attitude in view when he wrote of himself in the third person in *The Education of Henry Adams*. On the other hand, some writers of biography seek to identify themselves with their subjects in experience and psychology, to interpret them from the inside, as it were. The methods of psychoanalysis have naturally proved of assistance in this process, of which recent examples may be found in Miss Katharine Anthony's *Margaret Fuller* and Van Wyck Brooks's *The Ordeal of Mark Twain*.

Biography is properly a part of history, as Carlyle noted in the passage quoted at the head of the preceding section. When the biographer is in intimate association with his subject his value is largely that of the essential historian, the reporter. An example of the perfection of such art is seen in Boswell's *Life of Samuel Johnson*, which has been accepted universally as the greatest of all biographies. The success of this work is due, as Macaulay noted, to the willingness of the biographer to sacrifice his own personal dignity to the demands of his task, to accept the subordination of the satellite; but also, as Carlyle insisted, to his capacity for hero-worship, "his open and loving heart." Other great biographies which depend on the personal relation of the writer to the subject are Lockhart's *Life of Scott*, Forster's *Life of Dickens*, and Froude's *Carlyle*. In all serious biography the writings of the subject, formal and especially informal in the shape of personal letters, are evidence of high importance.

The popularity of biographies with the reading public has increased greatly in the last few years, until in publication they rival fiction, both in number issued and size of sales. When biographical writing approached in interest-rousing quality that of fiction, as in M. Maurois' *Ariel*, serious readers began to prefer the experience of a real person to that of an imaginary one. To take advantage of this disposition some biographers deliberately have used not only the style and method but the imaginative license of fiction, so that the fictionized biography has become a literary hybrid and a nuisance. Undoubtedly the scientific spirit of the time, its curiosity about experience, and its interest in reality are the causes of the rapidly growing importance of biography in contemporary literature.

This spirit is responsible for the qualities characteristic of modern, in distinction from conventional, biography. The latter, largely practiced in the nineteenth century, had as its object to minister to the dignity and importance of the subject. The innumerable "lives and times" of this or that person were like mortuary monuments erected to departed greatness or near-greatness. The first quality of a modern biography is that it should present a real character, not a flattering likeness. As an essential means to reality, frankness is a second quality. The biographies of the past prided themselves on being discreet. Even the loyalty of Lockhart to his father-in-law, Scott, was suspected on the ground of some very moderately revealing passages. Today the reaction against this gentlemanly tradition has gone so far that the term "debunking" has been coined to indicate certain biographies whose chief object seems to be to smash the stereotype by which their predecessors represented persons of respectability and distinction. While a certain overemphasis was inevitable in this enterprise, its value in setting standards of frankness for biography is incontestable. A third quality in modern biography, again the result of a scientific outlook, is accurate documentation. The suppression or alteration of documents in the interest of the sanctity of the subject, common enough in earlier times, destroys all claim of an author to be considered an honest biographer. Finally, in addition to the realism, frankness, and honesty of the record, a modern biographer is expected to furnish an interpretation of his subject. This explanation may be implicit in the narrative of experience, or it may be added as psychological analysis.

Miss Constance Mayfield Rourke's biography of P. T. Barnum from *Trumpets of Jubilee* (1927) illustrates the qualities noted above. The story is that of an actual experience which with all its extravagance contains much that may be regarded as typically American. There is the conventional beginning of the poor boy, making good by his wits until he stands forth as the embodiment of the American success story. There is the rapid oscillation of fortune which carried the hero from poverty to riches and power and back again, a process effected times without number. There is the relation of Barnum to his public, depending on the popular appeal of a personality which can be identified by striking qualities both surprising and expected. In these respects we see in Barnum but a crude anticipation of later American character and experience, the vicissitudes and success of the American business man, the popularity of the athlete or the moving picture star. Above all, Barnum was alive, and his vitality animates Miss Rourke's pages. He gave himself to his public with naïve frankness in many accounts of himself, from which Miss Rourke has quoted freely. And from her narrative emerges an interpretation which marks the subject as belonging especially to this country in the youthful period of its culture.

CONSTANCE MAYFIELD ROURKE

BORN in Cleveland in 1888, graduated from Vassar in 1907 (where she taught English, 1910–15), Constance Rourke has in a short time become one of the recognized interpreters of American life not so much in terms of historical events as in terms of national culture. Besides contributions to the *Dictionary of American Biography*, she has written three notable books, *Trumpets of Jubilee* (1927), *Troupers of the Gold Coast* (1928), and *American Humor* (1930).

P. T. BARNUM*

THE great Barnum was tireless in the practice of autobiography. His first volume appeared in 1855, in the full flower of his middle life; and the book was a flowing bowl of candor. In later years a friendly apologist declared that the narrative should never have been taken as the literal truth. "The soberer, matter-of-fact public did not see the Pickwickian sense of humor and the Orientalism of statement that pervaded it," protested this anxious gentleman. "The cold type could not carry with it the twinkling of the author's eye." But it was part of Barnum's genius that he could convey the twinkling of his eye whenever he chose; as for the soberer, matter-of-fact public, Barnum's friend had been misinformed as to its attitude. In England, a notable church quarterly was set quivering with decorous mirth by the volume, and found an excellent lesson of righteousness in the author's career; in this country Barnum's rise from humble origins, his struggles with adversity, his achievement of fortune were discovered as evidences of the American genius; he was hailed as a national example. The few captious critics were cried down.

Barnum soon outgrew this portrait. Fifteen years later he was moved to tell another and longer story; and as the years passed and brought fresh triumphs, he offered ample additions, sequels, and appendices, that the public might be kept apprised of his later phases. The book went on, a rising, swelling stream, under many titles and in many forms. The first volume had been homely, racy, naïve; in the second, with all its accumulations, Barnum blew the summoning trumpet note. "Few men in civil life have had a career more crowded with incident, enterprise, and various intercourse with the world than mine," he shouted. "With the alternations of success and defeat, extensive travel in this and foreign lands; a large acquaintance with the humble and honored; having held the pre-eminent place among all who have sought to furnish healthful entertainment to the American people, and, therefore, having had opportunities for garnering an ample storehouse of incident and anecdote...." On rolled his rhetoric: episodes were piled on episodes as though to provide a mountainous view

* From *Trumpets of Jubilee*, by Constance Mayfield Rourke. Copyright, 1927, by Harcourt, Brace and Company, Inc.

across a continent. As the public note salutes the ear for more than a thousand pages certain queries arise in the mind of the pigmy listener. Barnum had the public story-teller's habit; everything was his grist. In this semi-public performance of narration now and then he seized upon episodes which suited his taste or his purpose, and made himself the sublime hero, whether or not he was a leading figure in mortal fact. Here and there in his stories are obvious inflations, made with irresistible gusto. After describing the poverty and the miserable hardships which he had endured traveling in the South and West with a tiny circus during the thirties, he carelessly asserted that he purchased a steamboat for six thousand dollars and went down the Mississippi. After the great clock failure, when he had dismally pictured himself as at the lowest ebb of fortune and the dupe of shrewder men, he alertly explained to Thackeray that his wife possessed a neat fortune, which he may have sequestered; and he told the story, and the amount. In Barnum's long career remain innumerable small alleys or by-ways which it might be amusing or instructive for the humble student of character to follow. But such delights are forever barred: the regions which Barnum traversed were too obscure for easy penetration after the long lapse of years; his life was most often interwoven with mean or humble lives, which have left behind them no trace. And strangely enough, almost nothing substantial about him emerges from the ruck of contemporary evidence; scarcely another figure of equal proportions has left so little behind him by way of personal print. Necessarily he becomes a legend — an outcome he would have relished.

Perhaps, indeed, Barnum had no personal character. In a strict sense he had no private life. He lived in the midst of the crowd, in the peopled haunts of his great museum, on the road, on the lecture platform, on steamers, in caravans or circus trains, near the smell of sawdust or under the spreading lights of the city. He lived in public; at times it seemed he was the public. There was scarcely a murmur of popular taste or desire in his long era which he did not catch and use and fling back — magnified; his swelling cacophony became much of the noise of the nation, the smaller sounds mixing and mingling with the greater: he was carelessly orchestral. Yet, as we follow him over his widening course, we find that he was something more than a creator of emporiums to give the public what it wanted. He took his cues, he kept his ear to the ground; but he let play upon the faint stirrings of popular desires the energy of a sportive imagination, a fancy primitive but dramatic. There in the white glare of the public gaze, in his own proper figure of public middleman, he created an amused conglomerate. With numberless exhibits he traced patterns of his own, beginning with a familiar theme.

I

"As well attempt to revolutionize the Kingdom of Heaven as the State of Connecticut," cried Pierrepont Edwards in despair in the first decade of the last century. Clash after clash could be heard in the struggle to entrench Calvinism as a state established religion and to restrict the franchise to authenticated professors of its harsh dogmas. Lyman Beecher had lately come to Litchfield, and was in the thick of the bitter contention. Yet the small hamlets and villages of Connecticut, so often pictured as held remorselessly in the Puritan grip, contained a stirring admixture of other elements. There were Jeffersonian Democrats of all creeds or no creed who raised the cry of Toleration; there were indigenous Tories who were resentful but inarticulate; and there was a rabble. This last included tipplers and tavern-keepers, storekeepers, peddlers, tinkers, and an occasional squire: the unregenerate, the unheeding, unthrifty, or merely jovial of many orders and occupations. Artfully they eluded the severe legal restrictions upon personal conduct contained in the blue laws, kept a watchful, realistic eye upon the shortcomings of their God-fearing neighbors, and established a supremacy of their own. "In New Haven," said Timothy Dwight, "a trick in trade is rarely heard of; and when mentioned awakens alike surprise and indignation." But whatever the cool virtue of New Haven, in other Connecticut villages like Danbury and Bethel, Middletown and Norwalk, tricks in trade were not only frequently accomplished but boisterously enjoyed, alternating with rough practical jokes as a means of releasing lively wits and surplus energies. To trick a peddler or a storekeeper in a trade — still better a minister or an elder — was to achieve something like public prestige. To lead any neighbor into a home-made trap where he became ridiculous was to acquire an equal dominion. With high spirits this ruff-scuff made puppets of others and pulled the strings. There in Connecticut, under the awful shadow of the Calvinistic doom, the members of a casual brotherhood lived by their wits, and enjoyed their natural talents, and conducted their private anti-Puritan campaigns.

It was to such a loose community that young Taylor Barnum belonged by inheritance. He was born in the little village of Bethel near Danbury in the year 1810, of a numerous New England family which claimed Revolutionary connections, but upon whom dignity of any sort sat lightly. Barnum's grandfather and namesake, Phineas Taylor, was a Justice of the Peace, but he was also an incorrigible practical joker and trader who consorted by choice with the village wags and tricksters, and who relished a joke on a minister above all good jokes, and roared with laughter over adroit evasions of the blue laws. The Taylors and the Barnums were solidly on the defensive in Connecticut; their orthodoxy was questionable; and they had accepted the hated tenets of Democracy. Besides, in a frugal community, Barnum's father was thriftless. A farmer, a tailor, a tavern-keeper by turn, he improvidently died while his children were still young and left to his wife the rough and arduous business of keeping an inn. In this small hostelry our hero spent his earlier days — already in public life, a predestined anti-Puritan and born adventurer. At fourteen he was a tall limber lad with dark restless eyes and a quick tongue who was considered "up to snuff." His favorite companion was an older boy who pilfered horns from his employer, a comb-maker, and sold them for fair sums to the same person.

Young Barnum soon was pivoted in that prime location for the display

of equal talents — a general country store. All classes in the village came
and went. Yankee peddlers — outlaws even among the clever community
of village traders — bobbed up, tried their talents, and disappeared. Here
came farmers who offered corn and buckwheat, ax-helves and hickory nuts
for rum and tenpenny nails. Small manufacturers entered with their wares
— clocks, razors, and whetstones. The hatting industry had already sprung
up in Danbury; combs were made in Bethel; clocks were made everywhere.
There was a constant babble and the crack of many exchanges; young
Barnum himself drove many of the bargains, which were sharp and hard.
"Some of the smaller fry shaved us prodigiously," he admitted in candid
reminiscence. "The hatters mixed their inferior furs with a little of their
best, and sold us the hats for otter. We in turn mixed our teas and liquors
and gave them the most valuable names.... If we took our pay in clocks,
the chances were that they were no better than a chest of drawers for the
purpose — that they were like Pindar's razors, made to sell; and if half the
number of wheels necessary to form a clock could be found within the case,
it was as lucky as it was extraordinary." The changing miscellany of goods
was endless: feathers, flax, beeswax, bright calico and gay ribbons, hickory
nuts, oats and corn — novelties from the larger world, the spoils of the
seasons, and the fruit of country labor. Freely enough at the store flowed
Santa Cruz rum, Holland gin, and Jamaica spirits as well as many inferior
brews; everyone drank, even the clergy. "I suppose I have drawn and
bottled more rum than would be necessary to float a ship," said Barnum
afterward.

Barnum shifted from store to store, from Bethel to Danbury and back
again; he went to Brooklyn where he engaged in similar adventures on a
larger scale, and to New York, where still a youth, he opened a porter-house
for Danbury and Bethel hatters and comb-makers. From this he was obliged
to retreat; he had not yet reached the metropolitan pitch: he went back to
Bethel and entered into partnership in a general store with an uncle, Alanson
Taylor, painting a small frame building bright yellow, and laying in a large
stock of hardware, crockery, and notions. At about this time he married a
capable young tailoress named Charity Hallett. But he apparently felt that
none of these matters required all of his time or his talents. He launched a
lottery. Once as a boy he had acquired by a slip in trade a large consignment of worthless green glass bottles from a traveling peddler. He had
promptly made them up into lots with his employer's worthless stock of
fly-blown tin skimmers and shop-worn pie-pans, had advertised a prize for
everybody, sold chances, and recovered equally the loss in money and in
local reputation. Lotteries attracted him; he liked the jolts and surprises,
the air of public excitement, the effect of pulling off unaccountable feats.
He soon went into the lottery business on a considerable scale, with agencies
in the villages round about, and became a kind of peripatetic auctioneer,
crying his new and unstable wares from town to town and along country
roads, flinging broadcast a profusion of posters and advertising with staring
capitals and marks of wonder in the slender weekly papers of the region.
"As the curious letters of 'Joe Strickland' were highly popular at this time

I advertised my office as being under the special favor and protection of Dr. Peter Strickland, own blood cousin to the renowned Joe Strickland. In my bills and advertisements I rang all the possible changes upon the renowned name — 'The Ever Lucky Dr. Strickland,' 'Five More Capital Prizes Sold by Dr. Strickland,' 'A Fortune for a Dollar — apply to Fortune's Favorite, Dr. Strickland,' 'Another Mammoth Prize! — Huzza for Dr. Strickland.'

"Customers who brought their tickets and found them blanks, were told that their only wise plan was to 'look for money where they had lost it' — 'it was a long lane that never turned' — 'such bad luck could not continue long.'..."

Connecticut had at first innocently sanctioned lotteries, even using them as a means of raising money for churches and public works; but as they had grown in wild popularity the public conscience was sharply pricked. In truth, the business was scarcely reputable when Barnum embarked upon it. Suddenly his new and chequered enterprise was prohibited by law. The measure was a mesh through which the supple could slip, and young Barnum lacked nothing in flexibility, but he now found himself frankly and noisily ranged — where he had tacitly been before — against the stricter tenets of his community. Soon, through a quarrel with his uncle, Alanson Taylor, he plunged into battle. The exact cause of the dispute remains obscure; perhaps young Barnum played upon him too gross a practical joke; certainly his uncle proved to be a more solid citizen, a more rigorous Presbyterian than Barnum had supposed; and their differences quickly became set deep in the matrix of the ancient political and religious conflict. Alanson Taylor was as furiously stung to expression as was Barnum. Each promptly launched a newspaper and carried on a running fusillade of hot-headed personalities and arguments which made other Connecticut journals of the time look like academic ghosts. With a warm flourish Barnum gave to his paper the waving name of the *Herald of Freedom*. Freedom was his battle-cry; he attacked Calvinism, its ministers, indeed the entire Standing Order — as it was still fitly called — in the name of Freedom, insisting that a conspiracy was afoot to restore the old alliance of church and state in Connecticut, which would in the end abolish personal liberty. In this charge Barnum was evoking an empty bogey. The effort of the Puritans to keep the seat of government in Connecticut was long since over. Nearly fifteen years before, when Barnum was a boy of nine, the Standing Order had been swept away by the effectual means of a new constitution. Even Lyman Beecher, one of its best known leaders, had acknowledged the wisdom of its destruction, and was now, in the early thirties, off to the West with the light of a dozen new momentous issues before him. But Barnum kept up his attack, filling it with wind and fury, inflating it as if the mere act of blowing up a monstrous balloon were his pleasure. Shouting for freedom, he now upheld the scarcely respectable faith of Universalism, which abundantly offered hope and happiness for all, and had been a thorn in the Puritan side for twenty years. When Barnum's adoption of Universalism took place is not apparent; but in Bethel, at least, there was only one church, the Presbyterian; and his acknowledgment of a buoyant creed placed him in further antagonism to the older elements of his community. Likewise, in the midst of a growing Whiggery he cried up the hated Democracy, harking back to what he called the principles of the Republic.

Mixed and virulent as was his platform, some of these issues ran deep; with the onrush of the Jacksonian era was developing the first heady liberalism of the age. His paper was no mean achievement for a young man of twenty-two with the smallest education. Not its least features were reports of the important speeches in the campaign of 1832, and of the proceedings of the Connecticut legislature; and Barnum included a column of foreign news. But after all, what amused him most was the parry and thrust of personal attack; and at last he strained the patience of his respectable orthodox opponents. During the three years of his editorship, from 1831 to 1834, Barnum was three times arrested for libel. Once he was fined; once he succeeded in having the case against him dismissed. The third time, having accused an orthodox church officer in Bethel of extortion from an orphan, he was made to feel the accumulated wrath of the entrenched opposition. He was sentenced to pay a fine of one hundred dollars and to serve a term of sixty days in the Danbury jail.

Freedom! Again he shouted freedom! With a perfect adaptability and an easy stretch of terms, Barnum made the issue one of freedom of speech, and found an ally in the Reverend Theophilus Fisk, editor of the *Watch Tower of Freedom* at New Haven, a rampant speaker who was adding to the swelling note of early American oratory catchwords which had been the watchwords of the Revolution. Fisk was voluble; the pronouncement of the word liberty alone could stimulate him to salvo after salvo of praise, indignation, or melancholy, as the case might require. "Is it possible," queried the Reverend Theophilus in an open letter to Barnum, "an American — a Freeman — a Husband — has been torn from his family hearthstone, and by the strong arm of oppression has been incarcerated within the gloomy walls of a Common Jail!!! An American Citizen!! By the iron hand of power shut out from the glorious sunlight — and that too *for no crime!!!*... Amid the death struggles of prejudice, bigotry, and error to regain their palsying influence over the minds of men, the late desperate attempt to muzzle your press will be remembered when minor persecutions have been forgotten. The imprisonment of our friend and fellow-citizen involves more momentous consequences than that of any event within my recollection.... It tells us that the clouds which are thickening upon our borders are the fearful harbingers of an approaching storm! It tells us there is a demon rearing its hydra head in the midst of our peaceful valleys that has drenched the earth with gore! We must be up and doing. The deep silence, the hush, the awful stillness which pervades the moral atmosphere warns of approaching doom! Will men who love liberty — who prize our hallowed institutions, become, and continue to remain, the willing dupes of ecclesiastical domination? No. Let them, one and all, show to the world that they were not born with saddles on their backs for priests to ride.... Let them arise in the majesty of truth, and blow the trumpet of Zion!"

Barnum became a martyr. "The same spirit governs my enemies that imprisoned Sellick Osborn and burnt to death Michael Servetus by order of John Calvin," he wrote to Gideon Welles from jail in an impassioned letter. "The excitement in this and neighboring towns is very great, and it will have a grand effect." The grand effect he kept steadily in view; and though he seems not to have borrowed even the semblance of a fagot from the sad case of Michael Servetus, he took over intact the ritual which had attended Sellick Osborn, when, twenty years before, he had been released from the Litchfield jail. It was Osborn, from Danbury, who had invaded Litchfield in the desperate years when the foundations of the older Connecticut were first being shaken; the answer to his Democratic and anti-Puritan paper had been the cool one of imprisonment. The case had become famous up and down the land; Osborn had been made the very symbol of rebellion against the New England domination; and when he was released, a few noisy rebels had contrived a parade along the stately eminence of Litchfield Hill. Accordingly, at sunrise of the day on which Barnum's term was ended, the national flag was hoisted over a small gathering place. At the actual moment of his release the national salute was fired. The services, for so he expressly denominated them, were begun by the singing of an ode composed for the occasion. *Strike the Cymbal* was also sung, and a patriotic carol called *Jefferson and Liberty*; and the Reverend Theophilus Fisk, appropriately in the foreground, delivered a stirring oration on the freedom of the press in which he ascended to even higher flights of praise and denunciation than in his letter. After a feast, Barnum solemnly took his place in a coach. Drawn by six horses, preceded by forty men on horseback with a marshal bearing a flag, to the booming roar of cannon, and followed — so he said — by sixty carriages, he drove in state from Danbury the six miles to Bethel, where with his young wife he lived over the yellow store.

His account of this gala performance was entitled *The Triumph of the People*. Indeed, from the Reverend Theophilus Fisk — or from a sudden native spring of fancy — Barnum had learned the easy values of the baldly patriotic appeal. Thenceforward in his paper he sounded a national note. But in vain. The sentence for libel had left a deeper stigma than he ever was willing to admit; and in communities as small as Bethel and Danbury personal feeling was sharply militant. He was obliged to move *The Herald of Freedom* to Norwalk, and then to sell it; the paper never had been a paying venture. His store failed. He had continued his lotteries; but in 1834 lotteries were at last effectively prohibited; and the blue laws were being affirmed and enforced. If in the matter of government the Standing Order had gone down, the Puritan mode of conduct was now defined with increasing sharpness. Respectability and Puritanism were more than ever closely intertwined. Barnum had engaged in a reckless running warfare against the only society he knew; and he had lost. His defeat was unmistakable; he was ousted from employments which were greatly to his liking; and he was badly out of pocket. Money in itself he perhaps cared for very little; he was lavish; from the first there was nothing niggardly in his composition; in his simple scale of moral values hoarding was evil. He was one of those Americans of whom Harriet Martineau spoke, for whom the miser was "an antique classical kind of personage, pictured forth as having a high cap, a long gown, and sitting in a vaulted chamber, amidst money-bags." If Barnum had coin, he liked to feel it slipping through his fingers with a fillip of excitement; he enjoyed his adventures less for the returns they yielded than for their variety, or for the advantage they gave him over other people. Here was another rub. In small Connecticut communities thrift was a staple virtue, joined with the sterner moralities. At every point, it seemed, young Barnum had been reduced to ignominy. Small wonder that his high moment of conquest, that of the triumphal procession, should remain a flowing pattern in his mind! So it seemed; with his lusty ache for power, that forced and straggling episode took on enchantment; its outlines were to invite him in a hundred ways through many a long year, indeed, throughout his lifetime. Barnum went to New York with certain elementary conclusions which he never forgot; but penniless though he was, and something of an outcast, with a family to support, he apparently remained irrepressible; his spirits still bounded; and after a few mistrials he found an enterprise precisely fitted to his hand.

II

In any sort of exhibit Barnum was always to find pleasure; there was the happy combination of a public appearance and of pulling off a feat — in most cases a joke — of producing some preposterous object for public wonder or acclaim. But for his maiden effort in what he was invariably to call the show business he could have looked far without finding an object so well calculated to offer him a timely sense of triumph as the one he soon hit upon: this was the ancient negress named Joice Heth, who was said to be one hundred and sixty-one years old, and the nurse of George Washington. He bought the repulsive living mummy — thus becoming a slave-owner — placed her on exhibit at Niblo's Gardens, and easily and gayly strummed the patriotic note. But Joice Heth was something more than a means of extorting the sentiment of patriotism; indeed, her discourses on religion and her singing of hymns were the larger part of her program. Watching the simple solemn folk who came reverently to listen and observe, he achieved a primitive backslap at the organized religionists with whom he had done battle in Bethel and Danbury. When at last popular attention began to lag, a letter by a supposed visitor in one of the public prints declared that Joice Heth was an ingenious contraption of rubber, whalebones, and springs, that the proprietor was a ventriloquist, and that "all conversations held with the ancient lady are purely imaginary." This bouncing inversion and quick slide into burlesque Barnum enjoyed to the full; the cry of fraud was one which he was to raise against his own exhibits throughout most of his long career. It not only provided advertisement, but an effect of a contest which Barnum seemed to relish. Now, as later, the device was successful; many serious persons came for a second look, and to pass a wise judgment. When this new inquiry had run its course Barnum took the ancient creature to Boston, Philadelphia, and Albany; and when the American Institute was opened in New York — that early ambitious organization for the promotion of American industry and science — he arranged to be on hand once more with his exhibit, this time presenting Joice Heth in the guise of a physical curio, thus by chance, knowledge, or intuition hitting upon one of his surest claims for public attention — the scientific claim. Though the creature survived the sessions of the Institute, she was not immortal; she died soon afterward; and Barnum, still cultivating science, still tireless and unhurried, stimulated a prolonged controversy as to the question of her age, in which a few men of scientific pretensions took part, and Bennett of the *Herald* was twice hoodwinked. This was sheer gratuitous sport, as Barnum's own name was not brought into play; and he was not then before the New York public.

Again he was without an occupation. During a visit in Washington he had interviewed Anne Royall, that picturesque early female journalist, lobbyist, editor, and thorough-going terror of national legislators, whom John Quincy Adams described as going about "like a virago-errant in enchanted armor, redeeming herself from the cramps of indigence by the notoriety of her eccentricities and the forced currency they gave to her publication." A bitter anti-Calvinist, Anne Royall had her sharp opinions about the powerful in Connecticut, indeed the powerful in all the New England states, where she had traveled some years before gathering material for her piquant *Black Books*. She became the editor of a little sheet appropriately called *Paul Pry*. It was proof of his continued absorption in the anti-Puritan rebellion that Barnum now tried to persuade her to lecture under his direction on the principles of government. In the early thirties the lecture platform was still a rough scaffolding in this country; the lyceums had just begun; but their power was already manifest. Barnum, with his easy assimilation, was trenching upon a movement of a signal importance. However, Anne Royall was strongly attached to the pastime of stamping through the halls of the Capitol with her huge umbrella; in spite of Barnum's blandishments she declined to leave Washington, and for many years continued to torment the nation's servants.

At his wit's end Barnum engaged an Italian plate-spinner and stilt-walker, and boldly set out to conquer Connecticut. He failed; the shadow of the blue laws still lay thick. He traveled through other New England states, and dipped into New Jersey, but with meager returns. In Philadelphia he trumped up a rival performer to walk stilts and spin plates for a wager against his own man; and the scene grew tumultuous, the profits were large, the sly effect of doubling much to Barnum's taste; but elsewhere he seemed unable to contrive similar matches. Presently he transferred the plate-spinner, whom he had christened Vivalla, to Aaron Turner's small traveling circus, joined the company himself as ticket-seller, treasurer, and part owner, and again entered Connecticut. Shabby and insignificant as it was, the little troupe received an ample volume of attack there and in Massachusetts; bitter invectives were flung from the pulpit; and to the pulpit Barnum ascended one Sunday morning at Lenox, pushing his way thither with bland effrontery, and delivering a defense of circuses from the sacred elevation. He repeated these tactics. Once an enraged minister shouted throughout Barnum's discourse, commanding his people to leave. Yet even with Barnum's cross-fire the circus failed to prosper; and the company traveled south. It was a rough life, crammed to the brim with hardships, enlivened in the main by practical jokes — which were often cruel — played by all members of the company singly or in groups against the others. Barnum apparently liked the whole haphazard journey, opposition and all, perhaps because he still was captivated by the hint of rebellion, possibly because he found a faint effect of the triumphal march in the poor little procession. Undaunted by slight rewards and hard fare, in North Carolina he resolved to create a circus of his own. By what sleight of hand he paid Turner is not clear; but he took Vivalla, a fiddler, a clown, and a negro breakdown dancer from the original company, and equipped with a single wagon and a small tent, proceeded further south, calling his assemblage a Scientific Theater. The roads were bad, the distances long; Puritanism was not without its outposts in the South. As he made a slow and tortuous way through Alabama and Mississippi and northward through Kentucky and Tennessee into that mid-country which was still called the West, his audiences were drawn from the roughs and tag-ends of every community through which he passed; at the same time he was obliged to avoid their boisterous attentions. Perhaps these inclined to mount as his Yankee birth became apparent; in the wake of the Yankee peddler every traveling Yankee was fair game. Barnum was muscular enough for defense when necessary, and sharp enough to use his wits instead of his fists whenever possible. If he could begin the performance he could usually win his audience; a fiddler was wickedly enchanting, a breakdown dancer the host of a hundred forbidden antics. Finally, by good luck, Barnum was joined by Henry Hawley, a sleight of hand performer who left his audiences gaping with astonishment, and proved to be a companion well adapted to run the gauntlet of rough travel. Hawley was a prodigious teller of tall tales.

Suddenly the tall tale was everywhere, a beanstalk growth which had shot up almost without warning all over the land. In the middle twenties, indeed, something of the sort had been decorously imprisoned by covers, in such an uproarious satire as Paulding's *John Bull in America*; but for the most part the native talent had become an affair of improvisation by word of mouth or of occasional journalistic enterprise. Hoaxes of all sorts were the mode. The Moon Hoax had been perpetrated by the New York *Sun* in a series of articles which purported to delineate the inhabitants of the moon as discovered by Herschel at the Cape of Good Hope. A little earlier Poe had published his *Hans Pfaall*, fabricated upon the same basis. "Humbug" was a word now in sudden common use, as if it denoted a discovery. But perhaps the most extensive application of the novel faculty appeared in casual tales told in remote regions, of the kind which was to appear thirty years later with so unlikely an effect of novelty in *The Celebrated Jumping Frog of Calaveras County*. In the backwoods the simple tale of adventure was growing elongated, was ascending, becoming preposterous — and was accepted. In the realm of supposed hazards anything was believed, not, perhaps, because life itself was so strange, but because it was not strange enough, because in those unsettled regions, once the risks of the first pioneering were over, men were bored. Out of an immense isolation came an equal lassitude; any jolt was welcome; and to match credulity a solemn, imperturbable narration was developed which became as closely masked as the face of danger.

In later years, though Hawley dropped from sight like dozens of others briefly attached to his train, and though Barnum showed no more interest in his career than in that of the rest, he would repeat Hawley's tales with relish, and with a life-like touch was able to evoke him as an artist of the time and place. A young man, prematurely gray, Hawley possessed a quiet, formal dignity; he would take his place in the village bar-room with no particular insistence, and would gradually draw his hearers by strange tales which were known to be true. Step by mild deliberate step he proceeded to his preposterous heights. "Gentlemen," asked Hawley, "have any of you ever visited the Rocky Mountains?" They had not. "I have been there frequently," he continued; and he narrated his adventures in a region where all the trappers and hunters met to celebrate the Fourth of July, making an excellent ice-punch, the ice being obtained in cart-loads from a nearby cavern where the supply was perennial. On one occasion a couple of Irishmen who had been sent for a second load returned in terror, having come upon a pair of boots with legs in them. Through the efforts of the party, a little antiquated man was exhumed who wore short breeches and knee-buckles, an old-fashioned coat and a cocked hat, and who looked so life-like that many of the old trappers insisted that he must be merely dormant. Truly enough, by the aid of brandy, a hot bath, and woolen blankets, the quaint creature was brought to life and proved to be an officer of King George, sent on a mission to some Indian tribes during the Revolutionary War; he had tripped in the cave, and knew nothing more until rescued by the trappers seeking ice for their punch fifty years later, on the Fourth of July.

Hawley went on to tell of another strange phenomenon in the same region, an area some twenty miles square where the air was so pure that people never died, unless by accident. "Never died!" exclaimed several of his listeners. "No, gentlemen, it was quite impossible. The rare purity of the air prevented it. When persons got too old to be useful they would sometimes be blown away, and once outside the charmed circle they were lost." A literal member of his audience still raised a doubt. "A fact, upon my honor," declared Hawley. "Indeed, some years ago several philanthropic gentlemen erected a museum at that place, where persons who became too old for usefulness were put in sacks, labeled, registered at the office, and hung up. If at any subsequent period their friends wished to converse with them, for a fee of fifty cents the old friend would be taken down, placed in a kettle of tepid water, and would soon be enabled to hold a conversation of half an hour, when he would be taken out, wiped off and hung up again." Hawley himself had found an uncle there who had gone to the Rocky Mountains thirty years before and had not been heard of since; he proved to be the contents of Sack No. 367; he was taken down, conversed weakly, and was able to tell his nephew of the whereabouts of a large gun he had once owned. Hawley declared that he found the gun on the identical crossbeam which his uncle had described, a monstrous large weapon which required a pound of powder and four pounds of shot for loading, and with which he subsequently went hunting pigeons in a buckwheat field. He threw a stick to arouse the pigeons, and they arose as a single mass; but unfortunately he fired half a second too late, and succeeded only in shooting off the legs of the flock; he picked up four bushels and a half of feet and legs.

"That's a lie, by thunder!" exclaimed one of his audience. Possibly even in the thirties the tricks of a gargantuan fabrication were well known. Such tales had already been constructed around episodes in the lives of heroes like Davy Crockett and a dozen others whose heroism and skill are now lost to view. But if Hawley's audience was sophisticated in the matter of monstrous guns, it was intrigued by the discovery of King George's messenger and by the museum of rarefied old men; Barnum declared that several members of one group solemnly wrote down the number of the sack that contained Hawley's uncle. Whether or not they in turn were acting a tall tale, there was no doubt of their lust for magnitude; it was as if that sense of scale which was presently to overwhelm the American imagination in so many forms were now germinating obscurely in these scant and barren recesses of the backwoods. Again and again Hawley pulled his resilient long bow, and won the momentary pleased attention of many a little crowd as the circus moved on its precarious way. But alas! when the small caravan circled into the Ohio Valley even this device failed. Here once more was the New England public, if anything more deeply rooted in its standards, prejudices, and prepossessions than on its native soil. Stragglers and idlers and careless pleasure-seekers existed in plenty, truly enough; young Henry Ward Beecher, then beginning his career in southern Indiana, knew them well; perhaps Barnum's Grand Musical and Scientific Theater drifted through Lawrenceburg, and was enjoyed by a heedless little throng there. But in the main Barnum encountered that rigorous opposition of which young Beecher himself was soon to become the spokesman in his *Lectures to Young Men*.

Barnum tried his last resort, the direct attack, and began delivering a defense of the circus in the shape of religious or moral lectures of his own, in groves, in open fields, from the tail of his wagon. Never, even in the most exuberant moments of later years did he refer to these ventures with anything but a vague and tepid allusion, not — surely — because he was ashamed of them, but because they were unsuccessful. The dint which he made upon the surface of this half formulated small society was exceedingly slight; he was defeated in the second New England of the West. He was obliged to leave a wagon in one village, a horse in the next, a watch elsewhere, in order to pay his bills. Other ill luck pursued him. Vivalla departed without warning; the negro dancer was drowned; once Barnum was obliged to disband his company altogether. Contriving to assemble another small troupe, he started down the Mississippi; but even in the small hamlets along the great river the circus was fair game; the rough gangs that haunted the river-front tormented the players and threatened to break up the performances; on one occasion Barnum was run out of town at the point of pistols. At New Orleans he wheeled about, and returned to New York. "I was thoroughly disgusted with the life of the itinerant showman," he declared. Yet in a few months he was traveling into the South and West once more with another crude little circus, enduring the same hardships, meeting the same resistance; round and round over these long and arduous circuits he made his way: these early tours covered four or five years, persisting with enormous endurance, with the incredible stability of madness or genius, as if either in the crude surprises of his own little performances or in the small gaping audiences which viewed them he found an irresistible attraction. With other scattered showmen and the race of Yankee peddlers and a few revivalists Barnum belonged to the pioneer travelers of the time and place, and learned an obscure lore whose value even then he may well have apprehended. In his own manner he girdled and possessed the new country.

When he reached New Orleans early in 1841 Barnum retrieved his fortunes in part by arranging a dancing match between his own breakdown dancer and another, much after the fashion of the duel of the plate-spinners and stilt-walkers which he had contrived in Philadelphia; but by a series of mishaps he lost most of his profits on the journey to New York. For a brief time he turned to the project of selling illustrated Bibles. "I thus made another effort to quit the life of a showman altogether, and settle down into a respectable calling." He became, as he said, a "Bible-man." But at the same moment he was moved to lease the Vauxhall saloon, where he conducted semi-theatrical performances throughout the summer. The double rôle was not successful, though in it may have been contained the pattern of a plan to keep one hand upon solid recommendations and the other upon a lively adventure. Barnum was at the end of a long and slippery rope when he learned that Scudder's Museum was for sale, at the corner of Ann Street and Broadway, half a block from the small printing shop where Horace Greeley had launched the *Tribune* earlier in the year.

With one of those sudden decisions which represented what he called "tact," he decided to acquire the Museum. He was always to entertain a number of ambitions at a single moment, tossing them up juggler-wise and keeping them in rapid motion until they seemed a single chain. He wanted Scudder's for all reasons. Museums were respectable, though circuses and theaters were not. Nearly sixty years before at Yale College a quaint little collection of relics had been gathered by Dr. Ezra Stiles in the name of science, history, and the classics; Peale in Philadelphia, an odd and gentle genius, had long since created his huge mixed aggregation of exquisite portraits, historical records, anatomical specimens, and amazing rubbish. Even in the strict and simple West few cities of any pretensions lacked a museum; Cincinnati possessed two. At first these institutions had been mere abiding places for the spoils of time and adventure, handy repositories for the queer trophies of travelers, explorers, sea-captains; but gradually they had assumed scientific pretensions. Scudder's itself had won its earliest repute by means of a monster tortoise which had been exhibited as a marvel of nature and also as a patriotic emblem, since the creature had been nurtured and caught on American shores. Of late, from the scientific interest had come an easy transition to an absorption in the grotesque. A passion for the morbidly strange, perhaps always languidly sleeping in the human mind, suddenly had become devouring. Poe had written his *Tales of the Grotesque and Arabesque* at the end of the thirties; he was even now offering spectral chambers, other-worldly abysses, and shuddering catastrophes to hundreds of eager readers. In a more immediate world the legend perhaps was plainer; freaks and monsters of all kinds were a fashion; it was a poor museum which did not boast a Chamber of Horrors with a magnetic shock. Aberrations from the normal in anatomical specimens were shown everywhere, with teeth and bones or even more gruesome relics which evoked the scenes of Indian slaughter, or the hint of monstrous heathen rites.

Perhaps because the element of pleasure was successfully inverted, or heavily disguised, museums had remained respectable. In New York, moreover, there was at least a hint of moral latitudes which Barnum had not discovered in his endless travels in the West; New York had long since been called Gotham. And the enterprise of Scudder's was a gamble; for several years money had been lost there. Barnum's liking for any lottery remained; he believed that by sleight of hand of his own the place could be made to yield a golden stream. He succeeded in discrediting other prospective purchasers of the Museum. Lacking a penny, he aroused the owner of the building to buy the collection for him, giving him a lease and an option of purchase, and settled at once to a program of cold lunches and severe self-denial in order to meet his obligations. But his period of discipline was short; nor was he able to maintain his original intention of investing all his surplus in advertising, except a small sum needed for his family. The feat proved impossible. His returns were far too large; the golden stream had become a flood.

III

A small New York sprawled uncertainly into farms along the rivers; but even in 1841 opulence was lavishly spread over the town. Broadway was bright and confused, with posters and placards hung from wooden pillars and cross-beams outside the shops. Gaudy tokens of wealth appeared in the gayly painted and expensively upholstered equipages which brushed by. Velvets and furs and multi-colored silks were worn by men as well as by women. In the midst of this effervescent thoroughfare Barnum's Museum promptly became the showiest place of all, with its pennants and flags streaming from the four-storied building, its paintings of birds, beasts, and reptiles in serried parallels between the windows, its flamboyant posters or brilliant transparencies. With his huge gas lights that blazed at night up and down the street Barnum created a flood of prophetic illumination. On a balcony he posted a brass band — Music for the Million — and blared forth the attractions of the Museum by sheer noise. On the Fourth of July, without asking permission he had flags strung from the Museum to St. Paul's church opposite, and when he was ordered to remove them, staged a timely and noisy bit of drama, with brawny men in shirt sleeves asking the vestrymen to take down the national emblem if they dared, and inquiring loudly whether the rector was a Britisher. Crowds were drawn by the strange ritual of a man who set down single bricks at given places in the street and within the building, without a word, and who changed them for other bricks; he was steadily followed — through the Museum — by a respectful throng. Other throngs came with babies, with dogs, with flowers, and poultry, to compete in the many shows advertised by Barnum as a prime feature of the Museum; they came for fame, and for the appropriate rewards of diplomas, medals, and money, paying their twenty-five cents — children half price — to enter the Museum.

Inside the gaudy painted box came a sudden shock; instead of the colored illumination visible on Broadway were dark vistas, dim recesses, and strange forms and figures, with an atmosphere of solemnity. The awed spectator could climb broad staircases which had semblance of grandeur: where else in New York in the early forties could be found the effect of scale in a public building? He could enjoy a vague sense of possession, and suddenly be startled out of it by a hideous surprise as he rounded a corner at the top. On the walls or suspended in cases were freaks of nature, stuffed or in wax or in their skeletal bones, two-headed calves and two-headed chickens, the more terrifying natural specimens, snakes and the Gila monster, startling amphibians, and dangerous beasts of the jungle. Presently Barnum brought to the attention of the public a creature which outstripped any contemporary offering as a fantasy in the grotesque: the tiny wizened relic of fin and skin, varnish and bone, forever contorted into a posture of agony, which he dubbed the Feejee Mermaid. Assisted by the agent who had helped him display Joice Heth — another fantasy in the grotesque — he teased and jogged and jolted the public curiosity for weeks by a series of adroitly contrived newspaper notices: the mermaid came from Pernambuco, and had been procured for the Natural History Lyceum of London; then, in Philadelphia, a few persons had gazed upon the wonder; and at last, after many circumvolutions, changes, new hints, and proposals, the mermaid was advertised to appear for a short time at the Concert Hall. With amplitude Barnum now played upon the scientific importance of the discovery — anonymously. With the mermaid were to be shown other strange creatures in the great chain of animated nature, like the Ornitho-Rhyncus, the Proteus Anguinus, and the Paddle-Tail Snake. Barnum appealed to a memory of the classics, to the esthetic sense — and to what else? Full-blown mermaids combing their hair and disporting their charms in trios and groups and happy shoals figured on posters and transparencies. A newspaper woodcut showed a small sail-boat filled with a company of ascetic-looking men in tall hats and women in Shaker bonnets; their gaze was fixed upon a retreating mermaid while a clerical gentleman appeared to be delivering a harangue: yet strangely enough, with its bow headed toward safe horizons, the little vessel appeared to be following the siren. There was no question as to the unhallowed excitement which Barnum aroused in the fabulous and pagan race of sea-nymphs, or as to his gusto, or his deliberate skill. When after this long prelude, and the promised appearance at the Concert Hall, and a further shower of posters, pamphlets, and transparencies, the problematical creature was at last shown at the American Museum under Barnum's own ægis, multitudes came; the mermaid crowded into the newspapers again; indeed, the fame of the creature, Barnum said, was "wafted" from one end of the country to the other. Later the small horrid relic was sent on tour, and remained in Boston for some years; the excitement seemed deathless; as late as 1855 Barnum was successfully exhibiting the mermaid at the Museum.

Here was a practical joke on a grand scale. If by a crude contrivance the spectator was not bumped downstairs, or tripped into humiliating posture after the manner of country-made practical jokes, mentally the same effect was achieved; he went to see a siren of fair proportions, and was confronted by a hideous little monster. From the sharp contrast between its gaudy exterior and the portentous gloom within, to the mixed and changing char-latanry of its exhibits, the whole Museum constituted a practical joke. Its object was to reduce the beholder again and again to an abject bewilderment; he might be terrified or horrified, disappointed or in the end amused, but he was also submissive and beaten. Barnum had only to walk about the halls of his new domain to hear empty giggles and helpless laughter, to see the dropped jaw and the pointed finger. By luck or insight he had found that a great undeveloped audience awaited him, which was bored and dull and aimless, without standards of taste, cramped by its heritage yet willing to shift this to a convenient formalism, desiring liberation and laughter — if this was laughter — desiring above all, perhaps, a common enjoyment. That sheep-like docility, that inclination to follow the crowd which had been satir-ically noted by Poe as an American characteristic, had already had at least one sufficient demonstration in the popular festival of the Harrison campaign the year before Barnum had opened the Museum, when the country had gone mad with contagious imitation, when whole mobs had worn the same emblems, shouted the same songs, cried the same phrases in unison for the first time in American history. An aborted hope of union — of companion-ship — what indeed? — was abroad; it seemed necessary only to strike some quaint and common interest to have its slogans run like loud essential signals, and to draw the expectant crowd into a close knot or a throng.

With his eye upon far larger numbers than he could assemble in the Museum, Barnum presently ranged outside, seizing upon the growing con-sciousness of the pioneer West which had lately been materialized by the figure of General Harrison. He advertised a free buffalo hunt at Hoboken. There was no hunt; the buffaloes were timid yearlings; one man appeared in a western costume. The crowd got nothing — for nothing. Almost any prophet would have declared that they would grow frenzied with rage: but no, as the small thin young buffaloes trotted out and quickly huddled in a far corner, the big assemblage roared with mirth, roared at its own predicament, and went good-naturedly home, demanding to know the perpetrator of so excellent a hoax. After all, a hoax is an elaborate form of attention. Who indeed had taken the pains to delude them on so preposterous a scale before?

A few years later, when the western fever was at its height, Barnum turned to his own ends the romantic excitement which had centered about the figure of Colonel Frémont. "Colonel Frémont was lost among the trackless snows of the Rocky Mountains," he said afterward in half-hearted apology. "The public mind was excited. Serious apprehensions existed that the intrepid soldier and engineer had fallen a victim to the rigors of a severe winter. At last the mail brought intelligence of his safety. The public heart beat quick with joy. I now saw a chance for the woolly horse" — a small horse covered with wool like a sheep, and lacking both mane and tail, which he had purchased in Cincinnati some time earlier, and had hidden away until the suitable moment for exhibition should arise. Immediately after the announcement that Frémont was safe, another item appeared in the New York newspapers. "The public appetite was craving something tangible from Colonel Frémont," said Barnum. "The community was absolutely famishing. They were ravenous. They could have swallowed anything, and like a good genius, I threw them, not a bone, but a regular titbit, a bonbon — and they swallowed it at a single gulp." The second dispatch declared that on the Gila River Frémont and his band had discovered an amazing nondescript which resembled a horse, but which was undoubtedly made up of the elephant, the deer, the horse, the buffalo, the camel, and the sheep. According to further information, the creature had been sent by Frémont to a United States Quartermaster, and was to be exhibited in New York for a few days before being sent to London. Handbills appeared showing a huge horse in full flight, and making a terrific leap over a chasm which embraced, as Barnum said, at least five miles, with Frémont's men in full pursuit. Pamphlets were circulated about the horse, written in the unhurried descriptive style which still prevailed in public writing. These announcements came in rapid succession; the horse was brought on for exhibit — in an empty store — at a swift climax. After all, Colonel Frémont would not remain in the trackless snows of the Rocky Mountains forever; and United States Quartermasters were not wholly obscure figures. Indeed, when the horse was sent to Washington on exhibit — "to see if the wool could be pulled over the eyes of politicians" — the hot-tempered father-in-law of Frémont, Colonel Benton, sued Barnum's agent: but the case was dismissed.

At the outset Barnum's name was absent from public information about the woolly horse; but he calmly announced it when the rich returns were in. The venture was on the whole a minor sally; yet it represented — as did the Buffalo Hunt — a brisk tendency in Barnum's exhibits; he was still engaged in hoaxes, but more and more frequently these tended to come alive. Sitting among his show-cases, at the end of corridors, or in appropriate corners, were living monstrosities like giants, fat boys, albinos; to these were gradually added a sprinkling of Indians, Chinese, gypsies, and even a "live Yankee" — so the advertisement ran, though why he became an exhibit is not entirely clear, unless Barnum wished to pillory or exalt the type. Presently sprightlier surprises appeared, in occasional ventriloquists who disturbed the many

by uncanny sounds from unlikely quarters, in a pair of jugglers, a sleight of
hand performer, and even a troupe of rope-dancers. Here and there his
stuffed specimens were replaced by living animals in cages. "If I have
exhibited a questionable dead mermaid in my Museum it should not be
overlooked that I have also exhibited camelopards, a rhinoceros, grizzly
bears, orang-outangs, and great serpents, about which there could be no
mistake because they were alive." Here, indeed, were the scattered features
of that dubious entertainment, the circus: here was another hoax. Barnum
never mentioned the word circus; he hedged his diversions round with what
he called "a wilderness of realities" — knitting-machines, glass-blowers,
mummies, models of Dublin, Paris, Jerusalem, an anatomical Venus, numberless dissolving views, automatons, and an increasing quantity of strange
mementoes from all parts of the world.

"Bless me, what have we here? The hand and part of an arm, as I'm
alive," said one of the good little boys who figured in an illuminated pamphlet
describing the Museum. "Yes," said Uncle Find-Out in reply, "that is the
arm of the celebrated Tom Trouble, the pirate, who was taken after a severe
action, in which he lost the forefinger of his hand. He died in prison, at St.
Thomas, while under the sentence of death. He was afterward nailed to
a plank, and exposed in the harbor, when, strange to say, his whole body
became bleached and preserved, similar to this arm, which was cut off by
an American seaman, and brought to New York. Here, also, is a human
body, found in 1814, at Glasgow, in Kentucky, in a saltpetrous cave, nine
feet under ground. A very curious specimen, and in fine condition."

"I suppose the saline properties preserved the body, sir," said the wise
little nephew.

Despite such opportune instruction, the circus grew a little larger and
a little brisker year by year; and an even more equivocal amusement was
developed with an abundant energy. In truth, any wanderer through the
halls of the Museum might have surmised that drama would somewhere
prove a rightful climax; the dramatic was evoked at every turn, in the club
that killed Captain Cook, in the panoramic diorama of the obsequies of
Napoleon, in the wax models of famous murderers of the past and celebrated
heroes of the present, all life-size and shown in the act of introducing themselves to the spectator. Naturally enough, then, in a little room upstairs
the drama quickly bloomed. At first, as part of Scudder's, this place had
been devoted to lectures on the more puzzling exhibits; and Barnum kept
the covering name of Lecture Room to the end. He provided another
elaborate mask. The *moral drama*, as he emphatically called it, was approached through an avenue of Biblical waxworks, or scenes in wax illustrating the miseries of intemperance. "We must fetch the public somehow.
Cum the moral on 'em strong. If it's a temperance community tell 'em
I sined the pledge fifteen minutes after I'se born," said Artemus Ward afterward, drawing his episode, it seems, from the career of Barnum himself.
Actually, in the midst of these presentations Barnum did sign a total absti-
nence pledge, in 1847, shortly after the meeting of the first world's temperance congress in London; the movement had lately received an immense

impetus from the lectures of Gough. And in Philadelphia, where he had acquired Peale's Museum, and where the temperance harvest was ripe, Barnum not only displayed the pledge in the box-office, where he said thousands signed it, but brought forth both temperance waxworks and a temperance drama. But in New York, where reform sentiment was less pronounced, he offered Biblical drama, including scenes from the life of the early Christians.

Deftly and casually, along with these offerings appeared one of the early high examples of the ten-twenty-thirty shows, which were not to exist in their entire extravagance for another generation. On holidays there were continuous performances; Artemus Ward said that Barnum's actors could be seen going to the Museum as early as seven o'clock with their tin dinner pails; and their number included many who later appeared on a broader stage, like Sothern, who took comedy parts at Barnum's in the early fifties, having failed to please Boston with tragedy. Under the large enveloping domino were presented imitations of some of the more celebrated actors and actresses then in New York: Macready, Forrest, the elder Booth, Kean, and Fanny Kemble. Here, in fact, was the very substance of the feared and hated theater. This perhaps was to underscore Barnum's joke, but it blared forth in any case with incredible resonance. He now offered such opulent productions as *Love, or the Countess and the Serf*, which little Henry and William James witnessed, with other plays of the same order, when they were permitted to spend their Saturday afternoons at the Museum. In this production appeared Miss Emily Mestayer, said Henry James long afterward, "large, red in the face, coifed in a tangle of small, fine, damp-looking curls and clad in a light blue garment edged with swansdown, shouting at the top of her voice that a 'pur-s-se of gold' would be the fair guerdon of the minion who should start on the spot to do her bidding at some desperate crisis which I now forget.... I forget everybody but Miss Mestayer.... She had a hooked nose, a great play of nostril, a vast protuberance of bosom, and always the crop of close, moist ringlets.... She had a rusty, rasping, heaving and tossing authority of which the bitterness is still in my ears."

In a superabundant measure Miss Mestayer seemed to possess precisely those brave seductions which made the theater an abomination. The little Jameses were enchanted; doubtless other young people enjoyed a similar wedge of dubious pleasure. The little Jameses, indeed, were restrained by no narrow axioms; the only irony which hemmed them round lay in the fact that the elder Henry James politely and exquisitely detested what he called "flagrant morality." Flagrant enough it was at Barnum's, the mere blazing word and the adroit admixture covering the uproarious fact. Simple as the fraud was, Barnum's mere insistence turned the trick. The drama was still shunned by the great respectable public; the ministry still denounced it with entire regularity. Henry Ward Beecher, who had lately come to Brooklyn, avoided the theater to the end of his life though it offered much that fitted his taste and temperament, saying that attendance would involve him in endless explanations. Yet Beecher commended Barnum's, and perhaps was present at some of the programs of the Lecture Room, for he certainly wandered through the maze of curiosities. In fact, the ministry fairly contended to praise the Museum; and Barnum himself looked almost clerical in his long black coat and tall black hat — the notorious "emblem of equality." His countenance was bland and unbetraying; but as the curious and gullible swarmed to the Lecture Room he collected their remarks as he collected other grotesque exhibits; he was vastly entertained by the rapid discursive explanations of a maiden lady from New England who announced her prejudice against all amusements, and asked when the services were to begin. Barnum called his audience the congregation; the number of his private jokes on the ministry multiplied. His sheaf of Biblical quotations which played upon the word "pass" — "Thou shalt not pass" — was originally compiled as a neat and stabbing method of announcing to the clergy that henceforth, like other people, they would have to pay to enter his Museum.

His burlesque took on enormous proportions, and plumbed unsuspected depths. Perhaps more than any other single force or figure Barnum broke down the barriers which had long kept the American public from the theater; irresistibly his audience must have filtered into the unsanctioned playhouses. But if he opened a sluice, he also deepened a channel. Though his designation was a shell, and his drama itself a caricature, he magnified the notion that the play must teach a lesson. Barnum, the anti-Puritan, thus perpetuated the stringent influence. As if indeed he belonged to the concentrated opposition, he seemed bent upon diminishing all the arts, by ridicule, with a battering gusto. He burlesqued the dance, naming a monstrous orang-outang for the exquisite Fanny Elssler. As for his Music for the Million, "I took pains to select and maintain the poorest band I could find," he declared, "one whose discordant notes would drive the crowd into the Museum, out of earshot of my orchestra." In these years the romantic passion was abroad in forms both delicate and profound. A wish to explore other worlds, beyond the seas, beyond any earthly region, within strange or evil places of the human heart, was apparent even in crude and minor expression, and was flowering in the writings of Poe and Hawthorne and Melville. Clearly a wave of this absorption or its fainter ripples must have flowed through the Museum, in the absurd responses to the grotesque, and to the unlikely relics from far places so thickly crowded there. Even that loose impulse toward assemblage upon which Barnum so steadily drew may have contained the beginnings of an attitude which makes a plastic audience for all of the arts. Barnum turned the obscurer hopes of his time upside down, presented its finer pursuits with destructive grossness: the Museum was his palace and his temple, filled to the brim with contemporary wishes and frustrations. Triumph! not only over the ancient Puritan enemy but over a whole society: triumph was what he wanted. Other men lived with the public; Barnum vanquished the public. Something of an outcast, himself defeated or diminished at every turn in that long and halted progress out of Connecticut into the farther reaches of the mid-country, and back to the emporium of New York — he finally had become the great trickmaster. If once he had fancied the image of the procession and had tried to create it trailing through a barren land, now the procession passed him in review. It was Barnum who determined its pace and direction, its gestures and noises of astonishment; using his favorite arrangement of the match, he even played off one public against another, pitted one museum against another, quietly buying Peale's in New York, and offering in each of his two possessions burlesques of the other which kept the crowd racing to and fro. "You and I are like a pair of shears," his manager at Peale's said to Barnum. "We seem to cut each other, but we only cut what comes between."

When the match of the two museums had run its length Barnum announced the consolidation — two in one for the same price — and was able to drag a further multitude into his own flamboyant building. The public laughed at the device; they often laughed at his extravagant promises — after the event. "I should hope that a little clap-trap occasionally, in the way of transparencies, exaggerated pictures, and puffing advertisements, might find an offset in a wilderness of wonderful, instructive, and amusing realities," said Barnum in casual apology. "Indeed, I cannot doubt that the sort of clap-trap referred to is allowable, and that the public likes a little of it mixed up with the great realities which I provide." It was true: they seemed to like it. Somberly enough they wandered through his halls; foreign critics noticed the grave American countenance; perhaps in the American Museum this was another example of the impassive look of the pioneer in the face of danger — fearing — in search of what? But afterwards they laughed, or joked about old Barnum. "There's Barnum! That's old Barnum!" He frequently overheard the whispered excitement. One man paid his admission, asked for Barnum, stared at the famous showman a moment, and threw down his ticket. "It's all right. I've got my money's worth," he exclaimed, and left the Museum. As they came and went, arriving at sunrise or before breakfast, looking at Barnum, looking at his preposterous conglomeration, who can say what they found? The imagination of the forties or the fifties, like that of youth, is difficult to recover; and Barnum's greatest exhibit, the public, left little trace of its conclusions. Perhaps if he was bent upon conquest, his spectators caught only his indestructible gusto; if the arts were destroyed before their eyes, they may have discovered the tangible good of a livelier existence. A public for whom violence was not far in the background, either from remembrance of the past or because of the perpetual advances of a rough pioneering, may have craved violence, may have found a rough liberation in those boisterous jolts which Barnum perpetually offered. Fifty years later Henry James declared that his afternoons at the Museum were "flushed with the very complexion of romance," and that in the "stuffed and dim little hall of audience" he "plucked somehow the very flower of the ideal." It may be that he found there among the trooping hundreds something of that inveterate and questing innocence which long seemed to him the essence of the American character.

IV

"I myself relished a higher grade of amusement, and was a frequent attendant at the opera, first class concerts, lectures, and the like; but I worked for the million," said Barnum in later years. His labor for the million was not too severe. Against the background of his huge medley of exhibits he found time from the first to trace a few patterns that might have been created for sheer pleasure, like his fantasy with the midget Tom Thumb. Barnum's taste usually ran to magnitude, to excess: here was excess inverted, the extraordinary in diminution, exquisitely producing the favorite start of surprise. Barnum trained the child in monologues and dances, tricked him out in pretty costumes, and after a season at the Museum, hit upon the audacious notion of taking his tiny curiosity abroad. Though visitors of all tempers and temperaments had been interchanged between the old world and the new for half a century only a few foreign actors or singers or dancers had come to this country; and the notion of an American conquest of the old world in the realm of entertainment was unheard of. But hopefully enough, in 1844, Barnum started off with Tom Thumb, who was now widely proclaimed to be an American midget; and after the fewest obstacles, and a sufficient blaze of advertisement by a short exhibition in London, the two were established in a Grafton Street mansion, where notables came rolling up in carriages by the hundreds. Presently the Baroness Rothschild sent for the pair; and Barnum entered upon the thousand and one nights.

"We were received by half a dozen servants elegantly dressed in black coats and pantaloons, white vests and cravats, white kid gloves, and, in fact, wearing the *tout ensemble* of a gentleman. One old chap was dressed in livery — a heavy laced coat, breeches, a large, white powdered and curled wig, and everything else to match. The hall was brilliantly illuminated, and each side was graced with the most beautiful statuary. We were ushered up a broad flight of marble stairs, and our names announced at the door of the drawing-room by an elegantly dressed servant, who under other circumstances I might have supposed was a member of the noble family. As we entered the drawing-room, a glare of magnificence met my sight which it is impossible for me to describe. The Baroness was seated on a gorgeous couch covered with rich figured silk damask and several lords and ladies were seated in chairs elegantly carved and covered with gold, looking indeed like solid gold, except the bottoms, which were rich velvet. On each side of the mantelpiece were specimens of marble statuary — on the right of which stood glazed cabinets containing urns, vases, and a thousand other things of the most exquisite workmanship, made of gold, silver, diamonds, alabaster, pearl, etc. The center table, and several tables about the size and something like the shape of a pianoforte, all covered with gold, or made of ebony thickly inlaid with pearls of various hues, were loaded with *bijous* of every kind, surpassing in elegance anything I had ever dreamed of. The chairs at one end of the room were made of ebony, inlaid with pearl and gold, elegantly cushioned with damask. The walls were paneled and heavily gilt — the curtains and ornaments of the most costly kind. The immense chandeliers and candelabras exceeded all my powers of description. Here we spent about two hours. About twenty lords and ladies were present. On taking our leave, an elegant and well-filled purse was quietly slipped into my hand, and I felt that the golden shower was beginning to fall!"

Gold — gold — he saw the aureate metal everywhere, not only in money-bags but in royal appurtenances.

Through the impetus of a letter from Horace Greeley to Edward Everett, Barnum quickly found himself in the yellow drawing-room at Buckingham Palace, "a magnificent apartment, surpassing in splendor and gorgeousness anything of the kind I had ever seen.... It was hung with drapery of rich yellow satin damask, the couches, sofas, and chairs being covered with the same material. The bases, urns, and ornaments were all of modern patterns and the most exquisite workmanship. The room was paneled in gold, and the heavy cornices beautifully carved and gilt. The tables, pianos, etc., were mounted with gold, inlaid with pearl of various hues, and of the most elegant devices."

The young Queen Victoria — she was only twenty-five — received the tall showman and his tiny charge graciously, took Tom Thumb by the hand, introduced the little Princess Royal, and the smaller Prince of Wales, and at the end of the songs, dances and imitations, presented the midget with "an elegant and costly souvenir." A second audience was granted by the Queen, and a third. Queen Adelaide also requested a performance, at which the old Duke of Cambridge was present, and offered the sprightly little dwarf a pinch of snuff. "Dear little General," said the kind-hearted Queen, taking him in her lap, like a story-book queen, "I see you have got no watch. Will you permit me to present you with a watch and chain?" "I would like it very much," replied the General, his eyes glistening with joy as he spoke. "I will have them made expressly for you," responded the Queen Dowager; and she did. The Duke of Devonshire with quaint eighteenth century notions, gave him "an elegant little snuff-box mounted with turquoise," and there were many other "costly gifts from the nobility and gentry." For four months the midget (and Barnum) held levees in London at the Egyptian Hall. "I do not believe that a single nobleman in England failed to see Tom Thumb," said Barnum exultantly. In gilded triumph the two went to Paris, where equally royal scenes were enacted. "King Louis Philippe was minute in his inquiries about my country, and talked freely about his experiences when he wandered as an exile in America. He playfully alluded to the time when he earned his living as a tutor, and said he had roughed it generally and had even slept in Indian wigwams." At the end of two hours the King presented the little General with a large emerald brooch set with diamonds; and it was arranged that Tom Thumb's superb tiny carriage with four ponies and a powdered coachman and footman should appear at Long-champs in the midst of the avenue reserved for the court and the diplomatic corps. Paris was in a furor. Statuettes of *Tom Pouce* appeared in plaster and sugar and chocolate; the daily receipts at the exhibition hall were so heavy that Barnum was obliged to carry home bags of gold and silver at night.

Then began a posting tour through the provinces. Barnum, who less than half a dozen years before had made his precarious way through the rough American back-country, now traveled in a magnificent post chaise with a retinue. A large vehicle transported the General's four ponies and little carriage; another carried the "elegant little house and furniture set on the stage." There were outriders and postilions. From France they went to Belgium, and from Belgium back to England, where interest in the midget was by no means exhausted. They toured Scotland; and the little General learned the Scotch dialect and Scotch dances, and appeared in a kilt. The entire journey lasted three years, with Barnum making an occasional hasty trip to New York — as rapidly as he could go in a sailing-packet — and back again; and it included an effort to purchase Shakespeare's house and Mme. Tussaud's, and the positive acquisition of some Lancashire Bell-Ringers whom he promptly converted into Swiss, a Happy Family of unlikely birds and animals trained to dwell together in a single cage, and a myriad other new attractions for the Museum. But Barnum's richest gain was not these, nor the golden shower of which he perpetually talked, nor that contact with the nobility which he so deeply relished, but an idea — a dream of personal splendor.

After all, he had haunted palaces — why should he not possess one? The full bloom of the early American country house was not to begin for another dozen years or more; Barnum forecast it on a prodigious scale, creating an archetypal dwelling called "Iranistan," from which the myriad later jigsaw, cut-work, wooden cottages of the Hudson Valley and the Berkshires might have sprung. During his stay in England he had seen the Orientalized pavilion which George IV had built at Brighton; and in all his travels he found nothing which better suited his taste. He copied it, choosing for his sovereign residence the scene of his many battles — Connecticut; among its cities he decided upon Bridgeport, "because the town seemed destined to become the first in size and opulence," and he bought a sufficient tract of land overlooking the Sound. There the extravagant house — his homestead, he called it — arose, with serried balconies, wide wings, shining domes, spires, minarets, and a lacy fretwork wherever fretwork could be introduced, along the balconies, above the windows, at the cornices. Everything glittered; the edifice might have been washed with gold or silver; a huge fountain played outside; bronze deer appeared in clusters on the grounds; and beyond, lay the fair semblance of an English park. Within was the same luster and scale. Rooms already sufficiently large were magnified by paneled mirrors on every side; gilt and a gorgeous patterning shone on the walls, on the thick piled carpets, on the paintings, the abundant statuary, the furniture. Was it the trickery of the mirrors which gave the sudden notion that Barnum's palace was another more glowing Museum? Or was it the wide walnut staircase which wound straight upward to the conservatory in the central dome, a goal not wholly different from the little roof-garden with a wilted palm or two which Barnum maintained on top of the Museum, and mentioned in later years with apology? The huge pavilion even contained a kind of glorified office, what an admirer called "the bijou apartment of the villa," or Mr. Barnum's private study, the most golden of all the rooms, the walls and ceilings of which were hung with the richest orange satin, and with furniture, rugs, and hangings luxuriously made to match. If the Museum boasted a pictorial saloon, Barnum also had one in his dwelling; at every turn were cabinets full of curios; instead of a few bedraggled Chinese men, he had a whole Chinese library whose walls were entirely covered by Chinese paintings in oil. Here and there the arts were glorified — as if he must inevitably range among them — by rich panels which represented Music, Painting, and Poetry, and by a large apartment set aside for music and dancing. And, when the palace was at last completed, over a thousand persons trooped in for the housewarming.

Here Barnum sat like a sultan with the somewhat somber Charity and his four children; or he roamed through the gorgeous upper stories to command the view. He declared that he meant to "withdraw from the whirlpool of excitement." A friend of Horace Greeley's, he now exalted the occupation of the farmer; he became a member of the Fairfield Agricultural Society, and began to buy Alderney cattle, Suffolk swine, and fine specimens of poultry. But even in the midst of these pastoral pursuits he was drawn by his native calling. Discovering that the attendance at the Fairfield county fair was falling off, he arranged to exhibit a live pickpocket who had been captured on the grounds, and had appropriate handbills printed and circulated. Indeed, within his dazzling tranquility, Barnum grew restless. The Philadelphia Museum, like one in Baltimore, had proved a transient venture; and apparently the New York Museum moved by its own weight. Still young, hardly forty, with the conquest of Europe behind him, he looked about for new material upon which to exercise his talents, and found it in what he called "the Jenny Lind enterprise."

"Little did the public see the hand that indirectly pulled their heart-strings, preparatory to a relaxation of their purse-strings," he exultantly remarked. "I may as well state that although I relied prominently upon Jenny Lind's reputation as a great musical *artiste*, I also took largely into my estimate... her character for extraordinary benevolence and generosity. Without this peculiarity in her disposition, I never would have dared make the engagements which I did...." Her charitable enterprises, indeed, were famous; she was known for her piety, and for her rigorous moral standards in the midst of a dubious European world of art; she had refused to sing in opera because opera — she reasoned — was only a glorified theater. She was an exquisite Puritan. With an accomplished talent Barnum shouted all these circumstances through the public prints. He used subtler means. Since Jenny Lind represented song, he surrounded her by lyrics, using the prime means of a prize competition; and then with this sufficient impetus a hundred other poems sprang into being.

"Blest must their vocation be
Who with tones of melody
Charm the discord and the strife
And the railroad rush of life,
And with Orphean magic move
Souls inert to life and love,
But there's one that doth inherit
Angel gifts and angel spirit —"

Thus sang Mrs. Sigourney, one of the veterans among the poetesses who were now commanding public attention. The chorus mounted; the fever spread; presently there were Jenny Lind gloves, handkerchiefs, veils, shawls, riding habits, robes, mantillas, chairs, sofas, beds, and pianos — all the paraphernalia of imitation once more. At a punctual moment tickets for the first concert were auctioned off, with Genin the hatter as the highest bidder; the sum which he paid, well over two hundred dollars, was considered fabulous; the tale ran like wild-fire through the country; and according to Eyre Crowe, Thackeray's friend and companion, an enormous hat-brim was suspended over Jenny Lind's private box at the concert at Castle Garden.

For the public, the hat, if it existed, would always have remained phantasmal. In white — she invariably wore white — Jenny Lind seemed indeed the exquisite embodiment of a feminine vision which had been floating into consciousness in this country for half a dozen years, and was to remain a regnant fashion for a dozen more. She was an epitome of innocence, she was willowy, she suggested tears. "Sweet, tearful Jenny!" exclaimed an admirer. Through green arbors she had walked when she landed in New York — by Barnum's contrivance; now, in the midst of arbors she sang; she looked a sublime country maiden, sharing the cool marvel of her voice without premeditation. Around her Barnum kept a prismatic radiance, in the rainbow lights which illuminated the great hall, in the colored wands carried by the ushers; and he maintained as well, in that first novel multitude, a stringent perfection of order. Small matter that her figure was not truly graceful, that her character was not pliant and sweet, but stubborn and dogmatic. Small matter that a few critics were unmoved by her voice. Perhaps its unbroken coolness was the quality which completed the airy vision; a chilly purity was essential in those fragile heroines who were already drifting into fiction in passionless serenity. Those persons whom Barnum called "the fashionables" remained aloof for a time, but they too were captivated. "It was with some difficulty that I prevented the fashionables from monopolizing her altogether, and thus, as I believed, sadly marring my interests by cutting her off from the warm sympathies which she had awakened among the masses." It was the masses to which he constantly appealed by every known device in his armory; and he drew them by the thousands in a long tour over the country. When "the campaign closed," as Barnum said, fortunes had been earned both for Jenny Lind and for himself: how large these were it remains impossible to tell, for with a not uncustomary recession of candor he gave Miss Lind's net returns and his own in gross. But there was no question as to the magnitude of his accomplishment. Though a few dancers had come from Europe — Fanny Elssler foremost among them — Jenny Lind was the first of a long line of famous continental singers to conquer this continent. With that fascinated circling about the arts which Barnum seemed continually to maintain, he had broken down another prejudice, he had created the revolutionary notion that pleasure of the senses might be indulged without harm or danger and even with benefit. And since music was a luxury, by introducing that prim figure, he perhaps assisted in the birth of a new worldliness, and did so with his habitual skill at an opportune moment: at the brink of the ample fifties, when opulence was to have a riotous sway in a thousand new enjoyments which had long been denied.

If Barnum was aware of the effects of his tireless momentum he gave no sign except a single reference to the "most humanizing of all the arts." In all his voluminous commentary on Jenny Lind there is scarcely a line to suggest that he recognized her voice except as a means of making money; he spoke of her as "the greatest musical wonder in the world," as though she were an automatic singer and a museum exhibit. Indeed, during the two years consumed by his preparation for the concerts and the tour, he had become preoccupied with the plan of quite a different kind of circuit. In those months of leisure at his palace in Bridgeport he had had time for reflection; he may have gone back to his years of drudging failure with a tiny caravan in the West. Certainly the scheme of a new and monster circus might have been devised expressly to blot out the old memory of failure. Chartering a ship, he sent agents to Ceylon to procure at least a dozen living elephants and a herd of other wild animals; a crew of one hundred and sixty natives plunged into the jungle at his remote bidding; presently his elephants were parading up and down Broadway harnessed to chariots; and the circus was sent on tour, not yet acknowledged as a circus, however, but sonorously proclaimed as Barnum's Great Asiatic Caravan, Museum, and Menagerie. Whether he failed to supervise its progress closely, or whether the time was not yet ripe for circuses, he dropped the project at the end of four years, but insisted that it had yielded another fortune. As a symbol and a prophecy, he kept a single elephant on view near Bridgeport, with a keeper in an Oriental costume, on a tract of ground near the railroad to New York.

The elephant advertised the Museum; yet Barnum seemed to have forgotten that rich source of fortune; his efforts there had grown mechanical. He introduced new features, it is true; when *Uncle Tom's Cabin* made its momentous appearance, he appropriated the book, as did many others, and turned it into a play for his Lecture Room without compensation to Mrs. Stowe. But these were minor matters; again he was seeking an absorbing new scheme. With a few others he engaged in the enterprise of creating another Crystal Palace in New York, modeled after the great shell created by Prince Albert: but the project failed. He promoted the manufacture of a new fire annihilator, became part owner of a steamship, invested in a copper mine at Litchfield, became president of a Bridgeport bank, and launched a weekly paper called the *Illustrated News* with Rufus Griswold as the editor, and young Charles Godfrey Leland as an assistant, whose gypsy days were far in the future, and who had not yet published *Hans Breitmann's Ballads.* In the cramped quarters of their office Barnum spent hours, as though fascinated by the making of copy; he submitted jokes, and was enormously pleased with them. "I think I see him now, coming smiling in like a harvest moon, big with some new joke," said Leland long afterward, and recorded one of the few genial judgments on Barnum which remain from his contemporaries. He insisted that Barnum was "a brother of the same band" as Lincoln, expressing "vast problems, financial, intellectual, or natural, by the brief arithmetic of the joke. To engineer some grotesque and startling paradox into tremendous notoriety, to make something *immensely* puzzling with a stupendous *sell* as a postscript, was more of a motive with him than even the main chance," said Leland, and declared that of all the business men whom he met in those days Barnum was the freest from guile. Leland himself was a master of uproarious stories; the two apparently listened to each other's tales like children.

"Lewd did I live & evil did I dwel" —

Such simple inversions seemed to give Barnum prodigious pleasure. But for some reason a niggardly policy prevailed on the paper in the matter of money; and the *Illustrated News* hardly made an impression among the flourishing new journals in New York. Presently it was sold to another magazine. Barnum still kept a literary strain; he interviewed Thackeray, and afterward insisted that Thackeray often consulted him as to his American tour. Perhaps as result of his association with Jenny Lind he now moved in circles which might earlier have been closed to him. The Cary sisters had recently come to New York, and had established their cheerful *salon*; with Greeley, Leland, Griswold, Whittier, Mrs. Stanton, and many other writers and reformers, Barnum appeared there, and was cordially welcomed. In these years he too entered literature, and brought forth his autobiography. Leland said that Barnum asked him to write the book, and that he declined; he added that Griswold probably performed the task.

Rufus Wilmot Griswold, the transient friend of Horace Greeley and the lasting enemy of Poe, may very well have written Barnum's first autobiography. He was an editor by vocation; he had always done an immense bulk of unacknowledged hack work; in these years, the few before his death, he was in the thick of financial difficulties; and not least, Griswold had a liking for the extravagant and bizarre which found little outlet in his usual occupations. Indeed, most if not all of Barnum's books seem to have been written by humble servitors; it was his pleasure, perhaps, to command a literary style like any other exhibit. A little pamphlet containing a New Year's address, published in 1851, was written by a newspaperman; his stories for children were composed by his press-agent. To discuss his many progenitors in *Humbugs of the World*, and to let the reader decide in what manner he had surpassed them — this project, with the liberal lacing of anecdotes, surely belonged to Barnum himself; but it is incredible that he should have assembled the closely packed information on Cornelius Agrippa, Cagliostro, Riza Bey, Joanna Southcott, and a dozen others, or that he should have offered allusions to Virgil, Erasmus, Gulliver, Peter Wilkins, and Dr. Faustus, even though he had a considerable aptitude for appropriating picturesque information.

No doubt the schemes for all his books sprang from Barnum's own fertile fancy. His broad, thick-fingered hand must have shaped their substance. Surely he talked — talked by the hour to his hired scribes: the accent of speech breaks through the many styles. In his first autobiography, certainly, his own high voice was sharply lifted. If they read it, the Cary sisters must have considered the book an odd production, though Phoebe, who was witty, may have liked the jokes, and Alice, who was religious, may have accepted at their face value Barnum's frequent assertions that religion had always been one of his main preoccupations. What the little company which frequently met at the Carys thought of Joice Heth or the Feejee Mermaid might make a social document of superlative value, or their commentary on Barnum's unvarying insistence that his main purpose had been to make money. "My prime object has been to put money into my purse." In a dozen forms he fairly shouted the statement. But at the end, perhaps under the influence of the reformers, perhaps because he received the suggestion that his blatant insistence needed amelioration, at the end he discussed the grave American temperament.

"The great defect of our American civilization is a severe and drudging practicalness," he declared. "A practicalness which is not commendable, because it loses sight of the true aims of life, and concentrates itself upon dry and technical ideas of duty, and upon a sordid love of acquisition — leaving entirely out of view all those needful and proper relaxations and enjoyments which are interwoven through even the most humble conditions in other countries.... The consequence is, that with the most universal diffusion of the means of happiness ever known among any people, we are unhappy.... As a business man, undoubtedly, my prime object has been to put money in my purse. I succeeded beyond my most sanguine expectations, and am satisfied. But what I have here said, will prepare the reader for what I conceive to be a just and altogether reasonable claim, that I have been a public benefactor, to an extent seldom paralleled in the histories of professed and professional philanthropists...."

V

This peroration had the sound of benediction or farewell. In the bright parlors of the Cary sisters Barnum had found a happy goal; untethered or outcast for years, he now belonged to a society. He was pleased, he was immensely reverential: one can see him bending and smiling amid the sparkling Bohemian glass and the carved rosewood. And these were Universalist circles in the main: not only the Cary sisters but Greeley had accepted that broad and hopeful faith. His lines could scarcely have fallen in more agreeable places.

There was no doubt of his responsive gesture: but Barnum was making it with a slight sweep of his left hand; his real preoccupations ran far beyond the delights of literary conversation in the *salon* of two maiden ladies. He wanted more than a circle: he had conceived the idea of possessing a city, and had set out to create one east of Bridgeport, on a plateau which Timothy Dwight — whom he quoted — had long before called "a cheerful and elegant piece of ground." Securing more than two hundred acres, he laid out a park, lined the prospective streets with trees, had two bridges built across the river at a large cost, and began to sell alternate lots to workmen. A coach factory was built and leased to a company of coach makers; and Barnum moved a small clock factory from Litchfield to East Bridgeport, where business was

begun under the style of Terry and Barnum. Clocks! Barnum could hardly
have hit upon an industry more indigenous to Connecticut. Clocks had been
peddled and exchanged in his early days in a country store; wooden clocks
were a staple of the peddlers whose path he had crossed in the West and
South. Chauncey Jerome, with whom Barnum presently became associated,
admitted that wooden clocks were often classed with wooden nutmegs and
wooden cucumber seeds. But through his small factory Barnum had inherited the most honored name in the Connecticut clock industry and had
joined it to his own; soon he proposed to magnify his project by an alliance
with the Jerome Clock Company of New Haven. Jerome was also one of
the early makers of wooden clocks; he had peddled them as a youth; he had
contrived a bronze looking-glass clock which was six inches taller than
Terry's clock, could be made for a dollar less and could sell for a dollar more.
Later, with an eye upon the foreign trade, he had invented the one day brass
clock: wooden clocks could not be transported overseas. In the middle
fifties Jerome was still one of the best known names in the clock industry.

The tale of Barnum's alliance with Chauncey Jerome is mixed; and the
outcome remains obscure: but at least his entry into the mystery of clock-
making proved disastrous. Jerome declared that in the end he was swindled
by the huge failure which followed; and it was true that as an old man he was
obliged to begin life again without a penny. Barnum said that the first
advances for a merger of the two companies came from Jerome, and that he
was tempted to advance the large sum required, something over a hundred
thousand dollars, because of his desire to promote the new city of East
Bridgeport: the Jerome Company was to be moved there. Perhaps beneath
all these transactions ran confusion: Barnum, who could on occasion plan
precisely, lost his head. With his lust for public conquest he may have had
in dazzling view not so much a profitable commercial speculation as a dominating replica of an ancient situation. Long before he had fought his native
battles amid a medley of clocks; perhaps combs or hats would have been
more exact materials for a later triumph; but here at least was a part of the
early conglomerate — the substance of a native industry. With his own
clock factory in full blast in his own village he would repeat his youth and
achieve a perfect ascendancy.

Some such fevered purpose must have run through Barnum's mind;
a positive obsession must have compelled him, or he could hardly have taken
the wildly incautious steps which followed. He plunged into the merger of
the two companies with only the slightest knowledge of the financial condition of the Jerome Company; he was completely unaware of an outstanding
debt that far exceeded the amount which he had promised to lend. At the
end of three months the agent of the company requested twenty-five thousand
dollars more. This Barnum declined to furnish except in exchange for
canceled notes of his original loan. The canceled notes were shown him, he
said; but why these should have been in the hands of the company's agent at
cancellation rather than his own is not clear. In any case he renewed them;
the uncertain procedure was frequently repeated, "till finally my confidence
in the company became so established that I did not ask to see the notes that

had been taken up, but furnished new accommodation paper as it was called for." He declared that he not only furnished the new notes without assurance that the old ones were canceled, but wrote them without dates, allowing the agents of the Jerome Company to fill these in; and he seems to have been totally unconcerned with a financial situation which could interminably require his large original endorsement. At last a rumor reached him that the banks had grown doubtful of his paper. Then came the revelation that he had endorsed to the amount of half a million dollars for the Jerome Company; and he failed in 1856. Apparently a huge burden of debts had been adroitly transferred from the company to Barnum; and the clock company had not been moved to Bridgeport.

Barnum's subsequent strategy is far from clear. He declared that he found means to pay off every personal claim against him, and then failed: but the fact remains that even after the failure he still kept "Iranistan," and though the tract of land for his city of East Bridgeport was put up at auction, he found means for its re-purchase. The building of the American Museum stood in his wife's name; and it was announced that the collection had been sold a year before to one of Barnum's agents. If a valid transfer had been made and Barnum was no longer in control of the Museum, he would have had in train no other enterprises except those of the clock company and the promotion of East Bridgeport. His lapse in shrewdness thus became colossal, if not all but incredible. Indeed, a question remains whether with timely dexterity he had not put the Museum out of legal reach. He was reviled; he was praised; the press rang with his failure. Benefits were offered him, by Tom Thumb, by Cornelius Vanderbilt; he went through a long and teasing process of examination and cross-examination as to his assets. At length he found himself installed for the summer with his family in a farmhouse at West Hampton on Long Island. The scene must have appeared to him almost unbearably quiet; the upper end of Long Island had changed but little since the years that Lyman Beecher had spent there. But Barnum's familiar genius followed him even to that sequestered place. Strolling along the beach one morning, he discovered a young black whale that had been washed ashore. He sent it to the Museum, where it was placed on exhibition in a refrigerator for several days, and yielded sufficient returns to pay his expenses and those of his family for the entire summer.

If Barnum had scanned the American horizon he might have seen a phantom whale across the sky like a sign of the zodiac. A few years earlier that symbol of a monstrous warring universe had silently slipped into a lasting place through the epic of *Moby Dick*. With the turn of the decade, in truth, sheer size — very like a whale — had captured the American imagination. Like living emblems Barnum's own train of elephants had marched over the land in a series of long processions. In a dream of magnitude a drove of camels had been sent across the desert to San Francisco as pathfinders for a new and spacious travel. In poetry, like incantations, the first rolling numbers of *Leaves of Grass* were now heard, mounting and accumulating. On all sides, in the rush of oratory, in the growing clash of great regional forces the same huge blast was ascending. Did Barnum hear it? Did he observe the gigantic tokens — of size, of inflation?

Whether or not he gazed in clairvoyant revery upon his small black whale — which may after all have been a porpoise — a signal change came over Barnum's intention. His first movement was astute; it was clear that whatever he earned would now promptly be swallowed up by the clock debts. He went abroad, lectured on *The Art of Money-Getting* in England, exhibited Tom Thumb and little Cordelia Howard on the continent — though his connection as manager was kept secret because of the debts — spent two years, and collected an enormous new stock of attractions for the Museum. In the meantime his agents had gradually been purchasing the clock notes at a discount. Nearly free of debt he returned from Europe and re-purchased the Museum. Blazing posters announced to the city, "Barnum's himself again." Decorating the entire building with new flags, banners, and transparencies as for a holiday, he took the stage and received, as he said, an ovation which surpassed anything which he had ever witnessed in a public career of quarter of a century. And strangely enough, the Museum was hardly launched under his own management when he learned that a white whale had been captured at the mouth of the St. Lawrence. He promptly went to the little port, determined to secure two living white whales for the Museum. The attempt was preposterous, the result a miracle. Who had captured living whales and transhipped them? All that was necessary, after the whales were secured, was to place them in a box lined with sea-weed and partially filled with salt water, with an attendant at hand to keep their mouths and blow-holes moist. Barnum had arranged to have the progress of the car telegraphed from one station to the next, "creating a tremendous advertisement seven hundred miles long." Despatches as to the progress of the whales on their long journey were bulletined in front of the Museum every hour; the newspapers burst forth into dithyrambic advertisements, with the assurance that Barnum had built a small ocean in the Museum, and had filled it from the briny deep, where

THE TWO LIVING WHALES

measuring respectively fifteen and twenty feet in length, may be seen in their native element." The whales died, for despite the advertisement they were placed in fresh water: but Barnum had salt water piped from the bay, paid a thousand dollars to the aldermanic ring for the privilege, built a glass tank twenty-four feet square, and procured another pair of whales. Then came a hippopotamus, "the Sweating Behemoth of the Scriptures," living sharks, porpoises, sea horses, and tropical fish.

Barnum was back; and the great noise which was to last for thirty years — with how many long reverberations? — had begun. Gone were the earlier days of a sprightly fantasy and a precipitous humor. Gone were the sudden adventures into unknown regions, half a step ahead of the public enthusiasm. With a resistless sweep Barnum inaugurated a dozen clamorous public enterprises as a prelude or an accompaniment for an enormous intention. He entered the Connecticut legislature at the end of the war, fought the railroads in their endeavor to raise commuters' rates in Connecticut, and won opportunely, with the onset of the Erie scandal. He was on the popular side; and truly enough he believed in cheap rates, in expansion, in the million, and in East Bridgeport; diminished fares were an advantage for suburban residents. In the end he declared that he made a greater fortune out of his speculation in East Bridgeport than he had lost in the clock enterprise. His city grew by leaps and bounds, grew in the safe, precise pattern of the New England village, with small trim white houses with green blinds, under a regimen that would have delighted Lyman Beecher himself. He insisted that purchasers should sign and keep the temperance pledge, and forego the use of tobacco. He advertised the Puritan program; with increasing frequency and ardor he mounted the lecture platform in the temperance cause. There was an opposition, to be sure; a young man named John Fiske issued a manifesto in 1868 entitled *Tobacco and Alcohol: The Coming Man WILL Smoke; The Coming Man WILL Drink*. But Barnum was greeted by immense audiences which apparently accepted his exhortations, or listened with equal zest to his *Art of Money-Getting*, the lecture with which he had addressed England after his failure.

Even in the realm of his personal life Barnum tried to prune his old exuberance. "Iranistan" had burned after the clock failure; his next home, "Lindencroft," was a smaller, conventional residence "with no attempt at ostentation," as he explicitly said. "Elegance, pure and simple, predominated and permeated everywhere." Then he declared that Mrs. Barnum, whose health was failing, could not manage even the less pretentious establishment; he built another residence in Bridgeport, "Waldemere," which he said was still smaller. Yet after all Barnum could not forego size. An English newspaper-man observed that the new dwelling presented a front of one hundred and sixty feet. "On entering, one is pleasantly struck by the spaciousness of the hall and rooms. One can breathe as freely inside as out. Nothing is small or contracted." The house appears, indeed, to have been even larger than "Lindencroft," with more verandas, wings, and bay-windows than the earlier residence; it was described as "a curious but pleasant *mélange* of Gothic, Italian, and French architecture and decoration," and it was as crowded with strange curios as his first palace; but it never reached the preposterous splendor of "Iranistan." Barnum seemed possessed by a mania of house-building; a few years later he erected still another dwelling, "Marina." Was he seeking to conform to a style? To discover precisely the right accent in all that growing wilderness of expensive and elaborate establishments which now were rising everywhere about him? He insisted upon the simplicity of all these dwellings: but he could not be simple, and he could not be still. He purchased a mansion in New York; with a view to posterity he gave a park to Bridgeport; he was deeply engaged in the project of a cemetery. While he was addressing the legislature on his proposed railroad bill, a telegram was handed him which announced that the Museum was in flames. With that unruffled calm in the face of catastrophe which he probably first learned in the midst of the practical jokes of Bethel and Danbury, he betrayed not the slightest emotion and continued his speech. Within eight months he had assembled curiosities from all over the world, had purchased several large collections and hundreds of small ones, had gathered together his old companies of actors, actresses, and living curiosities, and inaugurated a new museum higher up on Broadway. Within a year and a half this Museum also burned. "During my whole life," he remarked, "I had been so much accustomed to operations of magnitude for or against my interests, that large losses or gains were not likely to disturb my equanimity." He found the ice-coated ruins by moonlight "sublime," and this time complacently announced that he would retire. But as he said afterward, "Everyone knows the history of the Emperor Charles the Fifth. His ambition gratified to satiety in the conquest of kingdoms, and the firm establishment of empire, he craved rest. He abdicated his throne.... I want a royal illustration; and the history of Charles the Fifth, in particular in advocating rest, I find very pertinent to my own experience. I took a formal, and as I then supposed, a last adieu of my readers on my fifty-ninth birthday. I was, as I flattered myself, through with travel, with adventure, and with business...."

He had only begun. In 1871 he had created his first mammoth circus, A Museum, Menagerie, Caravan, Hippodrome, and Circus in one — the name came out at last — whose tents covered three acres of ground, and could be filled by ten thousand spectators, and required five hundred men and battalions of horses to transport it through the country. He horrified his assistants by his extravagance. "Undaunted, I still expended thousands of dollars, and ship after ship brought me rare and valuable animals and works of art.... As no giraffe had ever lived two years in America, all other managers had given up any attempt to import them, but this only made me more determined to always have one on hand at any cost." For a few years he was obsessed by the towering absurd image of the giraffe. Indeed, Barnum, who cared nothing for animals, who never mentioned with pleasure even a dog or a horse, who showed not a quaver of interest when the many living creatures in his museums had burned, now added hundreds from all parts of the globe. He sent to Alaska to procure sea-lions and barking seals, and rejoiced that they devoured from sixty to a hundred pounds of fresh fish daily. His Italian goat had been taught to ride on horseback, leap through hoops and over banners, alighting on his feet on the back of a horse while going at full speed. He procured four wild Fiji cannibals, whom he declared to have been ransomed at great cost from a royal enemy — surely royal! — who was about to eat them. For the winter display he opened a Hippotheatron. Four weeks later the building burned; only two elephants and a camel were rescued. Barnum, who was in New Orleans, telegraphed for the purchase of new attractions for a larger circus, and went on eating his breakfast. By spring he had sent out on the road a circus which required double the tent space of the earlier one. He went to Europe, "to rest my over-worked brain, and see what could be picked up to instruct and edify my amusement patrons." He came back to establish a Roman Hippodrome, Zoological Institute, Aquarium, and Museum, and to inaugurate his "Congress of Nations, in a grand procession of gilded chariots and triumphal cars, conveying Kings, Queens, Emperors, and other potentates of the civilized world, costumed with historical correctness, royally surrounded, and accompanied and followed by their respective courts and splendid retinues.... Never since the days of the Cæsars has there been so grand and so interesting a public spectacle." He tried to purchase the right to exhibit Brigham Young.

In those black and bitter years which followed the war when men struggled for wealth and power, Barnum wanted both, attained both, and gave to his monstrous creation a fabulous air. Other men gambled with railroads, or caught a local government in a huge net, or piled fortunes into the millions. Barnum proved his magnitude by constantly dragging a huge and orderly mass of living creatures — men, women, birds, beasts, creatures of the wild and of the deep, in a triumphant procession round and round over the land with himself at the head. His friend Horace Greeley went down to tragedy. Barnum was numbered among his supporters; but otherwise he gave no sign. The Cary sisters died. Some years earlier rooms at "Waldemere" had been named for them, but did Barnum have a private or personal feeling? His life was in the circus. He was forever there; he was part of the show, and knew it. He made his own engagements even for performers in his side-shows, supervised such details as the printing of handbills and the new editions of his autobiographies, which now were sold at the gates; he employed his own musicians. With that extreme narrowing of judgment which often accompanies the achievement of enormous projects he grew sharply penurious in small matters, wrote out passes on the cheapest kind of paper, cut and saved at every tiny corner — and remained tirelessly extravagant in his large expenditures. Loss of life in his enormous companies hardly touched him; occasionally, in his old manner, he played drastic practical jokes; but these were the merest flicker on the face of his dream. Magnitude was piled on magnitude, conquest upon conquest. As a minor witticism he succeeded in drawing the king of the Sandwich Islands to his Hippodrome in New York, and then, by an adroit persuasion, drove him round the arena in a barouche while the crowd cheered. Barnum introduced the firing of Zazel from a cannon; he contrived Roman games and chariot races. Instead of a single midget he now had a company of midgets, with Tom Thumb still regnant, and with his marriage at Grace Church to the tiny Lavinia Warren staged as a huge public notice of Barnum's monster troupe. He blew a prodigious blast for the centennial year. By 1878 he was using the title the Greatest Show on Earth for the first time; the consummation of the idea was reached two years later by his union with Sanger's Great London circus, which had been purchased by Cooper, Bailey, and Hutchinson. Rivalry had been intense, and reached its climax over the matter of a baby elephant, born in the captivity of the opposite camp. Barnum found his own failure to possess a baby elephant unendurable: and in 1880, after suitable negotiations, he obtained the creature, and joined the two great circuses. He secured Jumbo from the Royal Zoological Gardens in London, and stirred two nations to an abysmal excitement by the transaction. Jumbo — Jumbo: the resonant sound and the vast image were battered back and forth across the sea. A cartoon of Nast's showed Barnum and Jumbo cheek to cheek.

Then Barnum wanted a white elephant, and obtained one, "whiter than King Theebaud's." The elephant had supplanted the whale; for after all elephants could comfortably travel overland, and so could camels, and giraffes, with the train of lesser animals.

Across the sea, over the land, around the world he went either by proxy or in person. The world was now a constant image in his speech. He tossed off a lecture on *The World and How to Live in It*, made new encirclements of the West, purchased a cattle ranch in Colorado, again traveled to the rim of the continent, collected sea-lions, returned for a reminiscent buffalo hunt on the plains of Kansas, and again sent out expeditions to the Orient, launching another and still larger circus, scattering handbills, lithographs, pictures of himself, and copies of his autobiography over the country by the ton. His music was now furnished by four brass bands, a calliope, chimes of bells, a steam organ, a squad of Scotch bagpipers, and a company of negro jubilee singers. Louder and louder rose his clangorous vociferation. Out of sheer noise — power! In that immense concourse, triumph — the triumph which tramples and obscures, tosses all things into abstractions of size and space.

There were brief interludes in this accumulated procession. Barnum became ill, then at length recovered and was welcomed back to New York by a vast torch-light parade which he said was witnessed by over half a million people, and pronounced the most brilliant display ever seen in America. He brought reporters in drawing-room cars from all the leading cities round about for the spectacle, lodged them at hotels, and sent them home the next day. As a minor conquest he at last went back to Bethel, upon invitation, discoursed on the blue laws, and presented the village with a fountain whose Triton could suggest what one chose — the whale, the hippopotamus, or even Barnum himself rising from the elements. Official recognition of his contributions to science was made by the Smithsonian Institution, whose directors asked for a life-mask from which to mold a bust; and Barnum helped to found a college, where at last the stuffed semblance of Jumbo was enshrined.

These, in the main, were minor excursions. By the union of the Barnum and Bailey companies the three ring circus was at hand: with Calliope, the muse of eloquence and heroic poetry, to herald the epos with shrill and blasting whistles, with the inevitable huge creatures of the wild which made man seem small, with the caprioles of trick horses, the procession of clowns, tumblers, aërial acrobats, a gaudy pilgrim's progress. In the triple ring the single actor with his tiny skill was lost; everything must be bold, whirling, changing: no brilliancy of lights can quite illuminate that monstrous top: flying color, the inevitable magenta and sky blue and silver stars, the grin of clowns and the swift turn of the acts, revolve and pass, projected against a void. Here at last was wonder, though Barnum never spoke of it — beauty amid that showy aggregation, an exquisite precision which seemed aërial, and informed the whole long march, and even the faint high fretwork overhead. A final gayety Barnum never saw or celebrated, though that was his creation. He still dragged the whole huge affair at his heels, took it to London, was observed by celebrities, and returned for final triumphs in his own country. In 1877, when the Greatest Show was yet to come, Barnum calculated his audiences as aggregating over eighty million persons. He had conquered an empire; and before the end he doubled it. Over and over his huge displays drew that friend — or enemy — to whom he had never capitulated, the public. Towns, cities, counties, the entire country poured into his huge tents. In his later years he heard that earnest if tepid satire on American tendencies called *Numbers*, and gave the hospitality of a night in Bridgeport to its author. Afterwards Arnold mentioned Barnum's remark that he meant to belong to the remnant; but Barnum perhaps knew as well as another that he had swallowed the remnant. Even in his own long, cumulative self-portrait scarcely a small and individualized quality appears. In that spreading design he comes forth with magnitude, energy, and an air of leisure: with all his nimbleness, which was often like that of a trapeze performer, apparently Barnum never hurried. These traits belong to the public: the crowd is also a reservoir of force, is large and slow-moving. With the bland and unbetraying smile which he seems to have kept to the end — a public smile — Barnum died in 1891, full of years, power, and unwitting romance. Fittingly enough, he has become a myth. His history grows into fable, mixed with the caprices of the time — not the great fable, perhaps, but a portion of what might be called the American legend.

PART TWO

REFLECTION, ESSAYS

REFLECTION, ESSAYS

As STATED in the Preface, the essay is the characteristic form of reflective writing. On its first appearance in England Francis Bacon gave the name to a series of "dispersed meditations" on such subjects as "Friendship," "Adversity," "Parents and Children." The French word *essai* derives from a Latin word that means to weigh, to examine, to test. In this sense the essay may be regarded as an informal weighing or testing of an idea or point of view — a trial balloon, so to speak, sent up by the author. In another sense, the essay is a composition intended to communicate "the ideas of men of rich intelligence" to their generation, usually without that formal and studied arrangement which constitutes a treatise or a monograph.

The formal essay is more definitely a work of mind in that it treats of a serious subject with a more organic and logical development of the topic discussed. Its modern popularity is due to journalism in the broad sense, that is, the relative quality of our thinking and the tentative nature of our conclusions. The modern magazine article is the characteristic form of the contemporary formal essay. But even the magazine article retains enough of its essay origins to be distinguished from the monograph, the treatise, or other more exhaustive forms of expository writing, by retaining something of the quality of weighing or testing conclusions in a manner more provisional than complete.

The formal essay may be an editorial, a magazine article, an argument, or even a "paper" or address to be delivered at a public gathering. It is more useful, however, to classify formal essays by their subject matter than by insisting upon purely theoretical categories. Thus in this book the informal essays are grouped together, followed by portraits or sketches of character, and finally by articles or formal essays which treat of scientific, economic, social, educational and literary problems.

THE INFORMAL ESSAY

THE original type of the essay is the informal or personal, as practiced by Montaigne in France of the sixteenth century, or by Bacon in England. The essay became the leading form of prose literature in the eighteenth century, in the hands of Addison and Steele. It was revived in the nineteenth century by Lamb, Hazlitt, and Thackeray, by Emerson and Stevenson. The informal essay tends to approach the tone and manner of the best conversation, or rather a heightened monologue by some cultured and amusing person; and though an informal essay generally has a central subject, the looseness of the form permits of digressions in the manner of good talk, provided always that the digressions express the personality of the writer, and that the personality is an interesting one. The subject matter of such a piece obviously may be anything or nothing, good essays having been written on subjects as impressive as the fear of death and on topics as trivial as the grocer's cat. There is no reason why an informal essay should not include dialogue or narrative.

Of the informal essays here included that by Stevenson shows the wide variety of subject matter and style possible within this form. It opens with a description of the fishing village where as a boy he passed his summer vacations, a description which is at first static in its listing of "the ingredients" of the place, but which becomes suddenly full of movement and action. This is followed by an account of the inhabitants, and particularly of the boys' game which gives the title to the essay. This in turn leads to a discussion of the element of romance in life, and finally to a piece of literary criticism. So skillfully has the reader been led along that he is unconscious of any awkward transition or change of subject.

The essay by Dr. Crothers, "Every Man's Natural Desire to be Somebody Else," deals with a single theme of Stevenson's essay, expressed in the sentence in which he speaks of those "who are meat salesmen to the external eye, and possibly to themselves are Shakespeares, Napoleons, or Beethovens." Dr. Crothers draws out this thought through a multitude of illustrations, giving the effect which the rhetoricians call abundance. Mr. Max Beerbohm, on the contrary, obtains emphasis through economy.   He points his theme by a single instance, of which the plausibility makes for the form of humor known as paradox.

The personal essay is a means of revelation of the volatile, evanescent group of qualities which we call personality.   It is the purpose of the author to give himself freely to his readers, and the successful personal essayists have in general been men like Montaigne, Goldsmith, Lamb, Thackeray, who have developed the art of personal communication to the point where literary style has the immediacy of talk.   Originality, vivacity, gaiety, good nature, humor are the gifts which the personal essayist brings to his writing, and he calls out in especial degree the personal response of his readers in terms of genuine affection.

ROBERT LOUIS STEVENSON

POET, novelist, essayist, or traveler, Robert Louis Stevenson (1850–1895) has at some time been the intimate companion of almost everyone to whom English literature is native. To some extent, Stevenson was an alchemist of illness. His childhood delicacy and later periods of invalidism strengthened the love of adventure and romance which found expression in those books that now seem as inevitable and as indispensable as boyhood: *Treasure Island*, *Kidnapped*, etc. It was his illness, also, which was responsible for the walking trip that furnished material for *Travels with a Donkey* and the canoe trip celebrated in *An Inland Voyage*. "The Lantern-Bearers" is one of a series of articles published in *Scribner's Magazine* in 1888.

THE LANTERN–BEARERS *

I

THESE boys congregated every autumn about a certain easterly fisher-village, where they tasted in a high degree the glory of existence. The place was created seemingly on purpose for the diversion of young gentlemen. A street or two of houses, mostly red and many of them tiled; a number of fine trees clustered about the manse and the kirkyard, and turning the chief street into a shady alley; many little gardens more than usually bright with flowers; nets a-drying, and fisher-wives scolding in the backward parts; a smell of fish, a genial smell of seaweed; whiffs of blowing sand at the street corners; shops with golf-balls and bottled lollipops; another shop with penny pickwicks (that remarkable cigar) and the *London Journal*, dear to me for its startling pictures, and a few novels, dear for their suggestive names: such, as well as memory serves me, were the ingredients of the town. These, you are to conceive posted on a spit between two sandy bays, and sparsely flanked with villas — enough for the boys to lodge in with their subsidiary parents, not enough (not yet enough) to cocknify the scene: a haven in the rocks in front: in front of that, a file of grey islets: to the left, endless links and sand-wreaths, a wilderness of hiding-holes, alive with popping rabbits and soaring gulls; to the right, a range of seaward crags, one rugged brow beyond another; the ruins of a mighty and ancient fortress on the brink of one; coves between — now charmed into sunshine quiet, now whistling with wind and clamorous with bursting surges; the dens and sheltered hollows redolent of thyme and southernwood, the air at the cliff's edge brisk and clean and pungent of the sea — in front of all, the Bass Rock, tilted seaward like a doubtful bather, the surf ringing it with white, the solangeese hanging round its summit like a great and glittering smoke. This choice piece of sea-board was sacred, besides, to the wrecker; and the Bass, in the eye of fancy, still flew the colors of King James; and in the ear of fancy the arches of Tantallon still rang with horse-shoe iron, and echoed to the commands of Bell-the-Cat.

* By permission of Charles Scribner's Sons.

There was nothing to mar your days, if you were a boy summering in that part, but the embarrassment of pleasure. You might golf if you wanted; but I seem to have been better employed. You might secrete yourself in the Lady's Walk, a certain sunless dingle of elders, all mossed over by the damp as green as grass, and dotted here and there by the stream-side with roofless walls, the cold homes of anchorites. To fit themselves for life, and with a special eye to acquire the art of smoking, it was even common for the boys to harbor there; and you might have seen a single penny pickwick, honestly shared in lengths with a blunt knife, bestrew the glen with these apprentices. Again, you might join our fishing-parties, where we sat perched as thick as solan-geese, a covey of little anglers, boy and girl, angling over each other's heads, to the much entanglement of lines and loss of podleys and consequent shrill recrimination — shrill as the geese themselves. Indeed, had that been all, you might have done this often; but though fishing be a fine pastime, the podley is scarce to be regarded as a dainty for the table; and it was a point of honor that a boy should eat all that he had taken. Or again, you might climb the Law, where the whale's jawbone stood landmark in the buzzing wind, and behold the face of many counties, and the smoke and spires of many towns, and the sails of distant ships. You might bathe, now in the flaws of fine weather, that we pathetically call our summer, now in a gale of wind, with the sand scourging your bare hide, your clothes thrashing abroad from underneath their guardian stone, the froth of the great breakers casting you headlong ere it had drowned your knees. Or you might explore the tidal rocks, above all in the ebb of spring, when the very roots of the hills were for the nonce discovered; following my leader from one group to another, groping in slippery tangle for the wreck of ships, wading in pools after the abominable creatures of the sea, and ever with an eye cast backward on the march of the tide and the menaced line of your retreat. And then you might go Crusoeing, a word that covers all extempore eating in the open air: digging perhaps a house under the margin of the links, kindling a fire of the sea-ware, and cooking apples there — if they were truly apples, for I sometimes suppose the merchant must have played us off with some inferior and quite local fruit, capable of resolving, in the neighborhood of fire, into mere sand and smoke and iodine; or perhaps pushing to Tantallon, you might lunch on sandwiches and visions in the grassy court, while the wind hummed in the crumbling turrets; or clambering along the coast, eat geans (the worst, I must suppose, in Christendom) from an adventurous gean-tree that had taken root under a cliff, where it was shaken with an ague of east wind, and silvered after gales with salt, and grew so foreign among its bleak surroundings that to eat of its produce was an adventure in itself.

There are mingled some dismal memories with so many that were joyous. Of the fisher-wife, for instance, who had cut her throat at Canty Bay; and of how I ran with the other children to the top of the Quadrant, and beheld a posse of silent people escorting a cart, and on the cart, bound in a chair, her throat bandaged, and the bandage all bloody — horror! — the fisher-wife herself, who continued thenceforth to hag-ride my thoughts, and even today (as I recall the scene) darkens daylight. She was lodged in the little old jail in the chief street; but whether or no she died there, with a wise terror of the worst, I never inquired. She had been tippling; it was but a dingy tragedy; and it seems strange and hard that, after all these years, the poor crazy sinner should be still pilloried on her cart in the scrap-book of my memory. Nor shall I readily forget a certain house in the Quadrant where a visitor died, and a dark old woman continued to dwell alone with the dead body; nor how this old woman conceived a hatred to myself and one of my cousins, and in the dread hour of the dusk, as we were clambering on the garden-walls, opened a window in that house of mortality and cursed us in a shrill voice and with a marrowy choice of language. It was a pair of very colorless urchins that fled down the lane from this remarkable experience! But I recall with a more doubtful sentiment, compounded out of fear and exultation, the coil of equinoctial tempests; trumpeting squalls, scouring flaws of rain; the boats with their reefed lug-sails scudding for the harbor mouth, where danger lay, for it was hard to make when the wind had any east in it; the wives clustered with blowing shawls at the pierhead, where (if fate was against them) they might see boat and husband and sons — their whole wealth and their whole family — engulfed under their eyes; and (what I saw but once) a troop of neighbors forcing such an unfortunate homeward, and she squalling and battling in their midst, a figure scarcely human, a tragic Mænad.

These are things that I recall with interest; but what my memory dwells upon the most I have been all this while withholding. It was a sport peculiar to the place, and indeed to a week or so of our two months' holiday there. Maybe it still flourishes in its native spot; for boys and their pastimes are swayed by periodic forces inscrutable to man; so that tops and marbles reappear in their due season, regular like the sun and moon; and the harmless art of knucklebones has seen the fall of the Roman Empire and the rise of the United States. It may still flourish in its native spot, but nowhere else, I am persuaded; for I tried myself to introduce it on Tweedside, and was defeated lamentably; its charm being quite local, like a country wine that cannot be exported.

The idle manner of it was this:

Toward the end of September, when school-time was drawing near and the nights were already black, we would begin to sally from our respective villas, each equipped with a tin bull's-eye lantern. The thing was so well known that it had worn a rut in the commerce of Great Britain; and the grocers, about the due time, began to garnish their windows with our particular brand of luminary. We wore them buckled to the waist upon a cricket belt, and over them, such was the rigor of the game, a buttoned top-coat. They smelled noisomely of blistered tin; they never burned aright, though they would always burn our fingers; their use was naught; the pleasure of them merely fanciful; and yet a boy with a bull's-eye under his top-coat asked for nothing more. The fishermen used lanterns about their boats, and it was from them, I suppose, that we had got the hint; but theirs were not bull's-eyes, nor did we ever play at being fishermen. The police carried them at their belts, and we had plainly copied them in that; yet we did not pretend to be policemen. Burglars, indeed, we may have had some haunting thoughts of; and we had certainly an eye to past ages when lanterns were more common, and to certain story-books in which we had found them to figure very largely. But take it for all in all, the pleasure of the thing was substantive; and to be a boy with a bull's-eye under his top-coat was good enough for us.

When two of these asses met, there would be an anxious "Have you got your lantern?" and a gratified "Yes!" That was the shibboleth, and very needful too; for, as it was the rule to keep our glory contained, none could recognize a lantern-bearer, unless (like the pole-cat) by the smell. Four or five would sometimes climb into the belly of a ten-man lugger, with nothing but the thwarts above them — for the cabin was usually locked; or choose out some hollow of the links where the wind might whistle overhead. There the coats would be unbuttoned and the bull's-eye discovered; and in the chequering glimmer, under the huge windy hall of the night, and cheered by a rich steam of toasting tinware, these fortunate young gentlemen would crouch together in the cold sand of the links or on the scaly bilges of the fishing-boat, and delight themselves with inappropriate talk. Woe is me that I may not give some specimens — some of their foresights of life, or deep inquiries into the rudiments of man and nature, these were so fiery and so innocent, they were so richly silly, so romantically young. But the talk, at any rate, was but a condiment; and these gatherings themselves only accidents in the career of the lantern-bearer. The essence of this bliss was to walk by yourself in the black night; the slide shut, the top-coat buttoned; not a ray escaping, whether to conduct your footsteps or to make your glory public; a mere pillar of darkness in the dark; and all the while, deep down in the privacy of your fool's heart, to know you had a bull's-eye at your belt, and to exult and sing over the knowledge.

2

It is said that a poet has died young in the breast of the most stolid. It may be contended, rather, that this (somewhat minor) bard in almost every case survives, and is the spice of life to his possessor. Justice is not done to the versatility and the unplumbed childishness of man's imagination. His life from without may seem but a rude mound of mud; there will be some golden chamber at the heart of it, in which he dwells delighted; and for as dark as his pathway seems to the observer, he will have some kind of a bull's-eye at his belt.

It would be hard to pick out a career more cheerless than that of Dancer, the miser, as he figures in the "Old Bailey Reports," a prey to the most sordid persecutions, the butt of his neighborhood, betrayed by his hired man, his house beleaguered by the impish school-boy, and he himself grinding and fuming and impotently fleeing to the law against these pin-pricks. You marvel at first that anyone should willingly prolong a life so destitute of charm and dignity; and then you call to memory that had he chosen, had he ceased to be a miser, he could have been freed at once from these trials, and might have built himself a castle and gone escorted by a squadron. For the love of more recondite joys, which we cannot estimate, which, it may be, we should envy, the man had willingly forgone both comfort and consideration. "His mind to him a kingdom was"; and sure enough, digging into that mind, which seems at first a dust-heap, we unearth some priceless jewels. For Dancer must have had the love of power and the disdain of using it, a noble character in itself; disdain of many pleasures, a chief part of what is commonly called wisdom; disdain of the inevitable end, that finest trait of mankind; scorn of men's opinions, another element of virtue; and at the back of all, a conscience just like yours and mine, whining like a cur, swindling like a thimble-rigger, but still pointing (there or thereabout) to some conventional standard. Here were a cabinet portrait to which Hawthorne perhaps had done justice; and yet not Hawthorne either, for he was mildly minded, and it lay not in him to create for us that throb of the miser's pulse, his fretful energy of gusto, his vast arms of ambition clutching in he knows not what: insatiable, insane, a god with a muck-rake. Thus, at least, looking in the bosom of the miser, consideration detects the poet in the full tide of life, with more, indeed, of the poetic fire than usually goes to epics; and tracing that mean man about his cold hearth, and to and fro in his discomfortable house, spies within him a blazing bonfire of delight. And so with others, who do not live by bread alone, but by some cherished and perhaps fantastic pleasure; who are meat salesmen to the external eye, and possibly to themselves are Shakespeares, Napoleons, or Beethovens; who have not one virtue to rub against another in the field of active life, and yet perhaps, in the life of contemplation, sit with the saints. We see them on the street, and we can count their buttons; but Heaven knows in what they pride themselves! Heaven knows where they have set their treasure!

There is one fable that touches very near the quick of life; the fable of the monk who passed into the woods, heard a bird break into song, hearkened for a trill or two, and found himself on his return a stranger at his convent gates; for he had been absent fifty years, and of all his comrades there survived but one to recognize him. It is not only in the woods that this enchanter carols, though perhaps he is native there. He sings in the most doleful places. The miser hears him and chuckles, and the days are moments. With no more apparatus than an ill-smelling lantern I have evoked him on the naked links. All life that is not merely mechanical is spun out of two strands: seeking for that bird and hearing him. And it is just this that makes life so hard to value, and the delight of each so incommunicable. And just a knowledge of this, and a remembrance of those fortunate hours in which the bird has sung to us, that fills us with such wonder when we turn the pages of the realist. There, to be sure, we find a picture of life in so far as it consists of mud and of old iron, cheap desires and cheap fears, that which we are ashamed to remember and that which we are careless whether we forget; but of the note of that time-devouring nightingale we hear no news.

The case of these writers of romance is most obscure. They have been boys and youths; they have lingered outside the window of the beloved, who was then most probably writing to someone else; they have sat before a sheet of paper, and felt themselves mere continents of congested poetry, not one line of which would flow; they have walked alone in the woods, they have walked in cities under the countless lamps; they have been to sea, they have hated, they have feared, they have longed to knife a man, and maybe done it; the wild taste of life has stung their palate. Or, if you deny them all the rest, one pleasure at least they have tasted to the full — their books are there to prove it — the keen pleasure of successful literary composition. And yet they fill the globe with volumes, whose cleverness inspires me with despairing admiration, and whose consistent falsity to all I care to call existence, with despairing wrath. If I had no better hope than to continue to revolve among the dreary and petty businesses, and to be moved by the paltry hopes and fears with which they surround and animate their heroes, I declare I would die now. But there has never an hour of mine gone quite so dully yet; if it were spent waiting at a railway junction, I would have some scattering thoughts, I could count some grains of memory, compared to which the whole of one of these romances seems but dross.

These writers would retort (if I take them properly) that this was very true; that it was the same with themselves and other persons of (what they call) the artistic temperament; that in this we were exceptional, and should apparently be ashamed of ourselves; but that our works must deal exclusively with (what they call) the average man, who was a prodigious dull fellow, and quite dead to all but the paltriest considerations. I accept the issue. We can only know others by ourselves. The artistic temperament (a plague on the expression!) does not make us different from our fellowmen, or it would make us incapable of writing novels; and the average man (a murrain on the word!) is just like you and me, or he would not be average. It was Whitman who stamped a kind of Birmingham sacredness upon the latter phrase; but Whitman knew very well, and showed very nobly, that the average man was full of joys and full of poetry of his own. And this harping on life's dulness and man's meanness is a loud profession of incompetence; it is one of two things; the cry of the blind eye, *I cannot see*, or the complaint of the dumb tongue, *I cannot utter*. To draw a life without delights is to prove I have not realized it. To picture a man without some sort of poetry — well, it goes near to prove my case, for it shows an author may have little enough. To see Dancer only as a dirty, old, small-minded, impotently fuming man, in a dirty house, besieged by Harrow boys, and probably beset by small attorneys, is to show myself as keen an observer as... The Harrow boys. But these young gentlemen (with a more becoming modesty) were content to pluck Dancer by the coat-tails; they did not suppose they had surprised his secret or could put him living in a book: and it is there my error would have lain. Or say that in the same romance — I continue to call these books romances, in the hope of giving pain — say that in the same romance, which now begins really to take shape, I should leave to speak of Dancer, and follow instead the Harrow boys; and say that I came on such business as that of my lantern-bearers on the links, and described the boys as very cold, spat upon by flurries of rain, and drearily surrounded, all of which they were; and their talk as silly and indecent, which it certainly was. I might upon these lines, and had I Zola's genius, turn out, in a page or so, a gem of literary art, render the lantern-light with the touches of a master, and lay on the indecency with the ungrudging hand of love; and when all was done, what a triumph would my picture be of shallowness and dulness! how it would have missed the point! how it would have belied the boys! To the ear of the stenographer, the talk is merely silly and indecent; but ask the boys themselves, and they are discussing (as it is highly proper they should) the possibilities of existence. To the eye of the observer they are wet and cold and drearily surrounded; but ask themselves, and they are in the heaven of recondite pleasure, the ground of which is an ill-smelling lantern.

3

For, to repeat, the ground of a man's joy is often hard to hit. It may hinge at times upon a mere accessory, like the lantern, it may reside, like Dancer's in the mysterious inwards of psychology. It may consist with perpetual failure, and find exercise in the continued chase. It has so little bond with externals (such as the observer scribbles in his note-book) that it may even touch them not; and the man's true life, for which he consents to live, lie altogether in the field of fancy. The clergyman, in his spare hours, may be winning battles, the farmer sailing ships, the banker reaping triumph in the arts: all leading another life, plying another trade from that they chose; like the poet's house-builder, who, after all, is cased in stone,

"By his fireside, as impotent fancy prompts,
Rebuilds it to his liking."

In such a case the poetry runs underground. The observer (poor soul, with his documents!) is all abroad. For to look at the man is but to court deception. We shall see the trunk from which he draws his nourishment; but he himself is above and abroad in the green dome of foliage, hummed through by winds and nested in by nightingales. And the true realism were that of the poets, to climb up after him like a squirrel, and catch some glimpse of the heaven for which he lives. And the true realism, always and everywhere, is that of the poets to find out where joy resides, and give it a voice far beyond singing.

For to miss the joy is to miss all. In the joy of the actors lies the sense of any action. That is the explanation, that the excuse. To one who has not the secret of the lanterns, the scene upon the links is meaningless. And hence the haunting and truly spectral unreality of realistic books. Hence, when we read the English realists, the incredulous wonder with which we observe the hero's constancy under the submerging tide of dulness, and how he bears up with his jibbing sweetheart, and endures the chatter of idiot girls, and stands by his whole unfeatured wilderness of an existence, instead of seeking relief in drink or foreign travel. Hence in the French, in that meat-market of middle-aged sensuality, the disgusted surprise with which we see the hero drift sidelong, and practically quite untempted, into every description of misconduct and dishonor. In each, we miss the personal poetry, the enchanted atmosphere, that rainbow work of fancy that clothes what is naked and seems to ennoble what is base; in each, life falls dead like dough, instead of soaring away like a balloon into the colors of the sunset; each is true, each inconceivable; for no man lives in the external truth, among salts and acids, but in the warm, phantasmagoric chamber of his brain, with the painted windows and the storied walls.

Of this falsity we have had a recent example from a man who knows far better — Tolstoy's *Powers of Darkness*. Here is a piece full of force and truth, yet quite untrue. For before Mikita was led into so dire a situation he was tempted, and temptations are beautiful at least in part; and a work which dwells on the ugliness of crime and gives no hint of any loveliness in the temptation, sins against the modesty of life, and even when a Tolstoy writes it, sinks to melodrama. The peasants are not understood; they saw their life in fairer colors; even the deaf girl was clothed in poetry for Mikita, or he had never fallen. And so, once again, even an Old Bailey melodrama, without some brightness of poetry and lustre of existence, falls into the inconceivable and ranks with fairy tales.

4

In nobler books we are moved with something like the emotions of life; and this emotion is very variously provoked. We are so moved when Levine labors in the field,[1] when André[2] sinks beyond emotion, when Richard Feverel and Lucy Desborough meet beside the river,[3] when Antony, "not cowardly, puts off his helmet,"[4] when Kent has infinite pity on the dying Lear, when, in Dostoieffsky's *Despised and Rejected*, the uncomplaining hero drains his cup of suffering and virtue. These are notes that please the great heart of man. Not only love, and the fields, and the bright face of danger, but sacrifice and death and unmerited suffering humbly supported, touch in us the vein of the poetic. We love to think of them, we long to try them, we are humbly hopeful that we may prove heroes also.

We have heard, perhaps, too much of lesser matters. Here is the door, here is the open air.

Itur in antiquam silvam.

[1] In Tolstoy's *Anna Karenina*.
[2] In Tolstoy's *War and Peace*.
[3] In Meredith's *The Ordeal of Richard Feverel*.
[4] In Shakespeare's *Antony and Cleopatra*.

SAMUEL McCHORD CROTHERS

THE writings of Samuel McChord Crothers (1857–1928) are a strong defense against the popular conception of the clergyman. Born in Illinois, Mr. Crothers studied at Wittenberg College, Princeton, Union Theological Seminary, and finally at Harvard. Later he returned to Cambridge as minister of the First Unitarian Church there. The suave and scholarly humor of his numerous essays has been compared to that of Charles Lamb. Mr. Crothers' essays have been collected under the titles: *Among Friends, The Cheerful Giver, The Gentle Reader, The Pardoner's Wallet* and *The Dame School of Experience,* from which the present selection is taken.

EVERY MAN'S NATURAL DESIRE TO BE SOMEBODY ELSE *

SEVERAL years ago a young man came to my study with a manuscript which he wished me to criticize.

"It is only a little bit of my work," he said modestly, "and it will not take you long to look it over. In fact it is only the first chapter, in which I explain the Universe."

I suppose that we have all had moments of sudden illumination when it occurred to us that we had explained the Universe, and it was so easy for us that we wondered why we had not done it before. Some thought drifted into our mind and filled us with vague forebodings of omniscience. It was not an ordinary thought, that explained only a fragment of existence. It explained everything. It proved one thing and it proved the opposite just as well. It explained why things are as they are, and if it should turn out that they are not that way at all, it would prove that fact also. In the light of our great thought chaos seemed rational.

Such thoughts usually occur about four o'clock in the morning. Having explained the Universe, we relapse into satisfied slumber. When, a few hours later, we rise, we wonder what the explanation was.

Now and then, however, one of these highly explanatory ideas remains to comfort us in our waking hours. Such a thought is that which I here throw out, and which has doubtless at some early hour occurred to most of my readers. It is that every man has a natural desire to be somebody else.

This does not explain the Universe, but it explains that perplexing part of it which we call Human Nature. It explains why so many intelligent people, who deal skillfully with matters of fact, make such a mess of it when they deal with their fellow creatures. It explains why we get on as well as we do with strangers, and why we do not get on better with our friends. It explains why people are so often offended when we say nice things about them, and why it is that, when we say harsh things about them, they take

* Copyright, Houghton Mifflin Company. By permission.

it as a compliment. It explains why people marry their opposites and why they live happily ever afterwards. It also explains why some people don't. It explains the meaning of tact and its opposite.

The tactless person treats a person according to a scientific method as if he were a thing. Now, in dealing with a thing, you must first find out what it is, and then act accordingly. But with a person, you must first find out what he is and then carefully conceal from him the fact that you have made the discovery. The tactless person can never be made to understand this. He prides himself on taking people as they are without being aware that that is not the way they want to be taken.

He has a keen eye for the obvious, and calls attention to it. Age, sex, color, nationality, previous condition of servitude, and all the facts that are interesting to the census-taker, are apparent to him and are made the basis of his conversation. When he meets one who is older than he, he is conscious of the fact, and emphasizes by every polite attention the disparity in years. He has an idea that at a certain period in life the highest tribute of respect is to be urged to rise out of one chair and take another that is presumably more comfortable. It does not occur to him that there may remain any tastes that are not sedentary. On the other hand, he sees a callow youth and addresses himself to the obvious callowness, and thereby makes himself thoroughly disliked. For, strange to say, the youth prefers to be addressed as a person of precocious maturity.

The literalist, observing that most people talk shop, takes it for granted that they like to talk shop. This is a mistake. They do it because it is the easiest thing to do, but they resent having attention called to their limitations. A man's profession does not necessarily coincide with his natural aptitude or with his predominant desire. When you meet a member of the Supreme Court you may assume that he is gifted with a judicial mind. But it does not follow that that is the only quality of mind he has; nor that when, out of court, he gives you a piece of his mind, it will be a piece of his judicial mind that he gives.

My acquaintance with royalty is limited to photographs of royal groups, which exhibit a high degree of domesticity. It would seem that the business of royalty when pursued as a steady job becomes tiresome, and that when they have their pictures taken they endeavor to look as much like ordinary folks as possible — and they usually succeed.

The member of one profession is always flattered by being taken for a skilled practitioner of another. Try it on your minister. Instead of saying, "That was an excellent sermon of yours this morning," say, "As I listened to your cogent argument, I thought what a successful lawyer you would have made." Then he will say, "I did think of taking to the law."

If you had belonged to the court of Frederick the Great you would have proved a poor courtier indeed if you had praised His Majesty's campaigns. Frederick knew that he was a Prussian general, but he wanted to be a French literary man. If you wished to gain his favor you should have told him that in your opinion he excelled Voltaire.

We do not like to have too much attention drawn to our present circumstances. They may be well enough in their way, but we can think of something which would be more fitting for us. We have either seen better days or we expect them.

Suppose you had visited Napoleon in Elba and had sought to ingratiate yourself with him.

"Sire," you would have said, "this is a beautiful little empire of yours, so snug and cozy and quiet. It is just such a domain as is suited to a man in your condition. The climate is excellent. Everything is peaceful. It must be delightful to rule where everything is arranged for you and the details are taken care of by others. As I came to your dominion I saw a line of British frigates guarding your shores. The evidences of such thoughtfulness are everywhere."

Your praise of his present condition would not have endeared you to Napoleon. You were addressing him as the Emperor of Elba. In his own eyes he was Emperor, though in Elba.

It is such a misapprehension which irritates any mature human being when his environment is taken as the measure of his personality.

The man with a literal mind moves in a perpetual comedy of errors. It is not a question of two Dromios. There are half a dozen Dromios under one hat.

How casually introductions are made, as if it were the easiest thing in the world to make two human beings acquainted! Your friend says, "I want you to know Mr. Stifflekin," and you say that you are happy to know him. But does either of you know the enigma that goes under the name of Stifflekin? You may know what he looks like and where he resides and what he does for a living. But that is all in the present tense. To really know him you must not only know what he is but what he used to be; what he used to think he was; what he used to think he ought to be and might be if he worked hard enough. You must know what he might have been if certain things had happened otherwise, and you must know what might have happened otherwise if he had been otherwise. All these complexities are a part of his own dim apprehension of himself. They are what make him so much more interesting to himself than he is to anyone else.

It is this consciousness of the inadequacy of our knowledge which makes us so embarrassed when we offer any service to another. Will he take it in the spirit in which it is given?

That was an awkward moment when Stanley, after all his hardships in his search for Dr. Livingstone, at last found the Doctor by a lake in Central Africa. Stanley held out his hand and said stiffly, "Dr. Livingstone, I presume?" Stanley had heroically plunged through the equatorial forests to find Livingstone and to bring him back to civilization. But Livingstone was not particularly anxious to be found, and had a decided objection to being brought back to civilization. What he wanted was a new adventure. Stanley did not find the real Livingstone till he discovered that the old man was as young at heart as himself. The two men became acquainted only when they began to plan a new expedition to find the source of the Nile.

The natural desire of every man to be somebody else explains many of the minor irritations of life. It prevents that perfect organization of society in which everyone should know his place and keep it. The desire to be somebody else leads us to practice on work that does not strictly belong to us. We all have aptitudes and talents that overflow the narrow bounds of our trade or profession. Every man feels that he is bigger than his job, and he is all the time doing what theologians called "works of supererogation."

The serious-minded housemaid is not content to do what she is told to do. She has an unexpected balance of energy. She wants to be a general household reformer. So she goes to the desk of the titular master of the house and gives it a thorough reformation. She arranges the papers according to her idea of neatness. When the poor gentleman returns and finds his familiar chaos transformed into a hateful order, he becomes a reactionary.

The serious manager of a street railway company is not content with the simple duty of transporting passengers cheaply and comfortably. He wants to exercise the functions of a lecturer in an ethical culture society. While the transport victim is swaying precariously from the end of a strap he reads a notice urging him to practice Christian courtesy and not to push. While the poor wretch pores over this counsel of perfection, he feels like answering as did Junius to the Duke of Grafton, "My Lord, injuries may be atoned for and forgiven, but insults admit of no compensation."

A man enters a barber shop with the simple desire of being shaved. But he meets with the more ambitious desires of the barber. The serious barber is not content with any slight contribution to human welfare. He insists that his client shall be shampooed, manicured, massaged, steamed beneath boiling towels, cooled off by electric fans, and, while all this is going on, that he shall have his boots blacked.

Have you never marveled at the patience of people in having so many things done to them that they don't want, just to avoid hurting the feelings of professional people who want to do more than is expected of them? You watch the stoical countenance of the passenger in a Pullman car as he stands up to be brushed. The chances are that he doesn't want to be brushed. He would prefer to leave the dust on his coat rather than be compelled to swallow it. But he knows what is expected of him. It is a part of the solemn ritual of traveling. It precedes the offering.

The fact that every man desires to be somebody else explains many of the aberrations of artists and literary men. The painters, dramatists, musicians, poets, and novelists are just as human as housemaids and railway managers and porters. They want to do "all the good they can to all the people they can in all the ways they can." They get tired of the ways they are used to and like to try new combinations. So they are continually mixing things. The practitioner of one art tries to produce effects that are proper to another art.

A musician wants to be a painter and use his violin as if it were a brush. He would have us see the sunset glories that he is painting for us. A painter wants to be a musician and paint symphonies, and he is grieved because the uninstructed cannot hear his pictures, although the colors do swear at each other. Another painter wants to be an architect and build up his picture as if it were made of cubes of brick. It looks like brick-work, but to the natural eye it doesn't look like a picture. A prose-writer gets tired of writing prose, and wants to be a poet. So he begins every line with a capital letter, and keeps on writing prose.

You go to the theater with the simple-minded Shakespearian idea that the play's the thing. But the playwright wants to be a pathologist. So you discover that you have dropped into a gruesome clinic. You sought innocent relaxation, but you are one of the non-elect and have gone to the place prepared for you. You must see the thing through. The fact that you have troubles of your own is not a sufficient claim for exemption.

Or you take up a novel expecting it to be a work of fiction. But the novelist has other views. He wants to be your spiritual adviser. He must do something to your mind, he must rearrange your fundamental ideas, he must massage your soul, and generally brush you off. All this in spite of the fact that you don't want to be brushed off and set to rights. You don't want him to do anything to your mind. It's the only mind you have and you need it in your own business.

But if the desire of every man to be somebody else accounts for many whimsicalities of human conduct and for many aberrations in the arts, it cannot be lightly dismissed as belonging only to the realm of comedy. It has its origin in the nature of things. The reason why every man wants to be somebody else is that he can remember the time when he was somebody else. What we call personal identity is a very changeable thing, as all of us realize when we look over old photographs and read old letters.

The oldest man now living is but a few years removed from the undifferential germ-plasm, which might have developed into almost anything. In the beginning he was a bundle of possibilities. Every actuality that is developed means a decrease in the rich variety of possibilities. In becoming one thing it becomes impossible to be something else.

The delight in being a boy lies in the fact that the possibilities are still manifold. The boy feels that he can be anything that he desires. He is conscious that he has capacities that would make him a successful banker. On the other hand, there are attractions in a life of adventure in the South Seas. It would be pleasant to lie under a bread-fruit tree and let the fruit drop into his mouth, to the admiration of the gentle savages who would gather about him. Or he might be a saint — not a commonplace modern saint who does chores and attends tiresome committee meetings, but a saint such as one reads about, who gives away his rich robes and his purse of gold to the first beggar he meets, and then goes on his carefree way through the forest to convert interesting robbers. He feels that he might practice that kind of unscientific charity, if his father would furnish him with the money to give away.

But by and by he learns that making a success in the banking business is not consistent with excursions to the South Seas or with the more picturesque and unusual forms of saintliness. If he is to be in a bank he must do as the bankers do.

Parents and teachers conspire together to make a man of him, which means making a particular kind of man of him. All mental processes which are not useful must be suppressed. The sum of their admonitions is that he must pay attention. That is precisely what he is doing. He is paying attention to a variety of things that escape the adult mind. As he wriggles on the bench in the schoolroom, he pays attention to all that is going on. He attends to what is going on out-of-doors; he sees the weak points of his fellow pupils, against whom he is planning punitive expeditions; and he is delightfully conscious of the idiosyncrasies of the teacher. Moreover, he is a youthful artist and his sketches from life give acute joy to his contemporaries when they are furtively passed around.

But the schoolmaster says sternly, "My boy, you must learn to pay attention; that is to say, you must not pay attention to so many things, but you must pay attention to one thing, namely the second declension."

Now the second declension is the least interesting thing in the room, but unless he confines his attention to it he will never learn it. Education demands narrowing of attention in the interest of efficiency.

A man may, by dint of application to a particular subject, become a successful merchant or real-estate man or chemist or overseer of the poor. But he cannot be all these things at the same time. He must make his choice. Having in the presence of witnesses taken himself for better for worse, he must, forsaking all others, cleave to that alone. The consequence is that, by the time he is forty, he has become one kind of a man, and is able to do one kind of work. He has acquired a stock of ideas true enough for his purposes, but not so transcendentally true as to interfere with his business. His neighbors know where to find him, and they do not need to take a spiritual elevator. He does business on the ground floor. He has gained in practicality, but has lost in the quality of interestingness.

The old prophet declared that the young men dream dreams and the old men see visions, but he did not say anything about the middle-aged men. *They* have to look after the business end.

But has the man whose working hours are so full of responsibilities changed so much as he seems to have done? When he is talking shop is he "all there"? I think not. There are elusive personalities that are in hiding. As the rambling mansions of the old Catholic families had secret panels into the "priest's hole," to which the family resorted for spiritual comfort, so in the mind of the most successful man there are secret chambers where are hidden his unsuccessful ventures, his romantic ambitions, his unfulfilled promises. All that he dreamed of as possible is somewhere concealed in the man's heart. He would not for the world have the public know how much he cares for the selves that have not had a fair chance to come into the light of day. You do not know a man until you know his lost Atlantis, and his Utopia for which he still hopes to set sail.

When Dogberry asserted that he was "as pretty a piece of flesh as any is in Messina" and "one that hath two gowns and everything handsome about him," he was pointing out what he deemed to be quite obvious. It was in a more intimate tone that he boasted, "and a fellow that hath had losses."

When Julius Caesar rode through the streets of Rome in his chariot, his laurel crown seemed to the populace a symbol of his present greatness. But gossip has it that Casear at that time desired to be younger than he was, and that before appearing in public he carefully arranged his laurel wreath so as to conceal the fact that he had had losses.

Much that passes for pride in the behavior of the great comes from the fear of the betrayal of emotions that belong to a simpler manner of life. When the sons of Jacob saw the great Egyptian officer to whom they appealed turn away from them, they little knew what was going on. "And Joseph made haste, for his bowels did yearn upon his brother: and he sought where to weep; and he entered into his chamber, and wept there. And he washed his face, and went out, and refrained himself." Joseph didn't want to be a great man. He wanted to be human. It was hard to refrain himself.

What of the lost arts of childhood, the lost audacities and romantic admirations of adolescence? What becomes of the sympathies which make us feel our kinship to all sorts of people? What becomes of the early curiosity in regard to things which were none of our business? We ask as Saint Paul asked of the Galatians, "Ye began well; who did hinder you?"

The answer is not wholly to our discredit. We do not develop all parts of our nature because we are not allowed to do so. Walt Whitman might exult over the Spontaneous Me. But nobody is paid for being spontaneous. A spontaneous switchman on the railway would be a menace to the traveling public. We prefer someone less temperamental.

As civilization advances and work becomes more specialized, it becomes impossible for anyone to find free and full development for all his natural powers in any recognized occupation. What then becomes of the other selves? The answer must be that playgrounds must be provided for them outside the confines of daily business. As work becomes more engrossing and narrowing the need is more urgent for recognized and carefully guarded periods of leisure.

The old Hebrew sage declared, "Wisdom cometh from the opportunity of leisure." It does not mean that a wise man must belong to what we call the leisure classes. It means that if one has only a little free time at his disposal, he must use that time for the refreshment of his hidden selves. If he cannot have a sabbath rest of twenty-four hours, he must learn to sanctify little sabbaths, it may be of ten minutes' length. In them he shall do no manner of work. It is not enough that the self that works and receives wages shall be recognized and protected; the world must be made safe for our other selves. Does not the Declaration of Independence say that every man has an inalienable right to the pursuit of happiness?

To realize that men are not satisfied with themselves requires imagination, and we have had a terrible example of what misfortunes come from the lack of imagination. The Prussian militarists had a painstaking knowledge of facts, but they had a contempt for human nature. Their tactlessness was almost beyond belief. They treated facts with deadly seriousness, but had no regard for feelings. They had spies all over the world to report all that could be seen, but they took no account of what could not be seen. So, while they were dealing scientifically with the obvious facts and forces, all the hidden powers of the human soul were being turned against them. Prussianism insisted on highly specialized men who have no sympathies to interfere with their efficiency. Having adopted a standard, all variation must be suppressed. It was against this effort to suppress the human variations that the world fought. We did not want all men to be reduced to one pattern. And against the effort to produce a monotonous uniformity we must keep on fighting. It was of little use to dethrone the Kaiser if we submit to other tyrants of our own making.

MAX BEERBOHM

"MY GIFTS are small," Max Beerbohm says of himself. "I've used them very well and discreetly, never straining them, and the result is that I've made a charming little reputation." But no one familiar with the sharp wit, exquisite style, and originality of his essays and his sometimes deadly caricatures will agree that his talents are slight, or that a reputation as a prime favorite of cultivated literary taste in the English reading world is a little one. He was born in London in 1872 and educated at Oxford (see his *Zuleika Dobson* for his now classic satire on Oxford life), but he has spent most of his life in Italy. His essays are published in volumes entitled characteristically *Works, More, And Even Now, Yet Again*, etc., from which the present selection is taken.

SEEING PEOPLE OFF *

I AM NOT good at it. To do it well seems to me one of the most difficult things in the world, and probably seems so to you, too.

To see a friend off from Waterloo to Vauxhall were easy enough. But we are never called on to perform that small feat. It is only when a friend is going on a longish journey, and will be absent for a longish time, that we turn up at the railway station. The dearer the friend, and the longer the journey, and the longer the likely absence, the earlier do we turn up, and the more lamentably do we fail. Our failure is in exact ratio to the seriousness of the occasion, and to the depth of our feeling.

In a room, or even on a doorstep, we can make the farewell quite worthily. We can express in our faces the genuine sorrow we feel. Nor do words fail us. There is no awkwardness, no restraint, on either side. The thread of our intimacy has not been snapped. The leave-taking is an ideal one. Why not, then, leave the leave-taking at that? Always, departing friends implore us not to bother to come to the railway station next morning. Always, we are deaf to these entreaties, knowing them to be not quite sincere. The departing friends would think it very odd of us if we took them at their words. Besides, they really do want to see us again. And that wish is heartily reciprocated. We duly turn up. And then, oh then, what a gulf yawns! We stretch our arms vainly across it. We have utterly lost touch. We have nothing at all to say. We gaze at each other as dumb animals gaze at human beings. We "make conversation" — and *such* conversation! We know that these are the friends from whom we parted overnight. They know that we have not altered. Yet, on the surface, everything is different; and the tension is such that we only long for the guard to blow his whistle and put an end to the farce.

On a bleak morning of last week I duly turned up at Euston, to see off an old friend who was starting for America.

Overnight, we had given him a farewell dinner, in which sadness was

---

* Reprinted from *Yet Again*, by Max Beerbohm, by permission of and special arrangement with Alfred A. Knopf, Inc., authorized publishers.

mingled with festivity. Years probably would elapse before his return. Some of us might never see him again. Not ignoring the shadow of the future, we gaily celebrated the past. We were as thankful to have known our guest as we were grieved to lose him; and both these emotions were made evident. It was a perfect farewell.

And now, here we were, stiff and self-conscious on the platform; and framed in the window of the railway-carriage was the face of our friend; but it was as the face of a stranger — a stranger anxious to please, an appealing stranger, an awkward stranger. "Have you got everything?" asked one of us, breaking the silence. "Yes, everything," said our friend, with a pleasant nod. "Everything," he repeated with the emphasis of an empty brain. "You'll be able to lunch on the train," said I, though this prophecy had already been made more than once. "Oh, yes," he said with conviction. He added that the train went straight through to Liverpool. This fact seemed to strike us as rather odd. We exchanged glances. "Doesn't it stop at Crewe?" asked one of us. "No," said our friend, briefly. He seemed almost disagreeable. There was a long pause. One of us, with a nod and a forced smile at the traveller, said "Well!" The nod, the smile, and the unmeaning monosyllable were returned conscientiously. Another pause was broken by one of us with a fit of coughing. It was an obviously assumed fit, but it served to pass the time. The bustle of the platform was unabated. There was no sign of the train's departure. Release — ours, and our friend's — was not yet.

My wandering eye alighted on a rather portly middle-aged man who was talking earnestly from the platform to a young lady at the next window but one to ours. His fine profile was vaguely familiar to me. The young lady was evidently American, and he was evidently English; otherwise I should have guessed from his impressive air that he was her father. I wished I could hear what he was saying. I was sure he was giving the very best advice; and the strong tenderness of his gaze was really beautiful. He seemed magnetic, as he poured out his final injunctions. I could feel something of his magnetism even where I stood. And the magnetism, like the profile, was vaguely familiar to me. Where had I experienced it?

In a flash I remembered. The man was Hubert le Ros. But how changed since last I saw him! That was seven or eight years ago, in the Strand. He was then (as usual) out of an engagement, and borrowed half-a-crown. It seemed a privilege to lend anything to him. He was always magnetic. And why his magnetism had never made him successful on the London stage was always a mystery to me. He was an excellent actor, and a man of sober habit. But, like many others of his kind, Hubert le Ros (I do not, of course, give the actual name by which he was known) drifted seedily away into the provinces; and I, like everyone else, ceased to remember him.

It was strange to see him, after all these years, here on the platform of Euston, looking so prosperous and solid. It was not only the flesh he had put on, but also the clothes, that made him hard to recognise. In the old days, an imitation fur coat had seemed to be as integral a part of him as were his ill-shorn lantern jaws. But now his costume was a model of rich and sombre moderation, drawing, not calling, attention to itself. He looked like a banker. Anyone would have been proud to be seen off by him.

"Stand back, please." The train was about to start, and I waved farewell to my friend. Le Ros did not stand back. He stood clasping in both hands the hands of the young American. "Stand back, sir, please!" He obeyed, but quickly darted forward again to whisper some final word. I think there were tears in her eyes. There certainly were tears in his when, at length, having watched the train out of sight, he turned round. He seemed, nevertheless, delighted to see me. He asked me where I had been hiding all these years; and simultaneously repaid me the half-crown as though it had been borrowed yesterday. He linked his arm in mine, and walked me slowly along the platform, saying with what pleasure he read my dramatic criticisms every Saturday.

I told him, in return, how much he was missed on the stage. "Ah, yes," he said, "I never act on the stage nowadays." He laid some emphasis on the word "stage," and I asked him where, then, he did act. "On the platform," he answered. "You mean," said I, "that you recite at concerts?" He smiled. "This," he whispered, striking his stick on the ground, "is the platform I mean." Had his mysterious prosperity unhinged him? He looked quite sane. I begged him to be more explicit.

"I suppose," he said presently, giving me a light for the cigar which he had offered me, "you have been seeing a friend off?" I assented. He asked me what I supposed *he* had been doing. I said that I had watched him doing the same thing. "No," he said gravely, "that lady was not a friend of mine. I met her for the first time this morning, less than half an hour ago, *here*," and again he struck the platform with his stick.

I confessed that I was bewildered. He smiled. "You may," he said, "have heard of the Anglo-American Social Bureau?" I had not. He explained to me that of the thousands of Americans who annually pass through England there are many hundreds who have no English friends. In the old days they used to bring letters of introduction. But the English are so inhospitable that these letters are hardly worth the paper they are written on. "Thus," said Le Ros, "the A.A.S.B. supplies a long-felt want. Americans are a sociable people, and most of them have plenty of money to spend. The A.A.S.B. supplies them with English friends. Fifty per cent of the fees is paid over to the friends. The other fifty is retained by the A.A.S.B. I am not, alas, a director. If I were, I should be a very rich man indeed. I am only an employé. But even so I do very well. I am one of the seers-off."

Again I asked for enlightenment. "Many Americans," he said, "cannot afford to keep friends in England. But they can all afford to be seen off. The fee is only five pounds (twenty-five dollars) for a single traveller; and eight pounds (forty dollars) for a party of two or more. They send that in to the Bureau, giving the date of their departure, and a description by which the seer-off can identify them on the platform. And then — well, then they are seen off."

"But is it worth it?" I exclaimed. "Of course it is worth it," said Le Ros. "It prevents them from feeling 'out of it.' It earns them the respect of the guard. It saves them from being despised by their fellow-passengers — the people who are going to be on the boat. It gives them a *footing* for the whole voyage. Besides, it is a great pleasure in itself. You saw me seeing that young lady off. Didn't you think I did it beautifully?" "Beautifully," I admitted. "I envied you. There was I ——" "Yes, I can imagine. There were you, shuffling from foot to foot, staring blankly at your friend, trying to make conversation. I know. That's how I used to be myself, before I studied, and went into the thing professionally. I don't say I'm perfect yet. I'm still a martyr to platform fright. A railway station is the most difficult of all places to act in, as you have discovered for yourself." "But," I said with resentment, "I wasn't trying to act. I really *felt*." "So did I, my boy," said Le Ros. "You can't act without feeling. What's his name, the Frenchman — Diderot, yes — said you could; but what did *he* know about it? Didn't you see those tears in my eyes when the train started? I hadn't forced them. I tell you I was *moved*. So were you, I dare say. But you couldn't have pumped up a tear to prove it. You can't express your feelings. In other words, you can't act. At any rate," he added kindly, "not in a railway station." "Teach me!" I cried. He looked thoughtfully at me. "Well," he said at length, "the seeing-off season is practically over. Yes, I'll give you a course. I have a good many pupils on hand already; but yes," he said, consulting an ornate note-book, "I could give you an hour on Thursdays and Fridays."

His terms, I confess, are rather high. But I do not grudge the investment.

PORTRAITS AND CHARACTERS

THE portrait or character sketch is to the biography what the personal essay is to the autobiography. Autobiography may contain reflection, and biography, interpretation of character, but both are mainly concerned with events. They move forward and find their natural expression in narrative. The character sketch may contain a story, somewhat as a painted portrait may present a piece of action in the background, but in the main it holds its subject fixed in space, as if for contemplation.

The best known character studies in English literature are the essays of Macaulay. His portraits are frequently biased by his own prepossessions as an English Whig, and by his rhetorical fondness for sharp contrasts of light and shade in the drawing of character, but by virtue of the vigor and vivacity of his style, he has, more than any other historian, determined the conventional view held by the Anglo-Saxon world of great figures, English and European, Bacon, Milton, Johnson, Clive, Hastings, Machiavelli. In the present day the tendency toward frankness in the revelation of character, leading to a correction or distortion of the conventional portraits in which the public recognized its heroes, showed itself notably in a series of essays by Lytton Strachey called *Eminent Victorians*, in which the saints of the Victorian Era, Doctor Thomas Arnold, Florence Nightingale, Cardinal Manning, and General Gordon were reduced to human stature. Naturally the methods of psychoanalysis have contributed to a sharper apprehension of the realities of human character as seen, for example, in the studies of Gamaliel Bradford in *Damaged Souls*.

The three character sketches represent different attitudes according to the position of the author in relation to the subject. Emerson knew Thoreau in Concord, boy and man, for thirty years, and summarizes a lifetime of companionship, experience, and understanding. Miss Sergeant had the advantage of interviews with Mr. Justice Holmes, who obligingly sat for his portrait. Finally, Mr. Nicolson writes of a single episode in which he was participant from start to finish. His sketch is narrative in method and might be called a short story out of real life, but as he has included it in a volume of character studies entitled *Some People* we take him at his word. That the sketch is one of Lord Curzon as well as of the titular hero is evident from reading Mr. Nicolson's book *Curzon, The Last Phase*, which depicts the statesman as Secretary of State for Foreign Affairs in the period to which "Arketall" refers.

In style the essays correspond to the mood of the writer and his attitude toward his subject. Emerson writes of Thoreau with affection and admiration, as representing an ideal to which he himself aspired. Miss Sergeant sees Mr. Justice Holmes in a brilliant and yet tragic light — the last of the Americans. Mr. Harold Nicolson writes of his chief with understanding tempered by affection, and affection pointed by irony.

RALPH WALDO EMERSON

Too much has been made of the supposed difficulty and obscurity of the essays of Ralph Waldo Emerson (1803–1882), the chief representative of a way of thinking known as New England Transcendentalism.   In his mystic moments Emerson is sometimes hard sledding for the inexperienced reader, but he had a saving sense of humor and a kind of common-sense and sanity which keep his feet on the ground.   Certainly there is nothing obscure or diffi- cult about the commemorative essay which he wrote about his friend and, in some sense, his follower, Henry David Thoreau (1817-1862), and which gives a vivid sense of Thoreau's personality.   Indeed, so interested was Emerson in trying to record the living man that he forgets to say in the essay that Thoreau has recently died.   Sympathy, the bringing together of revelatory personal detail, and a fine feeling for happy phrases make this essay one of the memorable commemorations in American letters.

THOREAU

A QUEEN rejoices in her peers,
And wary nature knows her own,
By court and city, dale and down,
And like a lover volunteers,
And to her son will treasures more,
And more to purpose, freely pour
In one wood walk, than learned men
Will find with glass in ten times ten.

It seemed as if the breezes brought him,
It seemed as if the sparrows taught him,
As if by secret sign he knew
Where in far fields the orchis grew.

Henry David Thoreau was the last male descendant of a French ancestor who came to this country from the Isle of Guernsey.   His character ex- hibited occasional traits drawn from this blood, in singular combination with a very strong Saxon genius.

He was born in Concord, Massachusetts, on the 12th of July, 1817.   He was graduated at Harvard College in 1837, but without any literary distinc- tion.   An iconoclast in literature, he seldom thanked colleges for their service to him, holding them in small esteem, whilst yet his debt to them was im- portant.   After leaving the University, he joined his brother in teaching a private school, which he soon renounced.   His father was a manufacturer of lead-pencils, and Henry applied himself for a time to this craft, believing he could make a better pencil than was then in use.   After completing his ex- periments, he exhibited his work to chemists and artists in Boston, and hav- ing obtained their certificates to its excellence and to its equality with the best London manufacture, he returned home contented.   His friends congratulated him that he had now opened his way to fortune. But he replied that he should never make another pencil. "Why should I? I would not do again what I have done once." He resumed his endless walks and miscellaneous studies, making every day some new acquaintance with Nature, though as yet never speaking of zoology or botany, since, though very studious of natural facts, he was incurious of technical and textual science.

At this time, a strong, healthy youth, fresh from college, whilst all his companions were choosing their profession, or eager to begin some lucrative employment, it was inevitable that his thoughts should be exercised on the same question, and it required rare decision to refuse all the accustomed paths and keep his solitary freedom at the cost of disappointing the natural expectations of his family and friends: all the more difficult that he had a perfect probity, was exact in securing his own independence, and in holding every man to the like duty. But Thoreau never faltered. He was a born protestant. He declined to give up his large ambition of knowledge and action for any narrow craft or profession, aiming at a much more comprehensive calling, the art of living well. If he slighted and defied the opinions of others, it was only that he was more intent to reconcile his practice with his own belief. Never idle or self-indulgent, he preferred, when he wanted money, earning it by some piece of manual labor agreeable to him, as building a boat or a fence, planting, grafting, surveying or other short work, to any long engagements. With his hardy habits and few wants, his skill in wood-craft, and his powerful arithmetic, he was very competent to live in any part of the world. It would cost him less time to supply his wants than another. He was therefore secure of his leisure.

A natural skill for mensuration, growing out of his mathematical knowledge and his habit of ascertaining the measures and distances of objects which interested him, the size of trees, the depth and extent of ponds and rivers, the height of mountains and the airline distance of his favorite summits — this, and his intimate knowledge of the territory about Concord, made him drift into the profession of land-surveyor. It had the advantage for him that it led him continually into new and secluded grounds, and helped his studies of Nature. His accuracy and skill in this work were readily appreciated, and he found all the employment he wanted.

He could easily solve the problems of the surveyor, but he was daily beset with graver questions, which he manfully confronted. He interrogated every custom, and wished to settle all his practice on an ideal foundation. He was a protestant *à outrance*, and few lives contain so many renunciations. He was bred to no profession; he never married; he lived alone; he never went to church; he never voted; he refused to pay a tax to the state; he ate no flesh, he drank no wine, he never knew the use of tobacco; and, though a naturalist, he used neither trap nor gun. He chose, wisely no doubt for himself, to be the bachelor of thought and Nature. He had no talent for wealth, and knew how to be poor without the least hint of squalor or inelegance. Perhaps he fell into his way of living without forecasting it much, but approved it with later wisdom. "I am often reminded," he wrote in his journal, "that if I had bestowed on me the wealth of Crœsus, my aims must be still the same, and my means essentially the same." He had no temptations to fight against — no appetites, no passions, no taste for elegant trifles. A fine house, dress, the manners and talk of highly cultivated people were all thrown away on him. He much preferred a good Indian, and considered these refinements as impediments to conversation, wishing to meet his companions on the simplest terms. He declined invitations to dinner-parties, because there each was in everyone's way, and he could not meet the individuals to any purpose. "They make their pride," he said, "in making their dinner cost much; I make my pride in making my dinner cost little." When asked at dinner what dish he preferred, he answered, "The nearest." He did not like the taste of wine, and never had a vice in his life. He said — "I have a faint recollection of pleasure derived from smoking dried lily-stems, before I was a man. I had commonly a supply of these. I have never smoked anything more noxious."

He chose to be rich by making his wants few, and supplying them himself. In his travels, he used the railroad only to get over so much country as was unimportant to the present purpose, walking hundreds of miles, avoiding taverns, buying a lodging in farmers' and fishermen's houses, as cheaper, and more agreeable to him, and because there he could better find the men and the information he wanted.

There was somewhat military in his nature, not to be subdued, always manly and able, but rarely tender, as if he did not feel himself except in op-position. He wanted a fallacy to expose, a blunder to pillory, I may say re-quired a little sense of victory, a roll of the drum, to call his powers into full exercise. It cost him nothing to say No; indeed he found it much easier than to say Yes. It seemed as if his first instinct on hearing a proposition was to controvert it, so impatient was he of the limitations of our daily thought. This habit, of course, is a little chilling to the social affections; and though the companion would in the end acquit him of any malice or un-truth, yet it mars conversation. Hence, no equal companion stood in af-fectionate relations with one so pure and guileless. "I love Henry," said one of his friends, "but I cannot like him; and as for taking his arm, I should as soon think of taking the arm of an elm-tree."

Yet, hermit and stoic as he was, he was really fond of sympathy, and threw himself heartily and childlike into the company of young people whom he loved, and whom he delighted to entertain, as he only could, with the varied and endless anecdotes of his experiences by field and river: and he was al-ways ready to lead a huckleberry-party or a search for chestnuts or grapes. Talking, one day, of a public discourse, Henry remarked that whatever suc-ceeded with the audience was bad. I said, "Who would not like to write something which all can read, like Robinson Crusoe? and who does not see with regret that his page is not solid with a right materialistic treatment, which delights everybody?" Henry objected, of course, and vaunted the better lectures which reached only a few persons. But, at supper, a young girl, understanding that he was to lecture at the Lyceum, sharply asked him, "Whether his lecture would be a nice interesting story, such as she wished to hear, or whether it was one of those old philosophical things that she did not care about." Henry turned to her, and bethought himself, and, I saw, was trying to believe that he had matter that might fit her and her brother, who were to sit up and go to the lecture, if it was a good one for them.

He was a speaker and actor of the truth, born such, and was ever running into dramatic situations from this cause. In any circumstance it interested all bystanders to know what part Henry would take, and what he would say; and he did not disappoint expectation, but used an original judgment on each emergency. In 1845 he built himself a small framed house on the shores of Walden Pond, and lived there two years alone, a life of labor and study. This action was quite native and fit for him. No one who knew him would tax him with affectation. He was more unlike his neighbors in his thought than in his action. As soon as he had exhausted the advantages of that solitude, he abandoned it. In 1847, not approving some uses to which the public expenditure was applied, he refused to pay his town tax, and was put in jail. A friend paid the tax for him, and he was released. The like annoyance was threatened the next year. But as his friends paid the tax, notwithstanding his protest, I believe he ceased to resist. No opposition or ridicule had any weight with him. He coldly and fully stated his opinion without affecting to believe that it was the opinion of the company. It was of no consequence if everyone present held the opposite opinion. On one occasion he went to the University Library to procure some books. The librarian refused to lend them. Mr. Thoreau repaired to the President, who stated to him the rules and usages, which permitted the loan of books to resident graduates, to clergymen who were alumni, and to some others resident within a circle of ten miles' radius from the College. Mr. Thoreau explained to the President that the railroad had destroyed the old scale of distances — that the library was useless, yes, and President and College useless, on the terms of his rules — that the one benefit he owed to the College was its library — that, at this moment, not only his want of books was imperative, but he wanted a large number of books, and assured him that he, Thoreau, and not the librarian, was the proper custodian of these. In short, the President found the petitioner so formidable, and the rules getting to look so ridiculous, that he ended by giving him a privilege which in his hands proved unlimited thereafter.

No truer American existed than Thoreau. His preference of his country and condition was genuine, and his aversion from English and European manners and tastes almost reached contempt. He listened impatiently to news or *bonmots* gleaned from London circles; and though he tried to be civil, these anecdotes fatigued him. The men were all imitating each other, and on a small mould. Why can they not live as far apart as possible, and each be a man by himself? What he sought was the most energetic nature; and he wished to go to Oregon, not to London. "In every part of Great Britain," he wrote in his diary, "are discovered traces of the Romans, their funereal urns, their camps, their roads, their dwellings. But New England, at least, is not based on any Roman ruins. We have not to lay the foundations of our houses on the ashes of a former civilization."

But idealist as he was, standing for abolition of slavery, abolition of tariffs, almost for abolition of government, it is needless to say he found himself not only unrepresented in actual politics, but almost equally opposed to every class of reformers. Yet he paid the tribute of his uniform respect to the Anti-Slavery party. One man, whose personal acquaintance he had formed, he honored with exceptional regard. Before the first friendly word had been spoken for Captain John Brown, he sent notices to most houses in Concord that he would speak in a public hall on the condition and character of John Brown, on Sunday evening, and invited all people to come. The Republican Committee, the Abolitionist Committee, sent him word that it was premature and not advisable. He replied — "I did not send to you for advice, but to announce that I am to speak." The hall was filled at an early hour by people of all parties, and his earnest eulogy of the hero was heard by all respectfully, by many with a sympathy that surprised themselves.

It was said of Plotinus that he was ashamed of his body, and 'tis very likely he had good reason for it — that his body was a bad servant, and he had not skill in dealing with the material world, as happens often to men of abstract intellect. But Mr. Thoreau was equipped with a most adapted and serviceable body. He was of short stature, firmly built, of light complexion, with strong, serious blue eyes, and a grave aspect — his face covered in the late years with a becoming beard. His senses were acute, his frame well-knit and hardy, his hands strong and skilful in the use of tools. And there was a wonderful fitness of body and mind. He could pace sixteen rods more accurately than another man could measure them with rod and chain. He could find his path in the woods at night, he said, better by his feet than his eyes. He could estimate the measure of a tree very well by his eye; he could estimate the weight of a calf or a pig, like a dealer. From a box containing a bushel or more of loose pencils, he could take up with his hands fast enough just a dozen pencils at every grasp. He was a good swimmer, runner, skater, boatman, and would probably outwalk most countrymen in a day's journey. And the relation of body to mind was still finer than we have indicated. He said he wanted every stride his legs made. The length of his walk uniformly made the length of his writing. If shut up in the house he did not write at all.

He had a strong common sense, like that which Rose Flammock, the weaver's daughter in Scott's romance, commends in her father, as resembling a yardstick, which, whilst it measures dowlas and diaper, can equally well measure tapestry and cloth of gold. He had always a new resource. When I was planting forest trees, and had procured half a peck of acorns, he said that only a small portion of them would be sound, and proceeded to examine them and select the sound ones. But finding this took time, he said, "I think if you put them all into water the good ones will sink"; which experiment we tried with success. He could plan a garden or a house or a barn; would have been competent to lead a "Pacific Exploring Expedition"; could give judicious counsel in the gravest private or public affairs.

He lived for the day, not cumbered and mortified by his memory. If he brought you yesterday a new proposition, he would bring you today another not less revolutionary. A very industrious man, and setting, like all highly organized men, a high value on his time, he seemed the only man of leisure in town, always ready for any excursion that promised well, or for conversation prolonged into late hours. His trenchant sense was never stopped by his rules of daily prudence, but was always up to the new occasion. He liked and used the simplest food, yet, when someone urged a vegetable diet, Thoreau thought all diets a very small matter, saying that "the man who shoots the buffalo lives better than the man who boards at the Graham House." He said — "You can sleep near the railroad, and never be disturbed: Nature knows very well what sounds are worth attending to, and has made up her mind not to hear the railroad-whistle. But things respect the devout mind, and a mental ecstasy was never interrupted." He noted what repeatedly befell him, that, after receiving from a distance a rare plant, he would presently find the same in his own haunts. And those pieces of luck which happen only to good players happened to him. One day, walking with a stranger, who inquired where Indian arrow-heads could be found, he replied, "Everywhere," and, stooping forward, picked one on the instant from the ground. At Mount Washington, in Tuckerman's Ravine, Thoreau had a bad fall, and sprained his foot. As he was in the act of getting up from his fall, he saw for the first time the leaves of the *Arnica mollis*.

His robust common sense, armed with stout hands, keen perceptions and strong will, cannot yet account for the superiority which shone in his simple and hidden life. I must add the cardinal fact, that there was an excellent wisdom in him, proper to a rare class of men, which showed him the material world as a means and symbol. This discovery, which sometimes yields to poets a certain casual and interrupted light, serving for the ornament of their writing, was in him an unsleeping insight; and whatever faults or obstructions of temperament might cloud it, he was not disobedient to the heavenly vision. In his youth, he said, one day, "The other world is all my art; my pencils will draw no others; my jack-knife will cut nothing else; I do not use it as a means." This was the muse and genius that ruled his opinions, conversation, studies, work and course of life. This made him a searching judge of men. At first glance he measured his companion, and, though insensible to some fine traits of culture, could very well report his weight and calibre. And this made the impression of genius which his conversation sometimes gave.

He understood the matter in hand at a glance, and saw the limitations and poverty of those he talked with, so that nothing seemed concealed from such terrible eyes. I have repeatedly known young men of sensibility converted in a moment to the belief that this was the man they were in search of, the man of men, who could tell them all they should do. His own dealing with them was never affectionate, but superior, didactic, scorning their petty ways — very slowly conceding, or not conceding at all, the promise of his society at their houses, or even at his own. "Would he not walk with them?" "He did not know. There was nothing so important to him as his walk; he had no walks to throw away on company." Visits were offered him from respectful parties, but he declined them. Admiring friends offered to carry him at their own cost to the Yellowstone River — to the West Indies — to South America. But though nothing could be more grave or considered than his refusals, they remind one, in quite new relations, of that fop Brummel's reply to the gentleman who offered him his carriage in a shower, "But where will *you* ride, then?" — and what accusing silences, and what searching and irresistible speeches, battering down all defences, his companions can remember!

Mr. Thoreau dedicated his genius with such entire love to the fields, hills and waters of his native town, that he made them known and interesting to all reading Americans, and to people over the sea. The river on whose banks he was born and died he knew from its springs to its confluence with the Merrimack. He had made summer and winter observations on it for many years, and at every hour of the day and night. The result of the recent survey of the Water Commissioners appointed by the State of Massachusetts he had reached by his private experiments, several years earlier. Every fact which occurs in the bed, on the banks or in the air over it; the fishes, and their spawning and nests, their manners, their food; the shad-flies which fill the air on a certain evening once a year, and which are snapped at by the fishes so ravenously that many of these die of repletion; the conical heaps of small stones on the river-shallows, the huge nests of small fishes, one of which will sometimes overfill a cart; the birds which frequent the stream, heron, duck, sheldrake, loon, osprey; the snake, muskrat, otter, woodchuck and fox, on the banks; the turtle, frog, hyla and cricket, which make the banks vocal — were all known to him, and, as it were, townsmen and fellow creatures; so that he felt an absurdity or violence in any narrative of one of these by itself apart, and still more of its dimensions on an inch-rule, or in the exhibition of its skeleton, or the specimen of a squirrel or a bird in brandy. He liked to speak of the manners of the river, as itself a lawful creature, yet with exactness, and always to an observed fact. As he knew the river, so the ponds in this region.

One of the weapons he used, more important to him than microscope or alcohol-receiver to other investigators, was a whim which grew on him by indulgence, yet appeared in gravest statement, namely, of extolling his own town and neighborhood as the most favored centre for natural observation. He remarked that the Flora of Massachusetts embraced almost all the important plants of America — most of the oaks, most of the willows, the best pines, the ash, the maple, the beech, the nuts. He returned Kane's *Arctic Voyage* to a friend of whom he had borrowed it, with the remark, that "Most of the phenomena noted might be observed in Concord." He seemed a little envious of the Pole, for the coincident sunrise and sunset, or five minutes' day after six months: a splendid fact, which Annursnuc had never afforded him. He found red snow in one of his walks, and told me that he expected to find yet the *Victoria regia* in Concord. He was the attorney of the indigenous plants, and owned to a preference of the weeds to the imported plants, as of the Indian to the civilized man, and noticed, with pleasure, that the willow bean-poles of his neighbor had grown more than his beans. "See these weeds," he said, "which have been hoed at by a million farmers all spring and summer, and yet have prevailed, and just now come out triumphant over all lanes, pastures, fields and gardens, such is their vigor. We have insulted them with low names, too — as Pigweed, Wormwood, Chickweed, Shad-blossom." He says, "They have brave names, too — Ambrosia, Stellaria, Amelanchier, Amaranth, etc."

I think his fancy for referring everything to the meridian of Concord did not grow out of any ignorance or depreciation of other longitudes or latitudes, but was rather a playful expression of his conviction of the indifference of all places, and that the best place for each is where he stands. He expressed it once in this wise: "I think nothing is to be hoped from you, if this bit of mould under your feet is not sweeter to you to eat than any other in this world, or in any world."

The other weapon with which he conquered all obstacles in science was patience. He knew how to sit immovable, a part of the rock he rested on, until the bird, the reptile, the fish, which had retired from him, should come back and resume its habits, nay, moved by curiosity, should come to him and watch him.

It was a pleasure and a privilege to walk with him. He knew the country like a fox or a bird, and passed through it as freely by paths of his own. He knew every track in the snow or on the ground, and what creature had taken this path before him. One must submit abjectly to such a guide, and the reward was great. Under his arm he carried an old music-book to press plants; in his pocket, his diary and pencil, a spy-glass for birds, microscope, jack-knife and twine. He wore a straw hat, stout shoes, strong gray trousers, to brave scrub-oaks and smilax, and to climb a tree for a hawk's or a squirrel's nest. He waded into the pool for the water-plants, and his strong legs were no insignificant part of his armor. On the day I speak of he looked for the Menyanthes, detected it across the wide pool, and, on examination of the florets, decided that it had been in flower five days. He drew out of his breast-pocket his diary, and read the names of all the plants that should bloom on this day, whereof he kept account as a banker when his notes fall due. The Cypripedium not due till tomorrow. He thought that, if waked up from a trance, in this swamp, he could tell by the plants what time of the year it was within two days. The redstart was flying about, and presently the fine grosbeaks, whose brilliant scarlet "makes the rash gazer wipe his eye," and whose fine clear note Thoreau compared to that of a tanager which has got rid of its hoarseness. Presently he heard a note which he called that of the night-warbler, a bird he had never identified, had been in search of twelve years, which always, when he saw it, was in the act of diving down into a tree or bush, and which it was vain to seek; the only bird which sings indifferently by night and by day. I told him he must beware of finding and booking it, lest life should have nothing more to show him. He said, "What you seek in vain for, half your life, one day you come full upon, all the family at dinner. You seek it like a dream, and as soon as you find it you become its prey."

His interest in the flower or the bird lay very deep in his mind, was connected with Nature — and the meaning of Nature was never attempted to be defined by him. He would not offer a memoir of his observations to the Natural History Society. "Why should I? To detach the description from its connections in my mind would make it no longer true or valuable to me: and they do not wish what belongs to it." His power of observation seemed to indicate additional senses. He saw as with microscope, heard as with ear-trumpet, and his memory was a photographic register of all he saw and heard. And yet none knew better than he that it is not the fact that imports, but the impression or effect of the fact on your mind. Every fact lay in glory in his mind, a type of the order and beauty of the whole.

His determination on Natural History was organic. He confessed that he sometimes felt like a hound or a panther, and, if born among Indians, would have been a fell hunter. But, restrained by his Massachusetts culture, he played out the game in this mild form of botany and ichthyology. His intimacy with animals suggested what Thomas Fuller records of Butler the apiologist, that "either he had told the bees things or the bees had told him." Snakes coiled round his legs; the fishes swam into his hand, and he took them out of the water; he pulled the woodchuck out of its hole by the tail, and took the foxes under his protection from the hunters. Our naturalist had perfect magnanimity; he had no secrets: he would carry you to the heron's haunt, or even to his most prized botanical swamp — possibly knowing that you could never find it again, yet willing to take his risks.

No college ever offered him a diploma, or a professor's chair; no academy made him its corresponding secretary, its discoverer or even its member. Perhaps these learned bodies feared the satire of his presence. Yet so much knowledge of Nature's secret and genius few others possessed; none in a more large and religious synthesis. For not a particle of respect had he to the opinions of any man or body of men, but homage solely to the truth itself; and as he discovered everywhere among doctors some leaning of courtesy, it discredited them. He grew to be revered and admired by his townsmen, who had at first known him only as an oddity. The farmers who employed him as a surveyor soon discovered his rare accuracy and skill, his knowledge of their lands, of trees, of birds, of Indian remains and the like, which enabled him to tell every farmer more than he knew before of his own farm; so that he began to feel a little as if Mr. Thoreau had better rights in his land than he. They felt, too, the superiority of character which addressed all men with a native authority.

Indian relics abound in Concord — arrowheads, stone chisels, pestles and fragments of pottery; and on the river-bank, large heaps of clam-shells and ashes mark spots which the savages frequented. These, and every circumstance touching the Indian, were important in his eyes. His visits to Maine were chiefly for love of the Indian. He had the satisfaction of seeing the manufacture of the bark canoe, as well as of trying his hand in its management on the rapids. He was inquisitive about the making of the stone arrow-head, and in his last days charged a youth setting out for the Rocky Mountains to find an Indian who could tell him that: "It was well worth a visit to California to learn it." Occasionally, a small party of Penobscot Indians would visit Concord, and pitch their tents for a few weeks in summer on the river-bank. He failed not to make acquaintance with the best of them; though he well knew that asking questions of Indians is like catechizing beavers and rabbits. In his last visit to Maine he had great satisfaction from Joseph Polis, an intelligent Indian of Oldtown, who was his guide for some weeks.

He was equally interested in every natural fact. The depth of his perception found likeness of law throughout Nature, and I know not any genius who so swiftly inferred universal law from the single fact. He was no pedant of a department. His eye was open to beauty, and his ear to music. He found these, not in rare conditions, but wheresoever he went. He thought the best of music was in single strains; and he found poetic suggestion in the humming of the telegraph-wire.

His poetry might be bad or good; he no doubt wanted a lyric facility and technical skill, but he had the source of poetry in his spiritual perception. He was a good reader and critic, and his judgment on poetry was to the ground of it. He could not be deceived as to the presence or absence of the poetic element in any composition, and his thirst for this made him negligent and perhaps scornful of superficial graces. He would pass by many delicate rhythms, but he would have detected every live stanza or line in a volume and knew very well where to find an equal poetic charm in prose. He was so enamoured of the spiritual beauty that he held all actual written poems in very light esteem in the comparison. He admired Aeschylus and Pindar; but when some one was commending them, he said that Aeschylus and the Greeks, in describing Apollo and Orpheus, had given no song, or no good one. "They ought not to have moved trees, but to have chanted to the gods such a hymn as would have sung all their old ideas out of their heads, and new ones in." His own verses are often rude and defective. The gold does not yet run pure, is drossy and crude. The thyme and marjoram are not yet honey. But if he want lyric fineness and technical merits, if he have not the poetic temperament, he never lacks the causal thought, showing that his genius was better than his talent. He knew the worth of the Imagination for the uplifting and consolation of human life, and liked to throw every thought into a symbol. The fact you tell is of no value, but only the impression. For this reason his presence was poetic, always piqued the curiosity to know more deeply the secrets of his mind. He had many reserves, an unwillingness to exhibit to profane eyes what was still sacred in his own, and knew well how to throw a poetic veil over his experience. All readers of *Walden* will remember his mythical record of his disappointments:

"I long ago lost a hound, a bay horse and a turtle-dove, and am still on their trail. Many are the travellers I have spoken concerning them, describing their tracks, and what calls they answered to. I have met one or two who have heard the hound, and the tramp of the horse, and even seen the dove disappear behind a cloud; and they seemed as anxious to recover them as if they had lost them themselves."

His riddles were worth the reading, and I confide that if at any time I do not understand the expression, it is yet just. Such was the wealth of his truth that it was not worth his while to use words in vain. His poem entitled "Sympathy" reveals the tenderness under that triple steel of stoicism, and the intellectual subtility it could animate. His classic poem on "Smoke" suggests Simonides, but is better than any poem of Simonides. His biography is in his verses. His habitual thought makes all his poetry a hymn to the Cause of causes, the Spirit which vivifies and controls his own:—

> "I hearing get, who had but ears,
> And sight, who had but eyes before;
> I moments live, who lived but years,
> And truth discern, who knew but learning's lore."

And still more in these religious lines: —

> "Now chiefly is my natal hour,
> And only now my prime of life;
> I will not doubt the love untold,
> Which not my worth nor want have bought,
> Which wooed me young, and wooes me old,
> And to this evening hath me brought."

Whilst he used in his writings a certain petulance of remark in reference to churches or churchmen, he was a person of a rare, tender and absolute religion, a person incapable of any profanation, by act or by thought. Of course, the same isolation which belonged to his original thinking and living detached him from the social religious forms. This is neither to be censured nor regretted. Aristotle long ago explained it, when he said, "One who surpasses his fellow citizens in virtue is no longer a part of the city. Their law is not for him, since he is a law to himself."

Thoreau was sincerity itself, and might fortify the convictions of prophets in the ethical laws by his holy living. It was an affirmative experience which refused to be set aside. A truth-speaker he, capable of the most deep and strict conversation; a physician to the wounds of any soul; a friend, knowing not only the secret of friendship, but almost worshipped by those few persons who resorted to him as their confessor and prophet, and knew the deep value of his mind and great heart. He thought that without religion or devotion of some kind nothing great was ever accomplished: and he thought that the bigoted sectarian had better bear this in mind.

His virtues, of course, sometimes ran into extremes. It was easy to trace to the inexorable demand on all for exact truth that austerity which made this willing hermit more solitary even than he wished. Himself of a perfect probity, he required not less of others. He had a disgust at crime, and no worldly success would cover it. He detected paltering as readily in dignified and prosperous persons as in beggars, and with equal scorn. Such dangerous frankness was in his dealing that his admirers called him "that terrible Thoreau," as if he spoke when silent, and was still present when he had departed. I think the severity of his ideal interfered to deprive him of a healthy sufficiency of human society.

The habit of a realist to find things the reverse of their appearance in-

clined him to put every statement in a paradox. A certain habit of antagonism defaced his earlier writings — a trick of rhetoric not quite outgrown
in his later, of substituting for the obvious word and thought its diametrical
opposite. He praised wild mountains and winter forests for their domestic
air, in snow and ice he would find sultriness, and commended the wilderness
for resembling Rome and Paris. "It was so dry, that you might call
it wet."

The tendency to magnify the moment, to read all the laws of Nature
in the one object or one combination under your eye, is of course comic to
those who do not share the philosopher's perception of identity. To him
there was no such thing as size. The pond was a small ocean; the Atlantic,
a large Walden Pond. He referred every minute fact to cosmical laws.
Though he meant to be just, he seemed haunted by a certain chronic assumption that the science of the day pretended completeness, and he had just
found out that the *savans* had neglected to discriminate a particular botanical
variety, had failed to describe the seeds or count the sepals. "That is to
say," we replied, "the blockheads were not born in Concord; but who said
they were? It was their unspeakable misfortune to be born in London, or
Paris, or Rome; but, poor fellows, they did what they could, considering
that they never saw Bateman's Pond, or Nine-Acre Corner, or Becky
Stow's Swamp; besides, what were you sent into the world for, but to add
this observation?"

Had his genius been only contemplative, he had been fitted to his life,
but with his energy and practical ability he seemed born for great enterprise
and for command; and I so much regret the loss of his rare powers of action,
that I cannot help counting it a fault in him that he had no ambition. Wanting this, instead of engineering for all America, he was the captain of a
huckleberry-party. Pounding beans is good to the end of pounding empires
one of these days; but if, at the end of years, it is still only beans!

But these foibles, real or apparent, were fast vanishing in the incessant
growth of a spirit so robust and wise, and which effaced its defeats with new
triumphs. His study of Nature was a perpetual ornament to him, and
inspired his friends with curiosity to see the world through his eyes, and to
hear his adventures. They possessed every kind of interest.

He had many elegancies of his own, whilst he scoffed at conventional
elegance. Thus, he could not bear to hear the sound of his own steps,
the grit of gravel; and therefore never willingly walked in the road, but in
the grass, on mountains and in woods. His senses were acute, and he
remarked that by night every dwelling-house gives out bad air, like a
slaughter-house. He liked the pure fragrance of melilot. He honored certain plants with special regard, and, over all, the pond-lily — then, the
gentian, and the *Mikania scandens*, and "life-everlasting," and a bass-tree
which he visited every year when it bloomed, in the middle of July. He
thought the scent a more oracular inquisition than the sight, — more oracular and trustworthy. The scent, of course, reveals what is concealed from
the other senses. By it he detected earthiness. He delighted in echoes,
and said they were almost the only kind of kindred voices that he heard.

He loved Nature so well, was so happy in her solitude, that he became very jealous of cities and the sad work which their refinements and artifices made with man and his dwelling. The axe was always destroying his forest. "Thank God," he said, "they cannot cut down the clouds!" "All kinds of figures are drawn on the blue ground with this fibrous white paint."

I subjoin a few sentences taken from his unpublished manuscripts, not only as records of his thought and feeling, but for their power of description and literary excellence: —

"Some circumstantial evidence is very strong, as when you find a trout in the milk."

"The chub is a soft fish, and tastes like boiled brown paper salted."

"The youth gets together his materials to build a bridge to the moon, or, perchance, a palace or temple on the earth, and, at length the middle-aged man concludes to build a wood-shed with them."

"The locust z-ing."

"Devil's-needles zigzagging along the Nut-Meadow brook."

"Sugar is not so sweet to the palate as sound to the healthy ear."

"I put on some hemlock-boughs, and the rich salt crackling of their leaves was like mustard to the ear, the crackling of uncountable regiments. Dead trees love the fire."

"The bluebird carries the sky on his back."

"The tanager flies through the green foliage as if it would ignite the leaves."

"If I wish for a horse-hair for my compass-sight I must go to the stable; but the hair-bird, with her sharp eyes, goes to the road."

"Immortal water, alive even to the superficies."

"Fire is the most tolerable third party."

"Nature made ferns for pure leaves, to show what she could do in that line."

"No tree has so fair a bole and so handsome an instep as the beech."

"How did these beautiful rainbow-tints get into the shell of the fresh-water clam, buried in the mud at the bottom of our dark river?"

"Hard are the times when the infant's shoes are second-foot."

"We are strictly confined to our men to whom we give liberty."

"Nothing is so much to be feared as fear. Atheism may comparatively be popular with God himself."

"Of what significance the things you can forget? A little thought is sexton to all the world."

"How can we expect a harvest of thought who have not had a seedtime of character?"

"Only he can be trusted with gifts who can present a face of bronze to expectations."

"I asked to be melted. You can only ask of the metals that they be tender to the fire that melts them. To nought else can they be tender."

There is a flower known to botanists, one of the same genus with our summer plant called "Life-Everlasting," a *Gnaphalium* like that, which grows on the most inaccessible cliffs of the Tyrolese mountains, where the chamois dare hardly venture, and which the hunter, tempted by its beauty, and by his love (for it is immensely valued by the Swiss maidens), climbs the cliffs to gather, and is sometimes found dead at the foot, with the flower in his hand. It is called by botanists the *Gnaphalium leontopodium*, but by the Swiss *Edelweisse*, which signifies *Noble Purity*. Thoreau seemed to me living in the hope to gather this plant, which belonged to him of right. The scale on which his studies proceeded was so large as to require longevity, and we were the less prepared for his sudden disappearance. The country knows not yet, or in the least part, how great a son it has lost. It seems an injury that he should leave in the midst his broken task which none else can finish, a kind of indignity to so noble a soul that he should depart out of Nature before yet he has been really shown to his peers for what he is. But he, at least, is content. His soul was made for the noblest society; he had in a short life exhausted the capabilities of this world; wherever there is knowledge, wherever there is virtue, wherever there is beauty, he will find a home.

ELIZABETH SHEPLEY SERGEANT

ELIZABETH SHEPLEY SERGEANT was born at Winchester, Massachusetts. She took her A.B. at Bryn Mawr College in 1903, having received the George W. Childs prize for essays. She was engaged for some years in social work and investigation. She acted as correspondent for the *New Republic* in France in 1917–18. She had already written *French Perspectives* (1916). The present selection appeared in *The New Republic* for December 8, 1921. Mr. Justice Holmes died March 6, 1935.

OLIVER WENDELL HOLMES *

JUSTICE TOUCHED WITH FIRE

HERE is a Yankee, strayed from Olympus. Olympians are reputed at ease in the universe; they know truth in flashes of fire, and reveal its immortal essence in cryptic phrase. How disturbing to the solemnities of average mortals, average lawyers, average judges even, is the swift, searching epigrammatic thought of Mr. Justice Holmes. Even the wise-cracks he loves to fling out are keyed to profundity and wit. He has lived through the most restless periods of American history since the American Revolution itself, yet his early divinations of the law, outlined nearly half a century ago, and his Supreme Court opinions, which have together recast American legal thinking, seem to have been formulated in the elegant leisure that we associate with the classics.

Oliver Wendell Holmes's tall and erect figure, which a ripe and white old age has scarcely stooped; his grand manner, at once noble and dazzling — those have never asked quarter of time. Watch his snowy head for a moment among his younger peers on the bench. Note the set of the shoulders in the gown, the oval contour of the face with its fine, angular New England features, the flow of the level white brows into the thin distinction of the nose, the martial mustachios, with their heavy guardsman's droop and their curved ends of punctilio. The eyes, the most striking feature, give off sparkles of scintillating grey-blue, and have more scepticism and gentle malice than mercy in their depths. Though at bottom Holmes is and looks a simple American gentleman of aristocratic rectitude, he has a spice of the Mephistophelean quality which he himself has recommended to the naïveté of judges.

The Justice is listening to a complex argument — listening till his mind, hovering and intent, like the wasp that paralyses the caterpillar, has driven straight to its heart. Then, while the other judges still patiently listen, he reads over the briefs, calls the pages to bring reports containing opinions

* Reprinted from *Fire Under the Andes*, by Elizabeth S. Sergeant, by permission of and special arrangement with Alfred A. Knopf, Inc., authorized publisher.

relied on by counsel, and is ready, by the time counsel is rising to his peroration, to draft an opinion that will not fail to "strike the jugular."

The jurist who, at fourscore years and five, can command this penetration of essentials, this intense focusing of mental powers, has some rare elixir in his veins. Is it not the true elixir of youth? The youth offered by a young Bostonian to his country in the most heroic of her wars, and thrice wounded, at Ball's Bluff, Antietam, and Fredericksburg? Judge Holmes's clearest genius — the sharp and supple functioning of his mind — in some nameless fashion draws its strength from his curiosity and awe in the face of the mystery of existence. It seems that the near presence of death in those three stern and shadowed years fused his intellect and his emotion in a single shaft of will. It made sceptical philosophy a necessity, but gave to fundamental doubt a practical idealism. It affirmed man's destiny on earth as battle, his chances those of war. But it discovered to him that the root of joy as of duty and the worth of life itself is to put out all one's powers to the full, though the end be dim and the plan of campaign little understood. "Men carry their signatures upon their persons," he has written, "although they may not always be visible at the first glance." The friends of the Justice all know the signature that the Civil War inscribed. It is that of a youthful fighter who somehow inspired the fate of the lonely thinker with the faith of the soldier.

The son of Dr. Oliver Wendell Holmes was a fortunate youth. Born in the flower of New England's cultural dominance, and at the dawn of the Darwinian age into a family at once brahminical, literary, and scientific, brought up at that "autocratic" breakfast-table where a bright saying gave a child a double help of marmalade, he must early have acquired the rich flavour of belles-lettres which in him has ever mellowed the scientific habit. Celebrated men were familiars at his father's house, and from the greatest among them — Emerson — he drew a priceless intellectual ferment. Yet, with his glancing wit and his worldly charm, he might have been tempted away from the isolated path of the original thinker but for the war of secession. It was, in his own view, his greatest good fortune to graduate from Harvard in the class of '61, at the age of twenty, just as this war was beginning, and to learn one day, as he was walking down Beacon Hill, with Hobbes's *Leviathan* in his hand, that he had a commission in the Twentieth Massachusetts Volunteers; a regiment commemorated at last in the Boston Public Library by one of the lions of St. Gaudens that guard the entrance stairway. So the young officer, whom we may see in his uniform at Langdell Hall, at the Harvard Law School, with his visored cap on his knee, in one of those touching little faded photographs which were a sop to parental love — a mere lad, trusting and vulnerable, like all lads who have fought all the great wars — went forth to a baptism that he has never forgotten.

It came at Ball's Bluff: an engagement where the Twentieth Massachusetts got its first crucial trial. There were tactical errors which cost dear. The blues, defeated but "too proud to surrender," as the greys declared, were driven down the cliff on the Virginia shore into the Potomac, where, dying, swimming, drowning in numbers, they yet struggled to transport the survivors and the wounded in the few sinking boats to the island in mid-stream, and then to the Maryland shore, while the river was whipped into a foam of bullets, and darkness fell. Lieutenant Holmes, apparently mortally wounded in the breast, was laid in a boat with dying men and ferried through the night. As he recovered consciousness, he heard the man next him groan and — thinking he probably had his own dose — said to himself:

"I suppose Sir Philip Sidney would say: 'Put that man ashore first.' I think I will let events take their course."

A story written down by the elder Holmes in the *Atlantic Monthly* (not altogether to the pleasure of the younger?) is indicative of another side of the Justice's character. This relates how, after the battle of Antietam, Dr. Holmes started out to search for a wounded son. But the doctor could not find his young hero, though he followed this clue and that. At last, in despair, he was taking a train for the north at Hagerstown, Maryland, when, "in the first car, on the fourth seat to the right, I saw my captain."

"Hullo, my boy!"

"Boy, nothing!" (The original tale does not run quite this way.) The "boy" had been spending a week much to his taste. "As he walked languidly along [in Hagerstown], some ladies saw him across the street and, seeing, were moved with pity and pitying, spoke such soft words that he was tempted to accept their invitation to rest awhile beneath their hospitable roof. The mansion was old, as the dwellings of gentlefolk should be; the ladies were some of them young, and all were full of kindness; there were gentle cares and unasked luxuries and pleasant talk, and music sprinklings for the piano, with a sweet voice to keep them company."

The words call up, along with other images of an America gone for ever, a quaint photograph found in a portfolio in the Memorial Alcove at the Boston Library: a bevy of devout young ladies in bustles and tight waists and long, flowing skirts, sewing together on a flag. Such a flag was presented, after Ball's Bluff, to Company E "by the sisters of Lieutenants Lowell and Putnam," with a polished letter from Charles Eliot Norton about the honour of the Bay State. The Colonel of the Twentieth, by the way, on first reaching headquarters, and asked by the commanding officer if he had arms, uniforms, and accoutrements, replied proudly: "My regiment, sir, came from Massachusetts."

Back to Massachusetts, then, came young Holmes, to the soil for whose outcropping rocks and barberry bushes and sand dunes and old towns built of brick and shingle he has confessed a rooted affection. He had no path to blaze unless he chose: the natural Puritan aristocracy from which he sprang awaited him with its pleasant securities. But there burned in this young man, as there burns in the Holmes of today, a sense of the valuable brevity of existence. Life was a rich but a responsible adventure, and he had a simple democratic conviction, denied to some who are born under the shadow of Beacon Hill, that "the deepest cause we have to love our country" is "that instinct, that spark, that makes the American unable to meet his fellow man otherwise than simply as a man, eye to eye, hand to hand, and foot to foot, wrestling naked on the sand." Holmes was recognizing fiery energies which later claimed mountain climbing as an outlet. A stern intellectual ambition, worthy substitute for the primitive and heroic, was taking shape. A sentence of his own conjures him up for me, standing apart even in his tested group: "In our youth our hearts were touched with fire. It was given us to learn at the outset that life is a profound and passionate thing."

It is hinted that among those young ladies of the best families who — Boston being truly a village in the sixties — "knew every carriage in town," the return of a handsome wounded soldier (also the class poet of the decimated '61) made a stir. "That lanky talker of a Wendell Holmes" was an old maid-servant's dictum. Holmes has always loved talking by a fire with a clever and gracious woman, and these ghostly maidens, if they yet lived, could probably tell us why a young man of varied and brilliant parts chose from several possible destinies to enter the Harvard Law School.

For there was also literature, there was above all philosophy. Holmes was not the man to follow in his father's footsteps, or even in Emerson's, though he had in fact qualities as a literary stylist far superior to the doctor's, and gifts as a philosopher which gave a universal impress to his legal thinking. The winds and waves of eternity beat through his writings. "Nerve and dagger," said Emerson, are lacking in the American genius. Holmes the writer has nerve and dagger, as he has in moral and intellectual issues a blade-like courage. But he did not dream, in those tormented days, of being named among great American writers and philosophers. In his twenties this profession of the law which he had elected seemed barren enough. Did he choose it, by a quirk common to New Englanders, for that very reason? Because it was hard, male, undesired? The law enforced more than thought: an activity in the world of men, a reality which the soldier felt bound to espouse, if only that it was so alien to his intuitive bent for inward brooding thought. "It cost me some years of doubt and unhappiness," the Justice has avowed, "before I could say to myself: 'The law is part of the universe — if the universe can be thought about, one part must reveal it as much as another to one who can see that part. It is only a question if you have the eyes.'"

The study of philosophy helped Holmes to find his legal eyes. He likes to tell how he began to read Plato, as an undergraduate at Harvard, and was admonished by Emerson: "Hold him at arm's length. You must say to yourself: 'Plato, you have pleased the world for two thousand years: let us see if you can please me.'" The sequel is pertinent. Young Holmes not only read, but turned off a critical essay which he showed expectantly to his mentor. "I have read your piece. When you strike at a king, you must *kill* him." That shaft went straight to the bull's eye. When Holmes graduated from the Law School he approached his profession in the spirit of scientific and philosophic inquiry. Not as do the practitioners "to whom the law is a rag-bag from which they pick out the piece and the colour that they want." Holmes had no consuming interest in practice, considered as winning cases and making money. But he had the hope, as yet scarce conscious, of shooting with true aim at some great intellectual marks. "I suppose the law is worthy of the interest of an intelligent man," he once hazarded, in his anguish of doubt whether it was, to Charles Francis Adams, the Minister to England.

That a philosopher could be, must be, a man of intelligence Holmes was morally certain. Was he not "twisting the tail of the cosmos" with his friend Bill James? One gets from the early letters of William James a fine series of images of two golden and impetuous youths, whetting thought on thought, doubt on doubt, in an upper chamber. In the year 1866, when "Bill" was twenty-four and studying medicine, and "Wendle" twenty-five and studying law, they exchanged acute argument on materialism. A year later, when James had gone to Germany to pursue philosophy, and Holmes had been admitted to the bar, discussions of "our dilapidated old friend the Kosmos" continued by letter — interspersed by affectionate reminiscence from James, of "your whitely lit-up room, drinking in your profound wisdom, your golden jibes, your costly imagery, listening to your shuddering laughter." "Why don't you join the Society for Psychical Research?" James is said to have inquired. To which Holmes: "Why don't you investigate Mohammedanism? There are millions of men who think you will be damned without it. Life is like an artichoke, you pull out a leaf, a tip only is edible. You pull out a day, only an hour or two is available for spiritual thoughts."

Holmes was looking, though he may not have realized it, for a personal philosophy that he could use as a raft from which to take the long, deep plunge into his legal-scholarly pursuits. It is typical — for his power of choice and exclusion, his economy of time and means are facets of his greatness — that he did not continue to flounder about in the philosophical waters, trying this system and that, cursing Jehovah and calling on his angels to save, but grasped the planks that he found near at hand and skilfully fitted them together into the aforementioned raft. *Raft* is too perishable a word. Holmes's philosophy was a tidy boat, formed, for all its pointed nails of scepticism, of sturdy Puritan oak, a shipshape bark, in which he could cruise safely about the cosmos among the other worlds and the stars.

Every speech, every personal letter, every opinion of Oliver Wendell Holmes rests on this hardy and lucid doctrine. Divergent though it was from the philosophy of James — who continued his search for a solution that would fit the fate of Man in general, and for himself tended toward those supernatural revelations and consolations which Holmes's scepticism impatiently repudiated, — the affectionate relation continued through life. And every distant interchange made the old philosophic quarrel flare up. The following statement of Holmes's "platform," — happily preserved in the James files — though written from the Supreme Court in 1901, "after reading your two pieces about Pragmatism (pedantic name)" might as well have been written in 1875, or, if William James had lived, in 1926.

"It is as absurd" (the Justice remarks, with familiar humility, before an expert) "for me to be spearing my old commonplaces at you as it would be for an outsider to instruct me in the theory of legal responsibility — but you see, *mon vieux*, although it is years since we have had any real talk together, I am rather obstinate in my adherence to ancient sympathies and enjoy letting out a little slack to you."

"I have been in the habit of saying that all I mean by truth is what I can't help thinking. The assumption of the validity of the thinking process seems to mean no more than that. But I have learned to surmise that my *can't helps* are not necessarily cosmic... philosophy seems to me generally speaking to sin through arrogance... I can't help preferring champagne to ditch water, but I doubt if the universe does... The great act of faith is when a man decides that he is not God.... If I did come out of it [the universe] or rather if I am in it, I see no wonder that I can't swallow it. If it fixed my bounds, as it gives me my powers, I have nothing to say about its possibilities or characteristics, except that it is the kind of a thing (using this phraseology sceptically and under protest) that has me in its belly and so is bigger than I. It seems to me that my only promising activity is to make *my* universe coherent and livable, not to babble about *the* universe."

These passages define a consistent character. Judge Holmes has, at eighty-five, an intellectual youth that most men of forty cannot boast. He lives greatly in the brilliant young legal minds of today; believes that there are more men of promise in the present than in his own youth, receives their ideas with the courtesy, admiration, and speculative curiosity accorded to honoured guests. One of his favourite aphorisms is that the average life of an idea is fifteen years, another, that the literature of the past is a bore. Yet it is to be noted (since the laity persist in labelling him a radical) that, though he admires Proust and finds *Nize Baby* richly droll, he is more often to be seen, in that dignified Washington study of his, with a volume of eighteenth-century memoirs in his hand than with a daily newspaper. His own universe, material, spiritual, or intellectual, is not subject to perpetual revision. His economics, like his philosophy and his literary tastes, were pretty well settled in the twenties. The foundations of his legal thinking were laid in the thirties. His domestic happiness, which continues unbroken to this day, was established at the age of thirty-one — fifty-four years ago.

Meanwhile he was taking his plunge into the deep waters of the law. In 1869 James comments that "Wendell" is working too hard, taking no vacation. In 1870 he assumes the editorship of the *American Law Review*. In 1873 appears his important edition of Kent's *Commentaries*, and in the same year he becomes a member of the firm of Shattuck, Holmes and Munroe. But he cannot have given much time to practice, for the years from thirty to forty were a period of intensive research: a time of lonely and original productivity, often hinted at in his speeches, when he learned "to lay his course by a star which he has never seen"; and, feeling around him "a black gulf of solitude more isolating than that which surrounds the dying man," learned also to trust his "own unshaken will." During these years he offered his life to the law as completely as he had offered it to his country; and, losing it, found it again in his classic *Common Law*, which dates an epoch in American legal history.

The chapters were written first, as a Boston classic should be, in the form of "Lowell Lectures," and delivered in 1880. Published as a learned volume in 1881, the book was hailed by those competent to judge, both in America and in England, as a great and even a prophetic work. "The law embodies the story of a nation's development through the centuries," we read at the outset, "and it cannot be dealt with as if it contained only the axioms and corollaries of a book of mathematics." "The life of the law has not been logic; it has been experience." Together with the legal essays published before and after in the journals of the period, the book established, as Dean Pound has pointed out, that "functional" and relative view of the law now generally accepted as replacing the anatomical and morphological. Jurisprudence had been considered a self-sufficient science, with traditions all but God-given. Holmes discovered, by following a "right" or some other legal symbol to its early source, that the tradition was based often on some unreasoned survival that had lost all meaning. "The common law" — the phrase, from a later opinion, is famous — "is not a brooding omnipresence in the sky." Holmes emphasized the need of "thinking things rather than words." Pound says that he anticipated the teachers of today by thirty years or more. "The Epigoni could easily forget whose armour they were wearing and whose weapons they were wielding."

Justice Holmes's career as a jurist covers eras of rapid and organic social change and his eminence owes much to the insight — an insight very different from the piling of fact on fact — with which he has held the balance between history, experience, and timely necessity. He scrutinized the historical texts not for antiquarian reasons, not to discover an absolute — for in law, as in philosophy, he knew that he was not God — but for a concrete revelation of "man's destiny upon this earth." And looking back, he began to see the law at last as his constant and all-inclusive mistress: "A princess mightier than she who once wrought at Bayeux, eternally weaving into her web dim figures out of the ever lengthening past.... disclosing every painful step and every world-shaking contest by which mankind has worked and fought its way from savage isolation to organic social life."

The fame that resulted from *The Common Law* led to a professorship at the Harvard Law School, and before the same year, 1882, was out, to an appointment to the Massachusetts Supreme Bench — "a stroke of lightning which changed all the course of my life." On this bench Holmes spent twenty fertile years, Associate Justice till 1899, Chief Justice till 1902. He managed his court with a practised hand. But through these Boston years, as now, he wore an air of detachment which marked him, in his native town, with a kind of uncommonness, and so, in certain quarters, with a kind of suspicion. The "village" never queries its failures: Tom Blank is a queer duck, but he is the son of John Blank, the banker. Now Oliver Wendell Holmes, Jr., was never the son of the doctor. He was a peacock with shining plumage; he flew afield and consorted with famous English jurists, like Bryce and Sir Frederick Pollock. He climbed Alps with Leslie Stephen. He enjoyed free spirits, whether Back Bay brahmins, or Jews, or Roman Catholic priests. He invited a labour leader to his home. (Said the man: "You have changed my feeling. I used to see an enemy in every house.") With women he had the ease and gaiety of a Parisian or a Viennese, and sought their company. He was impatient with dullness and long-windedness, suggesting, when Chief Justice, that the lawyers of the state would greatly oblige him by taking a course in risqué French novels and so learn to speak in innuendo rather than at length. Yet, all the while, he was more absorbed by the discoveries of his own mind than by the privileges or limitations of the world about him. The mind accompanied his tall and elegant figure, in Boston as elsewhere, a pervasive and sceptical presence at every feast.

At a dinner given by the Boston Bar Association two years before the nomination of Oliver Wendell Holmes by Roosevelt to the Supreme Bench of the United States, the Chief Justice, in his responsive speech, asked himself what he had to show for this half lifetime that had passed — "I look into my book, in which I keep a docket of the decisions... which fall to me to write, and find about a thousand cases, many of them upon trifling or transitory matters... a thousand cases, when one would have liked to study to the bottom and to say his say on every question which the law ever presented.... We are lucky enough if we can give a sample of our best and if in our hearts we can feel that it has been nobly done."

This reads like a peroration: it was a prelude to the richest maturity of Holmes's life. Twenty-five more years on the Supreme Bench, a thousand more cases, and the Justice still on the firing line. Nearly half a century altogether that Holmes has been "living through," as judge, the wisdom whose foundations were laid before forty. The phrase is his partner, Shattuck's, spoken in a moment when it seemed to Holmes, after many honours, that he had tasted the full feast of the law: "Now you must live it through." One may relate the words to a comment of Dean Wigmore that Justice Holmes is the only one of the long list of judges of the American Supreme Courts who framed for himself a system of legal truths and general truths of life, and composed his opinions in harmony with the system.

The system was flexible because at bottom it was an attitude of tolerance based on insight into the complexity of human affairs. It has done more than any system of orthodoxies to make the Supreme Court a tribunal, as Professor Felix Frankfurter has said, where inevitable frictions between the individual and society, between the expanding powers of the states and nation could be fought out, instead of a deistic chamber operating by scholastic formulae. Holmes's wish has been ever to harmonize conflicting interests; to see where man's social desires come from, and where they are tending. (He maintains that the "little decisions" frequently reveal more of interstitial change in the tissue of the law than famous disputes about a telephone company.) Though he proceeds from the general to the particular, he repudiates finalities. Behind his generalizations are intuitions of reality.

Minority decisions have probably made Mr. Justice Holmes's reputation with the rank and file. Yet his famous dissents as well as his majority decisions have frequently run counter to his personal prejudice. "The decision of a gentleman," says a Boston friend. The decision of a poet would be equally true. For to Holmes a fire smoulders at the core of things which makes them for ever plastic and mobile. *Plus ça change, plus c'est la même chose*, says the French sceptic. Holmes feels that the universe may be "too great a swell to condescend to have a meaning," but he is bound to accept the temporary pattern. "The best test of truth is the power of the thought to get itself accepted in the competition of the market.... Every year, if not every day, we have to wager our salvation upon some prophecy based upon imperfect knowledge." The Justice never refuses such a wager, but, taking it up, he uses his mind as guide rather than as dictator. His conservative critics cannot point to a single self-interested opinion. His best friends cannot boast that he has ever decided things their way. Indeed, President Roosevelt, who appointed him because he imagined Holmes had "the right ideas" — i.e., T. R.'s — soon was taught a lesson in true judicial-mindedness by Holmes's dissent in Roosevelt's pet case against the Northern Securities merger.

Roosevelt used to urge young men to fight for *their* ideas. So did President Eliot, whose prejudices were the defect of his passion. Holmes the sceptic thinks one idea very like another, but Holmes the New Englander knows well the difference between one aim and another. So his counsel to young lawyers is: Do the handsome thing, young feller! Don't be content to be a lawyer, be a lawyer in the grand manner. If you are sailing an intellectual bark, prepare for rigours, and head for the Pole. Forget subjectivities, be a willing instrument. Wreak yourself upon life. "If you want to hit a bird on the wing, you must have all your will in a focus.... Every achievement is a bird on the wing." Key sentences which reveal a freedom from passion that has made the ideal judicial temper.

A judge of the Federal bench tells of driving with Justice Holmes to the Capitol one morning some years ago, in that neat brougham drawn by a fat cob, with a highly respectable coloured coachman on the box, in which Holmes used to be recognised on the Washington streets. The Justice had got out of the carriage and was striding off, vigorous and loose-limbed, toward the dome when the younger man called out humorously: "Do justice, sir!" Holmes wheeled: "Come here, young feller!" and then, "I am not here to do justice. I am here to play the game according to the rules. When I was at the bar and Lowell used to beat, I'd say to him: 'Judge, your result may be good, but it's another game I undertook to play. I gave you a thrust in tierce and you countered with a bag of potatoes over my head.'"

When in some summer hour of ease in his home at Beverly Farms on the Massachusetts shore — an unpretentious Victorian house, with gravel drive and formal flower-beds set with cannas and geraniums — he turns to Pepys's *Diary* — "this and Walpole's *Letters* are the two books if you don't want ideas, and don't want to waste your time" — he looks misty at the duel of two friends who fought for love. When he finds himself in the dentist's chair he recalls that fear of pain and rattling musketry which only the brave admit preceded the attack. His intimate talk still breaks into Civil War slang — "Shut your trap!" — his speeches and letters are full of war metaphors and allusions to this past which he says he "cannot bear to read about," perhaps because his remembered picture is too final to bear the intervention of historians, who describe how Sherman kept Lincoln waiting, and why great battles failed. Writing to Henry James, he is "firing away at high pressure with breech-loading speed." In a speech: "When once the dead fifers of thirty years since begin to play in my head, the laws are silent." In another: "Life is a roar of bargain and battle, but in the very heart of it there rises a mystical spiritual tone.... It transmutes the dull details into romance. It reminds us that our only but wholly adequate significance is as parts of the unimaginable whole."

This seasoned judge, this gallant gentleman of the old New England, is the most romantic of contemporary Americans. He starts off for the court every morning at 11.30 as if on an errand for the gods — whereas he is to listen to argument from 12.00 to 2.00; lunch from 2.00 to 2.30; sit again from 2.30 to 4.30. Judge Cardozo has used, of his sentences, the word phosphorescence. Always Holmes gives out light. When he returns from the court to the sober dignity of his old house on I Street — formerly it was on foot; now the Chief Justice is likely to drive him a part of the distance; but who can be sure that, disdaining his elevator, he will not still take his stairs two steps at a time? — he will be able, with the young secretary who guards the book-lined antechamber of his library, with the visitor, to search thought and make it glow. The secretary — a new jewel of the Harvard Law School every year — wears an exalted air. He must promise not to get engaged during the period. "But I reserve the right," says the Justice with a twinkle, "to die or resign." With this young mind the Justice twists the tail of the still recalcitrant cosmos, engages in legal disputation, reads his opinions for criticism as modestly as if he were a novice. Sometimes, but rarely, there is a point of law to look up. For Holmes carries the law in his head, as a prophet the words of the Lord. And the Justice, in his own fine and ornamental script, answers every personal letter scrupulously, almost within the hour. "My messenger is waiting." Off it goes. The eye that falls upon the delicate missive in the cheap plethora of the morning mail has found treasure. Every page has some metaphysical touchstone, some literary epigram or casual heresy. "I must read *Twelfth Night* once more — a little girl tells me Shakespeare is long in getting to the point. I think we take ourselves too seriously."

Mr. Justice Holmes, who has permanently enriched our law, our literature, our philosophy — of whom another distinguished judge has said: "There is Holmes — and there are all the other judges" — takes himself far less seriously than any good Rotarian. That blithe nonchalance, that true humbleness in the face of acknowledged human vanities, seems to his friends a part of his unerring taste. But it provokes distrust in those who need the support of the rolling platitudes of the Fathers. Holmes bears his critics no grudge. His courtesy to his fellows, like his generosity, is basic, and he has an innocent heart. When one sees his gracious figure outlined against his bookshelves full of classics, with their spaces for the books the Lord will omit mentioning, and their gaps for the books of the future, one is struck by its unquenchable youth. The face has a fine fresh colour, the voice, with its humorous vain echo of hesitation — mmm — that seems to set off the sparks in the eyes, has clarity and fervour. Maliciously it expunges the name of a popular New England poet from the slate of time, honestly it admits that gentlemen prefer blondes. But it will never allow our modern American idol, publicity, a niche in this hospitable library. If glory is here, she is hidden, diffused into a clear serenity, a scent of tender memory, a vital intellectual replenishment.

Yet do not think of Oliver Wendell Holmes as meagrely recompensed. He has found it well, he says, to have philosophy "the main wind of his life blowing from the side, instead of from behind." He has had his reward in the inspired performance of a daily task, in the constant siege of the eternal verities. Holmes was an infantry officer, at Ball's Bluff, but in the field of ideas he belongs to an arm more mobile. I see him as a light horseman, a fabulous skirmisher, a cavalier for all his "cold Puritan passion," who carries a pennon as well as a lance, and with it "that little flutter which means ideals."

HAROLD NICOLSON

THE Honorable Harold Nicolson is the son of a distinguished diplomat, Arthur Nicolson, Lord Carnock, whose career he relates in *The Portrait of a Diplomatist*. After leaving Oxford he was himself connected with the Foreign Office and served in diplomatic posts in Spain, Turkey and Persia. He was a member of the British Delegation to the Peace Conference, of which he wrote an illuminating study. He has written also of Tennyson, Byron and Swinburne. The present selection is from a volume of personal reminiscences and character sketches entitled *Some People* (1927). He has written more fully of Lord Curzon in a recent book of that title.

ARKETALL *

I

THE train was waiting at Victoria Station and there remained but three minutes to the time when it was scheduled to leave. In front of the Pullman reserved for Lord Curzon clustered the photographers, holding their hooded cameras ungainlily. The stationmaster gazed towards the barrier. Already the two typists were ensconced in the saloon: Sir William Tyrrell in the next compartment had disappeared behind a newspaper: the red despatch boxes were piled upon the rack, and on the linoleum of the gangway Lord Curzon's armorial dressing-case lay cheek by jowl with the fibre of Miss Petticue's portmanteau. I waited with Allen Leeper on the platform. We were joined by Mr. Emmott of Reuter's. "Is the Marquis often as late as this?" he inquired. "Lord Curzon," I answered, "is never late," and as I said the words a slight stir was observable at the barrier. Majestically, and as if he were carrying his own howdah, Lord Curzon proceeded up the platform accompanied by the police, paused for a moment while the cameras clicked, smiled graciously upon the stationmaster, and entered the Pullman. A whistle shrieked, a flag fluttered, the crowd stood back from the train and began to wave expectantly. It was then that I first saw Arketall. He was running with haste but dignity along the platform: in his left hand he held his bowler, and in his right a green baize foot-rest. He jumped on to the step as the train was already moving. "Crakey," said Arketall, as he entered the saloon.

2

Leeper and I sat opposite each other, going through the telegrams which had been sent down to the station from the Foreign Office. We sat there in the green morocco chairs of the Southern Railway: the marquetry on the panels behind us squeaked softly: the metal reading lamp chinked ever so slightly against the glass top of the table: to our right the houses of Purley,

* Copyright, Houghton Mifflin Company. By permission.

to our left the houses of Lewisham, passed rapidly below us in the autumn sunshine: someone came and told Leeper that he was wanted by Lord Curzon. I pushed the telegrams aside and leant back in my chair. Miss Petticue was reading the *Royal* magazine; Miss Bridges was reading her own passport: I had ample time to study Arketall.

He sat opposite to me at the end of the saloon. A man, I should have said, of about fifty-five; a tall man, at first impression, with a large naked face and large white bony hands. The fine Victorian modelling of his brow and chin was marred by a puffy weakness around the eyes and mouth: at certain angles the thoughtful refinement of his features suggested a drawing of Mr. Galsworthy by George Richmond: he would then shift his position, the illusion would pass, there would be a touch of red ink around the eyelids, a touch of violet ink about the lips: the pallor of his cheeks, the little bleached ridges around his mouth, would lose all suggestion of asceticism: when he leant forward in the full light of the window he had the appearance of an aged and dissolute pro-consul. His face, if he will forgive my saying so, seemed at such moments, self-indulgent. "That man," I reflected, "drinks."

I was well aware of the circumstances in which at the last Lord Curzon had engaged Arketall as his valet. Three days before we were due to leave for Lausanne, I had walked across to Carlton House Terrace with some papers that were urgently required. The Secretary of State was undergoing one of his recurrent attacks of phlebitis and I was taken up to his bedroom. I gave him the papers and he began to look at them, his lips, as was his wont, moving rapidly in a faint, but not unpleasant, whisper as he read the documents. My eyes wandered around the room. It was a small room with but one window which looked over the park: there was a white washing-stand, a servant's chest of drawers, and a cheap brass bedstead: the walls were papered with a simple pattern of sweetpea, and there were some photographs and a brown wooden hair-brush upon the dressing-table: on the small mantelpiece beside me I noticed a washing-list, a bone collar-stud, and two pieces of string. It was like a single bedroom in one of the Gordon Hotels: the only luxuries were an elaborate telephone affixed to the wall beside the bed, and a large box of crystallised fruits upon a side-table. The problem of Lord Curzon's personality, which had become almost an obsession to me, was enhanced by the sight of these accessories. My eyes wandered round the room in mute surprise. They returned finally to the figure in the bed. He was no longer looking at the documents, he was looking at me. "You are observing," he said, "the simple squalor of my bedroom. I can assure you, however, that my wife's apartments are of the most unexămpled magnificence." And at this his shoulders shook with that infectious laughter of his, that rich eighteenth-century amusement. "You have also," he continued, "observed the telephone. A disăstrous invention, my dear Nicolson, but it has its uses. Thus if I make upon this ivory lever a slight pressure to deflect it to the right, a mere *exiguum clinamen*, the whole secrets of my household are revealed to me. I overhear. This morning, for instance, when thus switched on (I think that is the correct term) to the universe, the bell rang. A voice said, 'Is that you, Alf, and 'ow's it feeling this morning? I 'ad a devil of a time coming in with the milk like that.' 'My dear young lady,' I ănswered, 'you are singularly mistaken. You are not speaking to Mr. Alfred Horlick, you are speaking to Lord Curzon himself.' The noises, I may say, which greeted me from the other end indicated that my words had produced an effect which was positively blăsting. And Horlick, an excellent valet, leaves me tomorrow."

Victim of such coincidences did Arketall sit there that morning in the Pullman with a small and incongruous bowler perched upon his head. He became slightly uneasy at my scrutiny: he reached for his suitcase and extracted *John o' London's Weekly*: I returned to my telegrams. The train skimmed tinkling and direct above the Weald of Kent.

3

Our arrival at Dover somewhat disconcerted Arketall. It was evident that he was proud of his competence as a travelling valet and anxious to win confidence by a brisk display of merit. Before the train had come to a standstill he was out on the platform, his face assuming the expression of "Leave everything to me." He was at once brushed aside by an inspector of police and two Foreign Office messengers. A phalanx of porters stood behind the inspector and leapt upon our baggage. The Foreign Office messengers seized the despatch boxes. Before Aketall had realised what had happened, Lord Curzon was walking slowly towards the boat chatting to the inspector with not unconscious affability. We strolled behind. Arketall came up to me and murmured something about passports. I waved him aside. There was a man beside the gangway with a cinematograph, the handle of which he began to turn gently as we approached. I glanced behind me at Arketall. His attitude had stiffened suddenly into the processional. "Arketall," I said to him, "you have forgotten the foot-rest." "Crakey!" he exclaimed as he turned to run towards the train. The other passengers were by then beginning to dribble through the pens in which they had been herded: I leant over the taffrail, watching the single agitation meeting the multiple agitation: widows hurrying along searching frantically in their reticules for those yellow tickets which would take them to Bordighera: Arketall, in acute anxiety, breasting this fumbling torrent with his bowler in his hand. A policeman touched me on the shoulder: he was holding the foot-rest. "His lordship generally requires this with him on the voyage." But by then Arketall was but a distant dome-shaped head bobbing against a panic stream. The little cords that tied the awning above me were pattering against the stays in an off-shore wind: in the gap between the pierheads a swell tumbled into foam, the inner harbour was wrinkled with scudding frowns: clearly we were in for a rough crossing. I took the foot-rest to Lord Curzon. He was sitting at his cabin table writing on loose sheets of foolscap in a huge flowing hand: his pencil dashed over the paper with incredible velocity: his lips moved: from time to time he would impatiently throw a finished sheet upon the chintz settee beside him. I adjusted the foot-rest. He groaned slightly as he moved his leg. He was much too occupied to notice my ministrations. I returned to the deck outside. A voice wailed to me from the shore: "It's gone; it's gone." Arketall flung into the words that forlorn intensity which throbs in the earlier poems of Lord Tennyson. I replied by reassuring gestures indicative that he should come on board. He was mopping his forehead with a large linen handkerchief: little white drops were still forming on it as he stood panting beside me. "Crakey," he gasped. "You had better go downstairs," I answered, "it is going to be rough." He closed one eye at me. "A little peg ay don't think." His words, at the moment, had little apparent meaning.

4

I did not see Arketall again until we were approaching Calais. I found him talking to Sir William Tyrrell outside the cabin. "Now Ostend," he was saying, "that's another question. Nane francs a day and no questions asked." "And no questions asked," he repeated looking wistfully at the sand dunes. The inspector came up to me with a packet of passports: he said he would hand them over to the *commissaire de police* on arrival. I took them from him, desiring to solve a problem which had often assailed me, namely, whether Lord Curzon made out a passport for himself. It was there all right — "We George Nathaniel," and then his name written again in the blank spaces. That amused me, and I was still considering the curious associations evoked by such official Narcissism when we sidled up to the Calais landing-stage. The gangway was immediately opposite Lord Curzon's cabin: on the pier below stood the Consul in a top-hat, and some French officials. I went in to Lord Curzon and told him we were arriving: he was still writing hard, and paid no attention: on the settee beside him was a pile of foolscap and at least twenty envelopes stamped and addressed. A muffled jerk showed that we were already alongside. Sighing deeply Lord Curzon addressed and stamped the last envelope. "Send me that valet man," he said. I fetched Arketall, telling him to hurry as the other passengers were being kept waiting: there they were on my left secured by a cord across the deck, a serried wedge of passengers looking their part. Lord Curzon emerged genially from his cabin at the exact moment the gangway was fixed: Arketall followed with the foot-rest: he stumbled as he stepped on to the gangway and clasped the rail. "Yes, I thought he was drunk," said Sir W. Tyrrell as we followed in our correct order. Lord Curzon was being greeted by the Representative of the French Republic. He moved slowly towards the train, leaning on his ebony cane; behind him zigzagged Arketall, clasping the green baize foot-rest. "Hadn't we better warn the Marquis...?" I asked. "Oh, he'll notice it soon enough." Lord Curzon had paused by the train to say a few chosen words to the Consul. Behind him stood Arketall, very rigid as to the feet, but swaying slightly with the upper part of body, bending slowly forwards and then straightening himself with a jerk. We left for Paris.

5

The next thirty-six hours are somewhat of a blur in my memory. I can recall M. William Martin at the Gare du Nord and other top-hats raised

simultaneously, and the flash and subsequent smell of magnesium wire lighting rows of white featureless faces beyond the barrier: a group of Americans
pausing to stare at us, cocktail in hand, as we entered the Ritz — "Why,
look, Mrs. Cameron..." and then the figure of Mr. Ellis, pale and courtly,
standing erect beside Lord Curzon in the lift: the corridor stretching white,
airless, unwindowed, the little lighted globes in the ceiling, the four detectives
grouped together, a bottle of Evian and two glasses on a Saratoga trunk. I
remember also a late dinner and Olivier ministering to Lord Curzon and yet
not ignoring us — Olivier blending with a masterly precision the servile and
the protective, the deferential and the condescending. And then the following day the familiar conference atmosphere: the crackle of Rolls-Royces
upon the raked and watered gravel in front of the Affaires Étrangères: the
slow ascent, maps, despatch boxes, politeness, up the wide stone staircase:
the two huissiers in evening dress and silver chains, that huissier with a white
nose, that other huissier whose nose is red; the first anteroom, gold and
damask, the second soft-carpeted anteroom, damask and gold: the Salle de
l'Horloge — green rectangles of tables, a perspective of pink rectangles of
blotting-paper: M. Poincaré advancing from a group by the furthest window:
the symmetry of alignment broken suddenly by papers on the green cloth,
protruding edges of maps, despatch boxes with open lids, secretaries bending from behind over their employers, the interpreter sitting with his pencils
and notebook by himself: the soft hum of traffic along the Quai d'Orsay.
   We lunched that day with Madame Poincaré and afterwards the discussions continued: at 4 P.M. the chandeliers leapt in successive tiers to brilliance; the white and scarlet benches in the window recesses were hidden one
by one as the silk curtains were drawn across them, and at five we had tea
and macaroons in the large white room beyond. At nine we returned exhausted to our dinner; we were all to start for Lausanne next morning at
7:30.
   We gathered sleepily at 7.5 A.M. in the hall of the Ritz: the revolving glass
door was clamped open and a man in a striped apron was shaking an india-
rubber mat out on to the Place Vendôme: the luggage had already preceded
us, the typists were sitting in the third motor rather pinched and blue: we
waited for Lord Curzon. At 7.16 A.M. he appeared from the lift escorted by
Mr. Ellis. He climbed slowly into the motor, falling back on to the cushions
with a sigh of pain: he beckoned to me: "I shall want my foot-rest." I dashed
back into the hotel to search for Arketall. Mr. Ellis was standing by the
staircase, and as I approached him I could hear someone pattering above me
down the stairs: at the last turning there was a bump and a sudden exclamation, and Arketall shot round and down the staircase like a bob-sleigh, landing beside me with his feet in the air and the foot-rest raised above him.
"Crakey," he remarked. We had by then only eleven minutes in which to
reach the Gare de Lyon. The three motors swayed and dashed along the
boulevards like fire-escapes to an incessant noise of Claxons. Then very
slowly, processionally, sleepily we walked up through the station towards
the platform. M. Poincaré in a black silk cap with a peak was waiting, a
little irritably I thought, beside the train. There was a saloon for the French

Delegation, a saloon for the British Delegation, and separating them a satin-wood drawing-room carriage and a dining-car. The large white clocks marked 7.29 as we entered the train. At 7.30 we slid out into the grey morning past a stiff line of saluting police and railway officials. Arketall was standing beside me: "Ay left me 'at behind," he remarked in sudden dismay. I had a picture of that disgraceful bowler lying upwards on the stair carpet of the Ritz: "Tiens," they would exclaim, "le chapeau de Lord Curzon." "You can get another," I answered, "at Lausanne." Miss Petticue came up to me holding a bowler. "They threw this into our motor as we were leaving the Ritz." I handed it in silence to Arketall.

6

For the greater part of that twelve-hour journey we sat in the drawing-room carriage discussing with our French colleagues the procedure of the impending conference: from time to time a Frenchman would rise and retire to the back of the train to consult M. Poincaré: from time to time Allen Leeper or I would make our way to the front of the train to consult Lord Curzon: outside his door Arketall sat on a spring bracket-seat which let down on to the corridor: he would stand up when we came, and the seat would fly up smack against the wood-work: Arketall looked shaken and unwell. Lord Curzon in his *coupé* carriage reclined in a dove-coloured armchair with his leg stretched out on the foot-rest. On the table beside him were at least thirty envelopes stamped and addressed: he did not appear to relish our interruptions.

Towards evening the lights were lit in that satin-wood saloon. We sat there, M. Barrère, General Weygand, Admiral Lacaze, Sir William Tyrrell, Laroche, Massigli, Allen Leeper and myself. The discussion had by then become desultory: from time to time a station would leap up at us from the gathering dusk, flick past the train in a sudden rectangle of illuminated but unfocussed shapes, be lost again in the brooding glimmer of the Cotes d'Or. We stopped at Pontarlier and telephoned to M. Mussolini. He answered from Locarno. He wanted us to dine with him that night at Vevey. We pattered up and down the platform conveying messages from M. Poincaré to Lord Curzon, from Lord Curzon to M. Poincaré. It was agreed that they would both proceed to Vevey, and then the train slid onwards down upon Lausanne. Lord Curzon in his dove-coloured arm-chair was slightly petulant. He was all for dining with M. Mussolini but would have preferred another night. "And why Vevey?" he said. "Why indeed?" I echoed. Lord Curzon sighed deeply and went on writing, writing. I left him and stood in the corridor. Arketall had pulled up the blind, and as the train jigged off to the left over some points a row of distant lights swung round to us, low lying, coruscating, white and hard. "Evian," I said to Arketall. "Ho indeed," he answered. Ten minutes later, the train came to rest in the station of Lausanne: there was a pause and silence: the arc-lamps on the platform threw white shapes across the corridor, dimming our own lights, which but a few minutes before had seemed so garish against the darkness. I returned to Lord Curzon's compartment. "I think," he said, "that you and Leeper had

better get out here. It is quite unnecessary for you to come on to Vevey."
"Oh, but, sir..." I protested. "Quite unnecessary," he repeated. I usually
enjoyed an argument with Lord Curzon, but there was something in his voice
which indicated that any argument at that moment would be misplaced. I
went and told Leeper: we both seized our despatch boxes and climbed down
on to the platform. Bill Bentinck, who had been sent on two days before to
complete arrangements, came up to us, immaculate, adolescent and so reliable. "There are four motors," he said, "and a lorry for the luggage."
"The Marquis isn't coming," I informed him, "he and M. Poincaré are going
on to Vevey to dine with Mussolini. They won't get back here till midnight." "Oh Lud," he exclaimed, "and there's a vast crowd outside and
the Mayor of Lausanne." "Lud," I echoed, and at that the slim presidential train began to slide past us towards the night and Mussolini. It was
only then that I noticed that the platform was empty from excess rather
than from lack of public interest: behind the barrier, behind a double row of
police, stretched the expectant citizens of the Swiss Confederation. On the
wide bare desert of the platform stood Leeper in a little brown hat, myself
in a little black hat, and Arketall in his recovered bowler: Miss Petticue: Miss
Bridges: pitilessly the glare of forty arc-lamps beat down upon our isolation
and inadequacy. We walked (with dignity I feel) towards the barrier: at our
approach the magnesium wire flashed up into its own smoke and there was
a stir of excitement in the crowd: somebody cheered: Arketall raised his
bowler in acknowledgment: the cheers were repeated: he held his bowler
raised at exactly the correct angle above his head: the Mayor advanced
towards him. I intervened at that moment and explained the situation.
The Mayor turned from me, a little curtly perhaps, and said something to
the police inspector. The wide lane which had been kept open for us ceased
suddenly to be a lane and became a crowd leaving a station: we left with it.
In a few minutes we were hooting our way under the railway bridge and down
to Ouchy.

7

The hall of the Beau Rivage was crowded with hotel managers and journalists. The former bowed ingratiatingly at our entry: the latter, who had
been sitting together at little tables drinking sherry, rose as a man to greet
us. There was Mr. Walter, and Mr. Pirrie Gordon, and Mr. Ward Price,
and Mr. Ryall. There were a great many others whom I did not know:
they looked diverse and yet convivial: I like journalists in principle and
was extremely sorry to disappoint them: at no moment of my life have I
desired so acutely to be important. Through all this gratuitous humiliation
I was conscious, however, of a thin thread somewhere within me of self-
esteem. I lay idly in my bath trying to work this vaguely apprehended fibre
of pleasure into the central focus of my consciousness, which seemed in its
turn wholly occupied by pain: I tested myself in successive phases: the platform, solid pain: the exit from the platform, pain unrelieved: it was only
when I went back to the phase in the motor that I ceased inwardly to wince.
Leeper, rather tired and thinking silently about Rumania, had sat beside

me; but Arketall, on the strapontin opposite, was full of talk. "Very civil," he had said, "these Swiss people. Now ay remember when ay was with a Columbian gentleman, we went to Zurich. You know Zurich, sir? Well, it was lake this..." Yes, Arketall at that moment had called me "Sir": up to that moment he had treated me solely as a colleague. Something in the force of my personality or in Lord Curzon's absence had elevated me to a higher level of regard. I was gratified on discovering this, and lay back in my bath thinking affectionately of Lord Curzon, who at that moment must have been descending on to the platform at Vevey. Sir William Tyrrell would have to carry the foot-rest: I did so hope that, if Lord Curzon got tired, Sir William would be able to soothe him down.

We dined downstairs in the restaurant. The remainder of the Delegation had assembled by earlier trains. There was General Burnett-Stuart with a military staff, and Sir Roger Keyes with naval assistants: there was Mr. S. D. Waley of the Treasury, and Mr. Payne of the Board of Trade: our own Secretariat was under the charge of Tom Spring Rice: there was a young man of extreme elegance who looked after the maps: there was an accountant and two further lady typists, and there was Mr. McClure for the Press. Undoubtedly we were an imposing collection. M. Duca and M. Diamandy, the Rumanian representatives, were seated at a further table; they came across to us and gave us caviare out of a flat tin box. I was pleased at this, mainly for Allen Leeper's sake, since, although in general the most stimulating of companions, he is apt at moments to brood about Rumania in silent suffering: with their arrival his pang had found a voice. It was a pleasant dinner if I remember rightly, and when it was over, Leeper and I ascended to put the final touches to Lord Curzon's suite. A large drawing-room on the first floor gazing from its three high windows upon the lake: on the left a dining-room, on the right a bedroom with baths beyond. The drawing-room was sprinkled with little white arm-chairs and tables looking very occasional: there were palms and chrysanthemums in a large brass jardinière: there was a little bean-shaped bureau, and on the walls some coloured prints of ladies in green riding-habits descending the steps of Chambord, Chenonceaux and Blois. We removed these pictures and secured a larger writing-table. We sent for more flowers, and arranged some newspapers and brandy and soda upon a side table. In the bedroom next door Arketall was unpacking several trunks: I looked in on him: he was not inclined for conversation, but hiccoughed gently to himself as he swayed, now over the Marquis' black suits and now over his grey. It was by then 11.30: a telephone message came in from Vevey to say that Lord Curzon should reach Lausanne about midnight: we descended to the hall to await his arrival.

8

At 12.10 there was a stir at the front door and the managers dashed to the entrance. They returned in triumph, escorting a small brown gentleman in a brown suit and very white shirt-cuffs. He carried a brown bowler in his left hand and his right was thrust into his waistcoat. The iris of his eyes was entirely surrounded by white, a phenomenon which I had hitherto observed only in the photographs of distinguished mesmerists. He was followed by three or four other gentlemen and two boy-scouts in black shirts. An electric tremor ran through the assembled journalists. "Mussolini," they whispered in amazement. I turned to Allen Leeper. "Really," I remarked, "that was very odd indeed." "It was," he answered.

Ten minutes later the glass doors again gyrated and Lord Curzon, magnificent and smiling, stood upon the threshold. Slowly and benignly he bowed to the managers: to the journalists he made a friendly gesture at once welcoming and dismissive: he proceeded to the lift. Seizing the green foot-rest from Sir William Tyrrell, I hurried through the crowd towards the staircase: "Tiens," exclaimed a French journalist, indicating the foot-rest, "le trône de Bagdad." I pushed past him and arrived on the first floor just as Lord Curzon was leaving the lift. He paused at the doorway of his apartment and surveyed it. "How ghăstly!" he sighed. He walked towards the window, pulled aside the yellow cretonne curtain, and gazed across to the lights of Evian. "How positively ghăstly," he repeated. We helped him out of his large Lovat mixture greatcoat; we propped the ebony against the white wall: we pulled up the least diminutive of the sixteen armchairs, and we placed the foot-rest in position. He sank back, sipped at a brandy-and-soda, sighed deeply, and then embarked on a narrative of the Vevey conference.

Ah, those Curzonian dissertations! No small thing has passed from my life now they are silenced. As if some stately procession proceeding orderly through Arcs de Triomphe along a straight wide avenue: outriders, escorts, bands; the perfection of accoutrements, the precise marshalling of detail, the sense of conscious continuity, the sense of absolute control. The voice rising at moments in almost histrionic scorn, or dropping at moments into a hush of sudden emotion; and then a flash of March sunshine, a sudden dart of eighteenth-century humour, a pause while his wide shoulders rose and fell in rich amusement. And all this under a cloud of exhaustion, under a cloud of persistent pain.

The glamour of this particular discourse was somewhat dimmed for me by anxiety on behalf of Arketall. The door into the bedroom was open, and there came from it the sound of cupboards opening and shutting, the sound at intervals of a hiccough inadequately suppressed. "We had by then," Lord Curzon was saying, "reached the last point of the six which I have grouped under category A. Mussolini had as yet not fully grasped my intention; with the assistance of that dilapidated marmoset who acts as his mentor I regained my point of departure: the status of pertinenza, I explained..."

"'Ic" came loudly from the adjoining room. Lord Curzon paused. My eyes met those of Allen Leeper and I motioned to him to close the door.

"... the status of pertinenza, I explained, was in no way identical with what we regard as domicile. Poincaré, who on all such points, is exăsperatingly punctilious, insisted on interrupting. He maintained..."

"'Ic," said Arketall from the next room. Leeper had by then reached the doorway and closed it abruptly. "What was that?" said Lord Curzon, turning a petulant eye in my direction. "It is your servant, sir, unpacking some clothes."

"He maintained that the *droit d'etablissement* ..." The procession had reformed and continued its stately progress: it continued until 2 A.M.: the Marquis then dismissed us: he said he had letters to write as well as a report for the Cabinet; he had by then to our certain knowledge been working without interruption for nineteen hours; and yet in the morning there was a report of eight pages for the Cabinet, and on the table in the passage twenty-two letters addressed and stamped — or, as he himself would have said, "stamped and directed."

9

Next morning there was to be a meeting to continue the conversations begun at Vevey. We arranged a large table in Lord Curzon's room and placed paper and pencils at intervals. The Marquis sat at his desk writing rapidly. Punctually at eleven both doors were flung open by Arketall. "Excellence Poyncarry," he bawled, "and General Wiggand." Lord Curzon rose genially to meet them, and conducted them to the table. They sat down and waited for M. Mussolini. General Weygand began drawing little squares and triangles on the sheet before him. M. Poincaré rose and walked up and down the room in obvious impatience, flicking his pince-nez against his thumbnail. From time to time he would pause at one of the windows, looking at the grey fog which crept among the conifers. Lord Curzon kept on sending me with messages to the Duce urging him to come. I did not execute these missions, knowing them to be of no avail, but I had several pleasant chats in the passage with Mario Pansa, who was acting as M. Mussolini's personal secretary. From time to time I would return to Lord Curzon's room and assure them all that M. Mussolini was on his way. I would then resume my talks with Mario, whose gay Harrovian chatter relieved a situation which but for him I might have found a trifle tense. When, at 11.35, M. Mussolini actually did come, he came very quickly. Pushing Arketall aside, His Excellency shot into the room like a brown thunderbolt, stopped short, clicked his heels, bowed and exclaimed, "Je vous salue, Messieurs." They then sat down at the table, and we sat behind. The maps were spread in convenient places; the interpreter sharpened his pencil. The Vevey conversations were resumed.

That evening M. Poincaré returned to Paris, and M. Mussolini to Rome: Lord Curzon was left pre-eminent over a Conference consisting mostly of Ambassadors. There was M. Barrère and M. Bompard for France: and for Italy the aged Marchese Garroni: Ismet Pasha, deaf and boyish, coped with a large and resentful Turkish delegation: M. Venizelos, troubled but conciliatory, spoke for Greece: at moments, even, the mezzo-soprano of M. Tchicherine would quaver into our discussion. And as the days passed, Arketall, to my despair, entered visibly on a decline.

10

We found it difficult to induce Lord Curzon to treat the problem seriously. On the second morning Arketall, in helping his master on with his socks, had slipped and fallen. "Arketall," Lord Curzon had remonstrated, "you are either very ill or very drunk." "Both, m' Lord," Arketall had answered. Lord Curzon was so pleased with this response that his affection for Arketall became unassailable. We grew seriously uneasy. I found him one morning standing by the side-table in the dining-room pouring liqueur-brandy into a claret glass. He winked slowly at me and placed a shaky forefinger beside his nose. I was incensed at this gesture of confederacy: I told Bill Bentinck that the Marquis must again be warned. But unfortunately that morning Marchese Garroni had, in Lord Curzon's presence, mistaken Arketall for Sir Roger Keyes, had seized both his hands and had assured him in a torrent of Genoese French how great a debt, how unforgettable a debt, Italy owed to the noble and generous British Navy. Lord Curzon was so delighted by this incident that our warnings fell on even deafer ears. A catastrophe was imminent, and it came.

The Hôtel Beau Rivage at Ouchy consists of two wings joined together by a large suite of ball-rooms and dining-rooms. In the evening the natives of Lausanne and the visitors undergoing either education or treatment would gather in the foyer to listen to the band, to watch the dancing, and to observe the diplomatists and journalists passing backwards and forwards on hurried and mysterious errands. Saturday was the gala night, and on Saturdays I would generally slip down after eleven and sit there admiring the couples jerking together in the ball-room. There was an American woman of great distinction, who wore a stomacher of diamonds: there was a greedy-looking Cuban woman in a wheeled basket chair: there was Prince Nicholas of Russia, who was staying at a neighbouring pension and who danced with all the young ladies. It was a pleasant sight, and on the second Saturday I induced Lord Curzon to come and watch it. He stood there by the entrance to the ballroom leaning on his ebony cane, and smiling genially at the diverse couples who jigged and twirled before him. I observed the American lady syncopating towards us in the arms of a distinguished-looking gentleman in evening dress. I called Lord Curzon's attention to her, warning him to observe her stomacher as she passed. He glanced towards her and grasped my arm. "Surely," he said, "surely that can't be Arketall?" It was Arketall, and he recognised us at the same moment. In trying to wince away from the cold inquiry in Lord Curzon's eye, he slipped between the legs of the American lady and brought her down upon him. Lord Curzon had turned abruptly and was walking back across the foyer. I ran after him. "I think," he said, "that Arketall had better leave. He had better leave early to-morrow."

I returned to the ball-room and accompanied Arketall to his room. He was somewhat dazed by his experience and he followed me meekly. I told him that there was a train at 7.30 next morning and he had better leave by it. He plunged under the bed and began pulling out his portmanteau: it refused to move and he tugged at it viciously: three empty bottles of Benedictine and a bottle of Grand Marnier shot out into the room, followed by the trunk. Arketall sat on the floor, nodding at the empty bottles. "You must pull yourself together," I said. "You should at least assist us to minimise the scandal which your conduct has caused." "Never," he hiccoughed vaguely, "not no more."

II

I did not witness his departure. I merely heard next morning that he had gone. While having breakfast I received a message that Lord Curzon wished to see me urgently. I found him in his dressing-gown. He was half angry and half amused. "That indefinite Arketall," he said, "has stolen my trousers." "Not *all* your trousers?" I asked in some confusion. "Yes, *all* of them, except these." Lord Curzon was wearing his evening trousers of the night before. I glanced at my watch. There was still an hour before the meeting of the Conference, but by this time Arketall must have reached Pontarlier. I ran for Bill Bentinck and told him to telephone to the frontier police: "Don't say trousers," I shouted after him, "say 'quelques effets.'" I then secured the manager and proceeded to Arketall's room. We looked in, over and under the cupboard and into the chest of drawers: I peered under the bed; there were three more bottles of Benedictine against the wall, but otherwise the space was empty. The manager and I looked at each other in despair. "C'est inénarrable," he muttered, "complètement in'-é-narrable." I sat down wearily on the bed to consider our position. I jumped up again immediately and pulled back the bed-spread. Upon the crumpled bed-clothes lay a trouser-press bursting with Lord Curzon's trousers. I sent the manager to stop Bill Bentinck telephoning; myself I clasped the trouser-press and returned in triumph to Lord Curzon. He was seated at his writing-table, his pencil dashing across sheets of foolscap, his lips moving. I stood there waiting. When he had finished four or five sheets and cast them from him he turned to me indignantly. His face relaxed into a smile and then extended into that irresistible laugh of his, that endearing boyish sense of farce. "Thank you," he said, "I shall now complete my toilet. There will only be Leeper to dinner tonight, and as a reward I shall give you my cele-brated imitation of Tennyson reciting 'Tears, idle tears.'"

He kept his promise. It was an amazing performance. We expressed our admiration and our gratitude. A sudden wave of depression descended upon Lord Curzon. "Ah, yes," he sighed, "ah yes. I know. All that was years ago, when I was young and could still láugh at my elders. But all young men are remorseless. You will go upstairs this evening and cháff me behind my back. You will give imitations in after life of the old buffer imi-tating Tennyson. And so it continues." He sighed deeply. And then he grinned. "I am sorry," he said, "for Arketall. I liked that man."

THE FORMAL ESSAY: SCIENCE, SOCIAL SCIENCE, EDUCATION

THE use of the term "essay" for the formal and organized presentation of subject matter represents a more intellectual type of reflection. Pope entitled his philosophical poems "An Essay on Criticism" and "An Essay on Man." The establishment of the great reviews, *The Edinburgh* and *The Quarterly*, at the beginning of the nineteenth century gave opportunity for the writers of reviews which, taking a published work of importance as a starting point, proceeded to make an elaborate and independent survey of the whole subject involved. Macaulay's essays are the best examples of this type. Today the magazine has largely replaced the old-fashioned review as the vehicle for the presentation of serious subjects, treated more briefly and in a style for general reading. Frequently the magazine article which may be regarded in its tentative form as an essay passes over into a more assured and permanent existence as a chapter in a book. Illustrations have been selected from science, social science, and education.

The chief contemporary interest in science is the result of Professor Einstein's theory of relativity, replacing Newton's conception of the universe, and the new discoveries in physics relating to the structure of the atom, the so-called quantum theory. The effects of these changes in outlook at both ends of the scale, the inordinately vast and the infinitesimally little, on the conception of human knowledge and attitude toward existence, on philosophy and religion, are considered in the articles by Professor Bridgman and Mr. Ward.

One of the chief problems of human association today occurs in connection with national and racial differences for which science suggests a basis of consideration in Miss Benedict's *The Science of Custom*. Another set of problems is the result of the economic increase of productive capacity through the extension of machinery leading to dislocation of labor and consequent unemployment. Professor Boas's *In Defence of Machines* deals with the subject in a spirit of rational inquiry. A third social problem, which is as old as organized government itself, is the relation of the individual to the state, of liberty to social control. This subject has been especially important in English and American political thought and has given rise to many notable declarations, such as Milton's *Areopagitica*, John Stuart Mill's *On Liberty*, Thoreau's *Civil Disobedience*, among which Professor Becker's essay takes its place.

Writing in 1916, George Herbert Palmer said that "books on education are usually addressed to teachers, as those on sight to opticians." Whatever may have been true twenty years ago, the observation is not true of essays on college education today. Discussions of the purpose of education at the higher levels have left the academic platform and got into the magazines and thence into the public consciousness, at least at the more literate plane. In a confusing world, the question of the intellectual shape which the next generation is to take on is of more than "academic" interest.

In the essays which follow, it will be observed that the writers agree in assuming that the thinking process is to be trained. In "Self-Cultivation in English" Palmer shows that he who lacks words, lacks thoughts. President Meiklejohn declares that the business of the liberal college is to create and protect the intellectual life. This may seem like a platitude, but the primary purpose of college education has been so overlaid with well-meant secondary purposes it is important to return to its original idea. It is not sufficient for the faculty to believe in the intellectual life; the student body must believe in it also.

These two essays are included here not merely because what they say has permanent value, but because of the manner in which they say it. It is interesting to note that both of them were originally written as public addresses. In writing a public address on so vast and complex a topic as education the author cannot hope to exhaust his subject, but must decide to discuss a single phase of it; and of that single phase he can say only three or four important things. The rest of his manuscript will have to be built around these central ideas. His problem is to make general principles clear; but he can hope to do so only by being simple and direct and, wherever possible, specific, using illustration, witticism, and quotation. The tone throughout is that of the best type of public discourse; easy yet not undignified, colloquial but not vulgar, straightforward but not bare and lean and thin. The whole man speaks; and the man who discusses education must himself be a cultured and educated man.

PERCY WILLIAMS BRIDGMAN

THE academic career of Percy Williams Bridgman (1882–   ) has been spent at Harvard, first as student, then as teacher of Physics; now as Hollis Professor of Mathematics and Natural Philosophy. His *Logic of Modern Physics* is a contribution which only the scientist can evaluate; but the evaluation scientists have placed on his work enhances the lay reader's confidence in and appreciation of Dr. Bridgman's more popular writings. The present selection was published in *Harper's Magazine*, March, 1929.

THE NEW VISION OF SCIENCE *

THE attitude which the man in the street unconsciously adopts toward science is capricious and varied. At one moment he scorns the scientist for a highbrow, at another anathematizes him for blasphemously undermining his religion; but at the mention of a name like Edison he falls into a coma of veneration. When he stops to think, he does recognize, however, that the whole atmosphere of the world in which he lives is tinged by science, as is shown most immediately and strikingly by our modern conveniences and material resources. A little deeper thinking shows him that the influence of science goes much farther and colors the entire mental outlook of modern civilized man on the world about him. Perhaps one of the most telling evidences of this is his growing freedom from superstition. Freedom from superstition is the result of the conviction that the world is not governed by caprice, but that it is a world of order and can be understood by man if he will only try hard enough and be clever enough. This conviction that the world is understandable is, doubtless, the most important single gift of science to civilization. The widespread acceptance of this view can be dated to the discovery by Newton of the universal sway of the law of gravitation; and for this reason Newton may be justly regarded as the most important single contributor to modern life.

The point of view for which Newton is responsible is well exemplified by the remark often made that every particle of matter in the universe attracts to some extent every other particle, even though the attraction is almost inconceivably minute. There is thus presented to the mind a sublime picture of the interrelatedness of all things; all things are subject to law, and the universe is in this respect a unit. As a corollary to this conviction about the structure of the universe, an equally important conviction as to man's place in the universe has been growing up; man feels more and more that he is in a congenial universe, that he is part and parcel of everything around him, that the same laws that make things outside him go also make him go, and that, therefore, he can, by taking sufficient pains, understand these laws. These two theses so closely related — that the world is a world of order and that man can find the guiding motif of this order — have come to be the tacit cardinal articles of faith of the man of science, and from him have diffused through the entire social structure, so that now some such conviction essentially colors the thinking of every educated person. It is to be emphasized that the justification for this conviction is entirely in experience; it is true that, as man has grown older and acquired more extensive acquaintance with nature and pondered more deeply, he has been increasingly successful in reducing the world about him to order and understandability. It has been most natural to generalize this experience into the conviction that this sort of thing will always be possible, and to believe that as we delve constantly deeper we shall always be able to give a rational account of what we find, although very probably the difficulties will become continually greater.

The thesis of this article is that the age of Newton is now coming to a close, and that recent scientific discoveries have in store an even greater revolution in our entire outlook than the revolution effected by the discovery of universal gravitation by Newton. The revolution that now confronts us arises from the recent discovery of new facts, the only interpretation of which is that our conviction that nature is understandable and subject to law arose from the narrowness of our horizons, and that if we sufficiently extend our range we shall find that nature is intrinsically and in its elements neither understandable nor subject to law.

The task of the rest of this article is twofold. In the first place I shall try to give some suggestion of the nature of the physical evidence and of the reasoning that has forced the physicist to the conclusion that nature is constituted in this way. This task is by no means easy; for not only is it impossible to indicate more than very partially the physical evidence, but it is often necessary to compress into a few sentences steps in the reasoning that can be completely justified only by long and difficult mathematical or logical analysis. The second part of the task is to envisage a few of the far-reaching consequences on the whole outlook of mankind of the acceptance of the view that this is actually the structure of nature. This aspect of the situation can be appreciated without a detailed grasp of the preliminary analysis.

II

The new experimental facts are in the realm of quantum phenomena. Comparatively little has been written for popular consumption about this new realm which has opened in the last fifteen years. The man in the street has been much more interested in relativity, which to him has seemed extremely interesting and revolutionary. Occasionally, however, there has filtered down to him the news that nearly all the theoretical physicists are occupied with a new order of phenomena which they find very much more exciting and revolutionary than any in the realm of relativity. For after all is said and done, the practical effects of relativity, measured in dollars and cents or in centimeters and grams, are exceedingly small, and require specially designed experiments executed by men of the highest skill to show their existence at all. The phenomena with which quantum theory deals, on the other hand, are of the greatest practical importance and involve the simplest aspects of everyday life. For example, before the advent of quantum theory no one could explain why a tea kettle of water boiling on the stove should not give out enough light in virtue of its temperature to be visible in the dark; the accepted theories of optics demand that it should be visible, but every burned child knew that it was not.

One reason that the man in the street has not sensed this new domain is that it is much more difficult to explain than relativity; this is partly due to the nature of the subject, and partly also to the fact that the physicist himself does not understand the subject as well. I shall not in this article rush in where the angels have not ventured, but it is, nevertheless, necessary to try to give a glimmering of an idea of what it is all about.

Although all the phenomena of ordinary life are really quantum phenomena, they do not begin to stand out unequivocally in their quantum aspect and admit of no other interpretation until we have penetrated very far down into the realm of small things and have arrived at the atoms and electrons themselves. It must not be pretended that the nature of the quantum phenomena met in this realm of small things is by any means completely understood; but a suggestive characterization of the general situation is that atomicity or discontinuity is an even more pervading characteristic of the structure of the universe than had been previously supposed. In fact the name, "quantum," was suggested by the atomicity.

We were a long time in convincing ourselves of the atomic structure of ordinary matter; although this was guessed by the poets as early as the beginning of the Christian era, it was not generally accepted as proved, even by physicists, until the beginning of this century. The next step was the discovery of the atomic structure of electricity; there are indivisible units of positive and negative electricity, and the atoms of matter are constructed of atoms of electricity. This situation was not even guessed until about 1890; the proof and acceptance of the doctrine have taken place within the memory of the majority of the readers of this article. Finally comes the discovery that, not only is matter doubly atomic in its structure, but that there is an atomicity in the way in which one piece of matter acts on another. This is perhaps best understood in the case of optical phenomena. It used to be thought that light was infinitely subdivisible — that I could, for example, receive at pleasure on the film of my camera either the full intensity of the sun's radiation, or, by interposing a sufficiently small stop, that I could cut the intensity of the light down to anything this side of nothing at all. This is now known not to be true; but the light which we receive from the sun is atomic in structure, like an almost inconceivably fine rain composed of indivisible individual drops, rather than like the continuous flood of infinitely subdivisible radiation that we had supposed. If I close the stop of my camera too much I may receive nothing at all on the film, or I may receive a single one of the drops in the rain of radiation, but there is no step between one drop and nothing. The recognition that radiation has this property means that in some respects we have come back very close to Newton's ideas about light.

The proof that this is the structure of light can be given in many ways. Perhaps the most illuminating for our purpose is that discovered by Arthur

Compton, for which he received the Nobel prize. Compton's discovery consisted in finding that the drops of radiation behave in certain ways like the material drops of ordinary rain; they have energy and mass and momentum, which means that when they collide with matter they behave in some respects very much as ordinary bodies do. The laws which govern the interaction or collision of ordinary bodies are known to any graduate of a high-school course in physics; he could calculate what would happen after two billiard balls had collided provided we would tell him exactly how each of the balls was moving before the collision, and what were the elastic properties of the materials of which the balls are composed. In making the calculation he would use, among other things, the two fundamental principles of the conservation of energy and the conservation of momentum. Now Compton showed that what happens when a drop, or better a bullet, of radiation collides with an electron is also governed by the same two fundamental principles. The proof consisted in showing that the way in which the electron rebounds is connected with the way in which the bullet rebounds by equations deduced from these principles; this is one of the features which makes Compton's discovery of such a fundamental importance.

But Compton's experiment contains another feature, and it is this which seems destined to revolutionize the thinking of civilization. Go back to the billiard-ball analogy: An expert billiard player can, by proper manipulation of the cue ball, make the two balls rebound from the collision as he wishes; this involves the ability to predict how the balls will move after collision from their behavior before collision. We should expect by analogy to be able to do the same thing for a collision between a bullet of radiation and an electron; but the fact is that it never has been done and, if our present theories are correct, in the nature of things never can be done. It is true that, if someone will tell me how the electron bounces away, I can tell, on the basis of the equations given by Compton's theory, how the bullet of radiation bounces away, or conversely; but no one has ever been able to tell how both will bounce away. Billiards, played with balls like this, even by a player of infinite skill, would degenerate into a game of pure chance.

This unpredictable feature has been seized and incorporated as one of the corner stones in the new theory of quantum mechanics, which has so stirred the world of physicists in the last three years. It has received implicit formulation in the "Principle of Uncertainty" of Heisenberg, a principle which I believe is fraught with the possibility of greater change in mental outlook than was ever packed into an equal number of words. The exact formulation of the principle, which is very brief, is framed in too technical language to reproduce here, but I shall try to give the spirit of the principle. The essence of it is that there are certain inherent limitations to the accuracy with which a physical situation can be described. Of course we have always recognized that all our physical measurements are necessarily subject to error; but it has always been thought that, if we took pains enough and were sufficiently clever, no bounds could be set to the accuracy which we might some day achieve. Heisenberg's principle states, on the other hand, that the ultimately possible accuracy of our measurements is limited in a curious and unsuspected way. There is no limit to the accuracy with which we can describe (or measure) any one quality in a physical situation, but if we elect to measure one thing accurately we pay a price in our inability to measure some other thing accurately. Specifically, in Compton's experiment, the principle states that we can measure the position of the electron as accurately as we choose, but in so doing we must sacrifice by a compensating amount the possibility of accurately measuring its velocity. In particular, if we measure with perfect accuracy the position of the electron, we have thereby denied ourselves the possibility of making any measurement at all of its velocity.

The meaning of the fact that it is impossible to measure exactly both the position and velocity of the electron may be paradoxically stated to be that an electron cannot have both position and velocity. The justification of this is to be found in the logical analysis of the meaning of our physical concepts which has been stimulated by the relativity theory of Einstein. On careful examination the physicist finds that in the sense in which he uses language no meaning at all can be attached to a physical concept which cannot ultimately be described in terms of some sort of measurement. A body has position only in so far as its position can be measured; if its position cannot in principle be measured, the concept of position applied to the body is meaningless, or in other words, a position of the body does not exist. Hence if both the position and velocity of the electron cannot in principle be measured, the electron cannot have both position and velocity; position and velocity as expressions of properties which an electron can simultaneously have are meaningless. To carry the paradox one step farther, by choosing whether I shall measure the position or velocity of the electron I thereby determine whether the electron has position or velocity. The physical properties of the electron are not absolutely inherent in it, but involve also the choice of the observer.

Return to the analogy of the billiard ball. If we ask our high-school physicist what he must be told before he can predict how the billiard balls will rebound after collision, he will say that, unless he is told both how fast the balls are traveling when they collide, and also what their relative positions are at the moment of collision he can do very little. But this is exactly the sort of thing that the Heisenberg principle says no one can ever tell; so that our high-school computer would never be able to predict how a bullet of radiation and an electron behave after collision, and no more could we. This means that in general when we get down to fine-scale phenomena the detailed results of interaction between the individual elements of which our physical world are composed are essentially unpredictable.

This principle has been built into a theory, and the theory has been checked in many ways against experiment, and always with complete success. One of the consequences of which the man in the street has heard a good deal is that an electron has some of the properties of waves, as shown so strikingly in the experiments of Davisson and Germer. Of course no one can say that some day a fact may not be discovered contrary to the principle, but up to the present there is no evidence of it; and it is certain that something very much like this principle, if not this principle exactly, covers an enormously wide range of phenomena. In fact the principle probably governs every known type of action between different parts of our physical universe. One reason that this principle has not been formulated before is that the error which it tells us is inherent in all measurement is so small that only recently have methods become accurate enough to detect it. The error is unimportant, and indeed immeasurably small when we are dealing with the things of ordinary life. The extreme minuteness of the effect can be illustrated again with the billiard balls. Suppose that at the instant of collision the position of the balls is known with an uncertainty no greater than the diameter of a single atom, a precision very much higher than has ever been attained. Then the principle says that it is impossible to measure the velocity of the balls without a related uncertainty; but on figuring it out we find that this uncertainty is so small that after the lapse of one hundred thousand years, assuming a billiard table large enough for the balls to continue rolling for one hundred thousand years, the additional uncertainty in the position of the balls arising from the uncertainty in the velocity would again be only the diameter of a single atom. The error becomes important only when we are concerned with the ultimately small constituents of things, such as the action between one atom and another or between an atom of radiation and an electron.

III

It is easy to see why the discovery that nature is constituted in this way, and in particular is essentially unpredictable, has been so enormously upsetting. For the ability to predict a happening is tied up with our ideas of cause and effect. When we say that the future is causally determined by the present we mean that if we are given a complete description of the present the future is completely determined, or in other words, the future is the effect of the present, which is the cause. This causal relation is a bilateral relation; given the cause, the effect is determined, or given the effect, the cause may be deduced. But this means, in the particular case that we have been considering of collision between a bullet of radiation and an electron, that the causal connection does not exist, for if it did the way in which the electron rebounds after the collision would be determined, that is, it could be predicted, in terms of what happens before the collision. Conversely, it is of course impossible to reconstruct from the way in which the electron and the radiation rebound the way in which they were moving before collision. Hence the rebound of the electron is not causally connected with what goes before.

The same situation confronts the physicist everywhere; whenever he penetrates to the atomic or electronic level in his analysis, he finds things acting in a way for which he can assign no cause, for which he never can assign a cause, and for which the concept of cause has no meaning, if Heisenberg's principle is right. This means nothing more nor less than that the law of cause and effect must be given up. The precise reason that the law of cause and effect fails can be paradoxically stated; it is not that the future is not determined in terms of a complete description of the present, but that in the nature of things the present cannot be completely described.

The failure of the law of cause and effect has been exploited by a number of German physicists, who have emphasized the conclusion that we are thus driven to recognize that the universe is governed by pure chance; this conclusion does not, I believe, mean quite what appears on the surface, but in any event we need not trouble ourselves with the further implications of this statement, in spite of their evident interest.

One may be sure that a principle as revolutionary in its implications as this, which demands the sacrifice of what had become the cardinal article of faith of the physicist, has not been accepted easily, but there has been a great deal of pondering and searching of fundamentals.

The result of all this pondering has been to discover in the principle an inevitableness, which when once understood, is so convincing that we have already almost ceased to kick against the pricks. This inevitableness is rooted in the structure of knowledge. It is a commonplace that we can never know anything about anything without getting into some sort of connection with it, either direct or indirect. We, or someone else, must smell the object, or taste it, or touch it, or hear it, or see it, or it must affect some other object which can affect our senses either directly or indirectly, before we can know anything about it, even its existence. This means that no knowledge of any physical property or of even mere existence is possible without interaction; in fact these terms have no meaning apart from interaction. Formerly, if this aspect of the situation was thought of at all, it would have been dismissed as merely of academic interest, of no pertinence at all, and the justification of this would have been found in the supposed possibility of making the inevitable interaction as small as we pleased. The defender of the old point of view might have flippantly remarked that a cat may look at a king, by which he would have meant that the act of observation has no effect on the object. But even in the old days a captious critic might have objected to this easy self-satisfaction by pointing out that light exerts a pressure, so that light cannot pass from the king to the cat without the exercise of a certain amount of mechanical repulsion between them. This remark of the captious critic now ceases to be merely academic because of the discovery that light itself is atomic in structure, so that at least one bullet of radiation must pass if any light at all passes, and the king cannot be observed at all without the exertion of that minimum amount of mechanical repulsion which corresponds to a single bullet.

This evidently alters the entire situation. The mere act of giving meaning through observation to any physical property of a thing involves a certain minimum amount of interaction. Now if there are definite characteristics associated with the minimum interaction, it is conceivable that no observation of anything whatever can be made without entraining certain universal consequences, and this turns out to be the case. Let us return again to the useful billiard-ball analogy. What must our high-school calculator know in order completely to calculate the behavior of the balls after collision? Evidently, if he is to give a complete description of the motion, that is, give in addition to direction and velocity of motion the exact time at which the balls are in any particular location, he must know how long the collision lasts.

This means that the act of collision itself must be analyzed. This analysis is actually possible, and in fact rapid-moving pictures have been taken, showing in detail how the balls are deformed during their contact together.

Returning now to the collision between a bullet of radiation and an electron, in order to determine completely the behavior after collision we must similarly analyze the details of the process of collision. In particular, if we want to predict where the electron is after collision we must analyze the collision sufficiently to be able to say how fast the electron is moving at each instant of the collision. But how shall this analysis be made? If the analysis means anything, it must involve the possibility of observation; and observation involves interaction; and interaction cannot be reduced below a minimum. But the collision, or interaction, between the electron and radiation that we are analyzing is itself the minimum interaction. It is obvious that we cannot discover fine details with an instrument as coarse as the thing that we are trying to analyze, so that the necessary analysis of the minimum interaction can never be made, and hence has no meaning, because of our fundamental dictum that things which cannot in principle be measured have no meaning. Therefore, the act of collision cannot be analyzed, the electron and radiation during collision have no measurable properties, and the ordinary concepts, which depend on these properties, do not apply during collision, and have no meaning. In particular, the ordinary concept of velocity does not apply to the act of collision, and we are prepared to expect something curious as the result of the collision. In fact, the detailed working out of the theory shows that the meaninglessness of velocity during the act of collision carries with it the consequence that the electron emerges from the collision with a certain nebulosity or indefiniteness in properties such as position, which according to the old point of view depend on the velocity, and it is precisely this nebulosity which is described in Heisenberg's principle.

The infinitesimal world thus takes on a completely new aspect, and it will doubtless be a long while before the average human mind finds a way of dealing satisfactorily with a situation so foreign to ordinary experience. Almost the first necessity is a renunciation of our present verbal habits and of their implications. It is extraordinarily difficult to deal with this new situation with our present forms of expression, and the exposition of this paper is no exception. The temptation is almost irresistible to say and to think that the electron *really* has *both* position and velocity, only the trouble is that our methods of measurement are subject to some limitation which prevents us from measuring both simultaneously. An attitude like this is justified by all the experience of the past, because we have always been able hitherto to continue to refine our methods of measurement after we had apparently reached the end. But here we are confronted by a situation which in principle contains something entirely novel, and the old expectations are no longer valid. The new situation cannot be adequately dealt with until long-continued familiarity with the new facts produces in our subconsciousness as instinctive a grasp as that which we now have of the familiar relations of everyday experience.

IV

The implications of this discovery are evidently most far-reaching. Let us first consider the scientific implications and, in particular, the implications for physics. The physicist is here brought to the end of his domain. The record of physics up to the present has been one of continued expansion, ever penetrating deeper and deeper, and always finding structure on a finer and finer scale beyond previous achievement. Several times in the past even eminent physicists have permitted themselves the complacent announcement that we were in sight of the end, and that the explanation of all things was in our hands. But such predictions have always been set at naught by the discovery of finer details, until the average physicist feels an instinctive horror of the folly of prediction. But here is a situation new and unthought of. We have reached the point where knowledge must stop because of the nature of knowledge itself: beyond this point meaning ceases.

It may seem that we are getting back pretty close to the good Bishop Berkeley, but I think that actually nothing could be wider of the mark. We are not saying that nothing exists where there is no consciousness to perceive it; we are saying that existence has meaning only when there is interaction with other existence, but direct contact with consciousness need not come until the end of a long chain. The logician will have no trouble in showing that this description of the situation is internally self-contradictory and does not make sense; but I believe that, nevertheless, the sympathetic reader will be able to see what the situation is, and will perhaps subscribe to the opinion that to describe it the development of a new language is necessary.

The physicist thus finds himself in a world from which the bottom has dropped clean out; as he penetrates deeper and deeper it eludes him and fades away by the highly unsportsmanlike device of just becoming meaningless. No refinement of measurement will avail to carry him beyond the portals of this shadowy domain which he cannot even mention without logical inconsistency. A bound is thus forever set to the curiosity of the physicist. What is more, the mere existence of this bound means that he must give up his most cherished convictions and faith. The world is not a world of reason, understandable by the intellect of man, but as we penetrate ever deeper, the very law of cause and effect, which we had thought to be a formula to which we could force God Himself to subscribe, ceases to have meaning. The world is not intrinsically reasonable or understandable; it acquires these properties in ever-increasing degree as we ascend from the realm of the very little to the realm of everyday things; here we may eventually hope for an understanding sufficiently good for all practical purposes, but no more.

The thesis that this is the structure of the world was not reached by armchair meditation, but it is the interpretation of direct experiment. Now all experiment is subject to error, and no one can say that some day new experimental facts may not be found incompatible with our present interpretation; all we can say is that at present we have no glimmering of such a situation. But whether or not the present interpretation will survive, a vision has come to the physicist in this experience which he will never forget; the possibility that the world may fade away, elude him, and become meaningless because of the nature of knowledge itself, has never been envisaged before, at least by the physicist, and this possibility must forever keep him humble.

When this view of the structure of nature has once been accepted by physicists after a sufficiently searching experimental probe, it is evident that there will be a complete revolution in the aspect of all the other physical sciences. The mental outlook will change; the mere feeling that boundaries are set to man's inquiry will produce a subtle change of attitude no less comprehensive in its effects than the feeling, engendered by Newton's conquest of celestial mechanics, that the universe was a universe of order accessible to the mind of man. The immediate effect on scientific inquiry will be to divert effort away from the more obviously physical fields back to the fields of greater complication, which have been passed over by the physicist in his progress toward the ultimately little, especially the field of biology.

Another important result of the realization of the structure of the world is that the scientist will see that his program is finite. The scientist is perhaps only a passing phase in the evolution of man; after unguessable years it is not impossible that his work will be done, and the problems of mankind will become for each individual the problem of best ordering his own life. Or it may be that the program of the scientist, although finite, will turn out to need more time than the life of the world itself.

But doubtless by far the most important effect of this revolution will not be on the scientist, but on the man in the street. The immediate effect will be to let loose a veritable intellectual spree of licentious and debauched thinking. This will come from the refusal to take at its true value the statement that it is meaningless to penetrate much deeper than the electron, and will have the thesis that there *is really* a domain beyond, only that man with his present limitations is not fitted to enter this domain. The temptation to deal with the situation in this way is one that not many who have not been trained in careful methods of thinking will be able to resist — one reason is in the structure of language. Thought has a predisposition to certain tendencies merely because of the necessity of expressing itself in words. This has already been brought out sufficiently by the discussion above; we have seen how difficult it is to express in words the fact that the universe fades away from us by becoming meaningless without the implication that there really is something beyond the verge of meaning.

The man in the street will, therefore, twist the statement that the scientist has come to the end of meaning into the statement that the scientist has penetrated as far as he can with the tools at his command, and that there is something beyond the ken of the scientist. This imagined beyond, which the scientist has proved he cannot penetrate, will become the playground of the imagination of every mystic and dreamer. The existence of such a domain will be made the basis of an orgy of rationalizing. It will be made the substance of the soul; the spirits of the dead will populate it; God will lurk in its shadows; the principle of vital processes will have its seat here; and it will be the medium of telepathic communication. One group will find in the failure of the physical law of cause and effect the solution of the age-long problem of the freedom of the will; and on the other hand the atheist will find the justification of his contention that chance rules the universe.

Doubtless generations will be needed to adjust our thinking so that it will spontaneously and freely conform to our knowledge of the actual structure of the world. It is probable that new methods of education will have to be painfully developed and applied to very young children in order to inculcate the instinctive and successful use of habits of thought so contrary to those which have been naturally acquired in meeting the limited situations of everyday life. This does not mean at all that the new methods of thought will be less well adapted than those we now have to meet the situations of everyday life, but on the contrary, since thought will conform to reality, understanding and conquest of the world about us will proceed at an accelerated pace. I venture to think that there will also eventually be a favorable effect on man's character; the mean man will react with pessimism, but a certain courageous nobility is needed to look a situation like this in the face. And in the end, when man has fully partaken of the fruit of the tree of knowledge, there will be this difference between the first Eden and the last, that man will not become as a god, but will remain forever humble.

HENSHAW WARD

The books of Henshaw Ward (1872–1935) fall into two groups. The first of these is concerned with English Composition and Grammar and the teaching of them, which he himself practiced for many years. The second deals with a subject of immediate concern to every thinking person today: the implications of science, and their bearing on the beliefs of the layman. The first in this group, *Evolution for John Doe* was followed by *The Circus of the Intellect* (*Thobbing*) which aroused such violent discussion when it appeared. His most recent volume is *Builders of Delusion*.

SCIENCE HAS NOT GONE MYSTICAL *

I

IF AN inquiring microbe should ask me to explain what I know about the sun, he would understand part of my description. He could realize the distance almost as well as I can, because he is only a million times shorter than I am and could easily imagine his own length multiplied by that number. He could understand the heat of the sun about as well as I can, for his sensitiveness to heat is much the same as mine. I should find him an intelligent listener.

But when I began to tell him how the sun *looks*, he would give a disdainful wriggle and tell me to quit being mystical. In his mind there is nothing that corresponds to *looks*. For he has no sense of sight, no apparatus like an eye which can receive light rays and convert them into a feeling that he is acquainted with a distant object. Light rays do produce an effect on his consciousness, but only a vague, diffused feeling of discomfort. They do not create pictures in him. If I try to explain what they do to me — try to show by analogies what a picture of the sun is like — he will think that I have gone beyond common sense and am babbling metaphysics. It is not merely his ignorance that makes him unable to learn from me, but his unconsciousness of being ignorant.

So, in a similar way, if I could put a human inquiry about space to a seraph, and if he obligingly began to explain, I should soon find his talk intolerable. For he would have to say something like this: "Space is the force which brings time closer to my mind. It makes a separation between time and matter, so that I can avoid matter and fly only in time. Don't you see?" This would not sound like common sense. I should be impatient of it, not so much because of my ignorance as because of my unconsciousness that I am utterly ignorant of what space can do for a seraph. I have never been conscious that space is a force. It doesn't make any more contact with my mind than light does with a microbe's mind. Space, for me, is just emptiness; it is only a name for the fact that pieces of matter are not all together. I am powerless to imagine that space *is something* — a great force, a phase of matter that acts on the mind of a seraph and reveals to him a portion of the universe to which

* From *The Atlantic Monthly*, August, 1933. By permission of publisher and author.

my senses can make no response. I can no more perceive my ignorance of space than an oyster can realize that he does not know what rainbows look like.

It is the human unawareness of time and space that recent science is struggling with. It has found a clue to them which was furnished by an experiment with light, and it is trying to follow the clue, gropingly and falteringly, by the use of mathematics. Science is not at all sure of what it is doing or where it is going, but it is keeping hold of the clue and tracing its unimaginable course to — somewhere, perhaps. We can see these mathematicians working in the bright sunshine, fumbling about where eyesight is of no avail. They have no sixth sense that tells them anything about time and space — any more than a microbe has a sense of sight. They can see, everywhere, out through unnumbered galaxies that are millions of light years away, but they are not able to feel the time and space that are directly perceived by a seraph. They are groping for some slight, indirect knowledge, reaching here and there in the light that can reveal nothing. Hence their occupation seems mystical, not to say ludicrous; for they are putting out mathematical feelers *beyond their senses*.

II

If we wish to understand what the physicists have been feeling for, during the past twenty years, we must first be assured that this most recent form of science is not different in purpose or nature from what it has always been. It is exactly the same sort of mental operation that Huxley described eighty years ago, in his address at St. Martin's Hall "On the Educational Value of the Natural History Sciences": —

Science is nothing but trained and organized common sense, differing from the latter only as a veteran may differ from a raw recruit.... The vast results obtained by science are won by no mystical faculties, by no mental processes, other than those which are practised by every one of us, in the humblest and meanest affairs of life.... The man of science simply uses with scrupulous exactness the methods which we all, habitually and at every moment, use carelessly.

It was easier for Huxley to convince his audience of this truth in 1854 than it would be now. For during the past twenty years the scientists have discharged such a barrage of fanciful possibilities that they have not seemed to talk common sense. They have bewildered us with the free will of electrons, with a finite but unbounded universe, with expanding space, with space that would be destroyed by too much matter, with time that is only a phase of space, with matter that is only a form of energy, with the chance that a flame might turn water to ice, with the probability that a million monkeys leaping about on a million typewriters would reproduce the books in the British Museum. If Huxley were brought back to life in 1933 and, without any preparation, suddenly confronted with all those notions, he might well suspect that science had deserted its five senses and gone on a picnic with its fancies. He might naturally fear that common sense has become old-fashioned and that science is now a kaleidoscope of incredibilities.

But as soon as his first bewilderment was over he would recover his composure, ask for a cup of coffee, and request some professor at the Imperial College of Science to give him an account of how the weird things originated. He would not assume that science had gone crazy in the twentieth century, but would prepare himself to understand what its strange new language meant. The strangeness would not perturb him, for he would know that nothing recent and complicated could be essentially more mysterious than the oldest and simplest experience that primitive man had of the universe in which he found himself.

When an eye makes contact with a bull that is grazing on a hill a mile away, it gives us experience of a mystery so profound that anything proposed by relativity is simple in comparison. No philosopher or psychologist or physicist has the least understanding of what that contact is like: of what the distance is, or the motion is, or of what the correspondence is between the thing on the hill and the impression somewhere within a human skull. But we live *unconscious of this deepest ignorance*. We assume that of course the passage of a bull to a brain is a commonplace that may be taken for granted. Not till we hear of "a bull in the brain" do we recognize anything that needs explaining.

Huxley was aware that the simplest and oldest mystery is the deepest one; and he would not expect the most fantastic discovery of twentieth-century science to be harder to comprehend. He might say to the professor: "Let's put your free-will electrons and your typewriting monkeys to one side for the present. Begin at the beginning. Tell me what originated these quaint playthings of the intellect. For all their grotesqueness, I presume they are just phases of the same old common sense that I used to lecture about."

And the professor might begin with a matter-of-fact narrative like the following.

III

The first inkling that a human being ever got of space — an element of the universe which our senses cannot perceive — was detected by an American professor of physics at the Case School of Applied Science in Cleveland, in 1887. His name was Albert Abraham Michelson. He was as hard-headed and non-mystical an experimenter as ever wore a dirty apron in a laboratory. He had completed an investigation with a set of mirrors and a big stone that was floated in a vat of mercury. There had been no philosophy about his work. His apparatus and his reasoning were so simple in principle that any freshman in the Case School could understand them. Every freshman, like every professor of physics in the world at that time, would have bet a hundred to one that the result of the experiment would be positive. But it was negative. The negative result was just as astonishing to Michelson as it was to everybody else. It was as puzzling as if he had found that a man can row upstream as fast as he can row downstream.

That way of describing the situation is a literal statement of what had happened. Until Michelson's experiment was completed, the human mind had always known that when two speeds are added together they produce the sum of the speeds. If, for example, I am on an escalator which is taking me upstairs at the rate of four feet a second, and if I am in a hurry and add my walking speed of five feet a second to the speed of the escalator, I move upstairs at the rate of nine feet every second. A stop watch will prove that I actually do add the two speeds. Any boy can measure the addition of the speed of his rowing to the speed of a river current, and find that he moves ahead at the sum of the two speeds. If a man stands on the deck of a steamer and throws a baseball forward, the ball moves with the speed of the throw plus the speed of the steamer. Everybody knows that it does. Nobody can conceive that the sum of two motions is anything but the sum of them. Yet Michelson had found — if his measurements were correct — that something in his basement laboratory, impelled by two motions at once in the same direction, *had the speed of only one motion.*

The something was light. Michelson had measured the speeds of rays of light in many directions. His reasoning was this: If a light ray, traveling with its own proper speed, moves in the direction of the earth's motion through space, it will have the sum of the speeds; if it moves in a direction opposite to the earth's course, it will — like a man rowing upstream — have its speed diminished by the amount of the earth's speed. What could be simpler or more certain? For measuring the speed of the light rays he had an instrument so sensitive that it would have detected differences far smaller than the earth's motion around the sun would give. Thus he felt no doubt that by a series of measurements he could tell the direction of the earth's movement through space. The speed would be highest when the light traveled in the same direction as the earth; it would be slowest when the light traveled in the direction opposite to the earth's. The reasoning was flawless; the delicacy and reliability of the apparatus were beyond question. Yet the light did not respond as anything else on earth would have had to respond. Its speed remained the same at all angles, and would not reveal the direction of the earth's movement.

Later experiments of a far more elaborate kind only proved that the first one had been correct. No observer has ever been able to show any variation in the speed of light. Here is a fact of a different sort from anything else ever investigated by the human mind. It seemed at first a rather slight fact — remarkable, of course, and probably significant, but with nothing revolutionary about it.

As soon as it was established, the mathematicians began to reckon with it. "If," they said in effect, with all their symbols, "this is the fact about light, how must our explanations of other facts be adjusted to it?" For science has never found two facts in conflict; the mind cannot conceive that two facts could be in conflict. Science is a process of discovering how facts fit together. When science learned how light behaves, it inquired, "What must be the nature of the space and time in which such behavior is possible?" The result of fitting the new fact to the old ones was some breath-taking conclusions about space and time. The mathematics led far beyond our senses. But at one point after another the astronomers were able, most ingeniously, to check up the speculations by actual measurements of what their eyes could see. The Theory of Relativity was born, and grew, and increasingly persuaded the physicists, helped them forward, never failed them — until now it is the master conception of recent science.

It was not, in its origin, and has never become, philosophical. It made its triumphant way against the most skeptical opposition, because it was everywhere shown to correspond to common sense. It has given a hint of what lies beyond the senses, a little glimpse into the nature of time and space. Huxley would find it fitting perfectly into his definition of science. It has in it no tincture of the mystical.

IV

Another part of recent science has the appearance of being sheer mysticism — the field where men explore the insides of atoms. The space within an atom is so inconceivably minute that it is beyond the senses, beyond even the utmost stretch of imagination. Atoms are so small that a milllion of them placed side by side in a row would reach no farther than the thickness of the sheet of paper on which these words are printed. Yet rigorously careful scientists have contrived ways of putting out their mathematical tentacles into the infinite smallness of an atom, have measured the forces that sweep about there with inconceivable velocities, and have reported details of this sub-microscopic universe. After twenty years of painstaking exploration, they have unanimously agreed that they have been in contact with definite, measurable realities. They have given the world various hair-raising descriptions of the components of atoms.

The pioneer work was done by Max Planck at the beginning of this century. His genius was so deep that Einstein considers him the wisest and most fertile of modern physicists. His great achievement has been the Quantum Theory. In 1927 the brilliant Heisenberg extended this theory to a description of conditions inside an atom. Before we hear it we had best recall what "the inside of an atom" is like.

An atom, despite its inconceivable smallness, is a stable, lawful unit of matter. No one has ever intimated that it has any mystical qualities. Just what is inside of it nobody knows. In 1926 the general conception was that an atom is composed of definite particles of electricity whose size is extremely small compared with the diameter of the atom; by 1927 the fashion had changed, and the internals of the atom were conceived as a system of waves. But the older fashion is still respectable and will not be misleading. The particles are called electrons. They are estimated to be a hundred thousand times smaller than the atom. So the atom is mostly composed of empty space, in which electrons whirl with a rapidity that is too dizzying to name here. It would distract us from our proper business. What we have to fix our minds on is the fact that the study of electrons is a system of mathematics which deals with uncomprehended motions of electric particles that are extremely small compared with the infinitesimal dimensions of the atom.

How the Heisenbergs and Schrödingers secure their data for the exploration of electrons has never been explained to ordinary human beings, but we may feel assured that there is no nonsense about their work. The reason for assurance is that every scientist is eager to expose, pitilessly, the errors of any other scientist. So long as they agree that they are actually dealing in a common-sense way with actual formulas that can be verified, we can trust them. They are in complete agreement — at least for the present — about the actuality of electrons.

In 1927, Heisenberg announced, as a scientific principle, what every physicist accepts as indisputable, what is said on high authority "to rank in importance with the principle of relativity" — namely: Both the position and the velocity of an electron cannot be determined; the more accurately its position is determined, the less accurately its velocity can be determined, and vice versa.

V

The ingenious and delightful Eddington at once seized upon this principle, and from it deduced a mystical conclusion: Since the motions are "indeterminate," they are not caused as motions are caused in large bodies; therefore an electron may act spontaneously; and therefore "physics is no longer pledged to a scheme of deterministic law." Human will may be free from mechanism.

If this conclusion had been proposed to Huxley as soon as he returned to life, he would probably not have survived the shock, but would have had to quit breathing our twentieth-century scientific air. For the very foundation of science in Huxley's day was this law of cause and effect. In the very year when Michelson made his experiment, Huxley wrote: "All physical science starts from certain postulates. One of these is the law that nothing happens without a cause." Yet only forty years later it had become good form to declare that everything inside the atom happens without a cause.

If this statement had been confined to atoms, the world would never have felt much excitement about it. "Who cares whether the parts of an atom are lawless?" we should have said. "The poor particles haven't any real liberty, at that; for they are closely confined within a diameter of one sixty-three-millionth of an inch. Let the little things have their freedom." There would have been no human interest in the anarchy that was limited to such infinitesimal dimensions. But Eddington had discovered within the bounds of the atom a hope for human freedom. He issued — as a scientist reasoning scientifically — an emancipation proclamation for the human will. The philosophers read with glad amazement that their souls were not automatons acting solely by mechanical laws, but were uncontrolled, spontaneous, *free!* "Glory be to science!" said the philosophers. "Blessings be upon Eddington!" cried the theologians. A flood of sermons and essays conveyed to an eager populace the glad tidings that now the human will was free. Halleluiahs were the order of the day.

No frantic vagary of the mind of man has ever been more entertaining than this one, or has exhibited more clearly what emotional animals we are — what incurably superstitious animals. For six clamorous years we have been shouting the slogan of our new-found freedom: "Great is the Indeterminacy of Heisenberg!" The suddenness with which this theory arose, and the violent change it wrought in the modes of thinking, may be gauged by this one fact: The article on "Free Will" in the latest edition of the *Britannica* was prepared too early to make use of the atomic gospel; it therefore sounds flat and antiquated, because it lacks all the zest with which this most ancient puzzle is now brought to a picturesque solution.

Eddington's logic has been echoed with plaudits by all manner of intellectual people. It has been accepted by a few unwary scientists. But it has become stale and disreputable logic in 1933. Bridgman had patiently exploded it in the very year when Eddington preached it. In 1930, J. E. Turner showed that Eddington had merely been confused by two meanings in one word: "indeterminate" may mean "not caused," or it may mean "we cannot determine." In 1931, Bertrand Russell agreed that Eddington had merely been deceived by the first meaning, when he should have seen that the second was the true one. "The principle of indeterminacy," said Russell, "does nothing whatever to show that the course of nature is not determined." C. G. Darwin, in *The New Conceptions of Matter*, delivered a similar verdict: "It has been suggested that the new outlook will remove the well-known philosophical conflict between the doctrines of free will and determinism, and it has been welcomed by many for that reason. I would personally offer a most strenuous opposition to any such idea." In 1932, Herbert Dingle published a book which scornfully enlarged upon Eddington's error; the great Planck declared, "I have not been able to find the slightest reason which would force us to give up the assumption of a law-governed universe"; and Einstein was quoted in the same book as saying, "The idea of a free will in nature is preposterous." Before the year was out a philosopher, R. W. Sellars, in his most severely reasoned *The Philosophy of Physical Realism*, spoke thus of Eddington's epistemology: "I have the impression that physics is already getting its balance in these matters. The uncertainty is in our knowledge and not in the event.... There is no need of grasping at electronic spontaneity as at a straw." Early in 1933 appeared H. Levy's *Where is Science Going?* — a book which was written to show "the vicious features" of Eddington's argument from "a fictitious world of isolated electrons." And three months later, in *The New Background of Science*, Jeans concluded his masterly discussion with these words: "When we represent objects beyond our senses in space-time, their *apparent absence of determinism* may be merely the price we pay for trying to force a real world of nature into too cramped a framework."

So it appears that a few scientists, philosophizing beyond their knowledge, have veered toward mysticism. There is no evidence that real science has ever swerved an inch out of its road of accepting only what can be unanimously verified — and retaining it only so long as it continues to be verified.

VI

"The road of science" — what does that mean? It means that a bundle of electrons, calling itself "man," finds itself in a universe of energy and space and time, and tries to make acquaintance with its surroundings. It can receive impressions from one kind of energy, light; and so it says to itself, "I see the universe." But it has no understanding of what light is, or what seeing is. And as for space and time, man can receive only the most vague and indirect impressions from them. He tries to feel out these forces with his spectroscope and his mathematics — touches them, and calculates his touchings very ingeniously. But his senses cannot take hold of them directly. He has made some progress, so that now he can measure his length against his surroundings. In one direction he is so many quadrillion times the size of an intricate bundle of force that he has named an electron. In the opposite direction he measures a great aggregate of force that he names a star, and he finds that the star is the same number of quadrillion times larger than himself. This is something. He has reason to be proud of himself.

But he has gone only a fraction — he cannot make any guess at how small a fraction — of the whole way of knowledge that science is striving to cover. On either hand stretches an infinity; one he names "small," and the other he names "large." But he has no way of telling whether the large dimension is any greater than the small one; for both alike reach endlessly on and on beyond his power to follow the clues of the symbols that represent them. The more he advances, the greater seems to be the distance that unrolls before him. At present he has no intimation of any boundary to his search. He bumps into an obstruction that shows he must choose another direction, or he suddenly swoops forward a great way through clear space. But the impediment may reveal something; the far flight may land him in perplexity. He cannot find out what he is exploring or whether his road has any end. He can only push ahead, impelled by the curiosity that is instinctive in him.

Always, as he squirms along through the unknown, he imagines what may lie ahead, makes pictures for himself. Sometimes these pictures have been the luckiest aids he can contrive for himself — as when some genius fancied the earth going round the sun, or when Newton sketched a design of gravitation. It is this imagination of man, forever running in advance of the senses, which has shown him how to prospect for knowledge, which is now luring the astronomers onward beyond their calculations to places where more headway may be possible.

If these mental pictures are recognized as mere possibilities, they are harbingers that prepare a way through the mysteries. But more often they have been regarded as true just because they are so lifelike. "I see a picture," said Lamarck, "of a giraffe striving to reach higher and higher for food. By continued exercise the animal increases its power to elongate its neck, and this power is inherited by its children. I see all animals improving themselves in various ways by their efforts to fulfill their desires, and I see these improvements inherited by offspring. Look at the great picture that my mind shows you: organisms continually altering themselves for the better and passing on their acquirements to their descendants. This *is* the way animals developed into higher forms." The mind of Lamarck had seen a vivid picture and then declared that it represented reality. The minds of all men naturally do the same. They see an image take shape; they suppose that the image *is* a reality.

Science acts differently. It scrutinizes a mental picture with interest, and remarks: "This *may* be like reality. Let's test it." It tested Lamarck's vision by asking, "Where is some example of the kind of evolution that you describe?" For a century it sought the example. None was ever found. So evolution was discarded. When Darwin offered another picture, science was far more skeptical, even hostile. But the new form of evolution was gradually found to correspond more and more with all the realities that zoologists and botanists could discover. It stands until someone can discredit it — not a day longer.

"Evolution" is a word. It names a discarded notion; it also names an accepted theory. Within this one term there are two opposite meanings. We simians prefer to argue about the word and not trouble ourselves to sort out the meanings. Thus, we infallibly tend toward mysticism. It is the business of science to elude the tyranny of words, to examine what lies behind the words — to escape from mysticism.

VII

Many of our mental pictures are enshrined in words that contain opposite meanings. One of these is "faith." "I have a faith in the law of cause and effect," said Huxley. And a religious man says, "I have faith in a personal God." Whereupon some logician declares, "Religion rests on the same foundation as science; both rest on faith." It seldom occurs to us to ask for definitions of the word. If we defined Huxley's faith, and then defined religious faith, we should see that they have nothing in common. For one is universally verified; the other is agreed upon by only a small fraction of the race.

"I have an experience of God," says Eddington. Straightway the word "experience" forms a picture in millions of minds, and they seem to see a reality of science in contact with God. Then another astronomer announces, "I have an experience of Betelgeuse"; and, as soon as all other astronomers have examined his evidence and corroborated it, the world accepts as real a picture of a great mass of tenuous vapor 260,000,000 miles in diameter. Each man has used the same word, "experience"; our simian brain therefore assumes that the experience of God is the same thing as the experience of a red star; and we conclude that science is just as mystical as a mystical religion. A pair of definitions of the two utterly different uses of the term would reveal that the two experiences have nothing in common.

Thirty years ago, a prominent Yale physicist said to a colleague, "There is nothing of which we have so much knowledge as we have of the ether." Fifteen years later, the physicists discarded the ether and threw it into the lumber room of bygone hypotheses. This would be a pretty story for a college debater to use if he was arguing that science relies on faith as much as religion does. But there is no parallel between a belief in ether and a religious belief. The two kinds of mental operations are confused only because the same word is used for both. The mind of the physicist who thought he knew so much about ether worked thus: "All the evidence we have indicates that there is a substance pervading all space; all competent students agree about the evidence; not one of them can conceive that the ether does not exist; I shall therefore accept it as a probability until there is some new reason for doubting it; I am ready any day to consider any objection that comes from a reliable source." But a man who believes in Hell uses his mind quite differently. He says: "Only a fraction of the religious experts, and only a much smaller fraction of university professors, believe in Hell, but their disbelief means nothing to me; I feel assured that the majority is wrong."

The difference in those two attitudes is the difference between science and any other way of using the mind. No scientist ever "believed in" gravitation as a force of attraction. Every physicist has known that gravitation is a mental picture; he has thought that it probably corresponds with reality; but he has been ready at any hour to throw the picture away as soon as it became doubtful. Most physicists quickly threw it away as soon as they understood Einstein's theory of 1915.

A respectable scientist does not "believe in" the theory of probability which teaches that once in so many quintillion times a hot fire will cause a kettle of water to freeze, or that once in so many sextillion times a band of monkeys on a battery of typewriters would produce Washington's Farewell Address. He agrees that these mathematical conceptions may correspond to some form of reality, but he sees a stronger probability that the mathematicians have confused two different meanings of the word "probability."

Of course, there is a sense in which science "believes." It does not deny that there is some objective reality in the universe, or that our brain receives impressions from this reality, or that all motions of molecules are produced by some cause, or that heat always passes from a warmer body to a cooler one. Nor does science deny that the mind may be different from matter, or that a personal God directs the universe. But neither does science affirm these statements. For denying and affirming are warlike actions, suitable only for creatures who are unconscious of their ignorance, who are devoted to private dreams and empty logic. Science is the activity of persons who realize what ineffable mystery is, who are curious to explore it.

RUTH FULTON BENEDICT

RUTH FULTON BENEDICT (1887–   ) is now lecturer and assistant professor at Columbia, where she took her degree in Anthropology. She has also been since 1923 editor of the *Journal of American Folklore*. The material presented in her numerous articles and her recent book, *Patterns of Culture*, is based not only on literary research but also on extended field trips to the Indian settlements in the Southwest. In addition to her scientific work, Dr. Benedict has published a considerable amount of verse.

THE SCIENCE OF CUSTOM *

ANTHROPOLOGY is the study of human beings as creatures of society. It fastens its attention upon those physical characteristics and industrial techniques, those conventions and values, which distinguish one community from all others that belong to a different tradition.

The distinguishing mark of anthropology among the social sciences is that it includes for serious study other societies than our own. For its purposes any social regulation of mating and reproduction is as significant as our own, though it may be that of the Sea Dyaks, and have no possible historical relation to that of our civilization. To the anthropologist, our customs and those of a New Guinea tribe are two possible social schemes for dealing with a common problem, and in so far as he remains an anthropologist he is bound to avoid any weighting of one in favour of the other. He is interested in human behaviour, not as it is shaped by one tradition, our own, but as it has been shaped by any tradition whatsoever. He is interested in the great gamut of custom that is found in various cultures, and his object is to understand the way in which these cultures change and differentiate, the different forms through which they express themselves, and the manner in which the customs of any peoples function in the lives of the individuals who compose them.

Now custom has not been commonly regarded as a subject of any great moment. The inner workings of our own brains we feel to be uniquely worthy of investigation, but custom, we have a way of thinking, is behaviour at its most commonplace. As a matter of fact, it is the other way around. Traditional custom, taken the world over, is a mass of detailed behaviour more astonishing than what any one person can ever evolve in individual actions no matter how aberrant. Yet that is a rather trivial aspect of the matter. The fact of first-rate importance is the predominant rôle that custom plays in experience and in belief, and the very great varieties it may manifest.

No man ever looks at the world with pristine eyes. He sees it edited by a definite set of customs and institutions and ways of thinking. Even in his philosophical probings he cannot go behind these stereotypes; his very concepts of the true and the false will still have reference to his particular traditional customs. John Dewey has said in all seriousness that the part played by custom in shaping the behaviour of the individual as over against any way in which he can affect traditional custom, is as the proportion of the total vocabulary of his mother tongue over against those words of his own baby talk that are taken up into the vernacular of his family. When one seriously studies social orders that have had the opportunity to develop autonomously, the figure becomes no more than an exact and matter-of-fact observation. The life-history of the individual is first and foremost an accommodation to the patterns and standards traditionally handed down in his community. From the moment of his birth the customs into which he is born shape his experience and behaviour. By the time he can talk, he is the little creature of his culture, and by the time he is grown and able to take part in its activities, its habits are his habits, its beliefs his beliefs, its impossibilities his impossibilities. Every child that is born into his group will share them with him, and no child born into one on the opposite side of the globe can ever achieve the thousandth part. There is no social problem it is more incumbent upon us to understand than this of the rôle of custom. Until we are intelligent as to its laws and varieties, the main complicating facts of human life must remain unintelligible.

The study of custom can be profitable only after certain preliminary propositions have been accepted, and some of these propositions have been violently opposed. In the first place any scientific study requires that there be no preferential weighting of one or another of the items in the series it selects for its consideration. In all the less controversial fields like the study of cacti or termites or the nature of nebulae, the necessary method of study is to group the relevant material and to take note of all possible variant forms and conditions. In this way we have learned all that we know of the laws of astronomy, or of the habits of the social insects, let us say. It is only in the study of man himself that the major social sciences have substituted the study of one local variation, that of Western civilization.

Anthropology was by definition impossible as long as these distinctions between ourselves and the primitive, ourselves and the barbarian, ourselves and the pagan, held sway over people's minds. It was necessary first to arrive at that degree of sophistication where we no longer set our own belief over against our neighbour's superstition. It was necessary to recognize that those institutions which are based on the same premises, let us say the supernatural, must be considered together, our own among the rest.

In the first half of the nineteenth century this elementary postulate of anthropology could not occur to the most enlightened person of Western civilization. Man, all down his history, has defended his uniqueness like a point of honour. In Copernicus' time this claim to supremacy was so inclusive that it took in even the earth on which we live, and the fourteenth century refused with passion to have this planet subordinated to a place in the solar scheme. By Darwin's time, having granted the solar system to the enemy, man fought with all the weapons at his command for the uniqueness of the soul, an unknowable attribute given by God to man in such a manner that it disproved man's ancestry in the animal kingdom. No lack of con-

tinuity in the argument, no doubts of the nature of this "soul," not even the
fact that the nineteenth century did not care in the least to defend its brotherhood with any group of aliens — none of these facts counted against the
first-rate excitement that raged on account of the indignity evolution proposed against the notion of man's uniqueness.

Both these battles we may fairly count as won — if not yet, then soon; but
the fighting has only massed itself upon another front.   We are quite willing
to admit now that the revolution of the earth about the sun, or the animal
ancestry of man, has next to nothing to do with the uniqueness of our human
achievements.   If we inhabit one chance planet out of a myriad solar systems,
so much the greater glory, and if all the ill-assorted human races are linked
by evolution with the animal, the provable differences between ourselves
and them are the more extreme and the uniqueness of our institutions the
more remarkable.   But *our* achievements, *our* institutions are unique; they
are of a different order from those of lesser races and must be protected at
all costs.   So that today, whether it is a question of imperialism, or of race
prejudice, or of a comparison between Christianity and paganism, we are
still preoccupied with the uniqueness, not of the human institutions of the
world at large, which no one has ever cared about anyway, but of our own
institutions and achievements, our own civilization.

Western civilization, because of fortuitous historical circumstances, has
spread itself more widely than any other local group that has so far been
known.   It has standardized itself over most of the globe, and we have been
led, therefore, to accept a belief in the uniformity of human behaviour that
under other circumstances would not have arisen.   Even very primitive
peoples are sometimes far more conscious of the rôle of cultural traits than
we are, and for good reason.   They have had intimate experience of different
cultures.   They have seen their religion, their economic system, their marriage prohibitions, go down before the white man's.   They have laid down
the one and accepted the other, often uncomprehendingly enough, but they
are quite clear that there are variant arrangements of human life.   They
will sometimes attribute dominant characteristics of the white man to his
commercial competition, or to his institution of warfare, very much in the
fashion of the anthropologist.

The white man has had a different experience.   He has never seen an outsider, perhaps, unless the outsider has been already Europeanized.   If he
has travelled, he has very likely been around the world without ever staying
outside a cosmopolitan hotel.   He knows little of any ways of life but his
own.   The uniformity of custom, of outlook, that he sees spread about him
seems convincing enough, and conceals from him the fact that it is after all
an historical accident.   He accepts without more ado the equivalence of
human nature and his own cultural standards.

Yet the great spread of white civilization is not an isolated historical circumstance.   The Polynesian group, in comparatively recent times, has
spread itself from Ontong, Java, to Easter Island, from Hawaii to New
Zealand, and the Bantu-speaking tribes spread from the Sahara to southern
Africa.   But in neither case do we regard these peoples as more than an

overgrown local variation of the human species. Western civilization has had all its inventions in transportation and all its far-flung commercial arrangements to back up its great dispersion, and it is easy to understand historically how this came about.

The psychological consequences of this spread of white culture have been out of all proportion to the materialistic. This world-wide cultural diffusion has protected us as man had never been protected before from having to take seriously the civilizations of other peoples; it has given to our culture a massive universality that we have long ceased to account for historically, and which we read off rather as necessary and inevitable. We interpret our dependence, in our civilization, upon economic competition, as proof that this is the prime motivation that human nature can rely upon, or we read off the behaviour of small children as it is moulded in our civilization and recorded in child clinics, as child psychology or the way in which the young human animal is bound to behave. It is the same whether it is a question of our ethics or of our family organization. It is the inevitability of each familiar motivation that we defend, attempting always to identify our own local ways of behaving with Behaviour, or our own socialized habits with Human Nature.

Now modern man has made this thesis one of the living issues in his thought and in his practical behaviour, but the sources of it go far back into what appears to be, from its universal distribution among primitive peoples, one of the earliest of human distinctions, the difference in kind between "my own" closed group and the outsider. All primitive tribes agree in recognizing this category of the outsiders, those who are not only outside the provisions of the moral code which holds within the limits of one's own people, but who are summarily denied a place anywhere in the human scheme. A great number of the tribal names in common use, Zuñi, Déné, Kiowa, and the rest, are names by which primitive peoples know themselves, and are only their native terms for "the human beings," that is, themselves. Outside of the closed group there are no human beings. And this is in spite of the fact that from an objective point of view each tribe is surrounded by peoples sharing in its arts and material inventions, in elaborate practices that have grown up by a mutual give-and-take of behaviour from one people to another.

Primitive man never looked out over the world and saw "mankind" as a group and felt his common cause with his species. From the beginning he was a provincial who raised the barriers high. Whether it was a question of choosing a wife or of taking a head, the first and important distinction was between his own human group and those beyond the pale. His own group, and all its ways of behaving, was unique.

So modern man, differentiating into Chosen People and dangerous aliens, groups within his own civilization genetically and culturally related to one another as any tribes in the Australian bush are among themselves, has the justification of a vast historical continuity behind his attitude. The Pygmies have made the same claims. We are not likely to clear ourselves easily of so fundamental a human trait, but we can at least learn to recognize its history and its hydra manifestations.

One of these manifestations, and one which is often spoken of as primary and motivated rather by religious emotions than by this more generalized provincialism, is the attitude that has universally held in Western civilizations so long as religion remained a living issue among them. The distinction between any closed group and outside peoples, becomes in terms of religion that between the true believers and the heathen. Between these two categories for thousands of years there were no common meeting-points. No ideas or institutions that held in the one were valid in the other. Rather all institutions were seen in opposing terms according as they belonged to one or the other of the very often slightly differentiated religions: on the one side it was a question of Divine Truth and the true believer, of revelation and of God; on the other it was a matter of mortal error, of fables, of the damned and of devils. There could be no question of equating the attitudes of the opposed groups and hence no question of understanding from objectively studied data the nature of this important human trait, religion.

We feel a justified superiority when we read a description such as this of the standard religious attitude. At least we have thrown off that particular absurdity, and we have accepted the study of comparative religion. But considering the scope a similar attitude has had in our civilization in the form of race prejudices, for example, we are justified in a little scepticism as to whether our sophistication in the matter of religion is due to the fact that we have outgrown naïve childishness, or simply to the fact that religion is no longer the area of life in which the important modern battles are staged. In the really live issues of our civilization we seem to be far from having gained the detachment that we have so largely achieved in the field of religion.

There is another circumstance that has made the serious study of custom a late and often a half-heartedly pursued discipline, and it is a difficulty harder to surmount than those of which we have just spoken. Custom did not challenge the attention of social theorists because it was the very stuff of their own thinking: it was the lens without which they could not see at all. Precisely in proportion as it was fundamental, it had its existence outside the field of conscious attention. There is nothing mystical about this blindness. When a student has assembled the vast data for a study of international credits, or of the process of learning, or of narcissism as a factor in psychoneuroses, it is through and in this body of data that the economist or the psychologist or the psychiatrist operates. He does not reckon with the fact of other social arrangements where all the factors, it may be, are differently arranged. He does not reckon, that is, with cultural conditioning. He sees the trait he is studying as having known and inevitable manifestations, and he projects these as absolute because they are all the materials he has to think with. He identifies local attitudes of the 1930's with Human Nature, the description of them with Economics or Psychology.

Practically, it often does not matter. Our children must be educated in our pedagogical tradition, and the study of the process of learning in our schools is of paramount importance. There is the same kind of justification for the shrug of the shoulders with which we often greet a discussion of other economic systems. After all, we must live within the framework of mine and thine that our own culture institutionalizes.

That is true, and the fact that the varieties of culture can best be discussed as they exist in space gives colour to our nonchalance. But it is only limitation of historical material that prevents examples from being drawn rather from the succession of cultures in time. That succession we cannot escape if we would, and when we look back even a generation we realize the extent to which revision has taken place, sometimes in our most intimate behaviour. So far these revisions have been blind, the result of circumstances we can chart only in retrospect. Except for our unwillingness to face cultural change in intimate matters until it is forced upon us, it would not be impossible to take a more intelligent and directive attitude. The resistance is in large measure a result of our misunderstanding of cultural conventions, and especially an exaltation of those that happen to belong to our nation and decade. A very little acquaintance with other conventions, and a knowledge of how various these may be, would do much to promote a rational social order.

The study of different cultures has another important bearing upon present-day thought and behaviour. Modern existence has thrown many civilizations into close contact, and at the moment the overwhelming response to this situation is nationalism and racial snobbery. There has never been a time when civilization stood more in need of individuals who are genuinely culture-conscious, who can see objectively the socially conditioned behaviour of other peoples without fear and recrimination.

Contempt for the alien is not the only possible solution of our present contact of races and nationalities. It is not even a scientifically founded solution. Traditional Anglo-Saxon intolerance is a local and temporal culture-trait like any other. Even people as nearly of the same blood and culture as the Spanish have not had it, and race prejudice in the Spanish-settled countries is a thoroughly different thing from that in countries dominated by England and the United States. In this country it is obviously not an intolerance directed against the mixture of blood of biologically far-separated races, for upon occasion excitement mounts as high against the Irish Catholic in Boston, or the Italian in New England mill towns, as against the Oriental in California. It is the old distinction of the in-group and the out-group, and if we carry on the primitive tradition in this matter, we have far less excuse than savage tribes. We have travelled, we pride ourselves on our sophistication. But we have failed to understand the relativity of cultural habits, and we remain debarred from much profit and enjoyment in our human relations with peoples of different standards, and untrustworthy in our dealings with them.

The recognition of the cultural basis of race prejudice is a desperate need in present Western civilization. We have come to the point where we entertain race prejudice against our blood brothers the Irish, and where Norway and Sweden speak of their enmity as if they too represented different blood. The so-called race line, during a war in which France and Germany fight on opposite sides, is held to divide the peoples of Baden from those of Alsace, though in bodily form they alike belong to the Alpine sub-race. In a day of footloose movements of people and of mixed marriages in the ancestry of the most desirable elements of the community, we preach unabashed the gospel of the pure race.

To this anthropology makes two answers. The first is as to the nature of culture and the second is as to the nature of inheritance. The answer as to the nature of culture takes us back to prehuman societies. There are societies where Nature perpetuates the slightest mode of behaviour by biological mechanisms, but these are societies not of men but of the social insects. The queen ant, removed to a solitary nest, will reproduce each trait of sex behaviour, each detail of the nest. The social insects represent Nature in a mood when she was taking no chances. The pattern of the entire social structure she committed to the ant's instinctive behaviour. There is no greater chance that the social classes of an ant society, or its patterns of agriculture, will be lost by an ant's isolation from its group than that the ant will fail to reproduce the shape of its antennae or the structure of its abdomen.

For better or for worse, man's solution lies at the opposite pole. Not one item of his tribal social organization, of his language, of his local religion, is carried in his germ-cell. In Europe, in other centuries, when children were occasionally found who had been abandoned and had maintained themselves in forests apart from other human beings, they were all so much alike that Linnaeus classified them as a distinct species, *Homo ferus*, and supposed that they were a kind of gnome that man seldom ran across. He could not conceive that these half-witted brutes were born human, these creatures with no interest in what went on about them, rocking themselves rhythmically back and forth like some wild animal in a zoo, with organs of speech and hearing that could hardly be trained to do service, who withstood freezing weather in rags and plucked potatoes out of boiling water without discomfort. There is no doubt, of course, that they were children abandoned in infancy, and what they had all of them lacked was association with their kind, through which alone man's faculties are sharpened and given form.

We do not come across wild children in our more humane civilization. But the point is made as clearly in any case of adoption of an infant into another race and culture. An Oriental child adopted by an Occidental family learns English, shows toward its foster parents the attitudes current among the children he plays with, and grows up to the same professions that they elect.

He learns the entire set of the cultural traits of the adopted society, and the set of his real parents' group plays no part. The same process happens on a grand scale when entire peoples in a couple of generations shake off their traditional culture and put on the customs of an alien group. The culture of the American Negro in northern cities has come to approximate in detail that of the whites in the same cities. A few years ago, when a cultural survey was made of Harlem, one of the traits peculiar to the Negroes was their fashion of gambling on the last three unit figures of the next day's stock turnover. At least it cost less than the whites' corresponding predilection for gambling in the stocks themselves and was no less uncertain and exciting. It was a variation on the white pattern, though hardly a great departure. And most Harlem traits keep still closer to the forms that are current in white groups.

All over the world, since the beginning of human history, it can be shown that peoples have been able to adopt the culture of peoples of another blood. There is nothing in the biological structure of man that makes it even difficult. Man is not committed in detail by his biological constitution to any particular variety of behaviour. The great diversity of social solutions that man has worked out in different cultures in regard to mating, for example, or trade, are all equally possible on the basis of his original endowment. Culture is not a biologically transmitted complex.

What is lost in Nature's guaranty of safety is made up in the advantage of greater plasticity. The human animal does not, like the bear, grow himself a polar coat in order to adapt himself, after many generations, to the Arctic. He learns to sew himself a coat and put up a snow house. From all we can learn of the history of intelligence in pre-human as well as human societies, this plasticity has been the soil in which human progress began and in which it has maintained itself. In the ages of the mammoths, species after species without plasticity arose, overreached itself, and died out, undone by the development of the very traits it had biologically produced in order to cope with its environment. The beasts of prey and finally the higher apes came slowly to rely upon other than biological adaptations, and upon the consequent increased plasticity the foundations were laid, bit by bit, for the development of intelligence. Perhaps, as is often suggested, man will destroy himself by this very development of intelligence. But no one has suggested any means by which we can return to the biological mechanisms of the social insect, and we are left no alternative. The human cultural heritage, for better or for worse, is not biologically transmitted.

The corollary in modern politics is that there is no basis for the argument that we can trust our spiritual and cultural achievements to any selected hereditary germ-plasms. In our Western civilization, leadership has passed successively in different periods to the Semitic-speaking peoples, to the Hamitic, to the Mediterranean sub-group of the white race, and lately to the Nordic. There is no doubt about the cultural continuity of the civilization, no matter who its carriers were at the moment. We must accept all the implications of our human inheritance, one of the most important of which is the small scope of biologically transmitted behaviour, and the enormous rôle of the cultural process of the transmission of tradition.

The second answer anthropology makes to the argument of the racial purist concerns the nature of heredity. The racial purist is the victim of a mythology. For what is "racial inheritance"? We know roughly what heredity is from father to son. Within a family line the importance of heredity is tremendous. But heredity is an affair of family lines. Beyond that it is mythology. In small and static communities like an isolated Eskimo village, "racial" heredity and the heredity of child and parent are practically equivalent, and racial heredity therefore has meaning. But as a concept applied to groups distributed over a wide area, let us say, to Nordics, it has no basis in reality. In the first place, in all Nordic nations there are family lines which are represented also in Alpine or Mediterranean communities. Any analysis of the physical make-up of a European population shows overlapping: the dark-eyed, dark-haired Swede represents family lines that are more concentrated farther south, but he is to be understood in relation to what we know of these latter groups. His heredity, so far as it has any physical reality, is a matter of his family line, which is not confined to Sweden. We do not know how far physical types may vary without intermixture. We know that inbreeding brings about a local type. But this is a situation that in our cosmopolitan white civilization hardly exists, and when "racial heredity" is invoked, as it usually is, to rally a group of persons of about the same economic status, graduating from much the same schools, and reading the same weeklies, such a category is merely another version of the in- and the out-group and does not refer to the actual biological homogeneity of the group.

What really binds men together is their culture, — the ideas and the standards they have in common. If instead of selecting a symbol like a common blood heredity and making a slogan of it, the nation turned its attention rather to the culture that unites its people, emphasizing its major merits and recognizing the different values which may develop in a different culture, it would substitute realistic thinking for a kind of symbolism which is dangerous because it is misleading.

A knowledge of cultural forms is necessary in social thinking, and the present volume is concerned with this problem of culture. As we have just seen, bodily form, or race, is separable from culture, and can for our purposes be laid to one side except at certain points where for some special reason it becomes relevant. The chief requirement for a discussion of culture is that it should be based on a wide selection of possible cultural forms. It is only by means of such facts that we can possibly differentiate between those human adjustments that are culturally conditioned and those that are common and, so far as we can see, inevitable in mankind. We cannot discover by introspection or by observation of any one society what behaviour is "instinctive," that is, organically determined. In order to class any behaviour as instinctive, much more is necessary than that it should be proved to be automatic. The conditioned response is as automatic as the organically determined, and culturally conditioned responses make up the greater part of our huge equipment of automatic behaviour.

Therefore the most illuminating material for a discussion of cultural forms and processes is that of societies historically as little related as possible to our own and to one another. With the vast network of historical contact which has spread the great civilizations over tremendous areas, primitive cultures are now the one source to which we can turn. They are a laboratory in which we may study the diversity of human institutions. With their comparative isolation, many primitive regions have had centuries in which to elaborate the cultural themes they have made their own. They provide ready to our hand the necessary information concerning the possible great variations in human adjustments, and a critical examination of them is essential for any understanding of cultural processes. It is the only laboratory of social forms that we have or shall have.

This laboratory has another advantage. The problems are set in simpler terms than in the great Western civilizations. With the inventions that make for ease of transportation, international cables and telephones and radio transmission, those that ensure permanence and wide-spread distribution to the printed page, the development of competing professional groups and cults and classes and their standardization over the world, modern civilization has grown too complex for adequate analysis except as it is broken up for the purpose into small artificial sections. And these partial analyses are inadequate because so many outside factors cannot be controlled. A survey of any one group involves individuals out of opposed heterogeneous groups, with different standards, social aims, home relations, and morality. The interrelation of these groups is too complicated to evaluate in the necessary detail. In primitive society, the cultural tradition is simple enough to be contained within the knowledge of individual adults, and the manners and morals of the group are moulded to one well-defined general pattern. It is possible to estimate the interrelation of traits in this simple environment in a way which is impossible in the cross-currents of our complex civilization.

Neither of these reasons for stressing the facts of primitive culture has anything to do with the use that has been classically made of this material. This use had to do with a reconstruction of origins. Early anthropologists tried to arrange all traits of different cultures in an evolutionary sequence from the earliest forms to their final development in Western civilization. But there is no reason to suppose that by discussing Australian religion rather than our own we are uncovering primordial religion, or that by discussing Iroquoian social organization we are returning to the mating habits of man's early ancestors.

Since we are forced to believe that the race of man is one species, it follows that man everywhere has an equally long history behind him. Some primitive tribes may have held relatively closer to primordial forms of behaviour than civilized man, but this can only be relative and our guesses are as likely to be wrong as right. There is no justification for identifying some one contemporary primitive custom with the original type of human behaviour. Methodologically there is only one means by which we may gain an approximate knowledge of these early beginnings. That is by a study of the distribution of those few traits that are universal or near-universal in human society. There are several that are well known. Of these everyone agrees upon animism, and the exogamous restrictions upon marriage. The conceptions, diverse as they prove to be, of the human soul, and of an after-life, raise more question. Beliefs as nearly universal as these we may justifiably regard as exceedingly old human inventions. This is not equivalent to regarding them as biologically determined, for they may have been very early inventions of the human race, "cradle" traits which have become fundamental in all human thinking. In the last analysis they may be as socially conditioned as any local custom. But they have long since become automatic in human behaviour. They are old, and they are universal. All this, however, does not make the forms that can be observed today the original forms that arose in primordial times. Nor is there any way of reconstructing these origins from the study of their varieties. One may isolate the universal core of the belief and differentiate from this its local forms, but it is still possible that the trait took its rise in a pronounced local form and not in some original least common denominator of all observed traits.

For this reason the use of primitive customs to establish origins is speculative. It is possible to build up an argument for any origin that can be desired, origins that are mutually exclusive as well as those that are complementary. Of all the uses of anthropological material, this is the one in which speculation has followed speculation most rapidly, and where in the nature of the case no proof can be given.

Nor does the reason for using primitive societies for the discussion of social forms have necessary connection with a romantic return to the primitive. It is put forward in no spirit of poeticizing the simpler peoples. There are many ways in which the culture of one or another people appeals to us strongly in this era of heterogeneous standards and confused mechanical bustle. But it is not in a return to ideals preserved for us by primitive peoples that our society will heal itself of its maladies. The romantic Utopianism that reaches out toward the simpler primitive, attractive as it sometimes may be, is as often, in ethnological study, a hindrance as a help.

The careful study of primitive societies is important today rather, as we have said, because they provide case material for the study of cultural forms and processes. They help us to differentiate between those responses that are specific to local cultural types and those that are general to mankind. Beyond this, they help us to gauge and understand the immensely important rôle of culturally conditioned behaviour. Culture, with its processes and functions, is a subject upon which we need all the enlightenment we can achieve, and there is no direction in which we can seek with greater reward than in the facts of pre-literate societies.

GEORGE BOAS

When Professor Boas rises to speak urbanely for the machine he can hardly be accused of joining the side either of those who unthinkingly accept it or those materialists who hail it as the greatest of all possible goods. He looks at it as a philosopher who knows that in every age humanity has had to cope with the problems of its own kind of civilization, that the present issue is not the machine itself but wise use of its benefits. The author was born in Providence in 1891, was graduated from Brown University in 1913, and since 1921 has been Professor of Philosophy at Johns Hopkins University. He is the author of *Adventures in Human Thought*, and *Our New Ways of Thinking*.

IN DEFENSE OF MACHINES *

I

So much has been written about machines and the Machine Age that the very words are taboo in polite conversation. The Machine Age, like Freudianism and War Guilt and Flaming Youth, is a topic of which everyone is sick and tired. But so much that has been said on the subject is muddled or beside the point or both, that one who is interested in the analysis of ideas may be pardoned perhaps for continuing the conversation, even though the audience gets up and leaves when he begins.

It is in a way absurd to discuss any great social movement in logical terms. Social movements are made by psychology, not logic. Yet it is barely possible that if everyone caught in the current would stop and think he might find a way of crawling out on dry land. But as a matter of fact no one to speak of is going to stop and think. Some people stop and scream, like the poor English weavers when the Industrial Revolution began concentrating production in factories or the conscientious objectors during the War. But such screaming is rarely effective because it is bad form. All the more difficult is it for people to stop and think. For thinking is not only bad form but hard. There is, moreover, the possibility that society as a whole, or even its major sub-divisions, gets what it wants, and when large sections of society find that what they want is illegal — as is happening in American cities in regard to alcohol — they simply devise their own ways of nullifying laws or resisting change. Note the electoral status of the Negro in the South, the success of the Russian Revolution, the survival of Anglo-Saxon culture in England and, for that matter, the absorption of pagan divinities by institutionalized Christianity.

Thinking, therefore, may do no actual good in changing anything but men's minds, but it is at least harmless, which one cannot say of screaming.

To turn, then, to machines. We are first told that though man invented them to be his servants he has become theirs. The Frankenstein motif, as Mr. Stuart Chase pointed out in *Harper's* in March, 1929, seems to be the most prominent theme of the screamers. As Mr. Chase clearly indicated in

* From *Harper's Magazine*, June, 1932. By permission of the publisher.

that article, this argument is a gross exaggeration. Man is no more a slave of his machines now than he has ever been, or than he is to his body, of which they are — as I think Samuel Butler first suggested — an extension. A farmer is certainly as much of a slave to his primitive plow or sickle as a factory hand to his power loom or engine. Anyone who has ever lived on an old-fashioned farm knows how the farmer and his family get up at four in the morning to sharpen their instruments, filing, cutting, nailing, repairing, lest the machines on which their lives depend fall to pieces. I have lived closely enough to French peasants to observe them sweating and groaning over their tools. When they have no automatic binders and reapers they cut their wheat with sickles and bind it idyllically by hand. Are they who spend endless brutalizing hours in the fields because of the laziness and general inefficiency of their machines more free than our Western ranchmen with their tractors? I have seen milk become diseased and filthy because there was no ice or ice-machine and eggs wasted because there were no incubators and grain rotting because there were no reapers. The machines of primitive men, the handlooms, the sickles, the wooden plows, the animals — which modern machines have often replaced — tyrannize over their owners not by their power but by their very weakness. Primitive men, with the possible exception of the Bushman who strangles his prey and eats it raw and goes naked and sleeps in the open and has no family life — if there be such a creature — are like the dutiful husbands of professional invalids.

In the second place, so far as I know, no clear definition of a machine has ever been given. A steamboat is a machine, according to Silas Bent — and in his opinion indeed the beginning of the steam age is the beginning of the machine age. But what makes a steamboat a machine and a sailboat a non-machine? The fact that human beings had to freeze and half starve to catch the wind? But after all they roast and suffocate at least to boil the water to make the steam, if it is man-power one is thinking of. Steam undoubtedly produces much of the ugliness and dirt of our cities, but we are not for the moment discussing the æsthetic aspects of the question. Why steam is more mechanical than wind or falling water or muscle-driven hammers is somewhat obscure. A sailboat, a rowboat, an inflated goatskin, a log are all equally machines. A linotype, a handpress, a pen, a reed, a charred stick are all machines. They are all mechanical supplements to man's corporeal inadequacies. They differ in quantity of output, in excellence of production, in speed, i.e., in what is usually called efficiency. A stone hurled from a sling at an insolent neighbor is as mechanical as shrapnel hurled from a cannon. It does not kill so many men; it is a worse machine. But man has always relied in part on mechanical devices, although he has dreamed of a time in the distant past when they were unnecessary because of the fertility of the earth, the simplicity of human desires, the general health of humanity, and its blissfully divine ignorance. No one would call the time of Nero a machine age; but read Seneca's Ninetieth Epistle. Machines are precisely what differentiate us from the brutes. Some people of course would prefer that the differentiation be less marked.

When I have pointed this out in conversation with primitivistic friends

I have been invariably charged with sophistry. They have always insisted that my definition of "machine" was too broad. My answer is that the only alternative they offer arbitrarily identifies a machine with a bad machine. But any student of "Logic I" knows that either all machines are bad because they are machines or because of something else. And if only some and not all machines are bad, then their badness is not the fact that they are machines. Take the case of the woman who calls a player piano a machine but refuses to call a piano a machine. Yet a piano is a harp whose strings are struck, not plucked. This cannot be done by hand unless little hammers are attached to each finger. A harpsichord is a mechanical harp — that is a harp whose strings are plucked not by fingers but by little pieces of crow-quill or hard leather. The harpsichord does not do much more than could be done by hand. Does that put it in the class of player-pianos? The answer to this question does not lie in any principle of construction. It lies in what you want to get out of the instrument. People who call player-pianos machines feel that it is better to play a piece of music inaccurately so long as one has maximum responsibility for what is played than to reproduce even the good playing of someone else. People who call all three instruments machines want above all an accurately rendered piece of music. One group thinks of the producing, the other of the product.

But that is not a question of machines *vs*. non-machines. It is a question of whether producing or consuming is better. Romanticists tend to think that activity, doing, originality are the greatest goods, regardless of what one does. Anti-romanticists are likely to think in terms of ends. The ungracious answer is that there is plenty of room in the world for both producers and consumers, and that no one can be exclusively one or the other. As a matter of fact, the present age furnishes amazing possibilities for the producers. There has probably never been a time when artists and scientists were freer to satisfy their desires for creation. Think of the universities and learned foundations which support men not to teach others, not to think of utilitarian ends, but simply to pursue research. The most absurd investigations are sanctified by the superstition that pure research is noble and deserves free maintenance. It is taken for granted nowadays that artists "be true to themselves," and few would dream of minutely prescribing what a painter or poet should produce.

II

In fact the real clash in opinion is probably ethical. We are — a great many of us — unhappy today and, following a long tradition, we attribute our unhappiness to the economic structure of our civilization. But one can find such outcries of woe as early as eight hundred years before Christ in the works of Hesiod. The crop of cynicism and despair which we uncritically think of as modern is simply human. There has often in the past been as profound and as general despair among the articulate members of society. We read more books and essays of our own time than we do of other times. But those of us who know anything about the history of ideas can find the most striking analogues to our contemporary attitude from Hesiod — if not from Homer — down: yearning for the past, which was of course better than the present; yearning for a society without arts, sciences, or crafts, where the earth bears spontaneously and there is neither money, trade, nor private property; yearning for happy islands beyond the seas, praise of noble savages. The Golden Age took the place of the Age of Handicraft, the Scythians and the Hyperboreans of American Indians, pre-Conquest Mexicans, or South Sea Islanders. This unhappiness of ours, which in its literary form expresses itself in tirades against steam, electricity, urban life, manufactures, cannot, therefore, be attributed to machines.

Machines are not the cause either of happiness or unhappiness. They may be present or absent at the time when a man is miserable or blissful. They are irrelevant to what is called our spiritual welfare. Just because a man has a radio is no reason why a man should feel that he has been transported either to Heaven or Hell, unless a man wants to have or to brag of having what his fellows have. The same thing is true of our other possessions. Some of us snooty members of society feel a certain self-esteem in not having many of the right things to have. As for mechanized industry, it is simply not true that the farmer on his isolated farm in the old days in New England, without radio, telephone, automobile, tractor, reaper, and so on was any happier than the factory hand in Lowell or Lawrence — when there actually was industry in those cities. Some of them were probably happy; others were living a mean, stinted, swinish life, crabbed and thwarted, sickly in mind and body, full of the lowest motives that ever disgraced the human soul. If rustic life was so delightful, why did the rustic fly to the city as soon as he could find a city to fly to and the railroad fare? The pastoralist is usually either a genuine lover of rural things or a city dweller to whom the country means the spring gardens, the old swimming hole, barn dances, and corn husking, rather than winter, weeding and "cultivating," hauling water, the wood pile, drought, and insect pests.

To be sure factory hands can play a good second to farm hands so far as a dreary life goes. They are as a mass an unlovely lot. In my boyhood in Providence I used to see men, women, and children trudging to the mills at six-thirty in the morning, tin dinner pails in hand — and not so full at that, in spite of Mark Hanna — to return at six-thirty at night. They were pale and rickety, God knows, and nothing for the mill owners to look in the eyes. But that does not mean that their contemporaries on the farms were red-cheeked and stocky, effervescing with vitamines, sleeping late in the morning and going to bed early, delighting in robust rural pleasures.

Who has yet found the key to human happiness? Who knows whether there is a key to be found? We do know that it is not always produced by possessions — though it sometimes is. And, furthermore, we know that a man who has health is more likely to be capable of happiness than a man who is sickly. Can we attribute modern hygiene to anything other than our various 'scopes and 'graphs? Instruments of precision have been all important in producing modern longevity and health. For it was not unaided brains. The brains have always been there. But the brains could not see without lenses. I am no worshipper of mere hygiene nor am I extolling twofistedness and red-bloodedness and he-manship. But it simply does not make sense to say that the millennium would set in if we could all relapse into dirt and disease. It would make no difference to some of us, I admit, and doubtless the human race would get used to it in time. But the fact that Occidentals have spent such effort to eliminate the combination is some evidence of its lack of charm. Unless it was done for self-mortification.

This point needs no emphasis, although many of the opponents of the machine seem to think that Oriental squalor is a help to the inner life. There are, to be sure, greater opportunities for a would-be saint in filth than in cleanliness, but that is precisely because human beings dislike it so. But the inner life is not entirely an affair of corporeal asceticism. I venture to suggest that the inner life of a Noguchi or an Einstein is as fine as that of a St. Simeon Stylites. I admit that I cannot prove it. Still one could point to dozens of men and women today whose works show as noble a perception of human values as those of their ancestors in a supposed machineless age. We still have mystics, devoted scientists, great artists. Religion, love, creative power, intelligence seem to be no less in evidence today than they ever were, and the lack of them no less bewailed in literature. A period which has produced a new religion (Christian Science), seen the increasing hold of an old one (Roman Catholicism), the rise of pacifism and internationalism, a new physical science, an artistic style in painting, sculpture, architecture, music, and literature has not been deprived of its inner life.

Machines are as indifferent to the inner life as they are to happiness. The inner life — if the term indicates the ability to think and to dream and all that is entailed in thinking and dreaming — is independent of the presence or absence of machines. Introverts have been and still are able to crawl into themselves in spite of factory whistles and automobile horns, and extroverts had no difficulty in finding trees to chop down and men to fight when they could not swat flies or pilot airplanes. One of the best proofs of the irrelevancy of machinery to the spirit is the flood of anti-machine literature. How in the world do these writers find the time to compose their essays and sermons in a breath-taking age dominated by a soul-gobbling Moloch? It is true that many of their productions seem to have required a minimum of reflection. But the Twentieth Century has no corner on unintelligence. If people would only read past as well as present literature, they would understand why President Eliot was able to house what was worth salvaging of three thousand years of writing on a five-foot shelf. But when we think of the past we forget the fools and remember the sages. We reverse the process for our own time.

III

One of the points especially emphasized by the enemies of machines is that they substitute something lifeless for something vital and human. Concretely, this means that a farmer cannot love a tractor or an incubator as he could a horse or a hen. This is very probable, particularly if the farmer started farming with horses and hens. But it is not absolutely certain otherwise. Machines can be as lovable as animals. Who has not known engineers who literally love their locomotives, or boys who care for their radios, speed boats, and automobiles as if they were alive? People are constantly personifying their machines as they do boats. They brag about their accomplishments as if the machines were able to accomplish things independently of their operators. One can always love that with which one can identify oneself, and a man can identify himself with a power loom or a turbine as well as with a football team, his family, or his wife. Think of a musician and his beloved violin or flute about which so many romantic stories are invented. Some machines are lovable and some aren't. As a boy I used to hate the old coal furnace which I was delegated to feed and water and clean, and it required all the attention that a voracious and diarrhoeic infant might demand. Today I worship my gas furnace with its exquisite little thermostat and its complete autonomy. It costs as much as a steam yacht, but love is blind. It can go the limit as far as this doting old fool is concerned. Another man might hate it and love the now abandoned coal furnace. The lovableness and hatefulness of these things is not entirely a function of their mechanical nature. It is in large measure a function of the person who owns or tends them. The old debate on the relative merits of cats and dogs as pets is very much like this — and no more sensible. For emotional qualities are in popular speech attributed to the things that arouse them and not to us in whom they are aroused. So we say that a chair is comfortable, meaning that we are comfortable in the chair. And until human beings all react emotionally in the same way on all occasions to the same things — until women cease to ask, "What in the world could he see in her?" — there is no laying down the law about the inherent lovableness or hatefulness of anything.

Nor is it true that modern machines absorb us and make us part of them more than primitive machines did. A day laborer is as much part of his pick and shovel as the operator of a steam shovel is part of it. If a man is assumed to be his own boss, to be living on a small farm near the Equator, where we shall imagine that he can work or not without either starving or freezing, where there are no malevolent micro-organisms, and food drops from the skies like manna, then of course he can lay down his tools at any time and pick them up at any time, as a woman can lay down and pick up a piece of embroidery. But such an earthly paradise has not existed since Adam ate the apple, and there is no sense in arguing as if it had or could. The Gloucester fisherman out for cod off the Grand Banks is probably living as nonmechanical and primitive a life as is possible for modern Americans. Is he less a part of his boat, sails, and tackle than the factory hand is of his levers and belts and spindles and presses? He makes more different motions and he may find them more interesting — though it is questionable whether the factory hand would — but he is no less absorbed into his tools.

It will be said that the old machines, actuated by human muscles rather than by steam or electricity, at least helped a man's creative power. Friends of the machine are constantly being told that hand-weaving is creative whereas machine-weaving is not. The old French artisan, we are told, lived a life of creativity; he stamped things with his own individuality; he projected his personality into his products. The modern American factory hand is passive; he makes nothing; his product is standardized. This, within limits, is true of the factory hand. But it was also true of the artisan. He had certain styles and patterns which he reproduced endlessly, as our great-grandmothers reproduced world without end the same old quilting patterns. That man's products have always been standardized is proved by archaeology, and the history of taste. If there had not been standardization, how could archaeologists date works of art by their style, material, and subject matter? There is no more individuality in the cave drawings at Les Eyzies — which are the most primitive works of art we have — than in the photographs of today. Yet drawing and painting are practically free of mechanical fetters. Peruvian pre-Columbian weaving is hardly the product of the machine age, yet we see running through it the same standardized weaves, the same colors, the same designs. Artists up to modern times almost always were working on commission; they executed orders; and it is a sheer falsification of history to think of their carrying out in matter the fancies of their dream-life. We have so much evidence of this that there is an embarrassment of choice.

One who knows history knows that the love of the individual, the different, the original is modern, wherever it exists at all. Where we find standardization of taste today we find not a product of the machine age but the survival of a long tradition. People in general have always wanted to be like everyone else in their social group — have we not books of etiquette running back to the fourteenth century at least? There are undeniably a great many people today — perhaps even the majority for all I know — who still want to be indistinguishable from their fellows. At the same time it is possible, if not always easy, for people even to think differently, whereas a century or so ago it was literally impossible if one wished to save one's skin.

As one digs into this discussion one finds the instinctive hatred that many people have always had for innovation. We do not hate machines, we hate new machines. A woman will object to buying a dress cut out by machine, but will not object to buying one sewn by machine. The very person who objected to the player-piano had no objections to a phonograph; she grew up with one and learned all the music she knows from it. I find myself fuming at automobiles and yearning for the old bicycles. I can remember old folks shaking their heads over telephones as their juniors now curse out the dial phones. I have heard a gardener in France inveighing against chemical fertilizers which "*violent la terre*," as if horse manure were non-chemical. Sailors in the windjammers railed against the steamboat, and steamboat crews think none too kindly of the johnnies who sail oil-burners. Greek and Roman literature is full of invective against any kind of navigation, for it takes the pine tree off its mountain top and sends men wandering.

Obviously a new machine, like an old one, must be judged on its merits, not on its novelty. But the fact that it is novel should not condemn it. Here are two stalwart platitudes. But think of the fools who objected to anaesthesia, to aeronautics, even to cooked foods, because they were not "natural." The question cannot be settled by the wild use of question-begging epithets. We must each establish a system of values for ourselves or absorb that of our social group, and judge machines by it as we do everything else. There is no other way of evaluating anything.

As we all know — we have certainly heard it frequently enough — the real question is what to do with our leisure. There is no doubt that we can have more of it now than we ever could in the past — if we want it. If it be true that movie palaces, dance halls, and speakeasies are crowded, that radios are going night and day, and automobiles are whizzing about like whirling atoms, it would seem as if most people had found the answer. It is an answer which displeases the magazine writers. That is because writers are by nature people who enjoy and need quiet and solitude and cannot understand other people's enjoying and needing noise and society. But can they point to a time when the leisure class as a mass was less ignobly amused? We happen to have a very large leisure class. It acts as idle human beings have always acted: the theater, the gaming table, the divan. Did anyone seriously think that it would take to improving its mind or sit cross-legged in rapt contemplation of its collective navel? Leisure is man's one opportunity to satisfy whatever appetites he happens to have. And no one can say that he is forced by lack of libraries, educational institutions, museums, and the like to spend it staring at films or boozing and petting. The fact is that most people are what their cultured fellows would call sots and always have been. And the probability is that in modern times — whether because or in spite of machines — they have more chance to rise from the sty than they have ever had. The machine has neither given them wings nor cloven hooves. In the very nature of the case it could do neither.

CARL LOTUS BECKER

CARL LOTUS BECKER (1873–   ) has held several university positions in history and is now professor of that subject in Cornell University. He is a student and defender of the American tradition in politics. The present essay, first published in *The Nation*, January 24, 1934, is a modern examination of the liberal doctrine of freedom of speech, which received its classic formulation in John Stuart Mill's tractate *On Liberty*. For further exposition of the theme the student may turn to Professor Becker's *Our Great Experiment in Democracy*, and *The Declaration of Independence: A Study in the History of Political Ideas*.

FREEDOM OF SPEECH *

The worth of men consists in their liability to persuasion.   WHITEHEAD

I

THE nation's recent affirmation of faith in freedom of speech called forth an unusual number of protests, not against the principle, but against an unlimited application of it. A re-examination of the liberal doctrine is always in order, but never more so than now. The times are such that every liberal may well ask himself, not so much how far he is willing to carry the principle of free speech, but rather how far the principle is capable of carrying him.

It seems necessary to ask what we mean by freedom of speech, since people often have disconcerting ideas about it. A woman once asked me what all the pother was about. Weren't people always free to say what they thought? Of course one must be prepared to face the consequences. I didn't know the answer to that one. Last summer a Columbia University student explained to me that all governments, being based on force, were dictatorships, and that there was no more freedom of speech in the U.S.A. than in the U.S.S.R., the only difference being in the things one was permitted to say. I suggested that, supposing freedom of speech to be a good thing, a poor way of getting more of it than we already had would be to adopt a philosophy which denied that it was worth having. The editors of *The Nation* do not say that the laws guaranteeing freedom of speech are always effective. They say that freedom of speech, as defined in our fundamental law, is the foundation of free government, and should therefore never be denied to anyone — "even to the Nazis."

The fundamental law guaranteeing freedom of speech was well formulated in the Virginia constitution of 1780: "Any person may speak, write, and publish his sentiments on any subject, being responsible for the abuse [as defined by law] of that liberty." As thus defined, freedom of speech was the principal tenet of the eighteenth-century doctrine of liberal democracy. Its validity, for those who formulated it, rested upon presuppositions which may be put in the form of a syllogism. *Major premise:* The sole method of

---

* From *Everyman His Own Historian*. Copyright, 1935, F. S. Crofts & Co. By permission of *The Nation*, F. S. Crofts & Company, and the author.

arriving at truth is the application of human reason to the problems presented by the universe and the life of men in it. *Minor premise:* Men are rational creatures who can easily grasp and will gladly accept the truth once it is disclosed to them. *Conclusion:* By allowing men freedom of speech and the press, relevant knowledge will be made accessible, untrammeled discussion will reconcile divergent interests and opinions, and laws acceptable to all will be enacted. To the early prophets of democracy the syllogism seemed irrefutable; but to us, in the light of liberal democracy as we know it, the minor premise is obviously false, the conclusion invalid. There remains the major premise. What can we do with it?

II

The major premise, with reservations as to "human reason," we can accept — must do so in fact, since there is nothing else to cling to. Even if reason be not always Reason, even if, like Hitler, we have nothing better than our blood to think with, we must make the most of whatever thinking we can muster. "All our dignity," said Pascal, "consists in thought. Endeavor then to think well: that is the essence of morality." It was by taking thought that man first differentiated himself from the beasts; by taking more thought that he achieved whatever men have, by taking thought, judged worthy. What more he may achieve can be achieved, and whether it is worthy can be determined, only by taking still more thought. Since men must in any case think, and do what they think of doing, it seems axiomatic to say that they should be free to think and to express their thoughts as well as they can.

Nevertheless, the statement is not axiomatic — obviously not, since, if it were, *The Nation* would not bother to print articles about it. There is a catch somewhere. Perhaps we are too prone to think of freedom of speech in terms of Man and Speech. This was the way in which eighteenth-century liberals thought of it. Confronted with a social régime which hedged in the individual at every point, they found the obvious solution in the maximum of liberty for the individual — political liberty, economic liberty, liberty of speech and the press. Knowing little of these liberties in the concrete, they visualized them as ideal abstractions, so that all the spacious but unfurnished chambers in the Temple of Freedom could be brilliantly illuminated by turning on certain phrases — as, for example, Voltaire's epigram: "I disagree absolutely with what you say, but I will defend to the death your right to say it." Liberals still think of liberty somewhat too much in the eighteenth-century manner. Give us, in a mental test, the words "free speech," and we are apt to recall Voltaire's epigram, which then fades into a picture of two amiable, elderly gentlemen engaged in a rational discussion of the existence of the Deity.

Voltaire's epigram expresses a profound truth in the ideal world of knowledge. It would be equally relevant to the world of practical activities if society were a debating club of well-intentioned and reasonable men in which speech, being the only form of action, issued in nothing more dangerous than abstract propositions about reality. Since the activities of men are diverse, the ideal of a debating club is sometimes nearly realized. Mathematical physicists, discussing the nature of the atom, enjoy (at least in this country) the utmost freedom of speech without having (as yet) to call upon *The Nation* for first aid. Economists, historians, even biologists are more likely to encounter obstacles, since their activities have a more direct bearing on practical affairs. Where the principle of free speech has to fight for its life is in the realm of concrete political activities. Since the eighteenth century we have learned at least this much, that society is something more than a debating club of reasonable men in search of the truth. We know what use men actually make of their liberties. We are therefore in a position to estimate the principle of free speech in terms, not of Man and Speech, but of men and speeches — in terms of the best that has been thought and said by the Honorable Members we have elected, the Attorney-Generals we have known, the Insulls we have suffered, the fruity-throated announcers who, every day, for a profit, avail themselves of the Liberty of Lying.

Estimated in terms of its concrete manifestations, the principle of free speech is resolved into a diversity of oral and printed utterances, some of which need to be suppressed. No one has ever thought otherwise. Even the editors of *The Nation* do not approve of the freedom of speech that issues in slander and libel. Do they approve of the freedom of speech that issues in the lynching of Negroes? In the sale of poisoned cosmetics? The sale of worthless stock to honest but gullible people? They would say that of course there are, as the Virginia constitution recognizes, "abuses" to be defined by law; but that unless the law is careful, the definition may be a greater abuse than the speech it suppresses. True enough: the law is always in danger of being "a ass." But as soon as abuses appear, the principle of free speech is merged in another and broader principle: "Liberty is the right of everyone to do whatever does not injure others"; and we are at once confronted with the fundamental practical problem of all government: What individual acts, including the act that is speech, do here and now injure others?

By no formulation of principles beforehand can answers to this question be provided for concrete situations. The answers must wait on experience. Experience has taught us, or surely will teach us, that the eighteenth-century solution for social will ills no longer serve. Economic liberty, which was to have brought about equality of conditions, has contrived, with the aid of machines, to bring about a monstrous inequality of conditions. That there are rich and poor is nothing new, nor even disastrous. What is disastrous is that a great part of social wealth is owned by the many who do not control it, and controlled by the few who do not own it. Having well learned this, liberals find the obvious solution for social ills not in extending but in restricting the economic liberty of the individual. What we have not learned, or not sufficiently, is that the economic liberty of the individual is intimately associated with his political liberty, and that both are associated with his liberty of speech and the press. It will prove extremely difficult to restrict the one without restricting the others.

The speech that is socially vicious, to the point of endangering all our liberties, functions chiefly as an instrument of the competitive "business" economy. Such an instrument it has always been, no doubt; but never before so important an instrument, for the reason that modern methods of communicating thought are more subtle and effective than any ever before known, while the verification of the truth or relevance of the thought so communicated is far more difficult. The result is that there issues daily from the press and the radio a deluge of statements that are false in fact or misleading in implication, that are made for no other purpose than to fool most of the people most of the time for the economic advantage of a few of the people all of the time. This steady stream of falsification is called by various names which smell, if not too sweet, at least not foul — "advertising," "propaganda," "selling the public." Selling the public is an exact description of what is essential to the "successful" conduct of "business" — so essential that it is itself a business; and not the least of its evil consequences is that it is creating a state of mind disposed to regard anything as O.K. if you can get by with it. This manifestation of free speech is a far greater menace to liberal democracy than the freest dissemination of an alien political philosophy by Nazis or Communists is ever likely to be; and the only defense for it is that to restrict it would endanger the principle of free speech.

III

The danger is chiefly verbal, since the practical problem carries us beyond the speech we condemn to the practical activities that occasion it. The evil cannot of course be cured by creating a board of censors pledged to exclude lies from oral discourse and printed matter. But neither can it be cured by waiting while truth crushed to earth pulls itself up and assembles its battered armor. In the competitive business economy, as it now operates, those who largely control and extensively use the avenues of expression are not seeking truth but profits; and freedom of speech will not cease to be used for purposes that are socially vicious until it ceases to be profitable so to use it. It would seem, then, that the essential thing is either to abolish the profit motive or divert it into socially useful channels. Communists and fascists confidently assert that neither of these objects can be attained through the liberal democratic political mechanism. They may be right. Liberals who think otherwise must at least take account of a disturbing fact: the liberal democratic political mechanism functions by enacting into law the common will that emerges from free discussion. Thus the circle seems completed: for curing the evil effects of free speech we must rely upon a public opinion formed in large part by the speech that is evil.

The editors of *The Nation* admit that the situation is full of "uncomfortable possibilities," but they hold to the traditional liberal method of meeting them — the promotion, by appealing from free speech drunk to free speech sober, of a "healthy movement to the left." The uncomfortable possibilities, as seen by *The Nation*, are that "continued economic decline," and the "demand of a despairing people for drastic action," may enable a "well-directed [Nazi] propaganda" [free speech] to bring about the "triumph of fascism... with all its attendant horrors." Another uncomfortable possibility, as I see it, is that the "healthy" movement to the left may become "unhealthy," and end in the triumph of communism with all its attendant horrors. Among the attendant horrors, in either case, *The Nation* would no doubt include, as one of the drastic actions demanded by a despairing people, the drastic suppression of free speech as a political method. The logical dilemma involved in free speech for political objects is therefore this: if social ills cannot be alleviated by the democratic method of free speech, this very freedom of speech will be used by those whose avowed aim is the abolition of the democratic method, and free speech as a part of it. Am I expected to be loyal to the principle of free speech to the point of standing by while, writhing in pain among its worshipers, it commits suicide? It is asking a lot.

It is asking too much only so long as we remain in the realm of logical discourse. In demanding the privilege of free speech from a liberal government in order to convince its citizens that free speech is a present evil, neither Nazis nor Communists have any standing in logic. Their programs, so far as the preliminaries of social reform are concerned at least, are based on an appeal to force rather than to persuasion. Very well, since that is their program, let us cease talking, resort to force, and see which is the stronger. Their own principles teach us that it is logical for them to resist oppression but merely impudent to resent it. Nevertheless, the logic of events is not very logical, and I see no practical virtue in a syllogistic solution of the problem presented by Nazi and Communist propaganda. The freedom of speech which by their own logic I deny them, I am therefore quite willing to concede them in fact.

I concede it because, for one thing, there is a bare chance that the Nazis, or the Communists, or both of them may be, as they seem to claim, true prophets whom the world would not willingly have stoned — agents of the God Woden or the Dialectic duly accredited and predestined to establish truth and justice by a ruthless suppression of oppressors. I should dislike very much to put myself in opposition to the forces, not of persuasion, that make for righteousness, apart from the fact that it would be futile to do so if they are in any case to triumph. But perhaps a better reason for conceding freedom of speech to Nazis and Communists is that freedom of speech can neither be suppressed by argument nor maintained by suppressing argument. The principle of free speech must justify itself or go under. The real danger, from the liberal point of view, is not that Nazis and Communists will destroy liberal democracy by free speaking, but that liberal democracy, through its own failure to cure social ills, will destroy itself by breeding Nazis and Communists. If liberal democracy can sufficiently alleviate social ills, freedom of speech will have sufficiently justified itself; if not, freedom of speech will in any case be lost in the shuffle.

Whatever may be the virtues of freedom of speech in the abstract world of ideas, as a rule of political action it is like any other law — it works well only if the conditions are favorable. It works not too badly in a society in which the material conditions of life, being relatively easy, create no radical conflicts of interest, and in which there exists a common tradition of moral and social ideas, one of which is that just government rests upon the consent, freely expressed and freely given, of the governed.   A long-time view of human civilization discloses the fact that such favorable conditions have existed only in a few places or for short times.   Experience gives us slight ground for supposing that nineteenth-century liberal democracy is a permanent conquest of intelligence.   It may very well be but a passing phase, a cumbersome and extravagant form of government, practicable only in relatively simple agricultural societies suddenly dowered with unaccustomed wealth by the discovery of new instruments of power and the invention of new machines.

Present events do little to discredit this view.   Certain European countries have already abandoned liberal democracy — gladly by all accounts — for one or another form of dictatorship.   Even in this Land of the Free there are developing, under the pressure of continued economic distress, significant movements to the left and to the right.   These movements can surely not be checked by declaring a quarantine — by pronouncing them "unhealthy," and closing the mouths of Nazis and Communists in order to prevent the spread of verbal infection.   They can be checked only by removing the economic confusion and distress on which they thrive.   Perhaps this can be done by the methods of liberal democracy.   Perhaps not.   If not, it needs no prophet to tell us that sooner or later a "despairing people" will demand "drastic action."   The demand may assume the voice of communism, or of fascism, or of both.   It may conceivably lead to another "irreconcilable conflict," similar to that of 1861.   Outmoded liberals would not then need, any more than they did in 1861, to ask whether they should abandon the principle of free speech, since the principle of free speech would already have abandoned them.   The logic of events would present them — perhaps is already, without their knowing it, presenting them — with nothing better than that choice of evils which liberals always have to face in times when arms speak and laws are silent, the choice of joining one uncongenial armed camp or the other.

There would, it is true, be another way out for any liberal who wished to take it.   Any man might in desperation cry, "A plague on both your houses!" Withdrawing from the world of affairs, he might, as a non-resistant pacifist, still exercise the right of private judgment, having deliberately fortified himself to face, as the woman said, "the consequences."   In short, he might, as a last refuge from imbecility, turn Christian and practice the precept that it is better to suffer evil than to do it.   In that elevated spiritual retreat he would have leisure to meditate the bitter truth of Pascal's profound commonplace: "It is *right* to follow that which is just, it is *necessary* to follow that which is stronger."

GEORGE HERBERT PALMER

GEORGE HERBERT PALMER (1842–1933) was graduated at Harvard in the class of 1864 and was connected with that institution most of his life, as teacher of philosophy. His literary work covers a wide range, including a translation of the *Odyssey*, an edition of the works of George Herbert, the *Life of Alice Freeman Palmer*, and many essays on educational, literary, and social topics. "Self-Cultivation in English" was an address delivered at the University of Michigan in 1897. It is an example of Professor Palmer's lucid, easy style and orderly development of the topic. Other essays are "The New Education," "The Glory of the Imperfect."

SELF–CULTIVATION IN ENGLISH *

ENGLISH study has four aims: the mastery of our language as a science, as a history, as a joy, and as a tool. I am concerned with but one, the mastery of it as a tool. Philology and grammar present it as a science; the one attempting to follow its words, the other its sentences, through all the intricacies of their growth, and so to manifest laws which lie hidden in these airy products no less than in the moving stars or the myriad flowers of spring. Fascinating and important as all this is, I do not recommend it here. For I want to call attention only to that sort of English study which can be carried on without any large apparatus of books. For a reason similar, though less cogent, I do not urge historical study. Probably the current of English literature is more attractive through its continuity than that of any other nation. Notable works in verse and prose have appeared in long succession, and without gaps intervening, in a way that would be hard to parallel in any other language known to man. A bounteous endowment this for every English speaker, and one which should stimulate us to trace the marvellous and close-linked progress from the times of the Saxons to those of Tennyson and Kipling. Literature too has this advantage over every other species of art study, that everybody can examine the original masterpieces and not depend on reproductions, as in the cases of painting, sculpture, and architecture; or on intermediate interpretation, as in the case of music. Today most of these masterpieces can be bought for a trifle, and even a poor man can follow through centuries the thoughts of his ancestors. But even so, ready of access as it is, English can be studied as a history only at the cost of solid time and continuous attention, much more time than the majority of those for whom I am writing can afford. By most of us our mighty literature cannot be taken in its continuous current, the later stretches proving interesting through relation with the earlier. It must be taken fragmentarily, if at all, the attention delaying on those parts only which offer the greatest beauty or promise the best exhilaration. In other words, English may be possible as a joy where it is not possible as a history. In the endless wealth which our poetry,

* By permission of the publishers, Houghton Mifflin Company.

story, essay, and drama afford, every disposition may find its appropriate nutriment, correction, or solace. He is unwise, however busy, who does not have his loved authors, veritable friends with whom he takes refuge in the intervals of work and by whose intimacy he enlarges, refines, sweetens, and emboldens his own limited existence. Yet the fact that English as a joy must largely be conditioned by individual taste prevents me from offering general rules for its pursuit. The road which leads one man straight to this joy leads another to tedium. In all literary enjoyment there is something incalculable, something wayward, eluding the precision of rule, and rendering inexact the precepts of him who would point out the path to it. While I believe that many suggestions may be made, useful to the young enjoyer and promotive of his wise vagrancy, I shall not undertake here the complicated task of offering them. Let enjoyment go, let history go, let science go, and still English remains — English as a tool. Every hour our language is an engine for communicating with others, every instant for fashioning the thoughts of our own minds. I want to call attention to the means of mastering this curious and essential tool, and to lead everyone who reads me to become discontented with his employment of it.

The importance of literary power needs no long argument. Everybody acknowledges it, and sees that without it all other human faculties are maimed. Shakespeare says that death-bringing time "insults o'er dull and speechless tribes." It and all who live in it insult over the speechless person. So mutually dependent are we that on our swift and full communication with one another is staked the success of almost every scheme we form. He who can explain himself may command what he wants. He who cannot is left to the poverty of individual resource; for men do what we desire only when persuaded. The persuasive and explanatory tongue is, therefore, one of the chief levers of life. Its leverage is felt within us as well as without, for expression and thought are integrally bound together. We do not first possess completed thoughts and then express them. The very formation of the outward product extends, sharpens, enriches the mind which produces, so that he who gives forth little after a time is likely enough to discover that he has little to give forth. By expression too we may carry our benefits and our names to a far generation. This durable character of fragile language puts a wide difference of worth between it and some of the other great objects of desire, — health, wealth, and beauty, for example. These are notoriously liable to accident. We tremble while we have them. But literary power, once ours, is more likely than any other possession to be ours always. It perpetuates and enlarges itself by the very fact of its existence and perishes only with the decay of the man himself. For this reason, because more than health, wealth, and beauty, literary style may be called the man, good judges have found in it the final test of culture and have said that he, and he alone, is a well-educated person who uses his language with power and beauty. The supreme and ultimate product of civilization, it has well been said, is two or three persons talking together in a room. Between ourselves and our language there accordingly springs up an association peculiarly close. We are as sensitive to criticism of our speech as of our manners. The young man looks up with awe to him who has written a book, as already half divine; and the graceful speaker is a universal object of envy.

But the very fact that literary endowment is immediately recognized and eagerly envied has induced a strange illusion in regard to it. It is supposed to be something mysterious, innate in him who possesses it and quite out of the reach of him who has it not. The very contrary is the fact. No human employment is more free and calculable than the winning of language. Undoubtedly there are natural aptitudes for it, as there are for farming, seamanship, or being a good husband. But nowhere is straight work more effective. Persistence, care, discriminating observation, ingenuity, refusal to lose heart, — traits which in every other occupation tend toward excellence, — tend toward it here with special security. Whoever goes to his grave with bad English in his mouth has no one to blame but himself for the disagreeable taste; for if faulty speech can be inherited, it can be exterminated too. I hope to point out some of the methods of substituting good English for bad. And since my space is brief, and I wish to be remembered, I throw what I have to say into the form of four simple precepts which, if pertinaciously obeyed, will, I believe, give anybody effective mastery of English as a tool.

First then, "Look well to your speech." It is commonly supposed that when a man seeks literary power he goes to his room and plans an article for the press. But this is to begin literary culture at the wrong end. We speak a hundred times for every once we write. The busiest writer produces little more than a volume a year, not so much as his talk would amount to in a week. Consequently through speech it is usually decided whether a man is to have command of his language or not. If he is slovenly in his ninety-nine cases of talking, he can seldom pull himself up to strength and exactitude in the hundredth case of writing. A person is made in one piece, and the same being runs through a multitude of performances. Whether words are uttered on paper or to the air, the effect on the utterer is the same. Vigor or feebleness results according as energy or slackness has been in command. I know that certain adaptations to a new field are often necessary. A good speaker may find awkwardnesses in himself when he comes to write, a good writer when he speaks. And certainly cases occur where a man exhibits distinct strength in one of the two, speaking or writing, and not in the other. But such cases are rare. As a rule, language once within our control can be employed for oral or for written purposes. And since the opportunities for oral practice enormously outbalance those for written, it is the oral which are chiefly significant in the development of literary power. We rightly say of the accomplished writer that he shows a mastery of his own tongue.

This predominant influence of speech marks nearly all great epochs of literature. The Homeric poems are addressed to the ear, not to the eye. It is doubtful if Homer knew writing, certain that he knew profoundly every quality of the tongue, — veracity, vividness, shortness of sentence, simplicity of thought, obligation to insure swift apprehension. Writing and rigidity are apt to go together. In Homer's smooth-slipping verses one catches everywhere the voice. So too the aphorisms of Hesiod might naturally pass from mouth to mouth, and the stories of Herodotus be told by an old man at the fireside. Early Greek literature is plastic and garrulous. Its distinctive glory is that it contains no literary note; that it gives forth human feeling not in conventional arrangement, but with apparent spontaneity — in short, that it is speech literature, not book literature. And the same tendency continued long among the Greeks. At the culmination of their power the drama was their chief literary form, — the drama, which is but speech ennobled, connected, clarified. Plato too, following the dramatic precedent and the precedent of his talking master, accepted conversation as his medium for philosophy and imparted to it the vivacity, ease, waywardness even, which the best conversation exhibits. Nor was the experience of the Greeks peculiar. Our literature shows a similar tendency. Its bookish times are its decadent times, its talking times its glory. Chaucer, like Herodotus, is a story-teller, and follows the lead of those who on the Continent entertained courtly circles with pleasant tales. Shakespeare and his fellows in the spacious times of great Elizabeth did not concern themselves with publication. Marston in one of his prefaces thinks it necessary to apologize for putting his piece in print, and says he would not have done such a thing if unscrupulous persons, hearing the play at the theatre, had not already printed corrupt versions of it. Even the Queen Anne's men, far removed though they are from anything dramatic, still shape their ideals of literature by demands of speech. The essays of the Spectator, the poems of Pope, are the remarks of a cultivated gentleman at an evening party. Here is the brevity, the good taste, the light touch, the neat epigram, the avoidance of whatever might stir passion, controversy, or laborious thought, which characterize the conversation of a well-bred man. Indeed it is hard to see how any literature can be long vital which is based on the thought of a book and not on that of living utterance. Unless the speech notion is uppermost, words will not run swiftly to their mark. They delay in delicate phrasings while naturalness and a sense of reality disappear. Women are the best talkers. I sometimes please myself with noticing that three of the greatest periods of English literature coincide with the reigns of the three English queens.

Fortunate it is, then, that self-cultivation in the use of English must chiefly come through speech; because we are always speaking, whatever else we do. In opportunities for acquiring a mastery of language the poorest and busiest are at no large disadvantage as compared with the leisured rich. It is true the strong impulse which comes from the suggestion and approval of society may in some cases be absent, but this can be compensated by the sturdy purpose of the learner. A recognition of the beauty of well-ordered words, a strong desire, patience under discouragements, and promptness in counting every occasion as of consequence, — these are the simple agencies which sweep one on to power. Watch your speech then. That is all which is needed. Only it is desirable to know what qualities of speech to watch for. I find three, — accuracy, audacity, and range, — and I will say a few words about each.

Obviously, good English is exact English. Our words should fit our thoughts like a glove and be neither too wide nor too tight. If too wide, they will include much vacuity beside the intended matter. If too tight, they will check the strong grasp. Of the two dangers, looseness is by far the greater. There are people who say what they mean with such a naked precision that nobody not familiar with the subject can quickly catch the sense. George Herbert and Emerson strain the attention of many. But niggardly and angular speakers are rare. Too frequently words signify nothing in particular. They are merely thrown out in a certain direction to report a vague and undetermined meaning or even a general emotion. The first business of everyone who would train himself in language is to articulate his thought, to know definitely what he wishes to say, and then to pick those words which compel the hearer to think of this and only this. For such a purpose two words are often better than three. The fewer the words, the more pungent the impression. Brevity is the soul, not simply of a jest, but of wit in its finer sense where it is identical with wisdom. He who can put a great deal into a little is the master. Since firm texture is what is wanted, not embroidery or superposed ornament, beauty has been well defined as the purgation of superfluities. And certainly many a paragraph might have its beauty brightened by letting quiet words take the place of its loud words, omitting its "verys," and striking out its purple patches of fine writing. Here is Ben Jonson's description of Bacon's language: "There happened in my time one noble speaker who was full of gravity in his speech. No man ever spoke more neatly, more pressly, more weightily, or suffered less emptiness, less idleness, in what he uttered. No member of his speech but consisted of his own graces. His hearers could not cough or look aside without loss. He commanded when he spoke, and had his judges angry or pleased at his discretion." Such are the men who command, men who speak "neatly and pressly." But to gain such precision is toilsome business. While we are in training for it, no word must unpermittedly pass the portal of the teeth. Something like what we mean must never be counted equivalent to what we mean. And if we are not sure of our meaning or of our word, we must pause until we are sure. Accuracy does not come of itself. For persons who can use several languages, capital practice in acquiring it can be had by translating from one language to another and seeing that the entire sense is carried over. Those who have only their native speech will find it profitable often to attempt definitions of the common words they use. Inaccuracy will not stand up against the habit of definition. Dante boasted that no rhythmic exigency had ever made him say what he did not mean. We heedless and unintending speakers, under no exigency of rhyme or reason, say what we mean but seldom, and still more seldom mean what we say. To hold our thoughts and words in significant adjustment requires unceasing consciousness, a perpetual determination not to tell lies; for of course every inaccuracy is a bit of untruthfulness. We have something in mind, yet convey something else to our hearer. And no moral purpose will save us from this untruthfulness unless that purpose is sufficient to inspire the daily drill which brings the power to be true. Again and again we are shut up to evil because we have not acquired the ability of goodness.

But after all, I hope that nobody who hears me will quite agree. There is something enervating in conscious care. Necessary as it is in shaping our purposes, if allowed too direct and exclusive control consciousness breeds hesitation and feebleness. Action is not excellent, at least, until spontaneous. In piano-playing we begin by picking out each separate note; but we do not call the result music until we play our notes by the handful, heedless how each is formed. And so it is everywhere. Consciously selective conduct is elementary and inferior. People distrust it, or rather they distrust him who exhibits it. If anybody talking to us visibly studies his words, we turn away. What he says may be well enough as school exercise, but it is not conversation. Accordingly, if we would have our speech forcible, we shall need to put into it quite as much of audacity as we do of precision, terseness, or simplicity. Accuracy alone is not a thing to be sought, but accuracy and dash. It was said of Fox, the English orator and statesman, that he was accustomed to throw himself headlong into the middle of a sentence, trusting to God Almighty to get him out. So must we speak. We must not before beginning a sentence decide what the end shall be; for if we do, nobody will care to hear that end. At the beginning, it is the beginning which claims the attention of both speaker and listener, and trepidation about going on will mar all. We must give our thought its head, and not drive it with too tight a rein, nor grow timid when it begins to prance a bit. Of course we must retain coolness in courage, applying the results of our previous discipline in accuracy; but we need not move so slowly as to become formal. Pedantry is worse than blundering. If we care for grace and flexible beauty of language, we must learn to let our thought run. Would it, then, be too much of an Irish bull to say that in acquiring English we need to cultivate spontaneity? The uncultivated kind is not worth much; it is wild and haphazard stuff, unadjusted to its uses. On the other hand no speech is of much account, however just, which lacks the element of courage. Accuracy and dash, then, the combination of the two, must be our difficult aim; and we must not rest satisfied so long as either dwells with us alone.

But are the two so hostile as they at first appear? Or can, indeed, the first be obtained without the aid of the second? Supposing we are convinced that words possess no value in themselves, and are correct or incorrect only as they truly report experience, we shall feel ourselves impelled in the mere interest of accuracy to choose them freshly and to put them together in ways in which they never co-operated before, so as to set forth with distinctness that which just we, not other people, have seen or felt. The reason why we do not naturally have this daring exactitude is probably twofold. We let our experiences be blurred, not observing sharply, nor knowing with any minuteness what we are thinking about; and so there is no individuality in our language. And then, besides, we are terrorized by custom and inclined to adjust what we would say to what others have said before. The cure for the first of these troubles is to keep our eye on our object, instead of on our listener or ourselves; and for the second, to learn to rate the expressiveness of language more highly than its correctness. The opposite of this, the disposition to set correctness above expressiveness, produces that peculiarly vulgar diction known as "school-ma'am English," in which for the sake of a dull accord with usage all the picturesque, imaginative and forceful employment of words is sacrificed. Of course we must use words so that people can understand them, and understand them too with ease; but this once granted, let our language be our own, obedient to our special needs. "Whenever," says Thomas Jefferson, "by small grammatical negligences the energy of an idea can be condensed, or a word be made to stand for a sentence, I hold grammatical rigor in contempt." "Young man," said Henry Ward Beecher to one who was pointing out grammatical errors in a sermon of his, "when the English language gets in my way, it doesn't stand a chance." No man can be convincing, writer or speaker, who is afraid to send his words wherever they may best follow his meaning, and this with but little regard to whether any other person's words have ever been there before. In assessing merit let us not stupefy ourselves with using negative standards. What stamps a man as great is not freedom from faults, but abundance of powers.

Such audacious accuracy, however, distinguishing as it does noble speech from commonplace speech, can be practised only by him who has a wide range of words. Our ordinary range is absurdly narrow. It is important, therefore, for anybody who would cultivate himself in English to make strenuous and systematic efforts to enlarge his vocabulary. Our dictionaries contain more than a hundred thousand words. The average speaker employs about three thousand. Is this because ordinary people have only three or four thousand things to say? Not at all. It is simply due to dullness. Listen to the average schoolboy. He has a dozen or two nouns, half a dozen verbs, three or four adjectives, and enough conjunctions and prepositions to stick the conglomerate together. This ordinary speech deserves the description which Hobbes gave to his "State of Nature," that "it is solitary, poor, nasty, brutish and short." The fact is, we fall into the way of thinking that the wealthy words are for others and that they do not belong to us. We are like those who have received a vast inheritance, but who persist in the inconveniences of hard beds, scanty food, rude clothing, who never travel, and who limit their purchases to the bleak necessities of life. Ask such people why they endure niggardly living while wealth in plenty is lying in the bank, and they can only answer that they have never learned how to spend. But this is worth learning. Milton used eight thousand words, Shakespeare fifteen thousand. We have all the subjects to talk about that these early speakers had; and in addition we have bicycles and sciences and strikes and political combinations and all the complicated living of the modern world.

Why then do we hesitate to swell our words to meet our needs? It is a nonsense question. There is no reason. We are simply lazy, too lazy to make ourselves comfortable. We let our vocabularies be limited and get along rawly without the refinements of human intercourse, without refinements in our own thoughts; for thoughts are almost as dependent on words as words on thoughts. For example, all exasperations we lump together as "aggravating," not considering whether they may not rather be displeasing, annoying, offensive, disgusting, irritating, or even maddening; and without observing too that in our reckless usage we have burned up a word which might be convenient when we should need to mark some shading of the word "increase." Like the bad cook, we seize the frying-pan whenever we need to fry, broil, roast, or stew, and then we wonder why all our dishes taste alike while in the next house the food is appetizing. It is all unnecessary. Enlarge the vocabulary. Let anyone who wants to see himself grow resolve to adopt two new words each week. It will not be long before the endless and enchanting variety of the world will begin to reflect itself in his speech, and in his mind as well. I know that when we use a word for the first time we are startled, as if a fire-cracker went off in our neighborhood. We look about hastily to see if anyone has noticed. But finding that no one has, we may be emboldened. A word used three times slips off the tongue with entire naturalness. Then it is ours forever, and with it some phase of life which had been lacking hitherto. For each word presents its own point of view, discloses a special aspect of things, reports some little importance not otherwise conveyed, and so contributes its small emancipation to our tied-up minds and tongues.

But a brief warning may be necessary to make my meaning clear. In urging the addition of new words to our present poverty-stricken stock I am far from suggesting that we should seek out strange, technical or inflated expressions, which do not appear in ordinary conversation. The very opposite is my aim. I would put every man who is now employing a diction merely local and personal in command of the approved resources of the English language. Our poverty usually comes through provinciality, through accepting without criticism the habits of our special set. My family, my immediate friends, have a diction of their own. Plenty of other words, recognized as sound, are known to be current in books and to be employed by modest and intelligent speakers, only we do not use them. Our set has never said "diction," or "current," or "scope," or "scanty," or "hitherto," or "convey," or "lack." Far from unusual as these words are, to adopt them might seem to set me apart from those whose intellectual habits I share. From this I shrink. I do not like to wear clothes suitable enough for others, but not in the style of my own plain circle. Yet if each one of that circle does the same, the general shabbiness is increased. The talk of all is made narrow enough to fit the thinnest there. What we should seek is to contribute to each of the little companies with which our life is bound up a gently enlarging influence, such impulses as will not startle or create detachment, but which may save from humdrum, routine and dreary usualness. We cannot be really kind without being a little venturesome. The small shocks of our increasing vocabulary will in all probability be as helpful to our friends as to ourselves.

Such then are the excellences of speech. If we would cultivate ourselves in the use of English, we must make our daily talk accurate, daring and full. I have insisted on these points the more because in my judgment all literary power, especially that of busy men, is rooted in sound speech. But though the roots are here, the growth is also elsewhere. And I pass to my later precepts, which, if the earlier one has been laid well to heart, will require only brief discussion.

Secondly, "Welcome every opportunity for writing." Important as I have shown speech to be, there is much that it cannot do. Seldom can it teach structure. Its space is too small. Talking moves in sentences, and rarely demands a paragraph. I make my little remark, — a dozen or two words, — then wait for my friend to hand me back as many more. This gentle exchange continues by the hour; but either of us would feel himself unmannerly if he should grasp an entire five minutes and make it uninterruptedly his. That would not be speaking, but rather speech-making. The brief groupings of words which make up our talk furnish capital practice in precision, boldness and variety; but they do not contain room enough for exercising our constructive faculties. Considerable length is necessary if we are to learn how to set forth *B* in right relation to *A* on the one hand and to *C* on the other; and while keeping each a distinct part, are to be able through their smooth progression to weld all the parts together into a compacted whole. Such wholeness is what we mean by literary form. Lacking it, any piece of writing is a failure; because in truth it is not a piece, but pieces. For ease of reading, or for the attainment of an intended effect, unity is essential — the multitude of statements, anecdotes, quotations, arguings, gay sportings and appeals, all "bending one way their gracious influence." And this dominant unity of the entire piece obliges unity also in the subordinate parts. Not enough has been done when we have huddled together a lot of wandering sentences and penned them in a paragraph, or even when we have linked them together by the frailties of "and, and." A sentence must be compelled to say a single thing; a paragraph, a single thing; an essay, a single thing. Each part is to be a preliminary whole and the total a finished whole. But the ability to construct one thing out of many does not come by nature. It implies fecundity, restraint, an eye for effects, the forecast of finish while we are still working in the rough, obedience to the demands of development and a deaf ear to whatever calls us into the by-paths of caprice; in short it implies that the good writer is to be an artist.

Now something of this large requirement which composition makes, the young writer instinctively feels, and he is terrified. He knows how ill-fitted he is to direct "toil co-operant to an end"; and when he sits down to the desk and sees the white sheet of paper before him, he shivers. Let him know that the shiver is a suitable part of the performance. I well remember the pleasure with which, as a young man, I heard my venerable and practised professor of rhetoric say that he supposed there was no work known to man more difficult than writing. Up to that time I had supposed its severities peculiar to myself. It cheered me, and gave me courage to try again, to learn that I had all mankind for my fellow sufferers. Where this is not understood, writing is avoided. From such avoidance I would save the young writer by my precept to seek every opportunity to write. For most of us this is a new way of confronting composition — treating it as an opportunity, a chance, and not as a burden or compulsion. It saves from slavishness and takes away the drudgery of writing, to view each piece of it as a precious and necessary step in the pathway to power. To those engaged in bread-winning employments these opportunities will be few. Spring forward to them, then, using them to the full. Severe they will be because so few, for only practice breeds ease; but on that very account let no one of them pass with merely a second-best performance. If a letter is to be written to a friend, a report to an employer, a communication to a newspaper, see that it has a beginning, a middle and an end. The majority of writings are without these pleasing adornments. Only the great pieces possess them. Bear this in mind and win the way to artistic composition by noticing what should be said first, what second and what third.

I cannot leave this subject, however, without congratulating the present generation on its advantages over mine. Children are brought up today, in happy contrast with my compeers, to feel that the pencil is no instrument of torture, hardly indeed to distinguish it from the tongue. About the time they leave their mother's arms they take their pen in hand. On paper they are encouraged to describe their interesting birds, friends, adventures. Their written lessons are almost as frequent as their oral, and they learn to write compositions while not yet quite understanding what they are about. Some of these fortunate ones will, I hope, find the language I have sadly used about the difficulty of writing extravagant. And let me say too that since frequency has more to do with ease of writing than anything else, I count the newspaper men lucky because they are writing all the time, and I do not think so meanly of their product as the present popular disparagement would seem to require. It is hasty work undoubtedly and bears the marks of haste. But in my judgment, at no period of the English language has there been so high an average of sensible, vivacious and informing sentences written as appears in our daily press. With both good and evil results, the distinction between book literature and speech literature is breaking down. Everybody is writing, apparently in verse and prose; and if the higher graces of style do not often appear, neither on the other hand do the ruder awkwardnesses and obscurities. A certain straightforward English is becoming established. A whole nation is learning the use of its mother tongue. Under such circumstances it is doubly necessary that anyone who is conscious of feebleness in his command of English should promptly and earnestly begin the cultivation of it.

My third precept shall be, "Remember the other person." I have been urging self-cultivation in English as if it concerned one person alone, ourself. But every utterance really concerns two. Its aim is social. Its object is communication; and while unquestionably prompted halfway by the desire to ease our mind through self-expression, it still finds its only justification in the advantage somebody else will draw from what is said. Speaking or writing is, therefore, everywhere a double-ended process. It springs from me, it penetrates him; and both of these ends need watching. Is what I say precisely what I mean? That is an important question. Is what I say so shaped that it can readily be assimilated by him who hears? This is a question of quite as great consequence and much more likely to be forgotten. We are so full of ourselves that we do not remember the other person. Helter-skelter we pour forth our unaimed words merely for our personal relief, heedless whether they help or hinder him whom they still purport to address. For most of us are grievously lacking in imagination, which is the ability to go outside ourselves and take on the conditions of another mind. Yet this is what the literary artist is always doing. He has at once the ability to see for himself and the ability to see himself as others see him. He can lead two lives as easily as one life; or rather, he has trained himself to consider that other life as of more importance than his, and to reckon his comfort, likings and labors as quite subordinated to the service of that other. All serious literary work contains within it this readiness to bear another's burden. I must write with pains, that he may read with ease. I must

Find out men's wants and wills,
And meet them *there*.

As I write, I must unceasingly study what is the line of least intellectual resistance along which my thought may enter the differently constituted mind; and to that line I must subtly adjust, without enfeebling, my meaning. Will this combination of words or that make the meaning clear? Will this order of presentation facilitate swiftness of apprehension, or will it clog the movement? What temperamental perversities in me must be set aside in order to render my reader's approach to what I would tell him pleasant? What temperamental perversities in him must be accepted by me as fixed facts, conditioning all I say? These are the questions the skilful writer is always asking.

And these questions, as will have been perceived already, are moral questions no less than literary. That golden rule of generous service by which we do for others what we would have them do for us is a rule of writing too. Every writer who knows his trade perceives that he is a servant, that it is his business to endure hardship if only his reader may win freedom from toil, that no impediment to that reader's understanding is too slight to deserve diligent attention, that he has consequently no right to let a single sentence slip from him unsocialized — I mean, a sentence which cannot become as naturally another's possession as his own. In the very act of asserting himself he lays aside what is distinctively his. And because these qualifications of the writer are moral qualifications they can never be completely fulfilled so long as we live and write. We may continually approximate them more nearly, but there will still always be possible an alluring refinement of exercise beyond. The world of the literary artist and the moral man is interesting through its inexhaustibility; and he who serves his fellows by writing or by speech is artist and moral man in one. Writing a letter is a simple matter, but it is a moral matter and an artistic; for it may be done either with imagination or with raw self-centredness. What things will my correspondent wish to know? How can I transport him out of his properly alien surroundings into the vivid impressions which now are mine? How can I tell all I long to tell and still be sure the telling will be for him as lucid and delightful as for me? Remember the other person, I say. Do not become absorbed in yourself. Your interests cover only the half of any piece of writing; the other man's less visible half is necessary to complete yours. And if I have here discussed writing more than speech, that is merely because when we speak we utter our first thoughts, but when we write, our second, — or better still, our fourth; and in the greater deliberation which writing affords I have felt that the demands of morality and art, which are universally imbedded in language, could be more distinctly perceived. Yet none the less truly do we need to talk for the other person than to write for him.

But there remains a fourth weighty precept, and one not altogether detachable from the third. It is this: "Lean upon the subject." We have seen how the user of language, whether in writing or in speaking, works for himself; how he works for another individual too; but there is one more for whom his work is performed, one of greater consequence than any person, and that is his subject. From this comes his primary call. Those who in their utterance fix their thoughts on themselves, or on other selves, never reach power. That resides in the subject. There we must dwell with it and be content to have no other strength than its. When the frightened schoolboy sits down to write about Spring, he cannot imagine where the thoughts which are to make up his piece are to come from. He cudgels his brain for ideas. He examines his pen-point, the curtains, his inkstand, to see if perhaps ideas may not be had from these. He wonders what his teacher will wish him to say and he tries to recall how the passage sounded in the Third Reader. In every direction but one he turns, and that is the direction where lies the prime mover of his toil, his subject. Of that he is afraid. Now, what I want to make evident is that this subject is not in reality the foe, but the friend. It is his only helper. His composition is not to be, as he seems to suppose, a mass of his laborious inventions, but it is to be made up exclusively of what the subject dictates. He has only to attend. At present he stands in his own way, making such a din with his private anxieties that he cannot hear the rich suggestions of the subject. He is bothered with considering how he feels, or what he or somebody else will like to see on his paper. This is debilitating business. He must lean on his subject, if he would have his writing strong, and busy himself with what it says rather than with what he would say. Matthew Arnold, in the important preface to his poems of 1853, contrasting the artistic methods of Greek poetry and modern poetry, sums up the teaching of the Greeks in these words: "All depends upon the subject; choose a fitting action, penetrate yourself with the feeling of its situations; this done, everything else will follow." And he calls attention to the self-assertive and scatter-brained habits of our time. "How different a way of thinking from this is ours! We can hardly at the present day understand what Menander meant when he told a man who inquired as to the progress of his comedy that he had finished it, not having yet written a single line, because he had constructed the action of it in his mind. A modern critic would have assured him that the merit of his piece depended on the brilliant things which arose under his pen as he went along. I verily think that the majority of us do not in our hearts believe that there is such a thing as a total-impression to be derived from a poem or to be demanded from a poet. We permit the poet to select any action he pleases and to suffer that action to go as it will, provided he gratifies us with occasional bursts of fine writing and with a shower of isolated thoughts and images." Great writers put themselves and their personal imaginings out of sight. Their writing becomes a kind of transparent window on which reality is reflected, and through which people see, not them, but that of which they write. How much we know of Shakespeare's characters! How little of Shakespeare! Of him that might almost be said which Isaiah said of God, "He hideth himself." The best writer is the best mental listener, the one who peers farthest into his matter and most fully heeds its behests. Pre-eminently obedient is such a writer, — refinedly, energetically obedient. I once spent a day with a great novelist when the book which subsequently proved his masterpiece was only half written. I praised his mighty hero, but said I should think the life of an author would be miserable who, having created a character so huge, now had him in hand and must find something for him to do. My friend seemed puzzled by my remark, but after a moment's pause said, "I don't think you know how we work. I have nothing to do with the character. Now that he is created he will act as he will."

And such docility must be cultivated by everyone who would write well, such strenuous docility. Of course there must be energy in plenty; the imagination which I described in my third section, the passion for solid form as in my second, the disciplined and daring powers as in my first; but all these must be ready at a moment's notice to move where the matter calls and to acknowledge that all their worth is to be drawn from it. Religion is only enlarged good sense, and the words of Jesus apply as well to the things of earth as of heaven. I do not know where we could find a more compendious statement of what is most important for one to learn who would cultivate himself in English than the saying in which Jesus announces the source of his power, "The word which ye hear is not mine, but the Father's which sent me." Whoever can use such words will be a noble speaker indeed.

These then are the fundamental precepts which everyone must heed who would command our beautiful English language. There is of course a fifth. I hardly need name it; for it always follows after, whatever others precede. It is that we should do the work, and not think about it; do it day after day and not grow weary in bad doing. Early and often we must be busy and be satisfied to have a great deal of labor produce but a small result. I am told that early in life John Morley, wishing to engage in journalism, wrote an editorial and sent it to a paper every day for nearly a year before he succeeded in getting one accepted. We all know what a power he became in London journalism. I will not vouch for the truth of this story, but I am sure an ambitious author is wise who writes a weekly essay for his stove. Publication is of little consequence so long as one is getting one's self hammered into shape.

But before I close this paper let me acknowledge that in it I have neglected a whole class of helpful influences, probably quite as important as any I have discussed. Purposely I have passed them by. Because I wished to show what we can do for ourselves, I have everywhere assumed that our cultivation in English is to be effected by naked volition and a kind of dead lift. These are mighty agencies, but seldom in this interlocked world do they work well alone. They are strongest when backed by social suggestion and unconscious custom. Ordinarily the good speaker is he who keeps good company, but increases the helpful influence of that company by constant watchfulness along the lines I have marked out. So supplemented, my teaching is true. By itself it is not true. It needs the supplementation of others. Let him who would speak or write well seek out good speakers and writers. Let him live in their society, — for the society of the greatest writers is open to the most secluded, — let him feel the ease of their excellence, the ingenuity, grace and scope of their diction, and he will soon find in himself capacities whose development may be aided by the precepts I have given. Most of us catch better than we learn. We take up unconsciously from our surroundings what we cannot altogether create. All this should be remembered, and we should keep ourselves exposed to the wholesome words of our fellow men. Yet our own exertions will not on that account be rendered less important. We may largely choose the influences to which we submit; we may exercise a selective attention among these influences; we may enjoy, oppose, modify, or diligently ingraft what is conveyed to us, — and for doing any one of these things rationally we must be guided by some clear aim. Such aims, altogether essential even if subsidiary, I have sought to supply; and I would reiterate that he who holds them fast may become superior to linguistic fortune and be the wise director of his sluggish and obstinate tongue. It is as certain as anything can be that faithful endeavor will bring expertness in the use of English. If we are watchful of our speech, making our words continually more minutely true, free and resourceful; if we look upon our occasions of writing as opportunities for the deliberate work of unified construction; if in all our utterances we think of him who hears as well as of him who speaks; and above all, if we fix the attention of ourselves and our hearers on the matter we talk about and so let ourselves be supported by our subject — we shall make a daily advance not only in English study, but in personal power, in general serviceableness and in consequent delight.

ALEXANDER MEIKLEJOHN

ALEXANDER MEIKLEJOHN (1872–   ), an Englishman by birth, came to
the United States in 1880 and took his bachelor's degree at Brown University,
whither he returned as teacher of philosophy and dean. He was President
of Amherst College from 1912 to 1924. Later he was professor of philosophy
and Chairman of the Experimental College at the University of Wisconsin,
and is now director of the Center for Social Studies at San Francisco. Mr.
Meiklejohn is a leader in thought concerning higher education. He exempli-
fies the reaction against the elective system introduced at Harvard by President Eliot. The present essay, delivered as his inaugural address when he
became President of Amherst College (1912), is a plea for the older ideal of
intellectual discipline as fundamental in college training.

THE AIM OF A LIBERAL COLLEGE *

IN THE discussions concerning college education there is one voice which is
all too seldom raised and all too often disregarded. It is the voice of the
teacher and the scholar, of the member of the college faculty. It is my purpose to devote this address to a consideration of the ideals of the teacher, of
the problems of instruction as they present themselves to the men who are
giving the instruction. And I do this not because I believe that just now the
teachers are wiser than others who are dealing with the same questions, but
rather as an expression of a definite conviction with regard to the place of the
teacher in our educational scheme. It is, I believe, the function of the teacher
to stand before his pupils and before the community at large as the intellectual leader of his time. If he is not able to take this leadership, he is not
worthy of his calling. If the leadership is taken from him and given to
others, then the very foundations of the scheme of instruction are shaken.
He who in matters of teaching must be led by others is not the one to lead the
imitative undergraduate, not the one to inspire the confidence and loyalty
and discipleship on which all true teaching depends. If there are others who
can do these things better than the college teacher of today, then we must
bring them within the college walls. But if the teacher is to be deemed
worthy of his task, then he must be recognized as the teacher of us all, and
we must listen to his words as he speaks of the matters intrusted to his charge.

In the consideration of the educational creed of the teacher I will try to
give, first, a brief statement of his belief; second, a defense of it against other
views of the function of the college; third, an interpretation of its meaning
and significance; fourth, a criticism of what seem to me misunderstandings
of their own meaning prevalent among the teachers of our day; and, finally,
a suggestion of certain changes in policy which must follow if the belief of
the teacher is clearly understood and applied in our educational procedure.

* From *The Liberal College*, by Alexander Meiklejohn. Reprinted by permission of the
author and the publisher, Marshall Jones Company, Boston.

I

First, then, What do our teachers believe to be the aim of college instruction? Wherever their opinions and convictions find expression there is one contention which is always in the foreground, namely, that to be liberal a college must be essentially intellectual. It is a place, the teachers tell us, in which a boy, forgetting all things else, may set forth on the enterprise of learning. It is a time when a young man may come to awareness of the thinking of his people, may perceive what knowledge is and has been and is to be. Whatever light-hearted undergraduates may say, whatever the opinions of solicitous parents, of ambitious friends, of employers in search of workmen, of leaders in church or state or business — whatever may be the beliefs and desires and demands of outsiders — the teacher within the college, knowing his mission as no one else can know it, proclaims that mission to be the leading of his pupil into the life intellectual. The college is primarily not a place of the body, nor of the feelings, nor even of the will; it is, first of all, a place of the mind.

II

Against this intellectual interpretation of the college our teachers find two sets of hostile forces constantly at work. Outside the walls there are the practical demands of a busy commercial and social scheme; within the college there are the trivial and sentimental and irrational misunderstandings of its own friends. Upon each of these our college teachers are wont to descend as Samson upon the Philistines, and when they have had their will, there is little left for another to accomplish.

As against the immediate practical demands from without, the issue is clear and decisive. College teachers know that the world must have trained workmen, skilled operatives, clever buyers, and sellers, efficient directors, resourceful manufacturers, able lawyers, ministers, physicians, and teachers. But it is equally true that, in order to do its own work, the liberal college must leave the special and technical training for these trades and professions to be done in other schools and by other methods. In a word, the liberal college does not pretend to give all the kinds of teaching which a young man of college age may profitably receive; it does not even claim to give all the kinds of intellectual training which are worth giving. It is committed to intellectual training of the liberal type, whatever that may mean, and to that mission it must be faithful. One may safely say, then, on behalf of our college teachers, that their instruction is intended to be radically different from that given in the technical school or even in the professional school. Both these institutions are practical in a sense which the college, as an intellectual institution, is not. In the technical school the pupil is taught how to do some one of the mechanical operations which contribute to human welfare. He is trained to print, to weave, to farm, to build; and for the most part he is trained to do these things by practice rather than by theory. His possession when he leaves the school is not a stock of ideas, of scientific principles, but a measure of skill, a collection of rules of thumb. His primary function as a tradesman is not to understand but to do, and in doing what is needed he is following directions which have first been thought out by others and are now practised by him. The technical school intends to furnish training which, in the sense in which we use the term, is not intellectual but practical.

In a corresponding way the work of the professional school differs from that of the liberal college. In the teaching of engineering, medicine, or law we are or may be beyond the realm of mere skill and within the realm of ideas and principles. But the selection and the relating of these ideas is dominated by an immediate practical interest which cuts them off from the intellectual point of view of the scholar. If an undergraduate should take away from his studies of chemistry, biology, and psychology only those parts which have immediate practical application in the field of medicine, the college teachers would feel that they had failed to give to the boy the kind of instruction demanded of a college. It is not their purpose to furnish applied knowledge in this sense. They are not willing to cut up their sciences into segments and to allow the student to select those segments which may be of service in the practice of an art or a profession. In one way or another the teacher feels a kinship with the scientist and the scholar which forbids him to submit to this domination of his instruction by the demands of an immediate practical interest. Whatever it may mean, he intends to hold the intellectual point of view and to keep his students with him if he can. In response, then, to demands for technical and professional training our college teachers tell us that such training may be obtained in other schools; it is not to be had in a college of liberal culture.

In the conflict with the forces within the college our teachers find themselves fighting essentially the same battle as against the foes without. In a hundred different ways the friends of the college — students, graduates, trustees, and even colleagues — seem to them so to misunderstand its mission as to minimize or to falsify its intellectual ideals. The college is a good place for making friends; it gives excellent experience in getting on with men; it has exceptional advantages as an athletic club; it is a relatively safe place for a boy when he first leaves home; on the whole, it may improve a student's manners; it gives acquaintance with lofty ideals of character, preaches the doctrine of social service, exalts the virtues and duties of citizenship. All these conceptions seem to the teacher to hide or to obscure the fact that the college is fundamentally a place of the mind, a time for thinking, an opportunity for knowing. And perhaps in proportion to their own loftiness of purpose and motive they are the more dangerous as tending all the more powerfully to replace or to nullify the underlying principle upon which they all depend. Here again, when misconception clears away, one can have no doubt that the battle of the teacher is a righteous one. It is well that a boy should have four good years of athletic sport, playing his own games and watching the games of his fellows; it is well that his manners should be improved; it is worth while to make good friends; it is very desirable to develop the power of understanding and working with other men; it is surely good to grow in strength and purity of character, in devotion to the interests of society, in readiness to meet the obligations and opportunities of citizenship. If any one of these be lacking from the fruits of a college course we may well complain of the harvest. And yet is it not true that by sheer pressure of these, by the driving and pulling of the social forces within and without the college, the mind of the student is constantly torn from its chief concern? Do not our social and practical interests distract our boys from the intellectual achievements which should dominate their imagination and command their zeal? I believe that one may take it as the deliberate judgment of the teachers of our colleges today that the function of the college is constantly misunderstood, and that it is subjected to demands which, however friendly in intent, are yet destructive of its intellectual efficiency and success.

III

But now that the contention of the teacher has been stated and reaffirmed against objections, it is time to ask: What does it mean? And how can it be justified? By what might does a company of scholars invite young men to spend with them four years of discipleship? Do they, in their insistence upon the intellectual quality of their ideal, intend to give an education which is avowedly unpractical? If so, how shall they justify their invitation, which may perhaps divert young men from other interests and other companionships which are valuable to themselves and to their fellows? In a word, what is the underlying motive of the teacher, what is there in the intellectual interests and activities which seems to him to warrant their domination over the training and instruction of young men during the college years?

It is no fair answer to this question to summon us to faith in intellectual ideals, to demand of us that we live the life of the mind with confidence in the virtues of intelligence, that we love knowledge and because of our passion follow after it. Most of us are already eager to accept intellectual ideals, but our very devotion to them forbids that we accept them blindly. I have often been struck by the inner contradictoriness of the demand that we have faith in intelligence. It seems to mean, as it is so commonly made to mean, that we must unintelligently follow intelligence, that we must ignorantly pursue knowledge, that we must question everything except the business of asking questions, that we think about everything except the use of thinking itself. As Mr. F. H. Bradley would say, the dictum "Have faith in intelligence" is so true that it constantly threatens to become false. Our very conviction of its truth compels us to scrutinize and test it to the end.

How, then, shall we justify the faith of the teacher? What reason can we give for our exaltation of intellectual training and activity? To this question two answers are possible. First, knowledge and thinking are good in themselves. Secondly, they help us in the attainment of other values in life which without them would be impossible. Both these answers may be given and are given by college teachers. Within them must be found whatever can be said by way of explanation and justification of the work of the liberal college.

The first answer receives just now far less of recognition than it can rightly claim. When the man of the world is told that a boy is to be trained in thinking just because of the joys and satisfactions of thinking itself, just in order that he may go on thinking as long as he lives, the man of the world has been heard to scoff and to ridicule the idle dreaming of scholarly men. But if thinking is not a good thing in itself, if intellectual activity is not worth while for its own sake, will the man of the world tell us what is? There are those among us who find so much satisfaction in the countless trivial and vulgar amusements of a crude people that they have no time for the joys of the mind. There are those who are so closely shut up within a little round of petty pleasures that they have never dreamed of the fun of reading and conversing and investigating and reflecting. And of these one can only say that the difference is one of taste, and that their tastes seem to be relatively dull and stupid. Surely it is one function of the liberal college to save boys from that stupidity, to give them an appetite for the pleasures of thinking, to make them sensitive to the joys of appreciation and understanding, to show them how sweet and captivating and wholesome are the games of the mind. At the time when the play element is still dominant it is worth while to acquaint boys with the sport of facing and solving problems. Apart from some of the experiences of friendship and sympathy, I doubt if there are any human interests so permanently satisfying, so fine and splendid in themselves, as are those of intellectual activity. To give our boys that zest, that delight in things intellectual, to give them an appreciation of a kind of life which is well worth living, to make them men of intellectual culture — that certainly is one part of the work of any liberal college.

On the other hand, the creation of culture as so defined can never constitute the full achievement of the college. It is essential to awaken the impulses of inquiry, of experiment, of investigation, of reflection, the instinctive cravings of the mind. But no liberal college can be content with this. The impulse to thinking must be questioned and rationalized as must every other instinctive response. It is well to think, but what shall we think about? Are there any lines of investigation and reflection more valuable than others, and, if so, how is their value to be tested? Or again, if the impulse for thinking comes into conflict with other desires and cravings, how is the opposition to be solved? It has sometimes been suggested that our man of intellectual culture may be found, like Nero, fiddling with words while all the world about him is aflame. And the point of the suggestion is not that fiddling is a bad and worthless pastime, but rather that it is inopportune on such an occasion, that the man who does it is out of touch with his situation, that his fiddling does not fit his facts. In a word, men know with regard to thinking, as with regard to every other content of human experience, that it cannot be valued merely in terms of itself. It must be measured in terms of its relation to other contents and to human experience as a whole. Thinking is good in itself,— but what does it cost of other things; what does it bring of other values? Place it amid all the varied contents of our individual and social experience, measure it in terms of what it implies, fix it by means of its relations, and then you will know its worth not simply in itself but in that deeper sense which comes when human desires are rationalized and human lives are known in their entirety, as well as they can be known by those who are engaged in living them.

In this consideration we find the second answer of the teacher to the demand for justification of the work of the college. Knowledge is good, he tells us, not only in itself, but in its enrichment and enhancement of the other values of our experience. In the deepest and fullest sense of the words, knowledge pays. This statement rests upon the classification of human actions into two groups, those of the instinctive type and those of the intellectual type. By far the greater part of our human acts are carried on without any clear idea of what we are going to do or how we are going to do it. For the most part our responses to our situations are the immediate responses of feeling, of perception, of custom, of tradition. But slowly and painfully, as the mind has developed, action after action has been translated from the feeling to the ideational type; in wider and wider fields men have become aware of their own modes of action, more and more they have come to understanding, to knowledge of themselves and of their needs. And the principle underlying all our educational procedure is that, on the whole, actions become more successful as they pass from the sphere of feeling to that of understanding. Our educational belief is that in the long run, if men know what they are going to do and how they are going to do it and what is the nature of the situation with which they are dealing, their response to that situation will be better adjusted and more beneficial than are the responses of the feeling type in like situations.

It is all too obvious that there are limits to the validity of this principle. If men are to investigate, to consider, to decide, then action must be delayed, and we must pay the penalty of waiting. If men are to endeavor to understand and know their situations, then we must be prepared to see them make mistakes in their thinking, lose their certainty of touch, wander off into pitfalls and illusions and fallacies of thought, and, in consequence, secure for the time results far lower in value than those of the instinctive response which they seek to replace. The delays and mistakes and uncertainties of our thinking are a heavy price to pay, but it is the conviction of the teacher that the price is as nothing when compared with the goods which it buys. You may point out to him the loss when old methods of procedure give way before the criticism of understanding, you may remind him of the pain and suffering when old habits of thought and action are replaced, you may reprove him for all the blunders of the past; but in spite of it all he knows, and you know, that in human lives taken separately and in human life as a whole men's greatest lack is the lack of understanding, their greatest hope to know themselves and the world in which they live.

Within the limits of this general educational principle the place of the liberal college may easily be fixed. In the technical school pupils are prepared for a specific work and are kept for the most part on the plane of perceptual action, doing work which others understand. In the professional school, students are properly within the realm of ideas and principles, but they are still limited to a specific human interest with which alone their understanding is concerned. But the college is called liberal as against both of these because the instruction is dominated by no special interest, is limited to no single human task, but is intended to take human activity as a whole, to understand human endeavors not in their isolation, but in their relations to one another and to the total experience which we call the life of our people. And just as we believe that the building of ships has become more successful as men have come to a knowledge of the principles involved in their construction; just as the practice of medicine has become more successful as we have come to a knowledge of the human body, of the conditions within it and the influences without; — just so the teacher in the liberal college believes that life as a total enterprise, life as it presents itself to each one of us in his career as an individual — human living — will be more successful in so far as men come to understand it and to know it as they attempt to carry it on. To give boys an intellectual grasp on human experience — this it seems to me is the teacher's conception of the chief function of the liberal college.

May I call attention to the fact that this second answer of the teacher defines the aim of the college as avowedly and frankly practical? Knowledge is to be sought chiefly for the sake of its contribution to the other activities of human living. But, on the other hand, it is as definitely declared that in method the college is fully and unreservedly intellectual. If we can see that these two demands are not in conflict, but that they stand together in the harmonious relation of means and ends, of instrument and achievement, of method and result, we may escape many a needless conflict and keep our educational policy in singleness of aim and action. To do this we must show that the college is intellectual, not as opposed to practical interests and purposes, but as opposed to unpractical and unwise methods of work. The issue is not between practical and intellectual aims but between the immediate and the remote aim, between the hasty and the measured procedure, between the demand for results at once and the willingness to wait for the best results. The intellectual road to success is longer and more roundabout than any other, but they who are strong and willing for the climbing are brought to higher levels of achievement than they could possibly have attained had they gone straight forward in the pathway of quick returns. If this were not true the liberal college would have no proper place in our life at all. In so far as it is true the college has a right to claim the best of our young men to give them its preparation for the living they are to do.

IV

But now that we have attempted to interpret the intellectual mission of the college, it may be fair to ask: "Are the teachers and scholars of our day always faithful to that mission? Do their statements and their practice always ring in accord with the principle which has been stated?" It seems to me that at two points they are constantly off the key, constantly at variance with the reasons by which alone their teaching can be justified.

In the first place, it often appears as if our teachers and scholars were deliberately in league to mystify and befog the popular mind regarding this practical value of intellectual work. They seem not to wish too much said about the results and benefits. Their desire is to keep aloft the intellectual banner, to proclaim the intellectual gospel, to demand of student and public alike adherence to the faith. And in general when they are questioned as to results they give little satisfaction except to those who are already pledged to unwavering confidence in their *ipse dixits*. And largely as a result of this attitude the American people seem to me to have little understanding of the intellectual work of the college. Our citizens and patrons can see the value of games and physical exercises; they readily perceive the importance of the social give and take of a college democracy; they can appreciate the value of studies which prepare a young man for his profession and so anticipate or replace the professional school; they can even believe that if a boy is kept at some sort of thinking for four years his mind may become more acute, more systematic, more accurate, and hence more useful than it was before. But as for the content of a college course, as for the value of knowledge, what a boy gains by knowing Greek or economics, philosophy or literature, history or biology, except as they are regarded as having professional usefulness, I think our friends are in the dark and are likely to remain so until we turn on the light. When our teachers say, as they sometimes do say, that the effect of knowledge upon the character and life of the student must always be for the college an accident, a circumstance which has no essential connection with its real aim or function, then it seems to me that our educational policy is wholly out of joint. If there be no essential connection between instruction and life, then there is no reason for giving instruction except in so far as it is pleasant in itself, and we have no educational policy at all. As against this hesitancy, this absence of a conviction, we men of the college should declare in clear and unmistakable terms our creed — the creed that knowledge is justified by its results. We should say to our people so plainly that they cannot misunderstand: "Give us your boys, give us the means we need, and we will so train and inform the minds of those boys that their own lives and the lives of the men about them shall be more successful than they could be without our training. Give us our chance and we will show your boys what human living is, for we are convinced that they can live better in knowledge than they can in ignorance."

There is a second wandering from the faith which is so common among investigators that it may fairly be called the "fallacy of the scholar." It is the belief that all knowledge is so good that all parts of knowledge are equally good. Ask many of our scholars and teachers what subjects a boy should study in order that he may gain insight for human living, and they will say: "It makes no difference in what department of knowledge he studies; let him go into Sanscrit or bacteriology, into mathematics or history; if only he goes where men are actually dealing with intellectual problems, and if only he learns how to deal with problems himself, the aim of education is achieved, he has entered into intellectual activity." This point of view, running through all the varieties of elective system, seems to me hopelessly at variance with any sound educational doctrine. It represents the scholar of the day at his worst both as a thinker and as a teacher. In so far as it dominates a group of college teachers it seems to me to render them unfit to determine and to administer a college curriculum. It is an announcement that they have no guiding principles in their educational practice, no principles of selection in their arrangement of studies, no genuine grasp on the relationship between knowledge and life. It is the concerted statement of a group of men each of whom is lost within the limits of his own special studies, and who as a group seem not to realize the organic relationships between them nor the common task which should bind them together.

In bringing this second criticism against our scholars I am not urging that the principle of election of college studies should be entirely discontinued. But I should like to inquire by what right and within what limits it is justified. The most familiar argument in its favor is that if a student is allowed to choose along the lines of his own intellectual or professional interest he will have enthusiasm, the eagerness which comes with the following of one's own bent. Now just so far as this result is achieved, just so far as the quality of scholarship is improved, the procedure is good, and we may follow it if we do not thereby lose other results more valuable than our gain. But if the special interest comes into conflict with more fundamental ones, if what the student prefers is opposed to what he ought to prefer, then we of the college cannot leave the choice with him. We must say to him frankly: "If you do not care for liberal training you had better go elsewhere; we have a special and definite task assigned us which demands that we keep free from the domination of special or professional pursuits. So long as we are faithful to that task we cannot give you what you ask."

In my opinion, however, the fundamental motive of the elective system is not the one which has been mentioned. In the last resort our teachers allow students to choose their own studies, not in order to appeal to intellectual or to professional interest, but because they themselves have no choice of their own in which they believe with sufficient intensity to impose it upon their pupils. And this lack of a dominating educational policy is in turn an expression of an intellectual attitude, a point of view, which marks the scholars of our time. In a word, it seems to me that our willingness to allow students to wander about in the college curriculum is one of the most characteristic expressions of a certain intellectual agnosticism, a kind of intellectual bankruptcy, into which, in spite of all our wealth of information, the spirit of the time has fallen. Let me explain my meaning.

The old classical curriculum was founded by men who had a theory of the world and of human life. They had taken all the available content of human knowledge and had wrought it together into a coherent whole. What they knew was, as judged by our standards, very little in amount. But upon that little content they had expended all the infinite pains of understanding and interpretation. They had taken the separate judgments of science, philosophy, history, and the arts, and had so welded them together, so established their relationships with one another, so freed them from contradictions and ambiguities that, so far as might be in their day and generation, human life as a whole and the world about us were known, were understood, were rationalized. They had a knowledge of human experience by which they could live and which they could teach to others engaged in the activities of living.

But with the invention of methods of scientific investigation and discovery there came pouring into the mind of Europe great masses of intellectual material: astronomy, physics, chemistry. This content for a time it could not understand, could not relate to what it already knew. The old boundary lines did not enclose the new fields; the old explanations and interpretations would not fit the new facts. Knowledge had not grown; it had simply been enlarged; and the two masses of content, the old and the new, stood facing each other with no common ground of understanding. Here was the intellectual task of the great leaders of the early modern thought of Europe: to re-establish the unity of knowledge, to discover the relationships between these apparently hostile bodies of judgments, to know the world again, but with all the added richness of the new insights and the new information. This was the work of Leibnitz and Spinoza, of Kant and Hegel, and those who labored with them. And in a very considerable measure the task had been accomplished, order had been restored. But again with the inrush of the newer discoveries, first in the field of biology and then later in the world of human relationships, the difficulties have returned, multiplied a thousandfold. Every day sees a new field of facts opened up, a new method of investigation invented, a new department of knowledge established. And in the rush of it all these new sciences come merely as additions, not to be understood but simply numbered, not to be interpreted but simply listed in the great collection of separate fields of knowledge. If you will examine the work of any scientist within one of these fields, you will find him ordering, systematizing, reducing to principles — in a word, knowing every fact in terms of its relation to every other fact and to the whole field within which it falls. But at the same time these separate sciences, these separate groups of judgment, are left standing side by side with no intelligible connections, no establishment of relationships, no interpretation in the sense in which we insist upon it with each of the fields taken by itself. Is it not the characteristic statement of a scholar of our time to say: "I do not know what may be the ultimate significance of these facts and these principles; all that I know is that if you will follow my methods within my field you will find the facts coming into order, the principles coming into simple and coherent arrangement. With any problems apart from this order and this arrangement I have intellectually no concern"?

It has become an axiom with us that the genuine student labors within his own field. And if the student ventures forth to examine the relations of his field to the surrounding country he very easily becomes a popularizer, a littérateur, a speculator, and, worst of all, unscientific. Now I do not object to a man's minding his own intellectual business if he chooses to do so, but when a man minds his own business because he does not know any other business, because he has no knowledge whatever of the relationships which justify his business and make it worth while, then I think one may say that, though such a man minds his own affairs, he does not know them, he does not understand them. Such a man, from the point of view of the demands of a liberal education, differs in no essential respect from the trades-man who does not understand his trade or the professional man who merely practises his profession. Just as truly as they, he is shut up within a special interest; just as truly as they, he is making no intellectual attempt to under-stand his experience in its unity. And the pity of it is that more and more the chairs in our colleges are occupied by men who have only this special interest, this specialized information, and it is through them that we attempt to give our boys a liberal education, which the teachers themselves have not achieved.

I should not like to be misunderstood in making this railing accusation against our teachers and our time. If I say that our knowledge is at pres-ent a collection of scattered observations about the world rather than an understanding of it, fairness compels the admission that the failure is due to the inherent difficulties of the situation and to the novelty of the problems presented. If I cry out against the agnosticism of our people it is not as one who has escaped from it, nor as one who would point the way back to the older synthesis, but simply as one who believes that the time has come for a reconstruction, for a new synthesis. We have had time enough now to get some notion of our bearings, shocks enough to get over our nervousness and discomfiture when a new one comes along. It is the opportunity and the obligation of this generation to think through the content of our know-ing once again, to understand it, so far as we can. And in such a battle as this, surely it is the part of the college to take the lead. Here is the mission of the college teacher as of no other member of our common life. Surely he should stand before his pupils and before all of us as a man who has achieved some understanding of this human situation of ours, but, more than that, as one who is eager for the conflict with the powers' of darkness and who can lead his pupils in enthusiastic devotion to the common cause of enlightenment.

V

And now, finally, after these attacks upon the policies which other men have derived from their love of knowledge, may I suggest two matters of policy which seem to me to follow from the definition of education which we have taken? The first concerns the content of the college course; the second has to do with the method of its presentation to the under-graduate.

We have said that the system of free election is natural for those to whom knowledge is simply a number of separate departments. It is equally true that just in so far as knowledge attains unity, just so far as the relations of the various departments are perceived, freedom of election by the student must be limited. For it at once appears that on the one side there are vast ranges of information which have virtually no significance for the purposes of a liberal education, while on the other hand there are certain elements so fundamental and vital that without any one of them a liberal education is impossible.

I should like to indicate certain parts of human knowledge which seem to me so essential that no principle of election should ever be allowed to drive them out of the course of any college student.

First, a student should become acquainted with the fundamental motives and purposes and beliefs which, clearly or unclearly recognized, underlie all human experience and bind it together. He must perceive the moral strivings, the intellectual endeavors, the esthetic experiences of his race, and closely linked with these, determining and determined by them, the beliefs about the world which have appeared in our systems of religion. To investigate this field, to bring it to such clearness of formulation as may be possible, is the task of philosophy — an essential element in any liberal education. Secondly, as in human living, our motives, purposes, and beliefs have found expression in institutions — those concerted modes of procedure by which we work together — a student should be made acquainted with these. He should see and appreciate what is intended, what accomplished, and what left undone by such institutions as property, the courts, the family, the church, the mill. To know these as contributing and failing to contribute to human welfare is the work of our social or humanistic sciences, into which a boy must go on his way through the liberal college. Thirdly, in order to understand the motives and the institutions of human life one must know the conditions which surround it, the stage on which the game is played. To give this information is the business of astronomy, geology, physics, chemistry, biology, and the other descriptive sciences. These a boy must know, so far as they are significant and relevant to his purpose. Fourthly, as all three of these factors, the motives, the institutions, the natural processes, have sprung from the past and have come to be what they are by change upon change in the process of time, the student of human life must try to learn the sequence of events from which the present has come. The development of human thought and attitude, the development of human institutions, the development of the world and of the beings about us — all these must be known, as throwing light upon present problems, present instrumentalities, present opportunities in the life of human endeavor. And in addition to these four studies which render human experience in terms of abstract ideas, a liberal education must take account of those concrete representations of life which are given in the arts, and especially in the art of literature. It is well that a boy should be acquainted with his world not simply as expressed by the principles of knowledge, but also as depicted by the artist with all the vividness and definiteness which are possible in the portrayal of individual beings in individual relationships. These five elements, then, a young man must take from a college of liberal training: the contributions of philosophy, of humanistic science, of natural science, of history, and of literature. So far as knowledge is concerned, these at least he should have, welded together in some kind of interpretation of his own experience and of the world in which he lives.

My second suggestion is that our college curriculum should be so arranged and our instruction so devised that its vital connection with the living of men should be obvious even to an undergraduate. A little while ago I heard one of the most prominent citizens of this country speaking of his college days, and he said: "I remember so vividly those few occasions on which the professor would put aside the books and talk like a real man about real things." Oh, the bitterness of those words to the teacher! Our books are not dealing with the real things, and for the most part we are not real men either, but just old fogies and bookworms. And to be perfectly frank about the whole matter, I believe that in large measure our pupils are indifferent to their studies simply because they do not see that these are important.

Now if we really have a vital course of study to present I believe that this difficulty can in large measure be overcome. It is possible to make a freshman realize the need of translating his experience from the forms of feeling to those of ideas. He can and he ought to be shown that now, his days of mere tutelage being over, it is time for him to face the problems of his people, to begin to think about those problems for himself, to learn what other men have learned and thought before him — in a word, to get himself ready to take his place among those who are responsible for the guidance of our common life by ideas and principles and purposes. If this could be done, I think we should get from the reality-loving American boy something like an intellectual enthusiasm, something of the spirit that comes when he plays a game that seems to him really worth playing. But I do not believe that this result can be achieved without a radical reversal of the arrangement of the college curriculum. I should like to see every freshman at once plunged into the problems of philosophy, into the difficulties and perplexities about our institutions, into the scientific accounts of the world especially as they bear on human life, into the portrayals of human experience which are given by the masters of literature. If this were done by proper teaching, it seems to me the boy's college course would at once take on significance for him; he would understand what he is about; and though he would be a sadly puzzled boy at the end of the first year, he would still have before him three good years of study, of investigation, of reflection, and of discipleship, in which to achieve, so far as may be, the task to which he has been set. Let him once feel the problems of the present, and his historical studies will become significant; let him know what other men have discovered and thought about his problems, and he will be ready to deal with them himself. But in any case, the whole college course will be unified and dominated by a single interest, a single purpose — that of so understanding human life as to be ready and equipped for the practice of it. And this would mean for the college, not another seeking of the way of quick returns, but rather an escape from aimless wanderings in the mere bypaths of knowledge, a resolute climbing on the highroad to a unified grasp upon human experience.

I have taken so much of your time this morning that an apology seems due for the things I have omitted to mention. I have said nothing of the organization of the college, nothing of the social life of the students, nothing of the relations with the alumni, nothing of the needs and qualifications of the teachers, and even within the consideration of the course of study, noth-

ing of the value of specialization or of the disciplinary subjects or of the training in language and expression.   And I have put these aside deliberately,
for the sake of a cause which is greater than any of them — a cause which
lies at the very heart of the liberal college.   It is the cause of making clear
to the American people the mission of the teacher, of convincing them of
the value of knowledge: not the specialized knowledge which contributes
to immediate practical aims, but the unified understanding which is Insight.

LITERARY CRITICISM

THE three essays chosen to represent literary criticism are written from different points of view. Dr. Santayana deals with Dickens as the most enduringly popular of English novelists to deserve the title of classic. Mr. Henry Hazlitt in "Literature versus Opinion" discusses a general topic of wide interest at the present time. Mr. Max Eastman offers us an example of the immediately contemporary book review in the department of what may be called literary journalism.

When one sets out to discuss a familiar great figure in literature, one must be sure that one has something fresh to say. Note how Mr. Santayana takes for granted that any literate person knows not only something about Dickens, but something about the conventional things that have been said of Dickens. Dickens is a sentimentalist; Dickens is vulgar; Dickens is a great comic artist; Dickens is theatrical; Dickens loves to describe eating and drinking and coaching and the life of the lower classes. These are matters that anybody knows who knows Dickens at all; but this critic, not blinking any of these familiar comments, takes hold of them, puts them in fresh perspective, shows how they all spring out of a central point of view, a common sympathy that is Dickens; and then proceeds to show how necessary and healthy and true is the essential thing which lies at the heart of the great novelist. In short, he recreates a Dickens whom one recognizes to be quite true, and yet totally fresh; and the result of reading the essay is to make us want to read the novels.

Mr. Hazlitt writes with reference to a school of critics who have maintained that literature is sound in proportion as it mirrors what they call the class struggle. These critics go on to demand novels that shall, as they say, "tell the truth" about the class struggle. But the facts of social history are not necessarily the truth of literary art; and Mr. Hazlitt examines the premises of the argument and reveals from the point of view of literature what is good and what is bad about a theory which is advanced from the point of view of sociology and economics. We have, in sum, an examination of a bit of literary theory by a practicing literary critic.

Mr. Eastman set himself an analogous problem.   Unthinking readers having taken a noted contemporary writer at his face value, Mr. Eastman, with wonderful tact, examines the writer and shows that the writer is not doing at all what he thinks he is doing; that, in fact, his whole nature really moves him in quite an opposite direction.   The fact that Mr. Eastman admires Mr. Hemingway for certain qualities does not blind him as a literary critic to the fact that Mr. Hemingway may mistake his own virtues and misunderstand his own vices.   The resulting essay, with perfect good humor, quietly puts to death a totally false interpretation of a writer's merits.

GEORGE SANTAYANA

GEORGE SANTAYANA (1863–   ), born in Spain, came to Boston when nine years old. After his undergraduate course at Harvard and some years of study in Germany he returned to the former to teach philosophy. In 1915 he resigned, to live in Europe and write. His first published work was in poetry — the *Sonnets* in 1894. Philosophy has furnished the intellectual background for his poetry and literary criticism; in the latter category, *Interpretations of Poetry and Religion*, and *Three Philosophic Poets* may be mentioned. More recently he has published *Character and Opinion in the United States* and *Soliloquies in England*, from which the study of Dickens is taken. Mr. Santayana is a classicist in literary criticism, as witness his strictures on Whitman and Browning, in his essay "The Poetry of Barbarism." His appreciation of Dickens is the more noteworthy, since that author does not lend himself to definition by classical formulae. He has recently entered the field of fiction with a novel, *The Last Puritan*.

DICKENS *

IF CHRISTENDOM should lose everything that is now in the melting-pot, human life would still remain amiable and quite adequately human. I draw this comforting assurance from the pages of Dickens. Who could not be happy in his world? Yet there is nothing essential to it which the most destructive revolution would be able to destroy. People would still be as different, as absurd, and as charming as are his characters; the springs of kindness and folly in their lives would not be dried up. Indeed, there is much in Dickens which communism, if it came, would only emphasize and render universal. Those schools, those poorhouses, those prisons, with those surviving shreds of family life in them, show us what in the coming age (with some sanitary improvements) would be the nursery and home of everybody. Everybody would be a waif, like Oliver Twist, like Smike, like Pip, and like David Copperfield; and amongst the agents and underlings of social governement, to whom all these waifs would be entrusted, there would surely be a goodly sprinkling of Pecksniffs, Squeers and Fangs; whilst the Fagins would be everywhere commissioners of the people. Nor would there fail to be, in high places and in low, the occasional sparkle of some Pickwick or Cheeryble Brothers or Sam Weller or Mark Tapley; and the voluble Flora Finchings would be everywhere in evidence, and the strong-minded Betsey Trotwoods in office. There would also be, among the inefficient, many a Dora and Agnes and Little Emily — with her charm but without her tragedy, since this is one of the things which the promised social reform would happily render impossible; I mean, by removing all the disgrace of it. The only element in the world of Dickens which would become obsolete would be the setting, the atmosphere of material instru-

* By permission of the publisher, Charles Scribner's Sons, New York.

mentalities and arrangements, as travelling by coach is obsolete; but travelling by rail, by motor, or by airship will emotionally be much the same thing. It is worth noting how such instrumentalities, which absorb modern life, are admired and enjoyed by Dickens, as they were by Homer. The poets ought not to be afraid of them; they exercise the mind congenially, and can be played with joyfully. Consider the black ships and the chariots of Homer, the coaches and river-boats of Dickens, and the aeroplanes of today; to what extent would an unspoiled young mind turn with more interest? Dickens tells us little of English sports, but he shares the sporting nature of the Englishman, to whom the whole material world is a playing-field, the scene giving ample scope to his love of action, legality, and pleasant achievement. His art is to sport according to the rules of the game, and to do things for the sake of doing them, rather than for any ulterior motive.

It is remarkable, in spite of his ardent simplicity and openness of heart, how insensible Dickens was to the greater themes of the human imagination — religion, science, politics, art. He was a waif himself, and utterly disinherited. For example, the terrible heritage of contentious religions which fills the world seems not to exist for him. In this matter he was like a sensitive child, with a most religious disposition, but no religious ideas. Perhaps, properly speaking, he had no *ideas* on any subject; what he had was a vast sympathetic participation in the daily life of mankind; and what he saw of ancient institutions made him hate them, as needless sources of oppression, misery, selfishness, and rancour. His one political passion was philanthropy, genuine but felt only on its negative, reforming side; of positive utopias or enthusiasms we hear nothing. The political background of Christendom is only, so to speak, an old faded back-drop for his stage; a castle, a frigate, a gallows, and a large female angel with white wings standing above an orphan by an open grave — a decoration which has to serve for all the melodramas in his theatre, intellectually so provincial and poor. Common life as it is lived was varied and lovable enough for Dickens, if only the pests and cruelties could be removed from it. Suffering wounded him, but not vulgarity; whatever pleased his senses and whatever shocked them filled his mind alike with romantic wonder, with the endless delight of observation. Vulgarity — and what can we relish, if we recoil at vulgarity? — was innocent and amusing; in fact, for the humorist, it was the spice of life. There was more piety in being human than in being pious. In reviving Christmas, Dickens transformed it from the celebration of a metaphysical mystery into a feast of overflowing simple kindness and good cheer; the church bells were still there — in the orchestra; and the angels of Bethlehem were still there — painted on the back-curtain. Churches, in his novels, are vague, desolate places where one has ghastly experiences, and where only the pew-opener is human; and such religious and political conflicts as he depicts in *Barnaby Rudge* and in *A Tale of Two Cities* are street brawls and prison scenes and conspiracies in taverns, without any indication of the contrasts in mind or interests between the opposed parties. Nor had Dickens any lively sense for fine art, classical tradition, science, or even the manners and feelings of the upper classes in his own time and country: in his novels we may almost say there is no army, no navy, no church, no sport, no distant travel, no daring adventure, no feeling for the watery wastes and the motley nations of the planet, and — luckily, with his notion of them — no lords and ladies. Even love of the traditional sort is hardly in Dickens's sphere — I mean the soldierly passion in which a rather rakish gallantry was sobered by devotion, and loyalty rested on pride. In Dickens love is sentimental or benevolent or merry or sneaking or canine; in his last book he was going to describe a love that was passionate and criminal; but love for him was never chivalrous, never poetical. What he paints most tragically is a quasi-paternal devotion in the old to the young, the love of Mr. Peggotty for Little Emily, or of Solomon Gills for Walter Gay. A series of shabby little adventures, such as might absorb the interest of an average youth, were romantic enough for Dickens.

I say he was disinherited, but he inherited the most terrible negations. Religion lay on him like the weight of the atmosphere, sixteen pounds to the square inch, yet never noticed nor mentioned. He lived and wrote in the shadow of the most awful prohibitions. Hearts petrified by legality and falsified by worldliness offered, indeed, a good subject for a novelist, and Dickens availed himself of it to the extent of always contrasting natural goodness and happiness with whatever is morose; but his morose people were wicked, not virtuous in their own way; so that the protest of his temperament against his environment never took a radical form nor went back to first principles. He needed to feel, in his writing, that he was carrying the sympathies of every man with him. In him conscience was single, and he could not conceive how it could ever be divided in other men. He denounced scandals without exposing shams, and conformed willingly and scrupulously to the proprieties. Lady Dedlock's secret, for instance, he treats as if it were the sin of Adam, remote, mysterious, inexpiable. Mrs. Dombey is not allowed to deceive her husband except by pretending to deceive him. The seduction of Little Emily is left out altogether, with the whole character of Steerforth, the development of which would have been so important in the moral experience of David Copperfield himself. But it is not public prejudice alone that plays the censor over Dickens's art; his own kindness and even weakness of heart act sometimes as marplots. The character of Miss Mowcher, for example, so brilliantly introduced, was evidently intended to be shady, and to play a very important part in the story; but its original in real life, which was recognized, had to be conciliated, and the sequel was omitted and patched up with an apology — itself admirable — for the poor dwarf. Such a sacrifice does honour to Dickens's heart; but artists should meditate on their works in time, and it is easy to remove any too great likeness in a portrait by a few touches making it more consistent than real people are apt to be; and in this case, if the little creature had been really guilty, how much more subtle and tragic her apology for herself might have been, like that of the bastard Edmund in *King Lear*! So, too, in *Dombey and Son*, Dickens could not bear to let Walter Gay turn out badly, as he had been meant to do, and to break his uncle's heart as well as the heroine's; he was accordingly transformed into a stage hero miraculously saved from shipwreck, and Florence was not allowed to reward the admirable Toots, as she should have done, with her trembling hand.   But Dickens was no free artist; he had more genius than taste, a warm fancy not aided by a thorough understanding of complex characters.   He worked under pressure, for money and applause, and often had to cheapen in execution what his inspiration had so vividly conceived.

What, then, is there left, if Dickens has all these limitations?   In our romantic disgust we might be tempted to say, Nothing.   But in fact almost everything is left, almost everything that counts in the daily life of mankind, or that by its presence or absence can determine whether life shall be worth living or not; because a simple good life is worth living, and an elaborate bad life is not.   There remains in the first place eating and drinking; relished not bestially, but humanly, jovially, as the sane and exhilarating basis for everything else.   This is a sound English beginning; but the immediate sequel, as the England of that day presented it to Dickens, is no less delightful.   There is the ruddy glow of the hearth; the sparkle of glasses and brasses and well-scrubbed pewter; the savoury fumes of the hot punch, after the tingle of the wintry air; the coaching-scenes, the motley figures and absurd incidents of travel; the changing sights and joys of the road.   And then, to balance this, the traffic of ports and cities, the hubbub of crowded streets, the luxury of shop-windows and of palaces not to be entered; the procession of the passers-by, shabby or ludicrously genteel; the dingy look and musty smell of their lodgings; the labyrinth of back-alleys, courts, and mews, with their crying children, and scolding old women, and listless, half-drunken loiterers.   These sights, like fables, have a sort of moral in them to which Dickens was very sensitive; the important air of nobodies on great occasions, the sadness and preoccupation of the great as they hasten by in their mourning or on their pressing affairs; the sadly comic characters of the tavern; the diligence of shopkeepers, like squirrels turning in their cages; the children peeping out everywhere like grass in an untrodden street; the charm of humble things, the nobleness of humble people, the horror of crime, the ghastliness of vice, the deft hand and shining face of virtue passing through the midst of it all; and finally a fresh wind of indifference and change blowing across our troubles and clearing the most lurid sky.

I do not know whether it was Christian charity or naturalistic insight, or a mixture of both (for they are closely akin) that attracted Dickens particularly to the deformed, the half-witted, the abandoned, or those impeded or misunderstood by virtue of some singular inner consecration.   The visible moral of these things, when brutal prejudice does not blind us to it, comes very near to true philosophy; one turn of the screw, one flash of reflection, and we have understood nature and human morality and the relation between them.

In his love of roads and wayfarers, of river-ports and wharves and the idle or sinister figures that lounge about them, Dickens was like Walt Whitman; and I think a second Dickens may any day appear in America, when it is possible in that land of hurry to reach the same degree of saturation, the same unquestioning pleasure in the familiar facts.   The spirit of

Dickens would be better able to do justice to America than was that of Walt Whitman; because America, although it may seem nothing but a noisy nebula to the impressionist, is not a nebula but a concourse of very distinct individual bodies, natural and social, each with its definite interests and story. Walt Whitman had a sort of transcendental philosophy which swallowed the universe whole, supposing there was a universal spirit in things identical with the absolute spirit that observed them; but Dickens was innocent of any such clap-trap, and remained a true spirit in his own person. Kindly and clear-sighted, but self-identical and unequivocally human, he glided through the slums like one of his own little heroes, uncontaminated by their squalor and confusion, courageous and firm in his clear allegiances amid the flux of things, a pale angel at the Carnival, his heart aflame, his voice always flute-like in its tenderness and warning. This is the true relation of spirit to existence, not the other which confuses them; for this earth (I cannot speak for the universe at large) has no spirit of its own, but brings forth spirits only at certain points, in the hearts and brains of frail living creatures, who like insects flit through it, buzzing and gathering what sweets they can; and it is the spaces they traverse in this career, charged with their own moral burden, that they can report on or describe, not things rolling on to infinity in their vain tides. To be hypnotized by that flood would be a heathen idolatry. Accordingly Walt Whitman, in his comprehensive democratic vistas, could never see the trees for the wood, and remained incapable, for all his diffuse love of the human herd, of ever painting a character or telling a story; the very things in which Dickens was a master. It is this life of the individual, as it may be lived in a given nation, that determines the whole value of that nation to the poet, to the moralist, and to the judicious historian. But for the excellence of the typical single life, no nation deserves to be remembered more than the sands of the sea; and America will not be a success, if every American is a failure.

Dickens entered the theatre of this world by the stage door; the shabby little adventures of the actors in their private capacity replace for him the mock tragedies which they enact before a dreaming public. Mediocrity of circumstances and mediocrity of soul for ever return to the centre of his stage; a more wretched or a grander existence is sometimes broached, but the pendulum soon swings back, and we return, with the relief with which we put on our slippers after the most romantic excursion, to a golden mediocrity — to mutton and beer, and to love and babies in a suburban villa with one frowsy maid. Dickens is the poet of those acres of yellow brick streets which the traveller sees from the railway viaducts as he approaches London; they need a poet, and they deserve one, since a complete human life may very well be lived there. Their little excitements and sorrows, their hopes and humours are like those of the Wooden Midshipman in *Dombey and Son*; but the sea is not far off, and the sky — Dickens never forgets it — is above all those brief troubles. He had a sentiment in the presence of this vast flatness of human fates, in spite of their individual pungency, which I think might well be the dominant sentiment of mankind in the future; a sense of happy freedom in littleness, an open-eyed reverence and religion without words. This universal human anonymity is like a sea, an infinitive democratic desert, chock-full and yet the very image of emptiness, with nothing in it for the mind, except, as the Moslems say, the presence of Allah. Awe is the counterpart of humility — and this is perhaps religion enough. The atom in the universal vortex ought to be humble; he ought to see that, materially, he doesn't much matter, and that morally his loves are merely his own, without authority over the universe. He can admit without obloquy that he is what he is; and he can rejoice in his own being, and in that of all other things in so far as he can share it sympathetically. The apportionment of existence and of fortune is in Other Hands; his own portion is contentment, vision, love, and laughter.

Having humility, that most liberating of sentiments, having a true vision of human existence and joy in that vision, Dickens had in a superlative degree the gift of humour, of mimicry, of unrestrained farce. He was the perfect comedian. When people say that Dickens exaggerates, it seems to me they can have no eyes and no ears. They probably have only *notions* of what things and people are; they accept them conventionally, at their diplomatic value. Their minds run on in the region of discourse, where there are masks only and no faces, ideas and no facts; they have little sense for those living grimaces that play from moment to moment upon the countenance of the world. The world is a perpetual caricature of itself; at every moment it is the mockery and the contradiction of what it is pretending to be. But as it nevertheless intends all the time to be something different and highly dignified, at the next moment it corrects and checks and tries to cover up the absurd thing it was; so that a conventional world, a world of masks, is superimposed on the reality, and passes in every sphere of human interest for the reality itself. Humour is the perception of this illusion, the fact allowed to pierce here and there through the convention, whilst the convention continues to be maintained as if we had not observed its absurdity. Pure comedy is more radical, cruder, in a certain sense less human; because comedy throws the convention over altogether, revels for a moment in the fact, and brutally says to the notions of mankind, as if it slapped them in the face, There, take that! That's what you really are! At this the polite world pretends to laugh, not tolerantly as it does at humour, but a little angrily. It does not like to see itself by chance in the glass, without having had time to compose its features for demure self-contemplation. "What a bad mirror," it exclaims; "it must be concave or convex; for surely I never looked like that. Mere caricature, farce, and horse play. Dickens exaggerates; *I* never was so sentimental as that; *I* never saw anything so dreadful; *I* don't believe there were ever any people like Quilp, or Squeers, or Serjeant Buzfuz." But the polite world is lying; there *are* such people; we are such people ourselves in our true moments, in our veritable impulses; but we are careful to stifle and to hide those moments from ourselves and from the world; to purse and pucker ourselves in the mask of our conventional personality; and so simpering, we profess that it is very coarse and inartistic of Dickens to undo our life's work for us in an instant, and remind us of what we are. And as to other people, though we may allow that considered superficially

they are often absurd, we do not wish to dwell on their eccentricities, nor
to mimic them. On the contrary, it is good manners to look away quickly,
to suppress a smile, and to say to ourselves that the ludicrous figure in the
street is not at all comic, but a dull ordinary Christian, and that it is foolish
to give any importance to the fact that its hat has blown off, that it has
slipped on an orange-peel and unintentionally sat on the pavement, that it
has a pimple on its nose, that its one tooth projects over its lower lip, that it is
angry with things in general, and that it is looking everywhere for the penny
which it holds tightly in its hand. That may fairly represent the moral
condition of most of us at most times; but we do not want to think of it;
we do not want to see; we gloss the fact over; we console ourselves before
we are grieved, and reassert our composure before we have laughed. We
are afraid, ashamed, anxious to be spared. What displeases us in Dickens
is that he does not spare us; he mimics things to the full; he dilates and
exhausts and repeats; he wallows. He is too intent on the passing experience
to look over his shoulder, and consider whether we have not already understood, and had enough. He is not thinking of us; he is obeying the impulse
of the passion, the person, or the story he is enacting. This faculty, which
renders him a consummate comedian, is just what alienated from him a
later generation in which people of taste were aesthetes and virtuous people
were higher snobs; they wanted a mincing art, and he gave them copious
improvization, they wanted analysis and development, and he gave them
absolute comedy. I must confess, though the fault is mine and not his,
that sometimes his absoluteness is too much for me. When I come to the
death of Little Nell, or to What the Waves were always Saying, or even to
the incorrigible perversities of the pretty Dora, I skip. I can't take my liquor
neat in such draughts, and my inner man says to Dickens, Please don't. But
then I am a coward in so many ways! There are so many things in this
world that I skip, as I skip the undiluted Dickens! When I reach Dover on
a rough day, I wait there until the Channel is smoother; am I not travelling
for pleasure? But my prudence does not blind me to the admirable virtue
of the sailors that cross in all weathers, nor even to the automatic determination of the sea-sick ladies, who might so easily have followed my example,
if they were not the slaves of their railway tickets and of their labelled
luggage. They are loyal to their tour, and I to my philosophy. Yet as
wrapped in my great-coat and sure of a good dinner, I pace the windy pier
and soliloquize, I feel the superiority of the bluff tar, glad of breeze, stretching
a firm arm to the unsteady passenger, and watching with a masterful thrill
of emotion the home cliffs receding and the foreign coasts ahead. It is only
courage (which Dickens had without knowing it) and universal kindness
(which he knew he had) that are requisite to nerve us for a true vision of
this world. And as some of us are cowards about crossing the Channel,
and others about "crossing the bar," so almost everybody is a coward about
his own humanity. We do not consent to be absurd, though absurd we are.
We have no fundamental humility. We do not wish the moments of our
lives to be caught by a quick eye in their grotesque initiative, and to be
pilloried in this way before our own eyes. For that reason we don't like

Dickens, and don't like comedy, and don't like the truth.   Dickens could don the comic mask with innocent courage; he could wear it with a grace, ease, and irresistible vivacity seldom given to men.   We must go back for anything like it to the very greatest comic poets, to Shakespeare or to Aristophanes.   Who else, for instance, could have penned this:

> "It was all Mrs. Bumble.   She *would* do it," urged Mr. Bumble; first looking round to ascertain that his partner had left the room.
> "That is no excuse," replied Mr. Brownlow.   "You were present on the occasion of the destruction of these trinkets, and indeed are the more guilty of the two, in the eye of the law; for the law supposes that your wife acts under your direction."
> "If the law supposes that," said Mr. Bumble, squeezing his hat emphatically in both hands, "the law is a ass, a idiot.   If that's the eye of the law, the law is a bachelor; and the worst I wish the law is, that his eye may be opened by experience — by experience."
> Laying great stress on the repetition of these two words, Mr. Bumble fixed his hat on very tight, and putting his hands in his pockets, followed his helpmate downstairs.

This is high comedy; the irresistible, absurd, intense dream of the old fool, personifying the law in order to convince and to punish it.   I can understand that this sort of thing should not be common in English literature, nor much relished; because pure comedy is scornful, merciless, devastating, holding no door open to anything beyond.   Cultivated English feeling winces at this brutality, although the common people love it in clowns and in puppet shows; and I think they are right.   Dickens, who surely was tender enough, had so irresistible a comic genius that it carried him beyond the gentle humour which most Englishmen possess to the absolute grotesque reality. Squeers, for instance, when he sips the wretched dilution which he has prepared for his starved and shivering little pupils, smacks his lips and cries: "Here's richness!"   It is savage comedy; humour would come in if we understood (what Dickens does not tell us) that the little creatures were duly impressed and thought the thin liquid truly delicious.   I suspect that English sensibility prefers the humour and wit of Hamlet to the pure comedy of Falstaff; and that even in Aristophanes it seeks consolation in the lyrical poetry for the flaying of human life in the comedy itself.   Tastes are free; but we should not deny that in merciless and rollicking comedy life is caught in the act.   The most grotesque creatures of Dickens are not exaggerations or mockeries of something other than themselves; they arise because nature generates them, like toadstools; they exist because they can't help it, as we all do.   The fact that these perfectly self-justified beings are absurd appears only by comparison, and from outside; circumstances, or the expectations of other people, make them ridiculous and force them to contradict themselves; but in nature it is no crime to be exceptional.   Often, but for the savagery of the average man, it would not even be a misfortune.   The sleepy fat boy in *Pickwick* looks foolish; but in himself he is no more foolish, nor less solidly self-justified, than a pumpkin lying on the ground.   Toots seems ridiculous; and we laugh heartily at his incoherence, his beautiful waistcoats, and his extreme modesty; but when did anybody more obviously grow into what he is because he couldn't grow otherwise? So with Mr. Pickwick, and Sam Weller, and Mrs. Gamp, and Micawber, and all the rest of this wonderful gallery; they are ridiculous only by accident, and in a context in which they never intended to appear. If Oedipus and Lear and Cleopatra do not seem ridiculous, it is only because tragic reflection has taken them out of the context in which, in real life, they would have figured. If we saw them as facts, and not as emanations of a poet's dream, we should laugh at them till doomsday; what grotesque presumption, what silly whims, what mad contradiction of the simplest realities! Yet we should not laugh at them without feeling how real their griefs were; as real and terrible as the griefs of children and of dreams. But facts, however serious inwardly, are always absurd outwardly; and the just critic of life sees both truths at once, as Cervantes did in *Don Quixote*. A pompous idealist who does not see the ridiculous in *all* things is the dupe of his sympathy and abstraction; and a clown, who does not see that these ridiculous creatures are living quite in earnest, is the dupe of his egotism. Dickens saw the absurdity, and understood the life; I think he was a good philosopher.

It is usual to compare Dickens with Thackeray, which is like comparing the grape with the gooseberry; there are obvious points of resemblance, and the gooseberry has some superior qualities of its own; but you can't make red wine of it. The wine of Dickens is of the richest, the purest, the sweetest, the most fortifying to the blood; there is distilled in it, with the perfection of comedy, the perfection of morals. I do not mean, of course, that Dickens appreciated all the values that human life has or might have; that is beyond any man. Even the greatest philosophers, such as Aristotle, have not always much imagination to conceive forms of happiness or folly other than those which their age or their temperament reveals to them; their insight runs only to discovering the *principle* of happiness, that it is spontaneous life of any sort harmonized with circumstances. The sympathies and imagination of Dickens, vivid in their sphere, were no less limited in range; and of course it was not his business to find philosophic formulas; nevertheless I call his the perfection of morals for two reasons: that he put the distinction between good and evil in the right place, and that he felt this distinction intensely. A moralist might have excellent judgment, he might see what sort of life is spontaneous in a given being and how far it may be harmonized with circumstances, yet his heart might remain cold, he might not suffer nor rejoice with the suffering or joy he foresaw. Humanitarians like Bentham and Mill, who talked about the greatest happiness of the greatest number, might conceivably be moral prigs in their own persons, and they might have been chilled to the bone in their theoretic love of mankind, if they had had the wit to imagine in what, as a matter of fact, the majority would place their happiness. Even if their theory had been correct (which I think it was in intention, though not in statement) they would then not have been perfect moralists, because their maxims would not have expressed their hearts. In expressing their hearts, they ought to have embraced one of those forms of "idealism" by which men fortify themselves in their bitter passions or in their helpless commitments; for they do not wish mankind to be happy in its own way, but in theirs. Dickens was not one of those moralists who summon every man to do himself the greatest violence so that he may not offend them, nor defeat their ideas. Love of the good of others is something that shines in every page of Dickens with a truly celestial splendour. How entirely limpid is his sympathy with life — a sympathy uncontaminated by dogma or pedantry or snobbery or bias of any kind! How generous is this keen, light spirit, how pure this open heart! And yet, in spite of this extreme sensibility, not the least wobbling; no deviation from a just severity of judgment, from an uncompromising distinction between white and black. And this happens as it ought to happen; sympathy is not checked by a flatly contrary prejudice or commandment, by some categorical imperative irrelevant to human nature; the check, like the cheer, comes by tracing the course of spontaneous impulse amid circumstances that inexorably lead it to success or to failure. There is a bed to this stream, freely as the water may flow; when it comes to this precipice it must leap, when it runs over these pebbles it must sing, and when it spreads into that marsh it must become livid and malarial. The very sympathy with human impulse quickens in Dickens the sense of danger; his very joy in joy makes him stern to what kills it. How admirably drawn are his surly villains. No rhetorical vilification of them, as in a sermon; no exaggeration of their qualms or fears; rather a sense of how obvious and human all their courses seem from their own point of view; and yet no sentimental apology for them, no romantic worship of rebels in their madness or crime. The pity of it, the waste of it all, are seen not by a second vision but by the same original vision which revealed the lure and drift of the passion. Vice is a monster here of such sorry mien, that the longer we see it the more we deplore it; that other sort of vice which Pope found so seductive was perhaps only some innocent impulse artificially suppressed, and called a vice because it broke out inconveniently and displeased the company. True vice is human nature strangled by the suicide of attempting the impossible. Those so self-justified villains of Dickens never elude their fates. Bill Sikes is not let off, neither is Nancy; the oddly benevolent Magwitch does not escape from the net, nor does the unfortunate young Richard Carstone, victim of the Circumlocution Office. The horror and ugliness of their fall are rendered with the hand of a master; we see here, as in the world, that in spite of the romanticists it is not virtue to rush enthusiastically along any road. I think Dickens is one of the best friends mankind has ever had. He has held the mirror up to nature, and of its reflected fragments has composed a fresh world, where the men and women differ from real people only in that they live in a literary medium, so that all ages and places may know them. And they are worth knowing, just as one's neighbors are, for their picturesque characters and their pathetic fates. Their names should be in every child's mouth; they ought to be adopted members of every household. Their stories cause the merriest and the sweetest chimes to ring in the fancy, without confusing our moral judgment or alienating our interest from the motley commonplaces of daily life. In every English-speaking home, in the four quarters of the globe, parents and children will do well to read Dickens aloud of a winter's evening; they will love winter, and one another, and God the better for it. What a wreath that will be of ever-fresh holly, thick with bright berries, to hang to this poet's memory — the very crown he would have chosen!

HENRY HAZLITT

HENRY HAZLITT (born in Philadelphia, 1894) is both an economist and a literary critic, and his first-hand familiarity with the economic literature on which the so-called Marxist critics base their judgments of books gives force to his analysis of their weaknesses. He is a graduate of the College of the City of New York, and has written for the *Wall Street Journal*, the *Sun*, and other papers. He was until recently literary editor of the *Nation* and is now on the editorial staff of the New York *Times*. The selection below was the Hopwood Lecture of 1935 delivered at the University of Michigan.

LITERATURE VERSUS OPINION *

THE will of the late Avery Hopwood expressed the desire that the literary prizes for which he so generously provided should be especially used to encourage "the new, the unusual, and the radical." It is interesting to recall that the will was made in 1922. It was about that time that those whom we now think of as the older generation in American literature, symbolized by such figures as Theodore Dreiser and H. L. Mencken, emerged into real prominence. Just before that period the waters of literary discussion had been relatively stagnant. Mencken and his disciples, deserting the genteel tradition, began calling their opponents harsh and extraordinary names, and the attention of youth was arrested. A fight is always exciting: moreover, if literature was something worth fighting over, it might be worth looking into.

That particular battle has not continued, but a series of battles have followed each other with only the briefest intermission. Meanwhile the issues have altered and even the sides have changed, so that many of those who were previously on the left now somehow find themselves on the right. The battle lines, moreover, have become so widely extended that it is no longer clearly possible to tell the literary front from the political front. Whatever one may say of the present era, it is not stagnant. One result, at least, is that "the new, the unusual, and the radical" are today much more certain of a hearing than they were thirteen years ago. But another result, less happy, is that the growing bitterness of the battle, and the extent and depth of the issues involved, have placed the most serious obstacles in the way of a sober objective evaluation of the current literary product, whether new, unusual, radical, or otherwise.

The tone of political discussion in the last few years has been increasingly acrimonious. It is not merely that arguments have been growing more passionate and less reasonable; the extremists on both sides have been losing faith in the efficacy of reason itself. One should not attempt to persuade one's opponent; one should suppress or imprison or execute him. This is the

* *Address at the Award of the Avery Hopwood Prizes*, The University of Michigan. May 31, 1935.

philosophy of the rulers of Germany and of Russia; it is shared only to a lesser degree by other rulers who have not yet consolidated their power, and it has influenced the tone of political discussion even in the great democracies. It has spread to the field of letters, and it emerges there as the theory that no such thing as an objective judgment of literary work is possible: there are only proletarian, bourgeois, or Fascist judgments; and writers are praised or denounced in accordance with their political or economic sympathies and doctrines.

Now I cannot believe that this attitude is either a salutary or a lasting one. It is, of course, the most natural thing in the world to praise those who are on our side of any question and to denounce those who are against us. Some of the so-called Marxist critics have built up elaborate rationalizations of the process. But the critic of literature who yields to this temptation, whatever good he thinks he may thereby be doing for his particular "cause," betrays his function as a literary critic.

The great critics of the past have always recognized this fact, and have been great critics partly through that very recognition. One of the most interesting examples is William Hazlitt. Now few writers have ever had more violent and uncompromising political opinions than he had. He was an ardent and tireless defender of the French Revolution; the uncompromising vehemence of his Jacobinism, indeed, led him into constant quarrels with most of his friends. But these differences of opinion, or even violent personal antagonisms, seldom perverted his literary judgments. No better illustration of his sanity and insight in this respect appears than in his numerous discussions of Edmund Burke. Here was a writer who had thrown the whole weight of his eloquence and passion against that French Revolution which to Hazlitt was one of the great historic landmarks in the eternal struggle for human liberty. Yet Hazlitt almost never wrote of Burke except in terms of the most ungrudging praise. In an essay devoted to him in 1807, Hazlitt tells us that Burke "enriched every subject to which he applied himself"; that "he was the most eloquent man of his time, and his wisdom was greater than his eloquence." "It has always been with me," he added, "a test of the sense and candor of anyone belonging to the opposite party, whether he allowed Burke to be a great man." Hazlitt apparently had never met more than one or two political opponents who would make this concession; and he set their reluctance down either to the fact that party feelings ran too high to admit of any real candor, or to "an essential vulgarity in their habits of thinking."

Hazlitt's praise seems to have been misunderstood. In a later printing of his "Character of Mr. Burke" he inserted the following explanatory footnote: "This character was written in a fit of extravagant candor, at a time when I thought I could do justice, or more than justice, to an enemy, without betraying a cause." But the truth was that Hazlitt was always subject to such "fits of extravagant candor," and seldom had fits of any other kind. In his essay "On Reading Old Books," he tells us that when he first encountered Burke's writings he exclaimed to himself: "This is true eloquence: this is a man pouring out his mind on paper." "The most perfect prose style, the most powerful, the most dazzling, the most daring... was Burke's." It was "forked and playful as the lightning, crested like the serpent." And here Hazlitt wrote the sentences that may serve as a sort of text for the present lecture:

> I did not care for his doctrines. I was then, and am still, proof against their contagion; but I admired the author, and was considered as not a very staunch partisan of the opposite side, though I thought myself that an abstract proposition was one thing — a masterly transition, a brilliant metaphor, another. I conceived too that he might be wrong in his main argument, and yet deliver fifty truths in arriving at a false conclusion.

Let us look at some of the implications of this attitude, and see to what extent we can apply them to the literary controversies of our own day. One of the favorite slogans of the Marxist critics is that "art is a weapon." We need not ask, at the moment, in what sense or to what extent this is true. But I should like to point out that even if art *is* a weapon, and even if we grant also that we must all line up on one of two sides in wielding it, it is still possible for us to judge it objectively. Machine guns are certainly weapons, and we should prefer to have them all on our side, but a sensible man's preferences have nothing to do with his realistic observation. Allied military commentators during the World War were able to say quite objectively whether the Germans had better or worse rifles, artillery, airplanes, or gases, than they had, or whether they made more or less effective use of them. An objectivity that is possible in a war of bullets ought surely to be possible in a war of pamphlets. A Communist critic ought to be able to discuss the ability of a bourgeois or a Fascist writer with the same cool detachment with which the high command in a war must estimate the ability of the opposing leadership. Wars are not won by dismissing all the enemy's generals as scoundrels and fools.

Here, then, is one form of critical objectivity of which even the most embittered class-conscious critics should recognize the need. We must correctly estimate the skill and ability of our opponents. This correct estimate is one of the primary functions of literary criticism. The important question for such criticism is not which side a writer is on, but how able he is in the service of that side. For estimating him it is not the bald conclusion at which he arrives that counts, but the mental process by which he arrives at it. It is not what he nakedly contends; it is the persuasiveness with which he states it. There are dull minds on both sides of every great controversy — minds that deal only in stereotypes and clichés, minds that can only repeat, parrot-like, the phrases the leaders have coined. But there are also brilliant minds on both sides of every great controversy; it is these that develop the new arguments and put them forward with the greatest force. The cardinal business of literary criticism in such a situation is not to declare that side A is right and side B wrong; it is to distinguish, on whichever side, the brilliant and original writers from the empty ones.

In brief, it is the paradoxical function of the literary critic, *as* critic, to detach himself as completely as possible from the actual merits of the controversies of his own time. In appraising the comparative qualities of individual writers, he must judge not the controversies but the controversialists.

He will sometimes be obliged to say, at least to himself: "What A writes is perfectly sound, and I agree with it passionately; but I am obliged to add that it will be completely forgotten ten years from now." At other times he will have to say: "This man B is utterly wrong; his perversity sometimes infuriates me; but, damn it all, there is some quality in what he says that leads me to fear that a century from now it will still be quoted." Few people could be more thoroughly wrong-headed, according to most of our current standards, than Dr. Johnson, but his aphorisms live because they have this quality. As for the philosopher, there is almost as much disagreement today as in his own lifetime whether Berkeley, or Kant, or Hegel was right or wrong. It is not being right or wrong that counts: it is having an interesting and original and powerful mind.

But this brings us to a further question. There is a certain ambiguity about the phrase "being right." For there are several kinds of truth, and the truth of literature is not necessarily the truth of science. We recognize this as soon as we come to deal, in fiction, with the differences between realism and romanticism, naturalism and fantasy. "Gulliver's Travels" is a true book; but it is not true that there are midgets of six inches, or giants seventy feet high, or nations of horses. The truth of "Alice in Wonderland" is not the truth of Main Street. The truth of poetry is not the truth of prose. Departures from fact, even when not purposely made for a certain effect, must be judged by different standards, depending on where they occur. The recognition of this principle is as old as Aristotle. When an error has been made in poetry, he remarks, it is important to ask whether it is a matter directly or only accidentally connected with the poetic art. For example, he tells us, it is a lesser error in an artist not to know that the hind has no horns, than to produce an unrecognizable picture of one. To speak of stout Cortez and all his men, silent, upon a peak in Darien, may be bad history but excellent poetry.

What all this comes down to is that we cannot apply ordinary fact-standards or opinion-standards in any crude or direct way to the judgment of literature. We have first of all to recognize that the elements of literature are so various and complex, as Lytton Strachey once reminded us, that no writer can be damned on a mere enumeration of faults, because he may always possess merits which make up for everything. If this is true, as I believe it is, then it is surely still more absurd either to dismiss a writer, or to regard him as important, merely because he holds or rejects some specific doctrine.

I am afraid that most Marxist critics would disagree with this. They might say that this would doubtless be so if the doctrine were one of secondary importance, but that the question of the class struggle happens to be paramount and central. A writer must align himself either with the proletariat or with the bourgeoisie, either with the forces of light, or with the forces of darkness. In the first case, the effect of his work will be beneficent; in the second it must be pernicious. They might go even further, and hold that the abler a bourgeois or capitalistic writer is, the more harmful the effect of his writing will be.

Now when we examine this reasoning it begins to strike us as strangely familiar. The class struggle is not the first so-called paramount or central question to divide mankind. Historically there has always been some issue that partisans have declared to be the central one, and historically it is always a different issue. For centuries writers have been damned for not holding the correct religious or theological beliefs, or for not belonging to the right political party, or for not having the correct attitude toward sex. In the Victorian period, and during the nineteen twenties, we were accustomed to having novels judged by so-called moral standards, which usually referred to sexual morality. The Victorians condemned their predecessors, from Rabelais and Boccaccio to Wycherly and Congreve, for their indecency, and disapproved of the Voltaires and Swifts for their cynicism. Our critics of the twenties dismissed the Victorians for their prudery and puritanism, and derided them also because they were sentimental, and not, as they should have been, cynical. Our new Communist critics now dismiss contemporary writers who have only a "sterile cynicism" in place of a fighting faith.

There are two ways of dealing with Marxist criticism. One may begin by questioning its premises. Is it true that there is an inevitable class struggle? Is it true that social and economic classes divide themselves basically into just two? Is it true that this social cleavage is more important than any other? Even before we begin any close scrutiny of the matter we are entitled, certainly, to our suspicions. For it would be astonishing if the objective facts were to fit in so neatly with the requirements of drama. Immemorially playwrights have recognized that audiences want to see a clash of just two great contending forces. If the contending forces are three, four, five, or twenty, the audience is distracted and confused. Its attention is scattered, its sympathies dispersed. To economize attention and sympathy, it is necessary that there be essentially just two contending forces, and that the audience should wish to see one triumphant and the other crushed. The theory of the class struggle conforms providentially to this law of the theater. It is obliging enough to conform also to the requirements of Hegelian logic. This second conformity is perhaps not so surprising, because the Hegelian logic, by which Marx was so deeply influenced, was itself unconsciously created by Hegel to accord with the rules of dramatic appeal. Marx acquired from him the habit of looking in the actual world for the embodiment of logical categories, with sharp boundaries, clearly opposed to each other.

So we have presented to us in the Marxist drama a world consisting essentially of just two classes engaged in a death struggle: on the one side the capitalists and their hirelings; on the other the on-marching proletariat. When we look at the world, however, unencumbered by this rigid theory, we see that the borderline between economic classes, particularly in America, is vague and shifting. We see that the president of a great steel corporation, working on salary and holding little or no stock in his company, is technically an employee, while the owner of a fruit stand with one assistant is technically a capitalist and an employer. More importantly, we know that, for all the appalling contrasts in wealth and income at the two extremes, income classes in the United States shade gradually into each other. The National Bureau of Economic Research, a statistical organization of the highest standing, for example, recently divided the country, not into two, but into seventy-four separate "income classes."

Space will hardly permit an extensive examination of the postulates of Communism, and fortunately such an examination is not necessary. Let us for the moment, instead, accept some of the premises of Marxist literary criticism. Let us accept the premises that there are essentially just two economic classes, that the division between them is real and sharp, and that membership in one of these classes affects our whole point of view. Even if we cannot believe that our opinions are mere rationalizations of our class status, let us grant at least the large element of truth in the contention that our class status influences the opinions of nearly all of us in various unconscious and subtle ways — and sometimes even in pretty obvious ways.

The question we must then ask ourselves is this: Is it impossible for the exceptional writer to surmount these limitations? Is it impossible for him, once he has been brought to recognize this bias, to guard against it as he tries to guard against other forms of bias? For the limitations and biases that may affect the human mind are almost innumerable. There is the limitation imposed by a man's language and nationality. What can Thomas Mann and Spengler, and Proust and Gide, and Pareto and Knut Hamsun, and Dostoievsky and Tolstoy, have to say that could interest Americans with their so different experience? Yet somehow they seem to have a great deal to say to us. There are Americans who feel that they get more of value from some of these foreigners than from any of their own writers. Anatole France once regretted that we could not, like Tiresias, be men and remember having been women, that we are shut up in our personality as in a perpetual prison. But his own works, and the works of hundreds of other writers in all ages, of Shakespeare, of Flaubert, of Hardy, of Dreiser, prove otherwise. The great male writer, by the power of his imagination, can portray the soul of a woman more fully and truthfully, even in the opinion of women, than the overwhelming majority of women writers can. And the great woman novelist can tell us more of what goes on in the mind of a man than most men can.

To take but one more example, there is the limitation imposed upon a writer by the historic era in which he lives. If any limitation seems absolutely insuperable, this one does. How can Karl Marx, who died fifty years ago, who knew nothing of the immense social, political, scientific and technological changes that have taken place in the half century since then, how can Marx possibly have anything to tell us that is still of value? How can Shakespeare and Montaigne, in their graves three centuries and more, possibly have written words that we can still cherish for their wisdom or beauty, that may even come to us with a shock of delight? What could be more absurd than to suppose that Aristotle and Plato and Homer, who knew nothing at all of the knowledge and experience that a hundred generations of mankind have garnered in the years since they passed on, what could be more absurd than to suppose that any of them could have written works that can still give us intense pleasure, or a sense of encountering flashes of penetrating wisdom for the first time? Yet this miracle is achieved.

In brief, the great writer, with supreme imaginative gifts, can universalize himself. He can vault over the apparently insuperable barriers of race, sex, and time. And yet there is a new school of critics who tell us, in effect, that he cannot vault over the barrier of his class. This contention is an astonishing one. For while no writer can, in any literal or physical sense, change his race, his sex, or his historic era, the one thing he can and frequently does change is precisely his economic status. He can have the experience of being poor, as well as of being "comfortably off," not merely in imagination, but in actuality. Economic class boundaries are so uncertain, indeed, that even Marxists have difficulty in deciding upon which side of "the coming struggle for power" certain great groups will be aligned, or which "ideology" controls them.

We are obliged to conclude, then, that it is surely no more difficult for the great writer, in a functional sense, to transcend the barriers of class than to transcend those of nationality, sex, and time. And we are also entitled to conclude that the great upper or middle-class writers of the past, or even of the present, have as much to say to the intelligent proletarian as they have to the intelligent bourgeois. We may acknowledge that class bias sometimes enters into what these writers have written. Where it does, it is the duty of the critic to point to the extent and nature of the bias. The positive contribution of the literary Marxists is that they have sharpened our eyes in this respect. But it is not the duty of the critic to declare *a priori* that this class bias necessarily affects and invalidates everything that a middle-class writer has written; or to point to this bias to the exclusion of all others; or to make it the central theme of all his criticism. Such criticism merely rests on the ancient fallacy of the *argumentum ad hominem* — of trying to discredit an argument or an attitude (and thus to seem to prove the opposite) by abusing the one who advances the argument or who holds the attitude. Such criticism, moreover, must miss all the infinitely rich and subtle values that literature has to offer. It must end by being dreadfully monotonous and tiresome.

Now I must confess that some of the views I have been discussing up to now are extreme. They are by no means held by all critics who call themselves Marxist. For the more intelligent Marxists have been uneasily aware of the narrow and absurd judgments into which this type of reasoning must lead them. So they have sought to rescue themselves from their dilemma by making a distinction. They have, in fact, sawn literature itself into two sharply contrasted aspects as they have sawn society into two sharply contrasted classes. This might almost be called the official cleavage. The resolution on literature, for example, adopted by the Political Bureau of the Communist Party of the Soviet Union in 1924, begins by declaring that "such a thing as neutral art in a class society does not and cannot exist." It then divides literary works, however, into their "social-political contents" on the one hand, and their "form and style" on the other. On all questions of "content," it holds, the Party must take a firm and positive stand; but on questions of "form and style" it may permit considerable freedom. A similar division is made by a number of American Marxist writers when they distinguish between the "social significance" or the "ideas" of a literary work, and its "craftsmanship." Something of the same sort seems also to be in the mind of the English Marxist, Mr. John Strachey, in his somewhat confused volume called "Literature and Dialectical Materialism." After praising Mr. Granville Hicks, for example, as "the foremost Marxist literary critic of America," he adds that Mr. Hicks "hardly seems to pay enough attention to the merits of writers as writers."

This whole attempt to split literature into its "ideas" or "social significance" on the one hand, and its "form and style" or "craftsmanship" on the other, seems to me mistaken. Literature will simply not submit to such a violent bifurcation. "Style" and "form" are not separate qualities that can be thrown over "content" like a raincoat: they are determined by content. A work of literature is an organic whole. It is true that, for convenience of discussion, either "craftsmanship" or "social significance" can be discussed as if it existed in isolation — provided the critic always remembers that it does nothing of the kind. What is even more important for us to keep in mind, in relation to the present point, is that after we have discussed the "social-political contents" of a literary work on the one hand, and its "craftsmanship" on the other, we may still have left out what is chiefly important about the work — unless, of course, we happen to have stretched one or the other of these two terms far beyond its legitimate meaning.

Let us see what would happen if we applied these standards, for example, to "Hamlet." I am afraid that on the question of social-political content a Marxist critic would give that play a very low rating. For in the usual sense of the phrase, it seems simply to have no social-political content. It aims at no reform; it does not imply the need of any change in social-political institutions. It takes for granted the institution of monarchy, and the class relationships and moral code of Shakespeare's time.

Ah, says the sophisticated Marxist critic, but the value of "Hamlet" lies in its "craftsmanship," in its "style and form." Now, certainly, part of its value does reside in these qualities. To take but one example, in the way in which he leads us up to the scene in which Hamlet first sees his father's ghost, Shakespeare reveals a masterly technical adroitness. But if the reputation of "Hamlet" rested wholly on its "craftsmanship," as that word is ordinarily used, it would not be higher than that of hundreds of other plays. For it is full of what today would be thought of as technical crudities. It is a sprawling drama of five acts and twenty scenes, overloaded with improbable accidents and coincidences. Any second-rater today could probably do a neater job of mere carpentry.

In what, then, does the greatness of "Hamlet" consist? We might, if we wished, here begin to introduce further criteria. We might speak of "character delineation," which is not "social-political content" and which is surely something broader than mere "form and style." We might talk of the magnificent poetic imagery, which may mean "style," but which implies a good deal more than that. We might talk of the truth or wisdom of the ideas in the famous soliloquy, or in the advice of Polonius. But whatever our detailed analysis, we should be obliged to say, finally, that what made "Hamlet" great was the whole range and texture and quality of its creator's mind.

This is what counts, in the end, in literature — the quality and nobility of the author's mind — and not either mere technical excellence, or the author's social and political sympathies. If we were to judge authors by our agreement or disagreement with their leading doctrines, a very strange sort of criticism would result. But in recognizing this, as the more intelligent Marxist critics do as well as the rest of us, it is unnecessary to fall back upon so narrow a standard as "craftsmanship." We can, instead, recognize more completely than before the wisdom of William Hazlitt's criticism of Burke. "Burke must be allowed to have wanted judgment," he wrote, "by all those who think that he was wrong in his conclusion.... But if in arriving at one error he discovered a hundred truths, I should consider myself a hundred times more indebted to him than if, stumbling on what I consider as the right side of the question, he had committed a hundred absurdities in striving to establish his point."

So far we have been discussing the duty of the critic in the present situation. What shall we say of the duty of the creative writer? Supposing his sympathies to be radical, shall he devote himself to writing propagandistic novels, propagandistic plays, propagandistic poetry? Shall he plunge into the center of the fight, or shall he stand "above the battle"?

These questions are by no means easy to answer. There is, to begin with, the difficulty of determining exactly what "propaganda" is. There is a sense in which all art is propagandistic because it reflects and propagates some vision of the world. Propaganda, it has been argued, does not need to be conscious; it may express itself through the unconscious acceptance of existing values and institutions that have been taken for granted. And it is on this basis that Marxists hold that all "bourgeois art" is propaganda for capitalism.

Now while there is perhaps an element of truth in this contention, it seems to me that it does make a difference whether propaganda is conscious or unconscious. To say this, however, does not solve the problem, for it is sometimes difficult to say to what extent propaganda is conscious. Perhaps we can get at the question best by looking first at propaganda in the strict sense, then at the examples of literature which are difficult to classify in this respect, and finally at literature which can be called propagandistic only by the greatest possible extension of the term.

Strictly propagandistic art may be provisionally defined as art which is not regarded by its creator as a sufficient end in itself, but merely as a means of achieving some further end which its creator considers more important. It aims usually at some specific social or political reform: the abolition of capital punishment or of vivisection, a revision of the divorce laws or of sexual mores, the need for revolutionary action. Thus "Uncle Tom's Cabin" is clearly a propagandistic novel, as are most of the novels of Upton Sinclair and the later plays of Elmer Rice.

But now we begin to move into more doubtful territory. As the implied reform becomes broader and vaguer, as the implication itself becomes less definite, the propagandistic nature of a work of literary art becomes more doubtful. The mere fact of whether the work under consideration is good or bad does not always help us in deciding upon its propagandistic nature. Horatio Alger's novels seem propagandistic enough, for they very clearly imply the importance for material success of the virtues of ambition, pluck, hard work, and thrift. But there is a question even here. Alger was certainly not, in the ordinary sense, *advocating* material success; it was a value that he took for granted and assumed that his readers took for granted. Further, the question may be raised whether he was deliberately advocating these means toward material success, or was again merely utilizing the values he assumed his readers already to believe in, in order to secure the undivided sympathy for his heroes and the undivided hatred for his villains deemed essential to create interest and suspense.

Most of the plays of Shaw are propagandistic, as are many of the dramas of Ibsen: "Pillars of Society," "A Doll's House," "An Enemy of the People," "The Wild Duck," all imply a definite social philosophy, and the need of some sort of social renovation. But clearly we have begun here to move toward works that it is getting to be more difficult to classify. This doubtful field is a very broad one. It includes many of the novels of Dickens, which helped in the movement toward prison reform and the alteration of the debtor laws; it includes Hugo's "Les Misérables," which affected the French attitude toward criminals. And almost too propagandistic to be doubtful are the novels and plays of Dumas fils, which inculcate such morals as the duty of a seducer to marry the woman he has seduced, or the right of a husband to take the law into his own hands and kill the wife who has been unfaithful and worthless. The propaganda in a novel need not necessarily take the form of solemn advocacy of a given attitude: it may consist merely in derision of its opposite. Thus Voltaire's "Candide" is a clear piece of propaganda against the philosophy of optimism.

We come at length to those works of literature which are as free from propaganda as it is possible to imagine. They include some of the greatest works in the language and some of the worst. It would be a rash critic indeed who would venture to say that there is much propaganda in the poetry of Keats, or who could find much more than a shade of it in the plays of Shakespeare. Shakespeare, it is true, sometimes reveals a social attitude; he had, for example, a hardly disguised contempt for the mob. But for the most part his work merely reflects an acceptance of, or an indifference to, the dominant social values and institutions of his time; he portrays no interest in changing them. The average detective story of our own day is just as non-propagandistic.

What conclusions can we draw from this casual survey? We are entitled to conclude, I think, that no clear-cut division can be made between propagandistic and non-propagandistic work. But this absence of a clear boundary line does not mean that the distinction is unimportant. On the spectrum it is impossible to tell at precisely what point blue becomes green or green becomes yellow; but this does not mean that there is no difference between blue and yellow. And it is pointless in view of this survey to continue to argue that *all* literary work is basically propagandistic, whether definitely or vaguely, consciously or unconsciously, aggressively or passively, because even if we were to grant this it would still be necessary, for purposes of intelligible discussion, to distinguish between definitely, consciously, and aggressively propagandistic work and vaguely, passively, and unconsciously propagandistic work. It saves time to call the first propagandistic and the second non-propagandistic.

Making this distinction, then, what can we say about the duty of the writer? Shall he write propaganda or unflinchingly eschew it? I think we are obliged to say, after our perfunctory glance over the field, that it is folly to lay down any general rule. We can merely point to some of the possibilities and dangers of the alternative courses. The dangers of writing propaganda are almost too numerous to mention. At its lowest level the propagandistic novel or play is too unreal and mechanical to be convincing or even interesting: the sheep are all on one side and the goats on the other: the characters are either white or black. Close to this is the danger of falling into a shopworn formula: there is a picture of the oppression of the working class in the first two acts, for example, with a triumphant revolution or strike or a sudden outburst of proletarian consciousness in the third act. Even the best writer runs the danger of subordinating his characters to his thesis: instead of being interesting for their own sakes, instead of impressing you as living, breathing people that act on their own account, they then become obvious marionettes built to fit the plot and to prove the equation; and one is always conscious of the author pulling the strings. For all his cleverness, most of Bernard Shaw's plays suffer from this defect.

"I hate poetry," said Keats, "that has a palpable design upon me." That line points to the central difficulty of propaganda in all art. It has a design upon you, and the task of the writer is to prevent it from becoming a palpable one. It requires the highest skill to succeed in that task. It would be unfair to condemn all propagandistic work merely by pointing to the innumerable examples of bad propagandistic works, but they must forever stand as awful warnings to the new aspirant. He must never forget that he always has the direct pamphlet in which to agitate specific reforms, and that it is possible to keep them out of his art.

There are, on the other hand, especially in an eruptive period like the present, also dangers in avoiding propaganda. The artist has every right, if he wishes, to ignore the social and political upheavals of his time, and if he is a great artist, he may increase his chances for immortality by doing so. "The world," as Joseph Wood Krutch has eloquently reminded us, "has always been unjust as well as uncertain.... It is too bad that men had to be hungry and women had to be dying at the very moment when Newton was inventing the method of fluxions or Gibbon was composing the history of the downfall of Rome. It is too bad that these things had to be done then; but it was far better that they should have been done then than that they should never have been done at all."

There is only one rule: the writer should write about what most interests him, and in the way that he prefers to do it. Good literature is any literature that intensely interests his fellow man; and that is likely to mean, whatever most intensely interests the writer himself. A more narrowly propagandistic literature may interest more men now and fewer men later. A literature with broader aims, without conscious propaganda, on some theme that has little to do with economics or politics, may be neglected today but widely read by the next generation. But what in any case will finally save a work of literature, and make it worth reading, is not the specific doctrines held by its author, but the whole quality and texture of the thought and imagination that go into it.

MAX EASTMAN

AFTER studying and teaching philosophy at Columbia University, Max Forrester Eastman (1883–   ) joined the radical movement, becoming editor of *The Masses*, and of *The Liberator* in the stormy years 1913–1922. As editor of the former he made a brilliant and successful defense of himself and his colleagues when they were prosecuted in war time under the espionage act. He has written extensively on the Russian Revolution, as well as several volumes of verse and criticism of current literary phenomena, including *Enjoyment of Poetry*, *The Literary Mind; Its Place in an Age of Science*, *Artists in Uniform*, and *The Relations Between Art and Propaganda*. The present selection is an excellent example of his aggressive, hard-hitting style, admirably adapted to a group of writers known as the "hard-boiled" school. It was called forth by Mr. Ernest Hemingway's book about bullfighting, *Death in the Afternoon*.

BULL IN THE AFTERNOON *

THERE are gorgeous pages in Ernest Hemingway's book about bullfights — big humor and reckless straight talk of what things are, genuinely heavy ferocity against prattle of what they are not. Hemingway is a full-sized man hewing his way with flying strokes of the poet's broad axe which I greatly admire. Nevertheless, there is an unconscionable quantity of bull — to put it as decorously as possible — poured and plastered all over what he writes about bullfights. By bull I mean juvenile romantic gushing and sentimentalizing of simple facts.

For example, it is well known and fairly obvious that bulls do not run and gallop about the pasture; they stand solid "dominating the landscape with their confidence" as Hemingway brilliantly says. Therefore when they have dashed about the ring some minutes, tossed a few horses, repeatedly charged and attempted to gore a man and thrown their heads off because he turned out to be a rag, they soon get winded and their tongues hang out and they pant. Certain bulls, however, for reasons more or less accidental, go through the ordeal in a small area without much running and therefore get tired in the muscles before they get winded. These bulls do not hang their tongues out and pant. This plain fact, which would be obvious to anybody without smoke in his eyes, is romanticized by Hemingway to mean that some bulls are so "brave" that they will never let their tongues out, but hold their mouths "tight shut to keep the blood in" even after they are stabbed to death and until they drop. This is not juvenile romanticism, it is child's fairy-story writing. And yet Hemingway asks us to believe that what drew him to bullfights was the desire to learn to put down "what really happened

* Reprinted from *Art and the Life of Action*, by Max Eastman, by permission of and special arrangement with Alfred A. Knopf, Inc., authorized publishers.

in action; what the actual things were which produced the emotion that you experienced."

In pursuit of this rigorous aim he informs us that bullfights are "so well ordered and so strongly disciplined by ritual that a person feeling the whole tragedy cannot separate the minor comic-tragedy of the horse so as to feel it emotionally." And he generalizes: "The *aficionado*, or lover of the bullfight, may be said, broadly, then, to be one who has this sense of the tragedy and ritual of the fight so that the minor aspects are not important except as they relate to the whole." Which is just the kind of sentimental poppycock most regularly dished out by those Art nannies and pale-eyed professors of poetry whom Hemingway above all men despises. Hemingway himself makes plain all through his book that the performance itself is not an artistic tragedy as often as one time out of a hundred. When it is, there is about one man out of a thousand in the grandstand who would know what you were talking about if you started in on "the whole tragedy" as opposed to the "minor comic-tragedy of the horse." The *aficionado*, or bullfight fan, is the Spanish equivalent of the American baseball fan. He reacts the same way to the same kind of things. If you could get the authorization to put on a bullfight in the Yankee Stadium, you would see approximately the same crowd there that you do now, and they would behave, after a little instruction from our star reporters and radio announcers, just about the way the Spanish crowd behaves. And they would not be — "broadly" — the kind of people, if there are such people, who can see an infuriated bull charge across a bull ring, ram his horns into the private end of a horse's belly and rip him clear up to the ribs, lifting and tossing his rider bodily in the air and over against the fence with the same motion, and keep their attention so occupied with the "whole tragedy" that they cannot "separate" this enough to "feel it emotionally." Bullfights are not wholly bad, but sentimentalizing over them in the name of art-form and ritual is.

Whatever art may be, a bullfight is not art in exactly that particular which exempts art from those rules of decent conduct which make life possible and civilization a hope — namely, that its representations are not real. A bullfight — foolishly so called by the English for it does not except for a moment resemble a fight — is real life. It is men tormenting and killing a bull; it is a bull being tormented and killed.

And if it is not "art" in a sense to justify Hemingway's undiscriminating recourse to that notion, still less is it "tragedy" in a sense to sustain the elevated emotions which he hopes to pump over it with this portentous term.

Suppose that you attend a bullfight with your eyes and emotional receptors recklessly wide open, as a poet should. What do you see to admire and what to despise? Men moving in the risk of wounds and death with skill, grace, suavity and courage. That is something to admire — and the wild free fighting force of the animal as he charges into the arena, a sight so thrilling that words fail utterly. They fail Hemingway. Until Christians thought up the sickly idea of worshipping a lamb, this noble creature symbolized the beauty of divine power in a good half of the great religions of the earth.

Here, then, are two things to admire and they command admiration; they command sympathy. And then you see these admirable brave men begin to take down this noble creature and reduce him to a state where they can successfully run in and knife him, by a means which would be described in any other situation under the sun as a series of dirty tricks, these tricks being made possible by his well known and all too obvious stupidity — the limitations of his vision and rigidity of his instincts — this stupidity being further assured by breeding, by keeping him in a dim light before the running and by never giving him a second chance in the ring. You see this beautiful creature, whom you admire because he is so gorgeously equipped with power for wild life and despise for his stupidity, trapped in a ring where his power is nothing, and you see him put forth his utmost in vain to escape death at the hands of these spryer and more flexible monkeys, whose courage you admire and whose mean use of their wit you despise. You see him baffled, bewildered, insane with fright, fury and physical agony, jabbed, stabbed, haunted, hounded, steadily brought dreadfully down from his beauty of power, until he stands horribly torpid, sinking leadlike into his tracks, lacking the mere strength of muscle to lift his vast head, panting, gasping, gurgling, his mouth too little and the tiny black tongue hanging out too far to give him breath, and faint falsetto cries of anguish, altogether lost-babylike now and not bulllike, coming out of him, and you see one of these triumphant monkeys strike a theatrical pose, and dash in swiftly and deftly — yes, while there is still danger, still a staggering thrust left in the too heavy horns — and they have invented statistics, moreover, and know exactly how much and how little danger there is — dash in swiftly and deftly and plunge a sword into the very point where they accurately know — for they have also invented anatomy, these wonderful monkeys — that they will end that powerful and noble thing forever.

That is what a bullfight is, and that is all it is. To drag in notions of honor and glory here, and take them seriously, is ungrown-up enough and rather sophomoric. But to pump words over it like tragedy and dramatic conflict is mere romantic nonsense and self-deception crying to heaven. It is not tragic to die in a trap because although beautiful you are stupid; it is not tragic to play mean tricks on a beautiful thing that is stupid, and stab it when its power is gone. It is the exact opposite of tragedy in every high meaning that has ever been given to that word. It is killing made meaner, death more ignoble, bloodshed more merely shocking than it has need to be.

Fortunately it is no great trick to close one's receptors in a certain direction, to deaden sympathies that are unfruitful. We all go through life with these emotional blinders on; we could not go through otherwise. I remember an anxious mother in fits of anxiety because her husband had taken their infant son into one of those sidewalk horror exhibitions — it was an illuminated view of a "famous painting of Nero throwing Christians to the lions."

"George, George, how could you subject Bobby's tender little growing soul to that shocking experience? What *did* he do? What *did* he say?"

"He said, 'Oh, Papa, there's one poor lion hasn't got any Christian!'"

This being the nature of the human infant, it is obvious that if you grow up in a society which does not extend sympathy to bulls in the bull ring, barring some heightened consciousness or gift of reflection in you amounting to an eccentricity, you will not do so either. For this reason the idea that bullfights prove Spaniards to be cruel, or as Havelock Ellis says, "indifferent to pain both in themselves and others," seems to me — with all respect to that eminent authority — the veriest nonsense. The appetites to which bullfighting appeals are a universal human inheritance, and if its survival in Spain must have some explanation other than cultural accident, I should associate it with the almost feminine gentleness of character to be felt in that country which seems to have need of this stoical overprotest of courage without mercy. At any rate, we expect an American poet who goes down there to see more and not less than a Spanish adolescent, whose one-sided obtundity in this matter is as inevitable as the misshapen callous on the bottom of any man's foot.

Why then does our iron advocate of straight talk about what things are, our full-sized man, our ferocious realist, go blind and wrap himself up in clouds of juvenile romanticism the moment he crosses the border on his way to a Spanish bullfight? It is of course a commonplace that Hemingway lacks the serene confidence that he *is* a full-sized man. Most of us too delicately organized babies who grow up to be artists suffer at times from that small inward doubt. But some circumstance seems to have laid upon Hemingway a continual sense of the obligation to put forth evidences of red-blooded masculinity. It must be made obvious not only in the swing of the big shoulders and the clothes he puts on, but in the stride of his prose style and the emotions he permits to come to the surface there. This trait of his character has been strong enough to form the nucleus of a new flavor in English literature, and it has moreover begotten a veritable school of fiction-writers — a literary style, you might say, of wearing false hair on the chest — but, nevertheless, I think it is inadequate to explain the ecstatic adulation with which Hemingway approaches everything connected with the killing of bulls in the bull ring.

He says that he went to see these spectacles because he was trying to learn how to write, and he wanted something "simple" to write about; violent death, he thought, was one of the simplest things; he had seen a great deal of violent death in the War, but the War being over and he still learning to write, it seemed necessary to see some more. I do not think you can call it psychoanalysis to remark that the only simple thing here is Ernest Hemingway. A man writes about — and travels over the earth to see — what he likes to dwell on. Moreover, it is not death Hemingway writes about or travels to see, but killing. Nobody above fourteen years old will contend that he has got into his book that "feeling of life and death" which he says he was working for. He has got into it an enthusiasm for killing — for courage and dominating and killing. Hemingway cannot feel — he cannot even see — the hero of his "tragedy" staggering toward death in blood loss and bewilderment. He withdraws automatically from any participation in that central fact. He did once feel, he tells us, the surprise of pain which makes the animal toss awkwardly like a great inflexible box when the banderillas are jabbed into his withers, but this live feeling vanished instantly and by an extraordinary magic the moment he learned that the bull is more and not less dangerous after he has been "slowed" in this way, and will now make better aimed, because more desperate, efforts to defend his life. After learning that, Hemingway felt "no more sympathy" for the bull "than for a canvas or the marble a sculptor cuts or the dry powder snow your skis cut through." Which is a clear statement — is it not? — of indifference to "the feeling of life and death," and total preoccupation with the art of courageous killing.

A like numbness of imagination afflicts this poet when the life and death of the matador is in question. The climax of his enterprise of learning how to write, at least the last mention of it, occurs on page 20, where after seeing a matador gored by a bull, he wakes in the night and tries to remember "what it was that seemed just out of my remembering and that was the thing that I had really seen and, finally, remembering all around it, I got it. When he stood up, his face white and dirty and the silk of his breeches opened from waist to knee, it was the dirtiness of the rented breeches, the dirtiness of his slit underwear and the clean, clean, unbearably clean whiteness of the thigh bone that I had seen, and it was that which was important." Is the clean whiteness of a man's thigh bone the "important" thing to a poet working for the feeling of life and death, or is it merely the most shocking thing, and therefore the most sought after by an ecstatic in the rapture of killing?

"Do you know the sin it would be," he says, "to ruffle the arrangement of the feathers on a hawk's neck if they could never be replaced as they were? Well, that would be the sin it would be to kill El Gallo." And we turn the page with a shudder for El Gallo.

It seems, then, that our ferocious realist is so romantic about bullfights, and so blind to much of what they "actually are," because he is enraptured with courageous killing. He is athirst after this quality of act and emotion with that high-fevered thirst of the saint after the blood of the living God, so that little else can open its way into his eyes or down to his heartstrings. He is himself, moreover, courageous enough — and with a courage rarer than that of toreros — to state plainly that he loves killing, and try to state why. It is because killing makes him feel triumphant over death.

"Killing cleanly and in a way which gives you esthetic pride and pleasure," he says, "has always been one of the greatest enjoyments of a part of the human race.... One of its greatest pleasures... is the feeling of rebellion against death which comes from its administering. Once you accept the rule of death thou shalt not kill is an easily and a naturally obeyed commandment. But when a man is still in rebellion against death he has pleasure in taking to himself one of the godlike attributes; that of giving it. This is one of the most profound feelings in those men who enjoy killing."

Hemingway is quite right about the pleasure derived by a part of our race, and, in imagination, indeed, by all of it, from killing. One need only read the Old Testament to see how easy it was for our most pious ancestors in morality to cut a whole people out of the tiny circle of their tribal sympathy like the ring of light round a campfire, and enjoy with free hearts the delight of slaughtering them "so that there was none left in that city, man, woman or child." And one need only remark the popularity of murder stories — or of Hemingway's own book so gorgeously full of horse's blood and bull's blood, and matador's blood, and even the blood of "six carefully selected Christs" crucified in his riotous imagination to make a holiday for his readers, in order to see that this little-satisfied thirst is wellnigh universal.

Had men not enjoyed killing, they would not be here, and the bulls would be doing it all. That is a significant fact. But nevertheless the important part of the killing has been done, and the present tendency is to suppress, to sublimate in representative art, even in some measure to breed out this dangerous taste. For this we have the authority of Gene Tunney, a writer who stands at the opposite pole from Hemingway, having abundantly established his prowess in action, and in literature therefore being somewhat concerned, strangely enough, to establish his sensibility. Speaking in his biography of the "killer-instinct boys," he remarks that "the higher in human development one goes, the more controlled one finds this reaction." And if that is true in the prize ring, it is more certainly true among poets and artists and sensitive young men generally.

It is so true that the nervous horror of these young men, and their mental and moral sickness, after forcing themselves through the insensate butchery of the World War, may be said almost to have created an epoch in our literature. One by one they have recovered their tongues and stood up during these fifteen years, those stricken poets, and confessed that they were devastated and broken clear down and shattered by that forced discipline in the art of wholesale killing — those have who were not too shattered to speak. And their speech with the silence of the others is the true aftermath in poetry of the Great War — not the priggish trivialities of the Cult of Unintelligibility, not the cheap moral of decorum (that shallow cult so admirably exterminated root and branch by Ernest Hemingway in a paragraph of this book), not the new Bohemianism of the synthetic-gin period, not the poetry of the new scientific hope in Russia, for it has had no poetry — but the confession in language of blood and tears of the horror unendurable to vividly living nerves of the combination of civilized life with barbaric slaughter.

Will it be too much like a clinic if I point out that Ernest Hemingway is one of the most sensitive and vivid-living of these poets, one of the most passionately intolerant, too, of priggery and parlor triviality and old maids' morals and empty skulls hiding in unintelligibility? I am not strong for literary psychoanalysis, but I must record a guess rising toward the middle of his book and growing to conviction in the end, that *Death in the Afternoon* belongs also among those confessions of horror which are the true poetry and the only great poetry of this generation. It does not matter much whether Ernest Hemingway knows this fact or not. We may hope he will find out, for a man cannot grow to his height without self-knowledge. But the important thing is for us to know.

We took this young man with his sensitive genius for experience, for living all the qualities of life and finding a balance among them — and with that too obvious fear in him of proving inadequate — and we shoved him into our pit of slaughter, and told him to be courageous about killing. And we thought he would come out weeping and jittering. Well, he came out roaring for blood, shouting to the skies the joy of killing, the "religious ecstasy" of killing — and most pathetic, most pitiable, killing as a protest against death.

WAR

WAR or Peace is the most important and immediate subject of consideration at the present time in connection with science, social science, history, and education. Accordingly several articles representing different forms of discourse have been arranged under this title. Miss LaMotte's sketch of personal experience forms an appropriate introduction. Randolph Bourne's informal essay considers the subject from the individual's point of view. C. E. Montague's essay of the same type from a more general point of view expresses the disillusionment with war which is one of the lessons of recent experience. "Arms and the Men" is of the more formal type of essay approaching the monograph, dealing with a contributing factor to war. This section gives various forms of what is known as propaganda, a word which in its original definition of that which ought to be spread abroad, has a good, as well as the bad sense of common usage. That war is the greatest danger confronting the human race as a whole, even threatening its existence, is beyond controversy.

ELLEN NEWBOLD LaMOTTE

THE best writing is not always done by professional literary men. This truth is illustrated by Ellen LaMotte's *The Backwash of War*, first published in 1916 and then suppressed because it told the painful truth about war as seen from the hospitals. Re-issued in 1934, the vivid and horrible sketches it contains, utterly convincing in their unpretentious truthfulness, have made it one of the most moving of war books. The author was born in Louisville, Kentucky (1873), graduated from the nurses' training school of The Johns Hopkins University, and saw war at first hand when she was a nurse in the French army. Since then she has traveled and contributed to various American magazines. The following selection is representative of her volume.

POUR LA PATRIE *

THIS is how it was. It is pretty much always like this in a field hospital. Just ambulances rolling in, and dirty, dying men, and the guns off there in the distance! Very monotonous, and the same, day after day, till one gets so tired and bored. Big things may be going on over there, and here, on this side of them, it is always the same. The weariness of it — and the sameness of it! The same ambulances, and dirty men, and groans, or silence. The same hot operating rooms, the same beds, always full, in the wards. This is war. But it goes on and on, over and over, day after day, till it seems like life. Life in peace time. It might be life in a big city hospital, so alike is the routine. Only the city hospitals are bigger, and better equipped, and the ambulances are smarter, and the patients don't always come in ambulances — they walk in sometimes, or come in street cars, or in limousines, and they are of both sexes, men and women, and have ever so many things the matter with them — the hospitals of peace time are not nearly so stupid, so monotonous, as the hospitals of war. Bah! War's humane compared to peace! More spectacular, I grant you, more acute, — that's what interests us, — but for the sheer agony of life — oh, peace is way ahead!

War is so clean. Peace is so dirty. There are so many foul diseases in peace times. They drag on over so many years, too. No, war's clean! I'd rather see a man die in prime of life, in war time, than see him doddering along in peace time, broken hearted, broken spirited, life broken, and very weary, having suffered many things, — to die at last, at a good, ripe age! How they have suffered, those who drive up to our city hospitals in limousines, in peace time. What's been saved them, those who die young, and clean and swiftly, here behind the guns. In the long run it dots up just the same. Only war's spectacular, that's all.

Well, he came in like the rest, only older than most of them. A shock of iron-gray hair, a mane of it, above heavy, black brows, and the brows were

* From *The Backwash of War*, by Ellen N. LaMotte. Courtesy of G. P. Putnam's Sons, publishers, New York.

contracted in pain. Shot, as usual, in the abdomen. He spent three hours on the table after admission — the operating table — and when he came over to the ward, they said, not a dog's chance for him. No more had he. When he came out of ether, he said he didn't want to die. He said he wanted to live. Very much. He said he wanted to see his wife again and his children. Over and over he insisted on this, insisted on getting well. He caught hold of the doctor's hand and said he must get well, that the doctor must get him well. Then the doctor drew away his slim fingers from the rough, imploring grasp, and told him to be good and patient.

"Be good! Be patient!" said the doctor, and that was all he could say, for he was honest. What else could he say, knowing that there were eighteen little holes, cut by the bullets, leaking poison into that gashed, distended abdomen? When these little holes, that the doctor could not stop, had leaked enough poison into his system, he would die. Not today, no, but day after tomorrow. Three days more.

So all that first day, the man talked of getting well. He was insistent on that. He was confident. Next day, the second of the three days the doctor gave him, very much pain laid hold of him. His black brows bent with pain and he grew puzzled. How could one live with such pain as that?

That afternoon, about five o'clock, came the General. The one who decorates the men. He had no sword, just a riding whip, so he tossed the whip on the bed, for you can't do an accolade with anything but a sword. Just the *Médaille Militaire*. Not the other one. But the *Médaille Militaire* carries a pension of a hundred francs a year, so that's something. So the General said, very briefly: "In the name of the Republic of France, I confer upon you the *Médaille Militaire*." Then he bent over and kissed the man on his forehead, pinned the medal to the bedspread, and departed.

There you are! Just a brief little ceremony, and perfunctory. We all got that impression. The General has decorated so many dying men. And this one seemed so nearly dead. He seemed half-conscious. Yet the General might have put a little more feeling into it, not made it quite so perfunctory. Yet he's done this thing so many, many times before. It's all right, he does it differently when there are people about, but this time there was no one present — just the doctor, the dying man, and me. And so we four knew what it meant — just a widow's pension. Therefore there wasn't any reason for the accolade, for the sonorous, ringing phrases of a dress parade ——

We all knew what it meant. So did the man. When he got the medal, he knew too. He knew there wasn't any hope. I held the medal before him, after the General had gone, in its red plush case. It looked cheap, somehow. The exchange didn't seem even. He pushed it aside with a contemptuous hand sweep, a disgusted shrug.

"I've seen these things before!" he exclaimed. We all had seen them too. We all knew about them, he and the doctor, and the General and I. He knew and understood, most of all. And his tone was bitter.

After that, he knew the doctor couldn't save him, and that he should not see his wife and children again. Whereupon he became angry with the treatment, and protested against it. The *piqûres* — they hurt very much, and he did not want them. Moreover, they did no good, for his pain was now very intense, and he tossed and tossed to get away from it.

So the third day dawned, and he was alive, and dying, and knew that he was dying. Which is unusual and disconcerting. He turned over and over, and black fluid vomited from his mouth into the white enamel basin. From time to time, the orderly emptied the basin, but always there was more, and always he choked and gasped and knit his brows in pain. Once his face broke up as a child's breaks up when it cries. So he cried in pain and loneliness and resentment.

He struggled hard to hold on. He wanted very much to live, but he could not do it. He said, "*Je ne tiens plus.*"

Which was true. He couldn't hold on. The pain was too great. He clenched his hands and writhed, and cried out for mercy. But what mercy had we? We gave him morphia, but it did not help. So he continued to cry to us for mercy, he cried to us and to God. Between us, we let him suffer eight hours more like that, us and God.

Then I called the priest. We have three priests on the ward, as orderlies, and I got one of them to give him the Sacrament. I thought it would quiet him. We could not help him with drugs, and he had not got it quite in his head that he must die, and when he said, "I am dying," he expected to be contradicted. So I asked Capolarde to give him the Sacrament, and he said yes, and put a red screen around the bed, to screen him from the ward. Then Capolarde turned to me and asked me to leave. It was summer time. The window at the head of the bed was open, the hay outside was new cut and piled into little haycocks. Over in the distance the guns rolled. As I turned to go, I saw Capolarde holding a tray of Holy Oils in one hand, while with the other he emptied the basin containing black vomitus out the window.

No, it did not bring him comfort, or resignation. He fought against it. He wanted to live, and he resented Death, very bitterly. Down at my end of the ward — it was a silent, summer afternoon — I heard them very clearly. I heard the low words from behind the screen.

"*Dites:* '*Dieu je vous donne ma vie librement pour ma patrie*'" (God, I give you my life freely for my country). The priests usually say that to them, for death has more dignity that way. It is not in the ritual, but it makes a soldier's death more noble. So I suppose Capolarde said it. I could only judge by the response. I could hear the heavy, labored breath, the choking, wailing cry.

"*Oui! Oui!*" gasped out at intervals. "*Ah, mon Dieu! Oui!*"

Again the mumbling, guiding whisper.

"*Oui! — oui!*" came sobbing, gasping, in response.

So I heard the whispers, the priest's whispers, and the stertorous choke, the feeble, wailing, rebellious wailing in response. He was being forced into it. Forced into acceptance. Beaten into submission, beaten into resignation.

"*Oui, oui,*" came the protesting moans. "*Ah, oui!*"

It must be dawning upon him now. Capolarde is making him see.

"*Oui! Oui!*" The choking sobs reach me, "*Ah, mon Dieu, oui!*" Then very deep, panting, crying breaths:

"*Dieu — je — vous — donne — ma — vie — librement — pour — ma — patrie!*"

"*Librement! Librement! Ah, oui! Oui!*" He was beaten at last. The choking, dying, bewildered man had said the noble words.

"God, I give you my life freely for my country!"

After which came a volley of low toned Latin phrases, rattling in the stillness like the popping of a *mitrailleuse*.

Two hours later he was still live, restless, but no longer resentful. "It is difficult to go," he murmured, and then: "Tonight, I shall sleep well." A long pause followed, and he opened his eyes.

"Without doubt, the next world is more *chic* than this," he remarked, smiling, and then:

"I was mobilized against my inclination. Now I have won the *Médaille Militaire*. My Captain won it for me. He made me brave. He had a revolver in his hand."

RANDOLPH BOURNE

AFTER being graduated from Columbia University and studying abroad, Randolph Silliman Bourne (1886–1918) settled down to journalism in New York, where he was connected with *The New Republic*, *The Dial*, and *The Seven Arts*. He was interested especially in education, and was the author of two books on the subject, *Youth and Life* and *Education and Living*. An outspoken opponent of the entrance of the United States into the European War, he contributed a series of essays to *The Seven Arts*, of which the most famous was "The War and the Intellectuals." Bourne had a mind of extraordinary clearness and penetration in a terribly crippled body. Exempt himself from the demand of military service, he felt keenly the tragedy of the young men in whose school and college life he had taken such interest, who were called implacably to suffer and die in a cause which grew always more doubtful of value to humanity in whose name they fought. "Below the Battle" was written in a spirit of protest which is expressed freely today in the sentence: "It must never happen again." It was published in *The Seven Arts*, July, 1917.

BELOW THE BATTLE *
(JULY, 1917)

HE IS one of those young men who, because his parents happened to mate during a certain ten years of the world's history, has had now to put his name on a wheel of fate, thereby submitting himself to be drawn into a brief sharp course of military training before being shipped across the sea to kill Germans or be killed by them. He does not like this fate that menaces him, and he dislikes it because he seems to find nothing in the programme marked out for him which touches remotely his aspirations, his impulses, or even his desires. My friend is not a happy young man, but even the unsatisfactory life he is living seems supplemented at no single point by the life of the drill-ground or the camp or the stinking trench. He visualizes the obscenity of the battlefield and turns away in nausea. He thinks of the weary regimentation of young men, and is filled with disgust. His mind has turned sour on war and all that it involves. He is poor material for the military proclamation and the drill-sergeant.

I want to understand this friend of mine, for he seems rather typical of a scattered race of young Americans of today. He does not fall easily into the categories of patriot and coward which the papers are making popular. He feels neither patriotism nor fear, only an apathy toward the war, faintly warmed' into a smoldering resentment at the men who have clamped down the war-pattern upon him and that vague mass of people and ideas and workaday living around him that he thinks of as his country. Now that resentment has knotted itself into a tortured tangle of what he should do, how he can best be true to his creative self? I should say that his apathy cannot be imputed to cowardly ease. My friend earns about fifteen hundred dollars a year as an architect's assistant, and he lives alone in a little room over a fruitshop. He worked his way through college, and he has never known even a leisurely month. There is nothing Phaeacian about his life. It is scarcely to save his skin for riotous living that he is reluctant about war. Since he left college he has been trying to find his world. He is often seriously depressed and irritated with himself for not having hewed out a more glorious career for himself. His work is just interesting enough to save it from drudgery, and yet not nearly independent and exacting enough to give him a confident professional sense. Outside his work, life is deprived and limited rather than luxurious. He is fond of music and goes to cheap concerts. He likes radical meetings, but never could get in touch with the agitators. His friends are seeking souls just like himself. He likes midnight talks in cafés and studios, but he is not especially amenable to drink. His heart of course is hungry and turbid, but his two or three love-affairs have not clarified anything for him. He eats three rather poor restaurant meals a day. When he reads, it is philosophy — Nietzsche, James, Bergson — or the novels about youth — Rolland, Nexö, Cannan, Frenssen, Beresford. He has a rather constant mood of futility, though he is in unimpeachable health. There are moments when life seems quite without sense or purpose. He has enough friends, however, to be not quite lonely, and yet they are so various as to leave him always with an ache for some more cohesive, purposeful circle. His contacts with people irritate him without rendering him quite unhopeful. He is always expecting he doesn't know quite what, and always being frustrated of he doesn't quite know what would have pleased him. Perhaps he never had a moment of real external or internal ease in his life.

Obviously a creature of low vitality, with neither the broad vision to be stirred by the President's war message, nor the red blood to itch for the dummy bayonet-charge. Yet somehow he does not seem exactly weak, and there is a consistency about his attitude which intrigues me. Since he left college eight years ago, he has been through most of the intellectual and emotional fads of the day. He has always cursed himself for being so superficial and unrooted, and he has tried to write a little of the thoughts that stirred him. What he got down on paper was, of course, the usual large vague feeling of a new time that all of us feel. With the outbreak of the Great War, most of his socialist and pacifist theories were knocked flat. The world turned out to be an entirely different place from what he had thought it. Progress and uplift seemed to be indefinitely suspended, though it was a long time before he realized how much he had been corroded by the impact of news and the endless discussions he heard. I think he gradually worked himself into a truly neutral indifference. The reputable people and the comfortable classes who were having all the conventional emotions rather disgusted him. The neurotic fury about self-defense seemed to come from types and classes that he instinctively detested. He was not scared, and somehow he could not get enthusiastic about defending himself with "preparedness" unless he were badly scared. Things got worse. All that he valued seemed frozen until the horrible mess came to a close. He had gone to an unusually intelligent American college, and he had gotten a feeling for a humane civilization that had not left him. The war, it is true, bit away piece by piece every ideal that made this feeling seem plausible. Most of the big men — intellectuals — whom he thought he respected had had so much of their idealism hacked away and got their nerves so frayed that they became at last, in their panic, willing and even eager to adopt the war-technique in aid of their government's notions of the way to impose democracy on the world.

My poor young friend can best be understood as too naïve and too young to effect this metamorphosis. Older men might mix a marvelous intellectual brew of personal anger, fear, a sense of "dishonor," fervor for a League of Peace, and set going a machinery that crushed everything intelligent, humane and civilized. My friend was less flexible. War simply did not mix with anything that he had learned to feel was desirable. Something in his mind spewed it out whenever it was suggested as a cure for our grievous American neutrality. As I got all this from our talks, he did not seem weak. He merely had no notion of the patriotism that meant the springing of a nation to arms. He read conscientiously *The New Republic*'s feast of eloquent idealism, with its appealing harbingers of a cosmically efficacious and well-bred war. He would often say, This is all perfectly convincing; why, then, are we not all convinced? He seemed to understand the argument for American participation. We both stood in awe at the superb intellectual structure that was built up. But my friend is one of those unfortunate youths whose heart has to apprehend as well as his intellect, and it was his heart that inexorably balked. So he was in no mood to feel the worth of American participation, in spite of the infinite tact and Fabian strategy of the Executive and his intellectualist backers. He felt apart from it all. He had not the imagination to see a healed world-order built out of the rotten materials of armaments, diplomacy and "liberal" statesmanship. And he wasn't affected by the psychic complex of panic, hatred, rage, class-arrogance and patriotic swagger that was creating in newspaper editors and in the "jeunesse dorée" around us the authentic élan for war.

My friend is thus somehow in the nation but not of the nation. The war has as yet got no conceivable clutch on his soul. He knows that theoretically he is united with a hundred million in purpose, sentiment and deed for an idealistic war to defend democracy and civilization against predatory autocracy. Yet somehow, in spite of all the excitement, nobody has as yet been able to make this real to him. He is healthy, intelligent, idealistic. The irony is that the demand which his country now makes on him is one to which not one single cell or nerve of idealism or desire responds. The cheap and silly blare of martial life leaves him cold. The easy inflation of their will-to-power which is coming to so many people from their participation in volunteer or government service, or, better still, from their urging others to farm, enlist, invest, retrench, organize, — none of this allures him. His life is uninteresting and unadventurous, but it is not quite dull enough to make this activity or anything he knows about war seem a release into lustier expression. He has ideals but he cannot see their realization through a desperate struggle to the uttermost. He doubts the "saving" of an America which can only be achieved through world-suicide. He wants democracy, but he does not want the kind of democracy we will get by this war enough to pay the suicidal cost of getting it in the way we set about it.

Dulce et decorum est pro patria mori, sweet and becoming is it to die for one's country. This is the young man who is suddenly asked to die for his country. My friend was much concerned about registration. He felt coercive forces closing in upon him. He did not want to register for the purposes of being liable to conscription. It would be doing something positive when he felt only apathy. Furthermore, if he was to resist, was it not better to take a stand now than to wait to be drafted? On the other hand, was it not too much of a concession to rebel at a formality? He did not really wish to be a martyr. Going to prison for a year for merely refusing to register was rather a grotesque and futile gesture. He did not see himself as a hero, shedding inspiration by his example to his fellows. He did not care what others did. His objection to prison was not so much fear perhaps as contempt for a silly sacrifice. He could not keep up his pose of complete aliency from the war-enterprise, now that registration was upon him. Better submit stoically, he thought, to the physical pressure, mentally reserving his sense of spiritual aliency from the enterprise into which he was being remorselessly molded. Yet my friend is no arrant prig. He does not pretend to be a "world-patriot," or a servant of some higher law than his country's. Nor does he feel blatantly patriotic. With his groping philosophy of life, patriotism has merely died as a concept of significance for him. It is to him merely the emotion that fills the head when it imagines itself engaged in massed defense or massed attack. Having no such images, he has no feeling of patriotism. He still feels himself inextricably a part of this blundering, wistful, crass civilization we call America. All he asks is not to be identified with it for warlike ends. He does not feel pro-German. He tells me there is not a drop of any but British blood in his veins. He does not love the Kaiser. He is quite willing to believe that it is the German government and not the German people whom he is asked to fight, although it may be the latter whom he is obliged to kill. But he cannot forget that it is the American government rather than the American people who got up the animus to fight the German government. He does not forget that the American government, having through tragic failure slipped into the war-technique, is now trying to manipulate him into that war-technique. And my friend's idea of *patria* does not include the duty of warlike animus, even when the government decides such animus is necessary to carry out its theories of democracy and the future organization of the world. There are ways in which my friend would probably be willing to die for his country. If his death now meant the restoration of those ravaged lands and the bringing back of the dead, that would be a cause to die for. But he knows that the dead cannot be brought back or the brotherly currents restored. The work of madness will not be undone. Only a desperate war will be prolonged. Everything seems to him so mad that there is nothing left worth dying for. *Pro patria mori,* to my friend, means something different from lying gaunt as a conscript on a foreign battlefield, fallen in the last desperate fling of an interminable world-war.

Does this mean that if he is drafted he will refuse to serve? I do not know. It will not be any plea of "conscientious objection" that keeps him back. That phrase to him has already an archaic flavor which implies a ruling norm, a stiff familiar whom he must obey in the matter. It implies that one would be delighted to work up one's blood-lust for the business, except that this unaccountable conscience, like a godly grandmother, absolutely forbids. In the case of my friend, it will not be any objective "conscience." It will be something that is woven into his whole modern philosophic feel for life. This is what paralyzes him against taking one step toward the war-machine. If he were merely afraid of death, he would seek some alternative service. But he does not. He remains passive and apathetic, waiting for the knife to fall. There is a growing cynicism in him about the brisk and inept bustle of war-organization. His attitude suggests that if he is worked into war-service, he will have to be coerced every step of the way.

Yet he may not even rebel. He may go silently into the ranks in a mood of cold contempt. His horror of useless sacrifice may make even the bludgeoning of himself seem futile. He may go in the mood of so many young men in the other countries, without enthusiasm, without idealism, without hope and without belief, victims of a tragically blind force behind them. No other government, however, has had to face from the very start quite this appalling skepticism of youth. My friend is significant because all the shafts of panic, patriotism and national honor have been discharged at him without avail. All the seductions of "liberal" idealism leave him cold. He is to be susceptible to nothing but the use of crude, rough, indefeasible violence. Nothing could be more awkward for a "democratic" President than to be faced with this cold, staring skepticism of youth, in the prosecution of his war. The attitude of my friend suggests that there is a personal and social idealism in America which is out of reach of the most skillful and ardent appeals of the older order, an idealism that cannot be hurt by the taunts of cowardice and slacking or kindled by the slogans of capitalistic democracy. This is the cardinal fact of our war — the non-mobilization of the younger intelligentsia.

What will they do to my friend? If the war goes on they will need him. Pressure will change skepticism into bitterness. That bitterness will well and grow. If the country submissively pours month after month its wealth of life and resources into the work of annihilation, that bitterness will spread out like a stain over the younger American generation. If the enterprise goes on endlessly, the work, so blithely undertaken for the defense of democracy, will have crushed out the only genuinely precious thing in a nation, the hope and ardent idealism of its youth.

CHARLES EDWARD MONTAGUE

CHARLES EDWARD MONTAGUE (1867–1928) was one of those who endured the fiery apprenticeship of the War and emerged a master of disillusionment. Educated at Oxford and active on the *Manchester Guardian* during most of his writing career, Montague is best known for his satirical novels dealing with government and war; especially *Rough Justice* and *Right Off the Map*. He also published three collections of essays, including several war sketches and short stories, many of which had previously been printed in various periodicals. In striking contrast to the mordant bitterness of his dealings with the powers that make for corruption and bloodshed are his studies of the creation and appreciation of literature; on this subject he wrote with fastidiousness and charm, revealing among other things the basis of his own impeccable style. The following selection is from a volume of essays entitled *Disenchantment*.

THE OLD AGE OF THE WAR *

MEN wearing in trenches used to tell one another sometimes what they fancied the end of the war would be like. Each had his particular favourite vision. Some morning the Captain would come down the trench at "stand-to" and try to speak as if it were nothing. "All right, men," he would say, "you can go across and shake hands." Or the first thing we should hear would be some jubilant peal suddenly shaken out on the air from the nearest standing church in the rear. But the commonest vision was that of marching down a road to a wide, shining river. Once more the longing of a multitude struggling slowly across a venomous wilderness fixed itself on the first glimpse of a Jordan beyond; for most men the Rhine was the physical goal of effort, the term of endurance, the symbol of all attainment and rest.

To win what your youth had desired, and find the taste of it gone, is said to be one of the standard pains of old age. With a kind of blank space in their minds where the joy of fulfilment ought to have been, two British privates of 1914, now Captains attached to the Staff, emerged from the narrow and crowded High Street of Cologne on December 7, 1918, crossed the Cathedral square, and gained their first sight of the Rhine. As they stood on the Hohenzollern bridge and looked at the mighty breadth of rushing stream, each of them certainly gave his heart leave to leap up if it would and if it could. Had they not, by toil and entreaty, gained permission to enter the city with our first cavalry? Were they not putting their lips to the first glass of the sparkling vintage of victory? Neither of them said anything then. The heart that knoweth its own bitterness need not always avow it straight off. But they were friends; they told afterwards.

The first hours of that ultimate winding-up of the old, long-decaying estate of hopes and illusions were not the worst, either. The cavalry brigadier in command at Cologne, those first few days, was a man with a good fighting

* From *Disenchantment*, published by Coward McCann, Inc. Reprinted by permission.

record; and now his gesture towards the conquered was that of the happy warrior, that of Virgilian Rome, that of the older England in hours of victory. German civilians clearly expected some kind of maltreatment, such perhaps as their own scum had given to Belgians. They strove with desperate care to be correct in their bearing, neither to jostle us accidentally in the streets nor to shrink away from us pointedly. Soon, to their surprise and shame, they found that among the combatant English there lingered the hobby of acting like those whom the Germans had known through their Shakespeare: "We give express charge that in our marches through the country there be nothing compelled from the villages, nothing taken but paid for, none of the French upbraided or abused in disdainful language."

The "cease fire" order on Armistice Day had forbidden all "fraternizing." But any man who has fought with a sword, or its equivalent, knows more about that than the man who has only blown with a trumpet. To men who for years have lived like foxes or badgers, dodging their way from each day of being alive to the next, there comes back more easily, after a war, a sense of the tacit league that must, in mere decency, bind together all who cling precariously to life on a half-barren ball that goes spinning through space. All castaways together, all really marooned on the one desert island, they know that, however hard we may have to fight to sober a bully or guard to each man his share of the shell-fish and clams, we all have to come back at last to the joint work of making the island more fit to live on. The gesture of the decimated troops who held Cologne at the end of that year was, in essence, that of the cavalry brigadier. Sober or drunk, the men were contumaciously sportsmen, incorrigibly English. One night before Christmas I thought I heard voices outside my quarters long after curfew, and went to look out from my balcony high up in the Domhof into the moon-flooded expanse of the Cathedral square below. By rights there should have been no figures there at that hour, German or British. But there were three; two tipsy Highlanders — "Women from Hell," as German soldiers used to call the demonic stabbers in kilts — gravely dispensing the consolations of chivalry to a stout burgher of Cologne. "Och, dinna tak' it to hairrt, mon. I tell ye that your lads were grond." It was like a last leap of the flame that had burnt clear and high four years before.

II

For the day of the fighting man, him and his chivalric hobbies, was over. The guns had hardly ceased to fire before from the rear, from the bases, from London, there came flooding up the braves who for all those four years had been squealing threats and abuse, some of them begging off service in arms on the plea that squealing was indispensable national work. We had not been long in Cologne when there arrived in hot haste a young pressman from London, one of the first of a swarm. He looked a fine strong man. He seemed to be one of the male Vestals who have it for their trade to feed the eternal flame of hatred between nations, instead of cleaning out stables or doing some other work fit for a male. His train had fortunately brought him just in time for luncheon. This he ate and drank with goodwill, complaining only that the wine, which seemed to me good, was not better. He then slept on his bed until tea-time. Reanimated with tea, he said genially, "Well, I must be getting on with my mission of hate," and retired to his room to write a vivacious account of the wealth and luxury of Cologne, the guzzling in all cafés and restaurants, the fair round bellies of the working class, the sleek and rosy children of the poor. I read it, two days after, in his paper. Our men who had helped to fight Germany down were going short of food at the time, through feeding the children in houses where they were billeted. "Proper Zoo there is in this place," one of them told me. "Proper lions and tigers. Me and my friend are taking the kids from our billet soon's we've got them fatted up a bit. If you'll believe me, sir, them kiddies ain't safe in a Zoo. They could walk in through the bars and get patting the lions." I had just seen some of the major carnivora in their cages close to the Rhine, each a rectangular lamina of fur and bone like the tottering cats I had seen pass through incredible slits of space in Amiens a month after the people had fled from the city that spring. But little it mattered in London what he or I saw. The nimble scamps had the ear of the world; what the soldier said was not evidence.

Some Allied non-combatants did almost unthinkable things in the first ecstasy of the triumph that others had won. One worthy drove into Cologne in a car plastered over with Union Jacks, like a minor bookie going to Epsom. It passed the wit of man to make him understand that one does not do these things to defeated peoples. But he could understand, with some help, that our Commander-in-Chief alone was entitled to carry a Union Jack on his car. "We must show these fellows our power"; that was the form of the licence taken out by every churl in spirit who wanted to let his coltish nature loose on a waiter or barber in some German hotel. I saw one such gallant assert the majesty of the Allies by refusing to pay more than half the prices put down on the wine-list. Another would send a waiter across an hotel dining-room to order a quiet party of German men and women not to speak so loud. Another was all for inflicting little bullying indignities on the editor of the *Kölnische Zeitung* — making him print as matters of fact our versions of old cases of German misconduct, etc. Probably he did not even know that the intended exhibition-ground for these deplorable tricks was one of the great journals of Europe.

Not everybody, not even every non-combatant in the dress of a soldier, had caught that shabby epidemic of spite. But it was rife. It had become a fashion to have it, as in some raffish circles it is a fashion to have some rakish disease. In the German military cemetery at Lille I have heard a man reared at one of our most famous public schools and our most noble university, and then wearing our uniform, say that he thought the French might do well to desecrate the German soldiers' graves on French soil. Another, at Brussels, commended a Belgian who was said to have stripped his wife naked in one of the streets of that city and cut off her hair on some airy suspicion of an affair with a German officer during the enemy's occupation. A fine sturdy sneer at the notion of doing anything chivalrous was by this time the mode. "I hope to God," an oldish and highly non-combatant general said, in discussing the probable terms of peace with a younger general who had begun the war as a full lieutenant and fought hard all the way up, "that there's going to be no rot about not kicking a man when he's down." The junior general grunted. He did not agree. But he clearly felt shy of protesting. Worshippers of setting suns feel ill at ease in discussion with these bright, confident fellows who swear by the rising one.

III

The senior general need not have feared. The generous youth of the war, when England could carry, with no air of burlesque, the flag of St. George, was pretty well gone. The authentic flame might still flicker on in the minds of a few tired soldiers and disregarded civilians. Otherwise it was as dead as the half-million of good fellows whom it had fired four years ago, whose credulous hearts the maggots were now eating under so many shining and streaming square miles of wet Flanders and Picardy. They gone, their war had lived into a kind of dotage ruled by mean fears and desires. At home our places of honour were brown with shirkers masquerading in the dead men's clothes and licensed by careless authorities to shelter themselves from all danger under the titles of Colonel, Major, and Captain. Nimble politicians were rushing already to coin into votes for themselves — "the men who won the war" — the golden memory of the dead before the living could come home and make themselves heard. Sounds of a general election, the yells of political cheap-jacks, the bawling of some shabby promise, capped by some shabbier bawl, made their way out to Cologne.

"This way, gents, for the right sort of whip to give Germans!" "Rats, gentlemen, rats! Don't listen to *him*. Leave it to me and I'll chastise 'em with scorpions." "I'll devise the brave punishments for them." "Ah, but I'll sweat you more money out of the swine." That was the gist of the din that most of the gramophones of the home press gave out on the Rhine. Each little demagogue had got his little pots of pitch and sulphur on sale for the proper giving of hell to the enemy whom he had not faced. Germany lay at our feet, a world's wonder of downfall, a very Lucifer, fallen, broken, bereaved beyond all the retributive griefs which Greek tragedy shows you afflicting the great who were insolent, wilful, and proud. But it was not enough for our small epicures of revenge. They wanted to twist the enemy's wrists, where he lay bound, and to run pins into his eyes. And they had the upper hand of us now. The soldiers could only look on while the scurvy performance dragged itself out till the meanest of treaties was signed at Versailles. "Fatal Versailles!" as General Sir Ian Hamilton said for us all: "Not a line — not one line in your treaty to show that those boys (our friends who were dead) had been any better than the emperors; not one line to stand for the kindliness of England; not one word to bring back some memory of the generosity of her sons!"

"The freedom of Europe," "The war to end war," "The overthrow of militarism," "The cause of civilization" — most people believe so little now in anything or anyone that they would find it hard to understand the simplicity and intensity of faith with which these phrases were once taken among our troops, or the certitude felt by hundreds of thousand of men who are now dead that if they were killed their monument would be a new Europe not soured or soiled with the hates and greeds of the old. That the old spirit of Prussia might not infest our world any more; that they or, if not they, their sons might breathe a new, cleaner air they had willingly hung themselves up to rot on the uncut wire at Loos or wriggled to death, slow hour by hour, in the cold filth at Broodseinde. Now all was done that man could do, and all was done in vain. The old spirit of Prussia was blowing anew, from strange mouths. From several species of men who passed for English — as mongrels, curs, shoughs, water-rugs, and demi-wolves are all clept by the name of dogs — there was rising a chorus of shrill yelps for the outdoing of all the base folly committed by Prussia when drunk with her old conquest of France. Prussia, beaten out of the field, had won in the souls of her conquerors' rulers; they had become her pupils; they took her word for it that she, and not the older England, knew how to use victory.

IV

Sir Douglas Haig came to Cologne when we had been there a few days. On the grandiose bridge over the Rhine he made a short speech to a few of us. Most of it sounded as if the thing were a job he had got to get through with, and did not much care for. Perhaps the speech, like those of other great men who wisely hate making speeches, had been written for him by somebody else. But once he looked up from the paper and put in some words which I felt sure were his own; "I only hope that, now we have won, we shall not lose our heads, as the Germans did after 1870. It has brought them to this." He looked at the gigantic mounted statue of the Kaiser overhead, a thing crying out in its pride for fire from heaven to fall and consume it, and at the homely, squat British sentry moving below on his post. I think the speech was reported. But none of our foremen at home took any notice of it at all. They knew a trick worth two of Haig's. They were as moonstruck as any victorious Prussian.

So we had failed — had won the fight and lost the prize; the garland of the war was withered before it was gained. The lost years, the broken youth, the dead friends, the women's overshadowed lives at home, the agony and bloody sweat — all had gone to darken the stains which most of us had thought to scour out of the world that our children would live in. Many men felt, and said to each other, that they had been fooled. They had believed that their country was backing them. They had thought, as they marched into Germany, "Now we shall show old Fritz how you treat a man when you've thrashed him." They would let him into the English secret, the tip that the power and glory are not to the bully. As some of them looked at the melancholy performance which followed, our Press and our politicians parading at Paris in moral *pickelhauben* and doing the Prussianist goose-step by way of *pas de triomphe*, they could not but say in dismay to themselves: "This is our doing. We cannot wish the war unwon, and yet — if we had shirked, poor old England, for all we know, might not have come to this pass. So we come home draggle-tailed, sick of the mess that we were unwittingly helping to make when we tried to do well."

THE EDITORS OF FORTUNE MAGAZINE

FORTUNE MAGAZINE was established in 1932 under the editorship of Mr. Henry R. Luce. The article "Arms and the Men" appeared in the number for March, 1934. The article received mention in the Honor Roll of *The Nation*, January 2, 1935, "The Editorial Staff of *Fortune*, for their articles on the munitions industry, which stimulated the important Senatorial investigation of the subject." *The Nation* for January 23, 1935, contains an explanation by Mr. Archibald MacLeish: "*Fortune* articles are the result of the combined work of several members of the staff, and in this particular case the editor in charge was Associate Editor Eric Hodgkins, to whom all personal credit should go."

ARMS AND THE MEN *

A PRIMER ON EUROPE'S ARMAMENT MAKERS; THEIR MINES, THEIR SMELTERS, THEIR BANKS, THEIR HOLDING COMPANIES, THEIR ABILITY TO SUPPLY EVERYTHING YOU NEED FOR A WAR FROM CANNONS TO THE CASUS BELLI; THEIR AXIOMS, WHICH ARE (A) PROLONG WAR, (B) DISTURB PEACE

ACCORDING to the best accountancy figures, it cost about $25,000 to kill a soldier during the World War. There is one class of Big Business Men in Europe that never rose up to denounce the extravagance of its governments in this regard — to point out that when death is left unhampered as an enterprise for the individual initiative of gangsters the cost of a single killing seldom exceeds $100. The reason for the silence of these Big Business Men is quite simple: the killing is their business. Armaments are their stock in trade; governments are their customers; the ultimate consumers of their products are, historically, almost as often their compatriots as their enemies. That does not matter. The important point is that every time a burst shell fragment finds its way into the brain, the heart, or the intestines of a man in the front line, a great part of the $25,000, much of it profit, finds its way into the pocket of the armament maker.

The problem of European armaments is complex: if we are to get anywhere with it we must first park our emotions outside. Pacifists and militarists alike have indulged in a good deal of loose talk on the subject. Most pacifists are not sufficiently informed; their arguments and accusations frequently boil down to nothing more substantial than Sir Arthur Eddington's definition of the Quantum Theory — i.e., "Something unknown is doing we don't know what." Most militarists are insincere.

Anyone who talks about European armaments and their makers must inevitably oversimplify. But to oversimplify is not to overgeneralize — and we should start by ridding ourselves of one generality that will give us trouble as long as it stays in our heads.

* By permission of *Fortune*.

There is nothing that could, in any strict accuracy, be called an "Armament Ring" in Europe today. There is no perfectly homologous group of single-purposed individuals that sits down before a polished table in a soundproof room and plots new holocausts in Europe. Search through the armament makers as you will, you will find neither a Machiavelli nor a Dr. Fu Manchu. But that's all you *won't* find.

For without a shadow of doubt there is at the moment in Europe a huge and subversive force that lies behind the arming and counter-arming of nations: there are mines, smelters, armament works, holding companies, and banks, entangled in an international embrace, yet working inevitably for the destruction of such little internationalism as the world has achieved so far. The control of these myriad companies vests, finally, in not more than a handful of men whose power, in some ways, reaches above the power of the State itself. Thus, French interests not only sold arms to Hungary in flat violation of the Treaty of Trianon, but when Hungary defaulted on the bill the armorers got the French government to lend Hungary the money to pay the French armorers. Thus, too, the great Czechoslovakian armament company, controlled by Frenchmen, promoted the rise of Hitler in Germany and contributed millions of marks to Hitler's campaign. These same Frenchmen own newspapers that did more than any others to enrage France against Hitler. It is time we had a dramatis personæ of arms and the men.

KRUPP

Best known armament name in all the world is perhaps the name of Krupp. The Krupp who, despite early discouragements at the hands of his own government, built up the gigantic works at Essen and made his name a synonym for cannon was Alfred — a strange figure who wore wooden sabots when he visited his factory, opened the windows of his house only once a month, had a bathtub in his parlor, assembled his intimates in his home every few weeks to be weighed, for no discoverable reason, on scales of his own devising, and carried a steel walking stick. Alfred Krupp began as a humble petitioner of governments, coming hat in hand to ministers, kings, and emperors of assorted nationalities to beg orders for his guns. By the time of his death he was an intimate of Wilhelm I, the 1870 conqueror of France. He was also an officer of the French Legion of Honor (one of Napoleon III's earlier generosities) and a Knight of the Russian Order of Peter the Great.

Under his son, Friedrich Alfred Krupp, the house rose to higher and higher glories. Yet Friedrich Alfred failed in one important respect: he left no male heir to carry on. It took Kaiser Wilhelm II to solve this difficulty. When big buxom Bertha, Friedrich Alfred's daughter, came of marriageable age Wilhelm II betrothed her to the protégé of his own selection and training: Gustav von Bohlen und Halbach — and it was the groom, not his bride, whose name was changed by the betrothal. He became then *Krupp* von Bohlen und Halbach. Under this new head of the house, who took command in 1909, Krupp went further still, supplied fifty-two countries with arms before the war, and stood all but single-handed against the world during it.

What of Krupp now? In theory, Krupp smelts only peaceful ore, and forges its steels only into such benign shapes as locomotives, rails, bridge girders, and others purely industrial. Actually, Krupp is rearming Germany — the discoverable portion of whose annual armament bill is now about $80,000,000. Germany, forbidden by the Treaty of Versailles to import armaments, receives generous supplies from Sweden (where Krupp controls the armament firm of Bofors) and Holland; forbidden to export armaments, she ships to South America, the Far East, or to any European nation that will violate its own treaty by ordering from her. Yet for all the might of the Krupp works we must look elsewhere today to find the real heart of the armament business.

BETHLEHEM STEEL *et al*

To the United States, perhaps? After all, we have our Du Ponts, whose powder-making activities have not been without profit. We have an army and navy whose officers, according to the statement of a former Cabinet officer, are far more active than the officers of any other armed force against any sort of international understanding. We have an armament bill of over $200,000,000 a year.[1] We once had our Big Bass Drum, Mr. William B. Shearer, whose boast was that he wrecked the Naval Conference at Geneva in 1927. We have our Midvale Co. (controlled by the Baldwin Locomotive Works) which prospered mightily during the war and has continued the manufacture of guns and gun forgings, armor plate and projectiles; our Colt's Patent Firearms Mfg. Co. which supplies machine guns as well as squirrel rifles, which declared an extra dividend in 1933; our Remington Arms Co. (controlled by Du Pont) whose output of firearms and ammunition together is one third of U. S. production. And we have our Bethlehem Steel Co.

Bethlehem's Mr. Charles M. Schwab dismayed the cadets of West Point in 1927 by saying: "Today the Bethlehem Steel Company has definitely abandoned any thought of ever again engaging in the manufacture of ordnance except in times of great national emergency." Such times are apparently with us now — have, in fact, been continually with us since Mr. Schwab unloosed this shaft of oratory. In the official listing of Bethlehem's products (you need only turn to Standard Statistics or Bethlehem's own most recent annual report) you will find armor plate, projectiles, gun and shell forgings, battleships, battle cruisers, scout cruisers, destroyers, submarines, and airplane carriers all listed as products of Bethlehem's plants. The site at Bethlehem where cannon and armor plate are made is separate from the rest of the plant. No outsiders are allowed, and it may be that Mr. Schwab has never been able to evade the vigilance of his watchmen. But if he could once get inside he would see a triumph of inventiveness — for Bethlehem not only makes "armor-piercing" projectiles, but "nonpierceable" armor plate — which must sometimes cause slight confusion on the proving ground when anyone attempts to demonstrate the virtues of both at the same time.

Our own country is not, then, quite so virginally innocent in this business as we might like to suppose. But despite the size of our armament bill, our

[1] When we say armaments we mean here, and hereafter, only the actual implements and materials of war: cannon, guns, ammunition, tanks, military aircraft, and naval vessels.

armament and munitions exports to South and Central America and the Far East, we are essentially small fry in this game.

ENGLAND'S VICKERS-ARMSTRONGS

Much larger fry is England, where the firm of Vickers-Armstrongs is the brightest star in the armament firmament. The annual bills of Vickers-Armstrongs to nations for armaments purchased quite possibly amount to $100,000,000. For England's powerful position as one of the greatest exporters of the materials of war in the world, the bulk of the credit goes to Vickers-Armstrongs. It makes other things than armaments, true enough; such unwarlike products as sewing machines and golf clubs come from some of its factories. But its chairman, General the Hon. Sir Herbert Lawrence, G.C.B., onetime Chief of Staff of the B.E.F., has put himself on record as saying, "Vickers-Armstrongs, Ltd., relies very largely on armament orders for its existence." The Vickers research staffs work constantly to bring into mass production such bolsters to international comfort as the Vickers-Carden-Lloyd Light Amphibious Tank, or the Vickers Vildebeest Bombing Machine.

The sun never sets upon Vickers. It has its factories in Rumania where, for greater convenience, Sir Herbert Lawrence is a director of the Bank of Rumania (and Vickers to some degree allies itself with the Czechoslovakian armament firm of Skoda). In Italy it Latinizes its name to Società Vickers-Terni; in Japan it has as a subsidiary the Japan Steel Works, and thus allies itself with the Japanese armament and industrial firm of Mitsui. There are Vickers factories or subsidiary companies in Spain, Canada, Ireland, Holland (The Hague affords an appropriate site for some of the Vickers operations), and New Zealand.

Vickers directors are men of wide affairs. Sir Herbert Lawrence, besides being a director of the Bank of Rumania, is also a director of the Sun Insurance Office, Ltd., with which Vickers-Armstrongs had a curious agreement that "if the profits [of Vickers] in any year during the five years ending December 31, 1932, do not amount to £900,000, then a contribution not exceeding £200,000 will be made in each year." Sir Otto Niemeyer, the infant phenomenon of British finance who first entered His Majesty's Treasury at the age of twenty-three, is another Vickers director; he is, in addition, an officer of the Bank of England, a director of the Anglo-International Bank and the Bank of International Settlements.

Through these industrial and financial interlockings Vickers-Armstrongs conducts its affairs. They are profitable affairs — for as the agreement with Sun Insurance indicates a profit of some $4,500,000 a year is considered so unsatisfactory that insurance must be carried against it. And England's aristocracy takes pleasure in clipping its coupons. Among the more prominent shareholders, in 1932, of Vickers or other concerns associated with the production of materials of war were: Rt. Hon. Neville Chamberlain, Chancellor of the Exchequer, and Sir Austen Chamberlain, M.P., winner of the Nobel Peace Prize in 1925. In 1914 the list was even more imposing. It included that lofty philosopher Lord Balfour, that glittering snob Lord

Curzon, and also Lord Kinnaird (President of the Y.M.C.A.), three bishops, and Dean Inge of St. Paul's.   It was in that same year that Socialist Philip Snowden spoke in Parliament: "It would be impossible to throw a stone on the benches opposite without hitting a member who is a shareholder in one or other of these firms."

You will gather that England, peace-loving England, has been quite some time at the task of building up this organization.   She has.   The firm began in 1829.   Slowly, throughout the nineteenth century, the firm grew, changed its name, cast its outworn skins, grew fat, prosperous, and highly multi-cellular through the acquisition of *this* torpedo works, of *that* heavy ordnance factory.   And then there came along Mr. Basileios Zacharias.

He is known today as Sir Basil Zaharoff.   He was an intimate of Lloyd George during the war; a few relatively mild revelations of the degree to which he influenced Great Britain's armament, military, and foreign policies during and after the war were enough, in 1922, to send Lloyd George, who did more than any other man to win the war, out of office forever.   This strange character, the greatest armament salesman the world has ever known, struck a major spark in the world when he collided with an American of somewhat similar interests.   Zaharoff at that time was a salesman for the Nordenfeldt Guns & Ammunition Co., Ltd., of England and had done very well in profits out of the perpetual dogfights in the Balkans and the Near East, to which he was usually purveyor and of which he was frequently (it was an easy trick once he learned it) instigator.   The American that gladdened his heart was Hiram Maxim, whose new machine gun was incomparably the best killing machine Zaharoff had ever seen.   Zaharoff took Maxim to his bosom, with reservations.   First he used his wily, polyglot salesmanship to block the gun's sale in Austria as an impractical toy; then, when he had offered Maxim a partnership and got the sale of the gun firmly in his own hands, he swept over Europe and Asia selling such quantities that soon the new firm of the Maxim-Nordenfeldt Guns & Ammunition Co. was purchsed for some $6,000,000 (the year was 1897) by Vickers interests and became Vickers Sons & Maxim.   Sir Basil was established now as a power in armament affairs, hence in Great Britain's affairs, hence in world affairs.   He already enjoyed the distinction of having sold the first practical submarine ever used in naval operations to his native Greece, and the further distinction of having used this sale to frighten Turkey into buying *two* submarines. The Boer War added to his laurels: Boers shot Englishmen with Vickers guns and ammunition.   The Russo-Japanese War provided him with an even wider field for his gifts: Vickers sold as much war material (and possibly more) to Russia as it did to Japan, England's supposed ally.

But, naturally, it was the World War that gratified Sir Basil most.   The profits of war-time armament manufacture were practically incalculable; by the end of the war Sir Basil had a personal fortune that was estimated as low as $100,000,000 or $200,000,000 and as high as a billion.   And in 1917, when there seemed a possibility of peace through the intervention of the United States, Lord Bertie, British Ambassador to France, naïvely recorded in his diary: "Zaharoff is all for continuing the war *jusqu' au bout*." ...

So much for Germany and her Krupp, the United States and Bethlehem Steel, England and Vickers-Armstrongs, and the now withered and senile Sir Basil. Do these armament businesses seem Big Business? Then you must alter your sense of proportion before you go further. All the foregoing is a mere curtain raiser to the Big Show. The Big Show is France.

SCHNEIDER-CREUSOT

France stands at the very top. She stands at the top in the amount her government spends on armaments; at the top in the amount of arms she exports to other nations; at the top also by virtue of the billion francs she has spent to build a military Chinese wall of forts, many of them underground, along her eastern boundaries. But these mere quantitative details do not reveal the true significance of her position.

She stands today as a queer paradox: France, the democracy, a quiet pasture land for the world's most famous peasantry, coexisting with France, the greatest military power of modern times, with an army which all but equals in numbers and far surpasses in equipment Germany's vast militaristic machine in 1914.

At the head of this latter France stands the figure of General Maxime Weygand (Vice President of the Higher War Council, Inspector General of the Army, possessor of the Grand Cross of the Legion of Honor, Member of the French Academy), ruling an army (including Colonials) of 650,000 men. But despite his decorations, his medals and orders, and the power he has, once a new war begins, to order several million men to death, General Weygand, a devout Catholic, represents not the urge for war, on the contrary, France's desire for peace — by means of "security." The French threat to the peace of the world lies elsewhere — in France. For in France, and only in France, a new situation exists: the armament makers are no longer, like Alfred Krupp or Sir Basil Zaharoff in his younger days, humble petitioners of government, hat-in-hand solicitors of orders — their influence is so infiltrated into the industrial, social, and political affairs of the nation that they have power in some ways beyond the State; a power so mighty that they are all but able, for their own individualistic reasons, to sweep the State along in a course of action against its own will. They are all but anonymous, these men. They are displeased by publicity and are well able to enforce their displeasure. But we must now displease one of them and present the figure of M. Charles Prosper Eugène Schneider.

Charles Prosper Eugène Schneider is a man of many offices — the executive head of hundreds of armament firms throughout Europe. He is President of the Schneider-Creusot company, armament manufacturers with mines, smelters, and foundries scattered throughout France. He is director of the Banque de l'Union Parisienne, one of whose most profitable sources of business is the financing of loans for armaments. In 1920 he founded and became the President of the Union Européenne Industriale et Financière — a holding company, capitalized at 140,000,000 francs. Through it Schneider-Creusot controls 182 French companies that manufacture heavy ordnance, machine guns, tanks, shells, ammunition, and warfare chemicals.

Out of the $300,000,000 which, at the most conservative guess, represents the annual billing of France's armament concerns, Schneider-Creusot or subsidiaries takes the lion's share.

CZECH'S SKODA

But the Union Européenne has an even more important function. Through it, Schneider-Creusot reaches out to control 230 armament and allied enterprises *outside* France. The greatest of *these* concerns is that glittering jewel in the crown of the principal Ideal State that came into being in 1919 as the result of the self-determination of oppressed peoples. The state is Czechoslovakia, and its jewel is Skoda.

Skoda, although its main works are in Brno (which was once on Austrian territory), has factories scattered not only over Czechoslovakia but over Poland and Rumania as well. Upon the board of Skoda, which the Union Européenne controls through 56 per cent of its stock, M. Schneider sits with his friend André Vicaire, Director General of Schneider-Creusot; his brother-in-law, Arnaud de Saint-Sauveur; Eduard Benes, who, as Czechoslovakia's Foreign Minister, takes second place to no one in the vocal support he lends to the League of Nations; and two Czecho-Germans, Von Dutschnitz and Von Arthaber, who were, it is interesting to note in view of laser facts, very heavy financial contributors to Hitler's political success. Political France and political Germany may be at constant swords' points, the Polish Corridor may inflame the Nazis, France may quiver at her lack of "security" from another northern invasion — but the lion and the lamb never lie down together with more good fellowship than these French, German, Czech, and Polish gentlemen when they come together to discuss, as fellow directors, the problems of increasing Europe's consumption of armaments. Thanks to the activities of Skoda and its allies, arms form a full 10 per cent of all Czech exports — and 40 per cent of all Skoda's products are exported — to the extent of $30,000,000 worth a year.

BACK TO SCHNEIDER

M. Schneider's nationality is capable of any supple manipulation that a political emergency may call for. The founder of his dynasty was his grandfather, also named Eugène, who, with a brother Adolph, left Bidestroff in the then German territory of the Saar and came to France in 1836. More particularly Brothers Eugène and Adolph came to Le Creusot (literally "The Hollow" or "The Cruicible") where to the south of the Burgundy wine district a small foundry had been making cannon from the days of Louis XVI. With perfect impartiality it had supplied first the monarchy, then the republic, and then Napoleon's Empire with its products. With the aid of the French banking house of Seillière these German brothers bought the foundry (La Société Générale des Hauts Fourneaux) for 2,500,000 francs — and were then forced to wait for almost twenty years for their first major war. War-promotion methods in those days were not what they were to become later in the century, but that gap was neatly bridged by the demands that the new steamboats and the even newer railroads were making on the producers of iron and steel. Then, in 1854, the Crimean War broke out, and Eugène (alone now, following Adolph's death) converted Le Creusot almost exclusively to the manufacture of arms. The family fortune was founded; the family tradition was established.

In the few years that followed the Crimean War, Eugène Schneider had time to look about him for parliamentary posts. First he became a Member of the Chamber of Deputies; later he rose to be Minister of Agriculture, then of Commerce. By 1865 he had become President of the Chamber of Deputies (analogous to the Speaker of the U. S. House of Representatives).

It was from this vantage point that he was able to watch the sweep of events that led to the Franco-Prussian War. Alfred Krupp saw it coming, too. He, like Schneider, was capable of an internationalism far above the confines of narrow patriotism and was anxious to equip Napoleon III's armies with his own cannon — a suggestion not entirely without its logic or, even, its sportsmanship, for Krupp had borrowed in Paris (from the same banking house of Seillière as had set Eugène Schneider up in business) the money with which he made the guns that later humbled France at Metz and Sedan.

But in those days Schneider was jealous of Krupp's mounting power and persuaded Napoleon III that his patronage of Le Creusot would be more enlightened. The inferiority of the French cannon in 1870 was one factor that brought about the catastrophic ruin of the Second Empire.

Nothing in the career of the Schneider dynasty is more remarkable than the fact that it was able to overcome this shocking disgrace and actually to get the job of re-equipping the new armies of the Republic. This time Eugène Schneider supplied France with cannon modeled upon the designs of the victorious Krupps. It was not until some twenty years later that he died, full of years and his own sort of wisdom, to be succeeded by his son Henri.

It was under Henri's son — the present Eugène Schneider, now sixty-six years old, that the Schneider-Creusot company began to work upon a gigantic, world-wide scale. Its real expansion began with the turn of the century. Eugène Schneider acquired iron mines in Lorraine and began a program of mill, foundry, and shipyard building at Bordeaux and Toulon. And then, opportunely, the Russo-Japanese War arrived.

Not until after the close of this war did the real genius of the living Eugène Schneider begin to manifest itself. Russia needed rearming. The Krupps rushed in. The English firm of Vickers rushed in. Eugène Schneider rushed in. There ensued a brief jockeying for position among the three firms — and it was Schneider, perhaps, who captured the best. "Buy from us," he whispered gently into the proper ears, "and pay with *French* money." It was not hard to arrange. The French Ambassador to Imperial Russia was then Maurice Paléologue, who was likewise a director in the Schneider Banque de l'Union Parisienne. The Russians made a brief call on Paris and came back to St. Petersburg with money with which to pay for Schneider armaments. From that time until, in 1918, the Soviet government of Russia expressed its official uninterest in paying the debts of the Czarist régime, sixteen billion gold francs, drained slowly from the savings of the French people, were loaned to Russia, secured by bonds that have long since been tossed on the rubbish heap. Most of the profit in the sixteen billion found its way back to Schneider-Creusot and is today in their foundries and their bank accounts.

Yet the Czar's government was not wholly credulous. It seemed to have some qualms that so much Russian armament should be manufactured on foreign soil. This offered no problem to the armament makers. Schneider installed engineers and managers at the Putilov works in St. Petersburg. The Krupps did likewise. French newspapers screamed that the Krupps were spying. German newspapers screamed that the French were spying. But 1914 found Schneider and Krupp engineers side by side on terms of cordial friendship, overseeing ordnance manufacture on behalf of Nicholas II, Czar of all the Russias.

LOVE THINE ENEMY

The armorers, after all, are the true internationalists. Regardless of their nationalities, they work in concert at the two axioms of their trade — prolong wars, disturb peace. Between 1914 and 1918 they practiced constantly a neat practical way of prolonging war.

It was this: if your enemy is in danger of running short of a basic raw material that he needs in the business of destroying your troops, sell him some out of your own surplus stocks.

Such interchanges went on constantly during the war — always of course through a neutral intermediary. (The amenities of warfare must be observed, even at some inconvenience.) Throughout the war English and French industries maintained to Germany a steady stream of glycerin (for explosives), nickel, copper, oil, and rubber. Germany even returned the compliment: she sent France iron and steel and magnetos for gasoline engines. This constant traffic went on during the war via Sweden, Norway, Denmark, Switzerland, Spain, or Holland, by the simple process of transshipment — enemy to neutral to enemy.

It is no bristling Communist who supplies corroboration, but as conservative and well-considered a gentleman as Rear Admiral Montagu William Warcop Peter Consett, who was British Naval Attaché in Denmark between 1912 and 1917 and in Norway and Sweden between 1912 and 1919. He stated, in so many words, that if the "blockade" of Germany had been really effective during 1915 and 1916, Germany would have been forced to her knees long before the collapse of Russia permitted her to prolong the struggle by throwing more troops into the trenches of the Western Front. And it is he who is responsible for the following statement: "In 1915 England exported twice as much nickel to Sweden as in the two previous years put together. Of the total imports of 504 tons, seventy were reshipped to Germany. But it can be said that the total importation served the needs of Germany, for the remaining 434 tons were used in Sweden for the manufacture of munitions."

And so it went. Germany, throughout the war, had urgent need of nickel, aluminum, and chemicals like glycerin for explosives. France, because the rich Briey basin and other sources were out of her control, had to scratch hard for iron and steel. Continuously, therefore, what one nation lacked, the armament manufacturers of an enemy nation did their urgent best to provide. Month after month, during the war, German heavy industries exported an average of 150,000 tons of scrap iron, steel, or barbed wire to Switzerland, where, having been smelted to a more convenient form, it was then transshipped to France. France, in her turn, shipped chemicals to the Lonza Co. (a Swiss industrial concern, German controlled, but with directors who were French, Italian, and Austrian as well) from which they reached munitions works in Germany. It was all very profitable — and the splendid war went on and on.

EYE-OPENER: BRIEY

If you have a naïveté about the war, shed it now: the war in no way interrupted the cordiality of the armament makers. Throughout the years from 1914 to 1918 they stayed on jolly terms; they even emerged from the war better friends than they were when they went into it. One major wartime episode in particular revealed their unshakable solidarity.

Before 1914 the great iron mines and smelters in the Briey basin provided 70 per cent of the ore used by France. The German advance wrested them from the political control of France — and quite naturally the German artillery chiefs saw to it that the mines were so protected from shell fire that they could be taken over intact. Thenceforth the mines of the Briey basin were operated for the benefit of Germany — in association with other mines in Lorraine which had been in German hands since 1871 *they supplied Germany with some three quarters of the ore she consumed during the war.*

In 1916, some two years later, the Briey basin came once again within the potential grasp of the French. Throughout the second battle of Verdun, Briey was within range of the operations of the French Second Army. The Briey mines and smelters were turning out tons of raw materials per day which were being continuously turned into weapons of death against French troops, and the naïve civilian would therefore suppose that the French Second Army would now turn loose its bombing planes and blast out of existence a principal source of enemy supply.

The naïve civilian would be quite wrong. Bombs did not burst at Briey; nowhere near Briey did more than a few shells from either side fall during the entire course of the war. There were even line officers who shared civilian naïveté enough to question French G.H.Q. on the immunity of Briey. A reasonable explanation *could* have been that the French were withholding fire from Briey because they, in turn, hoped to recapture the basin and turn its products back to France. But this was not the explanation that emerged from headquarters; instead it was stated that if Briey were bombarded, the Germans, in reprisal, would turn their guns on Dombasle in Meurthe-et-Moselle, where equally large-scale mining operations were supplying the French with much of their own raw material for ordnance and ammunition. So long as the French left Briey alone the Germans would let Dombasle alone; what hothead was there who would want to upset the apple cart under these circumstances? Of course, if the French and Germans had each leveled the other's smelters, the war would have ended sooner. And so would war-time profits. That was that. Briey and Dombasle came unscathed through the war.

Here the proof of the international operations of the armament makers is open to no question at all. In corroboration there is spread upon the records the testimony of Deputy Pierre Etienne Flandin (scarcely a flaming Bolshevist, for he was later Finance Minister under Tardieu) to the effect that he, an artillery officer during the war, knew of his own knowledge that the artillery of the French Second Army had been expressly forbidden to bombard Briey when the chance existed, and when a ten-mile penetration of the sector would have come close to spelling German ruin. And the statement of his colleague, Deputy Barthe, in the Chamber on January 24, 1919, lost little of its significance in the long, loud, vicious debates and investigations which followed it: "I affirm that either by the fact of the international solidarity of the great metallurgy companies, or in order to safeguard private business interests, our military chiefs were ordered not to bombard the establishments of the Briey basin, which were being exploited by the enemy during the war. I affirm that our aviation service received instructions to respect the blast furnaces in which the enemy steel was being made, and that a general who wished to bombard them was reprimanded."

There is a quality of delirium about facts like these. Anyone who comes upon them for the first time is likely to feel a sense of incredulity that these can be facts at all; to feel that they must be, instead, some insane fiction of a super-Voltaire.

The sense of incredulity is quite excusable. Yet the facts *are* facts — and into the bargain they are quite easily explicable. In this present imperfect world nations have yet found no agreement upon practical methods of disarming. So long as they refuse to, the easiest way for them to stay armed is to permit a full exploitation of the private profit system in the manufacture of armaments. By this device nations avoid the expense and annoyance of maintaining plants and inventories of armaments throughout a period of twenty years when perhaps they may never be needed at all; the private armorer meanwhile is able to keep his plants oiled and humming by sales not only to his own government but to foreign markets in which he is able to foment enough suspicion to sell large bills of goods. Here is the rock upon which every private conference that precedes official disarmament conferences has split. Here the circle closes. So long as we must have armaments we must lend rein and scope to the business methods of the armorers. What happened at Briey, considered in this light, was very simple: the mere working out of the profit system in armaments to its perfect, logical, and ultimate conclusion.

CLIMAX: THE DE WENDELS

The episode of Briey brings us now to the pinnacle of the armament structure. Who held the impulsive line officers in check? Through whose influence was the general reprimanded?

We must look higher than to Schneider-Creusot for the final answer. For far overtopping Schneider-Creusot and its subsidiaries stands that great organization of iron and steel manufacturers, the Comité des Forges de France.

The Comité des Forges is not, as it has frequently been called, the "French Steel Trust." It is not a cartel. Individual French iron and steel companies are bound together by rigid agreements covering quotas and prices into great groups like the Comptoir Sidérurgique de France or into lesser ones like the Comptoir des Rails or the Comptoir des Demi-Produits. The Comité cannot be said to "combine" these organizations; in actuality, however, it remains the most powerful iron and steel organization in France. It does not sell; it does not produce. Its activities are more subtle, more delicate than that. Essentially, its field is in the strategy and tactics of the iron and steel industries; accordingly politics and propaganda are its principal concerns. It does not have subsidiaries; it has members that pay dues into its central treasury either upon a basis of their tonnage production or the number of their employees. Two hundred and fifty companies — mines, smelters, metallurgical establishments, foundries — make up its membership, and of these 250 companies, over 150 are armament concerns. The nominal capital stock of the member companies of the Comité totals some 7,500,000,-000 francs, yet some accountants have placed the figure for a true valuation as high as 40,000,000,000 francs. The chief officer of the Comité, the President, is a man of whom we are to hear much more in just a moment. He derives his power not only from being President of the Comité but as one of the principal owners of his own iron and steel concerns. Beneath him and his administrative board on the Comité there spread out six regional committees: the Loire, Nord, l'Est, Minière d'Alsace-Lorraine, Forges de Lorraine, and Champagne. The total tonnage that the members of the Comité produce in France in a typical year is, for pig iron, some 10,000,000 tons and, for steel, some 9,500,000 tons.

Membership begins with firms that may actually be as small and unimpressive as the capitalization would make them seem; it ends in the grand climax of Member No.1, Schneider-Creusot — whose capitalization of 100,-000,000 francs reflects only a fraction of its true importance. The great and the little, thus bound together, make up the power and the glory of the Comité. It controls the press; it has the ear of the foreign office. Former President Millerand has been its legal defender; former President Doumer was a director of one subsidiary; present President Albert Lebrun is a former director of another. So — most significantly of all — is former Premier André Tardieu, a great leader of the Right. There was no stronger influence upon former Premier Poincaré in his occupation of the Ruhr than the Comité; the present agitation over the Saar Basin springs from its headquarters. It is governed by a commission of directors, and upon this commission, as President (we must now displease another lover of anonymity), there sits the misty and cloud-wreathed figure of François de Wendel.

François de Wendel comes legitimately by his present power and position; his family have been Europe's armorers since before the French Revolution

— although the De Wendels have not always been French nor, even always the *De* Wendels. There was once a Johann Georg *von* Wendel, who in the seventeenth century was a colonel in the armies of Ferdinand III of Germany. Since his time, however, the family generally has preferred to remain out of uniform, on the theory that in uniform there is no higher title of power than that of general; whereas by the process of forgoing the title, the power may be vastly increased. The members of this family have always been uniquely international. When their vast Lorraine estates lay upon soil politically German they attached to their name the prefix *von* and turned their eyes toward Berlin; when the political frontier shifted under their rich deposits of coal and iron, they altered the prefix to *de* and looked to Paris.

Either capital was glad to claim them; the family was equally happy to serve either — or better, both. Today, for example, when political boundary lines throw most of their estates into France but leave a few in Germany, the family consists preponderantly of *De* Wendels, but with a sufficient number of *Von* Wendels in reserve to manage its German affairs. (Being a *De* Wendel, however, is no necessary barrier to the perquisites and profits still obtainable from the German armament business, as will later appear.) In 1914, the ranking member of the family was Humbert *von* Wendel, a member of the German Reichstag, living at Hayange in Moselle, near the Saar Basin. After the Treaty of Versailles he became Humbert *de* Wendel. He still lives at Hayange, but he is no longer a member of the Reichstag. A younger brother, Guy, is a French Senator, however — and of his other brother, the François of the Comité, more later.

This international hermaphroditism is not a new family trait. The son of Johann Georg *von* Wendel, who fought for the German Ferdinand III, blossomed into Christian *de* Wendel, who was a follower of Charles IV of Lorraine. For a good period of years the family retained the prefix *De*; Christian's grandson, Ignace, was the true founder of the family's fortune — and this, curiously enough, began when he established at Creusot the works that the Schneiders were later to buy. When the Bastille fell Ignace's close relations with the monarchy drove him from the country. His properties were sequestered, but they were managed by his mother and were bought back through dummies for the account of his two sons. During this turbulent period the sequestered properties were arming the revolutionists, to the De Wendel profit, while the properties beyond the wabbling frontiers of the Republic were arming the monarchists, trying to regain power, and their allies — also to the De Wendel profit.

Then, with the Napoleonic Empire rearing its magnificence upon the ruins of the monarchy, an earlier François de Wendel (Ignace's son) returned to Paris to provide the armaments of the Grande Armée. The tragedy of Waterloo was no tragedy to the De Wendels; a cartoon of them going home after the battle to count their profits from it would not have been far-fetched.

Today's members of the family were, therefore, well equipped by wealth and heredity for the task of riding the political horses of France and Germany in the later years, when Lorraine was to become one of the major circus rings for their virtuosity. Their long experience made Briey almost a minor episode to them. When a military advance turned a "French" possession into a "German" one, the De Wendels need have felt no great concern. Regardless of the national tag attached to these mines and smelters, they remained in the placid control of one or the other branches of the family.

The François de Wendel of the present day is a Pooh-Bah; his connections and directorships would fill a dozen of these pages. He is among other things a director not only of the French but of the German De Wendel companies. But that coincidence does not set forth his true qualities of being a Pooh-Bah. Is François de Wendel, President of the Comité des Forges, faced with a financial problem? Then let him consult François de Wendel, Regent of the Banque de France. Is he in need of political support? François de Wendel, Member of the Chamber of Deputies for Meurthe-et-Moselle, intimate and supporter of André Tardieu, onetime controller of some sixty deputies, is the man for him to see. Does this or the other piece of news need to be "interpreted"? He cannot do better than consult that powerful journalist, François de Wendel, who owns a majority interest in *Le Journal des Débats*, is the head of the group that in October, 1931 (jointly with the Comité des Houillères, the coal cartel), purchased the semiofficial newspaper of the French government, *Le Temps*, controls the *Journée Industrielle*, and is a power in the management of *Le Matin* and *L'Echo de Paris*. Yet for all the illustriousness of this multi-sided man, the newspapers of France almost never mention his name. He does not like publicity.

DOUBLE-EDGED SWORD

Conspirators is not an unfair word to apply to the armament makers of France — yet it must not be used with any melodramatic connotations. Probably the conspirators are not bad men at all in their personal lives and their individual contacts with society. Sir Basil Zaharoff, the passion of whose declining years is orchid culture, would probably *not* be aghast at the suggestion that he was the greatest murderer the world has ever known. He has heard it too often. And he may even enjoy the irony of his gifts (they took a few millions out of the hundreds of millions he made from the World War) for hospitalization of the war wounded. But probably Eugène Schneider and François de Wendel are lovable old gentlemen who weep at a Chopin ballade. If an Advance Angel of Judgment should undertake today to quiz the De Wendels or Eugène Schneider on the ethics of their business they would unquestionably answer: (a) they didn't invent the passions and cupidities that lead to war, (b) if they didn't supply the demand for armaments someone else would, and (c) they inherited the business, anyway.

All of which is perfectly true. Then why are these men conspirators? They are conspirators because they have no loyalties; because theirs is the sword that knows no brother. The rise of Hitler to power in Nazi Germany provides a neat example of this — and into the bargain shows what a double-edged sword it is that the armament makers wield.

In Germany the greatest steel company is the Vereinigte Stahlwerke A.-G. and for its head it has Fritz Thyssen, king of the Ruhr. It was Thyssen who was Hitler's angel; who, as one move in a battle to retain control of his industrial affairs (dealt a desperate blow by Germany's banking crisis of 1931), began pouring money into the treasury of the Nazis to assure to himself the help of a friendly government. So far, nothing improper; if Thyssen believed in the Nazi philosophy, or the good it might do him, there was no real reason why he should not lend Hitler all the financial support he wanted to. In 1932 old Fritz Thyssen capped many previous generosities with a single contribution of 3,000,000 marks for the German presidential campaign. But old Fritz, despite his personally violent nationalism, was not at all hostile to the De Wendel-Schneider interests in France. He favored, in fact, a working compact with them so long as he could retain unhampered control of his own properties. We see, then, the spectacle of a Nazi supporter on the one hand breathing fire against France, and on the other sitting down on terms of thorough understanding with the principal armament firm that represented the implacable political enemy of his country.

But that does not complete the picture. The Comité des Forges and Schneider-Creusot were not at all unwilling to see Hitler gain ascendancy in Germany. Here the documentary proof is lacking but the inferential proof is close to inescapable. In 1933 Hitler sued a German journalist for having made the statement that Skoda (and, through Skoda, Schneider-Creusot) had contributed to his campaign expenses. When, however, he was challenged to make a direct denial that this was so, he stormed from the witness stand, cursed the opposing lawyer for a Jew, never specifically answered the question, and was subsequently fined 1000 marks for contempt of court, as a result. De Wendel and Schneider, according to their immemorial custom, said nothing, and nowhere has a denial of the accusation ever been made.

In other words, as the record stands, the leading armament makers not only in Germany but in France united in their support behind the one man most capable of stirring up a new outbreak of international anarchy in Europe. And by a curious coincidence (here is where the sword presents its other gleaming edge) the De Wendel-controlled newspapers in Paris immediately broke out in a fever of denunciation against the Hitler régime and called for fresh guaranties of security against the menace of rearming Germany. Awake, La Patrie!

ARMORER'S PHILOSOPHY

In that one example the whole philosophy of the armament makers reveals itself. Keep Europe in a constant state of nerves. Publish periodical war scares. Impress governmental officials with the vital necessity of maintaining armaments against the "aggressions" of neighbor states. Bribe as necessary.[1] In every practical way create suspicion that security is threat-

---

[1] An example: In March, 1933, the Rumanian government discovered that the Skoda works had evaded taxes to the extent of 65,000,000 lei (something over $600,000). It looked into the safe of Bruno Seletski, Skoda's agent in Rumania, and discovered that he had distributed more than 1,000,000,000 lei (close to $10,000,000) among the "right" officials of both the government and the army, and their wives and mistresses, and that hundreds of thousands had gone to

ened. And if you do your job thoroughly enough you will be able to sink into your armchair and re-echo the contented words of Eugène Schneider, announcing a dividend to his shareholders: "The defense of our country has brought us satisfactions which cannot be ignored."

For the armament industry operates with one curious advantage over any other business in the world; the greater the competition the greater the amount of business for *all* competitors. Perhaps it was Sir Basil Zaharoff who first discovered this economic fact when he played his one-submarine-two-submarine game with Greece and Turkey. At any rate, salesmen for the armament industry know the fact well and build on it today. If a Schneider-Creusot salesman sells 100,000 rifles to Yugoslavia he has already eased the path of the Vickers-Armstrongs salesman in selling 200,000 rifles to Italy. "Under this strange system," the French economist, Delaisi, wrote not long ago, "the war potential of a great country, or of a group of countries, is strengthened by the development of the adverse military power. *The trade in arms is the only one in which an order obtained by a competitor increases that of his rivals.* The great armament firms of hostile powers oppose one another like pillars supporting the same arch. And the opposition of their governments makes their common prosperity."

WHO HOLDS THE BAG?

A very handsome prosperity it has been; one that has endured as few others during the stormy days since 1929. As a result of the operations of these highly international concerns the world's yearly armament bill stands now in the vicinity of a billion and a half dollars. During the last few years the Far East in particular has contributed much to satisfy the MM. de Wendel and Schneider — to say nothing of Vickers-Armstrongs' Sir Herbert Lawrence. Japan has been a highly profitable customer; the firm of Mitsui, allied to both Schneider-Creusot and Vickers-Armstrongs, served its country splendidly when Manchuria was flaming brightest. It also served China excellently. In 1930 China, the world's largest importer of arms, bought almost 40 per cent of its war materials from Japan. The European armament makers who were supplying this trade found the free port of Hamburg convenient: during one famous week in 1932 there cleared from Hamburg two ships loaded with dynamite, grenades, and airplane parts; another with 1000 cases of explosives, another with 1700 cases of ammunition, and still another, bringing up a triumphal rear, with 100,000,000 francs' worth of French machine guns.

The world traffic in arms has continued unceasingly since the war; the armament leopards have never changed their spots. Detail upon detail, incident upon incident, illustrate how well the armament makers apply the two axioms of their business. Let one incident suffice here.

"charity" and "entertainment" because the beneficiaries "will be used by us some day."
There was an intense amount of internal and international noise over the scandal, but it subsided in the general political turnover in Rumania last fall. And everything, including the bribes, is just about where it was, except General Popescu, who, in a fit of conscience, shot himself fatally through the head.

Inevitably, after the war, Hungary caught the itch to rearm. The Treaty of Trianon, by which she made peace with the Allies and Associated Powers, forbade it. Schneider-Creusot, however, was above treaties. Hungary got the money with which to place a large order with Skoda, the Schneider-Creusot subsidiary in Czechoslovakia — got it through the Banque Générale de Crédit Hongrois; which in turn is financed by the Banque de l'Union Parisienne, of which Eugène Schneider is a director. Thus it was that Schneider contrived once again to circumvent his government and rearm a nation that France had spent blood and treasure in the attempt to disarm.

But the story does not end here. When the Hungarian loan fell due it seemed inevitable that Hungary would default. Thereupon it was conveniently arranged that Hungary negotiate a loan from the French government. The plan went through like clockwork. The French government lent the Hungarian government just enough money to repay the Schneider firm. The money was transmitted through M. Schneider's Banque de l'Union Parisienne instead of, as one might have expected, through the Banque de France.

One voice crying in the wilderness was the voice of the French Deputy from the Creusot district, Paul Faure. Several times in 1931 and 1932 M. Faure made speeches to the Chamber. He raised the question of the Hungarian loan and asked, in essence, Who holds the bag? Obviously not Skoda; it had paid a dividend of 5 per cent in 1920 and a dividend of 28 ½ per cent in 1930, with never a recession in its steady year-by-year increases. He went further: he traced from the early days of the century the curious fashion in which French governmental loans insisted on relating themselves to Schneider-Creusot orders. Throughout these years France had made loans to Mexico, Greece, Japan, Russia, Spain, Italy, Rumania, Serbia, Bulgaria, and Turkey, and every one of these countries had thereupon placed armament orders with Schneider-Creusot. The last two countries had, in fact, pushed the return compliment as far as turning French guns, so bought, upon French troops at the outbreak of the war. Almost inevitably, M. Faure pointed out, there sat on the directorate of the financing bank of the country that bought the armaments a representative of Schneider-Creusot or some other member of the Comité. This precaution did not, however, prevent most of these loans from being in default. Coming to the present, said M. Faure, "we find M. Schneider arming Bulgaria, M. Schneider arming Turkey, Skoda supporting Hitler, Franco-Japanese, Franco-Argentine, and Franco-Mexican banks. "This is all" — he ended with a masterpiece of moderation — "extremely suspicious." Then, having made these revelations, M. Faure shortly after found himself defeated for re-election to the Chamber; he was, after all, a deputy from the Creusot district, and M. Schneider found it more convenient to bring about his defeat than to listen to more of his speeches.

RAY OF HOPE

Have governments ever taken any steps to confiscate the business of the armament makers? Very few. In the early days after the war, Europe's governments had small heart for proceeding against their betrayers, even though the waxen seals on the Treaty of Versailles were scarcely hard before they were once again busy disturbing the peace.

And although the conviction began later to grow among Europe's more enlightened statesmen that something had to be done about the De Wendels, the Schneiders, and their breed, governments were puzzled to know what it could be. A nation that suppresses or confiscates its private armament industry is faced with these alternatives: (a) it must disarm; (b) it must become exclusively an *importer* of arms; (c) it must make arms manufacturing a function of the state, which means, in effect, that the state must become (or inevitably *thinks* it must) a vast arsenal — since, having no opportunity to keep plants large and active by supplying an export trade, it must manufacture in quantities sufficiently large so that it could step, overnight, from a peace-time to a war-time, production schedule.

Therein lay one difficulty. But why could concerted action toward disarmament make so little progress? One important reason was first laid bare by Lord Robert Cecil. "There is a very sinister feature," he said, "to all the disarmament discussions. I refer to the tremendous power wielded against all the proposals by armament firms.... We must aim at getting rid of this immense instrument in the maintenance of suspicion." Yet in 1932 the Disarmament Conference was enriched by the presence of M. Charles Dumont of Schneider-Creusot, President of the Schneider-controlled Banque Franco-Japonaise, on the French delegation. The British delegation was similarly benefited by the advice of Colonel A. G. C. Dawnay, the brother of a director of Vickers-Armstrongs, and now the political supervisor of the British Broadcasting Corporation.

If the armament business were conducted by an outlawed band of international gangsters, the problem would be simple to define. The difficulty is that precisely the opposite is the case. The armament business is a part of the most essential industries of industrialized nations — steel and chemicals. But even so the problem does not become acute until you have a nation in which the biggest part or a very, very large part of these essential industries is the manufacture of the actual munitions of war. Such is the case in France, and also in Czechoslovakia. And, potentially, in Germany.

No American would be shocked to hear that the steel business and the coal business of Pennsylvania, owners and workers together, exercised big political influence in Pennsylvania, and, through Pennsylvania, upon the nation. Now put Detroit also in Pennsylvania. And then suppose that by far the most profitable part of the combined Steel-Coal-Motorcar Industry were the manufacture of munitions. And then try to imagine a Senator from Pennsylvania convincing himself that there is no possible chance of war with Japan and that therefore both the American navy and the American army are much too big.

While this may make it easy to understand why Messrs. de Wendel and Schneider should be so influential in France, it brings us no nearer a solution. To deal with the general problem of disarmament in all its phases would be impossible within the limits of this article. Suffice it to say, the simplest solution is to have the state take over all the manufacturing of munitions. But to do that, the state would have to take over most of the essential industries of modern life. And for anyone but a 100 per cent Socialist, that is not simple at all. Russia is today the only country in which there is no "private" manufacture and sale of armaments.[1]

Then is there no hope? Is Europe caught so tight in the steely grip of the armament makers that it can only do their bidding?

Well, the grip is pretty tight, yet there is some hope. Perhaps there is a war coming, but first there is a fight coming.

Recently that fight has loomed most noticeably in France. The Comité des Forges has decidedly not been a popular name in France. To be exact, it never *was* a popular name. Just as a politician in the United States was always against Wall Street during his campaign, so in France many a political victory has been won by accusing the opposition of being in the pay of the Comité des Forges. Of late, as political tension in France has grown hotter, so resentment against the De Wendels and the Schneiders has grown more bitter.

No country has more to gain from peace and the sanctity of treaties than France. So it is not surprising to find that many Frenchmen are now saying that France made a tragic mistake in supporting Japan (in a backhand manner) in the Manchurian affair. And they note, with bitterness, that it was the De Wendel press that wanted to let Japan have her imperial way.

To France's great credit it must also be said that, except in the Manchurian affair, France has been, for her own best interest, the stanchest supporter of the League. More than that, her Briand was unquestionably the greatest Peace Man of the post-war decade. Today, many a Frenchman is resentful of the fact that Briand's policies did not succeed in conciliating Germany, and while blaming Germany most, he wonders whether the failure was not helped along by the patriotic M. de Wendel.

If Herriot should again come to power it may well be that he will feel a mandate even more powerful than ever before to fight against the warriors of Europe — and to include among his enemies the armorers, greatest of whom are the greatest industrialists of his own land. For they are sometimes not *too* clever, these Schneiders and De Wendels. And they seem to miss one point: the fire trenches and shell holes that scar the countryside in war time are only the primary lesions of an international social disease. When the disease at last inevitably attacks the blood and bones of nations that have gone to war, even De Wendels, and Schneiders can suffer — suffer with their tottering banks, their dropsical holding companies, their shocked and collapsing industrial empires.

Within their long lives, however, neither François de Wendel nor Charles Prosper Eugène Schneider has ever let drop a word to indicate that he sees any connection between his business and an eventual ruin of his capitalistic industry. Only Sir Basil Zaharoff, doddering brokenly in his wheel chair,

---

[1] Parenthetically it will be recalled by those who have followed the dreary course of disarmament conferences that Russia, in the mouth of Comrade Maxim Litvinov, has been the most consistent and the loudest advocate of disarmament.

seems to give any outward evidence of disillusionment. That may be only because he gambled $20,000,000 of his personal fortune on the only war in which he ever took emotional sides — the Greco-Turkish War in 1921 — and lost it.

Or it might be because he was always the cleverest, anyway.

PART THREE
IMAGINATION

THE SHORT STORY

THE short fiction narrative is almost as old as the human appetite for vicarious experience. Throughout its long history, its form and purpose have varied. From the very beginning there have been stories told for sheer pleasure. Very early, however, there developed the story told to point a moral: the fable, the parable, the allegory, and the moral tale found even in the *Arabian Nights*, though less frequently than in Victorian periodicals.

The distinction between stories told for edification and stories told for pleasure has been maintained. To some extent it has merged with the distinction between realism, which seeks to reveal familiar scenes and characters, and romance, which offers the reader escape from his world. Social propaganda, in the short story as in the novel and drama, is intimately bound up with the history of realism. Adventure and mystery stories carry on the tradition of romance, but they too have benefited by the methods of realism, as is well illustrated in such an "Action" story as "Mute Fate," or a semi-mystery story like "An Episode at Pintail Lake."

In a discussion of the short story as a literary form, it soon becomes necessary to distinguish between any comparatively brief prose narrative, and the short story "proper," sometimes written Short Story or Short-Story. It is generally agreed that the short story came into its own in the latter half of the nineteenth century, immediately after Irving had polished to a high degree the more rambling tale. Poe published the first and most famous pronouncement on the short story. "Having conceived, with deliberate care, a certain unique or single *effect* to be wrought out,... [a skilful literary artist] then invents such incidents — he then combines such events as may best aid him in establishing this preconceived effect. If his very initial sentence tend not to the out-bringing of this effect, then he has failed in his first step. In the whole composition there should be no word written of which the tendency, direct or indirect, is not to the one pre-established design." The sketch is to the short story as a snapshot is to a cinema reel.

One basis for classifying a story is the extent to which actual events and experiences have been revised and composed by the author. Often, especially today, it is not a far cry from autobiography to fiction. When a story is a mere transcript of something that happened, it occupies that stage between straight personal experience and fiction which may be called journalistic or anecdotal. Formally, the transcript from experience may closely resemble the short story with its close-knit structure and logical climax, and the distinction between the two may be very difficult to fix. Many of O. Henry's stories seem to be on the borderline between the two types; some of them cross it, to one side or the other. "A Municipal Report," for example, is definitely on the *composed* side. Mr. Moffat's "Gendarmes and the Man," with all its vivacity and flavor, remains a personal transcript; it is material for fiction, rather than fiction out and out. It differs from many examples of its type in that its claim to interest lies not in the incidents recorded, but wholly in the manner of presenting them.

A short story must have fiction quality plus the architectural planning, the lucid development to a climax, which its first exponents called structure and the popular magazine of today knows as plot. "In Affection and Esteem," brief and simple as it is, comes close to the requirements of this particular form. An example of the short story *par excellence* is "A Jury of Her Peers," which shows that a single *effect* may have several facets. For all its clear-cut and cleverly devised plot, the chief interest is in character: the central character, who does not appear, and the women who define her traits. The plot itself grows out of her character, and its unfolding is the step-by-step revelation of how she would react to a situation which, again, is a product of her nature. That the construction of the typical short story is dramatic may be seen in the ease with which this one was converted into a one-act play.

Such a story suggests also the advantage of writing about people and places with which one is familiar. In this case the setting contributes what is known as local color, which may be either regional, historical, or occupational. The first type was an essential ingredient of the New England stories written by Mrs. Freeman and Miss Jewett in the later nineteenth century. Kipling is noted for his use of both the regional and the occupational varieties. In "High Water," as in Miss Glaspell's story, local color (occupational) is organic rather than, as is too often the case, merely decorative. Every step of "High Water" is built upon the technique of railroading; without his knowledge of this technique, the author could not have written the story. This type of local color has in recent years taken on new interest in stories of war, sport, big business, and in the growing body of "proletarian" literature.

"Point of view" — the angle of vision from which the action is seen — has always been of especial importance in the short story, partly as a means to unity; and we become increasingly aware of how much may be gained by skill and consistency in this rather technical matter of who is supposed to be telling the story and what is his relation to it. Much of the humor and tang in Ring Lardner's fiction is due to his deftness in handling point of view, as well as to his shrewd analysis of Americans and their speech. For his purposes, narrative in the first person offers obvious advantages, and this is his usual method. The first person is often the easiest for the author, since it

helps to obscure irregularities of structure, especially to cover up infringe-
ments on the classical unities of time, place, and action. But if used indis-
criminately or clumsily it pays for its advantages, sometimes at too great a
price.

Point of view has received much attention in the experimenting which the
short story has undergone of late; especially the modification known as the
stream-of-consciousness technique. In this technique, events are reported
only as perceived by someone in the story and colored by his reactions, and
the inner processes of a character's mind may be presented without the intermediary "He thought," or "It seemed to him." Recent changes have naturally gone hand in hand with those of the novel and with the changes in current attitudes and interests which are both reflected and influenced by current
fiction. Thus the general interest in psychology has modified the material,
the structure, the very style of the story, whether long or short. Increasing
awareness of action within the individual has made overt action no longer indispensable, and hence has altered our ideas of what a plot must be. The
ripening or merely the revealing of a state of mind may constitute the plot of
a story. It is for this variety of fiction that the stream-of-consciousness
technique has been developed, especially by such writers as Katherine Mansfield and Virginia Woolf. On the other hand, a detached and objective
method such as that of Ernest Hemingway and his "hard-boiled" school may
be highly effective for telling a story in which "nothing happens." In fiction
long and short there has been a growing sense for incongruity in action and
in character, an impatience with the former standard of unity which pictured
the normal person as self-consistent rather than as a field of inner conflicts,
and his experience as a well-ordered series of events building up into the required climax. In this, as in much else, the story of today has been deeply
influenced by the Russian Chekov and also by Henry James, who turned
aside from the novel to experiment with the short story and novelette. His
disciple, Edith Wharton, has employed both forms with greater popular success but with less experimentation.

Judged by the orthodox rules of form, present tendencies may seem to represent a back-sliding from the standard — and too often standardized —
short story. They by no means involve, however, discarding the short-
story ideals of unity, economy, craftsmanship. The difference lies chiefly in
the type of "effect" conceived by the author, and the means by which he
strives to achieve it. There is a difference also in the reader's role, which has
become less passive. Instead of finding conveniently set out at the beginning of a story all the essential information about preceding action and the
characters involved in it, he is supposed to glean it in scraps as he goes along,
just as in life such data are gradually collected. And as in life, much remains
unsaid — about characters, about events, about the intentions of the author
— for him to fathom if and as he can. So it may happen that the reader
finds a sketch in what the author conceived to be a short story, and that what
purports to be a short story may have the effect of an "implied" novel.

DONALD MOFFAT

DONALD MOFFAT graduated from Harvard in 1916, "without having done any writing," as he says, "except one story turned down by *The Advocate*." He went to France with the American Ambulance Corps, and later served in the army. He now lives in Brookline, Massachusetts, and writes for several magazines, especially *The New Yorker*. He has published a volume of short stories, *A Villa in Brittany*.

GENDARMES AND THE MAN *

ROSY was a second-hand Renault of eleven horsepower, a nice friendly machine, partly covered with second-hand paint and adorned with a high tonneau or bustle, like the poop of a galleon. Although really quite fond of Rosy, Mr. Mott, a sensitive man, didn't quite like to leave her hanging round outside the Hôtel Crillon, as he felt that the contrast between her out-moded raiment and that of her smartly dressed sisters might cause her (and him) mental anguish. She was perfectly at home in front of Mr. Mott's own hotel, however, and was undeniably an object of pride to Pierre, the combined valet, concierge, and chasseur, who loved to stand outside in his striped apron and felt slippers, with one hand resting affectionately on the fender, and open the door for the Motts and smile them out of sight.

Mr. Mott's first act after taking Rosy over from an Englishman named Wrightstoneham, her most recent protector, was to drive her the two blocks from her little *rez-de-chaussée*, or garage, to the hotel, proudly honking the squeaky little horn all the way like a real Parisian. There he left her by the sidewalk, and went upstairs for as long as it takes a man to recite "The Wreck of the Hesperus," and came down again with a song on his lips and a bright smile for Célie, known in the hotel as the maid-of-all-work because she did all the work. "*Monsieur va faire un petit tour?*" Ah-ha! Wasn't he just — and monsieur skipped out the door.

And immediately ceased being Monsieur.

A sinister figure in blue and red was leaning over Rosy. In his hand was a notebook, and he was moistening a pencil at his lips. Rosy looked furtive, as if this sort of thing had happened to her before, *en faisant le trottoir*.

Mr. Mott murmured: "What is it that it has, Mr. the Agent? She is to me, the carriage."

He turned his attention from Rosy. "Ha!" he stated. "She is to you, the carriage. Then!" Mr. Mott thought he had seldom seen a more unpleasant face.

"One has, maybe, committed a fault of which one is ignorant?"

"Evidently!"

"May one be permitted to inquire the nature of this fault?"

"Ha!" stated the gendarme again. "One has placed the carriage at the bad side of the street; see you, how can other carriages circulate in these old ways so contracted? Thus if all the world pleases but himself without consideration of no matter what other voyagers, what *tohu-bohu* does not then arrive, by example?"

Mr. Mott brightened. "But yesterday," he said, "I observed the carriage of the merchant of wine and carbon at the same side, here." A mistake.

"Yesterday! But yesterday is not today, figure to yourself." Mr. Mott bowed, with dignity.

"Show me then the gray card," the gendarme demanded sternly.

Mr. Mott unbuckled his portfolio of licenses and dealt a hand from the top of the deck. The gendarme sorted them skillfully and discarded onto the front seat, keeping only the gray registration card and the pink driving license. He read them attentively, then looked at the nickel plaque on Rosy's instrument board, which the law requires to be inscribed with the owner's name and address, and gave a sudden start.

"Then!" he thundered, pointing dramatically to the plaque. "The name on the gray card is not in rapport with the one on the plaque, evidently! That is your name engraved on the dashboard." And so it came about that Mr. Mott was known as Monsieur Vrrigstonhonh throughout the subsequent proceedings.

Mr. Mott tried to deny it, with some confidence at first. "But no, monsieur. That is the name of the old proprietor. I am the proprietor since fifteen days, and was even now on road to the graver for my proper plaque, already commanded."

"Make no histories," the gendarme ordered darkly. "I can read, I."

At this point the investigating committee was swelled by the arrival of a bicycle bearing another and more potent gendarme, and on his heels a little group consisting of a stubby patriarch with a long yellow beard, part of a bowler hat, and one half of a pair of suspenders; an old and respectable female in black, with a figure, who had been washing out a bit of flannel in the fresh current of the gutter; and a man-child with long bare legs, a downy beard, and serious tonsil trouble. The committee rose long enough for the ranking gendarme to suggest politely to this trio that possibly it had, then, other affairs to claim its attention than breathing on the foreign sir, a suggestion for which the prisoner was grateful. They drifted on a few yards, and the committee took up the minutes.

Mr. Mott's man said: "The carriage of this sir rest, evidently, at the bad side of the street. He pretends too that the carriage is to him, when see you, my sergeant, the name of another, a Monsieur Mott, is inscribed on the gray card."

The true owner of the name opened his mouth to take exception to this use of the word "pretend," but was interrupted by the sergeant, a tall, lean man with an apoplectic face who, like all his rank, believed in action: "Get the hell over there on the other side of the street where you belong, then we'll take up the paper work," and Mr. Mott, glad of something to do besides being talked at, sprang in, started the motor, and in order to turn round as quickly as possible, backed Rosy up.

Instantly he heard a gentle crashing, crumpling sound from behind, then two bellows, or screams, one hoarse and low, the other shrill and vibrant, which Mr. Mott traced quickly to the two gendarmes. He stopped and looked over the side, more in curiosity than apprehension....

A bicycle had been left leaning against the curb behind Rosy.

One had backed Rosy over the bicycle.

To whom was the bicycle?

The bicycle was to the tall gendarme with the hoarse voice.

What says the tall gendarme?

The words of the tall gendarme would have no meaning except to another Frenchman.

The tall gendarme angers himself of it, *hein?*

Yes, he angers himself of it formidably.

And the companion of the tall one, he too has choler not badly.

For the bicycle of the tall gendarme lies by the ground, riven by the foreign sir.

Eventually the filibuster, with gestures, began to simmer down, and Mr. Mott began to get his first tips on Paris traffic regulations; he learned for instance about the crime of backing up, with or without destruction of police bicycles. And there was something mysterious and obviously childish said about parking on the odd and even sides of the street, to the undisguised interest of the little group of assorted bystanders who had, it was apparent, nothing better to do that day after all than to breathe upon the foreign sir.

The gendarmes collared all Mr. Mott's documents, told him to follow in the car, and started to walk away, carrying the injured bicycle. This brought up what Mr. Mott considered a nice point of behaviour.

He bleated: "How then is one to follow, since it is forbidden to recoil and the way is too narrow to make a turn?"

"Drive round the block," they snarled over their shoulders, as who should say: Go take a running dive off the Eiffel Tower. "One awaits your return here."

Rosy and Mr. Mott obediently scuttled off down the street, took their first left, and instantly heard a whistle. They stopped, shuddering with emotion. A stout gendarme with a red beard and pince-nez was approaching with deliberate tread. He leaned affectionately over Rosy's shoulder.

"Attend, my little," he said indulgently. "Is it that one knows not how to read?" He pointed to a red disk high up on the corner building: " *Sens interdit.*" — One-way Street.

"My God!" thought Mr. Mott.

The gendarme said: "Let me see your gray card."

"Mr. the Agent," Mr. Mott replied, "I come from being arrested by two other agents of high rank who have taken all my papers and even now await my return from this voyage round the block. I now find that it is forbidden to advance further; nor can I retreat, as that too is forbidden. Must one then rest here forever, a mute inglorious warning to all other foreign conductors?"

The gendarme roared with dignified laughter. "Recoil then, my old," adding to himself, Mr. Mott felt sure, "and may heaven protect thee."

Mr. Mott backed up, or recoiled, while the gendarme held up three swiftly converging streams of taxis whose drivers honked their horns and bellowed personal remarks, and drove slowly back to his original captors. They were looking suggestively at their watches.

Mr. Mott followed them round the corner to the police station and left Rosy behind a taxi which heaven had sent to be his guide in the still mysterious matter of parking. He entered the building and, closely attended by his guards, approached the desk. A squat man with one evil eye and a face slashed with old scars, examined his papers and listened to the sergeant's story of his crimes. When the commissioner asked him his true name, then, he rashly reached across the desk to point it out on the gray card which the commissioner held in his hand. This proved to be an error. The commissioner shouted "*Halte!*", snatched the card away, and glared. The gendarmes each seized one of Mr. Mott's arms and glared; a huge black cat that had been sleeping quietly on the desk sprang to its feet, humped its back, glared, *and* spat at him. Mr. Mott waited, in terror, to be searched for arms.

Finally, after a prolonged discussion in which he took no part, as his French had utterly deserted him in the stress of emotion, Mr. Mott's true identity was established with the help of his passport, it was decided that he had an honest face, that very likely he had not actually stolen the car, and that he might be treated with indulgence on account of his ignorance of the ways of a civilized country. The parking mystery was not further explained. Nor was any mention made of the smashed bicycle. Mr. Mott learned why in the corridor outside, when the owner whispered that he had not mentioned it to the commissioner because he counted on Mr. Mott to make private reparation, and that fifty francs would be just about the right amount.

Mr. Mott paid the fifty francs, and after shaking hands all round they parted, the gendarmes on their wheels — the damage to the bicycle had apparently been exaggerated — and Mr. Mott to return Rosy temporarily to her garage, draw a deep breath or two, and hasten for something to restore his injured nerve tissues at the nearest café — a rather pleasant feature of Paris life which I won't go into just now because I think something has already been written on the subject.

RING LARDNER

RINGGOLD WILMER LARDNER, born in Michigan in 1885, attended local schools; then went for two years to the Armour Institute in Chicago. From 1907 to 1919 he contributed to the sporting pages of various leading papers, after which he joined a syndicate. Already he had begun his humorous skits and short stories, becoming most widely known through his *You Know Me Al* (1916), stories told in letters by an unforgettable, stupid, boastful, and amazing baseball player. Here, and in subsequent volumes, Lardner is unsurpassed in reproducing the speech and inflection of the semi-illiterate. His humor is often biting, but not contemptuous or pitiless, and though he has few illusions, he is not bitter. Two of his best collections are *The Love Nest and Other Stories* (1926) and *Round Up* (1929). He died in 1934.

ALIBI IKE *

I

His right name was Frank X. Farrell, and I guess the X stood for "Excuse me." Because he never pulled a play, good or bad, on or off the field, without apologizin' for it.

"Alibi Ike" was the name Carey wished on him the first day he reported down South. O' course we all cut out the "Alibi" part of it right away for the fear he would overhear it and bust somebody. But we called him "Ike" right to his face and the rest of it was understood by everybody on the club except Ike himself.

He ast me one time, he says:

"What do you all call me Ike for? I ain't no Yid."

"Carey give you the name," I says. "It's his nickname for everybody he takes a likin' to."

"He mustn't have only a few friends then," says Ike. "I never heard him say 'Ike' to nobody else."

But I was goin' to tell you about Carey namin' him. We'd been workin' out two weeks and the pitchers was showin' somethin' when this bird joined us. His first day out he stood up there so good and took such a reef at the old pill that he had everyone lookin'. Then him and Carey was together in left field, catchin' fungoes, and it was after we was through for the day that Carey told me about him.

"What do you think of Alibi Ike?" ast Carey.

"Who's that?" I says.

"This here Farrell in the outfield," says Carey.

"He looks like he could hit," I says.

* By permission of the publisher, Charles Scribner's Sons, New York.

"Yes," says Carey, "but he can't hit near as good as he can apologize."

Then Carey went on to tell me what Ike had been pullin' out there. He'd dropped the first fly ball that was hit to him and told Carey his glove wasn't broke in good yet, and Carey says the glove could easy of been Kid Gleason's gran'father. He made a whale of a catch out o' the next one and Carey says "Nice work!" or somethin' like that, but Ike says he could of caught the ball with his back turned only he slipped when he started after it and, besides that, the air currents fooled him.

"I thought you done well to get to the ball," says Carey.

"I ought to been settin' under it," says Ike.

"What did you hit last year?" Carey ast him.

"I had malaria most o' the season," says Ike. "I wound up with .356."

"Where would I have to go to get malaria?" says Carey, but Ike didn't wise up.

I and Carey and him set at the same table together for supper. It took him half an hour longer'n us to eat because he had to excuse himself every time he lifted his fork.

"Doctor told me I needed starch," he'd say, and then toss a shoveful o' potatoes into him. Or, "They ain't much meat on one o' these chops," he'd tell us, and grab another one. Or he'd say: "Nothin' like onions for a cold," and then he'd dip into the perfumery.

"Better try that apple sauce," says Carey. "It'll help your malaria."

"Whose malaria?" says Ike. He'd forgot already why he didn't only hit .356 last year.

I and Carey begin to lead him on.

"Whereabouts did you say your home was?" I ast him.

"I live with my folks," he says. "We live in Kansas City — not right down in the business part — outside a ways."

"How's that come?" says Carey. "I should think you'd get rooms in the post office."

But Ike was too busy curin' his cold to get that one.

"Are you married?" I ast him.

"No," he says. "I never run round much with girls, except to shows onct in a wile and parties and dances and roller skatin'."

"Never take 'em to the prize fights, eh?" says Carey.

"We don't have no real good bouts," says Ike. "Just bush stuff. And I never figured a boxin' match was a place for the ladies."

Well, after supper he pulled a cigar out and lit it. I was just goin' to ask him what he done it for, but he beat me to it.

"Kind o' rests a man to smoke after a good work-out," he says. "Kind o' settles a man's supper, too."

"Looks like a pretty good cigar," says Carey.

"Yes," says Ike. "A friend o' mine give it to me — a fella in Kansas City that runs a billiard room."

"Do you play billiards?" I ast him.

"I used to play a fair game," he says. "I'm all out o' practice now — can't hardly make a shot."

We coaxed him into a four-handed battle, him and Carey against Jack Mack and I. Say, he couldn't play billiards as good as Willie Hoppe; not quite. But to hear him tell it, he didn't make a good shot all evenin'. I'd leave him an awful-lookin' layout and he'd gather 'em up in one try and then run a couple o' hundred, and between every carom he'd say he'd put too much stuff on the ball, or the English didn't take, or the table wasn't true, or his stick was crooked, or somethin'. And all the time he had the balls actin' like they was Dutch soldiers and him Kaiser William. We started out to play fifty points, but we had to make it a thousand so as I and Jack and Carey could try the table.

The four of us set round the lobby a wile after we was through playin', and when it got along toward bedtime Carey whispered to me and says:

"Ike'd like to go to bed, but he can't think up no excuse."

Carey hadn't hardly finished whisperin' when Ike got up and pulled it:

"Well, good night, boys," he says. "I ain't sleepy, but I got some gravel in my shoes and it's killin' my feet."

We knowed he hadn't never left the hotel since we'd came in from the grounds and changed our clo'es. So Carey says:

"I should think they'd take them gravel pits out o' the billiard room."

But Ike was already on his way to the elevator, limpin'.

"He's got the world beat," says Carey to Jack and I. "I've knew lots o' guys that had an alibi for every mistake they made; I've heard pitchers say that the ball slipped when somebody cracked one off'n 'em; I've heard in-fielders complain of a sore arm after heavin' one into the stand, and I've saw outfielders, tooken sick with a dizzy spell when they've misjudged a fly ball. But this baby can't even go to bed without apologizin', and I bet he excuses himself to the razor when he gets ready to shave."

"And at that," says Jack, "he's goin' to make us a good man."

"Yes," says Carey, "unless rheumatism keeps his battin' average down to .400."

Well, sir, Ike kept whalin' away at the ball all through the trip till every-body knowed he'd won a job. Cap had him in there regular the last few ex-hibition games and told the newspaper boys a week before the season opened that he was goin' to start him in Kane's place.

"You're there, kid," says Carey to Ike, the night Cap made the 'nnounce-ment. "They ain't many boys that wins a big league berth their third year out."

"I'd of been up here a year ago," says Ike, "only I was bent over all season with lumbago."

II

It rained down in Cincinnati one day and somebody organized a little game o' cards. They was shy two men to make six and ast I and Carey to play.

"I'm with you if you get Ike and make it seven-handed," says Carey.

So they got a hold of Ike and we went up to Smitty's room.

"I pretty near forgot how many you deal," says Ike. "It's been a long wile since I played."

I and Carey give each other the wink, and sure enough, he was just as ig'orant about poker as billiards. About the second hand, the pot was opened two or three ahead of him, and they was three in when it come his turn. It cost a buck, and he throwed in two.

"It's raised, boys," somebody says.

"Gosh, that's right, I did raise it," says Ike.

"Take out a buck if you didn't mean to tilt her," says Carey.

"No," says Ike, "I'll leave it go."

Well, it was raised back at him and then he made another mistake and raised again. They was only three left in when the draw come. Smitty'd opened with a pair o' kings and he didn't help 'em. Ike stood pat. The guy that'd raised him back was flushin' and he didn't fill. So Smitty checked and Ike bet and didn't get no call. He tossed his hand away, but I grabbed it and give it a look. He had king, queen, jack and two tens. Alibi Ike he must have seen me peekin', for he leaned over and whispered to me.

"I overlooked my hand," he says. "I thought all the wile it was a straight."

"Yes," I says, "that's why you raised twice by mistake."

They was another pot that he come into with tens and fours. It was tilted a couple o' times and two o' the strong fellas drawed ahead of Ike. They each drawed one. So Ike threwed away his little pair and come out with four tens. And they was four treys against him. Carey'd looked at Ike's discards and then he says:

"This lucky bum busted two pair."

"No, no, I didn't," says Ike.

"Yes, yes, you did," says Carey, and showed us the two fours.

"What do you know about that?" says Ike. "I'd of swore one was a five spot."

Well, we hadn't had no pay day yet, and after a wile everybody except Ike was goin' shy. I could see him gettin' restless and I was wonderin' how he'd make the get-away. He tried two or three times. "I got to buy some collars before supper," he says.

"No hurry," says Smitty. "The stores here keeps open all night in April."

After a minute he opened up again.

"My uncle out in Nebraska ain't expected to live," he says. "I ought to send a telegram."

"Would that save him?" says Carey.

"No, it sure wouldn't," says Ike, "but I ought to leave my old man know where I'm at."

"When did you hear about your uncle?" says Carey.

"Just this mornin'," says Ike.

"Who told you?" ast Carey.

"I got a wire from my old man," says Ike.

"Well," says Carey, "your old man knows you're still here yet this afternoon if you was here this mornin'. Trains leavin' Cincinnati in the middle o' the day don't carry no ball clubs."

"Yes," says Ike, "that's true. But he don't know where I'm goin' to be next week."

"Ain't he got no schedule?" ast Carey.

"I sent him one openin' day," says Ike, "but it takes mail a long time to get to Idaho."

"I thought your old man lived in Kansas City," says Carey.

"He does when he's home," says Ike.

"But now," says Carey, "I s'pose he's went to Idaho so as he can be near your sick uncle in Nebraska."

"He's visitin' my other uncle in Idaho."

"Then how does he keep posted about your sick uncle?" ast Carey.

"He don't," says Ike. "He don't even know my other uncle's sick. That's why I ought to wire and tell him."

"Good night!" says Carey.

"What town in Idaho is your old man at?" I says.

Ike thought it over.

"No town at all," he says. "But he's near a town."

"Near what town?" I says.

"Yuma," says Ike.

Well, by this time he'd lost two or three pots and he was desperate. We was playin' just as fast as we could, because we seen we couldn't hold him much longer. But he was tryin' so hard to frame an escape that he couldn't pay no attention to the cards, and it looked like we'd get his whole pile away from him if we could make him stick.

The telephone saved him. The minute it begun to ring, five of us jumped for it. But Ike was there first.

"Yes," he says, answerin' it. "This is him. I'll come right down."

And he slammed up the receiver and beat it out o' the door without even sayin' good-by.

"Smitty'd ought to locked the door," says Carey.

"What did he win?" ast Carey.

We figured it up — sixty-odd bucks.

"And the next time we ask him to play," says Carey, "his fingers will be so stiff he can't hold the cards."

Well, we set round a wile talkin' it over, and pretty soon the telephone rung again. Smitty answered it. It was a friend of his'n from Hamilton and he wanted to know why Smitty didn't hurry down. He was the one that had called before and Ike had told him he was Smitty.

"Ike'd ought to split with Smitty's friend," says Carey.

"No," I says, "he'll need all he won. It costs money to buy collars and to send telegrams from Cincinnati to your old man in Texas and keep him posted on the health o' your uncle in Cedar Rapids, D.C."

III

And you ought to heard him out there on that field! They wasn't a day when he didn't pull six or seven, and it didn't make no difference whether he was goin' good or bad. If he popped up in the pinch he should of made a base hit and the reason he didn't was so-and-so. And if he cracked one for three bases he ought to had a home run, only the ball wasn't lively, or the wind brought it back, or he tripped on a lump o' dirt, roundin' first base.

They was one afternoon in New York when he beat all records. Big Marquard was workin' against us and he was good.

In the first innin' Ike hit one clear over that right field stand, but it was a few feet foul. Then he got another foul and then the count come to two and two. Then Rube slipped one acrost on him and he was called out.

"What do you know about that!" he says afterward on the bench. "I lost count. I thought it was three and one, and I took a strike."

"You took a strike all right," says Carey. "Even the umps knowed it was a strike."

"Yes," says Ike, "but you can bet I wouldn't of took it if I'd knew it was the third one. The score board had it wrong."

"That score board ain't for you to look at," says Cap. "It's for you to hit that old pill against."

"Well," says Ike, "I could of hit that one over the score board if I'd knew it was the third."

"Was it a good ball?" I says.

"Well, no, it wasn't," says Ike. "It was inside."

"How far inside?" says Carey.

"Oh, two or three inches or half a foot," says Ike.

"I guess you wouldn't of threatened the score board with it then," says Cap.

"I'd of pulled it down the right foul line if I hadn't thought he'd call it a ball," says Ike.

Well, in New York's part o' the innin' Doyle cracked one and Ike run back a mile and a half and caught it with one hand. We was all sayin' what a whale of a play it was, but he had to apologize just the same as for gettin' struck out.

"That stand's so high," he says, "that a man don't never see a ball till it's right on top o' you."

"Didn't you see that one?" ast Cap.

"Not at first," says Ike; "not till it raised up above the roof o' the stand."

"Then why did you start back as soon as the ball was hit?" says Cap.

"I knowed by the sound that he'd got a good hold of it," says Ike.

"Yes," says Cap, "but how'd you know what direction to run in?"

"Doyle usually hits 'em that way, the way I run," says Ike.

"Why don't you play blindfolded?" says Carey.

"Might as well, with that big high stand to bother a man," says Ike. "If I could of saw the ball all the time I'd of got it in my hip pocket."

Along in the fifth we was one run to the bad and Ike got on with one out. On the first ball throwed to Smitty, Ike went down. The ball was outside and Meyers throwed Ike out by ten feet.

You could see Ike's lips movin' all the way to the bench and when he got there he had his piece learned.

"Why didn't he swing?" he says.

"Why didn't you wait for his sign?" says Cap.

"He give me his sign," says Ike.

"What is his sign with you?" says Cap.

"Pickin' up some dirt with his right hand," says Ike.

"Well, I didn't see him do it," Cap says.

"He done it all right," says Ike.

Well, Smitty went out and they wasn't no more argument till they come in for the next innin'. Then Cap opened it up.

"You fellas better get your signs straight," he says.

"Do you mean me?" says Smitty.

"Yes," Cap says. "What's your sign with Ike?"

"Slidin' my left hand up to the end o' the bat and back," says Smitty.

"Do you hear that, Ike?" ast Cap.

"What of it?" says Ike.

"You says his sign was pickin' up dirt and he says it's slidin' his hand. Which is right?"

"I'm right," says Smitty. "But if you're arguin' about him goin' last innin', I didn't give him no sign."

"You pulled your cap down with your right hand, didn't you?" ast Ike.

"Well, s'pose I did," says Smitty. "That don't mean nothin'. I never told you to take that for a sign, did I?"

"I thought maybe you meant to tell me and forgot," says Ike.

They couldn't none of us answer that and they wouldn't of been no more said if Ike had of shut up. But wile we was settin' there Carey got on with two out and stole second clean.

"There!" says Ike. "That's what I was tryin' to do and I'd of got away with it if Smitty'd swang and bothered the Indian."

"Oh!" says Smitty. "You was tryin' to steal then, was you? I thought you claimed I give you the hit and run."

"I didn't claim no such a thing," says Ike. "I thought maybe you might of gave me a sign, but I was goin' anyway because I thought I had a good start."

Cap prob'ly would of hit him with a bat, only just about that time Doyle booted one on Hayes and Carey come acrost with the run that tied.

Well, we go into the ninth finally, one and one, and Marquard walks McDonald with nobody out.

"Lay it down," says Cap to Ike.

And Ike goes up there with orders to bunt and cracks the first ball into that right-field stand! It was fair this time, and we're two ahead, but I didn't think about that at the time. I was too busy watchin' Cap's face. First he turned pale and then he got red as fire and then he got blue and purple, and finally he just laid back and busted out laughin'. So we wasn't afraid to laugh ourselfs when we seen him doin' it, and when Ike come in everybody on the bench was in hysterics.

But instead o' takin' advantage, Ike had to try and excuse himself. His play was to shut up and he didn't know how to make it.

"Well," he says, "if I hadn't hit quite so quick at that one I bet it'd of cleared the center-field fence."

Cap stopped laughin'.

"It'll cost you plain fifty," he says.

"What for?" says Ike.

"When I say 'bunt' I mean 'bunt,'" says Cap.

"You didn't say 'bunt,'" says Ike.

"I says 'Lay it down,'" says Cap. "If that don't mean 'bunt,' what does it mean?"

"'Lay it down' means 'bunt' all right," says Ike, "but I understood you to say 'Lay on it.'"

"All right," says Cap, "and the little misunderstandin' will cost you fifty."

Ike didn't say nothin' for a few minutes. Then he had another bright idear.

"I was just kiddin' about misunderstandin' you," he says. "I knowed you wanted me to bunt."

"Well, then, why didn't you bunt?" ast Cap.

"I was goin' to on the next ball," says Ike. "But I thought if I took a good wallop I'd have 'em all fooled. So I walloped at the first one to fool 'em, and I didn't have no intention o' hittin' it."

"You tried to miss it, did you?" says Cap.

"Yes," says Ike.

"How'd you happen to hit it?" ast Cap.

"Well," Ike says, "I was lookin' for him to throw me a fast one and I was goin' to swing under it. But he come with a hook and I met it right square where I was swingin' to go under the fast one."

"Great!" says Cap. "Boys," he says, "Ike's learned how to hit Marquard's curve. Pretend a fast one's comin' and then try to miss it. It's a good thing to know and Ike'd ought to be willin' to pay for the lesson. So I'm goin' to make it a hundred instead o' fifty."

The game wound up 3 to 1. The fine didn't go, because Ike hit like a wild man all through that trip and we made pretty near a clean-up. The night we went to Philly I got him cornered in the car and I says to him:

"Forget them alibis for a wile and tell me somethin'. What'd you do that for, swing that time against Marquard when you was told to bunt?"

"I'll tell you," he says. "That ball he throwed me looked just like the one I struck out on in the first innin' and I wanted to show Cap what I could of done to that other one if I'd knew it was the third strike."

"But," I says, "the one you struck out on in the first innin' was a fast ball."

"So was the one I cracked in the ninth," says Ike.

IV

You've saw Cap's wife, o' course. Well, her sister's about twict as good-lookin' as her, and that's goin' some.

Cap took his missus down to St. Louis the second trip and the other one come down from St. Joe to visit her. Her name is Dolly, and some doll is right.

Well, Cap was goin' to take the two sisters to a show and he wanted a beau for Dolly. He left it to her and she picked Ike. He'd hit three on the nose that afternoon — off'n Sallee, too.

They fell for each other that first evenin'. Cap told us how it come off. She begin flatterin' Ike for the star game he'd played and o' course he begin excusin' himself for not doin' better. So she thought he was modest and it went strong with her. And she believed everything he said and that made her solid with him — that and her make-up. They was together every mornin' and evenin' for the five days we was there. In the afternoons Ike played the grandest ball you ever see, hittin' and runnin' the bases like a fool and catchin' everything that stayed in the park.

I told Cap, I says: "You'd ought to keep the doll with us and he'd make Cobb's figures look sick."

But Dolly had to go back to St. Joe and we come home for a long serious.

Well, for the next three weeks Ike had a letter to read every day and he'd set in the clubhouse readin' it till mornin' practice was half over. Cap didn't say nothin' to him, because he was goin' so good. But I and Carey wasted a lot of our time tryin' to get him to own up who the letters was from. Fine chanct!

"What are you readin'?" Carey'd say. "A bill?"

"No," Ike'd say, "not exactly a bill. It's a letter from a fella I used to go to school with."

"High school or college?" I'd ask him.

"College," he'd say.

"What college?" I'd say.

Then he'd stall a wile and then he'd say:

"I didn't go to the college myself, but my friend went there."

"How did it happen you didn't go?" Carey'd ask him.

"Well," he'd say, "they wasn't no colleges near where I lived."

"Didn't you live in Kansas City?" I'd say to him.

One time he'd say he did and another time he didn't. One time he says he lived in Michigan.

"Where at?" says Carey.

"Near Detroit," he says.

"Well," I says, "Detroit's near Ann Arbor and that's where they got the university."

"Yes," says Ike, "they got it there now, but they didn't have it there then."

"I come pretty near goin' to Syracuse," I says, "only they wasn't no railroads runnin' through there in them days."

"Where'd this friend o' yours go to college?" says Carey.

"I forget now," says Ike.

"Was it Carlisle?" ast Carey.

"No," says Ike, "his folks wasn't very well off."

"That's what barred me from Smith," I says.

"I was goin' to tackle Cornell's," says Carey, "but the doctor told me I'd have hay fever if I didn't stay up North."

"Your friend writes long letters," I says.

"Yes," says Ike; "he's tellin' me about a ball player."

"Where does he play?" ast Carey.

"Down in the Texas League — Fort Wayne," says Ike.

"It looks like a girl's writin'," Carey says.

"A girl wrote it," says Ike. "That's my friend's sister, writin' for him."

"Didn't they teach writin' at this here college where he went?" says Carey.

"Sure," Ike says, "they taught writin', but he got his hand cut off in a railroad wreck."

"How long ago?" I says.

"Right after he got out o' college," says Ike.

"Well," I says, "I should think he'd of learned to write with his left hand by this time."

"It's his left hand that was cut off," says Ike; "and he was left-handed."

"You get a letter every day," says Carey. "They're all the same writin'. Is he tellin' you about a different ball player every time he writes?"

"No," Ike says. "It's the same ball player. He just tells me what he does every day."

"From the size o' the letters, they don't play nothin' but double-headers down there," says Carey.

We figured that Ike spent most of his evenin's answerin' the letters from his "friend's sister," so we kept tryin' to date him up for shows and parties to see how he'd duck out of 'em. He was bugs over spaghetti, so we told him one day that they was goin' to be a big feed of it over to Joe's that night and he was invited.

"How long'll it last?" he says.

"Well," we says, "we're goin' right over there after the game and stay till they close up."

"I can't go," he says, "unless they leave me come home at eight bells."

"Nothin' doin'," says Carey. "Joe'd get sore."

"I can't go then," says Ike.

"Why not?" I ast him.

"Well," he says, "my landlady locks up the house at eight and I left my key home."

"You can come and stay with me," says Carey.

"No," he says, "I can't sleep in a strange bed."

"How do you get along when we're on the road?" says I.

"I don't never sleep the first night anywheres," he says. "After that I'm all right."

"You'll have time to chase home and get your key right after the game," I told him.

"The key ain't home," says Ike. "I lent it to one o' the other fellas and he's went out o' town and took it with him."

"Couldn't you borry another key off'n the landlady?" Carey ast him.

"No," he says, "that's the only one they is."

Well, the day before we started East again, Ike come into the clubhouse all smiles.

"Your birthday?" I ast him.

"No," he says.

"What do you feel so good about?" I says.

"Got a letter from my old man," he says. "My uncle's goin' to get well."

"Is that the one in Nebraska?" says I.

"Not right in Nebraska," says Ike. "Near there."

But afterwards we got the right dope from Cap. Dolly'd blew in from Missouri and was goin' to make the trip with her sister.

V

Well, I want to alibi Carey and I for what come off in Boston. If we'd of had any idear what we was doin', we'd never did it. They wasn't nobody outside o' maybe Ike and the dame that felt worse over it than I and Carey.

The first two days we didn't see nothin' of Ike and her except out to the park. The rest o' the time they was sight-seein' over to Cambridge and down to Revere and out to Brook-a-line and all the other places where the rubes go.

But when we come into the beanery after the third game Cap's wife called us over.

"If you want to see somethin' pretty," she says, "look at the third finger on Sis's left hand."

Well, o' course we knowed before we looked that it wasn't goin' to be no hangnail. Nobody was su'prised when Dolly blew into the dinin' room with it — a rock that Ike'd bought off'n Diamond Joe the first trip to New York. Only o' course it'd been set into a lady's-size ring instead o' the automobile tire he'd been wearin'.

Cap and his missus and Ike and Dolly ett supper together, only Ike didn't eat nothin', but just set there blushin' and spillin' things on the table-cloth. I heard him excusin' himself for not havin' no appetite. He says he couldn't never eat when he was clost to the ocean. He'd forgot about them sixty-five oysters he destroyed the first night o' the trip before.

He was goin' to take her to a show, so after supper he went upstairs to change his collar. She had to doll up, too, and o' course Ike was through long before her.

If you remember the hotel in Boston, they's a little parlor where the piano's at and then they's another little parlor openin' off o' that. Well, when Ike come down Smitty was playin' a few chords and I and Carey was harmonizin'. We seen Ike go up to the desk to leave his key and we called him in. He tried to duck away, but we wouldn't stand for it.

We ast him what he was all duded up for and he says he was goin' to the theayter.

"Goin' alone?" says Carey.

"No," he says, "a friend o' mine's goin' with me."

"What do you say if we go along?" says Carey.

"I ain't only got two tickets," he says.

"Well," says Carey, "we can go down there with you and buy our own seats; maybe we can all get together."

"No," says Ike. "They ain't no more seats. They're all sold out."

"We can buy some off'n the scalpers," says Carey.

"I wouldn't if I was you," says Ike. "They say the show's rotten."

"What are you goin' for, then?" I ast.

"I didn't hear about it bein' rotten till I got the tickets," he says.

"Well," I says, "if you don't want to go I'll buy the tickets from you."

"No," says Ike, "I wouldn't want to cheat you. I'm stung and I'll just have to stand for it."

"What are you goin' to do with the girl, leave her here at the hotel?" I says.

"What girl?" says Ike.

"The girl you ett supper with," I says.

"Oh," he says, "we just happened to go into the dinin' room together, that's all. Cap wanted I should set down with 'em."

"I noticed," says Carey, "that she happened to be wearin' that rock you bought off'n Diamond Joe."

"Yes," says Ike. "I lent it to her for a wile."

"Did you lend her the new ring that goes with it?" I says.

"She had that already," says Ike. "She lost the set out of it."

"I wouldn't trust no strange girl with a rock o' mine," says Carey.

"Oh, I guess she's all right," Ike says. "Besides, I was tired o' the stone. When a girl asks you for somethin', what are you goin' to do?"

He started out toward the desk, but we flagged him.

"Wait a minute!" Carey says. "I got a bet with Sam here, and it's up to you to settle it."

"Well," says Ike, "make it snappy. My friend'll be here any minute."

"I bet," says Carey, "that you and that girl was engaged to be married."

"Nothin' to it," says Ike.

"Now look here," says Carey, "this is goin' to cost me real money if I lose. Cut out the alibi stuff and give it to us straight. Cap's wife just as good as told us you was roped."

Ike blushed like a kid.

"Well, boys," he says, "I may as well own up. You win, Carey."

"Yatta boy!" says Carey. "Congratulations!"

"You got a swell girl, Ike," I says.

"She's a peach," says Smitty.

"Well, I guess she's O.K.," says Ike. "I don't know much about girls."

"Didn't you never run round with 'em?" I says.

"Oh, yes, plenty of 'em," says Ike. "But I never seen none I'd fall for."

"That is, till you seen this one," says Carey.

"Well," says Ike, "this one's O.K., but I wasn't thinkin' about gettin' married yet a wile."

"Who done the askin'— her?" says Carey.

"Oh, no," says Ike, "but sometimes a man don't know what he's gettin' into. Take a good-lookin' girl, and a man gen'ally almost always does about what she wants him to."

"They couldn't no girl lasso me unless I wanted to be lassoed," says Smitty.

"Oh, I don't know," says Ike. "When a fella gets to feelin' sorry for one of 'em it's all off."

Well, we left him go after shakin' hands all round. But he didn't take Dolly to no show that night. Some time wile we was talkin' she'd came into that other parlor and she'd stood there and heard us. I don't know how much she heard. But it was enough. Dolly and Cap's missus took the midnight train for New York. And from there Cap's wife sent her on her way back to Missouri.

She'd left the ring and a note for Ike with the clerk. But we didn't ask Ike if the note was from his friend in Fort Wayne, Texas.

VI

When we'd come to Boston Ike was hittin' plain .397. When we got back home he'd fell off to pretty near nothin'. He hadn't drove one out o' the infield in any o' them other Eastern parks, and he didn't even give no excuse for it.

To show you how bad he was, he struck out three times in Brooklyn one day and never opened his trap when Cap ast him what was the matter. Before, if he'd whiffed oncet in a game he'd of wrote a book tellin' why.

Well, we dropped from first place to fifth in four weeks and we was still goin' down. I and Carey was about the only ones in the club that spoke to each other, and all as we did was remind ourself o' what a boner we'd pulled.

"It's goin' to beat us out o' the big money," says Carey.

"Yes," I says. "I don't want to knock my own ball club, but it looks like a one-man team, and when that one man's dauber's down we couldn't trim our whiskers."

"We ought to knew better," says Carey.

"Yes," I says, "but why should a man pull an alibi for bein' engaged to such a bearcat as she was?"

"He shouldn't," says Carey. "But I and you knowed he would or we'd never started talkin' to him about it. He wasn't no more ashamed o' the girl than I am of a regular base hit. But he just can't come clean on no subjec'."

Cap had the whole story, and I and Carey was as pop'lar with him as an umpire.

"What do you want me to do, Cap?" Carey'd say to him before goin' up to hit.

"Use your own judgment," Cap'd tell him. "We want to lose another game."

But finally, one night in Pittsburgh, Cap had a letter from his missus and he come to us with it.

"You fellas," he says, "is the ones that put us on the bum, and if you're sorry I think they's a chancet for you to make good. The old lady's out to St. Joe and she's been tryin' her hardest to fix things up. She's explained that Ike don't mean nothin' with his talk; I've wrote and explained that to Dolly, too. But the old lady says that Dolly says that she can't believe it.

But Dolly's still stuck on this baby, and she's pinin' away just the same as Ike. And the old lady says she thinks if you two fellas would write to the girl and explain how you was always kiddin' with Ike and leadin' him on, and how the ball club was all shot to pieces since Ike quit hittin', and how he acted like he was goin' to kill himself, and this and that, she'd fall for it and maybe soften down. Dolly, the old lady says, would believe you before she'd believe I and the old lady, because she thinks it's her we're sorry for, and not him."

Well, I and Carey was only too glad to try and see what we could do. But it wasn't no snap. We wrote about eight letters before we got one that looked good. Then we give it to the stenographer and had it wrote out on a typewriter and both of us signed it.

It was Carey's idear that made the letter good. He stuck in somethin' about the world's serious money that our wives wasn't goin' to spend unless she took pity on a "boy who was so shy and modest that he was afraid to come right out and say that he had asked such a beautiful and handsome girl to become his bride."

That's prob'ly what got her, or maybe she couldn't of held out much longer anyway. It was four days after we sent the letter that Cap heard from his missus again. We was in Cincinnati.

"We've won," he says to us. "The old lady says that Dolly says she'll give him another chance. But the old lady says it won't do no good for Ike to write a letter. He'll have to go out there."

"Send him tonight," says Carey.

"I'll pay half his fare," I says.

"I'll pay the other half," says Carey.

"No," says Cap, "the club'll pay his expenses. I'll send him scoutin'."

"Are you goin' to send him tonight?"

"Sure," says Cap. "But I'm goin' to break the news to him right now. It's time we win a ball game."

So in the clubhouse, just before the game, Cap told him. And I certainly felt sorry for Rube Benton and Red Ames that afternoon! I and Carey was standin' in front o' the hotel that night when Ike come out with his suitcase.

"Sent home?" I says to him.

"No," he says, "I'm goin' scoutin'."

"Where to?" I says. "Fort Wayne?"

"No, not exactly," he says.

"Well," says Carey, "have a good time."

"I ain't lookin' for no good time," says Ike. "I says I was goin' scoutin'."

"Well, then," says Carey, "I hope you see somebody you like."

"And you better have a drink before you go," I says.

"Well," says Ike, "they claim it helps a cold."

MARY WEBB

MARY MEREDITH WEBB was born in Leighton, Shropshire, in 1881 and died in 1927. She was the daughter of a schoolmaster and in 1912 married another schoolmaster; and, what is more important, she spent most of her life in rural England, her husband having given up his school and turned market gardener. This close association with the English countryside helps to explain the extraordinary success of her fiction, which, though unknown for some time, caught the attention of leading British critics and public men just before her death. Of these books *Precious Bane* is the best known, a novel which, said Stanley Baldwin, is "haunted with the shadows of superstition, the legendary lore and phantasy" of the Welsh border. But Mrs. Webb wrote equally distinguished short stories, as the present selection testifies.

IN AFFECTION AND ESTEEM *

MISS MYRTLE BROWN had never, since she unwillingly began her earthly course, received the gift of a box or a bouquet of flowers. She used to think, as she trudged away to the underground station every day, to go and stitch buttonholes in a big London shop, that it would have been nice if, on one of her late returns, she had found a bunch of roses — red, with thick, lustrous petals, deeply sweet, or white, with their rare fragrance — awaiting her on her table. It was, of course, an impossible dream. She ought to be glad enough to have a table at all, and a loaf to put on it. She ought to be grateful to those above for letting her have a roof over her head.

"You might," she apostrophized herself, as she lit her gas-ring and put on the kettle, "not *have* a penny for this slot. You might, Myrtle Brown, not *have* a spoonful of tea to put in this pot. Be thankful!"

And she was thankful to Providence, to her landlady, to her employer, who sweated his workers, to the baker for bringing her loaf, to the milkman for leaving her half a pint of milk on Sundays, to the landlady's cat for refraining from drinking it.

To all these, in her anxious and sincere heart, she gave thanks. She had enough to keep body and soul together. How dared she, then, desire anything so inordinate as a bouquet?

"You might," she remarked, holding up the teapot to get the last drop, "be sleeping on the Embankment. Others as good as you, as industrious as you, sleep there every night, poor souls."

Yet she could not help thinking, when she put out her light and lay down, of the wonderful moment if she ever *did* receive a bouquet.

Think of unpacking the box! Think of seeing on the outside, "Cut Flowers Immediate," undoing the string, taking off the paper, lifting the lid! What then? Ah, violets, perhaps, or roses; lilies of the valley, whiter than

* From *Armour Wherein He Trusted*, by Mary Webb, published and copyrighted by E. P. Dutton & Co., Inc., New York.

belief in their startling bright leaves; lilac or pale pink peonies or mimosa with its benignant warm sweetness.

The little room would be like a greenhouse — like one of the beautiful greenhouses at Kew — with the passionate purity of tall lilies; with pansies, softly creased; with cowslips in tight bunches, and primroses edged with dark leaves, and daffodils with immense frail cups. She would borrow jam-pots from the landlady, and it would take all evening to arrange them. And the room would be wonderful — like heaven. The flowers would pour out incense, defeating the mustiness of the house and the permanent faint scent of cabbage.

To wake, slowly and luxuriously, on a Sunday morning, into that company — what bliss!

Red roses at the bed's head, white roses at the foot. On the table, pinks. Not a *few* flowers; not just a small box. Many, many flowers — all the sweetness the world owed her.

She dimly felt that it owed her something. All those buttonholes! Yes. There was a debt of much colour and perfume, golden petals, veined mauve chalices, velvet purples, passion flower, flower of the orange. She was its creditor for small daisies and immense sun-flowers; for pink water-lilies acquainted with liquid deeps; for nameless blooms, rich, streaked with strange fantastic hues, plucked in Elfland; for starred branches dripping with the honeys of Paradise.

"Dr. to Myrtle Brown, the World. Item, love and beauty. Item, leisure. Item, sunlight, laughter and the heart's desire."

She might, of course, out of her weekly wage, buy a bunch of flowers. She did occasionally. But that was not quite the perfect thing, not quite what she desired. The centre of all the wonder was to be the little bit of pasteboard with her name on it, and the sender's name, and perhaps a few words of greeting. She had heard that this was the custom in sending a bouquet to anyone — a great actress or prima donna. And on birthdays it was customary, and at funerals.

Birthdays! Suppose, now, she received such a parcel on her birthday. She had had so many birthdays, and they had all been so very much alike. A tomato with her tea, perhaps, and a cinema afterwards. Once it had been a pantomime, the landlady having been given a ticket, and having passed it on in consideration of some help with needlework.

Miss Brown liked the Transformation Scene. She liked the easy way in which the ladies who had been reclining on sharp, green peaks of ice in a snowbound country were suddenly, at the ringing of a bell, changed into languid, rosy summer nymphs with as many blossoms about them as even she could desire. She supposed they were only paper flowers and trees of cardboard, but still it would be pleasant to recline in a warm rosy light and see rows and rows of pleased faces. Yes. If she had been younger, she might have become a transformation fairy. She mentioned this when thanking the landlady for a pleasant evening.

"What? Go as one of those brazen girls? Dear me, Miss Brown, what next?"

"They only just lie there in a nice dress to be looked at," said Miss Brown, with spirit.

"There's some," replied the landlady darkly, "as do more harm, just lying still to be looked at, than respectable people would do in a thousand miles."

"I'm not young enough, anyway."

"No. You don't get any younger. Time soon passes."

She minced the meat for the first-floor diners as if Time and Death were on the chopping-board.

Myrtle Brown was depressed at the idea of Time and Death marching upon her. She realized that there would come a time when she could not make any more buttonholes. She knew she ought to be saving every penny against the rainy day which, once it came, would go on. Even a bunch of snowdrops would not do.

"There'll come a day," she said, as she washed her cup and saucer after a frugal tea, "when you'll *want* a penny, when a penny may be life or death. Save, and be thankful!"

Yet always in her heart was the longing for some great pageant, some splendid gift of radiance. How she could enjoy it! With what zest she would tell over every smallest bit of it! Nothing that they could give her would go unnoticed. Every petal, every leaf would be told over like a rosary.

But nobody seemed anxious to inaugurate any pageant. Nobody wanted to light a candle at Miss Brown's shrine. And at last, on a bleak winter day when everything had gone wrong and she had been quite unable to be grateful to anybody, she made a reckless decision. She would provide a pageant for herself. Before she began to save up for the rainy day, she would save up for the pageant.

"After that," she remarked, carefully putting crumbs on the window-sill for the birds, "you'll be quiet. You'll be truly thankful, Myrtle Brown."

She began to scrimp and save. Week by week the little hoard increased. A halfpenny here and a penny there — it was wonderful how soon she amassed a shilling. So great was her determination that, before her next birthday, she had got together two pounds.

"It's a wild and wicked thing to spend two pounds on what neither feeds nor clothes," she said. She knew it would be impossible to tell the landlady. She would never hear the last of it. No! It must be a dead secret. Nobody must know where those flowers came from. What was the word people used when you were not to know the name?

"Anon" — something. Yes. The flowers must be "anon." There was a little shop at Covent Garden where they would sell retail. Tuberoses, they sometimes had. Wonderful things were heaped in hampers. She would go there on the day before her birthday.

"You ought," she said, as she drank her cup of cocoa at five o'clock on a winter morning, "to be downright ashamed of what you're going to do this morning. Spending forty shillings on the lust of the eye!"

But this rather enhanced the enjoyment, and she was radiant as she surveyed early London from the bus.

Tomorrow morning, not much later than this, it would arrive — the alabaster box of precious nard.

She descended at Covent Garden, walking through the piled crates of greenstuff, the casks of fruit, the bursting sacks of potatoes, the large flat frails of early narcissi, exhaling fragrance. She came to her Mecca.

The shopkeeper was busy. He saw a shabby little woman with an expression of mingled rapture and anxiety.

"Well, ma'am, what is it?" he asked. "Cabbage?"

Cabbage! And she had come for the stored wealth of a hundred flower-gardens!

"No, sir!" she replied with some asperity. "I want some flowers. Good flowers. They are to be packed and sent to a lady I know, tonight."

"Vi'lets?"

"Yes. Vi'lets and tuberoses and lilies and pheasant-eye, and maidenhair and mimosa and a few dozen roses, and some of those early polyanthus and gilly-flowers."

"Wait a minute! Wait a minute! I suppose you know they'll cost a pretty penny?"

"I can pay for what I order," said Miss Brown with hauteur. "Write down what I say, add it up as you go on, put down box and postage, and I'll pay."

The shopkeeper did as he was told.

Miss Brown went from flower to flower, like a sad-coloured butterfly, softly touching a petal, softly sniffing a rose. She was bliss incarnate. The shopkeeper, realizing that something unusual was afoot, gave generous measure. At last the order was complete, the address given, the money — all two pounds — paid.

"Any card enclosed?" queried the shopman.

Triumphantly Miss Brown produced one.

"In affection and esteem."

"A good friend, likely?" queried the shopman.

"Almost my only friend," replied Miss Brown.

Through Covent Garden's peculiarly glutinous mud she went in a beatitude, worked in a beatitude, went home in a dream.

She slept brokenly, as children do on Christmas Eve, and woke early, listening for the postman's ring.

Hark! Yes! A ring.

But the landlady did not come up. It must have been only the milkman. Another wait. Another ring. No footsteps. The baker, she surmised.

Where was the postman? He was very late. If he only knew, how quick he would have been!

Another pause. An hour. Nothing. It was long past his time. She went down.

"Postman?" said the landlady, "why, the postman's been gone above an hour! Parcel? No, nothing for you. There did a parcel come for Miss Brown, but it was a great expensive box with "Cut Flowers" on it, so I knew it wasn't for you and I sent it on straight to Miss Elvira Brown the actress, who was used to lodge here. *She* was always getting stacks of flowers, so I knew it was for her."

SUSAN GLASPELL

Born in Iowa in 1882, Susan Glaspell attended Drake University and the University of Chicago; then, like many others, she began her literary career as a reporter. In association with her first husband, George Cram Cook, she was closely identified with the Provincetown Theater movement, where Eugene O'Neill and others since prominent in American drama served their first apprenticeship. She has never lost interest in the theater, her play *Alison's House* having been the Pulitzer Prize choice for 1930. Besides novels and accounts of personal experience, she has written many short stories, of which the one (1917) here given is among her best — a narrative of simple rural folk, a model of compression, of restrained drama, and of sympathetic characterization.

A JURY OF HER PEERS *

When Martha Hale opened the storm-door and got a cut of the north wind, she ran back for her big woolen scarf. As she hurriedly wound that round her head her eye made a scandalized sweep of her kitchen. It was no ordinary thing that called her away — it was probably farther from ordinary than anything that had ever happened in Dickson County. But what her eye took in was that her kitchen was in no shape for leaving: her bread all ready for mixing, half the flour sifted and half unsifted.

She hated to see things half done; but she had been at that when the team from town stopped to get Mr. Hale, and then the sheriff came running in to say his wife wished Mrs. Hale would come too — adding, with a grin, that he guessed she was getting scarey and wanted another woman along. So she had dropped everything right where it was.

"Martha!" now came her husband's impatient voice. "Don't keep folks waiting out here in the cold."

She again opened the storm-door, and this time joined the three men and the one woman waiting for her in the big two-seated buggy.

After she had the robes tucked around her she took another look at the woman who sat beside her on the back seat. She had met Mrs. Peters the year before at the county fair, and the thing she remembered about her was that she didn't seem like a sheriff's wife. She was small and thin and didn't have a strong voice. Mrs. Gorman, sheriff's wife before Gorman went out and Peters came in, had a voice that somehow seemed to be backing up the law with every word. But if Mrs. Peters didn't look like a sheriff's wife, Peters made it up in looking like a sheriff. He was to a dot the kind of man who could get himself elected sheriff — a heavy man with a big voice, who was particularly genial with the law-abiding, as if to make it plain that he knew the difference between criminals and non-criminals. And right there it came into Mrs. Hale's mind, with a stab, that this man who was so pleasant and lively with all of them was going to the Wrights' now as a sheriff.

* By permission of the author.

"The country's not very pleasant this time of year," Mrs. Peters at last ventured, as if she felt they ought to be talking as well as the men.

Mrs. Hale scarcely finished her reply, for they had gone up a little hill and could see the Wright place now, and seeing it did not make her feel like talking. It looked very lonesome this cold March morning. It had always been a lonesome-looking place. It was down in a hollow, and the poplar trees around it were lonesome-looking trees. The men were looking at it and talking about what had happened. The county attorney was bending to one side of the buggy, and kept looking steadily at the place as they drew up to it.

"I'm glad you came with me," Mrs. Peters said nervously, as the two women were about to follow the men in through the kitchen door.

Even after she had her foot on the door-step, her hand on the knob, Martha Hale had a moment of feeling she could not cross that threshold. And the reason it seemed she couldn't cross it now was simply because she hadn't crossed it before. Time and time again it had been in her mind, "I ought to go over and see Minnie Foster" — she still thought of her as Minnie Foster, though for twenty years she had been Mrs. Wright. And then there was always something to do and Minnie Foster would go from her mind. But *now* she could come.

The men went over to the stove. The women stood close together by the door. Young Henderson, the county attorney, turned around and said, "Come up to the fire, ladies."

Mrs. Peters took a step forward, then stopped. "I'm not — cold," she said.

And so the two women stood by the door, at first not even so much as looking around the kitchen.

The men talked for a minute about what a good thing it was the sheriff had sent his deputy out that morning to make a fire for them, and then Sheriff Peters stepped back from the stove, unbuttoned his outer coat, and leaned his hands on the kitchen table in a way that seemed to mark the beginning of official business. "Now, Mr. Hale," he said in a sort of semi-official voice, "before we move things about, you tell Mr. Henderson just what it was you saw when you came here yesterday morning."

The county attorney was looking around the kitchen.

"By the way," he said, "has anything been moved?" He turned to the sheriff. "Are things just as you left them yesterday?"

Peters looked from cupboard to sink; from that to a small worn rocker a little to one side of the kitchen table.

"It's just the same."

"Somebody should have been left here yesterday," said the county attorney.

"Oh — yesterday," returned the sheriff, with a little gesture as of yesterday having been more than he could bear to think of. "When I had to send Frank to Morris Center for that man who went crazy — let me tell you, I had my hands full *yesterday*. I knew you could get back from Omaha by today, George, and as long as I went over everything here myself —"

"Well, Mr. Hale," said the county attorney, in a way of letting what was past and gone go, "tell just what happened when you came here yesterday morning."

Mrs. Hale, still leaning against the door, had that sinking feeling of the mother whose child is about to speak a piece. Lewis often wandered along and got things mixed up in a story. She hoped he would tell this straight and plain, and not say unnecessary things that would just make things harder for Minnie Foster. He didn't begin at once, and she noticed that he looked queer — as if standing in that kitchen and having to tell what he had seen there yesterday morning made him almost sick.

"Yes, Mr. Hale?" the county attorney reminded.

"Harry and I had started to town with a load of potatoes," Mrs. Hale's husband began.

Harry was Mrs. Hale's oldest boy. He wasn't with them now, for the very good reason that those potatoes never got to town yesterday and he was taking them this morning, so he hadn't been home when the sheriff stopped to say he wanted Mr. Hale to come over to the Wright place and tell the county attorney his story there, where he could point it all out. With all Mrs. Hale's other emotions came the fear now that maybe Harry wasn't dressed warm enough — they hadn't any of them realized how that north wind did bite.

"We come along this road," Hale was going on, with a motion of his hand to the road over which they had just come, "and as we got in sight of the house I says to Harry, 'I'm goin' to see if I can't get John Wright to take a telephone.' You see," he explained to Henderson, "unless I can get somebody to go in with me they won't come out this branch road except for a price *I* can't pay. I'd spoke to Wright about it once before; but he put me off, saying folks talked too much anyway, and all he asked was peace and quiet — guess you know about how much he talked himself. But I thought maybe if I went to the house and talked about it before his wife, and said all the women-folks liked the telephones, and that in this lonesome stretch of road it would be a good thing — well, I said to Harry that that was what I was going to say — though I said at the same time that I didn't know as what his wife wanted made much difference to John —"

Now, there he was! — saying things he didn't need to say. Mrs. Hale tried to catch her husband's eye, but fortunately the county attorney interrupted with:

"Let's talk about that a little later, Mr. Hale. I do want to talk about that, but I'm anxious now to get along to just what happened when you got here."

When he began this time, it was very deliberately and carefully:

"I didn't see or hear anything. I knocked at the door. And still it was all quiet inside. I knew they must be up — it was past eight o'clock. So I knocked again, louder, and I thought I heard somebody say, 'Come in.' I wasn't sure — I'm not sure yet. But I opened the door — this door," jerking a hand toward the door by which the two women stood, "and there, in that rocker" — pointing to it — "sat Mrs. Wright."

Everyone in the kitchen looked at the rocker. It came into Mrs. Hale's mind that that rocker didn't look in the least like Minnie Foster — the Minnie Foster of twenty years before. It was a dingy red, with wooden rungs up the back, and the middle rung was gone, and the chair sagged to one side.

"How did she — look?" the county attorney was inquiring.

"Well," said Hale, "she looked — queer."

"How do you mean — queer?"

As he asked it he took out a note-book and pencil. Mrs. Hale did not like the sight of that pencil. She kept her eye fixed on her husband, as if to keep him from saying unnecessary things that would go into that note-book and make trouble.

Hale did speak guardedly, as if the pencil had affected him too.

"Well, as if she didn't know what she was going to do next. And kind of — done up."

"How did she seem to feel about your coming?"

"Why, I don't think she minded — one way or other. She didn't pay much attention. I said, 'Ho' do, Mrs. Wright? It's cold, ain't it?' And she said, 'Is it?' — and went on pleatin' at her apron.

"Well, I was surprised. She didn't ask me to come up to the stove, or to sit down, but just set there, not even lookin' at me. And so I said: 'I want to see John.'

"And then she — laughed. I guess you would call it a laugh.

"I thought of Harry and the team outside, so I said, a little sharp, 'Can I see John?' 'No,' says she — kind of dull like. 'Ain't he home?' says I. Then she looked at me. 'Yes,' says she, 'he's home.' 'Then why can't I see him?' I asked her, out of patience with her now. ''Cause he's dead,' says she, just as quiet and dull — and fell to pleatin' her apron. 'Dead?' says I, like you do when you can't take in what you've heard.

"She just nodded her head, not getting a bit excited, but rockin' back and forth.

"'Why — where is he?' says I, not knowing *what* to say.

"She just pointed upstairs — like this" — pointing to the room above.

"I got up, with the idea of going up there myself. By this time I — didn't know what to do. I walked from there to here; then I says: 'Why, what did he die of?'

"'He died of a rope round his neck,' says she; and just went on pleatin' at her apron."

Hale stopped speaking, and stood staring at the rocker, as if he were still seeing the woman who had sat there the morning before. Nobody spoke; it was as if everyone were seeing the woman who had sat there the morning before.

"And what did you do then?" the county attorney at last broke the silence.

"I went out and called Harry. I thought I might — need help. I got Harry in, and we went upstairs." His voice fell almost to a whisper. "There he was — lying over the ——"

"I think I'd rather have you go into that upstairs," the county attorney interrupted, "where you can point it all out. Just go on now with the rest of the story."

"Well, my first thought was to get that rope off. It looked ——"

He stopped, his face twitching.

"But Harry, he went up to him, and he said, 'No, he's dead all right, and we'd better not touch anything.' So we went downstairs.

"She was still sitting that same way. 'Has anybody been notified?' I asked. 'No,' says she, unconcerned.

"'Who did this, Mrs. Wright?' said Harry. He said it businesslike, and she stopped pleatin' at her apron. 'I don't know,' she says. 'You don't *know*?' says Harry. 'Weren't you sleepin' in the bed with him?' 'Yes,' says she, 'but I was on the inside.' 'Somebody slipped a rope round his neck and strangled him, and you didn't wake up?' says Harry. 'I didn't wake up,' she said after him.

"We may have looked as if we didn't see how that could be, for after a minute she said, 'I sleep sound.'

"Harry was going to ask her more questions, but I said maybe that weren't our business; maybe we ought to let her tell her story first to the coroner or the sheriff. So Harry went fast as he could over to High Road — the Rivers' place, where there's a telephone."

"And what did she do when she knew you had gone for the coroner?" The attorney got his pencil in his hand all ready for writing.

"She moved from that chair to this one over here" — Hale pointed to a small chair in the corner — "and just sat there with her hands held together and looking down. I got a feeling that I ought to make some conversation, so I said I had come in to see if John wanted to put in a telephone; and at that she started to laugh, and then she stopped and looked at me — scared."

At sound of a moving pencil the man who was telling the story looked up.

"I dunno — maybe it wasn't scared," he hastened; "I wouldn't like to say it was. Soon Harry got back, and then Dr. Lloyd came, and you, Mr. Peters, and so I guess that's all I know that you don't."

He said that last with relief, and moved a little, as if relaxing. Everyone moved a little. The county attorney walked toward the stair door.

"I guess we'll go upstairs first — then out to the barn and around there."

He paused and looked around the kitchen.

"You're convinced there was nothing important here?" he asked the sheriff. "Nothing that would — point to any motive?"

The sheriff too looked all around, as if to re-convince himself.

"Nothing here but kitchen things," he said, with a little laugh for the insignificance of kitchen things.

The county attorney was looking at the cupboard — a peculiar, ungainly structure, half closet and half cupboard, the upper part of it being built in the wall, and the lower part just the old-fashioned kitchen cupboard. As if its queerness attracted him, he got a chair and opened the upper part and looked in. After a moment he drew his hand away sticky.

"Here's a nice mess," he said resentfully.

The two women had drawn nearer, and now the sheriff's wife spoke.

"Oh — her fruit," she said, looking to Mrs. Hale for sympathetic under-standing. She turned back to the county attorney and explained: "She wor-ried about that when it turned so cold last night. She said the fire would go out and her jars might burst."

Mrs. Peters' husband broke into a laugh.

"Well, can you beat the women! Held for murder, and worrying about her preserves!"

The young attorney set his lips.

"I guess before we're through with her she may have something more serious than preserves to worry about."

"Oh, well," said Mrs. Hale's husband, with good-natured superiority, "women are used to worrying over trifles."

The two women moved a little closer together. Neither of them spoke. The county attorney seemed suddenly to remember his manners — and think of his future.

"And yet," said he, with the gallantry of a young politician, "for all their worries, what would we do without the ladies?"

The women did not speak, did not unbend. He went to the sink and began washing his hands. He turned to wipe them on the roller towel — whirled it for a cleaner place.

"Dirty towels! Not much of a housekeeper, would you say, ladies?"

He kicked his foot against some dirty pans under the sink.

"There's a great deal of work to be done on a farm," said Mrs. Hale stiffly.

"To be sure. And yet" — with a little bow to her — "I know there are some Dickson County farm-houses that do not have such roller towels." He gave it a pull to expose its full length again.

"Those towels get dirty awful quick. Men's hands aren't always as clean as they might be."

"Ah, loyal to your sex, I see," he laughed. He stopped and gave her a keen look. "But you and Mrs. Wright were neighbors. I suppose you were friends, too."

Martha Hale shook her head.

"I've seen little enough of her of late years. I've not been in this house — it's more than a year."

"And why was that? You didn't like her?"

"I liked her well enough," she replied with spirit. "Farmers' wives have their hands full, Mr. Henderson. And then —" She looked around the kitchen.

"Yes?" he encouraged.

"It never seemed a very cheerful place," said she, more to herself than to him.

"No," he agreed; "I don't think anyone would call it cheerful. I shouldn't say she had the home-making instinct."

"Well, I don't know as Wright had, either," she muttered.

"You mean they didn't get on very well?" he was quick to ask.

"No; I don't mean anything," she answered, with decision. As she turned a little away from him, she added: "But I don't think a place would be any the cheerfuler for John Wright's bein' in it."

"I'd like to talk to you about that a little later, Mrs. Hale," he said. "I'm anxious to get the lay of things upstairs now."

He moved toward the stair door, followed by the two men.

"I suppose anything Mrs. Peters does'll be all right?" the sheriff inquired. "She was to take in some clothes for her, you know — and a few little things. We left in such a hurry yesterday."

The county attorney looked at the two women whom they were leaving alone there among the kitchen things.

"Yes — Mrs. Peters," he said, his glance resting on the woman who was not Mrs. Peters, the big farmer woman who stood behind the sheriff's wife. "Of course Mrs. Peters is one of us," he said, in a manner of entrusting responsibility. "And keep your eye out, Mrs. Peters, for anything that might be of use. No telling; you women might come upon a clue to the motive — and that's the thing we need."

Mr. Hale rubbed his face after the fashion of a showman getting ready for a pleasantry.

"But would the women know a clue if they did come upon it?" he said; and, having delivered himself of this, he followed the others through the stair door.

The women stood motionless and silent, listening to the footsteps, first upon the stairs, then in the room above them.

Then, as if releasing herself from something strange, Mrs. Hale began to arrange the dirty pans under the sink, which the county attorney's disdainful push of the foot had deranged.

"I'd hate to have men comin' into my kitchen," she said testily — "snoopin' round and criticizin'."

"Of course it's no more than their duty," said the sheriff's wife, in her manner of timid acquiescence.

"Duty's all right," replied Mrs. Hale bluffly; "but I guess that deputy sheriff that come out to make the fire might have got a little of this on." She gave the roller towel a pull. "Wish I'd thought of that sooner! Seems mean to talk about her for not having things slicked up, when she had to come away in such a hurry."

She looked around the kitchen. Certainly it was not "slicked up." Her eye was held by a bucket of sugar on a low shelf. The cover was off the wooden bucket, and beside it was a paper bag — half full.

Mrs. Hale moved toward it.

"She was putting this in there," she said to herself — slowly.

She thought of the flour in her kitchen at home — half sifted, half not sifted. She had been interrupted, and had left things half done. What had interrupted Minnie Foster? Why had that work been left half done? She made a move as if to finish it — unfinished things always bothered her — and then she glanced around and saw that Mrs. Peters was watching her —

and she didn't want Mrs. Peters to get that feeling she had got of work begun and then — for some reason — not finished.

"It's a shame about her fruit," she said, and walked toward the cupboard that the county attorney had opened, and got on the chair, murmuring: "I wonder if it's all gone."

It was a sorry enough looking sight, but "Here's one that's all right," she said at last. She held it toward the light. "This is cherries, too." She looked again. "I declare I believe that's the only one."

With a sigh, she got down from the chair, went to the sink, and wiped off the bottle.

"She'll feel awful bad, after all her hard work in the hot weather. I remember the afternoon I put up my cherries last summer."

She set the bottle on the table, and, with another sigh, started to sit down in the rocker. But she did not sit down. Something kept her from sitting down in that chair. She straightened — stepped back, and, half turned away, stood looking at it, seeing the woman who had sat there "pleatin' at her apron."

The thin voice of the sheriff's wife broke in upon her: "I must be getting those things from the front room closet." She opened the door into the other room, started in, stepped back. "You coming with me, Mrs. Hale?" she asked nervously. "You — you could help me get them."

They were soon back — the stark coldness of that shut-up room was not a thing to linger in.

"My!" said Mrs. Peters, dropping the things on the table and hurrying to the stove.

Mrs. Hale stood examining the clothes the woman who was being detained in town had said she wanted.

"Wright was close!" she exclaimed, holding up a shabby black skirt that bore the marks of much making over. "I think maybe that's why she kept so much to herself. I s'pose she felt she couldn't do her part; and then, you don't enjoy things when you feel shabby. She used to wear pretty clothes and be lively — when she was Minnie Foster, one of the town girls, singing in the choir. But that — oh, that was twenty years ago."

With a carefulness in which there was something tender, she folded the shabby clothes and piled them at one corner of the table. She looked up at Mrs. Peters, and there was something in the other woman's look that irritated her.

"She don't care," she said to herself. "Much difference it makes to her whether Minnie Foster had pretty clothes when she was a girl."

Then she looked again, and she wasn't so sure; in fact, she hadn't at any time been perfectly sure about Mrs. Peters. She had that shrinking manner, and yet her eyes looked as if they could see a long way into things.

"This all you was to take in?" asked Mrs. Hale.

"No," said the sheriff's wife; "she said she wanted an apron. Funny thing to want," she ventured in her nervous little way, "for there's not much to get you dirty in jail, goodness knows. But I suppose just to make her feel more natural. If you're used to wearing an apron —. She said they were in the bottom drawer of this cupboard. Yes — here they are. And then her little shawl that always hung on the stair door."

She took the small gray shawl from behind the door leading upstairs, and stood a minute looking at it.

Suddenly Mrs. Hale took a quick step toward the other woman.

"Mrs. Peters!"

"Yes, Mrs. Hale?"

"Do you think she — did it?"

A frightened look blurred the other thing in Mrs. Peters' eyes.

"Oh, I don't know," she said, in a voice that seemed to shrink away from the subject.

"Well, I don't think she did," affirmed Mrs. Hale stoutly. "Asking for an apron, and her little shawl. Worryin' about her fruit."

"Mr. Peters says ——" Footsteps were heard in the room above; she stopped, looked up, then went on in a lowered voice: "Mr. Peters says — it looks bad for her. Mr. Henderson is awful sarcastic in a speech, and he's going to make fun of her saying she didn't — wake up."

For a moment Mrs. Hale had no answer. Then, "Well, I guess John Wright didn't wake up — when they was slippin' that rope under his neck," she muttered.

"No, it's *strange*," breathed Mrs. Peters. "They think it was such a — funny way to kill a man."

She began to laugh; at sound of the laugh, abruptly stopped.

"That's just what Mr. Hale said," said Mrs. Hale, in a resolutely natural voice. "There was a gun in the house. He says that's what he can't understand."

"Mr. Henderson said, coming out, that what was needed for the case was a motive. Something to show anger — or sudden feeling."

"Well, I don't see any signs of anger around here," said Mrs. Hale. "I don't ——"

She stopped. It was as if her mind tripped on something. Her eye was caught by a dish-towel in the middle of the kitchen table. Slowly she moved toward the table. One half of it was wiped clean, the other half messy. Her eyes made a slow, almost unwilling turn to the bucket of sugar and the half empty bag beside it. Things begun — and not finished.

After a moment she stepped back, and said, in that manner of releasing herself:

"Wonder how they're finding things upstairs? I hope she had it a little more red up up there. You know," — she paused, and feeling gathered — "it seems kind of *sneaking*: locking her up in town and coming out here to get her own house to turn against her!"

"But, Mrs. Hale," said the sheriff's wife, "the law is the law."

"I s'pose 'tis," answered Mrs. Hale shortly.

She turned to the stove, saying something about that fire not being much to brag of. She worked with it a minute, and when she straightened up she said aggressively:

"The law is the law — and a bad stove is a bad stove. How'd you like to cook on this?" — pointing with the poker to the broken lining. She opened the oven door and started to express her opinion of the oven; but she was swept into her own thoughts, thinking of what it would mean, year after year, to have that stove to wrestle with. The thought of Minnie Foster trying to bake in that oven — and the thought of her never going over to see Minnie Foster ——

She was startled by hearing Mrs. Peters say: "A person gets discouraged — and loses heart."

The sheriff's wife had looked from the stove to the sink — to the pail of water which had been carried in from outside. The two women stood there silent, above them the footsteps of the men who were looking for evidence against the woman who had worked in that kitchen. That look of seeing into things, of seeing through a thing to something else, was in the eyes of the sheriff's wife now. When Mrs. Hale next spoke to her, it was gently:

"Better loosen up your things, Mrs. Peters. We'll not feel them when we go out."

Mrs. Peters went to the back of the room to hang up the fur tippet she was wearing. A moment later she exclaimed, "Why, she was piecing a quilt," and held up a large sewing basket piled high with quilt pieces.

Mrs. Hale spread some of the blocks out on the table.

"It's log-cabin pattern," she said, putting several of them together. "Pretty, isn't it?"

They were so engaged with the quilt that they did not hear the footsteps on the stairs. Just as the stair door opened Mrs. Hale was saying:

"Do you suppose she was going to quilt it or just knot it?"

The sheriff threw up his hands.

"They wonder whether she was going to quilt it or just knot it!"

There was a laugh for the ways of women, a warming of hands over the stove, and then the county attorney said briskly:

"Well, let's go right out to the barn and get that cleared up."

"I don't see as there's anything so strange," Mrs. Hale said resentfully, after the outside door had closed on the three men — "our taking up our time with little things while we're waiting for them to get the evidence. I don't see as it's anything to laugh about."

"Of course they've got awful important things on their minds," said the sheriff's wife apologetically.

They returned to an inspection of the block for the quilt. Mrs. Hale was looking at the fine, even sewing, and preoccupied with thoughts of the woman who had done that sewing, when she heard the sheriff's wife say, in a queer tone:

"Why, look at this one."

She turned to take the block held out to her.

"The sewing," said Mrs. Peters, in a troubled way. "All the rest of them have been so nice and even — but — this one. Why, it looks as if she didn't know what she was about!"

Their eyes met — something flashed to life, passed between them; then, as if with an effort, they seemed to pull away from each other. A moment

Mrs. Hale sat there, her hands folded over that sewing which was so unlike all the rest of the sewing. Then she had pulled a knot and drawn the threads.

"Oh, what are you doing, Mrs. Hale?" asked the sheriff's wife, startled.

"Just pulling out a stitch or two that's not sewed very good," said Mrs. Hale mildly.

"I don't think we ought to touch things," Mrs. Peters said, a little helplessly.

"I'll just finish up this end," answered Mrs. Hale, still in that mild, matter-of-fact fashion.

She threaded a needle and started to replace bad sewing with good. For a little while she sewed in silence. Then, in that thin, timid voice, she heard:

"Mrs. Hale!"

"Yes, Mrs. Peters?"

"What do you suppose she was so — nervous about?"

"Oh, *I* don't know," said Mrs. Hale, as if dismissing a thing not important enough to spend much time on. "I don't know as she was — nervous. I sew awful queer sometimes when I'm just tired."

She cut a thread, and out of the corner of her eye looked up at Mrs. Peters. The small, lean face of the sheriff's wife seemed to have tightened up. Her eyes had that look of peering into something. But next moment she moved, and said in her thin, indecisive way:

"Well, I must get those clothes wrapped. They may be through sooner than we think. I wonder where I could find a piece of paper — and string."

"In that cupboard, maybe," suggested Mrs. Hale, after a glance around.

One piece of the crazy sewing remained unripped. Mrs. Peters' back turned, Martha Hale now scrutinized that piece, compared it with the dainty, accurate sewing of the other blocks. The difference was startling. Holding this block made her feel queer, as if the distracted thoughts of the woman who had perhaps turned to it to try and quiet herself were communicating themselves to her.

Mrs. Peters' voice roused her.

"Here's a bird-cage," she said. "Did she have a bird, Mrs. Hale?"

"Why, I don't know whether she did or not." She turned to look at the cage Mrs. Peters was holding up. "I've not been here in so long." She sighed. "There was a man round last year selling canaries cheap — but I don't know as she took one. Maybe she did. She used to sing real pretty herself."

Mrs. Peters looked around the kitchen.

"Seems kind of funny to think of a bird here." She half laughed — an attempt to put up a barrier. "But she must have had one — or why would she have a cage? I wonder what happened to it."

"I suppose maybe the cat got it," suggested Mrs. Hale, resuming her sewing.

"No; she didn't have a cat. She's got that feeling some people have about cats — being afraid of them. When they brought her to our house yesterday, my cat got in the room, and she was real upset and asked me to take it out."

"My sister Bessie was like that," laughed Mrs. Hale.

The sheriff's wife did not reply. The silence made Mrs. Hale turn round. Mrs. Peters was examining the bird-cage.

"Look at this door," she said slowly. "It's broke. One hinge has been pulled apart."

Mrs. Hale came nearer.

"Looks as if someone must have been — rough with it."

Again their eyes met — startled, questioning, apprehensive. For a moment neither spoke nor stirred. Then Mrs. Hale, turning away, said brusquely:

"If they're going to find any evidence, I wish they'd be about it. I don't like this place."

"But I'm awful glad you came with me, Mrs. Hale." Mrs. Peters put the bird-cage on the table and sat down. "It would be lonesome for me — sitting here alone."

"Yes, it would, wouldn't it?" agreed Mrs. Hale, a certain determined naturalness in her voice. She had picked up the sewing, but now it dropped in her lap, and she murmured in a different voice: "But I tell you what I *do* wish, Mrs. Peters. I wish I had come over sometimes when she was here I wish — I had."

"But of course you were awful busy, Mrs. Hale. Your house — and your children."

"I could've come," retorted Mrs. Hale shortly. "I stayed away because it weren't cheerful — and that's why I ought to have come. I" — she looked around — "I've never liked this place. Maybe because it's down in a hollow and you don't see the road. I don't know what it is, but it's a lonesome place, and always was. I wish I had come over to see Minnie Foster sometimes. I can see now —" She did not put it into words.

"Well, you mustn't reproach yourself," counseled Mrs. Peters. "Somehow, we just don't see how it is with other folks till — something comes up."

"Not having children makes less work," mused Mrs. Hale, after a silence, "but it makes a quiet house — and Wright out to work all day — and no company when he did come in. Did you know John Wright, Mrs. Peters?"

"Not to know him. I've seen him in town. They say he was a good man."

"Yes — good," conceded John Wright's neighbor grimly. "He didn't drink, and kept his word as well as most, I guess, and paid his debts. But he was a hard man, Mrs. Peters. Just to pass the time of day with him ——" She stopped, shivered a little. "Like a raw wind that gets to the bone." Her eye fell upon the cage on the table before her, and she added, almost bitterly: "I should think she would've wanted a bird!"

Suddenly she leaned forward, looking intently at the cage. "But what do you s'pose went wrong with it?"

"I don't know," returned Mrs. Peters; "unless it got sick and died."

But after she said it she reached over and swung the broken door. Both women watched it as if somehow held by it.

"You didn't know — her?" Mrs. Hale asked, a gentler note in her voice.

"Not till they brought her yesterday," said the sheriff's wife.

"She — come to think of it, she was kind of like a bird herself. Real sweet and pretty, but kind of timid and — fluttery. How — she — did — change." That held her for a long time. Finally, as if struck with a happy thought and relieved to get back to everyday things, she exclaimed:

"Tell you what, Mrs. Peters, why don't you take the quilt in with you? It might take up her mind."

"Why, I think that's a real nice idea, Mrs. Hale," agreed the sheriff's wife, as if she too were glad to come into the atmosphere of a simple kindness. "There couldn't possibly be any objection to that, could there? Now, just what will I take? I wonder if her patches are in here — and her things."

They turned to the sewing basket.

"Here's some red," said Mrs. Hale, bringing out a roll of cloth. Underneath that was a box. "Here, maybe her scissors are in here — and her things." She held it up. "What a pretty box! I'll warrant that was something she had a long time ago — when she was a girl."

She held it in her hand a moment; then, with a little sigh, opened it. Instantly her hand went to her nose.

"Why —!"

Mrs. Peters drew nearer — then turned away.

"There's something wrapped up in this piece of silk," faltered Mrs. Hale.

"This isn't her scissors," said Mrs. Peters, in a shrinking voice.

Her hand not steady, Mrs. Hale raised the piece of silk. "Oh, Mrs. Peters!" she cried. "Its —— "

Mrs. Peters bent closer.

"It's the bird," she whispered.

"But, Mrs. Peters!" cried Mrs. Hale. "*Look* at it! Its *neck* — look at its neck! It's all — other side *to*."

She held the box away from her.

The sheriff's wife again bent closer.

"Somebody wrung its neck," said she, in a voice that was slow and deep.

And then again the eyes of the two women met — this time clung together in a look of dawning comprehension, of growing horror. Mrs. Peters looked from the dead bird to the broken door of the cage. Again their eyes met. And just then there was a sound at the outside door.

Mrs. Hale slipped the box under the quilt pieces in the basket, and sank into the chair before it. Mrs. Peters stood holding to the table. The county attorney and the sheriff came in from outside.

"Well, ladies," said the county attorney, as one turning from serious things to little pleasantries, "have you decided whether she was going to quilt it or knot it?"

"We think," began the sheriff's wife in a flurried voice, "that she was going to — knot it."

He was too preoccupied to notice the change that came in her voice on that last.

"Well, that's very interesting, I'm sure," he said tolerantly. He caught sight of the bird-cage. "Has the bird flown?"

"We think the cat got it," said Mrs. Hale in a voice curiously even.

He was walking up and down, as if thinking something out.

"Is there a cat?" he asked absently.

Mrs. Hale shot a look up at the sheriff's wife.

"Well, not *now*," said Mrs. Peters. "They're superstitious, you know; they leave."

She sank into her chair.

The county attorney did not heed her. "No sign at all of anyone having come in from the outside," he said to Peters, in the manner of continuing an interrupted conversation. "Their own rope. Now let's go upstairs again and go over it, piece by piece. It would have to have been someone who knew just the ——"

The stair door closed behind them and their voices were lost.

The two women sat motionless, not looking at each other, but as if peering into something and at the same time holding back. When they spoke now it was as if they were afraid of what they were saying, but as if they could not help saying it.

"She liked the bird," said Martha Hale, low and slowly. "She was going to bury it in that pretty box."

"When I was a girl," said Mrs. Peters, under her breath, "my kitten — there was a boy took a hatchet, and before my eyes — before I could get there ——" She covered her face an instant. "If they hadn't held me back I would have" — she caught herself, looked upstairs where footsteps were heard, and finished weakly — "hurt him."

Then they sat without speaking or moving.

"I wonder how it would seem," Mrs. Hale at last began, as if feeling her way over strange ground — "never to have had any children around?" Her eyes made a slow sweep of the kitchen, as if seeing what that kitchen had meant through all the years. "No, Wright wouldn't like the bird," she said after that — "a thing that sang. She used to sing. He killed that too." Her voice tightened.

Mrs. Peters moved uneasily.

"Of course we don't know who killed the bird."

"I knew John Wright," was Mrs. Hale's answer.

"It was an awful thing was done in this house that night, Mrs. Hale," said the sheriff's wife. "Killing a man while he slept — slipping a thing round his neck that choked the life out of him."

Mrs. Hale's hand went out to the bird-cage.

"His neck. Choked the life out of him."

"We don't *know* who killed him," whispered Mrs. Peters wildly. "We don't *know*."

Mrs. Hale had not moved. "If there had been years and years of — nothing, then a bird to sing to you, it would be awful — still — after the bird was still."

It was as if something within her not herself had spoken, and it found in Mrs. Peters something she did not know as herself.

"I know what stillness is," she said, in a queer, monotonous voice. "When we homesteaded in Dakota, and my first baby died — after he was two years old — and me with no other then ——"

Mrs. Hale stirred.

"How soon do you suppose they'll be through looking for the evidence?"

"I know what stillness is," repeated Mrs. Peters, in just that same way. Then she too pulled back. "The law has got to punish crime, Mrs. Hale," she said in her tight little way.

"I wish you'd seen Minnie Foster," was the answer, "when she wore a white dress with blue ribbons, and stood up there in the choir and sang."

The picture of that girl, the fact that she had lived neighbor to that girl for twenty years, and had let her die for lack of life, was suddenly more than she could bear.

"Oh, I *wish* I'd come over here once in a while!" she cried. "That was a crime! That was a crime! Who's going to punish that?"

"We mustn't take on," said Mrs. Peters, with a frightened look toward the stairs.

"I might 'a' *known* she needed help! I tell you, it's *queer*, Mrs. Peters. We live close together, and we live far apart. We all go through the same things — it's all just a different kind of the same thing! If it weren't — why do you and I *understand*? Why do we *know* — what we know this minute?"

She dashed her hand across her eyes. Then, seeing the jar of fruit on the table, she reached for it and choked out:

"If I was you I wouldn't *tell* her her fruit was gone! Tell her it *ain't*. Tell her it's all right — all of it. Here — take this in to prove it to her! She — she may never know whether it was broke or not."

She turned away.

Mrs. Peters reached out for the bottle of fruit as if she were glad to take it — as if touching a familiar thing, having something to do, could keep her from something else. She got up, looked about for something to wrap the fruit in, took a petticoat from the pile of clothes she had brought from the front room, and nervously started winding that round the bottle.

"My!" she began, in a high, false voice, "it's a good thing the men couldn't hear us! Getting all stirred up over a little thing like a — dead canary." She hurried over that. "As if that could have anything to do with — with —— My, wouldn't they *laugh*?"

Footsteps were heard on the stairs.

"Maybe they would," muttered Mrs. Hale — "maybe they wouldn't."

"No, Peters," said the county attorney incisively; "it's all perfectly clear, except the reason for doing it. But you know juries when it comes to women. If there was some definite thing — something to show. Something to make a story about. A thing that would connect up with this clumsy way of doing it."

In a covert way Mrs. Hale looked at Mrs. Peters. Mrs. Peters was looking at her. Quickly they looked away from each other. The outer door opened and Mr. Hale came in.

"I've got the team round now," he said. "Pretty cold out there."

"I'm going to stay here awhile by myself," the county attorney suddenly announced. "You can send Frank out for me, can't you?" he asked the sheriff. "I want to go over everything. I'm not satisfied we can't do better."

Again, for one brief moment, the two women's eyes found one another.

The sheriff came up to the table.

"Did you want to see what Mrs. Peters was going to take in?"

The county attorney picked up the apron. He laughed.

"Oh, I guess they're not very dangerous things the ladies have picked out."

Mrs. Hale's hand was on the sewing basket in which the box was concealed. She felt that she ought to take her hand off the basket. She did not seem able to. He picked up one of the quilt blocks which she had piled on to cover the box. Her eyes felt like fire. She had a feeling that if he took up the basket she would snatch it from him.

But he did not take it up. With another little laugh, he turned away, saying:

"No; Mrs. Peters doesn't need supervising. For that matter, a sheriff's wife is married to the law. Ever think of it that way, Mrs. Peters?"

Mrs. Peters was standing beside the table. Mrs. Hale shot a look up at her; but she could not see her face. Mrs. Peters had turned away. When she spoke, her voice was muffled.

"Not — just that way," she said.

"Married to the law!" chuckled Mrs. Peters' husband. He moved toward the door into the front room, and said to the county attorney:

"I just want you to come in here a minute, George. We ought to take a look at these windows."

"Oh — windows," said the county attorney scoffingly.

"We'll be right out, Mr. Hale," said the sheriff to the farmer, who was still waiting by the door.

Hale went to look after the horses. The sheriff followed the county attorney into the other room. Again — for one final moment — the two women were alone in that kitchen.

Martha Hale sprang up, her hands tight together, looking at that other woman, with whom it rested. At first she could not see her eyes, for the sheriff's wife had not turned back since she turned away at that suggestion of being married to the law. But now Mrs. Hale made her turn back. Her eyes made her turn back. Slowly, unwillingly, Mrs. Peters turned her head until her eyes met the eyes of the other woman. There was a moment when they held each other in a steady, burning look in which there was no evasion nor flinching. Then Martha Hale's eyes pointed the way to the basket in which was hidden the thing that would make certain the conviction of the other woman — that woman who was not there and yet who had been there with them all through that hour.

For a moment Mrs. Peters did not move. And then she did it. With a rush forward, she threw back the quilt pieces, got the box, tried to put it in her handbag. It was too big. Desperately she opened it, started to take the bird out. But there she broke — she could not touch the bird. She stood there helpless, foolish.

There was the sound of a knob turning in the inner door. Martha Hale snatched the box from the sheriff's wife, and got it in the pocket of her big coat just as the sheriff and the county attorney came back into the kitchen.

"Well, Henry," said the county attorney facetiously, "at least we found out that she was not going to quilt it. She was going to — what is it you call it, ladies?"

Mrs. Hale's hand was against the pocket of her coat.

"We call it — knot it, Mr. Henderson."

A. W. SOMERVILLE

Mr. Somerville writes pleasantly and informingly: "As to facts about my-self, it is with difficulty that I restrain myself as to my sterling worth and the perilous paths of immortality including the usual crop of detours, byways and sunken roads, as well as the more humdrum statistics of birth, consciousness, urges, and pains from spiritual wounds, but as it is a railroad story it would perhaps be sensible to say that I worked some eight or nine years on railroads, mostly in Texas, functioning in various capacities such as machinist's helper, machinist, machinist inspector, car inspector, work train foreman. I was born June 9, 1900."

HIGH WATER *

Two long-limbed, slovenly-clothed, dirty-faced and unshaven telegraph men waded through a foot or more of water to the business car. They halted below the observation platform, in the drizzle and mud and water, and held a consultation.

"You got the most education," said the chief; "I'll let you tell him."

"He might not believe me," demurred his assistant, "and I wouldn't think of assuming so much authority, besides. You tell him and I'll stand right behind you, near the door."

"When I start to leave," warned the chief, "don't get in my way. I might wanta hurry." They entered the business car. A negro porter appeared. "Where's the Old Man?" demanded the chief.

"Mistah Childress jes' now wen' to bed," objected the porter. "He done been up all night, las' three nights. You gen'mun bes' wait till he get up."

"You go tell him," said the chief telegraph man heartlessly, "that the wires are down between Adelaide and Cloudy Bend, and that we wanta know what he wants to do about it."

"Ah don' think it am advisable," objected the negro politely. "Yuh see, Mistah Childress he done tol' me profoun'ly not tuh wake him up 'foh suppah lessen it am a emergency."

"This," mimicked the chief, "am a emergency, see? Go get him up. And where," continued the chief, "do you keep the hot coffee, Dudley?"

"Yes-suh," said Dudley, "got plenty hot coffee. Right this way, suh."

He showed the way respectfully. The two telegraph men were served two steaming cups of black coffee and two thick sandwiches. They ate with big bites and drank in noisy gulps.

"Go wake Mr. Childress," ordered the chief.

"Ef yuh insists," said the porter, "Ah'll go get him up. Ah'll say Mistah Allbright he says de wires is down 'tween Adelaide an' Cloudy Bend, an' what mus' he do — am that right?"

"That am right," assented Allbright. "Hurry up!"

Dudley departed on his mission. A moment later a growl was heard from

* From *The Saturday Evening Post*. By permission of the author and the publishers.

one of the state-rooms, followed shortly by a bellow. Dudley emerged with a wrinkled forehead and a meek but injured look in his eyes.

"De boss am sure mad," he confided. "He say somethin' about puttin' wires up. Heah he come!" Dudley disappeared toward the kitchen.

Mr. Childress stalked up. He ignored the telegraph men. "Dudley!" he bawled. He waited one-tenth of a half second. "Dudley!" he bawled again. He waited one-twentieth of a half second. "Where is that black scoundrel?" he demanded of no one in particular.

Dudley stuck his head unobtrusively around a corner.

"So there you are!" bawled the Old Man. "Do I have to wait all day for a cup of coffee? Everybody else around here gets coffee. Don't I get any? You got any more coffee?"

"Yes-suh," declared Dudley seriously.

"Well, don't stand there all day and talk about it!" shouted Childress. "Get me some!" Childress turned to Allbright. "What's the matter with your lousy wire?" he demanded.

"It's down," said Allbright briefly, "between Adelaide and Cloudy Bend."

"Put it up," said Childress ungraciously. Allbright grinned. "What're you laughin' at?" demanded the Old Man.

Allbright became serious. "The poles are twenty to twenty-five feet from the dump, some of 'em further," he answered. "We'll never get some of 'em up till the water goes down."

Dudley arrived with the coffee. Childress seized the cup, took a hefty swig, nearly burned the lining out of his throat. He glared at the retreating Dudley, took another swig.

"Why come an' tell me about it?" he snarled at the electrical men. "Go put something up — get us through somehow — that's what you're here for."

"We haven't any wire," replied the ill-smelling Allbright. He didn't smell any worse than the weary-eyed Childress; the business car *in toto* smelled like a wet pigsty. Business cars smell that way when the worn-out occupants flop down to a thirty-minute nap in soggy clothes covered to the belt line with mud and slime, when refugees from the high waters are given coffee, food and shelter until they can be got to safety.

"Haven't any wire?" demanded Childress crossly.

"No, sir," responded Allbright. "Used up the last we had today at noon running a line over to the telephone company to keep the line open through Ravenhead."

"How much wire you gotta have?"

"They're salvagin' what they can," answered Allbright, "but it's slow work. We lost sixteen thousand feet."

"What?" shouted Childress.

"Sixteen thousand feet," said the man gloomily. "Half of it's under water."

Childress drummed on the table before him. He sat down, shoved the coffee cup out of the way. He scratched several places that itched. Suddenly he raised his head sharply.

"Didn't we send about forty rolls down here for replacement on the branch?" he demanded suddenly. Allbright nodded. "Well, where is it?" came the aggressive demand.

Allbright said something about forty feet of water. A short fat man had entered and stood gulping down a sandwich as though he never expected to see food again. He was T. P. Patchbolt, division master mechanic. His bright blue eyes took in everything.

"Damn the water!" shouted Childress. "Here we got a million miles of drawn copper an' you holler for wire! You'd think it was ten feet of baling wire. Are ye afraid to get wet?"

"Listen, boss ——" began the electrician.

"Listen, hell!" stormed the official. "Go get me that wire!"

"Listen, boss ——" began the man again desperately.

"I'll listen to nothing!" answered the weary-eyed official. "You get that wire an' I'll listen to you. Understand? G'wan!"

The two telegraph men slouched out. Patchbolt started to follow them.

"Wait a minute, T. P.," said Childress. "I wanta talk to you."

The fat man waved his hand. "I'll be back in two shakes," he declared. He joined the two men out in the drizzle. "The boss sounded like he was mad," he observed. The two men snorted. "Would you like to get the wire now," said T. P., "or would you sooner wait till it stops raining?"

"A government dredge couldn't get that wire out," said the younger of the telegraph men, named Carter. "The storeroom's forty feet under water, an' the storeroom's got a roof on it. A submarine might help."

"What's the idea in standin' out here in the rain?" demanded Allbright. "Let's get under cover."

"I know where there's some wire," said T. P. calmly.

"Lay off the humor," suggested Allbright.

"No foolin'," said T. P.

"Where?" demanded Allbright.

T. P. told them — down the branch on the cotton platform at Tudow — about Mile Post 4.

"You sure?"

"Positive," declared T. P. "Eight new rolls of wire. I was there when they stashed it."

"Let's get a boat," said Allbright.

"I gotta go back an' talk to the Old Man," said T. P. "You let me know how you come out."

"Sure will," declared Allbright. "Much obliged too."

"Oh, don't mention it," said T. P. with a lordly gesture.

Allbright and Carter crossed the bridge, walked down the levee, came to the temporary wharf. There were two soldiers sitting in the comparative dryness of a rude shanty. Before the two soldiers were boats of all sizes and descriptions.

"Howdy," said Allbright.

"H'lo," said one of the soldiers suspiciously.

"We wanta get a motorboat," said Allbright. "We're railroad men. We gotta go down the Cadjin Branch an' get some material."

"Do tell," said the soldier.

"No funny stuff," answered the tired railroader. "We gotta have a boat. If you can't let us have a motorboat, let us have anything — anything that'll float."

"Well, well," said the soldier, "did you hear him, Jake?" He spoke to the second soldier. "I do believe it's Mr. Hoover. And he wants a boat. I'm so sorry, Mr. Hoover, but the yacht just now broke a G string, an' Mr. Coolidge warned all of us personally not to let you take no chances. An important fellah like you oughtn't to take no chances. I'm so sorry, Herbert, but Mr. Coolidge would fire all of us if we let you take the yacht out when it's rainin' an' with a G string broke."

"Listen," said Allbright, "I wanta boat, see? I don't wanta argue about it — what I want is a boat."

"Herbert," chided the soldier, "you shouldn't be so venturesome."

"Maybe you don't understand," spoke up Carter. "We've got to get some wire up the branch, and the only way we can get up there is in a boat. We want that wire for our main line — we've got to have it."

"This must be Herbert's secretary," observed the second soldier.

"We gotta have a boat," said Allbright desperately. "You half-wits think this is a swell joke. Well, it ain't no joke. We gotta have a boat."

"Why, Herbert," soothed the first soldier, "how you do talk! Tut-tut!"

"Don't Herbert me!" exploded Allbright. "I want a boat, see?"

"On your way, bums," said the first soldier aggressively. "You nor nobody else gets a boat to go joy-ridin' in. Not with the levee about ready to come down around our ears."

The two boat seekers finally retreated to the bridge head and sat down. Allbright asked Carter if he had ever known a soldier who had any brains. Carter said he didn't care to know any well enough to find out.

T. P. came clumping down the track from the direction of the station. They hailed him.

"I was lookin' for you," he said. "Get a boat?" They told him about the half-witted soldiers. "Yeah," said T. P. "Weather Bureau says she'll hit the top at six tonight. They commandeered everything, I guess. They wouldn't let Pershing have a canoe if he was here."

What could they do, demanded Allbright. T. P. fished a moldy cigar from his shapeless coat.

"Anybody got a dry match?" he asked. Allbright produced one from an old shotgun shell. "This cigar," said T. P., after much puffing and blowing, "don't seem to taste right."

Carter suggested that he squeeze the water out of it.

"This is one hell of a life," said T. P. moodily, looking glumly at the sad cigar.

"How we gonna get that wire?" demanded Allbright.

"I was just gonna suggest," said T. P., "that you boys come with me down the branch. I'm gonna take the 235 down there's soon as she's hot."

Allbright and Carter gave him incredulous stares. "Say that again," said Carter.

"I'm gonna take the 235 down the branch," said T. P., "an' I'll take you two wire experts along with me if you wanta go — in about twenty minutes."

Allbright and Carter looked at each other. "I think he's crazy," said Allbright.

"The strain's been too much for him," declared Carter.

"You're like a pair of old women," said T. P. "Now I'm goin' down the branch, an' what's more, I'm takin' a engine down there with me, an' I'm gonna bring out six box cars if I can, an' I don't know how many refugees on them box cars. While I was talkin' to the boss they phoned down from False River that a arryplane had seen 'em. So the boss says, 'T. P., we gotta get them people out.' An' I says, 'Boss, we sure gotta do that. But how we gonna do it?' I says. Then he says he wishes I wouldn't ask so many silly questions, but to see if I couldn't do somethin'. An' if I couldn't, to tell the soldiers down on the levee about it. So I went down an' told the nigger to get the 235 hot — she still had thirty pounds on her — an' I'm gonna hook a flat car behind her an' go down that branch. That's the dope. Now d'you wanta stay in good company?"

Neither of the men hesitated. "I'll go," said Carter.

"Me, too," said Allbright. "We've all gotta die some day."

"Fine!" said T. P. "We ain't gonna take no engine crew, no train crew. Ain't but one here — they need 'em here — an' I ain't got the gall to call a crew to go down that branch, nohow." They were walking down the track toward the station. They passed the station, came to the Y. Near the main-line switch stood the 235, a little ten-wheeled engine, a relic of better days. She was vomiting black smoke, with the blower kicking up an awful rumpus. The three men climbed into the shelter of the cab out of the drizzle.

The 235 was an oil burner. A negro sat on the left-hand side with one paw on the firing valve.

"What you tryin' to do, Jumbo — smoke up the parish?" demanded Patchbolt. "Get outta there an' let me fire this engine."

The negro slid off the seat hastily. T. P. adjusted the atomizer and cut down on the oil. There was one hundred and forty pounds of steam showing on the gauge.

"We'll go get some water," called T. P. to Carter. "Go let us out on the main line."

"Boss man," said Jumbo, "where is we gwine?"

"Goin' down the branch, Jumbo," answered T. P.

"De branch?" questioned Jumbo.

"The Cadjin Branch," answered T. P., reaching up and ringing the bell. He crossed over to the right-hand side and whipped two blasts out of the whistle. "Come here an' set her back for me," he ordered Jumbo.

They moved out on the main line, stopped. Carter threw the switch green, the negro threw the hand reverse forward for T. P. and they moved down to the water tank.

"Mistah Patchbolt," said Jumbo, "dis looks like a good place foh me to get off."

"You put some water in her," said T. P., "an' I don't much give a damn what you do. Get back there on the tank!"

The negro crawled back on the tank and helped T. P. spot for the spout. He then pulled the spout down over the manhole and yanked the valve open. T. P. found a piece of waste, pulled the oil-marker rod out of its slot, wiped it off, stuck it back down in the oil, pulled it into view again. It registered twenty-four hundred gallons.

"More than enough," he murmured.

A man in woebegone overalls came up the gangway. "Hello, Jim," said Patchbolt.

"Where you goin'?" demanded Jim.

"Down the branch," said T. P.

"What for?" asked the man.

"Refugees," answered the fat man.

"Oh," said Jim. He went over and motioned for Carter to get off the left-hand seat box. "I'll do the firin'," he said.

"We didn't call no crew," said T. P.

Jim shrugged. "I don't care," he said.

Jumbo came down from the tank above. "She's runnin' over," he reported.

T. P. crossed over to the right-hand side, pulled on the whistle cord. They picked up a flat car on their way to the branch-line switch, hooked it onto the tank. Jumbo dropped off here. Jim, a fireman in regular service, was over on the left-hand side, firing the engine. They came to the branch switch, backing up with the flat car first. They would back up going down the branch; when they returned the engine would be going forward.

"See you later, Jim," called T. P., as they stopped at the switch. Carter swung down and went ahead to bend the rail.

"I think I'll stay with you," called Jim.

"You better stay here," answered the fat man. "I can make out all right. This ain't no regular call."

"That nigger can fire for Sam if I don't get back," answered the fireman, crossing over to the right-hand side. Carter had thrown the switch, the 235 moved off the main line, stopped in the clear.

"You understand," said T. P., "that you take your own chances. If the levee goes here, we're up the creek with no paddle. We go down as far as Sugarland if we can, an' there's two feet of water over the rails that I know of. There's about one chance in ten that we can get through."

"Sugarland," said the fireman —"that where the refugees are?"

"Supposed to be," answered Patchbolt. "The boss figures they were left-overs from the Ravenhead crevasse."

The fireman nodded. "They can't stop us from tryin'," he said, and went back to the firing lever.

T. P. turned to Allbright. "Here's the dope," he said. "You an' your playmate go up on that flat car. You'll have to take turns walkin' ahead. Walk fast. If you get too tired, you let us know an' we'll try to help out. Jim here'll come up as soon as we see how she steams. I don't even know whether the dump's still here, but we'll find out in a few minutes."

Allbright climbed over the back of the tank, joined Carter on the flat car.

Carter agreed to walk first. The engine backed up until the flat car came to the edge of the muddy water that hid the tracks, and Carter got off and walked up the flooded dump.

Ahead of them stretched a flat expanse of muddy water. Two feet under lay the branch-line dump and rails, and because of the danger of a washout that no one could possibly see, someone had to walk ahead of the train to make sure the engine and cars could pass over.

"Why don't you try to get those refugees out in a boat?" demanded Jim of T. P.

"It's forty miles around to Sugarland by boat," answered the fat master mechanic.

"Huh?"

"You see," explained Patchbolt, "the only way to get in there is around by way of the river and down the crevasse at Ravenhead. Take a good boat to go down that crevasse. They can't follow our dump to Sugarland by boat on account of the old levee. We ain't in no danger unless the levee breaks in back of us; but, brother, if she comes through behind us, it's gonna be tough."

"No worse than some of 'em got," said the fireman somberly.

"That's true," admitted the fat man.

There was a steady swish-swish-swish of muddy water as they backed slowly down the branch. Both T. P. and Jim watched Carter closely. It wouldn't do to slip off the rails — it just wouldn't do. Although there was not more than two feet of water over the ties, it should not be forgotten that the dump was from eight to fifteen feet high. If the engine ever slid over the dump and lit in a soft spot, it would take a powerful lot of fishing even to find it, let alone rerail it. The branch line was built through a swamp.

Carter tired and Allbright took his place, and Carter came back to the cab to dry out. It was still raining — a cold, bone-chilling, spring drizzle. Allbright plodded along ahead of the little train.

After what seemed a long time, T. P. said: "You go up ahead, Jim. I can handle her; she's set about right." Jim climbed over the back of the tank, disappeared.

"Anything I can do, T. P.?" asked Carter.

"Yeah," said T. P., "get over on the left side an' watch those men up ahead. If any one of 'em says stop, holler your head off."

They went slopping through the water to the weak wuf-wuf-wuf of exhaust and the monotonous high-pitched roar of the blower. Allbright tired and they slowed, almost stopping, when the fireman took his place. Carter went back — or rather, ahead — to the flat car and Allbright came into the cab to dry out and get warm.

"Keep your eye on those men up ahead," ordered T. P.

They came to the cotton platform at Tudow, just past Mile Post 4, within the hour. The three men, Jim and Carter and Allbright, had taken turns walking ahead. All three were tired to almost utter weariness. None of them, including Patchbolt, could remember when a night of real sleep had been theirs. They were dirty of body and weary of eye.

Allbright was in the cab when they came to the cotton platform. "Let's stop an' put that wire aboard," he suggested.

"We'll pick it up comin' back," said T. P.

"Let's get it now," argued Allbright. "We may be drowned by the time we get back here. It'll be a supreme satisfaction just to get my paws on that wire."

Patchbolt grinned.

"All right," he agreed, "but throw your feet out. Go up an' tell Carter to bend that rail. We'll go right in the house track an' alongside the platform. Hurry it up!"

They moved very slowly onto the switch and into the house track.

"I'm a fool for doing this," muttered the fat man. "These lousy little house tracks wouldn't hold up a bag of beans. It won't hurt nothin', though, an' maybe it's a good hunch."

They oozed along the house track. All three men were wading through the water up ahead, checking up the track. The flat car came up even with the cotton platform, which stood well above the water. They stopped, spotted even with the little frame building at one end. T. P. cut his fire down and went up ahead to help.

Allbright kicked the padlocked door in with very few preliminaries. Allbright was a tough old veteran. The only job he had never tackled in the telegraph and telephone game was stringing submarine cable. Inside the shack they found eight rolls of wire — Number 9 copper wire, weighing two hundred and ten pounds to the roll and averaging about a mile in length. With the wire they found a pay-out reel. They loaded everything on the flat car.

They moved slowly back toward the branch main line, reached it without accident. Jim threw and locked the switch. Allbright went ahead, wading through the flood. Carter stayed on the flat car. Jim came up in the cab to dry out.

"It's only four more miles to the old levee and dry land," said T. P. "We'll be out of this slop from there till we get to Sugarland — I mean, jus' before we get to Sugarland. If those people are this side of Sugarland, we oughtta get 'em without no trouble."

"They won't be this side of Sugarland," said the fireman gloomily. "If they'd been this side, they'd of followed the dump back to the main line."

"Well," said T. P., "if they're below the old levee, I don't see how we can get to 'em. They tell me the Ravenhead crevasse cut a regular channel between the old levee an' Sugarland."

"That's what I heard," said the fireman moodily. The two men were silent for a moment. Finally Jim said, "We shouldda brought a boat."

"We couldn't get a boat," explained T. P. "Most all the boats went up to Ravenhead night before last when the levee busted there; what boats they got down around the bridge they won't part with. They think the levee's gonna go just east of the bridge, an' they're keepin' those boats to get the men out with."

Jim nodded gloomily. They slopped along through the dirty water.

"You live down here?" asked T. P.

"Yeah," said Jim shortly.

"Where?" asked the fat man.

"Just below Ravenhead," said Jim shortly.

"The hell!" said T. P. "Any of your people get caught?"

"I tried to find out," said Jim gloomily. "Nobody seemed to know. They took two relief trains out. I went through one of 'em — didn't see anybody. They may of been on the other one — I dunno."

"They?" questioned T. P.

"I'm a family man," said Jim gloomily.

They slowed, almost stopping, as Carter took Allbright's place in the lead. Jim went up ahead; Allbright came aboard shivering. The little ten-wheeler went slopping along. The three men changed places oftener now for the disagreeable task of wading ahead of the flat car. Carter was in the cab when they sighted dry land through the drizzling rain.

"That the old levee?" he called, pointing.

"That's it," said T. P. "It may not look like a monument, brother, but there's plenty of 'em down here that'd give a lot to be on it."

"I guess that's so," agreed Carter.

They finally came to the levee. It was a tremendous relief to be able to see the rails again. Everybody came back to the cab. They would be on this comparatively high ground for eight miles, until they came to Sugarland. No one knew for certain what they would find at Sugarland, but everyone expected the worst.

T. P. was glad to cut the blower off; he was sick of hearing it. They were running fast enough now so the exhaust created enough draft to take care of the fire. T. P. held her with the independent air and worked a heavy throttle while Jim tossed four or five scoopfuls of sand into the fire box to clean out the flues. When they had been coming through the water the boot under the fire box had been covered, and the bottom air inlets of the fire pan might just as well not have been there. The little engine didn't seem to appreciate the treatment and it had been found necessary to smoke her heavy in order to get her to steam.

But they'd been lucky, thought the fat man, as they went rolling along — mighty lucky. If their luck held, they might get these refugees out. Rescue boats must have missed them. It might be that the rescue boats couldn't get to them. The flood did some funny things.

"How'd they know they was anybody out there?" shouted Allbright.

"A arryplane saw 'em," answered the fat man.

"A arryplane," said Allbright. "H'm! So they fin'ly found a use for them things."

They came to the curve that led off the old levee onto the flats. There was a straightaway about a mile long before them, then nothing but water.

"I see something," called Carter. "Guess it must be the box cars."

When they came to the water's edge, all but T. P. were on the flat car. T. P. opened the whistle up for a long mournful bellow through the drizzling rain. The fat man left the air on service, methodically shut off the oil and the blower, left the atomizer barely cracked and clambered down. He proceeded to the flat car.

"Anybody on those cars?" he demanded, squinting through the rain.

"Somebody waved from up on top," declared Jim.

Over the yellow flood, slightly less than a half mile distant, could be discerned a short string of box cars. The fat man made out a figure on top the first of these cars. Near these cars was a small house, apparently turned over on its side. Beyond the box cars and the house, another half mile beyond, could be barely seen the refinery at Sugarland. The stack was easily visible, but little else.

"That's a woman on top that car," declared Carter.

"I'm gonna walk down the dump," declared Jim excitedly, jumping off the flat car into the slop and the wet. Carter followed.

The fat man and Allbright watched the pair wade out along the dump. They advanced some fifty feet, when Jim, who was in the lead, suddenly dropped from sight. Carter pulled him back. The pair stood for a moment shouting, then turned and came back.

"No track," said Jim to T. P., looking down at the ground.

"Thought so," said the fat man.

"Strong current," supplemented Carter.

"We could hear 'em call," said Jim.

"Whose name were you yellin' out there?" asked the fat man.

The fireman hesitated. "That's my wife's name," he answered shortly.

"Wonder if his wife could be out there," thought the fat man. The flood did funny things. That was probably a woman on top that car. "They've been out in this hell for at least a night and a day," he thought. "They must have floated down on that house." Hello, there were two figures on top that car! Now there were three. One of 'em must be a kid.

"I can tell you what's happened," declared T. P. "The flood's cut the dump out between them and here, and it's cut it out between them an' Sugarland. Those box cars are on a sort of island."

"How we gonna get 'em out?" demanded Jim.

"I can swim it easy," said Carter.

"He sure can," declared Allbright; "he's a regular fish."

"That's a mean current," warned the fat man.

"I can make it easy," declared Carter.

T. P. was silent for a moment. "Could you take a wire across?" he demanded.

Carter grinned. "I'll give it a big try," he answered.

Allbright slapped a heavy hand on a soggy thigh. "Here we go!" he cried.

Jim had been walking down to the deeper water. He returned. "Figure out a way?" he asked eagerly.

"Carter'll take a wire across," said T. P. "Says he can swim it."

"I can't swim," said Jim gloomily, as though accused.

T. P. clapped him on the shoulder. "That's all right, old-timer," he declared. They stood leaning up against the flat car. "Could you make out anything?"

"It looks like my house," declared Jim. "I won't leave here, Mr. Patch-bolt, until we get 'em out."

"Don't you worry," said the master mechanic; "we'll get 'em out."

Allbright and Carter had the pay-out reel on the track in front of them and had set a roll of wire on it.

"Don't let's get in too big a rush," said T. P. "We got to figure this thing out. That one wire ain't gonna get those people across. How stout is that wire, anyways?"

"We pull 'em up to four hundred pounds," answered Allbright promptly. "Four hundred pounds tensile strength. Got a big margin of safety too. If we hang five of these wires together, we can pull down a house."

"Let's get everything ready while we're all here," suggested T. P. "We ain't got but the one reel. It'll take a long time to unreel five of those rolls — six of 'em, if you count the one Carter's to take across."

"How d'you wanta do it?" demanded Allbright.

"If you think it'll work," said T. P., "we can anchor one end of the wire on the flat car and unreel it before you can bat an eye — run up the track about three-quarters of a mile. That's as long as they'll have to be."

Allbright grinned. "I never heard of no one unreeling telegraph wire with a locomotive before," he said, "but I'm willing to try it. Get up in the cab an' get ready; we're about all set."

T. P. clambered up in the cab and put a fire under the 235, and by the time he'd done that they were waiting on him. They had wrapped the free end of the wire around a stick, and Jim braced himself on the flat car and held this stick. Allbright and Carter held the reel and kept it running free, and they unreeled most of the first roll without a hitch. Allbright cut the wire when T. P. stopped on a hand signal, and they laid their product over to one side and stuck a fresh roll in the reel. Six times the 235 puffed up the track and returned, but they did the job in one-fifth the time it would have taken by hand.

Allbright and Carter bound five of the strands together at short distances and pulled the makeshift cable as far down the dump as they could. It wasn't a particularly beautiful cable, but it was strong enough to do the job for them. They brought the single piece of wire down to the end of the dump — the one that Carter was to carry across.

Carter slipped out of his soggy clothes, all except his underwear, took off his shoes. They bound the wire under his armpits, ran another piece over his shoulders so he couldn't lose his burden. After a hasty check-up, he slipped out into the dirty rainspecked flood.

Carter could swim, no question about that. He went angling across in an easy churning crawl; they paid out the wire behind him. Jim watched his every movement with anxious eyes. It seemed like hours — in reality it was only minutes — before they saw him, vaguely through the drizzle, come to land near the box cars, saw him stand up in two or more feet of water. Three figures met him.

They hooked the five-strand cable onto the single wire and Carter pulled it across.

"I told him," said T. P. to Jim, "to pry off a couple of box-car doors an' hook that wire on 'em — or any kind of raft — it don't matter so long as it'll hold them people up. An' boy, when the 235 starts down the railroad we'll bring the whole works home." The fireman said nothing, only watched intently across the water. "If he can find somethin' to pry with," muttered T. P., "he oughtn't to have no trouble."

Carter had disappeared near the first box car; they could recognize him easily because of his white underwear. It was a long time to the watchers — particularly Jim — before he reappeared.

"He's got somethin'," called Allbright.

The white figure disappeared again, reappeared after another age. The watchers could make out the four figures near the cars; they could see the white figure bend and straighten up, bend and straighten up. They had agreed, T. P. and Carter and the rest, that it would be best were there no shouting or waving until the raft was ready. They saw the white figure straighten, saw him wave, heard his faint shout. The other figures were waving too. Jim shouted in answer, T. P. and Allbright waved their hats.

"Come on, Jim!" exclaimed T. P., starting for the 235.

"You can run it," answered Jim excitedly. "I'm gonna stay right here!"

T. P. mounted to the cab, held the whistle cord down. Everything was set. The cable was hooked through a stake socket on the flat car. The fat man moved her ahead slowly, very carefully, half hanging out the cab window. Jim was giving him the go-ahead. "About ten miles an hour will do the trick," thought T. P., pulling the throttle a little wider. He could see Jim. The fireman was still giving him the highball. "He must want me to go faster," thought T. P.; "that current must be tough."

Jim was watching the makeshift raft with its burden of refugees breast the dirty water. Carter was swimming near it, losing distance apparently. No, he decided, Carter had hold of the back end of the raft.

The current caught the bobbing crazy craft with its human cargo, tipped it, swung it. Jim closed his eyes, turned, shouted and waved to T. P. to go faster. He turned to look at the raft again. He determined not to think who might be aboard. It was slipping downstream now, being carried downstream, but it was closer. There were still three figures on board, with Carter trailing behind. He kept pace with the raft as it slipped downstream; it drew closer and closer. He shouted suddenly, shouted again, danced, ran down to where the raft would land.

T. P. was thoroughly disgusted. If that Jim ain't a punk fireman, he decided, then he had never seen one. They were on their way back to the main line. Everybody had forgotten about T. P. being on the engine; in fact they had forgotten that there was such a thing as an engine numbered 235 when the raft grounded. And since T. P. couldn't see anything because the raft had drifted down, the 235 had kept right on going and pulled that confounded amateur boat two or three hundred yards through the woods — all because Allbright and Jim got excited. A swell way to railroad, thought T. P. And Allbright had the gall to gripe about his wire being all busted up, as though he couldn't tie knots in it.

And every few minutes Jim's wife would say to her husband, "Honey, I never expected to see you again," and start to sniffle. How was a man going to fire an engine properly with a woman hanging around his neck, thought T. P. indignantly, and a kid on the seat box with him? That woman with Jim's wife — a cousin; she better stay away from the right-hand side. He didn't have any time to monkey with women; if there was one thing that'd put the Indian sign on railroading, it was a woman.

They were rolling along the dry land near the old levee; they came to the flooded area. It was four P.M.; if their luck held, they would make the main line by six. T. P. was hungry enough to eat a car wheel.

There were seven people in the cab, most of them crowded up against the back boiler head. It was still raining. They slopped into the water, the rails disappeared. T. P. watched the main and side rods come up and go under, come up and go under. Slop, slop, slop. "Hell of a way to railroad," thought the fat man. The water came over the boot of the fire pan; T. P. reached over and opened the fire door. The blower was wide open, but they were wasting more oil than they used.

"Hey, you," called T. P. harshly to Jim, "put some water in her!"

Jim grinned happily at T. P. and put the injector on. They went slopping along. After about an hour they came to the cotton platform. T. P. applied the brakes.

"Listen, boys," he said, "when we come through here before there was a current in three or four places. We'll have to do like we done before — walk ahead to see if there's any washouts. Can't take chances."

There was a pause. It was very comfortable in the cab, out of the cold and drizzle.

"Well," said Allbright resignedly, "I'll lead off."

He went through the left-hand cab door, walked forward on the running board, descended over the pilot and walked up the flooded dump. The engine followed. Allbright walked — rather, waded — about a half mile and Carter took his place. Allbright came back to the cab shivering. After a little while, Jim arose.

"You watch the fire?" he called to T. P.; Patchbolt nodded.

"Where you goin'?" demanded Allbright.

"I'll take Carter's place," said the fireman.

"Sit down," said Allbright, "an' stay here with your wife an' kid. Carter an' I'll do the walkin'."

T. P. came waddling across the cab deck.

"Get over there an' run her," he rumbled. "I'll walk." The fireman protested. "Git over there," rumbled T. P.; "I'm tired of arguin'."

So the fireman ran the engine and T. P. replaced Carter out on the flooded dump. Allbright relieved Patchbolt as they came in sight of the main line.

They were all in the cab again. Jim and his wife and kid were all crowded together on the left-hand side. The woman and the boy were half asleep. Allbright and Carter and the other woman were on the cab deck, sitting on the cab deck in front of the fire door. T. P. was running the engine.

He could see the main-line dump clearly now, could T. P.   There was an
engine working just east of the station, pulling some box cars down toward
the bridge.   The 368, he decided.   They were certainly in one big hurry to
get those cars across the bridge.   He blinked.   The light was failing, the
drizzle continued.   Those must be people at the bridge, he decided.   He
looked over at the main-line dump.

That couldn't be water cascading over the top of the dump.   Why, the
main-line dump was only a foot or so lower than the levee.   But it was water.
Almost before his eyes the bank dissolved under the main-line rails and ties,
and the yellow flood was on them!

T. P. shouted and pointed, pulling the throttle wider.   The branch-line
rails curved to the right here and the break in the dump before them passed
from his view behind the boiler.   The water was rising, turbulent, under the
cab.   It covered the bottom of the fire pan, sizzling; it came flush with the
mud ring as the steam filtered into the cab from below.

"Cut your fire off!" bellowed Patchbolt.

The track was wavering under their drivers, the cab was a blur of steam.
They paralleled the main-line dump.   The main-line washout slid slowly
past the left-hand window and gangway.   If the track would hold, they had
a chance to get in, for the branch entered the main-line four hundred yards
east of the washout.   "Not too heavy on the throttle," T. P. warned himself.
"If she slips off it's curtains for us all.   Just a few hundred yards more —
stay on the rails, old-timer.   One hundred and twenty pounds on the gauge
— that's enough for any flat car and some lousy copper wire."

The water was even with the belly of the boiler, almost flush with the cab
deck.   The wheels were covered — you couldn't see the rods, couldn't see
the cylinders, couldn't even see the flat car behind them.

"Come on, old-timer," thought T. P., "they haven't got us licked yet."

Through the layers of steam in the cab T. P. could dimly make out the
fireman, one arm about his wife, the other holding his kid.   The two other
men and the woman were jammed in the left-hand gangway, staring at the
water, staring at the break in the dump.

T. P. shouted.   Allbright came over.   "We'll make the main line," said
T. P., "if the track holds.   I doubt if she'll pull up onto the main-line dump,
but we'll get up close enough so we can walk up.   You get these people off
— see that they get across the bridge.   The levee's gone on this side.   The
whole river's comin' through that break."

Allbright nodded.   He crossed over, made sure the fireman understood.
He talked to Carter — told him to take Jim's cousin over the bridge.

It was scary business, with the water sucking at the track beneath them.
But suddenly the water receded and they went swinging up the incline toward the main line and safety.   The 235 chuffed for the last time very solemnly and paid off.   They straggled up the incline, the fireman carrying
his youngster.   "Never heard a whimper out of that kid," thought the fat
master mechanic.   They came to the top of the dump and T. P. made a bee
line for the 368.   Allbright was on his heels.   Patchbolt clambered up the
gangway of the 368.

"Let's take her down the branch lead, Sam," he cried to the engineer. "The 235's stuck; we can pull her out."

"I got orders to go no farther west than the station," answered the engineer.

"You got some new ones now," said T. P. grimly. "Let's get down there. This is an emergency."

"You take the responsibility?" demanded the engineer.

"Hell, yes!" announced T. P.

"Here we go!" said the engineer.

Allbright was standing behind T. P. "I'll throw the switch," he said.

T. P. nodded, looked over at the fireman's seat. A very scared darky sat on the seat box, one quivering hand on the firing valve.

T. P. stepped over. "Get across the bridge, Jumbo," he rumbled. "I'll take your job."

The negro was down the gangway and gone before the fat man could sit down. They came to the branch-line switch. Allbright ran ahead and threw it; they went slowly down the grade and coupled into the 235. The water was over the valve stem, over the flat slide valves above the cylinders. They dragged her back to the main line, with the flat car behind.

A man swung up the gangway. He was the trainmaster. "What you doin' down here?" he demanded of the engineer.

T. P. came over. "We had to get the 235 out, Eddie," he explained.

"I ain't got nothin' to get out, I spose!" sneered Eddie.

"Well, whadda you want out?" demanded T. P. "Here we are."

"We'll get two coaches off the Y," snarled the trainmaster. "Step on it, Sam!"

They swung down on the Y. Allbright raced ahead to throw the switch. They hooked into the two day coaches, pulled them back on the main line. The dump was ready to slide from under the drivers; it was touch and go. Almost even with the break in the levee, only a scant hundred yards from where the yellow torrent was cutting the dump away in mammoth bites, they pulled the two day coaches off the Y and to safety. They backed down the main line and eased slowly across the bridge and the water beneath them was flush with the rails. They stopped on the east side of the bridge and watched the track they had come over eaten away, watched the station tilt up and slide from sight, watched the hungry river undermine the west piers of the bridge, watched the bridge itself slip majestically into the all-devouring flood — all in the space of less than thirty minutes.

"We don't know how lucky we were!" declared T. P.

"Pretty lucky," declared Allbright. "There was a couple of times when I didn't think we was gonna get back with that wire!"

T. P. surveyed him in utter disgust. "Say," he demanded, "don't you realize we damn near lost a engine?"

IRVIN S. COBB

HUMORIST, short-story writer, dramatist, and correspondent, Irvin S. Cobb
(born in Paducah, Kentucky, 1876) met his first success as a New York newspaper man in 1905, when his original reporting of the Russo-Japanese peace
negotiations at Portsmouth drew the attention of many editors and readers to
his work. During the World War he became one of the most widely read war
correspondents in the world. In his short stories, as with many writers following O. Henry, the manner rather than the matter is the more important, although his shrewd and humorous characterizations have given his work more
interest and durability than other "popular" writers enjoy. In the present
selection, which appeared in the *O. Henry Prize Stories of 1928*, Mr. Cobb re-
verses the usual procedure in the crime story by giving away the criminal at
once and emphasizing the ingenious and homely reasoning of the "correspondence school" detective in exposing the "perfect crime."

AN EPISODE AT PINTAIL LAKE *

THE gang at Starbuck's back a mile from the river were joking that comical
old cooter of a Joe Sam Flint about his prized new badge and his ten-dollar
diplomy, or whatever it was you called the fool contrapshun, just before this
stranger, young Gaul, ran up, dripping wet and panting, with the word that
his friend was drowned in Pintail Lake.

Their humour was of a primitive but searching order. They conceded
Uncle Joe Sam to be a master hand at tolling turkeys into range with a wing-
bone yelper; for the sake of the argument they admitted that he seemed to
understand the ways of fox-squirrels better than the fox-squirrels themselves
did. But granted that much, still they desired — as one inspired spokesman
put it — to know this: what excuse could an old, ignorant, red-necked, hard-
shelled, wool-hatted tarrypin of a hillbilly such as he was, that hadn't never
been nowheres and hadn't never seen nothing, have to go pestering around
aclaiming to be one of these here regular detecatives?

That was what these genial loafers desired to hear and asked for and loudly
clamoured for, with frequent interpolations of barbed elemental wit by this
homespun jester and that. As the startling interruption came, their indignant
prey stoutly was defending his authority as derived by mail and for a price
from the Argus International Detective Agency & Correspondence School at
Portland, Maine, U.S.A., and likewise his potential merits for the proposed
career of his declining but maturer years.

Conceded that he couldn't read very much, if at all, his daughter could; and
she had read to him what the printed instructions sent through the post office
said about detecting crime and catching criminals; and he had remembered a
good part of it; maybe half, possibly two thirds. Moreover, if a man devoted

* From Hearst's *International* combined with *Cosmopolitan*, October, 1927. Copyright, 1927.
Reprinted by permission of the author.

his lifetime to studying the secret habits of the wild things, it was only common sense to assume that he'd be able to figure out the hidden motives and the hidden doings of human creatures better than the run of people, now, wasn't it? Or, anyway, words to that effect.

Flurried but positive, he was diving head first into a counter tide of derisive laughter when just then there appeared this man, Herbert Gaul, all soaked and agitated, crying out of his friend's death and begging for help.

At that they all sobered down and jumped up from where they had been lounging at the front of the store and hurried back with the stranger over the Crooketty Creek road. Uncle Joe Sam went too, but at a slower gait than the rest, he having rheumatic swellings in his elderly legs. He carried along his old double-barrelled scatter gun. As a confirmed hunter he carried it about with him nearly everywhere. Now, though, he seemed to regard it as an added credential, a token, so to speak, signifying an armed and militant vigilance against lawbreaking.

He hobbled along the best he could, but by the time he got down to the fog-covered lake which lay in the lowland paralleling the river, plans for dragging already were under way. There was need for haste. According to the survivor the accident had occurred less than half an hour earlier, and several there professed to know of cases when the breath was pumped back into lungs which had been under water longer even than half an hour.

Immediately, with a sort of improvised dredge, they scraped and raked over a roughly designated area but brought up only mud and weedy stuff and dead branches of trees. Eventually the quest would take on a systematized aspect, with orderly direction to it, with groups working under the loose command of Wallie Starbuck, the storekeeper. That though was to follow after they had given up hope of saving a life and were moved by the size of the reward which Gaul offered for the recovery of the body.

Now, at this present confused and exciting stage, nearly every fellow offered suggestions which conflicted with nearly every other fellow's suggestions, and nobody was heeding any of them. In forty minutes enough advice to raise a sunken battleship went absolutely to waste. Starbuck did show some qualifications for leadership.

He sent a messenger back to his place for dynamite and adequate coils of rope — thus far they had been using a skiff's painter — and to the blacksmith's on beyond his place for bent iron to make proper grapnels of. He called for volunteers who would strip off and risk pneumonia by diving for the dead man.

While awaiting the runner's return, Gaul repeated for Uncle Joe Sam's benefit his account of the drowning. Coming down he already had told and retold it. But the oldest man of the lot had been trailing them far behind. Also, being spavined and slow-motioned, he had the wisdom to stay outside the orbits of active co-operations on the part of the crowd. At the first opportunity he engaged Gaul, saying he desired to learn the details, if it wasn't too much trouble, and Gaul, who had grown measurably calmer, very willingly obliged him.

"There's not very much to it, awful as it is," began Gaul, speaking in that curious foreign way of his.   He was from up North somewhere, as Uncle Joe Sam had heard, but even if he hadn't heard could have guessed from the other's manner of accenting and pronouncing his words.   "We were over in that blind there on the far side.   Two ducks came out of the fog and flew in toward us over the decoys — the second batch we'd seen this morning.   I shot twice and missed both times — I'm not much of a shot.   Mr. Pettigrew dropped his, though, with his second barrel.   Considering that he was sixty-five years old and wore glasses he was pretty good at that sort of thing — not an expert gunner but fair."

"Yep, I heard the shootin' back up on the bluff whar me and the other boys wuz," stated Uncle Joe Sam.   "You-all shot about a half-hour or so before that, though — three barrels that time, fust one, and then in a second or so two more, sort of clos't togither."

"Yes, we didn't get anything then — the fog was too thick to make them out," explained Gaul.   "Well, as I was saying, Mr. Pettigrew had one bird down.   I think that must be it floating off there."

His audience of one peered where he pointed to a seemingly faraway dot on the surface.   Distant objects were revealing themselves now as the fog shredded away.   It had been very heavy; now it was disappearing fast.

"That's it," pronounced Uncle Joe Sam after prolonged scrutiny; "looks small.   Must be a green-wing or mebbe one of these here summer ducks — what up in your country they'd likely call wood ducks.   It's drifted out a right smart piece frum whar it spilled, ain't it?"

"It started drifting as soon as it struck.   Besides, it wasn't quite dead then.   It fluttered and splashed, sort of kicked itself along; and after it died and quit kicking, the wind carried it still farther away.   Well, anyway, we crawled into that cranky little skiff that we borrowed, to go out and pick it up.   I was handling the oars.   Mr. Pettigrew was in the stern.   I manœuvred to get up alongside the dead duck.   It was about out there."   Again he aimed an index finger.   "Yes, as nearly as I can tell it was just about there that we caught up with it.   I let the skiff come around broadside and tried to scoop it in with one of the oars.   But I missed.   So I said to Mr. Pettigrew that he'd better grab it as it went by.

"He leaned over to the left — like this — trying to reach it.   He must've leaned too far, or it's possible that just at that second he had one of his attacks of dizziness.   He was subject to them — something like vertigo, I guess it was — if he over-exerted himself or even if he stooped his head.   At any rate, it tipped suddenly, the skiff, I mean, and began to dip water — a lot of water — over the gunwale.   And before I could think to throw my body in the other direction in an effort to right her I was in the lake and so was he, and the skiff was bottom-side up.

"I went clear under, and went down deep, too, being weighed down with these heavy hunting clothes and this pair of rubber hip boots.   He was dressed the same way.   When I came up he was gone — not a sign of him.   I swam around a little while — not very long, though — hoping his head would show.   I didn't dare try to dive for him, outfitted the way I was — I'm just a fair swimmer and I felt like I had tons hanging to me.   So when his head still didn't show I got hold of the capsized skiff and steered her across to this bank and ran up to the store for help.

"There's two fine guns lost, but I'm not thinking of them, of course. I'm thinking of the terrible finish of his trip and the fact that I've lost the best friend I ever had in this world, or ever expect to have. I've been his private secretary for twelve years, ever since I came out of college, and he was almost like a father to me. He didn't have any sons of his own or daughters either — only two nieces and one nephew and a few distant relatives."

"Pity you had to turn over out whar it's the deepest," commented Uncle Joe Sam, his face and voice gravely sympathetic. "Effen it'd 'a' happened ten rods clos'ter to the bank you could 'a' teched, standin' on your tiptoes."

"It must have been fate. Well, all I can hope for now is that they'll find the — the remains. You think they will, don't you?"

"Well, they oughter. Ef them hooks don't ketch onto his clothes a blast of dynamite mout fetch him up — it gin'elly does. And ef that should fail he oughter rise by hisself inside of three or four days even with the lake water ez coolish ez 'tis now — the gases, you know — they'll lift him. That is, without he gits lodged fast amongst some brush or wedged-in-like under a sunken log down in a deep part. I've knowed of sech things."

"I'm afraid of that myself," admitted Gaul. "I've got a sort of feeling about it."

He stole a covert quick glance at his present companion. The old man's face was seamed with lines of gravity; his faded-out eyes were pondering on the squads of searchers where in front yonder they circled in two boats — a tricky dugout and a small skiff which had been found upturned and oarless in a shallow near at hand. The oars had been picked up some distance away toward mid-lake. Absently Uncle Joe Sam lifted a flap of his unbuttoned vest, and breathed upon the preposterous lettered disk of imitation silver which he wore pinned over his left breast, and next he polished at it with the sleeve of his coat. He uttered a series of small clucks betokening regret and commiseration.

The man Gaul gave an inward heave of deep self-satisfaction. It was going to be no harder to hoodwink this hobbling ancient than it had been befooling those other deluded natives. Going to be? — that was wrong. It already was. A pack of innocents, that was what these yokels here in the bottoms of this Tennessee River were. Who was it said that murder must always out — that a murderer, no matter how shrewd his design or how finished his execution of it, always left some betraying clue behind? Whoever it was, he was wrong. Behold, here was one murder about which there had been no slip-up — or only one, and it didn't count — no mischance, no thing undone, no thing overdone. It had been snugly, surely accomplished and swiftly and accurately and completely.

This was what Herbert Gaul exultantly was saying to himself as now he sat him down on a log and drew off his sloshing boots. He did not feel as though he had just got through with committing premeditated murder. He felt like a man who has been bidden to a noble feast. A glow of pleasure for a perfect and balanced achievement flowed up out of him and spread through him and filled him, brain and heart and body. It was as though an artist sat and admired his own masterpiece.

At a certain stage of the undertaking he had been physically very sick; at another had been seized with quick, almost panicky misgivings as to the success of its outcome. And before that when he first was putting his hand to it a mounting swell of doubt, call it irresolution, had for a moment, but only a moment, threatened his forces of decision.

That, though, was all past and over and done with; that was all safely behind him. Within himself he tested his nerves. Taut but not too taut, they responded like violin strings that strum their answer to the finger of a musician. A great confidence, a great strength and steadiness possessed him. Also, and on fuller thought of the transaction, there was with this a fine proud sensation, a sense of self-appreciation for having so readily and so powerfully mastered two separate and difficult contingencies — really they had been unforeseen emergencies — which had arisen in the midst of his job. Why, he had been a regular calculating machine, clever at the preliminary forecasts, prompt to take up the slack ends of things.

All he had to do now was just stand fast and let the events, as he had provided both for and against them, take their natural courses, he meanwhile to counterfeit just the properest most plausible air of a man stricken with a great grief yet not stricken beyond powers of manly self-control and not shaken past the ability to meet a lamentable, tragical situation and still carry on. Like a chemist mixing a delicate compound in the peace of a quiet laboratory, he decided what looks to wear, what phrases to repeat, what emotional proportions to emphasize, and what ones to slight.

The inception of the plot dated back; had been months in the shaping and at first had worn a different face. To begin with, he uttered a false will for his patron, the man he today had killed. That was the germ idea. There was a true will accessible to him, in his keeping practically, but he had too much craft to destroy it. He had no fear of what might result from a comparison of signatures — he had worked too long to achieve a perfect imitation of Pettigrew's handwriting.

Likewise he had a better reason, which was this: By the real will nothing at all was given to most of Pettigrew's kins-people; ten thousand cash was given to the two nephews and the niece; fifteen thousand went to him, Gaul, in consideration of long and faithful service, and all the residue, amounting roughly to three millions, went to create a fund in perpetuity for the education of coloured youth in the South. Now, then, the newer will which he had forged left to both nephews and to the niece five hundred thousand dollars apiece; it left to him, Gaul, an equal amount; it reduced no lesser bequest but substantially increased most of them, and it devised the remainder, as shrunken to a few hundreds of thousands, to the cause of the young Negroes.

So doing, Gaul was manufacturing sympathy and influence and friendly aid for himself; he was destroying the prospect of jealousy against him. Regardless of whatever private suspicions anyone among them might entertain, it would be to the interests of every individual beneficiary to contend for the probating of the bogus will and the throwing out of the prior-dated genuine will.

Human nature, selfishness, greed — why, they'd all fight as strong and influential allies on his side. So much for step number one.

Originally he had not contemplated doing away with his benefactor by violence. If the tempting thought came he put it from him as being unnecessary and over-risky. Pettigrew was well along in years, was sickly, and despite his small meagre body, showed apoplectic tendencies. He had weak kidneys, too, or thought he had, which amounted practically to the same thing; was altogether a peevish failing dyspeptic bundle of walking symptoms, forever coddling himself and forever dosing himself. Surely Gaul should not have to wait long for his reward.

But perversely the hypochondriac hung on. He gave up active business; he gave himself over to playing seemingly conflicting parts — the part of a semi-invalid, and the part of a persistent gunner of wild fowl, which last was a sport of his youth, a thing dropped for business and now taken up again with almost a passionate avidity.

This naturally wore heavily on Gaul. It irked him, all this trapesing about to boggy, cheerless, isolated wild places; the lying out in all weathers; the uncongenial and uncomfortable surroundings; the banging away at shy but stupid web-footed birds; the enforced constant society of an irritable, peppery, intolerant master — for Pettigrew, who had few friends and no intimates, would have Gaul and none other for a companion on his expeditions.

Gaul's patience wore out. He thought of poison — some slowly consuming drug to be slipped into the medicines Pettigrew forever was taking. But he discarded that half-formed plan. He builded a better one, and he stayed his eager hand only until time and plan and conditions should match favourably with the purpose.

Largely through chance the opportunity came. Earlier in this present month of October Pettigrew took him to Reelfoot Lake for the beginning of the open season on migratory game. But the weather still was mild — too mild to stir the flocks out of the marshes of the Northern resting grounds.

At this juncture there happened along a fellow sportsman from somewhere in northern Alabama — a gentleman named Scopes — who told Mr. Pettigrew of a small unfrequented lake situate not very far above what he called the Big Bend of the Tennessee River, where for unfathomed reasons and despite climatic conditions there was a fairly dependable early flight of black duck and teal. Later would come swarms of the greenheads and the pintails, from which latter creatures this lake took its name. Within moderation he felt he could guarantee Mr. Pettigrew, going thither, would find satisfactory sport.

He went further. The town where he lived was not very many miles away from this lake. He paid a nominal sum yearly for the exclusive shooting privileges here. He offered to transfer his rights to Mr. Pettigrew and Mr. Gaul, to lend his equipment and to write a letter arranging with a widow who owned a farmhouse near by for their entertainment.

Mr. Pettigrew accepted with thanks. So the upshot was that he and Gaul packed up and travelled by train to Paducah and there boarded a stern-wheel packet, the *Lady Slidell*.

The *Lady Slidell* on the day before had delivered them at a small landing, and a native with a buckboard had carried them and their belongings to the homestead of the accommodating widow near a crossroads known as Starbuck's Store. In the afternoon they tramped through thick woods to the lake for a preliminary survey.

It revealed itself as a longish narrow body, encompassed with tall timber and around its edges with dense undergrowth in which there was but one tiny break and that where the footpath broke through. In times of high water it was joined, top and foot, to the river — not exactly a phenomenon in these parts, as they had learned. Very probably it once upon a prehistoric time had been a part of the bed of the river.

To Gaul's eyes it was a forbidding and altogether desolate spot, but Pettigrew liked the deserted looks of it. Its isolation should suit the wild fowl. Therefore it suited him.

It had at least one distinction not common to such waters but common enough to tidal estuaries. Offshore, above the solitary blind and therefore nearer the head, there stood a fish weir made, according to a familiar pattern, of tall poles set very closely together with one long slightly curved arm extending out across the current and the other bending in and forming an enclosed pouch, the whole being, roughly, in the shape of the Arabic numeral 9, with the joint not quite closed where the loop met the backbone.

Scopes had told them of the existence of this trapping device. A former owner of the place had built it, using the peeled trunks of straight willow saplings cut out of the adjacent swamps, his hope being that, in the time of the spring freshets, quantities of marketable large fish, schooling in from the river, would be pocketed here and held as prisoners, until he seined them out. The venture, though, had never paid and had been abandoned, but the ragged ramparts still stood.

Against their outer flanks driftwood had been deposited by succeeding overflows, until the accumulated mass formed rude rafts and platforms. The serried tips, standing yards above the present stage of water, were favourite perching places for fish-eating birds. Here they would sit, like sparrows on fence pickets, to watch with cocked heads and then to dart down and catch the impounded small fry.

On this afternoon nearly every slender pile had its feathered tenant. There were chuckling kingfishers not yet driven down country by the withheld threat of winter; there were silent herons, both great and small; there were a few pouncing herring gulls, they being the advance guards for the hosts which soon would swarm in from the regions of the Great Lakes; there were two dingy water turkeys, rare visitors these, from the semitropical bayous far south of here; there was an even rarer casual out of the same quarter — a lone brown pelican strayed far inland from his accustomed habitat in the brackish bays of the bitter salt of the Gulf. There was a pair of fish hawks cruising overhead, and there was a solitary largish black forager flapping about awkwardly, a creature of a species which Gaul, idly eyeing the greedy assemblage, could not identify. But then he was no ornithologist.

Money was what he loved, not nature; and especially he did not love such phases of nature as now presented themselves to his view. But in one regard he was pleased. For he saw that his chance was at hand. This lonesome unvisited place was as though made to order for his well-nursed and long-delayed design.

And when this morning he had awakened to find everything wrapped in thick woolly fogginess, a vapoury blanket against sight and a muffler for sound, he rejoiced inwardly. They had been called at four-thirty o'clock; had breakfasted in a lamplit kitchen with their sleepy hostess serving them, and long before the retarded daylight came had trudged through the cloaking grayness across a field and had entered a narrow trail where wet cold bushes whipped at their legs. He bore his gun, also a heavy case of shells, a luncheon and a jug of water for drinking. Old Pettigrew went ahead of him, carrying only a gun, and thereby the more surely sealed his own death warrant. His bottled hate made the laden and labouring Gaul fairly writhe as he followed close behind.

Coming down to the lake's margin they had to feel their way. It was by stumbling against it that Pettigrew, still in advance, found the skiff snubbed up to bank.

The older man climbed in and went astern. The younger cast off the tether, took the oars, and pulled out, aiming as best he could for a point diagonally opposite, where the well-sheltered blind should be. Largely by luck, they blundered headlong into it and disembarked and made ready against the further lifting of the fog and the coming of the game. Gaul set out the decoys.

The fog lifted, or at any rate it thinned. But it was after eight o'clock before in the murk about them they caught the *swish-swish*, like tough silk being torn crosswise, of swift wings. Directly overhead and, by reason of an optical illusion due to the atmospheric conditions, seeming to be twice their proper size, suddenly appeared a brace of ducks. They loomed an instant, swung, disappeared, then wheeled back into sight, poised and hovered, their pinions set and they ready to pitch in.

Pettigrew fired his right barrel, and the second bird crumpled and tumbled down with a splash perhaps ten yards in front of their ambush. He laid his empty gun aside, wriggled out from behind the blind, and splashed through the shallows.

"Well, anyhow, I got one," he said. "Why didn't you shoot?"

These were his last words. He stooped to pick up the dead bird and, with that, Gaul after just one lightning-swift fit of hesitation, one instantaneous flicker of his will, let him have it in back of the head and dropped him.

But strangely he lived. He must have a skull like iron. Face downward in the water, he wallowed and kicked spasmodically — like a speared frog, like a hooked fish. His shoulders heaved, he thrust up his mangled head and started a strangled gurgling cry. He began it, but he never finished it. Gaul broke through the blind, advanced, stood directly behind him and with the muzzle almost touching gave him the contents of the tight-choked left-hand barrel right between the shoulders. So of course after that he did not stir again.

Right there Gaul had displayed that first flash of quick-wittedness upon which, looking back on it, he might congratulate himself. How expedient he had been about reshaping the plan — how marvellously swift! For before-hand it had been his intention to claim he had killed by accident. The re-morseful grief-stricken explanation of it already had been framed and men-tally many times rehearsed — the fatal and ever-to-be regretted moment of carelessness, the stumbling of an unwary foot, the involuntary tightening of a numbed trigger finger on a touchy trigger. Every day nearly in the hunting season you read just that self-same story in the city papers. Some days you read it twice or oftener even.

But here was a difficulty: To account for one mortal wound in the dead body would be easy enough; to account for two such wounds and both of them inflicted from the rear, would be impossible. Instantly, though, or so now it in retrospect seemed to him, this most resourceful of assassins re-moulded his scheme. He would weight the body with the heavy shell box and sink it in a deep part of the lake. In places the lake was very deep. This fact he knew by hearsay; he would prove it by making soundings. Then he would hurry back to the crossroads with a tale of a boat overturned, of the drowning of his unfortunate benefactor, of his own narrow escape. Why, in-deed, this should make infinitely a better tale than the other.

He drew the skiff from its hiding in the slushy reed-grown herbage along-side the blind and shoved it out to where the flattened corpse was sprawled in shallows now vividly distempered. Taking care to get little or no blood on his garments, he lifted the body into the stern of the skiff. He had no trouble in huddling it on the floor below the level of the gunwale.

He put in also the shell case and the two guns, got in himself and took the oars, and pulled out through the cloaking fog which opaquely exaggerated everything — distances, the sizes of objects, the shapes of them. He meant to use the hitch rope of the skiff for fastening the shell case to Pettigrew's middle.

He pulled with steady strokes. He must be in the middle of the lake, or near it, when misgivings of a new and a terrible sort beset him. Suppose, dragging for the corpse, they grappled it fast and hauled up the dumb yet eloquent evidence to hang him? Suppose it somehow was freed from its anchorage and rose? Suppose there was a way of draining this lake? One overlapping another, these dreadful contingencies raced across his mind, and the blood flowing to his heart seemed suddenly to stop short and curdle.

He threw up his head as though to clear his brain of fumes, and by that motion found the answer for his problems, for in that same instant he re-membered having read somewhere, years and years before — perhaps it was in Dickens he read it — how formerly in England a suicide was buried where two highways met, with a stake driven through the heart.

Not a hundred yards from him and, by reason of a providential rift in the fog, more or less distinctly visible, a whole army of stakes showed themselves; a geometric pattern of them, protruding at gentle slants above the misted surface of the waters. They angled outward and toward him, forming a sort of irregular, slightly tilted palisade. A considerable number of them, especially those which formed the wing of the ruined weir, were shifted from true alignment with their fellows. Indeed a few had vanished altogether, leaving spaces like gaps in a row of snaggly teeth. If some were gone altogether it stood to reason that some of the others must be loosely rooted in the loamy bottom.

He pulled across there, frightening away a mixed flock of the birds which, as he had casually remarked yesterday, made this their hunting ground. Steering up alongside, he tried certain experiments. They were most gratifying experiments. The interwoven drift jam contained sizable saw logs, strayed cross ties, trunks of fallen trees. At this point and again at that it snugly was fixed. It teetered and quivered under pressure but would sustain him, would give him a reasonably secure footing. He tested it and knew it would.

Climbing out on it and balancing himself cautiously, he found that by exercising due care he could walk to and fro along it. He did this meanwhile, holding the painter of the burdened skiff securely, and at once dislodged from a crevice that special accessory to his new design for which he sought — a length of tree bough, water-soaked, solid enough to withstand hard strokes, heavy enough to serve him either as battering ram or hammer. And also by feeling, he discovered, just where accident or age had made those intermittent spaces between the stakes, one stake which could be lifted out of its present position.

He did lift it out in a series of tugs, after having forcibly freed it from its socketing in the tenacious mud of the lake bed. Heaving it up, foot by foot, he saw that at its base it was sharpened to a point, as he had expected it would be. It had been displaced; it could readily be replaced and with blows upon its top, given a firmer position than before, and no human eye, however keen, be ever the wiser. Finally, for the simplification of his task there was this to be said — the body he meant to pin and shove under and press flat at the foot of his stake already was bored through and through.

It was here that for a brief ghastly spell a surge of nausea made him weak and dizzy. It passed through, immediately, and did not return. At the end of twenty minutes or so, the main job being completed, he re-entered the rowboat, and drawing away a few yards, contemplated his handiwork for any betraying flaws. There was no flaw. There was not the slightest difference by which to distinguish that one particular pile from the piles which neighboured it right and left. What hideous transfixed secret it held so securely submerged ten, twelve feet down beneath the placid coffee-coloured waters would still be his secret and his alone long after the tissues vanished and the skeleton parted and the bones sank into the soft ooze. Now let them drag and probe and scrape to their deluded hearts' content.

He rowed back to mid-lake, diagonally fronting the blind, and thereabouts, with an oar plunged straight downward so that his arm was wetted to the shoulder. He made soundings until the paddle blade no longer touched bottom. By taking bearings from the shore, now more plainly seen as a rising breeze carded the mist, he marked this spot. He meant to return to it. He did return after he had rowed into a small eddy above the blind and, standing knee-deep in water, had tilted the skiff on its side and painstakingly had washed it clean of all its fresh red stains.

Then, once more taking along his gun and Pettigrew's and the shells, he went back where he had sounded the depths and cast these articles overboard. But before that, standing in the blind, he had reloaded both guns, and for support of his revised narrative had fired either set of barrels in rapid succession into the air.

He sent one oar adrift here. With the other he sculled his way nearer the bank and climbed overboard in water which was thigh-deep on him. He set the remaining oar free, capsized the skiff and gave it a strong push outward, then held his breath and stooped under, submerging himself entirely. His cap he allowed to lift off his head so that his scalp got thoroughly wet along with the rest of him. He waded ashore, being careful to emerge at a point where he stepped upon springy vegetation which recorded no foot traces, and ran, bareheaded, to give the alarm.

And now here he was, pouring the water out of his boots, and the thing was finished and it was all so fool-proof and so perfect!

Three days went by, then four, then five, and little happened except that Gaul sent messengers across country to the nearest railroad point with telegrams for divers of the dead man's kin and for the executors of the estate. Answers came back and were relayed to him, but none of the senders appeared. They would leave in Gaul's competent hands the melancholy efforts to reclaim the remains of deceased; the wires so stated. This suited Gaul.

He spent the daylight of these five days at Pintail. To the searchers he made it appear that merely a natural anxiety over their failure to recover his friend's body concerned him. He watched while they set off their futile, foolish blasts of dynamite, and inwardly laughed at them behind the mask of a face set to show a deep concern. The explosions created a heavy mortality among the fishes but that was all. A grapnel brought up one of the guns, but the other gun and the shell case remained unfound.

Also Gaul watched Uncle Joe Sam Flint. That venerable person took no active part in these vain proceedings but appeared content to moon about the shores of the lake, a solitary comic figure, always with his gun on his shoulder or in the crook of his elbow.

Once, on an afternoon toward the end of the week, Gaul suffered a passing qualm of apprehensiveness when he beheld the old man on the low bank immediately overlooking the abandoned fish trap. At once though he was able to convince himself that he had no cause for trepidation because about all Flint did — and he did it for at least two hours — was to sit near the water's edge and smoke a pipe and contemplate his surroundings.

He did do just one thing besides these things, and that, to Gaul's way of thinking, was a characteristically stupid thing. He pulled up and fired toward the flocks hovering and darting among the pilings. He didn't hit anything, though. At the shot the frightened birds sped away, but presently returned to their foraging, and shortly after this their disturber betook himself away.

This triviality befell on the afternoon of the fifth day. On the morning of the sixth day, it being a Saturday, only four volunteer searchers appeared, and they knocked off at noon and went to their homes to eat their dinners. Gaul himself was preparing to go to his boarding-place at the widow's when Uncle Joe Sam came trudging up and hailed him.

"Mister," he said, in his friendly nasal drawl, "I wonder would you mind much agoin' out thar jest onc't more with me and show me perzactly whar it were you turned over and all. I'll pull the boat. You see, I've got a kind of a new idee about this here."

Gaul didn't mind. So they boarded the skiff, he sitting in the stern facing the oarsman, and they cruised over a given radius, and patiently Gaul, perhaps for the fiftieth time that week, repeated his mythical narrative.

"I reckon thet'll be enough," Flint said presently, "and much oblige' to you, mister." He gave a hard shove on the oars, then another and a third.

"Hold on," said Gaul, glancing backward over his shoulders. "You're getting off your course, aren't you? We're going away from the bank, not for it."

"I aim to head this here way," explained Flint. "That there old fish-cage jest yonder — that's what I'm headin' fur."

"But why?" Gaul strove to keep any suggestion of uneasiness out of his query.

"Oh, I got another little idee, tha's all. Look at them there near'most stobs stickin' up thar. Count 'em, please, startin' frum this end till you come to the 'leventh."

"I see it — what of it?" Gaul's voice was steady, careless, but the beginnings of a terrible premonition smote on the killer's nerves.

"Well, I aim — ef you don't mind? — to land at that drift pile and let you out. And then, ez a special favour to me — you bein' younger'n I am and lots pearter — I'm agoin' to ast you, please, suh, to take holts of that there 'leventh stob and sort of rastle it loose fur me."

Gaul tensed himself for a spring. It was too late for that. Uncle Joe Sam had released his grips on the oars; they trailed in the oarlocks. He had his gun up ready to snap its butt to his shoulder; its muzzle, slowly lifting, almost brushed Gaul's breast.

"Mebbe" — the old man's tone was gentleness itself — "mebbe, mister, thar's some reason why you wouldn't keer to pull up that thar stob, heh? Well, then, which would you ruther do — have me hold this here fuzee on you and make you pull it up whether or no, or else whilst us two is settin' here with nobody else handy, would you ruther tell me whut's fastened down underneath at the foot of it?"

In the terror which had seized on him and was shaking him to pieces Gaul misinterpreted the motive behind this last. Could it mean this grim old man wanted pay for silence? It must mean that. It had to mean that. He caught at the hope it seemed to offer.

"I — I'll tell you," he cried, "tell you everything!" He did tell, in halting broken sentences, and by the time he had finished telling, the skiff before a puffy wind had drifted ashore at a point not very far from where the footpath broke through the frost-painted woods.

"This'll do fust rate fur a landin'," stated Flint. "Fur the time bein' I reckin we'll jest let that thar stob be. I reckin that'll suit you best. We'll get out here — you fust, please, and stand stiddy, till I kin crawl out." He made no threats, but his gun barrel was eloquent.

Had he tried, Gaul couldn't have run, though. His legs were like columns of soft gelatin under him, and in his ears, like a clashing gong he heard doom ringing, and he had a hideous choked feeling as though a noose was about his throat. In a way of speaking, a noose was.

Obeying a command — but it was in the form of a request most mildly and politely put — he set his hands behind his back and crossed them, and Uncle Joe Sam lashed them together with the tie rope of the skiff. So doing, his captor apologized for the lack of proper bonds:

"I ordered me a set of handcuffs the same time I got me my badge and all. Cost eight dollars, too. The badge come and the diplomy, but they ain't never sent them handcuffs, yit. I'm sorry."

He scooped a palmful of lake water and let it trickle on the knot to shrink it tighter. He wrapped the free end of the rope about his left wrist, leaving perhaps three yards of tether between him and his prisoner. They turned inland.

"Them boys up at the store — they certainly have been thinkin' they had the laugh on me." The old man chuckled softly. "They'll be laughin' t'other sides of their mouths!... Not that way, please, mister," he said then. They had come to where the trail forked under the bluff. "We take the righthand turn. You see," he added painstakingly, as though feeling an explanation were due, "you see, I wouldn't dast take you out past Starbuck's. Them boys mout not feel prone to string you up jest fur killin' yore friend the way you done, but I'm afeared they mout git the notion of takin' you away frum me and stringin' you up fur the way you treated him after he was dead. That would rile 'em up — and then them workin' so long and so hard on your say-so fur nuthin'.

"So we'll just dodge off here to the right and 'leven miles'll bring us to the county seat. We got a nice new county jail over thar. It's a right smart piece fur you to have to walk, but we'll jest jog along slow and take it easy. We'll have to, account of my old laigs."

But it was the old man and not the younger who shambled up the slope and on into the tall timber. Gaul's chin lolled on his breast, and at intervals hard shivers ran through him — through his legs, his body, his twisted pinioned arms. Not once again during the long journey to the new county jail did he speak.

Flint did, though, several times. For example, he presently said: "Mister, mebbe you'd like to know how 'twuz I come to ketch on? Well, I'll tell you. It wuzn't nothin' you said nor nothin' you done. You wuz purty smart, purty slick about it. I got to give you credit fur that. It was somethin' you didn't have no hand in, mister. It wuz a bird!

"Yes, suh, believe it or not, jest ez you're a mind to, that's whut it wuz — a bird. A crow, leastwise a kind of a crow. Not one of them reg'lar crows sich ez is so thick round these parts all the year round, but a bigger kind than whut they air and diffe'nt in his ways. F'r instance, now, he ain't so sharp after cawn and hen aigs ez they are. Seems like his taste runs more fur spiled vittles — carrion and stuff like that, same ez a buzzard's does. I reckin he ain't no keener eye than a buzzard's fur somethin' that's dead, but his smellin' powers is whar he seems to have the aidge on all of them. And smart — it's like ez ef he had second sight.

"He's an old residenter, same ez me. He's been hangin' 'round this lake fur years now — three or four anyways. He ain't got no mate, and I reckin he'd 'a' pulled out long before this, only he's got somethin' chronic the matter with one wing and can't fly so very good. It's a wonder to me how he come to git away in here in the fust place because he don't rightly belong to a country like this.

"A feller that was in here gunnin' two seasons ago, he told me about him. This here feller I'm speakin' of knowed the book names fur birds and all, even ef he hadn't steddied 'em clos't the way I have, and he says to me that this here crow rightly belonged fur away frum here — by the ocean side. Sea crow — that's whut he called him. He 'lowed he must 'a' strayed mighty fur frum headquarters. He marvelled about it, he did so.... Jest a minute, mister, I want to kind of ketch up with my breathin'. Got a kind of stitch in my laig, too."

There was a very short halt, then they went on, the leash drooping and swaying between them, and he droned on:

"Yes, suh, it's likely I wouldn't never 'spicioned nothin' out of the way ef it hadn't been fur that selfsame old crow. We've got to thank him. At the fust, I jest hung round because it seemed like to me, me havin' tuck up detecatin', that it wuz my place to be on hand whilst this here drowndin' business wuz goin' on. That's the main reason I stayed round. But nachelly I kept my eyes peeled, and day before yistiddy 'twas, I tuck note of him — the way he wuz actin' and all. I reckin ef I'd seen him onc't before that I'd seen him a thousand times, but now he wuz actin' funny — fur him.

"Here's whut he wuz doin'. He wuz settin' constant on one of them stobs on that old fish trap along with the kingfishers and the creek cranes and all like that. I knowed whut they wuz thar fur — to ketch 'em some live feed — but whut wuz he thar fur? That's whut floored me. Because he ain't no great hand fur minnows and sunfish. Ef he's goin' to eat fish he'd ruther it'd be washed up on the bank, good and dead.

"But thar he wuz, and somehow I couldn't keep frum watchin' him and I thinks to myself: 'Whut're you up to, anyway?' And after a spell I noticed yit another funny thing about him. I notice that he's stickin' to jest one stob all the time.

"The other birds is flappin' hither and yon, and lightin' fust one place and then another, but he ain't — no, suh. And by grannies, the next I sees is that he's peckin' away, peckin' away with that old big black bill of his'n at the top of that stob like he's tryin' to get at somethin' down in it.

"All that night it stuck in my haid. I like to figger out whut wild things mean when they do a seemin'ly curious thing, because, shore ez shootin', they've always got a sensible meanin' to it. So yestiddy when I come back I looked fur him right off. And shore enough thar he sets on that same stob of his'n and he's peckin' away harder'n ever, seems like. So in the evenin' I tuck a turn round the end of the lake and crope up clos't and now, I could hear him fussin' to himself between licks.

"I comes out in the open whar he kin see me, and still he don't fly away — which ain't like him. So I sets and I steddies and I steddies, and after while I says to myself: 'That there stob he's foolin' with wuz pethy to begin with, it bein' a willow, and its grain runs straight up and down. Mo'over, it's been asettin' thar in the water a long time so probably it's got deep seams in it and water cracks. It don't stand to reason,' I says to myself, 'that that thar old scound'el's tuck a sudden fancy fur willow chips.'

"And right then and thar the beginnin's of a big notion come to me. So I ups and shoots one barrel above him in the air but not clos't enough to hit him. Anyway he goes lickety-split, but, by grannies, he don't go clean away, and that ain't like his nature, neither. He flops round and round and round and then purty soon back he comes, like he's cravin' and can't stay away, and down he drops clos'ter and clos'ter ——"

It was as though by his homely words this old man created a dreadful picture. It penetrated even through his sweated agony of despair to the numbed brain of the murderer so that he saw it and the damnation that was in it — this winged and ravenous undertaker, this black dreadful bird of nemesis, cawing, circling, hovering, descending to worry and tear with a strong greedy beak at the porous tip of a willow stake — a certain stake, always one certain stake.

"Clos'ter and clos'ter he comes and lights ag'in and starts peckin' ag'in... And so that's how-come me to toll you out thar on the lake with me this mawnin' and try that little trick of mine on you, which it certainly worked out right, didn't it, now?... Them blame' boys back at Starbuck's —— Say, mister, I kin shut my eyes and see the fool looks on their faces!"

O. HENRY

SINCE his pen name is the one he is known by, it seems almost affected to call him William Sidney Porter (1862–1910). He was born in Greensboro, North Carolina, had little schooling, at twenty went to Texas, fled from there to Central America, returned to face trial for embezzlement, and upon conviction served three years in the Ohio Federal Penitentiary. He had had previous newspaper experience, but in prison he turned for the first time to fiction — sending out from there his first dozen stories. In 1902 he arrived in New York; by 1903, when he became short-story writer for the Sunday *World*, he had found his literary home and his own style. He is accused of having permanently damaged the short story by his almost mechanical formula — a careless, off-hand manner of telling overlaying a careful, artificial plot of no important substance, but he can be forgiven much for his humor, his keen eye for story material, his genius in making a story move, his creation of a *genre* which may not be the highest art but without which the American short story would be much poorer.

A MUNICIPAL REPORT *

Fancy a novel about Chicago or Buffalo, let us say, or Nashville, Tennessee! There are just three big cities in the United States that are "story cities" — New York, of course, New Orleans, and, best of the lot, San Francisco. — *Frank Norris.*

EAST is East, and West is San Francisco, according to Californians. Californians are a race of people; they are not merely inhabitants of a State. They are the Southerners of the West. Now, Chicagoans are no less loyal to their city; but when you ask them why, they stammer and speak of lake fish and the new Odd Fellows Building. But Californians go into detail.

Of course they have, in the climate, an argument that is good for half an hour while you are thinking of your coal bills and heavy underwear. But as soon as they come to mistake your silence for conviction, madness comes upon them, and they picture the city of the Golden Gate as the Bagdad of the New World. So far, as a matter of opinion, no refutation is necessary. But, dear cousins all (from Adam and Eve descended), it is a rash one who will lay his finger on the map and say: "In this town there can be no romance — what could happen here?" Yes, it is a bold and a rash deed to challenge in one sentence history, romance, and Rand and McNally.

NASHVILLE. — A city, port of delivery, and the capital of the State of Tennessee, is on the Cumberland River and on the N. C. & St. L. and the L. & N. railroads. This city is regarded as the most important educational center in the South.

I stepped off the train at 8 P.M. Having searched the thesaurus in vain for adjectives, I must, as a substitution, hie me to comparison in the form of a recipe.

* From *Strictly Business*, by O. Henry, copyright, 1910, by Doubleday, Doran and Company, Inc.

Take of London fog 30 parts; malaria 10 parts; gas leaks 20 parts; dew-drops gathered in a brick yard at sunrise, 25 parts; odor of honeysuckle 15 parts. Mix.

The mixture will give you an approximate conception of a Nashville drizzle. It is not so fragrant as a moth-ball nor as thick as pea-soup; but 'tis enough — 'twill serve.

I went to a hotel in a tumbril. It required strong self-suppression for me to keep from climbing to the top of it and giving an imitation of Sidney Carton. The vehicle was drawn by beasts of a bygone era and driven by something dark and emancipated.

I was sleepy and tired, so when I got to the hotel I hurriedly paid it the fifty cents it demanded (with approximate lagniappe, I assure you). I knew its habits; and I did not want to hear it prate about its old "marster" or anything that happened "befo' de wah."

The hotel was one of the kind described as "renovated." That means $20,000 worth of new marble pillars, tiling, electric lights and brass cuspidors in the lobby, and a new L. & N. time table and a lithograph of Lookout Mountain in each one of the great rooms above. The management was without reproach, the attention full of exquisite Southern courtesy, the service as slow as the progress of a snail and as good-humored as Rip Van Winkle. The food was worth traveling a thousand miles for. There is no other hotel in the world where you can get such chicken livers *en brochette*.

At dinner I asked a Negro waiter if there was anything doing in town. He pondered gravely for a minute, and then replied. "Well, boss, I don't really reckon there's anything at all doin' after sundown."

Sundown had been accomplished; it had been drowned in the drizzle long before. So that spectacle was denied me. But I went forth upon the streets in the drizzle to see what might be there.

It is built on undulating grounds; and the streets are lighted by electricity at a cost of $32,470 per annum.

As I left the hotel there was a race riot. Down upon me charged a company of freedmen, or Arabs, or Zulus, armed with — no, I saw with relief that they were not rifles, but whips. And I saw dimly a caravan of black, clumsy vehicles; and at the reassuring shouts, "Kyar you anywhere in the town, boss, fuh fifty cents," I reasoned that I was merely a "fare" instead of a victim.

I walked through long streets, all leading uphill. I wondered how those streets ever came down again. Perhaps they didn't until they were "graded." On a few of the "main streets" I saw lights in stores here and there; saw street cars go by conveying worthy burghers hither and yon; saw people pass engaged in the art of conversation, and heard a burst of semi-lively laughter issuing from a soda-water and ice-cream parlor. The streets other than "main" seemed to have enticed upon their borders houses conse-crated to peace and domesticity. In many of them lights shone behind dis-creetly drawn window shades; in a few pianos tinkled orderly and irreproachable music. There was, indeed, little "doing." I wished I had come before sundown. So I returned to my hotel.

> In November, 1864, the Confederate General Hood advanced against Nashville, where he shut up a National force under General Thomas. The latter then sallied forth and defeated the Confederates in a terrible conflict.

All my life I have heard of, admired, and witnessed the fine marksmanship of the South in its peaceful conflicts in the tobacco-chewing regions. But in my hotel a surprise awaited me. There were twelve bright, new, imposing, capacious brass cuspidors in the great lobby, tall enough to be called urns and so widemouthed that the crack pitcher of a lady baseball team should have been able to throw a ball into one of them at five paces distant. But, although a terrible battle had raged and was still raging, the enemy had not suffered. Bright, new, imposing, capacious, untouched, they stood. But, shades of Jefferson Brick! the tile floor — the beautiful tile floor! I could not avoid thinking of the battle of Nashville, and trying to draw, as is my foolish habit, some deductions about hereditary marksmanship.

Here I first saw Major (by misplaced courtesy) Wentworth Caswell. I knew him for a type the moment my eyes suffered from the sight of him. A rat has no geographical habitat. My old friend, A. Tennyson, said, as he so well said almost everything:

> Prophet, curse me the blabbing lip,
> And curse me the British vermin, the rat.

Let us regard the word "British" as interchangeable *ad lib*. A rat is a rat.

This man was hunting about the hotel lobby like a starved dog that had forgotten where he had buried a bone. He had a face of great acreage, red, pulpy, and with a kind of sleepy massiveness like that of Buddha. He possessed one single virtue — he was very smoothly shaven. The mark of the beast is not indelible upon a man until he goes about with a stubble. I think that if he had not used his razor that day I would have repulsed his advances, and the criminal calendar of the world would have been spared the addition of one murder.

I happened to be standing within five feet of a cuspidor when Major Caswell opened fire upon it. I had been observant enough to perceive that the attacking force was using Gatlings instead of squirrel rifles; so I side-stepped so promptly that the major seized the opportunity to apologize to a noncombatant. He had the blabbing lip. In four minutes he had become my friend and had dragged me to the bar.

I desire to interpolate here that I am a Southerner. But I am not one by profession or trade. I eschew the string tie, the slouch hat, the Prince Albert, the number of bales of cotton destroyed by Sherman, and plug chewing. When the orchestra plays Dixie I do not cheer. I slide a little lower on the leather-cornered seat and, well, order another Würzburger and wish that Longstreet had — but what's the use?

Major Caswell banged the bar with his fist, and the first gun at Fort Sumter re-echoed. When he fired the last one at Appomattox I began to hope. But then he began on family trees, and demonstrated that Adam was only a third cousin of a collateral branch of the Caswell family. Genealogy disposed of, he took up, to my distaste, his private family matters. He spoke of his wife, traced her descent back to Eve, and profanely denied any possible rumor that she may have had relations in the land of Nod.

By this time I began to suspect that he was trying to obscure by noise the fact that he had ordered the drinks, on the chance that I would be bewildered into paying for them. But when they were down he crashed a silver dollar loudly upon the bar. Then, of course, another serving was obligatory. And when I had paid for that I took leave of him brusquely; for I wanted no more of him. But before I had obtained my release he had prated loudly of an income that his wife received, and showed a handful of silver money.

When I got my key at the desk the clerk said to me courteously: "If that man Caswell has annoyed you, and if you would like to make a complaint, we will have him ejected. He is a nuisance, a loafer, and without any known means of support, although he seems to have some money most the time. But we don't seem to be able to hit upon any means of throwing him out legally."

"Why, no," said I, after some reflection; "I don't see my way clear to making a complaint. But I would like to place myself on record as asserting that I do not care for his company. Your town," I continued, "seems to be a quiet one. What manner of entertainment, adventure, or excitement have you to offer to the stranger within your gates?"

"Well, sir," said the clerk, "there will be a show here next Thursday. It is — I'll look it up and have the announcement sent up to your room with the ice water. Good night."

After I went up to my room I looked out the window. It was only about ten o'clock, but I looked upon a silent town. The drizzle continued, spangled with dim lights, as far apart as currants in a cake sold at the Ladies' Exchange.

"A quiet place," I said to myself, as my first shoe struck the ceiling of the occupant of the room beneath mine. "Nothing of the life here that gives color and variety to the cities in the East and West. Just a good, ordinary, humdrum, business town."

> Nashville occupies a foremost place among the manufacturing centers of the
> country. It is the fifth boot and shoe market in the United States, the largest
> candy and cracker manufacturing city in the South, and does an enormous
> wholesale drygoods, grocery, and drug business.

I must tell you how I came to be in Nashville, and I assure you the digression brings as much tedium to me as it does to you. I was traveling elsewhere on my own business, but I had a commission from a Northern literary magazine to stop over there and establish a personal connection between the publication and one of its contributors, Azalea Adair.

Adair (there was no clue to the personality except the handwriting) had sent in some essays (lost art!) and poems that had made the editors swear approvingly over their one o'clock luncheon. So they had commissioned me to round up said Adair and corner by contract his or her output at two cents a word before some other publisher offered her ten or twenty.

At nine o'clock the next morning, after my chicken livers *en brochette* (try them if you can find that hotel), I strayed out into the drizzle, which was still on for an unlimited run. At the first corner I came upon Uncle Caesar. He was a stalwart Negro, older than the pyramids, with gray wool and a face that reminded me of Brutus, and a second afterwards of the late King Ccttiwayo. He wore the most remarkable coat that I ever had seen or expect to see. It reached to his ankles and had once been a Confederate gray in colors. But rain and sun and age had so variegated it that Joseph's coat, beside it, would have faded to a pale monochrome. I must linger with that coat, for it has to do with the story — the story that is so long in coming, because you can hardly expect anything to happen in Nashville.

Once it must have been the military coat of an officer. The cape of it had vanished, but all adown its front it had been frogged and tasseled magnificently. But now the frogs and tassels were gone. In their stead had been patiently stitched (I surmised by some surviving "black mammy") new frogs made of cunningly twisted common hempen twine. This twine was frayed and disheveled. It must have been added to the coat as a substitute for vanished splendors, with tasteless but painstaking devotion, for it followed faithfully the curves of the long-missing frogs. And, to complete the comedy and pathos of the garment, all its buttons were gone save one. The second button from the top alone remained. The coat was fastened by other twine strings tied through the buttonholes and other holes rudely pierced in the opposite side. There was never such a weird garment so fantastically bedecked and of so many mottled hues. The lone button was the size of a half-dollar, made of yellow horn and sewed on with coarse twine.

This Negro stood by a carriage so old that Ham himself might have started a hack line with it after he left the ark with the two animals hitched to it. As I approached he threw open the door, drew out a feather duster, waved it without using it, and said in deep, rumbling tones:

"Step right in, suh; ain't a speck of dust in it — jus' got back from a funeral, suh."

I inferred that on such gala occasions carriages were given an extra cleaning. I looked up and down the street and perceived that there was little choice among the vehicles for hire that lined the curb. I looked in my memorandum book for the address of Azalea Adair.

"I want to go to 861 Jessamine Street," I said, and was about to step into the hack. But for an instant the thick, long, gorilla-like arm of the old Negro barred me. On his massive and saturnine face a look of sudden suspicion and enmity flashed for a moment. Then, with quickly returning conviction, he asked blandishingly, "What are you gwine there for, boss?"

"What is that to you?" I asked, a little sharply.

"Nothin', suh, jus' nothin'. Only it's a lonesome kind of part of town and few folks ever has business out there. Step right in. The seats is clean — jes' got back from a funeral, suh."

A mile and a half it must have been to our journey's end. I could hear nothing but the fearful rattle of the ancient hack over the uneven brick paving; I could smell nothing but the drizzle, now further flavored with coal smoke and something like a mixture of tar and oleander blossoms. All I could see through the streaming windows were two rows of dim houses.

> The city has an area of 10 square miles; 181 miles of streets, of which 137 miles are paved; a system of waterworks that cost $2,000,000, with 77 miles of mains.

Eight-sixty-one Jessamine Street was a decayed mansion. Thirty yards back from the street it stood, outmerged in a splendid grove of trees and untrimmed shrubbery. A row of box bushes overflowed and almost hid the paling fence from sight; the gate was kept closed by a rope noose that encircled the gate post and the first paling of the gate. But when you got inside you saw that 861 was a shell, a shadow, a ghost of former grandeur and excellence. But in the story, I have not yet got inside.

When the hack had ceased from rattling and the weary quadrupeds came to a rest I handed my jehu his fifty cents with an additional quarter, feeling a glow of conscious generosity, as I did so. He refused it.

"It's two dollars, suh," he said.

"How's that?" I asked. "I plainly heard you call out at the hotel: 'Fifty cents to any part of the town.'"

"It's two dollars, suh," he repeated obstinately. "It's a long ways from the hotel."

"It is within the city limits and well within them," I argued. "Don't think that you have picked up a greenhorn Yankee. Do you see those hills over there?" I went on, pointing toward the east (I could not see them, myself, for the drizzle); "well, I was born and raised on their other side. You old fool nigger, can't you tell people from other people when you see 'em?"

The grim face of King Cettiwayo softened. "Is you from the South, suh? I reckon it was them shoes of yourn fooled me. They is somethin' sharp in the toes for a Southern gen'l'man to wear."

"Then the charge is fifty cents, I suppose?" said I inexorably.

His former expression, a mingling of cupidity and hostility, returned, remained ten seconds, and vanished.

"Boss," he said, "fifty cents is right; but I *needs* two dollars, suh; I'm obleeged to have two dollars. I ain't *demandin'* it now, suh; after I knows whar you 's from; I'm jus' sayin' that I *has* to have two dollars tonight, and business is mighty po'."

Peace and confidence settled upon his heavy features. He had been luckier than he had hoped. Instead of having picked up a greenhorn, ignorant of rates, he had come upon an inheritance.

"You confounded old rascal," I said, reaching down to my pocket, "you ought to be turned over to the police."

For the first time I saw him smile. He knew; *he knew;* HE KNEW.

I gave him two one-dollar bills. As I handed them over I noticed that one of them had seen parlous times. Its upper right-hand corner was missing, and it had been torn through in the middle, but joined again. A strip of blue tissue paper, pasted over the split, preserved its negotiability.

Enough of the African bandit for the present: I left him happy, lifted the rope and opened the creaky gate.

The house, as I said, was a shell. A paint brush had not touched it in twenty years. I could not see why a strong wind should not have bowled it over like a house of cards until I looked again at the trees that hugged it close — the trees that saw the battle of Nashville and still drew their protecting branches around it against storm and enemy and cold.

Azalea Adair, fifty years old, white-haired, a descendant of the cavaliers, as thin and frail as the house she lived in, robed in the cheapest and cleanest dress I ever saw, with an air as simple as a queen's, received me.

The reception room seemed a mile square, because there was nothing in it except some rows of books, on unpainted white-pine bookshelves, a cracked marble-top table, a rag rug, a hairless horsehair sofa and two or three chairs. Yes, there was a picture on the wall, a colored crayon drawing of a cluster of pansies. I looked around for the portrait of Andrew Jackson and the pine-cone hanging basket but they were not there.

Azalea Adair and I had conversation, a little of which will be repeated to you. She was a product of the old South, gently nurtured in the sheltered life. Her learning was not broad, but was deep and of splendid originality in its somewhat narrow scope. She had been educated at home, and her knowledge of the world was derived from inference and by inspiration. Of such is the precious, small group of essayists made. While she talked to me I kept brushing my fingers, trying, unconsciously, to rid them guiltily of the absent dust from the half-calf backs of Lamb, Chaucer, Hazlitt, Marcus Aurelius, Montaigne and Hood. She was exquisite, she was a valuable discovery. Nearly everybody nowadays knows too much — oh, so much too much — of real life.

I could perceive clearly that Azalea Adair was very poor. A house and a dress she had, not much else, I fancied. So, divided between my duty to the magazine and my loyalty to the poets and essayists who fought Thomas in the valley of the Cumberland, I listened to her voice, which was like a harpsichord's, and found that I could not speak of contracts. In the presence of the nine Muses and the three Graces one hesitated to lower the topic to two cents. There would have to be another colloquy after I had regained my commercialism. But I spoke of my mission, and three o'clock of the next afternoon was set for the discussion of the business proposition.

"Your town," I said, as I began to make ready to depart (which is the time for smooth generalities), "seems to be a quiet, sedate place. A home town, I should say, where few things out of the ordinary ever happen."

It carries on an extensive trade in stoves and hollow ware with the West and South, and its flouring mills have a daily capacity of more than 2,000 barrels.

Azalea Adair seemed to reflect.

"I have never thought of it that way," she said, with a kind of sincere intensity that seemed to belong to her. "Isn't it in the still, quiet places that things do happen? I fancy that when God began to create the earth on the first Monday morning one could have leaned out one's window and heard the drops of mud splashing from His trowel as He built up the ever-lasting hills. What did the noisiest project in the world — I mean the build-ing of the tower of Babel — result in finally? A page and a half of Esperanto in the *North American Review.*"

"Of course," said I platitudinously, "human nature is the same every-where; but there is more color — er — more drama and movement and — er — romance in some cities than in others."

"On the surface," said Azalea Adair. I have traveled many times around the world in a golden airship wafted on two wings — print and dreams. I have seen (on one of my imaginary tours) the Sultan of Turkey bowstring with his own hands one of his wives who had uncovered her face in public. I have seen a man in Nashville tear up his theater tickets because his wife was going out with her face covered — with rice powder. In San Francisco's Chinatown I saw the slave girl Sing Yee dipped slowly, inch by inch, in boiling almond oil to make her swear she would never see her American lover again. She gave in when the boiling oil had reached three inches above her knee. At a euchre party in East Nashville the other night I saw Kitty Morgan cut dead by seven of her schoolmates and lifelong friends because she had married a house painter. The boiling oil was sizzling as high as her heart; but I wish you could have seen the fine little smile that she carried from table to table. Oh, yes, it is a humdrum town. Just a few miles of red brick houses and mud and stores and lumber yards."

Some one knocked hollowly at the back of the house. Azalea Adair breathed a soft apology and went to investigate the sound. She came back in three minutes with brightened eyes, a faint flush on her cheeks, and ten years lifted from her shoulders.

"You must have a cup of tea before you go," she said, "and a sugar cake."

She reached and shook a little iron bell. In shuffled a small Negro girl about twelve, barefoot, not very tidy, glowering at me with thumb in mouth and bulging eyes.

Azalea Adair opened a tiny, worn purse and drew out a dollar bill, a dollar bill with the upper right-hand corner missing, torn in two pieces and pasted together again with a strip of blue tissue paper. It was one of the bills I had given the piratical Negro — there was no doubt of it.

"Go up to Mr. Baker's store on the corner, Impy," she said, handing the girl the dollar bill, "and get a quarter of a pound of tea — the kind he always sends me — and ten cents worth of sugar cakes. Now, hurry. The supply of tea in the house happens to be exhausted," she explained to me.

Impy left by the back way. Before the scrape of her hard, bare feet had died away on the back porch, a wild shriek — I was sure it was hers — filled the hollow house. Then the deep, gruff tones of an angry man's voice mingled with the girl's further squeals and unintelligible words.

Azalea Adair rose without surprise or emotion and disappeared. For two minutes I heard the hoarse rumble of the man's voice; then something like an oath and a slight scuffle, and she returned calmly to her chair.

"This is a roomy house," she said, "and I have a tenant for part of it.

I am sorry to have to rescind my invitation to tea. It was impossible to get the kind I always use at the store. Perhaps tomorrow Mr. Baker will be able to supply me."

I was sure that Impy had not had time to leave the house. I inquired concerning street-car lines and took my leave. After I was well on my way I remembered that I had not learned Azalea Adair's name. But tomorrow would do.

That same day I started in on the course of iniquity that this uneventful city forced upon me. I was in the town only two days, but in that time I managed to lie shamelessly by telegraph, and to be an accomplice — after the fact, if that is the correct legal term — to a murder.

As I rounded the corner nearest my hotel the Afrite coachman of the polychromatic, nonpareil coat seized me, swung open the dungeony door of his peripatetic sarcophagus, flirted his feather duster and began his ritual: "Step right in, boss. Carriage is clean — jus' got back from a funeral. Fifty cents to any ——"

And then he knew me and grinned broadly. "'Scuse me, boss; you is de gen'l'man what rid out with me dis mawnin'. Thank you kindly, suh."

"I am going out to 861 again tomorrow afternoon at three," said I, "and if you will be here, I'll let you drive me. So you know Miss Adair?" I concluded, thinking of my dollar bill.

"I belonged to her father, Judge Adair, suh," he replied.

"I judge that she is pretty poor," I said. "She hasn't much money to speak of, has she?"

For an instant I looked again at the fierce countenance of King Cettiwayo, and then he changed back to an extortionate old Negro hack driver.

"She ain't gwine to starve, suh," he said slowly. "She has reso'ces, suh; she has reso'ces."

"I shall pay you fifty cents for the trip," said I.

"Dat is puffeckly correct, suh,' he answered humbly. "I jus' had to have dat two dollars dis mawnin', boss."

I went to the hotel and lied by electricity. I wired the magazine: "A. Adair holds out for eight cents a word."

The answer that came back was: "Give it to her quick, you duffer."

Just before dinner "Major" Wentworth Caswell bore down upon me with the greetings of a long-lost friend. I have seen few men whom I have so instantaneously hated, and of whom it was so difficult to be rid. I was standing at the bar when he invaded me; therefore I could not wave the white ribbon in his face. I would have paid gladly for the drinks, hoping, thereby, to escape another; but he was one of those despicable, roaring, advertising bibbers who must have brass bands and fireworks attend upon every cent that they waste in their follies.

With an air of producing millions he drew two one-dollar bills from a pocket and dashed one of them upon the bar. I looked once more at the dollar bill with the upper right-hand corner missing, torn through the middle, and patched with a strip of blue tissue paper. It was my dollar bill again. It could have been no other.

I went up to my room. The drizzle and the monotony of a dreary, eventless Southern town had made me tired and listless. I remember that just before I went to bed I mentally disposed of the mysterious dollar bill (which might have formed the clue to a tremendously fine detective story of San Francisco) by saying to myself sleepily: "Seems as if a lot of people here own stock in the Hack-Driver's Trust. Pays dividends promptly, too. Wonder if ——" Then I fell asleep.

King Cettiwayo was at his post the next day, and rattled my bones over the stones out to 861. He was to wait and rattle me back again when I was ready.

Azalea Adair looked paler and cleaner and frailer than she had looked on the day before. After she had signed the contract at eight cents per word she grew still paler and began to slip out of her chair. Without much trouble I managed to get her up on the antediluvian horsehair sofa and then I ran out to the sidewalk and yelled to the coffee-colored Pirate to bring a doctor. With a wisdom that I had not suspected in him, he abandoned his team and struck off up the street afoot, realizing the value of speed. In ten minutes he returned with a grave, gray-haired and capable man of medicine. In a few words (worth much less than eight cents each) I explained to him my presence in the hollow house of mystery. He bowed with stately understanding, and turned to the old Negro.

"Uncle Caesar," he said calmly, "run up to my house and ask Miss Lucy to give you a cream pitcher full of fresh milk and half a tumbler of port wine. And hurry back. Don't drive — run. I want you to get back sometime this week."

It occurred to me that Dr. Merriman also felt a distrust as to the speeding powers of the land-pirate's steeds. After Uncle Caesar was gone, lumberingly, but swiftly, up the street, the doctor looked me over with great politeness and as much careful calculation until he had decided that I might do.

"It is only a case of insufficient nutrition," he said. "In other words, the result of poverty, pride, and starvation. Mrs. Caswell has many devoted friends who would be glad to aid her, but she will accept nothing except from that old Negro, Uncle Caesar, who was once owned by her family."

"Mrs. Caswell!" said I, in surprise. And then I looked at the contract and saw that she had signed it "Azalea Adair Caswell."

"I thought she was Miss Adair," I said.

"Married to a drunken, worthless loafer, sir," said the doctor. "It is said that he robs her even of the small sums that her old servant contributes toward her support."

When the milk and wine had been brought the doctor soon revived Azalea Adair. She sat up and talked of the beauty of the autumn leaves that were then in season, and their height of color. She referred lightly to her fainting seizure as the outcome of an old palpitation of the heart. Impy fanned her as she lay on the sofa. The doctor was due elsewhere, and I followed him to the door. I told him that it was within my power and intentions to make a reasonable advance of money to Azalea Adair on future contributions to the magazine, and he seemed pleased.

"By the way," he said, "perhaps you would like to know that you have had royalty for a coachman. Old Caesar's grandfather was a king in Congo. Caesar himself has royal ways, as you may have observed."

As the doctor was moving off I heard Uncle Caesar's voice inside: "Did he git bofe of dem two dollars from you, Mis' Zalea?"

"Yes, Caesar," I heard Azalea Adair answer weakly. And then I went in and concluded business negotiations with our contributor. I assumed the responsibility of advancing fifty dollars, putting it as a necessary formality in binding our bargain. And then Uncle Caesar drove me back to the hotel.

Here ends all of the story as far as I can testify as a witness. The rest must be only bare statements of facts.

At about six o'clock I went out for a stroll. Uncle Caesar was at his corner. He threw open the door of his carriage, flourished his duster and began his depressing formula: "Step right in, suh. Fifty cents to anywhere in the city — hack's puffickly clean, suh — jus' got back from a funeral ——"

And then he recognized me. I think his eyesight was getting bad. His coat had taken on a few more faded shades of color, the twine strings were more frayed and ragged, the last remaining button — the button of yellow horn — was gone. A motley descendant of kings was Uncle Caesar!

About two hours later I saw an excited crowd besieging the front of a drug store. In a desert where nothing happens this was manna; so I edged my way inside. On an extemporized couch of empty boxes and chairs was stretched the mortal corporeality of Major Wentworth Caswell. A doctor was testing him for the immortal ingredient. His decision was that it was conspicuous by its absence.

The erstwhile Major had been found dead on a dark street and brought by curious and ennuied citizens to the drug store. The late human being had been engaged in terrific battle — the details showed that. Loafer and reprobate though he had been, he had been also a warrior. But he had lost. His hands were yet clinched so tightly that his fingers would not be opened. The gentle citizens who had known him stood about and searched their vocabularies to find some good words, if it were possible, to speak of him. One kind-looking man said, after much thought: "When 'Cas' was about fo'-teen he was one of the best spellers in school."

While I stood there the fingers of the right hand of "the man that was," which hung down the side of a white pine box, relaxed, and dropped something at my feet. I covered it with one foot quietly, and a little later on I picked it up and pocketed it. I reasoned that in his last struggle his hand must have seized that object unwittingly and held it in a death grip.

At the hotel that night the main topic of conversation, with the possible exceptions of politics and prohibition, was the demise of Major Caswell. I heard one man say to a group of listeners:

"In my opinion, gentlemen, Caswell was murdered by some of these no-account niggers for his money. He had fifty dollars this afternoon which he showed to several gentlemen in the hotel. When he was found the money was not on his person."

I left the city the next morning at nine, and as the train was crossing the bridge over the Cumberland River I took out of my pocket a yellow horn overcoat button the size of a fifty-cent piece, with frayed ends of coarse twine hanging from it, and cast it out of the window into the slow, muddy waters below.

I wonder what's doing in Buffalo!

MARTIN STORM

MARTIN STORM writes from Uruapan, Michoacán, Mexico, that he is prospecting in that country, after similar experience in Bolivia and Peru. He suggests the change of title of his story from "A Shipment of Mute Fate," under which name it originally appeared in *Esquire*.

MUTE FATE *

THOUGH the *Chancay* steamed placidly from La Guayra through oily waters, that drowsy afternoon, three of those aboard her were distinctly not themselves. For their several reasons they had lost the tranquillity proper to the captain, the chief steward, and to Mother Willis.

An engineer, humming on his way to wash up, raised a black champion's fist — "Why, Mother, I'm surprised! What's wrong today with my darlin'?" He peered reproachfully into the red eyes of his veteran shipmate. Mother was everybody's pet; a stewardess extraordinary, relic and treasure, she had not missed a voyage of the old *Chancay* for fifteen years.

"Oh, it's the same thing again, Charlie — It's Clara. Mr. Bowman won't stand for an extra cat aboard, but you would think that at a time like this, when she needs the kindest care... How could I help it if she came to me and just asked me to take her in, last winter? I tried to find her a good private home in New York — you know that."

"She was a dirty gray skunk, poor little feller." Feeley grinned at a memory. "Mangy, too. She sat there on the anchor chain, all covered with grease and oil. I says to Bowman, 'I'm afraid we'll have that object with us henceforward,' I says, 'moths and all,' and how he swore! Then she saw you."

"Well, it's only one of the exasperating things that's happened on this sailing day. There's no reason for Mr. Bowman to roar out at her. None of the other chief stewards ever used to say a word. He's too new, that's all! And it seems so cruel just at this time. If I only had her back I'd hide her."

"Where's Clara now?"

"He dumped her right off on the mole, before we pulled out. I better go now and fix supper for that lady's baby in 109. Good night, then, Charlie, dear boy."

Feeley patted her shoulder, staring sadly after the fading lights ashore. "Officers all seems to be cranky right at the start of the run — thassa bad sign. I heard that the old man himself was bawling out Bowman, so probably that's what killed the cat. Well, don't you worry, Mother. Night."

Mrs. Willis did worry as she carefully prepared trays for three baby passengers. She thought of the piteous way Clara had just sat there, abandoned, and glared up at the ship as if too miserable to meow or even move. How

* From *Esquire*, July, 1934. Reprinted here by permission of Martin Storm and of *Esquire*.

could she take care of herself now, on the eve of motherhood again? Something too terrible to imagine would happen to her — and why need all this be? Exactly as Charlie had said, everyone was plain cranky, even the captain, whose business it was to be calm, no matter if a particularly special relative of the company were aboard, pestering him with requests out of order.

What Mrs. Willis did not understand was that this young Warner in his way and despite his father's still ponderous fortune, was desperately in earnest about some things — the more wishful because of physical delicacy to distinguish himself for his own nerve and brains. That was why he had spent an insect-tormented and perilous vacation in hostile jungle above the Orinoco when he could have been at Sands Point. It was why he had made a silent, thrilling vow when the assistant in zoology, returning to New Haven from a spring reptile hunt, remarked to the group he was tutoring that while other poisonous snakes were a drug on the market, with everybody catching them and presenting them to collections, nowhere could you see a live bushmaster. When at Easter he casually asked his father to fix him up a passage on the *Chancay*, that gentleman had no idea that his listless son was already capturing bushmasters in his dreams, though as yet he did not even know what the creatures looked like.

To catch one alive proved a grimly different matter. Once, after weeks on the land and water trail, just once, he had an appalling sight of that mute death coiled upon the forest floor, waiting for them to take the next step, then shifting toward them. No one would help him try to bag it, and presently with insolent leisure it glided back into the depths of jungle. They did not come upon another, to the relief of everybody except Chris Warner, but on the way out the Indians of one unusually ambitious village agreed to see if they could get him any old bushmaster — for an irresistible price. Days after, they returned, bearing the horror in a rubber sack. With shuddering elation he transferred it to his ready canvas.

When the Customs officers learned of the nature of this portion of his baggage, however, they would only exclaim, "Impossible!" — "It is not to be arranged, unfortunately, señor." Since nothing got him any further, Chris wired New York and then went in anxious and indignant haste to his father's employe, Captain Wood of the *Chancay*. "Skipper, I seem to be in a little jam. Last thing I ever expected, any difficulty at this stage. I've spent a whole summer and a lot of money getting a prize I can't even take home! It looks like the whole expedition's wasted, as far as my part of it's concerned — and I can't tell you how much it means to me!"

"Mighty sorry, Christopher. I just cabled your father that I'd have done it for you if I possibly could. He asked me to."

The boy looked startled at this failure of his last recourse. "But I can't see your logic. You took a jaguar up last trip."

The captain glanced over toward the Customs pier where in a box with small, wire-covered openings, protected by an outer crate, his terrible passenger waited to embark. "The worst thing I know, to carry, is right there — the thing you want to take aboard a ship with women passengers. My judgment won't let me do it, even for you, son. Because something could happen, though I don't know what and there's only a chance in a thousand that it would. But those are just the things that do happen — know what I mean? I haven't a choice in the matter. Safety of passengers comes first."

"But with proper precautions? They carry snakes all the time."

"Not this snake they don't — I'd have obliged the scientists long ago — and they always want a bushmaster — if it was some other kind. Why are they so scarce, why are you so anxious now, if anybody'll transport one north? And I'm not superstitious, either, but I know what to be afraid of."

Young Warner left the cabin, seething. To be deprived at the last minute, by an old man's pig-headedness and exaggerated caution, of the one glory of his summer's labor! The unexpected obstacle chafed him intolerably. He made a hasty visit to the bank, then carefully composed a longer cable to New York. Within an hour of sailing time the captain sent ashore for him and with a face averted in displeasure laid down certain conditions. The company had cracklingly "desired" him to do this favor for Mr. Warner's son "if possible," which virtually meant, do it anyway.

"You'll have to put the thing into a box. That flimsy crate's no good."

"Tell you how I'll fix it, skipper." Chris was joyful and placatory. "The snake's got to have some air on this long hot voyage, of course, but I'll put the box with the wire-covered hole into another good stout box, quite a bit larger, with a chain and padlock. Then we can prop the lid up, just half an inch or so, with the box still locked."

"And in dirty weather the lid'll have to be fastened down tight. I'll take no chances."

"Right."

"And the whole thing will be kept during the entire run in my inner cabin, where I sleep. I won't have it in the baggage room." He thought, too late, that it would fortunately have suffocated in the hold.

"Just as you say, skipper, but I was planning to stick the box under my own berth."

As the three blasts of departure sounded from the ship's whistle Captain Wood remembered what was there in his room and his skin prickled, raising up the black hair on his wrists. Then he almost forgot about it, for the steward put a chintz table cover over the mysterious object and they had fine weather through the Caribbean. Not even Chico, the captain's boy, knew that a bushmaster was aboard.

Never for one peaceful instant could Chris Warner forget it. A vague distress brooded over his pleasure in the social life of the voyage. Yet, he kept telling himself, poisonous snakes were shipped often enough — rattlers, copperheads, coral snakes, even cobras could be negotiated if some one responsible were in charge. Why was it different with a bushmaster? Why did every skipper kick, as the captain said they did — and as the scarcity of the serpents proved, even to him — about taking aboard a bushmaster? What could be worse than a cobra? "Cobras will quiet down when they know they're caught," Dr. Sutton had told him last spring. "Some get quite dopey and docile if they're left alone. But a bushmaster's always alert and hostile, even after a feeding. I like most snakes, but not them. Still, I would to God I could get hold of one!"

That sudden glimpse of the creature in the forest returned to him: he saw it lying like a richly colored, horrible mat, with an undulant, S-shaped loop, ready to strike true and instantly at anything. Often it pursued animals not its natural prey with seeming sheer malignance. It boldly followed its own occasions along trails, fearing nothing — never fled. This was the most terrible of all snakes, pantomimed the Indian guide, because it would run right after a man! The natives never attempted a cure for the copious poison that flowed from those great fangs. It bore in earnest its chilling name — Lachesis muta.

On apparently social visits to the captain's quarters he would furtively peer in at his treasure, holding a flashlight to the wire-covered hole. Always he saw it coiled. This one was almost eleven feet long — reddish brown, adorned above with dark lozenges that showed lighter spots on either side, its rough skin glistened like a strange, beauteous fabric, the pale yellow scales on the under part revealing a porcelain glaze. He was sumptuously clad, this ominous minister of the Parcae. But the spade-shaped head was that of very Antichrist.

"You're as white as my apron, Mr. Warner. What's the matter, dear boy?" caressed Mother Willis, meeting him with a pile of towels on the way to lunch.

"Well, I didn't have such a soft time on that jungle hike, Mother. Anyway, weather like this makes you feel low." He went on into the dining-room and strove to take an interest in Roseanne Crane, who sat next at the captain's table. "You know, this is positively a peculiar ship!" she complained. "I don't know exactly what it is, but it's something solemn — even in the smoking-room. Coming down we were all so jolly — foolishness and fun every minute. These elderly new passengers must be to blame!"

"It'll be all right when we run into nice cool weather," he promised her. "They were getting ready for a hurricane last night, I guess, the way the glass dropped, but apparently it was just a false alarm. It's probably off in the Gulf of Mexico by now."

Fine days met them. The sunlit languors of the Indies vanished, and out on the open Atlantic — "Five miles deep here," an officer at taffrail murmured — played brisk winds and hurrying, foam-laced water. It was on a blowy day when the waves looked huge, yet not phenomenal, though mounted on long swells, that a monster green comber arose alone, slapped the ship terrifically to port and boarded her, racing hungrily over empty decks, carrying away a length of the rail, bashing in windows on the A-deck and falling with fury upon the exposed wheel-house of the old-fashioned liner. Water drove through closed doors and tumbled downstairs in little cataracts. Seamen were bruised and the third officer had his leg broken, being hurled across the bridge. But as the captain had ordered all passengers inside half an hour before, they were only shaken up and scared. The carpenter and the doctor went to work, the decks dried off, the sun smiled, and no brother of the awful wave crossed the subsiding sea. Ladies calmed themselves by dressing for dinner, once wardrobe trunks were righted and puddles mopped up.

At the captain's room Chico gave one look and then went to get mops and another steward to help him. It had almost been carried away, along with the wheelhouse, and water sloshed back and forth on the floor. The pillow on the bed was soaked and the mattress lay disarranged and sodden. The heavy desk had charged right across the room; a chest of drawers had fallen over, mixing bay rum with brine. "We'll be working half the night!" Grumpily they righted furniture. "Whole blooming ship's a mess, but we had to get the worst trick, as usual!"

"Poor old swivel-chair's busted for good. That desk must of carried some tonnage."

"It's what the old man's hoarded inside of it. A lifetime's plunder, if you only knew."

"God, look, what —?"

"What where?"

"Something went out over the sill then when the water sloshed. Like a hoseline or sumpin'."

"Search me. This box that the old man was so choice of, that's stove in too."

"Just put it outside. Tell him about it before it goes over."

They had been mopping for half an hour and the room was once more orderly if still very moist, when Captain Wood came in from the bridge, looking drawn and weary, and motioned them to get along.

"We got to bring you another chair, sir. That comber passed right through your bunk on its way out. There's been a good deal of damage done, sir."

"Let it all go till morning — jump below. I'll lie down for twenty minutes before we run into something else." Chico thought "He's getting old" as he took the wet uniform and closed the door behind him, feeling rather sorry. He was recalled by a bellow that brought the officer on watch as well. "What in Holy Jesse have you done with the box that was under this bed?"

"It must have gone slidin' and floatin' around, captain. Anyway, something's fell on it — the bureau maybe — or the old desk charged up against it. Anyway ——"

"Where is it?"

"We was just going to pitch it over. It's broke so it's no good now, captain."

"There were two boxes, one inside of the other."

"Only look for yourself, sir. Split like kindling."

The captain closed the door and alone faced a room which he believed held death. For a moment he could not stir from that one little space in the middle of the floor — where he could see. He switched on every light and took out his flashlight, but a cold and slowly mounting horror, goading his weariness into tense vigilance, half paralyzed him.

He bent over at last, drew back, waited though another interval, and then forced himself to pass the light along under the bed. With a ruler he pushed open the closet door, standing well away, but no lidless eyes reflected the searching beam. He knocked the cushions from the wall-bench, lifted up the chintz curtain, holding his revolver ready. Nothing was there. If only it had been there! If only he himself, the man responsible, could have been the first and the last to meet it!

He pulled on his heavy coat and gave an order. "Send the chief steward and the purser right up. The chief, too, if he can come. Call the first officer."

As he stood before the small, grave conference, telling them hastily what had happened, he hoped that somehow the thing might not seem so horrible to them as now it was to him. One of these resourceful and experienced men could perhaps think of something to do — together. With a plan of action made the horror would lessen. Over their heads he saw young Warner's white face appear in the open door. He told him to step in.

"It would be easier if we didn't have to let all the crew and passengers know," said the mate. "It's panic I'm scared of. That's the most dangerous thing there is at sea, in my experience. Then lots of people — the lady passengers, the ignorant black gang — they'll be sort of fanatical. Just one ordinary snake loose on board would be enough to drive the whole bunch..."

"Why do we have to tell?" suggested the purser.

"Think what you're saying, Mr. Kane. Who knows where it is, where it's gone? In fairness they've got to be put on guard, every one of 'em, passengers and crew."

"It might have crawled overboard."

"That's the one hope, sir."

"And then again there's not a place on the ship where it might not be, except the boilers and the galley stove. I had the Number Two hatch open, just now, to make sure no water had got through to that dry goods. It might have slid down there by this time."

"It might be in a fire-bucket, or one of the lifeboats — or a baby's bed."

Chris Warner had not spoken. He was arguing with himself, "But such a snake as that — it was so long, so awful to look at, how can it hide?" He turned hurriedly, but the captain detained him. "No one is to leave until we all decide exactly what to do."

"Captain," said Bowman, "all we can do is go now and look everywheres. I'll start now and take along a few boys I can trust for sense. Then if we haven't found anything by dark..."

"It's getting dark early tonight."

"Excuse me, captain — I don't think that's just." The purser was resolute. "Everyone aboard is in equal, constant danger. Everyone's got to look out for himself. Every living soul ought to be told right away. Or we might make one quick, thorough search."

"You don't know what the effect may be, to tell them — my God! I've seen passengers panicky at sea before."

"But it's right that everyone should be warned. At this minute that damned snake may be coiled under some woman's berth. We have to tell! There's nothing else to do."

"Anyway we can't make a search of the whole ship without giving reasons. Sooner or later someone will find out. We don't want it to be too late."

Captain Wood was surprised that he felt no real anger at Chris, sitting there so miserably without stirring or speaking, enduring a remorse that he alone could understand, along with the weight of the unuttered blame of the others: a feeling worse than fear. "We'll search now," he decided. "Afterward, if we have no luck, each steward will tell the passengers in his rooms, trying not to alarm them, and the officers will tell the crew. Don't worry so, Christopher — we'll give you one of the hardest places. Go take a look around the baggage room. It's been open — since?"

"Probably, sir. Some ladies usually want to get a trunk for something, just before dinner." The chief steward was actually making some notes. His wrist shook. The peculiar dread that now informed the atmosphere seemed to render all their movements stiff. It was difficult to step freely... to breathe...

Captain Wood apportioned the ship among them, and with a strained nonchalance that puzzled passengers who chanced to be watching they moved about decks, corridors and general rooms, interested, apparently, in everything.

But no long reddish body marked with dark lozenges glided at them over the carpet nor lay coiled in a corner nor outstretched above a curtain pole. No deadly viper's head lifted from the gathering shadows. Alone in the dusky baggage room with its numberless lurking places, Chris turned sick and stood still in the middle of the floor, just as the captain had done in his cabin. Then he too forced himself to step about, to poke, to look. "This with the blame besides!" How did they know before? — How did they know that something always happens if you take a bushmaster aboard a ship? What is there about this one snake... Trembling and sweating, he kept up the search. He did not leave one dark corner without thrusting in his long stick, always thinking that this time surely death must rush out after it.

They all met again in the captain's room. No one had found any sign. The passengers would have to be warned.

The slow nightmare that followed and grew more frightful hour by hour was rarely relieved by natural sleep. Soon they could hardly eat or rest. Fear was a heavy fog in the lungs of the whole ship's company: they dreaded to move. Only the babies played happily, not reading the terror in their parents' wakeful eyes.

But as yet it remained a quiet, freezing fear. It had not broken into panic. Then, in full sight of many passengers, two colored stokers raced along the deck and leaped yelling into the sea. They went right down in the smother. Everyone thought that they must have seen the snake, but it was not found, and Bowman decided that they had merely gone crazy thinking about it. A few hours afterward an elderly woman turned to the group beside her and remarked seriously, "If we could only get off this ship we could fumigate it." Then she, too, suddenly made for the sea, but a steward caught her. Down in her little dark inside room, which she could hardly bear to enter now, even with a bright light, Mother Willis tried to sip some good hot tea and keep going. The women passengers needed her more than ever before, and the poor babies.

Starboard on the bridge the captain stood in a whooping rain-squall and prayed into its rush. "Three days and we'll be in — Lord, let nothing happen for three more days!" A wireless to the office had brought back prompt instructions to "Keep quiet and keep coming." Such a situation lost horror, no doubt, in the safe office. Well, there was no use asking other ships for help, anyway. Short of taking off all the passengers what could they do? And then the crew wouldn't stay. To keep his head, he always tried to believe that the bushmaster had gone overboard. That, too, was what Mother Willis told hysterical women who could not spend a third night awake with all the lights on, and who yet could not sleep; who screamed at the dark. "But you don't know," jabbered Mrs. Crane at her, all at once an old woman. "Nobody knows! And if anyone goes to sleep it may come through a ventilator. It may drop from somewhere. It may be in the bathroom. I can't turn my back — to anything — I keep whirling around!" The inescapable pursuit ceaselessly wore at them, and by some it could no longer be borne. A Venezuelan woman gave quieting medicine to herself and her baby until both were safe forever. "I wish I could get out of this that easy," thought Chris, ready to crack as he kept at his awful job of listening, peering, leaping back from nothing.

There were no longer nights and days. Only the light became the intolerable darkness. Some felt that they were always being watched by lidless eyes; some knew that they had heard the long body flop to the floor. For everyone it lay coiled beneath his bunk. With men calm to the sea's dangers but almost driven to run amok under the strain of this unknown, invisible horror the officers fought to keep up ship's discipline, their own minds invaded and shaken by the fanged uncertainty.

Carrying his flashlight for any treacherous corner the chief steward went at seven bells to the galley to see if all had been left neat for the night. Yes — only the watchman's coffee-pot stood on the shining stove. He turned to leave, and from the pan closet that ran along the floor to his left he saw two unwinking eyes give back the light. The bushmaster waited there among the tins, and as Bowman hesitated for an instant it began slowly to undulate over the sill, between him and the door. He could hear the faint scratching of its long scales. No heavy object that a man could move was within reach to throw at it. He carried only the flashlight. The call button was over by the door. He longed to yell but did not dare, lest any sound or movement hasten the thing after him or cause it to vanish.

The snake paused with half of its length out of the cupboard, then taking its own time emerged entirely and lay coiled like a patterned kitchen mat by the stove. With wonder Bowman perceived that it was staring not at him but past him. And something else was moving, back under the sink. Despite himself he had to turn his head and look.

Slowly stepping toward the snake until she was just out of striking range came a gray, mangy skeleton of a cat. She confronted the coiled enemy, each gazing at the other with unwinking eyes.

Suddenly, and almost too quickly for sight, the bushmaster struck, and as quickly the cat evaded the lance-thrust of that spade-shaped head. Again and again it just missed her body and then as the snake began to tire a little she countered with one precise spat of a sharp-clawed paw. Now every time that the head shot out she caught it on her claws, just at the end of the lunge, bracing her absurdly meagre frame. Before Bowman grasped her strategy she had blinded the bushmaster in both lidless eyes.

It struck wildly and more rapidly, but always the countering paw was exactly there at the point and instant when its small strength could avail. The monster coiled no more, but slid after her in fury, eyes ripped, as she danced out of its way. With the agility of desperation Bowman made one leap above the melee and got his legs over the edge of the sink. Now the cat darted in among the twisting folds and fixed her teeth just in back of the great jaws; there with tooth and claw she clung. Lashing and flailing, striving to keep its crushing coils around her, the bushmaster thrashed about the galley, but both power and venom were used up; its wounds were mortal. The rough folds slackened at last.

In them Clara lay dead. Bowman saw, then, why she had challenged such an adversary and why she could not lose the fight, for out from under the sink, their tails straight as pokers, their eyes bright with curiosity, crept three new kittens. He gathered them up hastily and went with them toward Mother Willis's room.

DRAMA

THE first important fact to keep in mind when one reads a play is that it was written to be acted in a theater, not read in a book. Strictly speaking, drama is not a part of literature but rather an independent art, or better, a combination of arts, whose life depends upon the spoken word — sometimes (as in the case of pantomime) upon the implied word. If the manuscript of a play is printed, it is as if the manuscript of a musical composition is printed, with one important difference, since, whereas most people can read words, only a few highly trained persons can read a musical score silently and get out of it the color, the movement, the significance which the composer intended. Yet neither the symphony nor the tragedy comes to life until it is performed.

But because words are a better understood means of communication than the series of abstract and highly conventionalized signs which register music on the printed page, it is possible for most persons to imagine what a play will be like in the theater, provided that in reading its text they do not treat it like a work of fiction. In reading a work of fiction we have done enough if we permit the author to carry us along on a single plane of the imagination; we listen to a monologue, more or less entertaining; we see in our mind's eyes only as the author bids us see, hear only what he tells us to hear, and understand only what he wants us to understand. In reading a play, on the other hand, a greater responsibility rests upon us: the author has disappeared, and in his place are only the briefest of stage directions and the most compressed and essential parts of the characters' words.

These stage directions and these words it is the business of the reader to make "come alive" in his imagination. If he is blessed with a lively visual imagination, when he sits down to read a play, he should enter a tiny theater in his own mind. On this internal stage a strong light is suddenly snapped on; the curtain is raised; the stage is set for the first act according to the directions of the dramatist; and on this tiny stage the characters enter, speak their lines, gesticulate, smile, weep, or are silent according to the words and pauses set down for them. Indeed, so much more vivid and satisfactory was this mental theater to a man like Charles Lamb that, with all his love of the actual stage, he pretended that the plays of Shakespeare could not be as satisfactorily performed by living actors as they were in the theater of Lamb's imagination.

If one is not blessed with an imagination of this sort, the next best thing is to read the play aloud, assuming the various parts, and indicating by changes in one's voice (however unconvincing this may be to the unsympathetic ear of someone else) the various rôles and the various emotions. Thus it is that one can force one's self to enter into the separate personalities of the play. Or, if others can be persuaded to help, the rôles can be distributed, the stage directions followed as far as may be practicable; and suddenly that which was words before springs alive as drama and passes from the gray, one-dimensional form of badly constructed fiction to the vivid, three-dimensional, and completed form of drama. One does not need costumes and a theater to bring a printed play "alive," however desirable these things may be; as the younger Dumas said, when he was asked what is necessary for a play, "Four boards and two trestles, three actors and a passion."

As for the structure of drama, there are those who declare it is one of the most difficult of art forms, and those who say it is one of the simplest. Good plays have been written under both theories. A theatrical performance succeeds only when it holds people in the theater, whether it be trick bicycle riding (a perpetual dramatic conflict between the rider and the possibility of his fall, the hero usually being successful), or whether Hamlet in all the panoply of woe, mix philosophy, poetry, and melodrama in one of the immortal masterpieces of the stage. A play does not usually succeed unless it contain a probable and humanly important conflict — although even this principle has, on occasion, been successfully violated. The conflict of men with men, of man with nature, of human impulses and desires with laws or principles supposed to be universal or absolute — such are the themes of drama. These themes also appear in literature, as in fiction or poetry; in drama, however, the conflict is foreshortened, telescoped, compressed, made more vivid and laughable or more appalling and tragic, for the world of the theater is a world of compressed time, of narrower space, of more violent emotion and intenser life.

Until modern times the formal division of plays into comedies and tragedies long maintained, tragedy (in Europe at least) being a stately play in five acts of a grand order conforming to certain well-established aesthetic principles, and comedy, usually in three acts, having a less exalted manner, a more "realistic" tone, and a looser structure. In the course of years new kinds of plays arose, old distinctions tended to be blotted out, audiences were unwilling to spend as much time in the theater as they had formerly done, new modes of lighting and scenery rendered unnecessary much expository and descriptive material; and as a consequence one finds in the modern theater not comedy and tragedy in the older sense, but melodrama, farce comedy, comedy drama, and drama. One notes also theatrical performances which to a greater or less degree involve music, such as the musical review, musical comedy, comic opera, and, of course grand opera or music drama. The ancestry of each of these types may be traced backward almost as far as the inquirer wants to look.

Two types of modern dramatic entertainment are illustrated in this book: *The Green Goddess*, an excellent melodrama, turning on one of the oldest tricks of the theater, namely, the rescue of captives from a seemingly impossible and fatal situation; *Journey's End*, an example of that serious or tragic drama which has replaced formal tragedy in the modern theater.

In melodrama, the playwright, selecting a simple "strong" situation, exercises his ingenuity in pushing the boundaries of that situation to the utmost verge of probability. Here the attack upon the emotions of the audience is simple and direct, and there is no room for nuances of character. Strongly marked contrast is one of the dramatist's most useful devices. Thus in *The Green Goddess* the physical setting of the play offers such violent disharmonies as the Himalaya Mountains and a store of Parisian frocks, the fortress of the Raja, and the radio and the airplane. Character also exhibits these contrasts. The Raja is compounded of European sophistication and Oriental amoralism; Crespin, apparently a disagreeable reprobate, redeems himself by a shining death; Watkins, who first appears as comic relief, concludes by being an unspeakable villain justly punished by a violent end. Motives are simple; thus Mrs. Crespin is any woman of a certain class and type torn between a high concept of honor and mother-love, the conflict being satisfactorily resolved by the death of Crespin. The play is most ingenious in its mechanism. Note, for example, the recurrence of the green goddess in the various scenes, always in contrast with such "modern" devices as an airplane, the salon in the castle, and so on. Note how, from the opening group of "dark and rudely-clad natives, rather Mongolian in feature," to the using up of the (apparently) last possible moment of time, the dramatist cunningly insists upon the isolation of the Europeans. Note the "holding" of the final tableau: the rescuing force presents itself in the apparently inadequate shape of "a mere boy" and three soldiers; first one bomb, then another, and then a third have to explode; and even then the Raja does not yield until the priests themselves insist on giving up the captives. Note also the obvious but nonetheless adroit use of humor in the final speeches rapidly to let down tension.

In contrast to the elaborate mechanism of *The Green Goddess*, the plot of *Journey's End* is simplicity itself. A young and inexperienced officer seeks out an admired elder friend rendered morbid by the intolerable strain of life in the trenches; a series of misunderstandings arises, held in check by an older officer until his death; the young officer dies, leaving his friend without a single companion, but not before a reconciliation has taken place. Everything depends upon character, and with what insight, with what sympathy the dramatist has presented his men! We participate in their every emotion, we live equally the life of Osborne, of Stanhope, of Raleigh, even of Trotter, Private Mason, and the German soldier. We feel that each is himself, that the frictions which arise are inevitable; we cry out against the pitiless caprice of war when Osborne is killed and welcome the death of Raleigh with relief, since it is a cheap price to pay for the sense of calm, of peace, of reconciliation with which the final curtain ends the suffering of the characters — and our own.   Yet we feel that the human values — affection, duty, humor — transcend the trivial fact that these men die in a senseless bravura of stupidity.   The recurrence in act after act of the same setting, the ceaseless sound of the guns, the concentration upon a few characters, the elimination of the conventional love element from the play, so that everything arises from men's values — all these elements hold us to the simple and merciless fact of human tragedy.   The play is a well-nigh flawless example of its kind.

WILLIAM ARCHER

A GENUINE force in the English dramatic world for nearly fifty years, William Archer (1856–1924) was born in Scotland, received piecemeal schooling, but spent much of his early life in Norway, which he loved from the beginning, and where he learned the language thoroughly. This led to his early interest in Ibsen, whose works he later edited and whom he helped popularize in England. He began writing for newspapers in 1873, became dramatic critic for (London) *Figaro* in 1878, for the *World* in 1884, and for other leading papers in subsequent years, in the course of which he exerted a profound influence on dramatic affairs. In 1920, wishing to assure himself of an adequate retiring income, he tried his hand at his first play — *The Green Goddess*. A brilliant success from the start, it is still considered a model of play-making and a triumphant demonstration of Archer's dramatic theories.

THE GREEN GODDESS *

CHARACTERS

THE RAJA OF RUKH.
WATKINS, *his valet.*
MAJOR ANTONY CRESPIN.
LUCILLA, *his wife.*
DOCTOR BASIL TRAHERNE.
LIEUTENANT DENIS CARDEW.
  Priests, Villagers, Regular and Irregular Troops, Servants, and an unseen multitude.

SCENE — *A remote region at the back of the Himalayas.*

ACT I

SCENE. — *A region of gaunt and almost treeless mountains, uniformly grey in tone, except in so far as the atmosphere lends them colour. Clinging to the mountain wall in the background, at an apparent distance of about a mile, is a vast barbaric palace, with long stretches of unbroken masonry, crowned by arcades and turrets.*

The foreground consists of a small level space between two masses of rock. In the rock on the left a cave-temple has been roughly hewn. Two thick and rudely-carved pillars divide it into three sections. Between the pillars, in the middle section, can be seen the seated figure of a six-armed Goddess, of forbidding

---

* Reprinted with permission of and by special arrangement with Alfred A. Knopf, Inc., authorized publishers.

aspect, coloured dark green. In front of the figure is a low altar with five or six newly-severed heads of goats lying at its base. The temple is decorated with untidy and mouldering wreaths and other floral offerings.

The open space between the two rock masses forms a rudely-paved forecourt to the temple. It is bordered by smaller idols and three or four round-headed stone posts, painted green.

Mountain paths wind off behind the rocks, and through the low shrubs, both to right and left.

Projecting over the rock-mass on the right can be seen the wing of an aeroplane, the nacelle and under-carriage hidden. It has evidently just made a rather disastrous forced landing.

The pilot and two passengers are in the act of extricating themselves from the wreck, and clambering down the cliff. The pilot is DR. BASIL TRAHERNE; *the passengers are* MAJOR ANTONY CRESPIN *and his wife* LUCILLA. TRAHERNE *is a well set-up man, vigorous and in good training.* CRESPIN, *somewhat heavy and dissipated-looking, is in khaki.* LUCILLA *is a tall, slight, athletic-woman, wearing a tailor-made tweed suit. All three on their first appearance wear aviation helmets and leather coats. The coats they take off as occasion offers.*

Their proceedings are watched with wonder and fear by a group of dark and rudely-clad natives, rather Mongolian in feature. They chatter eagerly among themselves. A man of higher stature and more Aryan type, the PRIEST *of the temple, seems to have some authority over them.*

As soon as all three newcomers have descended, the PRIEST *gives some directions to a young man among the bystanders, who makes off at great speed. He is a messenger to the castle.*

LUCILLA [*to* CRESPIN, *who is at a difficult point, and about to jump*]. Take care, Antony! Let Dr. Traherne give you a hand.

TRAHERNE [*already on the ground*]. Yes.

CRESPIN. Hang it all, I'm not such a crock as all that. [*Jumps heavily, but safely.*]

TRAHERNE. Are you all right, Mrs. Crespin? Not very much shaken?

LUCILLA. Not a bit.

TRAHERNE. It was a nasty bump.

LUCILLA. You managed splendidly.

CRESPIN. Come on, Lu — sit on that ledge, and I can swing you down.

TRAHERNE. Let me ——

[CRESPIN *and* TRAHERNE *support her as she jumps lightly to the ground.*]

LUCILLA. Thank you.

CRESPIN. That last ten minutes was pretty trying. I don't mind owning that my nerves are all of a twitter. [*Producing a pocket flask, and pouring some of its contents into the cup.*] Have a mouthful, Traherne?

TRAHERNE. No, thank you.

CRESPIN [*to* LUCILLA]. You won't, I know. I will. [*Drinks off the brandy, then pours and drinks again.*] That's better! — And now — where are we, Doctor?

TRAHERNE. I have no notion.

CRESPIN. Let's ask the populace.

[*The natives have been standing at some distance, awestruck, but chattering eagerly among themselves. The* PRIEST, *intently watching, is silent.* CRESPIN *advances towards him, the natives meanwhile shrinking back in fear. The* PRIEST *salaams slightly and almost contemptuously.* CRESPIN *addresses him in Hindustani, which he evidently does not understand. He in turn pours forth a speech of some length, pointing to the temple and the palace.* CRESPIN *can make nothing of it. While this is proceeding:*]

TRAHERNE [*in a low voice, to* LUCILLA]. You were splendid, all through!

LUCILLA. I had perfect faith in *you.*

TRAHERNE. If I'd had another pint of petrol, I might have headed for that sort of esplanade behind the castle ——

LUCILLA. Yes, I saw it.

TRAHERNE. — and made an easy landing. But I simply *had* to try for this place, and trust to luck.

LUCILLA. It wasn't luck, but your skill, that saved us.

TRAHERNE. You are very good to me.

CRESPIN [*turning*]. It's no use — he doesn't understand a word of Hindustani. You know Russian, don't you, Doctor?

TRAHERNE. A little.

CRESPIN. We must be well on towards Central Asia. Suppose you try him in Russian. Ask him where the hell we are, and who owns the shooting-box up yonder. [TRAHERNE *says something to the* PRIEST *in Russian.*]

The PRIEST [*his face lighting up, points to the earth, and then makes an enveloping gesture to signify the whole country, saying:*] Rukh, Rukh, Rukh, Rukh.

CRESPIN. What the deuce is he Rooking about?

TRAHERNE. Goodness knows.

LUCILLA. I believe I know. Wait a minute. [*Feeling in her pockets.*] I thought I had the paper with me. I read in the *Leader*, just before we started, that the three men who murdered the Political Officer at Abdulabad came from a wild region at the back of the Himalayas, called Rukh.

TRAHERNE. Now that you mention it, I *have* heard of the place. [*He turns to the* PRIEST *and says a few more words in Russian, pointing to the palace. The* PRIEST *replies "Raja Sahib" several times over.*]

CRESPIN. Oh, it's Windsor Castle, is it? Well, we'd better make tracks for it. Come, Lucilla. [*The* PRIEST, *much excited, stops his way, pouring forth a stream of unintelligible language.* TRAHERNE *says something to him in Russian, whereupon he pauses and then says two or three words, slowly and with difficulty — one of them "Raja."*]

TRAHERNE. His Russian is even more limited than mine; but I gather that the Raja has been sent for and will come here.

CRESPIN [*lighting a cigarette*]. All right — then we'd better await developments. [*Seats himself on a green-painted stone. As the* PRIEST *sees this, he makes a rush, hustles* CRESPIN *off, with wild exclamations, and then, disregarding him, makes propitiatory gestures, and mutters formulas of deprecation, to the stone.*]

CRESPIN [*very angry, lays his hand on his revolver-case*].   Confound you, take care what you're doing!   You'd better treat us civilly, or ——

TRAHERNE [*laying a hand on his arm*].   Gently, gently, Major.   This is evidently some sort of sacred enclosure, and you were sitting on one of the gods.

CRESPIN.   Well damn him, he might have told me ——

TRAHERNE.   If he had, you wouldn't have understood.   The fellow seems to be the priest — you see, he's begging the god's pardon.

CRESPIN.   If I knew his confounded lingo, I'd jolly well make him beg mine.

TRAHERNE.   We'd better be careful not to tread on their corns.   We have Mrs. Crespin to think of.

CRESPIN.   Damn it, sir, do you think I don't know how to take care of my own wife?

TRAHERNE.   I think you're a little hasty, Major — that's all.   These are evidently queer people, and we're dependent on them to get us out of our hobble.

LUCILLA [*down, right*].   Do you think I could sit on this stone without giving offense to the deities?

TRAHERNE.   Oh, yes, that seems safe enough.   [*After* LUCILLA *is seated*.] I don't know how to apologize for having got you into this mess.

LUCILLA.   Don't talk nonsense, Dr. Traherne.   Who can foresee a Himalayan fog?

TRAHERNE.   The only thing to do was to get above it, and then, of course, my bearings were gone.

LUCILLA.   Now that we're safe, I should think it all great fun if it weren't for the children.

CRESPIN.   Oh, they don't expect us for a week, and surely it won't take us more than that to get back to civilization.

TRAHERNE.   Or, at all events, to a telegraph line.

LUCILLA.   I suppose there's no chance of flying back?

TRAHERNE.   Not the slightest, I'm afraid.   I fancy the old 'bus is done for.

LUCILLA.   Oh, Dr. Traherne, what a shame!   And you'd only had it a few weeks!

TRAHERNE.   What does it matter so long as *you* are safe?

LUCILLA.   What does it matter so long as we're *all* safe?

CRESPIN.   That's not what Traherne said.   Why pretend to be blind to his — chivalry?

TRAHERNE [*trying to laugh it off*].   Of course I'm glad you're all right, Major, and I'm not sorry to be in a whole skin myself.   But ladies first, you know.

CRESPIN.   The perfect knight errant, in fact!

TRAHERNE.   Decidedly "errant."   I couldn't well have gone more completely astray.

LUCILLA.   Won't you look at the machine and see if it's quite hopeless?

TRAHERNE.   Yes, at once.   [*He goes towards the wreck of the aeroplane and passes out of sight.   The populace clustered in and around the temple on the left are intent upon the marvel of the aeroplane, but the* PRIEST *fixes his gaze upon* CRESPIN *and* LUCILLA.]

CRESPIN [*sits beside* LUCILLA *on the stone*]. Well, Lucilla!

LUCILLA. Well?

CRESPIN. That was a narrow squeak.

LUCILLA. Yes, I suppose so.

CRESPIN. All's well that ends well, eh?

LUCILLA. Of course.

CRESPIN. You don't seem very grateful to Providence.

LUCILLA. For sending the fog?

CRESPIN. For getting us down safely — all three.

LUCILLA. It was Dr. Traherne's nerve that did that. If he hadn't kept his head ——

CRESPIN. We should have crashed. One or other of us would probably have broken his neck; and if Providence had played up, it might have been the right one.

LUCILLA. What do you mean?

CRESPIN. It might have been me. Then you'd have thanked God, right enough!

LUCILLA. Why *will* you talk like this, Antony? If I hadn't sent Dr. Traherne away just now, you'd have been saying these things in his hearing.

CRESPIN. Well, why not? He's quite one of the family? Don't tell me he doesn't know all about the "state of our relations," as they say in the divorce court.

LUCILLA. If he does, it's not from me. No doubt he knows what the whole station knows.

CRESPIN. And what does the whole station know? Why, that your deadly coldness drives me to drink. I've lived for three years in an infernal clammy fog like that we passed through. Who's to blame if I take a whiskey-peg now and then, to keep the chill out?

LUCILLA. Oh, Antony, why go over it all again? You know very well it was drink — and other things — that came between us; not my coldness, as you call it, that drove you to drink.

CRESPIN. Oh, you good women! You patter after the parson "Forgive us as we forgive those that trespass against us." But you don't know what forgiveness means.

LUCILLA. What's the use of it, Antony? Forgive? I have "forgiven" you. I don't try to take the children from you, though it might be better for them if I did. But to forgive is one thing, to forget another. When a woman has seen a man behave as you have behaved, do you think it is possible for her to forget it, and to love him afresh? There are women in novels, and perhaps in the slums, who have such short memories; but I am not one of them.

CRESPIN. No, by God, you're not! So a man's whole life is to be ruined ——

LUCILLA. Do you think yours is the only life to be ruined?

CRESPIN. Ah, there we have it! I've not only offended your sensibilities;

I am in your way. You love this other man, this model of all the virtues!

LUCILLA. You have no right to say that.

CRESPIN [*disregarding her protest*]. He's a paragon. He's a wonder. He's a mighty microbe-killer before the Lord; he's going to work Heaven knows what miracles, only he hasn't brought them off yet. And you're cursing the mistake you made in marrying a poor devil of a soldier-man instead of a first-class scientific genius. Come! Make a clean breast of it! You may as well!

LUCILLA. I have nothing to answer. While I continue to live with you, I owe you an account of my actions — but not of my thoughts.

CRESPIN. Your actions? Oh, I know very well you're too cold — too damned respectable — to kick over the traces. And then you have the children to think of.

LUCILLA. Yes; I have the children.

CRESPIN. Besides, there's no hurry. If you only have patience for a year or two, I'll do the right thing for once, and drink myself to death.

LUCILLA. You have only to keep yourself a little in hand to live to what they call "a good old age."

CRESPIN. 'Pon my soul, I've a mind to try to, though goodness knows my life is not worth living. I was a fool to come on this crazy expedition ——

LUCILLA. Why, it was you yourself that jumped at Dr. Traherne's proposal.

CRESPIN. I thought we'd get to the kiddies a week earlier. *They'd* be glad to see me, poor little things. *They* don't despise their daddy.

LUCILLA. It shan't be my fault, Antony, if they ever do. But you don't make it easy to keep up appearances.

CRESPIN. Oh, Lu, Lu, if you would treat me like a human being — if you would help me and make life tolerable for me, instead of a thing that won't bear looking at except through the haze of drink — we might retrieve the early days. God knows I never cared two pins for any woman but you ——

LUCILLA. No, the others, I suppose, only helped you, like whiskey, to see the world through a haze. *I* saw the world through a haze when I married you; but you have dispelled it once for all. Don't force me to tell you how impossible it is for me to be your wife again. I am the mother of your children — that gives you a terrible hold over me. Be content with that.

TRAHERNE. [*Still unseen, calls:*] Oh, Mrs. Crespin! [*He appears, clambering down from the aeroplane.*] I've found in the wreck the newspaper you spoke of — you were right about Rukh.

CRESPIN [*as* TRAHERNE *comes forward*]. What does it say?

TRAHERNE [*reads*]. "Abdulabad, Tuesday. Sentence of death has been passed on the three men found guilty of the murder of Mr. Haredale. It appears that these miscreants are natives of Rukh, a small and little-known independent state among the northern spurs of the Himalayas."

LUCILLA. Yes, that's what I read.

TRAHERNE. This news isn't the best possible passport for us in our present situation.

LUCILLA. But if we're hundreds of miles from anywhere, it can't be known here yet.

CRESPIN [*lighting a cigarette*]. In any case, they wouldn't dare to molest us.

TRAHERNE. All the same it might be safest to burn this paragraph in case there's anybody here that can read it. [*He tears a strip out of the paper, lights it at* CRESPIN'S *match, watches it burn till he has to drop the flaming remnant of it, upon which he stamps.* LUCILLA *takes the rest of the small local paper and lays it beside her leather coat on the stone, left. The* PRIEST *intently watches all these proceedings.*]

[*Meanwhile strange ululations, mingled with the throb of tom-toms and the clash of cymbals, have made themselves faintly heard from the direction of the mountain path, left.*]

CRESPIN. Hallo! What's this?

TRAHERNE. Sounds like the march of the Great Panjandrum.

[*The sounds rapidly approach. The natives all run to the point where the path debouches on the open space. They prostrate themselves, some on each side of the way. A wild procession comes down the mountain path. It is headed by a gigantic negro flourishing two naked sabres, and gyrating in a barbaric war-dance. Then come half a dozen musicians with tom-toms and cymbals. Then a litter carried by four bearers. Through its gauze curtains the figure of the* RAJA *can be indistinctly seen. Immediately behind the litter comes* WATKINS, *an English valet, demure and correct, looking as if he had just strolled in from St. James Street. The procession closes with a number of the* RAJA'S *bodyguard, in the most fantastic, parti-coloured attire, and armed with antique match-locks, some of them with barrels six or seven feet long. The* RAJA'S *litter is set down in front of the temple.* WATKINS *opens the curtains and gives his arm to the* RAJA *as he alights. The* RAJA *makes a step towards the European party in silence. He is a tall, well-built man of forty, dressed in the extreme of Eastern gorgeousness.* CRESPIN *advances and salutes.*]

CRESPIN. Does Your Highness speak English?

RAJA. Oh, yes, a little. [*As a matter of fact he speaks it irreproachably.*]

CRESPIN [*pulling himself together and speaking like a soldier and a man of breeding*]. Then I have to apologize for our landing uninvited in your territory.

RAJA. Uninvited, but, I assure you, not unwelcome.

CRESPIN. We are given to understand that this is the State of Rukh.

RAJA. The kingdom of Rukh, Major — if I rightly read the symbols on your cuff.

CRESPIN [*again salutes*]. Major Crespin. Permit me to introduce my wife ——

RAJA [*with a profound salaam*]. I am delighted, Madam, to welcome you to my secluded dominions. You are the first lady of your nation I have had the honour of receiving.

LUCILLA. Your Highness is very kind.

CRESPIN. And this is Dr. Basil Traherne, whose aeroplane — or what is left of it — you see.

RAJA. Doctor Traherne? *The* Doctor Traherne, whose name I have so often seen in the newspapers? "The Pasteur of Malaria."

TRAHERNE. The newspapers make too much of my work. It is very incomplete.

RAJA. But you are an aviator as well?

TRAHERNE. Only as an amateur.

RAJA. I presume it is some misadventure — a most fortunate misadventure for me — that has carried you so far into the wilds of the Himalayas?

TRAHERNE. Yes — we got lost in the clouds. Major and Mrs. Crespin were coming up from the plains to see their children at a hill station ——

RAJA. Pahari no doubt?

TRAHERNE. Yes, Pahari — and I was rash enough to suggest that I might save them three days' travelling by taking them up in my aeroplane.

RAJA. Madam is a sportswoman, then?

LUCILLA. Oh, I have been up many times.

CRESPIN [*with a tinge of sarcasm*]. Yes, many times.

LUCILLA. It was no fault of Dr. Traherne's that we went astray. The weather was impossible.

RAJA. Well, you have made a sensation here, I can assure you. My people have never seen an aeroplane. They are not sure — simple souls — whether you are gods or demons. But the fact of your having descended in the precincts of a temple of our local goddess — [*with a wave of his hand towards the idol*] allow me to introduce you to her — is considered highly significant.

CRESPIN. I hope, sir, that we shall find no difficulty in obtaining transport back to civ— to India.

RAJA. To civilization, you were going to say? Why hesitate, my dear sir? We know very well that we are barbarians. We are quite reconciled to the fact. We have had some five thousand years to accustom ourselves to it. This sword [*touching his scimitar*] is a barbarous weapon compared with your revolver; but it was worn by my ancestors when yours were daubing themselves blue and picking up a precarious livelihood in the woods. [*Breaking off hastily to prevent any reply.*] But Madam is standing all this time! Watkins, what are you thinking of? Some cushions. [WATKINS *piles some cushions from the litter so as to form a seat for* LUCILLA. *Meanwhile the* RAJA *continues.*] Another litter for Madam, and mountain-chairs for the gentlemen, will be here in a few minutes. Then I hope you will accept the hospitality of my poor house.

LUCILLA. We are giving a great deal of trouble, Your Highness.

RAJA. A great deal of pleasure, Madam.

CRESPIN. But I hope, sir, there will be no difficulty about transport back to — India.

RAJA. Time enough to talk of that, Major, when you have rested and recuperated after your adventure. You will do me the honour of dining with me this evening? I trust you will not find us altogether uncivilized.

LUCILLA [*lightly*]. Your Highness will have to excuse the barbarism of our attire. We have nothing to wear but what we stand up in.

RAJA. Oh, I think we can put that all right. Watkins!

WATKINS [*advancing*]. Your 'Ighness!

RAJA. You are in the confidence of our Mistress of the Robes. How does our wardrobe stand?

WATKINS. A fresh consignment of Paris models come in only last week, Your 'Ighness.

RAJA. Good! Then I hope, Madam, that you may find among them some rag that you will deign to wear.

LUCILLA. Paris models, Your Highness! And you talk of being uncivilized!

RAJA. We do what we can, Madam. I sometimes have the pleasure of entertaining European ladies — though not hitherto, Englishwomen — in my solitudes; and I like to mitigate the terrors of exile for them. Then as for civilization, you know, I have always at my elbow one of its most finished products. Watkins!

WATKINS [*stepping forward*]. Your 'Ighness!

RAJA. You will recognize in Watkins, gentlemen, another representative of the Ruling Race. [WATKINS, *with downcast eyes, touches his hat to* CRESPIN *and* TRAHERNE.] I assure you he rules me with an iron hand — not always in a velvet glove. Eh, Watkins?

WATKINS. Your 'Ighness will 'ave your joke.

RAJA. He is my Prime Minister and all my Cabinet — but more particularly my Lord Chamberlain. No one can touch him at mixing a cocktail or making a salad. My entire household trembles at his nod; even my *chef* quails before him. Nothing comes amiss to him; for he is, like myself, a man without prejudices. You may be surprised at my praising him to his face in this fashion; you may foresee some danger of — what shall I say? — swelled head. But I know my Watkins; there is not the slightest risk of his outgrowing that modest bowler. He knows his value to me, and he knows that he would never be equally appreciated elsewhere. I have guarantees for his fidelity — eh, Watkins?

WATKINS. I know when I'm well off, if that's what Your 'Ighness means.

RAJA. I mean a little more than that — but no matter. I have sometimes thought of instituting a peerage, in order that I might raise Watkins to it. But I mustn't let my admiration for British institutions carry me too far. — Those scoundrels of bearers are taking a long time, Watkins.

WATKINS. The lady's litter 'ad to 'ave fresh curtains, Your 'Ighness. They won't be a minute, now.

RAJA. You were speaking of transport, Major — is your machine past repair, Dr. Traherne?

TRAHERNE. Utterly, I'm afraid.

RAJA. Let us look at it. [*Turns and finds that his bodyguard are all clustered on the path, looking at it. He gives a sharp word of command. They scamper into a sort of loose order, up left.*] Ah, yes — propeller smashed — planes crumpled up ——

TRAHERNE. Under-carriage wrecked ——

RAJA. I'm afraid we can't offer to repair the damage for you.

TRAHERNE. I'm afraid not, sir.

RAJA. A wonderful machine! Yes, Europe has something to boast of. I wonder what the Priest here thinks of it. [*He says a few words to the* PRIEST, *who salaams, and replies volubly at some length.*] He says it is the great roc — the giant bird, you know, of our Eastern stories. And he declares that he plainly saw his Goddess hovering over you as you descended, and guiding you towards her temple.

TRAHERNE. I wish she could have guided us towards the level ground I saw behind your castle. I could have made a safe landing there.

RAJA. No doubt — on my parade ground — almost the only level spot in my dominions.

LUCILLA. These, I suppose, are your bodyguard?

RAJA. My household troops, Madam.

LUCILLA. How picturesque they are!

RAJA. Oh, a relic of barbarism, I know. I can quite understand the contempt with which my friend the Major is at this moment regarding them.

CRESPIN. Irregular troops, Raja. Often first-class fighting men.

RAJA. And you think that, if irregularity is the virtue of irregular troops, these — what is the expression, Watkins?

WATKINS. Tyke the cyke, Your 'Ighness?

RAJA. That's it — take the cake — that is what you are thinking?

CRESPIN. Well, they would be hard to beat, sir.

RAJA. I repeat — a relic of barbarism. You see, I have strong conservative instincts — I cling to the fashions of my fathers — and my people would be restive if I didn't. I maintain these fellows, as his Majesty the King-Emperor keeps up the Beefeaters in the Tower. But I also like to move with the times, as perhaps you will allow me to show you. [*He blows two short blasts on a silver whistle hanging round his neck. Instantly from behind every rock and shrub — from every bit of cover — there emerges a soldier, in spick-and-span European uniform (Russian in style), armed with the latest brand of magazine rifles. They stand like statues at attention.*]

CRESPIN. Good Lord!

TRAHERNE. Hallo!

RAJA [*to* LUCILLA, *who makes no move*]. I trust I did not startle you, Madam?

LUCILLA. Oh, not at all. I'm not nervous.

RAJA. You of course realize that this effect is not original. I have plagiarized it from the excellent Walter Scott:

> "These are Clan-Alpine's warriors true,
> And, Saxon, I am Roderick Dhu!"

But I think you'll admit, Major, that my men know how to take cover.

CRESPIN. By the Lord, sir, they must move like cats — for you can't have planted them there before we arrived.

RAJA. No, you had given me no notice of your coming.

LUCILLA. Perhaps the Goddess did.

RAJA. Not she, Madam. She keeps her own counsel. These men followed me down from the palace and have taken up position while we have been speaking. [*The* RAJA *gives a word of command, and the men rapidly assemble and form in two ranks, an officer on their flank.*]

CRESPIN. A very smart body of men, Raja. Allow me to congratulate you on their training.

RAJA. I am greatly flattered, Major. I superintend it myself. — Ah, here comes the litter. [*Down the path comes a litter borne, like the* RAJA'S, *by four men. It is followed by two mountain-chairs carried by two men apiece.*] Permit me, Madam, to hand you to your palanquin. [*He offers* LUCILLA *his hand. As she rises she picks up her leather coat, and the newspaper falls to the ground. The* RAJA *notices it.*] Forgive me, Madam. [*Picks up the paper and looks at it.*] A newspaper, only two days old! This is such a rarity you must allow me to glance at it. [*He opens the paper and sees that a strip has been torn out from the back page.*] Ah! the telegraphic news gone! What a pity! In my seclusion, I hunger for tidings from the civilized world. [*The* PRIEST *comes forward and speaks to him eagerly, suggesting in pantomime* TRAHERNE'S *action in burning the paper, and pointing to the ashes on the ground, at which the* RAJA *looks.*] You burned this column?

TRAHERNE. Unfortunately, I did.

RAJA. Ah! [*Pause.*] I know your motive, Dr. Traherne, and I appreciate it. You destroyed it out of consideration for my feelings, wishing to spare me a painful piece of intelligence. That was very thoughtful — but quite unnecessary. I already know what you tried to conceal.

CRESPIN. You know ——!

TRAHERNE. Your Highness knows ——!
　　[*Simultaneously.*]

RAJA. I know that three of my subjects, accused of a political crime, have been sentenced to death.

TRAHERNE. How is it possible ——?

RAJA. Bad news flies fast, Dr. Traherne. But one thing you can perhaps tell me — is there any chance of their sentences being remitted?

TRAHERNE. I am afraid not, Your Highness.

CRESPIN. Remitted? I should rather say not. It was a cold-blooded, unprovoked murder.

RAJA. Unprovoked, you think? Well, I won't argue the point. And the execution is to be ——?

TRAHERNE. I think tomorrow — or the day after.

RAJA. Tomorrow or the day after — yes. [*Turning to* LUCILLA.] Forgive me, Madam — I have kept you waiting.

TRAHERNE. Does Your Highness know anything of these men?

RAJA [*over his shoulder, as he hands* LUCILLA *into the litter*]. Know them? Oh, yes — they are my brothers. [*He seats himself on his own litter and claps his hands twice. Both litters are raised and move off,* LUCILLA'S *first. The regular soldiers line the way, in single rank. They salute as the litters pass.* WATKINS *follows the* RAJA'S. CRESPIN *and* TRAHERNE *seat themselves in their chairs. As they do so:*]

CRESPIN. His brothers? What did he mean?

TRAHERNE [*shrugging his shoulders*]. Heaven knows!

CRESPIN. I don't half like our host, Traherne. There's too much of the cat about him.

TRAHERNE. Or of the tiger. And how the devil had he got the news?

[*As the two chairs move off,* CRESPIN *first, the two ranks of soldiers close round them. The irregulars and musicians, headed by the dancing negro, bring up the rear. The* PRIEST *prostrates himself, as if in thanksgiving, before the Goddess.*]

ACT II

SCENE. — *A spacious and well-proportioned room, opening at the back upon a wide loggia. Beyond the loggia can be seen distant snow-peaks and a strip of sky. Late afternoon light.*

The room is furnished in a once splendid but now very old-fashioned and faded style. Furniture of black picked out with gold, and upholstered in yellow damask. A great crystal chandelier in the middle of the ceiling, and under it a circular ottoman. Left, a large two-leaved door; right, a handsome marble fire-place, with a mirror over it. Candlesticks with crystal pendants at each end of the mantelpiece, and in the middle a bronze statuette, some eighteen inches high, representing the many-armed Goddess. A wood fire laid, but unlighted. Near the fireplace, two quite modern saddle-bag arm-chairs, out of keeping with the stiffness of the remaining furniture. A small table near the door, left, with modern English and French books on it. A handsome gramophone in the corner, left. On the walls, left and right, some very bad paintings of fine-looking Orientals in gorgeous attire. Electric lights.

TRAHERNE *discovered at back, centre, looking out over the landscape. He does not go out upon the loggia (which can be entered both right and left without passing through the room) because two turbanned servants are there, under the direction of an old and dignified Major-domo, arranging a luxurious dinner table, with four covers.* TRAHERNE *stands motionless for a moment. Then* CRESPIN *enters by the door, right, ushered in by a servant, who salaams and retires.*]

CRESPIN. Ah, there you are, Doctor.

TRAHERNE [*turning*]. Hullo! How did you get on?

CRESPIN. All right. Had a capital tub. And you?

TRAHERNE. Feeling more like a human being. And what about Mrs. Crespin? I hope she's all right.

CRESPIN. She was taken off by an ayah as soon as we got in — presumably to the women's quarters.

TRAHERNE. And you let her go off alone?

CRESPIN. What the hell could I do? I couldn't thrust myself into the women's quarters.

TRAHERNE. You could have kept her with you.

CRESPIN. Do you think she'd have stayed? And, come to that, what business is it of yours?

TRAHERNE. It's any man's business to be concerned for a woman's safety.

CRESPIN. Well, well — all right. But there was nothing I could have done or that she would let me do. And I don't think there's any danger.

TRAHERNE. Let us hope not.

CRESPIN. It's a vast shanty this.

TRAHERNE. It's a palace and a fortress in one.

CRESPIN. A devilish strong place before the days of big guns. But a couple of howitzers would soon make it look pretty foolish.

TRAHERNE. No doubt; but how would you get them here?

CRESPIN [looking at the dinner table]. I say — it looks as if our friend were going to do us well. [One of the servants comes in with a wine-cooler. When the man has gone, CRESPIN picks up the bottle and looks at the label.] Perrier Jouet, nineteen-o-six, by the lord! [He strolls over to the ottoman, and seats himself, facing the fire-place.] It's a rum start this, Traherne. I suppose you intellectual chaps would call it romantic.

TRAHERNE [examining the figure of the Goddess on the mantelpiece]. More romantic than agreeable, I should say. I don't like the looks of this lady.

CRESPIN. What is she?

TRAHERNE. The same figure we saw in the little temple, where we landed.

CRESPIN. How many arms has she got?

TRAHERNE. Six.

CRESPIN. She could give you a jolly good hug, anyway.

TRAHERNE. You wouldn't want another.

CRESPIN. Where do you suppose we really are, Traherne?

TRAHERNE. On the map, you mean?

CRESPIN. Of course.

TRAHERNE. Oh, in the never-never land. Somewhere on the way to Bokhara. I've been searching my memory for all I ever heard about Rukh. I fancy very little is known, except that it seems to send forth a peculiarly poisonous breed of fanatics.

CRESPIN. Like those who did poor Haredale in?

TRAHERNE. Precisely.

CRESPIN. D'you think our host was serious when he said they were his brothers? Or was he only pulling our leg, curse his impudence?

TRAHERNE. He probably meant caste-brothers, or simply men of the same race. But, even so, it's awkward.

CRESPIN. I don't see what these beggars, living at the back of the north wind, have got to do with Indian politics. We've never interfered with them.

TRAHERNE. Oh, it's a case of Asia for the Asians. Ever since the Japanese beat the Russians, the whole continent has been itching to kick us out.

CRESPIN. So that they may cut each other's throats at leisure, eh?

TRAHERNE. We Westerners never cut each other's throats, do we?

[WATKINS has entered at the back, right, carrying a silver centre-piece for the table. He sets it down and is going out to the left, when CRESPIN catches sight of him and hails him.]

CRESPIN. Hallo! You there! What's your name! [WATKINS *stops.*] Just come here a minute, will you?

WATKINS. Meaning me, sir? [*He advances into the room. There is a touch of covert insolence in his manner.*]

CRESPIN. Yes, you, Mr. ——? Mr. ——?

WATKINS. Watkins is my name, sir.

CRESPIN. Right ho! Watkins. Can you tell us where we are, Watkins?

WATKINS. They calls the place Rukh, sir.

CRESPIN. Yes, yes, we know that. But where *is* Rukh?

WATKINS. I hunderstand these mountains is called the 'Imalayas, sir.

CRESPIN. Damn it, sir, we don't want a lesson in geography!

WATKINS. No, sir? My mistake, sir.

TRAHERNE. Major Crespin means that we want to know how far we are from the nearest point in India.

WATKINS. I really couldn't say, sir. Not so very far, I dessay, as the crow flies.

TRAHERNE. Unfortunately we're not in a position to fly with the crow. How long does the journey take?

WATKINS. They tell me it takes about three weeks to Cashmere.

CRESPIN. They tell you! Surely you must remember how long it took *you?*

WATKINS. No, sir, excuse me, sir — I've never been in India.

CRESPIN. Not been in India? And I was just thinking, as I looked at you, that I seemed to have seen you before.

WATKINS. Not in India, sir. We might 'ave met in England, but I don't call to mind having that pleasure.

CRESPIN. But if you haven't been in India, how the hell did you get here?

WATKINS. I came with 'Is 'Ighness, sir, by way of Tashkent. All our dealin's with Europe is by way of Russia.

TRAHERNE. But it's possible to get to India direct, and not by way of Central Asia?

WATKINS. Oh, yes, it's done, sir. But I'm told there are some very tight places to negotiate — like the camel and the needle's eye, as you might say.

TRAHERNE. Difficult travelling for a lady, eh?

WATKINS. Next door to himpossible, I should guess, sir.

CRESPIN. A nice look-out, Traherne! [*To* WATKINS.] Tell me, my man — is His Highness — h'm — married?

WATKINS. Oh, yessir — very much so, sir.

CRESPIN. Children?

WATKINS. He has fifteen sons, sir.

CRESPIN. The daughters don't count, eh?

WATKINS. I've never 'ad a hopportunity of counting 'em, sir.

TRAHERNE. He said the men accused of assassinating a political officer were his brothers ——

WATKINS [*quickly*]. Did 'e say that, sir?

TRAHERNE. Didn't you hear him? What did he mean?

WATKINS. I'm sure I couldn't say, sir. 'Is 'Ighness is what you'd call a very playful gentleman, sir.

TRAHERNE. But I don't see the joke in saying that.

WATKINS. No, sir? P'raps 'Is 'Ighness'll explain, sir.

[*A pause.*]

CRESPIN. Your master spoke of visits from European ladies — do *they* come from Russia?

WATKINS. From various parts, I understand, sir, — mostly from Paris.

CRESPIN. Any here now?

WATKINS. I really couldn't say, sir.

TRAHERNE. They don't dine with His Highness?

WATKINS. Oh, no, sir. 'Is 'Ighness sometimes sups with *them*.

CRESPIN. And my wife — Mrs. Crespin ——?

WATKINS. Make your mind easy, sir — the lady won't meet any hundesirable characters, sir. I give strict orders to the — the female what took charge of the lady.

TRAHERNE. She is to be trusted?

WATKINS. Habsolutely, sir. She is — in a manner of speakin' — my wife, sir.

CRESPIN. Mrs. Watkins, eh?

WATKINS. Yessir — I suppose you would say so.

TRAHERNE. But now look here, Watkins — you say we're three weeks away from Cashmere — yet the Raja knew of the sentence passed on these subjects of his who were tried only three days ago. How do you account for that?

WATKINS. I can't, sir. All I can say is, there's queer things goes on here.

TRAHERNE. Queer things? What do you mean?

WATKINS. Well, sir, them priests you know — they goes in a lot for what 'Is 'Ighness calls magic ——

TRAHERNE. Oh, come, Watkins — you don't *believe* in that!

WATKINS. Well, sir, p'raps not. I don't, not to say *believe* in it. But there's queer things goes on. I can't say no more, nor I can't say no less. If you'll excuse me, sir, I must just run my eye over the dinner-table. 'Is 'Ighness will be here directly.

[*He retires, inspects the table, makes one or two changes, and presently goes out by the back, right.*]

CRESPIN. That fellow's either a cunning rascal or a damned fool. Which do you think?

TRAHERNE. I don't believe he's the fool he'd like us to take him for. — Ah, here is Mrs. Crespin.

[*Enter* LUCILLA, *left, ushered in by a handsome* AYAH. *She is dressed in a gauzy gown of quite recent style, dark blue or crimson. Not in the least décolleté. At most the sleeves might be open, so as to show her arms to the elbow. No ornaments except a gold locket on a little gold chain round her neck. The costume is absolutely plain, but in striking contrast to her travelling dress. Her hair is beautifully arranged.*]

LUCILLA [*to the* AYAH]. Thank you. [*The* AYAH *disappears.* LUCILLA *advances, holding out her skirt a little.*] Behold the Paris model!

CRESPIN. My eye, Lu, what a ripping frock!

TRAHERNE. Talk of magic, Major! There's something in what our friend says.

LUCILLA. What is that? What about magic?

CRESPIN. We'll tell you afterwards. Let's have *your* adventures first.

LUCILLA. No adventures precisely — only a little excursion into the Arabian Nights.

TRAHERNE. Do tell us!

LUCILLA [*evidently a little nervous, yet not without enjoyment of the experience*]. Well, my guide — the woman you saw — led me along corridor after corridor, and upstairs and downstairs, till we came to a heavy bronze door where two villainous-looking blacks, with crooked swords, were on guard. I didn't like the looks of them a bit; but I was in for it and had to go on. They drew their swords and flourished a sort of salute, grinning with all their teeth. Then the ayah clapped her hands twice, someone inspected us through a grating in the door, and the ayah said a word or two ——

TRAHERNE. No doubt "Open sesame!"

LUCILLA. The door was opened by a hideous, hump-backed old woman, just like the wicked fairy in a pantomime. She didn't actually bite me, but she looked as if she'd like to — and we passed on. More corridors, with curtained doorways, where I had a feeling that furtive eyes were watching me — though I can't positively say I saw them. But I'm sure I heard whisperings and titterings ——

CRESPIN. Good Lord! If I'd thought they were going to treat you like that, I'd have ——

LUCILLA. Oh, there was nothing you could have done; and, you see, no harm came of it. At last the woman led me into a large sort of wardrobe room, lighted from above, and almost entirely lined with glazed presses full of frocks. Then she slid back a panel, and there was a marble-lined bathroom! — a deep pool, with a trickle of water flowing into it from a dolphin's head of gold — just enough to make the surface ripple and dance. And all around were the latest Bond Street luxuries — shampooing bowls and brushes, bottles of essences, towels on hot rails and all the rest of it. The only thing that was disagreeable was a sickly odour from some burning pastilles — oh, and a coal-black bath-woman.

TRAHERNE. It suggests a Royal Academy picture — "The Odalisque's Pool."

CRESPIN. Or a soap advertisement.

TRAHERNE. Same thing.

LUCILLA. Well, I wasn't sorry to play the odalisque for once; and when I had finished, lo and behold! the ayah had laid out for me half a dozen gorgeous and distinctly risky dinner-gowns. I had to explain to her in gestures that I couldn't live up to any of them, and would rather put on my old travelling dress. She seemed quite frightened at the idea ——

CRESPIN. Ha ha! She'd probably have got the sack — perhaps literally — if she'd let you do that.

LUCILLA. Anyway, she at last produced this comparatively inoffensive frock. She did my hair, and wanted to finish me off with all sorts of necklaces and bangles, but I stuck to my old locket with the babies' heads.

CRESPIN. Well, all's well that ends well, I suppose. But if I'd foreseen all this "Secrets of the Zenana" business, I'm dashed if I wouldn't ——

LUCILLA [cutting him short]. What were you saying about magic when I came in?

TRAHERNE. Only that this man, Watkins — he's the husband of your ayah, by the way — says queer things go on here, and pretends to believe in magic.

LUCILLA. Do you know, Antony, when the Raja was speaking about him down there, it seemed to me that his face was somehow familiar to me.

CRESPIN. There, Doctor! What did I say? I knew I'd seen him before, but I'm damned if I can place him.

LUCILLA. I wish I could get a good look at him.

[WATKINS enters, back, left, with something for the table.]

TRAHERNE. There he is. Shall I call him in?

LUCILLA. Say I want him to thank his wife from me.

TRAHERNE [calls]. Watkins.

WATKINS. Sir?

TRAHERNE. Mrs. Crespin would like to speak to you. [WATKINS comes forward.]

LUCILLA. I hear, Watkins, that the ayah who so kindly attended to me is your wife.

WATKINS. That's right, ma'am.

LUCILLA. She gave me most efficient assistance, and, as she seems to know no English, I couldn't thank her. Will you be good enough to tell her how much I appreciated all she did for me?

WATKINS. Thank you kindly, ma'am. She'll be proud to hear it. [Pause.] Is that all, ma'am?

LUCILLA. That's all, thank you, Watkins.

[He returns to the loggia, but goes to the other side of the dinner-table and keeps an eye on the three.]

CRESPIN. You've a good memory for faces, Lu. Do you spot him?

LUCILLA. Don't let him see we're talking about him. I believe I do know him, but I'm not quite sure. Do you remember, the first year we were in India, there was a man of the Dorsets that used often to be on guard outside the messroom?

CRESPIN. By God, you've hit it!

TRAHERNE. Take care! He's watching.

LUCILLA. You remember he deserted, and was suspected of having murdered a woman in the bazaar.

CRESPIN. I believe it's the very man.

LUCILLA. It's certainly very like him.

CRESPIN. And he swears he's never been in India!

TRAHERNE. Under the circumstances, he naturally would.

LUCILLA. At all events, he's not a man to be trusted.

[*At this moment the* RAJA *enters by the door, left. He is in faultless European evening dress — white waistcoat, white tie, etc. No jewels, except the ribbon and star of a Russian order. Nothing oriental about him except his turban and his complexion.*]

RAJA [*as he enters*]. Pray forgive me, Madam, for being the last to appear. The fact is, I had to hold a sort of Cabinet Council — or shall I say a conclave of prelates? — with regard to questions arising out of your most welcome arrival.

CRESPIN. May we hope, Raja, that you were laying a dawk for our return.

RAJA. Pray, pray, Major, let us postpone that question for the moment. First let us fortify ourselves; after dinner we will talk seriously. If you are in *too* great a hurry to desert me, must I not conclude, Madam, that you are dissatisfied with your reception?

LUCILLA. How could we possibly be so ungrateful, your Highness? Your hospitality overwhelms us.

RAJA. I trust my Mistress of the Robes furnished you with all you required?

LUCILLA. With all and more than all. She offered me quite a bewildering array of gorgeous apparel.

RAJA. Oh, I am glad. I had hoped that perhaps your choice might have fallen on something more —— [*He indicates by gestures, "décolleté."*] But no — I was wrong — Madam's taste is irreproachable.

[*A servant enters from behind with cocktails on a silver salver.* LUCILLA *refuses. The men accept.* LUCILLA *picks up a yellow French book on one of the tables.*]

RAJA. You see, Madam, we fall behind the age here. We are still in the Anatole France period. If he bores you, here [*picking up another book*] is a Maurice Barrès that you may find more amusing.

LUCILLA. Oh, I too am in the Anatole France period, I assure you. [*Reads.*] "Sur la Pierre Blanche" — isn't that the one you were recommending to me, Dr. Traherne?

TRAHERNE. Yes, I like it better than some of his later books.

RAJA [*picking up a silver-grey book*]. As for Bernard Shaw, I suppose he's quite a back number; but I confess his impudence entertains me. What do *you* say, Major?

CRESPIN. Never read a line of the fellow — except in *John Bull*.

LUCILLA and TRAHERNE [*simultaneously*]. In *John Bull!*

CRESPIN. Somebody told me he wrote in *John Bull* — doesn't he?

RAJA. Are you fond of music, Mrs. Crespin? [*Goes to the gramophone, and turns over some records, till he finds one which he lays on the top of the pile.*] Suppose we have some during dinner. [WATKINS *enters from the back, left.*] Watkins, just start this top record, will you? [WATKINS *does so.*]

[*At this moment the* MAJOR-DOMO *enters from the back, and says a few words.*]

RAJA. Ah! *Madame est servie!* Allow me ——

[*He offers* LUCILLA *his arm and leads her to the table. The others follow.*] Will you take this seat, Madam? You here, Major — Dr. Traherne!

[He himself sits to the left of the table; LUCILLA on his left; TRAHERNE opposite him; and CRESPIN opposite LUCILLA, with his back to the sunset, which is now flooding the scene.]

RAJA *[as the servants offer dishes]*. I can recommend this caviare, Major — and you'll take a glass of maraschino with it — Russian fashion.

[Just as they sit down the gramophone reels out the first bars of a piece of music.]

LUCILLA *[after listening a moment]*. Oh, what *is* that?

RAJA. Don't you know it?

LUCILLA. Oh, yes, but I can't think what it is.

RAJA. Gounod's "Funeral March of a Marionette" — a most humorous composition. May I pour you a glass of maraschino? *[He goes on talking as*

THE CURTAIN FALLS

When it rises again, the glow has faded, and some big stars are pulsing in the strip of purple sky. The party is just finishing dinner. Dessert is on the table, which is lighted by electric lamps. WATKINS stands behind the RAJA's chair. The MAJOR-DOMO and other servants hover round.

The RAJA has just finished a story, at which all laugh. A short pause.]

LUCILLA. What a heavenly night!

RAJA. Yes, our summer climate is far from bad.

LUCILLA. The air is like champagne.

RAJA. A little over frappé for some tastes. What do you say, Madam? Shall we have coffee indoors? There is an edge to the air at these altitudes, as soon as the sun has gone down.

LUCILLA *[shivers slightly]*. Yes, I do feel a little chilly.

RAJA. Watkins, send for a shawl for Madam. *[Rising.]* And ah — let us have the fire lighted. *[WATKINS goes off to the left. The RAJA says a word to the MAJOR-DOMO, who touches a switch in one of the pillars of the loggia opening. The chandelier and wall-lamps of the salon burst into brilliant light.]*

RAJA *[offering his arm to LUCILLA]*. Let me find you a comfortable seat, Madam. *[He leads her to the two armchairs further back.]* When the fire is lighted, I think you will find this quite pleasant. Take the other chair, Major. *[CRESPIN does so.]* I must really refurnish this salon. My ancestors had no notion of comfort. To tell the truth, I use the room only on state occasions, like the present. *[Bowing to LUCILLA.]* I have a much more modern snuggery upstairs, which I hope you will see tomorrow.

[Servants hand round coffee, liqueurs, cigars, cigarettes during what follows. One of them lights the fire, of aromatic wood.]

RAJA *[to TRAHERNE, who has remained at the loggia opening, looking out into the night]*. Star-gazing, Dr. Traherne?

TRAHERNE. I beg your pardon. *[Comes forward.]*

LUCILLA. Dr. Traherne is quite an astronomer.

RAJA. As much at home with the telescope as with the microscope, eh?

TRAHERNE. Oh, no. I'm no astronomer. I can pick out a few of the constellations, — that's all.

RAJA. For my part, I look at the stars as little as possible. As a spectacle they're monotonous, and they don't bear thinking of.

[The AYAH, *entering by door, left, brings* LUCILLA *a shawl, which the* RAJA *places on her shoulders*.]

LUCILLA. What an exquisite shawl!

RAJA. And most becoming — don't you think so, Doctor? [TRAHERNE *is gazing at* LUCILLA.] My Mistress of the Robes has chosen well! [*He makes a motion of noiseless applause to the* AYAH, *who grins and exits, left*.]

LUCILLA. Why won't the stars bear thinking of, Raja?

RAJA. Well, dear lady, don't you think they're rather ostentatious? *I* was guilty of a little showing-off today, when I played that foolish trick with my regular troops. But think of the Maharaja up yonder [*pointing upwards*] who night after night whistles up his glittering legions, and puts them through their deadly punctual drill, as much as to say "See what a devil of a fellow *I* am!" Do you think it quite in good taste, Madam?

TRAHERNE [*laughing*]. I'm afraid you're jealous, Raja. You don't like having to play second fiddle to a still more absolute ruler.

RAJA. Perhaps you're right, Doctor — perhaps it's partly that. But there's something more to it. I can't help resenting — [*To* CRESPIN *to whom a servant is offering liqueurs*.] Let me recommend the kümmel, Major. I think you'll find it excellent.

TRAHERNE. What is it you resent?

RAJA. Oh, the respect paid to mere size — to the immensity, as they call it, of the universe. Are we to worship a god because he's big?

TRAHERNE. If you resent his bigness, what do you say to his littleness? The microscope, you know, reveals him no less than the telescope.

RAJA. And reveals him in the form of death-dealing specks of matter, which you, I understand, Doctor, are impiously proposing to exterminate.

TRAHERNE. I am trying to marshal the life-saving against the death-dealing powers.

RAJA. To marshal God's right hand against his left, eh? or *vice versa?* But I admit you have the pull of the astronomers, in so far as you deal in life, not in dead mechanism. [*Killing a gnat on the back of his hand*.] This mosquito that I have just killed — I am glad to see you smoke, Madam: it helps to keep them off — this mosquito, or any smallest thing that has life in it, is to me far more admirable than a whole lifeless universe. What do *you* say, Major?

CRESPIN [*smoking a cigar*]. I say, Raja, that if you'll tell that fellow to give me another glass of kümmel, I'll let you have your own way about the universe. [*The* RAJA *says a word to one of the servants, who refills* CRESPIN'S *glass*.]

LUCILLA. But what if the mechanism, as you call it, isn't dead? What if the stars are swarming with life?

TRAHERNE. Yes — suppose there are planets, which of course we can't see, circling round each of the great suns we *do* see? And suppose they are all inhabited?

RAJA. I'd rather not suppose it. Isn't one inhabited world bad enough? Do we want it multiplied by millions?

LUCILLA. Haven't you just been telling us that a living gnat is more wonderful than a dead universe?

RAJA. Wonderful? Yes, by all means — wonderful as a device for torturing and being tortured. Oh, I'm neither a saint nor an ascetic — I take life as I find it — I am tortured and I torture. But there's one thing I'm really proud of — I'm proud to belong to the race of the Buddha, who first found out that life was a colossal blunder.

LUCILLA [*in a low voice*]. Should you like the sky to be starless? That seems to me — forgive me, Prince — the last word of impiety.

RAJA. Possibly, Madam. How my esteemed fellow-creatures were ever bluffed into piety is a mystery to me. Not that I'm complaining. If men could not be bluffed by the Raja above, much less would they be bluffed by us Rajas below. And though life is a contemptible business, I don't deny that *power* is the best part of it.

TRAHERNE. In short, your Highness is a Superman.

RAJA. Ah, you read Nietzsche? Yes, if I weren't of the kindred of the Buddha, I should like to be of the race of that great man.

[*The servants have now all withdrawn.*]

LUCILLA [*looking out*]. There is the moon rising over the snowfields. I hope you wouldn't banish *her* from the heavens?

RAJA. Oh, no — I like her silly, good-natured face. And she's useful to lovers and brigands and other lawless vagabonds, with whom I have great sympathy. Besides, I don't know that she's so silly either. She seems to be forever raising her eyebrows in mild astonishment at human folly.

CRESPIN. All this is out of my depth, your Highness. We've had a rather fatiguing day. Mightn't we ——?

RAJA. To be sure. I only waited till the servants had gone. Now, are you all quite comfortable?

LUCILLA. Quite.

TRAHERNE. Perfectly, thank you.

CRESPIN. Perfectly.

RAJA [*smoking a cigar, and standing with his back to the fire*]. Then we'll go into committee upon your position here.

CRESPIN. If you please, sir.

RAJA. I'm afraid you may find it rather disagreeable.

CRESPIN. Communications bad, eh? We have a difficult journey before us?

RAJA. A long journey, I fear — yet not precisely difficult.

CRESPIN. It surely can't be so very far, since you had heard of the sentence passed on those assassins.

RAJA. I am glad, Major, that you have so tactfully spared me the pain of re-opening that subject. We should have had to come to it, sooner or later. [*An embarrassing pause.*]

TRAHERNE. When your Highness said they were your brothers, you were of course speaking figuratively. You meant your tribesmen?

RAJA. Not at all. They are sons of my father — not of my mother.

LUCILLA. And we intrude upon you at such a time! How dreadful!

RAJA. Oh, pray don't apologize. Believe me, your arrival has given great satisfaction.

TRAHERNE. How do you mean?

RAJA. I'll explain presently. But first ——

CRESPIN [*interrupting*]. First let us understand each other. You surely can't approve of this abominable crime?

RAJA. My brothers are fanatics, and there is no fanaticism in me.

LUCILLA. How do they come to be so different from you?

RAJA. That is just what I was going to tell you. I was my father's eldest son, by his favourite wife. Through my mother's influence (my poor mother — how I loved her!) I was sent to Europe. My education was wholly European. I shed all my prejudices. I became the open-minded citizen of the world whom I hope you recognize in me. My brothers, on the other hand, turned to India for their culture. The religion of our people has always been a primitive idolatry. My brothers naturally fell in with adherents of the same superstition, and they worked each other up to a high pitch of frenzy against the European exploitation of Asia.

TRAHERNE. Had you no restraining influence upon them?

RAJA. Of course I might have imprisoned them — or had them strangled — the traditional form of argument in our family. But why should I? As I said, I have no prejudices — least of all in favour of the British raj. We are of Indian race, though long severed from the Motherland — and I do not love her tyrants.

CRESPIN [*who has had quite enough to drink*]. In short, sir, you defend this devilish murder?

RAJA. Oh, no — I think it foolish and futile. But there is a romantic as well as a practical side to my nature, and, from the romantic point of view, I rather admire it.

CRESPIN [*rising*]. Then, sir, the less we intrude on your hospitality the better. If you will be good enough to furnish us with transport tomorrow morning ——

RAJA. That is just where the difficulty arises ——

CRESPIN. No transport, hey?

RAJA. Materially it might be managed; but morally I fear it is — excuse the colloquialism, Madam — no go.

CRESPIN. What the devil do you mean, sir ——?

LUCILLA [*trying to cover his bluster*]. Will your Highness be good enough to explain?

RAJA. I mentioned that the religion of my people is a primitive superstition? Well, since the news has spread that three Feringhis have dropped from the skies precisely at the time when three princes of the royal house are threatened with death at the hands of the Feringhi government, — and dropped, moreover, in the precincts of a temple — my subjects have got

into their heads that you have been personally conducted hither by the
Goddess whom they especially worship.

LUCILLA. The Goddess ——?

RAJA [*turning to the statuette*]. Here is her portrait on the mantelpiece —
much admired by connoisseurs.

[LUCILLA *cannot repress a shudder.*]

RAJA. I need not say that I am far from sharing the popular illusion.
Your arrival is of course the merest coincidence — for me, a charming coincidence. But my people hold unphilosophic views. I understand that
even in England the vulgar are apt to see the Finger of Providence in
particularly fortunate — or unfortunate — occurrences.

CRESPIN. Then the upshot of all this palaver is that you propose to hold
us as hostages, to exchange for your brothers?

RAJA. That is not precisely the idea, my dear sir. My theologians do
not hold that an exchange is what the Goddess decrees. Nor, to be quite
frank, would it altogether suit my book.

LUCILLA. Not to get your brothers back again?

RAJA. You may have noted in history, Madam, that family affection is
seldom the strong point of Princes. Is it not Pope who remarks on their
lack of enthusiasm for "a brother near the throne"? My sons are mere
children, and were I to die — we are all mortal — there might be trouble
about the succession. In our family, uncles seldom love nephews.

LUCILLA. So you would raise no finger to save your brothers?

RAJA. That is not my only reason. Supposing it possible that I could
bully the Government of India into giving up my relatives, do you think it
would sit calmly down under the humiliation? No, no, dear lady. It might
wait a few years to find some decent pretext, but assuredly we should have a
punitive expedition. It would cost thousands of lives and millions of money,
but what would that matter? Prestige would be restored, and I should end
my days in a maisonette in Petrograd. It wouldn't suit me at all. Hitherto
I have escaped the notice of your Government by a policy of masterly in-
activity, and I propose to adhere to that policy.

CRESPIN. Then I don't see how ——

TRAHERNE [*simultaneously*]. Surely you don't mean ——?

RAJA. We are approaching the crux of the matter — a point which I fear
you may have some difficulty in appreciating. I would beg you to remember,
that, though I am what is commonly called an autocrat, there is no such
thing under the sun as real despotism. All government is government by
consent of the people. It is very stupid of them to consent — but they do.
I have studied the question — I took a pretty good degree at Cambridge,
in Moral and Political Science — and I assure you that, though I have
absolute power of life and death over my subjects, it is only their acquiescence that gives me that power. If I defied their prejudices or their passions, they could upset my throne tomorrow.

CRESPIN [*angrily*]. Will you be so kind as to come to the point, sir?

RAJA. Gently, Major! We shall reach it soon enough.

[*To* LUCILLA]. Please remember, too, Madam, that an autocracy is generally a theocracy to boot, and mine is a case in point. I am a slave to theology. The clerical party can do what it pleases with me, for there is no other party to oppose it. True, I am my own Archbishop of Canterbury — but "I have a partner: Mr. Jorkins" — I have a terribly exacting Archbishop of York. I fear I may have to introduce you to him tomorrow.

LUCILLA. You are torturing us, your Highness. Like my husband, I beg you to come to the point.

RAJA. The point is, dear lady, that the theology on which, as I say, my whole power is founded, has not yet emerged from the Mosaic stage of development: it demands an eye for an eye, a tooth for a tooth ——

[*A long pause.*]

a life for a life.

[*Another pause.*]

TRAHERNE. You mean to say ——

RAJA. Unfortunately, I do.

LUCILLA. You would kill us ——?

RAJA. Not I, Madam — the clerical party. And only if my brothers are executed. If not, I will merely demand your word of honour that what has passed between us shall never be mentioned to any human soul — and you shall go free.

CRESPIN. But if your brother assassins are hanged — as assuredly they will be — you will put to death in cold blood ——

RAJA [*interrupting.*] Oh, not in cold blood, Major. There is nothing cold-blooded about the clerical party when "white goats," as their phrase goes, are to be sacrificed to the Goddess.

TRAHERNE. Does your Goddess demand the life of a woman?

RAJA. Well, on that point she might not be too exacting. "On trouve avec le Ciel des accommodements." If Madam would be so gracious as to favour me with her — society ——

[LUCILLA *after gazing at him for a moment speechless, realizes his meaning and springs up with a cry of rage and shame.*]

TRAHERNE. Scoundrel!

CRESPIN [*draws his revolver*]. Another word, and I shoot you like a dog!

RAJA. Oh, no, Major — that wouldn't help a bit. You would only be torn to pieces instead of beheaded. Besides, I have had your teeth drawn. That precaution was taken while you were at your bath.

CRESPIN [*examines his revolver and finds it empty*]. Damnation!

LUCILLA [*raising her head and addressing both men*]. Promise you won't leave me alone! If we must die, let me die first.

RAJA. The order of the ceremony, Madam, will not be at these gentlemen's choice. [LUCILLA *makes a gesture of despair.*] But do not be alarmed. No constraint shall be put upon your inclinations. Dr. Traherne reproached me with lack of consideration for your sex, and I hinted that, if you so pleased, your sex should meet with every consideration. I gather that you do *not* so please? Well, I scarcely hoped you would — I do not press the point. None the less, the suggestion remains open. And now, I'm afraid I've been talking a great deal. You must be fatigued.

[*The* MAJOR-DOMO *appears at the door, left, with a slip of paper on a salver. The* RAJA *motions him to advance, goes to meet him, takes the paper and looks at it.*]

RAJA. Ah, this is interesting! If you will wait a few minutes, I may have some news for you. Excuse me.

[*Exit left, followed by the* MAJOR-DOMO.]

[*The three stare at each other for a moment in speechless horror.*]

LUCILLA. And we were saved this morning — only for this!

TRAHERNE. Courage! There must be some way out.

CRESPIN. The whole thing's a damned piece of bluff! Ha, ha, ha! The scoundrel almost took me in.

LUCILLA [*throwing herself down on the ottoman in a passion of tears*]. My babies! Oh, my babies! Never to see them again! To leave them all alone in the world! My Ronny! My little Iris! What can we do? What can we do? Antony! Dr. Traherne! Think of something — something ——

CRESPIN. Yes, yes, Lu — we'll think of something ——

TRAHERNE. There's that fellow Watkins — we might bribe him ——

LUCILLA. Oh, offer him every penny we have in the world ——

TRAHERNE. I'm afraid he's a malicious scoundrel. He must have known what was hanging over our heads, and, looking back, I seem to see him gloating over it.

LUCILLA. Still — still — perhaps he can be bought. Antony! Think of the children! Oh, do let us try.

CRESPIN. But even if he would, he couldn't guide us through the mountains.

LUCILLA. Oh, he could hire someone else.

TRAHERNE. I don't believe we can possibly be so far from the frontier as he makes out.

LUCILLA. How far did he say?

TRAHERNE. Three weeks' journey. Yet they know all about things that happened less than a week ago.

[*Suddenly all the lights in the room go down very perceptibly. All look round in surprise.*]

LUCILLA. What is that? [*A sort of hissing and chittering sound is heard faintly but unmistakably.*] What an odd sound!

TRAHERNE. Major! Do you hear that!

CRESPIN. Do I hear it? I should say so!

TRAHERNE. Wireless!

CRESPIN [*much excited*]. Wireless, by Jupiter! They're sending out a message!

TRAHERNE. That accounts for it! They're in wireless communication with India!

LUCILLA [*to* TRAHERNE]. Antony knows all about wireless.

CRESPIN. I should rather think so! Wasn't it my job all through the war! If I could hear more distinctly now — and if they're transmitting in clear — I could read their message.

TRAHERNE. That may be our salvation!

CRESPIN. If we could get control of the wireless for five minutes, and call up the aerodrome at Amil-Serai ——

LUCILLA. What then?

CRESPIN. Why, we'd soon bring the Raja to his senses.

LUCILLA [to CRESPIN]. Where do you suppose the installation is?

CRESPIN. Somewhere overhead I should say.

TRAHERNE. We must go very cautiously, Major. We must on no account let the Raja suspect that we know anything about wireless telegraphy, else he'd take care we should never get near the installation.

CRESPIN. Right you are, Traherne — I'll lie very low.

LUCILLA [tearing off the shawl]. And how are we to behave to that horrible man?

CRESPIN. We must keep a stiff upper lip, and play the game.

LUCILLA. You mean pretend to take part in his ghastly comedy of hospitality and politeness?

TRAHERNE. If you can, it would be wisest. His delight in showing off his European polish is all in our favour. But for that he might separate us and lock us up. We must avoid that at all costs.

LUCILLA. Oh, yes, yes ——

CRESPIN. You've always had plenty of pluck, Lu ——. Now's the time to show it.

LUCILLA [putting on the shawl again]. You can trust me. The thought of the children knocked me over at first; but I'm not afraid to die. [The chittering sound ceases, and the lights suddenly go up again.] The noise has stopped.

CRESPIN. Yes, they've left off transmitting, and ceased to draw on the electric current.

TRAHERNE. He'll be back presently. Don't let us seem to be consulting.

[TRAHERNE seats himself in an easy chair. LUCILLA sits on the ottoman. CRESPIN lights a cigar and takes the RAJA's place before the fire.]

CRESPIN. Curse it! I can't remember the wave-length and the call for Amil-Serai. I was constantly using it at one time.

TRAHERNE. It'll come back to you.

CRESPIN. I pray to the Lord it may!

[The RAJA enters, left.]

RAJA. I promised you news, and it has come.

CRESPIN. What news?

RAJA. My brothers' execution is fixed for the day after tomorrow.

LUCILLA. Then the day after tomorrow ——?

RAJA. Yes — at sunset. [A pause.] But meanwhile I hope you will regard my poor house as your own. This is Liberty Hall. My tennis courts, my billiard-room, my library are all at your disposal. I should not advise you to pass the palace gates — it would not be safe, for popular feeling, I must warn you, runs very high. Besides, where could you go? There are three hundred miles of almost impassable country between you and the nearest British post.

TRAHERNE. In that case, Prince, how do you communicate with India? How has this news reached you?

RAJA. Does that puzzle you?

TRAHERNE. Naturally.

RAJA. You don't guess?

TRAHERNE. We have been trying to. The only thing we could think of was that you must be in wireless communication.

RAJA. You observed nothing to confirm the idea?

TRAHERNE. Why no.

RAJA. Did you not notice that the lights suddenly went down?

TRAHERNE. Yes, and at the same time we heard a peculiar hissing sound.

RAJA. None of you knew what it meant?

TRAHERNE. No.

RAJA. Then you have no knowledge of wireless telegraphy?

TRAHERNE. None.

RAJA. I may tell you, then, that that hissing *is* the sound of wireless transmission. I *am* in communication with India.

TRAHERNE [*to the others*]. You see, I was right.

CRESPIN. You have a wireless expert here then?

RAJA. Watkins — that invaluable fellow — he is my operator.

TRAHERNE. And with whom do you communicate?

RAJA. Do you think that quite a fair question, Doctor? Does it show your usual tact? I have my agents — I can say no more. [*Pause.*] Shall I ring for the ayah, Madam, to see you to your room?

LUCILLA. If you please. [*As he has his finger on the bell, she says*] No; stay a moment. [*Rises and advances towards him.*] Prince, I have two children. If it weren't for them, don't imagine that any of us would beg a favour at your hands. But for their sakes won't you instruct your agent to communicate with Simla and try to bring about an exchange — your brothers' lives for ours?

RAJA. I am sorry, Madam, but I have already told you why that is impossible. Even if your Government agreed, it would assuredly take revenge on me for having extorted such a concession. No whisper of your presence here must ever reach India, or — again forgive the vulgarism — my goose is cooked.

LUCILLA. The thought of my children does not move you?

RAJA. My brothers have children — does the thought of them move the Government of India? No, Madam, I am desolated to have to refuse you, but you must not ask for the impossible. [*He presses the bell.*]

LUCILLA. Does it not strike you that, if you drive us to desperation, we may find means of cheating your Goddess? What is to prevent me, for instance, from throwing myself from that loggia?

RAJA. Nothing, dear lady, except that clinging to the known, and shrinking from the unknown, that all of us feel, even while we despise it. Besides, it would be foolishly precipitate, in every sense of the word. While there is life there is hope. You can't read my mind. For aught you can tell, I may have no intention of proceeding to extremities, and may only be playing a little joke upon you. I hope you have observed that I have a sense of humour. [*The* AYAH *enters.*] Ah, here is the ayah. Good night, Madam; sleep well. [*Bows her to the door. Exit* LUCILLA *with* AYAH.] Gentlemen, a whiskey and soda. No? Then good night, good night. [*Exeunt* CRESPIN *and* TRAHERNE.]

> [*The* RAJA *takes from the table a powerful electric torch, and switches it on. Then he switches off the lights of the room, which is totally dark except for the now moonlit background. He goes up to the idol on the mantelpiece, throws the light of the torch upon it, and makes it an ironic salaam. Then he lights himself towards the door, right.*]

ACT III

SCENE. — *The* RAJA'S *Snuggery. An entirely European and modern room; its comfort contrasting with the old-fashioned, comfortless spendour of the scene of Act II.*

A door in front, right, opens on the billiard-room; another, a little further back, leads to the rest of the palace. A large and solid folding door in the back wall, centre. To the left, a large open window with a shallow balcony, which has the effect of being at a great height, and commands a view across the valley to the snow-peaks beyond.

On the left, near the window, a handsome pedestal writing table, with a large and heavy swivel chair behind it. Silver fittings on the table, all in perfect order. Close to the nearer end of the writing table, a revolving bookcase, containing the Encyclopedia Britannica and other books of reference. On the top of it a tantalus with a syphon and glasses. Close up to the writing table, and about of equal length, a deeply upholstered green leather sofa. Further over towards the left, a small table with smoking appliances. On each side of the table a comfortable green leather arm-chair. No small chairs. Low bookcases, filled with serious-looking modern books, against the walls, wherever there is space for them. On the top of one of the bookcases a large bronze bust of Napoleon. A black and white portrait of Nietzsche on the wall, along with some sporting prints.

[CRESPIN *discovered alone, wandering around the room, nervous and irritable. He tries the door at back; it is locked. Opens the door down right, and closes it, muttering "Billiards, begad!" Crosses to the writing table, examines the articles upon it, and picks up a paper which proves to be "La Vie Parisienne." He throws it down with the comment, "French muck!" Notices a paper on the couch, picks it up and says with disgust, "Russian." Then he comes down to the revolving bookcase, glances at the books and spins it angrily. After a moment's hesitation, he pours some whiskey into a tumbler and fills it from the syphon. Is on the point of drinking, but hesitates, then says, "No!" Goes to the balcony and throws out the contents of the glass. As he is setting the glass down,* TRAHERNE *enters, second door right, ushered in by a* SOLDIER, *who salutes and exits.*]

CRESPIN. There! You think you've caught me!
TRAHERNE. Caught you?

CRESPIN. Lushing. But I haven't been. I threw the stuff out of the window. For Lucilla's sake, I must keep all my wits about me.

TRAHERNE. Yes, if we can all do that, we may pull through yet.

CRESPIN. Did you sleep?

TRAHERNE. Not a wink. And you?

CRESPIN. Dozed and woke again fifteen times in a minute. A hellish night.

TRAHERNE. Have you news of Mrs. Crespin?

CRESPIN. She sent me this chit. [*Hands him a scrap of paper.*]

TRAHERNE [*reads*]. "Have slept and am feeling better. Keep the flag flying." What pluck she has!

CRESPIN. Yes, she's game — always was.

TRAHERNE. She reminds me of the women in the French Revolution. We might all be in the Conciergerie, waiting to hear the tumbrils.

CRESPIN. It would be more endurable if we *were* in prison. It's this appearance of freedom — the scoundrel's damned airs of politeness and hospitality — that makes the thing such a nightmare. [*Mechanically mixing himself a whiskey and soda.*] Do you believe we're really awake, Traherne? If I were alone, I'd think the whole thing *was* a blasted nightmare; but Lucilla and you seem to be dreaming it too. [*Raising the glass to his lips, he remembers and puts it down again, saying:*] Damn!

TRAHERNE. Some day we may look back upon it as on a bad dream.

CRESPIN. He does you well, curse him! They served me a most dainty *chota hazri* this morning, and with it a glass of rare old *fine champagne*.

TRAHERNE [*pointing to the door, down left*]. Where does that door lead?

CRESPIN. To a billiard-room. Billiards! Ha, ha!

TRAHERNE [*at door, centre*]. And this one?

CRESPIN. I don't know. It's locked — and a very solid door, too.

TRAHERNE. Do you know what I think?

CRESPIN. Yes, and I agree with you.

TRAHERNE. Opening off the fellow's own sanctum ——

CRESPIN. It's probably the wireless room. [*They exchange significant glances.*]

TRAHERNE [*indicating the window*]. And what's out here?

CRESPIN. Take a look.

TRAHERNE [*looking over*]. A sheer drop of a hundred feet.

CRESPIN. And a dry torrent below. How if we were to pick up our host, Traherne, and gently drop him on those razor-edged rocks?

TRAHERNE [*shrugs his shoulders*]. As he said last night, they'd only tear us to pieces the quicker.

CRESPIN. If it weren't for Lucilla, I'm damned if I wouldn't do it all the same.

[*The RAJA enters, second door left, dressed in spick-and-span up-to-date riding attire. He crosses to the writing table.*]

RAJA. Good morning, Major; good morning, Doctor. How do you like my snuggery? I hope you have slept well? [*They make no answer.*] No? Ah, perhaps you find this altitude trying? Never mind. We have methods of dealing with insomnia.

CRESPIN. Come now, Raja, a joke's a joke, but this cat-and-mouse business gets on one's nerves. Make arrangements to send us back to the nearest British outpost, and we'll give you our Bible oath to say nothing about the — pleasantry you've played on us.

RAJA. Send you back, my dear Major? I assure you, if I were ever so willing, it would be as much as my place is worth. You don't know how my faithful subjects are looking forward to tomorrow's ceremony. If I tried to cancel it, there would be a revolution. You must be reasonable, my dear sir.

CRESPIN. Do you think we would truckle to you, damn you, if it weren't for my wife's sake? But for her we'll make any concession — promise you anything.

RAJA. What can you promise that is worth a brass farthing to me? [With sudden ferocity.] No. Asia has a long score against you swaggering, blustering, whey-faced lords of creation, and, by all the gods, I mean to see some of it paid tomorrow! [Resuming his suave manner.] But in the meantime there is no reason why we shouldn't behave like civilized beings. How would you like to pass the morning? I'm sorry I can't offer you any shooting. I mustn't lead you into temptation. What do you say to billiards? It soothes the nerves. [Opening the door.] Here is the billiard-room. I have a little business to attend to, but I'll join you presently.

CRESPIN. Of all the infernal purring devils ——!

RAJA. Dignity, Major, dignity!

[TRAHERNE interposes and shepherds the MAJOR off. The click of billiard-balls is presently heard. The RAJA seats himself at the writing table and presses a bell. Then he takes up a pad of paper and pencil, and taps his teeth, cogitating what to write. In a few moments WATKINS enters.]

WATKINS. Your 'Ighness rang?

RAJA. Come in, Watkins. Just close the billiard-room door, will you? [WATKINS looks into the billiard-room and then closes the door.]

WATKINS. They're good pluck'd uns, sir; I will say that.

RAJA. Yes, there's some satisfaction in handling them. I'm glad they're not abject — it would quite spoil the sport.

WATKINS. Quite so, sir.

RAJA. But it has occurred to me, Watkins, that perhaps it's not quite safe to have them so near the wireless room. Their one chance would be to get into communication with India. They appeared last night to know nothing about the wireless, but I have my doubts. Tell me, Watkins — have they made any attempt to bribe you?

WATKINS. Not yet, sir.

RAJA. Ha, that looks bad. It looks as if they had something else up their sleeves, and were leaving bribery to the last resort. I want to test their ignorance of wireless. I want you, in their presence, to send out some message that is bound to startle or enrage them, and see if they show any sign of understanding it.

WATKINS [grinning]. That's a notion, sir.

RAJA. But I can't think of a message.

[*The* AYAH *opens the second door, right, ushers in* LUCILLA, *and exits.* LUCILLA *has resumed her travelling dress. The* RAJA *has been examining the lock of the wireless room, and is thus partly concealed by the entrance door as it opens, so that* LUCILLA *is well into the room before she observes him. He comes forward.*]

RAJA. Ah, Mrs. Crespin, I was just thinking of you. Think of angels and you hear their wings. Won't you sit down?

LUCILLA [*ignoring his invitation*]. I thought my husband was here.

RAJA. He's not far off. [*To* WATKINS, *pointing to the centre door.*] Just wait in there for a few minutes; I may have instructions for you.

[WATKINS *produces a key-ring, selects a key, unlocks the door of the wireless-room, and goes in, closing the door behind him.*]

RAJA [*to* LUCILLA, *who has stood motionless*]. Do, pray, sit down. I want so much to have a chat with you. [LUCILLA *seats herself, in silence.*] I hope you had everything you required?

LUCILLA. Everything.

RAJA. The ayah?

LUCILLA. Was most attentive.

RAJA. And you slept ——?

LUCILLA. More or less.

RAJA. More rather than less, if one may judge by your looks.

LUCILLA. Does it matter?

RAJA. What can matter more than the looks of a beautiful woman?

LUCILLA [*listening*]. What's that?

RAJA. The click of billiard-balls. Your husband and Dr. Traherne are passing the time.

LUCILLA [*rising*]. If you'll excuse me, I'll join them.

RAJA. Oh, pray spare me a few moments. I want to speak to you seriously.

LUCILLA [*sitting down again*]. Well — I am listening.

RAJA. You are very curt, Mrs. Crespin. I'm afraid you bear me malice, — you hold me responsible for the doubtless trying situation in which you find yourself.

LUCILLA. Who else is responsible?

RAJA. Who? Why chance, fate, the gods, Providence — whoever, or whatever, pulls the strings of this unaccountable puppet-show. Did *I* bring you here? Did *I* conjure up the fog? Could *I* have prevented your dropping from the skies? And when once you had set foot in the Goddess's precinct, it was utterly out of my power to save you — at any rate the men of your party. If I raised a finger to thwart the Goddess, it would be the end of my rule — perhaps of my life.

LUCILLA. You know that is not true. You could easily smuggle us away, and then face the people out. What about your troops?

RAJA. A handful, dear lady — a toy army. It amuses me to play at soldiers. They could do nothing against priests and people, even if they were to be depended upon. And they, too, worship the Goddess.

LUCILLA. What you really mean, Raja, is that you dare not risk it — you haven't the courage.

RAJA. You take a mean advantage, Madam. You abuse the privilege of your sex in order to taunt me with cowardice.

LUCILLA. Let us say, then, that you haven't the *will* to save us.

RAJA. Reflect one moment, Madam — why *should* I have the will, at the risk of all I possess, to save Major Crespin and Dr. Traherne? Major Crespin is your husband — does *that* recommend him to me? Forgive me if I venture to guess that it doesn't greatly recommend him to *you*. He is an only too typical specimen of a breed I detest: pigheaded, bullnecked, blustering, overbearing. Dr. Traherne is an agreeable man enough — I daresay a man of genius ——

LUCILLA. If you kill him — if you cut short his work — you kill millions of your own race, whom he would have saved.

RAJA. I don't know that I care very much about the millions you speak of. Life is a weed that grows again as fast as death mows it down. At all events, he is an Englishman, a Feringhi — and, may I add, without indiscretion, that the interest you take in him — oh, the merest friendly interest, I am sure — does not endear him to me. One is, after all, a man, and the favour shown to another man by a beautiful woman —— [LUCILLA *rises and moves toward the billiard-room. The* RAJA *interposes*.] Please, please, Mrs. Crespin, bear with me if I transgress your Western conventions. Can I help being an Oriental? Believe me, I mean no harm; I wanted to talk to you about ——

LUCILLA. Well?

RAJA. You spoke last night of — your children. [LUCILLA *turns away, her self-control wavering*.] I think you said — a boy and a little girl.

LUCILLA [*throws herself down on the couch in a fit of weeping*]. My babies, my babies!

RAJA. I feel for you, Mrs. Crespin, I do indeed. I would do anything ——

LUCILLA [*looking up, vehemently*]. Prince, if I write them a letter of farewell, will you give me your word of honour that it shall reach them?

RAJA. Ah, there, Madam, you must pardon me! I have already said that the last thing I desire is to attract the attention of the Government of India.

LUCILLA. I will say nothing to show where I am, or what has befallen me. You shall read it yourself.

RAJA. An ingenious idea! You would have it come fluttering down out of the blue upon your children's heads, like a message from a Mahatma. But, the strength of my position, you see, is that no one will ever know what has become of you. You will simply disappear in the uncharted sea of the Himalayas, as a ship sinks with all hands in the ocean. If I permitted any word from you to reach India, the detective instinct, so deeply implanted in your race, would be awakened, and the Himalayas would be combed out with a toothcomb. No, Madam, I cannot risk it.

LUCILLA [*her calm recovered*]. Cannot? You dare not! But you can and dare kill defenceless men and women. Raja, you are a pitiful coward.

RAJA. Forgive me if I smile at your tactics. You want to goad me into chivalry. If every man were a coward who took life without risking his own, where would your British sportsmen be?

LUCILLA. I beg your pardon — a savage is not necessarily a coward. And now let me go to my husband.

RAJA. Not yet, Mrs. Crespin — one more word. You are a brave woman, and I sincerely admire you ——

LUCILLA. Please — please ——

RAJA. Listen to me. It will be worth your while. I could not undertake to send a letter to your children — but it would be very easy for me to have them carried off and brought to you here.

LUCILLA [*starts, and faces him*]. What do you mean?

RAJA. I mean that, in less than a month, you may have your children in your arms, uninjured, unsuspecting, happy — if ——

LUCILLA. If?

RAJA. If — oh, in your own time, of your own free will — you will accept the homage it would be my privilege to offer you.

LUCILLA. That!

RAJA. You have the courage to die, dear lady — why not have the courage to live? [*Pause.*] You believe, I daresay, that tomorrow, when the ordeal is over, you will awaken in a new life, and that there your children will rejoin you. Suppose it were so: suppose that in forty — fifty — sixty years, they passed over to you: would they be your children? Can God Himself give you back their childhood? What I offer you is a new life, not problematical, but assured; a new life, without passing through the shadow of death; a future utterly cut off from the past, except that your children will be with you, not as vague shades, but living and loving. They must be quite young; they would soon forget all that had gone before. They would grow to manhood and womanhood under your eyes; and ultimately, perhaps, when the whole story was forgotten, you might, if you wished it, return with them to what you call civilization.

And meanwhile, you are only on the threshold of the best years of your life. You would pass them, not as a memsahib in a paltry Indian cantonment, but as the absolute queen of an absolute king. I do not talk to you of romantic love. I respect you too much to think you accessible to silly sentiment. But that is just it: I respect as much as I admire you; and I have never pretended to respect any other woman. Therefore I say you should be my first and only Queen. Your son, if you gave me one, should be the prince of princes; my other sons should all bow down to him and serve him. For, though I hate the arrogance of Europe, I believe that from a blending of the flower of the East with the flower of the West, the man of the future — the Superman — may be born.

[LUCILLA *has sat motionless through all this speech, her elbows on the end of the couch, twisting her handkerchief in her hands and gazing straight in front of her. There is now a perceptible pause before she speaks in a toneless voice.*]

LUCILLA. Is that all? Have you quite done?

RAJA. I beg you to answer.

LUCILLA. I can't answer the greater part of what you have been saying, for I have not heard it; at least I have not understood it. All I have heard is "In less than a month you may have your children in your arms," and then again, "Can God Himself give you back their childhood?" These words have kept hammering at my brain till — [*Showing her handkerchief.*] you see — I have bit my lip to keep from shrieking aloud. I think the devil must have put them in your mouth ——

RAJA. Pooh! You don't believe in these old bugbears.

LUCILLA. Perhaps not. But there is such a thing as diabolical temptation, and you have stumbled upon the secret of it.

RAJA. Stumbled!

LUCILLA. Mastered the art of it, if you like — but not in your long harangue. All I can think of is, "Can God Himself give you back their childhood?" and "In a month you may have them in your arms."

RAJA [*eagerly*]. Yes, yes — think of that. In three or four weeks you may have your little ones ——

LUCILLA [*rising and interrupting him vehemently*]. Yes — but on what conditions? That I should desert my husband and my friend — should let them go alone to their death — should cower in some back room of this murderous house of yours, listening to the ticking of the clock, and thinking, "Now — now — the stroke has fallen" — stopping my ears so as not to hear the yells of your bloodthirsty savages — and yet, perhaps, hearing nothing else to my dying day. No, Prince! — you said something about not passing through the shadow of death; but if I did this I should not pass through it, but live in it, and bring my children into it as well. What would be the good of having them in my arms if I could not look them in the face? [*She passes to the billiard-room door.*]

RAJA. That is your answer?

LUCILLA. The only possible answer. [*She enters the billiard-room and closes the door.*]

RAJA [*looking after her, to himself*]. But not the last word, my lady!

[*He sits at the writing table, and begins to write, at the same time calling, not very loudly,* "WATKINS!" *The valet immediately appears, centre.*]

WATKINS. Yessir?

RAJA [*tearing a sheet off the pad and handing it to him*]. Read that.

WATKINS. A message to be sent out, sir?

RAJA. Yes.

WATKINS [*reading*]. "The lady has come to terms. She will enter His Highness's household." Quite so, sir. What suite will she occupy?

RAJA. My innocent Watkins! Do you think it's true? What have I to do with a stuck-up Englishwoman? It's only a bait for the Feringhis. You shall send it out in their hearing, and if either of them can read the Morse code, the devil's in it if he doesn't give himself away.

WATKINS. Beg pardon, sir; I didn't quite catch on.

RAJA. If they move an eyelash I'll take care they never see the inside of this room again.

WATKINS. Am I to send this to India, sir?

RAJA. To anywhere or nowhere. Reduce the current, so that no one can pick it up. So long as it's heard in this room, that's all I want.

WATKINS. But when am I to send it, sir?

RAJA. Listen. I'll get them in here on the pretext of a little wireless demonstration, and then I'll tell you to send out an order to Tashkent for champagne. That'll be your cue. Go ahead — and send slowly.

WATKINS. Shall I ask you whether I'm to code it, sir?

RAJA. You may as well. It'll give artistic finish to the thing.

WATKINS. Very good, Your 'Ighness. But afterwards, — if, as you was saying, they was to try to corrupt me, sir ——

RAJA. Corrupt *you?* That would be painting the lily with a vengeance.

WATKINS [*with a touch of annoyance*]. Suppose they tries to get at me, sir — what are your instructions?

RAJA. How do you mean?

WATKINS. Shall I let on to take the bait?

RAJA. You may do exactly as you please. I have the most implicit confidence in you, Watkins.

WATKINS. You are very good, sir.

RAJA. I know that anything they can offer you would have to be paid either in England or in India, and that you daren't show your nose in either country. You have a very comfortable job here ——

WATKINS. My grateful thanks to you, sir.

RAJA. And you don't want to give the hangman a job, either in Lahore or in London.

WATKINS. The case in a nutshell, sir. But I thought if I was to *pretend* to send a message for them, it might keep them quiet-like.

RAJA. Very true, Watkins. It would not only keep them quiet, but the illusion of security would raise their spirits, which would be a humane action. I am always on the side of humanity.

WATKINS. Just so, sir. Then I'll humour them.

RAJA. Yes, if they want you to send a message. If they try to "get at," not only you, but the instrument, call the guard and let me know at once.

WATKINS. Certainly, sir.

RAJA. Now open the door and stand by. You have the message?

WATKINS [*producing the slip from his pocket, reads*]. "The lady has come to terms. She ——"

RAJA [*interrupting*]. Yes, that's right. [*As* WATKINS *is opening the door.*] Oh, look here — when you've finished, you'd better lock the door, and say, "Any orders, sir?" If I say "No orders, Watkins," it'll mean I'm satisfied they don't understand. If I think they *do* understand, I'll give you what orders I think necessary.

WATKINS. Very good, sir.

[*He opens the folding doors wide, revealing a small room, in which is a wireless installation.*]

RAJA [*at billiard-room door*]. Oh, Major, you were saying you had no experience of wireless. If you've finished your game, it might amuse you to see it at work. Watkins is just going to send out a message. Would Mrs. Crespin care to come?

CRESPIN [*at door*]. Yes — why not? Will you come, Lucilla?

[CRESPIN *enters, followed by* LUCILLA *and* TRAHERNE. *The* RAJA *eyes them closely so that they have no opportunity to make any sign to each other.*]

RAJA. This, you see, is the apparatus. All ready, Watkins? [*To the others:*] Won't you sit down? [*To* WATKINS:] You have the order for Tashkent?

WATKINS [*producing paper*]. Yes, Your 'Ighness; but I haven't coded it.

RAJA. Oh, never mind; send it in clear. Even if some outsider does pick it up, I daresay we can order three cases of champagne without causing international complications.

[CRESPIN *and* TRAHERNE *sit in the arm-chairs, right.* LUCILLA *is about to sit on the couch, but seeing the* RAJA *make a move to sit beside her, she passes behind the writing table and sits in the swivel chair. The* RAJA *sits on the sofa.* WATKINS *begins to transmit, — pauses.*]

RAJA. He's waiting for the reply signal.

[*A pause.*]

CRESPIN. May I take one of your excellent cigars, Raja?

RAJA. By all means.

[CRESPIN *lights a cigar.*]

WATKINS. I've got them. [*Proceeds to send the message:* "*The lady has come to terms,*" *etc.*]

CRESPIN. [*A moment after the transmission has begun, says in a low voice to the* RAJA:] May we speak?

RAJA. Oh, yes — you won't be heard in Tashkent.

CRESPIN [*holding out his cigarette case*]. Have a cigarette, Traherne.

TRAHERNE. Thanks. [*He takes a cigarette.* CRESPIN *strikes a match and lights the cigarette, saying meanwhile:*]

CRESPIN. Let us smoke and drink, for tomorrow we —— [*Blows out the match.*]

[*Silence until the transmission ends.*]

RAJA. That's how it's done!

TRAHERNE. How many words did he send?

RAJA. What was it, Watkins? "Forward by tomorrow's caravan twelve cases champagne. Usual brand. Charge our account"; was that it?

WATKINS. That's right, sir.

RAJA. Twelve words.

CRESPIN. And can they really make sense out of these fireworks?

RAJA. I hope so — else we shall run short of champagne.

WATKINS [*locking the folding door*]. Any orders, Your 'Ighness?

RAJA. No orders, Watkins.

[*As he is going out,* WATKINS *meets at the door a* SOLDIER, *who says a few words to him.*]

WATKINS [*turning*]. The 'Igh Priest is waiting to see Your 'Ighness.

RAJA. Oh, show him in.

[WATKINS *ushers in the* HIGH PRIEST OF THE GODDESS, *and then exits.*

The HIGH PRIEST'S *personality is unmistakably sinister. The* RAJA, *after a word of greeting, turns to the others.*]

RAJA. I mentioned my Archbishop of York. This is he. Allow me to introduce you. Your Grace, Mrs. Crespin — Major Crespin — Dr. Traherne.

[*The* PRIEST, *understanding the situation, makes a sort of contemptuous salaam.*]

The Archbishop's manners are not good. You will excuse him. He regards you, I regret to say, as unclean creatures, whose very presence means pollution. He would be a mine of information for an anthropologist.

[*He exchanges a few words with the* PRIEST, *and turns again to his guests.*]

His Grace reminds me of some arrangements for tomorrow's ceremony, which, as Archbishop of Canterbury, I must attend to in person. You will excuse me for half an hour? Pray make yourselves at home. Tiffin at half past twelve.

[*He speaks a few words to the* PRIEST, *who replies in a sort of growl.*]

His Grace says *au revoir* — and so do I.

[*Exits, followed by the* PRIEST. *Both* TRAHERNE *and* LUCILLA *are about to speak.* CRESPIN *motions them to be cautious. He goes to the billiard-room, opens the door, looks around and closes it again.* LUCILLA *examines the balcony.* TRAHERNE *slips up to the centre door and noiselessly tests it.*]

TRAHERNE [*to* CRESPIN]. What was the message?

CRESPIN. It said that the lady had accepted her life — on his terms.

TRAHERNE. Oh! — a trap for us.

CRESPIN. Yes. A put-up job.

LUCILLA. You gave no sign, Antony. I think he must have been reassured.

TRAHERNE. Evidently; or he wouldn't have left us here.

CRESPIN. What to do now?

TRAHERNE. Can we break open the door?

CRESPIN. No good. It would make a noise. We'd be interrupted, and then it would be all up.

TRAHERNE. Well, then, the next step is to try to bribe Watkins.

CRESPIN. I don't believe it's a bit of good.

TRAHERNE. Nor I. The fellow's a thorough-paced scoundrel. But we *might* succeed, and if we don't even try, they'll suspect that we're plotting something else. If we can convince them that we're at our wits' end, we've the better chance of taking them off their guard.

LUCILLA. Yes — you see that, Antony?

CRESPIN. Perhaps you're right. But, even if the damned scoundrel can be bought, what good is it if I can't remember the wave-length and the call for Amil-Serai?

LUCILLA. You'll think of it all of a sudden.

CRESPIN. Not if I keep racking my brains for it. If I could get my mind off it, the damned thing might come back to me.

TRAHERNE. All the more reason for action. But first, we must settle what message to send if we get the chance.

LUCILLA [*sits at writing-table*]. Dictate — I'll write.

TRAHERNE. What about this? "Major Crespin, wife, Traherne imprisoned, Rukh, Raja's palace, lives in danger."

[LUCILLA *writes on an envelope which she takes from the paper-case.*]

CRESPIN. We want something more definite.

LUCILLA. How would this do? "Death threatened tomorrow evening. Rescue urgent."

TRAHERNE. Excellent.

[LUCILLA *finishes the message, and hands it to* CRESPIN.]

CRESPIN [*reads*]. "Major Crespin, wife, Traherne, imprisoned, Rukh, Raja's palace. Death threatened tomorrow evening. Rescue urgent." [*Takes the paper.*] Right. I'll keep it ready.

TRAHERNE. Now, how to get hold of Watkins?

LUCILLA [*at the table*]. There's a bell here. Shall I try it?

TRAHERNE. Hold on a moment. We have to decide what to do if he won't take money, and we have to use force in order to get his keys.

CRESPIN [*looking around*]. There's nothing here to knock him on the head with — not even a chair you can lift ——

TRAHERNE. Not a curtain cord to truss him up with ——

LUCILLA. The first thing would be to gag him, wouldn't it? [*Takes off her scarf.*] Would this do for that?

TRAHERNE. Capital! [*Takes the scarf, ties a knot in it, and places it on the upper end of the sofa.*]

CRESPIN. What about a billiard cue?

TRAHERNE. If he saw it around he'd smell a rat.

CRESPIN. Then there's only one thing ——

TRAHERNE. What? [CRESPIN *points to the balcony, and makes a significant gesture.*]

LUCILLA. Oh! [*Shrinks away from the window.*]

TRAHERNE. I'm afraid it can't be helped. There's a drop of a good hundred feet.

CRESPIN. None too much for him.

TRAHERNE. When he locked that door he put the key in his trousers' pocket. We must remember to get it before ——

LUCILLA. But if you kill him and still don't remember the call, we shall be no better off than we are now.

TRAHERNE. We shall be no worse off.

CRESPIN. Better, by Jove! For if I can get three minutes at that instrument, the Raja can't tell whether we have communicated or not. [*He takes up the glass of whiskey-and-soda which he has poured out before.*]

LUCILLA. Oh, Antony!

CRESPIN. Don't be a fool, Lu. [*Gulps down the drink, and says as he pours out more whiskey:*] It's because I'm so unnaturally sober that my brain won't work. [*Drinks the whiskey raw.*] Now ring that bell. [LUCILLA *does so.*] You do the talking, Traherne. The fellow's damned insolence gets on my nerves.

TRAHERNE. All right. [*Sits at the writing-table.*]

CRESPIN. Look out ——

[*Enter* WATKINS, *second door, right.*]

WATKINS. You rang, sir? [*Standing by the door.*]

TRAHERNE. Yes, Watkins, we want a few words with you. Do you mind coming over here? We don't want to speak loud.

WATKINS. There's no one understands English, sir.

TRAHERNE. Please oblige me, all the same.

WATKINS [*coming forward*]. Now, sir!

TRAHERNE. I daresay you can guess what we want with you.

WATKINS. I'm no 'and at guessin', sir. I'd rather you'd put it plain.

TRAHERNE. Well, you know that we've fallen into the hands of blood-thirsty savages? You know what is proposed for tomorrow?

WATKINS. I've 'eard as your numbers is up.

TRAHERNE. You surely don't intend to stand by and see us murdered — three of your own people, and one of them a lady?

WATKINS. My own people, is it? And a *lady* ——!

LUCILLA. A woman, then, Watkins.

WATKINS. What has my own people ever done for me — or women either — that I should lose a cushy job and risk my neck for the sake of the three of you? I wouldn't do it for all your bloomin' England, I tell you straight.

CRESPIN. It's no good, Traherne. Come down to tin tacks.

TRAHERNE. Only a sighting shot, Major. It was just possible we might have misread our man.

WATKINS. You did if you took 'im for a V. C. 'ero wot 'ud lay down his life for England, 'ome, and beauty. The first thing England ever done for me was to 'ave me sent to a reformatory for pinching a silver rattle off of a young haristocrat in a p'rambulator. That, and the likes of that, is wot I've got to thank England for. And why did I do it? Because my mother would have bashed my face in if I'd have come back empty-handed. That's wot 'ome and beauty has meant for me. W'y should I care more for a woman being scragged than what I do for a man?

TRAHERNE. Ah, yes, I quite see your point of view. But the question now is: What'll you *take* to get us out of this?

WATKINS. Get you out of this! If you was to offer me millions, 'ow could I do that?

TRAHERNE. By going into that room and sending this message through to the Amil-Serai aerodome.

[CRESPIN *hands* WATKINS *the message. He reads it through and places it on the table.*]

WATKINS. So that's the game, is it?

TRAHERNE. That, as you say, is the game.

WATKINS. You know what you're riskin'?

TRAHERNE. What do you mean?

WATKINS. W'y, if the Guv'nor suspected as you'd got a word through to India, ten to one he'd wipe you off the slate like that [*snapping his fingers*] without waiting for tomorrow.

CRESPIN. That makes no difference. We've got to face it.

TRAHERNE. Come now! On your own showing, Mr. Watkins, loyalty to your master oughtn't to stand in your way. I don't suppose gratitude is one of your weaknesses.

WATKINS. Gratitude! To 'im? What for? I'm not badly off here, to be sure, but it's nothing to wot I does for 'im; and I 'ate 'im for 'is funny little ways. D'you think I don't see that he's always pulling my leg?

TRAHERNE. Well, then, you won't mind selling him. We've only to settle the price.

WATKINS. That's all very fine, sir; but what price 'ave you gents to offer?

TRAHERNE. Nothing down — no spot cash — that's clear. You'll have to take our word for whatever bargain we come to.

WATKINS. Your word! How do I know ——?

TRAHERNE. Oh, our written word. We'll give it to you in writing.

WATKINS [after thinking for a moment]. If I was to 'elp you out, there must be no more fairy-tales about any of you 'avin' seen me in India.

TRAHERNE. All right. We accept your assurance that you never were there.

WATKINS. And see here, Dr. Traherne — you know very well I couldn't stay here after I'd helped you to escape — leastways, if I stayed, it'd be in my grave. You'll 'ave to take me with you — and for that I can only have your word. Supposing you could get the message through, and the English was to come, no writing could bind you if you chose to leave me in the lurch.

TRAHERNE. Quite true. I'm afraid you'll have to trust us for that. But I give you my word of honour that we would be as careful of your safety as if you were one of ourselves. I suppose you know that, strange as you may think it, there are people in the world that would rather die than break a solemn promise.

CRESPIN. Even to a hound like you, Watkins.

WATKINS. I advise you to keep a civil tongue in yer 'ead, Major. Don't forget that I 'ave you in the 'ollow of my 'and.

TRAHERNE. True, Watkins; and the hollow of your hand is a very disagreeable place to be in. That's why we're willing to pay well to get out of it. Come, now, what shall we say?

WATKINS. Well, what about a little first instalment? You ain't quite on your uppers, are you, now? You could come down with something, be it ever so humble?

TRAHERNE [examining his pocket-book]. I have 300 rupees and five ten-pound notes. [Places the money on the table.]

WATKINS. And you, Major?

CRESPIN. Two hundred and fifty rupees. [Crosses and lays the notes on the table.] Oh, and some loose change.

WATKINS [nobly]. Oh, never mind the chicken-feed! And the lady?

LUCILLA. I gave my last rupee to your wife, Watkins.

WATKINS. Well, that's about £120 to go on with.

TRAHERNE [placing his hand on the heap of notes]. There. That's your first instalment. Now what about the balance? Shall we say £1000 apiece?

WATKINS. A thousand apiece! Three thousand pounds! You're joking, Dr. Traherne! Wot would £3000 be to me in England? W'y, I'd 'ave to take to valeting again. No, no, sir! If I'm to do this job, I must 'ave enough to make a gentleman of me.

[CRESPIN, TRAHERNE, *and* LUCILLA *burst out laughing.*]

WATKINS. Well, you are the queerest lot as ever I come across. Your lives is 'anging by a 'air, and yet you can larf!

LUCILLA [*hysterically*]. It's your own fault, Watkins. Why *will* you be so funny? [*Her laughter turns to tears and she buries her face in the end of the couch, shaken with sobs.*]

TRAHERNE. I'm afraid what you ask is beyond our means, Watkins. But I double my bid — two thousand apiece.

WATKINS. You'll 'ave to double it again, sir, and a little more. You write me out an I.O.U. for fifteen thousand pounds, and I'll see wot can be done.

CRESPIN. Well, you *are* the most consummate ——

WATKINS. If your lives ain't worth five thousand apiece to you, there's nothing doing. For my place here is worth fifteen thousand to me. And there's all the risk, too — I'm not charging you nothing for that.

TRAHERNE. We appreciate your generosity, Watkins. Fifteen thousand be it!

WATKINS. Now you're talking.

[TRAHERNE *rapidly writes and signs the I.O.U. and hands it to* WATKINS.]

WATKINS. That's right, sir; but the Major must sign it, too.

CRESPIN [*crosses to the table, on which* WATKINS *places the paper, writes, throws down the pen*]. There you are, damn you!

TRAHERNE. Now get to work quick, and call up Amil-Serai.

WATKINS. Right you are, sir. [*Picks up the envelope and begins, in a leisurely way, unlocking the centre door.*]

CRESPIN. Isn't there some special call you must send out to get Amil-Serai?

WATKINS. Oh, yes, sir, I know it.

[WATKINS *takes his seat at the instrument, with his back to the snuggery, and begins to work it.*]

CRESPIN [*whispers*]. That's not a service call.

[*A pause.*]

WATKINS. Right! Got them, sir. Now the message.

CRESPIN [*as* WATKINS *works the key,* CRESPIN *spells out:*] "The — white — goats — are — ready — for ——" [*To* TRAHERNE.] No, but the black sheep is! Come on!

[CRESPIN *tiptoes up toward* WATKINS *followed by* TRAHERNE. *As he passes the upper end of the sofa* CRESPIN *picks up* LUCILLA'S *scarf and hands it to* TRAHERNE, *meantime producing his own handkerchief.* LUCILLA *rises, her hand pressed to her mouth. The men steal up close behind* WATKINS. *Suddenly* TRAHERNE *jams the gag in* WATKINS'S *mouth, and ties the ends of the scarf.* WATKINS *attempts a cry, but it trails off into a gurgle.* CRESPIN *meantime grips* WATKINS'S *arms behind, and ties the wrists with his handkerchief.* TRAHERNE *makes fast the gag, and the two lift him, struggling, and carry him towards the window.* WATKINS'S *head falls back, and his terror-stricken eyes can be seen over the swathing gag. They rest him for a moment on the balustrade.*]

TRAHERNE. Must we ——?

CRESPIN. Nothing else for it — one, two, three! [*They heave him over.* LUCILLA, *who has been watching, petrified, gives a gasping cry.*]

CRESPIN. At least we haven't taken it lying down! [*He pours out some whiskey and is about to drink when he pauses, puts down the glass, and then cries in great excitement:*] Hold on! Don't speak! [*A pause.*] I have it! [*Another pause.*] Yes, by God, I have it! I've remembered the call! Can you lock that door?

LUCILLA [*at second door, left*]. No key this side!

TRAHERNE [*whispering, and running to the door*]. Don't open it. There are soldiers in the passage. I'll hold it. [*He stations himself before the door.* CRESPIN *rushes to the instrument and rapidly examines it.*]

CRESPIN. The scoundrel had reduced the current. [*Makes an adjustment with feverish haste.*] Now the wave length! [*More adjustment. He begins to transmit. A pause.*]

TRAHERNE. Do you get any answer?

CRESPIN. No, no; I don't expect any — I'm sure they haven't the power. But it's an even chance that I get them all the same. [*He goes on transmitting hurriedly while* TRAHERNE *and* LUCILLA *stand breathless,* TRAHERNE *with his shoulder to the door.*]

TRAHERNE. Someone's coming up this passage! Go on! Go on! I'll hold the door.

[*Another slight pause, while* CRESPIN *transmits feverishly. Suddenly* TRAHERNE *braces himself against the door, gripping the handle. After a moment, there is a word of command outside, the sound of shoulders heaved against the door, and it is gradually pushed open by three guards.* TRAHERNE *is shoved back by its motion.*]

[*The* RAJA *enters, rushes forward and grasps the situation.*]

RAJA. Ah! When the cat's away ——

[*He whips out a revolver and fires.*]

CRESPIN. Got me, by God!

[*He falls forward over the instrument, but immediately recovers himself, and rapidly unmakes the adjustments.* LUCILLA *and* TRAHERNE *catch him as he staggers back from the instrument, and lay him on the couch.*]

TRAHERNE [*kneeling and supporting him*]. Brandy!

[LUCILLA *gets the glass. They put it to his lips.*]

[*The* RAJA *meanwhile goes to the wireless table, sees the draft message and reads it.*]

RAJA [*holding out the paper*]. How much of this did you get through?

CRESPIN [*raising himself a little*]. Damn you — none! [*Falls back dead.*]

LUCILLA [*crying out*]. Antony!

RAJA. All over, eh?

[TRAHERNE, *still kneeling, makes an affirmative sign.*]

[*At this moment a noise is heard outside, and three soldiers burst open the door and rush in. One of them speaks to the* RAJA, *pointing to the window, the other two rush up to* TRAHERNE, *seize him and drag him over to the left.* LUCILLA *remains kneeling by* CRESPIN'S *body. The* RAJA *goes calmly over to the window and looks out.*]

RAJA [*returning to centre*]. Tut tut — most inconvenient. And foolish on your part — for now, if my brothers should be reprieved, we cannot hear of it. [*Looks at the message reflectively.*] Otherwise, the situation remains unchanged. We adhere to our programme for tomorrow. The Major has only a few hours' start of you.

ACT IV

SCENE. — *A gloomy hall, its roof supported by four wooden columns, two in a row, rudely carved with distorted animal and human figures. The walls are also of rudely-carved wood, and are pierced all round, at the height of about twelve feet, by a sort of clerestory — a series of oblong slits or unglazed windows through which the sky can be seen. The general tone of the wood is dark brown, but the interstices between the carvings have here and there been filled in with dull red. There is a high curtained doorway, right, leading to a sort of robing-room. Opposite to it, left, a two-leaved wooden door, closed with a heavy wooden bolt. An oblong hole in the door, with a sliding shutter, enables the guard within to inspect whoever approaches from without. At the back, centre, is a wide opening, curtained at the beginning of the act. When the curtains are withdrawn, they reveal a sort of balcony or tribune, raised by two steps above the level of the hall, over the balustrade of which can be seen the head and shoulders of a colossal image of the Goddess, apparently at a distance of some fifty yards. Between the two foremost columns, on a dais of two steps, a wide throne, which has for its backing a figure of the Goddess carved in high relief, amid a good deal of barbaric tracery. The figure is green, but there are touches of gold in her crown, her ornaments, and in the tracery. A low brazier rests on the ground in front of the throne.*

The hall is a sort of anteroom to the public place of sacrifice without.

Late afternoon light comes in through the clerestory on the left.

When the curtain rises, a group of Priests is gathered round the doorway, right, while the CHIEF PRIEST *stands at the centre, holding the curtains a little way apart and looking out. A Priest is on guard at the door, left.*

For a moment after the rise of the curtain, there is a regular and subdued murmur from the crowd without. Then it swells into a chorus of execrations. The CHIEF PRIEST *gives an order to the other Priests, right, one of whom goes off through the doorway. The guard at the door, left, slips back the shutter and looks out, then unbolts the door, and admits* TRAHERNE, *strapped to a mountain chair, and guarded by two soldiers, who withdraw. At the same time, the* RAJA, *in splendid Eastern attire, enters, right.*

RAJA. Well, Doctor, it doesn't appear that any "god from the machine" is going to interfere with our programme.

TRAHERNE. You are bringing a terrible vengeance upon yourself.

RAJA. Think, my dear Doctor. If, as the Major said, he did *not* get your S.O.S. through, I have nothing to fear. If he lied, and *did* get it through, nothing can ultimately save me, and I may as well be hung for a sheep as for a lamb.

TRAHERNE [*writhing in his bonds*]. You might have spared me this!

RAJA. A ritual detail, Doctor; not quite without reason. Persons lacking in self-control might throw themselves to the ground or otherwise disarrange the ceremony. [*He speaks a word, and the bearers promptly release* TRAHERNE, *and carry the chair out, left.*]

TRAHERNE. What have you done with Mrs. Crespin?

RAJA. Don't be alarmed. She'll be here in due time.

TRAHERNE. Listen to me, Raja. Do what you will with me, but let Mrs. Crespin go. Send her to India or to Russia, and I am sure, for her children's sake, she will swear to keep absolute silence as to her husband's fate and mine.

RAJA. You don't believe, then, that I couldn't save you if I would?

TRAHERNE. Believe it? No!

RAJA. You are quite right, my dear Doctor. I am not a High Priest for nothing. I might work the oracle. I might get a command from the Goddess to hurt no hair upon your heads.

TRAHERNE. Then what devilish pleasure do you find in putting us to death?

RAJA. Pleasure? The pleasure of a double vengeance. Vengeance for today — my brothers — and vengeance for centuries of subjection and insult. Do you know what brought you here? It was not blind chance, any more than it was the Goddess. It was my will, my craving for revenge, that drew you here by a subtle, irresistible magnetism. My will is my religion — my god. And by that god I have sworn that you shall not escape me.

[*Yells from the crowd outside.*]

Ah, they are bringing Mrs. Crespin.

[*The* PRIEST *unbolts the door, right, and* LUCILLA *is carried in.*]

RAJA. I apologize, Madam, for the manners of my people. Their fanaticism is beyond my control.

[*He says a word to the bearers, who release* LUCILLA. TRAHERNE *gives her his hand, and she steps from the chair, which the bearers remove, left.*]

TRAHERNE. How long have we left?

RAJA. Till the sun's rim touches the crest of the mountain. A blast of our great mountain horn will announce the appointed hour, and you will be led out to the sacred enclosure. You saw the colossal image of the Goddess out yonder?

[*He points to the back. They look at each other in silence.*]

TRAHERNE. Will you grant us one last request?

RAJA. By all means, if it is in my power. In spite of your inconsiderate action of yesterday ——

TRAHERNE. Inconsiderate ——?

RAJA. Watkins, you know — poor Watkins — a great loss to me! But *à la guerre comme à la guerre!* I bear no malice for a fair act of war. I am anxious to show you every consideration.

TRAHERNE. Then you will leave us alone for the time that remains to us.

RAJA. Why, by all means. And oh, by the way, you need have no fear of the — ceremony — being protracted. It will be brief and — I trust — painless. The High Church Party are not incapable of cruelty; but I have resolutely set my face against it. [LUCILLA *has meanwhile stood stonily gazing straight in front of her. The* RAJA *reflects for a moment, and then goes up to her.*] Before I go, Madam, may I remind you of my offer of yesterday? It is not yet too late. [LUCILLA *takes no notice.*] Is it just to your children to refuse? [*She looks at him stonily, saying nothing. After a pause.*] Immovable? So be it! [*He turns to go. At this moment a great yell of triumphant hatred goes up from the populace.*]

RAJA. Your husband's body, Madam. They are laying it at the feet of the Goddess.

LUCILLA. You promised me ——

RAJA. That it should be burnt. I will keep my promise. But you see I had three brothers — a head for a head.

[*He goes into the inner chamber, encircled by his Priests. Only the* GUARD *at the door, left, remains, half hidden by the door jamb.*]

[LUCILLA *and* TRAHERNE *are left alone.* LUCILLA *sinks down upon the broad base of the foremost pillar, right.*]

LUCILLA. So this is the end!

TRAHERNE. What offer did that devil make you?

LUCILLA. Oh, I didn't mean to tell you, but I may as well. He is an ingenious tormentor. He offered yesterday to let me live, and to kidnap the children and bring them here to me — you know on what terms.

TRAHERNE. To bring the children here?

LUCILLA. He said in a month I might have them in my arms. Think of it! Ronny and Iris in my arms! [*A pause.* TRAHERNE *stands with his back to her.*]

TRAHERNE [*in a low and unsteady voice*]. Are you sure you did right to refuse?

LUCILLA. Do you mean ——?

TRAHERNE [*louder and almost harshly*]. Are you sure it is not wrong to refuse?

LUCILLA. Oh, how can you ——? Right? Wrong? What are right and wrong to me now? If I could see my children again, would any scruple of "right" or "wrong" make me shrink from anything that was possible? But this is so utterly, utterly impossible.

TRAHERNE. Forgive me. You know it would add an unspeakable horror to death if I had to leave you here. But I felt I must ask you whether you had fully considered ——

LUCILLA. I have thought of nothing else through all these torturing hours.

TRAHERNE. How brave you are!

LUCILLA. Not brave, not brave. If I *could* live, I *would* — there, I confess it! But I should die of shame and misery, and leave my children — to that man. Or, if *I did* live, what sort of a mother should I be to them? They would be much better without me! Oh, my precious, precious darlings! [*She clasps her arms across her breast, and rocks herself in agony. A short silence.*]

TRAHERNE [*lays his hand on her shoulder*]. Lucilla!

LUCILLA [*looking up*]. Oh, Basil, say you think it won't be altogether bad for them! They will never know anything of their father now, but what was good. And their mother will simply have vanished into the skies. They will think she has flown away to heaven — and who knows but it may be true? There may be *something* beyond this hell.

TRAHERNE. We shall know soon, Lucilla.

LUCILLA. But to go away and leave them without a word——! Poor little things, poor little things.

TRAHERNE. They will remember you as something very dear and beautiful. The very mystery will be like a halo about you.

LUCILLA. Shall I see them again, Basil? Tell me that.

[*A pause.*]

TRAHERNE. Who knows? Even to comfort you, I won't say I am certain. But I do sincerely think you may.

LUCILLA [*smiling woefully*]. You think there is a sporting chance?

TRAHERNE. More than that. This life is such a miracle — could any other be more incredible?

LUCILLA. But even if I should meet them in another world, they would not be *my* Ronny and Iris, but a strange man and a strange woman, built up of experiences in which I had had no share. Oh, it was cunning, cunning, what that devil said to me! He said "God Himself cannot give you back their childhood."

TRAHERNE. How do you know that God is going to take their childhood from you? You may be with them this very night — with them, unseen, but perhaps not unfelt, all the days of their life.

LUCILLA. You are saying that to make what poor Antony called a "haze" for me — to soften the horror of darkness that is waiting for us? Don't give me "dope," Basil — I can face things without it.

TRAHERNE. I mean every word of it. [*A pause.*] Why do you smile?

LUCILLA. At a thought that came to me — the thought of poor Antony as a filmy, purified spirit. It seems so unthinkable.

TRAHERNE. Why unthinkable? Why may he not still exist, though he has left behind him the nerves, the cravings, that tormented him — and you? You have often told me that there was something fine in the depths of his nature; and you know how he showed it yesterday.

LUCILLA. Oh, if I could only tell the children how he died!

TRAHERNE. But his true self was chained to a machine that was hopelessly out of gear. The chain is broken: the machine lies out there — scrapped. Do you think that he was just that machine, and nothing else?

LUCILLA. I don't know. I only feel that Antony spiritualized would not be Antony. And you, Basil — if Antony leaves his — failings, you must leave behind your work. Do you *want* another life in which there is no work to be done — no disease to be rooted out? [*With a mournful smile.*] Don't tell me you don't long to take your microscope with you wherever you may be going.

TRAHERNE. Perhaps there are microscopes awaiting me there.

LUCILLA. Spirit microscopes for spirit microbes? You don't believe that, Basil.

TRAHERNE. I neither believe nor disbelieve. In all we can say of another life we are like children blind from birth, trying to picture the forms and colours of the rainbow.

LUCILLA. But if the forms and colours we know are of no use to us, what comfort are we to find in formless, colourless possibilities? If we are freed from all human selfishness, shall I love my children more than any other woman's? Can I love a child I cannot kiss, that cannot look into my eyes and kiss me back again?

TRAHERNE [*starting up*]. Oh, Lucilla, don't!

LUCILLA. What do you mean?

TRAHERNE. Don't remind me of all we are losing! I meant to leave it all unspoken — the thought of *him* lying out there seemed to tie my tongue. But we have only one moment on this side of eternity. Lucilla, shall I go on?

[*After a perceptible pause,* LUCILLA *bows her head.*]

Do you think it is with a light heart that I turn my back upon the life of earth and all it might have meant for you and me — for you and me, Lucilla!

LUCILLA. Yes, Basil, for you and me.

TRAHERNE. Rather than live *without* you, I am glad to die *with* you; but oh, what a wretched gladness compared with that of living with you and loving you! I wonder if you guess what it has meant to me, ever since we met at Dehra Dun, to see you as another man's wife, bound to him by ties I couldn't ask you to break. It has been hell, hell! [*Looking up with a mournful smile.*] My love has not been quite selfish, Lucilla, since I can say I really do love your children, though I know they have stood between me and heaven.

LUCILLA. Yes, Basil, I know. I have known from the beginning.

TRAHERNE. Oh, Lucilla, have we not been fools, fools? We have sacrificed to an idol as senseless as that — [*with a gesture towards the image*] all the glory and the beauty of life! What do I care for a bloodless, shadowy life — life in the abstract, with all the senses extinct? Is there not something in the depths of our hearts that cries out "We don't want it! Better eternal sleep!"

LUCILLA. Oh, Basil — you are going back to your own wisdom.

TRAHERNE. Wisdom! What has wisdom to say to love, thwarted and unfulfilled? You were right when you said that it is a mockery to speak of love without hands to clasp, without lips to kiss. We may be going to some pale parody of life; but in our cowardice we have killed love for ever and ever.

LUCILLA. No, Basil, don't call it cowardice. I, too, regret — perhaps as much as you — that things were — as they were. But not even your love could have made up to me for my children.

[*A trumpet-blast is heard — a prolonged deep, wailing sound.*]

There is the signal! Good-bye, dear love.

[*She holds out her hands to him. They kiss and stand embraced, until, at a sound of tom-toms and a low muttered chant from behind the curtains, right, they part, and stand hand in hand, facing the doorway.*]

[*Suddenly, at a great shattering note from a gong, the curtains of the doorway part, and a procession of chanting Priests enters, all wearing fantastic robes and headdresses, and all, except the* CHIEF PRIEST, *masked. The* RAJA *follows them, also wearing a priestly headdress, and gorgeously robed. Behind him came three dark-robed and masked figures, carrying heavy swords. Musicians bring up the rear. The Priests group themselves round the throne.*]

RAJA [*to* TRAHERNE *and* LUCILLA, *who are standing in front of the throne*]. May I trouble you to move a little aside? I am, for the moment, not a king, but a priest, and must observe a certain dignity. Ridiculous, isn't it?

[*They move over to the left of the throne. He advances in stately fashion and seats himself on it.*]

RAJA [*to Lucilla*]. Must I do violence to my feelings, Madam, by including you in the approaching ceremony? There is still time.

[LUCILLA *is silent.*]

We autocrats are badly brought up. We are not accustomed to having our desires, or even our whims, thwarted.

TRAHERNE [*interrupting*]. Will you never cease tormenting this lady?

RAJA [*totally disregarding him*]. Remember my power. If I may not take you back to my palace as my Queen, I can send you back as my slave.

[*A pause.*]

Have you nothing to say?

LUCILLA. Nothing.

RAJA. I repeat my offer as to your children.

LUCILLA. I would die a hundred times rather than see them in your hands.

RAJA. Remember, too, that, if I so will it, you cannot save them by dying. I can have them kidnapped — or — I can have them killed.

[LUCILLA *shrieks.* TRAHERNE, *with a cry of "Devil" makes a leap at the* RAJA's *throat, pinning him against the back of the throne. The Priests instantly pull* TRAHERNE *off, pinion him, and drag him over to the right. They talk furiously to each other, and the* CHIEF PRIEST *prostrates himself before the* RAJA, *apparently in urgent supplication. The* RAJA, *who is now to the right of the throne,* LUCILLA *remaining on the left, quits them with some difficulty, and then turns to* TRAHERNE.]

RAJA. Chivalrous but ill-advised, Dr. Traherne. I regret it, and so will you. My colleagues here insist that, as you have laid impious hands on the chief of their sacred caste, your death alone will not appease the fury of the Goddess. They insist on subjecting you to a process of expiation — a ritual of great antiquity — but ——

TRAHERNE. You mean torture?

RAJA. Well — yes.

[LUCILLA *rushes forward with a cry.*]

Not you, Madam — not you ——

LUCILLA. I must speak to you — speak to you alone! Send Dr. Traherne away.

TRAHERNE. Lucilla! What are you thinking of! Lucilla ——!

[*The* RAJA *motions to the Priests, who do something to* TRAHERNE *which causes him to crumple up, and his voice dies away.*]

LUCILLA. I beg you — I beg you! One minute — no more!

[*The* RAJA *looks at her for a moment, then shrugs his shoulders and gives an order.* TRAHERNE *is dragged through the doorway, right.*]

[LUCILLA, *in her desperation, has rushed up the steps of the throne. She now sinks, exhausted, upon the end of the throne itself.*]

LUCILLA. Let him go, send him back to India unharmed, and — it shall be as you wish.

RAJA. Soho! You will do for your lover — to save him a little additional pain — what you would not do to have your children restored to you! Suppose I agree — would *he* accept this sacrifice?

LUCILLA. No, no, he wouldn't — but he must have no choice. That is part of the bargain. Send him — bound hand and foot, if need be — down to Kashmir, and put him over the frontier ——

RAJA. You don't care what he thinks of you?

LUCILLA. He will know what to think.

RAJA. And I too, Madam, know what to think. [*Kneeling with one knee on the throne, he seizes her by the shoulders and turns her face towards him.*] Come, look me in the eyes and tell me that you honestly intend to fulfil your bargain! [*Her head droops.*] I knew it! You are playing with me! But the confiding barbarian is not so simple as you imagine. No woman has ever tried to fool me that has not repented it. You think, when you have to pay up, you will fob me off with your dead body. Let me tell you, I have no use for you dead — I want you with all the blood in your veins, with all the pride in that damned sly brain of yours. I want to make my plaything of your beauty, my mockery of your pride. I want to strip off the delicate English lady, and come down to the elemental woman, the handmaid and the instrument of man. [*Changing his tone.*] Come now, I'll make you a plain offer. I *will* put Dr. Traherne over the frontier, and, as they set him free, my people shall hand him a letter written by you at my dictation. You will tell him that you have determined to accept my protection and make this your home. Consequently you wish to have your children conveyed to you here ——

LUCILLA. Never — never — never! I will make no bargain that involves my children.

RAJA. You see! You will give me no hostages for the fulfillment of your bond. But a pledge of your good faith I must have. For without a pledge, Madam, I don't believe in it one little bit.

LUCILLA. What pledge?

RAJA. Only one is left — Dr. Traherne himself. I may — though it will strain my power to the uttermost — save his life, while keeping him in prison. Then, when you have fulfilled your bond — fulfilled it to the uttermost, mark you! — when you have borne me a child — I will let him go free.

But the moment you attempt to evade your pledge, by death or by escape, I will hand him over to the priests to work their will with; and I will put no restraint upon their savage instincts. [*Pause.*] Choose, my dear lady, choose!

> [*The subdued murmur of the crowd below, which has been faintly audible during the foregoing scene, ceases, and in the silence is heard a faint, but rapidly increasing, whirr and throb.*]

> [LUCILLA, *who has been crouching on the steps of the throne, looks up slowly, hope dawning in her face. For a few seconds she says nothing, waiting to assure herself that she can believe her ears. Then she says in a low voice, with a sort of sob of relief:*]

LUCILLA. Aeroplanes! [*She springs up with a shriek.*] The aeroplanes! Basil! Basil! The aeroplanes! [*She rushes out through the doorway, right, thrusting aside the incoming Priests, who are too amazed to oppose her.*]

> [*The* RAJA *does not at first alter his attitude but looks up and listens intently. The curtains shutting off the balcony at the back are violently torn apart by the guard outside, who shout to the* RAJA *and point upward. Sounds of consternation and terror proceed from the unseen crowd.*]

> [*The* RAJA *goes to the back and looks out. At the same moment* LUCILLA *and* TRAHERNE *rush in from the doorway, right.*]

LUCILLA. See! See! They are circling lower and lower! Is it true, Basil? Are we saved?

TRAHERNE. Yes, Lucilla, we are saved.

LUCILLA. Oh, thank God! thank God! I shall see my babies again!

> [*She sways, almost fainting.* TRAHERNE *supports her.*]

RAJA. So the Major lied like a gentleman! Good old Major! I didn't think he had it in him.

> [*The Guards call his attention; he looks out from the balcony, and gives an order, then turns down again.*]

One of the machines has landed. An officer is coming this way — he looks a mere boy.

TRAHERNE. The conquerors of the air have all been mere boys.

RAJA. I have given orders that he shall be brought here unharmed. Perhaps I had better receive him with some ceremony.

> [*He goes back to the throne and seats himself, cross-legged. At his command the Priests range themselves about him.*]

RAJA. You said just now, Dr. Traherne, that you were saved. Are you so certain of that?

TRAHERNE. Certain.

RAJA. How many men does each of these humming-birds carry?

TRAHERNE. Two or three, but ——

RAJA. I counted six planes — say at the outside twenty men. Even my toy army can cope with that number.

> [*There is a growing clamour outside. The* RAJA *gives an order to the Priest at the door, right. He throws it wide open.*]

> [FLIGHT-LIEUTENANT CARDEW *saunters in, escorted by three soldiers.*]

RAJA. Who are you, sir?

CARDEW. One moment! [*Crosses to* LUCILLA, *who holds out both her hands. He takes them cordially but coolly.*] Mrs. Crespin! I'm very glad we're in time. [*Turns to* TRAHERNE.] Dr. Traherne, I presume? [*Shakes hands with him.*] And Major Crespin?

TRAHERNE. Shot while transmitting our message.

CARDEW. I'm so sorry, Mrs. Crespin. [*To* TRAHERNE.] By whom?
[TRAHERNE *indicates the* RAJA, *who has meanwhile watched the scene impassively.*]

RAJA. I am sorry to interrupt these effusions, but ——

CARDEW. Who are you, sir?

RAJA. I am the Raja of Rukh. And you?

CARDEW. Flight-Lieutenant Cardew. I have the honour to represent his Majesty, the King-Emperor.

RAJA. The King-Emperor? Who is that, pray? We live so out of the world here, I don't seem to have heard of him.

CARDEW. You will in a minute, Raja, if you don't instantly hand over his subjects.

RAJA. His subjects? Ah, I see you mean the King of England. What terms does his Majesty propose?

CARDEW. We make no terms with cut-throats. [*Looks at his wrist watch.*] If I do not signal your submission within three minutes of our landing ——
    [*A bomb is heard to fall at some distance. Great consternation among the Priests, etc.*]

RAJA [*unperturbed*]. Ah! bombs!

CARDEW. Precisely.

RAJA. I fancied your Government affected some scruple as to the slaughter of innocent civilians.

CARDEW. There has been no slaughter — as yet. That bomb fell in the ravine, where it could do no harm. So will the next one ——
    [*Bomb — nearer.* Increasing hubbub without.]
But the third — well if you're wise you'll throw up the sponge, and there won't be a third.

RAJA. Throw up the sponge, Lieutenant ——? I didn't quite catch your name?

CARDEW. Cardew.

RAJA. Ah, yes, Lieutenant Cardew. Why on earth should I throw up the sponge? Your comrades up yonder can no doubt massacre quite a number of my subjects — a brave exploit! — but when they've spent their thunderbolts, they'll just have to fly away again — if they can. A bomb may drop on this temple, you say? In that case, you and your friends will escort me — in fragments — to my last abode. Does that prospect allure you? I call your bluff, Lieutenant Cardew.
    [*A third bomb — very loud.*]
    [*The Priests rush up to the* RAJA, *and fall before him in panic-stricken supplication, with voluble remonstrances, pointing to the Idol in the background. The* RAJA *hesitates for a moment, then proceeds:*]

RAJA. My priests, however, have a superstitious dread of these eggs of the Great Roc. They fear injury to the Sacred Image. For myself, I am always averse from bloodshed. You may, if you please, signal to your squadron commander my acceptance of your terms.

CARDEW. I thought you would come to reason. [*Shaking out his flag in preparation for signalling, he hurries across to where the white beam of a search-light is visible outside the doorway, right. He disappears for a moment.*]

RAJA. This comes of falling behind the times. If I had had anti-aircraft guns ——

TRAHERNE. Thank your stars you hadn't!

CARDEW [*returning*]. All clear for the moment, Raja. You have no further *immediate* consequences to fear.

RAJA. What am I to conclude from your emphasis on *immediate?*

CARDEW [*after whispering to* TRAHERNE]. I need scarcely remind you, sir, that you can hand over only the *body* of one of your prisoners.

RAJA. Major Crespin murdered a faithful servant of mine. His death at my hands was a fair act of war.

CARDEW. His Majesty's Government will scarcely view it in that light.

RAJA. His Majesty's Government has today, I believe, taken the lives of three kinsmen of mine. Your side has the best of the transaction by four lives to one.

CARDEW [*shrugging his shoulders*]. Will you assign us an escort through the crowd?

RAJA. Certainly. [*Gives an order to the officer of regulars, who hurries out, right.*] The escort will be here in a moment. [*To* LUCILLA *and* TRAHERNE.] It only remains for me to speed the parting guest. I hope we may one day renew our acquaintance — Oh, not here! I plainly foresee that I shall have to join the other Kings in Exile. Perhaps we may meet at Homburg or Monte Carlo, and talk over old times. Ah, here is the escort.

[*The escort has formed at the door, right.* TRAHERNE, LUCILLA, *and* CARDEW *cross to it, the* RAJA *following them up.*]

RAJA. Good-bye, dear lady. I lament the Major's end. Perhaps I was hasty; but, you know, "'Tis better to have loved and lost," etc. And oh — Mrs. Crespin! [*As she is going out,* LUCILLA *looks back at him with horror.*] My love to the children!

[*The Priests and others are all clustered on the balcony, looking at the aeroplanes. The* RAJA *turns back from the door, lights a cigarette at the brazier, takes a puff, and says:*]

Well, well — she'd probably have been a damned nuisance.

ROBERT CEDRIC SHERRIFF

THE author of one of the most sensationally successful plays of our time, Robert Sherriff, born just outside London in 1896, had no primary interest in the stage at all. After he left public school, he went into the insurance business, but all his spare hours were given to sports; and it was for one of his athletic groups that he first began to write dramatic pieces. *Journey's End* grew out of letters sent home from the trenches, but as it was found too difficult for the rowing club to act, it was offered to many theatrical agents, all of whom rejected it. Through the none too enthusiastic efforts of George Bernard Shaw, the play was produced by a struggling little organization, the London Stage Society, but Maurice Browne, the well-known producer, realized its merits too well to allow it to remain in obscurity. He gave it its first important production in January, 1929, at the Savoy Theatre, London, where it became an instant success and enjoyed a long run. It has been effectively filmed and may be read in more than twenty languages.

JOURNEY'S END *

THE SCENE

A dug-out in the British trenches before St. Quentin.

A few rough steps lead into the trench above, through a low doorway. A table occupies a good space of the dug-out floor. A wooden frame, covered with wire netting, stands against the left wall and serves the double purpose of a bed and a seat for the table. A wooden bench against the back wall makes another seat, and two boxes serve for the other sides.

Another wire-covered bed is fixed in the right corner beyond the doorway.

Gloomy tunnels lead out of the dug-out to left and right.

Except for the table, beds, and seats, there is no furniture save the bottles holding the candles, and a few tattered magazine pictures pinned to the wall of girls in flimsy costumes.

The earth walls deaden the sounds of war, making them faint and far away, although the front line is only fifty yards ahead. The flames of the candles that burn day and night are steady in the still, damp air.

ACT ONE
Evening on Monday, the 18th March, 1918

ACT TWO

SCENE I: *Tuesday morning*   SCENE II: *Tuesday afternoon*

ACT THREE

SCENE I: *Wednesday afternoon*   SCENE II: *Wednesday night*
SCENE III: *Thursday, towards dawn*

* Reprinted by special permission of Coward-McCann, Inc. No amateur or professional performance may be given without permission in writing from Samuel French, Inc., 25 West 45th St., New York, N.Y.

ACT ONE

The evening of a March day. A pale glimmer of moonlight shines down the narrow steps into one corner of the dug-out. Warm yellow candle-flames light the other corner from the necks of two bottles on the table. Through the doorway can be seen the misty grey parapet of a trench and a narrow strip of starlit sky. A bottle of whiskey, a jar of water, and a mug stand on the table amongst a litter of papers and magazines. An officer's equipment hangs in a jumbled mass from a nail in the wall.

CAPTAIN HARDY, a red-faced, cheerful-looking man is sitting on a box by the table, intently drying a sock over a candle-flame. He wears a heavy trench-boot on his left leg, and his right foot, which is naked, is held above the damp floor by resting it on his left knee. His right boot stands on the floor beside him. As he carefully turns the sock this way and that — feeling it against his face to see if it is dry — he half sings, half hums a song — humming when he is not quite sure of the words, and marking time with the toes of his right foot.

HARDY.   One and Two it's with Maud and Lou;
            Three and Four, two girls more;
            Five and Six it's with — hm — hm — hm —
            Seven, Eight, Clara and Caroline ——
[*He lapses into an indefinite humming, and finishes with a lively burst.*]
            Tick! — Tock! — wind up the clock,
            And we'll start the day over again.
[*A man's legs appear in the moonlit trench above, and a tall, thin man comes slowly down the dug-out steps, stooping low to avoid the roof. He takes his helmet off and reveals a fine head, with close-cropped, iron-grey hair. He looks about forty-five — physically as hard as nails.*]
HARDY. [*Looking round.*] Hullo, Osborne! Your fellows arriving?
OSBORNE. [*Hitching off his pack and dropping it in a corner.*] Yes. They're just coming in.
HARDY. Splendid! Have a drink.
OSBORNE. Thanks. [*He crosses and sits on the left-hand bed.*]
HARDY. [*Passing the whiskey and a mug.*] Don't have too much water. It's rather strong today.
OSBORNE. [*Slowly mixing a drink.*] I wonder what it *is* they put in the water.
HARDY. Some sort of disinfectant, I suppose.
OSBORNE. I'd rather have the microbes, wouldn't you?
HARDY. *I* would — yes ——
OSBORNE. Well, cheero.
HARDY. Cheero. Excuse my sock, won't you?
OSBORNE. Certainly. It's a nice-looking sock.
HARDY. It is rather, isn't it? Guaranteed to keep the feet dry. Trouble is, it gets so wet doing it.

OSBORNE. Stanhope asked me to come and take over. He's looking after the men coming in.

HARDY. Splendid! You know, I'm awfully glad you've come.

OSBORNE. I heard it was a quiet bit of line up here.

HARDY. Well, yes — in a *way*. But you never know. Sometimes nothing happens for hours on end; then — all of a sudden — "over she comes!" — rifle grenades — Minnies — and those horrid little things like pineapples — you know.

OSBORNE. I know.

HARDY. Swish — swish — swish — swish — BANG!

OSBORNE. All right — all right — I know.

HARDY. They simply blew us to bits yesterday. Minnies — enormous ones; about twenty. Three bang in the trench. I really *am* glad you've come; I'm not simply being polite.

OSBORNE. Do much damage?

HARDY. Awful. A dug-out got blown up and came down in the men's tea. They were frightfully annoyed.

OSBORNE. I know. There's nothing worse than dirt in your tea.

HARDY. By the way, you know the big German attack's expected any day now?

OSBORNE. It's been expected for the last month.

HARDY. Yes, but it's very near now; there's funny things happening over in the Boche country. I've been out listening at night when it's quiet. There's more transport than usual coming up — you can hear it rattling over the *pavé* all night; more trains in the distance — puffing up and going away again, one after another, bringing up loads and loads of men ——

OSBORNE. Yes. It's coming — pretty soon now.

HARDY. Are you here for six days?

OSBORNE. Yes.

HARDY. Then I should think you'll get it — right in the neck.

OSBORNE. Well, you won't be far away. Come along, let's do this handing over. Where's the map?

HARDY. Here we are. [*He gropes among the papers on the table and finds a tattered map.*] We hold about two hundred yards of front line. We've got a Lewis gun just here — and one here, in this little sap. Sentry posts where the crosses are ——

OSBORNE. Where do the men sleep?

HARDY. *I* don't know. The sergeant-major sees to that. [*He points off to the left.*] The servants and signallers sleep in there. Two officers in here, and three in there. [*He points to the right hand tunnel.*] That is, if you've *got* five officers.

OSBORNE. We've only got four at present, but a new man's coming up tonight. He arrived at transport lines a day or two ago.

HARDY. I hope you get better luck than I did with *my* last officer. He got lumbago the first night and went home. Now he's got a job lecturing young officers on "Life in the Front Line."

OSBORNE. Yes. They do send some funny people over here nowadays.

I hope we're lucky and get a youngster straight from school. They're the kind that do best.

HARDY. I suppose they are, really.

OSBORNE. Five beds, you say? [*He examines the one he is sitting on.*] Is this the best one?

HARDY. Oh, no. [*He points to the bed in the right corner.*] *That's* mine. The ones in the other dug-out haven't got any bottoms to them. You keep yourself in by hanging your arms and legs over the sides. Mustn't hang your legs too low, or the rats gnaw your boots.

OSBORNE. You got many rats here?

HARDY. I should say — roughly — about two million; but then, of course, I don't see them all. [*He begins to put on his sock and draw on his boot.*] Well, there's nothing else you want to know, is there?

OSBORNE. You haven't told me anything yet.

HARDY. What else do you *want* to know?

OSBORNE. Well, what about trench stores?

HARDY. You *are* a fussy old man. Anybody'd think you were in the Army. [*He finds a tattered piece of paper.*] Here you are: 115 rifle grenades — I shouldn't use them if I were you; they upset Jerry and make him offensive. Besides, they are rusty, in any case. Then there's 500 Mills bombs, 34 gum boots ——

OSBORNE. That's seventeen pairs ——

HARDY. Oh, no; 25 right leg, and 9 left leg. But everything's down here. [*He hands the list to* OSBORNE.]

OSBORNE. Did you check it when you took over?

HARDY. No. I think the sergeant-major did. It's quite all right.

OSBORNE. I expect Stanhope would like to see you before you go. He always likes a word with the company commander he's relieving.

HARDY. How *is* the dear young boy? Drinking like a fish, as usual?

OSBORNE. Why do you say that?

HARDY. Well, damn it, it's just the natural thing to ask about Stanhope. [*He pauses, and looks curiously at* OSBORNE.] Poor old man. It must be pretty rotten for you, being his second in command, and you such a quiet, sober old thing.

OSBORNE. He's a long way the best company commander we've got.

HARDY. Oh, he's a good chap, I know. But I never *did* see a youngster put away the whiskey he does. D'you know, the last time we were out resting at Valennes he came to supper with us and drank a whole bottle in one hour fourteen minutes — we timed him.

OSBORNE. I suppose it amused everybody; I suppose everybody cheered him on, and said what a splendid achievement it was.

HARDY. He didn't want any "cheering" on ——

OSBORNE. No, but everybody thought it was a big thing to do. [*There is a pause.*] Didn't they?

HARDY. Well, you can't help, somehow, *admiring* a fellow who can do that — and then pick out his own hat all by himself and walk home ——

OSBORNE. When a boy like Stanhope gets a reputation out here for drinking, he turns into a kind of freak show exhibit. People pay with a bottle of whiskey for the morbid curiosity of seeing him drink it.

HARDY. Well, naturally, you're biased. You have to put him to bed when he gets home.

OSBORNE. It rather reminds you of bear-baiting — or cock-fighting — to sit and watch a boy drink himself unconscious.

HARDY. Well, damn it, it's pretty dull without *something* to liven people up. I mean, after all — Stanhope really *is* a sort of freak; I mean it *is* jolly fascinating to see a fellow drink like he does — glass after glass. He didn't go home on his last leave, did he?

OSBORNE. No.

HARDY. I suppose he didn't think he was fit to meet papa. [*A pause.*] You know his father's vicar of a country village?

OSBORNE. I know.

HARDY. [*Laughing.*] Imagine Stanhope spending his leave in a country vicarage sipping tea! He spent his last leave in Paris, didn't he?

OSBORNE. Yes.

HARDY. I bet it was *some* leave!

OSBORNE. Do you know how long he's been out here?

HARDY. A good time, I know.

OSBORNE. Nearly three years. He came out straight from school — when he was eighteen. He's commanded this company for a year — in and out of the front line. He's never had a rest. Other men come over here and go home again ill, and young Stanhope goes on sticking it, month in, month out.

HARDY. Oh, I know he's a jolly good fellow ——

OSBORNE. I've seen him on his back all day with trench fever — then on duty all night ——

HARDY. Oh, I know; he's a splendid chap!

OSBORNE. And because he's stuck it till his nerves have got battered to bits, he's called a drunkard.

HARDY. Not a drunkard; just a — just a hard drinker; but you're quite right about his nerves. They *are* all to blazes. Last time out resting we were playing bridge and something happened — I don't remember what it was; some silly little argument — and all of a sudden he jumped up and knocked all the glasses off the table! Lost control of himself; and then he — sort of — came to — and cried ——

OSBORNE. Yes, I know.

HARDY. You heard about it?

OSBORNE. He told me.

HARDY. Did he? We tried to hush it up. It just shows the state he's in. [*He rises and puts on his pack. There is a pause.*] You know, Osborne, you ought to be commanding this company.

OSBORNE. Rubbish!

HARDY. Of course you ought. It sticks out a mile. I know he's got pluck and all that, but, damn it, man, you're twice his age — and think what a dear, level-headed old thing you are.

OSBORNE. Don't be an ass. He was out here before I joined up. His experience alone makes him worth a dozen people like me.

HARDY. You know as well as I do, you ought to be in command.

OSBORNE. There isn't a man to touch him as a commander of men. He'll command the battalion one day if —

HARDY. Yes, if! [*He laughs.*]

OSBORNE. You don't know him as I do; I love that fellow. I'd go to hell with him.

HARDY. Oh, you sweet, sentimental old darling!

OSBORNE. Come along. Finish handing over and stop blithering.

HARDY. There's nothing else to do.

OSBORNE. What about the log-book?

HARDY. God! you are a worker. Oh, well. Here we are. [*He finds a tattered little book among the papers on the table.*] Written right up to date; here's my last entry: "5 P.M. to 8 P.M. All quiet. German airman flew over trenches. Shot a rat."

OSBORNE. Did he?

HARDY. No. I shot the rat, you ass. Well, finish up your whiskey. I want to pack my mug. I'll leave you that drop in the bottle.

OSBORNE. Thanks. [*He drinks up his whiskey and hands* HARDY *the mug.*]

HARDY. [*Tucking the mug into his pack.*] I'll be off.

OSBORNE. Aren't you going to wait and see Stanhope?

HARDY. Well, no, I don't specially want to see him. He's so fussy about the trenches. I expect they *are* rather dirty. He'll talk for hours if he catches me. [*He hitches his pack over his shoulders, hangs on his gas satchel, map-case, binoculars, compass-case, until he looks like a travelling pedlar. As he dresses:*] Well, I hope you have a nice six days. Don't forget to change your clothes if you get wet.

OSBORNE. No, papa.

HARDY. And don't forget about the big attack.

OSBORNE. Oh, Lord, no, I mustn't miss that; I'll make a note in my diary.

HARDY. [*Fully dressed.*] There we are! Do I look every inch a soldier?

OSBORNE. Yes. I should get quite a fright if I were a German and met you coming round a corner.

HARDY. I should bloody well hope you would.

OSBORNE. Shouldn't be able to run away for laughing.

HARDY. Now don't be rude. [*He leans over to light a cigarette from a candle, and looks down on the table.*] Well, I'm damned. Still at it!

OSBORNE. What is?

HARDY. Why, that little cockroach. It's been running round and round that candle since tea-time; must have done a mile.

OSBORNE. I shouldn't hang about here if I were a cockroach.

HARDY. Nor should I. I'd go home. Ever had cockroach races?

OSBORNE. No.

HARDY. Great fun. We've had 'em every evening.

OSBORNE. What are the rules?

HARDY. Oh, you each have a cockroach, and start 'em in a line. On the word "Go" you dig your cockroach in the ribs and steer him with a match across the table. I won ten francs last night — had a *splendid* cockroach. I'll give you a tip.

OSBORNE. Yes?

HARDY. Promise not to let it go any farther?

OSBORNE. Yes.

HARDY. Well, if you want to get the best pace out of a cockroach, dip it in whiskey — makes 'em go like hell!

OSBORNE. Right. Thanks awfully.

HARDY. Well, I must be off. Cheero!

OSBORNE. Cheero!

HARDY. [*Goes up the narrow steps into the trench above, singing softly and happily to himself.*]

> "One and Two, it's with Maud and Lou;
> Three and Four, two girls more ——"

[*The words trail away into the night.*]

[OSBORNE *rises and takes his pack from the floor to the bed by the table. While he undoes it a* SOLDIER SERVANT *comes out of the tunnel from the left with a table-cloth over his arm and a plate with half a loaf of bread on it.*]

MASON. Excuse me, sir. Can I lay supper?

OSBORNE. Yes, do. [*He shuffles up the papers from the table and puts them on the bed.*]

MASON. Thank you, sir. [*He lays the table.*]

OSBORNE. What are you going to tempt us with tonight, Mason?

MASON. Soup, sir — cutlets — and pineapple.

OSBORNE. [*Suspiciously.*] Cutlets?

MASON. Well, sir — well, yes, sir — cutlets.

OSBORNE. What sort of cutlets?

MASON. Now, sir, you've got me. I shouldn't like to commit meself too deep, sir.

OSBORNE. Ordinary ration meat?

MASON. Yes, sir. Ordinary ration meat, but a noo shape, sir. Smells like liver, sir, but it 'asn't got that smooth, wet look that liver's got.

[MASON *leaves the dug-out.*]

[OSBORNE *sits up to the table and examines the map. Voices come from the trench above; a gruff voice says:*] "This is 'C' Company 'Eadquarters, sir."

[*A boyish voice replies.*] "Oh, thanks."

[*There is a pause, then the gruff voice says:*] "Better go down, sir."

[*The boyish voice replies.*] "Yes. Righto."

[*An* OFFICER *comes groping down the steps and stands in the candlelight. He looks round, a little bewildered. He is a well-built, healthy-looking boy of about eighteen, with the very new uniform of a 2nd lieutenant.* OSBORNE *looks up from the trench map, surprised and interested to see a stranger.*]

OSBORNE. Hullo!

RALEIGH. Good evening [*He notices* OSBORNE'S *grey hair and adds*] sir.

OSBORNE. You the new officer?

RALEIGH. Er — yes. I've been to Battalion Headquarters. They told me to report here.

OSBORNE. Good. We've been expecting you. Sit down, won't you?

RALEIGH. Thanks. [*He sits gingerly on the box opposite* OSBORNE.]

OSBORNE. I should take your pack off.

RALEIGH. Oh, right. [*He slips his pack from his shoulders.*]

OSBORNE. Will you have a drink?

RALEIGH. Er — well ——

OSBORNE. You don't drink whiskey?

RALEIGH. [*Hastily.*] Oh, yes — er — just a small one, sir.

OSBORNE. [*Pouring out a small whiskey and adding water.*] Whiskey takes away the taste of the water ——

RALEIGH. Oh, yes? [*He pauses, and laughs nervously.*]

OSBORNE. — and the water takes away the taste of the whiskey. [*He hands* RALEIGH *the drink.*] Just out from England?

RALEIGH. Yes, I landed a week ago.

OSBORNE. Boulogne?

RALEIGH. Yes. [*A pause, then he self-consciously holds up his drink.*] Well, here's luck, sir.

OSBORNE. [*Taking a drink himself.*] Good luck. [*He takes out a cigarette case.*] Cigarette?

RALEIGH. Thanks.

OSBORNE. [*Holding a bottle across so that* RALEIGH *can light his cigarette from the candle in it.*] Ever been up in the line before?

RALEIGH. Oh, no. You see, I only left school at the end of last summer term.

OSBORNE. I expect you find it a bit strange.

RALEIGH. [*Laughing.*] Yes — I do — a bit ——

OSBORNE. My name's Osborne. I'm second in command of the company. You only call me "sir" in front of the men.

RALEIGH. I see. Thanks.

OSBORNE. You'll find the other officers call me "Uncle."

RALEIGH. Oh, yes? [*He smiles.*]

OSBORNE. What's *your* name?

RALEIGH. Raleigh.

OSBORNE. I knew a Raleigh. A master at Rugby.

RALEIGH. Oh? He may be a relation. I don't know. I've got lots of uncles — and things like that.

OSBORNE. We've only just moved into these trenches. Captain Stanhope commands the company.

RALEIGH. [*Suddenly brightening up.*] I know. It's a frightful bit of luck.

OSBORNE. Why? D'you know him?

RALEIGH. Yes, rather! We were at school together — at least — of course — I was only a kid and he was one of the big fellows; he's three years older than I am.

[*There is a pause;* Osborne *seems to be waiting for* Raleigh *to go on, then suddenly he says.*]

Osborne. He's up in the front line at present, looking after the relief. [*Another pause.*] He's a splendid chap.

Raleigh. *Isn't* he? He was skipper of football at Barford, and kept wicket for the eleven. A jolly good bat, too.

Osborne. Did you play football — and cricket?

Raleigh. Oh, yes. Of course, I wasn't in the same class as Dennis — I say, I suppose I ought to call him Captain Stanhope?

Osborne. Just "Stanhope."

Raleigh. I see. Thanks.

Osborne. Did you get your colours?

Raleigh. I did for football. Not cricket.

Osborne. Football and cricket seem a long way from here.

Raleigh. [*Laughing.*] They do, rather.

Osborne. We play a bit when we're out of the line.

Raleigh. Good!

Osborne. [*Thoughtfully.*] So you were at school with Stanhope. [*Pause.*] I wonder if he'll remember you? I expect you've grown in the last three years.

Raleigh. Oh, I think he'll remember me. [*He stops, and goes on rather awkwardly.*] You see, it wasn't only that we were just at school together; our fathers were friends, and Dennis used to come and stay with us in the holidays. Of course, at school I didn't see much of him, but in the holidays we were terrific pals.

Osborne. He's a fine company commander.

Raleigh. I bet he is. Last time he was on leave he came down to the school; he'd just got his M.C. and been made a captain. He looked splendid! It — sort of — made me feel ——

Osborne. — keen?

Raleigh. Yes. Keen to get out here. I was frightfully keen to get into Dennis's regiment. I thought, perhaps, with a bit of luck I might get to the same battalion.

Osborne. It's a big fluke to have got to the same company.

Raleigh. I know. It's an amazing bit of luck. When I was at the base I did an awful thing. You see, my uncle's at the base — he has to detail officers to regiments ——

Osborne. General Raleigh?

Raleigh. Yes. I went to see him on the quiet and asked him if he could get me into this battalion. He bit my head off, and said I'd got to be treated like everybody else ——

Osborne. Yes?

Raleigh. — and next day I was told I *was* coming to this battalion. Funny, wasn't it?

Osborne. Extraordinary coincidence!

Raleigh. And when I got to Battalion Headquarters, and the colonel told me to report to "C" Company, I could have cheered. I expect Dennis'll be frightfully surprised to see me. I've got a message for him.

OSBORNE. From the colonel?

RALEIGH. No. From my sister.

OSBORNE. Your sister?

RALEIGH. Yes. You see, Dennis used to stay with us, and naturally my sister [*he hesitates*] — well — perhaps I ought not ——

OSBORNE. That's all right. I didn't actually know that Stanhope ——

RALEIGH. They're not — er — officially engaged ——

OSBORNE. No?

RALEIGH. She'll be awfully glad I'm with him here; I can write and tell her all about him. He doesn't say much in his letters; can we write often?

OSBORNE. Oh, yes. Letters are collected every day.

[*There is a pause.*]

RALEIGH. You don't think Dennis'll mind my — sort of — forcing myself into his company? I never thought of that; I was so keen.

OSBORNE. No, of course he won't. [*Pause.*] You say it's — it's a good time since you last saw him?

RALEIGH. Let's see. It was in the summer last year — nearly a year ago.

OSBORNE. You know, Raleigh, you mustn't expect to find him — quite the same.

RALEIGH. Oh?

OSBORNE. You see, he's been out here a long time. It — it tells on a man — rather badly ——

RALEIGH. [*Thinking.*] Yes, of course, I suppose it does.

OSBORNE. You may find he's — he's a little bit quick-tempered.

RALEIGH. [*Laughing.*] Oh, I know old Dennis's temper! I remember once at school he caught some chaps in a study with a bottle of whiskey. Lord! the roof nearly blew off. He gave them a dozen each with a cricket stump. [OSBORNE *laughs.*] He was so keen on the fellows in the house keeping fit. He was frightfully down on smoking — and that sort of thing.

OSBORNE. You must remember he's commanded this company for a long time — through all sorts of rotten times. It's — it's a big strain on a man.

RALEIGH. Oh, it must be.

OSBORNE. If you notice a — difference in Stanhope — you'll know it's only the strain ——

RALEIGH. Oh, yes.

[OSBORNE *rouses himself and speaks briskly.*]

OSBORNE. Now, let's see. We've got five beds here — one each. Two in here and three in that dug-out there. I'm afraid you'll have to wait until the others come and pick the beds they want.

RALEIGH. Righto!

OSBORNE. Have you got a blanket?

RALEIGH. Yes, in my pack. [*He rises to get it.*]

OSBORNE. Better wait and unpack when you know where you are sleeping.

RALEIGH. Righto! [*He sits down again.*]

OSBORNE. We never undress when we're in the line. You can take your boots off now and then in the daytime, but it's better to keep pretty well dressed always.

RALEIGH. I see. Thanks.

OSBORNE. I expect we shall each do about three hours on duty at a time and then six off. We all go on duty at stand-to. That's at dawn and dusk.

RALEIGH. Yes.

OSBORNE. I expect Stanhope'll send you on duty with one of us at first — till you get used to it.

[*There is a pause.* RALEIGH *turns, and looks curiously up the steps into the night.*]

RALEIGH. Are we in the front line here?

OSBORNE. No. That's the support line outside. The front line's about fifty yards farther on.

RALEIGH. How frightfully quiet it is!

OSBORNE. It's often quiet — like this.

RALEIGH. I thought there would be an awful row here — all the time.

OSBORNE. Most people think that.

[*Pause.*]

RALEIGH. I've never known anything so quiet as those trenches we came by; just now and then I heard rifle firing, like the range at Bisley, and a sort of rumble in the distance.

OSBORNE. Those are the guns up north — up Wipers way. The guns are always going up there; it's never quiet like this. [*Pause.*] I expect it's all very strange to you?

RALEIGH. It's — it's not exactly what I thought. It's just this — this quiet that seems so funny.

OSBORNE. A hundred yards from here the Germans are sitting in *their* dug-outs, thinking how quiet it is.

RALEIGH. Are they as near as that?

OSBORNE. About a hundred yards.

RALEIGH. It seems — uncanny. It makes me feel we're — we're all just waiting for something.

OSBORNE. We are, generally, just waiting for something. When anything happens, it happens quickly. Then we just start waiting again.

RALEIGH. I never thought it was like that.

OSBORNE. You thought it was fighting all the time?

RALEIGH. [*Laughing.*] Well, yes, in a way.

OSBORNE. [*After puffing at his pipe in silence for a while.*] Did you come up by trench tonight — or over the top?

RALEIGH. By trench. An amazing trench — turning and twisting for miles, over a sort of plain.

OSBORNE. Lancer's Alley it's called.

RALEIGH. Is it? It's funny the way it begins — in that ruined village, a few steps down into the cellar of a house — then right under the house and through a little garden — and then under the garden wall — then alongside an enormous ruined factory place — then miles and miles of plains, with those green lights bobbing up and down ahead — all along the front as far as you can see.

OSBORNE. Those are the Very lights. Both sides fire them over No Man's Land — to watch for raids and patrols.

RALEIGH. I knew they fired lights. [*Pause.*] I didn't expect so many — and to see them so far away.

OSBORNE. I know. [*He puffs at his pipe.*] There's something rather romantic about it all.

RALEIGH. [*Eagerly.*] Yes, I thought that, too.

OSBORNE. You must always think of it like that if you can. Think of it all as — as romantic. It helps.

[MASON *comes in with more dinner utensils.*]

MASON. D'you expect the captain soon, sir? The soup's 'ot.

OSBORNE. He ought to be here very soon now. This is Mr. Raleigh, Mason.

MASON. Good evening, sir.

RALEIGH. Good evening.

MASON. [*To* OSBORNE.] I've 'ad rather a unpleasant surprise, sir.

OSBORNE. What's happened?

MASON. You know that tin o' pineapple chunks I got, sir?

OSBORNE. Yes?

MASON. Well, sir, I'm sorry to say it's apricots.

OSBORNE. Good heavens! It must have given you a turn.

MASON. I distinctly said "pineapple chunks" at the canteen.

OSBORNE. Wasn't there a label on the tin?

MASON. No, sir. I pointed that out to the men. I said was 'e *certain* it was pineapple chunks?

OSBORNE. I suppose he said he was.

MASON. Yes, sir. 'E said a leopard can't change its spots, sir.

OSBORNE. What have leopards got to do with pineapple?

MASON. That's just what *I* thought, sir. Made me *think* there was something fishy about it. You see, sir, I know the captain can't stand the sight of apricots. 'E said next time we 'ad them 'e'd wring my neck.

OSBORNE. Haven't you anything else?

MASON. There's a pink blancmange I've made, sir. But it ain't anywhere near stiff yet.

OSBORNE. Never mind. We must have the apricots and chance it.

MASON. Only I thought I'd tell you, sir, so as the captain wouldn't blame me.

OSBORNE. All right, Mason. [*Voices are heard in the trench above.*] That sounds like the captain coming now.

MASON. [*Hastening away.*] I'll go and dish out the soup, sir.

[*The voices grow nearer; two figures appear in the trench above and grope down the steps — the leading figure tall and thin, the other short and fat. The tall figure is* CAPTAIN STANHOPE. *At the bottom of the steps he straightens himself, pulls off his pack, and drops it on the floor. Then he takes off his helmet and throws it on the right-hand bed. Despite his stars of rank he is no more than a boy; tall, slimly built, but broad-shouldered. His dark hair is carefully brushed; his uniform, though old and war-stained, is well cut and cared for. He is good-looking, rather from attractive features than the healthy good looks of* RALEIGH. *Although tanned by months in the open air, there is a pallor under his skin and dark shadows under his eyes. His short and fat companion — 2ND LIEUTENANT TROTTER — is middle-aged and homely looking. His face is red, fat, and round; apparently he has put on weight during his war service, for his tunic appears to be on the verge of bursting at the waist. He carries an extra pack belonging to the officer left on duty in the line.]*

STANHOPE. [*As he takes off his pack, gas satchel, and belt.*] Has Hardy gone?

OSBORNE. Yes. He cleared off a few minutes ago.

STANHOPE. Lucky for him he did. I had a few words to say to Master Hardy. You never saw the blasted mess those fellows left the trenches in. Dug-outs smell like cesspits; rusty bombs; damp rifle grenades; it's perfectly foul. Where are the servants?

OSBORNE. In there.

STANHOPE. [*Calling into* MASON's *dug-out.*] Hi! Mason!

MASON. [*Outside.*] Coming, sir! Just bringing the soup, sir.

STANHOPE. [*Taking a cigarette from his case and lighting it.*] Damn the soup! Bring some whiskey!

OSBORNE. Here's a new officer, Stanhope — just arrived.

STANHOPE. Oh, sorry. [*He turns and peers into the dim corner where* RALEIGH *stands smiling awkwardly.*] I didn't see you in this miserable light. [*He stops short at the sight of* RALEIGH. *There is silence.*]

RALEIGH. Hullo, Stanhope!

[STANHOPE *stares at* RALEIGH *as though dazed.* RALEIGH *takes a step forward, half raises his hand, then lets it drop to his side.*]

STANHOPE. [*In a low voice.*] How did you — get here?

RALEIGH. I was told to report to your company, Stanhope.

STANHOPE. Oh. I see. Rather a coincidence.

RALEIGH. [*With a nervous laugh.*] Yes.

[*There is a silence for a moment, broken by* OSBORNE *in a matter-of-fact voice.*]

OSBORNE. I say, Stanhope, it's a terrible business. We thought we'd got a tin of pineapple chunks; it turns out to be apricots.

TROTTER. Ha! Give me apricots every time! I 'ate pineapple chunks; too bloomin' sickly for me!

RALEIGH. I'm awfully glad I got to your company, Stanhope.

STANHOPE. When did you get here?

RALEIGH. Well, I've only just come.

OSBORNE. He came up with the transport while you were taking over.

STANHOPE. I see.

[MASON *brings in a bottle of whiskey, a mug, and two plates of soup — so precariously that* OSBORNE *has to help with the soup plates on to the table.*]

STANHOPE. [*With sudden forced gaiety.*] Come along, Uncle! Come and sit here. [*He waves towards the box on the right of the table.*] You better sit there, Raleigh.

RALEIGH. Right!

TROTTER. [*Taking a pair of pince-nez from his tunic pocket, putting them on, and looking curiously at* RALEIGH.] You Raleigh?

RALEIGH. Yes.

[*Pause.*]

TROTTER. I'm Trotter.

RALEIGH. Oh, yes?

[*Pause.*]

TROTTER. How *are* you?

RALEIGH. Oh, all right, thanks.

TROTTER. Been out 'ere before?

RALEIGH. No.

TROTTER. Feel a bit odd, I s'pose?

RALEIGH. Yes. A bit.

TROTTER. [*Getting a box to sit on.*] Oh, well, you'll soon get used to it; you'll feel you've been 'ere a year in about an hour's time. [*He puts the box on its side and sits on it. It is too low for the table, and he puts it on its end. It is then too high. He tries the other side, which is too low: he finally contrives to make himself comfortable by sitting on his pack, placed on the side of the box.*]

[MASON *arrives with two more plates of soup.*]

OSBORNE. What kind of soup is this, Mason?

MASON. It's yellow soup sir.

OSBORNE. It's got a very deep yellow flavour.

TROTTER. [*Taking a melodious sip.*] It wants some pepper; bring some pepper, Mason.

MASON. [*Anxiously.*] I'm very sorry, sir. When the mess box was packed the pepper was omitted, sir.

TROTTER. [*Throwing his spoon with a clatter into the plate.*] Oh, I say, but damn it!

OSBORNE. We must have pepper. It's a disinfectant.

TROTTER. You must have pepper in soup!

STANHOPE. [*Quietly.*] Why wasn't it packed, Mason?

MASON. It — it was missed, sir.

STANHOPE. Why?

MASON. [*Miserably.*] Well, sir, I left it to ——

STANHOPE. Then I advise you never to leave it to anyone else again — unless you want to rejoin your platoon out there. [*He points into the moonlit trench.*]

MASON. I'm — I'm very sorry, sir.

STANHOPE. Send one of the signallers.

MASON. Yes, sir. [*He hastens to the tunnel entrance and calls.*] Bert, you're wanted!

[A SOLDIER *appears, with a rifle slung over his shoulder. He stands stiffly to attention.*]

STANHOPE. Do you know "A" Company Headquarters?

SOLDIER. Yes, sir.

STANHOPE. Go there at once and ask Captain Willis, with my compliments, if he can lend me a little pepper.

SOLDIER. Very good, sir.

[*He turns smartly and goes up the steps,* MASON *stopping him for a moment to say confidentially:* "A *screw* of pepper, you ask for."]

OSBORNE. We must have pepper.

TROTTER. I mean — after all — war's bad enough with pepper — [*noisy sip*] — but war without pepper — it's — it's bloody awful!

OSBORNE. What's it like outside?

TROTTER. Quiet as an empty 'ouse. There's a nasty noise going on up north.

OSBORNE. Wipers, I expect. I believe there's trouble up there. I wish we knew more of what's going on.

TROTTER. So do I. Still, my wife reads the papers every morning and writes and tells me.

OSBORNE. Hardy says they had a lively time here yesterday. Three big Minnies right in the trench.

TROTTER. I know. And they left the bloomin' 'oles for us to fill in. [MASON *arrives with cutlets on enamel plates.*] What's this?

MASON. Meat, sir.

TROTTER. I know that. What sort?

MASON. Sort of cutlet, sir.

TROTTER. Sort of cutlet, is it? You know, Mason, there's cutlets and cutlets.

MASON. I know, sir; that one's a cutlet.

TROTTER. Well, it won't let me cut it.

MASON. No, sir?

TROTTER. That's a joke.

MASON. Oh. Right, sir. [*He goes out.*]

OSBORNE. [*Studying the map.*] There's a sort of ruin marked on this map — just in front of here, in No Man's Land — called Beauvais Farm.

TROTTER. That's what we saw sticking up, skipper. I wondered what it was.

STANHOPE. Better go out and look at it tonight.

TROTTER. I 'ate ruins in No Man's Land; too bloomin' creepy for me.

OSBORNE. There's only about sixty yards of No Man's Land, according to this map — narrower on the left, from the head of this sap; only about fifty.

TROTTER. [*Who has been looking curiously at* STANHOPE, *eating his meal with lowered head.*] Cheer up, skipper. You *do* look glum!

STANHOPE. I'm tired.

OSBORNE. I should turn in and get some sleep after supper.

STANHOPE. I've got hours of work before I sleep.

OSBORNE. I'll do the duty roll and see the sergeant-major — and all that.

STANHOPE. That's all right, Uncle. I'll see to it. [*He turns to* RALEIGH *for the first time.*] Trotter goes on duty directly he's had supper. You better go on with him — to learn.

RALEIGH. Oh, right.

TROTTER. Look 'ere, skipper, it's nearly eight now; couldn't we make it 'alf-past?

STANHOPE. No. I told Hibbert he'd be relieved at eight. Will you take from eleven till two, Uncle?

OSBORNE. Right.

STANHOPE. Hibbert can do from two till four, and I'll go on from then till stand-to. That'll be at six.

TROTTER. Well, boys! 'Ere we are for six days again. Six bloomin' eternal days. [*He makes a calculation on the table.*] That's a hundred and forty-four hours; eight thousand six 'undred and forty minutes. *That* doesn't sound so bad; we've done twenty of 'em already. I've got an idea! I'm going to draw a hundred and forty-four little circles on a bit o' paper, and every hour I'm going to black one in; that'll make the time go all right.

STANHOPE. It's five to eight now. You better go and relieve Hibbert. Then you can come back at eleven o'clock and black in three of your bloody little circles.

TROTTER. I 'aven't 'ad my apricots yet!

STANHOPE. We'll keep your apricots till you come back.

TROTTER. I never knew anything like a war for upsetting meals. I'm always down for dooty in the middle of one.

STANHOPE. That's because you never stop eating.

TROTTER. Any'ow, let's 'ave some coffee. Hi! Mason! Coffee!

MASON. Coming, sir!

TROTTER. [*Getting up.*] Well, I'll get dressed. Come on, Raleigh.

RALEIGH. [*Rising quickly.*] Right!

TROTTER. Just wear your belt with revolver case on it. Must have your revolver to shoot rats. And your gas mask — come here — I'll show you. [*He helps* RALEIGH.] You wear it sort of tucked up under your chin like a serviette.

RALEIGH. Yes. I was shown the way at home.

TROTTER. Now your hat. That's right. You don't want a walking-stick. It gets in your way if you have to run fast.

RALEIGH. Why — er — do you have to run fast?

TROTTER. Oh, Lord, yes, often! If you see a Minnie coming — that's a big trench-mortar shell, you know — short for *Minnywerfer* — you see 'em coming right out of the Boche trenches, right up in the air, then down, down, down; and you have to judge it and run like stink sometimes.

[MASON *comes in with two cups of coffee.*]

MASON. Coffee, sir?

TROTTER. Thanks. [*He takes the cup and drinks standing up.*]

RALEIGH. Thanks.

TROTTER. You might leave my apricots out, Mason. Put 'em on a separate plate and keep 'em in there. [*He points to* MASON'S *dug-out.*]

MASON. Very good, sir.

TROTTER. If you bring 'em in 'ere you never know *what* might 'appen to 'em.

MASON. No, sir.

TROTTER. "B" Company on our right, aren't they, skipper?

STANHOPE. Yes. There's fifty yards of undefended area between. You better patrol that a good deal.

TROTTER. Aye, aye, sir.

STANHOPE. Have a look at that Lewis gun position on the left. See what field of fire they've got.

TROTTER. Aye, aye, sir. You don't want me to go out and look at that blinkin' ruin?

STANHOPE. I'll see to that.

TROTTER. Good. I don't fancy crawling about on my belly after that cutlet. [*To* RALEIGH.] Well, come on, my lad, let's go and see about this 'ere war.

[*The two go up the steps, leaving* STANHOPE *and* OSBORNE *alone.* MASON *appears at his dug-out door.*]

MASON. Will you take apricots, sir?

STANHOPE. No, thanks.

MASON. Mr. Osborne?

OSBORNE. No, thanks.

MASON. I'm sorry about them being apricots, sir. I explained to Mr. Osborne ——

STANHOPE. [*Curtly.*] That's all right, Mason — thank you.

MASON. Very good, sir. [*He goes out.*]

OSBORNE. [*Over by the right-hand bed.*] Will you sleep here? This was Hardy's bed.

STANHOPE. No. You sleep there. I'd rather sleep by the table here. I can get up and work without disturbing you.

OSBORNE. This is a better one.

STANHOPE. You take it. Must have a little comfort in your old age, Uncle.

OSBORNE. I wish you'd turn in and sleep for a bit.

STANHOPE. Sleep? — I can't sleep. [*He takes a whiskey and water. A man appears in the trench and comes down the steps — a small, slightly built man in the early twenties, with a little moustache and a pallid face.*]

STANHOPE. [*Looking hard at the newcomer.*] Well, Hibbert?

HIBBERT. Everything's fairly quiet. Bit of sniping somewhere to our left; some rifle grenades coming over just on our right.

STANHOPE. I see. Mason's got your supper.

HIBBERT. [*Gently rubbing his forehead.*] I don't think I can manage any supper tonight, Stanhope. It's this beastly neuralgia. It seems to be right inside this eye. The beastly pain gets worse every day.

STANHOPE. Some hot soup and a good tough chop'll put that right.

HIBBERT. I'm afraid the pain rather takes my appetite away. I'm damn sorry to keep on talking about it, Stanhope, only I thought you'd wonder why I don't eat anything much.

STANHOPE. Try and forget about it.

HIBBERT. [*With a little laugh.*] Well — I wish I could.

STANHOPE. Get tight.

HIBBERT. I think I'll turn straight in for a rest — and try and get some sleep.

STANHOPE. All right. Turn in. You're in that dug-out there. Here's your pack. [*He picks up the pack that* TROTTER *brought down.*] You go on duty at two. I take over from you at four. I'll tell Mason to call you.

HIBBERT. [*Faintly.*] Oh, right — thanks, Stanhope — cheero.

STANHOPE. Cheero. [*He watches* HIBBERT *go down the tunnel into the dark.*]

HIBBERT. [*Returning.*] Can I have a candle?

STANHOPE. [*Taking one from the table.*] Here you are.

HIBBERT. Thanks.

[*He goes out again. There is silence.* STANHOPE *turns to* OSBORNE.]

STANHOPE. Another little worm trying to wriggle home.

OSBORNE. [*Filling his pipe.*] I wonder if he really is bad. He looks rotten.

STANHOPE. Pure bloody funk, that's all. He could eat if he wanted to; he's starving himself purposely. Artful little swine! Neuralgia's a splendid idea. No proof, as far as I can see.

OSBORNE. You can't help feeling sorry for him. I think he's tried hard.

STANHOPE. How long's he been out here? Three months, I suppose. Now he's decided he's done his bit. He's decided to go home and spend the rest of the war in comfortable nerve hospitals. Well, he's mistaken. I let Warren get away like that, but no more.

OSBORNE. I don't see how you can prevent a fellow going sick.

STANHOPE. I'll have a quiet word with the doctor before *he* does. He thinks he's going to wriggle off before the attack. We'll just see about that. No man of mine's going sick before the attack. They're going to take an equal chance — together.

OSBORNE. Raleigh looks a nice chap.

STANHOPE. [*Looking hard at* OSBORNE *before replying.*] Yes.

OSBORNE. Good-looking youngster. At school with you, wasn't he?

STANHOPE. Has he been talking already?

OSBORNE. He just mentioned it. It was a natural thing to tell me when he knew you were in command. [STANHOPE *is lounging at the table with his back to the wall.* OSBORNE, *sitting on the right-hand bed, begins to puff clouds of smoke into the air as he lights his pipe.*] He's awfully pleased to get into your company. [STANHOPE *makes no reply. He picks up a pencil and scribbles on the back of a magazine.*] He seems to think a lot of you.

STANHOPE. [*Looking up quickly at* OSBORNE *and laughing.*] Yes, I'm his hero.

OSBORNE. It's quite natural.

STANHOPE. You think so?

OSBORNE. Small boys at school generally have their heroes.

STANHOPE. Yes. Small boys at school do.

OSBORNE. Often it goes on as long as ——

STANHOPE. — as long as the hero's a hero.

OSBORNE. It often goes on all through life.

STANHOPE. I wonder. How many battalions are there in France?

OSBORNE. Why?

STANHOPE. We'll say fifty divisions. That's a hundred and fifty brigades — four hundred and fifty battalions. That's one thousand eight hundred companies. [*He looks up at* OSBORNE *from his calculations on the magazine cover.*] There are one thousand eight hundred companies in France, Uncle.

Raleigh might have been sent to any one of those, and, my God! he comes to mine.

OSBORNE. You ought to be glad. He's a good-looking youngster. I like him.

STANHOPE. I knew you'd like him. Personality, isn't it? [*He takes a worn leather case from his breast pocket and hands a small photograph to* OSBORNE.] I've never shown you that, have I?

OSBORNE. [*Looking at the photograph.*] No. [*Pause.*] Raleigh's sister, isn't it?

STANHOPE. How did you know?

OSBORNE. There's a strong likeness.

STANHOPE. I suppose there is.

OSBORNE. [*Intent on the picture.*] She's an awfully nice-looking girl.

STANHOPE. A photo doesn't show much, really. Just a face.

OSBORNE. She looks awfully nice. [*There is silence.* STANHOPE *lights a cigarette.* OSBORNE *hands the photo back.*] You're a lucky chap.

STANHOPE. [*Putting the photo back into his case.*] I don't know why I keep it, really.

OSBORNE. Why? Isn't she — I thought ——

STANHOPE. What did you think?

OSBORNE. Well, I thought that perhaps she was waiting for you.

STANHOPE. Yes. She is waiting for me — and she doesn't know. She thinks I'm a wonderful chap — commanding a company. [*He turns to* OSBORNE *and points up the steps into the line.*] She doesn't know that if I went up those steps into the front line — without being doped with whiskey — I'd go mad with fright.

[*There is a pause.* OSBORNE *stirs himself to speak.*]

OSBORNE. Look here, old man. I've meant to say it, for a long time, but it sounds damned impudence. You've done longer out here than any man in the battalion. It's time you went away for a rest. It's due to you.

STANHOPE. You suggest that I go sick, like that little worm in there — neuralgia in the eye? [*He laughs and takes a drink.*]

OSBORNE. No. Not that. The colonel would have sent you down long ago, only ——

STANHOPE. Only — what?

OSBORNE. Only he can't spare you.

STANHOPE. [*Laughing.*] Oh, rot!

OSBORNE. He told me.

STANHOPE. He thinks I'm in such a state I want a rest, is that it?

OSBORNE. No. He thinks it's due to you.

STANHOPE. It's all right, Uncle. I'll stick it out now. It may not be much longer now. I've had my share of luck — more than my share. There's not a man left who was here when I came. But it's rather damnable for that boy — of all the boys in the world — to have come to *me*. I might at least have been spared that.

OSBORNE. You're looking at things in rather a black sort of way.

STANHOPE. I've just told you. That boy's a hero-worshipper. I'm three years older than he is. You know what that means at school. I was skipper of football and all that sort of thing. It doesn't sound much to a man out here — but it does at school with a kid of fourteen. Damn it, Uncle, you're a schoolmaster; you know.

OSBORNE. I've just told you what I think of hero-worship.

STANHOPE. Raleigh's father knew mine, and I was told to keep an eye on the kid. I rather liked the idea of looking after him. I made him keen on the right things — and all that. His people asked me to stay with them one summer. I met his sister then ——

OSBORNE. Yes?

STANHOPE. At first I thought of her as another kid like Raleigh. It was just before I came out here for the first time that I realised what a topping girl she was. Funny how you realise it suddenly. I just prayed to come through the war — and — and *do* things — and keep absolutely fit for her.

OSBORNE. You've done pretty well. An M.C. and a company.

STANHOPE. [*Taking another whiskey.*] It was all right at first. When I went home on leave after six months it was jolly fine to feel I'd done a little to make her pleased. [*He takes a gulp of his drink.*] It was after I came back here — in that awful affair on Vimy Ridge. I knew I'd go mad if I didn't break the strain. I couldn't bear being fully conscious all the time — *you've* felt that, Uncle, haven't you?

OSBORNE. Yes, often.

STANHOPE. There were only two ways of breaking the strain. One was pretending I was ill — and going home; the other was this. [*He holds up his glass.*] Which would you pick, Uncle?

OSBORNE. I haven't been through as much as you. I don't know yet.

STANHOPE. I thought it all out. It's a slimy thing to go home if you're not really ill, isn't it?

OSBORNE. I think it is.

STANHOPE. Well, then. [*He holds his glass up to* OSBORNE.] Cheero, and long live the men who go home with neuralgia. [*He puts his glass down.*] I didn't go home on my last leave. I couldn't bear to meet her, in case she realised ——

OSBORNE. When the war's over — and the strain's gone — you'll soon be as fit as ever, at your age.

STANHOPE. I've hoped that all the time. I'd go away for months and live in the open air — and get fit — and then go back to her.

OSBORNE. And so you can.

STANHOPE. If Raleigh had gone to one of those other one thousand eight hundred companies.

OSBORNE. I don't see why you should think ——

STANHOPE. Oh, for Lord's sake don't be a damn fool. *You* know! You know he'll write and tell her I reek of whiskey all day.

OSBORNE. Why should he? He's not a ——

STANHOPE. Exactly. He's not a damned little swine who'd deceive his sister.

OSBORNE. He's very young; he's got hundreds of strange things to learn; he'll realise that men are — *different* — out here.

STANHOPE. It's no good, Uncle. Didn't you see him sitting there at supper? — staring at me? — and wondering? He's up in those trenches now — still wondering — and beginning to understand. And all these months he's wanted to be with me out here. Poor little devil!

OSBORNE. I believe Raleigh'll go on liking you — and looking up to you — through everything. There's something very deep, and rather fine, about hero-worship.

STANHOPE. Hero-worship be damned! [*He pauses, then goes on, in a strange, high-pitched voice.*] You know, Uncle, I'm an *awful* fool. I'm *captain* of this company. What's that bloody little prig of a boy matter? D'you see? He's a little prig. Wants to write home and tell Madge all about *me*. Well, he won't; d'you see, Uncle? He *won't* write. Censorship! I censor his letters — cross out all he says about me.

OSBORNE. You can't read his letters.

STANHOPE. [*Dreamily.*] Cross out all he says about me. Then we all go west in the big attack — and she goes on thinking I'm a fine fellow for ever — and ever — and ever. [*He pours out a drink, murmuring "Ever — and ever — and ever."*]

OSBORNE. [*Rising from his bed.*] It's not as bad as all that. Turn in and have a sleep.

STANHOPE. Sleep! Catch *me* wasting my time with sleep.

OSBORNE. [*Picking up* STANHOPE's *pack and pulling out the blanket.*] Come along, old chap. You come and lie down here. [*He puts the pack as a pillow on* STANHOPE's *bed, and spreads out the blanket.*]

STANHOPE. [*With his chin in his hands.*] Little prig — that's what he is. Did *I* ask him to force his way into my company? No! I didn't. Very well, he'll pay for his damn cheek. [OSBORNE *lays his hand gently on* STAN-HOPE's *shoulder to persuade him to lie down.*] Go away! [*He shakes* OS-BORNE's *hand off.*] What the hell are you trying to do?

OSBORNE. Come and lie down and go to sleep.

STANHOPE. Go sleep y'self. I censor his letters, d'you see, Uncle? You watch and see he doesn't smuggle any letters away.

OSBORNE. Righto. Now come and lie down. You've had a hard day of it.

STANHOPE. [*Looking up suddenly.*] Where's Hardy? D'you say he's gone?

OSBORNE. Yes. He's gone.

STANHOPE. Gone, has he? Y'know, I had a word to say to Master Hardy. He *would* go, the swine! Dirty trenches — everything dirty — I wanner tell him to keep his trenches clean.

OSBORNE. [*Standing beside* STANHOPE *and putting his hand gently on his shoulder again.*] We'll clean them up tomorrow.

[STANHOPE *looks up at* OSBORNE *and laughs gaily.*]

STANHOPE. Dear old Uncle! Clean trenches up — with little dustpan and brush. [*He laughs.*] Make you little apron — with lace on it.

OSBORNE. That'll be fine. Now then, come along, old chap. I'll see you get called at two o'clock. [*He firmly takes* STANHOPE *by the arm and draws him over to the bed.*] You *must* be tired.

STANHOPE. [*In a dull voice.*] God, I'm bloody tired; ache — all over — feel sick —

[OSBORNE *helps him on to the bed, takes the blanket and puts it over him.*]

OSBORNE. You'll feel all right in a minute. How's that? Comfortable?

STANHOPE. Yes. Comfortable. [*He looks up into* OSBORNE's *face and laughs again.*] Dear old Uncle. Tuck me up.

[OSBORNE *fumbles the blankets round* STANHOPE.]

OSBORNE. There we are.

STANHOPE. Kiss me, Uncle.

OSBORNE. Kiss you be blowed! You go to sleep.

STANHOPE. [*Closing his eyes.*] Yes — I go sleep. [*He turns slowly on to his side with his face to the earth wall.*]

[OSBORNE *stands watching for a while, then blows out the candle by* STANHOPE's *bed.* STANHOPE *gives a deep sigh, and begins to breathe heavily.* OSBORNE *crosses to the servant's dug-out and calls softly.*]

OSBORNE. Mason!

MASON. [*Appearing with unbuttoned tunic at the tunnel entrance.*] Yessir?

OSBORNE. Will you call me at ten minutes to eleven — and Mr. Hibbert at ten minutes to two? I'm going to turn in for a little while.

MASON. Very good, sir. [*Pause.*] The pepper's come, sir.

OSBORNE. Oh, good.

MASON. I'm very sorry about the pepper, sir.

OSBORNE. That's all right, Mason.

MASON. Good night, sir.

OSBORNE. Good night.

[MASON *leaves the dugout.* OSBORNE *turns, and looks up the narrow steps into the night, where the Very lights rise and fade against the starlit sky. He glances once more at* STANHOPE, *then crosses to his own bed, takes out from his tunic pocket a large, old-fashioned watch, and quietly winds it up. Through the stillness comes the low rumble of distant guns.*]

THE CURTAIN FALLS

ACT TWO

SCENE I

Early next morning.

A pale shaft of sunlight shines down the steps, but candles still burn in the dark corner where OSBORNE *and* RALEIGH *are at breakfast.* MASON *has put a large plate of bacon before each, and turns to go as* TROTTER *comes down the steps, whistling gaily and rubbing his hands.*

TROTTER. What a lovely smell of bacon!

MASON. Yes, sir. I reckon there's enough smell of bacon in 'ere to last for dinner.

TROTTER. Well, there's nothing like a good fat bacon rasher when you're as empty as I am.

MASON. I'm glad you like it fat, sir.

TROTTER. Well, I like a bit o' lean, too.

MASON. There *was* a bit of lean in the middle of yours, sir, but it's kind of shrunk up in the cooking.

TROTTER. Bad cooking, that's all. Any porridge?

MASON. Oh, yes, sir. There's porridge.

TROTTER. Lumpy, I s'pose?

MASON. Yes, sir. Quite nice and lumpy.

TROTTER. Well, take the lumps out o' mine.

MASON. And just bring you the gravy, sir? Very good, sir.

[MASON *goes out.* TROTTER *looks after him suspiciously.*]

TROTTER. You know, that man's getting familiar.

OSBORNE. He's not a bad cook.

[TROTTER *has picked up his coffee mug, and is smelling it.*]

TROTTER. I say, d'you realise he's washed his dish-cloth?

OSBORNE. I know. I told him about it.

TROTTER. Did you really? You've got some pluck. 'Ow did you go about it?

OSBORNE. I wrote and asked my wife for a packet of Lux. Then I gave it to Mason and suggested he try it on something.

TROTTER. Good man. No, he's not a bad cook. Might be a lot worse. When I was in the ranks we 'ad a prize cook — used to be a plumber before the war. Ought to 'ave seen the stew 'e made. Thin! Thin wasn't the word. Put a bucketful of 'is stew in a bath and pull the plug, and the whole lot would go down in a couple of gurgles.

[MASON *brings* TROTTER'S *porridge.*]

MASON. I've took the lumps out.

TROTTER. Good. Keep 'em and use 'em for dumplings next time we 'ave boiled beef.

MASON. Very good, sir. [*He goes out.*]

TROTTER. Yes. That plumber was a prize cook, 'e was. Lucky for us one day 'e set 'imself on fire making the tea. 'E went 'ome pretty well fried. Did Mason get that pepper?

OSBORNE. Yes.

TROTTER. Good. Must 'ave pepper.

OSBORNE. I thought you were on duty now.

TROTTER. I'm supposed to be. Stanhope sent me down to get my breakfast. He's looking after things till I finish.

OSBORNE. He's got a long job then.

TROTTER. Oh, no. I'm a quick eater. Hi! Mason! Bacon!

MASON. [*Outside.*] Coming, sir!

OSBORNE. It's a wonderful morning.

TROTTER. Isn't it lovely? Makes you feel sort of young and 'opeful. I was up in that old trench under the brick wall just now, and damned if a bloomin' little bird didn't start singing! Didn't 'arf sound funny. Sign of spring, I s'pose. [MASON *arrives with* TROTTER'S *bacon.*] That looks all right.

MASON. If you look down straight on it from above, sir, you can see the bit o' lean quite clear.

TROTTER. Good Lord, yes! That's it, isn't it?

MASON. No, sir; that's a bit o' rust off the pan.

TROTTER. Ah! *That's* it, then!

MASON. You've got it, sir. [*He goes out.*]

TROTTER. Cut us a chunk of bread, Uncle.

[OSBORNE *cuts him off a chunk.*]

OSBORNE. How are things going up there?

TROTTER. I don't like the look of things a bit.

OSBORNE. You mean — the quiet?

TROTTER. Yes. Standing up there in the dark last night there didn't seem a thing in the world alive — except the rats squeaking and my stomach grumbling about that cutlet.

OSBORNE. It's quiet even now.

TROTTER. Too damn quiet. You can bet your boots the Boche is up to something. The big attack soon, I reckon. I don't like it, Uncle. Pass the jam.

OSBORNE. It's strawberry.

TROTTER. Is it? I'm glad we've got rid o' that raspberry jam. Can't stand raspberry jam. Pips get be'ind your plate.

OSBORNE. Did Stanhope tell you he wants two wiring parties out tonight?

TROTTER. Yes. He's fixing it up now. [*He pauses, and goes on in a low voice.*] My goodness, Uncle, doesn't he look ill!

OSBORNE. I'm afraid he's not well.

TROTTER. Nobody'd be well who went on like he does. [*There is another pause.*] You know when you came up to relieve me last night?

OSBORNE. Yes?

TROTTER. Well, Raleigh and me came back here, and there was Stanhope sitting on that bed drinking a whiskey. He looked as white as a sheet. God, he looked awful; he'd drunk the bottle since dinner. I said, "'Ullo!" and he didn't seem to know who I was. Uncanny wasn't it, Raleigh?

RALEIGH. [*With lowered head.*] Yes.

TROTTER. He just said, "Better go to bed, Raleigh" — just as if Raleigh'd been a school kid.

OSBORNE. Did he? [*There is a pause.*] Look at the sun. It'll be quite warm soon.

[*They look at the pale square of sunlight on the floor.*]

TROTTER. It's warm now. You can feel it on your face outside if you stand in it. First time this year. 'Ope we 'ave an 'ot summer.

OSBORNE. So do I.

TROTTER. Funny about that bird. Made me feel quite braced up. Sort of made me think about my garden of an evening — walking round in me slippers after supper, smoking me pipe.

OSBORNE. You keen on gardening?

TROTTER. Oh, I used to do a bit of an evening. I 'ad a decent little grass plot in front, with flower-borders — geraniums, lobelia, and calsularia — you know, red, white, and blue. Looked rather nice in the summer.

OSBORNE. Yes.

TROTTER. 'Ad some fine 'olly'ocks out the back. One year I 'ad one eight feet 'igh. Took a photer of it. [*He fumbles in his pocket case.*] Like to look at it?

OSBORNE. I would. [*He looks at the photo.*] By Jove, it's a beauty.

TROTTER. [*Looking over* OSBORNE'S *shoulder.*] You see that, just there?

OSBORNE. Yes?

TROTTER. That's the roof of the summer-'ouse.

OSBORNE. Is it really!

TROTTER. Just shows the 'ite of the 'olly'ock.

OSBORNE. It does. [*He shows the photo to* RALEIGH.] A beauty, isn't it?

RALEIGH. Rather!

TROTTER. It never wanted no stick to keep it straight, neether. [*There is a pause.*] You keen on gardening?

OSBORNE. Yes. A bit. I made a rockery when I was home on leave. I used to cycle out to the woods and get primroses and things like that, and try and get 'em to grow in my garden.

TROTTER. I don't suppose they would!

OSBORNE. They would if you pressed a bit of moss round them ——

TROTTER. — to make 'em feel at 'ome, eh? [*He laughs.*]

OSBORNE. They'll be coming out again soon if they've got this sun at home.

TROTTER. I reckon they will. I remember one morning last spring — we was coming out of the salient. Just when it was getting light in the morning — it was at the time when the Boche was sending over a lot of that gas that smells like pear-drops, you know?

OSBORNE. I know. Phosgene.

TROTTER. That's it. We were scared to hell of it. All of a sudden we smelt that funny sweet smell, and a fellow shouted "Gas!" — and we put on our masks; and then I spotted what it was.

OSBORNE. What was it?

TROTTER. Why, a blinkin' may-tree! All out in bloom, growing beside the path! We did feel a lot of silly poops — putting on gas masks because of a damn may-tree! [*He stretches himself and tries to button his tunic.*] Lord! I *must* get my fat down. [*He gets up.*] Well, I better go and relieve Stanhope. He'll curse like hell if I don't. I bet he's got a red-hot liver this morning.

OSBORNE. I relieve you at eleven.

TROTTER. That's right. I don't like this time of day in the line. The old Boche 'as just 'ad 'is breakfast, and sends over a few whizz-bangs and rifle grenades to show 'e ain't forgotten us. Still, I'd rather 'ave a bang or two than this damn quiet. [*He puts on his helmet and gas mask satchel and goes up the steps.*] Cheero!

OSBORNE. Cheero!

RALEIGH. Cheero!

OSBORNE. [*To* RALEIGH.] I expect Stanhope'll let you go on duty alone now.

RALEIGH. Will he? About what time?

OSBORNE. Well, after me, I expect. From about two till four.

RALEIGH. I see.

[*There is a pause. Then* OSBORNE *looks at* RALEIGH *and laughs.*]

OSBORNE. What do you think about it all?

RALEIGH. Oh, all right, thanks. [*He laughs.*] I feel I've been here ages.

OSBORNE. [*Filling his pipe.*] I expect you do. The time passes, though.

RALEIGH. Are we here for six days?

OSBORNE. Yes. Seems a long time, doesn't it?

RALEIGH. [*Laughing shortly.*] It does rather. I can't imagine — the end of six days here ——

OSBORNE. Anyhow, we've done twelve hours already. It's fine when you are relieved and go down the line to billets, and have a good hot bath, and sit and read under trees.

RALEIGH. Good Lord, I feel I haven't seen a tree for ages — not a real tree with leaves and branches — and yet I've only been here twelve hours.

OSBORNE. How did you feel — in the front line?

RALEIGH. Oh, all right. It seemed so frightfully quiet and uncanny — everybody creeping about and talking in low voices. I suppose you've *got* to talk quietly when you're so near the German front line — only about seventy yards, isn't it?

OSBORNE. Yes. About the breadth of a football field.

RALEIGH. It's funny to think of it like that.

OSBORNE. I always measure distances like that out here. Keeps them in proportion.

RALEIGH. Did you play football?

OSBORNE. Yes. But mostly reffing at school in the last few years.

RALEIGH. Are you a schoolmaster, then?

OSBORNE. Yes. I must apologise.

RALEIGH. Oh, I don't mind schoolmasters. [*Hastily.*] I — I mean, I never met one outside a school.

OSBORNE. They do get out sometimes.

RALEIGH. [*Laughing.*] Who did you play for?

OSBORNE. The Harlequins.

RALEIGH. I say, really!

OSBORNE. I played for the English team on one great occasion.

RALEIGH. What! For *England!*

OSBORNE. I was awfully lucky to get the chance. It's a long time ago now.

RALEIGH. [*With awe.*] Oh, but, good Lord! that must have been simply topping. Where did you play?

OSBORNE. Wing three.

RALEIGH. I say, I — I never realised — you'd played for England?

OSBORNE. Tuppence to talk to me now! Anyhow, don't breeze it about.

RALEIGH. Don't the others know?

OSBORNE. We never talk about football.

RALEIGH. They ought to know. It'd make them feel jolly bucked.

OSBORNE. [*Laughing.*] It doesn't make much difference out here!

RALEIGH. It must be awfully thrilling, playing in front of a huge crowd — all shouting and cheering ——

OSBORNE. You don't notice it when the game begins.

RALEIGH. You're too taken up with the game?

OSBORNE. Yes.

RALEIGH. I used to get wind up playing at school with only a few kids looking on.

OSBORNE. You feel it more when there are only a few. [*He has picked up a slip of paper from the table; suddenly he laughs.*] Look at this!

RALEIGH. [*Looking at it curiously.*] What is it?

OSBORNE. Trotter's plan to make the time pass quickly. One hundred and forty-four little circles — one for each hour of six days. He's blacked in six already. He's six hours behind.

RALEIGH. It's rather a good idea. I like Trotter.

OSBORNE. He's a good chap.

RALEIGH. He makes things feel — natural.

OSBORNE. He's a genuine sort of chap.

RALEIGH. That's it. He's genuine. [*There is a pause. He has been filling a new pipe.* OSBORNE *is puffing at his old one.*] How topping — to have played for England!

OSBORNE. It was rather fun.

[*There is a pause.*]

RALEIGH. The Germans are really quite decent, aren't they? I mean, outside the newspapers?

OSBORNE. Yes. [*Pause.*] I remember up at Wipers we had a man shot when he was out on patrol. Just at dawn. We couldn't get him in that night. He lay out there groaning all day. Next night three of our men crawled out to get him in. It was so near the German trenches that they could have shot our fellows one by one. But, when our men began dragging the wounded man back over the rough ground, a big German officer stood up in their trenches and called out: "Carry him!" — and our fellows stood up and carried the man back, and the German officer fired some lights for them to see by.

RALEIGH. How topping!

OSBORNE. Next day we blew each other's trenches to blazes.

RALEIGH. It all seems rather — *silly*, doesn't it?

OSBORNE. It does, rather.

[*There is silence for a while.*]

RALEIGH. I started a letter when I came off duty last night. How do we send letters?

OSBORNE. The quartermaster-sergeant takes them down after he brings rations up in the evenings.

[STANHOPE *is coming slowly down the steps.* RALEIGH *rises.*]

RALEIGH. I think I'll go and finish it now — if I go on duty soon.

OSBORNE. Come and write it in here. It's more cheery.

RALEIGH. It's all right, thanks; I'm quite comfortable in there. I've rigged up a sort of little table beside my bed.

OSBORNE. Righto.

[RALEIGH *goes into his dug-out.* STANHOPE *is slowly taking off his equipment.*]

STANHOPE. What a foul smell of bacon.

OSBORNE. Yes. We've got bacon for breakfast.

STANHOPE. So I gather. Have you told Raleigh about rifle inspection?

OSBORNE. No.

STANHOPE. [*At the entrance to* RALEIGH'S *dug-out.*]   Raleigh!

RALEIGH. [*Appearing.*] Yes?

STANHOPE. You inspect your platoon's rifles at nine o'clock.

RALEIGH. Oh, righto, Stanhope. [*He goes again.*]

STANHOPE. [*Sitting at the table.*] I've arranged two wiring parties to begin at eight o'clock tonight — Corporal Burt with two men and Sergeant Smith with two.   I want them to strengthen the wire all along the front.

OSBORNE. It's very weak at present.

STANHOPE. Every company leaves it for the next one to do.   There're great holes blown out weeks ago.

OSBORNE. I know.

STANHOPE. Next night we'll start putting a belt of wire down both sides of us.

OSBORNE. Down the sides?

STANHOPE. Yes.   We'll wire ourselves right in.   If this attack comes, I'm not going to trust the companies on our sides to hold their ground.

[MASON *has come in, and stands diffidently in the background.*]

MASON. Would you like a nice bit o' bacon, sir?

STANHOPE. No, thanks.   I'll have a cup of tea.

MASON. Right, sir. [*He goes out.*]

STANHOPE. I've been having a good look round.   We've got a strong position here — if we wire ourselves right in.   The colonel's been talking to me up there.

OSBORNE. Oh.   Has he been round?

STANHOPE. Yes.   He says a German prisoner gave the day of attack as the 21st.

OSBORNE. That's Thursday?

STANHOPE. Yes.   Today's Tuesday.

OSBORNE. That means about dawn the day after tomorrow.

STANHOPE. The second dawn from now.

[*There is a pause.*]

OSBORNE. Then it'll come while we're here.

STANHOPE. Yes.   It'll come while we're here.   And we shall be in the front seats.

OSBORNE. Oh, well ——

[*In the silence that follows,* MASON *enters with a cup of tea.*]

MASON. Would you like a nice plate of sardines, sir?

STANHOPE. I should loathe it.

MASON. Very good, sir. [*He goes out.*]

OSBORNE. Did the colonel have much to say?

STANHOPE. Only that when the attack comes we can't expect any help from behind.   We're not to move from here.   We've got to stick it.

OSBORNE. I see.

STANHOPE. We'll wire ourselves in as strongly as possible. I've got to arrange battle positions for each platoon and section this afternoon.

OSBORNE. Well, I'm glad it's coming at last. I'm sick of waiting.

STANHOPE. [*Looking at* TROTTER'S *chart.*] What's this extraordinary affair?

OSBORNE. Trotter's plan to make the time pass by. A hundred and forty-four circles — one for each hour of six days.

STANHOPE. How many hours are there till dawn on the 21st?

OSBORNE. Goodness knows. Not many, I hope.

STANHOPE. Nearly nine o'clock now. Twenty-four till nine tomorrow; twelve till nine at night — that's thirty-six; nine till six next morning; that's forty-five altogether. [*He begins to count off forty-five circles on* TROTTER'S *chart.*]

OSBORNE. What are you going to do?

STANHOPE. At the end of the forty-fifth circle I'm going to draw a picture of Trotter being blown up in four pieces.

OSBORNE. Don't spoil his chart. It took him an hour to make that.

STANHOPE. He won't see the point. He's no imagination.

OSBORNE. I don't suppose he has.

STANHOPE. Funny not to have any imagination. Must be rather nice.

OSBORNE. A bit dull, I should think.

STANHOPE. It must be, rather. I suppose all his life Trotter feels like you and I do when we're drowsily drunk.

OSBORNE. Poor chap!

STANHOPE. I suppose if Trotter looks at that wall he just sees a brown surface. He doesn't see into the earth beyond — the worms wandering about round the stones and roots of trees. I wonder how a worm knows when it's going up or down.

OSBORNE. When it's going down I suppose the blood runs into its head and makes it throb.

STANHOPE. Worms haven't got any blood.

OSBORNE. Then I don't suppose it ever does know.

STANHOPE. Rotten if it didn't — and went on going down when it thought it was coming up.

OSBORNE. Yes, I expect that's the one thing worms dread.

STANHOPE. D'you think this life sharpens the imagination?

OSBORNE. It must.

STANHOPE. Whenever I look at anything nowadays I see right through it. Looking at you now there's your uniform — your jersey — shirt — vest — then beyond that ——

OSBORNE. Let's talk about something else — croquet, or the war.

STANHOPE. [*Laughing.*] Sorry! It's a habit that's grown on me lately — to look right through things, and on and on — till I get frightened and stop.

OSBORNE. I suppose everybody out here —*feels* more keenly.

STANHOPE. I hope so. I wondered if there was anything wrong with me. D'you ever get a sudden feeling that everything's going farther and farther away — till you're the only thing in the world — and then the world begins going away — until you're the only thing in — in the universe — and you struggle to get back — and can't?

OSBORNE. Bit of nerve strain, that's all.

STANHOPE. You don't think I'm going potty?

OSBORNE. Oh, Lord, no!

STANHOPE. [*Throwing back his head and laughing.*] Dear old Uncle! you don't really know, do you? You just pretend you do, to make me feel all right.

OSBORNE. When people are going potty they never talk about it; they keep it to themselves.

STANHOPE. Oh, well, that's all right, then. [*There is silence for a while.*] I had that feeling this morning, standing out there in the line while the sun was rising. By the way, did you see the sunrise? Wasn't it gorgeous?

OSBORNE. Splendid — this morning.

STANHOPE. I was looking across at the Boche trenches and right beyond — not a sound or a soul; just an enormous plain, all churned up like a sea that's got muddier and muddier till it's so stiff that it can't move. You could have heard a pin drop in the quiet; yet you knew thousands of guns were hidden there, all ready cleaned and oiled — millions of bullets lying in pouches — thousands of Germans, waiting and thinking. Then, gradually, that feeling came ——

OSBORNE. I never knew the sun could rise in so many ways till I came out here. Green, and pink, and red, and blue, and grey. Extraordinary, isn't it?

STANHOPE. Yes. Hi! Mason!

MASON. [*Outside.*] Yessir!

STANHOPE. Bring some mugs and a bottle of whiskey.

MASON. Yessir.

OSBORNE. [*Smiling.*] So early in the morning?

STANHOPE. Just a spot. It's damn cold in here.

OSBORNE. [*Turning over the pages of a magazine.*] This show at the Hippodrome has been running a long time.

STANHOPE. What? *Zig-zag?*

OSBORNE. Yes. George Robey's in it.

STANHOPE. Harper saw it on leave. Says it's damn good. Robey's pricelessly funny.

[MASON *brings whiskey and mugs and water.*]

OSBORNE. Wish I'd seen a show on leave.

STANHOPE. D'you mean to say you didn't go to any shows?

OSBORNE. [*Laughing.*] No. I spent all the time in the garden, making a rockery. In the evenings I used to sit and smoke and read — and my wife used to knit socks and play the piano a bit. We pretended there wasn't any war at all — till my two youngsters made me help in a tin-soldier battle on the floor.

STANHOPE. Poor old Uncle! You can't get away from it, can you?

OSBORNE. I wish I knew how to fight a battle like those boys of mine.

You ought to have seen the way they lured my men under the sofa and mowed them down.

STANHOPE. [*Laughing and helping himself to a drink.*] You going to have one?

OSBORNE. Not now, thanks.

STANHOPE. You go on duty at eleven, don't you?

OSBORNE. Yes. I relieve Trotter.

STANHOPE. Raleigh better go on at one o'clock and stay with you for an hour. Then he can stay on alone till four. Hibbert relieves him at four.

OSBORNE. Righto.

STANHOPE. What's Raleigh doing now?

OSBORNE. Finishing a letter.

STANHOPE. Did you tell him?

OSBORNE. About what?

STANHOPE. Censorship.

OSBORNE. You don't mean that seriously?

STANHOPE. Mean it? Of course I mean it.

OSBORNE. You can't do that.

STANHOPE. Officially I'm supposed to read all your letters. Damn it all, Uncle! Imagine yourself in my place — a letter going away from here — from that boy ——

OSBORNE. He'll say nothing — rotten — about you.

STANHOPE. You think so? [*There is a pause.*] I heard you go on duty last night. After you'd gone, I got up. I was feeling bad. I forgot Raleigh was out there with Trotter. I'd forgotten all about him. I was sleepy. I just knew something beastly had happened. Then he came in with Trotter — and looked at me. After coming in out of the night air, this place must have reeked of candle-grease, and rats — and whiskey. One thing a boy like that can't stand is a smell that isn't fresh. He looked at me as if I'd hit him between the eyes — as if I'd spat on him ——

OSBORNE. You imagine things.

STANHOPE. [*Laughing.*] Imagine things! No need to imagine!

OSBORNE. Why can't you treat him like any other youngster?

[RALEIGH *comes in from his dug-out with a letter in his hand. He stops short as he notices the abrupt silence that follows his entry.*]

RALEIGH. I'm sorry.

OSBORNE. It's all right, Raleigh. Going to inspect rifles?

RALEIGH. Yes.

OSBORNE. You needn't bother if the wood's a bit dirty — just the barrels and magazines and all the metal parts.

RALEIGH. Righto.

OSBORNE. See there's plenty of oil on it. And look at the ammunition in the men's pouches.

RALEIGH. Right. [*He crosses towards the door and turns.*] Where do we put the letters to be collected?

OSBORNE. Oh, just on the table.

RALEIGH. Thanks. [*He begins to lick the flap of the envelope.*]

STANHOPE. [*In a quiet voice.*] You leave it open.

RALEIGH. [*Surprised.*] Open?

STANHOPE. Yes. I have to censor all letters.

RALEIGH. [*Stammering.*] Oh, but — I haven't said anything about — where we are ——

STANHOPE. It's the rule that letters must be read.

RALEIGH. [*Nervously.*] Oh, I — I didn't realise that. [*He stands embarrassed; then gives a short laugh.*] I — I think — I'll just leave it, then. [*He unbuttons his tunic pocket to put the letter away.*]

[STANHOPE *rises, crosses slowly and faces* RALEIGH.]

STANHOPE. Give me that letter!

RALEIGH. [*Astonished.*] But — Dennis ——

STANHOPE. [*Trembling.*] Give me that letter!

RALEIGH. But it's — it's private. I didn't know ——

STANHOPE. D'you understand an order? Give me that letter!

RALEIGH. But I tell you — there's nothing — [STANHOPE *clutches* RALEIGH'S *wrist and tears the letter from his hand.*] Dennis — I'm ——

STANHOPE. Don't "Dennis" me! Stanhope's my name! You're not at school! Go and inspect your rifles.

[RALEIGH *stands in amazement at the foot of the steps.*]

STANHOPE. [*Shouting.*] D'you understand an order?

[*For a moment* RALEIGH *stares wide-eyed at* STANHOPE, *who is trembling and breathing heavily, then almost in a whisper he says:* "Right," *and goes quietly up the narrow steps.* STANHOPE *turns toward the table.*]

OSBORNE. Good heavens, Stanhope!

STANHOPE. [*Wheeling furiously on* OSBORNE.] Look here, Osborne, *I'm* commanding this company. I ask for advice when I want it!

OSBORNE. Very well.

[STANHOPE *sinks down at the table with the letter in his hand. There is silence for a moment. Then he throws the letter on the table and rests his head between his hands.*]

STANHOPE. Oh, God! I don't want to read the blasted thing!

OSBORNE. You'll let it go then?

STANHOPE. I don't care. [*There is a pause.*]

OSBORNE. Shall I glance through it — for you?

STANHOPE. If you like.

OSBORNE. I don't *want* to.

STANHOPE. You better. I can't.

[OSBORNE *takes the letter from the table and opens it.* STANHOPE *sits with his head in his hand, digging a magazine with a pencil. After a while,* OSBORNE *glances up at* STANHOPE.]

OSBORNE. D'you want to hear?

STANHOPE. I suppose I better know.

OSBORNE. He begins with a description of his getting here — he doesn't mention the names of any places.

STANHOPE. What does he say then?

OSBORNE. The last piece is about you.

STANHOPE. Go on.

OSBORNE. [*Reading.*] He says: "And now I come to the great news. I reported at Battalion Headquarters, and the colonel looked in a little book, and said, 'You report to "C" Company — Captain Stanhope.' Can't you imagine what I felt? I was taken along some trenches and shown a dug-out. There was an awfully nice officer there — quite old — with grey hair" — [OSBORNE *clears his throat*] — "and then later Dennis came in. He looked tired, but that's because he works so frightfully hard, and because of the responsibility. Then I went on duty in the front line, and a sergeant told me all about Dennis. He said that Dennis is the finest officer in the battalion, and the men simply love him. He hardly ever sleeps in the dug-out; he's always up in the front line with the men, cheering them on with jokes, and making them keen about things, like he did the kids at school. I'm awfully proud to think he's my friend." [*There is silence.* STANHOPE *has not moved while* OSBORNE *has read.*] That's all. [*Pause.*] Shall I stick it down?

[STANHOPE *sits with lowered head. He murmurs something that sounds like* "Yes, please." *He rises heavily and crosses to the shadows by* OS-BORNE'S *bed. The sun is shining quite brightly in the trench outside.*]

THE CURTAIN FALLS

SCENE II

Afternoon on the same day. The sunlight has gone from the dug-out floor, out still shines brightly in the trench.

STANHOPE *is lying on his bed reading by the light of a candle on the table beside him. A burly* FIGURE *comes groping down the steps and stands blinking in the shadows of the dug-out. A huge man, with a heavy black moustache, a fat red face, and massive chin.*

STANHOPE *puts the magazine down, rises and sits up to the table.*

STANHOPE. I want to talk with you, sergeant-major.

S.-M. [*Standing stolidly by the steps.*] Yes, sir?

STANHOPE. Sit down. Have a whiskey?

S.-M. [*A suspicion of brightness in his voice.*] Thank you, sir.

[*The* SERGEANT-MAJOR *diffidently takes a small tot.*]

STANHOPE. I say. You won't taste that. Take a proper one.

S.-M. Well — sir — [STANHOPE *reaches over, helps the* SERGEANT-MAJOR *to a large tot, and takes one himself.*] Turning chilly again, sir. Quite warm this morning.

STANHOPE. Yes.

S.-M. Well, here's your very good health, sir. [*He raises his glass and drinks.*]

STANHOPE. Cheero. [*He puts down his glass and abruptly changes his tone.*] Now, look here, sergeant-major. We must expect this attack on Thursday morning, at dawn. That's the second dawn from now.

[*The* SERGEANT-MAJOR *takes a very dirty little notebook from his pocket and jots down notes with a very small stub of pencil.*]

S.-M. Thursday morning. Very good, sir.

STANHOPE. We're to hold these trenches, and no man's to move from here.

S.-M. Very good, sir.

STANHOPE. It may happen that companies on our sides will give way, leaving our flanks exposed; so I want a screen of wire put down both flanks till it meets the wire in the support line.

S.-M. [*Writing hurriedly.*] Both flanks — yes, sir.

STANHOPE. When the attack begins, I shall take charge of the left, and Mr. Osborne the right. You will be with Mr. Osborne, and Sergeant Baker with me; 9 and 10 Platoons will move over here. [*He points out the position on the trench map.*] 11 and 12 Platoons to the left.

S.-M. I see, sir.

STANHOPE. Is there anything you're not clear about?

S.-M. [*Looking at his notes.*] Seems all clear, sir.

STANHOPE. Anything you want to know?

S.-M. Well, sir [*clears his throat*] — when the attack comes, of course, we beat 'em off — but what if they keep on attacking?

STANHOPE. Then we keep on beating them off.

S.-M. Yes, sir. But what I mean is — they're bound to make a big thing of it.

STANHOPE. [*Cheerily.*] Oh, I think they will!

S.-M. Well, then, sir. If they don't get through the first day, they'll attack the next day and the next ——

STANHOPE. They're bound to.

S.-M. Then oughtn't we to fix up something about, well [*he gropes for the right words*] — er — falling back?

STANHOPE. There's no need to — you see, this company's a lot better than "A" and "B" Companies on either side of us.

S.-M. Quite, sir.

STANHOPE. Well, then, if anyone breaks, "A" and "B" will break before we do. As long as we stick here when the other companies have given way, we can fire into the Boche as they try and get through the gaps on our sides — we'll make a hell of a mess of them. We might delay the advance a whole day.

S.-M. [*Diffidently.*] Yes, sir, but what 'appens when the Boche 'as all got round the back of us?

STANHOPE. Then we advance and win the war.

S.-M. [*Pretending to make a note.*] Win the war. Very good, sir.

STANHOPE. But you understand exactly what I mean, sergeant-major. Our orders are to stick here. If you're told to stick where you are you don't make plans to retire.

S.-M. Quite, sir.

[OSBORNE'S *voice is calling down the steps.* SERGEANT-MAJOR *rises.*]

OSBORNE. Are you there, Stanhope?

STANHOPE. [*Rising quickly.*] Yes. What's the matter?

OSBORNE. The colonel's up here. Wants to see you ——

STANHOPE. Oh, right, I'll come up.

COLONEL. [*From above.*] All right, Stanhope — I'll come down.

S.-M. [*Who has risen.*] Anything more, sir?

STANHOPE. I don't think so. I'll see you at stand-to this evening.

S.-M. Very good, sir.

[*He stands back a pace and salutes* STANHOPE *smartly.* STANHOPE'S *eye falls on the* SERGEANT-MAJOR'S *nearly finished drink on the table. He points to it.*]

STANHOPE. Hoy! What about that?

S.-M. Thank you, sir. [*He finishes the drink.*]

[*The* COLONEL *comes down the steps.*]

COLONEL. Good morning, sergeant-major.

S.-M. Good morning, sir.

[*The* SERGEANT-MAJOR *goes up the steps.*]

STANHOPE. Hullo, sir!

COLONEL. Hullo, Stanhope! [*He sniffs.*] Strong smell of bacon.

STANHOPE. Yes, sir. We had some bacon for breakfast.

COLONEL. Hangs about, doesn't it?

STANHOPE. Yes, sir. Clings to the walls.

COLONEL. Lovely day.

STANHOPE. Splendid, sir.

COLONEL. Spring's coming. [*There is a pause.*] I'm glad you're alone. I've got some rather serious news.

STANHOPE. I'm sorry to hear that, sir. Will you have a drink?

COLONEL. Well, thanks — just a spot. [STANHOPE *mixes a drink for the* COLONEL *and himself.*] Here's luck.

STANHOPE. Cheero, sir. [*Bringing forward a box.*] Sit down, sir.

COLONEL. Thanks.

STANHOPE. What's the news, sir?

COLONEL. The brigadier came to see me this morning. [*He pauses.*] It seems almost certain the attack's to come on Thursday morning. They've got information from more than one source — but they don't know where it's going to fall the hardest. The Boche began relieving his front-line troops yesterday. They're bound to put in certain regiments where they intend to make the hardest push ——

STANHOPE. Naturally ——

COLONEL. And the general wants us to make a raid to find out who's come into the line opposite here.

[*There is a pause.*]

STANHOPE. I see. When?

COLONEL. As soon as possible. He said tonight.

STANHOPE. Oh, but that's absurd!

COLONEL. I told him so. I said the earliest would be tomorrow afternoon. A surprise daylight raid under a smoke screen from the trench-mortar people. I think daylight best. There's not much moon now, and it's vitally important to get hold of a Boche or two.

STANHOPE. Quite.

COLONEL. I suggest sending two officers and ten men. Quite enough for the purpose. Just opposite here there's only seventy yards of No Man's Land. Tonight the trench-mortars can blow a hole in the Boche wire and you can cut a hole in yours. Harrison of the trench-mortars is coming in to dinner with me this evening to discuss everything. I'd like you to come too. Eight o'clock suit you?

STANHOPE. Very good, sir.

COLONEL. I'll leave you to select the men.

STANHOPE. You want me to go with them, sir?

COLONEL. Oh, no, Stanhope. I — I can't let you go. No. I want one officer to direct the raid and one to make the dash in and collar some Boche.

STANHOPE. Who do you suggest, sir?

COLONEL. Well, I suggest Osborne, for one. He's a very level-headed chap. He can direct it.

STANHOPE. And who else?

COLONEL. Well, there's Trotter — but he's a bit fat, isn't he? Not much good at dashing in?

STANHOPE. No. D'you suggest Hibbert?

COLONEL. Well, what do *you* think of Hibbert?

STANHOPE. I don't think so.

COLONEL. No.

> [*There is a pause.*]

STANHOPE. Why not send a good sergeant, sir?

COLONEL. No. I don't think a sergeant. The men expect officers to lead a raid.

STANHOPE. Yes. There is that.

COLONEL. As a matter of fact, Stanhope, I'm thinking of that youngster I sent up to you last night.

STANHOPE. Raleigh?

COLONEL. Yes. Just the type. Plenty of guts ——

STANHOPE. He's awfully new to it all ——

COLONEL. All to the good. His nerves are sound.

STANHOPE. It's rotten to send a fellow who's only just arrived.

COLONEL. Well, who else is there? I could send an officer from another company ——

STANHOPE. [*Quickly.*] Oh, Lord, no. We'll do it.

COLONEL. Then I suggest Osborne to direct the raid and Raleigh to make the dash — with ten good men. We'll meet Harrison at supper and arrange the smoke bombs — and blowing a hole in the wire. You select the men and talk to Osborne and Raleigh about it in the meantime.

STANHOPE. Very well, sir.

COLONEL. Better send Osborne and Raleigh down to me in the morning to talk things over. Or, better still — I'll come up here first thing tomorrow morning.

STANHOPE. Right, sir.

Colonel. It's all a damn nuisance; but, after all — it's necessary.

Stanhope. I suppose it is.

Colonel. Well, so long, Stanhope. I'll see you at eight o'clock. Do you like fish?

Stanhope. Fish, sir?

Colonel. Yes. We've had some fresh fish sent up from railhead for supper tonight.

Stanhope. Splendid, sir!

Colonel. Whiting, I think it is.

Stanhope. Good!

Colonel. Well, bye-bye. [*The* Colonel *goes up the steps.*]

 [Stanhope *stands watching for a moment, then turns and walks slowly to the table.* Hibbert *comes quietly into the dug-out from the tunnel leading from his sleeping quarters.*]

Stanhope. Hullo! I thought you were asleep.

Hibbert. I just wanted a word with you, Stanhope.

Stanhope. Fire away.

Hibbert. This neuralgia of mine. I'm awfully sorry. I'm afraid I can't stick it any longer ——

Stanhope. I know. It's rotten, isn't it? I've got it like hell ——

Hibbert. [*Taken aback.*] *You* have?

Stanhope. Had it for weeks.

Hibbert. Well, I'm sorry, Stanhope. It's no good. I've tried damned hard; but I must go down ——

Stanhope. Go down — where?

Hibbert. Why, go sick — go down the line. I must go into hospital and have some kind of treatment. [*There is a silence for a moment.* Stanhope *is looking at* Hibbert — *till* Hibbert *turns away and walks towards his dug-out.*] I'll go right along now, I think ——

Stanhope. [*Quietly.*] You're going to stay here.

Hibbert. I'm going down to see the doctor. He'll send me to hospital when he understands ——

Stanhope. I've seen the doctor. I saw him this morning. He won't send you to hospital, Hibbert; he'll send you back here. He promised me he would. [*There is silence.*] So you can save yourself a walk.

Hibbert. [*Fiercely.*] What the hell ——!

Stanhope. Stop that!

Hibbert. I've a perfect right to go sick if I want to. The men can — why can't an officer?

Stanhope. No man's sent down unless he's very ill. There's nothing wrong with you, Hibbert. The German attack's on Thursday; almost for certain. You're going to stay here and see it through with the rest of us.

Hibbert. [*Hysterically.*] I tell you, I can't — the pain's nearly sending me mad. I'm going! I've got all my stuff packed. I'm going now — you can't stop me! [*He goes excitedly into the dug-out.* Stanhope *walks slowly towards the steps, turns, and undoes the flap of his revolver holster. He takes out his revolver, and stands casually examining it.*]

[HIBBERT *returns with his pack slung on his back and a walking-stick in his hand. He pauses at the sight of* STANHOPE *by the steps.*]

HIBBERT. Let's get by, Stanhope.

STANHOPE. You're going to stay here and do your job.

HIBBERT. Haven't I *told* you? I *can't!* Don't you understand? Let — let me get by.

STANHOPE. Now look here, Hibbert. I've got a lot of work to do and no time to waste. Once and for all, you're going to stay here and see it through with the rest of us.

HIBBERT. I shall die of this pain if I don't go!

STANHOPE. Better die of pain than be shot for deserting.

HIBBERT. [*In a low voice.*] What do you mean?

STANHOPE. You know what I mean ——

HIBBERT. I've a right to see the doctor!

STANHOPE. Good God! Don't you understand! — he'll send you back here. Dr. Preston's never let a shirker pass him yet — and he's not going to start now — two days before the attack —

HIBBERT. [*Pleadingly.*] Stanhope — if you only *knew* how awful I feel —— Please do let me go by ——

[*He walks slowly round behind* STANHOPE. STANHOPE *turns and thrusts him roughly back. With a lightning movement* HIBBERT *raises his stick and strikes blindly at* STANHOPE, *who catches the stick, tears it from* HIBBERT'S *hands, smashes it across his knee, and throws it on the ground.*]

STANHOPE. God! — you little swine. You know what that means — don't you? Striking a superior officer! [*There is silence.* STANHOPE *takes hold of his revolver as it swings from its lanyard.* HIBBERT *stands quivering in front of* STANHOPE.] Never mind, though. I won't have you shot for that ——

HIBBERT. Let me go ——

STANHOPE. If you went, I'd have you shot — for deserting. It's a hell of a disgrace — to die like that. I'd rather spare you the disgrace. I give you half a minute to think. You either stay here and try and be a man — or you try to get out of that door — to desert. If you do that, there's going to be an accident. D'you understand? I'm fiddling with my revolver, d'you see? — cleaning it — and it's going off by accident. It often happens out here. It's going off, and it's going to shoot you between the eyes.

HIBBERT. [*In a whisper.*] You daren't ——

STANHOPE. You don't deserve to be shot by accident — but I'd save you the disgrace of the other way — I give you half a minute to decide. [*He holds up his wrist to look at his watch.*] Half a minute from now —

[*There is silence: a few seconds go by. Suddenly* HIBBERT *burst into a high-pitched laugh.*]

HIBBERT. Go on, then, shoot! You won't let me go to hospital. I swear I'll never go into those trenches again. Shoot! — and thank God ——

STANHOPE. [*With his eyes on his watch.*] Fifteen more seconds ——

HIBBERT. Go on! I'm ready ——

STANHOPE. Ten. [*He looks up at* HIBBERT, *who has closed his eyes.*] Five.

[*Again* STANHOPE *looks up. After a moment he quietly drops his revolver into its holster and steps towards* HIBBERT, *who stands with lowered head and eyes tightly screwed up, his arms stretched stiffly by his sides, his hands tightly clutching the edges of his tunic. Gently* STANHOPE *places his hands on* HIBBERT'S *shoulders.* HIBBERT *starts violently and gives a little cry. He opens his eyes and stares vacantly into* STANHOPE'S *face.* STANHOPE *is smiling.*]

STANHOPE. Good man, Hibbert. I liked the way you stuck that.

HIBBERT. [*Hoarsely.*] Why didn't you shoot?

STANHOPE. Stay here, old chap — and see it through ——

[HIBBERT *stands trembling, trying to speak. Suddenly he breaks down and cries.* STANHOPE *takes his hands from his shoulders and turns away.*]

HIBBERT. Stanhope! I've tried like hell — I swear I have. Ever since I came out here I've hated and loathed it. Every sound up there makes me all — cold and sick. I'm different to — to the others — you don't understand. It's got worse and worse, and now I can't bear it any longer. I'll never go up those steps again — into the line — with the men looking at me — and knowing — I'd rather die here.

[*He is sitting on* STANHOPE'S *bed, crying without effort to restrain himself.*]

STANHOPE. [*Pouring out a whiskey.*] Try a drop of this, old chap ——

HIBBERT. No, thanks.

STANHOPE. Go on. Drink it. [HIBBERT *takes the mug and drinks.* STANHOPE *sits down beside* HIBBERT *and puts an arm round his shoulder.*] I know what you feel, Hibbert. I've known all along ——

HIBBERT. How *can* you know?

STANHOPE. Because I feel the same — exactly the same! Every little noise up there makes me feel — just as you feel. Why didn't you tell me instead of talking about neuralgia? We *all* feel like you do sometimes, if you only knew. I hate and loathe it all. Sometimes I feel I could just lie down on this bed and pretend I was paralysed or something — and couldn't move — and just lie there till I died — or was dragged away.

HIBBERT. I can't bear to go up into those awful trenches again.

STANHOPE. When are you due to go on?

HIBBERT. Quite soon. At four.

STANHOPE. Shall we go on together? We know how we both feel now. Shall we see if we can stick it together?

HIBBERT. I can't ——

STANHOPE. Supposing I said *I* can't — supposing we *all* say we can't — what would happen then?

HIBBERT. I don't care. What does it matter? It's all so — so beastly — nothing matters ——

STANHOPE. Supposing the worst happened — supposing we were knocked right out. Think of all the chaps who've gone already. It can't be very lonely there — with all those fellows. Sometimes I think it's lonelier here. [*He pauses.* HIBBERT *is sitting quietly now, his eyes roving vacantly in front of him.*] Just go and have a quiet rest. Then we'll go out together.

HIBBERT. Do please let me go, Stanhope ——

STANHOPE. If you went — and left Osborne and Trotter and Raleigh and all those men up there to do your work — could you ever look a man straight in the face again — in all your life? [*There is silence again.*] You may be wounded. Then you can go home and feel proud — and if you're killed you — you won't have to stand this hell any more. I might have fired just now. If I had you would have been dead now. But you're still alive — with a straight fighting chance of coming through. Take the chance, old chap, and stand in with Osborne and Trotter and Raleigh. Don't you think it worth standing in with men like that? — when you know they all feel like you do — in their hearts — and just go on sticking it because they know it's —it's the only thing a decent man can do. [*Again there is silence.*] What about it?

HIBBERT. I'll — I'll try ——

STANHOPE. Good man!

HIBBERT. You — you won't say anything, Stanhope — about this?

STANHOPE. If you promise not to tell anyone what a blasted funk *I* am.

HIBBERT. [*With a little laugh.*] No.

STANHOPE. Splendid! Now go and have ten minutes' rest and a smoke — then we'll go up together and hold each other's hands — and jump every time a rat squeaks. [HIBBERT *rises and blows his nose.*] We've all got a good fighting chance. *I* mean to come through — don't you?

HIBBERT. Yes. Rather. [*He goes timidly towards his dug-out, and turns at the doorway.*] It's awfully decent of you, Stanhope — [STANHOPE *is pouring himself out a whiskey.*] And thanks most awfully for ——

STANHOPE. That's all right.

[HIBBERT *goes away.* STANHOPE *takes a drink and sits down at the table to write.* MASON *comes in.*]

MASON. Will you have a nice cup of tea, sir?

STANHOPE. Can you guarantee it's nice?

MASON. Well, sir — it's a bit oniony, but that's only because of the saucepan.

STANHOPE. In other words, it's onion soup with tea-leaves in it?

MASON. Not till dinner-time, sir.

STANHOPE. All right, Mason. Bring two cups of onion tea. One for Mr. Hibbert.

MASON. Very good, sir. [*Going towards the door, he meets* OSBORNE *coming in.*] Will you have a nice cup of tea, sir?

OSBORNE. Please, Mason — and plenty of bread and butter and strawberry jam.

MASON. Very good, sir.

STANHOPE. Well, Uncle — how are things going on up there?

OSBORNE. Two lonely rifle grenades came over just now.

STANHOPE. I heard them. Where did they pitch?

OSBORNE. Just over the front line on the left. Otherwise nothing doing.
[*Pause.*]

STANHOPE. The colonel's been talking to me.

OSBORNE. About the attack?

STANHOPE. Partly. We've got to make a raid, Uncle.

OSBORNE. Oh? When?

STANHOPE. Tomorrow afternoon. Under a smoke screen. Two officers and ten men.

OSBORNE. Who's going?

STANHOPE. You and Raleigh.

[*Pause.*]

OSBORNE. Oh. [*There is another pause.*] Why Raleigh?

STANHOPE. The colonel picked you to direct and Raleigh to dash in.

OSBORNE. I see.

STANHOPE. The brigade wants to know who's opposite here.

OSBORNE. Tomorrow? What time?

STANHOPE. I suggest about five o'clock. A little before dusk ——

OSBORNE. I see.

STANHOPE. I'm damn sorry.

OSBORNE. That's all right, old chap.

STANHOPE. I'm dining with the colonel to arrange everything. Then I'll come back and go through it with you.

OSBORNE. Where do we raid from?

STANHOPE. Out of the sap on our left. Straight across.

OSBORNE. Where's the map?

STANHOPE. Here we are. Look. Straight across to this sentry post of the Boche. Sixty yards. Tonight we'll lay out a guiding tape as far as possible. After dark the toch-emmas are going to break the Boche wire and we'll cut a passage in ours.

OSBORNE. Will you fix up the men who are to go?

STANHOPE. Are you keen on any special men?

OSBORNE. Can I take a corporal?

STANHOPE. Sure.

OSBORNE. May I have young Crooks?

STANHOPE. Righto.

OSBORNE. You'll ask for volunteers, I suppose?

STANHOPE. Yes. I'll see the sergeant-major and get him to go round for names. [*He crosses to the doorway as* MASON *comes in with the tea.*]

MASON. Your tea, sir!

STANHOPE. Keep it hot, Mason.

MASON. Will you take this cup, Mr. Osborne?

STANHOPE. Take the other in to Mr. Hibbert, in there.

MASON. Very good, sir. [*He goes in to* HIBBERT'S *dug-out.*]

STANHOPE. Shan't be long, Uncle. [*He goes up the steps.*]

OSBORNE. Righto.

[MASON *returns.*]

MASON. Will you have cut bread and butter — or shall I bring the loaf, sir?

OSBORNE. Cut it, Mason, please.

MASON. Just bringing the jam separately?

OSBORNE. Yes.

MASON. Very good, sir.

[MASON *goes out.* OSBORNE *take a small leather bound book from his pocket, opens it at a marker, and begins to read.* TROTTER *appears from the sleeping dug-out looking very sleepy.*]

TROTTER. Tea ready?

OSBORNE. Yes.

TROTTER. Why's Hibbert got his tea in there?

OSBORNE. I don't know.

TROTTER. [*Rubbing his eyes.*] Oh, Lord, I do feel frowsy. 'Ad a fine sleep, though.

[MASON *brings more tea and a pot of jam.*]

MASON. Bread just coming, sir. 'Ere's the strawberry jam, sir.

TROTTER. [*Reciting.*] "'Tell me, mother, what is that
That looks like strawberry jam?'
'Hush, hush, my dear; 'tis only Pa
Run over by a tram ——'"

OSBORNE. The colonel came here while you were asleep.

TROTTER. Oh?

OSBORNE. We've got to make a raid tomorrow afternoon.

TROTTER. Oh, Lord! What — All of us?

OSBORNE. Two officers and ten men.

TROTTER. Who's got to do it?

OSBORNE. Raleigh and I.

TROTTER. Raleigh!

OSBORNE. Yes.

TROTTER. But 'e's only just come!

OSBORNE. Apparently that's the reason.

TROTTER. And you're going too?

OSBORNE. Yes.

TROTTER. Let's 'ear all about it.

OSBORNE. I know nothing yet. Except that it's got to be done.

TROTTER. What a damn nuisance!

OSBORNE. It is, rather.

TROTTER. I reckon the Boche are all ready waiting for it. Did you 'ear about the raid just south of 'ere the other night?

OSBORNE. Nothing much.

TROTTER. The trench-mortars go and knock an 'ole in the Boche wire to let our fellers through — and in the night the Boche went out and tied bits o' red rag on each side of the 'ole!

OSBORNE. Yes. I heard about that.

TROTTER. And even then our fellers 'ad to make the raid. It was murder. Doesn't this tea taste of onions?

OSBORNE. It does a bit.

TROTTER. Pity Mason don't clean 'is pots better. [MASON *brings some bread on a plate.*] This tea tastes of onions.

MASON. I'm sorry, sir. Onions do 'ave such a way of cropping up again.

TROTTER. Yes, but we 'aven't 'ad onions for days!

MASON. I know, sir. That's what makes it so funny.

TROTTER. Well, you better do something about it.

MASON. I'll look into it, sir. [*He goes out.*]

[OSBORNE *and* TROTTER *prepare themselves slices of bread and jam.*]

TROTTER. Joking apart. It's damn ridiculous making a raid when the Boche are expecting it.

OSBORNE. We're not doing it for fun.

TROTTER. I know.

OSBORNE. You might avoid talking to Raleigh about it.

TROTTER. Why? How do you mean?

OSBORNE. There's no need to tell him it's murder ——

TROTTER. Oh, Lord! no. [*He pauses.*] I'm sorry 'e's got to go. 'E's a nice young feller —— [OSBORNE *turns to his book. There is silence.*] What are you reading?

OSBORNE. [*Wearily.*] Oh, just a book.

TROTTER. What's the title?

OSBORNE. [*Showing him the cover.*] Ever read it?

TROTTER. [*Leaning over and reading the cover.*] *Alice's Adventures in Wonderland* — why, that's a kid's book!

OSBORNE. Yes.

TROTTER. You aren't *reading* it?

OSBORNE. Yes.

TROTTER. What — a *kid's* book?

OSBORNE. Haven't you read it?

TROTTER. [*Scornfully.*] No!

OSBORNE. You ought to. [*Reads*]:

> "How doth the little crocodile
> Improve his shining tail,
> And pour the waters of the Nile
> On every golden scale?

> "How cheerfully he seems to grin
> And neatly spread his claws,
> And welcomes little fishes in
> With gently smiling jaws!"

TROTTER. [*After a moment's thought.*] I don't see no point in that.

OSBORNE. [*Wearily.*] Exactly. That's just the point.

TROTTER. [*Looking curiously at* OSBORNE.] You are a funny chap!

[STANHOPE *returns.*]

STANHOPE. The sergeant-major's getting volunteers.

OSBORNE. Good!

TROTTER. Sorry to 'ear about the raid, skipper.

STANHOPE. [*Shortly.*] So am I. What do you make the time?

TROTTER. Just on four.

[MASON *brings in more tea.*]

STANHOPE. [*Taking the mug of tea.*] Was Hibbert asleep when you came out of there?

TROTTER. No. 'E was just lying on 'is bed, smoking.

STANHOPE. [*Going to the sleeping dug-out.*] Hibbert!

HIBBERT. [*Coming out.*] I'm ready, Stanhope.

STANHOPE. Had some tea?

HIBBERT. Yes, thanks.

TROTTER. I reckon Raleigh'll be glad to be relieved. Rotten being on dooty for the first time alone.

OSBORNE. I don't think he minds.

STANHOPE. I shall be up there sometime, Uncle.

OSBORNE. I say, why don't you have a rest — you've been on the go all day.

STANHOPE. There's too much to do. This raid's going to upset the arrangements of the wiring party tonight. Can't have men out there while the toch-emmas are blowing holes in the Boche wire. [*He drinks up his tea.*] Ready, Hibbert? Come on, my lad.

[STANHOPE *and* HIBBERT *leave the dug-out together.* TROTTER *looks after them curiously, and turns to* OSBORNE.]

TROTTER. Can't understand that little feller, can you?

OSBORNE. Who?

TROTTER. Why, 'Ibbert. D'you see, 'is eyes? All red. 'E told me in there 'e'd got 'ay-fever.

OSBORNE. Rotten thing, hay-fever.

TROTTER. If you ask me, 'e's been crying ——

[OSBORNE *is writing at the table.*]

OSBORNE. Maybe.

TROTTER. Funny little bloke, isn't 'e?

OSBORNE. Yes. I say — d'you mind? I just want to get a letter off.

TROTTER. Oh, sorry. They 'aven't collected the letters yet, then?

OSBORNE. Not yet.

TROTTER. I'll get one off to my old lady. [*He goes towards his dug-out.*] She's wrote and asked if I've got fleas.

OSBORNE. Have you?

TROTTER. [*Gently rotating his shoulders.*] I wish it *was* fleas.

[TROTTER *goes into his dug-out;* OSBORNE *continues his letter.* RALEIGH *comes down the steps from the trench.*]

RALEIGH. [*Excitedly.*] I say, Stanhope's told me about the raid.

OSBORNE. Has he?

RALEIGH. Just you and me, isn't it — and ten men?

OSBORNE. Yes, tomorrow. Just before dusk. Under a smoke cloud.

RALEIGH. I say — it's most frightfully exciting!

OSBORNE. We shall know more about it after Stanhope sees the colonel tonight.

RALEIGH. Were you and I picked — specially?

OSBORNE. Yes.

RALEIGH. I — say!

THE CURTAIN FALLS

ACT THREE

SCENE I

The following day, towards sunset. The earth wall of the trench outside glows with a light that slowly fades with the sinking sun.

STANHOPE *is alone, wandering to and fro across the dug-out. He looks up the steps for a moment, crosses to the table, and glances down at the map. He looks anxiously at his watch, and, going to the servants' dug-out, calls:*

STANHOPE. Mason!

MASON. [*Outside.*] Yessir!

STANHOPE. Are you making the coffee?

MASON. Yessir!

STANHOPE. Make it hot and strong. Ready in five minutes. I'll call when it's wanted.

MASON. Very good, sir.

[*Again* STANHOPE *wanders restlessly to and fro. The* COLONEL *comes down the steps.*]

COLONEL. Everything ready?

STANHOPE. Yes, sir. [*There is silence.*] You've no news, then?

COLONEL. I'm afraid not. It's got to be done.

STANHOPE. [*After a pause.*] I see.

COLONEL. The brigadier says the Boche did the same thing just south of here the other day.

STANHOPE. I know; but didn't you suggest we altered our plans and made a surprise raid farther up the line after dark?

COLONEL. Yes. I suggested that.

STANHOPE. What did he say?

COLONEL. He said the present arrangements have got to stand.

STANHOPE. But surely he must realise ——?

COLONEL. [*Impatiently breaking in.*] Look here, Stanhope, I've done all I can, but my report's got to be at headquarters by seven this evening. If we wait till it's dark we shall be too late.

STANHOPE. Why seven?

COLONEL. They've got some conference to arrange the placing of reserves.

STANHOPE. They can't have it later because of dinner, I suppose.

COLONEL. Lots of raids have taken place along the line today. With the attack tomorrow morning, headquarters naturally want all the information they can get as early as possible.

STANHOPE. Meanwhile the Boche are sitting over there with a dozen machine-guns trained on that hole — waiting for our fellows to come.

COLONEL. Well, I can't disobey orders.

STANHOPE. Why didn't the trench-mortars blow a dozen holes in different places — so the Boche wouldn't know which we were going to use?

COLONEL. It took three hours to blow that one. How could they blow a dozen in the time? It's no good worrying about that now. It's too late. Where's Osborne and Raleigh?

STANHOPE. They're up in the sap, having a last look round. What d'you make the time, sir?

COLONEL. Exactly nineteen minutes to.

STANHOPE. I'm thirty seconds behind you.

COLONEL. Funny. We checked this morning.

STANHOPE. Still, it's near enough. We shan't go till the smoke blows across.

COLONEL. The smoke ought to blow across nicely. The wind's just right. I called on the trench-mortars on the way up. Everything's ready. They'll drop the bombs thirty yards to the right.

STANHOPE. Are you going to stay here?

COLONEL. I'll watch from the trench just above, I think. Bring the prisoners straight back here. We'll question them right away.

STANHOPE. Why not take them straight down to your headquarters?

COLONEL. Well, the Boche are bound to shell pretty heavily. I don't want the risk of the prisoners being knocked out before we've talked to them.

STANHOPE. All right. I'll have them brought back here.

[*There is a pause. The* COLONEL *sucks hard at his pipe.* STANHOPE *roves restlessly about, smoking a cigarette.*]

COLONEL. It's no good getting depressed. After all, it's only sixty yards. The Boche'll be firing into a blank fog. Osborne's a cool, level-headed chap, and Raleigh's the very man to dash in. You've picked good men to follow them?

STANHOPE. The best. All youngsters. Strong, keen chaps.

COLONEL. Good. [*Another pause.*] You know quite well I'd give anything to cancel the beastly affair.

STANHOPE. I know you would, sir.

COLONEL. Have these red rags on the wire upset the men at all?

STANHOPE. It's hard to tell. They naturally take it as a joke. They say the rags are just what they want to show them the way through the gap.

COLONEL. That's the spirit, Stanhope. [OSBORNE *and* RALEIGH *come down the steps.*] Well, Osborne. Everything ready?

OSBORNE. Yes, I think we're all ready, sir. I make it just a quarter to.

COLONEL. That's right.

OSBORNE. The men are going to stand by at three minutes to.

COLONEL. The smoke bombs drop exactly on the hour. You'll give the word to go when the smoke's thick enough?

OSBORNE. That's right, sir.

STANHOPE. [*At the servants' dug-out.*] Mason!

MASON. Coming, sir!

STANHOPE. Were the men having their rum, Uncle?

OSBORNE. Yes. Just as we left. It gives it a quarter of an hour to soak in.

COLONEL. That's right. Are they cheerful?

OSBORNE. Yes. Quite.

[MASON *brings in two cups of coffee and puts them on table.*]

STANHOPE. Would you like to go up and speak to them, sir?

COLONEL. Well, don't you think they'd rather be left alone?

STANHOPE. I think they would appreciate a word or two.

COLONEL. All right. If you think they would.

OSBORNE. They're all in the centre dug-out, sir.

COLONEL. Right. You coming, Stanhope?

STANHOPE. Yes. I'll come, sir.

[*The* COLONEL *lingers a moment. There is an awkward pause. Then the* COLONEL *clears his throat and speaks.*]

COLONEL. Well, good luck, Osborne. I'm certain you'll put up a good show.

OSBORNE. [*Taking the* COLONEL's *hand.*] Thank you, sir.

COLONEL. And, Raleigh, just go in like blazes. Grab hold of the first Boche you see and bundle him across here. One'll do, but bring more if you see any handy.

RALEIGH. [*Taking the* COLONEL's *offered hand.*] Right, sir.

COLONEL. And, if you succeed, I'll recommend you both for the M.C. [OSBORNE *and* RALEIGH *murmur their thanks.*] Remember, a great deal may depend on bringing in a German. It may mean the winning of the whole war. You never know. [*Another pause.*] Well, good luck to you both. [*Again* OSBORNE *and* RALEIGH *murmur their thanks. The* COLONEL *and* STANHOPE *go towards the door.*]

COLONEL. [*Over his shoulder.*] Don't forget to empty your pockets of papers and things.

RALEIGH. Oh, no. [*He goes into his dug-out, taking letters and papers from his pockets.*]

[STANHOPE *is about to follow the* COLONEL *up the steps when* OSBORNE *calls him back.*]

OSBORNE. Er — Stanhope — just a moment.

STANHOPE. [*Returning.*] Hullo!

OSBORNE. I say, don't think I'm being morbid, or anything like that, but would you mind taking these?

STANHOPE. Sure. Until you come back, old man.

OSBORNE. It's only just in case —— [*He takes his watch and a letter from his tunic pocket and puts them on the table. Then he pulls off his ring.*] If anything should happen, would you send these along to my wife? [*He pauses, and gives an awkward little laugh.*]

STANHOPE. [*Putting the articles together on the table.*] You're coming back, old man. Damn it! what on earth should I do without you?

OSBORNE. [*Laughing.*] Goodness knows!

STANHOPE. Must have somebody to tuck me up in bed. [*There is a pause.*] Well, I'll see you up in the sap, before you go. Just have a spot of rum in that coffee.

OSBORNE. Righto.

[STANHOPE *goes to the steps and lingers for a moment.*]

STANHOPE. Cheero!

[*For a second their eyes meet; they laugh.* STANHOPE *goes slowly up the steps.* *There is silence in the dug-out.* OSBORNE *has been filling his pipe, and stands lighting it as* RALEIGH *returns.*]

OSBORNE. Just time for a small pipe.

RALEIGH. Good. I'll have a cigarette, I think. [*He feels in his pocket.*]

OSBORNE. Here you are. [*He offers his case to* RALEIGH.]

RALEIGH. I say, I'm always smoking yours.

OSBORNE. That's all right. [*Pause.*] What about this coffee?

RALEIGH. Sure. [*They sit at the table.*]

OSBORNE. Are you going to have a drop of rum in it?

RALEIGH. Don't you think it might make us a — a bit muzzy?

OSBORNE. I'm just having the coffee as it is.

RALEIGH. I think I will, too.

OSBORNE. We'll have the rum afterwards — to celebrate.

RALEIGH. That's a much better idea.

[*They stir their coffee in silence.* OSBORNE'S *eyes meet* RALEIGH'S. *He smiles.*]

OSBORNE. How d'you feel?

RALEIGH. All right.

OSBORNE. I've got a sort of empty feeling inside.

RALEIGH. That's just what I've got!

OSBORNE. Wind up!

RALEIGH. I keep wanting to yawn.

OSBORNE. That's it. Wind up. I keep wanting to yawn too. It'll pass off directly we start.

RALEIGH. [*Taking a deep breath.*] I wish we could go now.

OSBORNE. [*Looking at his watch on the table.*] We've got eight minutes yet.

RALEIGH. Oh, Lord!

OSBORNE. Let's just have a last look at the map. [*He picks up the map and spreads it out.*] Directly the smoke's thick enough, I'll give the word. You run straight for this point here ——

RALEIGH. When I get to the Boche wire I lie down and wait for you.

OSBORNE. Don't forget to throw your bombs.

RALEIGH. [*Patting his pocket.*] No. I've got them here.

OSBORNE. When I shout "Righto!" — in you go with your eight men. I shall lie on the Boche parapet, and blow my whistle now and then to show you where I am. Pounce on the first Boche you see and bundle him out to me.

RALEIGH. Righto.

OSBORNE. Then we come back like blazes.

RALEIGH. The whole thing'll be over quite quickly?

OSBORNE. I reckon with luck we shall be back in three minutes.

RALEIGH. As quick as that?

OSBORNE. I think so. [*He folds up the map.*] And now let's forget all about it for — [*he looks at his watch*] — for six minutes.

RALEIGH. Oh, Lord, I can't!

OSBORNE. You must.

RALEIGH. How topping if we both get the M.C.!

OSBORNE. Yes. [*Pause.*] Your coffee sweet enough?

RALEIGH. Yes, thanks. It's jolly good coffee. [*Pause.*] I wonder what the Boche are doing over there now?

OSBORNE. I don't know. D'you like coffee better than tea?

RALEIGH. I do for breakfast. [*Pause.*] Do these smoke bombs make much row when they burst?

OSBORNE. Not much. [*Pause.*] Personally, I like cocoa for breakfast.

RALEIGH. [*Laughing.*] I'm sorry!

OSBORNE. Why sorry? Why shouldn't I have cocoa for breakfast?

RALEIGH. I don't mean that. I — mean — I'm sorry to keep talking about the raid. It's so difficult to — to talk about anything else. I was just wondering — will the Boche retaliate in any way after the raid?

OSBORNE. Bound to — a bit.

RALEIGH. Shelling?

OSBORNE. "'The time has come,' the Walrus said,
  'To talk of many things:
  Of shoes — and ships — and sealing-wax —
  Of cabbages — and kings.'"

RALEIGH. "'And why the sea is boiling hot —
  And whether pigs have wings.'"

OSBORNE. Now we're off! Quick, let's talk about pigs! Black pigs or white pigs?

RALEIGH. Black pigs. In the New Forest you find them, quite wild.

OSBORNE. You know the New Forest?

RALEIGH. Rather! My home's down there. A little place called Allum Green just outside Lyndhurst.

OSBORNE. I know Lyndhurst well.

RALEIGH. It's rather nice down there.

OSBORNE. I like it more than any place I know.

RALEIGH. I think I do, too. Of course, it's different when you've always lived in a place.

OSBORNE. You like it in a different way.

RALEIGH. Yes. Just behind our house there's a stream called the Highland; it runs for miles — right through the middle of the forest. Dennis and I followed it once as far as we could.

OSBORNE. I used to walk a lot round Lyndhurst.

RALEIGH. I wish we'd known each other then. You could have come with Dennis and me.

OSBORNE. I wish I had. I used to walk alone.

RALEIGH. You must come and stay with us one day.

OSBORNE. I should like to — awfully.

RALEIGH. I can show you places in the forest that nobody knows about except Dennis and me. It gets thicker and darker and cooler, and you stir up all kinds of funny wild animals.

OSBORNE. They say there are ruins, somewhere in the forest, of villages that William the Conqueror pulled down to let the forest grow.

RALEIGH. I know. We often used to look for them, but we haven't found them yet. [*Pause.*] You must come and help look one day.

OSBORNE. I'll find them all right!

RALEIGH. Then you can write to the papers. "Dramatic Discovery of Professor Osborne!"

[OSBORNE *laughs*.]

OSBORNE. I did go exploring once — digging up Roman remains.

RALEIGH. Where was that?

OSBORNE. Near my home in Sussex there's a Roman road called Stane Street; it runs as straight as a line from the coast to London.

RALEIGH. I know it.

OSBORNE. Near where I live the road runs over Bignor Hill, but in recent times a new road's been cut round the foot of the hill, meeting the old road again farther on. The old road over the hill hasn't been used for years and years — and it's all grown over with grass, and bushes and trees grow in the middle of it.

RALEIGH. Can you still see where it runs?

OSBORNE. Quite easily, in places.

RALEIGH. Did you dig a bit of it up, then?

OSBORNE. Yes. We got permission to dig out a section. It was in wonderful condition.

RALEIGH. Did you find anything?

OSBORNE. We found a horseshoe — and a Roman penny.

RALEIGH. [*Laughing*.] Splendid!

OSBORNE. It's awfully fascinating, digging like that.

RALEIGH. It must be. [OSBORNE *glances at his watch*.] Is it time yet?

OSBORNE. Two minutes. Then we must go up. I wish we had a good hot bath waiting for us when we get back.

RALEIGH. So do I. [*Pause*.] We're having something special for dinner, aren't we?

OSBORNE. How did you know? It's supposed to be a secret.

RALEIGH. Mason dropped a hint.

OSBORNE. Well, we've had a fresh chicken sent up from Noyelle Farm.

RALEIGH. I say!

OSBORNE. And a most awful luxury — two bottles of champagne and half a dozen cigars! One each, and one spare one in case one explodes.

RALEIGH. I've never smoked a cigar.

OSBORNE. It's bound to make you sick.

[RALEIGH *notices* OSBORNE's *ring on the table; he picks it up*.]

RALEIGH. I say, here's your ring.

OSBORNE. Yes. I'm — I'm leaving it here. I don't want the risk of losing it.

RALEIGH. Oh! [*There is silence. He puts the ring slowly down*.]

OSBORNE. [*Rising*.] Well, I think perhaps we ought to get ready.

RALEIGH. Yes. Righto. [*He also rises*.]

OSBORNE. I'm not going to wear a belt — just my revolver, with the lanyard round my neck.

RALEIGH. I see. [*He puts his lanyard round his neck and grips his revolver*.] I feel better with this in my hand, don't you?

OSBORNE. Yes. Something to hold. Loaded all right?

RALEIGH. Yes.

[*They put on their helmets.* OSBORNE *takes his pipe from his mouth and lays it carefully on the table.*]

OSBORNE. I do hate leaving a pipe when it's got a nice glow on the top like that.

RALEIGH. [*With a short laugh.*] What a pity!

[*There is another pause.* OSBORNE *glances at his watch as it lies on the table.*]

OSBORNE. Three minutes to. I think we'd better go.

RALEIGH. Righto.

[*Their eyes meet as* OSBORNE *turns from the table.*]

OSBORNE. I'm glad it's you and I — together, Raleigh.

RALEIGH. [*Eagerly.*] Are you — really?

OSBORNE. Yes.

RALEIGH. So am I — awfully.

OSBORNE. We must put up a good show.

RALEIGH. Yes. Rather!

[*There is a short pause.*]

OSBORNE. Let's go along, shall we?

RALEIGH. Righto. [*They go towards the steps.*]

[MASON *comes to the entrance of his dug-out as they pass.*]

MASON. Good luck, sir.

OSBORNE. Thanks, Mason.

MASON. It's a lovely chicken for dinner, sir.

OSBORNE. [*Slowly going up the steps.*] Splendid!

MASON. Good luck, Mr. Raleigh.

RALEIGH. Thanks.

[OSBORNE *and* RALEIGH *go up together into the pale evening sun.* MASON *tidies the papers on the table; picks up the two coffee mugs, and goes away. There is silence in the trenches above the deserted dug-out. Then, suddenly, there comes the dull "crush" of bursting smoke bombs, followed in a second by the vicious rattle of machine-guns. The red and green glow of German alarm rockets comes faintly through the dug-out door. Then comes the thin whistle and crash of falling shells; first one by itself, then two, almost together. Quicker and quicker they come, till the noise mingles together in confused turmoil. Yet the noise is deadened by the earth walls of the tiny dug-out, and comes quite softly till the whine of one shell rises above the others to a shriek and a crash. A dark funnel of earth leaps up beyond the parapet of the trench outside; earth falls and rattles down the steps, and a black cloud of smoke rises slowly out of sight. Gradually the noise dies away — there is a longer pause between the crash of each bursting shell. The machine-guns stop — rattle again and stop — rattle for the last time — and stop. Voices are calling in the trench outside;* STANHOPE's *voice is heard.*]

STANHOPE. All right, sir. Come down quickly!

COLONEL. How many?

STANHOPE. Only one. [*Another shell whines and shrieks and crashes near by. There is silence for a moment, then* STANHOPE *speaks again.*] Hurt, sir?

COLONEL. No. It's all right.

[STANHOPE, *pale and haggard, comes down the steps, followed by the* COLONEL.]

STANHOPE. [*Calling up the steps.*] Bring him down, sergeant-major.

S.-M. [*Above.*] Coming, sir.

STANHOPE. [*To the* COLONEL.] You won't want me, will you?

COLONEL. Well — er ——

STANHOPE. I want to go and see those men.

COLONEL. Oh, all right.

[STANHOPE *goes to the door, making way for the* SERGEANT-MAJOR *to come down, followed by a bare-headed* GERMAN BOY, *in field grey, sobbing bitterly. Behind come two* SOLDIERS *with fixed bayonets.* STANHOPE *goes up the steps. The* SERGEANT-MAJOR *takes the* GERMAN BOY *by the arm and draws him into the centre of the dug-out to face the* COLONEL, *who has seated himself at the table. The two* SOLDIERS *stand behind.*]

S.-M. [*Soothingly to the* GERMAN BOY.] All right, sonny, we ain't going to 'urt you.

[*Suddenly the* BOY *falls on his knees and sobs out some words in broken English.*]

GERMAN. Mercy — mister — mercy!

S.-M. Come on, lad, get up. [*With a huge fist he takes the* BOY *by the collar and draws him to his feet.*]

[*The* BOY *sobs hysterically. The* COLONEL *clears his throat and begins in somewhat poor German.*]

COLONEL. Was ist sein Regiment?

GERMAN. Wurtembergisches.

COLONEL. Was ist der nummer von sein Regiment?

GERMAN. Zwanzig.

COLONEL. [*Making a note.*] Twentieth Wurtembergers. [*He looks up again.*] Wann kommen sie hier?

GERMAN. Gestern abend.

COLONEL. [*Making a note and looking up again.*] Wo kommen sie her?

GERMAN. [*After a moment's thought.*] Mein Geburtsort?

COLONEL. [*Forgetting himself for a moment.*] What's that?

GERMAN. [*In halting English.*] You — wish — to know — where I was — born?

COLONEL. No! What town did you come up to the line from?

GERMAN. [*After a little hesitation.*] I — do not tell you.

COLONEL. Oh, well, that's all right. [*To the* SERGEANT-MAJOR.] Search him.

[*The* SERGEANT-MAJOR'S *big fists grope over the* BOY'S *pockets. He produces a small book.*]

S.-M. [*Giving it to the* COLONEL.] Looks like 'is pay-book, sir.

COLONEL. [*Looking eagerly into the book.*] Good.

[*The* SERGEANT-MAJOR *has found a pocket-book; the* GERMAN BOY *clutches at it impulsively.*]

S.-M. 'Ere, stop that!

GERMAN. Lass mich! [*He pauses.*] Let — me — please — keep — that.

S.-M. [*Very embarrassed.*] You let go! [*He wrenches the case away and gives it to the* COLONEL.]

COLONEL. [*Glancing at the papers in the case.*] Look like letters. May be useful. Is that all, sergeant-major?

S.-M. [*Looking at a few articles in his hands.*] 'Ere's a few oddments, sir — bit o' string, sir; little box o' fruit drops; pocket-knife; bit o'cedar pencil — and a stick o' chocolate, sir.

COLONEL. Let him have those back, except the pocket-knife.

S.-M. Very good, sir. [*He turns to the* GERMAN BOY *with a smile.*] 'Ere you are, sonny.

[*The* GERMAN BOY *takes back the oddments.*]

COLONEL. All right, sergeant-major. Send him straight back to my head-quarters. I'll question him again there.

S.-M. Very good, sir. [*He turns to the* GERMAN.] Come on, sonny, up you go. [*He points up the steps.*]

[*The* GERMAN BOY, *calm now, bows stiffly to the* COLONEL *and goes away, followed by the two* SOLDIERS *and the* SERGEANT-MAJOR. *The* COLONEL *is deeply absorbed in the* GERMAN'S *pay-book. He mutters "Splendid!" to himself, then looks at his watch and rises quickly.* STANHOPE *comes slowly down the steps.*]

COLONEL. [*Excitedly.*] Splendid, Stanhope! We've got all we wanted — 20th Wurtembergers! His regiment came into the line last night. I must go right away and 'phone the brigadier. He'll be very pleased about it. It's a feather in our cap, Stanhope.

[STANHOPE *has given one look of astonishment at the* COLONEL *and strolled past him. He turns at the table and speaks in a dead voice.*]

STANHOPE. How awfully nice — if the brigadier's pleased.

[*The* COLONEL *stares at* STANHOPE *and suddenly collects himself.*]

COLONEL. Oh — er — what about the raiding-party — are they all safely back?

STANHOPE. Did you expect them to be all safely back, sir?

COLONEL. Oh — er — what — er ——

STANHOPE. Four men and Raleigh came safely back, sir.

COLONEL. Oh, I say, I'm sorry! That's — er — six men and — er — Osborne?

STANHOPE. Yes, sir.

COLONEL. I'm very sorry. Poor Osborne!

STANHOPE. Still it'll be awfully nice if the brigadier's pleased.

COLONEL. Don't be silly, Stanhope. Do you know — er — what happened to Osborne?

STANHOPE. A hand grenade — while he was waiting for Raleigh.

COLONEL. I'm very sorry. And the six men?

STANHOPE. Machine-gun bullets, I suppose.

COLONEL. Yes. I was afraid — er —— [*His words trail away; he fidgets uneasily as* STANHOPE *looks at him with a pale, expressionless face.* RALEIGH *comes slowly down the steps, walking as though he were asleep; his hands are bleeding. The* COLONEL *turns to the boy with enthusiasm.*] Very well done, Raleigh. Well done, my boy. I'll get you a Military Cross for this! Splendid! [RALEIGH *looks at the* COLONEL *and tries to speak. He raises his hand to his forehead and sways. The* COLONEL *takes him by the arm.*] Sit down here, my boy. [RALEIGH *sits on the edge of* OSBORNE'S *bed.*] Have a good rest. Well, I must be off. [*He moves towards the steps, and turns once more to* RALEIGH *as he leaves.*] Very well done. [*With a quick glance at* STANHOPE, *the* COLONEL *goes away.*]

    [*There is silence now in the trenches outside; the last shell has whistled over and crashed. Dusk is beginning to fall over the German lines. The glow of Very lights begins to rise and fade against the evening sky.* STANHOPE *is staring dumbly at the table — at* OSBORNE'S *watch and ring. Presently he turns his haggard face towards* RALEIGH, *who sits with lowered head, looking at the palms of his hands.* STANHOPE *moves slowly across towards the doorway, and pauses to look down at* RALEIGH. RALEIGH *looks up into* STANHOPE'S *face, and their eyes meet. When* STANHOPE *speaks, his voice is still expressionless and dead.*]

STANHOPE. Must you sit on Osborne's bed?

    [*He turns and goes slowly up the steps.* RALEIGH *rises unsteadily, murmurs "sorry" — and stands with lowered head. Heavy guns are booming miles away.*]

THE CURTAIN FALLS

SCENE II

Late evening on the same day.

    The dug-out is lit quite festively by an unusual number of candles. Two champagne bottles stand prominently on the table. Dinner is over.

    STANHOPE, *with a cigar between his teeth, lounges across the table, one elbow among the plates and mugs. His hair is ruffled; there is a bright red flush on his cheeks. He has just made a remark which has sent* HIBBERT *and* TROTTER *into uproarious laughter; he listens with a smile.* TROTTER *is sitting on the box to the right of the table, leaning back against the wall. A cigar is embedded in his podgy fingers; his face is a shiny scarlet, with deep red patches below the ears. The three bottom buttons of his tunic are undone, and now and then his hand steals gently over his distended stomach.* HIBBERT *sits on the bed to the left, his thin white fingers nervously twitching the ash from his cigar. His pale face is shiny with sweat from the heat of the candles; his laugh is high-pitched and excited.* TROTTER *speaks in a husky voice as the laughter dies away.*

TROTTER. And what did she say to that?

STANHOPE. She said, "Not in these trousers" — in French.

    [TROTTER *and* HIBBERT *burst into laughter again.*]

TROTTER. [*Coughing and wheezing.*] Oh — dear-o-dear!

STANHOPE. I simply drew myself up and said, "Very well, mam'sel, have it your own way."

TROTTER. And she did?

STANHOPE. No. She didn't.

[*Again the others laugh.* TROTTER *wipes a tear from his eye.*]

TROTTER. Oh, skipper, you *are* a scream — and no mistake!

HIBBERT. I never forget picking up a couple of tarts one night and taking 'em out to dinner.

TROTTER. [*Winking at* STANHOPE.] 'E's orf again.

HIBBERT. We drank enough bubbly to sink a battleship ——

STANHOPE. To *float* a battleship.

HIBBERT. Well — to float a battleship. Then I took 'em for a joy-ride out to Maidenhead — did sixty all the way. We danced a bit at Skindles, and drank a lot of port and muck. Then damned if I didn't lose the way coming back — got landed miles from anywhere. And those tarts began cursing me like hell — said I'd done it on purpose. I said if they didn't damn well shut up I'd chuck 'em both out in the road and leave 'em.

STANHOPE. [*Ironically.*] Hurrah! That's the idea! Treat 'em rough!

HIBBERT. [*Giggling.*] That shut 'em up all right! Then I started doing about sixty down all sorts of roads — I went round a corner on two wheels with those girls' hair on end — didn't have any more trouble from *them!* [*He chuckles at the memory, and takes an unsteady gulp of champagne.*]

STANHOPE. You're the sort of fellow who makes girls hard to please.

TROTTER. [*Heavily.*] Well, I never 'ad no motorcar; my old lady and me used to walk; legs is good enough for me.

STANHOPE. You satisfied with legs?

TROTTER. *I* am — yes!

STANHOPE. Much cheaper.

HIBBERT. [*Laughing delightedly.*] That's damn good!

STANHOPE. [*Raising his mug.*] Well, here's a toast to legs — God bless 'em!

HIBBERT. [*Raising his mug.*] Good old legs!

TROTTER. [*Raising his mug.*] Shanks's mare.

STANHOPE. Shanks's *what?*

TROTTER. Shanks's mare, they call 'em.

STANHOPE. Call what?

TROTTER. Why — legs.

HIBBERT. [*Almost screaming with delight.*] Oh, Trotter! you're a *dream!*

TROTTER. [*Turning a baleful eye on* HIBBERT.] You've 'ad too much champagne, you 'ave.

[HIBBERT *takes a leather case from his pocket and produces some picture post-cards.*]

HIBBERT. I say, I've never shown you these, have I?

[*He hands them one by one to* STANHOPE, *smiling up into* STANHOPE's *face for approval.*]

STANHOPE. Where did you get these from?

HIBBERT. In Bethune. [*He hands up a card.*] She's all right, isn't she?

STANHOPE. Too fat.

HIBBERT. [*Looking over* STANHOPE's *shoulder.*] Oh, I don't know.

STANHOPE. Much too fat. [*He hands the card to* TROTTER.] What do you think, Trotter?

[TROTTER *takes a pair of pince-nez from his pocket, balances them on his fat nose, and looks at the picture.*]

HIBBERT. All right, isn't she?

TROTTER. Well, I don't know. If you ask me I'd rather 'ave a decent picture of Margate Pier.

HIBBERT. [*Impatiently.*] Oh, you don't understand *art*. [*He hands another card to* STANHOPE.] There's a nice pair of legs for you.

STANHOPE. Too thin — aren't they, Trotter? [*He hands* TROTTER *the card.*]

TROTTER. [*After some thought.*] Scraggy, I call 'em.

HIBBERT. [*Handing* STANHOPE *another card.*] *That's* the one I like best.

STANHOPE. Not bad.

HIBBERT. Glorious bedroom eyes.

STANHOPE. She's all right.

HIBBERT. Ever seen that show *Zip* at the Hippodrome? Couple of damn fine girls in that — twins. Did you see 'em, skipper?

STANHOPE. [*Wearily.*] I don't know — seen stacks of shows — can't remember them all. [*He brightens up.*] Now then, swallow up that bubbly! Hi! Mason!

MASON. Yessir!

[MASON *appears.*]

STANHOPE. Bring some whiskey.

MASON. Yessir. [*He disappears.*]

TROTTER. What? Whiskey on top of champagne?

STANHOPE. Why not? It's all right.

TROTTER. Well, I don't know; doesn't sound right to me. I feel as if somebody's blown me up with a bicycle pump.

STANHOPE. You look it, too.

TROTTER. [*Blowing a stream of cigar smoke up to the dark ceiling.*] Any'ow, it was a jolly bit o' chicken — and I'd go a mile any day for a chunk o' that jam pudding.

[MASON *brings a bottle of whiskey.*]

STANHOPE. Your pudding's made Mr. Trotter feel all blown out, Mason.

MASON. I'm sorry, sir; it wasn't meant, sir.

TROTTER. It was all right, Mason, take it from me. I know a decent bit o' pudden when I see it.

MASON. It was only boiled ration biscuits and jam, sir. [*He turns to* STANHOPE.] I thought I better tell you, sir — this is the last bottle.

STANHOPE. The last bottle! Why, damn it, we brought six!

MASON. I know, sir. But five's gone.

STANHOPE. Where the devil's it gone to?

MASON. Well, sir, you remember there was one on the first night — and then one ——

STANHOPE. Oh, for Lord's sake don't go through them one by one; this'll last till sunrise. [*He turns to* TROTTER *and* HIBBERT.] Sunrise tomorrow, my lads!

TROTTER. Oh, forget that.

STANHOPE. You bet we will! Now then! Who's for a spot of whiskey?

TROTTER. I reckon I'm about full up. I'd like a nice cup o' tea, Mason.

MASON. Very good, sir. [*He goes out.*]

STANHOPE. Tea!

TROTTER. Yes. That's what I want. Decent cup o' tea. Still, I'll just 'ave about a spoonful o' whiskey — got a touch of pulpitations.

STANHOPE. Here you are — say when!

TROTTER. Wo! That's enough!

STANHOPE. You'll have a decent spot, won't you, Hibbert?

HIBBERT. Yes. I'm game!

TROTTER. [*Stifling a hiccup.*] Just a cup o' tea — then I'll go and relieve young Raleigh. Pity 'e didn't come down to supper.

STANHOPE. I told him to. I told him to come down for an hour and let the sergeant-major take over.

TROTTER. I wonder why 'e didn't come.

HIBBERT. That lad's too keen on his "duty." He told me he liked being up there with the men better than down here with us.

STANHOPE. [*Quietly.*] He *said* that?

HIBBERT. Yes. I told him about the chicken and champagne and cigars — and he stared at me and said, "You're not having that, are you?" — just as if he thought we were going to chuck it away!

TROTTER. I reckon that raid shook 'im up more'n we thought. I like that youngster. 'E's got pluck. Strong lad, too — the way he came back through the smoke after that raid, carrying that Boche under 'is arm like a baby.

HIBBERT. Did you see him afterwards, though? He came into that dug-out and never said a word — didn't seem to know where he was.

TROTTER. Well, 'e's only a lad.

STANHOPE. [*To* HIBBERT.] He actually told you he preferred being up with the men better than down here?

HIBBERT. That's what he said.

TROTTER. Well, I 'ope 'e gets the M.C., that's all; 'e's just the kid I'd like if ever I 'ave a kid — strong and plucky.

STANHOPE. Oh, for God's sake forget that bloody raid! Think I want to talk about it?

TROTTER. [*Surprised.*] No — but, after all ——

STANHOPE. Well — shut up!

TROTTER. [*Uneasily.*] All right — all right.

STANHOPE. We were having a jolly decent evening till you started blabbing about the war.

TROTTER. *I* didn't start it.

STANHOPE. You did.

TROTTER. You began it about ——

STANHOPE. Well, for God's sake stop it, then!

TROTTER. All right — all right.

HIBBERT. Did I ever tell you the story about the girl I met in Soho?

STANHOPE. I don't know — I expect you did.

HIBBERT. [*Undismayed.*] It'll amuse you. I'd been to a dance, and I was coming home quite late ——

STANHOPE. Yes, and it's late now. You go on duty at eleven. You better go and get some sleep.

HIBBERT. It's all right. I'm as fresh as a daisy.

STANHOPE. You may be. But go to bed.

HIBBERT. What?

STANHOPE. [*Louder.*] I said, "Go to bed!"

HIBBERT. I say, that's a nice end to a jolly evening!

STANHOPE. I'm sorry. I'm tired.

HIBBERT. [*Perkily.*] Well, *you* better go to bed!

[*There is silence.* STANHOPE *looks at* HIBBERT, *who sniggers.*]

STANHOPE. What was that you said?

HIBBERT. I was only joking.

STANHOPE. I asked you what you said.

HIBBERT. I said, "*You* better go to bed."

[STANHOPE's *flushed face is looking full into* HIBBERT's. HIBBERT *gives the ghost of a snigger.*]

STANHOPE. Clear out of here!

HIBBERT. [*Rising unsteadily.*] What — what d'you mean?

STANHOPE. Get out of here, for God's sake!

HIBBERT. [*Blustering.*] I say — look here ——

STANHOPE. Get out of my sight! [*With a frightened glance at* STANHOPE, HIBBERT *sneaks quietly away into his dug-out. There is silence, and the guns can be heard — deep and ominous.*] Little worm gets on my nerves.

TROTTER. Poor little bloke. Never seen 'im so cheerful before out 'ere.

STANHOPE. Doesn't he nearly drive you mad?

TROTTER. I reckon 'e only wanted to keep cheerful.

STANHOPE. Doesn't his repulsive little mind make you *sick*? [MASON *brings* TROTTER's *mug of tea and goes away.*] I envy you, Trotter. Nothing upsets you, does it? You're always the same.

TROTTER. Always the same, am I? [*He sighs.*] Little you know ——

STANHOPE. You never get sick to death of everything, or so happy you want to sing.

TROTTER. I don't know — I whistle sometimes.

STANHOPE. But you always *feel* the same.

TROTTER. I feel all blown out now. [*There is a pause.* TROTTER *sips his tea and* STANHOPE *takes a whiskey.*] 'Ere's 'Ibbert's post-cards. Funny a bloke carrying pictures like this about. Satisfies 'is lust, I s'pose — poor little feller. [*He rises.*] Well, I'll go and relieve young Raleigh. Pity 'e didn't come down to supper. [*He tries to button his tunic, without success. He buckles his webbing belt over his unbuttoned tunic, puts on his helmet, and slings his respirator over his shoulder.*] Well, cheero!

STANHOPE. You realise you're my second-in-command now, don't you?

TROTTER. Well, you 'adn't said nothing about it, but ——

STANHOPE. Well, you are.

TROTTER. Righto, skipper. [*He pauses.*] Thanks. [*He goes towards the door.*] I won't let you down.

STANHOPE. After your duty, have a decent sleep. We must be ready at half-past five.

TROTTER. Righto, skipper. Well, I'll be going up. Give me a chance to cool off up there. It's as 'ot as 'ell in 'ere, with all them damn candles burning.

STANHOPE. I suppose it is. My head's nearly splitting. [*He blows out three of the candles, leaving the dim light of one.*]

TROTTER. [*Half up the steps.*] There's a bit of a mist rising.

STANHOPE. [*Dully.*] Is there? [TROTTER *disappears into the night.* STANHOPE *broods over the table.*] Mason!

MASON. [*Outside.*] Yessir!

STANHOPE. You can bring Mr. Raleigh's dinner.

MASON. Very good, sir.

[MASON *brings a plate of steaming food, gathering up and taking away some of the used crockery. Presently* RALEIGH *comes slowly down the steps. He pauses at the bottom, takes off his helmet, and hesitates.* STANHOPE *is sitting at the table puffing at the remains of his cigar. There is silence except for the rumble of the guns.*]

STANHOPE. I thought I told you to come down to dinner at eight o'clock?

RALEIGH. Oh, I'm sorry. I didn't think you — er ——

STANHOPE. Well? You didn't think I — er — what?

RALEIGH. I didn't think you'd — you'd mind — if I didn't.

STANHOPE. I see. And why do you think I asked you — if I didn't mind?

RALEIGH. I'm sorry.

STANHOPE. Well, we've kept your dinner. It's ready for you here.

RALEIGH. Oh, it's awfully good of you to have kept it for me, but — I — I had something to eat up there.

STANHOPE. You — had something to eat up there? What do you mean, exactly?

RALEIGH. They brought the tea round while I was on duty. I had a cup, and some bread and cheese.

STANHOPE. Are you telling me — you've been feeding with the men?

RALEIGH. Well, Sergeant Baker suggested ——

STANHOPE. So you take your orders from Sergeant Baker, do you?

RALEIGH. No, but ——

STANHOPE. You eat the men's rations when there's barely enough for each man?

RALEIGH. They asked me to share.

STANHOPE. Now, look here. I know you're new to this, but I thought you'd have the common sense to leave the men alone to their meals. Do you think they want an officer prowling round eating their rations, and sucking up to them like that? My officers are here to be respected — not laughed at.

RALEIGH. Why did they ask me — if they didn't mean it?

STANHOPE. Don't you realise they were making a fool of you?

RALEIGH. Why should they?

STANHOPE. So you know more about my men than I do?

[*There is silence.* RALEIGH *is facing* STANHOPE *squarely*.]

RALEIGH. I'm sorry then — if I was wrong.

STANHOPE. Sit down.

RALEIGH. It's all right, thanks.

STANHOPE. [*Suddenly shouting*.] *Sit down!* [RALEIGH *sits on the box to the right of the table.* STANHOPE *speaks quietly again*.] I understand you prefer being up there with the men than down here with us?

RALEIGH. I don't see what you mean.

STANHOPE. What did you tell Hibbert?

RALEIGH. Hibbert? I — I didn't say ——

STANHOPE. Don't lie.

RALEIGH. [*Rising*.] I'm not lying! Why should I — lie?

STANHOPE. Then why didn't you come down to supper when I told you to?

RALEIGH. I — I wasn't hungry. I had rather a headache. It's cooler up there.

STANHOPE. You insulted Trotter and Hibbert by not coming. You realise that, I suppose?

RALEIGH. I didn't mean to do anything like that.

STANHOPE. Well, you did. You know now — don't you? [RALEIGH *makes no reply. He is trying to understand why* STANHOPE'S *temper has risen to a trembling fury.* STANHOPE *can scarcely control his voice. Loudly*.] I say — you *know* now, don't you?

RALEIGH. Yes. I'm sorry.

STANHOPE. My officers work *together*. I'll have no damn prigs.

RALEIGH. I'll speak to Trotter and Hibbert. I didn't realise ——

[STANHOPE *raises his cigar. His hand trembles so violently that he can scarcely take the cigar between his teeth.* RALEIGH *looks at* STANHOPE, *fascinated and horrified*.]

STANHOPE. What are you looking at?

RALEIGH. [*Lowering his head*.] Nothing.

STANHOPE. Anything — *funny* about me?

RALEIGH. No. [*After a moment's silence,* RALEIGH *speaks in a low, halting voice*.] I'm awfully sorry, Dennis, if — if I annoyed you by coming to your company.

STANHOPE. What on *earth* are you talking about? What do you mean?

RALEIGH. You resent my being here.

STANHOPE. Resent you *being* here?

RALEIGH. Ever since I came ——

STANHOPE. I don't know what you mean. I resent you being a damn fool, that's all. [*There is a pause*.] Better eat your dinner before it's cold.

RALEIGH. I'm not hungry, thanks.

STANHOPE. Oh, for God's sake, sit down and eat it like a man!

RALEIGH. I can't eat it, thanks.

STANHOPE. [*Shouting*.] Are you going to eat your dinner?

RALEIGH. Oh! Good God! Don't you understand? How *can* I sit down and eat that — when — [*his voice is nearly breaking*] — when Osborne's — lying — out there ——

[STANHOPE *rises slowly. His eyes are wide and staring; he is fighting for breath, and his words come brokenly.*]

STANHOPE. My God! You bloody little swine! You think I don't care — you think you're the only soul that cares!

RALEIGH. And yet you can sit there and drink champagne — and smoke cigars ——

STANHOPE. The one man I could trust — my best friend — the one man I could talk to as man to man — who understood everything — and you think I don't care ——

RALEIGH. But how can you when ——?

STANHOPE. To forget, you little fool — to forget! D'you understand? To forget! You think there's no limit to what a man can bear? [*He turns quickly from* RALEIGH *and goes to the dark corner by* OSBORNE'S *bed. He stands with his face towards the wall, his shoulders heaving as he fights for breath.*]

RALEIGH. I'm awfully sorry, Dennis. I — I didn't understand. [STANHOPE *makes no reply.*] You don't know how — I ——

STANHOPE. Go away, please — leave me alone.

RALEIGH. Can't I ——

[STANHOPE *turns wildly upon* RALEIGH.]

STANHOPE. Oh, get out! For God's sake, get out!

[RALEIGH *goes away into his dug-out, and* STANHOPE *is alone. The Very lights rise and fall outside, softly breaking the darkness with their glow — sometimes steel-blue, sometimes grey. Through the night there comes the impatient grumble of gunfire that never dies away.*]

THE CURTAIN FALLS

SCENE III

Towards dawn. The candles are no longer burning. The intense darkness of the dug-out is softened by the glow of the Very lights in the sky beyond the doorway. There is no sound except the distant mutter of the guns.

A man comes from the servants' dug-out; for a moment his head and shoulders stand out black against the glowing sky, then he passes on into the darkness by the table. There comes the rasp of a striking match — a tiny flame — and a candle gleams. MASON *blinks in the light and turns to* STANHOPE'S *bed.* STANHOPE *lies huddled with his blanket drawn tightly round him.*

MASON. [*Softly.*] Sir —— [STANHOPE *does not move;* MASON *shakes him gently by the knee. A little louder.*] Sir ——

STANHOPE. Yes? [*There is a pause.*] That you, Mason?

MASON. 'Arf-past five, sir.

STANHOPE. Oh, right. [*He raises himself on his elbow.*] I was only half asleep. I keep on waking up. It's so frightfully cold in here.

MASON. It's a cold dug-out, this one, sir. I've made some 'ot tea.

STANHOPE. Good. You might bring me some.

MASON. Right you are, sir.

STANHOPE. And take some to the officers in there — and wake them up.

MASON. Very good, sir.

[MASON *goes to his dug-out.* STANHOPE *rises stiffly from his bed, shudders from the cold, and slowly begins putting his equipment on.* TROTTER *wanders in from his dug-out vigorously lathering his face. He is dressed, except for his collar.*]

TROTTER. Wash and brush-up, tuppence!

STANHOPE. [*Looking up, surprised.*] Hullo! I thought you were asleep.

TROTTER. I 'ad a decent sleep when I come off dooty. What's the time?

STANHOPE. Half-past five. It'll be getting light soon. You better buck up.

TROTTER. All right. *I* shan't be long. Sounds quiet enough out there.

STANHOPE. Yes.

[MASON *brings four mugs of tea.*]

TROTTER. Ah! that's what I want. A decent cup of tea.

MASON. [*Putting a mug on the table for* STANHOPE.] Nice and 'ot, sir. I've cut a packet of sambridge for each gentleman, sir.

STANHOPE. Good.

[MASON *takes the other mugs of tea into the right-hand dug-out.* TROTTER *follows, lathering with gusto.*]

STANHOPE. You might give Hibbert and Raleigh a call.

TROTTER. I woke 'em up, skipper. They're getting their things on.

[MASON *returns.*]

STANHOPE. When you've cleared up your kitchen, you must dress and join your platoon in the line.

MASON. Very good, sir.

STANHOPE. If things are going well at eleven o'clock, come down here and do your best to get some lunch for us. We shall come down in turn as we can.

MASON. Very good, sir.

[STANHOPE *sits at the table and begins to write a short report. The first sign of dawn is beginning to gleam in the dark sky.* STANHOPE *calls "Runner!" as he writes. A* SOLDIER *comes from the servants' dug-out.*]

STANHOPE. [*Folding the note.*] Take this to Battalion Headquarters. There's no reply.

SOLDIER. Yessir.

[*The* SOLDIER *salutes and goes up the steps. A plaintive noise comes from the other dug-out.* TROTTER *is singing "There's a long, long trail a-winding."* STANHOPE *listens for a moment, then rises, takes a few small coins from his pocket, and throws them into* TROTTER'S *dug-out. The singing stops abruptly. After a moment* TROTTER'S *voice comes.*]

TROTTER. Thank you kindly, gov'nor!

[*The* SERGEANT-MAJOR *comes down the steps.*]

STANHOPE. Morning, sergeant-major.

S.-M. Morning, sir. Wiring parties are just in, sir. Made a decent job of it — right down to the support line.

STANHOPE. Good. Everything quiet?

S.-M. It's all right opposite 'ere, sir, but the guns are goin' 'ard down south. 'Eavy bombardment. Not sure if it ain't spreading up this way, sir.

STANHOPE. Very likely it is. The officers are coming up in a minute. They'll stand by with their platoons. I must stay here awhile in case of messages. I shall come up directly things begin to happen.

S.-M. Very good, sir.

STANHOPE. Are the men having their tea?

S.-M. Yessir.

STANHOPE. Let 'em have a decent drop of rum.

S.-M. About 'arf again, sir?

STANHOPE. Yes.

S.-M. If the attack don't come, sir, 'ow long are we to stand-to?

STANHOPE. We must expect the attack any time up till midday. After then I don't think it'll come till tomorrow.

S.-M. Very good, sir.

STANHOPE. We must naturally make our plans to meet things as they happen.

S.-M. Quite, sir.

STANHOPE. All right, sergeant-major. I'll see you up there soon.

S.-M. Yessir. [*He salutes and goes away.*]

[MASON *brings in four little packets of sandwiches, and puts one packet on the table for* STANHOPE.]

MASON. Your sambridges, sir. 'Arf bully beef and 'arf sardine. Sardine on top, sir.

STANHOPE. How delicious. No *pâté de foie gras?*

MASON. No what, sir?

STANHOPE. No *pâté de foie gras?*

MASON. No, sir. The milkman 'asn't been yet.

[MASON *takes the other parcels to the left-hand dug-out.* STANHOPE *pours a little whiskey into his tea and the remainder of the contents of the bottle into his flask.* MASON *returns.*]

STANHOPE. Get dressed as soon as you can.

MASON. Yessir.

[MASON *goes out.* TROTTER *comes in, fully dressed for the line.*]

TROTTER. All ready, skipper. Want me to go up?

STANHOPE. Yes. I think so. Go right round the line and see everything's all right. I'll be up soon.

[*Suddenly there comes the faint whistle and thud of falling shells — a few seconds between each.* STANHOPE *and* TROTTER *listen intently, four shells fall, then silence.*]

TROTTER. 'Ullo, 'ullo.

[STANHOPE *strides to the doorway, goes up a few steps, and looks out into the night. He comes slowly back.*]

STANHOPE. Over on Lancer's Alley — somewhere by the reserve line.

[*There comes the louder thud of three more shells.*]

TROTTER. That's nearer.

STANHOPE. Better go up, Trotter. Call the others.

TROTTER. [*At the left-hand dug-out.*] 'Ibbert! Raleigh! come on! [*He lights a cigarette over the candle — lingers a moment, and slowly goes up the steps.*] Cheero, skipper. See you later.

STANHOPE. Send your runner down to tell me how things are going.

TROTTER. Righto.

[TROTTER *disappears into the dark. A vague white line of dawn is broadening above the dark trench wall outside.* STANHOPE *sits at the table and sips his tea. He takes a cigarette and lights it with a quivering hand.* RALEIGH *comes from his dug-out.* STANHOPE *lowers his head and writes in his note-book.*]

RALEIGH. Do you want me to go up?

STANHOPE. [*Without looking up.*] Yes. Trotter's gone.

RALEIGH. Right. [*He goes to the steps and turns shyly.*] Cheero — Stanhope.

STANHOPE. [*Still writing with lowered head.*] Cheero, Raleigh. I shall be coming up soon. [RALEIGH *goes up the steps.* STANHOPE *stops writing, raises his head, and listens. The shells are falling steadily now. He glances towards the left-hand dug-out and calls.*] Hibbert! [*There is no reply. He slowly rises and goes to the left-hand dug-out doorway. He calls again — louder.*] Hibbert!! [*He looks into the doorway and says.*] What are you doing? [HIBBERT *appears. He is very pale; he moves as if half asleep.*] Come along, man!

HIBBERT. You want me to go up now?

STANHOPE. Of course I do. The others have gone.

HIBBERT. Got a drop of water?

STANHOPE. What d'you want water for?

HIBBERT. I'm so frightfully thirsty. All that champagne and stuff — dried my mouth up.

[STANHOPE *pours a drop of water into a mug and gives it to* HIBBERT.]

STANHOPE. Here you are. Didn't you have any tea?

HIBBERT. Yes. It was a bit sweet, though.

[*The shelling is steadily increasing, and now, above the lighter "crush" of the smaller shells, there comes the deep, resounding "boom" of Minenwerfer.* HIBBERT *sips his water very slowly, rinsing his mouth deliberately with each sip.* STANHOPE *is by the doorway, looking up into the trench. He has just turned away as a sonorous drawn-out call comes floating through the dawn:* "Stretcher bear-ers!" STANHOPE *half turns, then faces* HIBBERT.]

STANHOPE. Come on. Buck up.

HIBBERT. There's no appalling hurry, is there?

STANHOPE. No hurry! Why d'you think the others have gone up?

HIBBERT. [*Slowly.*] What? Trotter and Raleigh?

STANHOPE. [*Sharply.*] Wake up, man! What the devil's the matter with you?

[HIBBERT *slowly puts down his mug.*]

HIBBERT. Champagne dries the mouth up so. Makes the tongue feel like a bit of paper.

[*There is a slight pause.*]

STANHOPE. The longer you stay here, the harder it'll be to go up.

HIBBERT. Good Lord! You don't think I'm ——

STANHOPE. You're just wasting as much time as you can.

HIBBERT. Well, damn it, it's no good going up till I feel fit. Let's just have another spot of water.

[HIBBERT *takes the jug and pours out a little more water. He is the picture of misery.* STANHOPE *stands impatiently beside him.* MASON *appears from his dugout, fully dressed for the line, his rifle slung over his shoulder.*]

MASON. I'll go right along, sir. I've made up the fire to last a good three hours — if you don't mind me popping down about nine o'clock to 'ave a look at it.

STANHOPE. All right, Mason. Mr. Hibbert's coming up now. You can go along with him.

MASON. [*To* HIBBERT.] I'd like to come along of you if you don't mind, sir. I ain't bin up in this part of the front line. Don't want to get lorst.

STANHOPE. Mr. Hibbert'll show you the way up. [*He turns to* HIBBERT.] Keep your men against the back wall of the trench as long as the shells are dropping behind. Cheero! [HIBBERT *looks at* STANHOPE *for a moment, then with a slight smile, he goes slowly up the steps and into the trench,* MASON *following behind. A dark figure stands out against the pale sky; comes hurrying down the steps — a* PRIVATE SOLDIER, *out of breath and excited.*] Yes?

SOLDIER. Message from Mr. Trotter, sir. Shells falling mostly behind support line. Minnies along front line.

STANHOPE. Who's just been hit?

SOLDIER. Corporal Ross, I think it was, sir. Minnie dropped in the trench at the corner — just as I come away.

[*The* SERGEANT-MAJOR *comes down the steps, very much out of breath.*]

STANHOPE. [*To the* SOLDIER.] All right, thanks.

[*The* SOLDIER *salutes, and goes up the steps slower than he came.*]

S.-M. Beginning to get 'ot, sir.

STANHOPE. Corporal Ross hit?

S.-M. Yessir.

STANHOPE. Badly?

S.-M. Pretty badly, sir.

STANHOPE. Most of the shelling's going over, isn't it?

S.-M. Most of the *shells* is be'ind, sir, but there's Minnies and rifle grenades along the front line. Pretty 'ot it's getting, sir. They're attacking down south — there's rifle fire.

STANHOPE. All right, sergeant-major; thanks.

S.-M. What I come to ask, sir — what about the wounded — getting 'em down, sir? The shelling's pretty thick over Lancer's Alley.

STANHOPE. What about Fosse Way?

S.-M. Pretty bad there, too, sir.

STANHOPE. Don't try then. Take anyone badly hit down into the big dug-out on the right. Let the stretcher-bearers do what they can there.

S.-M. Very good, sir.

STANHOPE. Only Corporal Ross hit?

S.-M. That's all, sir ——

[*Again there comes the drawn-out call — several times as it is passed from man to man:* "Stretcher bear-ers!" *The* SERGEANT-MAJOR'S *eyes meet* STANHOPE'S. *He turns and goes up the steps.* STANHOPE *is alone. Flying fragments of shell whistle and hiss and moan overhead. The sharp "crack" of the rifle grenades, the thud of the shells, and the boom of the Minenwerfer mingle together in a muffled roar.* STANHOPE *takes his belt from the table and buckles it on, puts his revolver lanyard round his neck, and drops his flask and sandwiches into his pocket. The* SERGEANT-MAJOR *reappears and comes hurrying down the steps.*]

STANHOPE. [*Turning quickly.*] What is it, sergeant-major?

S.-M. Mr. Raleigh, sir ——

STANHOPE. What!

S.-M. Mr. Raleigh's been 'it, sir. Bit of shell's got 'im in the back.

STANHOPE. Badly?

S.-M. 'Fraid it's broke 'is spine, sir; can't move 'is legs.

STANHOPE. Bring him down here.

S.-M. Down 'ere, sir?

STANHOPE. [*Shouting.*] Yes! Down here — quickly!

[*The* SERGEANT-MAJOR *hurries up the steps. A shell screams and bursts very near. The* SERGEANT-MAJOR *shrinks back and throws his hand across his face, as though a human hand could ward off the hot flying pieces. He stumbles on again into the trench, and hurriedly away.* STANHOPE *is by* OSBORNE'S *bed, fumbling a blanket over it. He takes a trench coat off the wall and rolls it for a pillow. He goes to his own bed, takes up his blanket, and turns as the* SERGEANT-MAJOR *comes carefully down the steps carrying* RALEIGH *like a child in his huge arms.*]

STANHOPE. [*With blanket ready.*] Lay him down there.

S.-M. 'E's fainted, sir. 'E was conscious when I picked 'im up.

[*The* SERGEANT-MAJOR *lays the boy gently on the bed; he draws away his hands, looks furtively at the palms, and wipes the blood on the sides of his trousers.* STANHOPE *covers* RALEIGH *with his blanket, looks intently at the boy, and turns to the* SERGEANT-MAJOR.]

STANHOPE. Have they dressed the wound?

S.-M. They've just put a pad on it, sir. Can't do no more.

STANHOPE. Go at once and bring two men with a stretcher.

S.-M. We'll never get 'im down, sir, with them shells falling on Lancer's Alley.

STANHOPE. Did you hear what I said? Go and get two men with a stretcher.

S.-M. [*After a moment's hesitation.*] Very good, sir.

[*The* SERGEANT-MAJOR *goes slowly away.* STANHOPE *turns to* RALEIGH *once more, then goes to the table, pushes his handkerchief into the water-jug,*

and brings it, wringing wet, to RALEIGH'S *bed. He bathes the boy's face.*
Presently RALEIGH *gives a little moan, opens his eyes, and turns his head.*]
RALEIGH. Hullo — Dennis ——
STANHOPE. Well, Jimmy — [*he smiles*] — you got one quickly.
    [*There is silence for a while.* STANHOPE *is sitting on a box beside*
    RALEIGH. *Presently* RALEIGH *speaks again — in a wondering voice.*]
RALEIGH. Why — how did I get down here?
STANHOPE. Sergeant-major brought you down.
    [RALEIGH *speaks again, vaguely, trying to recollect.*]
RALEIGH. Something — hit me in the back — knocked me clean over —
sort of — winded me —— I'm all right now. [*He tries to rise.*]
STANHOPE. Steady, old boy. Just lie there quietly for a bit.
RALEIGH. I'll be better if I get up and walk about. It happened once be-
fore — I got kicked in just the same place at football; it — it soon wore off.
It — it just numbs you a bit. [*There is a pause.*] What's that rumbling
noise?
STANHOPE. The guns are making a bit of a row.
RALEIGH. Our guns?
STANHOPE. No. Mostly theirs.
    [*Again there is silence in the dug-out. A very faint rose light is beginning*
    to glow in the dawn sky. RALEIGH *speaks again — uneasily.*]
RALEIGH. I say — Dennis ——
STANHOPE. Yes, old boy?
RALEIGH. It — it hasn't gone through, has it? It only just hit me? — and
knocked me down?
STANHOPE. It's just gone through a bit, Jimmy.
RALEIGH. I won't have to — go on lying here?
STANHOPE. I'm going to have you taken away.
RALEIGH. Away? Where?
STANHOPE. Down to the dressing-station — then hospital — then home.
[*He smiles.*] You've got a Blighty one, Jimmy.
RALEIGH. But I — I can't go home just for — for a knock in the back.
[*He stirs restlessly.*] I'm certain I'll be better if — if I get up. [*He tries to*
raise himself, and gives a sudden cry.] Oh — God! It does hurt!
STANHOPE. It's bound to hurt, Jimmy.
RALEIGH. What's — on my legs? Something holding them down ——
STANHOPE. It's all right, old chap; it's just the shock — numbed them.
    [*Again there is a pause. When* RALEIGH *speaks, there is a different*
    note in his voice.]
RALEIGH. It's awfully decent of you to bother, Dennis. I feel rotten
lying here — everybody else — up there.
STANHOPE. It's not your fault, Jimmy.
RALEIGH. So — damn — silly — getting hit. [*Pause.*] Is there — just
a drop of water?
STANHOPE. [*Rising quickly.*] Sure. I've got some here. [*He pours some*
water into the mug and brings it to RALEIGH. *Cheerfully.*] Got some tea-
leaves in it. D'you mind?

RALEIGH. No. That's all right — thanks —— [STANHOPE *holds the mug to* RALEIGH's *lips, and the boy drinks.*] I say, Dennis, don't you wait — if — if you want to be getting on.

STANHOPE. It's quite all right, Jimmy.

RALEIGH. Can you stay for a bit?

STANHOPE. Of course I can.

RALEIGH. [*Faintly.*] Thanks awfully. [*There is quiet in the dug-out for a long time.* STANHOPE *sits with one hand on* RALEIGH's *arm, and* RALEIGH *lies very still. Presently he speaks again — hardly above a whisper.*] Dennis ——

STANHOPE. Yes, old boy?

RALEIGH. Could we have a light? It's — it's so frightfully dark and cold.

STANHOPE. [*Rising.*] Sure! I'll bring a candle and get another blanket.

[STANHOPE *goes to the left-hand dug-out, and* RALEIGH *is alone, very still and quiet, on* OSBORNE's *bed. The faint rosy glow of the dawn is deepening to an angry red. The grey night sky is dissolving, and the stars begin to go. A tiny sound comes from where* RALEIGH *is lying — something between a sob and a moan.* STANHOPE *comes back with a blanket. He takes a candle from the table and carries it to* RALEIGH's *bed. He puts it on the box beside* RALEIGH *and speaks cheerfully.*] Is that better, Jimmy? [RALEIGH *makes no sign.*] Jimmy ——

[*Still* RALEIGH *is quiet.* STANHOPE *gently takes his hand. There is a long silence.* STANHOPE *lowers* RALEIGH's *hand to the bed, rises, and takes the candle back to the table. He sits on the bench behind the table with his back to the wall, and stares listlessly across at the boy on* OSBORNE's *bed. The solitary candle-flame throws up the lines on his pale, drawn face, and the dark shadows under his tired eyes. The thudding of the shells rises and falls like an angry sea. A* PRIVATE SOLDIER *comes scrambling down the steps, his round, red face wet with perspiration, his chest heaving for breath.*]

SOLDIER. Message from Mr. Trotter, sir — will you come at once. [STANHOPE *gazes round at the* SOLDIER *— and makes no other sign.*] Mr. Trotter, sir — says will you come at once!

[STANHOPE *rises stiffly and takes his helmet from the table.*]

STANHOPE. All right, Broughton, I'm coming.

[*The* SOLDIER *turns and goes away.* STANHOPE *pauses for a moment by* OSBORNE's *bed and lightly runs his fingers over* RALEIGH's *tousled hair. He goes stiffly up the steps, his tall figure black against the dawn sky. The shelling has risen to a great fury. The solitary candle burns with a steady flame; and* RALEIGH *lies in the shadows. The whine of a shell rises to a shriek and bursts on the dug-out roof. The shock stabs out the candle-flame: the timber props of the door cave slowly in, sandbags fall and block the passage to the open air. There is darkness in the dug-out. Here and there the red dawn glows through the jagged holes of the broken doorway. Very faintly there comes the dull rattle of machine-guns and the fevered spatter of rifle fire.*]

THE PLAY ENDS

THE TALE

THE simple narrative of event and adventure is the earliest form of story-telling. It appears in verse in the ballad, in prose in the chronicle, and thence becomes the ancestor of such dignified literary forms as the epic and history. Subsequently, the tale was shaped into the short story and elaborated into the novel. Sometimes within its simple outline writers have dealt with themes of philosophic significance as in the famous apologues of the eight-eenth century, Voltaire's *Candide* and Johnson's *Rasselas,* but in general the tale is suited to the primitive stuff of legend and folklore as in Irving's *Rip Van Winkle* and *The Legend of Sleepy Hollow.* Sometimes, again, the tale is given a pattern which brings it within the scope of more sophisticated fiction, as a short novel or novelette, of which Prosper Merimée gave two notable ex-amples in *Carmen* and *Colomba,* and Henry James a large number including his powerful story of the supernatural, *The Turn of the Screw.*

The tale was a favorite form of Joseph Conrad. It fitted his material of adventure, and gave him an opportunity to develop character on simple lines. Fine conduct in the face of adverse circumstances, he has said, is the chief contribution which a man can make to the common life of humanity, and to Conrad as to Stevenson the essence of romance is in that. To Conrad the sea was the great school of human character and conduct, "the only world that counted, and ships, the test of manliness, of temperament, of courage and fidelity — and of love." He has made superb use of the sea as the source of danger and trial in *Youth,* the tale of a voyage from London to the South Seas in which persistence overcomes every conceivable mischance. In *Typhoon* and *The Nigger of the "Narcissus"* occur unforgettable accounts of storms at sea, and in *The Shadow Line* is pictured the no less threatening mood of calm. The force of these and other triumphs lies first in Conrad's reliance on the senses. "My task," he wrote, "is by the power of the written word to make you hear, to make you feel, it is, before all, to make you see." And next it lies in making the reader enter into the inner experience of the character concerned. The world of man's making, he explains in *A Personal Record,* "rests in a few very simple ideas.... It rests notably among others on the idea of fidelity." This theme of fidelity is the animating force of *Lord Jim*, and its opposite, betrayal, is the tragic burden of *The Heart of Darkness*. *The Nigger of the "Narcissus"* published in 1897 ranks with these among Conrad's masterpieces. He has explained his purpose and literary theory in the preface which is an important piece of criticism from the hand of a great artist.

JOSEPH CONRAD

THE man who under the name of Joseph Conrad became one of the notable writers of fiction in the early twentieth century was born in Poland in 1857 and known as Teodor Josef Konrad Korzeniowski. His father was a Polish patriot, exiled because of participation in the independence movement to a small Russian village where Josef grew up. He became a sailor and voyaged over the world, chiefly in the South Seas. He was concerned in the Carlist rising in Spain, and for a time employed in the Congo region. Thus revolution and adventure by sea and land gave him material for fiction which contributed to the serious revival of romanticism for which Stevenson argued in "The Lantern-Bearers." In the islands of the Archipelago Conrad laid the scene of his first stories, *Almayer's Folly* (1895), *An Outcast of the Islands* (1896), *Lord Jim* (1900), and his later more elaborate novels *Victory* (1915) and *The Rescue* (1920). The Congo gave him the background for one of his most powerful tales, *The Heart of Darkness* (1902), and the coast of South America was the scene of *Nostromo* (1904). He was interested in fiction as an art, in its theory and technique, including style, of which Henry James was the chief expositor. On his death in 1924 he was recognized as one of the leading English writers.

THE NIGGER OF THE "NARCISSUS" *

TO MY READERS IN AMERICA

FROM that evening when James Wait joined the ship — late for the muster of the crew — to the moment when he left us in the open sea, shrouded in sailcloth, through the open port, I had much to do with him. He was in my watch. A negro in a British forecastle is a lonely being. He has no chums. Yet James Wait, afraid of death and making her his accomplice, was an impostor of some character — mastering our compassion, scornful of our sentimentalism, triumphing over our suspicions.

But in the book he is nothing; he is merely the centre of the ship's collective psychology and the pivot of the action. Yet he, who in the family circle and amongst my friends is familiarly referred to as the Nigger, remains very precious to me. For the book written round him is not the sort of thing that can be attempted more than once in a life-time. It is the book by which, not as a novelist perhaps, but as an artist striving for the utmost sincerity of expression, I am willing to stand or fall. Its pages are the tribute of my unalterable and profound affection for the ships, the seamen, the winds and the great sea — the moulders of my youth, the companions of the best years of my life.

After writing the last words of that book, in the revulsion of feeling before the accomplished task, I understood that I had done with the sea, and that henceforth I had to be a writer. And almost without laying down the pen I wrote a preface, trying to express the spirit in which I was entering on the

* By permission of Doubleday, Doran and Company, publishers.

task of my new life. That preface on advice (which I now think was wrong) was never published with the book. But the late W. E. Henley, who had the courage at that time (1897) to serialize my "Nigger" in the *New Review* judged it worthy to be printed as an afterword at the end of the last instalment of the tale.

I am glad that this book which means so much to me is coming out again, under its proper title of "The Nigger of the 'Narcissus'" and under the auspices of my good friends and publishers Messrs. Doubleday, Page & Co. into the light of publicity.

Half the span of a generation has passed since W. E. Henley, after reading two chapters, sent me a verbal message: "Tell Conrad that if the rest is up to the sample it shall certainly come out in the *New Review*." The most gratifying recollection of my writer's life!

And here is the Suppressed Preface.

JOSEPH CONRAD

1914

PREFACE

A WORK that aspires, however humbly, to the condition of art should carry its justification in every line. And art itself may be defined as a single-minded attempt to render the highest kind of justice to the visible universe, by bringing to light the truth, manifold and one, underlying its every aspect. It is an attempt to find in its forms, in its colours, in its light, in its shadows, in the aspects of matter and in the facts of life what of each is fundamental, what is enduring and essential — their one illuminating and convincing quality — the very truth of their existence. The artist, then, like the thinker or the scientist, seeks the truth and makes his appeal. Impressed by the aspect of the world the thinker plunges into ideas, the scientist into facts — whence, presently, emerging they make their appeal to those qualities of our being that fit us best for the hazardous enterprise of living. They speak authoritatively to our common-sense, to our intelligence, to our desire of peace or to our desire of unrest; not seldom to our prejudices, sometimes to our fears, often to our egoism — but always to our credulity. And their words are heard with reverence, for their concern is with weighty matters: with the cultivation of our minds and the proper care of our bodies, with the attainment of our ambitions, with the perfection of the means and the glorification of our precious aims.

It is otherwise with the artist.

Confronted by the same enigmatical spectacle the artist descends within himself, and in that lonely region of stress and strife, if he be deserving and fortunate, he finds the terms of his appeal. His appeal is made to our less obvious capacities: to that part of our nature which, because of the warlike conditions of existence, is necessarily kept out of sight within the more resisting and hard qualities — like the vulnerable body within a steel armour. His appeal is less loud, more profound, less distinct, more stirring — and sooner forgotten. Yet its effect endures forever. The changing wisdom of successive generations discards ideas, questions facts, demolishes theories. But the artist appeals to that part of our being which is not dependent on wisdom: to that in us which is a gift and not an acquisition — and, therefore, more permanently enduring. He speaks to our capacity for delight and wonder, to the sense of mystery surrounding our lives; to our sense of pity, and beauty, and pain; to the latent feeling of fellowship with all creation — and to the subtle but invincible conviction of solidarity that knits together the loneliness of innumerable hearts, to the solidarity in dreams, in joy, in sorrow, in aspirations, in illusions, in hope, in fear, which binds men to each other, which binds together all humanity — the dead to the living and the living to the unborn.

It is only some such train of thought, or rather of feeling, that can in a measure explain the aim of the attempt, made in the tale which follows, to present an unrestful episode in the obscure lives of a few individuals out of all the disregarded multitude of the bewildered, the simple and the voiceless. For, if any part of truth dwells in the belief confessed above, it becomes evident that there is not a place of splendour or a dark corner of the earth that does not deserve, if only a passing glance of wonder and pity. The motive then, may be held to justify the matter of the work; but this preface, which is simply an avowal of endeavour, cannot end here — for the avowal is not yet complete.

Fiction — if it at all aspires to be art — appeals to temperament. And in truth it must be, like painting, like music, like all art, the appeal of one temperament to all the other innumerable temperaments whose subtle and resistless power endows passing events with their true meaning, and creates the moral, the emotional atmosphere of the place and time. Such an appeal to be effective must be an impression conveyed through the senses; and, in fact, it cannot be made in any other way, because temperament, whether individual or collective, is not amenable to persuasion. All art, therefore, appeals primarily to the senses, and the artistic aim when expressing itself in written words must also make its appeal through the senses, if its high desire is to reach the secret spring of responsive emotions. It must strenuously aspire to the plasticity of sculpture, to the colour of painting, and to the magic suggestiveness of music — which is the art of arts. And it is only through complete, unswerving devotion to the perfect blending of form and substance; it is only through an unremitting never-discouraged care for the shape and ring of sentences that an approach can be made to plasticity, to colour, and that the light of magic suggestiveness may be brought to play for an evanescent instant over the commonplace surface of words: of the old, old words, worn thin, defaced by ages of careless usage.

The sincere endeavour to accomplish that creative task, to go as far on that road as his strength will carry him, to go undeterred by faltering, weariness or reproach, is the only valid justification for the worker in prose. And if his conscience is clear, his answer to those who in the fullness of a wisdom which looks for immediate profit, demand specifically to be edified, consoled, amused; who demand to be promptly improved, or encouraged, or frightened, or shocked, or charmed, must run thus: — My task which I am trying to achieve is, by the power of the written word to make you hear, to make you feel — it is, before all, to make you *see*. That — and no more, and it is everything. If I succeed, you shall find there according to your deserts: encouragement, consolation, fear, charm — all you demand — and, perhaps, also that glimpse of truth for which you have forgotten to ask.

To snatch in a moment of courage, from the remorseless rush of time, a passing phase of life, is only the beginning of the task. The task approached in tenderness and faith is to hold up unquestioningly, without choice and without fear, the rescued fragment before all eyes in the light of a sincere mood. It is to show its vibration, its colour, its form; and through its movement, its form, and its colour, reveal the substance of its truth — disclose its inspiring secret: the stress and passion within the core of each convincing moment. In a single-minded attempt of that kind, if one be deserving and fortunate, one may perchance attain to such clearness of sincerity that at last the presented vision of regret or pity, of terror or mirth, shall awaken in the hearts of the beholders that feeling of unavoidable solidarity; of the solidarity in mysterious origin, in toil, in joy, in hope, in uncertain fate, which binds men to each other and all mankind to the visible world.

It is evident that he who, rightly or wrongly, holds by the convictions expressed above cannot be faithful to any one of the temporary formulas of his craft. The enduring part of them — the truth which each only imperfectly veils — should abide with him as the most precious of his possessions, but they all: Realism, Romanticism, Naturalism, even the unofficial sentimentalism (which like the poor, is exceedingly difficult to get rid of,) all these gods must, after a short period of fellowship, abandon him — even on the very threshold of the temple — to the stammerings of his conscience and to the outspoken consciousness of the difficulties of his work. In that uneasy solitude the supreme cry of Art for Art itself, loses the exciting ring of its apparent immorality. It sounds far off. It has ceased to be a cry, and is heard only as a whisper, often incomprehensible, but at times and faintly encouraging.

Sometimes, stretched at ease in the shade of a roadside tree, we watch the motions of a labourer in a distant field, and after a time, begin to wonder languidly as to what the fellow may be at. We watch the movements of his body, the waving of his arms, we see him bend down, stand up, hesitate, begin again. It may add to the charm of an idle hour to be told the purpose of his exertions. If we know he is trying to lift a stone, to dig a ditch, to uproot a stump, we look with a more real interest at his efforts; we are disposed to condone the jar of his agitation upon the restfulness of the landscape; and even, if in a brotherly frame of mind, we may bring ourselves to forgive his failure. We understood his object, and, after all, the fellow has tried, and perhaps he had not the strength — and perhaps he had not the knowledge. We forgive, go on our way — and forget.

And so it is with the workman of art. Art is long and life is short, and success is very far off. And thus, doubtful of strength to travel so far, we talk a little about the aim — the aim of art, which, like life itself, is inspiring, difficult — obscured by mists. It is not in the clear logic of a triumphant conclusion; it is not in the unveiling of one of those heartless secrets which are called the Laws of Nature. It is not less great, but only more difficult.

To arrest, for the space of a breath, the hands busy about the work of the earth, and compel men entranced by the sight of distant goals to glance for a moment at the surrounding vision of form and colour, of sunshine and shadows; to make them pause for a look, for a sigh, for a smile — such is the aim, difficult and evanescent, and reserved only for a very few to achieve. But sometimes, by the deserving and the fortunate, even that task is accomplished. And when it is accomplished — behold! — all the truth of life is there: a moment of vision, a sigh, a smile — and the return to an eternal rest.

1897   J. C.

CHAPTER ONE

MR. BAKER, chief mate of the ship *Narcissus*, stepped in one stride out of his lighted cabin into the darkness of the quarter-deck. Above his head, on the break of the poop, the night-watchman rang a double stroke. It was nine o'clock. Mr. Baker, speaking up to the man above him, asked: — "Are all the hands aboard, Knowles?"

The man limped down the ladder, then said reflectively: —

"I think so, sir. All our old chaps are there, and a lot of new men has come.... They must be all there."

"Tell the boatswain to send all hands aft," went on Mr. Baker; "and tell one of the youngsters to bring a good lamp here. I want to muster our crowd."

The main deck was dark aft, but halfway from forward, through the open doors of the forecastle, two streaks of brilliant light cut the shadow of the quiet night that lay upon the ship. A hum of voices was heard there, while port and starboard, in the illuminated doorways, silhouettes of moving men appeared for a moment, very black, without relief, like figures cut out of sheet tin. The ship was ready for sea. The carpenter had driven in the last wedge of the main-hatch battens, and, throwing down his maul, had wiped his face with great deliberation, just on the stroke of five. The decks had been swept, the windlass oiled and made ready to heave up the anchor; the big tow-rope lay in long bights along one side of the main deck, with one end carried up and hung over the bows, in readiness for the tug that would come paddling and hissing noisily, hot and smoky, in the limpid, cool quietness of the early morning. The captain was ashore, where he had been engaging some new hands to make up his full crew; and, the work of the day over, the ship's officers had kept out of the way, glad of a little breathing-time. Soon after dark the few liberty-men and the new hands began to arrive in shore-boats rowed by white-clad Asiatics, who clamoured fiercely for payment before coming alongside the gangway-ladder. The feverish and shrill babble of Eastern language struggled against the masterful tones of tipsy seamen, who argued against brazen claims and dishonest hopes by profane shouts. The resplendent and bestarred peace of the East was torn into squalid tatters by howls of rage and shrieks of lament raised over sums ranging from five annas to half a rupee; and every soul afloat in Bombay Harbour became aware that the new hands were joining the *Narcissus*.

Gradually the distracting noise had subsided. The boats came no longer in splashing clusters of three or four together, but dropped alongside singly, in a subdued buzz of expostulation cut short by a "Not a pice more! You go to the devil!" from some man staggering up the accommodation-ladder — a dark figure, with a long bag poised on the shoulder. In the forecastle the newcomers, upright and swaying amongst corded boxes and bundles of bedding, made friends with the old hands, who sat one above another in the two tiers of bunks, gazing at their future shipmates with glances critical but friendly. The two forecastle lamps were turned up high, and shed an intense hard glare; shore-going round hats were pushed far on the backs of heads, or rolled about on the deck amongst the chain-cables; white collars, undone, stuck out on each side of red faces; big arms in white sleeves gesticulated; the growling voices hummed steady amongst bursts of laughter and hoarse calls. "Here, sonny, take that bunk!... Don't you do it!... What's your last ship?... I know her.... Three years ago, in Puget Sound.... This here berth leaks, I tell you!... Come on; give us a chance to swing that chest!... Did you bring a bottle, any of you shore toffs?... Give us a bit of 'baccy.... I know her; her skipper drank himself to death.... He was a dandy boy!... Liked his lotion inside, he did!... No!... Hold your row, you chaps! ... I tell you, you came on board a hooker, where they get their money's worth out of poor Jack by ——!...

A little fellow, called Craik and nicknamed Belfast, abused the ship violently, romancing on principle, just to give the new hands something to think over. Archie, sitting aslant on his sea-chest, kept his knees out of the way, and pushed the needle steadily through a white patch in a pair of blue trousers. Men in black jackets and stand-up collars, mixed with men barefooted, bare-armed, with coloured shirts open on hairy chests, pushed against one another in the middle of the forecastle. The group swayed, reeled, turning upon itself with the motion of a scrimmage, in a haze of tobacco smoke. All were speaking together, swearing at every second word. A Russian Finn, wearing a yellow shirt with pink stripes, stared upwards, dreamy-eyed, from under a mop of tumbled hair. Two young giants with smooth, baby faces — two Scandinavians — helped each other to spread their bedding, silent, and smiling placidly at the tempest of good-humoured and meaningless curses. Old Singleton, the oldest able seaman in the ship, sat apart on the deck right under the lamps, stripped to the waist, tattooed like a cannibal chief all over his powerful chest and enormous biceps. Between the blue and red patterns his white skin gleamed like satin; his bare back was propped against the heel of the bowsprit, and he held a book at arm's length before his big, sunburnt face. With his spectacles and a venerable white beard, he resembled a learned and savage patriarch, the incarnation of barbarian wisdom serene in the blasphemous turmoil of the world. He was intensely absorbed, and as he turned the pages an expression of grave surprise would pass over his rugged features. He was reading "Pelham." The popularity of Bulwer Lytton in the forecastles of Southern-going ships is a wonderful and bizarre phenomenon. What ideas do his polished and so curiously insincere sentences awaken in the simple minds of the big children who people those dark and wandering places of the earth? What meaning can their rough, inexperienced souls find in the elegant verbiage of his pages? What excitement? — what forgetfulness? — what appeasement? Mystery! Is it the fascination of the incomprehensible? — is it the charm of the impossible? Or are those beings who exist beyond the pale of life stirred by his tales as by an enigmatical disclosure of a resplendent world that exists within the frontier of infamy and filth, within that border of dirt and hunger, of misery and dissipation, that comes down on all sides to the water's edge of the incorruptible ocean, and is the only thing they know of life, the only thing they see of surrounding land — those life-long prisoners of the sea? Mystery!

Singleton, who had sailed to the southward since the age of twelve, who in the last forty-five years had lived (as we had calculated from his papers) no more than forty months ashore — old Singleton, who boasted, with the mild composure of long years well spent, that generally from the day he was paid off from one ship till the day he shipped in another he seldom was in a condition to distinguish daylight — old Singleton sat unmoved in the clash of voices and cries, spelling through "Pelham" with slow labour, and lost in an absorption profound enough to resemble a trance. He breathed regularly. Every time he turned the book in his enormous and blackened hands the muscles of his big white arms rolled slightly under the smooth skin. Hidden by the white moustache, his lips, stained with tobacco-juice that trickled down the long beard, moved in inward whisper. His bleared eyes gazed fixedly from behind the glitter of black-rimmed glasses. Opposite to him, and on a level with his face, the ship's cat sat on the barrel of the windlass in the pose of a crouching chimera, blinking its green eyes at its old friend. It seemed to meditate a leap on to the old man's lap over the bent back of the ordinary seaman who sat at Singleton's feet. Young Charley was lean and long-necked. The ridge of his backbone made a chain of small hills under the old shirt. His face of a street-boy — a face precocious, sagacious, and ironic, with deep downward folds on each side of the thin, wide mouth — hung low over his bony knees. He was learning to make a lanyard knot with a bit of an old rope. Small drops of perspiration stood out on his bulging forehead; he sniffed strongly from time to time, glancing out of the corners of his restless eyes at the old seaman, who took no notice of the puzzled youngster muttering at his work.

The noise increased. Little Belfast seemed, in the heavy heat of the forecastle, to boil with facetious fury. His eyes danced; in the crimson of his face, comical as a mask, the mouth yawned black, with strange grimaces. Facing him, a half-undressed man held his sides, and, throwing his head back, laughed with wet eyelashes. Others stared with amazed eyes. Men sitting doubled up in the upper bunks smoked short pipes, swinging bare brown feet above the heads of those who, sprawling below on sea-chests, listened, smiling stupidly or scornfully. Over the white rims of berths stuck out heads with blinking eyes; but the bodies were lost in the gloom of those places, that resembled narrow niches for coffins in a whitewashed and lighted mortuary. Voices buzzed louder. Archie, with compressed lips, drew himself in, seemed to shrink into a smaller space, and sewed steadily, industrious and dumb. Belfast shrieked like an inspired Dervish: — "... So I seez to him, boys, seez I, 'Beggin' yer pardon, sorr,' seez I to that second mate of that steamer — 'beggin' your-r-r pardon, sorr, the Board of Trade must 'ave been drunk when they granted you your certificate!' 'What do you say, you ——!' seez he, comin' at me like a mad bull... all in his white clothes; and I up with my tar-pot and capsizes it all over his blamed lovely face and his lovely jacket.... 'Take that!' seez I. 'I am a sailor, anyhow, you nosing, skipper-licking, useless, sooperfloos bridge-stanchion, you! That's the kind of man I am!' shouts I.... You should have seed him skip, boys! Drowned, blind with tar, he was! So..."

"Don't 'ee believe him! He never upset no tar; I was there!" shouted somebody. The two Norwegians sat on a chest side by side, alike and placid, resembling a pair of love-birds on a perch, and with round eyes stared innocently; but the Russian Finn, in the racket of explosive shouts and rolling laughter, remained motionless, limp and dull, like a deaf man without a backbone. Near him Archie smiled at his needle. A broad-chested, slow-eyed newcomer spoke deliberately to Belfast during an exhausted lull in the noise: — "I wonder any of the mates here are alive yet with such a chap as you on board! I concloode they ain't that bad now, if you had the taming of them, sonny."

"Not bad! Not bad!" screamed Belfast. "If it wasn't for us sticking together.... Not bad! They ain't never bad when they ain't got a chawnce, blast their black 'arts...." He foamed, whirling his arms, then suddenly grinned and, taking a tablet of black tobacco out of his pocket, bit a piece off with a funny show of ferocity. Another new hand — a man with shifty eyes and a yellow hatchet face, who had been listening open-mouthed in the shadow of the midship locker — observed in a squeaky voice: — "Well, it's a 'omeward trip, anyhow. Bad or good, I can do it on my 'ed — s'long as I get 'ome. And I can look after my rights! I will show 'em!" All the heads turned towards him. Only the ordinary seaman and the cat took no notice. He stood with arms akimbo, a little fellow with white eyelashes. He looked as if he had known all the degradations and all the furies. He looked as if he had been cuffed, kicked, rolled in the mud; he looked as if he had been scratched, spat upon, pelted with unmentionable filth... and he smiled with a sense of security at the faces around. His ears were bending down under the weight of his battered felt hat. The torn tails of his black coat flapped in fringes about the calves of his legs. He unbuttoned the only two buttons that remained and everyone saw that he had no shirt under it. It was his deserved misfortune that those rags which nobody could possibly be supposed to own looked on him as if they had been stolen. His neck was long and thin; his eyelids were red; rare hairs hung about his jaws; his shoulders were peaked and drooped like the broken wings of a bird; all his left side was caked with mud which showed that he had lately slept in a wet ditch. He had saved his inefficient carcass from violent destruction by running away from an American ship where, in a moment of forgetful folly, he had dared to engage himself; and he had knocked about for a fortnight ashore in the native quarter, cadging for drinks, starving, sleeping on rubbish-heaps, wandering in sunshine: a startling visitor from a world of nightmares. He stood repulsive and smiling in the sudden silence. This clean white forecastle was his refuge; the place where he could be lazy; where he could wallow, and lie and eat — and curse the food he ate; where he could display his talents for shirking work, for cheating, for cadging; where he could find surely someone to wheedle and someone to bully — and where he would be paid for doing all this. They all knew him. Is there a spot on earth where such a man is unknown, an ominous survival testifying to the eternal fitness of lies and impudence? A taciturn long-armed shellback, with hooked fingers, who had been lying on his back smoking, turned in his bed to examine him dispassionately, then, over his head, sent a long jet of clear saliva towards the door. They all knew him! He was the man that cannot steer, that cannot splice, that dodges the work on dark nights; that, aloft, holds on frantically with both arms and legs, and swears at the wind, the sleet, the darkness; the man who curses the sea while others work. The man who is the last out and the first in when all hands are called. The man who can't do most things and won't do the rest. The pet of philanthropists and self-seeking landlubbers. The sympathetic and deserving creature that knows all about his rights, but knows nothing of courage, of endurance, and of the unexpressed faith, of the unspoken loyalty that knits together a ship's company. The independent offspring of the ignoble freedom of the slums full of disdain and hate for the austere servitude of the sea.

Someone cried at him: "What's your name?" — "Donkin," he said, looking round with cheerful effrontery. — "What are you?" asked another voice. — "Why, a sailor like you, old man," he replied, in a tone that meant to be hearty but was impudent. — "Blamme if you don't look a blamed sight worse than a broken-down fireman," was the comment in a convinced mutter. Charley lifted his head and piped in a cheeky voice: "He is a man and a sailor" — then wiping his nose with the back of his hand bent down industriously over his bit of rope. A few laughed. Others stared doubtfully. The ragged newcomer was indignant — "That's a fine way to welcome a chap into a fo'c'sle," he snarled. "Are you men or a lot of 'artless cannybals?" — "Don't take your shirt off for a word, shipmate," called out Belfast, jumping up in front, fiery, menacing, and friendly at the same time. — "Is that 'ere bloke blind?" asked the indomitable scarecrow, looking right and left with affected surprise. "Can't 'ee see I 'aven't got no shirt?"

He held both his arms out crosswise and shook the rags that hung over his bones with dramatic effect.

"'Cos why?" he continued very loud. "The bloody Yankees been tryin' to jump my guts out 'cos I stood up for my rights like a good 'un. I am an

Englishman, I am. They set upon me an' I 'ad to run. That's why. A'n't yer never seed a man 'ard up? Yah! What kind of blamed ship is this? I'm dead broke. I 'aven't got nothink. No bag, no bed, no blanket, no shirt — not a bloomin' rag but what I stand in. But I 'ad the 'art to stand up agin' them Yankees. 'As any of you 'art enough to spare a pair of old pants for a chum?"

He knew how to conquer the naïve instincts of that crowd. In a moment they gave him their compassion, jocularly, contemptuously, or surlily; and at first it took the shape of a blanket thrown at him as he stood there with the white skin of his limbs showing his human kinship through the black fantasy of his rags. Then a pair of old shoes fell at his muddy feet. With a cry: — "From under," a rolled-up pair of canvas trousers, heavy with tar stains, struck him on the shoulder. The gust of their benevolence sent a wave of sentimental pity through their doubting hearts. They were touched by their own readiness to alleviate a shipmate's misery. Voices cried: — "We will fit you out, old man." Murmurs: "Never seed seech a hard case.... Poor beggar.... I've got an old singlet.... Will that be of any use to you?... Take it, matey...." Those friendly murmurs filled the forecastle. He pawed around with his naked foot, gathering the things in a heap and looked about for more. Unemotional Archie perfunctorily contributed to the pile an old cloth cap with the peak torn off. Old Singleton, lost in the serene regions of fiction, read on unheeding. Charley, pitiless with the wisdom of youth, squeaked: — "If you want brass buttons for your new unyforms I've got two for you." The filthy object of universal charity shook his fist at the youngster. — "I'll make you keep this 'ere fo'c'sle clean, young feller," he snarled viciously. "Never you fear. I will learn you to be civil to an able seaman, you ignerant ass." He glared harmfully, but saw Singleton shut his book, and his little beady eyes began to roam from berth to berth. — "Take that bunk by the door there — it's pretty fair," suggested Belfast. So advised, he gathered the gifts at his feet, pressed them in a bundle against his breast, then looked cautiously at the Russian Finn, who stood on one side with an unconscious gaze, contemplating, perhaps, one of those weird visions that haunt the men of his race. — "Get out of my road, Dutchy," said the victim of Yankee brutality. The Finn did not move — did not hear. "Get out, blast ye," shouted the other, shoving him aside with his elbow. "Get out, you blanked deaf and dumb fool. Get out." The man staggered, recovered himself, and gazed at the speaker in silence. — "Those damned furriners should be kept under," opined the amiable Donkin to the forecastle. "If you don't teach 'em their place they put on you like any-think." He flung all his worldly possessions into the empty bed-place, gauged with another shrewd look the risks of the proceeding, then leaped up to the Finn, who stood pensive and dull. — "I'll teach you to swell around," he yelled. "I'll plug your eyes for you, you blooming square-head." Most of the men were now in their bunks and the two had the forecastle clear to themselves. The development of the destitute Donkin aroused interest. He danced all in tatters before the amazed Finn, squaring from a distance at the heavy, unmoved face. One or two men cried encouragingly: "Go it,

Whitechapel!" settling themselves luxuriously in their beds to survey the fight. Others shouted: "Shut yer row!... Go an' put yer 'ed in a bag!..." The hubbub was recommencing. Suddenly many heavy blows struck with a handspike on the deck above boomed like discharges of small cannon through the forecastle. Then the boatswain's voice rose outside the door with an authoritative note in its drawl: — "D'ye hear, below there? Lay aft! Lay aft to muster all hands!"

There was a moment of surprised stillness. Then the forecastle floor disappeared under men whose bare feet flopped on the planks as they sprang clear out of their berths. Caps were rooted for amongst tumbled blankets. Some, yawning, buttoned waistbands. Half-smoked pipes were knocked hurriedly against woodwork and stuffed under pillows. Voices growled: — "What's up?... Is there no rest for us?" Donkin yelped: — "If that's the way of this ship, we'll 'ave to change all that.... You leave me alone.... I will soon...." None of the crowd noticed him. They were lurching in twos and threes through the doors, after the manner of merchant Jacks who cannot go out of a door fairly, like mere landsmen. The votary of change followed them. Singleton, struggling into his jacket, came last, tall and fatherly, bearing high his head of a weather-beaten sage on the body of an old athlete. Only Charley remained alone in the white glare of the empty place, sitting between the two rows of iron links that stretched into the narrow gloom forward. He pulled hard at the strands in a hurried endeavour to finish his knot. Suddenly he started up, flung the rope at the cat, and skipped after the black tom which went off leaping sedately over chain compressors, with its tail carried stiff and upright, like a small flag pole.

Outside the glare of the steaming forecastle the serene purity of the night enveloped the seamen with its soothing breath, with its tepid breath flowing under the stars that hung countless above the mastheads in a thin cloud of luminous dust. On the town side the blackness of the water was streaked with trails of light which undulated gently on slight ripples, similar to filaments that float rooted to the shore. Rows of other lights stood away in straight lines as if drawn up on parade between towering buildings; but on the other side of the harbour sombre hills arched high their black spines, on which, here and there, the point of a star resembled a spark fallen from the sky. Far off, Byculla way, the electric lamps at the dock gates shone on the end of lofty standards with a glow blinding and frigid like captive ghosts of some evil moons. Scattered all over the dark polish of the roadstead, the ships at anchor floated in perfect stillness under the feeble gleam of their riding-lights, looming up, opaque and bulky, like strange and monumental structures abandoned by men to an everlasting repose.

Before the cabin door Mr. Baker was mustering the crew. As they stumbled and lurched along past the mainmast, they could see aft his round, broad face with a white paper before it, and beside his shoulder the sleepy head, with dropped eyelids, of the boy, who held, suspended at the end of his raised arm, the luminous globe of a lamp. Even before the shuffle of naked soles had ceased along the decks, the mate began to call over the names. He called distinctly in a serious tone befitting this roll-call to unquiet loneliness, to inglorious and obscure struggle, or to the more trying endurance of small privations and wearisome duties. As the chief mate read out a name, one of the men would answer: "Yes, sir!" or "Here!" and, detaching himself from the shadowy mob of heads visible above the blackness of starboard bulwarks, would step barefooted into the circle of light, and in two noiseless strides pass into the shadows on the port side of the quarter-deck. They answered in divers tones: in thick mutters, in clear, ringing voices; and some, as if the whole thing had been an outrage on their feelings, used an injured intonation: for discipline is not ceremonious in merchant ships, where the sense of hierarchy is weak, and where all feel themselves equal before the unconcerned immensity of the sea and the exacting appeal of the work.

Mr. Baker read on steadily: — "Hansen — Campbell — Smith — Wamibo. Now, then, Wamibo. Why don't you answer? Always got to call your name twice." The Finn emitted at last an uncouth grunt, and, stepping out, passed through the patch of light, weird and gaudy, with the face of a man marching through a dream. The mate went on faster: — "Craik — Singleton — Donkin.... O Lord!" he involuntarily ejaculated as the incredibly dilapidated figure appeared in the light. It stopped; it uncovered pale gums and long, upper teeth in a malevolent grin. — "Is there anything wrong with me, Mister Mate?" it asked, with a flavour of insolence in the forced simplicity of its tone. On both sides of the deck subdued titters were heard. — "That'll do. Go over," growled Mr. Baker, fixing the new hand with steady blue eyes. And Donkin vanished suddenly out of the light into the dark group of mustered men, to be slapped on the back and to hear flattering whispers: — "He ain't afeard, he'll give sport to 'em, see if he don't.... Reg'lar Punch and Judy show.... Did ye see the mate start at him?... Well! Damme, if I ever!..."

The last man had gone over, and there was a moment of silence while the mate peered at his list. — "Sixteen, seventeen," he muttered. "I am one hand short, bo'sen," he said aloud. The big west-countryman at his elbow, swarthy and bearded like a gigantic Spaniard, said in a rumbling bass: — "There's no one left forward, sir. I had a look round. He ain't aboard, but he may turn up before daylight." — "Ay. He may or he may not," commented the mate, "can't make out that last name. It's all a smudge.... That will do, men. Go below."

The distinct and motionless group stirred, broke up, began to move forward.

"Wait!" cried a deep, ringing voice.

All stood still. Mr. Baker, who had turned away yawning, spun round open-mouthed. At last, furious, he blurted out: — "What's this? Who said 'Wait'? What..."

But he saw a tall figure standing on the rail. It came down and pushed through the crowd, marching with a heavy tread towards the light on the quarter-deck. Then again the sonorous voice said with insistence: — "Wait!" The lamplight lit up the man's body. He was tall. His head was away up in the shadows of lifeboats that stood on skids above the deck. The whites of his eyes and his teeth gleamed distinctly, but the face was indistinguishable. His hands were big and seemed gloved.

Mr. Baker advanced intrepidly. "Who are you? How dare you..." he began.

The boy, amazed like the rest, raised the light to the man's face. It was black. A surprised hum — a faint hum that sounded like the suppressed mutter of the word "Nigger" — ran along the deck and escaped out into the night. The nigger seemed not to hear. He balanced himself where he stood in a swagger that marked time. After a moment he said calmly: — "My name is Wait — James Wait."

"Oh!" said Mr. Baker. Then, after a few seconds of smouldering silence, his temper blazed out. "Ah! Your name is Wait. What of that? What do you want? What do you mean, coming shouting here?"

The nigger was calm, cool, towering, superb. The men had approached and stood behind him in a body. He overtopped the tallest by half a head. He said: "I belong to the ship." He enunciated distinctly, with soft precision. The deep, rolling tones of his voice filled the deck without effort. He was naturally scornful, unaffectedly condescending, as if from his height of six foot three he had surveyed all the vastness of human folly and had made up his mind not to be too hard on it. He went on: — "The captain shipped me this morning. I couldn't get aboard sooner. I saw you all aft as I came up the ladder, and could see directly you were mustering the crew. Naturally I called out my name. I thought you had it on your list, and would understand. You misapprehended." He stopped short. The folly around him was confounded. He was right as ever, and as ever ready to forgive. The disdainful tones had ceased, and, breathing heavily, he stood still, surrounded by all these white men. He held his head up in the glare of the lamp — a head vigorously modelled into deep shadows and shining lights — a head powerful and misshapen with a tormented and flattened face — a face pathetic and brutal: the tragic, the mysterious, the repulsive mask of a nigger's soul.

Mr. Baker, recovering his composure, looked at the paper close. "Oh, yes; that's so. All right, Wait. Take your gear forward," he said.

Suddenly the nigger's eyes rolled wildly, became all whites. He put his hand to his side and coughed twice, a cough metallic, hollow, and tremendously loud; it resounded like two explosions in a vault; the dome of the sky rang to it, and the iron plates of the ship's bulwarks seemed to vibrate in unison, then he marched off forward with the others. The officers lingering by the cabin door could hear him say: "Won't some of you chaps lend a hand with my dunnage? I've got a chest and a bag." The words, spoken sonorously, with an even intonation, were heard all over the ship, and the question was put in a manner that made refusal impossible. The short, quick shuffle of men carrying something heavy went away forward, but the tall figure of the nigger lingered by the main hatch in a knot of smaller shapes. Again he was heard asking: "Is your cook a coloured gentleman?" Then a disappointed and disapproving "Ah! h'm!" was his comment upon the information that the cook happened to be a mere white man. Yet, as they went all together towards the forecastle, he condescended to put his head through the galley door and boom out inside a magnificent "Good evening, doctor!"

that made all the saucepans ring. In the dim light the cook dozed on the coal locker in front of the captain's supper. He jumped up as if he had been cut with a whip, and dashed wildly on deck to see the backs of several men going away laughing. Afterwards, when talking about that voyage, he used to say: — "The poor fellow had scared me. I thought I had seen the devil." The cook had been seven years in the ship with the same captain. He was a serious-minded man with a wife and three children, whose society he enjoyed on an average one month out of twelve. When on shore he took his family to church twice every Sunday. At sea he went to sleep every evening with his lamp turned up full, a pipe in his mouth, and an open Bible in his hand. Someone had always to go during the night to put out the light, take the book from his hand, and the pipe from between his teeth. "For" — Belfast used to say, irritated and complaining — "some night, you stupid cookie, you'll swallow your ould clay, and we will have no cook." — "Ah! sonny, I am ready for my Maker's call... wish you all were," the other would answer with a benign serenity that was altogether imbecile and touching. Belfast outside the galley door danced with vexation. "You holy fool! I don't want you to die," he howled, looking up with furious, quivering face and tender eyes. "What's the hurry? You blessed wooden-headed ould heretic, the divvle will have you soon enough. Think of Us... of Us... of Us!" And he would go away, stamping, spitting aside, disgusted and worried; while the other, stepping out, saucepan in hand, hot, begrimed and placid, watched with a superior, cock-sure smile the back of his "queer little man" reeling in a rage. They were great friends.

Mr. Baker, lounging over the after-hatch, sniffed the humid night in the company of the second mate. — "Those West India niggers run fine and large — some of them... Ough!... Don't they? A fine, big man that, Mr. Creighton. Feel him on a rope. Hey? Ough! I will take him into my watch, I think." The second mate, a fair, gentlemanly young fellow, with a resolute face and a splendid physique, observed quietly that it was just about what he expected. There could be felt in his tone some slight bitterness which Mr. Baker very kindly set himself to argue away. "Come, come, young man," he said, grunting between the words. "Come! Don't be too greedy. You had that big Finn in your watch all the voyage. I will do what's fair. You may have those two young Scandinavians and I... Ough! ... I get the nigger, and will take that... Ough! that cheeky costermonger chap in a black frock-coat. I'll make him... Ough!... make him toe the mark, or my... Ough!... name isn't Baker. Ough! Ough! Ough!"

He grunted thrice — ferociously. He had that trick of grunting so between his words and at the end of sentences. It was a fine, effective grunt that went well with his menacing utterance, with his heavy, bull-necked frame, his jerky, rolling gait; with his big, seamed face, his steady eyes, and sardonic mouth. But its effect had been long ago discounted by the men. They liked him; Belfast — who was a favourite, and knew it — mimicked him, not quite behind his back. Charley — but with greater caution — imitated his rolling gait. Some of his sayings became established, daily quotations in the forecastle. Popularity can go no farther! Besides, all hands were ready to admit that on a fitting occasion the mate could "jump down a fellow's throat in a reg'lar Western Ocean style."

Now he was giving his last orders. "Ough!... You, Knowles! Call all hands at four. I want... Ough!... to heave short before the tug comes. Look out for the captain. I am going to lie down in my clothes.... Ough!... Call me when you see the boat coming. Ough! Ough!... The old man is sure to have something to say when he gets aboard," he remarked to Creighton. "Well, good-night.... Ough! A long day before us tomorrow.... Ough!... Better turn in now. Ough! Ough!"

Upon the dark deck a band of light flashed, then a door slammed, and Mr. Baker was gone into his neat cabin. Young Creighton stood leaning over the rail, and looked dreamily into the night of the East. And he saw in it a long country lane, a lane of waving leaves and dancing sunshine. He saw stirring boughs of old trees outspread, and framing in their arch the tender, the caressing blueness of an English sky. And through the arch a girl in a light dress, smiling under a sunshade, seemed to be stepping out of the tender sky.

At the other end of the ship the forecastle, with only one lamp burning now, was going to sleep in a dim emptiness traversed by loud breathings, by sudden short sighs. The double row of berths yawned black, like graves tenanted by uneasy corpses. Here and there a curtain of gaudy chintz, half drawn, marked the resting-place of a sybarite. A leg hung over the edge very white and lifeless. An arm stuck straight out with a dark palm turned up, and thick fingers half closed. Two light snores, that did not synchronise, quarrelled in funny dialogue. Singleton stripped again — the old man suffered much from prickly heat — stood cooling his back in the doorway, with his arms crossed on his bare and adorned chest. His head touched the beam of the deck above. The nigger, half undressed, was busy casting adrift the lashing of his box, and spreading his bedding in an upper berth. He moved about in his socks, tall and noiseless, with a pair of braces beating about his calves. Amongst the shadows of stanchions and bowsprit, Donkin munched a piece of hard ship's bread, sitting on the deck with up-turned feet and restless eyes; he held the biscuit up before his mouth in the whole fist and snapped his jaws at it with a raging face. Crumbs fell between his outspread legs. Then he got up.

"Where's our water-cask?" he asked in a contained voice.

Singleton, without a word, pointed with a big hand that held a short smouldering pipe. Donkin bent over the cask, drank out of the tin, splashing the water, turned round and noticed the nigger looking at him over the shoulder with calm loftiness. He moved up sideways.

"There's a blooming supper for a man," he whispered bitterly. "My dorg at 'ome wouldn't 'ave it. It's fit enouf for you an' me. 'Ere's a big ship's fo'c'sle!... Not a blooming scrap of meat in the kids. I've looked in all the lockers...."

The nigger stared like a man addressed unexpectedly in a foreign language. Donkin changed his tone: — "Giv' us a bit of 'baccy, mate," he breathed out confidentially, "I 'aven't 'ad smoke or chew for the last month. I am rampin' mad for it. Come on, old man!"

"Don't be familiar," said the nigger. Donkin started and sat down on a chest near by, out of sheer surprise. "We haven't kept pigs together," continued James Wait in a deep undertone. "Here's your tobacco." Then, after a pause, he inquired: — "What ship?" — "*Golden State*," muttered Donkin indistinctly, biting the tobacco. The nigger whistled low. — "Ran?" he said curtly. Donkin nodded: one of his cheeks bulged out. "In course I ran," he mumbled. "They booted the life hout of one Dago chap on the passage 'ere, then started on me. I cleared hout 'ere. — "Left your dunnage behind?" — "Yes, dunnage and money," answered Donkin, raising his voice a little; "I got nothink. No clothes, no bed. A bandy-legged little Hirish chap 'ere 'as give me a blanket.... Think I'll go an' sleep in the fore topmast staysail tonight."

He went on deck trailing behind his back a corner of the blanket. Singleton, without a glance, moved slightly aside to let him pass. The nigger put away his shore togs and sat in clean working clothes on his box, one arm stretched over his knees. After staring at Singleton for some time he asked without emphasis: — "What kind of ship is this? Pretty fair? Eh?"

Singleton didn't stir. A long while after he said, with unmoved face: — "Ship!... Ships are all right. It is the men in them!"

He went on smoking in the profound silence. The wisdom of half a century spent in listening to the thunder of the waves had spoken unconsciously through his old lips. The cat purred on the windlass. Then James Wait had a fit of roaring, rattling cough, that shook him, tossed him like a hurricane, and flung him panting with staring eyes headlong on his sea-chest. Several men woke up. One said sleepily out of his bunk: "'Struth! what a blamed row!" — "I have a cold on my chest," gasped Wait. — "Cold! you call it," grumbled the man; "should think 'twas something more...." — "Oh! you think so," said the nigger upright and loftily scornful again. He climbed into his berth and began coughing persistently while he put his head out to glare all round the forecastle. There was no further protest. He fell back on the pillow, and could be heard there wheezing regularly like a man oppressed in his sleep.

Singleton stood at the door with his face to the light and his back to the darkness. And alone in the dim emptiness of the sleeping forecastle he appeared bigger, colossal, very old; old as Father Time himself, who should have come there into this place as quiet as a sepulchre to contemplate with patient eyes the short victory of sleep, the consoler. Yet he was only a child of time, a lonely relic of a devoured and forgotten generation. He stood, still strong, as ever unthinking; a ready man with a vast empty past and with no future, with his childlike impulses and his man's passions already dead within his tattooed breast. The men who could understand his silence were gone — those men who knew how to exist beyond the pale of life and within sight of eternity. They had been strong, as those are strong who know neither doubts nor hopes. They had been impatient and enduring, turbulent and devoted, unruly and faithful. Well-meaning people had tried to represent those men as whining over every mouthful of their food; as going about their work in fear of their lives. But in truth they had been men who knew toil, privation, violence, debauchery — but knew not fear, and had no desire of spite in their hearts. Men hard to manage, but easy to inspire; voiceless men — but men enough to scorn in their hearts the sentimental voices that bewailed the hardness of their fate. It was a fate unique and their own; the capacity to bear it appeared to them the privilege of the chosen! Their generation lived inarticulate and indispensable, without knowing the sweetness of affections or the refuge of a home — and died free from the dark menace of a narrow grave. They were the everlasting children of the mysterious sea. Their successors are the grown-up children of a discontented earth. They are less naughty, but less innocent; less profane, but perhaps also less believing; and if they have learned how to speak they have also learned how to whine. But the others were strong and mute; they were effaced, bowed and enduring, like stone caryatides that hold up in the night the lighted halls of a resplendent and glorious edifice. They are gone now — and it does not matter. The sea and the earth are unfaithful to their children: a truth, a faith, a generation of men goes — and is forgotten, and it does not matter! Except, perhaps, to the few of those who believed the truth, confessed the faith — or loved the men.

A breeze was coming. The ship that had been lying tide-rode swung to a heavier puff; and suddenly the slack of the chain cable between the windlass and the hawse-pipe clinked, slipped forward an inch, and rose gently off the deck with a startling suggestion as of unsuspected life that had been lurking stealthily in the iron. In the hawse-pipe the grinding links sent through the ship a sound like a low groan of a man sighing under a burden. The strain came on the windlass, the chain tautened like a string, vibrated — and the handle of the screw-brake moved in slight jerks. Singleton stepped forward.

Till then he had been standing meditative and unthinking, reposeful and hopeless, with a face grim and blank — a sixty-year-old child of the mysterious sea. The thoughts of all his lifetime could have been expressed in six words, but the stir of those things that were as much part of his existence as his beating heart called up a gleam of alert understanding upon the sternness of his aged face. The flame of the lamp swayed, and the old man, with knitted and bushy eyebrows, stood over the brake, watchful and motionless in the wild saraband of dancing shadows. Then the ship, obedient to the call of her anchor, forged ahead slightly and eased the strain. The cable relieved, hung down, and after swaying imperceptibly to and fro dropped with a loud tap on the hard wood planks. Singleton seized the high lever, and, by a violent throw forward of his body, wrung out another half-turn from the brake. He recovered himself, breathed largely, and remained for a while glaring down at the powerful and compact engine that squatted on the deck at his feet like some quiet monster — a creature amazing and tame.

"You... hold!" he growled at it masterfully, in the incult tangle of his white beard.

CHAPTER TWO

NEXT morning, at daylight, the *Narcissus* went to sea.

A slight haze blurred the horizon. Outside the harbour the measureless expanse of smooth water lay sparkling like a floor of jewels, and as empty as the sky. The short black tug gave a pluck to windward, in the usual way, then let go the rope, and hovered for a moment on the quarter with her engines stopped; while the slim, long hull of the ship moved ahead slowly under lower topsails. The loose upper canvas blew out in the breeze with soft round contours, resembling small white clouds snared in the maze of ropes. Then the sheets were hauled home, the yards hoisted, and the ship became a high and lonely pyramid, gliding, all shining and white, through the sunlit mist. The tug turned short round and went away towards the land. Twenty-six pairs of eyes watched her low broad stern crawling languidly over the smooth swell between the two paddle-wheels that turned fast, beating the water with fierce hurry. She resembled an enormous and aquatic black beetle, surprised by the light, overwhelmed by the sunshine, trying to escape with ineffectual effort into the distant gloom of the land. She left a lingering smudge of smoke on the sky, and two vanishing trails of foam on the water. On the place where she had stopped a round black patch of soot remained, undulating on the swell — an unclean mark of the creature's rest.

The *Narcissus* left alone, heading south, seemed to stand resplendent and still upon the restless sea, under the moving sun. Flakes of foam swept past her sides; the water struck her with flashing blows; the land glided away slowly fading; a few birds screamed on motionless wings over the swaying mastheads. But soon the land disappeared, the birds went away; and to the west the pointed sail of an Arab dhow running for Bombay, rose triangular and upright above the sharp edge of the horizon, lingered and vanished like an illusion. Then the ship's wake, long and straight, stretched itself out through a day of immense solitude. The setting sun, burning on the level of the water, flamed crimson below the blackness of heavy rain clouds. The sunset squall, coming up from behind, dissolved itself into the short deluge of a hissing shower. It left the ship glistening from trucks to water-line, and with darkened sails. She ran easily before a fair monsoon, with her decks cleared for the night; and, moving along with her, was heard the sustained and monotonous swishing of the waves, mingled with the low whispers of men mustered aft for the setting of watches; the short plaint of some block aloft; or, now and then, a loud sigh of wind.

Mr. Baker, coming out of his cabin, called out the first name sharply before closing the door behind him. He was going to take charge of the deck. On the homeward trip, according to an old custom of the sea, the chief officer takes the first night-watch — from eight till midnight. So Mr. Baker, after he had heard the last "Yes, sir!" said moodily, "Relieve the wheel and look-out"; and climbed with heavy feet the poop ladder to windward. Soon after Mr. Creighton came down, whistling softly, and went into the cabin. On the doorstep the steward lounged, in slippers, meditative, and with his shirt-sleeves rolled up to the armpits. On the main deck the cook, locking up the galley doors, had an altercation with young Charley about a pair of socks. He could be heard saying impressively, in the darkness amidships: "You don't deserve a kindness. I've been drying them for you, and now you complain about the holes — and you swear, too! Right in front of me! If I hadn't been a Christian — which you ain't, you young ruffian — I would give you a clout on the head.... Go away!" Men in couples or threes stood pensive or moved silently along the bulwarks in the waist. The first busy day of a homeward passage was sinking into the dull peace of resumed routine. Aft, on the high poop, Mr. Baker walked shuffling and grunted to himself in the pauses of his thoughts. Forward, the look-out man, erect between the flukes of the two anchors, hummed an endless tune, keeping his eyes fixed dutifully ahead in a vacant stare. A multitude of stars coming out into the clear night peopled the emptiness of the sky. They glittered, as if alive above the sea; they surrounded the running ship on all sides; more intense than the eyes of a staring crowd, and as inscrutable as the souls of men.

The passage had begun, and the ship, a fragment detached from the earth, went on lonely and swift like a small planet. Round her the abysses of sky and sea met in an unattainable frontier. A great circular solitude moved with her, ever changing and ever the same, always monotonous and always imposing. Now and then another wandering white speck, burdened with life, appeared far off — disappeared; intent on its own destiny. The sun looked upon her all day, and every morning rose with a burning, round stare of undying curiosity. She had her own future; she was alive with the lives of those beings who trod her decks; like that earth which had given her up to the sea, she had an intolerable load of regrets and hopes. On her lived timid truth and audacious lies; and, like the earth, she was unconscious, fair to see — and condemned by men to an ignoble fate. The august loneliness of her path lent dignity to the sordid inspiration of her pilgrimage. She drove foaming to the southward, as if guided by the courage of a high endeavour. The smiling greatness of the sea dwarfed the extent of time. The days raced after one another, brilliant and quick like the flashes of a lighthouse, and the nights, eventful and short, resembled fleeting dreams.

The men had shaken into their places, and the half-hourly voice of the bells ruled their life of unceasing care. Night and day the head and shoulders of a seaman could be seen aft by the wheel, outlined high against sunshine or starlight, very steady above the stir of revolving spokes. The faces changed, passing in rotation. Youthful faces, bearded faces, dark faces; faces serene, or faces moody, but all akin with the brotherhood of the sea; all with the same attentive expression of eyes, carefully watching the compass or the sails. Captain Allistoun, serious, and with an old red muffler round his throat, all day long pervaded the poop. At night, many times he rose out of the darkness of the companion, such as a phantom above a grave, and stood watchful and mute under the stars, his night-shirt fluttering like a flag — then, without a sound, sank down again. He was born on the shores of the Pentland Firth. In his youth he attained the rank of harpooner in

Peterhead whalers. When he spoke of that time his restless grey eyes became still and cold, like the loom of ice. Afterwards he went into the East Indian trade for the sake of change. He had commanded the *Narcissus* since she was built. He loved his ship, and drove her unmercifully; for his secret ambition was to make her accomplish some day a brilliantly quick passage which would be mentioned in nautical papers. He pronounced his owner's name with a sardonic smile, spoke but seldom to his officers, and reproved errors in a gentle voice, with words that cut to the quick. His hair was iron-grey, his face hard and of the colour of pump-leather. He shaved every morning of his life — at six — but once (being caught in a fierce hurricane eighty miles southwest of Mauritius) he had missed three consecutive days. He feared naught but an unforgiving God, and wished to end his days in a little house, with a plot of ground attached — far in the country — out of sight of the sea.

He, the ruler of that minute world, seldom descended from the Olympian heights of his poop. Below him — at his feet, so to speak — common mortals led their busy and insignificant lives. Along the main deck, Mr. Baker grunted in a manner bloodthirsty and innocuous; and kept all our noses to the grindstone, being — as he once remarked — paid for doing that very thing. The men working about the deck were healthy and contented — as most seamen are, when once well out to sea. The true peace of God begins at any spot a thousand miles from the nearest land; and when He sends there the messengers of His might it is not in terrible wrath against crime, presumption, and folly, but paternally, to chasten simple hearts — ignorant hearts that know nothing of life, and beat undisturbed by envy or greed.

In the evening the cleared decks had a reposeful aspect, resembling the autumn of the earth. The sun was sinking to rest, wrapped in a mantle of warm clouds. Forward, on the end of the spare spars, the boatswain and the carpenter sat together with crossed arms; two men friendly, powerful, and deep-chested. Beside them the short, dumpy sailmaker — who had been in the Navy — related, between the whiffs of his pipe, impossible stories about Admirals. Couples tramped backwards and forwards, keeping step and balance without effort, in a confined space. Pigs grunted in the big pigstye. Belfast, leaning thoughtfully on his elbow, above the bars, communed with them through the silence of his meditation. Fellows with shirts open wide on sunburnt breasts sat upon the mooring bits, and all up the steps of the forecastle ladders. By the foremast a few discussed in a circle the characteristics of a gentleman. One said: — "It's money as does it." Another maintained: — "No, it's the way they speak." Lame Knowles stumped up with an unwashed face (he had the distinction of being the dirty man of the forecastle), and showing a few yellow fangs in a shrewd smile, explained craftily that he "had seen some of their pants." The backsides of them — he had observed — were thinner than paper from constant sitting down in offices, yet otherwise they looked first-rate and would last for years. It was all appearance. "It was," he said, "bloomin' easy to be a gentleman when you had a clean job for life." They disputed endlessly, obstinate and childish; they repeated in shouts and with inflamed faces their amazing arguments; while the soft breeze, eddying down the enormous cavity of the foresail, distended above their bare heads, stirred the tumbled hair with a touch passing and light like an indulgent caress.

They were forgetting their toil, they were forgetting themselves. The cook approached to hear, and stood by, beaming with the inward consciousness of his faith, like a conceited saint unable to forget his glorious reward; Donkin, solitary and brooding over his wrongs on the forecastle-head, moved closer to catch the drift of the discussion below him; he turned his sallow face to the sea, and his thin nostrils moved, sniffing the breeze, as he lounged negligently by the rail. In the glow of sunset faces shone with interest, teeth flashed, eyes sparkled. The walking couples stood still suddenly, with broad grins; a man, bending over a washtub, sat up, entranced, with the soapsuds flecking his wet arms. Even the three petty officers listened leaning back, comfortably propped, and with superior smiles. Belfast left off scratching the ear of his favourite pig, and, open mouthed, tried with eager eyes to have his say. He lifted his arms, grimacing and baffled. From a distance Charley screamed at the ring: — "I know about gentlemen more'n any of you. I've been intermit with 'em.... I've blacked their boots." The cook, craning his neck to hear better, was scandalised. "Keep your mouth shut when your elders speak, you impudent young heathen — you." "All right, old Hallelujah, I'm done," answered Charley, soothingly. At some opinion of dirty Knowles, delivered with an air of supernatural cunning, a ripple of laughter ran along, rose like a wave, burst with a startling roar. They stamped with both feet; they turned their shouting faces to the sky; many, spluttering, slapped their thighs; while one or two, bent double, gasped, hugging themselves with both arms like men in pain. The carpenter and the boatswain, without changing their attitude, shook with laughter where they sat; the sailmaker, charged with an anecdote about a Commodore, looked sulky; the cook was wiping his eyes with a greasy rag; and lame Knowles, astonished at his own success, stood in their midst showing a slow smile.

Suddenly the face of Donkin leaning high-shouldered over the after-rail became grave. Something like a weak rattle was heard through the forecastle door. It became a murmur; it ended in a sighing groan. The washerman plunged both his arms into the tub abruptly; the cook became more crestfallen than an exposed backslider; the boatswain moved his shoulders uneasily; the carpenter got up with a spring and walked away — while the sailmaker seemed mentally to give his story up, and began to puff at his pipe with sombre determination. In the blackness of the doorway a pair of eyes glimmered white, and big, and staring. Then James Wait's head protruding, became visible, as if suspended between the two hands that grasped a doorpost on each side of the face. The tassel of his blue woollen nightcap, cocked forward, danced gaily over his left eyelid. He stepped out in a tottering stride. He looked powerful as ever, but showed a strange and affected unsteadiness in his gait; his face was perhaps a trifle thinner, and his eyes appeared rather startlingly prominent. He seemed to hasten the retreat of departing light by his very presence; the setting sun dipped sharply, as though fleeing before our nigger; a black mist emanated from him; a subtle and dismal influence; a something cold and gloomy that floated out and settled on all the faces like a mourning veil. The circle broke up. The joy of laughter died on stiffened lips. There was not a smile left among all the ship's company. Not a word was spoken. Many turned their backs, trying to look unconcerned; others, with averted heads, sent half-reluctant glances out of the corners of their eyes. They resembled criminals conscious of misdeeds more than honest men distracted by doubt; only two or three stared frankly, but stupidly, with lips slightly open. All expected James Wait to say something, and, at the same time, had the air of knowing before-hand what he would say. He leaned his back against the doorpost, and with heavy eyes swept over them a glance domineering and pained, like a sick tyrant overawing a crowd of abject but untrustworthy slaves.

No one went away. They waited in fascinated dread. He said ironically, with gasps between the words: —

"Thank you... chaps. You... are nice... and... quiet... you are! Yelling so... before... the door...."

He made a longer pause, during which he worked his ribs in an exaggerated labour of breathing. It was intolerable. Feet were shuffled. Belfast let out a groan; but Donkin above blinked his red eyelids with invisible eye-lashes, and smiled bitterly over the nigger's head.

The nigger went on again with surprising ease. He gasped no more, and his voice rang, hollow and loud, as though he had been talking in an empty cavern. He was contemptuously angry.

"I tried to get a wink of sleep. You know I can't sleep o'nights. And you come jabbering near the door here like a blooming lot of old women.... You think yourselves good shipmates. Do you?... Much you care for a dying man!"

Belfast spun away from the pigstye. "Jimmy," he cried tremulously, "if you hadn't been sick I would ——"

He stopped. The nigger waited awhile, then said, in a gloomy tone: — "You would.... What? Go an' fight another such one as yourself. Leave me alone. It won't be for long. I'll soon die.... It's coming right enough!"

Men stood around very still and with exasperated eyes. It was just what they had expected, and hated to hear, that idea of a stalking death, thrust at them many times a day like a boast and like a menace by this obnoxious nigger. He seemed to take a pride in that death which, so far, had attended only upon the ease of his life; he was overbearing about it, as if no one else in the world had ever been intimate with such a companion; he paraded it unceasingly before us with an affectionate persistence that made its presence indubitable, and at the same time incredible. No man could be suspected of such monstrous friendship! Was he a reality — or was he a sham — this ever-expected visitor of Jimmy's? We hesitated between pity and mistrust, while, on the slightest provocation, he shook before our eyes the bones of his bothersome and infamous skeleton. He was for ever trotting him out. He would talk of that coming death as though it had been already there, as if it had been walking the deck outside, as if it would presently come in to sleep in the only empty bunk; as if it had sat by his side at every meal. It interfered daily with our occupations, with our leisure, with our amusements. We had no songs and no music in the evening, because Jimmy (we all lovingly called him Jimmy, to conceal our hate of his accomplice) had managed, with that prospective decease of his, to disturb even Archie's mental balance. Archie was the owner of the concertina; but after a couple of stinging lectures from Jimmy he refused to play any more. He said: — "Yon's an uncanny joker. I dinna ken what's wrang wi' him, but there's something verra wrang, verra wrang. It's nae manner of use asking me. I won't play." Our singers became mute because Jimmy was a dying man. For the same reason no chap — as Knowles remarked — could "drive in a nail to hang his few poor rags upon," without being made aware of the enormity he committed in disturbing Jimmy's interminable last moments. At night, instead of the cheerful yell, "One bell! Turn out! Do you hear there? Hey! hey! hey! Show leg!" the watches were called man by man, in whispers, so as not to interfere with Jimmy's, possibly, last slumber on earth. True, he was always awake, and managed, as we sneaked out on deck, to plant in our backs some cutting remark that, for the moment, made us feel as if we had been brutes, and afterwards made us suspect ourselves of being fools. We spoke in low tones within that fo'c'sle as though it had been a church. We ate our meals in silence and dread, for Jimmy was capricious with his food, and railed bitterly at the salt meat, at the biscuits, at the tea, as at articles unfit for human consumption — "let alone for a dying man!" He would say: — "Can't you find a better slice of meat for a sick man who's trying to get home to be cured — or buried? But there! If I had a chance, you fellows would do away with it. You would poison me. Look at what you have given me!" We served him in his bed with rage and humility, as though we had been the base courtiers of a hated prince; and he rewarded us by his unconciliating criticism. He had found the secret of keeping for ever on the run the fundamental imbecility of mankind; he had the secret of life, that confounded dying man, and he made himself master of every moment of our existence. We grew desperate, and remained submissive. Emotional little Belfast was for ever on the verge of assault or on the verge of tears. One evening he confided to Archie: — "For a ha'penny I would knock his ugly black head off — the skulking dodger!" And the straightforward Archie pretended to be shocked! Such was the infernal spell which that casual St. Kitt's nigger had cast upon our guileless manhood! But the same night Belfast stole from the galley the officers' Sunday fruit pie, to tempt the fastidious appetite of Jimmy. He endangered not only his long friendship with the cook but also — as it appeared — his eternal welfare. The cook was overwhelmed with grief; he did not know the culprit but he knew that wickedness flourished; he knew that Satan was abroad amongst those men, whom he looked upon as in some way under his spiritual care. Whenever he saw three or four of us standing together he would leave his stove, to run out and preach. We fled from him; and only Charley (who knew the thief) affronted the cook with a candid gaze which irritated the good man.

"It's you, I believe," he groaned, sorrowful and with a patch of soot on his chin. "It's you. You are a brand for the burning! No more of YOUR socks in my galley." Soon, unofficially, the information was spread about that, should there be another case of stealing, our marmalade (an extra allowance: half a pound per man) would be stopped. Mr. Baker ceased to heap jocular abuse upon his favourites, and grunted suspiciously at all. The captain's cold eyes, high up on the poop, glittered mistrustful, as he surveyed us trooping in a small mob from halyards to braces for the usual evening pull at all the ropes. Such stealing in a merchant ship is difficult to check, and may be taken as a declaration by men of their dislike for their officers. It is a bad symptom. It may end in God knows what trouble. The *Narcissus* was still a peaceful ship, but mutual confidence was shaken. Donkin did not conceal his delight. We were dismayed.

Then illogical Belfast reproached our nigger with great fury. James Wait, with his elbow on the pillow, choked, gasped out: — "Did I ask you to bone the dratted thing? Blow your blamed pie. It has made me worse — you little Irish lunatic, you!" Belfast, with scarlet face and trembling lips, made a dash at him. Every man in the forecastle rose with a shout. There was a moment of wild tumult. Someone shrieked piercingly: — "Easy, Belfast! Easy!..." We expected Belfast to strangle Wait without more ado. Dust flew. We heard through it the nigger's cough, metallic and explosive like a gong. Next moment we saw Belfast hanging over him. He was saying plaintively: — "Don't! Don't, Jimmy! Don't be like that. An angel couldn't put up with ye — sick as ye are." He looked round at us from Jimmy's bedside, his comical mouth twitching, and through tearful eyes; then he tried to put straight the disarranged blankets. The unceasing whisper of the sea filled the forecastle. Was James Wait frightened, or touched, or repentant? He lay on his back with a hand to his side, and as motionless as if his expected visitor had come at last. Belfast fumbled about his feet, repeating with emotion: — "Yes. We know. Ye are bad, but.... Just say what ye want done, and.... We all know ye are bad — very bad...." No! Decidedly James Wait was not touched or repentant. Truth to say, he seemed rather startled. He sat up with incredible suddenness and ease. "Ah! You think I am bad, do you?" he said gloomily, in his clearest baritone voice (to hear him speak sometimes you would never think there was anything wrong with that man). "Do you?... Well, act according! Some of you haven't sense enough to put a blanket shipshape over a sick man. There! Leave it alone! I can die anyhow!" Belfast turned away limply with a gesture of discouragement. In the silence of the forecastle, full of interested men, Donkin pronounced distinctly: — "Well, I'm blowed!" and sniggered. Wait looked at him. He looked at him in a quite friendly manner. Nobody could tell what would please our incomprehensible invalid: but for us the scorn of that snigger was hard to bear.

Donkin's position in the forecastle was distinguished but unsafe. He stood on the bad eminence of a general dislike. He was left alone; and in his isolation he could do nothing but think of the gales of the Cape of Good Hope and envy us the possession of warm clothing and waterproofs. Our sea-boots, our oilskin coats, our well-filled sea-chests, were to him so many causes for bitter meditation: he had none of those things, and he felt instinctively that no man, when the need arose, would offer to share them with him. He was impudently cringing to us and systematically insolent to the officers. He anticipated the best results, for himself, from such a line of conduct — and was mistaken. Such natures forget that under extreme provocation men will be just — whether they want to be so or not. Donkin's insolence to long-suffering Mr. Baker became at last intolerable to us, and we rejoiced when the mate, one dark night, tamed him for good. It was done neatly, with great decency and decorum, and with little noise. We had been called — just before midnight — to trim the yards, and Donkin — as usual — made insulting remarks. We stood sleepily in a row with the forebrace in our hands waiting for the next order, and heard in the darkness a scuffly trampling of feet, an exclamation of surprise, sounds of cuffs and slaps, suppressed, hissing whispers: — "Ah! Will you!"... "Don't!... Don't!"... "Then behave."... "Oh! Oh!..." Afterwards there were soft thuds mixed with the rattle of iron things as if a man's body had been tumbling helplessly amongst the main-pump rods. Before we could realise the situation, Mr. Baker's voice was heard very near and a little impatient: — "Haul away, men! Lay back on that rope!" And we did lay back on the rope with great alacrity. As if nothing had happened, the chief mate went on trimming the yards with his usual and exasperating fastidiousness. We didn't at the time see anything of Donkin, and did not care. Had the chief officer thrown him overboard, no man would have said as much as "Hallo! he's gone!" But, in truth, no great harm was done — even if Donkin did lose one of his front teeth. We perceived this in the morning, and preserved a ceremonious silence: the etiquette of the forecastle commanded us to be blind and dumb in such a case, and we cherished the decencies of our life more than ordinary landsmen respect theirs. Charley, with unpardonable want of *savoir vivre*, yelled out: — "'Ave you been to your dentyst?... Hurt ye, didn't it?" He got a box on the ear from one of his best friends. The boy was surprised, and remained plunged in grief for at least three hours. We were sorry for him, but youth requires even more discipline than age. Donkin grinned venomously. From that day he became pitiless; told Jimmy that he was a "black fraud"; hinted to us that we were an imbecile lot, daily taken in by a vulgar nigger. And Jimmy seemed to like the fellow!

Singleton lived untouched by human emotions. Taciturn and unsmiling, he breathed amongst us — in that alone resembling the rest of the crowd. We were trying to be decent chaps, and found it jolly difficult; we oscillated between the desire of virtue and the fear of ridicule; we wished to save ourselves from the pain of remorse, but did not want to be made the contemptible dupes of our sentiment. Jimmy's hateful accomplice seemed to have blown with his impure breath undreamt-of subtleties into our hearts. We were disturbed and cowardly. That we knew. Singleton seemed to know nothing, understand nothing. We had thought him till then as wise as he looked, but now we dared, at times, suspect him of being stupid — from old age. One day, however, at dinner, as we sat on our boxes round a tin dish that stood on the deck within the circle of our feet, Jimmy expressed his general disgust with men and things in words that were particularly disgusting. Singleton lifted his head. We became mute. The old man, addressing Jimmy, asked: — "Are you dying?" Thus interrogated, James Wait appeared horribly startled and confused. We all were startled. Mouths remained open; hearts thumped, eyes blinked; a dropped tin fork rattled in the dish; a man rose as if to go out, and stood still. In less than a minute Jimmy pulled himself together: — "Why? Can't you see I am?" he answered shakily. Singleton lifted a piece of soaked biscuit ("his teeth" — he declared — "had no edge on them now") to his lips. — "Well, get on with your dying," he said with venerable mildness; "don't raise a blamed fuss with us over that job. We can't help you." Jimmy fell back in his bunk, and for a long time lay very still wiping the perspiration off his chin. The dinner-tins were put away quickly. On deck we discussed the incident in whispers. Some showed a chuckling exultation. Many looked grave. Wamibo, after long periods of staring dreaminess, attempted abortive smiles; and one of the young Scandinavians, much tormented by doubt, ventured in the second dog-watch to approach Singleton (the old man did not encourage us much to speak to him) and ask sheepishly: — "You think he will die?" Singleton looked up. — "Why, of course he will die," he said deliberately. This seemed decisive. It was promptly imparted to everyone by him who had consulted the oracle. Shy and eager, he would step up and with averted gaze recite his formula: — "Old Singleton says he will die." It was a relief! At last we knew that our compassion would not be misplaced, and we could again smile without misgivings — but we reckoned without Donkin. Donkin "didn't want to 'ave no truck with 'em dirty furriners." When Nilsen came to him with the news: "Singleton says he will die," he answered him by a spiteful "And so will you — you fat-headed Dutchman. Wish you Dutchmen were all dead — 'stead comin' takin' our money inter your starvin' country." We were appalled. We perceived that after all Singleton's answer meant nothing. We began to hate him for making fun of us. All our certitudes were going; we were on doubtful terms with our officers; the cook had given us up for lost; we had overheard the boatswain's opinion that "we were a crowd of softies." We suspected Jimmy, one another, and even our very selves. We did not know what to do. At every insignificant turn of our humble life we met Jimmy overbearing and blocking the way, arm-in-arm with his awful and veiled familiar. It was a weird servitude.

It began a week after leaving Bombay and came on us stealthily like any other great misfortune. Everyone had remarked that Jimmy from the first was very slack at his work; but we thought it simply the outcome of his philosophy of life. Donkin said: — "You put no more weight on a rope than a bloody sparrer." He disdained him. Belfast, ready for a fight, exclaimed provokingly: — "You don't kill yourself, old man!" — "Would YOU?" he retorted with extreme scorn — and Belfast retired. One morning, as we were washing decks, Mr. Baker called to him: — "Bring your broom over here, Wait." He strolled languidly. "Move yourself! Ough!"

grunted Mr. Baker; "what's the matter with your hind legs?" He stopped dead short. He gazed slowly with eyes that bulged out with an expression audacious and sad. — "It isn't my legs," he said, "it's my lungs." Everybody listened. — "What's... Ough!... What's wrong with them?" inquired Mr. Baker. All the watch stood around on the wet deck, grinning, and with brooms or buckets in their hands. He said mournfully: — "Going — or gone. Can't you see I'm a dying man? I know it!" Mr. Baker was disgusted. — "Then why the devil did you ship aboard here?" — "I must live till I die — mustn't I?" he replied. The grins became audible. — "Go off the deck — get out of my sight," said Mr. Baker. He was nonplussed. It was a unique experience. James Wait, obedient, dropped his broom, and walked slowly forward. A burst of laughter followed him. It was too funny. All hands laughed.... They laughed!... Alas!

He became the tormentor of all our moments; he was worse than a nightmare. You couldn't see that there was anything wrong with him: a nigger does not show. He was not very fat — certainly — but then he was no leaner than other niggers we had known. He coughed often, but the most prejudiced person could perceive that, mostly, he coughed when it suited his purpose. He wouldn't, or couldn't, do his work — and he wouldn't lie-up. One day he would skip aloft with the best of them, and next time we would be obliged to risk our lives to get his limp body down. He was reported, he was examined; he was remonstrated with, threatened, cajoled, lectured. He was called into the cabin to interview the captain. There were wild rumours. It was said he had cheeked the old man; it was said he had frightened him. Charley maintained that the "skipper, weepin', 'as giv' 'im 'is blessin' an' a pot of jam." Knowles had it from the steward that the unspeakable Jimmy had been reeling against the cabin furniture; that he had groaned; that he had complained of general brutality and disbelief; and had ended by coughing all over the old man's meteorological journals which were then spread on the table. At any rate, Wait returned forward supported by the steward, who, in a pained and shocked voice, entreated us: — "Here! Catch hold of him, one of you. He is to lie-up." Jimmy drank a tin mugful of coffee, and, after bullying first one and then another, went to bed. He remained there most of the time, but when it suited him would come on deck and appear amongst us. He was scornful and brooding; he looked ahead upon the sea, and no one could tell what was the meaning of that black man sitting apart in a meditative attitude and as motionless as a carving.

He refused steadily all medicine; he threw sago and cornflour overboard till the steward got tired of bringing it to him. He asked for paregoric. They sent him a big bottle; enough to poison a wilderness of babies. He kept it between his mattress and the deal lining of the ship's side; and nobody ever saw him take a dose. Donkin abused him to his face, jeered at him while he gasped; and the same day Wait would lend him a warm jersey. Once Donkin reviled him for half an hour; reproached him with the extra work his malingering gave to the watch; and ended by calling him "a black-faced swine." Under the spell of our accursed perversity we were horror-struck. But Jimmy positively seemed to revel in that abuse. It made him look cheerful — and Donkin had a pair of old sea boots thrown at him. "Here, you East-end trash," boomed Wait, "you may have that."

At last Mr. Baker had to tell the captain that James Wait was disturbing the peace of the ship. "Knock discipline on the head — he will, Ough," grunted Mr. Baker. As a matter of fact, the starboard watch came as near as possible to refusing duty, when ordered one morning by the boatswain to wash out their forecastle. It appears Jimmy objected to a wet floor — and that morning we were in a compassionate mood. We thought the boatswain a brute, and, practically, told him so. Only Mr. Baker's delicate tact prevented an all-fired row: he refused to take us seriously. He came bustling forward, and called us many unpolite names but in such a hearty and seaman-like manner that we began to feel ashamed of ourselves. In truth, we thought him much too good a sailor to annoy him willingly: and after all Jimmy might have been a fraud — probably was! The forecastle got a clean up that morning; but in the afternoon a sick-bay was fitted up in the deck-house. It was a nice little cabin opening on deck, and with two berths. Jimmy's belongings were transported there, and then — notwithstanding his protests — Jimmy himself. He said he couldn't walk. Four men carried him on a blanket. He complained that he would have to die there alone, like a dog. We grieved for him, and were delighted to have him removed from the forecastle. We attended him as before. The galley was next door, and the cook looked in many times a day. Wait became a little more cheerful. Knowles affirmed having heard him laugh to himself in peals one day. Others had seen him walking about on deck at night. His little place, with the door ajar on a long hook, was always full of tobacco smoke. We spoke through the crack cheerfully, sometimes abusively, as we passed by, intent on our work. He fascinated us. He would never let doubt die. He over-shadowed the ship. Invulnerable in his promise of speedy corruption he trampled on our selfrespect, he demonstrated to us daily our want of moral courage; he tainted our lives. Had we been a miserable gang of wretched immortals, unhallowed alike by hope and fear, he could not have lorded it over us with a more pitiless assertion of his sublime privilege.

CHAPTER THREE

MEANTIME the *Narcissus*, with square yards, ran out of the fair monsoon. She drifted slowly, swinging round and round the compass, through a few days of baffling light airs. Under the patter of short warm showers, grumbling men whirled the heavy yards from side to side; they caught hold of the soaked ropes with groans and sighs, while their officers, sulky and dripping with rain water, unceasingly ordered them about in wearied voices. During the short respites they looked with disgust into the smarting palms of their stiff hands, and asked one another bitterly: — "Who would be a sailor if he could be a farmer?" All the tempers were spoilt, and no man cared what he said. One black night, when the watch, panting in the heat and half-drowned with the rain, had been through four mortal hours hunted from brace to brace, Belfast declared that he would "chuck the sea for ever and go in a steamer." This was excessive, no doubt. Captain Allistoun, with great self-control, would mutter sadly to Mr. Baker: — "It is not so bad — not so bad," when he had managed to shove, and dodge, and manœuvre his smart ship through sixty miles in twenty-four hours. From the doorstep of the little cabin, Jimmy, chin in hand, watched our distasteful labours with insolent and melancholy eyes. We spoke to him gently — and out of his sight exchanged sour smiles.

Then, again, with a fair wind and under a clear sky, the ship went on piling up the South Latitude. She passed outside Madagascar and Mauritius without a glimpse of the land. Extra lashings were put on the spare spars. Hatches were looked to. The steward in his leisure moments and with a worried air tried to fit washboards to the cabin doors. Stout canvas was bent with care. Anxious eyes looked to the westward, towards the cape of storms. The ship began to dip into a southwest swell, and the softly luminous sky of low latitudes took on a harder sheen from day to day above our heads: it arched high above the ship vibrating and pale, like an immense dome of steel, resonant with the deep voice of freshening gales. The sunshine gleamed cold on the white curls of black waves. Before the strong breath of westerly squalls the ship, with reduced sail, lay slowly over, obstinate and yielding. She drove to and fro in the unceasing endeavour to fight her way through the invisible violence of the winds: she pitched headlong into dark smooth hollows; she struggled upwards over the snowy ridges of great running seas; she rolled, restless, from side to side, like a thing in pain. Enduring and valiant, she answered to the call of men; and her slim spars waving for ever in abrupt semicircles, seemed to beckon in vain for help towards the stormy sky.

It was a bad winter off the Cape that year. The relieved helmsmen came off flapping their arms, or ran stamping hard and blowing into swollen, red fingers. The watch on deck dodged the sting of cold sprays or, crouching in sheltered corners, watched dismally the high and merciless seas boarding the ship time after time in unappeasable fury. Water tumbled in cataracts over the forecastle doors. You had to dash through a waterfall to get into your damp bed. The men turned in wet and turned out stiff to face the redeeming and ruthless exactions of their glorious and obscure fate. Far aft, and peering watchfully to windward, the officers could be seen through the mist of squalls. They stood by the weather-rail, holding on grimly, straight and glistening in their long coats; and in the disordered plunges of the hard-driven ship, they appeared high up, attentive, tossing violently above the grey line of a clouded horizon in motionless attitudes.

They watched the weather and the ship as men on shore watch the momentous chances of fortune. Captain Allistoun never left the deck, as though he had been part of the ship's fittings. Now and then the steward, shivering, but always in shirt sleeves, would struggle towards him with some hot coffee, half of which the gale blew out of the cup before it reached the master's lips. He drank what was left gravely in one long gulp, while heavy sprays pattered loudly on his oilskin coat, the seas swishing broke about his high boots; and he never took his eyes off the ship. He kept his gaze riveted upon her as a loving man watches the unselfish toil of a delicate woman upon the slender thread of whose existence is hung the whole meaning and joy of the world. We all watched her. She was beautiful and had a weakness. We loved her no less for that. We admired her qualities aloud, we boasted of them to one another, as though they had been our own, and the conscious- ness of her only fault we kept buried in the silence of our profound affection. She was born in the thundering peal of hammers beating upon iron, in black eddies of smoke, under a grey sky, on the banks of the Clyde. The clamor- ous and sombre stream gives birth to things of beauty that float away into the sunshine of the world to be loved by men. The *Narcissus* was one of that perfect brood. Less perfect than many perhaps, but she was ours, and, consequently, incomparable. We were proud of her. In Bombay, ignorant landlubbers alluded to her as that "pretty grey ship." Pretty! A scurvy meed of commendation! We knew she was the most magnificent sea-boat ever launched. We tried to forget that, like many good sea-boats, she was at times rather crank. She was exacting. She wanted care in loading and handling, and no one knew exactly how much care would be enough. Such are the imperfections of mere men! The ship knew, and sometimes would correct the presumptuous human ignorance by the wholesome discipline of fear. We had heard ominous stories about past voyages. The cook (technically a seaman, but in reality no sailor) — the cook, when un- strung by some misfortune, such as the rolling over of a saucepan, would mutter gloomily while he wiped the floor: — "There! Look at what she has done! Some voy'ge she will drown all hands! You'll see if she won't." To which the steward, snatching in the galley a moment to draw breath in the hurry of his worried life, would remark philosophically: — "Those that see won't tell, anyhow. I don't want to see it." We derided those fears. Our hearts went out to the old man when he pressed her hard so as to make her hold her own, hold to every inch gained to windward; when he made her, under reefed sails, leap obliquely at enormous waves. The men, knitted together aft into a ready group by the first sharp order of an officer coming to take charge of the deck in bad weather: — "Keep handy the watch," stood admiring her valiance. Their eyes blinked in the wind; their dark faces were wet with drops of water more salt and bitter than human tears; beards and moustaches, soaked, hung straight and dripping like fine seaweed. They were fantastically misshapen; in high boots, in hats like helmets, and swaying clumsily, stiff and bulky in glistening oilskins, they resembled men strangely equipped for some fabulous adventure. Whenever she rose easily to a towering green sea, elbows dug ribs, faces brightened, lips murmured: — "Didn't she do it cleverly," and all the heads turning like one watched with sardonic grins the foiled wave go roaring to leeward, white with the foam of a monstrous rage. But when she had not been quick enough and, struck heavily, lay over trembling under the blow, we clutched at ropes, and looking up at the narrow bands of drenched and strained sails waving desperately aloft, we thought in our hearts: — "No wonder. Poor thing!"

The thirty-second day out of Bombay began inauspiciously. In the morning a sea smashed one of the galley doors. We dashed in through lots of steam and found the cook very wet and indignant with the ship: — "She's getting worse every day. She's trying to drown me in front of my own stove!" He was very angry. We pacified him, and the carpenter, though washed away twice from there, managed to repair the door. Through that accident our dinner was not ready till late, but it didn't matter in the end because Knowles, who went to fetch it, got knocked down by a sea and the dinner went over the side. Captain Allistoun, looking more hard and thin-lipped than ever, hung on to full topsails and foresail, and would not notice that the ship, asked to do too much, appeared to lose heart altogether for the first time since we knew her. She refused to rise, and bored her way sullenly through the seas. Twice running, as though she had been blind or weary of life, she put her nose deliberately into a big wave and swept the decks from end to end. As the boatswain observed with marked annoyance, while we were splashing about in a body to try and save a worthless wash-tub: — "Every blooming thing in the ship is going overboard this afternoon." Venerable Singleton broke his habitual silence and said with a glance aloft: — "The old man's in a temper with the weather, but it's no good bein' angry with the winds of heaven." Jimmy had shut his door, of course. We knew he was dry and comfortable within his little cabin, and in our absurd way were pleased one moment, exasperated the next, by that certitude. Donkin skulked shamelessly, uneasy and miserable. He grumbled: — "I'm perishin' with cold outside in bloomin' wet rags, an' that 'ere black sojer sits dry on a blamed chest full of bloomin' clothes; blank his black soul!" We took no notice of him; we hardly gave a thought to Jimmy and his bosom friend. There was no leisure for idle probing of hearts. Sails blew adrift. Things broke loose. Cold and wet, we were washed about the deck while trying to repair damages. The ship tossed about, shaken furiously, like a toy in the hand of a lunatic. Just at sunset there was a rush to shorten sail before the menace of a sombre hail cloud. The hard gust of wind came brutal like the blow of a fist. The ship relieved of her canvas in time received it pluckily: she yielded reluctantly to the violent onset; then, coming up with a stately and irresistible motion, brought her spars to windward in the teeth of the screeching squall. Out of the abysmal darkness of the black cloud overhead white hail streamed on her, rattled on the rigging, leaped in handfuls off the yards, rebounded on the deck — round and gleaming in the murky turmoil like a shower of pearls. It passed away. For a moment a livid sun shot horizontally the last rays of sinister light between the hills of steep, rolling waves. Then a wild night rushed in — stamped out in a great howl that dismal remnant of a stormy day.

There was no sleep on board that night. Most seamen remember in their life one or two such nights of a culminating gale. Nothing seems left of the whole universe but darkness, clamour, fury — and the ship. And like the last vestige of a shattered creation she drifts, bearing an anguished remnant of sinful mankind, through the distress, tumult, and pain of an avenging terror. No one slept in the forecastle. The tin oil-lamp suspended on a long string, smoking, described wide circles; wet clothing made dark heaps on the glistening floor; a thin layer of water rushed to and fro. In the bed-places men lay booted, resting on elbows and with open eyes. Hung-up suits of oilskin swung out and in, lively and disquieting like reckless ghosts of decapitated seamen dancing in a tempest. No one spoke and all listened. Outside the night moaned and sobbed to the accompaniment of a continuous loud tremor as of innumerable drums beating far off. Shrieks passed through the air. Tremendous dull blows made the ship tremble while she rolled under the weight of the seas toppling on her deck. At times she soared up swiftly as if to leave this earth for ever, then during interminable moments fell through a void with all the hearts on board of her standing still, till a frightful shock, expected and sudden, started them off again with a big thump. After every dislocating jerk of the ship, Wamibo, stretched full length, his face on the pillow, groaned slightly with the pain of his tormented universe. Now and then, for the fraction of an intolerable second, the ship, in the fiercer burst of a terrible uproar, remained on her side, vibrating and still, with a stillness more appalling than the wildest motion. Then upon all those prone bodies a stir would pass, a shiver of suspense. A man would protrude his anxious head and a pair of eyes glistened in the sway of light glaring wildly. Some moved their legs a little as if making ready to jump out. But several, motionless on their backs and with one hand gripping hard the edge of the bunk, smoked nervously with quick puffs, staring up-wards; immobilised in a great craving for peace.

At midnight, orders were given to furl the fore and mizen topsails. With immense efforts men crawled aloft through a merciless buffeting, saved the canvas and crawled down almost exhausted, to bear in panting silence the cruel battering of the seas. Perhaps for the first time in the history of the merchant service the watch, told to go below, did not leave the deck, as if compelled to remain there by the fascination of a venomous violence. At every heavy gust men, huddled together, whispered to one another:— "It can blow no harder"— and presently the gale would give them the lie with a piercing shriek, and drive their breath back into their throats. A fierce squall seemed to burst asunder the thick mass of sooty vapours; and above the wrack of torn clouds glimpses could be caught of the high moon rushing backwards with frightful speed over the sky, right into the wind's eye. Many hung their heads, muttering that it "turned their inwards out" to look at it. Soon the clouds closed up and the world again became a raging, blind dark-ness that howled, flinging at the lonely ship salt sprays and sleet.

About half-past seven the pitchy obscurity round us turned a ghastly grey, and we knew that the sun had risen. This unnatural and threatening daylight, in which we could see one another's wild eyes and drawn faces, was only an added tax on our endurance. The horizon seemed to have come on all sides within arm's length of the ship. Into that narrowed circle furious seas leaped in, struck, and leaped out. A rain of salt, heavy drops flew aslant like mist. The main-topsail had to be goose-winged, and with stolid resig-nation everyone prepared to go aloft once more; but the officers yelled, pushed back, and at last we understood that no more men would be allowed to go on the yard than were absolutely necessary for the work. As at any moment the masts were likely to be jumped out or blown overboard, we concluded that the captain didn't want to see all his crowd go over the side at once. That was reasonable. The watch then on duty, led by Mr. Creighton, began to struggle up the rigging. The wind flattened them against the rat-lines; then, easing a little, would let them ascend a couple of steps; and again, with a sudden gust, pin all up the shrouds the whole crawling line in attitudes of crucifixion. The other watch plunged down on the main deck to haul up the sail. Men's heads bobbed up as the water flung them irresistibly from side to side. Mr. Baker grunted encouragingly in our midst, spluttering and blowing amongst the tangled ropes like an energetic porpoise. Favoured by an ominous and untrustworthy lull, the work was done without anyone being lost either off the deck or from the yard. For the moment the gale seemed to take off, and the ship, as if grateful for our efforts, plucked up heart and made better weather of it.

At eight the men off duty, watching their chance, ran forward over the flooded deck to get some rest. The other half of the crew remained aft for their turn of "seeing her through her trouble," as they expressed it. The two mates urged the master to go below. Mr. Baker grunted in his ear: — "Ough! surely now... Ough!... confidence in us... nothing more to do... she must lay it out or go. Ough! Ough!" Tall young Mr. Creighton smiled down at him cheerfully: — "...She's as right as a trivet! Take a spell, sir." He looked at them stonily with bloodshot, sleepless eyes. The rims of his eyelids were scarlet, and he moved his jaws unceasingly with a slow effort, as though he had been masticating a lump of india-rubber. He shook his head. He repeated: — "Never mind me. I must see it out — I must see it out," but he consented to sit down for a moment on the skylight, with his hard face turned unflinchingly to windward. The sea spat at it — and stoical, it streamed with water as though he had been weeping. On the weather side of the poop the watch, hanging on to the mizen rigging and to one another, tried to exchange encouraging words. Singleton, at the wheel, yelled out: — "Look out for yourselves!" His voice reached them in a warning whisper. They were startled.

A big, foaming sea came out of the mist; it made for the ship, roaring wildly, and in its rush it looked as mischievous and discomposing as a madman with an axe. One or two, shouting, scrambled up the rigging; most, with a convulsive catch of the breath, held on where they stood. Singleton dug his knees under the wheel-box, and carefully eased the helm to the headlong pitch of the ship, but without taking his eyes off the coming wave. It towered close-to and high, like a wall of green glass topped with snow. The ship rose to it as though she had soared on wings, and for a moment rested poised upon the foaming crest as if she had been a great sea-bird. Before we could draw breath a heavy gust struck her, another roller took her unfairly under the weather bow, she gave a toppling lurch, and filled her decks. Captain Allistoun leaped up, and fell; Archie rolled over him, screaming: — "She will rise!" She gave another lurch to leeward; the lower deadeyes dipped heavily; the men's feet flew from under them, and they hung kicking above the slanting poop. They could see the ship putting her side in the water, and shouted all together: — "She's going!" Forward the forecastle doors flew open, and the watch below were seen leaping out one after another, throwing their arms up; and, falling on hands and knees, scrambled aft on all fours along the high side of the deck, sloping more than the roof of a house. From leeward the seas rose, pursuing them; they looked wretched in a hopeless struggle, like vermin fleeing before a flood; they fought up the weather ladder of the poop one after another, half naked and staring wildly; and as soon as they got up they shot to leeward in clusters, with closed eyes, till they brought up heavily with their ribs against the iron stanchions of the rail; then, groaning, they rolled in a confused mass. The immense volume of water thrown forward by the last scend of the ship had burst the lee door of the forecastle. They could see their chests, pillows, blankets, clothing, come out floating upon the sea. While they struggled back to windward they looked in dismay. The straw beds swam high, the blankets, spread out, undulated; while the chests, waterlogged and with a heavy list, pitched heavily like dismasted hulks, before they sank; Archie's big coat passed with outspread arms, resembling a drowned seaman floating with his head under water. Men were slipping down while trying to dig their fingers into the planks; others, jammed in corners, rolled enormous eyes. They all yelled unceasingly: — "The masts! Cut! Cut!..." A black squall howled low over the ship, that lay on her side with the weather yard-arms pointing to the clouds; while the tall masts, inclined nearly to the horizon, seemed to be of an immeasurable length. The carpenter let go his hold, rolled against the skylight, and began to crawl to the cabin entrance, where a big axe was kept ready for just such an emergency. At that moment the topsail sheet parted, the end of the heavy chain racketed aloft, and sparks of red fire steamed down through the flying sprays. The sail flapped once with a jerk that seemed to tear our hearts out through our teeth, and instantly changed into a bunch of fluttering narrow ribbons that tied themselves into knots and became quiet along the yard. Captain Allistoun struggled, managed to stand up with his face near the deck, upon which men swung on the ends of ropes, like nest robbers upon a cliff. One of his feet was on somebody's chest; his face was purple; his lips moved. He yelled also; he yelled, bending down: — "No! No!" Mr. Baker, one leg over the binnacle-stand, roared out: — "Did you say no? Not cut?" He shook his head madly. "No! No!" Between his legs the crawling carpenter heard, collapsed at once, and lay full length in the angle of the skylight. Voices took up the shout — "No! No!" Then all became still. They waited for the ship to turn over altogether, and shake them out into the sea; and upon the terrific noise of wind and sea not a murmur of remonstrance came out from those men, who each would have given ever so many years of life to see "them damned sticks go overboard!" They all believed it their only chance; but a little hard-faced man shook his grey head and shouted "No!" without giving them as much as a glance. They were silent, and gasped. They gripped rails, they had wound ropes'-ends under their arms; they clutched ringbolts, they crawled in heaps where there was foothold; they held on with both arms, hooked themselves to anything to windward with elbows, with chins, almost with their teeth: and some, unable to crawl away from where they had been flung, felt the sea leap up, striking against their backs as they struggled upwards. Singleton had stuck to the wheel. His hair flew out in the wind; the gale seemed to take its life-long adversary by the beard and shake his old head. He wouldn't let go, and, with his knees forced between the spokes, flew up and down like a man on a bough. As Death appeared unready, they began to look about. Donkin, caught by one foot in a loop of some rope, hung, head down, below us, and yelled, with his face to the deck: — "Cut! Cut!" Two men lowered themselves cautiously to him; others hauled on the rope. They caught him up, shoved him into a safer place, held him. He shouted curses at the master, shook his fist at him with horrible blasphemies, called upon us in filthy words to "Cut! Don't mind that murdering fool! Cut, some of you!" One of his rescuers struck him a back-handed blow over the mouth; his head banged on the deck, and he became suddenly very quiet, with a white face, breathing hard, and with a few drops of blood trickling from his cut lip. On the lee side another man could be seen stretched out as if stunned; only the washboard prevented him from going over the side. It was the steward. We had to sling him up like a bale, for he was paralysed with fright. He had rushed up out of the pantry when he felt the ship go over, and had rolled down helplessly, clutching a china mug. It was not broken. With difficulty we tore it away from him, and when he saw it in our hands he was amazed. "Where did you get that thing?" he kept on asking us in a trembling voice. His shirt was blown to shreds; the ripped sleeves flapped like wings. Two men made him fast, and, doubled over the rope that held him, he resembled a bundle of wet rags. Mr. Baker crawled along the line of men, asking: — "Are you all there?" and looking them over. Some blinked vacantly, others shook convulsively; Wamibo's head hung over his breast; and in painful attitudes, cut by lashings, exhausted with clutching, screwed up in corners, they breathed heavily. Their lips twitched, and at every sickening heave of the overturned ship they opened them wide as if to shout. The cook, embracing a wooden stanchion, unconsciously repeated a prayer. In every short interval of the fiendish noises around he could be heard there, without cap or slippers, imploring in that storm the Master of our lives not to lead him into temptation. Soon he also became silent. In all that crowd of cold and hungry men, waiting wearily for a violent death, not a voice was heard; they were mute, and in sombre thoughtfulness listened to the horrible imprecations of the gale.

Hours passed. They were sheltered by the heavy inclination of the ship from the wind that rushed in one long unbroken moan above their heads, but cold rain showers fell at times into the uneasy calm of their refuge. Under the torment of that new infliction a pair of shoulders would writhe a little. Teeth chattered. The sky was clearing, and bright sunshine gleamed over the ship. After every burst of battering seas, vivid and fleeting rainbows arched over the drifting hull in the flick of sprays. The gale was ending in a clear blow, which gleamed and cut like a knife. Between two bearded shellbacks Charley, fastened with somebody's long muffler to a deck ring-bolt, wept quietly, with rare tears wrung out by bewilderment, cold, hunger, and general misery. One of his neighbours punched him in the ribs asking roughly: — "What's the matter with your cheek? In fine weather there's no holding you, youngster." Turning about with prudence he worked himself out of his coat and threw it over the boy. The other man closed up, muttering: — "'Twill make a bloomin' man of you, sonny." They flung their arms over and pressed against him. Charley drew his feet up and his eyelids dropped. Sighs were heard, as men, perceiving that they were not to be "drowned in a hurry," tried easier positions. Mr. Creighton, who had hurt his leg, lay amongst us with compressed lips. Some fellows belonging to his watch set about securing him better. Without a word or a glance he lifted his arms one after another to facilitate the operation, and not a muscle moved in his stern, young face. They asked him with solicitude: — "Easier now, sir?" He answered with a curt: — "That'll do." He was a hard young officer, but many of his watch used to say they liked him well enough because he had "such a gentlemanly way of damning us up and down the deck." Others unable to discern such fine shades of refinement, respected him for his smartness. For the first time since the ship had gone on her beam ends Captain Allistoun gave a short glance down at his men. He was almost upright — one foot against the side of the skylight, one knee on the deck; and with the end of the vang round his waist swung back and forth with his gaze fixed ahead, watchful, like a man looking out for a sign. Before his eyes the ship, with half her deck below water, rose and fell on heavy seas that rushed from under her flashing in the cold sunshine. We began to think she was wonderfully buoyant — considering. Confident voices were heard shouting: — "She'll do, boys!" Belfast exclaimed with fervour: — "I would giv' a month's pay for a draw at a pipe!" One or two, passing dry tongues on their salt lips, muttered something about a "drink of water." The cook, as if inspired, scrambled up with his breast against the poop water-cask and looked in. There was a little at the bottom. He yelled, waving his arms, and two men began to crawl backwards and forwards with the mug. We had a good mouthful all round. The master shook his head impatiently, refusing. When it came to Charley one of his neighbours shouted: — "That bloomin' boy's asleep." He slept as though he had been dosed with narcotics. They let him be. Singleton held to the wheel with one hand while he drank, bending down to shelter his lips from the wind. Wamibo had to be poked and yelled at before he saw the mug held before his eyes. Knowles said sagaciously: — "It's better'n a tot o' rum." Mr. Baker grunted: — "Thank ye." Mr. Creighton drank and nodded. Donkin gulped greedily, glaring over the rim. Belfast made us laugh when with grimacing mouth he shouted: — "Pass it this way. We're all taytottlers here." The master, presented with the mug again by a crouching man, who screamed up at him: — "We all had a drink, captain," groped for it without ceasing to look ahead, and handed it back stiffly as though he could not spare half a glance away from the ship. Faces brightened. We shouted to the cook: — "Well done, doctor!" He sat to leeward, propped by the water-cask and yelled back abundantly, but the seas were breaking in thunder just then, and we only caught snatches that sounded like: "Providence" and "born again." He was at his old game of preaching. We made friendly but derisive gestures at him, and from below he lifted one arm, holding on with the other, moved his lips; he beamed up to us, straining his voice — earnest, and ducking his head before the sprays.

Suddenly someone cried: — "Where's Jimmy?" and we were appalled once more. On the end of the row the boatswain shouted hoarsely: — "Has anyone seed him come out?" Voices exclaimed dismally: — "Drowned — is he?... No! In his cabin!... Good Lord!... Caught like a bloomin' rat in a trap.... Couldn't open his door... Aye! She went over too quick and the water jammed it... Poor beggar!... No help for 'im.... Let's go and see..." "Damn him, who could go?" screamed Donkin. — "Nobody expects you to," growled the man next to him: "you're only a thing." — "Is there half a chance to get at 'im?" inquired two or three men together. Belfast untied himself with blind impetuosity, and all at once shot down to leeward quicker than a flash of lightning. We shouted all together with dismay; but with his legs overboard he held and yelled for a rope. In our extremity nothing could be terrible; so we judged him funny kicking there, and with his scared face. Someone began to laugh, and, as if hysterically infected with scream- ing merriment, all those haggard men went off laughing, wild-eyed, like a lot of maniacs tied up on a wall. Mr. Baker swung off the binnacle-stand and tendered him one leg. He scrambled up rather scared, and consigning us with abominable words to the "divvle." "You are.... Ough! You're a foul-mouthed beggar, Craik," grunted Mr. Baker. He answered, stutter- ing with indignation: — "Look at 'em, sorr. The bloomin' dirty images! laughing at a chum going overboard. Call themselves men, too." But from the break of the poop the boatswain called out: — "Come along," and Bel- fast crawled away in a hurry to join him. The five men, poised and gazing over the edge of the poop, looked for the best way to get forward. They seemed to hesitate. The others, twisting in their lashings, turning painfully, stared with open lips. Captain Allistoun saw nothing; he seemed with his eyes to hold the ship up in a superhuman concentration of effort. The wind screamed loud in sunshine; columns of spray rose straight up; and in the glitter of rainbows bursting over the trembling hull the men went over cautiously, disappearing from sight with deliberate movements.

They went swinging from belaying pin to cleat above the seas that beat the half-submerged deck. Their toes scraped the planks. Lumps of green cold water toppled over the bulwark and on their heads. They hung for a moment on strained arms, with the breath knocked out of them, and with closed eyes — then, letting go with one hand, balanced with lolling heads, trying to grab some rope or stanchion further forward. The long-armed and athletic boatswain swung quickly, gripping things with a fist hard as iron, and remembering suddenly snatches of the last letter from his "old woman." Little Belfast scrambled in a rage spluttering "cursed nigger." Wamibo's tongue hung out with excitement; and Archie, intrepid and calm, watched his chance to move with intelligent coolness.

When above the side of the house, they let go one after another, and falling heavily, sprawled, pressing their palms to the smooth teak wood. Round them the backwash of waves seethed white and hissing. All the doors had become trap-doors, of course. The first was the galley door. The galley extended from side to side, and they could hear the sea splashing with hollow noises in there. The next door was that of the carpenter's shop. They lifted it, and looked down. The room seemed to have been devastated by an earthquake. Everything in it had tumbled on the bulkhead facing the door, and on the other side of that bulkhead there was Jimmy dead or alive. The bench, a half-finished meat-safe, saws, chisels, wire rods, axes, crowbars, lay in a heap besprinkled with loose nails. A sharp adze stuck up with a shining edge that gleamed dangerously down there like a wicked smile. The men clung to one another, peering. A sickening, sly lurch of the ship nearly sent them overboard in a body. Belfast howled "Here goes!" and leaped down. Archie followed cannily, catching at shelves that gave way with him, and eased himself in a great crash of ripped wood. There was hardly room for three men to move. And in the sunshiny blue square of the door, the boatswain's face, bearded and dark, Wamibo's face, wild and pale, hung over — watching.

Together they shouted: "Jimmy! Jim!" From above the boatswain contributed a deep growl: "You... Wait!" In a pause, Belfast entreated: "Jimmy, darlin', are ye aloive?" The boatswain said: "Again! All together, boys!" All yelled excitedly. Wamibo made noises resembling loud barks. Belfast drummed on the side of the bulkhead with a piece of iron. All ceased suddenly. The sound of screaming and hammering went on thin and distinct — like a solo after a chorus. He was alive. He was screaming and knocking below us with the hurry of a man prematurely shut up in a coffin. We went to work. We attacked with desperation the abominable heap of things heavy, of things sharp, of things clumsy to handle. The boatswain crawled away to find somewhere a flying end of a rope; and Wamibo, held back by shouts: — "Don't jump!... Don't come in here, muddlehead!" — remained glaring above us — all shining eyes, gleaming fangs, tumbled hair; resembling an amazed and half-witted fiend gloating over the extraordinary agitation of the damned. The boatswain adjured us to "bear a hand," and a rope descended. We made things fast to it and they went up spinning, never to be seen by man again. A rage to fling things overboard possessed us. We worked fiercely, cutting our hands and speaking brutally to one another. Jimmy kept up a distracting row; he screamed piercingly, without drawing breath, like a tortured woman; he banged with hands and feet. The agony of his fear wrung our hearts so terribly that we longed to abandon him, to get out of that place deep as a well and swaying like a tree, to get out of his hearing, back on the poop where we could wait passively for death in incomparable repose. We shouted to him to "shut up, for God's sake." He redoubled his cries. He must have fancied we could not hear him. Probably he heard his own clamour but faintly. We could picture him crouching on the edge of the upper berth, letting out with both fists at the wood, in the dark, and with his mouth wide open for that unceasing cry. Those were loathsome moments. A cloud driving across the sun would darken the doorway menacingly. Every movement of the ship was pain. We scrambled about with no room to breathe, and felt frightfully sick. The boatswain yelled down at us: — "Bear a hand! Bear a hand! We two will be washed away from here directly if you ain't quick!" Three times a sea leaped over the high side and flung bucketfuls of water on our heads. Then Jimmy, startled by the shock, would stop his noise for a moment — waiting for the ship to sink, perhaps — and began again, distressingly loud, as if invigorated by the gust of fear. At the bottom the nails lay in a layer several inches thick. It was ghastly. Every nail in the world, not driven in firmly somewhere, seemed to have found its way into that carpenter's shop. There they were, of all kinds, the remnants of stores from seven voyages. Tin-tacks, copper tacks (sharp as needles); pump nails with big heads, like tiny iron mushrooms; nails without any heads (horrible); French nails polished and slim. They lay in a solid mass more inabordable than a hedgehog. We hesitated, yearning for a shovel, while Jimmy below us yelled as though he had been flayed. Groaning, we dug our fingers in, and very much hurt, shook our hands, scattering nails and drops of blood. We passed up our hats full of assorted nails to the boatswain, who, as if performing a mysterious and appeasing rite, cast them wide upon a raging sea.

We got to the bulkhead at last. Those were stout planks. She was a ship, well finished in every detail — the *Narcissus* was. They were the stoutest planks ever put into a ships' bulkhead — we thought — and then we perceived that, in our hurry, we had sent all the tools overboard. Absurd little Belfast wanted to break it down with his own weight, and with both feet leaped straight up like a springbok, cursing the Clyde shipwrights for not scamping their work. Incidentally he reviled all North Britain, the rest of the earth, the sea — and all his companions. He swore, as he alighted heavily on his heels, that he would never, never any more associate with any fool that "hadn't savee enough to know his knee from his elbow." He managed by his thumping to scare the last remnant of wits out of Jimmy. We could hear the object of our exasperated solicitude darting to and fro under the planks. He had cracked his voice at last, and could only squeak miserably. His back or else his head rubbed the planks, now here, now there, in a puzzling manner. He squeaked as he dodged the invisible blows. It was more heartrending even than his yells. Suddenly Archie produced a crowbar. He had kept it back; also a small hatchet. We howled with satisfaction. He struck a mighty blow and small chips flew at our eyes. The boatswain above shouted: — "Look out! Look out there. Don't kill the man. Easy does it!" Wamibo, maddened with excitement, hung head down and insanely urged us: — "Hoo! Strook 'im! Hoo! Hoo!" We were afraid he would fall in and kill one of us and, hurriedly, we entreated the boatswain to "shove the blamed Finn overboard." Then, all together, we yelled down at the planks: — "Stand from under! Get forward," and listened. We only heard the deep hum and moan of the wind above us, the mingled roar and hiss of the seas. The ship, as if overcome with despair, wallowed lifelessly, and our heads swam with that unnatural motion. Belfast clamoured: — "For the love of God, Jimmy, where are ye?... Knock! Jimmy darlint!... Knock! You bloody black beast! Knock!" He was as quiet as a dead man inside a grave; and, like men standing above a grave, we were on the verge of tears — but with vexation, the strain, the fatigue; with the great longing to be done with it, to get away, and lie down to rest somewhere where we could see our danger and breathe. Archie shouted: — "Gi'e me room!" We crouched behind him, guarding our heads, and he struck time after time in the joint of planks. They cracked. Suddenly the crowbar went halfway in through a splintered oblong hole. It must have missed Jimmy's head by less than an inch. Archie withdrew it quickly, and that infamous nigger rushed at the hole, put his lips to it, and whispered "Help" in an almost extinct voice; he pressed his head to it, trying madly to get out through that opening one inch wide and three inches long. In our disturbed state we were absolutely paralysed by his incredible action. It seemed impossible to drive him away. Even Archie at last lost his composure. "If ye don't clear oot I'll drive the crowbar thro' your head," he shouted in a determined voice. He meant what he said, and his earnestness seemed to make an impression on Jimmy. He disappeared suddenly, and we set to prising and tearing at the planks with the eagerness of men trying to get at a mortal enemy, and spurred by the desire to tear him limb from limb. The wood split, cracked, gave way. Belfast plunged in head and shoulders and groped viciously. "I've got 'im! Got 'im," he shouted. "Oh! There!... He's gone; I've got 'im!... Pull at my legs!... Pull!" Wamibo hooted unceasingly. The boatswain shouted directions: — "Catch hold of his hair, Belfast; pull straight up, you two!... Pull fair!" We pulled fair. We pulled Belfast out with a jerk, and dropped him with disgust. In a sitting posture, purple-faced, he sobbed despairingly: — "How can I hold on to 'is blooming short wool?" Suddenly Jimmy's head and shoulders appeared. He stuck halfway, and with rolling eyes foamed at our feet. We flew at him with brutal impatience, we tore the shirt off his back, we tugged at his ears, we panted over him; and all at once he came away in our hands as though somebody had let go his legs. With the same movement, without a pause, we swung him up. His breath whistled, he kicked our upturned faces, he grasped two pairs of arms above his head, and he squirmed up with such precipitation that he seemed positively to escape from our hands like a bladder full of gas. Steaming with perspiration, we swarmed up the rope, and, coming into the blast of cold wind, gasped like men plunged into icy water. With burning faces we shivered to the very marrow of our bones. Never before had the gale seemed to us more furious, the sea more mad, the sunshine more merciless and mocking, and the position of the ship more hopeless and appalling. Every movement of her was ominous of the end of her agony and of the beginning of ours. We staggered away from the door, and, alarmed by a sudden roll, fell down in a bunch. It appeared to us that the side of the house was more smooth than glass and more slippery than ice. There was nothing to hang on to but a long brass hook used sometimes to keep back an open door. Wamibo held on to it and we held on to Wamibo, clutching our Jimmy. He had completely collapsed now. He did not seem to have the strength to close his hand. We stuck to him blindly in our fear. We were not afraid of Wamibo letting go (we remembered that the brute was stronger than any three men in the ship), but we were afraid of the hook giving away, and we also believed that the ship had made up her mind to turn over at last. But she didn't. A sea swept over us. The boatswain spluttered: — "Up and away. There's a lull. Away aft with you, or we will all go to the devil here." We stood up surrounding Jimmy. We begged him to hold up, to hold on, at least. He glared with his bulging eyes, mute as a fish, and with all the stiffening knocked out of him. He wouldn't stand; he wouldn't even as much as clutch at our necks; he was only a cold black skin loosely stuffed with soft cotton wool; his arms and legs swung jointless and pliable; his head rolled about; the lower lip hung down, enormous and heavy. We pressed round him, bothered and dismayed; sheltering him we swung here and there in a body; and on the very brink of eternity we tottered all together with concealing and absurd gestures, like a lot of drunken men embarrassed with a stolen corpse.

Something had to be done. We had to get him aft. A rope was tied slack under his armpits, and, reaching up at the risk of our lives, we hung him on the foresheet cleet. He emitted no sound; he looked as ridiculously lament-able as a doll that had lost half its sawdust, and we started on our perilous journey over the main deck, dragging along with care that pitiful, that limp, that hateful burden. He was not very heavy, but had he weighed a ton he could not have been more awkward to handle. We literally passed him from hand to hand. Now and then we had to hang him up on a handy belaying-pin, to draw a breath and reform the line. Had the pin broken he would have irretrievably gone into the Southern Ocean, but he had to take his chance of that; and after a little while, becoming apparently aware of it, he groaned slightly, and with a great effort whispered a few words. We listened eagerly. He was reproaching us with our carelessness in letting him run such risks: "Now, after I got myself out from there," he breathed out weakly. "There" was his cabin. And he got himself out. We had nothing to do with it apparently!... No matter.... We went on and let him take his chances, simply because we could not help it; for though at that time we hated him more than ever — more than anything under heaven — we did not want to lose him. We had so far saved him; and it had become a per-sonal matter between us and the sea. We meant to stick to him. Had we (by an incredible hypothesis) undergone similar toil and trouble for an empty cask, that cask would have become as precious to us as Jimmy was. More precious, in fact, because we would have had no reason to hate the cask. And we hated James Wait. We could not get rid of the monstrous suspicion that this astounding black-man was shamming sick, had been malingering heartlessly in the face of our toil, of our scorn, of our patience — and now was malingering in the face of our devotion — in the face of death. Our vague and imperfect morality rose with disgust at his unmanly lie. But he stuck to it manfully — amazingly. No! It couldn't be. He was at all extremity. His cantankerous temper was only the result of the provoking invincibleness of that death he felt by his side. Any man may be angry with such a masterful chum. But, then, what kind of men were we — with our thoughts! Indignation and doubt grappled within us in a scuffle that trampled upon the finest of our feelings. And we hated him because of the suspicion; we detested him because of the doubt. We could not scorn him safely — neither could we pity him without risk to our dignity. So we hated him, and passed him carefully from hand to hand. We cried, "Got him?" — "Yes. All right. Let go." And he swung from one enemy to another, showing about as much life as an old bolster would do. His eyes made two narrow white slits in the black face. The air escaped through his lips with a noise like the sound of bellows. We reached the poop ladder at last, and it being a comparatively safe place, we lay for a moment in an exhausted heap to rest a little. He began to mutter. We were always incurably anxious to hear what he had to say. This time he mumbled peevishly, "It took you some time to come. I began to think the whole smart lot of you had been washed overboard. What kept you back? Hey? Funk?" We said nothing. With sighs we started again to drag him up. The secret and ardent desire of our hearts was the desire to beat him viciously with our fists about the head; and we handled him as tenderly as though he had been made of glass....

The return on the poop was like the return of wanderers after many years amongst people marked by the desolation of time. Eyes were turned slowly in their sockets, glancing at us. Faint murmurs were heard, "Have you got 'im after all?" The well-known faces looked strange and familiar; they seemed faded and grimy; they had a mingled expression of fatigue and eagerness. They seemed to have become much thinner during our absence, as if all these men had been starving for a long time in their abandoned attitudes. The captain, with a round turn of a rope on his wrist, and kneeling on one knee, swung with a face cold and stiff; but with living eyes he was still holding the ship up, heeding no one, as if lost in the unearthly effort of that endeavour. We fastened up James Wait in a safe place. Mr. Baker scrambled along to lend a hand. Mr. Creighton, on his back, and very pale, muttered, "Well done," and gave us, Jimmy and the sky, a scornful glance, then closed his eyes slowly. Here and there a man stirred a little, but most of them remained apathetic, in cramped positions, muttering between shivers. The sun was setting. A sun enormous, unclouded and red, declining low as if bending down to look into their faces. The wind whistled across long sunbeams that, resplendent and cold, struck full on the dilated pupils of staring eyes without making them wink. The wisps of hair and the tangled beards were grey with the salt of the sea. The faces were earthy, and the dark patches under the eyes extended to the ears, smudged into the hollows of sunken cheeks. The lips were livid and thin, and when they moved it was with difficulty, as though they had been glued to the teeth. Some grinned sadly in the sunlight, shaking with cold. Others were sad and still. Charley, subdued by the sudden disclosure of the insignificance of his youth, darted fearful glances. The two smooth-faced Norwegians resembled decrepit children, staring stupidly. To leeward, on the edge of the horizon, black seas leaped up towards the glowing sun. It sank slowly, round and blazing, and the crests of waves splashed on the edge of the luminous circle. One of the Norwegians appeared to catch sight of it, and, after giving a violent start, began to speak. His voice, startling the others, made them stir. They moved their heads stiffly, or turning with difficulty, looked at him with surprise, with fear, or in grave silence. He chattered at the setting sun, nodding his head, while the big seas began to roll across the crimson disc; and over miles of turbulent waters the shadows of high waves swept with a running darkness the faces of men. A crested roller broke with a loud hissing roar, and the sun, as if put out, disappeared. The chattering voice faltered, went out together with the light. There were sighs. In the sudden lull that follows the crash of a broken sea a man said wearily, "Here's that blooming Dutchman gone off his chump." A seaman, lashed by the middle, tapped the deck with his open hand with unceasing quick flaps. In the gathering greyness of twilight a bulky form was seen rising aft, and began marching on all fours with the movements of some big cautious beast. It was Mr. Baker passing along the line of men. He grunted encouragingly over everyone, felt their fastenings. Some, with half-opened eyes, puffed like men oppressed by heat; others mechanically and in dreamy voices answered him, "Aye! aye! sir!" He went from one to another grunting, "Ough!... See her through it yet"; and unexpectedly, with loud angry outbursts, blew up Knowles for cutting off a long piece from the fall of the relieving tackle. "Ough!—— Ashamed of yourself —— Relieving tackle —— Don't you know better! —— Ough! —— Able seaman! Ough!" The lame man was crushed. He muttered, "Get som'think for a lashing for myself, sir." — "Ough! Lashing —— yourself. Are you a tinker or a sailor —— What? Ough! —— May want that tackle directly —— Ough! —— More use to the ship than your lame carcass. Ough! —— Keep it! —— Keep it, now you've done it." He crawled away slowly, muttering to himself about some men being "worse than children." It had been a comforting row. Low exclamations were heard: "Hallo... Hallo."... Those who had been painfully dozing asked with convulsive starts: "What's up?... What is it?" The answers came with unexpected cheerfulness: "The mate is going bald-headed for lame Jack about something or other." "No!"... "What 'as he done?" Someone even chuckled. It was like a whiff of hope, like a reminder of safe days. Donkin, who had been stupefied with fear, revived suddenly and began to shout: — "'Ear 'im; that's the way they tawlk to us. Vy donch 'ee 'it 'im — one ov yer? 'It 'im. 'It 'im! Comin' the mate over us. We are as good men as 'ee! We're all goin' to 'ell now. We 'ave been starved in this rotten ship, an' now we're goin' to be drowned for them black 'earted bullies! 'It 'im!" He shrieked in the deepening gloom, he blubbered and sobbed, screaming: — "'It 'im! 'It 'im!" The rage and fear of his disregarded right to live tried the steadfastness of hearts more than the menacing shadows of the night that advanced through the unceasing clamour of the gale. From aft Mr. Baker was heard: — "Is one of you men going to stop him — must I come along?" "Shut up!"... "Keep quiet!" cried various voices, exasperated, trembling with cold. — "You'll get one across the mug from me directly," said an invisible seaman, in a weary tone, "I won't let the mate have the trouble." He ceased and lay still with the silence of despair. On the black sky the stars, coming out, gleamed over an inky sea that, speckled with foam, flashed back at them the evanescent and pale light of a dazzling whiteness born from the black turmoil of the waves. Remote in the eternal calm they glittered hard and cold above the uproar of the earth; they surrounded the vanquished and tormented ship on all sides: more pitiless than the eyes of a triumphant mob, and as unapproachable as the hearts of men.

The icy south wind howled exultingly under the sombre splendour of the sky. The cold shook the men with a resistless violence as though it had tried to shake them to pieces. Short moans were swept unheard off the stiff lips. Some complained in mutters of "not feeling themselves below the waist;" while those who had closed their eyes, imagined they had a block of ice on their chests. Others, alarmed at not feeling any pain in their fingers, beat the deck feebly with their hands — obstinate and exhausted. Wamibo stared vacant and dreamy. The Scandinavians kept on a meaningless mutter through chattering teeth. The spare Scotchmen, with determined efforts, kept their lower jaws still. The West-country men lay big and stolid in an invulnerable surliness. A man yawned and swore in turns. Another breathed with a rattle in his throat. Two elderly hard-weather shellbacks, fast side by side, whispered dismally to one another about the landlady of a boarding-house in Sunderland, whom they both knew. They extolled her motherliness and her liberality; they tried to talk about the joint of beef and the big fire in the downstairs kitchen. The words dying faintly on their lips, ended in light sighs. A sudden voice cried into the cold night, "O Lord!" No one changed his position or took any notice of the cry. One or two passed, with a repeated and vague gesture, their hand over their faces, but most of them kept very still. In the benumbed immobility of their bodies they were excessively wearied by their thoughts, which rushed with the rapidity and vividness of dreams. Now and then, by an abrupt and startling exclamation, they answered the weird hail of some illusion; then, again, in silence contemplated the vision of known faces and familiar things. They recalled the aspect of forgotten shipmates and heard the voice of dead and gone skippers. They remembered the noise of gaslit streets, the steamy heat of tap-rooms or the scorching sunshine of calm days at sea.

Mr. Baker left his insecure place, and crawled, with stoppages, along the poop. In the dark and on all fours he resembled some carnivorous animal prowling amongst corpses. At the break, propped to windward of a stanchion, he looked down on the main deck. It seemed to him that the ship had a tendency to stand up a little more. The wind had eased a little, he thought, but the sea ran as high as ever. The waves foamed viciously, and the lee side of the deck disappeared under a hissing whiteness as of boiling milk, while the rigging sang steadily with a deep vibrating note, and, at every upward swing of the ship, the wind rushed with a long-drawn clamour amongst the spars. Mr. Baker watched very still. A man near him began to make a blabbing noise with his lips, all at once and very loud, as though the cold had broken brutally through him. He went on: — "Ba — ba —

ba — brrr — brr — ba — ba." — "Stop that!" cried Mr. Baker, groping in the dark. "Stop it!" He went on shaking the leg he found under his hand. — "What is it, sir?" called out Belfast, in the tone of a man awakened suddenly; "we are looking after that 'ere Jimmy." — "Are you? Ough! Don't make that row then. Who's that near you?" — "It's me — the boatswain, sir," growled the West-country man; "we are trying to keep life in that poor devil." — "Aye, aye!" said Mr. Baker. "Do it quietly, can't you?" — "He wants us to hold him up above the rail," went on the boatswain, with irritation, "says he can't breathe here under our jackets." — "If we lift 'im, we drop 'im overboard," said another voice, "we can't feel our hands with cold." — "I don't care. I am choking!" exclaimed James Wait in a clear tone. — "Oh, no, my son," said the boatswain, desperately, "you don't go till we all go on this fine night." — "You will see yet many a worse," said Mr. Baker, cheerfully. — "It's no child's play, sir!" answered the boatswain. "Some of us further aft, here, are in a pretty bad way." — "If the blamed sticks had been cut out of her she would be running along on her bottom now like any decent ship, an' giv' us all a chance," said someone, with a sigh. — "The old man wouldn't have it... much he cares for us," whispered another. — "Care for you!" exclaimed Mr. Baker, angrily. "Why should he care for you? Are you a lot of women passengers to be taken care of? We are here to take care of the ship — and some of you ain't up to that. Ough!... What have you done so very smart to be taken care of? Ough!... Some of you can't stand a bit of a breeze without crying over it." — "Come, sorr. We ain't so bad," protested Belfast, in a voice shaken by shivers; "we ain't... brr..." — "Again," shouted the mate, grabbing at the shadowy form; "again!... Why, you're in your shirt! What have you done?" — "I've put my oilskin and jacket over that half-dead nayggur — and he says he chokes," said Belfast, complainingly. — "You wouldn't call me nigger if I wasn't half dead, you Irish beggar!" boomed James Wait, vigorously. — "You... brr... You wouldn't be white if you were ever so well... I will fight you... brrrr... in fine weather... brrr... with one hand tied behind my back... brrrrrr..." — "I don't want your rags — I want air," gasped out the other faintly, as if suddenly exhausted.

The sprays swept over whistling and pattering. Men disturbed in their peaceful torpor by the pain of quarrelsome shouts, moaned, muttering curses. Mr. Baker crawled off a little way to leeward where a watercask loomed up big, with something white against it. "Is it you, Podmore?" asked Mr. Baker. He had to repeat the question twice before the cook turned, coughing feebly. — "Yes, sir. I've been praying in my mind for a quick deliverance; for I am prepared for any call.... I ———" — "Look here, cook," interrupted Mr. Baker, "the men are perishing with cold." — "Cold!" said the cook, mournfully; "they will be warm enough before long." — "What?" asked Mr. Baker, looking along the deck into the faint sheen of frothing water. — "They are a wicked lot," continued the cook solemnly, but in an unsteady voice, "about as wicked as any ship's company in this sinful world! Now, I" — he trembled so that he could hardly speak; his was an exposed place, and in a cotton shirt, a thin pair of trousers, and with his knees under his nose, he received, quaking, the flicks of stinging, salt drops; his voice sounded exhausted — "now, I — any time... My eldest youngster, Mr. Baker... a clever boy... last Sunday on shore before this voyage he wouldn't go to church, sir. Says I, 'You go and clean yourself, or I'll know the reason why!' What does he do?... Pond, Mr. Baker — fell into the pond in his best rig, sir!... Accident?... 'Nothing will save you, fine scholar though you are!' says I.... Accident!... I whopped him, sir, till I couldn't lift my arm...." His voice faltered. "I whopped 'im!" he repeated, rattling his teeth; then, after a while, let out a mournful sound that was half a groan, half a snore. Mr. Baker shook him by the shoulders. "Hey! Cook! Hold up, Podmore! Tell me — is there any fresh water in the galley tank? The ship is lying along less, I think; I would try to get forward. A little water would do them good. Hallo! Look out! Look out!" The cook struggled. — "Not you, sir — not you!" He began to scramble to windward. "Galley!... my business!" he shouted. — "Cook's going crazy now," said several voices. He yelled: — "Crazy, am I? I am more ready to die than any of you, officers incloosive — there! As long as she swims I will cook! I will get you coffee." — "Cook, ye are a gentleman!" cried Belfast. But the cook was already going over the weather-ladder. He stopped for a moment to shout back on the poop: — "As long as she swims I will cook!" and disappeared as though he had gone overboard. The men who had heard sent after him a cheer that sounded like a wail of sick children. An hour or more afterwards someone said distinctly: "He's gone for good." — "Very likely," assented the boatswain; "even in fine weather he was as smart about the deck as a milch-cow on her first voyage. We ought to go and see." Nobody moved. As the hours dragged slowly through the darkness Mr. Baker crawled back and forth along the poop several times. Some men fancied they had heard him exchange murmurs with the master, but at that time the memories were incomparably more vivid than anything actual, and they were not certain whether the murmurs were heard now or many years ago. They did not try to find out. A mutter more or less did not matter. It was too cold for curiosity, and almost for hope. They could not spare a moment or a thought from the great mental occupation of wishing to live. And the desire of life kept them alive, apathetic and enduring, under the cruel persistence of wind and cold; while the bestarred black dome of the sky revolved slowly above the ship, that drifted, bearing their patience and their suffering, through the stormy solitude of the sea.

Huddled close to one another, they fancied themselves utterly alone. They heard sustained loud noises, and again bore the pain of existence through long hours of profound silence. In the night they saw sunshine, felt warmth, and suddenly, with a start, thought that the sun would never rise upon a freezing world. Some heard laughter, listened to songs; others, near the end of the poop, could hear loud human shrieks, and opening their eyes, were surprised to hear them still, though very faint, and far away. The boatswain said: — "Why, it's the cook, hailing from forward, I think." He hardly believed his own words or recognised his own voice. It was a long time before the man next to him gave a sign of life. He punched hard his other neighbour and said: — "The cook's shouting!" Many did not understand, others did not care; the majority further aft did not believe. But the boatswain and another man had the pluck to crawl away forward to see. They seemed to have been gone for hours, and were very soon forgotten. Then suddenly men who had been plunged in a hopeless resignation became as if possessed with a desire to hurt. They belaboured one another with fists. In the darkness they struck persistently anything soft they could feel near, and, with a greater effort than for a shout, whispered excitedly: — "They've got some hot coffee.... Boss'en got it...." "No!... Where?"... "It's coming! Cook made it." James Wait moaned. Donkin scrambled viciously, caring not where he kicked, and anxious that the officers should have none of it. It came in a pot, and they drank in turns. It was hot, and while it blistered the greedy palates, it seemed incredible. The men sighed out parting with the mug: — "How 'as he done it?" Some cried weakly: — "Bully for you, doctor!"

He had done it somehow. Afterwards Archie declared that the thing was "meeraculous." For many days we wondered, and it was the one ever-interesting subject of conversation to the end of the voyage. We asked the cook, in fine weather, how he felt when he saw his stove "reared up on end." We inquired, in the north-east trade and on serene evenings, whether he had to stand on his head to put things right somewhat. We suggested he had used his bread-board for a raft, and from there comfortably had stoked his grate; and we did our best to conceal our admiration under the wit of fine irony. He affirmed not to know anything about it, rebuked our levity, declared himself, with solemn animation, to have been the object of a special mercy for the saving of our unholy lives. Fundamentally he was right, no doubt; but he need not have been so offensively positive about it — he need not have hinted so often that it would have gone hard with us had he not been there, meritorious and pure, to receive the inspiration and the strength for the work of grace. Had we been saved by his recklessness or his agility, we could have at length become reconciled to the fact; but to admit our obligation to anybody's virtue and holiness alone was as difficult for us as for any other handful of mankind. Like many benefactors of humanity, the cook took himself too seriously, and reaped the reward of irreverence. We were not ungrateful, however. He remained heroic. His saying — *the* saying of his life — became proverbial in the mouth of men as are the sayings of conquerors or sages. Later, whenever one of us was puzzled by a task and advised to relinquish it, he would express his determination to persevere and to succeed by the words: — "As long as she swims I will cook!"

The hot drink helped us through the bleak hours that precede the dawn. The sky low by the horizon took on the delicate tints of pink and yellow like the inside of a rare shell. And higher, where it glowed with a pearly sheen, a small black cloud appeared, like a forgotten fragment of the night set in a border of dazzling gold. The beams of light skipped on the crests of waves. The eyes of men turned to the eastward. The sunlight flooded their weary faces. They were giving themselves up to fatigue as though they had done for ever with their work.   On Singleton's black oilskin coat the dried salt glistened like hoar frost.   He hung on by the wheel, with open and lifeless eyes.   Captain Allistoun, unblinking, faced the rising sun.   His lips stirred, opened for the first time in twenty-four hours, and with a fresh firm voice he cried, "Wear ship!"

The commanding sharp tones made all these torpid men start like a sudden flick of a whip.   Then again, motionless where they lay, the force of habit made some of them repeat the order in hardly audible murmurs.   Captain Allistoun glanced down at his crew, and several, with fumbling fingers and hopeless movements, tried to cast themselves adrift.   He repeated impatiently, "Wear ship.   Now then, Mr. Baker, get the men along.   What's the matter with them?" — "Wear ship.   Do you hear there? — Wear ship!" thundered out the boatswain suddenly.   His voice seemed to break through a deadly spell.   Men began to stir and crawl. — "I want the fore-top-mast stay-sail run up smartly," said the master, very loudly; "if you can't manage it standing up you must do it lying down — that's all.   Bear a hand!" — "Come along!   Let's give the old girl a chance," urged the boatswain. — "Aye! aye!   Wear ship!" exclaimed quavering voices.   The forecastle men, with reluctant faces, prepared to go forward.   Mr. Baker pushed ahead, grunting, on all fours to show the way, and they followed him over the break. The others lay still with a vile hope in their hearts of not being required to move till they got saved or drowned in peace.

After some time they could be seen forward appearing on the forecastle head, one by one in unsafe attitudes; hanging on to the rails, clambering over the anchors; embracing the cross-head of the windlass or hugging the fore-capstan.   They were restless with strange exertions, waved their arms, knelt, lay flat down, staggered up, seemed to strive their hardest to go overboard. Suddenly a small white piece of canvas fluttered amongst them, grew larger, beating.   Its narrow head rose in jerks — and at last it stood distended and triangular in the sunshine. — "They have done it!" cried the voices aft. Captain Allistoun let go the rope he had round his wrist and rolled to leeward headlong.   He could be seen casting the lee main braces off the pins while the backwash of waves splashed over him. — "Square the main yard!" he shouted up to us — who stared at him in wonder.   We hesitated to stir. "The main brace, men.   Haul! haul anyhow!   Lay on your backs and haul!" he screeched, half drowned down there.   We did not believe we could move the main yard, but the strongest and the less discouraged tried to execute the order.   Others assisted half-heartedly.   Singleton's eyes blazed suddenly as he took a fresh grip of the spokes.   Captain Allistoun fought his way up to windward. — "Haul, men!   Try to move it!   Haul, and help the ship." His hard face worked suffused and furious.   "Is she going off, Singleton?" he cried. — "Not a move yet, sir," croaked the old seaman in a horribly hoarse voice. — "Watch the helm, Singleton," spluttered the master. "Haul, men!   Have you no more strength than rats?   Haul, and earn your salt."   Mr. Creighton, on his back, with a swollen leg and a face as white as a piece of paper, blinked his eyes; his bluish lips twitched.   In the wild scramble men grabbed at him, crawled over his hurt leg, knelt on his chest.

He kept perfectly still, setting his teeth without a moan, without a sigh. The master's ardour, the cries of that silent man inspired us. We hauled and hung in bunches on the rope. We heard him say with violence to Donkin, who sprawled abjectly on his stomach, — "I will brain you with this belaying pin if you don't catch hold of the brace," and that victim of men's injustice, cowardly and cheeky, whimpered: — "Are you goin' to murder us now?" while with sudden desperation he gripped the rope. Men sighed, shouted, hissed meaningless words, groaned. The yards moved, came slowly square against the wind, that hummed loudly on the yard-arms. — "Going off, sir," shouted Singleton, "she's just started." — "Catch a turn with that brace. Catch a turn!" clamoured the master. Mr. Creighton, nearly suffocated and unable to move, made a mighty effort, and with his left hand managed to nip the rope — "All fast!" cried someone. He closed his eyes as if going off into a swoon, while huddled together about the brace we watched with scared looks what the ship would do now.

She went off slowly as though she had been weary and disheartened like the men she carried. She paid off very gradually, making us hold our breath till we choked, and as soon as she had brought the wind abaft the beam she started to move, and fluttered our hearts. It was awful to see her, nearly overturned, begin to gather way and drag her submerged side through the water. The dead-eyes of the rigging churned the breaking seas. The lower half of the deck was full of mad whirlpools and eddies; and the long line of the lee rail could be seen showing black now and then in the swirls of a field of foam as dazzling and white as a field of snow. The wind sang shrilly amongst the spars; and at every slight lurch we expected her to slip to the bottom sideways from under our backs. When dead before it she made the first distinct attempt to stand up, and we encouraged her with a feeble and discordant howl. A great sea came running up aft and hung for a moment over us with a curling top; then crashed down under the counter and spread out on both sides into a great sheet of bursting froth. Above its fierce hiss we heard Singleton's croak: — "She is steering!" He had both his feet now planted firmly on the grating, and the wheel spun fast as he eased the helm. — "Bring the wind on the port quarter and steady her!" called out the master, staggering to his feet, the first man up from amongst our prostrate heap. One or two screamed with excitement: — "She rises!" Far away forward, Mr. Baker and three others were seen erect and black on the clear sky, lifting their arms, and with open mouths as though they had been shouting all together. The ship trembled, trying to lift her side, lurched back, seemed to give up with a nerveless dip, and suddenly with an unexpected jerk swung violently to windward, as though she had torn herself out from a deadly grasp. The whole immense volume of water, lifted by her deck, was thrown bodily across to starboard. Loud cracks were heard. Iron ports breaking open thundered with ringing blows. The water topped over the starboard rail with the rush of a river falling over a dam. The sea on deck, and the seas on every side of her, mingled together in a deafening roar. She rolled violently. We got up and were helplessly run or flung about from side to side. Men, rolling over and over, yelled, — "The house will go!" — "She clears herself!" Lifted by a towering sea she ran along with it for a moment, spouting thick streams of water through every opening of her wounded sides. The lee braces having been carried away or washed off the pins, all the ponderous yards on the fore swung from side to side and with appalling rapidity at every roll. The men forward were seen crouching here and there with fearful glances upwards at the enormous spars that whirled about over their heads. The torn canvas and the ends of broken gear streamed in the wind like wisps of hair. Through the clear sunshine, over the flashing turmoil and uproar of the seas, the ship ran blindly, dishevelled and headlong, as if fleeing for her life; and on the poop we spun, we tottered about, distracted and noisy. We all spoke at once in a thin babble; we had the aspect of invalids and the gestures of maniacs. Eyes shone, large and haggard, in smiling, meagre faces that seemed to have been dusted over with powdered chalk. We stamped, clapped our hands, feeling ready to jump and do anything; but in reality hardly able to keep on our feet. Captain Allistoun, hard and slim, gesticulated madly from the poop at Mr. Baker: "Steady these fore-yards! Steady them the best you can!" On the main deck, men excited by his cries, splashed, dashing aimlessly here and there with the foam swirling up to their waists. Apart, far aft, and alone by the helm, old Singleton had deliberately tucked his white beard under the top button of his glistening coat. Swaying upon the din and tumult of the seas, with the whole battered length of the ship launched forward in a rolling rush before his steady old eyes, he stood rigidly still, forgotten by all, and with an attentive face. In front of his erect figure only the two arms moved crosswise with a swift and sudden readiness, to check or urge again the rapid stir of circling spokes. He steered with care.

CHAPTER FOUR

ON MEN reprieved by its disdainful mercy, the immortal sea confers in its justice the full privilege of desired unrest. Through the perfect wisdom of its grace they are not permitted to meditate at ease upon the complicated and acrid savour of existence. They must without pause justify their life to the eternal pity that commands toil to be hard and unceasing, from sunrise to sunset, from sunset to sunrise; till the weary succession of nights and days tainted by the obstinate clamour of sages, demanding bliss and an empty heaven, is redeemed at last by the vast silence of pain and labour, by the dumb fear and the dumb courage of men obscure, forgetful, and enduring.

The master and Mr. Baker coming face to face stared for a moment, with the intense and amazed looks of men meeting unexpectedly after years of trouble. Their voices were gone, and they whispered desperately at one another. — "Anyone missing?" asked Captain Allistoun. — "No. All there." — "Anybody hurt?" — "Only the second mate." — "I will look after him directly. We're lucky." — "Very," articulated Mr. Baker, faintly. He gripped the rail and rolled bloodshot eyes. The little grey man made an effort to raise his voice above a dull mutter, and fixed his chief mate with a cold gaze, piercing like a dart. — "Get sail on the ship," he said, speaking authoritatively and with an inflexible snap of his thin lips. "Get sail on her as soon as you can. This is a fair wind. At once, sir — Don't give the men time to feel themselves. They will get done up and stiff, and we will never … We must get her along now" … He reeled to a long heavy roll; the rail dipped into the glancing, hissing water. He caught a shroud, swung helplessly against the mate… "now we have a fair wind at last —— Make —— sail." His head rolled from shoulder to shoulder. His eyelids began to beat rapidly. "And the pumps —— pumps, Mr. Baker." He peered as though the face within a foot of his eyes had been half a mile off. "Keep the men on the move to —— to get her along," he mumbled in a drowsy tone, like a man going off into a doze. He pulled himself together suddenly. "Mustn't stand. Won't do," he said with a painful attempt at a smile. He let go his hold, and, propelled by the dip of the ship, ran aft unwillingly, with small steps, till he brought up against the binnacle stand. Hanging on there he looked up in an aimless manner at Singleton, who, unheeding him, watched anxiously the end of the jib-boom — "Steering gear works all right?" he asked. There was a noise in the old seaman's throat, as though the words had been rattling together before they could come out. — "Steers… like a little boat," he said, at last, with hoarse tenderness, without giving the master as much as half a glance — then, watchfully, spun the wheel down, steadied, flung it back again. Captain Allistoun tore himself away from the delight of leaning against the binnacle, and began to walk the poop, swaying and reeling to preserve his balance.…

The pump-rods, clanking, stamped in short jumps while the fly-wheels turned smoothly, with great speed, at the foot of the mainmast, flinging back and forth with a regular impetuosity two limp clusters of men clinging to the handles. They abandoned themselves, swaying from the hip with twitching faces and stony eyes. The carpenter, sounding from time to time, exclaimed mechanically: "Shake her up! Keep her going!" Mr. Baker could not speak, but found his voice to shout; and under the goad of his objurgations, men looked to the lashings, dragged out new sails; and thinking themselves unable to move, carried heavy blocks aloft — overhauled the gear. They went up the rigging with faltering and desperate efforts. Their heads swam as they shifted their hold, stepped blindly on the yards like men in the dark; or trusted themselves to the first rope at hand with the negligence of exhausted strength. The narrow escapes from falls did not disturb the languid beat of their hearts; the roar of the seas seething far below them sounded continuous and faint like an indistinct noise from another world: the wind filled their eyes with tears, and with heavy gusts tried to push them off from where they swayed in insecure positions. With streaming faces and blowing hair they flew up and down between sky and water, bestriding the ends of yard-arms, crouching on footropes, embracing lifts to have their hands free, or standing up against chain ties. Their thoughts floated vaguely between the desire of rest and the desire of life, while their stiffened fingers cast off head-earrings, fumbled for knives, or held with tenacious grip against the violent shocks of beating canvas. They glared savagely at one another, made frantic signs with one hand while they held their life in the other, looked down on the narrow strip of flooded deck, shouted along to leeward: "Light-to!"... "Haul out!"... "Make fast!" Their lips moved, their eyes started, furious and eager with the desire to be understood, but the wind tossed their words unheard upon the disturbed sea. In an unendurable and unending strain they worked like men driven by a merciless dream to toil in an atmosphere of ice or flame. They burnt and shivered in turns. Their eyeballs smarted as if in the smoke of a conflagration; their heads were ready to burst with every shout. Hard fingers seemed to grip their throats. At every roll they thought: Now I must let go. It will shake us all off — and thrown about aloft they cried wildly: "Look out there — catch the end."... "Reeve clear"... "Turn this block...." They nodded desperately; shook infuriated faces, "No! No! From down up." They seemed to hate one another with a deadly hate. The longing to be done with it all gnawed their breasts, and the wish to do things well was a burning pain. They cursed their fate, contemned their life, and wasted their breath in deadly imprecations upon one another. The sailmaker, with his bald head bared, worked feverishly, forgetting his intimacy with so many admirals. The boatswain, climbing up with marlinspikes and bunches of spunyarn rovings, or kneeling on the yard and ready to take a turn with the midship-stop, had acute and fleeting visions of his old woman and the youngsters in a moorland village. Mr. Baker, feeling very weak, tottered here and there, grunting and inflexible, like a man of iron. He waylaid those who, coming from aloft, stood gasping for breath. He ordered, encouraged, scolded. "Now then — to the main topsail now! Tally on to that gantline. Don't stand about there!" — "Is there no rest for us?" muttered voices. He spun round fiercely, with a sinking heart. — "No! No rest till the work is done. Work till you drop. That's what you're here for." A bowed seaman at his elbow gave a short laugh. — "Do or die," he croaked bitterly, then spat into his broad palms, swung up his long arms, and grasping the rope high above his head sent out a mournful, wailing cry for a pull all together. A sea boarded the quarter-deck and sent the whole lot sprawling to leeward. Caps, handspikes floated. Clenched hands, kicking legs, with here and there a spluttering face, stuck out of the white hiss of foaming water. Mr. Baker, knocked down with the rest, screamed — "Don't let go that rope! Hold on to it! Hold!" And sorely bruised by the brutal fling, they held on to it, as though it had been the fortune of their life. The ship ran, rolling heavily, and the topping crests glanced past port and starboard flashing their white heads. Pumps were freed. Braces were rove. The three topsails and foresail were set. She spurted faster over the water, outpacing the swift rush of waves. The menacing thunder of distanced seas rose behind her — filled the air with the tremendous vibrations of its voice. And devastated, battered, and wounded she drove foaming to the northward, as though inspired by the courage of a high endeavour....

The forecastle was a place of damp desolation. They looked at their dwelling with dismay. It was slimy, dripping; it hummed hollow with the wind, and was strewn with shapeless wreckage like a half-tide cavern in a rocky and exposed coast. Many had lost all they had in the world, but most of the starboard watch had preserved their chests; thin streams of water trickled out of them, however. The beds were soaked; the blankets spread out and saved by some nail squashed under foot. They dragged wet rags from evil-smelling corners, and wringing the water out, recognised their property. Some smiled stiffly. Others looked round blank and mute. There were cries of joy over old waistcoats, and groans of sorrow over shapeless things found among the splinters of smashed bed boards. One lamp was discovered jammed under the bowsprit. Charley whimpered a little. Knowles stumped here and there, sniffing, examining dark places for salvage. He poured dirty water out of a boot, and was concerned to find the owner. Those who, overwhelmed by their losses, sat on the forepeak hatch, remained elbows on knees, and, with a fist against each cheek, disdained to look up. He pushed it under their noses. "Here's a good boot. Yours?" They snarled, "No — get out." One snapped at him, "Take it to hell out of this." He seemed surprised. "Why? It's a good boot," but remembering suddenly that he had lost every stitch of his clothing, he dropped his find and began to swear. In the dim light cursing voices clashed. A man came in and, dropping his arms, stood still, repeating from the doorstep, "Here's a bloomin' old go! Here's a bloomin' old go!" A few rooted anxiously in flooded chests for tobacco. They breathed hard, clamoured with heads down. "Look at that Jack!"... "Here! Sam! Here's my shore-going rig spoilt for ever." One blasphemed tearfully, holding up a pair of dripping trousers. No one looked at him. The cat came out from somewhere. He had an ovation. They snatched him from hand to hand, caressed him in a murmur of pet names. They wondered where he had "weathered it out"; disputed about it. A squabbling argument began. Two men brought in a bucket of fresh water, and all crowded round it; but Tom, lean and mewing, came up with every hair astir and had the first drink. A couple of hands went aft for oil and biscuits.

Then in the yellow light and in the intervals of mopping the deck they crunched hard bread, arranging to "worry through somehow." Men chummed as to beds. Turns were settled for wearing boots and having the use of oilskin coats. They called one another "old man" and "sonny" in cheery voices. Friendly slaps resounded. Jokes were shouted. One or two stretched on the wet deck, slept with heads pillowed on their bent arms, and several, sitting on the hatch, smoked. Their weary faces appeared through a thin blue haze, pacified and with sparkling eyes. The boatswain put his head through the door. "Relieve the wheel, one of you" — he shouted inside — "it's six. Blamme if that old Singleton hasn't been there more'n thirty hours. You are a fine lot." He slammed the door again. "Mate's watch on deck," said someone. "Hey, Donkin, it's your relief!" shouted three or four together. He had crawled into an empty bunk and on wet planks lay still. "Donkin, your wheel." He made no sound. "Donkin's dead," guffawed someone. "Sell 'is bloomin' clothes," shouted another. "Donkin, if ye don't go to the bloomin' wheel they will sell your clothes — d'ye hear?" jeered a third. He groaned from his dark hole. He complained about pains in all his bones, he whimpered pitifully. "He won't go," exclaimed a contemptuous voice, "your turn, Davis." The young seaman rose painfully, squaring his shoulders. Donkin stuck his head out, and it appeared in the yellow light, fragile and ghastly. "I will giv' yer a pound of tobaccer," he whined in a conciliating voice, "so soon as I draw it from aft. I will — s'elp me..." Davis swung his arm backhanded and the head vanished. "I'll go," he said, "but you will pay for it." He walked unsteady but resolute to the door. "So I will," yelped Donkin, popping out behind him. "So I will — s'elp me... a pound... three bob they chawrge." Davis flung the door open. "You will pay my price... in fine weather," he shouted over his shoulder. One of the men unbuttoned his wet coat rapidly, threw it at his head. "Here, Taffy — take that, you thief!" "Thank you!" he cried from the darkness above the swish of rolling water. He could be heard splashing; a sea came on board with a thump. "He's got his bath already," remarked a grim shellback. "Aye, aye!" grunted others. Then, after a long silence, Wamibo made strange noises. "Hallo, what's up with you?" said someone grumpily. "He says he would have gone for Davy," explained Archie, who was the Finn's interpreter generally. "I believe him!" cried voices.... "Never mind, Dutchy... You'll do, muddle-head.... Your turn will come soon enough... You don't know when ye're well off." They ceased, and all together turned their faces to the door. Singleton stepped in, advanced two paces, and stood swaying slightly. The sea hissed, flowed roaring past the bows, and the forecastle trembled, full of deep murmurs; the lamp flared, swinging like a pendulum. He looked with a dreamy and puzzled stare, as though he could not distinguish the still men from their restless shadows. There were awestruck exclamations: — "Hallo, hallo"... "How does it look outside now, Singleton?" Those who sat on the hatch lifted their eyes in silence, and the next oldest seaman in the ship (those two understood one another, though they hardly exchanged three words in a day) gazed up at his friend attentively for a moment, then taking a short clay pipe out of his mouth, offered it without a word. Singleton put out his arm towards it, missed, staggered, and suddenly fell forward, crashing down, stiff and headlong like an uprooted tree. There was a swift rush. Men pushed, crying: — "He's done!"... "Turn him over!"... "Stand clear there!" Under a crowd of startled faces bending over him he lay on his back, staring upwards in a continuous and intolerable manner. In the breathless silence of a general consternation, he said in a grating murmur: — "I am all right," and clutched with his hands. They helped him up. He mumbled despondently: — "I am getting old... old." — "Not you," cried Belfast, with ready tact. Supported on all sides, he hung his head. — "Are you better?" they asked. He glared at them from under his eyebrows with large black eyes, spreading over his chest the bushy whiteness of a beard long and thick. — "Old! old!" he repeated sternly. Helped along, he reached his bunk. There was in it a slimy soft heap of something that smelt, as does at dead low water a muddy foreshore. It was his soaked straw bed. With a convulsive effort he pitched himself on it, and in the darkness of the narrow place could be heard growling angrily, like an irritated and savage animal uneasy in its den: — "Bit of breeze... small thing... can't stand up... old!" He slept at last, high-booted, sou'wester on head, and his oilskin clothes rustled, when with a deep sighing groan he turned over. Men conversed about him in quiet, concerned whispers. "This will break 'im up"... "Strong as a horse" ... "Aye. But he ain't what he used to be."... In sad murmurs they gave him up. Yet at midnight he turned out to duty as if nothing had been the matter, and answered to his name with a mournful "Here!" He brooded alone more than ever, in an impenetrable silence and with a saddened face. For many years he had heard himself called "Old Singleton," and had serenely accepted the qualification, taking it as a tribute of respect due to a man who through half a century had measured his strength against the favours and the rages of the sea. He had never given a thought to his mortal self. He lived unscathed, as though he had been indestructible, surrendering to all the temptations, weathering many gales. He had panted in sunshine, shivered in the cold; suffered hunger, thirst, debauch; passed through many trials — known all the furies. Old! It seemed to him he was broken at last. And like a man bound treacherously while he sleeps, he woke up fettered by the long chain of disregarded years. He had to take up at once the burden of all his existence, and found it almost too heavy for his strength. Old! He moved his arms, shook his head, felt his limbs. Getting old... and then? He looked upon the immortal sea with the awakened and groping perception of its heartless might; he saw it unchanged, black and foaming under the eternal scrutiny of the stars; he heard its impatient voice calling for him out of a pitiless vastness full of unrest, of turmoil, and of terror. He looked afar upon it, and he saw an immensity tormented and blind, moaning and furious, that claimed all the days of his tenacious life, and, when life was over, would claim the worn-out body of its slave....

This was the last of the breeze. It veered quickly, changed to a black south-easter, and blew itself out, giving the ship a famous shove to the north-ward into the joyous sunshine of the trade. Rapid and white she ran home-wards in a straight path, under a blue sky and upon the plain of a blue sea. She carried Singleton's completed wisdom, Donkin's delicate susceptibilities, and the conceited folly of us all. The hours of ineffective turmoil were for-gotten; the fear and anguish of these dark moments were never mentioned in the glowing peace of fine days. Yet from that time our life seemed to start afresh as though we had died and had been resuscitated. All the first part of the voyage, the Indian Ocean on the other side of the Cape, all that was lost in a haze, like an ineradicable suspicion of some previous existence. It had ended — then there were blank hours: a livid blurr — and again we lived! Singleton was possessed of sinister truth; Mr. Creighton of a damaged leg; the cook of fame — and shamefully abused the opportunities of his distinction. Donkin had an added grievance. He went about repeating with insistence: — "'E said 'e would brain me — did yer 'ear? They are goin' to murder us now for the least little thing." We began at last to think it was rather awful. And we were conceited! We boasted of our pluck, of our capacity for work, of our energy. We remembered honourable episodes:

our devotion, our indomitable perseverance — and were proud of them as though they had been the outcome of our unaided impulses. We remembered our danger, our toil — and conveniently forgot our horrible scare. We decried our officers — who had done nothing — and listened to the fascinating Donkin. His care for our rights, his disinterested concern for our dignity, were not discouraged by the invariable contumely of our words, by the disdain of our looks. Our contempt for him was unbounded — and we could not but listen with interest to that consummate artist. He told us we were good men — a "bloomin' condemned lot of good men." Who thanked us? Who took any notice of our wrongs? Didn't we lead a "dorg's loife for two poun' ten a month?" Did we think that miserable pay enough to compensate us for the risk to our lives and for the loss of our clothes? "We've lost every rag!" he cried. He made us forget that he, at any rate, had lost nothing of his own. The younger men listened, thinking — this 'ere Donkin's a long-headed chap, though no kind of man, anyhow. The Scandinavians were frightened at his audacities; Wamibo did not understand; and the older seamen thoughtfully nodded their heads making the thin gold earrings glitter in the fleshy lobes of hairy ears. Severe, sunburnt faces were propped meditatively on tattooed forearms. Veined, brown fists held in their knotted grip the dirty white clay of smouldering pipes. They listened, impenetrable, broad-backed, with bent shoulders, and in grim silence. He talked with ardour, despised and irrefutable. His picturesque and filthy loquacity flowed like a troubled stream from a poisoned source. His beady little eyes danced, glancing right and left, ever on the watch for the approach of an officer. Sometimes Mr. Baker going forward to take a look at the head sheets would roll with his uncouth gait through the sudden stillness of the men; or Mr. Creighton limped along, smooth-faced, youthful, and more stern than ever, piercing our short silence with a keen glance of his clear eyes. Behind his back Donkin would begin again darting stealthy, sidelong looks. — "'Ere's one of 'em. Some of yer 'as made 'im fast that day. Much thanks yer got for it. Ain't 'ee a-drivin' yer wusse'n ever?... Let 'im slip overboard.... Vy not? It would 'ave been less trouble. Vy not?" He advanced confidentially, backed away with great effect; he whispered, he screamed, waved his miserable arms no thicker than pipe-stems — stretched his lean neck — spluttered — squinted. In the pauses of his impassioned orations the wind sighed quietly aloft, the calm sea unheeded murmured in a warning whisper along the ship's side. We abominated the creature and could not deny the luminous truth of his contentions. It was all so obvious. We were indubitably good men; our deserts were great and our pay small. Through our exertions we had saved the ship and the skipper would get the credit of it. What had he done? we wanted to know. Donkin asked: — "What 'ee could do without hus?" and we could not answer. We were oppressed by the injustice of the world, surprised to perceive how long we had lived under its burden without realising our unfortunate state, annoyed by the uneasy suspicion of our undiscerning stupidity. Donkin assured us it was all our "good 'eartedness," but we would not be consoled by such shallow sophistry. We were men enough to courageously admit to ourselves our intellectual shortcomings; though from that time we refrained from kicking him, tweaking his nose, or from accidentally knocking him about, which last, after we had weathered the Cape, had been rather a popular amusement. Davis ceased to talk at him provokingly about black eyes and flattened noses. Charley, much subdued since the gale, did not jeer at him. Knowles deferentially and with a crafty air propounded questions such as: — "Could we all have the same grub as the mates? Could we all stop ashore till we got it? What would be the next thing to try for if we got that?" He answered readily with contemptuous certitude; he strutted with assurance in clothes that were much too big for him as though he had tried to disguise himself. These were Jimmy's clothes mostly — though he would accept anything from anybody; but nobody, except Jimmy, had anything to spare. His devotion to Jimmy was unbounded. He was for ever dodging in the little cabin, ministering to Jimmy's wants, humouring his whims, submitting to his exacting peevishness, often laughing with him. Nothing could keep him away from the pious work of visiting the sick, especially when there was some heavy hauling to be done on deck. Mr. Baker had on two occasions jerked him out from there by the scruff of the neck to our inexpressible scandal. Was a sick chap to be left without attendance? Were we to be ill-used for attending a shipmate? — "What?" growled Mr. Baker, turning menacingly at the mutter, and the whole half-circle like one man stepped back a pace. "Set the topmast stunsail. Away aloft, Donkin, overhaul the gear," ordered the mate inflexibly. "Fetch the sail along; bend the down-haul clear. Bear a hand." Then, the sail set, he would go slowly aft and stand looking at the compass for a long time, careworn, pensive, and breathing hard as if stifled by the taint of unaccountable ill-will that pervaded the ship. "What's up amongst them?" he thought. "Can't make out this hanging back and growling. A good crowd, too, as they go nowadays." On deck the men exchanged bitter words, suggested by a silly exasperation against something unjust and irremediable that would not be denied, and would whisper into their ears long after Donkin had ceased speaking. Our little world went on its curved and unswerving path carrying a discontented and aspiring population. They found comfort of a gloomy kind in an interminable and conscientious analysis of their unappreciated worth; and inspired by Donkin's hopeful doctrines they dreamed enthusiastically of the time when every lonely ship would travel over a serene sea, manned by a wealthy and well-fed crew of satisfied skippers.

It looked as if it would be a long passage. The south-east trades, light and unsteady, were left behind; and then, on the equator and under a low grey sky, the ship, in close heat, floated upon a smooth sea that resembled a sheet of ground glass. Thunder squalls hung on the horizon, circled round the ship, far off and growling angrily, like a troop of wild beasts afraid to charge home. The invisible sun, sweeping above the upright masts, made on the clouds a blurred stain of rayless light, and a similar patch of faded radiance kept pace with it from east to west over the unglittering level of the waters. At night, through the impenetrable darkness of earth and heaven, broad sheets of flame waved noiselessly; and for half a second the becalmed craft stood out with its masts and rigging, with every sail and every rope distinct and black in the centre of a fiery outburst, like a charred ship enclosed in a globe of fire. And, again, for long hours she remained lost in a vast universe of night and silence where gentle sighs wandering here and there like forlorn souls, made the still sails flutter as in sudden fear, and the ripple of a beshrouded ocean whisper its compassion afar — in a voice mournful, immense, and faint....

When the lamp was put out, and through the door thrown wide open, Jimmy, turning on his pillow, could see vanishing beyond the straight line of top-gallant rail, the quick, repeated visions of a fabulous world made up of leaping fire and sleeping water. The lightning gleamed in his big sad eyes that seemed in a red flicker to burn themselves out in his black face, and then he would lie blinded and invisible in the midst of an intense darkness. He could hear on the quiet deck soft footfalls, the breathing of some man lounging on the doorstep; the low creak of swaying masts; or the calm voice of the watch-officer reverberating aloft, hard and loud, amongst the unstirring sails. He listened with avidity, taking a rest in the attentive perception of the slightest sound from the fatiguing wanderings of his sleeplessness. He was cheered by the rattling of blocks, reassured by the stir and murmur of the watch, soothed by the slow yawn of some sleepy and weary seaman settling himself deliberately for a snooze on the planks. Life seemed an indestructible thing. It went on in darkness, in sunshine, in sleep; tireless, it hovered affectionately round the imposture of his ready death. It was bright, like the twisted flare of lightning, and more full of surprises than the dark night. It made him safe, and the calm of its overpowering darkness was as precious as its restless and dangerous light.

But in the evening, in the dog-watches, and even far into the first night-watch, a knot of men could always be seen congregated before Jimmy's cabin. They leaned on each side of the door peacefully interested and with crossed legs; they stood astride the doorstep discoursing, or sat in silent couples on his sea-chest; while against the bulwark along the spare topmast, three or four in a row stared meditatively; with their simple faces lit up by the projected glare of Jimmy's lamp. The little place, repainted white, had, in the night, the brilliance of a silver shrine where a black idol, reclining stiffly under a blanket, blinked its weary eyes and received our homage. Donkin officiated. He had the air of a demonstrator showing a phenomenon, a manifestation bizarre, simple, and meritorious that, to the beholders, should be a profound and an everlasting lesson. "Just look at 'im, 'ee knows what's what — never fear!" he exclaimed now and then, flourishing a hand hard and fleshless like the claw of a snipe. Jimmy, on his back, smiled with reserve and without moving a limb. He affected the languor of extreme weakness, so as to make it manifest to us that our delay in hauling him out from his horrible confinement, and then that night spent on the poop among our selfish neglect of his needs, had "done for him." He rather liked to talk about it, and of course we were always interested. He spoke spasmodically, in fast rushes with long pauses between, as a tipsy man walks.

... "Cook had just given me a pannikin of hot coffee.... Slapped it down there, on my chest — banged the door to.... I felt a heavy roll coming; tried to save my coffee, burnt my fingers... and fell out of my bunk.... She went over so quick.... Water came in through the ventilator.... I couldn't move the door... dark as a grave... tried to scramble up into the upper berth.... Rats... a rat bit my finger as I got up.... I could hear him swimming below me.... I thought you would never come.... I thought you were all gone overboard... of course... Could hear nothing but the wind.... Then you came... to look for the corpse, I suppose. A little more and..."

"Man! But ye made a rare lot of noise in here," observed Archie, thoughtfully.

"You chaps kicked up such a confounded row above.... Enough to scare anyone.... I didn't know what you were up to.... Bash in the blamed planks ... my head.... Just what a silly, scary gang of fools would do.... Not much good to me anyhow.... Just as well... drown.... Pah."

He groaned, snapped his big white teeth, and gazed with scorn. Belfast lifted a pair of dolorous eyes, with a broken-hearted smile, clenched his fists stealthily; blue-eyed Archie caressed his red whiskers with a hesitating hand; the boatswain at the door stared a moment, and brusquely went away with a loud guffaw. Wamibo dreamed.... Donkin felt all over his sterile chin for the few rare hairs, and said, triumphantly, with a sidelong glance at Jimmy: — "Look at 'im! Wish I was 'arf has 'ealthy as 'ee is — I do." He jerked a short thumb over his shoulder towards the after end of the ship. "That's the blooming way to do 'em!" he yelped, with forced heartiness. Jimmy said: — "Don't be a dam' fool," in a pleasant voice. Knowles, rubbing his shoulder against the doorpost, remarked shrewdly: — "We can't all go an' be took sick — it would be mutiny." — "Mutiny — gawn!" jeered Donkin, "there's no bloomin' law against bein' sick." — "There's six weeks' hard for refoosing dooty," argued Knowles, "I mind I once seed in Cardiff the crew of an overloaded ship — leastways she weren't overloaded, only a fatherly old gentleman with a white beard and an umbreller came along the quay and talked to the hands. Said as how it was crool hard to be drownded in winter just for the sake of a few pounds more for the owner — he said. Nearly cried over them — he did; and he had a square mainsail coat, and a gaff-topsail hat too — all proper. So they chaps they said they wouldn't go to be drownded in winter — depending upon that 'ere Plimsoll man to see 'em through the court. They thought to have a bloomin' lark and two or three days' spree. And the beak giv' 'em six weeks — coss the ship warn't overloaded. Anyways they made it out in court that she wasn't. There wasn't one overloaded ship in Penarth Dock at all. 'Pears that old coon he was only on pay and allowance from some kind people, under orders to look for overloaded ships, and he couldn't see no further than the length of his umbreller. Some of us in the boarding-house, where I live when I'm looking for a ship in Cardiff, stood by to duck that old weeping spunger in the dock. We kept a good look-out, too — but he topped his boom directly he was outside the court.... Yes. They got six weeks' hard...."

They listened, full of curiosity, nodding in the pauses their rough pensive faces. Donkin opened his mouth once or twice, but restrained himself. Jimmy lay still with open eyes and not at all interested. A seaman emitted the opinion that after a verdict of atrocious partiality "the bloomin' beaks go an' drink at the skipper's expense." Others assented. It was clear, of course. Donkin said: — "Well, six weeks ain't much trouble. You sleep all night in, reg'lar, in chokey. Do it on my 'ead." "You are used to it ainch'ee, Donkin?" asked somebody. Jimmy condescended to laugh. It cheered up everyone wonderfully. Knowles, with surprising mental agility, shifted his ground. "If we all went sick what would become of the ship? eh?" He posed the problem and grinned all round. — "Let 'er go to 'ell," sneered Donkin. "Damn 'er. She ain't yourn." — "What? Just let her drift?" insisted Knowles in a tone of unbelief. — "Aye! Drift, an' be blowed," affirmed Donkin with fine recklessness. The other did not see it — meditated. — "The stores would run out," he muttered, "and... never get anywhere... and what about pay-day?" he added with greater assurance. — "Jack likes a good pay-day," exclaimed a listener on the doorstep. "Aye, because then the girls put one arm round his neck an' t'other in his pocket, and call him ducky. Don't they, Jack?" — "Jack, you're a terror with the gals." — "He takes three of 'em in tow to once, like one of 'em Watkinses two-funnel tugs waddling away with three schooners behind." — "Jack, you're a lame scamp." — "Jack, tell us about that one with a blue eye and a black eye. Do." — "There's plenty of girls with one black eye along the Highway by..." — "No, that's a speshul one — come, Jack." Donkin looked severe and disgusted; Jimmy very bored; a grey-haired sea-dog shook his head slightly, smiling at the bowl of his pipe, discreetly amused. Knowles turned about bewildered; stammered first at one, then at another. — "No!... I never!... can't talk sensible sense midst you.... Always on the kid." He retired bashfully — muttering and pleased. They laughed, hooting in the crude light, around Jimmy's bed, where on a white pillow his hollowed black face moved to and fro restlessly. A puff of wind came, made the flame of the lamp leap, and outside, high up, the sails fluttered, while near by the block of the foresheet struck a ringing blow on the iron bulwark. A voice far off cried, "Helm up!" another, more faint, answered, "Hard-up, sir!" They became silent — waited expectantly. The grey-haired seaman knocked his pipe on the doorstep and stood up. The ship leaned over gently and the sea seemed to wake up, murmuring drowsily. "Here's a little wind comin'," said someone very low. Jimmy turned over slowly to face the breeze. The voice in the night cried loud and commanding: — "Haul the spanker out." The group before the door vanished out of the light. They could be heard tramping aft while they repeated with varied intonations: — "Spanker out!"... "Out spanker, sir!" Donkin remained alone with Jimmy. There was a silence. Jimmy opened and shut his lips several times as if swallowing draughts of fresher air; Donkin moved the toes of his bare feet and looked at them thoughtfully.

"Ain't you going to give them a hand with the sail?" asked Jimmy.

"No. If six ov 'em ain't 'nough beef to set that blamed, rotten spanker, they ain't fit to live," answered Donkin in a bored, far-away voice, as though he had been talking from the bottom of a hole. Jimmy considered the conical, fowl-like profile with a queer kind of interest; he was leaning out of his bunk with the calculating, uncertain expression of a man who reflects how best to lay hold of some strange creature that looks as though it could sting or bite. But he said only: — "The mate will miss you — and there will be ructions."

Donkin got up to go. "I will do for 'im some dark night; see if I don't," he said over his shoulder.

Jimmy went on quickly: — "You're like a poll-parrot, like a screechin' poll-parrot." Donkin stopped and cocked his head attentively on one side. His big ears stood out, transparent and veined, resembling the thin wings of a bat.

"Yuss?" he said, with his back towards Jimmy.

"Yes! Chatter out all you know — like... like a dirty white cockatoo."

Donkin waited. He could hear the other's breathing, long and slow; the breathing of a man with a hundredweight or so on the breastbone. Then he asked calmly: — "What do I know?"

"What?... What I tell you... not much. What do you want... to talk about my health so..."

"It's a blooming imposyshun. A bloomin', stinkin', first-class imposy-shun — but it don't tyke me in. Not it."

Jimmy kept still. Donkin put his hands in his pockets, and in one slouch-ing stride came up to the bunk.

"I talk — what's the odds. They ain't men 'ere — sheep they are. A driven lot of sheep. I 'old you up... Vy not? You're well orf."

"I am... I don't say anything about that...."

"Well. Let 'em see it. Let 'em larn what a man can do. I am a man, I know all about yer...." Jimmy threw himself further away on the pillow; the other stretched out his skinny neck, jerked his bird face down at him as though pecking at the eyes. "I am a man. I've seen the inside of every chokey in the Colonies rather'n give up my rights...."

"You are a jail-prop," said Jimmy, weakly.

"I am... an' proud of it, too. You! You 'aven't the bloomin' nerve — so you inventyd this 'ere dodge...." He paused; then with marked after-thought accentuated slowly: — "Yer ain't sick — are yer?"

"No," said Jimmy, firmly. "Been out of sorts now and again this year," he mumbled with a sudden drop in his voice.

Donkin closed one eye, amicable and confidential. He whispered: — "Ye 'ave done this afore 'aven'tchee?" Jimmy smiled — then as if unable to hold back he let himself go: — "Last ship — yes. I was out of sorts on the passage. See? It was easy. They paid me off in Calcutta, and the skipper made no bones about it either.... I got my money all right. Laid up fifty-eight days! The fools! O Lord! The fools! Paid right off." He laughed spasmodically. Donkin chimed in giggling. Then Jimmy coughed violently. "I am as well as ever," he said, as soon as he could draw breath.

Donkin made a derisive gesture. "In course," he said, profoundly, "any-one can see that." — "They don't," said Jimmy, gasping like a fish. —

"They would swallow any yarn," affirmed Donkin. — "Don't you let on too much," admonished Jimmy in an exhausted voice. — "Your little gyme? Eh?" commented Donkin, jovially. Then with sudden disgust: "Yer all for yerself, s'long as ye're right...."

So charged with egoism James Wait pulled the blanket up to his chin and lay still for a while. His heavy lips protruded in an everlasting black pout. "Why are you so hot on making trouble?" he asked without much interest.

"'Cos it's a bloomin' shayme. We are put upon... bad food, bad pay... I want us to kick up a bloomin' row; a blamed 'owling row that would make 'em remember! Knocking people about... brain us... indeed! Ain't we men?" His altruistic indignation blazed. Then he said calmly: — "I've been airing yer clothes." — "All right," said Jimmy, languidly, "bring them in." — "Giv' us the key of your chest, I'll put 'em away for yer," said Donkin with friendly eagerness. — "Bring 'em in, I will put them away myself," answered James Wait with severity. Donkin looked down, muttering.... "What d'you say? What d'you say?" inquired Wait anxiously. — "Nothink. The night's dry, let 'em 'ang out till the morning," said Donkin, in a strangely trembling voice, as though restraining laughter or rage. Jimmy seemed satisfied. — "Give me a little water for the night in my mug — there," he said. Donkin took a stride over the doorstep. — "Git it yerself," he replied in a surly tone. "You can do it, unless you *are* sick." — "Of course I can do it," said Wait, "only..." — "Well, then, do it," said Donkin, viciously, "if yer can look after yer clothes, yer can look after yerself." He went on deck without a look back.

Jimmy reached out for the mug. Not a drop. He put it back gently with a faint sigh — and closed his eyes. He thought: — That lunatic Belfast will bring me some water if I ask. Fool. I am very thirsty.... It was very hot in the cabin, and it seemed to turn slowly round, detach itself from the ship, and swing out smoothly into a luminous, arid space where a black sun shone, spinning very fast. A place without any water! No water! A policeman with the face of Donkin drank a glass of beer by the side of an empty well, and flew away flapping vigorously. A ship whose mastheads protruded through the sky and could not be seen, was discharging grain, and the wind whirled the dry husks in spirals along the quay of a dock with no water in it. He whirled along with the husks — very tired and light. All his inside was gone. He felt lighter than the husks — and more dry. He expanded his hollow chest. The air streamed in, carrying away in its rush a lot of strange things that resembled houses, trees, people, lamp-posts.... No more! There was no more air — and he had not finished drawing his long breath. But he was in jail! They were locking him up. A door slammed. They turned the key twice, flung a bucket of water over him — Phoo! What for?

He opened his eyes, thinking the fall had been very heavy for an empty man — empty — empty. He was in his cabin. Ah! All right! His face was streaming with perspiration, his arms heavier than lead. He saw the cook standing in the doorway, a brass key in one hand and a bright tin hook-pot in the other.

"I have locked up the galley for the night," said the cook, beaming benevolently. "Eight bells just gone. I brought you a pot of cold tea for your night's drinking, Jimmy. I sweetened it with some white cabin sugar, too. Well — it won't break the ship."

He came in, hung the pot on the edge of the bunk, asked perfunctorily, "How goes it?" and sat down on the box. — "H'm," grunted Wait, inhospitably. The cook wiped his face with a dirty cotton rag, which, afterwards, he tied round his neck. — "That's how them firemen do in steamboats," he said, serenely, and much pleased with himself. "My work is as heavy as theirs — I'm thinking — and longer hours. Did you ever see them down the stokehold? Like fiends they look — firing — firing — firing — down there."

He pointed his forefinger at the deck. Some gloomy thought darkened his shining face, fleeting, like the shadow of a travelling cloud over the light of a peaceful sea. The relieved watch tramped noisily forward, passing in a body across the sheen of the doorway. Someone cried, "Good-night!" Belfast stopped for a moment and looked at Jimmy, quivering and speechless with repressed emotion. He gave the cook a glance charged with dismal foreboding, and vanished. The cook cleared his throat. Jimmy stared upwards and kept as still as a man in hiding.

The night was clear, with a gentle breeze. Above the mastheads the resplendent curve of the Milky Way spanned the sky like a triumphal arch of eternal light, thrown over the dark pathway of the earth. On the forecastle head a man whistled with loud precision a lively jig, while another could be heard faintly, shuffling and stamping in time. There came from forward a confused murmur of voices, laughter — snatches of song. The cook shook his head, glanced obliquely at Jimmy, and began to mutter. "Aye. Dance and sing. That's all they think of. I am surprised that Providence don't get tired.... They forget the day that's sure to come... but you...."

Jimmy drank a gulp of tea, hurriedly, as though he had stolen it, and shrank under his blanket, edging away towards the bulkhead. The cook got up, closed the door, then sat down again and said distinctly: —

"Whenever I poke my galley fire I think of you chaps — swearing, stealing, lying, and worse — as if there was no such thing as another world.... Not bad fellows, either, in a way," he conceded, slowly; then, after a pause of regretful musing, he went on in a resigned tone: — "Well, well. They will have a hot time of it. Hot! Did I say? The furnaces of one of them White Star boats ain't nothing to it."

He kept very quiet for a while. There was a great stir in his brain; an addled vision of bright outlines; an exciting row of rousing songs and groans of pain. He suffered, enjoyed, admired, approved. He was delighted, frightened, exalted — as on that evening (the only time in his life — twenty-seven years ago; he loved to recall the number of years) when as a young man he had — through keeping bad company — become intoxicated in an East-end music-hall. A tide of sudden feeling swept him clean out of his body. He soared. He contemplated the secret of the hereafter. It commended itself to him. It was excellent; he loved it, himself, all hands, and Jimmy. His heart overflowed with tenderness, with comprehension, with the desire to meddle, with anxiety for the soul of that black man, with the pride of possessed eternity, with the feeling of might. Snatch him up in his arms and pitch him right into the middle of salvation.... The black soul — blacker — body — rot — Devil. No! Talk — strength — Samson.... There was a great din as of cymbals in his ears; he flashed through an ecstatic jumble of shining faces, lilies, prayer-books, unearthly joy, white skirts, gold harps, black coats, wings. He saw flowing garments, clean shaved faces, a sea of light — a lake of pitch. There were sweet scents, a smell of sulphur — red tongues of flame licking a white mist. An awesome voice thundered!... It lasted three seconds.

"Jimmy!" he cried in an inspired tone. Then he hesitated. A spark of human pity glimmered yet through the infernal fog of his supreme conceit.

"What?" said James Wait, unwillingly. There was a silence. He turned his head just the least bit, and stole a cautious glance. The cook's lips moved without a sound; his face was rapt, his eyes turned up. He seemed to be mentally imploring deck beams, the brass hook of the lamp, two cockroaches.

"Look here," said Wait, "I want to go to sleep. I think I could."

"This is no time for sleep!" exclaimed the cook, very loud. He had prayerfully divested himself of the last vestige of his humanity. He was a voice — a fleshless and sublime thing, as on that memorable night — the night when he went walking over the sea to make coffee for perishing sinners. "This is no time for sleeping," he repeated with exaltation. "*I* can't sleep."

"Don't care damn," said Wait, with factitious energy. "I can. Go an' turn in."

"Swear... in the very jaws!... In the very jaws! Don't you see the everlasting fire... don't you feel it? Blind, chockfull of sin! Repent, repent! I can't bear to think of you. I hear the call to save you. Night and day. Jimmy, let me save you!" The words of entreaty and menace broke out of him in a roaring torrent. The cockroaches ran away. Jimmy perspired, wriggling stealthily under his blanket. The cook yelled.... "Your days are numbered!..." — "Get out of this," boomed Wait, courageously. — "Pray with me!..." — "I won't!..." The little cabin was as hot as an oven. It contained an immensity of fear and pain; an atmosphere of shrieks and moans; prayers vociferated like blasphemies and whispered curses. Outside, the men called by Charley, who informed them in tones of delight that there was a holy row going on in Jimmy's place, crowded before the closed door, too startled to open it. All hands were there. The watch below had jumped out on deck in their shirts, as after a collision. Men running up, asked: — "What is it?" Others said: — "Listen!" The muffled screaming went on: — "On your knees! On your knees!" — "Shut up!" — "Never! You are delivered into my hands.... Your life has been saved.... Purpose.... Mercy.... Repent." — "You are a crazy fool!..." — "Account of you... you... Never sleep in this world, if I..." — "Leave off." — "No!... stokehold... only think!..." Then an impassioned screeching babble where words pattered like hail. — "No!" shouted Wait. — "Yes. You are!

... No help.... Everybody says so." — "You lie!" — "I see you dying this minnyt... before my eyes... as good as dead already." — "Help!" shouted Jimmy, piercingly. — "Not in this valley.... look upwards," howled the other. — "Go away! Murder! Help!" clamoured Jimmy. His voice broke. There were moanings, low mutters, a few sobs.

"What's the matter now?" said a seldom-heard voice. — "Fall back, men! Fall back, there!" repeated Mr. Creighton, sternly, pushing through. — "Here's the old man," whispered some. — "The cook's in there, sir," exclaimed several, backing away. The door clattered open; a broad stream of light darted out on wondering faces; a warm whiff of vitiated air passed. The two mates towered head and shoulders above the spare, grey-haired man who stood revealed between them, in shabby clothes, stiff and angular, like a small carved figure, and with a thin, composed face. The cook got up from his knees. Jimmy sat high in the bunk, clasping his drawn-up legs. The tassel of the blue night-cap almost imperceptibly trembled over his knees. They gazed astonished at his long, curved back, while the white corner of one eye gleamed blindly at them. He was afraid to turn his head, he shrank within himself; and there was an aspect astounding and animal-like in the perfection of his expectant immobility. A thing of instinct — the unthinking stillness of a scared brute.

"What are you doing here?" asked Mr. Baker, sharply. — "My duty," said the cook, with ardour. — "Your... what?" began the mate. Captain Allistoun touched his arm lightly. — "I know his caper," he said, in a low voice. "Come out of that, Podmore," he ordered, aloud.

The cook wrung his hands, shook his fists above his head, and his arms dropped as if too heavy. For a moment he stood distracted and speechless. — "Never," he stammered, "I... he... I." — "What — do — you — say?" pronounced Captain Allistoun. "Come out at once — or..." — "I am going," said the cook, with a hasty and sombre resignation. He strode over the door-step firmly — hesitated — made a few steps. They looked at him in silence. — "I make you responsible!" he cried, desperately, turning half round. "That man is dying. I make you..." — "You there yet?" called the master in a threatening tone. — "No, sir," he exclaimed, hurriedly, in a startled voice. The boatswain led him away by the arm; someone laughed; Jimmy lifted his head for a stealthy glance, and in one unexpected leap sprang out of his bunk; Mr. Baker made a clever catch and felt him very limp in his arms; the group at the door grunted with surprise. — "He lies," gasped Wait, "he talked about black devils — he is a devil — a white devil — I am all right." He stiffened himself, and Mr. Baker, experimentally, let him go. He staggered a pace or two; Captain Allistoun watched him with a quiet and penetrating gaze; Belfast ran to his support. He did not appear to be aware of anyone near him; he stood silent for a moment, battling single-handed with a legion of nameless terrors, amidst the eager looks of excited men who watched him far off, utterly alone in the impenetrable solitude of his fear. The sea gurgled through the scuppers as the ship heeled over to a short puff of wind.

"Keep him away from me," said James Wait at last in his fine baritone voice, and leaning with all his weight on Belfast's neck. "I've been better this last week... I am well... I was going back to duty... tomorrow — now if you like — Captain." Belfast hitched his shoulders to keep him upright.

"No," said the master, looking at him, fixedly.

Under Jimmy's armpit Belfast's red face moved uneasily. A row of eyes gleaming stared on the edge of light. They pushed one another with elbows, turned their heads, whispered. Wait let his chin fall on his breast and, with lowered eyelids, looked round in a suspicious manner.

"Why not?" cried a voice from the shadows, "the man's all right, sir."

"I am all right," said Wait, with eagerness. "Been sick... better... turn-to now." He sighed. — "Howly Mother!" exclaimed Belfast with a heave of the shoulders, "stand up, Jimmy." — "Keep away from me then," said Wait, giving Belfast a petulant push, and reeling fetched against the doorpost. His cheekbones glistened as though they had been varnished. He snatched off his night-cap, wiped his perspiring face with it, flung it on the deck. "I am coming out," he declared without stirring.

"No. You don't," said the master, curtly. Bare feet shuffled, disapproving voices murmured all round; he went on as if he had not heard: — "You have been skulking nearly all the passage and now you want to come out. You think you are near enough to the pay-table now. Smell the shore, hey?"

"I've been sick... now — better," mumbled Wait, glaring in the light. — "You have been shamming sick," retorted Captain Allistoun with severity; "Why..." he hesitated for less than half a second. "Why, anybody can see that. There's nothing the matter with you, but you choose to lie-up to please yourself — and now you shall lie-up to please me. Mr. Baker, my orders are that this man is not to be allowed on deck to the end of the passage."

There were exclamations of surprise, triumph, indignation. The dark group of men swung across the light. "What for?" "Told you so..." "Bloomin' shame..." — "We've got to say somethink about that," screeched Donkin from the rear. — "Never mind, Jim — we will see you righted," cried several together. An elderly seaman stepped to the front. "D'ye mean to say, sir," he asked, ominously, "that a sick chap ain't allowed to get well in this 'ere hooker?" Behind him Donkin whispered excitedly amongst a staring crowd where no one spared him a glance, but Captain Allistoun shook a forefinger at the angry bronzed face of the speaker. — "You — you hold your tongue," he said, warningly. — "This isn't the way," clamoured two or three younger men. — "Are we bloomin' masheens?" inquired Donkin in a piercing tone, and dived under the elbows of the front rank. — "Soon show 'im we ain't boys..." — "The man's a man if he is black." — "We ain't goin' to work this bloomin' ship shorthanded if Snowball's all right..." — "He says he is." — "Well then, strike, boys, strike!" — "That's the bloomin' ticket." Captain Allistoun said sharply to the second mate: "Keep quiet, Mr. Creighton," and stood composed in the tumult, listening with profound attention to mixed growls and screeches, to every exclamation and every curse of the sudden outbreak. Somebody slammed the cabin door to with a kick; the darkness full of menacing mutters leaped with a short clatter over the streak of light, and the men became gesticulating shadows that growled, hissed, laughed excitedly. Mr. Baker whispered: — "Get away from them, sir." The big shape of Mr. Creighton hovered silently about the slight figure of the master. — "We have been hymposed upon all this voyage," said a gruff voice, "but this 'ere fancy takes the cake." — "That man is a shipmate." — "Are we bloomin' kids?" — "The port watch will refuse duty." Charley carried away by his feeling whistled shrilly, then yelped: — "Giv' us our Jimmy!" This seemed to cause a variation in the disturbance. There was a fresh burst of squabbling uproar. A lot of quarrels were set going at once. — "Yes." — "No." — "Never been sick." — "Go for them to once." — "Shut yer mouth, youngster — this is men's work." — "Is it?" muttered Captain Allistoun, bitterly. Mr. Baker grunted: "Ough! They're gone silly. They've been simmering for the last month." — "I did notice," said the master. — "They have started a row amongst themselves now," said Mr. Creighton with disdain, "better get aft, sir. We will soothe them." — "Keep your temper, Creighton," said the master. And the three men began to move slowly towards the cabin door.

In the shadows of the fore rigging a dark mass stamped, eddied, advanced, retreated. There were words of reproach, encouragement, unbelief, execration. The elder seamen, bewildered and angry, growled their determination to go through with something or other; but the younger school of advanced thought exposed their and Jimmy's wrongs with confused shouts, arguing amongst themselves. They clustered round that moribund carcass, the fit emblem of their aspirations, and encouraging one another they swayed, they tramped on one spot, shouting that they would not be "put upon." Inside the cabin, Belfast, helping Jimmy into his bunk, twitched all over in his desire not to miss all the row, and with difficulty restrained the tears of his facile emotion. James Wait, flat on his back under the blanket, gasped complaints. — "We will back you up, never fear," assured Belfast, busy about his feet. — "I'll come out tomorrow morning —— take my chance —— you fellows must ——" mumbled Wait, "I come out tomorrow —— skipper or no skipper." He lifted one arm with great difficulty, passed the hand over his face; "Don't you let that cook..." he breathed out. — "No, no," said Belfast, turning his back on the bunk, "I will put a head on him if he comes near you." — "I will smash his mug!" exclaimed faintly Wait, enraged and weak; "I don't want to kill a man, but..." He panted fast like a dog after a run in sunshine. Someone just outside the door shouted, "He's as fit as any ov us!" Belfast put his hand on the door-handle. — "Here!" called James Wait, hurriedly, and in such a clear voice that the other spun round with a start. James Wait, stretched out black and deathlike in the dazzling light, turned his head on the pillow. His eyes stared at Belfast, appealing and impudent. "I am rather weak from lying-up so long," he said, distinctly. Belfast nodded. "Getting quite well now," insisted Wait. — "Yes. I noticed you getting better this... last month," said Belfast, looking down. "Hallo! What's this?" he shouted and ran out.

He was flattened directly against the side of the house by two men who lurched against him. A lot of disputes seemed to be going on all round. He got clear and saw three indistinct figures standing along in the fainter darkness under the arched foot of the mainsail, that rose above their heads like a convex wall of a high edifice. Donkin hissed: — "Go for them... it's dark!" The crowd took a short run aft in a body — then there was a check. Donkin, agile and thin, flitted past with his right arm going like a windmill — and then stood still suddenly with his arm pointing rigidly above his head. The hurtling flight of some heavy object was heard; it passed between the heads of the two mates, bounded heavily along the deck, struck the after hatch with a ponderous and deadened blow. The bulky shape of Mr. Baker grew distinct. "Come to your senses, men!" he cried, advancing at the arrested crowd. "Come back, Mr. Baker!" called the master's quiet voice. He obeyed unwillingly. There was a minute of silence, then a deafening hubbub arose. Above it Archie was heard energetically: — "If ye do oot ageen I wull tell!" There were shouts. "Don't!" "Drop it!" — "We ain't that kind!" The black cluster of human forms reeled against the bulwark, back again towards the house. Ringbolts rang under stumbling feet. — "Drop it!" "Let me!" — "No!" — "Curse you... hah!" Then sounds as of someone's face being slapped; a piece of iron fell on the deck; a short scuffle, and someone's shadowy body scuttled rapidly across the main hatch before the shadow of a kick. A raging voice sobbed out a torrent of filthy language... — "Throwing things — good God!" grunted Mr. Baker in dismay. — "That was meant for me," said the master, quietly; "I felt the wind of that thing; what was it — an iron belaying-pin?" — "By Jove!" muttered Mr. Creighton. The confused voices of men talking amidships mingled with the wash of the sea, ascended between the silent and distended sails — seemed to flow away into the night, further than the horizon, higher than the sky. The stars burned steadily over the inclined mastheads. Trails of light lay on the water, broke before the advancing hull, and, after she had passed, trembled for a long time as if in awe of the murmuring sea.

Meantime the helmsman, anxious to know what the row was about, had let go the wheel, and, bent double, ran with long, stealthy footsteps to the break of the poop. The *Narcissus*, left to herself, came up gently to the wind without anyone being aware of it. She gave a slight roll, and the sleeping sails woke suddenly, coming all together with a mighty flap against the masts, then filled again one after another in a quick succession of loud reports that ran down the lofty spars, till the collapsed mainsail flew out last with a violent jerk. The ship trembled from trucks to keel; the sails kept on rattling like a discharge of musketry; the chain sheets and loose shackles jingled aloft in a thin peal; the gin blocks groaned. It was as if an invisible hand had given the ship an angry shake to recall the men that peopled her decks to the sense of reality, vigilance, and duty. — "Helm up!" cried the master, sharply. "Run aft, Mr. Creighton, and see what that fool there is up to." — "Flatten in the head sheets. Stand by the weather fore-braces," growled Mr. Baker. Startled men ran swiftly repeating the orders. The watch below, abandoned all at once by the watch on deck, drifted towards the forecastle in twos and threes, arguing noisily as they went — "We shall see tomorrow!" cried a loud voice, as if to cover with a menacing hint an inglorious retreat. And then only orders were heard, the falling of heavy coils of rope, the rattling of blocks. Singleton's white head flitted here and there in the night, high above the deck, like the ghost of a bird. — "Going off, sir!" shouted Mr. Creighton from aft. — "Full again." — "All right..." — "Ease off the head sheets. That will do the braces. Coil the ropes up," grunted Mr. Baker, bustling about.

Gradually the tramping noises, the confused sound of voices, died out, and the officers, coming together on the poop, discussed the events. Mr. Baker was bewildered and grunted; Mr. Creighton was calmly furious; but Captain Allistoun was composed and thoughtful. He listened to Mr. Baker's growling argumentation, to Creighton's interjected and severe remarks, while looking down on the deck he weighed in his hand the iron belaying-pin — that a moment ago had just missed his head — as if it had been the only tangible fact of the whole transaction. He was one of those commanders who speak little, seem to hear nothing, look at no one — and know everything, hear every whisper, see every fleeting shadow of their ship's life. His two big officers towered above his lean, short figure; they talked over his head; they were dismayed, surprised, and angry, while between them the little quiet man seemed to have found his taciturn serenity in the profound depths of a larger experience. Lights were burning in the forecastle; now and then a loud gust of babbling chatter came from forward, swept over the decks, and became faint, as if the unconscious ship, gliding gently through the great peace of the sea, had left behind and for ever the foolish noise of turbulent mankind. But it was renewed again and again. Gesticulating arms, profiles of heads with open mouths appeared for a moment in the illuminated squares of doorways; black fists darted — withdrew... "Yes. It was most damnable to have such an unprovoked row sprung on one," assented the master.... A tumult of yells rose in the light, abruptly ceased.... He didn't think there would be any further trouble just then.... A bell was struck aft, another, forward, answered in a deeper tone, and the clamour of ringing metal spread round the ship in a circle of wide vibrations that ebbed away into the immeasurable night of an empty sea.... Didn't he know them! Didn't he! In past years. Better men, too. Real men to stand by one in a tight place. Worse than devils too sometimes — downright, horned devils. Pah! This — nothing. A miss as good as a mile.... The wheel was being relieved in the usual way. — "Full and by," said, very loud, the man going off. — "Full and by," repeated the other, catching hold of the spokes. — "This head wind is my trouble," exclaimed the master, stamping his foot in sudden anger; "head wind! all the rest is nothing." He was calm again in a moment. "Keep them on the move tonight, gentlemen; just to let them feel we've got hold all the time — quietly, you know. Mind you keep your hands off them, Creighton. Tomorrow I will talk to them like a Dutch Uncle. A crazy crowd of tinkers! Yes, tinkers! I could count the real sailors amongst them on the fingers of one hand. Nothing will do but a row — if — you — please." He paused. "Did you think I had gone wrong there, Mr. Baker?" He tapped his forehead, laughed short. "When I saw him standing there, three parts dead and so scared — black amongst that gaping lot — no grit to face what's coming to us all — the notion came to me all at once, before I could think. Sorry for him — like you would be for a sick brute. If ever creature was in a mortal funk to die!... I thought I would let him go out in his own way. Kind of impulse. It never came into my head, those fools.... H'm! Stand to it now — of course." He stuck the belaying-pin in his pocket, seemed ashamed of himself, then sharply: — "If you see Podmore at his tricks again tell him I will have him put under the pump. Had to do it once before. The fellow breaks out like that now and then. Good cook tho'." He walked away quickly, came back to the companion. The two mates followed him through the starlight with amazed eyes. He went down three steps, and changing his tone, spoke with his head near the deck: — "I shan't turn in tonight, in case of anything; just call out if... Did you see the eyes of that sick nigger, Mr. Baker? I fancied he begged me for something. What? Past all help. One lone black beggar amongst the lot of us, and he seemed to look through me into the very hell. Fancy, this wretched Podmore! Well, let him die in peace. I am master here after all. Let him be. He might have been half a man once... Keep a good look-out." He disappeared down below, leaving his mates facing one another, and more impressed than if they had seen a stone image shed a miraculous tear of compassion over the incertitudes of life and death....

In the blue mist spreading from twisted threads that stood upright in the bowls of pipes, the forecastle appeared as vast as a hall. Between the beams a heavy cloud stagnated; and the lamps surrounded by halos burned each at the core of a purple glow in two lifeless flames without rays. Wreaths drifted in denser wisps. Men sprawled about on the deck, sat in negligent poses, or, bending a knee, drooped with one shoulder against a bulkhead. Lips moved, eyes flashed, waving arms made sudden eddies in the smoke. The murmur of voices seemed to pile itself higher and higher as if unable to run out quick enough through the narrow doors. The watch below in their shirts, and striding on long white legs, resembled raving somnambulists; while now and then one of the watch on deck would rush in, looking strangely over-dressed, listen a moment, fling a rapid sentence into the noise and run out again; but a few remained near the door, fascinated, and with one ear turned to the deck. "Stick together, boys," roared Davis. Belfast tried to make himself heard. Knowles grinned in a slow, dazed way. A short fellow with a thick clipped beard kept on yelling periodically: — "Who's afeard? Who's afeard?" Another one jumped up, excited, with blazing eyes, sent out a string of unattached curses and sat down quietly. Two men discussed familiarly, striking one another's breast in turn, to clinch arguments. Three others, with their heads in a bunch, spoke all together with a confidential air, and at the top of their voices. It was a stormy chaos of speech where intelligible fragments tossing, struck the ear. One could hear: — "In the last ship" — "Who cares? Try it on any one of us if ——." "Knock under" — "Not a hand's turn" — "He says he is all right" — "I always thought" — "Never mind...." Donkin, crouching all in a heap against the bowsprit, hunched his shoulder blades as high as his ears, and hanging a peaked nose, resembled a sick vulture with ruffled plumes. Belfast, straddling his legs, had a face red with yelling, and with arms thrown up, figured a Maltese cross. The two Scandinavians, in a corner, had the dumbfounded and distracted aspect of men gazing at a cataclysm. And, beyond the light, Singleton stood in the smoke, monumental, indistinct, with his head touching the beam; like a statue of heroic size in the gloom of a crypt.

He stepped forward, impassive and big. The noise subsided like a broken wave: but Belfast cried once more with uplifted arms: — "The man is dying I tell ye!" then sat down suddenly on the hatch and took his head between his hands. All looked at Singleton, gazing upwards from the deck, staring out of dark corners, or turning their heads with curious glances. They were expectant and appeased as if that old man, who looked at no one, had possessed the secret of their uneasy indignations and desires, a sharper vision, a clearer knowledge. And indeed standing there amongst them, he had the uninterested appearance of one who had seen multitudes of ships, had listened many times to voices such as theirs, had already seen all that could happen on the wide seas. They heard his voice rumble in his broad chest as though the words had been rolling towards them out of a rugged past. "What do you want to do?" he asked. No one answered. Only Knowles muttered — "Aye, aye," and somebody said low: — "It's a bloomin' shame." He waited, made a contemptuous gesture. — "I have seen rows aboard ship before some of you were born," he said, slowly, "for something or nothing; but never for such a thing." — "The man is dying, I tell ye," repeated Belfast, woefully, sitting at Singleton's feet. — "And a black fellow, too," went on the old seaman, "I have seen them die like flies." He stopped, thoughtful, as if trying to recollect gruesome things, details of horrors, hecatombs of niggers. They looked at him fascinated. He was old enough to remember slavers, bloody mutinies, pirates perhaps; who could tell through what violences and terrors he had lived! What would he say? He said: — "You can't help him; die he must." He made another pause. His moustache and beard stirred. He chewed words, mumbled behind tangled white hairs; incomprehensible and exciting, like an oracle behind a veil.... — "Stop ashore —— sick. —— Instead —— bringing all this head wind. Afraid. The sea will have her own. —— Die in sight of land. Always so. They know it —— long passage —— more days, more dollars. —— You keep quiet. —— What do you want? Can't help him." He seemed to wake up from a dream. "You can't help yourselves," he said, austerely. "Skipper's no fool. He has something in his mind. Look out — I say! I know 'em!" With eyes fixed in front he turned his head from right to left, from left to right, as if inspecting a long row of astute skippers. — "'Ee said 'ee would brain me!" cried Donkin in a heartrending tone. Singleton peered downwards with puzzled attention, as though he couldn't find him. — "Damn you!" he said, vaguely, giving it up. He radiated unspeakable wisdom, hard unconcern, the chilling air of resignation. Round him all the listeners felt themselves somehow completely enlightened by their disappointment, and mute, they lolled about with the careless ease of men who can discern perfectly the irremediable aspect of their existence. He, profound and unconscious, waved his arm once, and strode out on deck without other word.

Belfast was lost in a round-eyed meditation. One or two vaulted heavily into upper berths, and, once there, sighed; others dived head first inside lower bunks — swift, and turning round instantly upon themselves, like animals going into lairs. The grating of a knife scraping burnt clay was heard. Knowles grinned no more. Davis said, in a tone of ardent conviction; "Then our skipper's looney." Archie muttered: "My faith! we haven't heard the last of it yet!" Four bells were struck. — "Half our watch below gone!" cried Knowles in alarm, then reflected. "Well, two hours' sleep is something towards a rest," he observed, consolingly. Some already pretended to slumber; and Charley, sound asleep, suddenly said a few slurred words in an arbitrary, blank voice. — "This blamed boy has worrums!" commented Knowles from under a blanket, in a learned manner. Belfast got up and approached Archie's berth. — "We pulled him out," he whispered, sadly. — "What?" said the other, with sleepy discontent. — "And now we will have to chuck him overboard," went on Belfast, whose lower lip trembled. — "Chuck what?" asked Archie. — "Poor Jimmy," breathed out Belfast. — "He be blowed!" said Archie with untruthful brutality, and sat up in his bunk; "It's all through him. If it hadn't been for me, there would have been murder on board this ship!" — "'Tain't his fault, is it?" argued Belfast, in a murmur; "I've put him to bed... an' he ain't no heavier than an empty beef-cask," he added, with tears in his eyes. Archie looked at him steadily, then turned his nose to the ship's side with determination. Belfast wandered about as though he had lost his way in the dim forecastle, and nearly fell over Donkin. He contemplated him from on high for a while. "Ain't ye going to turn in?" he asked. Donkin looked up hopelessly. — "That black'earted Scotch son of a thief kicked me!" he whispered from the floor, in a tone of utter desolation. — "And a good job, too!" said Belfast, still very depressed; "You were as near hanging as damn-it tonight, sonny. Don't you play any of your murthering games around my Jimmy! You haven't pulled him out. You just mind! 'Cos if I start to kick you" — he brightened up a bit — "if I start to kick you, it will be Yankee fashion — to break something!" He tapped lightly with his knuckles the top of the bowed head. "You moind that, my bhoy!" he concluded, cheerily. Donkin let it pass. — "Will they split on me?" he asked, with pained anxiety. — "Who — split?" hissed Belfast, coming back a step. "I would split your nose this minyt if I hadn't Jimmy to look after! Who d'ye think we are?" Donkin rose and watched Belfast's back lurch through the doorway. On all sides invisible men slept, breathing calmly. He seemed to draw courage and fury from the peace around him. Venomous and thin-faced, he glared from the ample misfit of borrowed clothes as if looking for something he could smash. His heart leaped wildly in his narrow chest. They slept! He wanted to wring necks, gouge eyes, spit on faces. He shook a dirty pair of meagre fists at the smoking lights. "Ye're no men!" he cried, in a deadened tone. No one moved. "Yer 'aven't the pluck of a mouse!" His voice rose to a husky screech. Wamibo darted out a dishevelled head, and looked at him wildly. "Ye're sweepings ov ships! I 'ope you will all rot before you die!" Wamibo blinked, uncomprehending but interested. Donkin sat down heavily; he blew with force through quivering nostrils, he ground and snapped his teeth, and, with the chin pressed hard against the breast, he seemed busy gnawing his way through it, as if to get at the heart within....

In the morning the ship, beginning another day of her wandering life, had an aspect of sumptuous freshness, like the spring-time of the earth. The washed decks glistened in a long clear stretch; the oblique sunlight struck the yellow brasses in dazzling splashes, darted over the polished rods in lines of gold, and the single drops of salt water forgotten here and there along the rail were as limpid as drops of dew, and sparkled more than scattered diamonds. The sails slept, hushed by a gentle breeze. The sun, rising lonely and splendid in the blue sky, saw a solitary ship gliding close-hauled on the blue sea.

The men pressed three deep abreast of the mainmast and opposite the cabin-door. They shuffled, pushed, had an irresolute mien and stolid faces. At every slight movement Knowles lurched heavily on his short leg. Donkin glided behind backs, restless and anxious, like a man looking for an ambush. Captain Allistoun came out on the quarter-deck suddenly. He walked to and fro before the front. He was grey, slight, alert, shabby in the sunshine, and as hard as adamant. He had his right hand in the side-pocket of his jacket, and also something heavy in there that made folds all down that side. One of the seamen cleared his throat ominously. — "I haven't till now found fault with you men," said the master, stopping short. He faced them with his worn, steely gaze, that by a universal illusion looked straight into every individual pair of the twenty pairs of eyes before his face. At his back Mr. Baker, gloomy and bull-necked, grunted low; Mr. Creighton, fresh as paint, had rosy cheeks and a ready, resolute bearing. "And I don't now," continued the master; "but I am here to drive this ship and keep every man-jack aboard of her up to the mark. If you knew your work as well as I do mine, there would be no trouble. You've been braying in the dark about 'See to-morrow morning!' Well, you see me now. What do you want?" He waited, stepping quickly to and fro, giving them searching glances. What did they want? They shifted from foot to foot, they balanced their bodies; some, pushing back their caps, scratched their heads. What did they want? Jimmy was forgotten; no one thought of him, alone forward in his cabin, fighting great shadows, clinging to brazen lies, chuckling painfully over his transparent deceptions. No, not Jimmy; he was more forgotten than if he had been dead. They wanted great things. And suddenly all the simple words they knew seemed to be lost for ever in the immensity of their vague and burning desire. They knew what they wanted, but they could not find anything worth saying. They stirred on one spot, swinging, at the end of muscular arms, big tarry hands with crooked fingers. A murmur died out. — "What is it — food?" asked the master, "you know the stores have been spoiled off the Cape." — "We know that, sir," said a bearded shell-back in the front rank. — "Work too hard — eh? Too much for your strength?" he asked again. There was an offended silence. — "We don't want to go shorthanded, sir," began at last Davis in a wavering voice, "and this 'ere black — ..." — "Enough!" cried the master. He stood scanning them for a moment, then walking a few steps this way and that began to storm at them coldly, in gusts violent and cutting like the gales of those icy seas that had known his youth. — "Tell you what's the matter? Too big for your boots. Think yourselves damn good men. Know half your work. Do half your duty. Think it too much. If you did ten times as much it wouldn't be enough." — "We did our best by her, sir," cried someone with shaky exasperation. — "Your best," stormed on the master; "You hear a lot on shore, don't you? They don't tell you there your best isn't much to boast of. I tell you — your best is no better than bad. You can do no more? No, I know, and say nothing. But you stop your caper or I will stop it for you. I am ready for you! Stop it!" He shook a finger at the crowd. "As to that man," he raised his voice very much; "as to that man, if he puts his nose out on deck without my leave I will clap him in irons. There!" The cook heard him forward, ran out of the galley lifting his arms, horrified, unbelieving, amazed, and ran in again. There was a moment of profound silence during which a bow-legged seaman, stepping aside, expectorated decorously into the scupper. "There is another thing," said the master, calmly. He made a quick stride and with a swing took an iron belaying-pin out of his pocket. "This!" His movement was so unexpected and sudden that the crowd stepped back. He gazed fixedly at their faces, and some at once put on a surprised air as though they had never seen a belaying-pin before. He held it up. "This is my affair. I don't ask you any questions, but you all know it; it has got to go where it came from." His eyes became angry. The crowd stirred uneasily. They looked away from the piece of iron, they appeared shy, they were embarrassed and shocked as though it had been something horrid, scandalous, or indelicate, that in common decency should not have been flourished like this in broad daylight. The master watched them attentively. "Donkin," he called out in a short, sharp tone.

Donkin dodged behind one, then behind another, but they looked over their shoulders and moved aside. The ranks kept on opening before him, closing behind, till at last he appeared alone before the master as though he had come up through the deck. Captain Allistoun moved close to him. They were much of a size, and at short range the master exchanged a deadly glance with the beady eyes. They wavered. — "You know this?" asked the master. — "No, I don't," answered the other, with cheeky trepidation. — "You are a cur. Take it," ordered the master. Donkin's arms seemed glued to his thighs; he stood, eyes front, as if drawn on parade. "Take it," repeated the master, and stepped closer; they breathed on one another. "Take it," said Captain Allistoun again, making a menacing gesture. Donkin tore away one arm from his side. — "Vy are yer down on me?" he mumbled with effort and as if his mouth had been full of dough. — "If you don't..." began the master. Donkin snatched at the pin as though his intention had been to run away with it, and remained stock still holding it like a candle. "Put it back where you took it from," said Captain Allistoun, looking at him fiercely. Donkin stepped back opening wide eyes. "Go, you blackguard, or I will make you," cried the master, driving him slowly backwards by a menacing advance. He dodged, and with the dangerous iron tried to guard his head from a threatening fist. Mr. Baker ceased grunting for a moment. — "Good! By Jove," murmured appreciatively Mr. Creighton in the tone of a connoisseur. — "Don't tech me," snarled Donkin, backing away. — "Then go. Go faster." — "Don't yer 'it me.... I will pull yer up afore the magistryt.... I'll show yer up." Captain Allistoun made a long stride, and Donkin, turning his back fairly, ran off a little, then stopped and over his shoulder showed yellow teeth. — "Further on, fore-rigging," urged the master, pointing with his arm. — "Are yer goin' to stand by and see me bullied?" screamed Donkin at the silent crowd that watched him. Captain Allistoun walked at him smartly. He started off again with a leap, dashed at the fore-rigging, rammed the pin into its hole violently. "I'll be even with yer yet," he screamed at the ship at large and vanished beyond the foremast. Captain Allistoun spun round and walked back aft with a composed face, as though he had already forgotten the scene. Men moved out of his way. He looked at no one. — "That will do, Mr. Baker. Send the watch below," he said, quietly. "And you men try to walk straight for the future," he added in a calm voice. He looked pensively for a while at the backs of the impressed and retreating crowd. "Breakfast, steward," he called in a tone of relief through the cabin door. — "I didn't like to see you — Ough! — give that pin to that chap, sir," observed Mr. Baker; "he could have bust — Ough! — bust your head like an eggshell with it. — "O! he!" muttered the master, absently. "Queer lot," he went on in a low voice. "I suppose it's all right now. Can never tell tho', nowadays, with such a... Years ago; I was a young master then — one China voyage I had a mutiny; real mutiny, Baker. Different men tho'. I knew what they wanted: they wanted to broach the cargo and get at the liquor. Very simple.... We knocked them about for two days, and when they had enough — gentle as lambs. Good crew. And a smart trip I made." He glanced aloft at the yards braced sharp up. "Head wind day after day," he exclaimed, bitterly. "Shall we never get a decent slant this passage?" — "Ready, sir," said the steward, appearing before them as if by magic and with a stained napkin in his hand. — "Ah! All right. Come along, Mr. Baker — it's late — with all this nonsense."

CHAPTER FIVE

A HEAVY atmosphere of oppressive quietude pervaded the ship. In the afternoon men went about washing clothes and hanging them out to dry in the unprosperous breeze with the meditative languor of disenchanted philosophers. Very little was said. The problem of life seemed too voluminous for the narrow limits of human speech, and by common consent it was abandoned to the great sea that had from the beginning enfolded it in its immense grip; to the sea that knew all, and would in time infallibly unveil to each the wisdom hidden in all the errors, the certitude that lurks in doubts, the realm of safety and peace beyond the frontiers of sorrow and fear. And in the confused current of impotent thoughts that set unceasingly this way and that through bodies of men, Jimmy bobbed up upon the surface, compelling attention, like a black buoy chained to the bottom of a muddy stream. Falsehood triumphed. It triumphed through doubt, through stupidity, through pity, through sentimentalism. We set ourselves to bolster it up, from compassion, from recklessness, from a sense of fun. Jimmy's steadfastness to his untruthful attitude in the face of the inevitable truth had the proportions of a colossal enigma — of a manifestation grand and incomprehensible that at times inspired a wondering awe; and there was also, to many, something exquisitely droll in fooling him thus to the top of his bent. The latent egoism of tenderness to suffering appeared in the developing anxiety not to see him die. His obstinate non-recognition of the only certitude whose approach we could watch from day to day was as disquieting as the failure of some law of nature. He was so utterly wrong about himself that one could not but suspect him of having access to some source of supernatural knowledge. He was absurd to the point of inspiration. He was unique, and as fascinating as only something inhuman could be; he seemed to shout his denials already from beyond the awful border. He was becoming immaterial like an apparition; his cheekbones rose, the forehead slanted more; the face was all hollows, patches of shade; and the fleshless head resembled a disinterred black skull, fitted with two restless globes of silver in the sockets of eyes. He was demoralising. Through him we were becoming highly humanised, tender, complex, excessively decadent: we understood the subtlety of his fear, sympathised with all his repulsions, shrinkings, evasions, delusions — as though we had been overcivilised, and rotten, and without any knowledge of the meaning of life. We had the air of being initiated in some infamous mysteries; we had the profound grimaces of conspirators, exchanged meaning glances, significant short words. We were inexpressibly vile and very much pleased with ourselves. We lied to him with gravity, with emotion, with unction, as if performing some moral trick with a view to an eternal reward. We made a chorus of affirmation to his wildest assertions, as though he had been a millionaire, a politician, or a reformer — and we a crowd of ambitious lubbers. When we ventured to question his statements we did it after the manner of obsequious sycophants, to the end that his glory should be augmented by the flattery of our dissent. He influenced the moral tone of our world as though he had it in his power to distribute honours, treasures, or pain; and he could give us nothing but his contempt. It was immense; it seemed to grow gradually larger, as his body day by day shrank a little more, while we looked. It was the only thing about him — of him — that gave the impression of durability and vigour. It lived within him with an unquenchable life. It spoke through the eternal pout of his black lips; it looked at us through the impertinent mournfulness of his languid and enormous stare. We watched him intently. He seemed unwilling to move, as if distrustful of his own solidity. The slightest gesture must have disclosed to him (it could not surely be otherwise) his bodily weakness, and caused a pang of mental suffering. He was chary of movements. He lay stretched out, chin on blanket, in a kind of sly, cautious immobility. Only his eyes roamed over faces: his eyes disdainful, penetrating and sad.

It was at that time that Belfast's devotion — and also his pugnacity — secured universal respect. He spent every moment of his spare time in Jimmy's cabin. He tended him, talked to him; was as gentle as a woman, as tenderly gay as an old philanthropist, as sentimentally careful of his nigger as a model slave-owner. But outside he was irritable, explosive as gunpowder, sombre, suspicious, and never more brutal than when most sorrowful. With him it was a tear and a blow: a tear for Jimmy, a blow for anyone who did not seem to take a scrupulously orthodox view of Jimmy's case. We talked about nothing else. The two Scandinavians, even, discussed the situation — but it was impossible to know in what spirit, because they quarrelled in their own language. Belfast suspected one of them of irreverence, and in this incertitude thought that there was no option but to fight them both. They became very much terrified by his truculence, and henceforth lived amongst us, dejected, like a pair of mutes. Wamibo never spoke intelligibly, but he was as smileless as an animal — seemed to know much less about it all than the cat — and consequently was safe. Moreover, he had belonged to the chosen band of Jimmy's rescuers, and was above suspicion. Archie was silent generally, but often spent an hour or so talking to Jimmy quietly with an air of proprietorship. At any time of the day and often through the night some man could be seen sitting on Jimmy's box. In the evening, between six and eight, the cabin was crowded, and there was an interested group at the door. Everyone stared at the nigger.

He basked in the warmth of our interest. His eyes gleamed ironically, and in a weak voice he reproached us with our cowardice. He would say, "If you fellows had stuck out for me I would be now on deck." We hung our heads. "Yes, but if you think I am going to let them put me in irons just to show you sport.... Well, no.... It ruins my health, this lying-up, it does. You don't care." We were as abashed as if it had been true. His superb impudence carried all before it. We would not have dared to revolt. We didn't want to, really. We wanted to keep him alive till home — to the end of the voyage.

Singleton as usual held aloof, appearing to scorn the insignificant events of an ended life. Once only he came along, and unexpectedly stopped in the doorway. He peered at Jimmy in profound silence, as if desirous to add that black image to the crowd of Shades that peopled his old memory. We kept very quiet, and for a long time Singleton stood there as though he had come by appointment to call for someone, or to see some important event. James Wait lay perfectly still, and apparently not aware of the gaze scrutinising him with a steadiness full of expectation. There was a sense of a contest in the air. We felt the inward strain of men watching a wrestling bout. At last Jimmy with perceptible apprehension turned his head on the pillow. — "Good evening," he said in a conciliating tone. — "H'm," answered the old seaman, grumpily. For a moment longer he looked at Jimmy with severe fixity, then suddenly went away. It was a long time before anyone spoke in the little cabin, though we all breathed more freely as men do after an escape from some dangerous situation. We all knew the old man's ideas about Jimmy, and nobody dared to combat them. They were unsettling, they caused pain; and, what was worse, they might have been true for all we knew. Only once did he condescend to explain them fully, but the impression was lasting. He said that Jimmy was the cause of head winds. Mortally sick men — he maintained — linger till the first sight of land, and then die; and Jimmy knew that the very first land would draw his life from him. It is so in every ship. Didn't we know it? He asked us with austere contempt: what did we know? What would we doubt next? Jimmy's desire encouraged by us and aided by Wamibo's (he was a Finn — wasn't he? Very well!) by Wamibo's spells delayed the ship in the open sea. Only lubberly fools couldn't see it. Whoever heard of such a run of calms and head winds? It wasn't natural.... We could not deny that it was strange. We felt uneasy. The common saying, "More days, more dollars," did not give the usual comfort because the stores were running short. Much had been spoiled off the Cape, and we were on half allowance of biscuit. Peas, sugar and tea had been finished long ago. Salt meat was giving out. We had plenty of coffee but very little water to make it with. We took up another hole in our belts and went on scraping, polishing, painting the ship from morning to night. And soon she looked as though she had come out of a band-box; but hunger lived on board of her. Not dead starvation, but steady, living hunger that stalked about the decks, slept in the forecastle; the tormentor of waking moments, the disturber of dreams. We looked to windward for signs of change. Every few hours of night and day we put her round with the hope that she would come up on that tack at last! She didn't. She seemed to have forgotten the way home; she rushed to and fro, heading northwest, heading east; she ran backwards and forwards, distracted, like a timid creature at the foot of a wall. Sometimes, as if tired to death, she would wallow languidly for a day in the smooth swell of an unruffled sea. All up the swinging masts the sails thrashed furiously through the hot stillness of the calm. We were weary, hungry, thirsty; we commenced to believe Singleton, but with unshaken fidelity dissembled to Jimmy. We spoke to him with jocose allusiveness, like cheerful accomplices in a clever plot; but we looked to the westward over the rail with longing eyes for a sign of hope, for a sign of fair wind; even if its first breath should bring death to our reluctant Jimmy. In vain! The universe conspired with James Wait. Light airs from the northward sprang up again; the sky remained clear; and round our weariness the glittering sea, touched by the breeze, basked voluptuously in the great sunshine, as though it had forgotten our life and trouble.

Donkin looked out for a fair wind along with the rest. No one knew the venom of his thoughts now. He was silent, and appeared thinner, as if consumed slowly by an inward rage at the injustice of men and of fate. He was ignored by all and spoke to no one, but his hate for every man dwelt in his furtive eyes. He talked with the cook only, having somehow persuaded the good man that he — Donkin — was a much calumniated and persecuted person. Together they bewailed the immorality of the ship's company. There could be no greater criminals than we, who by our lies conspired to send the unprepared soul of a poor ignorant black man to everlasting perdition. Podmore cooked what there was to cook, remorsefully, and felt all the time that by preparing the food of such sinners he imperilled his own salvation. As to the Captain — he had sailed with him for seven years, now, he said, and would not have believed it possible that such a man... "Well. Well... There it was... Can't get out of it. Judgment capsized all in a minute... Struck in all his pride... More like a sudden visitation than anything else." Donkin, perched sullenly on the coallocker, swung his legs and concurred. He paid in the coin of spurious assent for the privilege to sit in the galley; he was disheartened and scandalised; he agreed with the cook; could find no words severe enough to criticise our conduct; and when in the heat of reprobation he swore at us, Podmore, who would have liked to swear also if it hadn't been for his principles, pretended not to hear. So Donkin, unrebuked, cursed enough for two, cadged for matches, borrowed tobacco, and loafed for hours, very much at home, before the stove. From there he could hear us on the other side of the bulkhead, talking to Jimmy. The cook knocked the saucepans about, slammed the oven door, muttered prophesies of damnation for all the ship's company; and Donkin, who did not admit of any hereafter (except for purposes of blasphemy) listened, concentrated and angry, gloating fiercely over a called-up image of infinite torment — as men gloat over the accursed images of cruelty and revenge, of greed, and of power....

On clear evenings the silent ship, under the cold sheen of the dead moon, took on a false aspect of passionless repose resembling the winter of the earth. Under her a long band of gold barred the black disc of the sea. Footsteps echoed on her quiet decks. The moonlight clung to her like a frosted mist, and the white sails stood out in dazzling cones as of stainless snow. In the magnificence of the phantom rays the ship appeared pure like a vision of ideal beauty, illusive like a tender dream of serene peace. And nothing in her was real, nothing was distinct and solid but the heavy shadows that filled her decks with their unceasing and noiseless stir: the shadows darker than the night and more restless than the thoughts of men.

Donkin prowled spiteful and alone amongst the shadows, thinking that Jimmy too long delayed to die. That evening land had been reported from aloft, and the master, while adjusting the tubes of the long glass, had observed with quiet bitterness to Mr. Baker that, after fighting our way inch by inch to the Western Islands, there was nothing to expect now but a spell of calm. The sky was clear and the barometer high. The light breeze dropped with the sun, and an enormous stillness, forerunner of a night without wind, descended upon the heated waters of the ocean. As long as daylight lasted, the hands collected on the forecastle-head watched on the eastern sky the island of Flores, that rose above the level expanse of the sea with irregular and broken outlines like a sombre ruin upon a vast and deserted plain. It was the first land seen for nearly four months. Charley was excited, and in the midst of general indulgence took liberties with his betters. Men strangely elated without knowing why, talked in groups, and pointed with bared arms. For the first time that voyage Jimmy's sham existence seemed for a moment forgotten in the face of a solid reality. We had got so far anyhow. Belfast discoursed, quoting imaginary examples of short homeward runs from the Islands. "Them smart fruit schooners do it in five days," he affirmed. "What do you want? — only a good little breeze." Archie maintained that seven days was the record passage, and they disputed amicably with insulting words. Knowles declared he could already smell home from there, and with a heavy list on his short leg laughed fit to split his sides. A group of grizzled sea-dogs looked out for a time in silence and with grim absorbed faces. One said suddenly — "'Tain't far to London now." — "My first night ashore, blamme if I haven't steak and onions for supper... and a pint of bitter," said another. — "A barrel ye mean," shouted someone. — "Ham an' eggs three times a day. That's the way I live!" cried an excited voice. There was a stir, appreciative murmurs; eyes began to shine; jaws champed; short, nervous laughs were heard. Archie smiled with reserve all to himself. Singleton came up, gave a careless glance, and went down again without saying a word, indifferent, like a man who had seen Flores an incalculable number of times. The night travelling from the East blotted out of the limpid sky the purple stain of the high land. "Dead calm," said somebody quietly. The murmur of lively talk suddenly wavered, died out; the clusters broke up; men began to drift away one by one, descending the ladders slowly and with serious faces as if sobered by that reminder of their dependence upon the invisible. And when the big yellow moon ascended gently above the sharp rim of the clear horizon it found the ship wrapped up in a breathless silence; a fearless ship that seemed to sleep profoundly, dreamlessly on the bosom of the sleeping and terrible sea.

Donkin chafed at the peace — at the ship — at the sea that stretching away on all sides merged into the illimitable silence of all creation. He felt himself pulled up sharp by unrecognised grievances. He had been physically cowed, but his injured dignity remained indomitable, and nothing could heal his lacerated feelings. Here was land already — home very soon — a bad pay-day — no clothes — more hard work. How offensive all this was. Land. The land that draws away life from sick sailors. That nigger there had money — clothes — easy times; and would not die. Land draws life away.... He felt tempted to go and see whether it did. Perhaps already... It would be a bit of luck. There was money in the beggar's chest. He stepped briskly out of the shadows into the moonlight, and, instantly, his craving, hungry face from sallow became livid. He opened the door of the cabin and had a shock. Sure enough, Jimmy was dead! He moved no more than a recumbent figure with clasped hands, carved on the lid of a stone coffin. Donkin glared with avidity. Then Jimmy, without stirring, blinked his eyelids, and Donkin had another shock. Those eyes were rather startling. He shut the door behind his back with gentle care, looking intently the while at James Wait as though he had come in there at a great risk to tell some secret of startling importance. Jimmy did not move but glanced languidly out of the corners of his eyes. — "Calm?" he asked. — "Yuss," said Donkin, very disappointed, and sat down on the box.

Jimmy was used to such visits at all times of night or day. Men succeeded one another. They spoke in clear voices, pronounced cheerful words, repeated old jokes, listened to him; and each, going out, seemed to leave behind a little of his own vitality, surrender some of his own strength, renew the assurance of life — the indestructible thing! He did not like to be alone in his cabin, because, when he was alone, it seemed to him as if he hadn't been there at all. There was nothing. No pain. Not now. Perfectly right — but he couldn't enjoy his healthful repose unless someone was by to see it. This man would do as well as anybody. Donkin watched him stealthily: — "Soon home now," observed Wait. — "Vy d'yer whisper?" asked Donkin with interest, "can't yer speak up?" Jimmy looked annoyed and said nothing for a while; then in a lifeless, unringing voice: — "Why should I shout? You ain't deaf that I know." — "Oh! I can 'ear right enough," answered Donkin in a low tone, and looked down. He was thinking sadly of going out when Jimmy spoke again. — "Time we did get home ... to get something decent to eat... I am always hungry." Donkin felt angry all of a sudden. — "What about me," he hissed, "I am 'ungry too an' got ter work. You, 'ungry!" — "Your work won't kill you," commented Wait, feebly; "there's a couple of biscuits in the lower bunk there — you may have one. I can't eat them." Donkin dived in, groped in the corner and when he came up again his mouth was full. He munched with ardour. Jimmy seemed to doze with open eyes. Donkin finished his hard bread and got up. — "You're not going?" asked Jimmy, staring at the ceiling. — "No," said Donkin, impulsively, and instead of going out leaned his back against the closed door. He looked at James Wait, and saw him long, lean, dried up, as though all his flesh had shrivelled on his bones in the heat of a white furnace; the meagre fingers of one hand moved lightly upon the edge of the bunk playing an endless tune. To look at him was irritating and fatiguing; he could last like this for days; he was outrageous — belonging wholly neither to death nor life, and perfectly invulnerable in his apparent ignorance of both. Donkin felt tempted to enlighten him. — "What are yer thinkin' of?" he asked, surlily. James Wait had a grimacing smile that passed over the death-like impassiveness of his bony face, incredible and frightful as would, in a dream, have been the sudden smile of a corpse.

"There is a girl," whispered Wait.... "Canton Street girl. —— She chucked a third engineer of a Rennie boat —— for me. Cooks oysters just as I like... She says —— she would chuck —— any toff —— for a coloured gentleman.... That's me. I am kind to wimmen," he added, a shade louder.

Donkin could hardly believe his ears. He was scandalised — "Would she? Yer wouldn't be any good to 'er," he said with unrestrained disgust. Wait was not there to hear him. He was swaggering up the East India Dock Road; saying kindly, "Come along for a treat," pushing glass swing-

doors, posing with superb assurance in the gaslight above a mahogany counter. — "D'yer think yer will ever get ashore?" asked Donkin, angrily.
Wait came back with a start. — "Ten days," he said, promptly, and returned at once to the regions of memory that know nothing of time. He
felt untired, calm, and safely withdrawn within himself beyond the reach of
every grave incertitude. There was something of the immutable quality
of eternity in the slow moments of his complete restfulness. He was very
quiet and easy amongst his vivid reminiscences which he mistook joyfully
for images of an undoubted future. He cared for no one. Donkin felt this
vaguely like a blind man feeling in his darkness the fatal antagonism of all
the surrounding existences, that to him shall for ever remain irrealisable,
unseen and enviable. He had a desire to assert his importance, to break,
to crush; to be even with everybody for everything; to tear the veil, unmask,
expose, leave no refuge — a perfidious desire of truthfulness! He laughed
in a mocking splutter and said:

"Ten days. Strike me blind if I ever!... You will be dead by this time
tomorrow p'r'aps. Ten days!" He waited for a while. "D'ye 'ear me?
Blamme if yer don't look dead already."

Wait must have been collecting his strength, for he said almost aloud —
"You're a stinking, cadging liar. Everyone knows you." And sitting up,
against all probability, startled his visitor horribly. But very soon Donkin
recovered himself. He blustered,

"What? What? Who's a liar? You are — the crowd are — the skipper
— everybody. I ain't! Putting on airs! Who's yer?" He nearly choked
himself with indignation. "Who's yer to put on airs," he repeated, trembling. "'Ave one — 'ave one, says 'ee — an' cawn't eat 'em 'isself. Now
I'll 'ave both. By Gawd — I will! Yer nobody!"

He plunged into the lower bunk, rooted in there and brought to light another dusty biscuit. He held it up before Jimmy — then took a bite defiantly.

"What now?" he asked with feverish impudence. "Yer may take one
— says yer. Why not giv' me both? No. I'm a mangy dorg. One fur a
mangy dorg. I'll tyke both. Can yer stop me? Try. Come on. Try."

Jimmy was clasping his legs and hiding his face on the knees. His shirt
clung to him. Every rib was visible. His emaciated back was shaken in
repeated jerks by the panting catches of his breath.

"Yer won't? Yer can't! What did I say?" went on Donkin, fiercely.
He swallowed another dry mouthful with a hasty effort. The other's silent
helplessness, his weakness, his shrinking attitude exasperated him. "Ye're
done!" he cried. "Who's yer to be lied to; to be waited on 'and an' foot like
a bloomin' ymperor. Yer nobody. Yer no one at all!" he spluttered with
such a strength of unerring conviction that it shook him from head to foot
in coming out, and left him vibrating like a released string.

James Wait rallied again. He lifted his head and turned bravely at
Donkin, who saw a strange face, an unknown face, a fantastic and grimacing
mask of despair and fury. Its lips moved rapidly; and hollow, moaning,
whistling sounds filled the cabin with a vague mutter full of menace, com-

plaint and desolation, like the far-off murmur of a rising wind. Wait shook his head; rolled his eyes; he denied, cursed, threatened — and not a word had the strength to pass beyond the sorrowful pout of those black lips. It was incomprehensible and disturbing; a gibberish of emotions, a frantic dumb show of speech pleading for impossible things, promising a shadowy vengeance. It sobered Donkin into a scrutinising watchfulness.

"Yer can't 'oller. See? What did I tell yer?" he said, slowly, after a moment of attentive examination. The other kept on headlong and un- heard, nodding passionately, grinning with grotesque and appalling flashes of big white teeth. Donkin, as if fascinated by the dumb eloquence and anger of that black phantom, approached, stretching his neck out with distrustful curiosity; and it seemed to him suddenly that he was looking only at the shadow of a man crouching high in the bunk on the level with his eyes. — "What? What?" he said. He seemed to catch the shape of some words in the continuous panting hiss. "Yer will tell Belfast! Will yer? Are yer a bloomin' kid?" He trembled with alarm and rage, "Tell yer gran'mother! Yer afeard! Who's yer ter be afeard more'n anyone?" His passionate sense of his own importance ran away with a last remnant of caution. "Tell an' be damned! Tell, if yer can!" he cried. "I've been treated worser'n a dorg by your blooming back-lickers. They 'as set me on, only to turn aginst me. I am the only man 'ere. They clouted me, kicked me — an' yer laffed — yer black, rotten incumbrance, you! You will pay fur it. They giv' yer their grub, their water — yer will pay fur it to me, by Gawd! Who axed me ter 'ave a drink of water? They put their bloomin' rags on yer that night, an' what did they giv' ter me — a clout on the bloomin' mouth — blast their... S'elp me!... Yer will pay fur it with yer money. I'm goin' ter 'ave it in a minyte; as soon has ye're dead, yer bloomin' useless fraud. That's the man I am. An' ye're a thing — a bloody thing. Yah — you corpse!"

He flung at Jimmy's head the biscuit he had been all the time clutching hard, but it only grazed, and striking with a loud crack the bulkhead beyond burst like a hand-grenade into flying pieces. James Wait, as if wounded mortally, fell back on the pillow. His lips ceased to move and the rolling eyes became quiet and stared upwards with an intense and steady persist- ence. Donkin was surprised; he sat suddenly on the chest, and looked down, exhausted and gloomy. After a moment, he began to mutter to him- self, "Die, you beggar — die. Somebody'll come in... I wish I was drunk ... Ten days... oysters..." He looked up and spoke louder. "No... No more for yer... no more bloomin' gals that cook oysters... Who's yer? It's my turn now... I wish I was drunk; I would soon giv' you a leg up. That's where yer bound to go. Feet fust, through a port... Splash! Never see yer any more. Overboard! Good 'nuff fur yer."

Jimmy's head moved slightly and he turned his eyes to Donkin's face; a gaze unbelieving, desolated and appealing, of a child frightened by the menace of being shut up alone in the dark. Donkin observed him from the chest with hopeful eyes; then, without rising, tried the lid. Locked. "I wish I was drunk," he muttered and getting up listened anxiously to the distant sound of footsteps on the deck. They approached — ceased. Some one yawned interminably just outside the door, and the footsteps went away shuffling lazily. Donkin's fluttering heart eased its pace, and when he looked towards the bunk again Jimmy was staring as before at the white beam. — "'Ow d'yer feel now?" he asked. — "Bad," breathed out Jimmy.

Donkin sat down patient and purposeful. Every half-hour the bells spoke to one another ringing along the whole length of the ship. Jimmy's respiration was so rapid that it couldn't be counted, so faint that it couldn't be heard. His eyes were terrified as though he had been looking at unspeakable horrors; and by his face one could see that he was thinking of abominable things. Suddenly with an incredibly strong and heart-breaking voice he sobbed out:

"Overboard!... I!... My God!"

Donkin writhed a little on the box. He looked unwillingly. James Wait was mute. His two long bony hands smoothed the blanket upwards, as though he had wished to gather it all up under his chin. A tear, a big solitary tear, escaped from the corner of his eye and, without touching the hollow cheek, fell on the pillow. His throat rattled faintly.

And Donkin, watching the end of that hateful nigger, felt the anguishing grasp of a great sorrow on his heart at the thought that he himself, some day, would have to go through it all — just like this — perhaps! His eyes became moist. "Poor beggar," he murmured. The night seemed to go by in a flash; it seemed to him he could hear the irremediable rush of precious minutes. How long would this blooming affair last? Too long surely. No luck. He could not restrain himself. He got up and approached the bunk. Wait did not stir. Only his eyes appeared alive and his hands continued their smoothing movement with a horrible and tireless industry. Donkin bent over.

"Jimmy," he called low. There was no answer, but the rattle stopped. "D'yer see me?" he asked, trembling. Jimmy's chest heaved. Donkin, looking away, bent his ear to Jimmy's lips, and heard a sound like the rustle of a single dry leaf driven along the smooth sand of a beach. It shaped itself.

"Light... the lamp... and... go," breathed out Wait.

Donkin, instinctively, glanced over his shoulder at the brilliant flame; then, still looking away, felt under the pillow for a key. He got it at once and for the next few minutes remained on his knees shakily but swiftly busy inside the box. When he got up, his face — for the first time in his life — had a pink flush — perhaps of triumph.

He slipped the key under the pillow again, avoiding to glance at Jimmy, who had not moved. He turned his back squarely from the bunk, and started to the door as though he were going to walk a mile. At his second stride he had his nose against it. He clutched the handle cautiously, but at that moment he received the irresistible impression of something happening behind his back. He spun round as though he had been tapped on the shoulder. He was just in time to see Wait's eyes blaze up and go out at once, like two lamps overturned together by a sweeping blow. Something resembling a scarlet thread hung down his chin out of the corner of his lips — and he had ceased to breathe.

Donkin closed the door behind him gently but firmly. Sleeping men, huddled under jackets, made on the lighted deck shapeless dark mounds that had the appearance of neglected graves. Nothing had been done all through the night and he hadn't been missed. He stood motionless and perfectly astounded to find the world outside as he had left it; there was the sea, the ship — sleeping men; and he wondered absurdly at it, as though he had expected to find the men dead, familiar things gone for ever: as though, like a wanderer returning after many years, he had expected to see bewildering changes. He shuddered a little in the penetrating freshness of the air, and hugged himself forlornly. The declining moon drooped sadly in the western board as if withered by the cold touch of a pale dawn. The ship slept. And the immortal sea stretched away, immense and hazy, like the image of life, with a glittering surface and lightless depths. Donkin gave it a defiant glance and slunk off noiselessly as if judged and cast out by the august silence of its might.

Jimmy's death, after all, came as a tremendous surprise. We did not know till then how much faith we had put in his delusions. We had taken his chances of life so much at his own valuation that his death, like the death of an old belief, shook the foundations of our society. A common bond was gone; the strong, effective and respectable bond of a sentimental lie. All that day we mooned at our work, with suspicious looks and a disabused air. In our hearts we thought that in the matter of his departure Jimmy had acted in a perverse and unfriendly manner. He didn't back us up, as a shipmate should. In going he took away with himself the gloomy and solemn shadow in which our folly had posed, with humane satisfaction, as a tender arbiter of fate. And now we saw it was no such thing. It was just common foolishness; a silly and ineffectual meddling with issues of majestic import — that is, if Podmore was right. Perhaps he was? Doubt survived Jimmy; and, like a community of banded criminals disintegrated by a touch of grace, we were profoundly scandalised with each other. Men spoke unkindly to their best chums. Others refused to speak at all. Singleton only was not surprised. "Dead — is he? Of course," he said, pointing at the island right abeam; for the calm still held the ship spell-bound within sight of Flores. Dead — of course. *He* wasn't surprised. Here was the land, and there, on the forehatch and waiting for the sailmaker — there was that corpse. Cause and effect. And for the first time that voyage, the old seaman became quite cheery and garrulous, explaining and illustrating from the stores of experience how, in sickness, the sight of an island (even a very small one) is generally more fatal than the view of a continent. But he couldn't explain why.

Jimmy was to be buried at five, and it was a long day till then — a day of mental disquiet and even of physical disturbance. We took no interest in our work and, very properly, were rebuked for it. This, in our constant state of hungry irritation, was exasperating. Donkin worked with his brow bound in a dirty rag, and looked so ghastly that Mr. Baker was touched with compassion at the sight of this plucky suffering. — "Ough! You, Donkin!

Put down your work and go lay-up this watch. You look ill." — "I am bad, sir — in my 'ead," he said in a subdued voice, and vanished speedily. This annoyed many, and they thought the mate "bloomin' soft today." Captain Allistoun could be seen on the poop watching the sky to the southwest, and it soon got to be known about the decks that the barometer had begun to fall in the night, and that a breeze might be expected before long. This, by a subtle association of ideas, led to violent quarrelling as to the exact moment of Jimmy's death. Was it before or after "that 'ere glass started down?" It was impossible to know, and it caused much contemptuous growling at one another. All of a sudden there was a great tumult forward. Pacific Knowles and good-tempered Davis had come to blows over it. The watch below interfered with spirit, and for ten minutes there was a noisy scrimmage round the hatch, where, in the balancing shade of the sails, Jimmy's body, wrapped up in a white blanket, was watched over by the sorrowful Belfast, who, in his desolation, disdained the fray. When the noise had ceased, and the passions had calmed into surly silence, he stood up at the head of the swathed body, lifting both arms on high, cried with pained indignation: — "You ought to be ashamed of yourselves!..." We were.

Belfast took his bereavement very hard. He gave proofs of unextinguishable devotion. It was he, and no other man, who would help the sailmaker to prepare what was left of Jimmy for a solemn surrender to the insatiable sea. He arranged the weights carefully at the feet: two holystones, an old anchor-shackle without its pin, some broken links of a worn-out stream cable. He arranged them this way, then that. "Bless my soul! you aren't afraid he will chafe his heel?" said the sailmaker, who hated the job. He pushed the needle, puffing furiously, with his head in a cloud of tobacco smoke; he turned the flaps over, pulled at the stitches, stretched at the canvas. — "Lift his shoulders.... Pull to you a bit.... So — o — o. Steady." Belfast obeyed, pulled, lifted, overcome with sorrow, dropping tears on the tarred twine. — "Don't you drag the canvas too taut over his poor face, Sails," he entreated, tearfully. — "What are you fashing yourself for? He will be comfortable enough," assured the sailmaker, cutting the thread after the last stitch, which came about the middle of Jimmy's forehead. He rolled up the remaining canvas, put away the needles. "What makes you take on so?" he asked. Belfast looked down at the long package of grey sailcloth. — "I pulled him out," he whispered, "and he did not want to go. If I had sat up with him last night he would have kept alive for me... but something made me tired." The sailmaker took vigorous draws at his pipe and mumbled: — "When I... West India Station... In the *Blanche* frigate... Yellow Jack... sewed in twenty men a week... Portsmouth-Devonport men — townies — knew their fathers, mothers, sisters — the whole boiling of 'em. Thought nothing of it. And these niggers like this one — you don't know where it comes from. Got nobody. No use to nobody. Who will miss him?" — "I do — I pulled him out," mourned Belfast dismally.

On two planks nailed together and apparently resigned and still under the folds of the Union Jack with a white border, James Wait, carried aft by four men, was deposited slowly, with his feet pointing at an open port. A swell had set in from the westward, and following on the roll of the ship, the red ensign, at halfmast, darted out and collapsed again on the grey sky, like a tongue of flickering fire; Charley tolled the bell; and at every swing to starboard the whole vast semicircle of steely waters visible on that side seemed to come up with a rush to the edge of the port, as if impatient to get at our Jimmy. Everyone was there but Donkin, who was too ill to come; the Captain and Mr. Creighton stood bareheaded on the break of the poop; Mr. Baker, directed by the master, who had said to him gravely: — "You know more about the prayer book than I do," came out of the cabin door quickly and a little embarrassed. All the caps went off. He began to read in a low tone, and with his usual harmlessly menacing utterance, as though he had been for the last time reproving confidentially that dead seaman at his feet. The men listened in scattered groups; they leaned on the fife rail, gazing on the deck; they held their chins in their hands thoughtfully, or, with crossed arms and one knee slightly bent, hung their heads in an attitude of upright meditation. Wamibo dreamed. Mr. Baker read on, grunting reverently at the turn of every page. The words, missing the unsteady hearts of men, rolled out to wander without a home upon the heartless sea; and James Wait, silenced for ever, lay uncritical and passive under the hoarse murmur of despair and hopes.

Two men made ready and waited for those words that send so many of our brothers to their last plunge. Mr. Baker began the passage. "Stand by," muttered the boatswain. Mr. Baker read out: "To the deep," and paused. The men lifted the inboard end of the planks, the boatswain snatched off the Union Jack, and James Wait did not move. — "Higher," muttered the boatswain angrily. All the heads were raised; every man stirred uneasily, but James Wait gave no sign of going. In death and swathed up for all eternity, he yet seemed to cling to the ship with the grip of an undying fear. "Higher! Lift!" whispered the boatswain, fiercely. — "He won't go," stammered one of the men, shakily, and both appeared ready to drop everything. Mr. Baker waited, burying his face in the book, and shuffling his feet nervously. All the men looked profoundly disturbed; from their midst a faint humming noise spread out — growing louder.... "Jimmy!" cried Belfast in a wailing tone, and there was a second of shuddering dismay.

"Jimmy, be a man!" he shrieked, passionately. Every mouth was wide open, not an eyelid winked. He stared wildly, twitching all over; he bent his body forward like a man peering at an horror. "Go!" he shouted, and sprang out of the crowd with his arm extended. "Go, Jimmy! — Jimmy, go! Go!" His fingers touched the head of the body, and the grey package started reluctantly to whizz off the lifted planks all at once, with the suddenness of a flash of lightning. The crowd stepped forward like one man; a deep Ah — h — h! came out vibrating from the broad chests. The ship rolled as if relieved of an unfair burden; the sails flapped. Belfast, supported by Archie, gasped hysterically; and Charley, who anxious to see Jimmy's last dive, leaped headlong on the rail, was too late to see anything but the faint circle of a vanishing ripple.

Mr. Baker, perspiring abundantly, read out the last prayer in a deep rumour of excited men and fluttering sails. "Amen!" he said in an unsteady growl, and closed the book.

"Square the yards!" thundered a voice above his head. All hands gave a jump; one or two dropped their caps; Mr. Baker looked up surprised. The master, standing on the break of the poop, pointed to the westward. "Breeze coming," he said, "Man the weather braces." Mr. Baker crammed the book hurriedly into his pocket. "Forward, there — let go the foretack!" he hailed joyfully, bareheaded and brisk; "Square the foreyard, you portwatch!" — "Fair wind — fair wind," muttered the men going to the braces. — "What did I tell you?" mumbled old Singleton, flinging down coil after coil with hasty energy; "I knowed it — he's gone, and here it comes."

It came with the sound of a lofty and powerful sigh. The sails filled, the ship gathered way, and the waking sea began to murmur sleepily of home to the ears of men.

That night, while the ship rushed foaming to the Northward before a freshening gale, the boatswain unbosomed himself to the petty officers' berth: — "The chap was nothing but trouble," he said, "from the moment he came aboard — d'ye remember — that night in Bombay? Been bullying all that softy crowd — cheeked the old man — we had to go fooling all over a half drowned ship to save him. Dam' nigh a mutiny all for him — and now the mate abused me like a pickpocket for forgetting to dab a lump of grease on them planks. So I did, but you ought to have known better, too, than to leave a nail sticking up — hey, Chips?"

"And you ought to have known better than to chuck all my tools overboard for 'im, like a skeary greenhorn," retorted the morose carpenter. "Well — he's gone after 'em now," he added in an unforgiving tone. — "On the China Station, I remember once, the Admiral he says to me..." began the sailmaker.

A week afterwards the *Narcissus* entered the chops of the Channel.

Under white wings she skimmed low over the blue sea like a great tired bird speeding to its nest. The clouds raced with her mastheads; they rose astern enormous and white, soared to the zenith, flew past, and falling down the wide curve of the sky, seemed to dash headlong into the sea — the clouds swifter than the ship, more free, but without a home. The coast to welcome her stepped out of space into the sunshine. The lofty headlands trod masterfully into the sea; the wide bays smiled in the light; the shadows of homeless clouds ran along the sunny plains, leaped over valleys, without a check darted up the hills, rolled down the slopes; and the sunshine pursued them with patches of running brightness. On the brows of dark cliffs white lighthouses shone in pillars of light. The Channel glittered like a blue mantle shot with gold and starred by the silver of the capping seas. The *Narcissus* rushed past the headlands and the bays. Outward-bound vessels crossed her track, lying over, and with their masts stripped for a slogging fight with the hard sou'wester. And, inshore, a string of smoking steamboats waddled, hugging the coast, like migrating and amphibious monsters, distrustful of the restless waves.

At night the headlands retreated, the bays advanced into one unbroken line of gloom. The lights of the earth mingled with the lights of heaven; and above the tossing lanterns of a trawling fleet a great lighthouse shone steadily, like an enormous riding light burning above a vessel of fabulous dimensions. Below its steady glow, the coast, stretching away straight and black, resembled the high side of an indestructible craft riding motionless upon the immortal and unresting sea. The dark land lay alone in the midst of waters, like a mighty ship bestarred with vigilant lights — a ship carrying the burden of millions of lives — a ship freighted with dross and with jewels, with gold and with steel. She towered up immense and strong, guarding priceless traditions and untold suffering, sheltering glorious memories and base forgetfulness, ignoble virtues and splendid transgressions. A great ship! For ages had the ocean battered in vain her enduring sides; she was there when the world was vaster and darker, when the sea was great and mysterious, and ready to surrender the prize of fame to audacious men. A ship mother of fleets and nations! The great flagship of the race; stronger than the storms! and anchored in the open sea.

The *Narcissus*, heeling over to off-shore gusts, rounded the South Foreland, passed through the Downs, and, in tow, entered the river. Shorn of the glory of her white wings, she wound obediently after the tug through the maze of invisible channels. As she passed them the red-painted light-vessels, swung at their moorings, seemed for an instant to sail with great speed in the rush of tide, and the next moment were left hopelessly behind. The big buoys on the tails of banks slipped past her sides very low, and, dropping in her wake, tugged at their chains like fierce watchdogs. The reach narrowed; from both sides the land approached the ship. She went steadily up the river. On the riverside slopes the houses appeared in groups — seemed to stream down the declivities at a run to see her pass, and, checked by the mud of the foreshore, crowded on the banks. Further on, the tall factory chimneys appeared in insolent bands and watched her go by, like a straggling crowd of slim giants, swaggering and upright under the black plummets of smoke, cavalierly aslant. She swept round the bends; an impure breeze shrieked a welcome between her stripped spars; and the land, closing in, stepped between the ship and the sea.

A low cloud hung before her — a great opalescent and tremulous cloud, that seemed to rise from the steaming brows of millions of men. Long drifts of smoky vapours soiled it with livid trails; it throbbed to the beat of millions of hearts, and from it came an immense and lamentable murmur — the murmur of millions of lips praying, cursing, sighing, jeering — the undying murmur of folly, regret, and hope exhaled by the crowds of the anxious earth. The *Narcissus* entered the cloud; the shadows deepened; on all sides there was the clang of iron, the sound of mighty blows, shrieks, yells. Black barges drifted stealthily on the murky stream. A mad jumble of begrimed walls loomed up vaguely in the smoke, bewildering and mournful, like a vision of disaster. The tugs backed and filled in the stream, to hold the ship steady at the dock-gates; from her bows two lines went through the air whistling, and struck at the land viciously, like a pair of snakes. A bridge broke in two before her, as if by enchantment; big hydraulic capstans began to turn all by themselves, as though animated by a mysterious and unholy spell. She moved through a narrow lane of water between two low walls of granite, and men with check-ropes in their hands kept pace with her, walking on the broad flagstones. A group waited impatiently on each side of the vanished bridge: rough heavy men in caps; sallow-faced men in high hats; two bareheaded women; ragged children, fascinated, and with wide eyes. A cart coming at a jerky trot pulled up sharply. One of the women screamed at the silent ship — "Hallo, Jack!" without looking at anyone in particular, and all hands looked at her from the forecastle head. — "Stand clear! Stand clear of that rope!" cried the dockmen, bending over stone posts. The crowd murmured, stamped where they stood. — "Let go your quarter-checks! Let go!" sang out a ruddy-faced old man on the quay. The ropes splashed heavily falling in the water, and the *Narcissus* entered the dock.

The stony shores ran away right and left in straight lines, enclosing a sombre and rectangular pool. Brick walls rose high above the water — soulless walls, staring through hundreds of windows as troubled and dull as the eyes of over-fed brutes. At their base monstrous iron cranes crouched, with chains hanging from their long necks, balancing cruel-looking hooks over the decks of lifeless ships. A noise of wheels rolling over stones, the thump of heavy things falling, the racket of feverish winches, the grinding of strained chains, floated on the air. Between high buildings the dust of all the continents soared in short flights; and a penetrating smell of perfumes and dirt, of spices and hides, of things costly and of things filthy, pervaded the space, made for it an atmosphere precious and disgusting. The *Narcissus* came gently into her berth; the shadows of soulless walls fell upon her, the dust of all the continents leaped upon her deck, and a swarm of strange men, clambering up her sides, took possession of her in the name of the sordid earth. She had ceased to live.

A toff in a black coat and high hat scrambled with agility, came up to the second mate, shook hands, and said: — "Hallo, Herbert." It was his brother. A lady appeared suddenly. A real lady, in a black dress and with a parasol. She looked extremely elegant in the midst of us, and as strange as if she had fallen there from the sky. Mr. Baker touched his cap to her. It was the master's wife. And very soon the Captain, dressed very smartly and in a white shirt, went with her over the side. We didn't recognise him at all till, turning on the quay, he called to Mr. Baker: — "Don't forget to wind up the chronometers tomorrow morning." An underhand lot of seedy-looking chaps with shifty eyes wandered in and out of the forecastle looking for a job — they said. — "More likely for something to steal," commented Knowles, cheerfully. Poor beggars. Who cared? Weren't we home! But Mr. Baker went for one of them who had given him some cheek, and we were delighted. Everything was delightful. — "I've finished aft, sir," called out Mr. Creighton. — "No water in the well, sir," reported for the last time the carpenter, sounding-rod in hand. Mr. Baker glanced along the decks at the expectant group of sailors, glanced aloft at the yards.

— "Ough! That will do, men," he grunted. The group broke up. The voyage was ended.

Rolled-up beds went flying over the rail; lashed chests went sliding down the gangway — mighty few of both at that. "The rest is having a cruise off the Cape," explained Knowles enigmatically to a dock-loafer with whom he had struck a sudden friendship. Men ran, calling to one another, hailing utter strangers to "lend a hand with the dunnage," then with sudden decorum approached the mate to shake hands before going ashore. — "Good-bye, sir," they repeated in various tones. Mr. Baker grasped hard palms, grunted in a friendly manner at everyone, his eyes twinkled. — "Take care of your money, Knowles. Ough! Soon get a nice wife if you do." The lame man was delighted. — "Good-bye, sir," said Belfast, with emotion, wringing the mate's hand, and looked up with swimming eyes. "I thought I would take 'im ashore with me," he went on, plaintively. Mr. Baker did not understand, but said kindly: — "Take care of yourself, Craik," and the bereaved Belfast went over the rail mourning and alone.

Mr. Baker, in the sudden peace of the ship, moved about solitary and grunting, trying door-handles, peering into dark places, never done — a model chief mate! No one waited for him ashore. Mother dead; father and two brothers, Yarmouth fishermen, drowned together on the Dogger Bank; sister married and unfriendly. Quite a lady. Married to the leading tailor of a little town, and its leading politician, who did not think his sailor brother-in-law quite respectable enough for him. Quite a lady, quite a lady, he thought, sitting down for a moment's rest on the quarter-hatch. Time enough to go ashore and get a bite and sup, and a bed somewhere. He didn't like to part with a ship. No one to think about then. The darkness of a misty evening fell, cold and damp, upon the deserted deck; and Mr. Baker sat smoking, thinking of all the successive ships to whom through many long years he had given the best of a seaman's care. And never a command in sight. Not once! — "I haven't somehow the cut of a skipper about me," he meditated, placidly, while the shipkeeper (who had taken possession of the galley), a wizened old man with bleared eyes, cursed him in whispers for "hanging about so." — "Now, Creighton," he pursued the unenvious train of thought, "quite a gentleman... swell friends... will get on. Fine young fellow... a little more experience." He got up and shook himself. "I'll be back first thing tomorrow morning for the hatches. Don't you let them touch anything before I come, shipkeeper," he called out. Then, at last, he also went ashore — a model chief mate!

The men scattered by the dissolving contact of the land came together once more in the shipping office. — "The *Narcissus* pays off," shouted outside a glazed door a brass-bound old fellow with a crown and the capitals B. T. on his cap. A lot trooped in at once but many were late. The room was large, white-washed, and bare; a counter surmounted by a brass-wire grating fenced off a third of the dusty space, and behind the grating a pasty-faced clerk, with his hair parted in the middle, had the quick, glittering eyes and the vivacious, jerky movements of a caged bird. Poor Captain Allistoun also in there, and sitting before a little table with piles of gold and notes on it, appeared subdued by his captivity. Another Board of Trade bird was perching on a high stool near the door: an old bird that did not mind the chaff of elated sailors. The crew of the *Narcissus*, broken up into knots, pushed in the corners. They had new shore togs, smart jackets that looked as if they had been shaped with an axe, glossy trousers that seemed made of crumpled sheet-iron, collarless flannel shirts, shiny new boots. They tapped on shoulders, button-holed one another, asked: — "Where did you sleep last night?" whispered gaily, slapped their thighs with bursts of subdued laughter. Most had clean, radiant faces; only one or two turned up dishevelled and sad; the two young Norwegians looked tidy, meek, and altogether of a promising material for the kind ladies who patronise the Scandinavian Home. Wamibo, still in his working clothes, dreamed, upright and burly in the middle of the room, and, when Archie came in, woke up for a smile. But the wide-awake clerk called out a name, and the paying-off business began.

One by one they came up to the pay-table to get the wages of their glorious and obscure toil. They swept the money with care into broad palms, rammed it trustfully into trousers' pockets, or, turning their backs on the table, reckoned with difficulty in the hollow of their stiff hands. — "Money right? Sign the release. There — there," repeated the clerk, impatiently. "How stupid those sailors are!" he thought. Singleton came up, venerable — and uncertain as to daylight; brown drops of tobacco juice hung in his white beard; his hands, that never hesitated in the great light of the open sea, could hardly find the small pile of gold in the profound darkness of the shore. "Can't write?" said the clerk, shocked. "Make a mark, then." Singleton painfully sketched in a heavy cross, blotted the page. "What a disgusting old brute," muttered the clerk. Somebody opened the door for him, and the patriarchal seaman passed through unsteadily, without as much as a glance at any of us.

Archie displayed a pocket-book. He was chaffed. Belfast, who looked wild, as though he had already luffed up through a public-house or two, gave signs of emotion and wanted to speak to the captain privately. The master was surprised. They spoke through the wires, and we could hear the Captain saying: — "I've given it up to the Board of Trade." "I should've liked to get something of his," mumbled Belfast. "But you can't, my man. It's given up, locked and sealed, to the Marine Office," expostulated the master; and Belfast stood back, with drooping mouth and troubled eyes. In a pause of the business we heard the master and the clerk talking. We caught: "James Wait — deceased — found no papers of any kind — no relations — no trace — the Office must hold his wages then." Donkin entered. He seemed out of breath, was grave, full of business. He went straight to the desk, talked with animation to the clerk, who thought him an intelligent man. They discussed the account, dropping h's against one another as if for a wager — very friendly. Captain Allistoun paid. "I give you a bad discharge," he said, quietly. Donkin raised his voice: — "I don't want your bloomin' discharge — keep it. I'm goin' ter 'ave a job ashore." He turned to us. "No more bloomin' sea fur me," he said, aloud. All looked at him. He had better clothes, had an easy air, appeared more at home than any of us; he stared with assurance, enjoying the effect of his declaration. "Yuss. I 'ave friends well off. That's more'n you got. But I am a man. Yer shipmates for all that. Who's comin' fur a drink?"

No one moved. There was a silence; a silence of blank faces and stony looks. He waited a moment, smiled bitterly, and went to the door. There he faced round once more. "You won't? You bloomin' lot of yrpocrits. No? What 'ave I done to yer? Did I bully yer? Did I 'urt yer? Did I?... You won't drink?... No!... Then may ye die of thirst, every mother's son of yer! Not one of yer 'as the sperrit of a bug. Ye're the scum of the world. Work and starve!"

He went out, and slammed the door with such violence that the old Board of Trade bird nearly fell off his perch.

"He's mad," declared Archie. "No! No! He's drunk," insisted Belfast, lurching about, and in a maudlin tone. Captain Allistoun sat smiling thoughtfully at the cleared pay-table.

Outside, on Tower Hill, they blinked, hesitated clumsily, as if blinded by the strange quality of the hazy light, as if discomposed by the view of so many men; and they who could hear one another in the howl of gales seemed deafened and distracted by the dull roar of the busy earth. — "To the Black Horse! To the Black Horse!" cried some. "Let us have a drink together before we part." They crossed the road, clinging to one another. Only Charley and Belfast wandered off alone. As I came up I saw a red-faced, blowsy woman, in a grey shawl, and with dusty, fluffy hair, fall on Charley's neck. It was his mother. She slobbered over him: — "O, my boy! My boy!" — "Leggo of me," said Charley, "Leggo, mother!" I was passing him at the time, and over the untidy head of the blubbering woman he gave me a humorous smile and a glance ironic, courageous, and profound, that seemed to put all my knowledge of life to shame. I nodded and passed on, but heard him say again, good-naturedly: — "If you leggo of me this minyt — ye shall 'ave a bob for a drink out of my pay." In the next few steps I came upon Belfast. He caught my arm with tremulous enthusiasm. — "I couldn't go wi' 'em," he stammered, indicating by a nod our noisy crowd, that drifted slowly along the other sidewalk. "When I think of Jimmy... Poor Jim! When I think of him I have no heart for drink. You were his chum, too... but I pulled him out... didn't I? short wool he had.... Yes. And I stole the blooming pie.... He wouldn't go.... He wouldn't go for nobody." He burst into tears. "I never touched him — never — never!" he sobbed. "He went for me like... like... a lamb."

I disengaged myself gently. Belfast's crying fits generally ended in a fight with some one, and I wasn't anxious to stand the brunt of his inconsolable sorrow. Moreover, two bulky policemen stood near by, looking at us with a disapproving and incorruptible gaze. — "So long!" I said, and went on my way.

But at the corner I stopped to take my last look at the crew of the *Narcissus*. They were swaying irresolute and noisy on the broad flagstones before the Mint. They were bound for the Black Horse, where men, in fur caps with brutal faces and in shirt sleeves, dispense out of varnished barrels the illusions of strength, mirth, happiness; the illusion of splendour and poetry of life, to the paid-off crews of southern-going ships. From afar I saw them discoursing, with jovial eyes and clumsy gestures, while the sea of life thundered into their ears ceaseless and unheeded. And swaying about there on the white stones, surrounded by the hurry and clamour of men, they appeared to be creatures of another kind — lost, alone, forgetful, and doomed; they were like castaways, like reckless and joyous castaways, like mad castaways making merry in the storm and upon an insecure ledge of a treacherous rock. The roar of the town resembled the roar of topping breakers, merciless and strong, with a loud voice and cruel purpose; but overhead the clouds broke; a flood of sunshine streamed down the walls of grimy houses. The dark knot of seamen drifted in sunshine. To the left of them the trees in Tower Gardens sighed, the stones of the Tower gleaming, seemed to stir in the play of light, as if remembering suddenly all the great joys and sorrows of the past, the fighting prototypes of these men; press-gangs; mutinous cries; the wailing of women by the riverside, and the shouts of men welcoming victories. The sunshine of heaven fell like a gift of grace on the mud of the earth, on the remembering and mute stones, on greed, selfishness; on the anxious faces of forgetful men. And to the right of the dark group the stained front of the Mint, cleansed by the flood of light, stood out for a moment dazzling and white like a marble palace in a fairy tale. The crew of the *Narcissus* drifted out of sight.

I never saw them again. The sea took some, the steamers took others, the graveyards of the earth will account for the rest. Singleton has no doubt taken with him the long record of his faithful work into the peaceful depths of an hospitable sea. And Donkin, who never did a decent day's work in his life, no doubt earns his living by discoursing with filthy eloquence upon the right of labour to live. So be it! Let the earth and the sea each have its own.

A gone shipmate, like any other man, is gone for ever; and I never met one of them again. But at times the spring-flood of memory sets with force up the dark River of the Nine Bends. Then on the waters of the forlorn stream drifts a ship — a shadowy ship manned by a crew of Shades. They pass and make a sign, in a shadowy hail. Haven't we, together and upon the immortal sea, wrung out a meaning from our sinful lives? Good-bye, brothers! You were a good crowd. As good a crowd as ever fisted with wild cries the beating canvas of a heavy foresail; or tossing aloft, invisible in the night, gave back yell for yell to a westerly gale.

THE NOVEL

THE novel is the most popular and characteristic form of literature of the present day. One reason for this fact is that the novel has never had a definite and prescribed form, but adapts itself readily to many uses and tastes. The general conception of the novel as a long narrative in prose is, however, at once too broad and too narrow. In the first place a novel may be written in verse; and in the second place we require a certain pattern to distinguish the novel from the mere narrative, somewhat as the short story is distinguished from the tale. This pattern is figured in the relation of the characters to one another, and among such relations that of love between the sexes has always been the most prominent, though by no means the only determining factor.

The original elements of the novel, then, are human characters drawn together in some sort of pattern or plot which unfolds with the narrative. At moments when the characters are brought together in a situation deeply charged with feeling they are presented dramatically, as if on a stage, by a device known as dramatic scene. It is necessary that they exist in a definite place or places, which furnish the physical or geographical scene. And finally there is usually an intellectual content to the story, sometimes a definite moral purpose or social reform, sometimes a philosophy or an attitude toward life, sometimes merely a pervading mood or "atmosphere."

All these elements are employed significantly in *The Return of the Native*. Hardy knew the peasants of Dorsetshire from boyhood, and it has been said that no one since Shakespeare has presented this type with such characteristic qualities. In dealing with such simple persons he uses an external method known as "behaviorism": the characters reveal themselves by action and speech. Grandfer Cantle is always gay and boastful, breaking out into song and dance, and his son Christian is constantly fearful and shrinking. They are as persistent in attitude as figures in the *Pilgrim's Progress*. With more complex characters Hardy uses the method of George Eliot, who at the time was regarded as the leading novelist of England, that of psychological analysis. The sustained portrait of Eustacia Vye in her outward form and inward thought is one of the masterpieces of this method, and may be compared with George Eliot's characterization of Lydgate in *Middlemarch*. It is interesting to consider how a modern novelist like D. H. Lawrence, who uses the methods of psychoanalysis, would have treated Eustacia. In comparison with this heroine the chief male characters are rather undeveloped. Clym Yeobright becomes clear by virtue of his fundamental peasant simplicity, but Wildeve remains an ambiguous and conventional figure.

The plot in which these persons are involved is typical of Hardy. The force which animates them is love in various forms, the uncertain and volatile inclination of Wildeve toward Eustacia and Thomasin, the passion of Clym and Eustacia, the steadfast devotion of Diggory Venn, the mother love of Mrs. Yeobright. This force is inherent in the biological structure of humanity; it is independent of reason and gives a suggestion of an overmastering fate, as in Greek tragedy. It is assisted in bringing its victims to a tragic downfall by a series of accidents such as the innocent delay of Eustacia in opening the door to Mrs. Yeobright on her visit of reconciliation to her son, the failure of delivery of Clym's letter to Eustacia, and the grotesque catastrophe in the weir in which Eustacia and Wildeve meet their death. These mischances emphasize the feeling that human life is subject to a kind of fatal irony, the victim of a kind of malevolent power which rules its destiny. It may seem that in these passages the hand of the novelist is a bit heavy. It is to be remembered, however, that Hardy, on beginning his career as a novelist, was first directed to the school of Dickens and Wilkie Collins. These writers believed that the chief service of fiction was to relieve the tedium of life and promote escape from its commonplace routine by emphasizing its strange, exciting, sensational occurrences which provide romance in the midst of realism. Improbable as the series of accidents in Hardy's novels often are, they are always possible, and as Hardy himself remarked, "It is not improbabilities of incident but improbabilities of character that matter." More important than physical mischances are the misunderstandings which hamper the characters in their relation to one another. The main plot of *The Return of the Native* has an inevitability about it which makes the novel one of the most impressive in nineteenth-century literature. It realizes perfectly Hardy's definition, "A tragedy exhibits a state of things in the life of an individual which unavoidably causes some natural aim or desire of his to end in a catastrophe when carried out."

Hardy's novel abounds in dramatic scene when characters are brought together under the influence of a dominating force. Almost at the outset we have the brilliant ensemble scene of the peasants celebrating Guy Fawkes Day with a bonfire. Here Hardy uses the method of the painter to draw and color his picture. Later we have the fateful meeting of Clym and Eustacia at the mumming of the old play of Saint George; we have the striking episode of Wildeve and Diggory Venn throwing dice for Mrs. Yeobright's guineas by the light of the assembled glow-worms; and the tragic moment in the cottage when, as Clym sleeps on the floor, Wildeve and Eustacia are startled by the knocking, and Eustacia through the window sees Mrs. Yeobright outside. It is true, some of the scenes of love or anger do not approach our contemporary standard, chiefly owing to Hardy's stylized conversational manner. The art of reproducing human speech has advanced beyond Hardy with the American novelists Sinclair Lewis and Ernest Hemingway.

It has long been recognized that Hardy stands first among English novelists in the handling of scene. The description of Egdon Heath at the opening of the novel is one of the masterpieces of English prose description. The keenness of his senses in perceiving phenomena of nature, which was his inheritance as a country boy, was intensified by his literary feeling for that development which, from Wordsworth on, has given to English poetry the body of imaginative material most characteristic of the nineteenth century. Hardy's senses of hearing, smell and touch re-enforced that of sight. *Far from the Madding Crowd* begins with a description at night in which the wind in the trees and grasses pictures the landscape in sound as a musical composer like Debussy might do. A comparable reference occurs in *The Return of the Native* to "the intonation of a pollard thorn a little way to windward, the breezes filtering through its unyielding twigs as through a strainer. It was as if the night sang dirges through clenched teeth." Throughout the novel, Egdon Heath, responding to the changes of day and night, the seasons and the weather, is a kind of chorus setting the mood of the drama.

Hardy makes his natural background carry the mood, and even the fundamental philosophy of his story. He was temperamentally a pessimist. The belief in the domination of the universe by a cosmic process which was indifferent to man, his desires and aspirations, was a possible conclusion from Darwin's theory of evolution, propounded in 1859. While Hardy's great contemporary, George Meredith, saw in evolution promise of infinite achievement for man through the development of his intellectual faculties, Hardy saw in man's consciousness only an adventitious circumstance for which nature had made no provision and had no use. Hence, while Meredith represents mind as the great force in man's career, Hardy discounts the intellect and the conscious, in favor of instinct and the unconscious. Clym Yeobright is but one among many characters who represent this distrust of reason. His real strength lies in his submission to nature. Egdon Heath typifies the enduring force against which man vainly pits his puny strength. Hardy is fond of the metaphor of man as a parasite, "— a mere parasite of the heath fretting its surface in his daily labor as a moth frets a garment." Only the characters who accept Egdon and live near to it survive. Eustacia in her flaming hostility to it and Wildeve in his indifference pay the penalty of their defeat.

Hardy's pessimism grew upon him with the years. His last novels, *Tess of the D'Urbervilles* and *Jude the Obscure*, are bitter arraignments of a human society which reflects the indifference and cruelty of the cosmos. *The Return of the Native*, however, closes on a pastoral note of reconciliation and simple happiness. Diggory Venn, the reddleman, who throughout has acted as a kind of tutelary deity of the heath, borrowing something of a supernatural character from his calling, which makes him seem a red ghost to the peasants, and Thomasin, who has been in the most passive and affectionate conformity with nature about her, undoubtedly carry the theme of this book to its justified conclusion.

Hardy's novels reflect to a high degree the characteristics and interests of fiction in the later nineteenth century. On the one hand, he belongs to the group of novelists of ideas, including George Eliot and George Meredith, who felt the stimulus of the scientific movement, who gave to the novel a serious meaning and an intellectual content, beyond the range of Scott, Dickens, or Thackeray. On the other hand Hardy kept a firm hold of reality through his contact with simple people of the countryside. He limited his background to the region which he called Wessex, of which the city of Dorchester, known in the novels as Casterbridge, was the center. Here he grew up familiar with the customs, stories, and songs of the peasants. Later, as an architect's assistant, he traveled much in the district, restoring old churches and repairing old mansions, hearing tales which record the melodrama of country life. *The Return of the Native* is rich in local color. The bonfire scene on Guy Fawkes Day, the mumming at Christmas, the community hair cutting, the grappling for the lost bucket in the well, the burning of the wax image to ward off witchcraft — these are folk stuff which adds not only drama to the novel but also interest to the student of rural life. Hardy became the chief of the school of regional novelists. He made Wessex as famous as Scott's Highlands. He has been followed by Miss Sheila Kaye-Smith in her novels of Sussex, by Eden Phillpotts in Dartmoor, by Mary Webb in Shropshire. He influenced Joseph Conrad who took the islands of the South Seas for his province, and in this setting developed a fiction which expresses a philosophy somewhat similar to Hardy's with more artistic workmanship.

THOMAS HARDY

THOMAS HARDY was born in 1840 in the village of Upper Bockhampton, near Dorchester, in the region which he was to make famous as Wessex. He was apprenticed to an architect but turned to fiction as a profession which he followed for twenty-five years. His first published novel, *Desperate Remedies* (1871), was in the melodramatic style made popular by Dickens and Collins, but his second, *Under the Greenwood Tree* (1872), was a simple idyl of country life. *A Pair of Blue Eyes* (1873) showed a mingling of the two strains, with the ironical play of circumstance and coincidence which marked his later work, among which *Far from the Madding Crowd* (1874), *The Return of the Native* (1878), *The Mayor of Casterbridge* (1886), and *The Woodlanders* (1887) are notable. In *Tess of the D'Urbervilles* (1891) and *Jude the Obscure* (1895) Hardy wrote two powerful novels of social protest, which aroused such a storm of opposition that he forsook fiction. Henceforth he devoted himself to a vast epic drama, *The Dynasts*, based on the history of the Napoleonic wars, and to lyric poetry, of which some examples are given in the final section of this book. He died in 1928.

THE RETURN OF THE NATIVE

BOOK FIRST: THE THREE WOMEN

I

A FACE ON WHICH TIME MAKES BUT LITTLE IMPRESSION

A SATURDAY afternoon in November was approaching the time of twilight, and the vast tract of unenclosed wild known as Egdon Heath embrowned itself moment by moment. Overhead the hollow stretch of whitish cloud shutting out the sky was as a tent which had the whole heath for its floor.

The heaven being spread with this pallid screen and the earth with the darkest vegetation, their meeting-line at the horizon was clearly marked. In such contrast the heath wore the appearance of an instalment of night which had taken up its place before its astronomical hour was come: darkness had to a great extent arrived hereon, while day stood distinct in the sky. Looking upwards, a furze-cutter would have been inclined to continue work; looking down, he would have decided to finish his faggot and go home. The distant rims of the world and of the firmament seemed to be a division in time no less than a division in matter. The face of the heath by its mere complexion added half an hour to evening; it could in like manner retard the dawn, sadden noon, anticipate the frowning of storms scarcely generated, and intensify the opacity of a moonless midnight to a cause of shaking and dread.

In fact, precisely at this transitional point of its nightly roll into darkness the great and particular glory of the Egdon waste began, and nobody could be said to understand the heath who had not been there at such a time. It could best be felt when it could not clearly be seen, its complete effect and explanation lying in this and the succeeding hours before the next dawn: then, and only then, did it tell its true tale. The spot was, indeed, a near relation of night, and when night showed itself an apparent tendency to gravitate together could be perceived in its shades and the scene. The sombre stretch of rounds and hollows seemed to rise and meet the evening gloom in pure sympathy, the heath exhaling darkness as rapidly as the heavens precipitated it. And so the obscurity in the air and the obscurity in the land closed together in a black fraternization towards which each advanced half-way.

The place became full of a watchful intentness now; for when other things sank brooding to sleep the heath appeared slowly to awake and listen. Every night its Titanic form seemed to await something; but it had waited thus, unmoved, during so many centuries, through the crises of so many things, that it could only be imagined to await one last crisis — the final overthrow.

It was a spot which returned upon the memory of those who loved it with an aspect of peculiar and kindly congruity. Smiling champaigns of flowers and fruit hardly do this, for they are permanently harmonious only with an existence of better reputation as to its issues than the present. Twilight combined with the scenery of Egdon Heath to evolve a thing majestic without severity, impressive without showiness, emphatic in its admonitions, grand in its simplicity. The qualifications which frequently invest the façade of a prison with far more dignity than is found in the façade of a palace double its size lent to this heath a sublimity in which spots renowned for beauty of the accepted kind are utterly wanting. Fair prospects wed happily with fair times; but alas, if times be not fair! Men have oftener suffered from the mockery of a place too smiling for their reason than from the oppression of surroundings oversadly tinged. Haggard Egdon appealed to a subtler and scarcer instinct, to a more recently learnt emotion, than that which responds to the sort of beauty called charming and fair.

Indeed, it is a question if the exclusive reign of this orthodox beauty is not approaching its last quarter. The new Vale of Tempe may be a gaunt waste in Thule: human souls may find themselves in closer and closer harmony with external things wearing a sombreness distasteful to our race when it was young. The time seems near, if it has not actually arrived, when the chastened sublimity of a moor, a sea, or a mountain will be all of nature that is absolutely in keeping with the moods of the more thinking among mankind. And ultimately, to the commonest tourist, spots like Iceland may become what the vineyards and myrtle-gardens of South Europe are to him now; and Heidelberg and Baden be passed unheeded as he hastens from the Alps to the sand-dunes of Scheveningen.

The most thorough-going ascetic could feel that he had a natural right to wander on Egdon: he was keeping within the line of legitimate indulgence when he laid himself open to influences such as these. Colours and beauties so far subdued were, at least, the birthright of all. Only in summer days of highest feather did its mood touch the level of gaiety. Intensity was more usually reached by way of the solemn than by way of the brilliant, and such a sort of intensity was often arrived at during winter darkness, tempests, and mists. Then Egdon was aroused to reciprocity; for the storm was its lover, and the wind its friend. Then it became the home of strange phantoms; and it was found to be the hitherto unrecognized original of those wild regions of obscurity which are vaguely felt to be compassing us about in midnight dreams of flight and disaster, and are never thought of after the dream till revived by scenes like this.

It was at present a place perfectly accordant with man's nature — neither ghastly, hateful, nor ugly: neither commonplace, unmeaning, nor tame; but, like man, slighted and enduring; and withal singularly colossal and mysterious in its swarthy monotony. As with some persons who have long lived apart, solitude seemed to look out of its countenance. It had a lonely face, suggesting tragical possibilities.

This obscure, obsolete, superseded country figures in Domesday. Its condition is recorded therein as that of healthy, furzy, briary wilderness — "Bruaria." Then follows the length and breadth in leagues; and, though some uncertainty exists as to the exact extent of this ancient lineal measure, it appears from the figures that the area of Egdon down to the present day has but little diminished. "Turbaria Bruaria" — the right of cutting heath-turf — occurs in charters relating to the district. "Overgrown with heth and mosse," says Leland of the same dark sweep of country.

Here at least were intelligible facts regarding landscape — far-reaching proofs productive of genuine satisfaction. The untameable, Ishmaelitish thing that Egdon now was it always had been. Civilization was its enemy; and ever since the beginning of vegetation its soil had worn the same antique brown dress, the natural and invariable garment of the particular formation. In its venerable one coat lay a certain vein of satire on human vanity in clothes. A person on a heath in raiment of modern cut and colours has more or less an anomalous look. We seem to want the oldest and simplest human clothing where the clothing of the earth is so primitive.

To recline on a stump of thorn in the central valley of Egdon, between afternoon and night, as now, where the eye could reach nothing of the world outside the summits and shoulders of heathland which filled the whole circumference of its glance, and to know that everything around and underneath had been from prehistoric times as unaltered as the stars overhead, gave ballast to the mind adrift on change, and harassed by the irrepressible New. The great inviolate place had an ancient permanence which the sea cannot claim. Who can say of a particular sea that it is old? Distilled by the sun, kneaded by the moon, it is renewed in a year, in a day, or in an hour. The sea changed, the fields changed, the rivers, the villages, and the people changed, yet Egdon remained. Those surfaces were neither so steep as to be destructible by weather, nor so flat as to be the victims of floods and deposits. With the exception of an aged highway, and a still more aged barrow presently to be referred to — themselves almost crystallized to natural products by long continuance — even the trifling irregularities were not caused by pick-axe, plough, or spade, but remained as the very finger-touches of the last geological change.

The above-mentioned highway traversed the lower levels of the heath, from one horizon to another. In many portions of its course it overlaid an old vicinal way, which branched from the great Western road of the Romans, the Via Iceniana, or Ikenild Street, hard by. On the evening under consideration it would have been noticed that, though the gloom had increased sufficiently to confuse the minor features of the heath, the white surface of the road remained almost as clear as ever.

II

HUMANITY APPEARS UPON THE SCENE, HAND IN HAND WITH TROUBLE

ALONG the road walked an old man. He was white-headed as a mountain, bowed in the shoulders, and faded in general aspect. He wore a glazed hat, an ancient boat-cloak, and shoes; his brass buttons bearing an anchor upon their face. In his hand was a silver-headed walking-stick, which he used as a veritable third leg, perseveringly dotting the ground with its point at every few inches' interval. One would have said that he had been, in his day, a naval officer of some sort or other.

Before him stretched the long, laborious road, dry, empty, and white. It was quite open to the heath on each side, and bisected that vast dark surface like the parting-line on a head of black hair, diminishing and bending away on the furthest horizon.

The old man frequently stretched his eyes ahead to gaze over the tract that he had yet to traverse. At length he discerned, a long distance in front of him, a moving spot, which appeared to be a vehicle, and it proved to be going the same way as that in which he himself was journeying. It was the single atom of life that the scene contained, and it only served to render the general loneliness more evident. Its rate of advance was slow, and the old man gained upon it sensibly.

When he drew nearer he perceived it to be a spring van, ordinary in shape, but singular in colour, this being a lurid red. The driver walked beside it; and, like his van, he was completely red. One dye of that tincture covered his clothes, the cap upon his head, his boots, his face, and his hands. He was not temporarily overlaid with the colour: it permeated him.

The old man knew the meaning of this. The traveller with the cart was a reddleman — a person whose vocation it was to supply farmers with redding for their sheep. He was one of a class rapidly becoming extinct in Wessex, filling at present in the rural world the place which, during the last century, the dodo occupied in the world of animals. He is a curious, interesting, and nearly perished link between obsolete forms of life and those which generally prevail.

The decayed officer, by degrees, came up alongside his fellow wayfarer, and wished him good evening. The reddleman turned his head, and replied in sad and occupied tones. He was young, and his face, if not exactly handsome, approached so near to handsome that nobody would have contradicted an assertion that it really was so in its natural colour. His eye, which glared so strangely through his stain, was in itself attractive — keen as that of a bird of prey, and blue as autumn mist. He had neither whisker nor moustache, which allowed the soft curves of the lower part of his face to be apparent. His lips were thin, and though, as it seemed, compressed by thought, there was a pleasant twitch at their corners now and then. He was clothed throughout in a tight-fitting suit of corduroy, excellent in quality, not much worn, and well-chosen for its purpose; but deprived of its original colour by his trade. It showed to advantage the good shape of his figure. A certain well-to-do air about the man suggested that he was not poor for his degree. The natural query of an observer would have been, Why should such a promising being as this have hidden his prepossessing exterior by adopting that singular occupation?

After replying to the old man's greeting he showed no inclination to continue in talk, although they still walked side by side, for the elder traveller seemed to desire company. There were no sounds but that of the booming wind upon the stretch of tawny herbage around them, the crackling wheels, the tread of the men, and the footsteps of the two shaggy ponies which drew the van. They were small, hardy animals, of a breed between Galloway and Exmoor, and were known as "heath-croppers" here.

Now, as they thus pursued their way, the reddleman occasionally left his companion's side, and, stepping behind the van, looked into its interior through a small window. The look was always anxious. He would then return to the old man, who made another remark about the state of the country and so on, to which the reddleman again abstractedly replied, and then again they would lapse into silence. The silence conveyed to neither any sense of awkwardness; in these lonely places wayfarers, after a first greeting, frequently plod on for miles without speech; contiguity amounts to a tacit conversation where, otherwise than in cities, such contiguity can be put an end to on the merest inclination, and where not to put an end to it is intercourse in itself.

Possibly these two might not have spoken again till their parting, had it not been for the reddleman's visits to his van. When he returned from his fifth time of looking in the old man said, "You have something inside there besides your load?"

"Yes."

"Somebody who wants looking after?"

"Yes."

Not long after this a faint cry sounded from the interior. The reddleman hastened to the back, looked in, and came away again.

"You have a child there, my man?"

"No, sir, I have a woman."

"The deuce you have! Why did she cry out?"

"Oh, she has fallen asleep, and not being used to travelling, she's uneasy, and keeps dreaming."

"A young woman?"

"Yes, a young woman."

"That would have interested me forty years ago. Perhaps she's your wife?"

"My wife!" said the other bitterly. "She's above mating with such as I. But there's no reason why I should tell you about that."

"That's true. And there's no reason why you should not. What harm can I do to you or to her?"

The reddleman looked in the old man's face. "Well, sir," he said at last, "I knew her before today, though perhaps it would have been better if I had not. But she's nothing to me, and I am nothing to her; and she wouldn't have been in my van if any better carriage had been there to take her."

"Where, may I ask?"

"At Anglebury."

"I know the town well. What was she doing there?"

"Oh, not much — to gossip about. However, she's tired to death now, and not at all well, and that's what makes her so restless. She dropped off into a nap about an hour ago, and 'twill do her good."

"A nice-looking girl, no doubt?"

"You would say so."

The other traveller turned his eyes with interest towards the van window, and, without withdrawing them, said, "I presume I might look in upon her?"

"No," said the reddleman abruptly. "It is getting too dark for you to see much of her; and, more than that, I have no right to allow you. Thank God she sleeps so well: I hope she won't wake till she's home."

"Who is she? One of the neighbourhood?"

"'Tis no matter who, excuse me."

"It is not that girl of Blooms-End, who has been talked about more or less lately? If so, I know her; and I can guess what has happened."

"'Tis no matter.... Now, sir, I am sorry to say that we shall soon have to part company. My ponies are tired, and I have further to go, and I am going to rest them under this bank for an hour."

The elder traveller nodded his head indifferently, and the reddleman turned his horses and van in upon the turf, saying, "Good night." The old man replied, and proceeded on his way as before.

The reddleman watched his form as it diminished to a speck on the road and became absorbed in the thickening films of night. He then took some hay from a truss which was slung up under the van, and, throwing a portion of it in front of the horses, made a pad of the rest, which he laid on the ground beside his vehicle. Upon this he sat down, leaning his back against the wheel. From the interior a low soft breathing came to his ear. It appeared to satisfy him, and he musingly surveyed the scene, as if considering the next step that he should take.

To do things musingly, and by small degrees, seemed indeed, to be a duty in the Egdon valleys at this transitional hour, for there was that in the condition of the heath itself which resembled protracted and halting dubiousness. It was the quality of the repose appertaining to the scene. This was not the repose of actual stagnation, but the apparent repose of incredible slowness. A condition of healthy life so nearly resembling the torpor of death is a noticeable thing of its sort; to exhibit the inertness of the desert, and at the same time to be exercising powers akin to those of the meadow, and even of the forest, awakened in those who thought of it the attentiveness usually engendered by understatement and reserve.

The scene before the reddleman's eyes was a gradual series of ascents from the level of the road backward into the heart of the heath. It embraced hillocks, pits, ridges, acclivities, one behind the other, till all was finished by a high hill cutting against the still light sky. The traveller's eye hovered about these things for a time, and finally settled upon one noteworthy object up there. It was a barrow. This bossy projection of earth above its natural level occupied the loftiest ground of the loneliest height that the heath contained. Although from the vale it appeared but as a wart on an Atlantean brow, its actual bulk was great. It formed the pole and axis of this heathery world.

As the resting man looked at the barrow he became aware that its summit, hitherto the highest object in the whole prospect round, was surmounted by something higher. It rose from the semi-globular mound like a spike from a helmet. The first instinct of an imaginative stranger might have been to suppose it the person of one of the Celts who built the barrow, so far had all of modern date withdrawn from the scene. It seemed a sort of last man among them, musing for a moment before dropping into eternal night with the rest of his race.

There the form stood, motionless as the hill beneath. Above the plain rose the hill, above the hill rose the barrow, and above the barrow rose the figure. Above the figure was nothing that could be mapped elsewhere than on a celestial globe.

Such a perfect, delicate, and necessary finish did the figure give to the dark pile of hills that it seemed to be the only obvious justification of their outline. Without it, there was the dome without the lantern; with it the architectural demands of the mass were satisfied. The scene was strangely homogeneous. The vale, the upland, the barrow, and the figure above it amounted only to unity. Looking at this or that member of the group was not observing a complete thing, but a fraction of a thing.

The form was so much like an organic part of the entire motionless structure that to see it move would have impressed the mind as a strange phenomenon. Immobility being the chief characteristic of that whole which the person formed portion of, the discontinuance of immobility in any quarter suggested confusion.

Yet that is what happened. The figure perceptibly gave up its fixity, shifted a step or two, and turned round. As if alarmed, it descended on the right side of the barrow, with the glide of a water-drop down a bud, and then vanished. The movement had been sufficient to show more clearly the characteristics of the figure, and that it was a woman's.

The reason of her sudden displacement now appeared. With her dropping out of sight on the right side, a newcomer, bearing a burden, protruded into the sky on the left side, ascended the tumulus, and deposited the burden on the top. A second followed, then a third, a fourth, a fifth, and ultimately the whole barrow was peopled with burdened figures.

The only intelligible meaning in this sky-backed pantomime of silhouettes was that the woman had no relation to the forms who had taken her place, was sedulously avoiding these, and had come thither for another object than theirs. The imagination of the observer clung by preference to that vanished, solitary figure, as to something more interesting, more important, more likely to have a history worth knowing than these new-comers, and unconsciously regarded them as intruders. But they remained, and established themselves; and the lonely person who hitherto had been queen of the solitude did not at present seem likely to return.

III

THE CUSTOM OF THE COUNTRY

HAD a looker-on been posted in the immediate vicinity of the barrow, he would have learned that these persons were boys and men of the neighbouring hamlets. Each, as he ascended the barrow, had been heavily laden with furze-faggots, carried upon the shoulder by means of a long stake sharpened at each end for impaling them easily — two in front and two behind. They came from a part of the heath a quarter of a mile to the rear, where furze almost exclusively prevailed as a product.

Every individual was so involved in furze by his method of carrying the faggots that he appeared like a bush on legs till he had thrown them down. The party had marched in trail, like a travelling flock of sheep; that is to say, the strongest first, the weak and young behind.

The loads were all laid together, and a pyramid of furze thirty feet in circumference now occupied the crown of the tumulus, which was known as Rainbarrow for many miles round. Some made themselves busy with matches, and in selecting the driest tufts of furze, others in loosening the bramble bonds which held the faggots together. Others, again, while this was in progress, lifted their eyes and swept the vast expanse of country commanded by their position, now lying nearly obliterated by shade. In the valleys of the heath nothing save its own wild face was visible at any time of day; but this spot commanded a horizon enclosing a tract of far extent, and in many cases lying beyond the heath country. None of its features could be seen now, but the whole made itself felt as a vague stretch of remoteness.

While the men and lads were building the pile, a change took place in the mass of shade which denoted the distant landscape. Red suns and tufts of fire one by one began to arise, flecking the whole country round. They were the bonfires of other parishes and hamlets that were engaged in the same sort of commemoration. Some were distant, and stood in a dense atmosphere, so that bundles of pale strawlike beams radiated around them in the shape of a fan. Some were large and near, glowing scarlet-red from the shade, like wounds in a black hide. Some were Mænades, with winy faces and blown hair. These tinctured the silent bosom of the clouds above them and lit up their ephemeral caves, which seemed thenceforth to become scalding caldrons. Perhaps as many as thirty bonfires could be counted within the whole bounds of the district; and as the hour may be told on a clock face when the figures themselves are invisible, so did the men recognize the locality of each fire by its angle and direction, though nothing of the scenery could be viewed.

The first tall flame from Rainbarrow sprang into the sky, attracting all eyes that had been fixed on the distant conflagrations back to their own attempt in the same kind. The cheerful blaze streaked the inner surface of the human circle — now increased by other stragglers, male and female — with its own gold livery, and even overlaid the dark turf around with a lively luminousness, which softened off into obscurity where the barrow rounded downwards out of sight. It showed the barrow to be the segment of a globe, as perfect as on the day when it was thrown up, even the little ditch remaining from which the earth was dug. Not a plough had ever disturbed a grain of that stubborn soil. In the heath's barrenness to the farmer lay its fertility to the historian. There had been no obliteration, because there had been no tending.

It was as if the bonfire-makers were standing in some radiant upper storey of the world, detached from and independent of the dark stretches below. The heath down there was now a vast abyss, and no longer a continuation of what they stood on; for their eyes, adapted to the blaze, could see nothing of the deeps beyond its influence. Occasionally, it is true, a more vigorous flare than usual from their faggots sent darting lights like aides-de-camp down the inclines to some distant bush, pool, or patch of white sand, kindling these to replies of the same colour, till all was lost in darkness again. Then the whole black phenomenon beneath represented Limbo as viewed from the brink by the sublime Florentine in his vision, and the muttered articulations of the wind in the hollows were as complaints and petitions from the "souls of mighty worth" suspended therein.

It was as if these men and boys had suddenly dived into past ages, and fetched therefrom an hour and deed which had before been familiar with this spot. The ashes of the original British pyre which blazed from that summit lay fresh and undisturbed in the barrow beneath their tread. The flames from funeral piles long ago kindled there had shone down upon the lowlands as these were shining now. Festival fires to Thor and Woden had followed on the same ground and duly had their day. Indeed, it is pretty well known that such blazes as this the heathmen were now enjoying are rather the lineal descendants from jumbled Druidical rites and Saxon ceremonies than the invention of popular feeling about Gunpowder Plot.

Moreover to light a fire is the instinctive and resistant act of man when, at the winter ingress, the curfew is sounded throughout Nature. It indicates a spontaneous, Promethean rebelliousness against the fiat that this recurrent season shall bring foul times, cold darkness, misery and death. Black chaos comes, and the fettered gods of the earth say, Let there be light.

The brilliant lights and sooty shades which struggled upon the skin and clothes of the persons standing round caused their lineaments and general contours to be drawn with Dureresque vigour and dash. Yet the permanent moral expression of each face it was impossible to discover, for as the nimble flames towered, nodded, and swooped through the surrounding air, the blots

of shade and flakes of light upon the countenances of the group changed shape
and position endlessly.   All was unstable; quivering as leaves, evanescent as
lightning.   Shadowy eye-sockets, deep as those of a death's head, suddenly
turned into pits of lustre: a lantern-jaw was cavernous, then it was shining;
wrinkles were emphasized to ravines, or obliterated entirely by a changed ray.
Nostrils were dark wells; sinews in old necks were gilt mouldings; things with
no particular polish on them were glazed; bright objects, such as the tip of a
furze-hook one of the men carried, were as glass; eyeballs glowed like little
lanterns.   Those whom Nature had depicted as merely quaint became
grotesque, the grotesque became preternatural; for all was in extremity.

Hence it may be that the face of an old man, who had like others been
called to the heights by the rising flames, was not really the mere nose and
chin that it appeared to be, but an appreciable quantity of human countenance.   He stood complacently sunning himself in the heat.   With a speäker,
or stake, he tossed the outlying scraps of fuel into the conflagration, looking at
the midst of the pile, occasionally lifting his eyes to measure the height of the
flame, or to follow the great sparks which rose with it and sailed away into
darkness.   The beaming sight, and the penetrating warmth, seemed to breed
in him a cumulative cheerfulness, which soon amounted to delight.   With his
stick in his hand he began to jig a private minuet, a bunch of copper seals
shining and swinging like a pendulum from under his waistcoat: he also began
to sing, in the voice of a bee up a flue —

> "The king' call'd down' his no-bles all',
> By one', by two', by three';
> Earl Mar'-shal, I'll' go shrive' the queen',
> And thou' shalt wend' with me'.
>
> A boon', a boon', quoth Earl' Mar-shal',
> And fell' on his bend'-ded knee',
> That what'-so-e'er' the queen' shall say',
> No harm' there-of' may be'."

Want of breath prevented a continuance of the song; and the breakdown
attracted the attention of a firm-standing man of middle age, who kept each
corner of his crescent-shaped mouth rigorously drawn back into his cheek, as
if to do away with any suspicion of mirthfulness which might erroneously
have attached to him.

"A fair stave, Grandfer Cantle; but I am afeard 'tis too much for the
mouldy weasand of such a old man as you," he said to the wrinkled reveller.
"Doesn't wish th' wast three sixes again, Grandfer, as you was when you first
learnt to sing it?"

"Hey?" said Grandfer Cantle, stopping in his dance.

"Dostn't wish was young again, I say?   There's a hole in thy poor bellows
nowadays seemingly."

"But there's good art in me.   If I couldn't make a little wind go a long ways
I should seem no younger than the most aged man, should I, Timothy?"

"And how about the new-married folks down there at the Quiet Woman

Inn?" the other inquired, pointing towards a dim light in the direction of the distant highway, but considerably apart from where the reddleman was at that moment resting. "What's the rights of the matter about 'em? You ought to know, being an understanding man."

"But a little rakish, hey? I own to it. Master Cantle is that, or he's nothing. Yet 'tis a gay fault, neighbour Fairway, that age will cure."

"I heard that they were coming home tonight. By this time they must have come. What besides?"

"The next thing is for us to go and wish 'em joy, I suppose?"

"Well, no."

"No? Now, I thougnt we must. *I* must, or 'twould be very unlike me — the first in every spree that's going!

'Do thou' put on' a fri'-ar's coat',
And I'll' put on' a-no'-ther,
And we' will to' Queen Ele'anor go',
Like Fri'ar and' his bro'-ther.'

I met Mis'ess Yeobright, the young bride's aunt, last night, and she told me that her son Clym was coming home a' Christmas. Wonderful clever, 'a believe — ah, I should like to have all that's under that young man's hair. Well, then, I spoke to her in my well-known merry way, and she said, 'O that what's shaped so venerable should talk like a fool!' — that's what she said to me. I don't care for her, be jowned if I do, and so I told her. 'Be jowned if I care for 'ee,' I said. I had her there — hey?"

"I rather think she had you," said Fairway.

"No," said Grandfer Cantle, his countenance slightly flagging. "'Tisn't so bad as that with me?"

"Seemingly 'tis; however, is it because of the wedding that Clym is coming home a' Christmas — to make a new arrangement because his mother is now left in the house alone?"

"Yes, yes — that's it. But, Timothy, hearken to me," said the Grandfer earnestly. "Though known as such a joker, I be an understanding man if you catch me serious, and I am serious now. I can tell 'ee lots about the married couple. Yes, this morning at six o'clock they went up the country to do the job, and neither vell nor mark have been seen of 'em since, though I reckon that this afternoon has brought 'em home again, man and woman — wife, that is. Isn't it spoke like a man, Timothy, and wasn't Mis'ess Yeobright wrong about me?"

"Yes, it will do. I didn't know the two had walked together since last fall, when her mother forbad the banns. How long has this new set-to been in mangling then? Do you know, Humphrey?"

"Yes, how long?" said Grandfer Cantle smartly, likewise turning to Humphrey. "I ask that question."

"Ever since her aunt altered her mind, and said she might hae the man after all," replied Humphrey, without removing his eyes from the fire. He was a somewhat solemn young fellow, and carried the hook and leather gloves of a furze-cutter, his legs, by reason of that occupation, being sheathed in bulging leggings as stiff as the Philistine's greaves of brass. "That's why they went away to be married, I count. You see, after kicking up such a nunny-watch and forbidding the banns 'twould have made Mis'ess Yeobright seem foolish-like to have a banging wedding in the same parish all as if she'd never gainsaid it."

"Exactly — seem foolish-like; and that's very bad for the poor things that be so, though I only guess as much, to be sure," said Grandfer Cantle, still strenuously preserving a sensible bearing and mien.

"Ah, well, I was at church that day," said Fairway, "which was a very curious thing to happen."

"If 'twasn't my name's Simple," said the Grandfer emphatically. "I ha'n't been there to-year; and now the winter is a'coming on I won't say I shall."

"I ha'n't been these three years," said Humphrey; "for I'm so dead sleepy of a Sunday; and 'tis so terrible far to get there; and when you do get there 'tis such a mortal poor chance that you'll be chose for up above, when so many bain't, that I bide at home and don't go at all."

"I not only happened to be there," said Fairway, with a fresh collection of emphasis, "but I was sitting in the same pew as Mis'ess Yeobright. And though you may not see it as such, it fairly made my blood run cold to hear her. Yes, it is a curious thing; but it made my blood run cold, for I was close at her elbow." The speaker looked round upon the bystanders, now drawing closer to hear him, with his lips gathered tighter than ever in the rigorousness of his descriptive moderations.

"'Tis a serious job to have things happen to 'ee there," said a woman behind.

"'Ye are to declare it,' wez the parson's words," Fairway continued. "And then up stood a woman at my side — a touching of me. 'Well, be damned if there isn't Mis'ess Yeobright a-standing up,' I said to myself. Yes, neighbours, though I was in the temple of prayer that's what I said. 'Tis against my conscience to curse and swear in company, and I hope any woman here will overlook it. Still what I did say I did say, and 'twould be a lie if I didn't own it."

"So 'twould, neighbour Fairway."

"'Be damned if there isn't Mis'ess Yeobright a-standing up,' I said," the narrator repeated, giving out the bad word with the same passionless severity of face as before, which proved how entirely necessity and not gusto had to do with the iteration. "And the next thing I heard was, 'I forbid the banns,' from her. 'I'll speak to you after the service,' said the parson, in quite a homely way — yes, turning all at once into a common man no holier than you or I. Ah, her face was pale! Maybe you can call to mind that monument in church — the cross-legged soldier that have had his nose knocked away by the school-children? Well, he would about have matched that woman's face, when she said, 'I forbid the banns.'"

The audience cleared their throats and tossed a few stalks into the fire, not because these deeds were urgent, but to give themselves time to weigh the moral of the story.

"I'm sure when I heard they'd been forbid I felt as glad as if anybody had gied me sixpence," said an earnest voice — that of Olly Dowden, a woman who lived by making heath brooms, or besoms. Her nature was to be civil to enemies as well as to friends, and grateful to all the world for letting her remain alive.

"And now the maid have married him just the same," said Humphrey.

"After that Mis'ess Yeobright came round and was quite agreeable," Fairway resumed, with an unheeding air, to show that his words were no appendage to Humphrey's, but the result of independent reflection.

"Supposing they were ashamed, I don't see why they shouldn't have done it here-right," said a wide-spread woman whose stays creaked like shoes whenever she stooped or turned. "'Tis well to call the neighbours together and to hae a good racket once now and then; and it may as well be when there's a wedding as at tide-times. I don't care for close ways."

"Ah, now, you'd hardly believe it, but I don't care for gay weddings," said Timothy Fairway, his eyes again travelling round. "I hardly blame Thomasin Yeobright and neighbour Wildeve for doing it quiet, if I must own it. A wedding at home means five and six-handed reels by the hour; and they do a man's legs no good when he's over forty."

"True. Once at the woman's house you can hardly say nay to being one in a jig, knowing all the time that you be expected to make yourself worth your victuals."

"You be bound to dance at Christmas because 'tis the time o' year; you must dance at weddings because 'tis the time o' life. At christenings folk will even smuggle in a reel or two, if 'tis no further on than the first or second chiel. And this is not naming the songs you've got to sing.... For my part I like a good hearty funeral as well as anything. You've as splendid victuals and drink as at other parties, and even better. And it don't wear your legs to stumps in talking over a poor fellow's ways as it do to stand up in horn-pipes."

"Nine folks out of ten would own 'twas going too far to dance then, I suppose?" said Grandfer Cantle inquiringly.

"'Tis the only sort of party a staid man can feel safe at after the mug have been round a few times."

"Well, I can't understand a quiet lady-like little body like Tamsin Yeo-bright caring to be married to such a mean way," said Susan Nunsuch, the wide woman, who preferred the original subject. "'Tis worse than the poorest do. And I shouldn't have cared about the man, though some may say he's good-looking."

"To give him his due he's a clever, learned fellow in his way — a'most as clever as Clym Yeobright used to be. He was brought up to better things than keeping the Quiet Woman. An engineer — that's what the man was, as we know; but he threw away his chance, and so 'a took a public-house to live. His learning was no use to him at all."

"Very often the case," said Olly, the besom-maker. "And yet how people do strive after it and get it! The class of folk that couldn't use to make a round O to save their bones from the pit can write their names now without a sputter of the pen, oftentimes without a single blot: what do I say? — why, almost without a desk to lean their stomachs and elbows upon."

"True: 'tis amazing what a polish the world have been brought to," said Humphrey.

"Why, afore I went a soldier in the Bang-up Locals (as we was called), in the year four," chimed in Grandfer Cantle brightly, "I didn't know no more what the world was like than the commonest man among ye. And now, jown it all, I won't say what I bain't fit for, hey?"

"Couldst sign the book, no doubt," said Fairway, "if wast young enough to join hands with a woman again, like Wildeve and Mis'ess Tamsin, which is more than Humph there could do, for he follows his father in learning. Ah, Humph, well I can mind when I was married how I zid thy father's mark staring me in the face as I went to put down my name. He and your mother were the couple married just afore we were, and there stood thy father's cross with arms stretched out like a great banging scarecrow. What a terrible black cross that was — thy father's very likeness in en! To save my soul I couldn't help laughing when I zid en, though all the time I was as hot as dog-days, what with the marrying, and what with the woman a-hanging to me, and what with Jack Changley and a lot more chaps grinning at me through church window. But the next moment a strawmote would have knocked me down, for I called to mind that if thy father and mother had had high words once, they'd been at it twenty times since they'd been man and wife, and I zid myself as the next poor stunpoll to get into the same mess.... Ah — well, what a day 'twas!"

"Wildeve is older than Tamsin Yeobright by a good-few summers. A pretty maid too she is. A young woman with a home must be a fool to tear her smock for a man like that."

The speaker, a peat or turf-cutter, who had newly joined the group, carried across his shoulder the singular heart-shaped spade of large dimensions used in that species of labour; and its well-whetted edge gleamed like a silver bow in the beams of the fire.

"A hundred maidens would have had him if he'd asked 'em," said the wide woman.

"Didst ever know a man, neighbour, that no woman at all would marry?" inquired Humphrey.

"I never did," said the turf-cutter.

"Nor I," said another.

"Nor I," said Grandfer Cantle.

"Well, now, I did once," said Timothy Fairway, adding more firmness to one of his legs. "I did know of such a man. But only once, mind." He gave his throat a thorough rake round, as if it were the duty of every person not to be mistaken through thickness of voice. "Yes, I knew of such a man," he said.

"And what ghastly gallicrow might the poor fellow have been like, Master Fairway?" asked the turf-cutter.

"Well, 'a was neither a deaf man, nor a dumb man, nor a blind man. What 'a was I don't say."

"Is he known in these parts?" said Olly Dowden.

"Hardly," said Timothy; "but I name no name.... Come, keep the fire up there, youngsters."

"Whatever is Christian Cantle's teeth a-chattering for?" said a boy from amid the smoke and shades on the other side of the blaze. "Be ye a-cold, Christian?"

A thin jibbering voice was heard to reply, "No, not at all."

"Come forward, Christian, and show yourself. I didn't know you were here," said Fairway, with a humane look across towards that quarter.

Thus requested, a faltering man, with reedy hair, no shoulders, and a great quantity of wrist and ankle beyond his clothes, advanced a step or two by his own will, and was pushed by the will of others half a dozen steps more. He was Grandfer Cantle's youngest son.

"What be ye quaking for, Christian?" said the turf-cutter kindly.

"I'm the man."

"What man?"

"The man no woman will marry."

"The deuce you be!" said Timothy Fairway, enlarging his gaze to cover Christian's whole surface and a great deal more; Grandfer Cantle meanwhile staring as a hen stares at the duck she has hatched.

"Yes, I be he; and it makes me afeared," said Christian. "D'ye think 'twill hurt me? I shall always say I don't care, and swear to it, though I do care all the while."

"Well, be damned if this isn't the queerest start ever I know'd," said Mr. Fairway. "I didn't mean you at all. There's another in the country, then! Why did ye reveal yer misfortune, Christian?"

"'Twas to be if 'twas, I suppose. I can't help it, can I?" He turned upon them his painfully circular eyes, surrounded by concentric lines like targets.

"No, that's true. But 'tis a melancholy thing, and my blood ran cold when you spoke, for I felt there were two poor fellows where I had thought only one. 'Tis a sad thing for ye, Christian. How'st know the women won't hae thee?"

"I've asked 'em."

"Sure I should never have thought you had the face. Well, and what did the last one say to ye? Nothing that can't be got over, perhaps, after all?"

"'Get out of my sight, you slack-twisted, slim-looking fool,' was the woman's words to me."

"Not encouraging, I own," said Fairway. "'Get out of my sight, you slack-twisted, slim-looking fool,' is rather a hard way of saying No. But even that might be overcome by time and patience, so as to let a few grey hairs show themselves in the hussy's head. How old be you, Christian?"

"Thirty-one last tatie-digging, Mister Fairway."

"Not a boy — not a boy. Still there's hope yet."

"That's my age by baptism, because that's put down in the great book of the Judgment — that they keep down in church vestry; but mother told me I was born some time afore I was christened."

"Ah!"

"But she couldn't tell when, to save her life, except that there was no moon."

"No moon: that's bad. Hey, neighbours, that's bad for him!"

"Yes, 'tis bad," said Grandfer Cantle, shaking his head.

"Mother know'd 'twas no moon, for she asked another woman that had an almanac, as she did whenever a boy was born to her, because of the saying, 'No moon, no man,' which made her afeard every man-child she had. Do ye really think it serious, Mister Fairway, that there was no moon?"

"Yes; 'No moon, no man.' 'Tis one of the truest sayings ever spit out. The boy never comes to anything that's born at new moon. A bad job for thee, Christian, that you should have showed your nose then of all days in the month."

"I suppose the moon was terrible full when you were born?" said Christian, with a look of hopeless admiration at Fairway.

"Well, 'a was not new," Mr. Fairway replied, with a disinterested gaze.

"I'd sooner go without drink at Lammas-tide than be a man of no moon," continued Christian, in the same shattered recitative. "'Tis said I be only the rames of a man, and no good for my race at all; and I suppose that's the cause o't."

"Ay," said Grandfer Cantle, somewhat subdued in spirit; "and yet his mother cried for scores of hours when 'a was a boy, for fear he should outgrow hisself and go for a soldier."

"Well, there's many just as bad as he," said Fairway. "Wethers must live their time as well as other sheep, poor soul."

"So perhaps I shall rub on? Ought I to be afeard o' nights, Master Fairway?"

"You'll have to lie alone all your life; and 'tis not to married couples but to single sleepers that a ghost shows hisself when 'a do come. One has been seen lately, too. A very strange one."

"No — don't talk about it if 'tis agreeable of ye not to! 'Twill make my skin crawl when I think of it in bed alone. But you will — ah, you will, I know, Timothy; and I shall dream all night o't! A very strange one? What sort of a spirit did ye mean when ye said, a very strange one, Timothy? — no, no — don't tell me."

"I don't half believe in spirits myself. But I think it ghostly enough — what I was told. 'Twas a little boy that zid it."

"What was it like? — no, don't ——"

"A red one. Yes, most ghosts be white; but this is as if it had been dipped in blood."

Christian drew a deep breath without letting it expand his body, and Humphrey said, "Where has it been seen?"

"Not exactly here; but in this same heth. But 'tisn't a thing to talk about. What do ye say," continued Fairway in brisker tones, and turning upon them as if the idea had not been Grandfer Cantle's — "what do you say to giving the new man and wife a bit of a song tonight afore we go to bed — being their wedding-day? When folks are just married 'tis as well to look glad o't, since looking sorry won't unjoin 'em. I am no drinker, as we know, but when the womenfolk and youngsters have gone home we can drop down across to the Quiet Woman, and strike up a ballet in front of the married folks' door. 'Twill please the young wife, and that's what I should like to do, for many's the skinful I've had at her hands when she lived with her aunt at Blooms-End."

"Hey? And so we will!" said Grandfer Cantle, turning so briskly that his copper seals swung extravagantly. "I'm as dry as a kex with biding up here in the wind, and I haven't seen the colour of drink since nammet-time today. 'Tis said that the last brew at the Woman is very pretty drinking. And, neighbours, if we should be a little late in the finishing, why, to-morrow's Sunday, and we can sleep it off!"

"Grandfer Cantle! you take things very careless for an old man," said the wide woman.

"I take things careless; I do — too careless to please the women! Klk! I'll sing the 'Jovial Crew,' or any other song, when a weak old man would cry his eyes out. Jown it; I am up for anything.

'The king' look'-d o'-ver his left' shoul-der',
     And a grim' look look'-ed hee',
Earl Mar'-shal, he said', but for' my oath'
     Or hang'-ed thou' shouldst bee'.'"

"Well, that's what we'll do," said Fairway. "We'll give 'em a song, an' it please the Lord. What's the good of Thomasin's cousin Clym a-coming home after the deed's done? He should have come afore, if so be he wanted to stop it, and marry her himself."

"Perhaps he's coming to bide with his mother a little time, as she must feel lonely now the maid's gone."

"Now, 'tis very odd, but I never feel lonely — no, not at all," said Grandfer Cantle. "I am as brave in the night-time as a' admiral!"

The bonfire was by this time beginning to sink low, for the fuel had not been of that substantial sort which can support a blaze long. Most of the other fires within the wide horizon were also dwindling weak. Attentive observation of their brightness, colour, and length of existence would have revealed the quality of the material burnt; and through that, to some extent the natural produce of the district in which each bonfire was situate. The clear, kingly effulgence that had characterized the majority expressed a heath and furze country like their own, which in one direction extended an un-limited number of miles: the rapid flares and extinctions at other points of the compass showed the lightest of fuel — straw, beanstalks, and the usual waste from arable land. The most enduring of all — steady unaltering eyes like planets — signified wood, such as hazel-branches, thorn-faggots, and stout billets. Fires of the last-mentioned materials were rare, and, though comparatively small in magnitude beside the transient blazes, now began to get the best of them by mere long-continuance. The great ones had perished, but these remained. They occupied the remotest visible positions

— sky-backed summits rising out of rich coppice and plantation districts to the north, where the soil was different, and heath foreign and strange.

Save one; and this was the nearest of any, the moon of the whole shining throng. It lay in a direction precisely opposite to that of the little window in the vale below. Its nearness was such that, notwithstanding its actual smallness, its glow infinitely transcended theirs.

This quiet eye had attracted attention from time to time; and when their own fire had become sunken and dim it attracted more; some even of the wood fires more recently lighted had reached their decline, but no change was perceptible here.

"To be sure, how near that fire is!" said Fairway. "Seemingly, I can see a fellow of some sort walking round it. Little and good must be said of that fire, surely."

"I can throw a stone there," said the boy.

"And so can I!" said Grandfer Cantle.

"No, no, you can't, my sonnies. That fire is not much less than a mile and a half off, for all that 'a seems so near."

"'Tis in the heath, but not furze," said the turf-cutter.

"'Tis cleft-wood, that's what 'tis," said Timothy Fairway. "Nothing would burn like that except clean timber. And 'tis on the knap afore the old captain's house at Mistover. Such a queer mortal as that man is! To have a little fire inside your own bank and ditch, that nobody else may enjoy it or come anigh it! And what a zany an old chap must be, to light a bonfire when there's no youngsters to please."

"Cap'n Vye has been for a long walk today, and is quite tired out," said Grandfer Cantle, "so 'tisn't likely to be he."

"And he would hardly afford good fuel like that," said the wide woman.

"Then it must be his grand-daughter," said Fairway. "Not that a body of her age can want a fire much."

"She is very strange in her ways, living up there by herself, and such things please her," said Susan.

"She's a well-favoured maid enough," said Humphrey the furze-cutter; "especially when she's got one of her dandy gowns on."

"That's true," said Fairway. "Well, let her bonfire burn an't will. Ours is well-nigh out by the look o't."

"How dark 'tis now the fire's gone down!" said Christian Cantle, looking behind him with his hare eyes. "Don't ye think we'd better get home-along, neighbours? The heth isn't haunted, I know; but we'd better get home.... Ah, what was that?"

"Only the wind," said the turf-cutter.

"I don't think Fifth-of-Novembers ought to be kept up by night except in towns. It should be by day in outstep, ill-accounted places like this!"

"Nonsense, Christian. Lift up your spirits like a man! Susy, dear, you and I will have a jig — hey, my honey? — before 'tis quite too dark to see how well-favoured you be still, though so many summers have passed since your husband, a son of a witch, snapped you up from me."

This was addressed to Susan Nunsuch; and the next circumstance of which the beholders were conscious was a vision of the matron's broad form whisking off towards the space whereon the fire had been kindled.   She was lifted bodily by Mr. Fairway's arm, which had been flung round her waist before she had become aware of his intention.   The site of the fire was now merely a circle of ashes flecked with red embers and sparks, the furze having burnt completely away.   Once within the circle he whirled her round and round in a dance.   She was a woman noisily constructed; in addition to her enclosing framework of whalebone and lath, she wore pattens summer and winter, in wet weather and in dry, to preserve her boots from wear; and when Fairway began to jump about with her, the clicking of the pattens, the creaking of the stays, and her screams of surprise, formed a very audible concert.

"I'll crack thy numskull for thee, you mandy chap," said Mrs. Nunsuch, as she helplessly danced round with him, her feet playing like drumsticks among the sparks.   "My ancles were all in a fever afore, from walking through that prickly furze, and now you must make 'em worse with these vlankers!"

The vagary of Timothy Fairway was infectious.   The turf-cutter seized old Olly Dowden, and, somewhat more gently, poussetted with her likewise. The young men were not slow to imitate the example of their elders, and seized the maids; Grandfer Cantle and his stick jigged in the form of a three-legged object among the rest; and in half a minute all that could be seen on Rainbarrow was a whirling of dark shapes amid a boiling confusion of sparks, which leapt around the dancers as high as their waists.   The chief noises were women's shrill cries, men's laughter, Susan's stays and pattens, Olly Dowden's "heu-heu-heu!" and the strumming of the wind upon the furze-bushes, which formed a kind of tune to the demoniac measure they trod. Christian alone stood aloof, uneasily rocking himself as he murmured, "They ought not to do it — how the vlankers do fly! 'tis tempting the Wicked one, 'tis."

"What was that?" said one of the lads, stopping.

"Ah — where?" said Christian, hastily closing up to the rest.

The dancers all lessened their speed.

"'Twas behind you, Christian, that I heard it — down there."

"Yes — 'tis behind me!" Christian said.   "Matthew, Mark, Luke, and John, bless the bed that I lie on; four angels guard ——"

"Hold your tongue.   What is it?" said Fairway.

"Hoi-i-i-i!" cried a voice from the darkness.

"Halloo-o-o-o!" said Fairway.

"Is there any cart-track up across here to Mis'ess Yeobright's, of Blooms-End?" came to them in the same voice, as a long, slim, indistinct figure approached the barrow.

"Ought we not to run home as hard as we can, neighbours, as 'tis getting late?" said Christian.   "Not run away from one another, you know; run close together, I mean."

"Scrape up a few stray locks of furze, and make a blaze, so that we can see who the man is," said Fairway.

When the flame arose it revealed a young man in tight raiment, and red from top to toe. "Is there a track across here to Mis'ess Yeobright's house?" he repeated.

"Ay — keep along the path down there."

"I mean a way two horses and a van can travel over?"

"Well, yes; you can get up the vale below here with time. The track is rough, but if you've got a light your horses may pick along wi' care. Have ye brought your cart far up, neighbour reddleman?"

"I've left it in the bottom, about half a mile back. I stepped on in front to make sure of the way, as 'tis night-time, and I haven't been here for so long."

"Oh, well, you can get up," said Fairway. "What a turn it did give me when I zid him!" he added to the whole group, the reddleman included. "Lord's sake, I thought, whatever fiery mommet is this come to trouble us? No slight to your looks, reddleman, for ye bain't bad-looking in the ground-work, though the finish is queer. My meaning is just to say how curious I felt. I half thought it 'twas the devil or the red ghost the boy told of."

"It gied me a turn likewise," said Susan Nunsuch, "for I had a dream last night of a death's head."

"Don't ye talk o't no more," said Christian. "If he had a handkerchief over his head he'd look for all the world like the Devil in the picture of the Temptation."

"Well, thank you for telling me," said the young reddleman, smiling faintly. "And good night t'ye all."

He withdrew from their sight down the barrow.

"I fancy I've seen that young man's face before," said Humphrey. "But where, or how, or what his name is, I don't know."

The reddleman had not been gone more than a few minutes when another person approached the partially revived bonfire. It proved to be a well-known and respected widow of the neighbourhood, of a standing which can only be expressed by the word genteel. Her face, encompassed by the blackness of the receding heath, showed whitely, and without half-lights, like a cameo.

She was a woman of middle-age, with well-formed features of the type usually found where perspicacity is the chief quality enthroned within. At moments she seemed to be regarding issues from a Nebo denied to others around. She had something of an estranged mien: the solitude exhaled from the heath was concentrated in this face that had arisen from it. The air with which she looked at the heathmen betokened a certain unconcern at their presence, or at what might be their opinions of her for walking in that lonely spot at such an hour, thus indirectly implying that in some respect or other they were not up to her level. The explanation lay in the fact that though her husband had been a small farmer she herself was a curate's daughter, who had once dreamt of doing better things.

Persons with any weight of character carry, like planets, their atmospheres along with them in their orbits; and the matron who entered now upon the scene could, and usually did, bring her own tone into a company. Her normal manner among the heathfolk had that reticence which results from the consciousness of superior communicative power. But the effect of coming into society and light after lonely wandering in darkness is a sociability in the comer above its usual pitch, expressed in the features even more than in the words.

"Why, 'tis Mis'ess Yeobright," said Fairway. "Mis'ess Yeobright, not ten minutes ago a man was here asking for you — a reddleman."

"What did he want?" said she.

"He didn't tell us."

"Something to sell, I suppose; what it can be I am at a loss to understand."

"I am glad to hear that your son Mr. Clym is coming home at Christmas, ma'am," said Sam, the turf-cutter. "What a dog he used to be for bonfires!"

"Yes. I believe he is coming," she said.

"He must be a fine fellow by this time," said Fairway.

"He is a man now," she replied quietly.

"'Tis very lonesome for 'ee in the heth tonight, mis'ess," said Christian, coming from the seclusion he had hitherto maintained. "Mind you don't get lost. Egdon Heth is a bad place to get lost in, and the winds do huffle queerer tonight than ever I heard 'em afore. Them that know Egdon best have been pixy-led here at times."

"Is that you, Christian?" said Mrs. Yeobright. "What made you hide away from me?"

"'Twas that I didn't know you in this light, mis'ess; and being a man of the mournfullest make, I was scared a little, that's all. Oftentimes if you could see how terrible down I get in my mind, 'twould make 'ee quite nervous for fear I should die by my hand."

"You don't take after your father," said Mrs. Yeobright, looking towards the fire, where Grandfer Cantle, with some want of originality, was dancing by himself among the sparks, as the others had done before.

"Now, Grandfer," said Timothy Fairway, "we are ashamed of ye. A reverent old patriarch man as you be — seventy if a day — to go hornpiping like that by yourself!"

"A harrowing old man, Mis'ess Yeobright," said Christian despondingly. "I wouldn't live with him a week, so playward as he is, if I could get away."

"'Twould be more seemly in ye to stand still and welcome Mis'ess Yeobright, and you the venerablest here, Grandfer Cantle," said the besom-woman.

"Faith, and so it would," said the reveller, checking himself repentantly. "I've such a bad memory, Mis'ess Yeobright, that I forget how I'm looked up to by the rest of 'em. My spirits must be wonderful good, you'll say? But not always. 'Tis a weight upon a man to be looked up to as commander, and I often feel it."

"I am sorry to stop the talk," said Mrs. Yeobright. "But I must be leaving you now. I am crossing the heath towards my niece's new home, who is returning tonight with her husband; and hearing Olly's voice I came up here to ask her if she would soon be going home; I should like her to walk with me, as her way is mine."

"Ay, sure, ma'am, I'm just thinking of moving," said Olly.

"Why, you'll be safe to meet the reddleman that I told ye of," said Fairway. "He's only gone back to get his van. We heard that your niece and her husband were coming straight home as soon as they were married, and we are going down there shortly, to give 'em a song o' welcome."

"Thank you indeed," said Mrs. Yeobright.

"But we shall take a shorter cut through the furze than you can go with long clothes; so we won't trouble you to wait."

"Very well — are you ready, Olly?"

"Yes, ma'am. And there's a light shining from your niece's window, see. It will help to keep us in the path."

She indicated the faint light at the bottom of the valley which Fairway had pointed out; and the two women descended the barrow.

IV

THE HALT ON THE TURNPIKE ROAD

Down, downward they went, and yet further down — their descent at each step seeming to outmeasure their advance. Their skirts were scratched noisily by the furze, their shoulders brushed by the ferns, which, though dead and dry, stood erect as when alive, no sufficient winter weather having as yet arrived to beat them down. Their Tartarean situation might by some have been called an imprudent one for two unattended women. But these shaggy recesses were at all seasons a familiar surrounding to Olly and Mrs. Yeobright; and the addition of darkness lends no frightfulness to the face of a friend.

"And so Tamsin has married him at last," said Olly, when the incline had become so much less steep that their footsteps no longer required undivided attention.

Mrs. Yeobright answered slowly, "Yes: at last."

"How you will miss her — living with ye as a daughter, as she always have."

"I do miss her."

Olly, though without the tact to perceive when remarks were untimely, was saved by her very simplicity from rendering them offensive. Questions that would have been resented in others she could ask with impunity. This accounted for Mrs. Yeobright's acquiescence in the revival of an evidently sore subject.

"I was quite strook to hear you'd agreed to it, ma'am, that I was," continued the besom-maker.

"You were not more struck by it than I should have been last year this time, Olly. There are a good many sides to that wedding. I could not tell you all of them, even if I tried."

"I felt myself that he was hardly solid-going enough to mate with your family. Keeping an inn — what is it? But 'a's clever, that's true, and they say he was an engineering gentleman once, but has come down by being too outwardly given."

"I saw that, upon the whole, it would be better she should marry where she wished."

"Poor little thing, her feelings got the better of her, no doubt. 'Tis nature. Well, they may call him what they will — he've several acres of heath ground broke up here, besides the public-house, and the heth-croppers, and his manners be quite like a gentleman's. And what's done cannot be undone."

"It cannot," said Mrs. Yeobright. "See, here's the waggon-track at last. Now we shall get along better."

The wedding subject was no further dwelt upon; and soon a faint diverging path was reached, where they parted company, Olly first begging her companion to remind Mr. Wildeve that he had not sent her sick husband the bottle of wine promised on the occasion of his marriage. The besom-maker turned to the left towards her own house, behind a spur of the hill, and Mrs. Yeobright followed the straight track, which further on joined the highway by the Quiet Woman Inn, whither she supposed her niece to have returned with Wildeve from their wedding at Anglebury that day.

She first reached Wildeve's Patch, as it was called, a plot of land redeemed from the heath, and after long and laborious years brought into cultivation. The man who had discovered that it could be tilled died of the labour: the man who succeeded him in possession ruined himself in fertilizing it. Wildeve came like Amerigo Vespucci, and received the honours due to those who had gone before.

When Mrs. Yeobright had drawn near to the inn, and was about to enter, she saw a horse and vehicle some two hundred yards beyond it, coming towards her, a man walking alongside with a lantern in his hand. It was soon evident that this was the reddleman who had inquired for her. Instead of entering the inn at once, she walked by it and towards the van.

The conveyance came close, and the man was about to pass her with little notice, when she turned to him and said, "I think you have been inquiring for me? I am Mrs. Yeobright of Blooms-End."

The reddleman started, and held up his finger. He stopped the horses, and beckoned to her to withdraw with him a few yards aside, which she did, wondering.

"You don't know me, ma'am, I suppose?" he said.

"I do not," said she. "Why, yes, I do! You are young Venn — your father was a dairyman somewhere here?"

"Yes; and I knew your niece, Miss Tamsin, a little. I have something bad to tell you."

"About her — no? She has just come home, I believe, with her husband. They arranged to return this afternoon — to the inn beyond here?"

"She's not there."

"How do you know?"

"Because she's here. She's in my van," he added slowly.

"What new trouble has come?" murmured Mrs. Yeobright, putting her hand over her eyes.

"I can't explain much, ma'am. All I know is that, as I was going along the road this morning, about a mile out of Anglebury, I heard something trotting after me like a doe, and looking round there she was, white as death itself. 'Oh, Diggory Venn!' she said, 'I thought 'twas you: will you help me? I am in trouble.'"

"How did she know your Christian name?" said Mrs. Yeobright doubtingly.

"I had met her as a lad before I went away in this trade. She asked then if she might ride, and then down she fell in a faint. I picked her up and put her in, and there she has been ever since. She has cried a good deal, but she has hardly spoke; all she has told me being that she was to have been married this morning. I tried to get her to eat something, but she couldn't; and at last she fell asleep."

"Let me see her at once," said Mrs. Yeobright, hastening towards the van.

The reddleman followed with the lantern, and, stepping up first, assisted Mrs. Yeobright to mount beside him. On the door being opened she perceived at the end of the van an extemporized couch, around which was hung apparently all the drapery that the reddleman possessed, to keep the occupant of the little couch from contact with the red materials of his trade. A young girl lay thereon, covered with a cloak. She was asleep, and the light of the lantern fell upon her features.

A fair, sweet, and honest country face was revealed, reposing in a nest of wavy chestnut hair. It was between pretty and beautiful. Though her eyes were closed, one could easily imagine the light necessarily shining in them as the culmination of the luminous workmanship around. The groundwork of the face was hopefulness; but over it now lay like a foreign substance a film of anxiety and grief. The grief had been there so shortly as to have abstracted nothing of the bloom which had as yet but given a dignity to what it might eventually undermine. The scarlet of her lips had not had time to abate, and just now it appeared still more intense by the absence of the neighbouring and more transient colour of her cheek. The lips frequently parted, with a murmur of words. She seemed to belong rightly to a madrigal — to require viewing through rhyme and harmony.

One thing at least was obvious: she was not made to be looked at thus. The reddleman had appeared conscious of as much, and, while Mrs. Yeobright looked in upon her, he cast his eyes aside with a delicacy which well became him. The sleeper apparently thought so too, for the next moment she opened her eyes.

The lips then parted with something of anticipation, something more of doubt; and her several thoughts and fractions of thoughts, as signalled by the changes on her face, were exhibited by the light to the utmost nicety. An ingenuous, transparent life was disclosed; as if the flow of her existence could be seen passing within her. She understood the scene in a moment.

"O yes, it is I, aunt," she cried. "I know how frightened you are, and how you cannot believe it; but all the same, it is I who have come home like this!"

"Tamsin, Tamsin!" said Mrs. Yeobright, stooping over the young woman and kissing her. "O my dear girl!"

Thomasin was now on the verge of a sob; but by an unexpected self-command she uttered no sound. With a gentle panting breath she sat upright.

"I did not expect to see you in this state, any more than you me," she went on quickly. "Where am I, aunt?"

"Nearly home, my dear. In Egdon Bottom. What dreadful thing is it?"

"I'll tell you in a moment. So near, are we? Then I will get out and walk. I want to go home by the path."

"But this kind man who has done so much will, I am sure, take you right on to my house?" said the aunt, turning to the reddleman, who had withdrawn from the front of the van on the awakening of the girl, and stood in the road.

"Why should you think it necessary to ask me? I will, of course," said he.

"He is indeed kind," murmured Thomasin. "I was once acquainted with him, aunt, and when I saw him today I thought I should prefer his van to any conveyance of a stranger. But I'll walk now. Reddleman, stop the horses, please."

The man regarded her with tender reluctance, but stopped them.

Aunt and niece then descended from the van, Mrs. Yeobright saying to its owner, "I quite recognize you now. What made you change from the nice business your father left you?"

"Well, I did," he said, and looked at Thomasin, who blushed a little. "Then you'll not be wanting me any more tonight, ma'am?"

Mrs. Yeobright glanced around at the dark sky, at the hills, at the perishing bonfires, and at the lighted window of the inn they had neared. "I think not," she said, "since Thomasin wishes to walk. We can soon run up the path and reach home: we know it well."

And after a few further words they parted, the reddleman moving onwards with his van, and the two women remaining standing in the road. As soon as the vehicle and its driver had withdrawn so far as to be beyond all possible reach of her voice, Mrs. Yeobright turned to her niece.

"Now, Thomasin," she said sternly, "what's the meaning of this disgraceful performance?"

V

PERPLEXITY AMONG HONEST PEOPLE

THOMASIN looked as if quite overcome by her aunt's change of manner. "It means just what it seems to mean: I am — not married," she replied faintly. "Excuse me — for humiliating you, aunt, by this mishap: I am sorry for it. But I cannot help it."

"Me? Think of yourself first."

"It was nobody's fault. When we got there the parson wouldn't marry us because of some trifling irregularity in the licence."

"What irregularity?"

"I don't know. Mr. Wildeve can explain. I did not think when I went away this morning that I should come back like this." It being dark, Thomasin allowed her emotion to escape her by the silent way of tears, which could roll down her cheek unseen.

"I could almost say that it serves you right — if I did not feel that you don't deserve it," continued Mrs. Yeobright, who, possessing two distinct moods in close contiguity, a gentle mood and an angry, flew from one to the other without the least warning. "Remember, Thomasin, this business was none of my seeking; from the very first, when you began to feel foolish about that man, I warned you he would not make you happy. I felt it so strongly that I did what I would never have believed myself capable of doing — stood up in the church, and made myself the public talk for weeks. But having once consented, I don't submit to these fancies without good reason. Marry him you must after this."

"Do you think I wish to do otherwise for one moment?" said Thomasin, with a heavy sigh. "I know how wrong it was of me to love him, but don't pain me by talking like that, aunt! You would not have had me stay there with him, would you? — and your house is the only home I have to return to. He says we can be married in a day or two."

"I wish he had never seen you."

"Very well; then I will be the miserablest woman in the world, and not let him see me again. No, I won't have him!"

"It is too late to speak so. Come with me. I am going to the inn to see if he has returned. Of course I shall get to the bottom of this story at once. Mr. Wildeve must not suppose he can play tricks upon me, or any belonging to me."

"It was not that. The licence was wrong, and he couldn't get another the same day. He will tell you in a moment how it was, if he comes."

"Why didn't he bring you back?"

"That was me!" again sobbed Thomasin. "When I found we could not be married I didn't like to come back with him, and I was very ill. Then I saw Diggory Venn, and was glad to get him to take me home. I cannot explain it any better, and you must be angry with me if you will."

"I shall see about that," said Mrs. Yeobright; and they turned towards the inn, known in the neighbourhood as the Quiet Woman, the sign of which represented the figure of a matron carrying her head under her arm. The front of the house was towards the heath and Rainbarrow, whose dark shape seemed to threaten it from the sky. Upon the door was a neglected brass plate, bearing the unexpected inscription, "Mr. Wildeve, Engineer" — a useless yet cherished relic from the time when he had been started in that profession in an office at Budmouth by those who had hoped much from him, and had been disappointed. The garden was at the back, and behind this ran a still deep stream, forming the margin of the heath in this direction, meadow-land appearing beyond the stream.

But the thick obscurity permitted only sky-lines to be visible of any scene at present. The water at the back of the house could be heard, idly spinning whirlpools in its creep between the rows of dry featherheaded reeds which formed a stockade along each bank. Their presence was denoted by sounds as of a congregation praying humbly, produced by their rubbing against each other in the slow wind.

The window, whence the candlelight had shone up the vale to the eyes of the bonfire group, was uncurtained, but the sill lay too high for a pedestrian on the outside to look over it into the room. A vast shadow, in which could be dimly traced portions of a masculine contour, blotted half the ceiling.

"He seems to be at home," said Mrs. Yeobright.

"Must I come in, too, aunt?" asked Thomasin, faintly. "I suppose not; it would be wrong."

"You must come, certainly — to confront him, so that he may make no false representations to me. We shall not be five minutes in the house, and then we'll walk home."

Entering the open passage, she tapped at the door of the private parlour, unfastened it, and looked in.

The back and shoulders of a man came between Mrs. Yeobright's eyes and the fire. Wildeve, whose form it was, immediately turned, arose, and advanced to meet his visitors.

He was quite a young man, and of the two properties, form and motion, the latter first attracted the eye in him. The grace of his movement was singular: it was the pantomimic expression of a lady-killing career. Next came into notice the more material qualities, among which was a profuse crop of hair impending over the top of his face, lending to his forehead the high-cornered outline of an early Gothic shield; and a neck which was smooth and round as a cylinder. The lower half of his figure was of light build. Altogether he was one in whom no man would have seen anything to admire, and in whom no woman would have seen anything to dislike.

He discerned the young girl's form in the passage, and said, "Thomasin, then, has reached home. How could you leave me in that way, darling?" And turning to Mrs. Yeobright: "It was useless to argue with her. She would go, and go alone."

"But what's the meaning of it all?" demanded Mrs. Yeobright haughtily.

"Take a seat," said Wildeve, placing chairs for the two women. "Well, it was a very stupid mistake, but such mistakes will happen. The licence was useless at Anglebury. It was made out for Budmouth, but as I didn't read it I wasn't aware of that."

"But you had been staying at Anglebury?"

"No. I had been at Budmouth — till two days ago — and that was where I had intended to take her; but when I came to fetch her we decided upon Anglebury, forgetting that a new licence would be necessary. There was not time to get to Budmouth afterwards."

"I think you are very much to blame," said Mrs. Yeobright.

"It was quite my fault we chose Anglebury," Thomasin pleaded. "I proposed it because I was not known there."

"I know so well that I am to blame that you need not remind me of it," replied Wildeve shortly.

"Such things don't happen for nothing," said the aunt. "It is a great slight to me and my family; and when it gets known there will be a very unpleasant time for us. How can she look her friends in the face tomorrow? It is a very great injury, and one I cannot easily forgive. It may even reflect on her character."

"Nonsense," said Wildeve.

Thomasin's large eyes had flown from the face of one to the face of the other during this discussion, and she now said anxiously, "Will you allow me, aunt, to talk it over alone with Damon for five minutes? Will you, Damon?"

"Certainly, dear," said Wildeve, "if your aunt will excuse us." He led her into an adjoining room, leaving Mrs. Yeobright by the fire.

As soon as they were alone, and the door closed, Thomasin said, turning up her pale, tearful face to him. "It is killing me, this, Damon! I did not mean to part from you in anger at Anglebury this morning; but I was frightened, and hardly knew what I said. I've not let aunt know how much I have suffered today; and it is so hard to command my face and voice, and to smile as if it were a slight thing to me; but I try to do so, that she may not be still more indignant with you. I know you could not help it, dear, whatever aunt may think."

"She is very unpleasant."

"Yes," Thomasin murmured, "and I suppose I seem so now. . . . Damon, what do you mean to do about me?"

"Do about you?"

"Yes. Those who don't like you whisper things which at moments make me doubt you. We mean to marry, I suppose, don't we?"

"Of course we do. We have only to go to Budmouth on Monday, and we may marry at once."

"Then do let us go! — O Damon, what you make me say!" She hid her face in her handkerchief. "Here am I asking you to marry me; when by rights you ought to be on your knees imploring me, your cruel mistress, not to refuse you, and saying it would break your heart if I did. I used to think it would be pretty and sweet like that; but how different!"

"Yes, real life is never at all like that."

"But I don't care personally if it never takes place," she added with a little dignity; "no, I can live without you. It is aunt I think of. She is so proud, and thinks so much of her family respectability, that she will be cut down with mortification if this story should get abroad before — it is done. My cousin Clym, too, will be much wounded."

"Then he will be very unreasonable. In fact, you are all rather unreasonable."

Thomasin coloured a little, and not with love. But whatever the momentary feeling which caused that flush in her, it went as it came, and she humbly said, "I never mean to be, if I can help it. I merely feel that you have my aunt to some extent in your power at last."

"As a matter of justice it is almost due to me," said Wildeve. "Think what I have gone through to win her consent; the insult that it is to any man to have the banns forbidden: the double insult to a man unlucky enough to be cursed with sensitiveness, and blue demons, and Heaven knows what, as I am. I can never forget those banns. A harsher man would rejoice now in the power I have of turning upon your aunt by going no further in the business."

She looked wistfully at him with her sorrowful eyes as he said those words, and her aspect showed that more than one person in the room could deplore the possession of sensitiveness. Seeing that she was really suffering he seemed disturbed and added, "This is merely a reflection, you know. I have not the least intention to refuse to complete the marriage, Tamsie mine — I could not bear it."

"You could not, I know!" said the fair girl, brightening. "You, who cannot bear the sight of pain in even an insect, or any disagreeable sound, or unpleasant smell even, will not long cause pain to me and mine."

"I will not, if I can help it."

"Your hand upon it, Damon."

He carelessly gave her his hand.

"Ah, by my crown, what's that?" he said suddenly.

There fell upon their ears the sound of numerous voices singing in front of the house. Among these, two made themselves prominent by their peculiarity: one was a very strong bass, the other a wheezy thin piping. Thomasin recognized them as belonging to Timothy Fairway and Grandfer Cantle respectively.

"What does it mean — it is not skimmity-riding, I hope?" she said, with a frightened gaze at Wildeve.

"Of course not; no, it is that the heath-folk have come to sing to us a welcome. This is intolerable!" He began pacing about, the men outside singing cheerily —

> "He told' her that she' was the joy' of his life',
> And if' she'd con-sent' he would make her his wife';
> She could' not refuse' him; to church' so they went',
> Young Will' was forgot', and young Sue' was con-tent';
> And then' was she kiss'd' and set down' on his knee',
> No man' in the world' was so lov'-ing as he'!"

Mrs. Yeobright burst in from the outer room. "Thomasin, Thomasin!" she said, looking indignantly at Wildeve; "here's a pretty exposure! Let us escape at once. Come!"

It was, however, too late to get away by the passage. A rugged knocking had begun upon the door of the front room. Wildeve, who had gone to the window, came back.

"Stop!" he said imperiously, putting his hand upon Mrs. Yeobright's arm. "We are regularly besieged. There are fifty of them out there if there's one. You stay in this room with Thomasin; I'll go out and face them. You must stay now, for my sake, till they are gone, so that it may seem as if all was right. Come, Tamsie dear, don't go making a scene — we must marry after this; that you can see as well as I. Sit still, that's all — and don't speak much. I'll manage them. Blundering fools!"

He pressed the agitated girl into a seat, returned to the outer room and opened the door. Immediately outside, in the passage, appeared Grandfer

Cantle singing in concert with those still standing in front of the house. He came into the room and nodded abstractedly to Wildeve, his lips still parted, and his features excruciatingly strained in the emission of the chorus. This being ended, he said heartily, "Here's welcome to the new-made couple, and God bless 'em!"

"Thank you," said Wildeve, with dry resentment, his face as gloomy as a thunderstorm.

At the Grandfer's heels now came the rest of the group, which included Fairway, Christian, Sam the turf-cutter, Humphrey, and a dozen others. All smiled upon Wildeve, and upon his tables and chairs likewise, from a general sense of friendliness towards the articles as well as towards their owner.

"We be not here afore Mrs. Yeobright after all," said Fairway, recognizing the matron's bonnet through the glass partition which divided the public apartment they had entered from the room where the women sat. "We struck down across, d'ye see, Mr. Wildeve, and she went round by the path."

"And I see the young bride's little head!" said Grandfer, peeping in the same direction, and discerning Thomasin, who was waiting beside her aunt in a miserable and awkward way. "Not quite settled yet — well, well, there's plenty of time."

Wildeve made no reply; and probably feeling that the sooner he treated them the sooner they would go, he produced a stone jar, which threw a warm halo over matters at once.

"That's a drop of the right sort, I can see," said Grandfer Cantle, with the air of a man too well-mannered to show any hurry to taste it.

"Yes," said Wildeve, "'tis some old mead. I hope you will like it."

"Oh ay," replied the guests, in the hearty tones natural when the words demanded by politeness coincide with those of deepest feeling. "There isn't a prettier drink under the sun."

"I'll take my oath there isn't," added Grandfer Cantle. "All that can be said against mead is that 'tis rather heady, and apt to lie about a man a good while. But tomorrow's Sunday, thank God."

"I feel'd for all the world like some bold soldier after I had had some once," said Christian.

"You shall feel so again," said Wildeve, with condescension. "Cups or glasses, gentlemen?"

"Well, if you don't mind, we'll have the beaker, and pass 'em round; 'tis better than heling it out in dribbles."

"Jown the slippery glasses," said Grandfer Cantle. "What's the good of a thing that you can't put down in the ashes to warm, hey, neighbours; that's what I ask?"

"Right, Grandfer," said Sam; and the mead then circulated.

"Well," said Timothy Fairway, feeling demands upon his praise in some form or other, "'tis a worthy thing to be married, Mr. Wildeve; and the woman you've got is a dimant, so says I. Yes," he continued, to Grandfer Cantle, raising his voice so as to be heard through the partition; "her father (inclining his head towards the inner room) was as good a feller as ever lived. He always had his great indignation ready against anything underhand."

"Is that very dangerous?" said Christian.

"And there were few in these parts that were upsides with him," said Sam. "Whenever a club walked he'd play the clarinet in the band that marched before 'em as if he'd never touched anything but a clarinet all his life. And then, when they got to church-door he'd throw down the clarinet, mount the gallery, snatch up the bass-viol, and rozum away as if he'd never played anything but a bass-viol. Folk would say — folk that knowed what a true stave was — 'Surely, surely that's never the same man that I zid handling the clarinet so masterly by now!'"

"I can mind it," said the furze-cutter. "'Twas a wonderful thing that one body could hold it all and never mix the fingering."

"There was Kingsbere church likewise," Fairway recommenced, as one opening a new vein of the same mine of interest.

Wildeve breathed the breath of one intolerably bored, and glanced through the partition at the prisoners.

"He used to walk over there of a Sunday afternoon to visit his old acquaintance Andrew Brown, the first clarinet there; a good man enough, but rather screechy in his music, if you can mind?"

"'A was."

"And neighbour Yeobright would take Andrey's place for some part of the service, to let Andrey have a bit of a nap, as any friend would naturally do."

"As any friend would," said Grandfer Cantle, the other listeners expressing the same accord by the shorter way of nodding their heads.

"No sooner was Andrey asleep and the first whiff of neighbour Yeobright's wind had got inside Andrey's clarinet than everyone in church feeled in a moment there was a great soul among 'em. All heads would turn, and they'd say, 'Ah, I thought 'twas he!' One Sunday I can well mind — a bass-viol day that time, and Yeobright had brought his own. 'Twas the Hundred-and-thirty-third to 'Lydia'; and when they'd come to, 'Ran down his beard and o'er his robes its costly moisture shed,' neighbour Yeobright, who had just warmed to his work, drove his bow into them strings that glorious grand that he e'en a'most sawed the bass-viol into two pieces. Every winder in church rattled as if 'twere a thunderstorm. Old Pa'son Gibbons lifted his hands in his great holy surplice as natural as if he'd been in common clothes, and seemed to say to hisself, 'Oh for such a man in our parish!' But not a soul in Kingsbere could hold a candle to Yeobright."

"Was it quite safe when the winder shook?" Christian inquired.

He received no answer; all for the moment sitting rapt in admiration of the performance described. As with Farinelli's singing before the princesses, Sheridan's renowned Begum Speech, and other such examples, the fortunate condition of its being for ever lost to the world invested the deceased Mr. Yeobright's *tour de force* on that memorable afternoon with a cumulative glory which comparative criticism, had that been possible, might considerably have shorn down.

"He was the last you'd have expected to drop off in the prime of life," said Humphrey.

"Ah, well: he was looking for the earth some months afore he went. At that time women used to run for smocks and gown-pieces at Greenhill Fair, and my wife that is now, being a long-legged slittering maid, hardly husband-high, went with the rest of the maidens, for 'a was a good runner afore she got so heavy. When she came home I said — we were then just beginning to walk together — 'What have ye got, my honey?' 'I've won — well, I've won — a gown-piece,' says she, her colours coming up in a moment. 'Tis a smock for a crown, I thought; and so it turned out. Ay, when I think what she'll say to me now without a mossel of red in her face, it do seem strange that 'a wouldn't say such a little thing then.... However, then she went on, and that's what made me bring up the story, 'Well, whatever clothes I've won, white or figured, for eyes to see or for eyes not to see' ('a could do a pretty stroke of modesty in those days), 'I'd sooner have lost it than have seen what I have. Poor Mr. Yeobright was took bad directly he reached the fair ground, and was forced to go home again.' That was the last time he ever went out of the parish."

"'A faltered on from one day to another, and then we heard he was gone."

"D'ye think he had great pain when 'a died?" said Christian.

"O no: quite different. Nor any pain of mind. He was lucky enough to be God A'mighty's own man."

"And other folk — d'ye think 'twill be much pain to 'em, Master Fairway?"

"That depends on whether they be afeard."

"I bain't afeard at all, I thank God!" said Christian strenuously. "I'm glad I hain't, for then 'twon't pain me.... I don't think I be afeard — or if I be I can't help it, and I don't deserve to suffer. I wish I was not afeard at all!"

There was a solemn silence, and looking from the window, which was unshuttered and unblinded, Timothy said, "Well, what a fess little bonfire that one is, out by Cap'n Vye's! 'Tis burning just the same now as ever, upon my life."

All glances went through the window, and nobody noticed that Wildeve disguised a brief, tell-tale look. Far away up the sombre valley of heath, and to the right of Rainbarrow, could indeed be seen the light, small, but steady and persistent as before.

"It was lighted before ours was," Fairway continued; "and yet everyone in the country round is out afore 'n."

"Perhaps there's meaning in it!" murmured Christian.

"How meaning?" said Wildeve sharply.

Christian was too scattered to reply, and Timothy helped him.

"He means, sir, that the lonesome dark-eyed creature up there that some say is a witch — ever I should call a fine young woman such a name — is always up to some odd conceit or other; and so perhaps 'tis she."

"I'd be very glad to ask her in wedlock, if she'd hae me, and take the risk of her wild dark eyes ill-wishing me," said Grandfer Cantle staunchly.

"Don't ye say it, father!" implored Christian.

"Well, be dazed if he who do marry the maid won't hae an uncommon picture for his best parlour," said Fairway in a liquid tone, placing down the cup of mead at the end of a good pull.

"And a partner as deep as the North Star," said Sam, taking up the cup and finishing the little that remained.

"Well, really, now I think we must be moving," said Humphrey, observing the emptiness of the vessel.

"But we'll gie 'em another song?" said Grandfer Cantle. "I'm as full of notes as a bird!"

"Thank you, Grandfer," said Wildeve. "But we will not trouble you now. Some other day must do for that — when I have a party."

"Be jown'd if I don't learn ten new songs for't, or I won't learn a line!" said Grandfer Cantle. "And you may be sure I won't disappoint ye by biding away, Mr. Wildeve."

"I quite believe you," said that gentleman.

All then took their leave, wishing their entertainer long life and happiness as a married man, with recapitulations which occupied some time. Wildeve attended them to the door, beyond which the deep-dyed upward stretch of heath stood awaiting them, an amplitude of darkness reigning from their feet almost to the zenith, where a definite form first became visible in the lowering forehead of Rainbarrow. Diving into the dense obscurity in a line headed by Sam the turf-cutter, they pursued their trackless way home.

When the scratching of the furze against their leggings had fainted upon the ear, Wildeve returned to the room where he had left Thomasin and her aunt. The women were gone.

They could only have left the house in one way, by the back window; and this was open.

Wildeve laughed to himself, remained a moment thinking, and idly returned to the front room. Here his glance fell upon a bottle of wine which stood on the mantelpiece. "Ah — old Dowden!" he murmured; and going to the kitchen door shouted, "Is anybody here who can take something to old Dowden?"

There was no reply. The room was empty, the lad who acted as his factotum having gone to bed. Wildeve came back, put on his hat, took the bottle, and left the house, turning the key in the door, for there was no guest at the inn tonight. As soon as he was on the road the little bonfire on Mistover Knap again met his eye.

"Still waiting, are you, my lady?" he murmured.

However, he did not proceed that way just then; but leaving the hill to the left of him, he stumbled over a rutted road that brought him to a cottage which, like all other habitations on the heath at this hour, was only saved from being invisible by a faint shine from its bedroom window. This house was the home of Olly Dowden, the besom-maker, and he entered.

The lower room was in darkness; but by feeling his way he found a table, whereon he placed the bottle, and a minute later emerged again upon the heath. He stood and looked north-east at the undying little fire — high up above him, though not so high as Rainbarrow.

We have been told what happens when a woman deliberates; and the epigram is not always terminable with woman, provided that one be in the case, and that a fair one. Wildeve stood, and stood longer, and breathed perplexedly, and then said to himself with resignation, "Yes — by Heaven, I must go to her, I suppose!"

Instead of turning in the direction of home, he pressed on rapidly by a path under Rainbarrow towards what was evidently a signal light.

VI

THE FIGURE AGAINST THE SKY

WHEN the whole Egdon concourse had left the site of the bonfire to its accustomed loneliness, a closely wrapped female figure approached the barrow from that quarter of the heath in which the little fire lay. Had the reddleman been watching he might have recognized her as the woman who had first stood there so singularly, and vanished at the approach of strangers. She ascended to her old position at the top, where the red coals of the perishing fire greeted her like living eyes in the corpse of day. There she stood still, around her stretching the vast night atmosphere, whose incomplete darkness in comparison with the total darkness of the heath below it might have represented a venial beside a mortal sin.

That she was tall and straight in build, that she was ladylike in her movements, was all that could be learnt of her just now, her form being wrapped in a shawl folded in the old cornerwise fashion, and her head in a large kerchief, a protection not superfluous at this hour and place. Her back was towards the wind, which blew from the north-west; but whether she had avoided that aspect because of the chilly gusts which played about her exceptional position, or because her interest lay in the south-east, did not at first appear.

Her reason for standing so dead still as the pivot of this circle of heath-country was just as obscure. Her extraordinary fixity, her conspicuous loneliness, her heedlessness of night, betokened among other things an utter absence of fear. A tract of country unaltered from that sinister condition which made Cæsar anxious every year to get clear of its glooms before the autumnal equinox, a kind of landscape and weather which leads travellers from the South to describe our island as Homer's Cimmerian land, was not, on the face of it, friendly to women.

It might reasonably have been supposed that she was listening to the wind, which rose somewhat as the night advanced, and laid hold of the attention. The wind, indeed, seemed made for the scene, as the scene seemed made for the hour. Part of its tone was quite special; what was heard there could be heard nowhere else. Gusts in innumerable series followed each other from the north-west, and when each one of them raced past the sound of its progress resolved into three. Treble, tenor, and bass notes were to be found therein. The general ricochet of the whole over pits and prominences had the gravest pitch of the chime. Next there could be heard the baritone buzz of a holly tree. Below these in force, above them in pitch, a dwindled voice strove hard at a husky tune, which was the peculiar local sound alluded to. Thinner and less immediately traceable than the other two, it was far more impressive than either. In it lay what may be called the linguistic peculiarity of the heath; and being audible nowhere on earth off a heath, it afforded a shadow of reason for the woman's tenseness, which continued as unbroken as ever.

Throughout the blowing of these plaintive November winds that note bore a great resemblance to the ruins of human song which remain to the throat of fourscore and ten. It was a worn whisper, dry and papery, and it brushed so distinctly across the ear that, by the accustomed, the material minutiæ in which it originated could be realized as by touch. It was the united products of infinitesimal vegetable causes, and these were neither stems, leaves, fruit, blades, prickles, lichen, nor moss.

They were the mummied heath-bells of the past summer, originally tender and purple, now washed colourless by Michaelmas rains, and dried to dead skins by October suns. So low was an individual sound from these that a combination of hundreds only just emerged from silence, and the myriads of the whole declivity reached the woman's ear but as a shrivelled and intermittent recitative. Yet scarcely a single accent among the many afloat tonight could have such power to impress a listener with thoughts of its origin. One inwardly saw the infinity of those combined multitudes; and perceived that each of the tiny trumpets was seized on, entered, scoured and emerged from by the wind as thoroughly as if it were as vast as a crater.

"The spirit moved them." A meaning of the phrase forced itself upon the attention; and an emotional listener's fetichistic mood might have ended in one of more advanced quality. It was not, after all, that the left-hand expanse of old blooms spoke, or the right-hand, or those of the slope in front; but it was the single person of something else speaking through each in turn.

Suddenly, on the barrow, there mingled with all this wild rhetoric of night a sound which modulated so naturally into the rest that its beginning and ending were hardly to be distinguished. The bluffs, and the bushes, and the heather-bells had broken silence; at last, so did the woman; and her articulation was but as another phrase of the same discourse as theirs. Thrown out on the winds it became twined in with them, and with them it flew away.

What she uttered was a lengthened sighing, apparently at something in her mind which had led to her presence here. There was a spasmodic abandonment about it as if, in allowing herself to utter the sound, the woman's brain had authorized what it could not regulate. One point was evident in this; that she had been existing in a suppressed state, and not in one of languor, or stagnation.

Far away down the valley the faint shine from the window of the inn still lasted on; and a few additional moments proved that the window, or what was within it, had more to do with the woman's sigh than had either her own actions or the scene immediately around. She lifted her left hand, which held a closed telescope. This she rapidly extended, as if she were well accustomed to the operation, and raising it to her eye directed it towards the light beaming from the inn.

The handkerchief which had hooded her head was now a little thrown back, her face being somewhat elevated. A profile was visible against the dull monochrome of cloud around her; and it was as though side shadows from the features of Sappho and Mrs. Siddons had converged upwards from the tomb to form an image like neither but suggesting both. This, however, was mere superficiality. In respect of character a face may make certain admissions by its outline; but it fully confesses only in its changes. So much is this the case that what is called the play of the features often helps more in understanding a man or woman than the earnest labours of all the other members together. Thus the night revealed little of her whose form it was embracing, for the mobile parts of her countenance could not be seen.

At last she gave up her spying attitude, closed the telescope, and turned to the decaying embers. From these no appreciable beams now radiated, except when a more than usually smart gust brushed over their faces and raised a fitful glow which came and went like the blush of a girl. She stooped over the silent circle, and selecting from the brands a piece of stick which bore the largest live coal at its end, brought it to where she had been standing before.

She held the brand to the ground, blowing the red coal with her mouth at the same time; till it faintly illuminated the sod, and revealed a small object, which turned out to be an hour-glass, though she wore a watch. She blew long enough to show that the sand had all slipped through.

"Ah!" she said, as if surprised.

The light raised by her breath had been very fitful, and a momentary irradiation of flesh was all that it had disclosed of her face. That consisted of two matchless lips and a cheek only, her head being still enveloped. She threw away the stick, took the glass in her hand, the telescope under her arm, and moved on.

Along the ridge ran a faint foot-track, which the lady followed. Those who knew it well called it a path; and, while a mere visitor would have passed it unnoticed even by day, the regular haunters of the heath were at no loss for it at midnight. The whole secret of following these incipient paths, when there was not light enough in the atmosphere to show a turn-pike-road, lay in the development of the sense of touch in the feet, which comes with years of night-rambling in little-trodden spots. To a walker practised in such places a difference between impact on maiden herbage, and on the crippled stalks of a slight footway, is perceptible through the thickest boot or shoe.

The solitary figure who walked this beat took no notice of the windy tune still played on the dead heath-bells. She did not turn her head to look at a group of dark creatures further on, who fled from her presence as she skirted a ravine where they fed. They were about a score of the small wild ponies known as heath-croppers. They roamed at large on the undulations of Egdon, but in numbers too few to detract much from the solitude.

The pedestrian noticed nothing just now, and a clue to her abstraction was afforded by a trivial incident. A bramble caught hold of her skirt, and checked her progress. Instead of putting it off and hastening along, she yielded herself up to the pull, and stood passively still. When she began to extricate herself it was by turning round and round, and so unwinding the prickly switch. She was in a desponding reverie.

Her course was in the direction of the small undying fire which had drawn the attention of the men on Rainbarrow and of Wildeve in the valley below. A faint illumination from its rays began to glow upon her face, and the fire soon revealed itself to be lit, not on the level ground, but on a salient corner or redan of earth, at the junction of two converging bank fences. Outside was a ditch, dry except immediately under the fire, where there was a large pool, bearded all round by heather and rushes. In the smooth water of the pool the fire appeared upside down.

The banks meeting behind were bare of a hedge, save such as was formed by disconnected tufts of furze, standing upon stems along the top, like impaled heads above a city wall. A white mast, fitted up with spars and other nautical tackle, could be seen rising against the dark clouds whenever the flames played brightly enough to reach it. Altogether the scene had much the appearance of a fortification upon which had been kindled a beacon fire.

Nobody was visible; but ever and anon a whitish something moved above the bank from behind, and vanished again. This was a small human hand, in the act of lifting pieces of fuel into the fire; but for all that could be seen the hand, like that which troubled Belshazzar, was there alone. Occasionally an ember rolled off the bank, and dropped with a hiss into the pool.

At one side of the pool rough steps built of clods enabled anyone who wished to do so to mount the bank; which the woman did. Within was a paddock in an uncultivated state, though bearing evidence of having once been tilled; but the heath and fern had insidiously crept in, and were reasserting their old supremacy. Further ahead were dimly visible an irregular dwelling-house, garden, and outbuildings, backed by a clump of firs.

The young lady — for youth had revealed its presence in her buoyant bound up the bank — walked along the top instead of descending inside, and came to the corner where the fire was burning. One reason for the permanence of the blaze was now manifest: the fuel consisted of hard pieces of wood, cleft and sawn — the knotty boles of old thorn trees which grew in twos and threes about the hillsides. A yet unconsumed pile of these lay in the inner angle of the bank; and from this corner the upturned face of a little boy greeted her eyes. He was dilatorily throwing up a piece of wood into the fire every now and then, a business which seemed to have engaged him a considerable part of the evening, for his face was somewhat weary.

"I am glad you have come, Miss Eustacia," he said, with a sigh of relief. "I don't like biding by myself."

"Nonsense. I have only been a little way for a walk. I have been gone only twenty minutes."

"It seemed long," murmured the sad boy. "And you have been so many times."

"Why, I thought you would be pleased to have a bonfire. Are you not much obliged to me for making you one?"

"Yes; but there's nobody here to play wi' me."

"I suppose nobody has come while I've been away!"

"Nobody except your grandfather: he looked out of doors once for 'ee. I told him you were walking round upon the hill to look at the other bonfires."

"A good boy."

"I think I hear him coming again, miss."

An old man came into the remoter light of the fire from the direction of the homestead. He was the same who had overtaken the reddleman on the road that afternoon. He looked wistfully to the top of the bank at the woman who stood there, and his teeth, which were quite unimpaired, showed like parian from his parted lips.

"When are you coming indoors, Eustacia?" he asked. "'Tis almost bedtime. I've been home these two hours, and am tired out. Surely 'tis somewhat childish of you to stay out playing at bonfires so long, and wasting such fuel. My precious thorn roots, the rarest of all firing, that I laid by on purpose for Christmas — you have burnt 'em nearly all!"

"I promised Johnny a bonfire, and it pleases him not to let it go out just yet," said Eustacia, in a way which told at once that she was absolute queen here. "Grandfather, you go in to bed. I shall follow you soon. You like the fire, don't you, Johnny?"

The boy looked up doubtfully at her and murmured, "I don't think I want it any longer."

Her grandfather had turned back again, and did not hear the boy's reply. As soon as the white-haired man had vanished she said in a tone of pique to the child, "Ungrateful little boy, how can you contradict me? Never shall you have a bonfire again unless you keep it up now. Come, tell me you like to do things for me, and don't deny it."

The repressed child said, "Yes, I do, miss," and continued to stir the fire perfunctorily.

"Stay a little longer and I will give you a crooked sixpence," said Eustacia, more gently. "Put in one piece of wood every two or three minutes, but not too much at once. I am going to walk along the ridge a little longer, but I shall keep on coming to you. And if you hear a frog jump into the pond with a flounce, like a stone thrown in, be sure you run and tell me, because it is a sign of rain."

"Yes, Eustacia."

"Miss Vye, sir."

"Miss Vy — stacia."

"That will do. Now put in one stick more."

The little slave went on feeding the fire as before. He seemed a mere automaton, galvanized into moving and speaking by the wayward Eustacia's will. He might have been the brass statue which Albertus Magnus is said to have animated just so far as to make it chatter, and move, and be his servant.

Before going on her walk again the young girl stood still on the bank for a few instants and listened. It was to the full as lonely a place as Rainbarrow, though at rather a lower level; and it was more sheltered from wind and weather on account of the few firs to the north. The bank which enclosed the homestead, and protected it from the lawless state of the world without, was formed of thick square clods, dug from the ditch on the outside, and built up with a slight batter or incline, which forms no slight defence where hedges will not grow because of the wind and the wilderness, and where wall materials are unattainable. Otherwise the situation was quite open, commanding the whole length of the valley which reached to the river behind Wildeve's house. High above this to the right, and much nearer thitherward than the Quiet Woman Inn, the blurred contour of Rainbarrow obstructed the sky.

After her attentive survey of the wild slopes and hollow ravines a gesture of impatience escaped Eustacia. She vented petulant words every now and then; but there were sighs between her words, and sudden listenings between her sighs. Descending from her perch she again sauntered off towards Rainbarrow, though this time she did not go the whole way.

Twice she reappeared at intervals of a few minutes, and each time she said —

"Not any flounce into the pond yet, little man?"

"No, Miss Eustacia," the child replied.

"Well," she said at last, "I shall soon be going in; and then I will give you the crooked sixpence, and let you go home."

"Thank'ee, Miss Eustacia," said the tired stoker, breathing more easily. And Eustacia again strolled away from the fire, but this time not towards Rainbarrow. She skirted the bank and went round to the wicket before the house, where she stood motionless looking at the scene.

Fifty yards off rose the corner of the two converging banks, with the fire upon it: within the bank, lifting up to the fire one stick at a time, just as before, the figure of the little child. She idly watched him as he occasionally climbed up in the nook of the bank and stood beside the brands. The wind blew the smoke, and the child's hair, and the corner of his pinafore, all in the same direction: the breeze died, and the pinafore and hair lay still, and the smoke went up straight.

While Eustacia looked on from this distance the boy's form visibly started; he slid down the bank and ran across towards the white gate.

"Well?" said Eustacia.

"A hop-frog have jumped into the pond. Yes, I heard 'en!"

"Then it is going to rain, and you had better go home. You will not be afraid?" She spoke hurriedly, as if her heart had leapt into her throat at the boy's words.

"No, because I shall hae the crooked sixpence."

"Yes, here it is. Now run as fast as you can — not that way — through the garden here. No other boy in the heath has had such a bonfire as yours."

The boy, who clearly had had too much of a good thing, marched away into the shadows with alacrity. When he was gone Eustacia, leaving her telescope and hour-glass by the gate, brushed forward from the wicket towards the angle of the bank, under the fire.

Here, screened by the outwork, she waited. In a few moments a splash was audible from the pond outside. Had the child been there he would have said that a second frog had jumped in; but by most people the sound would have been likened to the fall of a stone into the water. Eustacia stepped upon the bank.

"Yes?" she said, and held her breath.

Thereupon the contour of a man became dimly visible against the low-reaching sky over the valley, beyond the outer margin of the pool. He came round it and leapt upon the bank beside her. A low laugh escaped her — the third utterance which the girl had indulged in tonight. The first, when she stood upon Rainbarrow, had expressed anxiety; the second, on the ridge, had expressed impatience; the present was one of triumphant pleasure. She let her joyous eyes rest upon him without speaking, as upon some wondrous thing she had created out of chaos.

"I have come," said the man, who was Wildeve. "You give me no peace. Why do you not leave me alone? I have seen your bonfire all the evening." The words were not without emotion, and retained their level tone as if by a careful equipoise between imminent extremes.

At this unexpectedly repressing manner in her lover the girl seemed to repress herself also. "Of course you have seen my fire," she answered with languid calmness, artificially maintained. "Why shouldn't I have a bonfire on the Fifth of November, like other denizens of the heath?"

"I knew it was meant for me."

"How did you know it? I have had no word with you since you — you chose her, and walked about with her, and deserted me entirely, as if I had never been yours body and soul so irretrievably!"

"Eustacia! could I forget that last autumn at this same day of the month and at this same place you lighted exactly such a fire as a signal for me to come and see you? Why should there have been a bonfire again by Captain Vye's house if not for the same purpose?"

"Yes, yes — I own it," she cried under her breath, with a drowsy fervour of manner and tone which was quite peculiar to her. "Don't begin speaking to me as you did, Damon; you will drive me to say words I would not wish to say to you. I had given you up, and resolved not to think of you any more; and then I heard the news, and I came out and got the fire ready because I thought that you had been faithful to me."

"What have you heard to make you think that?" said Wildeve, astonished.

"That you did not marry her!" she murmured exultingly. "And I knew it was because you loved me best, and couldn't do it.... Damon, you have been cruel to me to go away, and I have said I would never forgive you. I do not think I can forgive you entirely, even now — it is too much for a woman of any spirit to quite overlook."

"If I had known you wished to call me up here only to reproach me, I wouldn't have come."

"But I don't mind it, and I do forgive you now that you have not married her, and have come back to me!"

"Who told you that I had not married her?"

"My grandfather. He took a long walk today, and as he was coming home he overtook some person who told him of a broken-off wedding: he thought it might be yours; and I knew it was."

"Does anybody else know?"

"I suppose not. Now, Damon, do you see why I lit my signal fire? You did not think I would have lit it if I had imagined you to have become the husband of this woman. It is insulting my pride to suppose that."

Wildeve was silent: it was evident that he had supposed as much.

"Did you indeed think I believed you were married?" she again demanded earnestly. "Then you wronged me; and upon my life and heart I can hardly bear to recognize that you have such ill thoughts of me! Damon, you are not worthy of me: I see it, and yet I love you. Never mind: let it go — I must bear your mean opinion as best I may.... It is true, is it not," she added, with ill-concealed anxiety, on his making no demonstration, "that you could not bring yourself to give me up, and are still going to love me best of all?"

"Yes; or why should I have come?" he said touchily. "Not that fidelity will be any great merit in me after your kind speech about my unworthiness, which should have been said by myself if by anybody, and comes with an ill grace from you. However, the curse of inflammability is upon me, and I must live under it, and take any snub from a woman. It has brought me down from engineering to innkeeping: what lower stage it has in store for me I have yet to learn." He continued to look upon her gloomily.

She seized the moment, and throwing back the shawl so that the firelight shone full upon her face and throat, said with a smile, "Have you seen anything better than that in your travels?"

Eustacia was not one to commit herself to such a position without good ground. He said quietly, "No."

"Not even on the shoulders of Thomasin?"

"Thomasin is a pleasing and innocent woman."

"That's nothing to do with it," she cried with quick passionateness. "We will leave her out; there are only you and me now to think of." After a long look at him she resumed with the old quiescent warmth: "Must I go on weakly confessing to you things a woman ought to conceal; and own that no words can express how gloomy I have been because of that dreadful belief I held till two hours ago — that you had quite deserted me?"

"I am sorry I caused you that pain."

"But perhaps it is not wholly because of you that I get gloomy," she archly added. "It is in my nature to feel like that. It was born in my blood, I suppose."

"Hypochondriasis."

"Or else it was coming into this wild heath. I was happy enough at Budmouth. O the times, O the days at Budmouth! But Egdon will be brighter again now."

"I hope it will," said Wildeve moodily. "Do you know the consequence of this recall to me, my old darling? I shall come to see you again as before, at Rainbarrow."

"Of course you will."

"And yet I declare that until I got here tonight I intended, after this one good-bye, never to meet you again."

"I don't thank you for that," she said, turning away, while indignation spread through her like subterranean heat. "You may come again to Rainbarrow if you like, but you won't see me; and you may call, but I shall not listen; and you may tempt me, but I won't give myself to you any more."

"You have said as much before, sweet; but such natures as yours don't so easily adhere to their words. Neither, for the matter of that, do such natures as mine."

"This is the pleasure I have won by my trouble," she whispered bitterly. "Why did I try to recall you? Damon, a strange warring takes place in my mind occasionally. I think when I become calm after your woundings, 'Do I embrace a cloud of common fog after all?' You are a chameleon, and now you are at your worst colour. Go home, or I shall hate you!"

He looked absently towards Rainbarrow while one might have counted twenty, and said, as if he did not much mind all this, "Yes, I will go home. Do you mean to see me again?"

"If you own to me that the wedding is broken off because you love me best."

"I don't think it would be good policy," said Wildeve, smiling. "You would get to know the extent of your power too clearly."

"But tell me!"

"You know."

"Where is she now?"

"I don't know. I prefer not to speak of her to you. I have not yet married her: I have come in obedience to your call. That is enough."

"I merely lit that fire because I was dull, and thought I would get a little excitement by calling you up and triumphing over you as the Witch of Endor called up Samuel. I determined you should come; and you have come! I have shown my power. A mile and half hither, and a mile and half back again to your home — three miles in the dark for me. Have I not shown my power?"

He shook his head at her. "I know you too well, my Eustacia; I know you too well. There isn't a note in you which I don't know; and that hot little bosom couldn't play such a cold-blooded trick to save its life. I saw a woman on Rainbarrow at dusk looking down towards my house. I think I drew out you before you drew out me."

The revived embers of an old passion glowed clearly in Wildeve now; and he leant forward as if about to put his face towards her cheek.

"O no," she said, intractably moving to the other side of the decayed fire. "What did you mean by that?"

"Perhaps I may kiss your hand?"

"No, you may not."

"Then I may shake your hand?"

"No."

"Then I wish you good-night without caring for either. Good-bye, good-bye."

She returned no answer, and with the bow of a dancing-master he vanished on the other side of the pool as he had come.

Eustacia sighed: it was no fragile maiden sigh, but a sigh which shook her like a shiver. Whenever a flash of reason darted like an electric light upon her lover — as it sometimes would — and showed his imperfections, she shivered thus. But it was over in a second, and she loved on. She knew that he trifled with her; but she loved on. She scattered the half-burnt brands, went indoors immediately, and up to her bedroom without a light. Amid the rustles which denoted her to be undressing in the darkness other heavy breaths frequently came; and the same kind of shudder occasionally moved through her when, ten minutes later, she lay on her bed asleep.

VII

QUEEN OF NIGHT

EUSTACIA VYE was the raw material of a divinity. On Olympus she would have done well with a little preparation. She had the passions and instincts which make a model goddess, that is, those which make not quite a model woman. Had it been possible for the earth and mankind to be entirely in her grasp for a while, had she handled the distaff, the spindle, and the shears at her own free will, few in the world would have noticed the change of government. There would have been the same inequality of lot, the same heaping up of favours here, of contumely there, the same generosity before the justice, the same perpetual dilemmas, the same captious alternation of caresses and blows that we endure now.

She was in person full-limbed and somewhat heavy; without ruddiness, as without pallor; and soft to the touch as a cloud. To see her hair was to fancy that a whole winter did not contain darkness enough to form its shadow: it closed over her forehead like nightfall extinguishing the western glow.

Her nerves extended into those tresses, and her temper could always be softened by stroking them down. When her hair was brushed she would instantly sink into stillness and look like the Sphinx. If, in passing under one of the Egdon banks, any of its thick skeins were caught, as they sometimes were, by a prickly tuft of the large *Ulex Europæus* — which will act as a sort of hairbrush — she would go back a few steps, and pass against it a second time.

She had Pagan eyes, full of nocturnal mysteries. Their light, as it came and went, and came again, was partially hampered by their oppressive lids and lashes; and of these the under lid was much fuller than it usually is with English women. This enabled her to indulge in reverie without seeming to do so: she might have been believed capable of sleeping without closing them up. Assuming that the souls of men and women were visible essences, you could fancy the colour of Eustacia's soul to be flame-like. The sparks from it that rose into her dark pupils gave the same impression.

The mouth seemed formed less to speak than to quiver, less to quiver than to kiss. Some might have added, less to kiss than to curl. Viewed sideways, the closing-line of her lips formed, with almost geometric precision, the curve so well known in the arts of design as the cima-recta, or ogee. The sight of such a flexible bend as that on grim Egdon was quite an apparition. It was felt at once that that mouth did not come over from Sleswig with a band of Saxon pirates whose lips met like the two halves of a muffin. One had fancied that such lip-curves were mostly lurking underground in the South as fragments of forgotten marbles. So fine were the lines of her lips that, though full, each corner of her mouth was as clearly cut as the point of a spear. This keenness of corner was only blunted when she was given over to sudden fits of gloom, one of the phases of the night-side of sentiment which she knew too well for her years.

Her presence brought memories of such things as Bourbon roses, rubies, and tropical midnights; her moods recalled lotus-eaters and the march in "Athalie"; her motions, the ebb and flow of the sea; her voice, the viola. In a dim light, and with a slight rearrangement of her hair, her general figure might have stood for that of either of the higher female deities. The new moon behind her head, an old helmet upon it, a diadem of accidental dew-drops round her brow, would have been adjuncts sufficient to strike the note of Artemis, Athena, or Hera respectively, with as close an approximation to the antique as that which passes muster on many respected canvases.

But celestial imperiousness, love, wrath, and fervour had proved to be somewhat thrown away on netherward Egdon. Her power was limited, and the consciousness of this limitation had biassed her development. Egdon was her Hades, and since coming there she had imbibed much of what was dark in its tone, though inwardly and eternally unreconciled thereto. Her appearance accorded well with this smouldering rebelliousness, and the shady splendour of her beauty was the real surface of the sad and stifled warmth within her. A true Tartarean dignity, sat upon her brow, and not factitiously or with marks of constraint, for it had grown in her with years.

Across the upper part of her head she wore a thin fillet of black velvet, restraining the luxuriance of her shady hair, in a way which added much to this class of majesty by irregularly clouding her forehead. "Nothing can embellish a beautiful face more than a narrow band drawn over the brow," says Richter. Some of the neighbouring girls wore coloured ribbon for the same purpose, and sported metallic ornaments elsewhere; but if anyone suggested coloured ribbon and metallic ornaments to Eustacia Vye she laughed and went on.

Why did a woman of this sort live on Egdon Heath? Budmouth was her native place, a fashionable seaside resort at that date. She was the daughter of the bandmaster of a regiment which had been quartered there — a Corfiote by birth, and a fine musician — who met his future wife during her trip thither with her father the captain, a man of good family. The marriage was scarcely in accord with the old man's wishes, for the bandmaster's pockets were as light as his occupation. But the musician did his best; adopted his wife's name, made England permanently his home, took great trouble with his child's education, the expenses of which were defrayed by the grandfather, and throve as the chief local musician till her mother's death, when he left off thriving, drank, and died also. The girl was left to the care of her grandfather, who, since three of his ribs became broken in a shipwreck, had lived in this airy perch on Egdon, a spot which had taken his fancy because the house was to be had for next to nothing, and because a remote blue tinge on the horizon between the hills, visible from the cottage door, was traditionally believed to be the English Channel. She hated the change; she felt like one banished; but here she was forced to abide.

Thus it happened that in Eustacia's brain were juxtaposed the strangest assortment of ideas, from old time and from new. There was no middle distance in her perspective: romantic recollections of sunny afternoons on an esplanade, with military bands, officers, and gallants around, stood like gilded letters upon the dark tablet of surrounding Egdon. Every bizarre effect that could result from the random intertwining of watering-place glitter with the grand solemnity of a heath, was to be found in her. Seeing nothing of human life now, she imagined all the more of what she had seen.

Where did her dignity come from? By a latent vein from Alcinous' line, her father hailing from Phæacia's isle? — or from Fitzalan and De Vere, her maternal grandfather having had a cousin in the peerage? Perhaps it was the gift of Heaven — a happy convergence of natural laws. Among other things opportunity had of late years been denied her of learning to be undignified, for she lived lonely. Isolation on a heath renders vulgarity wellnigh impossible. It would have been as easy for the heath-ponies, bats, and snakes to be vulgar as for her. A narrow life in Budmouth might have completely demeaned her.

The only way to look queenly without realms or hearts to queen it over is to look as if you had lost them; and Eustacia did that to a triumph. In the captain's cottage she could suggest mansions she had never seen. Perhaps that was because she frequented a vaster mansion than any of them, the open hills. Like the summer condition of the place around her, she was an embodiment of the phrase "a populous solitude" — apparently so listless, void, and quiet, she was really busy and full.

To be loved to madness — such was her great desire. Love was to her the one cordial which could drive away the eating loneliness of her days. And she seemed to long for the abstraction called passionate love more than for any particular lover.

She could show a most reproachful look at times, but it was directed less against human beings than against certain creatures of her mind, the chief of these being Destiny, through whose interference she dimly fancied it arose that love alighted only on gliding youth — that any love she might win would sink simultaneously with the sand in the glass. She thought of it with an ever-growing consciousness of cruelty, which tended to breed actions of reckless unconventionality, framed to snatch a year's, a week's, even an hour's passion from anywhere while it could be won. Through want of it she had sung without being merry, possessed without enjoying, outshone without triumphing. Her loneliness deepened her desire. On Egdon, coldest and meanest kisses were at famine prices; and where was a mouth matching hers to be found?

Fidelity in love for fidelity's sake had less attraction for her than for most women: fidelity because of love's grip had much. A blaze of love, and extinction, was better than a lantern glimmer of the same which should last long years. On this head she knew by prevision what most women learn only by experience: she had mentally walked round love, told the towers thereof, considered its palaces; and concluded that love was but a doleful joy. Yet she desired it, as one in a desert would be thankful for brackish water.

She often repeated her prayers; not at particular times, but, like the unaffectedly devout, when she desired to pray. Her prayer was always spontaneous, and often ran thus, "O deliver my heart from this fearful gloom and loneliness: send me great love from somewhere, else I shall die."

Her high gods were William the Conqueror, Strafford, and Napoleon Buonaparte, as they had appeared in the Lady's History used at the establishment in which she was educated. Had she been a mother she would have christened her boys such names as Saul or Sisera in preference to Jacob or David, neither of whom she admired. At school she had used to side with the Philistines in several battles, and had wondered if Pontius Pilate were as handsome as he was frank and fair.

Thus she was a girl of some forwardness of mind, indeed, weighed in relation to her situation among the very rereward of thinkers, very original. Her instincts towards social nonconformity were at the root of this. In the matters of holidays, her mood was that of horses who, when turned out to grass, enjoy looking upon their kind at work on the highway. She only valued rest to herself when it came in the midst of other people's labour. Hence she hated Sundays when all was at rest, and often said they would be the death of her. To see the heathmen in their Sunday condition, that is, with their hands in their pockets, their boots newly oiled, and not laced up (a particularly Sunday sign), walking leisurely among the turves and furze-faggots they had cut during the week, and kicking them critically as if their use were unknown, was a fearful heaviness to her. To relieve the tedium of this untimely day she would overhaul the cupboards containing her grandfather's old charts and other rubbish, humming Saturday-night ballads of the country people the while. But on Saturday nights she would frequently sing a psalm, and it was always on a week-day that she read the Bible, that she might be unoppressed with a sense of doing her duty.

Such views of life were to some extent the natural begettings of her situation upon her nature. To dwell on a heath without studying its meanings was like wedding a foreigner without learning his tongue. The subtle beauties of the heath were lost to Eustacia; she only caught its vapours. An environment which would have made a contented woman a poet, a suffering woman a devotee, a pious woman a psalmist, even a giddy woman thoughtful, made a rebellious woman saturnine.

Eustacia had got beyond the vision of some marriage of inexpressible glory; yet, though her emotions were in full vigour, she cared for no meaner union. Thus we see her in a strange state of isolation. To have lost the god-like conceit that we may do what we will, and not to have acquired a homely zest for doing what we can, shows a grandeur of temper which cannot be objected to in the abstract, for it denotes a mind that, though disappointed, forswears compromise. But, if congenial to philosophy, it is apt to be dangerous to the commonwealth. In a world where doing means marrying, and the commonwealth is one of hearts and hands, the same peril attends the condition.

And so we see our Eustacia — for at times she was not altogether unlovable — arriving at that stage of enlightenment which feels that nothing is worth while, and filling up the spare hours of her existence by idealizing Wildeve for want of a better object. This was the sole reason of his ascendency: she knew it herself. At moments her pride rebelled against her passion for him, and she even had longed to be free. But there was only one circumstance which could dislodge him, and that was the advent of a greater man.

For the rest, she suffered much from depression of spirits, and took slow walks to recover them, in which she carried her grandfather's telescope and her grandmother's hour-glass — the latter because of a peculiar pleasure she derived from watching a material representation of time's gradual glide away. She seldom schemed, but when she did scheme, her plans showed rather the comprehensive strategy of a general than the small arts called womanish, though she could utter oracles of Delphian ambiguity when she did not choose to be direct. In heaven she will probably sit between the Héloïses and the Cleopatras.

VIII

THOSE WHO ARE FOUND WHERE THERE IS SAID TO BE NOBODY

As soon as the sad little boy had withdrawn from the fire he clasped the money tight in the palm of his hand, as if thereby to fortify his courage, and began to run. There was really little danger in allowing a child to go home alone on this part of Egdon Heath. The distance to the boy's house was not more than three-eighths of a mile, his father's cottage, and one other a few yards further on, forming part of the small hamlet of Mistover Knap: the third and only remaining house was that of Captain Vye and Eustacia, which stood quite away from the small cottages, and was the loneliest of lonely houses on these thinly populated slopes.

He ran until he was out of breath, and then, becoming more courageous, walked leisurely along, singing in an old voice a little song about a sailor-boy and a fair one, and bright gold in store. In the middle of this the child stopped: from a pit under the hill ahead of him shone a light, whence proceeded a cloud of floating dust and a smacking noise.

Only unusual sights and sounds frightened the boy. The shrivelled voice of the heath did not alarm him, for that was familiar. The thorn-bushes which arose in his path from time to time were less satisfactory, for they whistled gloomily, and had a ghastly habit after dark of putting on the shapes of jumping madmen, sprawling giants, and hideous cripples. Lights were not uncommon this evening, but the nature of all of them was different from this. Discretion rather than terror prompted the boy to turn back instead of passing the light, with a view of asking Miss Eustacia Vye to let her servant accompany him home.

When the boy had reascended to the top of the valley he found the fire to be still burning on the bank, though lower than before. Beside it, instead of Eustacia's solitary form, he saw two persons, the second being a man. The boy crept along under the bank to ascertain from the nature of the proceedings if it would be prudent to interrupt so splendid a creature as Miss Eustacia on his poor trivial account.

After listening under the bank for some minutes to the talk he turned in a perplexed and doubting manner and began to withdraw as silently as he had come. That he did not, upon the whole, think it advisable to interrupt her conversation with Wildeve, without being prepared to bear the whole weight of her displeasure, was obvious.

Here was a Scyllæo-Charybdean position for a poor boy. Pausing when again safe from discovery he finally decided to face the pit phenomenon as the lesser evil. With a heavy sigh he retraced the slope, and followed the path he had followed before.

The light had gone, the rising dust had disappeared — he hoped for ever. He marched resolutely along, and found nothing to alarm him till, coming within a few yards of the sandpit, he heard a slight noise in front, which led him to halt. The halt was but momentary, for the noise resolved itself into the steady bites of two animals grazing.

"Two he'th-croppers down here," he said aloud. "I have never known 'em come down so far afore."

The animals were in the direct line of his path, but that the child thought little of; he had played round the fetlocks of horses from his infancy. On coming nearer, however, the boy was somewhat surprised to find that the little creatures did not run off, and that each wore a clog, to prevent his going astray; this signified that they had been broken in. He could now see the interior of the pit, which, being in the side of the hill, had a level entrance. In the innermost corner the square outline of a van appeared, with its back towards him. A light came from the interior, and threw a moving shadow upon the vertical face of gravel at the further side of the pit into which the vehicle faced.

The child assumed that this was the cart of a gipsy, and his dread of those wanderers reached but to that mild pitch which titillates rather than pains. Only a few inches of mud wall kept him and his family from being gipsies themselves. He skirted the gravel-pit at a respectful distance, ascending the slope, and came forward upon the brow, in order to look into the open door of the van and see the original of the shadow.

The picture alarmed the boy. By a little stove inside the van sat a figure red from head to heels — the man who had been Thomasin's friend. He was darning a stocking, which was red like the rest of him. Moreover, as he darned he smoked a pipe, the stem and bowl of which were red also.

At this moment one of the heath-croppers feeding in the outer shadows was audibly shaking off the clog attached to its foot. Aroused by the sound, the reddleman laid down his stocking, lit a lantern which hung beside him, and came out from the van. In sticking up the candle he lifted the lantern to his face, and the light shone into the whites of his eyes and upon his ivory teeth, which, in contrast with the red surrounding, lent him a startling aspect enough to the gaze of a juvenile. The boy knew too well for his peace of mind upon whose lair he had lighted. Uglier persons than gipsies were known to cross Egdon at times, and a reddleman was one of them.

"How I wish 'twas only a gipsy!" he murmured.

The man was by this time coming back from the horses. In his fear of being seen the boy rendered detection certain by nervous motion. The heather and peat stratum overhung the brow of the pit in mats, hiding the actual verge. The boy had stepped beyond the solid ground; the heather now gave way, and down he rolled over the scarp of grey sand to the very foot of the man.

The red man opened the lantern and turned it upon the figure of the prostrate boy.

"Who be ye?" he said.

"Johnny Nunsuch, master!"

"What were you doing up there?"

"I don't know."

"Watching me, I suppose?"

"Yes, master."

"What did you watch me for?"

"Because I was coming home from Miss Vye's bonfire."

"Beest hurt?"

"No."

"Why, yes, you be: your hand is bleeding. Come under my tilt and let me tie it up."

"Please let me look for my sixpence."

"How did you come by that?"

"Miss Vye gied it to me for keeping up her bonfire."

The sixpence was found, and the man went to the van, the boy behind, almost holding his breath.

The man took a piece of rag from a satchel containing sewing materials, tore off a strip, which, like everything else, was tinged red, and proceeded to bind up the wound.

"My eyes have got foggy-like — please may I sit down, master?" said the boy.

"To be sure, poor chap. 'Tis enough to make you feel fainty. Sit on that bundle."

The man finished tying up the gash, and the boy said, "I think I'll go home now, master."

"You are rather afraid of me. Do you know what I be?"

The child surveyed his vermilion figure up and down with much misgiving, and finally said, "Yes."

"Well, what?"

"The reddleman!" he faltered.

"Yes, that's what I be. Though there's more than one. You little children think there's only one cuckoo, one fox, one giant, one devil, and one reddleman, when there's lots of us all."

"Is there? You won't carry me off in your bags, will ye, master? 'Tis said that the reddleman will sometimes."

"Nonsense. All that reddlemen do is sell reddle. You see all these bags at the back of my cart? They are not full of little boys — only full of red stuff."

"Was you born a reddleman?"

"No, I took to it. I should be as white as you if I were to give up the trade — that is, I should be white in time — perhaps six months: not at first, because 'tis grow'd into my skin and won't wash out. Now, you'll never be afraid of a reddleman again, will ye?"

"No, never. Willy Orchard said he seed a red ghost here t'other day — perhaps that was you?"

"I was here t'other day."

"Were you making that dusty light I saw by now?"

"O yes: I was beating out some bags. And have you had a good bonfire up there? I saw the light. Why did Miss Vye want a bonfire so bad that she should give you sixpence to keep it up?"

"I don't know. I was tired, but she made me bide and keep up the fire just the same, while she kept going up across Rainbarrow way."

"And how long did that last?"

"Until a hopfrog jumped into the pond."

The reddleman suddenly ceased to talk idly. "A hopfrog?" he inquired. "Hopfrogs don't jump into ponds this time of year."

"They do, for I heard one."

"Certain-sure?"

"Yes. She told me afore that I should hear'n; and so I did. They say she's clever and deep, and perhaps she charmed 'en to come."

"And what then?"

"Then I came down here, and I was afeard, and I went back; but I didn't like to speak to her, because of the gentleman, and I came on here again."

"A gentleman — ah! What did she say to him, my man?"

"Told him she supposed he had not married the other woman because he liked his old sweetheart best; and things like that."

"What did the gentleman say to her, my sonny?"

"He only said he did like her best, and how he was coming to see her again under Rainbarrow o' nights."

"Ha!" cried the reddleman, slapping his hand against the side of his van so that the whole fabric shook under the blow. "That's the secret o't!"

The little boy jumped clean from the stool.

"My man, don't you be afraid," said the dealer in red, suddenly becoming gentle. "I forgot you were here. That's only a curious way reddlemen have of going mad for a moment; but they don't hurt anybody. And what did the lady say then?"

"I can't mind. Please, Master Reddleman, may I go home-along now?"

"Ay, to be sure you may. I'll go a bit of ways with you."

He conducted the boy out of the grave-pit and into the path leading to his mother's cottage. When the little figure had vanished in the darkness the reddleman returned, resumed his seat by the fire, and proceeded to darn again.

IX

LOVE LEADS A SHREWD MAN INTO STRATEGY

REDDLEMEN of the old school are now but seldom seen. Since the introduction of railways Wessex farmers have managed to do without these Mephistophelian visitants, and the bright pigment so largely used by shepherds in preparing sheep for the fair is obtained by other routes. Even those who yet survive are losing the poetry of existence which characterized them when the pursuit of the trade meant periodical journeys to the pit whence the material was dug, a regular camping out from month to month, except in the depth of winter, a peregrination among farms which could be counted by the hundred, and in spite of this Arab existence the preservation of that respectability which is insured by the never-failing production of a well-lined purse.

Reddle spreads its lively hues over everything it lights on, and stamps unmistakably, as with the mark of Cain, any person who has handled it half an hour.

A child's first sight of a reddleman was an epoch in his life. That blood-coloured figure was a sublimation of all the horrid dreams which had afflicted the juvenile spirit since imagination began. "The reddleman is coming for you!" had been the formulated threat of Wessex mothers for many generations. He was successfully supplanted for a while, at the beginning of the present century, by Buonaparte; but as process of time rendered the latter personage stale and ineffective the older phrase resumed its early prominence. And now the reddleman has in his turn followed Buonaparte to the land of worn-out bogeys, and his place is filled by modern inventions.

The reddleman lived like a gipsy; but gipsies he scorned. He was about as thriving as travelling basket and mat makers; but he had nothing to do with them. He was more decently born and brought up than the cattle-drovers who passed and repassed him in his wanderings; but they merely nodded to him. His stock was more valuable than that of pedlars; but they did not think so, and passed his cart with eyes straight ahead. He was such an unnatural colour to look at that the men of round-abouts and wax-work shows seemed gentlemen beside him; but he considered them low company, and remained aloof. Among all these squatters and folks of the road the reddleman continually found himself; yet he was not of them. His occupation tended to isolate him, and isolated he was mostly seen to be.

It was sometimes suggested that reddlemen were criminals for whose misdeeds other men had wrongfully suffered: that in escaping the law they had not escaped their own consciences, and had taken to the trade as a lifelong penance. Else why should they have chosen it? In the present case such a question would have been particularly apposite. The reddleman who had entered Egdon that afternoon was an instance of the pleasing being wasted to form the ground-work of the singular, when an ugly foundation would have done just as well for that purpose. The one point that was forbidding about this reddleman was his colour. Freed from that he would have been as agreeable a specimen of rustic manhood as one would often see. A keen observer might have been inclined to think — which was, indeed, partly the truth — that he had relinquished his proper station in life for want of interest in it. Moreover, after looking at him one would have hazarded the guess that goodnature, and an acuteness as extreme as it could be without verging on craft, formed the framework of his character.

While he darned the stockings his face became rigid with thought. Softer expressions followed this, and then again recurred the tender sadness which had sat upon him during his drive along the highway that afternoon. Presently his needle stopped. He laid down the stocking, arose from his seat, and took a leathern pouch from a hook in the corner of the van. This contained among other articles a brown-paper packet, which, to judge from the hinge-like character of its worn folds, seemed to have been carefully opened and closed a good many times. He sat down on a three-legged milking-stool that formed the only seat in the van, and, examining his packet by the light of a candle, took thence an old letter and spread it open. The writing had originally been traced on white paper, but the letter had now assumed a pale red tinge from the accident of his situation; and the black strokes of writing thereon looked like the twigs of a winter hedge against a vermilion sunset. The letter bore a date some two years previous to that time, and was signed "Thomasin Yeobright." It ran as follows:

DEAR DIGGORY VENN — The question you put when you overtook me coming home from Pond-close gave me such a surprise that I am afraid I did not make you exactly understand what I meant. Of course, if my aunt had not met me I could have explained all then at once, but as it was there was no chance. I have been quite uneasy since, as you know I do not wish to pain you, yet I fear I shall be doing so now in contradicting what I seemed to say then. I cannot, Diggory, marry you, or think of letting you call me your sweetheart. I could not, indeed, Diggory. I hope you will not much mind my saying this, and feel in a great pain. It makes me very sad when I think it may, for I like you very much, and I always put you next to my cousin Clym in my mind. There are so many reasons why we cannot be married that I can hardly name them all in a letter. I did not in the least expect that you were going to speak on such a thing when you followed me, because I had never thought of you in the sense of a lover at all. You must not becall me for laughing when you spoke; you mistook when you thought I laughed at you as a foolish man. I laughed because the idea was so odd, and not at you at all. The great reason with my own personal self for not letting you court me is, that I do not feel the things a woman ought to feel who consents to walk with you with the meaning of being your wife. It is not as you think, that I have another in my mind, for I do not encourage anybody, and never have in my life. Another reason is my aunt. She would not, I know, agree to it, even if I wished to have you. She likes you very well, but she will want me to look a little higher than a small dairy-farmer, and marry a professional man. I hope you will not set your heart against me for writing plainly, but I felt you might try to see me again, and it is better that we should not meet. I shall always think of you as a good man, and be anxious for your well-doing. I send this by Jane Orchard's little maid — And remain, Diggory, your faithful friend,

THOMASIN YEOBRIGHT.

To Mr. VENN, Dairy-farmer.

Since the arrival of that letter, on a certain autumn morning long ago, the reddleman and Thomasin had not met till today. During the interval he had shifted his position even further from hers than it had originally been, by adopting the reddle trade; though he was really in very good circumstances still. Indeed, seeing that his expenditure was only one-fourth of his income, he might have been called a prosperous man.

Rejected suitors take to roaming as naturally as unhived bees; and the business to which he had cynically devoted himself was in many ways congenial to Venn. But his wanderings, by mere stress of old emotions, had frequently taken an Egdon direction, though he never intruded upon her who attracted him thither. To be in Thomasin's heath, and near her, yet unseen, was the one ewe-lamb of pleasure left to him.

Then came the incident of that day, and the reddleman, still loving her well, was excited by this accidental service to her at a critical juncture to vow an active devotion to her cause, instead of, as hitherto, sighing and holding aloof. After what had happened it was impossible that he should not doubt the honesty of Wildeve's intentions. But her hope was apparently centered upon him; and dismissing his regrets Venn determined to aid her to be happy in her own chosen way. That this way was, of all others, the most distressing to himself, was awkward enough; but the reddleman's love was generous.

His first active step in watching over Thomasin's interest was taken about seven o'clock the next evening, and was dictated by the news which he had learnt from the sad boy. That Eustacia was somehow the cause of Wildeve's carelessness in relation to the marriage had at once been Venn's conclusion on hearing of the secret meeting between them. It did not occur to his mind that Eustacia's love-signal to Wildeve was the tender effect upon the deserted beauty of the intelligence which her grandfather had brought home. His instinct was to regard her as a conspirator against rather than as an antecedent obstacle to Thomasin's happiness.

During the day he had been exceedingly anxious to learn the condition of Thomasin; but he did not venture to intrude upon a threshold to which he was a stranger, particularly at such an unpleasant moment as this. He had occupied his time in moving with his ponies and load to a new point in the heath, eastward to his previous station; and here he selected a nook with a careful eye to shelter from wind and rain, which seemed to mean that his stay there was to be a comparatively extended one. After this he returned on foot some part of the way that he had come; and, it being now dark, he diverged to the left till he stood behind a holly-bush on the edge of a pit not twenty yards from Rainbarrow.

He watched for a meeting there, but he watched in vain. Nobody except himself came near the spot that night.

But the loss of his labour produced little effect upon the reddleman. He had stood in the shoes of Tantalus, and seemed to look upon a certain mass of disappointment as the natural preface to all realizations, without which preface they would give cause for alarm.

The same hour the next evening found him again at the same place; but Eustacia and Wildeve, the expected trysters, did not appear.

He pursued precisely the same course yet four nights longer, and without success. But on the next, being the day-week of their previous meeting, he saw a female shape floating along the ridge and the outline of a young man ascending from the valley. They met in the little ditch encircling the barrow — the original excavation from which it had been thrown up by the ancient British people.

The reddleman, stung with suspicion of wrong to Thomasin, was aroused to strategy in a moment. He instantly left the bush and crept forward on his hands and knees. When he had got as close as he might safely venture without discovery he found that, owing to a cross-wind, the conversation of the trysting pair could not be overheard.

Near him, as in divers places about the heath, were areas strewn with large turves, which lay edgeways and upside-down awaiting removal by Timothy Fairway, previous to the winter weather. He took two of these as he lay, and dragged them over him till one covered his head and shoulders, the other his back and legs. The reddleman would now have been quite invisible, even by daylight; the turves, standing upon him with the heather upwards, looked precisely as if they were growing. He crept along again, and the turves upon his back crept with him. Had he approached without any covering the chances are that he would not have been perceived in the dusk; approaching thus, it was as though he burrowed underground. In this manner he came quite close to where the two were standing.

"Wish to consult me on the matter?" reached his ears in the rich, impetuous accents of Eustacia Vye. "Consult me? It is an indignity to me to talk so: I won't bear it any longer!" She began weeping. "I have loved you, and have shown you that I loved you, much to my regret; and yet you can come and say in that frigid way that you wish to consult with me whether it would not be better to marry Thomasin. Better — of course it would be. Marry her: she is nearer to your own position in life than I am!"

"Yes, yes; that's very well," said Wildeve peremptorily. "But we must look at things as they are. Whatever blame may attach to me for having brought it about, Thomasin's position is at present much worse than yours. I simply tell you that I am in a strait."

"But you shall not tell me! You must see that it is only harassing me. Damon, you have not acted well; you have sunk in my opinion. You have not valued my courtesy — the courtesy of a lady in loving you — who used to think of far more ambitious things. But it was Thomasin's fault. She won you away from me, and she deserves to suffer for it. Where is she staying now? Not that I care, nor where I am myself. Ah, if I were dead and gone how glad she would be! Where is she, I ask?"

"Thomasin is now staying at her aunt's shut up in a bedroom, and keeping out of everybody's sight," he said indifferently.

"I don't think you care much about her even now," said Eustacia with sudden joyousness; "for if you did you wouldn't talk so coolly about her. Do you talk so coolly to her about me? Ah, I expect you do! Why did you originally go away from me? I don't think I can ever forgive you, except on one condition, that whenever you desert me, you come back again, sorry that you served me so."

"I never wish to desert you."

"I do not thank you for that. I should hate it to be all smooth. Indeed, I think I like you to desert me a little once now and then. Love is the dismallest thing where the lover is quite honest. O, it is a shame to say so; but it is true!" She indulged in a little laugh. "My low spirits begin at the very idea. Don't you offer me tame love, or away you go!"

"I wish Tamsie were not such a confoundedly good little woman," said Wildeve, "so that I could be faithful to you without injuring a worthy person. It is I who am the sinner after all; I am not worth the little finger of either of you."

"But you must not sacrifice yourself to her from any sense of justice," replied Eustacia quickly. "If you do not love her it is the most merciful thing in the long run to leave her as she is. That's always the best way. There, now I have been unwomanly, I suppose. When you have left me, I am always angry with myself for things that I have said to you."

Wildeve walked a pace or two among the heather without replying. The pause was filled up by the intonation of a pollard thorn a little way to windward, the breezes filtering through its unyielding twigs as through a strainer. It was as if the night sang dirges with clenched teeth.

She continued, half sorrowfully, "Since meeting you last, it has occurred to me once or twice that perhaps it was not for love of me you did not marry her. Tell me, Damon: I'll try to bear it. Had I nothing whatever to do with the matter?"

"Do you press me to tell?"

"Yes, I must know. I see I have been too ready to believe in my own power."

"Well, the immediate reason was that the licence would not do for the place, and before I could get another she ran away. Up to that point you had nothing to do with it. Since then her aunt has spoken to me in a tone which I don't at all like."

"Yes, yes! I am nothing in it — I am nothing in it. You only trifle with me. Heaven, what can I, Eustacia Vye, be made of to think so much of you!"

"Nonsense; do not be so passionate…. Eustacia, how we roved among these bushes last year, when the hot days had got cool, and the shades of the hills kept us almost invisible in the hollows!"

She remained in moody silence till she said, "Yes; and how I used to laugh at you for daring to look up to me! But you have well made me suffer for that since."

"Yes, you served me cruelly enough until I thought I had found some one fairer than you. A blessed find for me, Eustacia."

"Do you still think you found somebody fairer?"

"Sometimes I do, sometimes I don't. The scales are balanced so nicely that a feather would turn them."

"But don't you really care whether I meet you or whether I don't?" she said slowly.

"I care a little, but not enough to break my rest," replied the young man languidly. "No, all that's past. I find there are two flowers where I thought there was only one. Perhaps there are three, or four, or any number as good as the first.... Mine is a curious fate. Who would have thought that all this could happen to me?"

She interrupted with a suppressed fire of which either love or anger seemed an equally possible issue, "Do you love me now?"

"Who can say?"

"Tell me; I will know it!"

"I do, and I do not," said he mischievously. "That is, I have my times and my seasons. One moment you are too tall, another moment you are too do-nothing, another too melancholy, another too dark, another I don't know what, except — that you are not the whole world to me that you used to be, my dear. But you are a pleasant lady to know, and nice to meet, and I dare say as sweet as ever — almost."

Eustacia was silent, and she turned from him, till she said, in a voice of suspended mightiness, "I am for a walk, and this is my way."

"Well, I can do worse than follow you."

"You know you can't do otherwise, for all your moods and changes!" she answered defiantly. "Say what you will; try as you may; keep away from me all that you can — you will never forget me. You will love me all your life long. You would jump to marry me!"

"So I would!" said Wildeve. "Such strange thoughts as I've had from time to time, Eustacia; and they come to me this moment. You hate the heath as much as ever; that I know."

"I do," she murmured deeply. "'Tis my cross, my misery, and will be my death!"

"I abhor it too," said he. "How mournfully the wind blows round us now!"

She did not answer. Its tone was indeed solemn and pervasive. Compound utterances addressed themselves to their senses, and it was possible to view by ear the features of the neighbourhood. Acoustic pictures were returned from the darkened scenery; they could hear where the tracts of heather began and ended; where the furze was growing stalky and tall; where it had been recently cut; in what direction the fir-clump lay, and how near was the pit in which the hollies grew; for these differing features had their voices no less than their shapes and colours.

"God, how lonely it is!" resumed Wildeve. "What are picturesque ravines and mists to us who see nothing else? Why should we stay here? Will you go with me to America? I have kindred in Wisconsin."

"That wants consideration."

"It seems impossible to do well here, unless one were a wild bird or a land-scape-painter. Well?"

"Give me time," she softly said, taking his hand. "America is so far away. Are you going to walk with me a little way?"

As Eustacia uttered the latter words she retired from the base of the bar-row, and Wildeve followed her, so that the reddleman could hear no more.

He lifted the turves and arose. Their black figures sank and disappeared from against the sky. They were as two horns which the sluggish heath had put forth from its crown, like a mollusc, and had now again drawn in.

The reddleman's walk across the vale, and over into the next where his cart lay, was not sprightly for a slim young fellow of twenty-four. His spirit was perturbed to aching. The breezes that blew around his mouth in that walk carried off in them the accents of a commination.

He entered the van, where there was a fire in a stove. Without lighting his candle he sat down at once on the three-legged stool, and pondered on what he had seen and heard touching that still loved-one of his. He uttered a sound which was neither sigh nor sob, but was even more indicative than either of a troubled mind.

"My Tamsie," he whispered heavily. "What can be done? Yes, I will see that Eustacia Vye."

X

A DESPERATE ATTEMPT AT PERSUASION

THE next morning, at the time when the height of the sun appeared very insignificant from any part of the heath as compared with the altitude of Rainbarrow, and when all the little hills in the lower levels were like an archipelago in a fog-formed Ægean, the reddleman came from the brambled nook which he had adopted as his quarters and ascended the slopes of Mist-over Knap.

Though these shaggy hills were apparently so solitary, several keen round eyes were always ready on such a wintry morning as this to converge upon a passer-by. Feathered species sojourned here in hiding which would have created wonder if found elsewhere. A bustard haunted the spot, and not many years before this five and twenty might have been seen in Egdon at one time. Marsh-harriers looked up from the valley by Wildeve's. A cream-coloured courser had used to visit this hill, a bird so rare that not more than a dozen have ever been seen in England; but a barbarian rested neither night nor day till he had shot the African truant, and after that event cream-coloured coursers thought fit to enter Egdon no more.

A traveller who should walk and observe any of these visitants as Venn observed them now could feel himself to be in direct communication with regions unknown to man. Here in front of him was a wild mallard — just arrived from the home of the north wind. The creature brought within him an amplitude of Northern knowledge. Glacial catastrophes, snow-storm episodes, glittering auroral effects, Polaris in the zenith, Franklin underfoot — the category of his commonplaces was wonderful. But the bird, like many other philosophers, seemed as he looked at the reddleman to think that a present moment of comfortable reality was worth a decade of memories.

Venn passed on through these towards the house of the isolated beauty who lived up among them and despised them. The day was Sunday; but as going to church, except to be married or buried, was exceptional at Egdon, this made little difference. He had determined upon the bold stroke of asking for an interview with Miss Vye — to attack her position as Thomasin's rival either by art or by storm, showing therein, somewhat too conspicuously, the want of gallantry characteristic of a certain astute sort of men, from clowns to kings. The great Frederick making war on the beautiful Archduchess, Napoleon refusing terms to the beautiful Queen of Prussia, were not more dead to difference of sex than the reddleman was, in his peculiar way, in planning the displacement of Eustacia.

To call at the captain's cottage was always more or less an undertaking for the inferior inhabitants. Though occasionally chatty, his moods were erratic, and nobody could be certain how he would behave at any particular moment. Eustacia was reserved, and lived very much to herself. Except the daughter of one of the cotters, who was their servant, and a lad who worked in the garden and stable, scarcely anyone but themselves ever entered the house. They were the only genteel people of the district except the Yeobrights, and though far from rich, they did not feel that necessity for preserving a friendly face towards every man, bird, and beast which influenced their poorer neighbours.

When the reddleman entered the garden the old man was looking through his glass at the stain of blue in the distant landscape, the little anchors on his buttons twinkling in the sun. He recognized Venn as his companion on the highway, but made no remark on that circumstance, merely saying, "Ah, reddleman — you here? Have a glass of grog?"

Venn declined, on the plea of it being too early, and stated that his business was with Miss Vye. The captain surveyed him from cap to waistcoat and from waistcoat to leggings for a few moments, and finally asked him to go indoors.

Miss Vye was not to be seen by anybody just then; and the reddleman waited in the window-bench of the kitchen, his hands hanging across his divergent knees, and his cap hanging from his hands.

"I suppose the young lady is not up yet?" he presently said to the servant.

"Not quite yet. Folks never call upon ladies at this time of day."

"Then I'll step outside," said Venn. "If she is willing to see me, will she please send out word, and I'll come in."

The reddleman left the house and loitered on the hill adjoining. A considerable time elapsed, and no request for his presence was brought. He was beginning to think that his scheme had failed, when he beheld the form of Eustacia herself coming leisurely towards him. A sense of novelty in giving audience to that singular figure had been sufficient to draw her forth.

She seemed to feel, after a bare look at Diggory Venn, that the man had come on a strange errand, and that he was not so mean as she had thought him; for her close approach did not cause him to writhe uneasily, or shift his feet, or show any of those little signs which escape an ingenuous rustic at the advent of the uncommon in womankind. On his inquiring if he might have a conversation with her she replied, "Yes, walk beside me"; and continued to move on.

Before they had gone far it occurred to the perspicacious reddleman that he would have acted more wisely by appearing less unimpressionable, and he resolved to correct the error as soon as he could find opportunity.

"I have made so bold, miss, as to step across and tell you some strange news which has come to my ears about that man."

"Ah! what man?"

He jerked his elbow to south-east — the direction of the Quiet Woman. Eustacia turned quickly to him. "Do you mean Mr. Wildeve?"

"Yes, there is trouble in a household on account of him, and I have come to let you know of it, because I believe you might have power to drive it away."

"I? What is the trouble?"

"It is quite a secret. It is that he may refuse to marry Thomasin Yeobright after all."

Eustacia, though set inwardly pulsing by his words, was equal to her part in such a drama as this. She replied coldly, "I do not wish to listen to this, and you must not expect me to interfere."

"But, miss, you will hear one word?"

"I cannot. I am not interested in the marriage, and even if I were I could not compel Mr. Wildeve to do my bidding."

"As the only lady on the heath I think you might," said Venn with subtle indirectness. "This is how the case stands. Mr. Wildeve would marry Thomasin at once, and make all matters smooth, if so be there were not another woman in the case. This other woman is some person he has picked up with, and meets on the heath occasionally, I believe. He will never marry her, and yet through her he may never marry the woman who loves him dearly. Now, if you, miss, who have so much sway over us men-folk, were to insist that he should treat your young neighbour Tamsin with honourable kindness and give up the other woman, he would perhaps do it, and save her a good deal of misery."

"Ah, my life!" said Eustacia, with a laugh which unclosed her lips, so that the sun shone into her mouth as into a tulip, and lent it a similar scarlet fire. "You think too much of my influence over men-folk indeed, reddleman. If I had such a power as you imagine I would go straight and use it for the good of anybody who has been kind to me — which Thomasin Yeobright has not particularly, to my knowledge."

"Can it be that you really don't know of it — how much she has always thought of you?"

"I have never heard a word of it. Although we live only two miles apart I have never been inside her aunt's house in my life."

The superciliousness that lurked in her manner told Venn that thus far he had utterly failed. He inwardly sighed and felt it necessary to unmask his second argument.

"Well, leaving that out of the question, 'tis in your power, I assure you, Miss Vye, to do a great deal of good to another woman."

She shook her head.

"Your comeliness is law with Mr. Wildeve. It is law with all men who see ye. They say, 'This well-favoured lady coming — what's her name? How handsome!' Handsomer than Thomasin Yeobright," the reddleman persisted, saying to himself, "God forgive a rascal for lying!" And she was handsomer, but the reddleman was far from thinking so. There was a certain obscurity in Eustacia's beauty, and Venn's eye was not trained. In her winter dress, as now, she was like the tiger-beetle, which, when observed in dull situations, seems to be of the quietest neutral colour, but under a full illumination blazes with dazzling splendour.

Eustacia could not help replying, though conscious that she endangered her dignity thereby. "Many women are lovelier than Thomasin," she said; "so not much attaches to that."

The reddleman suffered the wound and went on: "He is a man who notices the looks of women, and you could twist him to your will like withywind, if you only had the mind."

"Surely what she cannot do who has been so much with him I cannot do living up here away from him."

The reddleman wheeled and looked her in the face. "Miss Vye!" he said.

"Why do you say that — as if you doubted me?" She spoke faintly, and her breathing was quick. "The idea of your speaking in that tone to me!" she added, with a forced smile of hauteur. "What could have been in your mind to lead you to speak like that?"

"Miss Vye, why should you make-believe, that you don't know this man? — I know why, certainly. He is beneath you, and you are ashamed."

"You are mistaken. What do you mean?"

The reddleman had decided to play the card of truth. "I was at the meeting by Rainbarrow last night and heard every word," he said. "The woman that stands between Wildeve and Thomasin is yourself."

It was a disconcerting lift of the curtain, and the mortification of Candaules' wife glowed in her. The moment had arrived when her lip would tremble in spite of herself, and when the gasp could no longer be kept down.

"I am unwell," she said hurriedly. "No — it is not that — I am not in a humour to hear you further. Leave me, please."

"I must speak, Miss Vye, in spite of paining you. What I would put before you is this. However it may come about — whether she is to blame, or you — her case is without doubt worse than yours. Your giving up Mr. Wildeve will be a real advantage to you, for how could you marry him?

Now she cannot get off so easily — everybody will blame her if she loses him. Then I ask you — not because her right is best, but because her situation is worse — to give him up to her."

"No — I won't, I won't!" she said impetuously, quite forgetful of her previous manner towards the reddleman as an underling. "Nobody has ever been served so! It was going on well — I will not be beaten down — by an inferior woman like her. It is very well for you to come and plead for her, but is she not herself the cause of all her own trouble? Am I not to show favour to any person I may choose without asking permission of a parcel of cottagers? She has come between me and my inclination, and now that she finds herself rightly punished she gets you to plead for her!"

"Indeed," said Venn earnestly, "she knows nothing whatever about it. It is only I who ask you to give him up. It will be better for her and you both. People will say bad things if they find out that a lady secretly meets a man who has ill-used another woman."

"I have *not* injured her: he was mine before he was hers! He came back — because — because he liked me best!" she said wildly. "But I lose all self-respect in talking to you. What am I giving way to!"

"I can keep secrets," said Venn gently. "You need not fear. I am the only man who knows of your meetings with him. There is but one thing more to speak of, and then I will be gone. I heard you say to him that you hated living here — that Egdon heath was a jail to you."

"I did say so. There is a sort of beauty in the scenery, I know; but it is a jail to me. The man you mention does not save me from that feeling, though he lives here. I should have cared nothing for him had there been a better person near."

The reddleman looked hopeful: after these words from her his third attempt seemed promising. "As we have now opened our minds a bit, miss," he said, "I'll tell you what I have got to propose. Since I have taken to the reddle trade I travel a good deal, as you know."

She inclined her head, and swept round so that her eyes rested in the misty vale beneath them.

"And in my travels I go near Budmouth. Now Budmouth is a wonderful place — wonderful — a great salt sheening sea bending into the land like a bow — thousands of gentlepeople walking up and down — bands of music playing — officers by sea and officers by land walking among the rest — out of every ten folk you meet nine of 'em in love."

"I know it," she said disdainfully. "I know Budmouth better than you. I was born there. My father came to be a military musician there from abroad. Ah, my soul, Budmouth! I wish I was there now."

The reddleman was surprised to see how a slow fire could blaze on occasion. "If you were, miss," he replied, "in a week's time you would think no more of Wildeve than of one of those he'th-croppers that we see yond. Now, I could get you there."

"How?" said Eustacia, with intense curiosity in her heavy eyes.

"My uncle has been for five and twenty years the trusty man of a rich widow-lady who has a beautiful house facing the sea. This lady has become old and lame, and she wants a young company-keeper to read and sing to her, but can't get one to her mind to save her life, though she've advertised in the papers, and tried half a dozen. She would jump to get you, and uncle would make it all easy."

"I should have to work, perhaps?"

"No, not real work: you'd have a little to do, such as reading and that. You would not be wanted till New Year's Day."

"I knew it meant work," she said, drooping to languor again.

"I confess there would be a trifle to do in the way of amusing her; but though idle people might call it work, working people would call it play. Think of the company and the life you'd lead, miss; the gaiety you'd see, and the gentleman you'd marry. My uncle is to inquire for a trustworthy young lady from the country, as she don't like town girls."

"It is to wear myself out to please her! and I won't go. O, if I could live in a gay town as a lady should, and go my own ways, and do my own doings, I'd give the wrinkled half of my life! Yes, reddleman, that would I."

"Help me to get Thomasin happy, miss, and the chance shall be yours," urged her companion.

"Chance! — 'tis no chance," she said proudly. "What can a poor man like you offer me, indeed? — I am going indoors. I have nothing more to say. Don't your horses want feeding, or your reddlebags want mending, or don't you want to find buyers for your goods, that you stay idling here like this?"

Venn spoke not another word. With his hands behind him he turned away, that she might not see the hopeless disappointment in his face. The mental clearness and power he had found in this lonely girl had indeed filled his manner with misgiving even from the first few minutes of close quarters with her. Her youth and situation had led him to expect a simplicity quite at the beck of his method. But a system of inducement which might have carried weaker country lasses along with it had merely repelled Eustacia. As a rule, the word Budmouth meant fascination on Egdon. That rising port and watering-place, if truly mirrored in the minds of the heath-folk, must have combined, in a charming and indescribable manner, a Carthaginian bustle of building with Tarentine luxuriousness and Baian health and beauty. Eustacia felt little less extravagantly about the place; but she would not sink her independence to get there.

When Diggory Venn had gone quite away, Eustacia walked to the bank and looked down the wild and picturesque vale towards the sun, which was also in the direction of Wildeve's. The mist had now so far collapsed that the tips of the trees and bushes around his house could just be discerned, as if boring upwards through a vast white cobweb which cloaked them from the day. There was no doubt that her mind was inclined thitherward; indefinitely, fancifully — twining and untwining about him as the single object within her horizon on which dreams might crystallize. The man who had begun by being merely her amusement, and would never have been more than her hobby but for his skill in deserting her at the right moments, was now again her desire. Cessation in his love-making had revivified her love.

Such feeling as Eustacia had idly given to Wildeve was dammed into a flood by Thomasin. She had used to tease Wildeve, but that was before another had favoured him. Often a drop of irony into an indifferent situation renders the whole piquant.

"I will never give him up — never!" she said impetuously.

The reddleman's hint that rumour might show her to disadvantage had no permanent terror for Eustacia. She was as unconcerned at that contingency as a goddess at a lack of linen. This did not originate in inherent shamelessness, but in her living too far from the world to feel the impact of public opinion. Zenobia in the desert could hardly have cared what was said about her at Rome. As far as social ethics were concerned Eustacia approached the savage state, though in emotion she was all the while an epicure. She had advanced to the secret recesses of sensuousness, yet had hardly crossed the threshold of conventionality.

XI

THE DISHONESTY OF AN HONEST WOMAN

THE reddleman had left Eustacia's presence with desponding views on Thomasin's future happiness; but he was awakened to the fact that one other channel remained untried by seeing, as he followed the way to his van, the form of Mrs. Yeobright slowly walking towards the Quiet Woman. He went across to her; and could almost perceive in her anxious face that this journey of hers to Wildeve was undertaken with the same object as his own to Eustacia.

She did not conceal the fact. "Then," said the reddleman, "you may as well leave it alone, Mrs. Yeobright."

"I half think so myself," she said. "But nothing else remains to be done besides pressing the question upon him."

"I should like to say a word first," said Venn, firmly. "Mr. Wildeve is not the only man who has asked Thomasin to marry him; and why should not another have a chance? Mrs. Yeobright, I should be glad to marry your niece, and would have done it any time these last two years. There, now it is out, and I have never told anybody before but herself."

Mrs. Yeobright was not demonstrative, but her eyes involuntarily glanced towards his singular though shapely figure.

"Looks are not everything," said the reddleman, noticing the glance. "There's many a calling that don't bring in so much as mine, if it comes to money; and perhaps I am not so much worse off than Wildeve. There is nobody so poor as these professional fellows who have failed; and if you shouldn't like my redness — well, I am not red by birth, you know; I only took to this business for a freak; and I might turn my hand to something else in good time."

"I am much obliged to you for your interest in my niece; but I fear there would be objections. More than that, she is devoted to this man."

"True; or I shouldn't have done what I have this morning."

"Otherwise there would be no pain in the case, and you would not see me going to his house now. What was Thomasin's answer when you told her of your feelings?"

"She wrote that you would object to me; and other things."

"She was in a measure right. You must not take this unkindly: I merely state it as a truth. You have been good to her, and we do not forget it. But as she was unwilling on her own account to be your wife, that settles the point without my wishes being concerned."

"Yes. But there is a difference between then and now, ma'am. She is distressed now, and I have thought that if you were to talk to her about me, and think favourably of me yourself, there might be a chance of winning her round, and getting her quite independent of this Wildeve's backward and forward play, and his not knowing whether he'll have her or no."

Mrs. Yeobright shook her head. "Thomasin thinks, and I think with her, that she ought to be Wildeve's wife, if she means to appear before the world without a slur upon her name. If they marry soon, everybody will believe that an accident did really prevent the wedding. If not, it may cast a shade upon her character — at any rate make her ridiculous. In short, if it is anyhow possible they must marry now."

"I thought that till half an hour ago. But, after all, why should her going off with him to Anglebury for a few hours do her any harm? Anybody who knows how pure she is will feel any such thought to be quite unjust. I have been trying this morning to help on this marriage with Wildeve — yes, I, ma'am — in the belief that I ought to do it, because she was so wrapped up in him. But I much question if I was right, after all. However, nothing came of it. And now I offer myself."

Mrs. Yeobright appeared disinclined to enter further into the question. "I fear I must go on," she said. "I do not see that anything else can be done."

And she went on. But though this conversation did not divert Thomasin's aunt from her purposed interview with Wildeve, it made a considerable difference in her mode of conducting that interview. She thanked God for the weapon which the reddleman had put into her hands.

Wildeve was at home when she reached the inn. He showed her silently into the parlour, and closed the door. Mrs. Yeobright began —

"I have thought it my duty to call today. A new proposal has been made to me, which has rather astonished me. It will affect Thomasin greatly; and I have decided that it should at least be mentioned to you."

"Yes? What is it?" he said civilly.

"It is, of course, in reference to her future. You may not be aware that another man has shown himself anxious to marry Thomasin. Now, though I have not encouraged him yet, I cannot conscientiously refuse him a chance any longer. I don't wish to be short with you; but I must be fair to him and to her."

"Who is the man?" said Wildeve with surprise.

"One who has been in love with her longer than she has with you. He proposed to her two years ago. At that time she refused him."

"Well?"

"He has seen her lately, and has asked me for permission to pay his addresses to her. She may not refuse him twice."

"What is his name?"

Mrs. Yeobright declined to say. "He is a man Thomasin likes," she added, "and one whose constancy she respects at least. It seems to me that what she refused then she would be glad to get now. She is much annoyed at her awkward position."

"She never once told me of this old lover."

"The gentlest women are not such fools as to show *every* card."

"Well, if she wants him I suppose she must have him."

"It is easy enough to say that; but you don't see the difficulty. He wants her much more than she wants him; and before I can encourage anything of the sort I must have a clear understanding from you that you will not interfere to injure an arrangement which I promote in the belief that it is for the best. Suppose, when they are engaged, and everything is smoothly arranged for their marriage, that you should step between them and renew your suit? You might not win her back, but you might cause much unhappiness."

"Of course I should do no such thing," said Wildeve. "But they are not engaged yet. How do you know that Thomasin would accept him?"

"That's a question I have carefully put to myself; and upon the whole the probabilities are in favour of her accepting him in time. I flatter myself that I have some influence over her. She is pliable, and I can be strong in my recommendations of him."

"And in your disparagement of me at the same time."

"Well, you may depend upon my not praising you," she said drily. "And if this seems like manoeuvring, you must remember that her position is peculiar, and that she has been hardly used. I shall also be helped in making the match by her own desire to escape from the humiliation of her present state; and a woman's pride in these cases will lead her a very great way. A little managing may be required to bring her round; but I am equal to that, provided that you agree to the one thing indispensable; that is, to make a distinct declaration that she is to think no more of you as a possible husband. That will pique her into accepting him."

"I can hardly say that just now, Mrs. Yeobright. It is so sudden."

"And so my whole plan is interfered with! It is very inconvenient that you refuse to help my family even to the small extent of saying distinctly you will have nothing to do with us."

Wildeve reflected uncomfortably. "I confess I was not prepared for this," he said. "Of course I'll give her up if you wish, if it is necessary. But I thought I might be her husband."

"We have heard that before."

"Now, Mrs. Yeobright, don't let us disagree. Give me a fair time. I don't want to stand in the way of any better chance she may have; only I wish you had let me know earlier. I will write to you or call in a day or two. Will that suffice?"

"Yes," she replied, "provided you promise not to communicate with Thomasin without my knowledge."

"I promise that," he said. And the interview then terminated, Mrs. Yeobright returning homeward as she had come.

By far the greatest effect of her simple strategy on that day was, as often happens, in a quarter quite outside her view when arranging it. In the first place, her visit sent Wildeve the same evening after dark to Eustacia's house at Mistover.

At this hour the lonely dwelling was closely blinded and shuttered from the chill and darkness without. Wildeve's clandestine plan with her was to take a little gravel in his hand and hold it to the crevice at the top of the window-shutter, which was on the outside, so that it should fall with a gentle rustle, resembling that of a mouse, between shutter and glass. This precaution in attracting her attention was to avoid arousing the suspicions of her grandfather.

The soft words, "I hear; wait for me," in Eustacia's voice from within told him that she was alone.

He waited in his customary manner by walking round the enclosure and idling by the pool, for Wildeve was never asked into the house by his proud though condescending mistress. She showed no sign of coming out in a hurry. The time wore on, and he began to grow impatient. In the course of twenty minutes she appeared from round the corner, and advanced as if merely taking an airing.

"You would not have kept me so long had you known what I come about," he said with bitterness. "Still, you are worth waiting for."

"What has happened?" said Eustacia. "I did not know you were in trouble. I too am gloomy enough."

"I am not in trouble," said he. "It is merely that affairs have come to a head, and I must take a clear course."

"What course is that?" she asked with attentive interest.

"And can you forget so soon what I proposed to you the other night? Why, take you from this place, and carry you away with me abroad."

"I have not forgotten. But why have you come so unexpectedly to repeat the question, when you only promised to come next Saturday? I thought I was to have plenty of time to consider."

"Yes, but the situation is different now."

"Explain to me."

"I don't want to explain, for I may pain you."

"But I must know the reason of this hurry."

"It is simply my ardour, dear Eustacia. Everything is smooth now."

"Then why are you so ruffled?"

"I am not aware of it. All is as it should be. Mrs. Yeobright — but she is nothing to us."

"Ah, I knew she had something to do with it! Come, I don't like reserve."

"No — she has nothing. She only says she wishes me to give up Thomasin because another man is anxious to marry her. The woman, now she no longer needs me, actually shows off!" Wildeve's vexation had escaped him in spite of himself.

Eustacia was silent a long while. "You are in the awkward position of an official who is no longer wanted," she said in a changed tone.

"It seems so. But I have not yet seen Thomasin."

"And that irritates you. Don't deny it, Damon. You are actually nettled by this slight from an unexpected quarter."

"Well?"

"And you come to get me because you cannot get her. This is certainly a new position altogether. I am to be a stop-gap."

"Please remember that I proposed the same thing the other day."

Eustacia again remained in a sort of stupefied silence. What curious feeling was this coming over her? Was it really possible that her interest in Wildeve had been so entirely the result of antagonism that the glory and the dream departed from the man with the first sound that he was no longer coveted by her rival? She was, then, secure of him at last. Thomasin no longer required him. What a humiliating victory! He loved her best, she thought; and yet — dared she to murmur such treacherous criticism ever so softly? — what was the man worth whom a woman inferior to herself did not value? The sentiment which lurks more or less in all animate nature — that of not desiring the undesired of others — was lively as a passion in the supersubtle, epicurean heart of Eustacia. Her social superiority over him, which hitherto had scarcely ever impressed her, became unpleasantly insistent, and for the first time she felt that she had stooped in loving him.

"Well, darling, you agree?" said Wildeve.

"If it could be London, or even Budmouth, instead of America," she murmured languidly. "Well, I will think. It is too great a thing for me to decide offhand. I wish I hated the heath less — or loved you more."

"You can be painfully frank. You loved me a month ago warmly enough to go anywhere with me."

"And you loved Thomasin."

"Yes, perhaps that was where the reason lay," he returned, with almost a sneer. "I don't hate her now."

"Exactly. The only thing is that you can no longer get her."

"Come — no taunts, Eustacia, or we shall quarrel. If you don't agree to go with me, and agree shortly, I shall go by myself."

"Or try Thomasin again. Damon, how strange it seems that you could have married her or me indifferently, and only have come to me because I am — cheapest! Yes, yes — it is true. There was a time when I should have exclaimed against a man of that sort, and been quite wild; but it is all past now."

"Will you go, dearest? Come secretly with me to Bristol, marry me, and turn our backs upon this doghole of England for ever? Say yes."

"I want to get away from here at almost any cost," she said with weariness, "but I don't like to go with you. Give me more time to decide."

"I have already," said Wildeve. "Well, I give you one more week."

"A little longer, so that I may tell you decisively. I have to consider so many things. Fancy Thomasin being anxious to get rid of you! I cannot forget it."

"Never mind that. Say Monday week. I will be here precisely at this time."

"Let it be at Rainbarrow," said she. "This is too near home; my grandfather may be walking out."

"Thank you, dear. On Monday week at this time I will be at the Barrow. Till then good-bye."

"Good-bye. No, no, you must not touch me now. Shaking hands is enough till I have made up my mind."

Eustacia watched his shadowy form till it had disappeared. She placed her hand to her forehead and breathed heavily; and then her rich, romantic lips parted under that homely impulse — a yawn. She was immediately angry at having betrayed even to herself the possible evanescence of her passion for him. She could not admit at once that she might have over-estimated Wildeve, for to perceive his mediocrity now was to admit her own great folly heretofore. And the discovery that she was the owner of a disposition so purely that of the dog in the manger, had something in it which at first made her ashamed.

The fruit of Mrs. Yeobright's diplomacy was indeed remarkable, though not as yet of the kind she had anticipated. It had apparently influenced Wildeve, but it was influencing Eustacia far more. Her lover was no longer to her an exciting man whom many women strove for, and herself could only retain by striving with them. He was a superfluity.

She went indoors in that peculiar state of misery which is not exactly grief, and which especially attends the dawnings of reason in the latter days of an ill-judged, transient love. To be conscious that the end of the dream is approaching, and yet has not absolutely come, is one of the most wearisome as well as the most curious stages along the course between the beginning of a passion and its end.

Her grandfather had returned, and was busily engaged in pouring some gallons of newly arrived rum into the square bottles of his square cellaret. Whenever these home supplies were exhausted he would go to the Quiet Woman, and, standing with his back to the fire, grog in hand, tell remarkable stories of how he had lived seven years under the water-line of his ship, and other naval wonders, to the natives, who hoped too earnestly for a treat of ale from the teller to exhibit any doubts of his truth.

He had been there this evening. "I suppose you have heard the Egdon news, Eustacia?" he said, without looking up from the bottles. "The men have been talking about it at the Woman as if it were of national importance."

"I have heard none," she said.

"Young Clym Yeobright, as they call him, is coming home next week to spend Christmas with his mother. He is a fine fellow by this time, it seems. I suppose you remember him?"

"I never saw him in my life."

"Ah, true; he left before you came here. I well remember him as a promising boy."

"Where has he been living all these years?"

"In that rookery of pomp and vanity, Paris, I believe."

BOOK SECOND: THE ARRIVAL

I

TIDINGS OF THE COMER

ON FINE days at this time of the year, and earlier, certain ephemeral operations were apt to disturb, in their trifling way, the majestic calm of Egdon Heath. They were activities which, besides those of a town, a village, or even a farm, would have appeared as the ferment of stagnation merely, a creeping of the flesh of somnolence. But here, away from comparisons, shut in by the stable hills, among which mere walking had the novelty of pageantry, and where any man could imagine himself to be Adam without the least difficulty, they attracted the attention of every bird within eyeshot, every reptile not yet asleep, and set the surrounding rabbits curiously watching from hillocks at a safe distance.

The performance was that of bringing together and building into a stack the furze-faggots which Humphrey had been cutting for the captain's use during the foregoing fine days. The stack was at the end of the dwelling, and the men engaged in building it were Humphrey and Sam, the old man looking on.

It was a fine and quiet afternoon, about three o'clock; but the winter solstice having stealthily come on, the lowness of the sun caused the hour to seem later than it actually was, there being little here to remind an inhabitant that he must unlearn his summer experience of the sky as a dial. In the course of many days and weeks sunrise had advanced its quarters from north-east to south-east, sunset had receded from north-west to south-west; but Egdon had hardly heeded the change.

Eustacia was indoors in the dining-room, which was really more like a kitchen, having a stone floor and a gaping chimney-corner. The air was still, and while she lingered a moment here alone sounds of voices in conversation came to her ears directly down the chimney. She entered the recess, and, listening, looked up the old irregular shaft, with its cavernous hollows, where the smoke blundered about on its way to the square bit of sky at the top, from which the daylight struck down with a pallid glare upon the tatters of soot draping the flue as sea-weed drapes a rocky fissure.

She remembered: the furze-stack was not far from the chimney, and the voices were those of the workers.

Her grandfather joined in the conversation. "That lad ought never to have left home. His father's occupation would have suited him best, and the boy should have followed on. I don't believe in these new moves in families. My father was a sailor, so was I, and so should my son have been if I had had one."

"The place he's been living at is Paris," said Humphrey, "and they tell me 'tis where the king's head was cut off years ago. My poor mother used to tell me about that business. 'Hummy,' she used to say, 'I was a young maid then, and as I was at home ironing mother's caps one afternoon the parson came in and said, "They've cut the king's head off, Jane; and what 'twill be next God knows."'

"A good many of us knew as well as He before long," said the captain, chuckling. "I lived seven years under water on account of it in my boyhood — in that damned surgery of the *Triumph*, seeing men brought down to the cockpit with their legs and arms blown to Jericho.... And so the young man has settled in Paris. Manager to a diamond merchant, or some such thing, is he not?"

"Yes, sir, that's it. 'Tis a blazing great business that he belongs to, so I've heard his mother say — like a king's palace, so far as diments go."

"I can well mind when he left home," said Sam.

"'Tis a good thing for the feller," said Humphrey. "A sight of times better to be selling diments than nobbling about here."

"It must cost a good few shillings to deal at such a place."

"A good few indeed, my man," replied the captain. "Yes, you may make away with a deal of money and be neither drunkard nor glutton."

"They say, too, that Clym Yeobright is become a real perusing man, with the strangest notions about things. There, that's because he went to school early, such as the school was."

"Strange notions, has he?" said the old man. "Ah, there's too much of that sending to school in these days! It only does harm. Every gatepost and barn's door you come to is sure to have some bad word or other chalked upon it by the young rascals: a woman can hardly pass for shame sometimes. If they'd never been taught how to write they wouldn't have been able to scribble such villainy. Their fathers couldn't do it, and the country was all the better for it."

"Now, I should think, cap'n, that Miss Eustacia had about as much in her head that comes from books as anybody about here?"

"Perhaps if Miss Eustacia, too, had less romantic nonsense in her head it would be better for her," said the captain shortly; after which he walked away.

"I say, Sam," observed Humphrey when the old man was gone, "she and Clym Yeobright would make a very pretty pigeon pair — hey? If they wouldn't I'll be dazed! Both of one mind about niceties for certain, and learned in print, and always thinking about high doctrine — there couldn't be a better couple if they were made o' purpose. Clym's family is as good as hers. His father was a farmer, that's true; but his mother was a sort of lady, as we know. Nothing would please me better than to see them two man and wife."

"They'd look very natty, arm-in-crook together, and their best clothes on, whether or no, if he's at all the well-favoured fellow he used to be."

"They would, Humphrey. Well, I should like to see the chap terrible much after so many years. If I knew for certain when he was coming I'd stroll out three or four miles to meet him and help carry anything for'n; though I suppose he's altered from the boy he was. They say he can talk French as fast as a maid can eat blackberries; and if so, depend upon it we who have stayed at home shall seem no more than scroff in his eyes."

"Coming across the water to Budmouth by steamer, isn't he?"

"Yes; but how he's coming from Budmouth I don't know."

"That's a bad trouble about his cousin Thomasin. I wonder such a nice-notioned fellow as Clym likes to come home into it. What a nunnywatch we were in, to be sure, when we heard they weren't married at all, after singing to 'em as man and wife that night! Be dazed if I should like a relation of mine to have been made such a fool of by a man. It makes the family look small."

"Yes. Poor maid, her heart has ached enough about it. Her health is suffering from it, I hear, for she will bide entirely indoors. We never see her out now, scampering over the furze with a face as red as a rose, as she used to do."

"I've heard she wouldn't have Wildeve now if he asked her."

"You have? 'Tis news to me."

While the furze-gatherers had desultorily conversed thus Eustacia's face gradually bent to the hearth in a profound reverie, her toe unconsciously tapping the dry turf which lay burning at her feet.

The subject of their discourse had been keenly interesting to her. A young and clever man was coming into that lonely heath from, of all contrasting places in the world, Paris. It was like a man coming from heaven. More singular still, the heathmen had instinctively coupled her and this man together in their minds as a pair born for each other.

That five minutes of overhearing furnished Eustacia with visions enough to fill the whole blank afternoon. Such sudden alternations from mental vacuity do sometimes occur thus quietly. She could never have believed in the morning that her colourless inner world would before night become as animated as water under a microscope, and that without the arrival of a single visitor. The words of Sam and Humphrey on the harmony between the unknown and herself had on her mind the effect of the invading Bard's prelude in the "Castle of Indolence," at which myriads of imprisoned shapes arose where had previously appeared the stillness of a void.

Involved in these imaginings she knew nothing of time. When she became conscious of externals it was dusk. The furze-rick was finished; the men had gone home. Eustacia went upstairs, thinking that she would take a walk at this her usual time; and she determined that her walk should be in the direction of Blooms-End, the birthplace of young Yeobright and the present home of his mother. She had no reason for walking elsewhere, and why should she not go that way? The scene of a day-dream is sufficient for a pilgrimage at nineteen. To look at the palings before the Yeobrights' house had the dignity of a necessary performance. Strange that such a piece of idling should have seemed an important errand.

She put on her bonnet, and, leaving the house, descended the hill on the side towards Blooms-End, where she walked slowly along the valley for a distance of a mile and a half. This brought her to a spot in which the green bottom of the dale began to widen, the furze bushes to recede yet further from the path on each side, till they were diminished to an isolated one here and there by the increasing fertility of the soil. Beyond the irregular carpet of grass was a row of white palings, which marked the verge of the heath in this latitude. They showed upon the dusky scene that they bordered as distinctly as white lace on velvet. Behind the white palings was a little garden; behind the garden an old, irregular, thatched house, facing the heath, and commanding a full view of the valley. This was the obscure, removed spot to which was about to return a man whose latter life had been passed in the French capital — the centre and vortex of the fashionable world.

II

THE PEOPLE AT BLOOMS-END MAKE READY

ALL that afternoon the expected arrival of the subject of Eustacia's ruminations created a bustle of preparation at Blooms-End. Thomasin had been persuaded by her aunt, and by an instinctive impulse of loyalty towards her cousin Clym, to bestir herself on his account with an alacrity unusual in her during these most sorrowful days of her life. At the time that Eustacia was listening to the rick-makers' conversation on Clym's return, Thomasin was climbing into a loft over her aunt's fuel-house, where the store-apples were kept, to search out the best and largest of them for the coming holiday time.

The loft was lighted by a semicircular hole, through which the pigeons crept to their lodgings in the same high quarters of the premises; and from this hole the sun shone in a bright yellow patch upon the figure of the maiden as she knelt and plunged her naked arms into the soft brown fern, which, from its abundance, was used on Egdon in packing away stores of all kinds. The pigeons were flying about her head with the greatest unconcern, and the face of her aunt was just visible above the floor of the loft, lit by a few stray motes of light, as she stood half-way up the ladder, looking at a spot into which she was not climber enough to venture.

"Now a few russets, Tamsin. He used to like them almost as well as ribstones."

Thomasin turned and rolled aside the fern from another nook, where more mellow fruit greeted her with its ripe smell. Before picking them out she stopped a moment.

"Dear Clym, I wonder how your face looks now?" she said, gazing abstractedly at the pigeon-hole, which admitted the sunlight so directly upon her brown hair and transparent tissues that it almost seemed to shine through her.

"If he could have been dear to you in another way," said Mrs. Yeobright from the ladder, "this might have been a happy meeting."

"Is there any use in saying what can do no good, aunt?"

"Yes," said her aunt, with some warmth. "To thoroughly fill the air with the past misfortune, so that other girls may take warning and keep clear of it."

Thomasin lowered her face to the apples again. "I am a warning to others, just as thieves and drunkards and gamblers are," she said in a low voice. "What a class to belong to! Do I really belong to them? 'Tis absurd! Yet why, aunt, does everybody keep on making me think that I do, by the way they behave towards me? Why don't people judge me by my acts? Now, look at me as I kneel here, picking up these apples — do I look like a lost woman?... I wish all good women were as good as I!" she added vehemently.

"Strangers don't see you as I do," said Mrs. Yeobright; "they judge from false report. Well, it is a silly job, and I am partly to blame."

"How quickly a rash thing can be done!" replied the girl. Her lips were quivering, and tears so crowded themselves into her eyes that she could hardly distinguish apples from fern as she continued industriously searching to hide her weakness.

"As soon as you have finished getting the apples," her aunt said, descending the ladder, "come down, and we'll go for the holly. There is nobody on the heath this afternoon, and you need not fear being stared at. We must get some berries, or Clym will never believe in our preparations."

Thomasin came down when the apples were collected, and together they went through the white palings to the heath beyond. The open hills were airy and clear, and the remote atmosphere appeared, as it often appears on a fine winter day, in distinct planes of illumination independently toned, the rays which lit the nearer tracts of landscape streaming visibly across those further off: a stratum of ensaffroned light was imposed on a stratum of deep blue, and behind these lay still remoter scenes wrapped in frigid grey.

They reached the place where the hollies grew, which was in a conical pit, so that the tops of the trees were not much above the general level of the ground. Thomasin stepped up into a fork of one of the bushes, as she had done under happier circumstances on many similar occasions, and with a small chopper that they had brought she began to lop off the heavily berried boughs.

"Don't scratch your face," said her aunt, who stood at the edge of the pit, regarding the girl as she held on amid the glistening green and scarlet masses of the tree. "Will you walk with me to meet him this evening?"

"I should like to. Else it would seem as if I had forgotten him," said Thomasin, tossing out a bough. "Not that that would matter much; I belong to one man; nothing can alter that. And that man I must marry, for my pride's sake."

"I am afraid ——" began Mrs. Yeobright.

"Ah, you think, 'That weak girl — how is she going to get a man to marry her when she chooses?' But let me tell you one thing, aunt: Mr. Wildeve is not a profligate man, any more than I am an improper woman. He has an unfortunate manner, and doesn't try to make people like him if they don't wish to do it of their own accord."

"Thomasin," said Mrs. Yeobright quietly, fixing her eye upon her niece, "do you think you deceive me in your defence of Mr. Wildeve?"

"How do you mean?"

"I have long had a suspicion that your love for him has changed its colour since you have found him not to be the saint you thought him, and that you act a part to me."

"He wished to marry me, and I wish to marry him."

"Now, I put it to you: would you at this present moment agree to be his wife if that had not happened to entangle you with him?"

Thomasin looked into the tree and appeared much disturbed. "Aunt," she said presently, "I have, I think, a right to refuse to answer that question."

"Yes, you have."

"You may think what you choose. I have never implied to you by word or deed that I have grown to think otherwise of him, and I never will. And I shall marry him."

"Well, wait till he repeats his offer. I think he may do it, now that he knows — something I told him. I don't for a moment dispute that it is the most proper thing for you to marry him. Much as I have objected to him in bygone days, I agree with you now, you may be sure. It is the only way out of a false position, and a very galling one."

"What did you tell him?"

"That he was standing in the way of another lover of yours."

"Aunt," said Thomasin, with round eyes, "what *do* you mean?"

"Don't be alarmed; it was my duty. I can say no more about it now, but when it is over I will tell you exactly what I said, and why I said it."

Thomasin was perforce content.

"And you will keep the secret of my would-be marriage from Clym for the present?" she next asked.

"I have given my word to. But what is the use of it? He must soon know what has happened. A mere look at your face will show him that something is wrong."

Thomasin turned and regarded her aunt from the tree. "Now, hearken to me," she said, her delicate voice expanding into firmness by a force which was other than physical. "Tell him nothing. If he finds out that I am not worthy to be his cousin, let him. But, since he loved me once, we will not pain him by telling him my trouble too soon. The air is full of the story, I know; but gossips will not dare to speak of it to him for the first few days. His closeness to me is the very thing that will hinder the tale from reaching him early. If I am not made safe from sneers in a week or two I will tell him myself."

The earnestness with which Thomasin spoke prevented further objections. Her aunt simply said, "Very well. He should by rights have been told at the time that the wedding was going to be. He will never forgive you for your secrecy."

"Yes, he will, when he knows it was because I wished to spare him, and that I did not expect him home so soon. And you must not let me stand in the way of your Christmas party. Putting it off would only make matters worse."

"Of course I shall not. I do not wish to show myself beaten before all Egdon, and the sport of a man like Wildeve. We have enough berries now, I think, and we had better take them home. By the time we have decked the house with this and hung up the mistletoe, we must think of starting to meet him."

Thomasin came out of the tree, shook from her hair and dress the loose berries which had fallen thereon, and went down the hill with her aunt, each woman bearing half the gathered boughs. It was now nearly four o'clock, and the sunlight was leaving the vales. When the west grew red the two relatives came again from the house and plunged into the heath in a different direction from the first, towards a point in the distant highway along which the expected man was to return.

III

HOW A LITTLE SOUND PRODUCED A GREAT DREAM

Eustacia stood just within the heath, straining her eyes in the direction of Mrs. Yeobright's house and premises. No light, sound, or movement was perceptible there. The evening was chilly; the spot was dark and lonely. She inferred that the guest had not yet come; and after lingering ten or fifteen minutes she turned again towards home.

She had not far retraced her steps when sounds in front of her betokened the approach of persons in conversation along the same path. Soon their heads became visible against the sky. They were walking slowly; and though it was too dark for much discovery of character from aspect, the gait of them showed that they were not workers on the heath. Eustacia stepped a little out of the foot-track to let them pass. They were two women and a man; and the voices of the women were those of Mrs. Yeobright and Thomasin.

They went by her, and at the moment of passing appeared to discern her dusky form. There came to her ears in a masculine voice, "Good night!"

She murmured a reply, glided by them, and turned round. She could not, for a moment, believe that chance, unrequested, had brought into her presence the soul of the house she had gone to inspect, the man without whom her inspection would not have been thought of.

She strained her eyes to see them, but was unable. Such was her intentness, however, that it seemed as if her ears were performing the functions of seeing as well as hearing. This extension of power can almost be believed in at such moments. The deaf Dr. Kitto was probably under the influence of a parallel fancy when he described his body as having become, by long endeavour, so sensitive to vibrations that he had gained the power of perceiving by it as by ears.

She could follow every word that the ramblers uttered. They were talking no secrets. They were merely indulging in the ordinary vivacious chat of relatives who have long been parted in person though not in soul. But it was not to the words that Eustacia listened; she could not even have recalled, a few minutes later, what the words were. It was to the alternating voice that gave out about one-tenth of them — the voice that had wished her good night. Sometimes this throat uttered Yes, sometimes it uttered No; sometimes it made inquiries about a timeworn denizen of the place. Once it surprised her notions by remarking upon the friendliness and geniality written in the faces of the hills around.

The three voices passed on, and decayed and died out upon her ear. Thus much had been granted her; and all besides withheld. No event could have been more exciting. During the greater part of the afternoon she had been entrancing herself by imagining the fascination which must attend a man come direct from beautiful Paris — laden with its atmosphere, familiar with its charms. And this man had greeted her.

With the departure of the figures the profuse articulations of the women wasted away from her memory; but the accents of the other stayed on. Was there anything in the voice of Mrs. Yeobright's son — for Clym it was — startling as a sound? No: it was simply comprehensive. All emotional things were possible to the speaker of that "good night." Eustacia's imagination supplied the rest — except the solution to one riddle. What *could* the tastes of that man be who saw friendliness and geniality in these shaggy hills?

On such occasions as this a thousand ideas pass through a highly charged woman's head; and they indicate themselves on her face; but the changes, though actual, are minute. Eustacia's features went through a rhythmical succession of them. She glowed; remembering the mendacity of the imagination, she flagged; then she freshened; then she fired; then she cooled again. It was a cycle of aspects, produced by a cycle of visions.

Eustacia entered her own house; she was excited. Her grandfather was enjoying himself over the fire, raking about the ashes and exposing the red-hot surface of the turves, so that their lurid glare irradiated the chimney-corner with the hues of a furnace.

"Why is it that we are never friendly with the Yeobrights?" she said, coming forward and stretching her soft hands over the warmth. "I wish we were. They seem to be very nice people."

"Be hanged if I know why," said the captain. "I liked the old man well enough, though he was as rough as a hedge. But you would never have cared to go there, even if you might have, I am well sure."

"Why shouldn't I?"

"Your town tastes would find them far too countrified. They sit in the kitchen, drink mead and elderwine, and sand the floor to keep it clean. A sensible way of life; but how would you like it?"

"I thought Mrs. Yeobright was a ladylike woman? A curate's daughter, was she not?"

"Yes; but she was obliged to live as her husband did; and I suppose she has taken kindly to it by this time. Ah, I recollect that I once accidentally offended her, and I have never seen her since."

That night was an eventful one to Eustacia's brain, and one which she hardly ever forgot. She dreamt a dream; and few human beings, from Nebuchadnezzar to the Swaffham tinker, ever dreamed a more remarkable one. Such an elaborately developed, perplexing, exciting dream was certainly never dreamed by a girl in Eustacia's situation before. It had as many ramifications as the Cretan labyrinth, as many fluctuations as the Northern Lights, as much colour as a parterre in June, and was as crowded with figures as a coronation. To Queen Scheherazade the dream might have seemed not far removed from commonplace; and to a girl just returned from all the courts of Europe it might have seemed not more than interesting. But amid the circumstances of Eustacia's life it was as wonderful as a dream could be.

There was, however, gradually evolved from its transformation scenes a less extravagant episode, in which the heath dimly appeared behind the general brilliancy of the action. She was dancing to wondrous music, and her partner was the man in silver armour, who had accompanied her through the previous fantastic changes, the visor of his helmet being closed. The mazes of the dance were ecstatic. Soft whispering came into her ear from under the radiant helmet, and she felt like a woman in Paradise. Suddenly these two wheeled out from the mass of dancers, dived into one of the pools of the heath, and came out somewhere beneath into an iridescent hollow, arched with rainbows. "It must be here," said the voice by her side, and blushingly looking up she saw him removing his casque to kiss her. At that moment there was a cracking noise, and his figure fell into fragments like a pack of cards.

She cried aloud, "O that I had seen his face!"

Eustacia awoke. The cracking had been that of the window-shutter downstairs, which the maid-servant was opening to let in the day, now slowly increasing to Nature's meagre allowance at this sickly time of the year. "O that I had seen his face!" she said again. "'Twas meant for Mr. Yeobright!"

When she became cooler she perceived that many of the phases of the dream had naturally arisen out of the images and fancies of the day before. But this detracted little from its interest, which lay in the excellent fuel it provided for newly kindled fervour. She was at the modulating point between indifference and love, at the stage called "having a fancy for." It occurs once in the history of the most gigantic passions, and it is a period when they are in the hands of the weakest will.

The perfervid woman was by this time half in love with a vision. The fantastic nature of her passion, which lowered her as an intellect, raised her as a soul. If she had had a little more self-control she would have attenuated the emotion to nothing by sheer reasoning, and so have killed it off. If she had had a little less pride she might have gone and circumambulated the Yeobrights' premises at Blooms-End at any maidenly sacrifice until she had seen him. But Eustacia did neither of these things. She acted as the most exemplary might have acted, being so influenced; she took an airing twice or thrice a day upon the Egdon hills, and kept her eyes employed.

The first occasion passed, and he did not come that way.

She promenaded a second time, and was again the sole wanderer there.

The third time there was a dense fog: she looked around, but without much hope. Even if he had been walking within twenty yards of her she could not have seen him.

At the fourth attempt to encounter him it began to rain in torrents, and she turned back.

The fifth sally was in the afternoon: it was fine, and she remained out long, walking to the very top of the valley in which Blooms-End lay. She saw the white paling about half a mile off; but he did not appear. It was almost with heart-sickness that she came home, and with a sense of shame at her weakness. She resolved to look for the man from Paris no more.

But Providence is nothing if not coquettish; and no sooner had Eustacia formed this resolve than the opportunity came which, while sought, had been entirely withholden.

IV

EUSTACIA IS LED ON TO AN ADVENTURE

IN THE evening of this last day of expectation, which was the twenty-third of December, Eustacia was at home alone. She had passed the recent hour in lamenting over a rumour newly come to her ears — that Yeobright's visit to his mother was to be of short duration, and would end some time the next week. "Naturally," she said to herself. A man in the full swing of his activities in a gay city could not afford to linger long on Egdon Heath. That she would behold face to face the owner of the awakening voice within the limits of such a holiday was most unlikely, unless she were to haunt the environs of his mother's house like a robin, to do which was difficult and unseemly.

The customary expedient of provincial girls and men in such circumstances is churchgoing. In an ordinary village or country town one can safely calculate that, either on Christmas-day or the Sunday contiguous, any native home for the holidays, who has not through age or *ennui* lost the appetite for seeing and being seen, will turn up in some pew or other, shining with hope, self-consciousness, and new clothes. Thus the congregation on Christmas morning is mostly a Tussaud collection of celebrities who have been born in the neighbourhood. Hither the mistress, left neglected at home all the year, can steal and observe the development of the returned lover who has forgotten her, and think as she watches him over her prayer-book that he may throb with a renewed fidelity when novelties have lost their charm. And hither a comparatively recent settler like Eustacia may betake herself to scrutinize the person of a native son who left home before her advent upon the scene, and consider if the friendship of his parents be worth cultivating during his next absence in order to secure a knowledge of him on his next return.

But these tender schemes were not feasible among the scattered inhabitants of Egdon Heath. In name they were parishioners, but virtually they belonged to no parish at all. People who came to these few isolated houses to keep Christmas with their friends remained in their friends' chimney-corners drinking mead and other comforting liquors till they left again for good and all. Rain, snow, ice, mud everywhere around, they did not care to trudge two or three miles to sit wet-footed and splashed to the nape of their necks among those who, though in some measure neighbours, lived close to the church, and entered it clean and dry. Eustacia knew it was ten to one that Clym Yeobright would go to no church at all during his few days of leave, and that it would be a waste of labour for her to go driving the pony and gig over a bad road in hope to see him there.

It was dusk, and she was sitting by the fire in the dining-room or hall, which they occupied at this time of the year in preference to the parlour, because of its large hearth, constructed for turf-fires, a fuel the captain was partial to in the winter season. The only visible articles in the room were those on the window-sill, which showed their shapes against the low sky: the middle article being the old hour-glass, and the other two a pair of ancient British urns which had been dug from a barrow near, and were used as flower-pots for two razor-leaved cactuses. Somebody knocked at the door. The servant was out; so was her grandfather. The person, after waiting a minute, came in and tapped at the door of the room.

"Who's there?" said Eustacia.

"Please, Cap'n Vye, will you let us ——"

Eustacia arose and went to the door. "I cannot allow you to come in so boldly. You should have waited."

"The cap'n said I might come in without any fuss," was answered in a lad's pleasant voice.

"Oh, did he?" said Eustacia, more gently. "What do you want, Charley?"

"Please will your grandfather lend us his fuel-house to try over our parts in, tonight at seven o'clock?"

"What, are you one of the Egdon mummers for this year?"

"Yes, miss. The cap'n used to let the old mummers practise here."

"I know it. Yes, you may use the fuel-house if you like," said Eustacia languidly.

The choice of Captain Vye's fuel-house at the scene of rehearsal was dictated by the fact that his dwelling was nearly in the centre of the heath. The fuel-house was as roomy as a barn, and was a most desirable place for such a purpose. The lads who formed the company of players lived at different scattered points around, and by meeting in this spot the distances to be traversed by all the comers would be about equally proportioned.

Of mummers and mumming Eustacia had the greatest contempt. The mummers themselves were not afflicted with any such feeling for their art, though at the same time they were not enthusiastic. A traditional pastime is to be distinguished from a mere revival in no more striking feature than in this, that while in the revival all is excitement and fervour, the survival is carried on with a stolidity and absence of stir which sets one wondering why a thing that is done so perfunctorily should be kept up at all. Like Balaam and other unwilling prophets, the agents seem moved by an inner compulsion to say and do their allotted parts whether they will or no. This unweeting manner of performance is the true ring by which, in this refurbishing age, a fossilized survival may be known from a spurious reproduction.

The piece was the well-known play of "Saint George," and all who were behind the scenes assisted in the preparations, including the women of each household. Without the co-operation of sisters and sweethearts the dresses were likely to be a failure; but on the other hand, this class of assistance was not without its drawbacks. The girls could never be brought to respect tradition in designing and decorating the armour; they insisted on attaching loops and bows of silk and velvet in any situation pleasing to their taste. Gorget, gusset, basinet, cuirass, gauntlet, sleeve, all alike in the view of these feminine eyes were practicable spaces whereon to sew scraps of fluttering colour.

It might be that Joe, who fought on the side of Christendom, had a sweetheart, and that Jim, who fought on the side of the Moslem, had one likewise. During the making of the costumes it would come to the knowledge of Joe's sweetheart that Jim's was putting brilliant silk scallops at the bottom of her lover's surcoat, in addition to the ribbons of the visor, the bars of which, being invariably formed of coloured strips about half an inch wide hanging before the face, were mostly of that material. Joe's sweetheart straightway placed brilliant silk on the scallops of the hem in question, and, going a little further, added ribbon tufts to the shoulder-pieces. Jim's not to be outdone, would affix bows and rosettes everywhere.

The result was that in the end the Valiant Soldier, of the Christian army, was distinguished by no peculiarity of accoutrement from the Turkish Knight; and what was worse, on a casual view Saint George himself might be mistaken for his deadly enemy, the Saracen. The guisers themselves, though inwardly regretting this confusion of persons, could not afford to offend those by whose assistance they so largely profited, and the innovations were allowed to stand.

There was, it is true, a limit to this tendency to uniformity. The Leech or Doctor preserved his character intact: his darker habiliments, peculiar hat, and the bottle of physic slung under his arm, could never be mistaken. And the same might be said of the conventional figure of Father Christmas, with his gigantic club, an older man, who accompanied the band as general protector in long night journeys from parish to parish, and was bearer of the purse.

Seven o'clock, the hour of the rehearsal, came round, and in a short time Eustacia could hear voices in the fuel-house. To dissipate in some trifling measure her abiding sense of the murkiness of human life she went to the "linhay" or lean-to shed, which formed the rootstore of their dwelling and abutted on the fuel-house. Here was a small rough hole in the mud wall, originally made for pigeons, through which the interior of the next shed could be viewed. A light came from it now; and Eustacia stepped upon a stool to look in upon the scene.

On a ledge in the fuel-house stood three tall rushlights, and by the light of them seven or eight lads were marching about, haranguing, and confusing each other, in endeavours to perfect themselves in the play. Humphrey and Sam, the furze and turf-cutters, were there looking on, so also was Timothy Fairway, who leant against the wall and prompted the boys from memory, interspersing among the set words remarks and anecdotes of the superior days when he and others were the Egdon mummers-elect that these lads were now.

"Well, ye be as well up to it as ever ye will be," he said. "Not that such mumming would have passed in our time. Harry as the Saracen should strut a bit more, and John needn't holler his inside out. Beyond that perhaps you'll do. Have you got all your clothes ready?"

"We shall by Monday."

"Your first outing will be Monday night, I suppose?"

"Yes. At Mrs. Yeobright's."

"Oh, Mrs. Yeobright's. What makes her want to see ye? I should think a middle-aged woman was tired of mumming."

"She's got up a bit of a party, because 'tis the first Christmas that her son Clym has been home for a long time."

"To be sure, to be sure — her party! I am going myself. I almost forgot it, upon my life."

Eustacia's face flagged. There was to be a party at the Yeobrights'; she, naturally, had nothing to do with it. She was a stranger to all such local gatherings, and had always held them as scarcely appertaining to her sphere. But had she been going, what an opportunity would have been afforded her of seeing the man whose influence was penetrating her like summer sun! To increase that influence was coveted excitement; to cast it off might be to regain serenity; to leave it as it stood was tantalizing.

The lads and men prepared to leave the premises, and Eustacia returned to her fireside. She was immersed in thought, but not for long. In a few minutes the lad Charley, who had come to ask permission to use the place, returned with the key to the kitchen. Eustacia heard him, and opening the door into the passage said, "Charley, come here."

The lad was surprised. He entered the front room, not without blushing; for he, like many, had felt the power of this girl's face and form.

She pointed to a seat by the fire, and entered the other side of the chimney-corner herself. It could be seen in her face that whatever motive she might have had in asking the youth indoors would soon appear.

"Which part do you play, Charley — the Turkish Knight, do you not?" inquired the beauty, looking across the smoke of the fire to him on the other side.

"Yes, miss, the Turkish Knight," he replied diffidently.

"Is yours a long part?"

"Nine speeches, about."

"Can you repeat them to me? If so I should like to hear them."

The lad smiled into the glowing turf and began —

> "Here come I, a Turkish Knight,
> Who learnt in Turkish land to fight,"

continuing the discourse throughout the scenes to the concluding catastrophe of his fall by the hand of Saint George.

Eustacia had occasionally heard the part recited before. When the lad
ended she began, precisely in the same words, and ranted on without hitch
or divergence till she too reached the end. It was the same thing, yet
how different. Like in form, it had the added softness and finish of a
Raffaelle after Perugino, which, while faithfully reproducing the original
subject, entirely distances the original art.

Charley's eyes rounded with surprise. "Well, you be a clever lady!" he
said, in admiration. "I've been three weeks learning mine."

"I have heard it before," she quietly observed. "Now, would you do
anything to please me, Charley?"

"I'd do a good deal, miss."

"Would you let me play your part for one night?"

"O, miss! But your woman's gown — you couldn't."

"I can get boy's clothes — at least all that would be wanted besides
the mumming dress. What should I have to give you to lend me your
things, to let me take your place for an hour or two on Monday night,
and on no account to say a word about who or what I am? You would,
of course, have to excuse yourself from playing that night, and to say that
somebody — a cousin of Miss Vye's — would act for you. The other
mummers have never spoken to me in their lives, so that it would be safe
enough; and if it were not, I should not mind. Now, what must I give
you to agree to this? Half a crown?"

The youth shook his head.

"Five shillings?"

He shook his head again. "Money won't do it," he said, brushing the
iron head of the fire-dog with the hollow of his hand.

"What will, then, Charley?" said Eustacia in a disappointed tone.

"You know what you forbade me at the maypoling, miss," murmured
the lad, without looking at her, and still stroking the fire-dog's head.

"Yes," said Eustacia, with a little more hauteur. "You wanted to
join hands with me in the ring, if I recollect?"

"Half an hour of that, and I'll agree, miss."

Eustacia regarded the youth steadfastly. He was three years younger
than herself, but apparently not backward for his age. "Half an hour
of what?" she said, though she guessed what.

"Holding your hand in mine."

She was silent. "Make it a quarter of an hour," she said.

"Yes, Miss Eustacia — I will, if I may kiss it too. A quarter of an
hour. And I'll swear to do the best I can to let you take my place without
anybody knowing. Don't you think somebody might know your tongue,
miss?"

"It is possible. But I will put a pebble in my mouth to make it less
likely. Very well; you shall be allowed to have my hand as soon as you
bring the dress and your sword and staff. I don't want you any longer
now."

Charley departed, and Eustacia felt more and more interest in life. Here was something to do: here was someone to see, and a charmingly adventurous way to see him. "Ah," she said to herself, "want of an object to live for — that's all is the matter with me!"

Eustacia's manner was as a rule of a slumberous sort, her passions being of the massive rather than the vivacious kind. But when aroused she would make a dash which, just for the time, was not unlike the move of a naturally lively person.

On the question of recognition she was somewhat indifferent. By the acting lads themselves she was not likely to be known. With the guests who might be assembled she was hardly so secure. Yet detection, after all, would be no such dreadful thing. The fact only could be detected, her true motive never. It would be instantly set down as the passing freak of a girl whose ways were already considered singular. That she was doing for an earnest reason what would most naturally be done in jest was at any rate a safe secret.

The next evening Eustacia stood punctually at the fuel-house door, waiting for the dusk which was to bring Charley with the trappings. Her grandfather was at home tonight, and she would be unable to ask her confederate indoors.

He appeared on the dark ridge of heathland, like a fly on a negro, bearing the articles with him, and came up breathless with his walk.

"Here are the things," he whispered, placing them upon the threshold. "And now, Miss Eustacia ——"

"The payment. It is quite ready. I am as good as my word."

She leant against the door-post, and gave him her hand. Charley took it in both his own with a tenderness beyond description, unless it was like that of a child holding a captured sparrow.

"Why, there's a glove on it!" he said in a deprecating way.

"I have been walking," she observed.

"But, miss!"

"Well — it is hardly fair." She pulled off the glove, and gave him her bare hand.

They stood together minute after minute, without further speech, each looking at the blackening scene, and each thinking his and her own thoughts.

"I think I won't use it all up tonight," said Charley devotedly, when six or eight minutes had been passed by him caressing her hand. "May I have the other few minutes another time?"

"As you like," said she without the least emotion. "But it must be over in a week. Now, there is only one thing I want you to do: to wait while I put on the dress, and then to see if I do my part properly. But let me look first indoors."

She vanished for a minute or two, and went in. Her grandfather was safely asleep in his chair. "Now, then," she said, on returning, "walk down the garden a little way, and when I am ready I'll call you."

Charley walked and waited, and presently heard a soft whistle. He returned to the fuel-house door.

"Did you whistle, Miss Vye?"

"Yes; come in," reached him in Eustacia's voice from a back quarter. "I must not strike a light till the door is shut, or it may be seen shining. Push your hat into the hole through to the wash-house, if you can feel your way across."

Charley did as commanded, and she struck the light, revealing herself to be changed in sex, brilliant in colours, and armed from top to toe. Perhaps she quailed a little under Charley's vigorous gaze, but whether any shyness at her male attire appeared upon her countenance could not be seen by reason of the strips of ribbon which used to cover the face in mumming costumes, representing the barred visor of the mediæval helmet.

"It fits pretty well," she said, looking down at the white overalls, "except that the tunic, or whatever you call it, is long in the sleeve. The bottom of the overalls I can turn up inside. Now pay attention."

Eustacia then proceeded in her delivery, striking the sword against the staff or lance at the minatory phrases, in the orthodox mumming manner, and strutting up and down. Charley seasoned his admiration with criticism of the gentlest kind, for the touch of Eustacia's hand yet remained with him.

"And now for your excuse to the others," she said. "Where do you meet before you go to Mrs. Yeobright's?"

"We thought of meeting here, miss, if you have nothing to say against it. At eight o'clock, so as to get there by nine."

"Yes. Well, you of course must not appear. I will march in about five minutes late, ready-dressed, and tell them that you can't come. I have decided that the best plan will be for you to be sent somewhere by me, to make a real thing of the excuse. Our two heath-croppers are in the habit of straying into the meads, and tomorrow evening you can go and see if they are gone there. I'll manage the rest. Now you may leave me."

"Yes, miss. But I think I'll have one minute more of what I am owed, if you don't mind."

Eustacia gave him her hand as before.

"One minute," she said, and counted on till she reached seven or eight minutes. Hand and person she then withdrew to a distance of several feet, and recovered some of her old dignity. The contract completed, she raised between them a barrier impenetrable as a wall.

"There, 'tis all gone; and I didn't mean quite all," he said, with a sigh.

"You had good measure," said she, turning away.

"Yes, miss. Well, 'tis over, and now I'll get home-along."

V

THROUGH THE MOONLIGHT

The next evening the mummers were assembled in the same spot, awaiting the entrance of the Turkish Knight.

"Twenty minutes after eight by the Quiet Woman, and Charley not come."

"One minute past by Blooms-End."

"It wants ten minutes to, by Grandfer Cantle's watch."

"And 'tis five minutes past by the captain's clock."

On Egdon there was no absolute hour of the day. The time at any moment was a number of varying doctrines professed by the different hamlets, some of them having originally grown up from a common root, and then become divided by secession, some having been alien from the beginning. West Egdon believed in Blooms-End time, East Egdon in the time of the Quiet Woman Inn. Grandfer Cantle's watch had numbered many followers in years gone by, but since he had grown older faiths were shaken. Thus, the mummers having gathered hither from scattered points, each came with his own tenets on early and late; and they waited a little longer as a compromise.

Eustacia had watched the assemblage through the hole; and seeing that now was the proper moment to enter, she went from the "linhay" and boldly pulled the bobbin of the fuel-house door. Her grandfather was safe at the Quiet Woman.

"Here's Charley at last! How late you be, Charley."

"'Tis not Charley," said the Turkish Knight from within his visor. "'Tis a cousin of Miss Vye's, come to take Charley's place from curiosity. He was obliged to go and look for the heath-croppers that have got into the meads, and I agreed to take his place, as he knew he couldn't come back here again tonight. I know the part as well as he."

Her graceful gait, elegant figure, and dignified manner in general won the mummers to the opinion that they had gained by the exchange, if the newcomer were perfect in his part.

"It don't matter — if you be not too young," said Saint George. Eustacia's voice had sounded somewhat more juvenile and fluty than Charley's.

"I know every word of it, I tell you," said Eustacia decisively. Dash being all that was required to carry her triumphantly through, she adopted as much as was necessary. "Go ahead, lads, with the try-over. I'll challenge any of you to find a mistake in me."

The play was hastily rehearsed, whereupon the other mummers were delighted with the new knight. They extinguished the candles at half-past eight, and set out upon the heath in the direction of Mrs. Yeobright's house at Blooms-End.

There was a slight hoar-frost that night, and the moon, though not more than half full, threw a spirited and enticing brightness upon the fantastic figures of the mumming band, whose plumes and ribbons rustled in their walk like autumn leaves. Their path was not over Rainbarrow now, but down a valley which left that ancient elevation a little to the east. The bottom of the vale was green to a width of ten yards or thereabouts, and the shining facets of frost upon the blades of grass seemed to move on with the shadows of those they surrounded. The masses of furze and heath to the right and left were dark as ever; a mere half-moon was powerless to silver such sable features as theirs.

Half-an-hour of walking and talking brought them to the spot in the valley where the grass riband widened and led up to the front of the house. At sight of the place Eustacia, who had felt a few passing doubts during her walk with the youths, again was glad that the adventure had been undertaken. She had come out to see a man who might possibly have the power to deliver her soul from a most deadly oppression. What was Wildeve? Interesting, but inadequate. Perhaps she would see a sufficient hero tonight.

As they drew nearer to the front of the house the mummers became aware that music and dancing were briskly flourishing within. Every now and then a long low note from the serpent, which was the chief wind instrument played at these times, advanced further into the heath than the thin treble part, and reached their ears alone; and next a more than usually loud tread from a dancer would come the same way. With nearer approach these fragmentary sounds became pieced together, and were found to be the salient points of the tune called "Nancy's Fancy."

He was there, of course. Who was she that he danced with? Perhaps some unknown woman, far beneath herself in culture, was by that most subtle of lures sealing his fate this very instant. To dance with a man is to concentrate a twelvemonth's regulation fire upon him in the fragment of an hour. To pass to courtship without acquaintance, to pass to marriage without courtship, is a skipping of terms reserved for those alone who tread this royal road. She would see how his heart lay by keen observation of them all.

The enterprising lady followed the mumming company through the gate in the white paling, and stood before the open porch. The house was encrusted with heavy thatchings, which dropped between the upper windows: the front, upon which the moonbeams directly played, had originally been white; but a huge pyracanth now darkened the greater portion.

It became at once evident that the dance was proceeding immediately within the surface of the door, no apartment intervening. The brushing of skirts and elbows, sometimes the bumping of shoulders, could be heard against the very panels. Eustacia, though living within two miles of the place, had never seen the interior of this quaint old habitation. Between Captain Vye and the Yeobrights there had never existed much acquaintance, the former having come as a stranger and purchased the long-empty house at Mistover Knap not long before the death of Mrs. Yeobright's husband; and with that event and the departure of her son such friendship as had grown up became quite broken off.

"Is there no passage inside the door, then?" asked Eustacia as they stood within the porch.

"No," said the lad who played the Saracen. "The door opens right upon the front sitting-room, where the spree's going on."

"So that we cannot open the door without stopping the dance."

"That's it. Here we must bide till they have done, for they always bolt the back door after dark."

"They won't be much longer," said Father Christmas.

This assertion, however, was hardly borne out by the event. Again the instruments ended the tune; again they recommenced with as much fire and pathos as if it were the first strain. The air was now that one without any particular beginning, middle, or end, which perhaps, among all the dances

which throng an inspired fiddler's fancy, best conveys the idea of the interminable — the celebrated "Devil's Dream." The fury of personal movement
that was kindled by the fury of the notes could be approximately imagined
by these outsiders under the moon, from the occasional kicks of toes and heels
against the door, whenever the whirl round had been of more than customary
velocity.

The first five minutes of listening was interesting enough to the mummers.
The five minutes extended to ten minutes, and these to a quarter of an hour;
but no signs of ceasing were audible in the lively Dream. The bumping
against the door, the laughter, the stamping, were all as vigorous as ever, and
the pleasure in being outside lessened considerably.

"Why does Mrs. Yeobright give parties of this sort?" Eustacia asked, a
little surprised to hear merriment so pronounced.

"It is not one of her bettermost parlour-parties. She's asked the plain
neighbours and workpeople without drawing any lines, just to give 'em a
good supper and such like. Her son and she wait upon the folks."

"I see," said Eustacia.

"'Tis the last strain, I think," said Saint George, with his ear to the panel.
"A young man and woman have just swung into this corner, and he's saying
to her, 'Ah, the pity; 'tis over for us this time, my own.'"

"Thank God," said the Turkish Knight, stamping, and taking from the
wall the conventional staff that each of the mummers carried. Her boots
being thinner than those of the young men, the hoar had damped her feet and
made them cold.

"Upon my song 'tis another ten minutes for us," said the Valiant Soldier,
looking through the keyhole as the tune modulated into another without
stopping. "Grandfer Cantle is standing in this corner, waiting his turn."

"'Twon't be long; 'tis a six-handed reel," said the Doctor.

"Why not go in, dancing or no? They sent for us," said the Saracen.

"Certainly not," said Eustacia authoritatively, as she paced smartly up
and down from door to gate to warm herself. "We should burst into the
middle of them and stop the dance, and that would be unmannerly."

"He thinks himself somebody because he has had a bit more schooling
than we," said the Doctor.

"You may go to the deuce!" said Eustacia.

There was a whispered conversation between three or four of them, and
one turned to her.

"Will you tell us one thing?" he said, not without gentleness. "Be you
Miss Vye? We think you must be."

"You may think what you like," said Eustacia slowly. "But honourable
lads will not tell tales upon a lady."

"We'll say nothing, miss. That's upon our honour."

"Thank you," she replied.

At this moment the fiddles finished off with a screech, and the serpent
emitted a last note that nearly lifted the roof. When, from the comparative
quiet within, the mummers judged that the dancers had taken their seats,
Father Christmas advanced, lifted the latch, and put his head inside the door.

"Ah, the mummers, the mummers!" cried several guests at once. "Clear a space for the mummers."

Hump-backed Father Christmas then made a complete entry, swinging his huge club, and in a general way clearing the stage for the actors proper, while he informed the company in smart verse that he was come, welcome or welcome not; concluding his speech with

> "Make room, make room, my gallant boys,
>   And give us space to rhyme;
> We've come to show Saint George's play,
>   Upon this Christmas time."

The guests were now arranging themselves at one end of the room, the fiddler was mending a string, the serpent-player was emptying his mouthpiece, and the play began. First of those outside the Valiant Soldier entered, in the interest of Saint George —

> "Here come I, the Valiant Soldier;
>   Slasher is my name";

and so on. This speech concluded with a challenge to the infidel, at the end of which it was Eustacia's duty to enter as the Turkish Knight. She, with the rest who were not yet on, had hitherto remained in the moonlight which streamed under the porch. With no apparent effort or backwardness she came in, beginning —

> "Here come I, a Turkish Knight,
>   Who learnt in Turkish land to fight;
> I'll fight this man with courage bold:
>   If his blood's hot I'll make it cold!"

During her declamation Eustacia held her head erect, and spoke as roughly as she could, feeling pretty secure from observation. But the concentration upon her part necessary to prevent discovery, the newness of the scene, the shine of the candles, and the confusing effect upon her vision of the ribboned visor which hid her features, left her absolutely unable to perceive who were present as spectators. On the further side of a table bearing candles she could faintly discern faces, and that was all.

Meanwhile Jim Starks as the Valiant Soldier had come forward, and, with a glare upon the Turk, replied —

> "If then, thou art that Turkish Knight,
>   Draw out thy sword, and let us fight!"

And fight they did; the issue of the combat being that the Valiant Soldier was slain by a preternaturally inadequate thrust from Eustacia, Jim, in his ardour for genuine histrionic art, coming down like a log upon the stone floor with force enough to dislocate his shoulder. Then, after more words from the Turkish Knight, rather too faintly delivered, and statements that he'd fight Saint George and all his crew, Saint George himself magnificently entered with the well-known flourish —

"Here come I, Saint George, the valiant man,
    With naked sword and spear in hand,
Who fought the dragon and brought him to the slaughter,
And by this won fair Sabra, the King of Egypt's daughter;
    What mortal man would dare to stand
    Before me with my sword in hand?"

This was the lad who had first recognized Eustacia; and when she now, as the Turk, replied with suitable defiance, and at once began the combat, the young fellow took especial care to use his sword as gently as possible. Being wounded, the Knight fell upon one knee, according to the direction. The Doctor now entered, restored the Knight by giving him a draught from the bottle which he carried, and the fight was again resumed, the Turk sinking by degrees until quite overcome — dying as hard in this venerable drama as he is said to do at the present day.

This gradual sinking to the earth was, in fact, one reason why Eustacia had thought that the part of the Turkish Knight, though not the shortest, would suit her best. A direct fall from upright to horizontal, which was the end of the other fighting characters, was not an elegant or decorous part for a girl. But it was easy to die like a Turk, by a dogged decline.

Eustacia was now among the number of the slain, though not on the floor, for she had managed to retire into a sitting position against the clock-case, so that her head was well elevated. The play proceeded between Saint George, the Saracen, the Doctor, and Father Christmas; and Eustacia, having no more to do, for the first time found leisure to observe the scene around, and to search for the form that had drawn her hither.

VI

THE TWO STAND FACE TO FACE

THE room had been arranged with a view to the dancing, the large oak table having been moved back till it stood as a breastwork to the fireplace. At each end, behind, and in the chimney-corner were grouped the guests, many of them being warm-faced and panting, among whom Eustacia cursorily recognized some well-to-do persons from beyond the heath. Thomasin, as she had expected, was not visible, and Eustacia recollected that a light had shone from an upper window when they were outside — the window, probably, of Thomasin's room. A nose, chin, hands, knees, and toes projected from the seat within the chimney opening, which members she found to unite in the person of Grandfer Cantle, Mrs. Yeobright's occasional assistant in the garden, and therefore one of the invited. The smoke went up from an Etna of turf in front of him, played round the notches of the chimney-crook, struck against the salt-box, and got lost among the flitches.

Another part of the room soon riveted her gaze. At the other side of the chimney stood the settle, which is the necessary supplement to a fire so open that nothing less than a strong breeze will carry up the smoke. It is, to the hearths of old-fashioned cavernous fireplaces, what the east belt of trees is to the exposed country estate, or the north wall to the garden. Outside the settle candles gutter, locks of hair wave, young women shiver, and old men sneeze. Inside is Paradise. Not a symptom of a draught disturbs the air; the sitters' backs are as warm as their faces, and songs and old tales are drawn from the occupants by the comfortable heat, like fruit from melon-plants in a frame.

It was, however, not with those who sat in the settle that Eustacia was concerned. A face showed itself with marked distinctness against the dark-tanned wood of the upper part. The owner, who was leaning against the settle's outer end, was Clement Yeobright, or Clym, as he was called here; she knew it could be nobody else. The spectacle constituted an area of two feet in Rembrandt's intensest manner. A strange power in the lounger's appearance lay in the fact that though his whole figure was visible, the ob-server's eye was only aware of his face.

To one of middle age the countenance was that of a young man, though a youth might hardly have seen any necessity for the term of immaturity. But it was really one of those faces which convey less the idea of so many years as its age than of so much experience as its store. The number of their years may have adequately summed up Jared, Mahalaleel, and the rest of the antediluvians, but the age of a modern man is to be measured by the intensity of his history.

The face was well shaped, even excellently. But the mind within was beginning to use it as a mere waste tablet whereon to trace its idiosyncrasies as they developed themselves. The beauty here visible would in no long time be ruthlessly overrun by its parasite, thought, which might just as well have fed upon a plainer exterior where there was nothing it could harm. Had Heaven preserved Yeobright from a wearing habit of meditation, peo-ple would have said, "A handsome man." Had his brain unfolded under sharper contours they would have said, "A thoughtful man." But an inner strenuousness was preying upon an outer symmetry, and they rated his look as singular.

Hence people who began by beholding him ended by perusing him. His countenance was overlaid with legible meanings. Without being thought-worn he yet had certain marks derived from a perception of his surroundings, such as are not unfrequently found on men at the end of the four or five years of endeavour which follow the close of placid pupilage. He already showed that thought is a disease of flesh, and indirectly bore evidence that ideal physical beauty is incompatible with emotional development and a full recognition of the coil of things. Mental luminousness must be fed with the oil of life, even though there is already a physical need for it; and the pitiful sight of two demands on one supply was just showing itself here.

When standing before certain men the philosopher regrets that thinkers are but perishable tissue, the artist that perishable tissue has to think. Thus to deplore, each from his point of view, the mutually destructive interdependence of spirit and flesh would have been instinctive with these in critically observing Yeobright.

As for his look, it was a natural cheerfulness striving against depression from without, and not quite succeeding. The look suggested isolation, but it revealed something more. As is usual with bright natures, the deity that lies ignominiously chained within an ephemeral human carcase shone out of him like a ray.

The effect upon Eustacia was palpable. The extraordinary pitch of excitement that she had reached beforehand would, indeed, have caused her to be influenced by the most commonplace man. She was troubled at Yeobright's presence.

The remainder of the play ended: the Saracen's head was cut off, and Saint George stood as victor. Nobody commented, any more than they would have commented on the fact of mushrooms coming in autumn or snowdrops in spring. They took the piece as phlegmatically as did the actors themselves. It was a phase of cheerfulness which was, as a matter of course, to be passed through every Christmas; and there was no more to be said.

They sang the plaintive chant which follows the play, during which all the dead men rise to their feet in a silent and awful manner, like the ghosts of Napoleon's soldiers in the Midnight Review. Afterwards the door opened, and Fairway appeared on the threshold, accompanied by Christian and another. They had been waiting outside for the conclusion of the play, as the players had waited for the conclusion of the dance.

"Come in, come in," said Mrs. Yeobright; and Clym went forward to welcome them. "How is it you are so late? Grandfer Cantle has been here ever so long, and we thought you'd have come with him, as you live so near one another."

"Well, I should have come earlier," Mr. Fairway said, and paused to look along the beam of the ceiling for a nail to hang his hat on; but, finding his accustomed one to be occupied by the mistletoe, and all the nails in the walls to be burdened with bunches of holly, he at last relieved himself of the hat by ticklishly balancing it between the candle-box and the head of the clock-case. "I should have come earlier, ma'am," he resumed, with a more composed air, "but I know what parties be, and how there's none too much room in folks' houses at such times, so I thought I wouldn't come till you'd got settled a bit."

"And I thought so too, Mrs. Yeobright," said Christian earnestly; "but father there was so eager that he had no manners at all, and left home almost afore 'twas dark. I told him 'twas barely decent in a' old man to come so oversoon; but words be wind."

"Klk! I wasn't going to bide waiting about till half the game was over! I'm as light as a kite when anything's going on!" crowed Grandfer Cantle from the chimney-seat.

Fairway had meanwhile concluded a critical gaze at Yeobright. "Now, you may not believe it," he said to the rest of the room, "but I should never have knowed this gentleman if I had met him anywhere off his own he'th: he's altered so much."

"You too have altered, and for the better, I think, Timothy," said Yeobright, surveying the firm figure of Fairway.

"Master Yeobright, look me over too. I have altered for the better, haven't I, hey?" said Grandfer Cantle, rising, and placing himself something above half an inch from Clym's eye, to induce the most searching criticism.

"To be sure we will," said Fairway, taking the candle and moving it over the surface of the Grandfer's countenance, the subject of his scrutiny irradiating himself with light and pleasant smiles, and giving himself jerks of juvenility.

"You haven't changed much," said Yeobright.

"If there's any difference, Grandfer is younger," appended Fairway decisively.

"And yet not my own doing, and I feel no pride in it," said the pleased ancient. "But I can't be cured of my vagaries; them I plead guilty to. Yes, Master Cantle always was that, as we know. But I am nothing by the side of you, Mister Clym."

"Nor any o' us," said Humphrey, in a low rich tone of admiration, not intended to reach anybody's ears.

"Really, there would have been nobody here who could have stood as decent second to him, or even third, if I hadn't been a soldier in the Bang-up Locals (as we was called for our smartness)," said Grandfer Cantle. "And even as 'tis we all look a little scammish beside him. But in the year four 'twas said there wasn't a finer figure in the whole South Wessex than I, as I looked when dashing past the shop-winders with the rest of our company on the day we ran out o' Budmouth because it was thoughted that Boney had landed round the point. There was I, straight as a young poplar, wi' my firelock, and my bagnet, and my spatterdashes, and my stock sawing my jaws off, and my accoutrements sheening like the seven stars! Yes, neighbours, I was a pretty sight in my soldiering days. You ought to have seen me in four!"

"'Tis his mother's side where Master Clym's figure comes from, bless ye," said Timothy. "I know'd her brothers well. Longer coffins were never made in the whole country of Wessex, and 'tis said that poor George's knees were crumpled up a little e'en as 'twas."

"Coffins, where?" inquired Christian, drawing nearer. "Have the ghost of one appeared to anybody, Master Fairway?"

"No, no. Don't let your mind so mislead your ears, Christian; and be a man," said Timothy reproachfully.

"I will," said Christian. "But now I think o't my shadder last night seemed just the shape of a coffin. What is it a sign of when your shade's like a coffin, neighbours? It can't be nothing to be afeard of, I suppose?"

"Afeard, no!" said the Grandfer. "Faith, I was never afeard of nothing except Boney, or I shouldn't ha' been the soldier I was. Yes, 'tis a thousand pities you didn't see me in four!"

By this time the mummers were preparing to leave; but Mrs. Yeobright stopped them by asking them to sit down and have a little supper. To this invitation Father Christmas, in the name of them all, readily agreed.

Eustacia was happy in the opportunity of staying a little longer. The cold and frosty night without was doubly frigid to her. But the lingering was not without its difficulties. Mrs. Yeobright, for want of room in the larger apartment, placed a bench for the mummers immediately inside the pantry-door, which opened from the sitting-room. Here they seated themselves in a row, the door being left open: thus they were still virtually in the same apartment. Mrs. Yeobright now murmured a few words to her son, who crossed the room to the pantry, striking his head against the mistletoe as he passed, and brought the mummers beef and bread, cake, pastry, mead, and elder-wine, the waiting being done by him and his mother, that the little maid-servant might sit as guest. The mummers doffed their helmets, and began to eat and drink.

"But you will surely have some?" said Clym to the Turkish Knight, as he stood before that warrior, tray in hand. She had refused, and still sat covered, only the sparkle of her eyes being visible between the ribbons which covered her face.

"None, thank you," replied Eustacia.

"He's quite a youngster," said the Saracen apologetically, "and you must excuse him. He's not one of the old set, but have jined us because t'other couldn't come."

"But he will take something?" persisted Yeobright. "Try a glass of mead or elder-wine."

"Yes, you had better try that," said the Saracen. "It will keep the cold out going home-along."

Though Eustacia could not eat without uncovering her face she could drink easily enough beneath her disguise. The elder-wine was accordingly accepted, and the glass vanished inside the ribbons.

At moments during this performance Eustacia was half in doubt about the security of her position; yet it had a fearful joy. A series of attentions paid to her, and yet not to her but to some imaginary person, by the first man she had ever been inclined to adore, complicated her emotions indescribably. She had loved him partly because he was exceptional in this scene, partly because she had determined to love him, chiefly because she was in desperate need of loving somebody after wearying of Wildeve. Believing that she must love him in spite of herself, she had been influenced after the fashion of the second Lord Lyttleton and other persons, who have dreamed that they were to die on a certain day, and by stress of a morbid imagination have actually brought about that event. Once let a maiden admit the possibility of her being stricken with love for someone at a certain hour and place, and the thing is as good as done.

Did anything at this moment suggest to Yeobright the sex of the creature whom that fantastic guise inclosed, how extended was her scope both in feeling and in making others feel, and how far her compass transcended that of her companions in the band? When the disguised Queen of Love appeared before Æneas a preternatural perfume accompanied her presence and betrayed her quality. If such a mysterious emanation ever was projected by the emotions of an earthly woman upon their object, it must have signified

Eustacia's presence to Yeobright now. He looked at her wistfully, then seemed to fall into a reverie, as if he were forgetting what he observed. The momentary situation ended, he passed on, and Eustacia sipped her wine without knowing what she drank. The man for whom she had predetermined to nourish a passion went into the small room, and across it to the further extremity.

The mummers, as has been stated, were seated on a bench, one end of which extended into the small apartment, or pantry, for want of space in the outer room. Eustacia, partly from shyness, had chosen the innermost seat, which thus commanded a view of the interior of the pantry as well as the room containing the guests. When Clym passed down the pantry her eyes followed him in the gloom which prevailed there. At the remote end was a door which, just as he was about to open it for himself, was opened by somebody within; and light streamed forth.

The person was Thomasin, with a candle, looking anxious, pale, and interesting. Yeobright appeared glad to see her, and pressed her hand. "That's right, Tamsie," he said heartily, as though recalled to himself by the sight of her; "you have decided to come down. I am glad of it."

"Hush — no, no," she said quickly. "I only came to speak to you."

"But why not join us?"

"I cannot. At least I would rather not. I am not well enough, and we shall have plenty of time together now you are going to be home a good long holiday."

"It isn't nearly so pleasant without you. Are you really ill?"

"Just a little, my old cousin — here," she said, playfully sweeping her hand across her heart.

"Ah, mother should have asked somebody else to be present tonight, perhaps?"

"O no, indeed. I merely stepped down, Clym, to ask you ——" Here he followed her through the doorway into the private room beyond, and, the door closing, Eustacia and the mummer who sat next to her, the only other witness of the performance, saw and heard no more.

The heat flew to Eustacia's head and cheeks. She instantly guessed tnat Clym, having been home only these two or three days, had not as yet been made acquainted with Thomasin's painful situation with regard to Wildeve; and seeing her living there just as she had been living before he left home, he naturally suspected nothing. Eustacia felt a wild jealousy of Thomasin on the instant. Though Thomasin might possibly have tender sentiments towards another man as yet, how long could they be expected to last when she was shut up here with this interesting and travelled cousin of hers? There was no knowing what affection might not soon break out between the two, so constantly in each other's society, and not a distracting object near. Clym's boyish love for her might have languished, but it might easily be revived again.

Eustacia was nettled by her own contrivances. What a sheer waste of herself to be dressed thus while another was shining to advantage! Had she known the full effect of the encounter she would have moved heaven and earth to get here in a natural manner. The power of her face all lost, the charm of her emotions all disguised, the fascinations of her coquetry denied existence, nothing but a voice left to her: she had a sense of the doom of Echo. "Nobody here respects me," she said. She had overlooked the fact that, in coming as a boy among other boys, she would be treated as a boy. The slight, though of her own causing, and self-explanatory, she was unable to dismiss as unwittingly shown, so sensitive had the situation made her.

Women have done much for themselves in histrionic dress. To look far below those who, like a certain fair personator of Polly Peachum early in the last century, and another of Lydia Languish early in this, have won not only love but ducal coronets into the bargain, whole shoals of them have reached to the initial satisfaction of getting love almost whence they would. But the Turkish Knight was denied even the chance of achieving this by the fluttering ribbons which she dared not brush aside.

Yeobright returned to the room without his cousin. When within two or three feet of Eustacia he stopped, as if again arrested by a thought. He was gazing at her. She looked another way, disconcerted, and wondered how long this purgatory was to last. After lingering a few seconds he passed on again.

To court their own discomfiture by love is a common instinct with certain perfervid women. Conflicting sensations of love, fear, and shame reduced Eustacia to a state of the utmost uneasiness. To escape was her great and immediate desire. The other mummers appeared to be in no hurry to leave; and murmuring to the lad who sat next to her that she preferred waiting for them outside the house, she moved to the door as imperceptibly as possible, opened it, and slipped out.

The calm, lone scene reassured her. She went forward to the palings and leant over them, looking at the moon. She had stood thus but a little time when the door again opened. Expecting to see the remainder of the band Eustacia turned; but no — Clym Yeobright came out as softly as she had done, and closed the door behind him.

He advanced and stood beside her. "I have an odd opinion," he said, "and should like to ask you a question. Are you a woman — or am I wrong?"

"I am a woman."

His eyes lingered on her with great interest. "Do girls often play as mummers now? They never used to."

"They don't now."

"Why did you?"

"To get excitement and shake off depression," she said in low tones.

"What depressed you?"

"Life."

"That's a cause of depression a good many have to put up with."

"Yes."

A long silence. "And do you find excitement?" asked Clym at last.

"At this moment, perhaps."

"Then you are vexed at being discovered?"

"Yes; though I thought I might be."

"I would gladly have asked you to our party had I known you wished to come. Have I ever been acquainted with you in my youth?"

"Never."

"Won't you come in again, and stay as long as you like?"

"No. I wish not to be further recognized."

"Well, you are safe with me." After remaining in thought a minute he added gently, "I will not intrude upon you longer. It is a strange way of meeting, and I will not ask why I find a cultivated woman playing such a part as this."

She did not volunteer the reason which he seemed to hope for, and he wished her good night, going thence round to the back of the house, where he walked up and down by himself for some time before re-entering.

Eustacia, warmed with an inner fire, could not wait for her companions after this. She flung back the ribbons from her face, opened the gate, and at once struck into the heath. She did not hasten along. Her grandfather was in bed at this hour, for she so frequently walked upon the hills on moonlight nights that he took no notice of her comings and goings, and, enjoying himself in his own way, left her to do likewise. A more important subject than that of getting indoors now engrossed her. Yeobright, if he had the least curiosity, would infallibly discover her name. What then? She first felt a sort of exultation at the way in which the adventure had terminated, even though at moments between her exultations she was abashed and blushful. Then this consideration recurred to chill her: What was the use of her exploit? She was at present a total stranger to the Yeobright family. The unreasonable nimbus of romance with which she had encircled that man might be her misery. How could she allow herself to become so infatuated with a stranger? And to fill the cup of her sorrow there would be Thomasin, living day after day in inflammable proximity to him; for she had just learnt that, contrary to her first belief, he was going to stay at home some considerable time.

She reached the wicket at Mistover Knap, but before opening it she turned and faced the heath once more. The form of Rainbarrow stood above the hills, and the moon stood above Rainbarrow. The air was charged with silence and frost. The scene reminded Eustacia of a circumstance which till that moment she had totally forgotten. She had promised to meet Wildeve by the Barrow this very night at eight, to give a final answer to his pleading for an elopement.

She herself had fixed the evening and the hour. He had probably come to the spot, waited there in the cold, and been greatly disappointed.

"Well, so much the better: it did not hurt him," she said serenely. Wildeve had at present the rayless outline of the sun through smoked glass, and she could say such things as that with the greatest facility.

She remained deeply pondering; and Thomasin's winning manner towards her cousin arose again upon Eustacia's mind.

"O that she had been married to Damon before this!" she said. "And she would if it hadn't been for me! If I had only known — if I had only known!"

Eustacia once more lifted her deep stormy eyes to the moonlight, and, sighing that tragic sigh of hers which was so much like a shudder, entered the shadow of the roof. She threw off her trappings in the out-house, rolled them up, and went indoors to her chamber.

VII

A COALITION BETWEEN BEAUTY AND ODDNESS

The old captain's prevailing indifference to his granddaughter's movements left her free as a bird to follow her own courses; but it so happened that he did take upon himself the next morning to ask her why she had walked out so late.

"Only in search of events, grandfather," she said, looking out of the window with that drowsy latency of manner which discovered so much force behind it whenever the trigger was pressed.

"Search of events — one would think you were one of the bucks I knew at one and twenty."

"It is so lonely here."

"So much the better. If I were living in a town my whole time would be taken up in looking after you. I fully expected you would have been home when I returned from the Woman."

"I won't conceal what I did. I wanted an adventure, and I went with the mummers. I played the part of the Turkish Knight."

"No, never? Ha, ha! Good gad! I didn't expect it of you, Eustacia."

"It was my first performance, and it certainly will be my last. Now I have told you — and remember it is a secret."

"Of course. But, Eustacia, you never did — ha! ha! Dammy, how 'twould have pleased me forty years ago! But remember, no more of it, my girl. You may walk on the heath night or day, as you choose, so that you don't bother me; but no figuring in breeches again."

"You need have no fear for me, grandpapa."

Here the conversation ceased, Eustacia's moral training never exceeding in severity a dialogue of this sort, which, if it ever became profitable to good works, would be a result not dear at the price. But her thoughts soon strayed far from her own personality; and, full of a passionate and indescribable solicitude for one to whom she was not even a name, she went forth into the amplitude of tanned wild around her, restless as Ahasuerus the Jew. She was about half a mile from her residence when she beheld a sinister redness arising from a ravine a little way in advance — dull and lurid like a flame in sunlight, and she guessed it to signify Diggory Venn.

When the farmers who had wished to buy in a new stock of reddle during the last month had inquired where Venn was to be found, people replied, "On Egdon Heath." Day after day the answer was the same. Now, since Egdon was populated with heath-croppers and furze-cutters rather than with sheep and shepherds, and the downs where most of the latter were to be found lay some to the north, some to the west of Egdon, his reason for camping about there like Israel in Zin was not apparent. The position was central and occasionally desirable. But the sale of reddle was not Diggory's primary object in remaining on the heath, particularly at so late a period of the year, when most travellers of his class had gone into winter quarters.

Eustacia looked at the lonely man. Wildeve had told her at their last meeting that Venn had been thrust forward by Mrs. Yeobright as one ready and anxious to take his place as Thomasin's betrothed. His figure was perfect, his face young and well outlined, his eye bright, his intelligence keen, and his position one which he could readily better if he chose. But in spite of possibilities it was not likely that Thomasin would accept this Ishmaelitish creature while she had a cousin like Yeobright at her elbow, and Wildeve at the same time not absolutely indifferent. Eustacia was not long in guessing that poor Mrs. Yeobright, in her anxiety for her niece's future, had mentioned this lover to stimulate the zeal of the other. Eustacia was on the side of the Yeobrights now, and entered into the spirit of the aunt's desire.

"Good morning, miss," said the reddleman, taking off his cap of hareskin, and apparently bearing her no ill-will from recollection of their last meeting.

"Good morning, reddleman," she said, hardly troubling to lift her heavily shaded eyes to his. "I did not know you were so near. Is your van here too?"

Venn moved his elbow towards a hollow in which a dense brake of purple-stemmed brambles had grown to such vast dimensions as almost to form a dell. Brambles, though churlish when handled, are kindly shelter in early winter, being the latest of the deciduous bushes to lose their leaves. The roof and chimney of Venn's caravan showed behind the tracery and tangles of the brake.

"You remain near this part?" she asked with more interest.

"Yes, I have business here."

"Not altogether the selling of reddle?"

"It has nothing to do with that."

"It has to do with Miss Yeobright?"

Her face seemed to ask for an armed peace, and he therefore said frankly, "Yes, miss; it is on account of her."

"On account of your approaching marriage with her?"

Venn flushed through his stain. "Don't make sport of me, Miss Vye," he said.

"It isn't true?"

"Certainly not."

She was thus convinced that the reddleman was a mere *pis aller* in Mrs. Yeobright's mind; one, moreover, who had not even been informed of his promotion to that lowly standing. "It was a mere notion of mine," she said quietly; and was about to pass by without further speech, when, looking round to the right, she saw a painfully well-known figure serpentining upwards by one of the little paths which led to the top where she stood. Owing to the necessary windings of his course his back was at present towards them. She glanced quickly round; to escape that man there was only one way. Turning to Venn, she said, "Would you allow me to rest a few minutes in your van? The banks are damp for sitting on."

"Certainly, miss; I'll make a place for you."

She followed him behind the dell of brambles to his wheeled dwelling, into which Venn mounted, placing the three-legged stool just within the door.

"That is the best I can do for you," he said, stepping down and retiring to the path, where he resumed the smoking of his pipe as he walked up and down.

Eustacia bounded into the vehicle and sat on the stool, ensconced from view on the side towards the trackway. Soon she heard the brushing of other feet than the reddleman's, a not very friendly "Good day" uttered by two men in passing each other, and then the dwindling of the footfall of one of them in a direction onwards. Eustacia stretched her neck forward till she caught a glimpse of a receding back and shoulders; and she felt a wretched twinge of misery, she knew not why. It was the sickening feeling which, if the changed heart has any generosity at all in its composition, accompanies the sudden sight of a once-loved one who is beloved no more.

When Eustacia descended to proceed on her way the reddleman came near. "That was Mr. Wildeve who passed, miss," he said slowly, and expressed by his face that he expected her to feel vexed at having been sitting unseen.

"Yes, I saw him coming up the hill," replied Eustacia. "Why should you tell me that?" It was a bold question, considering the reddleman's knowledge of her past love; but her undemonstrative manner had power to repress the opinions of those she deemed remote from her.

"I am glad to hear that you can ask it," said the reddleman bluntly. "And, now I think of it, it agrees with what I saw last night."

"Ah — what was that?" Eustacia wished to leave him, but wished to know.

"Mr. Wildeve stayed at Rainbarrow a long time waiting for a lady who didn't come."

"You waited too, it seems?"

"Yes, I always do. I was glad to see him disappointed. He will be there again tonight."

"To be again disappointed. The truth is, reddleman, that that lady, so far from wishing to stand in the way of Thomasin's marriage with Mr. Wildeve, would be very glad to promote it."

Venn felt much astonishment at this avowal, though he did not show it clearly; that exhibition may greet remarks which are one remove from expectation, but it is usually withheld in complicated cases of two removes and upwards. "Indeed, miss," he replied.

"How do you know that Mr. Wildeve will come to Rainbarrow again tonight?" she asked.

"I heard him say to himself that he would. He's in a regular temper."

Eustacia looked for a moment what she felt, and she murmured, lifting her deep dark eyes anxiously to his, "I wish I knew what to do. I don't want to be uncivil to him; but I don't wish to see him again; and I have some few little things to return to him."

"If you choose to send 'em by me, miss, and a note to tell him that you wish to say no more to him, I'll take it for you quite privately. That would be the most straightforward way of letting him know your mind."

"Very well," said Eustacia. "Come towards my house, and I will bring it out to you."

She went on, and as the path was an infinitely small parting in the shaggy locks of the heath, the reddleman followed exactly in her trail. She saw from a distance that the captain was on the bank sweeping the horizon with his telescope; and bidding Venn to wait where he stood, she entered the house alone.

In ten minutes she returned with a parcel and a note, and said, in placing them in his hand, "Why are you so ready to take these for me?"

"Can you ask that?"

"I suppose you think to serve Thomasin in some way by it. Are you as anxious as ever to help on her marriage?"

Venn was a little moved. "I would sooner have married her myself," he said in a low voice. "But what I feel is that if she cannot be happy without him I will do my duty in helping her to get him, as a man ought."

Eustacia looked curiously at the singular man who spoke thus. What a strange sort of love, to be entirely free from that quality of selfishness which is frequently the chief constituent of the passion, and sometimes its only one! The reddleman's disinterestedness was so well deserving of respect that it overshot respect by being barely comprehended; and she almost thought it absurd.

"Then we are both of one mind at last," she said.

"Yes," replied Venn gloomily. "But if you would tell me, miss, why you take such an interest in her, I should be easier. It is so sudden and strange."

Eustacia appeared at a loss. "I cannot tell you that, reddleman," she said coldly.

Venn said no more. He pocketed the letter, and, bowing to Eustacia, went away.

Rainbarrow had again become blended with night when Wildeve ascended the long acclivity at its base. On his reaching the top a shape grew up from the earth immediately behind him. It was that of Eustacia's emissary. He slapped Wildeve on the shoulder. The feverish young innkeeper and ex-engineer started like Satan at the touch of Ithuriel's spear.

"The meeting is always at eight o'clock, at this place," said Venn, "and here we are — we three."

"We three?" said Wildeve, looking quickly round.

"Yes; you, and I, and she. This is she." He held up the letter and parcel. Wildeve took them wonderingly. "I don't quite see what this means," he said. "How do you come here? There must be some mistake."

"It will be cleared from your mind when you have read the letter. Lanterns for one." The reddleman struck a light, kindled an inch of tallow-candle which he had brought, and sheltered it with his cap.

"Who are you?" said Wildeve, discerning by the candle-light an obscure rubicundity of person in his companion. "You are the reddleman I saw on the hill this morning — why, you are the man who ——"

"Please read the letter."

"If you had come from the other one I shouldn't have been surprised," murmured Wildeve as he opened the letter and read. His face grew serious.

To Mr. WILDEVE.

After some thought I have decided once and for all that we must hold no further communication. The more I consider the matter the more I am convinced that there must be an end to our acquaintance. Had you been uniformly faithful to me throughout these two years you might now have some ground for accusing me of heartlessness; but if you calmly consider what I bore during the period of your desertion, and how I passively put up with your courtship of another without once interfering, you will, I think, own that I have a right to consult my own feelings when you come back to me again. That these are not what they were towards you may, perhaps, be a fault in me, but it is one which you can scarcely reproach me for when you remember how you left me for Thomasin.

The little articles you gave me in the early part of our friendship are returned by the bearer of this letter. They should rightly have been sent back when I first heard of your engagement to her.

EUSTACIA

By the time that Wildeve reached her name the blankness with which he had read the first half of the letter intensified to mortification. "I am made a great fool of, one way and another," he said pettishly. "Do you know what is in this letter?"

The reddleman hummed a tune.

"Can't you answer me?" asked Wildeve warmly.

"Ru-um-tum-tum," sang the reddleman.

Wildeve stood looking on the ground beside Venn's feet, till he allowed his eyes to travel upwards over Diggory's form, as illuminated by the candle, to his head and face. "Ha-ha! Well, I suppose I deserve it, considering how I have played with them both," he said at last, as much to himself as to Venn. "But of all the odd things that ever I knew, the oddest is that you should so run counter to your own interests as to bring this to me."

"My interests?"

"Certainly. 'Twas your interest not to do anything which would send me courting Thomasin again, now she has accepted you — or something like it. Mrs. Yeobright says you are to marry her. 'Tisn't true, then?"

"Good Lord! I heard of this before, but didn't believe it. When did she say so?"

Wildeve began humming as the reddleman had done.

"I don't believe it now," cried Venn.

"Ru-um-tum-tum," sang Wildeve.

"O Lord — how we can imitate!" said Venn contemptuously. "I'll have this out. I'll go straight to her."

Diggory withdrew with an emphatic step, Wildeve's eye passing over his form in withering derision, as if he were no more than a heath-cropper. When the reddleman's figure could no longer be seen, Wildeve himself descended and plunged into the rayless hollow of the vale.

To lose the two women — he who had been the well-beloved of both —

was too ironical an issue to be endured. He could only decently save himself by Thomasin; and once he became her husband, Eustacia's repentance, he thought, would set in for a long and bitter term. It was no wonder that Wildeve, ignorant of the new man at the back of the scene, should have supposed Eustacia to be playing a part. To believe that the letter was not the result of some momentary pique, to infer that she really gave him up to Thomasin, would have required previous knowledge of her transfiguration by that man's influence. Who was to know that she had grown generous in the greediness of a new passion, that in coveting one cousin she was dealing liberally with another, that in her eagerness to appropriate she gave way?

Full of this resolve to marry in haste, and wring the heart of the proud girl, Wildeve went his way.

Meanwhile Diggory Venn had returned to his van, where he stood looking thoughtfully into the stove. A new vista was opened up to him. But, however promising Mrs. Yeobright's views of him might be as a candidate for her niece's hand, one condition was indispensable to the favour of Thomasin herself, and that was a renunciation of his present wild mode of life. In this he saw little difficulty.

He could not afford to wait till the next day before seeing Thomasin and detailing his plan. He speedily plunged himself into toilet operations, pulled a suit of cloth clothes from a box, and in about twenty minutes stood before the van-lantern as a reddleman in nothing but his face, the vermilion shades of which were not to be removed in a day. Closing the door and fastening it with a padlock Venn set off towards Blooms-End.

He had reached the white palings and laid his hand upon the gate when the door of the house opened, and quickly closed again. A female form had glided in. At the same time a man, who had seemingly been standing with the woman in the porch, came forward from the house till he was face to face with Venn. It was Wildeve again.

"Man alive, you've been quick at it," said Diggory sarcastically.

"And you slow, as you will find," said Wildeve. "And," lowering his voice, "you may as well go back again now. I've claimed her, and got her. Good night, reddleman!" Thereupon Wildeve walked away.

Venn's heart sank within him, though it had not risen unduly high. He stood leaning over the palings in an indecisive mood for nearly a quarter of an hour. Then he went up the garden-path, knocked, and asked for Mrs. Yeobright.

Instead of requesting him to enter, she came to the porch. A discourse was carried on between them in low measured tones for the space of ten minutes or more. At the end of the time Mrs. Yeobright went in, and Venn sadly retraced his steps into the heath. When he had again regained his van he lit the lantern, and with an apathetic face at once began to pull off his best clothes, till in the course of a few minutes he reappeared as the confirmed and irretrievable reddleman that he had seemed before.

VIII

FIRMNESS IS DISCOVERED IN A GENTLE HEART

ON THAT evening the interior of Blooms-End, though cosy and comfortable, had been rather silent. Clym Yeobright was not at home. Since the Christmas party he had gone on a few days' visit to a friend about ten miles off.

The shadowy form seen by Venn to part from Wildeve in the porch, and quickly withdraw into the house, was Thomasin's. On entering she threw down a cloak which had been carelessly wrapped round her, and came forward to the light, where Mrs. Yeobright sat at her work-table, drawn up within the settle, so that part of it projected into the chimney-corner.

"I don't like your going out after dark alone, Tamsin," said her aunt quietly, without looking up from her work.

"I have only been just outside the door."

"Well?" inquired Mrs. Yeobright, struck by a change in the tone of Thomasin's voice, and observing her. Thomasin's cheek was flushed to a pitch far beyond that which it had reached before her troubles, and her eyes glittered.

"It was *he* who knocked," she said.

"I thought as much."

"He wishes the marriage to be at once."

"Indeed! What — is he anxious?" Mrs. Yeobright directed a searching look upon her niece. "Why did not Mr. Wildeve come in?"

"He did not wish to. You are not friends with him, he says. He would like the wedding to be the day after tomorrow, quite privately; at the church of his parish — not at ours."

"Oh! And what did you say?"

"I agreed to it," Thomasin answered firmly. "I am a practical woman now. I don't believe in hearts at all. I would marry him under any circumstances since — since Clym's letter."

A letter was lying on Mrs. Yeobright's work-basket, and at Thomasin's words her aunt reopened it, and silently read for the tenth time that day: —

"What is the meaning of this silly story that people are circulating about Thomasin and Mr. Wildeve? I should call such a scandal humiliating if there was the least chance of its being true. How could such a gross falsehood have arisen? It is said that one should go abroad to hear news of home, and I appear to have done it. Of course I contradict the tale everywhere; but it is very vexing, and I wonder how it could have originated. It is too ridiculous that such a girl as Thomasin could so mortify us as to get jilted on the wedding-day. What has she done?"

"Yes," Mrs. Yeobright said sadly, putting down the letter. "If you think you can marry him, do so. And since Mr. Wildeve wishes it to be unceremonious, let it be that too. I can do nothing. It is all in your own hands now. My power over your welfare came to an end when you left this house to go with him to Budmouth." She continued, half in bitterness, "I may almost ask, why do you consult me in the matter at all? If you had gone and married him without saying a word to me, I could hardly have been angry — simply because, poor girl, you can't do a better thing."

"Don't say that and dishearten me."

"You are right; I will not."

"I do not plead for him, aunt. Human nature is weak, and I am not a blind woman to insist that he is perfect. I did think so, but I don't now. But I know my course, and you know that I know it. I hope for the best."

"And so do I, and we will both continue to," said Mrs. Yeobright, rising and kissing her. "Then the wedding, if it comes off, will be on the morning of the very day Clym comes home?"

"Yes. I decided that it ought to be over before he came. After that you can look him in the face, and so can I. Our concealments will matter nothing."

Mrs. Yeobright moved her head in thoughtful assent, and presently said, "Do you wish me to give you away? I am willing to undertake that, you know, if you wish, as I was last time. After once forbidding the banns, I think I can do no less."

"I don't think I will ask you to come," said Thomasin reluctantly, but with decision. "It would be unpleasant, I am almost sure. Better let there be only strangers present, and none of my relations at all. I would rather have it so. I do not wish to do anything which may touch your credit, and I feel that I should be uncomfortable if you were there, after what has passed. I am only your niece, and there is no necessity why you should concern yourself more about me."

"Well, he has beaten us," her aunt said. "It really seems as if he had been playing with you in this way in revenge for my humbling him as I did by standing up against him at first."

"O no, aunt," murmured Thomasin.

They said no more on the subject then. Diggory Venn's knock came soon after; and Mrs. Yeobright, on returning from her interview with him in the porch, carelessly observed, "Another lover has come to ask for you."

"No?"

"Yes; that queer young man Venn."

"Asks to pay his addresses to me?"

"Yes; and I told him he was too late."

Thomasin looked silently into the candle-flame. "Poor Diggory!" she said, and then aroused herself to other things.

The next day was passed in mere mechanical deeds of preparation, both the women being anxious to immerse themselves in these to escape the emotional aspect of the situation. Some wearing apparel and other articles were collected anew for Thomasin, and remarks on domestic details were frequently made, so as to obscure any inner misgivings about her future as Wildeve's wife.

The appointed morning came. The arrangement with Wildeve was that he should meet her at the church, to guard against any unpleasant curiosity which might have affected them had they been seen walking off together in the usual country way.

Aunt and niece stood together in the bedroom where the bride was dressing. The sun, where it could catch it, made a mirror of Thomasin's hair, which she always wore braided. It was braided according to a calendric system: the more important the day the more numerous the strands in the braid. On ordinary working-days she braided it in threes; on ordinary Sundays in fours; at May-polings, gipsyings, and the like, she braided it in fives. Years ago she had said that when she married she would braid it in sevens. She had braided it in sevens today.

"I have been thinking that I will wear my blue silk after all," she said. "It *is* my wedding day, even though there may be something sad about the time. I mean," she added, anxious to correct any wrong impression, "not sad in itself, but in its having had great disappointment and trouble before it."

Mrs. Yeobright breathed in a way which might have been called a sigh. "I almost wish Clym had been at home," she said. "Of course you chose the time because of his absence."

"Partly. I have felt that I acted unfairly to him in not telling him all; but, as it was done not to grieve him, I thought I would carry out the plan to its end, and tell the whole story when the sky was clear."

"You are a practical little woman," said Mrs. Yeobright, smiling. "I wish you and he — no, I don't wish anything. There, it is nine o'clock," she interrupted, hearing a whizz and a dinging downstairs.

"I told Damon I would leave at nine," said Thomasin, hastening out of the room.

Her aunt followed. When Thomasin was going down the little walk from the door to the wicket-gate, Mrs. Yeobright looked reluctantly at her, and said, "It is a shame to let you go alone."

"It is necessary," said Thomasin.

"At any rate," added her aunt with forced cheerfulness, "I shall call upon you this afternoon, and bring the cake with me. If Clym has returned by that time he will perhaps come too. I wish to show Mr. Wildeve that I bear him no ill-will. Let the past be forgotten. Well, God bless you! There, I don't believe in old superstitions, but I'll do it." She threw a slipper at the retreating figure of the girl, who turned, smiled, and went on again.

A few steps further, and she looked back. "Did you call me, aunt?" she tremulously inquired. "Good-bye!"

Moved by an uncontrollable feeling as she looked upon Mrs. Yeobright's worn, wet face, she ran back, when her aunt came forward, and they met again. "O — Tamsie," said the elder, weeping, "I don't like to let you go."

"I — I am ——" Thomasin began, giving way likewise. But, quelling her grief, she said "Good-bye!" again and went on.

Then Mrs. Yeobright saw a little figure wending its way between the scratching furze-bushes, and diminishing far up the valley — a pale-blue spot in a vast field of neutral brown, solitary and undefended except by the power of her own hope.

But the worst feature in the case was one which did not appear in the landscape; it was the man.

The hour chosen for the ceremony by Thomasin and Wildeve had been so timed as to enable her to escape the awkwardness of meeting her cousin Clym, who was returning the same morning. To own to the partial truth of what he had heard would be distressing as long as the humiliating position resulting from the event was unimproved. It was only after a second and successful journey to the altar that she could lift up her head and prove the failure of the first attempt a pure accident.

She had not been gone from Blooms-End more than half an hour when Yeobright came up the road from the other direction and entered the house. "I had an early breakfast," he said to his mother after greeting her. "Now I could eat a little more."

They sat down to the repeated meal, and he went on in a low, anxious voice, apparently imagining that Thomasin had not yet come downstairs, "What's this I have heard about Thomasin and Mr. Wildeve?"

"It is true in many points," said Mrs. Yeobright quietly; "but it is all right now, I hope." She looked at the clock.

"True?"

"Thomasin is gone to him today."

Clym pushed away his breakfast. "Then there is a scandal of some sort, and that's what's the matter with Thomasin. Was it this that made her ill?"

"Yes. Not a scandal: a misfortune. I will tell you all about it, Clym. You must not be angry, but you must listen, and you'll find that what we have done has been done for the best."

She then told him the circumstances. All that he had known of the affair before he had returned from Paris was that there had existed an attachment between Thomasin and Wildeve, which his mother had at first discountenanced, but had since, owing to the arguments of Thomasin, looked upon in a little more favourable light. When she, therefore, proceeded to explain all he was greatly surprised and troubled.

"And she determined that the wedding should be over before you came back," said Mrs. Yeobright, "that there might be no chance of her meeting you, and having a very painful time of it. That's why she has gone to him; they have arranged to be married this morning."

"But I can't understand it," said Yeobright, rising. "'Tis so unlike her. I can see why you did not write to me after her unfortunate return home. But why didn't you let me know when the wedding was going to be — the first time?"

"Well, I felt vexed with her just then. She seemed to me to be obstinate; and when I found that you were nothing in her mind I vowed that she should be nothing in yours. I felt that she was only my niece after all; I told her she might marry, but that I should take no interest in it, and should not bother you about it either."

"It wouldn't have been bothering me. Mother, you did wrong."

"I thought it might disturb you in your business, and that you might throw up your situation, or injure your prospects in some way because of it, so I said nothing. Of course, if they had married at that time in a proper manner, I should have told you at once."

"Tamsin actually being married while we are sitting here!"

"Yes. Unless some accident happens again, as it did the first time. It may, considering he's the same man."

"Yes, and I believe it will. Was it right to let her go? Suppose Wildeve is really a bad fellow?"

"Then he won't come, and she'll come home again."

"You should have looked more into it."

"It is useless to say that," his mother answered, with an impatient look of sorrow. "You don't know how bad it has been here with us all these weeks, Clym. You don't know what a mortification anything of that sort is to a woman. You don't know the sleepless nights we've had in this house, and the almost bitter words that have passed between us since that Fifth of November. I hope never to pass seven such weeks again. Tamsin has not gone outside the door, and I have been ashamed to look anybody in the face; and now you blame me for letting her do the only thing that can be done to set that trouble straight."

"No," he said slowly. "Upon the whole I don't blame you. But just consider how sudden it seems to me. Here was I, knowing nothing; and then I am told all at once that Tamsie is gone to be married. Well, I suppose there was nothing better to do. Do you know, mother," he continued after a moment or two, looking suddenly interested in his own past history, "I once thought of Tamsin as a sweetheart? Yes, I did. How odd boys are! And when I came home and saw her this time she seemed so much more affectionate than usual, that I was quite reminded of those days, particularly on the night of the party, when she was unwell. We had the party just the same — was not that rather cruel to her?"

"It made no difference. I had arranged to give one, and it was not worth while to make more gloom than necessary. To begin by shutting ourselves up and telling you of Tamsin's misfortunes would have been a poor sort of welcome."

Clym remained thinking. "I almost wish you had not had that party," he said; "and for other reasons. But I will tell you in a day or two. We must think of Tamsin now."

They lapsed into silence. "I'll tell you what," said Yeobright again, in a tone which showed some slumbering feeling still. "I don't think it kind to Tamsin to let her be married like this, and neither of us there to keep up her spirits or care a bit about her. She hasn't disgraced herself, or done anything to deserve that. It is bad enough that the wedding should be so hurried and unceremonious, without our keeping away from it in addition. Upon my soul, 'tis almost a shame. I'll go."

"It is over by this time," said his mother with a sigh; "unless they were late, or he ——"

"Then I shall be soon enough to see them come out. I don't quite like your keeping me in ignorance, mother, after all. Really, I half hope he has failed to meet her!"

"And ruined her character?"

"Nonsense: that wouldn't ruin Thomasin."

He took up his hat and hastily left the house. Mrs. Yeobright looked ra-

ther unhappy, and sat still, deep in thought.   But she was not long left
alone.   A few minutes later Clym came back again, and in his company came
Diggory Venn.

"I find there isn't time for me to get there," said Clym.

"Is she married?" Mrs. Yeobright inquired, turning to the reddleman a
face in which a strange strife of wishes, for and against, was apparent.

Venn bowed.   "She is, ma'am."

"How strange it sounds," murmured Clym.

"And he didn't disappoint her this time?" said Mrs. Yeobright.

"He did not.   And there is now no slight on her name.   I was hastening
ath'art to tell you at once, as I saw you were not there."

"How came you to be there?   How did you know it?" she asked.

"I have been in that neighbourhood for some time, and I saw them go in,"
said the reddleman.   "Wildeve came up to the door, punctual as the clock.
I didn't expect it of him."   He did not add, as he might have added, that how
he came to be in that neighbourhood was not by accident; that, since Wildeve's resumption of his right to Thomasin, Venn, with the thoroughness
which was part of his character, had determined to see the end of the episode.

"Who was there?" said Mrs. Yeobright.

"Nobody hardly.   I stood right out of the way, and she did not see me."
The reddleman spoke huskily, and looked into the garden.

"Who gave her away?"

"Miss Vye."

"How very remarkable!   Miss Vye!   It is to be considered an honour, I
suppose."

"Who's Miss Vye?" said Clym.

"Captain Vye's granddaughter, of Mistover Knap."

"A proud girl from Budmouth," said Mrs. Yeobright.   "One not much
to my liking.   People say she's a witch, but of course that's absurd."

The reddleman kept to himself his acquaintance with that fair personage,
and also that Eustacia was there because he went to fetch her, in accordance
with a promise he had previously given as soon as he learnt that the marriage
was to take place.   He merely said, in continuation of the story —

"I was sitting on the churchyard-wall when they came up, one from one
way, the other from the other; and Miss Vye was walking thereabouts,
looking at the head-stones.   As soon as they had gone in I went to the door,
feeling I should like to see it, as I knew her so well.   I pulled off my boots
because they were so noisy, and went up into the gallery.   I saw then that
the parson and clerk were already there."

"How came Miss Vye to have anything to do with it, if she was only on
a walk that way?"

"Because there was nobody else.   She had gone into the church just before me, not into the gallery.   The parson looked round before beginning,
and as she was the only one near he beckoned to her, and she went up to the
rails.   After that, when it came to signing the book, she pushed up her veil
and signed; and Tamsin seemed to thank her for her kindness."   The reddle-

man told the tale thoughtfully, for there lingered upon his vision the changing colour of Wildeve, when Eustacia lifted the thick veil which had concealed her from recognition and looked calmly into his face. "And then," said Diggory sadly, "I came away, for her history as Tamsin Yeobright was over."

"I offered to go," said Mrs. Yeobright regretfully. "But she said it was not necessary."

"Well, it is no matter," said the reddleman. "The thing is done at last as it was meant to be at first, and God send her happiness. Now I'll wish you good morning."

He placed his cap on his head and went out.

From that instant of leaving Mrs. Yeobright's door, the reddleman was seen no more in or about Egdon Heath for a space of many months. He vanished entirely. The nook among the brambles where his van had been standing was as vacant as ever the next morning, and scarcely a sign remained to show that he had been there, excepting a few straws, and a little redness on the turf, which was washed away by the next storm of rain.

The report that Diggory had brought of the wedding, correct as far as it went, was deficient in one significant particular, which had escaped him through his being at some distance back in the church. When Thomasin was tremblingly engaged in signing her name Wildeve had flung towards Eustacia a glance that said plainly, "I have punished you now." She had replied in a low tone — and he little thought how truly — "You mistake; it gives me sincerest pleasure to see her your wife today."

BOOK THIRD: THE FASCINATION

I

"MY MIND TO ME A KINGDOM IS"

IN CLYM YEOBRIGHT's face could be dimly seen the typical countenance of the future. Should there be a classic period to art hereafter, its Pheidias may produce such faces. The view of life as a thing to be put up with, replacing that zest for existence, which was so intense in early civilizations, must ultimately enter so thoroughly into the constitution of the advanced races that its facial expression will become accepted as a new artistic departure. People already feel that a man who lives without disturbing a curve of feature, or setting a mark of mental concern anywhere upon himself, is too far removed from modern perceptiveness to be a modern type. Physically beautiful men — the glory of the race when it was young — are almost an anachronism now; and we may wonder whether, at some time or other, physically beautiful women may not be an anachronism likewise.

The truth seems to be that a long line of disillusive centuries has permanently displaced the Hellenic idea of life, or whatever it may be called. What the Greeks only suspected we know well; what their Æschylus imagined our nursery children feel. That old-fashioned revelling in the general situation grows less and less possible as we uncover the defects of natural laws, and see the quandary that man is in by their operation.

The lineaments which will get embodied in ideals based upon this new recognition will probably be akin to those of Yeobright. The observer's eye was arrested, not by his face as a picture but by his face as a page; not by what it was, but by what it recorded. His features were attractive in the light of symbols, as sounds intrinsically common become attractive in language, and as shapes intrinsically simple became interesting in writing.

He had been a lad of whom something was expected. Beyond this all had been chaos. That he would be successful in an original way, or that he would go to the dogs in an original way, seemed equally probable. The only absolute certainty about him was that he would not stand still in the circumstances amid which he was born.

Hence, when his name was casually mentioned by neighbouring yeomen, the listener said, "Ah, Clym Yeobright: what is he doing now?" When the instinctive question about a person is, What is he doing? it is felt that he will not be found to be, like most of us, doing nothing in particular. There is an indefinite sense that he must be invading some region of singularity, good or bad. The devout hope is that he is doing well. The secret faith is that he is making a mess of it. Half a dozen comfortable market-men, who were habitual callers at the Quiet Woman as they passed by in their carts, were partial to the topic. In fact, though they were not Egdon men, they could hardly avoid it while they sucked their long clay tubes and regarded the heath through the window. Clym had been so inwoven with the heath in his boyhood that hardly anybody could look upon it without thinking of him. So the subject recurred: if he were making a fortune and a name, so much the better for him; if he were making a tragical figure in the world, so much the better for a narrative.

The fact was that Yeobright's fame had spread to an awkward extent before he left home. "It is bad when your fame outruns your means," said the Spanish Jesuit, Gracian. At the age of six he had asked a Scripture riddle: "Who was the first man known to wear breeches?" and applause had resounded from the very verge of the heath. At seven he painted the Battle of Waterloo with tiger-lily pollen and black-currant juice, in the absence of water-colours. By the time he reached twelve he had in this manner been heard of as artist and scholar for at least two miles round. An individual whose fame spreads three or four thousand yards in the time taken by the fame of others similarly situated to travel six or eight hundred, must of necessity have something in him. Possibly Clym's fame, like Homer's, owed something to the accidents of his situation; nevertheless famous he was.

He grew up and was helped out in life. That waggery of fate which started Clive as a writing clerk, Gay as a linen-draper, Keats as a surgeon, and a thousand others in a thousand other odd ways, banished the wild and ascetic heath lad to a trade whose sole concern was with the especial symbols of self-indulgence and vainglory.

The details of this choice of a business for him it is not necessary to give. At the death of his father a neighbouring gentleman had kindly undertaken to give the boy a start; and this assumed the form of sending him to Bud-mouth. Yeobright did not wish to go there, but it was the only feasible open-ing. Thence he went to London; and thence, shortly after, to Paris, where he had remained till now.

Something being expected of him, he had not been at home many days before a great curiosity as to why he stayed on so long began to arise in the heath. The natural term of a holiday had passed, yet he still remained. On the Sunday morning following the week of Thomasin's marriage a discussion on this subject was in progress at a hair-cutting before Fairway's house. Here the local barbering was always done at this hour on this day; to be fol-lowed by the great Sunday wash of the inhabitants at noon, which in its turn was followed by the great Sunday dressing an hour later. On Egdon Heath Sunday proper did not begin till dinner-time, and even then it was a somewhat battered specimen of the day.

These Sunday-morning hair-cuttings were performed by Fairway; the victim sitting on a chopping-block in front of the house, without a coat, and the neighbours gossiping around, idly observing the locks of hair as they rose upon the wind after the snip, and flew away out of sight to the four quarters of the heavens. Summer and winter the scene was the same, unless the wind were more than usually blusterous, when the stool was shifted a few feet round the corner. To complain of cold in sitting out of doors, hatless and coatless, while Fairway told true stories between the cuts of the scissors, would have been to pronounce yourself no man at once. To flinch, exclaim, or move a muscle of the face at the small stabs under the ear received from those instruments, or at scarifications of the neck by the comb, would have been thought a gross breach of good manners, considering that Fairway did it all for nothing. A bleeding about the poll on Sunday afternoons was amply accounted for by the explanation, "I have had my hair cut, you know."

The conversation on Yeobright had been started by a distant view of the young man rambling leisurely across the heath before them.

"A man who is doing well elsewhere wouldn't bide here two or three weeks for nothing," said Fairway. "He's got some project in 's head — depend upon that."

"Well, 'a can't keep a diment shop here," said Sam.

"I don't see why he should have had them two heavy boxes home if he had not been going to bide; and what there is for him to do here the Lord in heaven knows."

Before many more surmises could be indulged in Yeobright had come near; and seeing the hair-cutting group he turned aside to join them. Marching up, and looking critically at their faces for a moment, he said, without in-troduction, "Now, folks, let me guess what you have been talking about."

"Ay, sure, if you will," said Sam.

"About me."

"Now, it is a thing I shouldn't have dreamed of doing, otherwise," said Fairway in a tone of integrity; "but since you have named it, Master Yeo-bright, I'll own that we was talking about 'ee. We were wondering what could keep you home here mollyhorning about when you have made such a world-wide name for yourself in the nick-nack trade — now, that's the truth o't."

"I'll tell you," said Yeobright, with unexpected earnestness. "I am not sorry to have the opportunity. I've come home because, all things considered, I can be a trifle less useless here than anywhere else. But I have only lately found this out. When I first got away from home I thought this place was not worth troubling about. I thought our life here was contemptible. To oil your boots instead of blacking them, to dust your coat with a switch instead of a brush: was there ever anything more ridiculous? I said."

"So 'tis; so 'tis!"

"No, no — you are wrong; it isn't."

"Beg your pardon, we thought that was your maning?"

"Well, this became very depressing as time went on. I found that I was trying to be like people who had hardly anything in common with myself. I was endeavouring to put off one sort of life for another sort of life, which was not better than the life I had known before. It was simply different."

"True; a sight different," said Fairway.

"Yes, Paris must be a taking place," said Humphrey. "Grand shop-winders, trumpets, and drums; and here be we out of doors in all winds and weathers ——"

"But you mistake me," pleaded Clym. "All this was very depressing. But not so depressing as something I next perceived — that my business was the idlest, vainest, most effeminate business that ever a man could be put to. That decided me: I would give it up and try to follow some rational occupation among the people I knew best, and to whom I could be of most use. I have come home; and this is how I mean to carry out my plan. I shall keep a school as near to Egdon as possible, so as to be able to walk over here and have a night-school in my mother's house. But I must study a little at first, to get properly qualified. Now, neighbours, I must go."

And Clym resumed his walk across the heath.

"He'll never carry it out in the world," said Fairway. "In a few weeks he'll learn to see things otherwise."

"'Tis good-hearted of the young man," said another. "But, for my part, I think he had better mind his business."

II

THE NEW COURSE CAUSES DISAPPOINTMENT

YEOBRIGHT loved his kind. He had a conviction that the want of most men was knowledge of a sort which brings wisdom rather than affluence. He wished to raise the class at the expense of individuals rather than individuals at the expense of the class. What was more, he was ready at once to be the first unit sacrificed.

In passing from the bucolic to the intellectual life the intermediate stages are usually two at least, frequently many more; and one of these stages is almost sure to be worldly advance. We can hardly imagine bucolic placidity quickening to intellectual aims without imagining social aims as the transitional phase. Yeobright's local peculiarity was that in striving at high thinking he still cleaved to plain living — nay, wild and meagre living in many respects, and brotherliness with clowns.

He was a John the Baptist who took ennoblement rather than repentance for his text. Mentally he was in a provincial future, that is, he was in many points abreast with the central town thinkers of his date. Much of this development he may have owed to his studious life in Paris, where he had become acquainted with ethical systems popular at the time.

In consequence of this relatively advanced position, Yeobright might have been called unfortunate. The rural world was not ripe for him. A man should be only partially before his time: to be completely to the vanward in aspirations is fatal to fame. Had Philip's warlike son been intellectually so far ahead as to have attempted civilization without bloodshed, he would have been twice the godlike hero that he seemed, but nobody would have heard of an Alexander.

In the interests of renown the forwardness should lie chiefly in the capacity to handle things. Successful propagandists have succeeded because the doctrine they bring into form is that which their listeners have for some time felt without being able to shape. A man who advocates aesthetic effort and deprecates social effort is only likely to be understood by a class to which social effort has become a stale matter. To argue upon the possibility of culture before luxury to the bucolic world may be to argue truly, but it is an attempt to disturb a sequence to which humanity has been long accustomed. Yeobright preaching to the Egdon eremites that they might rise to a serene comprehensiveness without going through the process of enriching themselves, was not unlike arguing to ancient Chaldeans that in ascending from earth to the pure empyrean it was not necessary to pass first into the intervening heaven of ether.

Was Yeobright's mind well-proportioned? No. A well-proportioned mind is one which shows no particular bias; one of which we may safely say that it will never cause its owner to be confined as a madman, tortured as a heretic, or crucified as a blasphemer. Also, on the other hand, that it will never cause him to be applauded as a prophet, revered as a priest, or exalted as a king. Its usual blessings are happiness and mediocrity. It produces the poetry of Rogers, the paintings of West, the statecraft of North, the spiritual guidance of Sumner; enabling its possessors to find their way to wealth, to wind up well, to step with dignity off the stage, to die comfortably in their beds, and to get the decent monument which, in many cases, they deserve. It never would have allowed Yeobright to do such a ridiculous thing as throw up his business to benefit his fellow-creatures.

He walked along towards home without attending to paths. If any one knew the heath well, it was Clym. He was permeated with its scenes, with its substance, and with its odours. He might be said to be its product. His eyes had first opened thereon; with its appearance all the first images of his memory were mingled; his estimate of life had been coloured by it; his toys had been the flint knives and arrow-heads which he found there, wondering why stones should "grow" to such odd shapes; his flowers, the purple bells and yellow gorse; his animal kingdom, the snakes and croppers; his society, its human haunters. Take all the varying hates felt by Eustacia Vye towards the heath, and translate them into loves, and you have the heart of Clym. He gazed upon the wide prospect as he walked, and was glad.

To many persons this Egdon was a place which had slipped out of its century generations ago, to intrude as an uncouth object into this. It was an obsolete thing, and few cared to study it. How could this be otherwise in the days of square fields, plashed hedges, and meadows watered on a plan so rectangular that on a fine day they look like silver gridirons? The farmer, in his ride, who could smile at artificial grasses, look with solicitude at the coming corn, and sigh with sadness at the fly-eaten turnips, bestowed upon the distant upland of heath nothing better than a frown. But as for Yeobright, when he looked from the heights on his way he could not help indulging in a barbarous satisfaction at observing that, in some of the attempts at reclamation from the waste, tillage, after holding on for a year or two, had receded again in despair, the ferns and furze-tufts stubbornly reasserting themselves.

He descended into the valley, and soon reached his home at Blooms-End. His mother was snipping dead leaves from the window-plants. She looked up at him as if she did not understand the meaning of his long stay with her; her face had worn that look for several days. He could perceive that the curiosity which had been shown by the hair-cutting group amounted in his mother to concern. But she had asked no question with her lips, even when the arrival of his trunks suggested that he was not going to leave her soon. Her silence besought an explanation of him more loudly than words.

"I am not going back to Paris again, mother," he said. "At least, in my old capacity. I have given up the business."

Mrs. Yeobright turned in pained surprise. "I thought something was amiss, because of the boxes. I wonder you did not tell me sooner."

"I ought to have done it. But I have been in doubt whether you would be pleased with my plan. I was not quite clear on a few points myself. I am going to take an entirely new course."

"I am astonished, Clym. How can you want to do better than you've been doing?"

"Very easily. But I shall not do better in the way you mean; I suppose it will be called doing worse. But I hate that business of mine, and I want to do some worthy thing before I die. As a schoolmaster I think to do it — a schoolmaster to the poor and ignorant, to teach them what nobody else will."

"After all the trouble that has been taken to give you a start, and when there is nothing to do but to keep straight on towards affluence, you say you will be a poor man's schoolmaster. Your fancies will be your ruin, Clym."

Mrs. Yeobright spoke calmly, but the force of feeling behind the words was but too apparent to one who knew her as well as her son did. He did not answer. There was in his face that hopelessness of being understood which comes when the objector is constitutionally beyond the reach of a logic that, even under favouring conditions, is almost too coarse a vehicle for the subtlety of the argument.

No more was said on the subject till the end of dinner. His mother then began, as if there had been no interval since the morning. "It disturbs me, Clym, to find that you have come home with such thoughts as those. I hadn't the least idea that you meant to go backward in the world by your own free choice. Of course, I have always supposed you were going to push straight on, as other men do — all who deserve the name — when they have been put in a good way of doing well."

"I cannot help it," said Clym, in a troubled tone. "Mother, I hate the flashy business. Talk about men who deserve the name, can any man deserving the name waste his time in that effeminate way, when he sees half the world going to ruin for want of somebody to buckle to and teach them how to breast the misery they are born to? I get up every morning and see the whole creation groaning and travailing in pain, as St. Paul says, and yet there am I, trafficking in glittering splendours with wealthy women and titled libertines, and pandering to the meanest vanities — I, who have health and strength enough for anything. I have been troubled in my mind about it all the year, and the end is that I cannot do it any more."

"Why can't you do it as well as others?"

"I don't know, except that there are many things other people care for which I don't; and that's partly why I think I ought to do this. For one thing, my body does not require much of me. I cannot enjoy delicacies; good things are wasted upon me. Well, I ought to turn that defect to advantage, and by being able to do without what other people require I can spend what such things cost upon anybody else."

Now, Yeobright, having inherited some of these very instincts from the woman before him, could not fail to awaken a reciprocity in her through her feelings, if not by arguments, disguise it as she might for his good. She spoke with less assurance. "And yet you might have been a wealthy man if you had only persevered. Manager to that large diamond establishment — what better can a man wish for? What a post of trust and respect! I suppose you will be like your father; like him, you are getting weary of doing well."

"No," said her son; "I am not weary of that, though I am weary of what you mean by it. Mother, what is doing well?"

Mrs. Yeobright was far too thoughtful a woman to be content with ready definitions, and, like the "What is wisdom?" of Plato's Socrates, and the "What is truth?" of Pontius Pilate, Yeobright's burning question received no answer.

The silence was broken by the clash of the garden gate, a tap at the door, and its opening. Christian Cantle appeared in the room in his Sunday clothes.

It was the custom on Egdon to begin the preface to a story before absolutely entering the house, so as to be well in for the body of the narrative by the time visitor and visited stood face to face. Christian had been saying to them while the door was leaving its latch, "To think that I, who go from home but once in a while, and hardly then, should have been there this morning!"

"'Tis news you have brought us, then, Christian?" said Mrs. Yeobright.

"Ay, sure, about a witch, and ye must overlook my time o' day; for, says I, 'I must go and tell 'em, though they won't have half done dinner.' I assure ye it made me shake like a driven leaf. Do ye think any harm will come o't?"

"Well — what?"

"This morning at church we was all standing up, and the pa'son said, 'Let us pray.' 'Well,' thinks I, 'one may as well kneel as stand'; so down I went; and, more than that, all the rest were as willing to oblige the man as I. We hadn't been hard at it for more than a minute when a most terrible screech sounded through church, as if somebody had just gied up their heart's blood. All the folk jumped up, and then we found that Susan Nunsuch had pricked Miss Vye with a long stocking-needle, as she had threatened to do as soon as ever she could get the young lady to church, where she don't come very often. She've waited for this chance for weeks, so as to draw her blood and put an end to the bewitching of Susan's children that has been carried on so long. Sue followed her into church, sat next to her, and as soon as she could find a chance in went the stocking-needle into my lady's arm."

"Good heaven, how horrid!" said Mrs. Yeobright.

"Sue pricked her that deep that the maid fainted away; and as I was afeard there might be some tumult among us, I got behind the bass-viol and didn't see no more. But they carried her out into the air, 'tis said; but when they looked round for Sue she was gone. What a scream that girl gied, poor thing! There were the pa'son in his surplice holding up his hand and saying, 'Sit down, my good people, sit down!' But the deuce a bit would they sit down. O, and what d'ye think I found out, Mrs. Yeobright? The pa'son wears a suit of clothes under his surplice! — I could see his black sleeve when he held up his arm."

"'Tis a cruel thing," said Yeobright.

"Yes," said his mother.

"The nation ought to look into it," said Christian. "Here's Humphrey coming, I think."

In came Humphrey. "Well, have ye heard the news? But I see you have. 'Tis a very strange thing that whenever one of Egdon folk goes to church some rum job or other is sure to go on. The last time one of us was there was when neighbour Fairway went in the fall; and that was the day you forbad the banns, Mrs. Yeobright."

"Has this cruelly treated girl been able to walk home?" said Clym.

"They say she got better, and went home very well. And now I've told it I must be moving homeward myself."

"And I," said Humphrey. "Truly now we shall see if there's anything in what folks say about her."

When they were gone into the heath again Yeobright said quietly to his mother, "Do you think I have turned teacher too soon?"

"It is right that there should be schoolmasters, and missionaries, and all such men," she replied. "But it is right, too, that I should try to lift you out of this life into something richer, and that you should not come back again, and be as if I had not tried at all."

Later in the day Sam, the turf-cutter, entered. "I've come a-borrowing, Mrs. Yeobright. I suppose you have heard what's been happening to the beauty on the hill?"

"Yes, Sam: half a dozen have been telling us."

"Beauty?" said Clym.

"Yes, tolerably well-favoured," Sam replied. "Lord! all the country owns that 'tis one of the strange things in the world that such a woman should have come to live up there."

"Dark or fair?"

"Now, though I've seen her twenty times, that's a thing I cannot call to mind."

"Darker than Tamsin," murmured Mrs. Yeobright.

"A woman who seems to care for nothing at all, as you may say."

"She is melancholy then?" inquired Clym.

"She mopes about by herself, and don't mix in with the people."

"Is she a young lady inclined for adventures?"

"Not to my knowledge."

"Doesn't join in with the lads in their games, to get some sort of excitement in this lonely place?"

"No."

"Mumming, for instance?"

"No. Her notions be different. I should rather say her thoughts were far away from here, with lords and ladies she'll never know, and mansions she'll never see again."

Observing that Clym appeared singularly interested Mrs. Yeobright said rather uneasily to Sam, "You see more in her than most of us do. Miss Vye is to my mind too idle to be charming. I have never heard that she is of any use to herself or to other people. Good girls don't get treated as witches even on Egdon."

"Nonsense — that proves nothing either way," said Yeobright.

"Well, of course I don't understand such niceties," said Sam, withdrawing from a possibly unpleasant argument; "and what she is we must wait for time to tell us. The business that I have really called about is this, to borrow the longest and strongest rope you have. The captain's bucket has dropped into the well, and they are in want of water; and as all the chaps are at home today we think we can get it out for him. We have three cart-ropes already, but they won't reach to the bottom."

Mrs. Yeobright told him that he might have whatever ropes he could find in the outhouse, and Sam went out to search. When he passed by the door Clym joined him, and accompanied him to the gate.

"Is this young witch-lady going to stay long at Mistover?" he asked.

"I should say so."

"What a cruel shame to ill-use her! She must have suffered greatly — more in mind than in body."

"'Twas a graceless trick — such a handsome girl, too. You ought to see her, Mr. Yeobright, being a young man come from far, and with a little more to show for your years than most of us."

"Do you think she would like to teach children?" said Clym.

Sam shook his head. "Quite a different sort of body from that, I reckon."

"O, it was merely something which occurred to me. It would of course be necessary to see her and talk it over — not an easy thing, by the way, for my family and hers are not very friendly."

"I'll tell you how you mid see her, Mr. Yeobright," said Sam. "We are going to grapple for the bucket at six o'clock tonight at her house, and you could lend a hand. There's five or six coming, but the well is deep, and another might be useful, if you don't mind appearing in that shape. She's sure to be walking round."

"I'll think of it," said Yeobright; and they parted.

He thought of it a good deal; but nothing more was said about Eustacia inside the house at that time. Whether this romantic martyr to superstition and the melancholy mummer he had conversed with under the full moon were one and the same person remained as yet a problem.

III

THE FIRST ACT IN A TIMEWORN DRAMA

The afternoon was fine, and Yeobright walked on the heath for an hour with his mother. When they reached the lofty ridge which divided the valley of Blooms-End from the adjoining valley they stood still and looked round. The Quiet Woman Inn was visible on the low margin of the heath in one direction, and afar on the other hand rose Mistover Knap.

"You mean to call on Thomasin?" he inquired.

"Yes. But you need not come this time," said his mother.

"In that case I'll branch off here, mother. I am going to Mistover."

Mrs. Yeobright turned to him inquiringly.

"I am going to help them get the bucket out of the captain's well," he continued. "As it is so very deep I may be useful. And I should like to see this Miss Vye — not so much for her good looks as for another reason."

"Must you go?" his mother asked.

"I thought to."

And they parted. "There is no help for it," murmured Clym's mother gloomily as he withdrew. "They are sure to see each other. I wish Sam would carry his news to other houses than mine."

Clym's retreating figure got smaller and smaller as it rose and fell over the hillocks on his way. "He is tender-hearted," said Mrs. Yeobright to herself while she watched him; "otherwise it would matter little. How he's going on!"

He was, indeed, walking with a will over the furze, as straight as a line, as if his life depended upon it. His mother drew a long breath, and turned to go back by the way she had come. The evening films began to make nebulous pictures of the valleys, but the high lands still were raked by the declining rays of the winter sun, which glanced on Clym as he walked forward, eyed by every rabbit and fieldfare around, a long shadow advancing in front of him.

On drawing near to the furze-covered bank and ditch which fortified the captain's dwelling he could hear voices within, signifying that operations had been already begun. At the side-entrance gate he stopped and looked over.

Half a dozen able-bodied men were standing in a line from the well-mouth, holding a rope which passed over the well-roller into the depths below. Fairway, with a piece of smaller rope round his body, made fast to one of the standards, to guard against accidents, was leaning over the opening, his right hand clasping the vertical rope that descended into the well.

"Now, silence, folks," said Fairway.

The talking ceased, and Fairway gave a circular motion to the rope, as if he were stirring batter. At the end of a minute a dull splashing reverberated from the bottom of the well; the helical twist he had imparted to the rope had reached the grapnel below.

"Haul!" said Fairway; and the men who held the rope began to gather it over the wheel.

"I think we've got sommat," said one of the haulers-in.

"Then pull steady," said Fairway.

They gathered up more and more, till a regular dripping into the well could be heard below. It grew smarter with the increasing height of the bucket, and presently a hundred and fifty feet of rope had been pulled in.

Fairway then lit a lantern, tied it to another cord, and began lowering it into the well beside the first. Clym came forward and looked down. Strange humid leaves, which knew nothing of the seasons of the year, and quaint-natured moss were revealed on the well-side as the lantern descended; till its rays fell upon a confused mass of rope and bucket dangling in the dank, dark air.

"We've only got en by the edge of the hoop — steady, for God's sake!" said Fairway.

They pulled with the greatest gentleness, till the wet bucket appeared about two yards below them, like a dead friend come to earth again. Three or four hands were stretched out, then jerk went the rope, whizz went the wheel, the two foremost haulers fell backward, the beating of a falling body was heard, receding down the sides of the well, and a thunderous uproar arose at the bottom. The bucket was gone again.

"Damn the bucket!" said Fairway.

"Lower again," said Sam.

"I'm as stiff as a ram's horn stooping so long," said Fairway, standing up and stretching himself till his joints creaked.

"Rest a few minutes, Timothy," said Yeobright. "I'll take your place."

The grapnel was again lowered. Its smart impact upon the distant water reached their ears like a kiss, whereupon Yeobright knelt down, and leaning over the well began dragging the grapnel round and round as Fairway had done.

"Tie a rope round him — it is dangerous!" cried a soft and anxious voice somewhere above them.

Everybody turned. The speaker was a woman, gazing down upon the group from an upper window, whose panes blazed in the ruddy glare from the west. Her lips were parted and she appeared for the moment to forget where she was.

The rope was accordingly tied round his waist, and the work proceeded. At the next haul the weight was not heavy, and it was discovered that they had only secured a coil of the rope detached from the bucket. The tangled mass was thrown into the background; Humphrey took Yeobright's place, and the grapnel was lowered again.

Yeobright retired to the heap of recovered rope in a meditative mood. Of the identity between the lady's voice and that of the melancholy mummer he had not a moment's doubt. "How thoughtful of her!" he said to himself.

Eustacia, who had reddened when she perceived the effect of her exclamation upon the group below, was no longer to be seen at the window, though Yeobright scanned it wistfully. While he stood there the men at the well succeeded in getting up the bucket without a mishap. One of them then went to inquire for the captain, to learn what orders he wished to give for mending the well-tackle. The captain proved to be away from home; and Eustacia appeared at the door and came out. She had lapsed into an easy and dignified calm, far removed from the intensity of life in her words of solicitude for Clym's safety.

"Will it be possible to draw water here tonight?" she inquired.

"No, miss; the bottom of the bucket is clean knocked out. And as we can do no more now we'll leave off, and come again tomorrow morning."

"No water," she murmured, turning away.

"I can send you up some from Blooms-End," said Clym, coming forward and raising his hat as the men retired.

Yeobright and Eustacia looked at each other for one instant, as if each had in mind those few moments during which a certain moonlit scene was common to both. With the glance the calm fixity of her features sublimed itself to an expression of refinement and warmth: it was like garish noon rising to the dignity of sunset in a couple of seconds.

"Thank you; it will hardly be necessary," she replied.

"But if you have no water?"

"Well, it is what I call no water," she said, blushing, and lifting her long-lashed eyelids as if to lift them were a work requiring consideration. "But my grandfather calls it water enough. This is what I mean."

She moved away a few yards, and Clym followed. When she reached the corner of the enclosure, where the steps were formed for mounting the boundary bank, she sprang up with a lightness which seemed strange after her listless movement towards the well. It incidentally showed that her apparent languor did not arise from lack of force.

Clym ascended behind her, and noticed a circular burnt patch at the top of the bank. "Ashes?" he said.

"Yes," said Eustacia. "We had a little bonfire here last Fifth of November, and those are the marks of it."

On that spot had stood the fire she had kindled to attract Wildeve.

"That's the only kind of water we have," she continued, tossing a stone into the pool, which lay on the outside of the bank like the white of an eye without its pupil. The stone fell with a flounce, but no Wildeve appeared on the other side, as on a previous occasion there. "My grandfather says he lived for more than twenty years at sea on water twice as bad as that," she went on, "and considers it quite good enough for us here on an emergency."

"Well, as a matter of fact there are no impurities in the water of these pools at this time of the year. It has only just rained into them."

She shook her head. "I am managing to exist in a wilderness, but I cannot drink from a pond," she said.

Clym looked towards the well, which was now deserted, the men having gone home. "It is a long way to send for spring-water," he said, after a silence. "But since you don't like this in the pond, I'll try to get you some myself." He went back to the well. "Yes, I think I could do it by tying on this pail."

"But, since I would not trouble the men to get it, I cannot in conscience let you."

"I don't mind the trouble at all."

He made fast the pail to the long coil of rope, put it over the wheel, and allowed it to descend by letting the rope slip through his hands. Before it had gone far, however, he checked it.

"I must make fast the end first, or we may lose the whole," he said to Eustacia, who had drawn near. "Could you hold this a moment, while I do it — or shall I call your servant?"

"I can hold it," said Eustacia; and he placed the rope in her hands, going then to search for the end.

"I suppose I may let it slip down?" she inquired.

"I would advise you not to let it go far," said Clym. "It will get much heavier, you will find."

However, Eustacia had begun to pay out. While he was tying she cried, "I cannot stop it!"

Clym ran to her side, and found he could only check the rope by twisting the loose part round the upright post, when it stopped with a jerk. "Has it hurt you?"

"Yes," she replied.

"Very much?"

"No; I think not." She opened her hands. One of them was bleeding; the rope had dragged off the skin. Eustacia wrapped it in her handkerchief.

"You should have let go," said Yeobright. "Why didn't you?"

"You said I was to hold on.... This is the second time I have been wounded today."

"Ah, yes; I have heard of it. I blush for my native Egdon. Was it a serious injury you received in church, Miss Vye?"

There was such an abundance of sympathy in Clym's tone that Eustacia slowly drew up her sleeve and disclosed her round white arm. A bright red spot appeared on its smooth surface, like a ruby on Parian marble.

"There it is," she said, putting her finger against the spot.

"It was dastardly of the woman," said Clym. "Will not Captain Vye get her punished?"

"He is gone from home on that very business. I did not know that I had such a magic reputation."

"And you fainted?" said Clym, looking at the scarlet little puncture as if he would like to kiss it and make it well.

"Yes, it frightened me. I had not been to church for a long time. And now I shall not go again for ever so long — perhaps never. I cannot face their eyes after this. Don't you think it dreadfully humiliating? I wished I was dead for hours after, but I don't mind now."

"I have come to clean away these cobwebs," said Yeobright. "Would you like to help me — by high class teaching? We might benefit them much."

"I don't quite feel anxious to. I have not much love for my fellow-creatures. Sometimes I quite hate them."

"Still I think that if you were to hear my scheme you might take an interest in it. There is no use in hating people — if you hate anything, you should hate what produced them."

"Do you mean Nature? I hate her already. But I shall be glad to hear your scheme at any time."

The situation had now worked itself out, and the next natural thing was for them to part. Clym knew this well enough, and Eustacia made a move of conclusion; yet he looked at her as if he had one word more to say. Perhaps if he had not lived in Paris it would never have been uttered.

"We have met before," he said, regarding her with rather more interest than was necessary.

"I do not own it," said Eustacia, with a repressed, still look.

"But I may think what I like."

"Yes."

"You are lonely here."

"I cannot endure the heath, except in its purple season. The heath is a cruel taskmaster to me."

"Can you say so?" he asked. "To my mind it is most exhilarating, and strengthening, and soothing. I would rather live on these hills than anywhere else in the world."

"It is well enough for artists; but I never would learn to draw."

"And there is a very curious Druidical stone just out there." He threw a pebble in the direction signified. "Do you often go to see it?"

"I was not even aware that there existed any such curious Druidical stone. I am aware that there are Boulevards in Paris."

Yeobright looked thoughtfully on the ground. "That means much," he said.

"It does indeed," said Eustacia.

"I remember when I had the same longing for town bustle. Five years of a great city would be a perfect cure for that."

"Heaven send me such a cure! Now, Mr. Yeobright, I will go indoors and plaster my wounded hand."

They separated, and Eustacia vanished in the increasing shade. She seemed full of many things. Her past was a blank, her life had begun. The effect upon Clym of this meeting he did not fully discover till some time after. During his walk home his most intelligible sensation was that his scheme had somehow become glorified. A beautiful woman had been intertwined with it.

On reaching the house he went up to the room which was to be made his study, and occupied himself during the evening in unpacking his books from the boxes and arranging them on shelves. From another box he drew a lamp and a can of oil. He trimmed the lamp, arranged his table, and said, "Now, I am ready to begin."

He rose early the next morning, read two hours before breakfast by the light of his lamp — read all the morning, all the afternoon. Just when the sun was going down his eyes felt weary, and he leant back in his chair.

His room overlooked the front of the premises and the valley of the heath beyond. The lowest beams of the winter sun threw the shadow of the house over the palings, across the grass margin of the heath, and far up the vale, where the chimney outlines and those of the surrounding tree-tops stretched forth in long dark prongs. Having been seated at work all day, he decided to take a turn upon the hills before it got dark; and, going out forthwith, he struck across the heath towards Mistover.

It was an hour and a half later when he again appeared at the garden gate. The shutters of the house were closed, and Christian Cantle, who had been wheeling manure about the garden all day, had gone home. On entering he found that his mother, after waiting a long time for him, had finished her meal.

"Where have you been, Clym?" she immediately said. "Why didn't you tell me that you were going away at this time?"

"I have been on the heath."

"You'll meet Eustacia Vye if you go up there."

Clym paused a minute. "Yes, I met her this evening," he said, as though it were spoken under the sheer necessity of preserving honesty.

"I wondered if you had."

"It was no appointment."

"No; such meetings never are."

"But you are not angry, mother?"

"I can hardly say that I am not. Angry? No. But when I consider the usual nature of the drag which causes men of promise to disappoint the world I feel uneasy."

"You deserve credit for the feeling, mother. But I can assure you that you need not be disturbed by it on my account."

"When I think of you and your new crotchets," said Mrs. Yeobright, with some emphasis, "I naturally don't feel so comfortable as I did a twelvemonth ago. It is incredible to me that a man accustomed to the attractive women of Paris and elsewhere should be so easily worked upon by a girl in a heath. You could just as well have walked another way."

"I had been studying all day."

"Well, yes," she added more hopefully, "I have been thinking that you might get on as a schoolmaster, and rise that way, since you really are determined to hate the course you were pursuing."

Yeobright was unwilling to disturb this idea, though his scheme was far enough removed from one wherein the education of youth should be made a mere channel of social ascent. He had no desires of that sort. He had reached the stage in a young man's life when the grimness of the general human situation first becomes clear; and the realization of this causes ambition to halt awhile. In France it is not uncustomary to commit suicide at this stage; in England we do much better, or much worse, as the case may be.

The love between the young man and his mother was strangely invisible now. Of love it may be said, the less earthly the less demonstrative. In its absolutely indestructible form it reaches a profundity in which all exhibition of itself is painful. It was so with these. Had conversations between them been overheard, people would have said, "How cold they are to each other!"

His theory and his wishes about devoting his future to teaching had made an impression on Mrs. Yeobright. Indeed, how could it be otherwise when he was a part of her — when their discourses were as if carried on between the right and the left hands of the same body? He had despaired of reaching her by argument; and it was almost as a discovery to him that he could reach her by a magnetism which was as superior to words as words are to yells.

Strangely enough he began to feel now that it would not be so hard to persuade her who was his best friend that comparative poverty was essentially the higher course for him, as to reconcile to his feelings the act of persuading her. From every provident point of view his mother was so undoubtedly right, that he was not without a sickness of heart in finding he could shake her.

She had a singular insight into life, considering that she had never mixed with it. There are instances of persons who, without clear ideas of the things they criticize, have yet had clear ideas of the relations of those things. Blacklock, a poet blind from his birth, could describe visual objects with accuracy; Professor Sanderson, who was also blind, gave excellent lectures on colour, and taught others the theory of ideas which they had and he had not. In the social sphere these gifted ones are mostly women; they can watch a world which they never saw, and estimate forces of which they have only heard. We call it intuition.

What was the great world to Mrs. Yeobright? A multitude whose tendencies could be perceived, though not its essences. Communities were seen by her as from a distance; she saw them as we see the throngs which cover the canvases of Sallaert, Van Alsloot, and others of that school — vast masses of beings, jostling, zigzagging, and processioning in definite directions, but whose features are indistinguishable by the very comprehensiveness of the view.

One could see that, as far as it had gone, her life was very complete on its reflective side. The philosophy of her nature, and its limitation by circumstances, was almost written in her movements. They had a majestic foundation, though they were far from being majestic; and they had a groundwork of assurance, but they were not assured. As her once elastic walk had become deadened by time, so had her natural pride of life been hindered in its blooming by her necessities.

The next slight touch in the shaping of Clym's destiny occurred a few days after. A barrow was opened on the heath, and Yeobright attended the operation, remaining away from his study during several hours. In the afternoon Christian returned from a journey in the same direction, and Mrs. Yeobright questioned him.

"They have dug a hole, and they have found things like flower-pots upside down, Mis'ess Yeobright; and inside these be real charnel bones. They have carried 'em off to men's houses; but I shouldn't like to sleep where they will bide. Dead folks have been known to come and claim their own. Mr. Yeobright had got one pot of the bones, and was going to bring 'em home — real skellington bones — but 'twas ordered otherwise. You'll be relieved to hear that he gave away his, pot and all, on second thoughts; and a blessed thing for ye, Mis'ess Yeobright, considering the wind o' nights."

"Gave it away?"

"Yes. To Miss Vye. She has a cannibal taste for such churchyard furniture seemingly."

"Miss Vye was there too?"

"Ay, 'a b'lieve she was."

When Clym came home, which was shortly after, his mother said, in a curious tone, "The urn you had meant for me you gave away."

Yeobright made no reply; the current of her feeling was too pronounced to admit it.

The early weeks of the year passed on. Yeobright certainly studied at home, but he also walked much abroad, and the direction of his walk was always towards some point of a line between Mistover and Rainbarrow.

The month of March arrived, and the heath showed its first faint signs of awakening from winter trance. The awakening was almost feline in its stealthiness. The pool outside the bank by Eustacia's dwelling, which seemed as dead and desolate as ever to an observer who moved and made noises in his observation, would gradually disclose a state of great animation when silently watched awhile. A timid animal world had come to life for the season. Little tadpoles and efts began to bubble up through the water, and to race along beneath it; toads made noises like very young ducks, and advanced to the margin in twos and threes; overhead, bumble-bees flew hither and thither in the thickening light, their drone coming and going like the sound of a gong.

On an evening such as this Yeobright descended into the Blooms-End valley from beside that very pool, where he had been standing with another person quite silently and quite long enough to hear all this puny stir of resurrection in nature; yet he had not heard it. His walk was rapid as he came down, and he went with a springy tread. Before entering upon his mother's premises he stopped and breathed. The light which shone forth on him from the window revealed that his face was flushed and his eye bright. What it did not show was something which lingered upon his lips like a seal set there. The abiding presence of this impress was so real that he hardly dared to enter the house, for it seemed as if his mother might say, "What red spot is that glowing upon your mouth so vividly?"

But he entered soon after. The tea was ready, and he sat down opposite his mother. She did not speak many words; and as for him, something had been just done and some words had been just said on the hill which prevented him from beginning a desultory chat. His mother's taciturnity was not without ominousness, but he appeared not to care. He knew why she said so little, but he could not remove the cause of her bearing towards him. These half-silent sittings were far from uncommon with them now. At last Yeobright made a beginning of what was intended to strike at the whole root of the matter.

"Five days have we sat like this at meals with scarcely a word. What's the use of it, mother?"

"None," said she, in a heart-swollen tone. "But there is only too good a reason."

"Not when you know all. I have been wanting to speak about this, and I am glad the subject is begun. The reason, of course, is Eustacia Vye. Well, I confess I have seen her lately, and have seen her a good many times."

"Yes, yes; and I know what that amounts to. It troubles me, Clym. You are wasting your life here; and it is solely on account of her. If it had not been for that woman you would never have entertained this teaching scheme at all."

Clym looked hard at his mother. "You know that is not it," he said.

"Well, I know you had decided to attempt it before you saw her; but that would have ended in intentions. It was very well to talk of, but ridiculous to put in practice. I fully expected that in the course of a month or two you would have seen the folly of such self-sacrifice, and would have been by this time back again to Paris in some business or other. I can understand objections to the diamond trade — I really was thinking that it might be inadequate to the life of a man like you even though it might have made you a millionaire. But now I see how mistaken you are about this girl I doubt if you could be correct about other things."

"How am I mistaken in her?"

"She is lazy and dissatisfied. But that is not all of it. Supposing her to be as good a woman as any you can find, which she certainly is not, why do you wish to connect yourself with anybody at present?"

"Well, there are practical reasons," Clym began, and then almost broke off under an overpowering sense of the weight of argument which could be brought against his statement. "If I take a school an educated woman would be invaluable as a help to me."

"What! you really mean to marry her?"

"It would be premature to state that plainly. But consider what obvious advantages there would be in doing it. She ——"

"Don't suppose she has any money. She hasn't a farthing."

"She is excellently educated, and would make a good matron in a boarding-school. I candidly own that I have modified my views a little, in deference to you; and it should satisfy you. I no longer adhere to my intention of giving with my own mouth rudimentary education to the lowest class. I can do better. I can establish a good private school for farmers' sons, and without stopping the school I can manage to pass examinations. By this means, and by the assistance of a wife like her ——"

"O, Clym!"

"I shall ultimately, I hope, be at the head of one of the best schools in the country."

Yeobright had enunciated the word "her" with a fervour which, in conversation with a mother, was absurdly indiscreet. Hardly a maternal heart within the four seas could, in such circumstances, have helped being irritated at that ill-timed betrayal of feeling for a new woman.

"You are blinded, Clym," she said warmly. "It was a bad day for you when you first set eyes on her. And your scheme is merely a castle in the air built on purpose to justify this folly which has seized you, and to salve your conscience on the irrational situation you are in."

"Mother, that's not true," he firmly answered.

"Can you maintain that I sit and tell untruths, when all I wish to do is to save you from sorrow? For shame, Clym! But it is all through that woman — a hussy!"

Clym reddened like fire and rose. He placed his hand upon his mother's shoulder and said, in a tone which hung strangely between entreaty and command, "I won't hear it. I may be led to answer you in a way which we shall both regret."

His mother parted her lips to begin some other vehement truth, but on looking at him she saw that in his face which led her to leave the words unsaid. Yeobright walked once or twice across the room, and then suddenly went out of the house. It was eleven o'clock when he came in, though he had not been further than the precincts of the garden. His mother was gone to bed. A light was left burning on the table, and supper was spread. Without partaking of any food he secured the doors and went upstairs.

IV

AN HOUR OF BLISS AND MANY HOURS OF SADNESS

THE next day was gloomy enough at Blooms-End. Yeobright remained in his study, sitting over the open books; but the work of those hours was miserably scant. Determined that there should be nothing in his conduct towards his mother resembling sullenness, he had occasionally spoken to her on passing matters, and would take no notice of the brevity of her replies.

With the same resolve to keep up a show of conversation he said, about seven o'clock in the evening, "There's an eclipse of the moon tonight. I am going out to see it." And, putting on his overcoat, he left her.

The low moon was not as yet visible from the front of the house, and Yeobright climbed out of the valley until he stood in the full flood of her light. But even now he walked on, and his steps were in the direction of Rainbarrow.

In half an hour he stood at the top. The sky was clear from verge to verge, and the moon flung her rays over the whole heath, but without sensibly lighting it, except where paths and water-courses had laid bare the white flints and glistening quartz sand, which made streaks upon the general shade. After standing awhile he stooped and felt the heather. It was dry, and he flung himself down upon the barrow, his face towards the moon, which depicted a small image of herself in each of his eyes.

He had often come up here without stating his purpose to his mother; but this was the first time that he had been ostensibly frank as to his purpose while really concealing it. It was a moral situation which, three months earlier, he could hardly have credited of himself. In returning to labour in this sequestered spot he had anticipated an escape from the chafing of social necessities; yet behold they were here also. More than ever he longed to be in some world where personal ambition was not the only recognized form of progress — such, perhaps, as might have been the case at some time or other in the silvery globe then shining upon him. His eye travelled over the length and breadth of that distant country — over the Bay of Rainbows, the sombre Sea of Crises, the Ocean of Storms, the Lake of Dreams, the vast Walled Plains, and the wondrous Ring Mountains — till he almost felt himself to be voyaging bodily through its wild scenes, standing on its hollow hills, traversing its deserts, descending its vales and old sea bottoms, or mounting to the edges of its craters.

While he watched the far-removed landscape a tawny stain grew into being on the lower verge: the eclipse had begun. This marked a preconcerted moment: for the remote celestial phenomenon had been pressed into sublunary service as a lover's signal. Yeobright's mind flew back to earth at the sight; he arose, shook himself, and listened. Minute after minute passed by, perhaps ten minutes passed, and the shadow on the moon perceptibly widened. He heard a rustling on his left hand, a cloaked figure with an upturned face appeared at the base of the Barrow, and Clym descended. In a moment the figure was in his arms, and his lips upon hers.

"My Eustacia!"

"Clym, dearest!"

Such a situation had less than three months brought forth.

They remained long without a single utterance, for no language could reach the level of their condition: words were as the rusty implements of a by-gone barbarous speech, and only to be occasionally tolerated.

"I began to wonder why you did not come," said Yeobright, when she had withdrawn a little from his embrace.

"You said ten minutes after the first mark of shade on the edge of the moon; and that's what it is now."

"Well, let us only think that here we are."

Then, holding each other's hand, they were again silent, and the shadow on the moon's disc grew a little larger.

"Has it seemed long since you last saw me?" she asked.

"It has seemed sad."

"And not long? That's because you occupy yourself, and so blind yourself to my absence. To me, who can do nothing, it has been like living under stagnant water."

"I would rather bear tediousness, dear, than have time made short by the means that mine has been shortened."

"In what way is that? You have been thinking you wished you did not love me."

"How can a man wish that, and yet love on? No, Eustacia."

"Men can, women cannot."

"Well, whatever I may have thought, one thing is certain — I do love you — past all compass and description. I love you to oppressiveness — I, who have never before felt more than a pleasant passing fancy for any woman I have ever seen. Let me look right into your moonlit face, and dwell on every line and curve in it! Only a few hair-breadths make the difference between this face and faces I have seen many times before I knew you; yet what a difference — the difference between everything and nothing at all. One touch on that mouth again! there, and there, and there. Your eyes seem heavy, Eustacia."

"No, it is my general way of looking. I think it arises from my feeling sometimes an agonizing pity for myself that I ever was born."

"You don't feel it now?"

"No. Yet I know that we shall not love like this always. Nothing can insure the continuance of love. It will evaporate like a spirit, and so I feel full of fears."

"You need not."

"Ah, you don't know. You have seen more than I, and have been into cities and among people that I have only heard of, and have lived more years than I; but yet I am older at this than you. I loved another man once, and now I love you."

"In God's mercy don't talk so, Eustacia!"

"But I do not think I shall be the one who wearies first. It will, I fear, end in this way: your mother will find out that you meet me, and she will influence you against me!"

"That can never be. She knows of these meetings already."

"And she speaks against me?"

"I will not say."

"There, go away! Obey her. I shall ruin you. It is foolish of you to meet me like this. Kiss me, and go away for ever. For ever — do you hear? — for ever!"

"Not I."

"It is your only chance. Many a man's love has been a curse to him."

"You are desperate, full of fancies, and wilful; and you misunderstand. I have an additional reason for seeing you tonight besides love of you. For though, unlike you, I feel our affection may be eternal, I feel with you in this, that our present mode of existence cannot last."

"O! 'tis your mother. Yes, that's it! I knew it."

"Never mind what it is. Believe this, I cannot let myself lose you. I must have you always with me. This very evening I do not like to let you go. There is only one cure for this anxiety, dearest — you must be my wife."

She started: then endeavoured to say calmly, "Cynics say that cures the anxiety by curing the love."

"But you must answer me. Shall I claim you some day — I don't mean at once?"

"I must think," Eustacia murmured. "At present speak of Paris to me. Is there any place like it on earth?"

"It is very beautiful. But will you be mine?"

"I will be nobody else's in the world — does that satisfy you?"

"Yes, for the present."

"Now tell me of the Tuilleries, and the Louvre," she continued evasively.

"I hate talking of Paris! Well, I remember one sunny room in the Louvre which would make a fitting place for you to live in — the Galerie d'Apollon. Its windows are mainly east; and in the early morning, when the sun is bright, the whole apartment is in a perfect blaze of splendour. The rays bristle and dart from the encrustations of gilding to the magnificent inlaid coffers, from the coffers to the gold and silver plate, from the plate to the jewels and precious stones, from these to the enamels, till there is a perfect network of light which quite dazzles the eye. But now, about our marriage ——"

"And Versailles — the King's Gallery is some such gorgeous room, is it not?"

"Yes. But what's the use of talking of gorgeous rooms? By the way, the Little Trianon would suit us beautifully to live in, and you might walk in the gardens in the moonlight and think you were in some English shrubbery; it is laid out in English fashion."

"I should hate to think that!"

"Then you could keep to the lawn in front of the Grand Palace. All about there you would doubtless feel in a world of historical romance."

He went on, since it was all new to her, and described Fontainebleau, St. Cloud, the Bois, and many other familiar haunts of the Parisians; till she said —

"When used you to go to these places?"

"On Sundays."

"Ah, yes. I dislike English Sundays. How I should chime in with their manners over there! Dear Clym, you'll go back again?"

Clym shook his head, and looked at the eclipse.

"If you'll go back again I'll — be something," she said tenderly, putting her head near his breast. "If you'll agree I'll give my promise, without making you wait a minute longer."

"How extraordinary that you and my mother should be of one mind about this!" said Yeobright. "I have vowed not to go back, Eustacia. It is not the place I dislike; it is the occupation."

"But you can go in some other capacity."

"No. Besides, it would interfere with my scheme. Don't press that, Eustacia. Will you marry me?"

"I cannot tell."

"Now — never mind Paris; it is no better than other spots. Promise, sweet!"

"You will never adhere to your education plan, I am quite sure; and then it will be all right for me; and so I promise to be yours for ever and ever."

Clym brought her face towards his by a gentle pressure of the hand, and kissed her.

"Ah! but you don't know what you have got in me," she said. "Sometimes I think there is not that in Eustacia Vye which will make a good homespun wife. Well, let it go — see how our time is slipping, slipping, slipping!" She pointed towards the half eclipsed moon.

"You are too mournful."

"No. Only I dread to think of anything beyond the present. What is, we know. We are together now, and it is unknown how long we shall be so: the unknown always fills my mind with terrible possibilities, even when I may reasonably expect it to be cheerful.... Clym, the eclipsed moonlight shines upon your face with a strange foreign colour, and shows its shape as if it were cut out in gold. That means that you should be doing better things than this."

"You are ambitious, Eustacia — no, not exactly ambitious, luxurious. I ought to be of the same vein, to make you happy, I suppose. And yet, far from that, I could live and die in a hermitage here, with proper work to do."

There was that in his tone which implied distrust of his position as a solicitous lover, a doubt if he were acting fairly towards one whose tastes touched his own only at rare and infrequent points. She saw his meaning, and whispered, in a low, full accent of eager assurance, "Don't mistake me, Clym: though I should like Paris, I love you for yourself alone. To be your wife and live in Paris would be heaven to me; but I would rather live with you in a hermitage here than not be yours at all. It is gain to me either way, and very great gain. There's my too candid confession."

"Spoken like a woman. And now I must soon leave you. I'll walk with you towards your house."

"But must you go home yet?" she asked. "Yes, the sand has nearly slipped away, I see, and the eclipse is creeping on more and more. Don't go yet! Stop till the hour has run itself out; then I will not press you any more. You will go home and sleep well; I keep sighing in my sleep! Do you ever dream of me?"

"I cannot recollect a clear dream of you."

"I see your face in every scene of my dreams, and hear your voice in every sound. I wish I did not. It is too much what I feel. They say such love never lasts. But it must! And yet once, I remember, I saw an officer of the

Hussars ride down the street at Budmouth, and though he was a total stranger and never spoke to me, I loved him till I thought I should really die of love — but I didn't die, and at last I left off caring for him. How terrible it would be if a time should come when I could not love you, my Clym!"

"Please don't say such reckless things. When we see such a time at hand we will say, 'I have outlived my faith and purpose,' and die. There, the hour has expired: now let us walk on."

Hand in hand they went along the path towards Mistover. When they were near the house he said, "It is too late for me to see your grandfather tonight. Do you think he will object to it?"

"I will speak to him. I am so accustomed to be my own mistress that it did not occur to me that we should have to ask him."

Then they lingeringly separated, and Clym descended towards Blooms-End.

And as he walked further and further from the charmed atmosphere of his Olympian girl his face grew sad with a new sort of sadness. A perception of the dilemma in which his love had placed him came back in full force. In spite of Eustacia's apparent willingness to wait through the period of an unpromising engagement, till he should be established in his new pursuit, he could not but perceive at moments that she loved him rather as a visitant from a gay world to which she rightly belonged than as a man with a purpose opposed to that recent past of his which so interested her. Often at their meetings a word or a sigh escaped her. It meant that, though she made no conditions as to his return to the French capital, this was what she secretly longed for in the event of marriage; and it robbed him of many an otherwise pleasant hour. Along with that came the widening breach between himself and his mother. Whenever any little occurrence had brought into more prominence than usual the disappointment that he was causing her it had sent him on lone and moody walks; or he was kept awake a great part of the night by the turmoil of spirit which such a recognition created. If Mrs. Yeobright could only have been led to see what a sound and worthy purpose this purpose of his was and how little it was being affected by his devotion to Eustacia, how differently would she regard him!

Thus as his sight grew accustomed to the first blinding halo kindled about him by love and beauty, Yeobright began to perceive what a strait he was in. Sometimes he wished that he had never known Eustacia, immediately to retract the wish as brutal. Three antagonistic growths had to be kept alive: his mother's trust in him, his plan for becoming a teacher, and Eustacia's happiness. His fervid nature could not afford to relinquish one of these, though two of the three were as many as he could hope to preserve. Though his love was as chaste as that of Petrarch for his Laura, it had made fetters of what previously was only a difficulty. A position which was not too simple when he stood whole-hearted had become indescribably complicated by the addition of Eustacia. Just when his mother was beginning to tolerate one scheme he had introduced another still bitterer than the first, and the combination was more than she could bear.

V

SHARP WORDS ARE SPOKEN AND A CRISIS ENSUES

WHEN Yeobright was not with Eustacia he was sitting slavishly over his books; when he was not reading he was meeting her. These meetings were carried on with the greatest secrecy.

One afternoon his mother came home from a morning visit to Thomasin. He could see from a disturbance in the lines of her face that something had happened.

"I have been told an incomprehensible thing," she said mournfully. "The captain has let out at the Woman that you and Eustacia Vye are engaged to be married."

"We are," said Yeobright. "But it may not be yet for a very long time."

"I should hardly think it *would* be yet for a very long time! You will take her to Paris, I suppose?" She spoke with weary hopelessness.

"I am not going back to Paris."

"What will you do with a wife, then?"

"Keep a school in Budmouth, as I have told you."

"That's incredible! The place is overrun with schoolmasters. You have no special qualifications. What possible chance is there for such as you?"

"There is no chance of getting rich. But with my system of education, which is as new as it is true, I shall do a great deal of good to my fellow-creatures."

"Dreams, dreams! If there had been any system left to be invented they would have found it out at the universities long before this time."

"Never, mother. They cannot find it out, because their teachers don't come in contact with the class which demands such a system — that is, those who have had no preliminary training. My plan is one for instilling high knowledge into empty minds without first cramming them with what has to be uncrammed again before true study begins."

"I might have believed you if you had kept yourself free from entanglements; but this woman — if she had been a good girl it would have been bad enough; but being ——"

"She is a good girl."

"So you think. A foreign bandmaster's daughter! What has her life been? Her surname even is not her true one."

"She is Captain Vye's granddaughter, and her father merely took her mother's name. And she is a lady by instinct."

"They call him 'captain,' but anybody is captain."

"He was in the Royal Navy!"

"No doubt he has been to sea in some tub or other. Why doesn't he look after her? No lady would rove about the heath at all hours of the day and night as she does. But that's not all of it. There was something queer between her and Thomasin's husband at one time — I am as sure of it as that I stand here."

"Eustacia has told me. He did pay her a little attention a year ago; but there's no harm in that. I like her all the better."

"Clym," said his mother with firmness, "I have no proofs against her, unfortunately. But if she makes you a good wife, there has never been a bad one."

"Believe me, you are almost exasperating," said Yeobright vehemently. "And this very day I had intended to arrange a meeting between you. But you give me no peace; you try to thwart my wishes in everything."

"I hate the thought of any son of mine marrying badly! I wish I had never lived to see this; it is too much for me — it is more than I thought!" She turned to the window. Her breath was coming quickly, and her lips were pale, parted, and trembling.

"Mother," said Clym, "whatever you do, you will always be dear to me — that you know. But one thing I have a right to say, which is, that at my age I am old enough to know what is best for me."

Mrs. Yeobright remained for some time silent and shaken, as if she could say no more. Then she replied, "Best? Is it best for you to injure your prospects for such a voluptuous, idle woman as that? Don't you see that by the very fact of your choosing her you prove that you do not know what is best for you? You give up your whole thought — you set your whole soul — to please a woman."

"I do. And that woman is you."

"How can you treat me so flippantly!" said his mother, turning again to him with a tearful look. "You are unnatural, Clym, and I did not expect it."

"Very likely," said he cheerlessly. "You did not know the measure you were going to mete me, and therefore did not know the measure that would be returned to you again."

"You answer me; you think only of her. You stick to her in all things."

"That proves her to be worthy. I have never yet supported what is bad. And I do not care only for her. I care for you and for myself, and for anything that is good. When a woman once dislikes another she is merciless!"

"O Clym! please don't go setting down as my fault what is your obstinate wrong-headedness. If you wished to connect yourself with an unworthy person why did you come home here to do it? Why didn't you do it in Paris? — it is more the fashion there. You have come only to distress me, a lonely woman, and shorten my days! I wish that you would bestow your presence where you bestow your love!"

Clym said huskily, "You are my mother. I will say no more — beyond this, that I beg your pardon for having thought this my home. I will no longer inflict myself upon you; I'll go." And he went out with tears in his eyes.

It was a sunny afternoon at the beginning of summer, and the moist hollows of the heath had passed from their brown to their green stage. Yeobright walked to the edge of the basin which extended down from Mistover and Rainbarrow. By this time he was calm, and he looked over the landscape. In the minor valleys, between the hillocks which diversified the contour of the vale, the fresh young ferns were luxuriantly growing up, ultimately to reach a height of five or six feet. He descended a little way, flung himself down in a spot where a path emerged from one of the small hollows, and waited. Hither it was that he had promised Eustacia to bring his mother this afternoon, that they might meet and be friends. His attempt had utterly failed.

He was in a nest of vivid green. The ferny vegetation round him, though so abundant, was quite uniform: it was a grove of machine-made foliage, a world of green triangles with saw-edges, and not a single flower. The air was warm with vaporous warmth, and the stillness was unbroken. Lizards, grasshoppers, and ants were the only living things to be beheld. The scene seemed to belong to the ancient world of the carboniferous period, when the forms of plants were few, and of the fern kind; when there was neither bud nor blossom, nothing but a monotonous extent of leafage, amid which no bird sang.

When he had reclined for some considerable time, gloomily pondering, he discerned above the ferns a drawn bonnet of white silk approaching from the left, and Yeobright knew directly that it covered the head of her he loved. His heart awoke from its apathy to a warm excitement, and, jumping to his feet, he said aloud, "I knew she was sure to come."

She vanished in a hollow for a few moments, and then her whole form unfolded itself from the brake.

"Only you here?" she exclaimed, with a disappointed air, whose hollowness was proved by her rising redness and her half-guilty low laugh. "Where is Mrs. Yeobright?"

"She has not come," he replied in a subdued tone.

"I wish I had known that you would be here alone," she said seriously, "and that we were going to have such an idle, pleasant time as this. Pleasure not known beforehand is half wasted; to anticipate it is to double it. I have not thought once today of having you all to myself this afternoon, and the actual moment of a thing is so soon gone."

"It is indeed."

"Poor Clym!" she continued, looking tenderly into his face. "You are sad. Something has happened at your home. Never mind what is — let us only look at what seems."

"But, darling, what shall we do?" said he.

"Still go on as we do now — just live on from meeting to meeting, never minding about another day. You, I know, are always thinking of that — I can see you are. But you must not — will you, dear Clym?"

"You are just like all women. They are ever content to build their lives on any incidental position that offers itself; whilst men would fain make a globe to suit them. Listen to this, Eustacia. There is a subject I have determined to put off no longer. Your sentiment on the wisdom of *Carpe diem* does not impress me today. Our present mode of life must shortly be brought to an end."

"It is your mother!"

"It is. I love you none the less in telling you; it is only right you should know."

"I have feared my bliss," she said, with the merest motion of her lips. "It has been too intense and consuming."

"There is hope yet. There are forty years of work in me yet, and why should you despair? I am only at an awkward turning. I wish people wouldn't be so ready to think that there is no progress without uniformity."

"Ah — your mind runs off to the philosophical side of it. Well, these sad and hopeless obstacles are welcome in one sense, for they enable us to look with indifference upon the cruel satires that Fate loves to indulge in. I have heard of people, who, upon coming suddenly into happiness, have died from anxiety lest they should not live to enjoy it. I felt myself in that whimsical state of uneasiness lately; but I shall be spared it now. Let us walk on."

Clym took the hand which was already bared for him — it was a favourite way with them to walk bare hand in bare hand — and led her through the ferns. They formed a very comely picture of love at full flush, as they walked along the valley that late afternoon, the sun sloping down on their right, and throwing their thin spectral shadows, tall as poplar trees, far out across the furze and fern. Eustacia went with her head thrown back fancifully, a certain glad and voluptuous air of triumph pervading her eyes at having won by her own unaided self a man who was her perfect complement in attainments, appearance, and age. On the young man's part, the paleness of face wh'ch he had brought with him from Paris, and the incipient marks of time and thought, were less perceptible than when he returned, the healthful and energetic sturdiness which was his by nature having partially recovered its original proportions. They wandered onward till they reached the nether margin of the heath, where it became marshy, and merged in moorland.

"I must part from you here, Clym," said Eustacia.

They stood still and prepared to bid each other farewell. Everything before them was on a perfect level. The sun, resting on the horizon line, streamed across the ground from between copper-coloured and lilac clouds, stretched out in flats beneath a sky of pale soft green. All dark objects on the earth that lay towards the sun were overspread by a purple haze, against which groups of wailing gnats shone out, rising upwards and dancing about like sparks of fire.

"O! this leaving you is too hard to bear!" exclaimed Eustacia in a sudden whisper of anguish. "Your mother will influence you too much; I shall not be judged fairly, it will get afloat that I am not a good girl, and the witch story will be added to make me blacker!"

"They cannot. Nobody dares to speak disrespectfully of you or of me."

"O how I wish I was sure of never losing you — that you could not be able to desert me anyhow!"

Clym stood silent a moment. His feelings were high, the moment was passionate, and he cut the knot.

"You shall be sure of me, darling," he said, folding her in his arms. "We will be married at once."

"O Clym!"

"Do you agree to it?"

"If — if we can."

"We certainly can, both being of full age. And I have not followed my occupation all these years without having accumulated money; and if you will agree to live in a tiny cottage somewhere on the heath, until I take a house in Budmouth for the school, we can do it at a very little expense."

"How long shall we have to live in the tiny cottage, Clym?"

"About six months. At the end of that time I shall have finished my reading — yes, we will do it, and this heart-aching will be over. We shall, of course, live in absolute seclusion, and our married life will only begin to outward view when we take the house in Budmouth, where I have already addressed a letter on the matter. Would your grandfather allow you?"

"I think he would — on the understanding that it should not last longer than six months."

"I will guarantee that, if no misfortune happens."

"If no misfortune happens," she repeated slowly.

"Which is not likely. Dearest, fix the exact day."

And then they consulted on the question, and the day was chosen. It was to be a fortnight from that time.

This was the end of their talk, and Eustacia left him. Clym watched her as she retired towards the sun. The luminous rays wrapped her up with her increasing distance, and the rustle of her dress over the sprouting sedge and grass died away. As he watched, the dead flat of the scenery overpowered him, though he was fully alive to the beauty of that untarnished early summer green which was worn for the nonce by the poorest blade. There was something in its oppressive horizontality which too much reminded him of the arena of life; it gave him a sense of bare equality with, and no superiority to, a single living thing under the sun.

Eustacia was now no longer the goddess but the woman to him, a being to fight for, support, help, be maligned for. Now that he had reached a cooler moment he would have preferred a less hasty marriage; but the card was laid, and he determined to abide by the game. Whether Eustacia was to add one other to the list of those who love too hotly to love long and well, the forthcoming event was certainly a ready way of proving.

VI

YEOBRIGHT GOES, AND THE BREACH IS COMPLETE

ALL that evening smart sounds denoting an active packing up came from Yeobright's room to the ears of his mother downstairs.

Next morning he departed from the house and again proceeded across the heath. A long day's march was before him, his object being to secure a dwelling to which he might take Eustacia when she became his wife. Such a house, small, secluded, and with its windows boarded up, he had casually observed a month earlier, near a village about five miles off; and thither he directed his steps today.

The weather was far different from that of the evening before. The yellow and vapoury sunset which had wrapped up Eustacia from his parting gaze had presaged change. It was one of those not infrequent days of an English June which are as wet and boisterous as November. The cold clouds hastened on in a body, as if painted on a moving slide. Vapours from other continents arrived upon the wind, which curled and parted round him as he walked on.

At length Clym reached the margin of a fir and beech plantation that had been enclosed from heath land in the year of his birth. Here the trees, laden heavily with their new and humid leaves, were now suffering more damage than during the highest winds of winter, when the boughs are specially disencumbered to do battle with the storm. The wet young beeches were undergoing amputations, bruises, cripplings, and harsh lacerations, from which the wasting sap would bleed for many a day to come, and which would leave scars visible till the day of their burning. Each stem was wrenched at the root, where it moved like a bone in its socket, and at every onset of the gale convulsive sounds came from the branches, as if pain were felt. In a neighbouring brake a finch was trying to sing; but the wind blew under his feathers till they stood on end, twisted round his little tail, and made him give up his song.

Yet a few yards to Yeobright's left, on the open heath, how ineffectively gnashed the storm! Those gusts which tore the trees merely waved the furze and heather in a light caress. Egdon was made for such times as these.

Yeobright reached the empty house about mid-day. It was almost as lonely as that of Eustacia's grandfather, but the fact that it stood near a heath was disguised by a belt of firs which almost enclosed the premises. He journeyed on about a mile further to the village in which the owner lived, and, returning with him to the house, arrangements were completed, and the man undertook that one room at least should be ready for occupation the next day. Clym's intention was to live there alone until Eustacia should join him on their wedding-day.

Then he turned to pursue his way homeward through the drizzle that had so greatly transformed the scene. The ferns, among which he had lain in comfort yesterday, were dripping moisture from every frond, wetting his legs through as he brushed past; and the fur of the rabbits leaping around him was clotted into dark locks by the same watery surrounding.

He reached home damp and weary enough after his ten-mile walk. It had hardly been a propitious beginning, but he had chosen his course, and would show no swerving. The evening and the following morning were spent in concluding arrangements for his departure. To stay at home a minute longer than necessary after having once come to his determination would be, he felt, only to give new pain to his mother by some word, look, or deed.

He had hired a conveyance and sent off his goods by two o'clock that day. The next step was to get some furniture, which, after serving for temporary use in the cottage, would be available for the house at Budmouth when increased by goods of a better description. A mart extensive enough for the purpose existed at Anglebury, some miles beyond the spot chosen for his residence, and there he resolved to pass the coming night.

It now only remained to wish his mother good-bye. She was sitting by the window as usual when he came downstairs.

"Mother, I am going to leave you," he said, holding out his hand.

"I thought you were, by your packing," replied Mrs. Yeobright in a voice from which every particle of emotion was painfully excluded.

"And you will part friends with me?"

"Certainly, Clym."

"I am going to be married on the twenty-fifth."

"I thought you were going to be married."

"And then — and then you must come and see us. You will understand me better after that, and our situation will not be so wretched as it is now."

"I do not think it likely I shall come to see you."

"Then it will not be my fault or Eustacia's, mother. Good-bye!"

He kissed her cheek, and departed in great misery, which was several hours in lessening itself to a controllable level. The position had been such that nothing more could be said without, in the first place, breaking down a barrier; and that was not to be done.

No sooner had Yeobright gone from his mother's house than her face changed its rigid aspect for one of blank despair. After a while she wept, and her tears brought some relief. During the rest of the day she did nothing but walk up and down the garden path in a state bordering on stupefaction. Night came, and with it but little rest. The next day, with an instinct to do something which should reduce prostration to mournfulness, she went to her son's room, and with her own hands arranged it in order, for an imaginary time when he should return again. She gave some attention to her flowers, but it was perfunctorily bestowed, for they no longer charmed her.

It was a great relief when, early in the afternoon, Thomasin paid her an unexpected visit. This was not the first meeting between the relatives since Thomasin's marriage; and past blunders having been in a rough way rectified, they could always greet each other with pleasure and ease.

The oblique band of sunlight which followed her through the door became the young wife well. It illuminated her as her presence illuminated the heath. In her movements, in her gaze, she reminded the beholder of the feathered creatures who lived around her home. All similes and allegories concerning her began and ended with birds. There was as much variety in her motions as in their flight. When she was musing she was a kestrel, which hangs in the air by an invisible motion of its wings. When she was in a high wind her light body was blown against trees and banks like a heron's. When she was frightened she darted noiselessly like a kingfisher. When she was serene she skimmed like a swallow, and that is how she was moving now.

"You are looking very blithe, upon my word, Tamsie," said Mrs. Yeobright, with a sad smile. "How is Damon?"

"He is very well."

"Is he kind to you, Thomasin?" And Mrs. Yeobright observed her narrowly.

"Pretty fairly."

"Is that honestly said?"

"Yes, aunt. I would tell you if he were unkind." She added, blushing, and with hesitation, "He — I don't know if I ought to complain to you about this, but I am not quite sure what to do. I want some money, you know, aunt — some to buy little things for myself — and he doesn't give me any. I don't like to ask him; and yet, perhaps, he doesn't give it me because he doesn't know. Ought I to mention it to him, aunt?"

"Of course you ought. Have you never said a word on the matter?"

"You see, I had some of my own," said Thomasin evasively; "and I have not wanted any of his until lately. I did just say something about it last week; but he seems — not to remember."

"He must be made to remember. You are aware that I have a little box full of spade-guineas, which your uncle put into my hands to divide between yourself and Clym whenever I chose. Perhaps the time has come when it should be done. They can be turned into sovereigns at any moment."

"I think I should like to have my share — that is, if you don't mind."

"You shall, if necessary. But it is only proper that you should first tell your husband distinctly that you are without any, and see what he will do."

"Very well, I will.... Aunt, I have heard about Clym. I know you are in trouble about him, and that's why I have come."

Mrs. Yeobright turned away, and her features worked in her attempt to conceal her feelings. Then she ceased to make any attempt, and said, weeping, "O Thomasin, do you think he hates me? How can he bear to grieve me so, when I have lived only for him through all these years?"

"Hate you — no," said Thomasin soothingly. "It is only that he loves her too well. Look at it quietly — do. It is not so very bad of him. Do you know, I thought it not the worst match he could have made. Miss Vye's family is a good one on her mother's side; and her father was a romantic wanderer — a sort of Greek Ulysses."

"It is no use, Thomasin; it is no use. Your intention is good; but I will not trouble you to argue. I have gone through the whole that can be said on either side times, and many times. Clym and I have not parted in anger; we have parted in a worse way. It is not a passionate quarrel that would have broken my heart; it is the steady opposition and persistence in going wrong that he has shown. O Thomasin, he was so good as a little boy — so tender and kind!"

"He was, I know."

"I did not think one whom I called mine would grow up to treat me like this. He spoke to me as if I opposed him to injure him. As though I could wish him ill!"

"There are worse women in the world than Eustacia Vye."

"There are too many better; that's the agony of it. It was she, Thomasin, and she only, who led your husband to act as he did: I would swear it!"

"No," said Thomasin eagerly. "It was before he knew me that he thought of her, and it was nothing but a mere flirtation."

"Very well; we will let it be so. There is little use in unravelling that now. Sons must be blind if they will. Why is it that a woman can see from a distance what a man cannot see close? Clym must do as he will — he is nothing more to me. And this is maternity — to give one's best years and best love to ensure the fate of being despised!"

"You are too unyielding. Think how many mothers there are whose sons have brought them to public shame by real crimes before you feel so deeply a case like this."

"Thomasin, don't lecture me — I can't have it. It is the excess above what we expect that makes the force of the blow, and that may not be greater in their case than in mine: they may have foreseen the worst.... I am wrongly made, Thomasin," she added, with a mournful smile. "Some widows can guard against the wounds their children give them by turning their hearts to another husband and beginning life again. But I always was a poor, weak, one-idea'd creature — I had not the compass of heart nor the enterprise for that. Just as forlorn and stupefied as I was when my husband's spirit flew away I have sat ever since — never attempting to mend matters at all. I was comparatively a young woman then, and I might have had another family by this time, and have been comforted by them for the failure of this one son."

"It is more noble in you that you did not."

"The more noble, the less wise."

"Forget it, and be soothed, dear aunt. And I shall not leave you alone for long. I shall come and see you every day."

And for one week Thomasin literally fulfilled her word. She endeavoured to make light of the wedding; and brought news of the preparations, and that she was invited to be present. The next week she was rather unwell, and did not appear. Nothing had as yet been done about the guineas, for Thomasin feared to address her husband again on the subject, and Mrs. Yeobright had insisted upon this.

One day just before this time, Wildeve was standing at the door of the Quiet Woman. In addition to the upward path through the heath to Rainbarrow and Mistover, there was a road which branched from the highway a short distance below the inn, and ascended to Mistover by a circuitous and easy incline. This was the only route on this side for vehicles to the captain's retreat. A light cart from the nearest town descended the road, and the lad who was driving pulled up in front of the inn for something to drink.

"You come from Mistover?" said Wildeve.

"Yes. They are taking in good things up there. Going to be a wedding." And the driver buried his face in his mug.

Wildeve had not received an inkling of the fact before, and a sudden expression of pain overspread his face. He turned for a moment into the passage to hide it. Then he came back again.

"Do you mean Miss Vye?" he said. "How is it — that she can be married so soon?"

"By the will of God and a ready young man, I suppose."

"You don't mean Mr. Yeobright?"

"Yes. He has been creeping about with her all the spring."

"I suppose — she was immensely taken with him?"

"She is crazy about him, so their general servant of all work tells me. And that lad Charley that looks after the horse is all in a daze about it. The stun-poll has got fond-like of her."

"Is she lively — is she glad? Going to be married so soon — well!"

"It isn't so very soon."

"No; not so very soon."

Wildeve went indoors to the empty room, a curious heart-ache within him. He rested his elbow upon the mantelpiece and his face upon his hand. When Thomasin entered the room he did not tell her of what he had heard. The old longing for Eustacia had reappeared in his soul: and it was mainly because he had discovered that it was another man's intention to possess her.

To be yearning for the difficult, to be weary of that offered; to care for the remote, to dislike the near; it was Wildeve's nature always. This is the true mark of the man of sentiment. Though Wildeve's fevered feeling had not been elaborated to real poetical compass, it was of the standard sort. He might have been called the Rousseau of Egdon.

VII

THE MORNING AND THE EVENING OF A DAY

The wedding morning came. Nobody would have imagined from appearances that Blooms-End had any interest in Mistover that day. A solemn stillness prevailed around the house of Clym's mother, and there was no more animation indoors. Mrs. Yeobright, who had declined to attend the ceremony, sat by the breakfast-table in the old room which communicated immediately with the porch, her eyes listlessly directed towards the open door. It was the room in which, six months earlier, the merry Christmas party had met, to which Eustacia came secretly and as a stranger. The only living thing that entered now was a sparrow; and seeing no movements to cause alarm, he hopped boldly round the room, endeavoured to go out by the window, and fluttered among the pot-flowers. This roused the lonely sitter, who got up, released the bird, and went to the door. She was expecting Thomasin, who had written the night before to state that the time had come when she would wish to have the money, and that she would if possible call this day.

Yet Thomasin occupied Mrs. Yeobright's thoughts but slightly as she looked up the valley of the heath alive with butterflies, and with grasshoppers whose husky noises on every side formed a whispered chorus. A domestic drama, for which the preparations were now being made a mile or two off, was but little less vividly present to her eyes than if enacted before her. She tried to dismiss the vision, and walked about the garden-plot; but her eyes ever and anon sought out the direction of the parish church to which Mistover belonged, and her excited fancy clove the hills which divided the building from her eyes. The morning wore away. Eleven o'clock struck: could it be that the wedding was then in progress? It must be so. She went on imagining the scene at the church to which he had by this time taken his bride. She pictured the little group of children by the gate as the pony-carriage drove up, in which, as Thomasin had learnt, they were going to perform the short journey. Then she saw them enter and proceed to the chancel and kneel; and the service seemed to go on.

She covered her face with her hands. "O, it is a mistake!" she groaned. "And he will rue it some day, and think of me!"

While she remained thus, overcome by her forebodings, the old clock indoors whizzed forth twelve strokes. Soon after, faint sounds floated to her ear from afar over the hills. The breeze came from that quarter, and it had brought with it the notes of distant bells, gaily starting off in a peal: one, two, three, four, five. The ringers at East Egdon were announcing the nuptials of Eustacia and her son.

"Then it is over," she murmured. "Well, well! and life too will be over soon. And why should I go on scalding my face like this? Cry about one thing in life, cry about all; one thread runs through the whole piece. And yet we say, 'a time to laugh!'"

Towards evening Wildeve came. Since Thomasin's marriage Mrs. Yeobright had shown towards him that grim friendliness which at last arises in all such cases of undesired affinity. The vision of what ought to have been is thrown aside in sheer weariness, and browbeaten human endeavour listlessly makes the best of the fact that is. Wildeve, to do him justice, had behaved very courteously to his wife's aunt; and it was with no surprise that she saw him enter now.

"Thomasin has not been able to come, as she promised to do," he replied to her inquiry, which had been anxious, for she knew that her niece was badly in want of money. "The captain came down last night and personally pressed her to join them today. So, not to be unpleasant, she determined to go. They fetched her in the pony-chaise, and are going to bring her back."

"Then it is done," said Mrs. Yeobright. "Have they gone to their new home?"

"I don't know. I have had no news from Mistover since Thomasin left to go."

"You did not go with her?" said she, as if there might be good reasons why.

"I could not," said Wildeve, reddening slightly. "We could not both leave the house; it was rather a busy morning, on account of Anglebury Great Market. I believe you have something to give to Thomasin? If you like, I will take it."

Mrs. Yeobright hesitated, and wondered if Wildeve knew what the something was. "Did she tell you of this?" she inquired.

"Not particularly. She casually dropped a remark about having arranged to fetch some article or other."

"It is hardly necessary to send it. She can have it whenever she chooses to come."

"That won't be yet. In the present state of her health she must not go on walking so much as she has done." He added, with a faint twang of sarcasm, "What wonderful thing is it that I cannot be trusted to take?"

"Nothing worth troubling you with."

"One would think you doubted my honesty," he said, with a laugh, though his colour rose in a quick resentfulness frequent with him.

"You need think no such thing," said she drily. "It is simply that I, in common with the rest of the world, feel that there are certain things which had better be done by certain people than by others."

"As you like, as you like," said Wildeve laconically. "It is not worth arguing about. Well, I think I must turn homeward again, as the inn must not be left long in charge of the lad and the maid only."

He went his way, his farewell being scarcely so courteous as his greeting. But Mrs. Yeobright knew him thoroughly by this time, and took little notice of his manner, good or bad.

When Wildeve was gone Mrs. Yeobright stood and considered what would be the best course to adopt with regard to the guineas, which she had not liked to entrust to Wildeve. It was hardly credible that Thomasin had told him to ask for them, when the necessity for them had arisen from the difficulty of obtaining money at his hands. At the same time Thomasin really wanted them, and might be unable to come to Blooms-End for another week at least. To take or send the money to her at the inn would be impolitic, since Wildeve would pretty surely be present, or would discover the transaction; and if, as her aunt suspected, he treated her less kindly than she deserved to be treated, he might then get the whole sum out of her gentle hands. But on this particular evening Thomasin was at Mistover, and anything might be conveyed to her there without the knowledge of her husband. Upon the whole the opportunity was worth taking advantage of.

Her son, too, was there, and was now married. There could be no more proper moment to render him his share of the money than the present. And the chance that would be afforded her, by sending him this gift, of showing how far she was from bearing him ill-will, cheered the sad mother's heart.

She went upstairs and took from a locked drawer a little box, out of which she poured a hoard of broad unworn guineas that had lain there many a year. There were a hundred in all, and she divided them into two heaps, fifty in each. Tying up these in small canvas bags, she went down to the garden and called to Christian Cantle, who was loitering about in hope of a supper which was not really owed him. Mrs. Yeobright gave him the money-bags, charged him to go to Mistover, and on no account to deliver them into any one's hands save her son's and Thomasin's. On further thought she deemed it advisable to tell Christian precisely what the two bags contained, that he might be fully impressed with their importance. Christian pocketed the money-bags, promised the great carefulness, and set out on his way.

"You need not hurry," said Mrs. Yeobright. "It will be better not to get there till after dusk, and then nobody will notice you. Come back here to supper, if it is not too late."

It was nearly nine o'clock when he began to ascend the vale towards Mistover; but the long days of summer being at their climax, the first obscurity of evening had only just begun to tan the landscape. At this point of his journey Christian heard voices, and found that they proceeded from a company of men and women who were traversing a hollow ahead of him, the tops only of their heads being visible.

He paused and thought of the money he carried. It was almost too early even for Christian seriously to fear robbery; nevertheless he took a precaution which ever since his boyhood he had adopted whenever he carried more than two or three shillings upon his person — a precaution somewhat like that of the owner of the Pitt Diamond when filled with similar misgivings. He took off his boots, untied the guineas, and emptied the contents of one little bag into the right boot, and of the other into the left, spreading them as flatly as possible over the bottom of each, which was really a spacious coffer by no means limited to the size of the foot. Pulling them on again and lacing them to the very top, he proceeded on his way, more easy in his head than under his soles.

His path converged towards that of the noisy company, and on coming nearer he found to his relief that they were several Egdon people whom he knew very well, while with them walked Fairway, of Blooms-End.

"What! Christian going too?" said Fairway as soon as he recognized the new-comer. "You've got no young woman nor wife to your name to gie a gown-piece to, I'm sure."

"What d'ye mean?" said Christian.

"Why, the raffle. The one we go to every year. Going to the raffle as well as ourselves?"

"Never knew a word o't. Is it like cudgel-playing or other sportful forms of bloodshed? I don't want to go, thank you, Mister Fairway, and no of-fence."

"Christian don't know the fun o't, and 'twould be a fine sight for him," said a buxom woman. "There's no danger at all, Christian. Every man puts in a shilling apiece, and one wins a gown-piece for his wife or sweetheart if he's got one."

"Well, as that's not my fortune there's no meaning in it to me. But I should like to see the fun, if there's nothing of the black art in it, and if a man may look on without cost or getting into any dangerous wrangle?"

"There will be no uproar at all," said Timothy. "Sure, Christian, if you'd like to come we'll see there's no harm done."

"And no ba'dy gaieties, I suppose? You see, neighbours, if so, it would be setting father a bad example, as he is so light moral'd. But a gown-piece for a shilling, and no black art — 'tis worth looking in to see, and it wouldn't hinder me half an hour. Yes, I'll come, if you'll step a little way towards Mistover with me afterwards, supposing night should have closed in, and nobody else is going that way?"

One or two promised; and Christian, diverging from his direct path, turned round to the right with his companions towards the Quiet Woman.

When they entered the large common room of the inn they found assembled there about ten men from among the neighbouring population, and the group was increased by the new contingent to double that number. Most of them were sitting round the room in seats divided by wooden elbows like those of crude cathedral stalls, which were carved with the initials of many an illustrious drunkard of former times who had passed his days and his nights between them, and now lay as an alcoholic cinder in the nearest churchyard. Among the cups on the long table before the sitters lay an open parcel of light drapery — the gown-piece, as it was called — which was to be raffled for. Wildeve was standing with his back to the fireplace, smoking a cigar; and the promoter of the raffle, a packman from a distant town, was expatiating upon the value of the fabric as material for a summer dress.

"Now, gentlemen," he continued, as the new-comers drew up to the table, there's five have entered, and we want four more to make up the number. I think, by the faces of those gentlemen who have just come in, that they are shrewd enough to take advantage of this rare opportunity of beautifying their ladies at a very trifling expense."

Fairway, Sam, and another placed their shillings on the table, and the man turned to Christian.

"No, sir," said Christian, drawing back, with a quick gaze of misgiving. "I am only a poor chap come to look on, an it please ye, sir. I don't so much as know how you do it. If so be I was sure of getting it I would put down the shilling; but I couldn't otherwise."

"I think you might almost be sure," said the pedlar. "In fact, now I look into your face, even if I can't say you are sure to win, I can say that I never saw anything look more like winning in my life."

"You'll anyhow have the same chance as the rest of us," said Sam.

"And the extra luck of being the last comer," said another.

"And I was born wi' a caul, and perhaps can be no more ruined than drowned?" Christian added, beginning to give way.

Ultimately Christian laid down his shilling, the raffle began, and the dice went round. When it came to Christian's turn he took the box with a trembling hand, shook it fearfully, and threw a pair-royal. Three of the others had thrown common low pairs, and all the rest mere points.

"The gentleman looked like winning, as I said," observed the chapman, blandly. "Take it, sir; the article is yours."

"Haw-haw-haw!" said Fairway. "I'm damned if this isn't the quarest start that ever I knowed!"

"Mine?" asked Christian, with a vacant stare from his target eyes. "I — I haven't got neither maid, wife, nor widder belonging to me at all, and I'm afeard it will make me laughed at to ha'e it, Master Traveller. What with being curious to join in I never thought of that! What shall I do wi' a woman's clothes in my bedroom, and not lose my decency!"

"Keep 'em, to be sure," said Fairway, "if it is only for luck. Perhaps 'twill tempt some woman that thy poor carcase had no power over when standing empty-handed."

"Keep it, certainly," said Wildeve, who had idly watched the scene from a distance.

The table was then cleared of the articles, and the men began to drink.

"Well, to be sure!" said Christian, half to himself. "To think I should have been born so lucky as this, and not have found it out until now! What curious creatures these dice be — powerful rulers of us all, and yet at my command! I am sure I never need be afeard of anything after this." He handled the dice fondly one by one. "Why, sir," he said in a confidential whisper to Wildeve, who was near his left hand, "if I could only use this power that's in me of multiplying money I might do some good to a near relation of yours, seeking what I've got about me of hers — eh?" He tapped one of his money-laden boots upon the floor.

"What do you mean?" said Wildeve.

"That's a secret. Well, I must be going now." He looked anxiously towards Fairway.

"Where are you going?" Wildeve asked.

"To Mistover Knap. I have to see Mrs. Thomasin there — that's all."

"I am going there, too, to fetch Mrs. Wildeve. We can walk together."

Wildeve became lost in thought, and a look of inward illumination came into his eyes. It was money for his wife that Mrs. Yeobright could not trust him with. "Yet she could trust this fellow," he said to himself. "Why doesn't that which belongs to the wife belong to the husband too?"

He called to the pot-boy to bring him his hat, and said, "Now, Christian, I am ready."

"Mr. Wildeve," said Christian timidly, as he turned to leave the room, "would you mind lending me them wonderful little things that carry my luck inside 'em, that I might practise a bit by myself, you know?" He looked wistfully at the dice and box lying on the mantelpiece.

"Certainly," said Wildeve carelessly. "They were only cut out by some lad with his knife, and are worth nothing." And Christian went back and privately pocketed them.

Wildeve opened the door and looked out. The night was warm and cloudy. "By Gad! 'tis dark," he continued. "But I suppose we shall find our way."

"If we should lose the path it might be awkward," said Christian. "A lantern is the only shield that will make it safe for us."

"Let's have a lantern by all means." The stable-lantern was fetched and lighted. Christian took up his gown-piece, and the two set out to ascend the hill.

Within the room the men fell into chat till their attention was for a moment drawn to the chimney-corner. This was large, and, in addition to its proper recess, contained within its jambs, like many on Egdon, a receding seat, so that a person might sit there absolutely unobserved, provided there was no fire to light him up, as was the case now and throughout the summer. From the niche a single object protruded into the light from the candles on the table. It was a clay pipe, and its colour was reddish. The men had been attracted to this object by a voice behind the pipe asking for a light.

"Upon my life, it fairly startled me when the man spoke!" said Fairway, handing a candle. "Oh — 'tis the reddleman! You've kept a quiet tongue, young man."

"Yes, I had nothing to say," observed Venn. In a few minutes he arose and wished the company good night.

Meanwhile Wildeve and Christian had plunged into the heath.

It was a stagnant, warm, and misty night, full of all the heavy perfumes of new vegetation not yet dried by hot sun, and among these particularly the scent of the fern. The lantern, dangling from Christian's hand, brushed the feathery fronds in passing by, disturbing moths and other winged insects, which flew out and alighted upon its horny panes.

"So you have money to carry to Mrs. Wildeve?" said Christian's companion, after a silence. "Don't you think it very odd that it shouldn't be given to me?"

"As man and wife be one flesh, 'twould have been all the same, I should think," said Christian. "But my strict documents was, to give the money into Mrs. Wildeve's hand: and 'tis well to do things right."

"No doubt," said Wildeve. Any person who had known the circumstances might have perceived that Wildeve was mortified by the discovery that the matter in transit was money, and not, as he had supposed when at Blooms-End, some fancy nicknack which only interested the two women themselves. Mrs. Yeobright's refusal implied that his honour was not considered to be of sufficiently good quality to make him a safe bearer of his wife's property.

"How very warm it is tonight, Christian!" he said, panting, when they were nearly under Rainbarrow. "Let us sit down for a few minutes, for Heaven's sake."

Wildeve flung himself down on the soft ferns; and Christian, placing the lantern and parcel on the ground, perched himself in a cramped position hard by, his knees almost touching his chin. He presently thrust one hand into his coat-pocket and began shaking it about.

"What are you rattling in there?" said Wildeve.

"Only the dice, sir," said Christian, quickly withdrawing his hand. "What magical machines these little things be, Mr. Wildeve! 'Tis a game I should never get tired of. Would you mind my taking 'em out and looking at 'em for a minute, to see how they are made? I didn't like to look close before the other men, for fear they should think it bad manners in me." Christian took them out and examined them in the hollow of his hand by the lantern light. "That these little things should carry such luck, and such charm, and such a spell, and such power in 'em, passes all I ever heard or zeed," he went on, with a fascinated gaze at the dice, which, as is frequently the case in country places, were made of wood, the points being burnt upon each face with the end of a wire.

"They are a great deal in a small compass, you think?"

"Yes. Do ye suppose they really be the devil's playthings, Mr. Wildeve? If so, 'tis no good sign that I be such a lucky man."

"You ought to win some money, now that you've got them. Any woman would marry you then. Now is your time, Christian, and I would recommend you not to let it slip. Some men are born to luck, some are not. I belong to the latter class."

"Did you ever know anybody who was born to it besides myself?"

"O yes. I once heard of an Italian, who sat down at a gaming-table, with only a louis (that's a foreign sovereign) in his pocket. He played on for twenty-four hours, and won ten thousand pounds, stripping the bank he had played against. Then there was another man who had lost a thousand pounds, and went to the broker's next day to sell stock, that he might pay the debt. The man to whom he owed the money went with him in a hackney-coach; and to pass the time they tossed who should pay the fare. The ruined man won, and the other was tempted to continue the game, and they played all the way. When the coachman stopped he was told to drive home again: the whole thousand pounds had been won back by the man who was going to sell."

"Ha — ha — splendid!" exclaimed Christian. "Go on — go on!"

"Then there was a man of London, who was only a waiter at White's club-house. He began playing first half-crown stakes, and then higher and higher, till he became very rich, got an appointment in India, and rose to be Governor of Madras. His daughter married a member of parliament, and the Bishop of Carlisle stood godfather to one of the children."

"Wonderful! wonderful!"

"And once there was a young man in America who gambled till he had lost his last dollar. He staked his watch and chain; and lost as before: staked his umbrella; lost again: staked his hat; lost again: staked his coat and stood in his shirt-sleeves; lost again. Began taking off his breeches, and then a look-er-on gave him a trifle for his pluck. With this he won. Won back his coat, won back his hat, won back his umbrella, his watch, his money, and went out of the door a rich man."

"O, 'tis too good — it takes away my breath! Mr. Wildeve, I think I will try another shilling with you, as I am one of that sort; no danger can come o't, and you can afford to lose."

"Very well," said Wildeve, rising. Searching about with the lantern, he found a large flat stone, which he placed between himself and Christian, and sat down again. The lantern was opened to give more light, and its rays directed upon the stone. Christian put down a shilling, Wildeve another, and each threw. Christian won. They played for two. Christian won again. "Let us try four," said Wildeve. They played for four. This time the stakes were won by Wildeve.

"Ah, those little accidents will, of course, sometimes happen to the luckiest man," he observed.

"And now I have no more money!" exclaimed Christian excitedly. "And yet, if I could go on, I should get it back again, and more. I wish this was mine." He struck his boot upon the ground, so that the guineas chinked within.

"What! you have not put Mrs. Wildeve's money there?"

"Yes. 'Tis for safety. Is it any harm to raffle with a married lady's money when, if I win, I shall only keep my winnings, and give her her own all the same; and if t'other man wins, her money will go to the lawful owner?"

"None at all."

Wildeve had been brooding ever since they started on the mean estimation in which he was held by his wife's friend; and it cut his heart severely. As the minutes passed he had gradually drifted into a revengeful intention without knowing the precise moment of forming it. This was to teach Mrs. Yeobright a lesson, as he considered it to be; in other words, to show her, if he could, that her niece's husband was the proper guardian of her niece's money.

"Well, here goes!" said Christian, beginning to unlace one boot. "I shall dream of it nights and nights, I suppose; but I shall always swear my flesh don't crawl when I think o't!"

He thrust his hand into the boot and withdrew one of poor Thomasin's precious guineas, piping hot. Wildeve had already placed a sovereign on the stone. The game was then resumed. Wildeve won first, and Christian ventured another, winning himself this time. The game fluctuated, but the average was in Wildeve's favour. Both men became so absorbed in the game that they took no heed of anything but the pigmy objects immediately beneath their eyes; the flat stone, the open lantern, the dice, and the few illuminated fern-leaves which lay under the light, were the whole world to them.

At length Christian lost rapidly; and presently, to his horror, the whole fifty guineas belonging to Thomasin had been handed over to his adversary.

"I don't care — I don't care!" he moaned, and desperately set about untying his left boot to get at the other fifty. "The devil will toss me into the flames on his three-pronged fork for this night's work, I know! But perhaps I shall win yet, and then I'll get a wife to sit up with me o' nights, and I won't be afeard, I won't! Here's another for'ee, my man!" He slapped another guinea down upon the stone, and the dice-box was rattled again.

Time passed on. Wildeve began to be as excited as Christian himself. When commencing the game his intention had been nothing further than a bitter practical joke on Mrs. Yeobright. To win the money, fairly or otherwise, and to hand it contemptuously to Thomasin in her aunt's presence, had been the dim outline of his purpose. But men are drawn from their intentions even in the course of carrying them out, and it was extremely doubtful, by the time the twentieth guinea had been reached, whether Wildeve was conscious of any other intention than that of winning for his own personal benefit. Moreover, he was now no longer gambling for his wife's money, but for Yeobright's; though of this fact Christian, in his apprehensiveness, did not inform him till afterwards.

It was nearly eleven o'clock, when, with almost a shriek, Christian placed Yeobright's last bright guinea upon the stone. In thirty seconds it had gone the way of its companions.

Christian turned and flung himself on the ferns in a convulsion of remorse. "O, what shall I do with my wretched self?" he groaned. "What shall I do? Will any good Heaven hae mercy upon my wicked soul?"

"Do? Live on just the same."

"I won't live on just the same! I'll die! I say you are a — a ——"

"A man sharper than my neighbour."

"Yes, a man sharper than my neighbour; a regular sharper!"

"Poor chips-in-porridge, you are very unmannerly."

"I don't know about that! And I say you be unmannerly! You've got money that isn't your own. Half the guineas are poor Mr. Clym's."

"How's that?"

"Because I had to gie fifty of 'em to him. Mrs. Yeobright said so."

"Oh?... Well, 'twould have been more graceful of her to have given them to his wife Eustacia. But they are in my hands now."

Christian pulled on his boots, and with heavy breathings, which could be heard to some distance, dragged his limbs together, arose, and tottered away out of sight. Wildeve set about shutting the lantern to return to the house, for he deemed it too late to go to Mistover to meet his wife, who was to be driven home in the captain's four-wheel. While he was closing the little horn door a figure rose from behind a neighbouring bush and came forward into the lantern light. It was the reddleman approaching.

VIII

A NEW FORCE DISTURBS THE CURRENT

WILDEVE stared. Venn looked coolly towards Wildeve, and, without a word being spoken, he deliberately sat himself down where Christian had been seated, thrust his hand into his pocket, drew out a sovereign, and laid it on the stone.

"You have been watching us from behind that bush?" said Wildeve.

The reddleman nodded. "Down with your stake," he said. "Or haven't you pluck enough to go on?"

Now, gambling is a species of amusement which is much more easily begun with full pockets than left off with the same; and though Wildeve in a cooler temper might have prudently declined this invitation, the excitement of his recent success carried him completely away. He placed one of the guineas on the slab beside the reddleman's sovereign. "Mine is a guinea," he said.

"A guinea that's not your own," said Venn sarcastically.

"It is my own," answered Wildeve haughtily. "It is my wife's, and what is hers is mine."

"Very well; let's make a beginning." He shook the box, and threw eight, ten, and nine; the three casts amounted to twenty-seven.

This encouraged Wildeve. He took the box; and his three casts amounted to forty-five.

Down went another of the reddleman's sovereigns against his first one which Wildeve laid. This time Wildeve threw fifty-one points, but no pair. The reddleman looked grim, threw a raffle of aces, and pocketed the stakes.

"Here you are again," said Wildeve contemptuously. "Double the stakes." He laid two of Thomasin's guineas, and the reddleman his two pounds. Ven won again. New stakes were laid on the stone, and the gamblers proceeded as before.

Wildeve was a nervous and excitable man; and the game was beginning to tell upon his temper. He writhed, fumed, shifted his seat; and the beating of his heart was almost audible. Venn sat with lips impassively closed and eyes reduced to a pair of unimportant twinkles; he scarcely appeared to breathe. He might have been an Arab, or an automaton; he would have been like a red-sandstone statue but for the motion of his arm with the dice-box.

The game fluctuated now in favour of one, now in favour of the other, without any great advantage on the side of either. Nearly twenty minutes were passed thus. The light of the candle had by this time attracted heath-flies, moths, and other winged creatures of night, which floated round the lantern, flew into the flame, or beat about the faces of the two players.

But neither of the men paid much attention to these things, their eyes being concentrated upon the little flat stone, which to them was an arena vast and important as a battle-field. By this time a change had come over the game; the reddleman won continually. At length sixty guineas — Thomasin's fifty and ten of Clym's — had passed into his hands. Wildeve was reckless, frantic, exasperated.

"'Won back his coat,'" said Venn slily.

Another throw, and the money went the same way.

"'Won back his hat,'" continued Venn.

"Oh, oh!" said Wildeve.

"'Won back his watch, won back his money, and went out of the door a rich man,'" added Venn sentence by sentence, as stake after stake passed over to him.

"Five more!" shouted Wildeve, dashing down the money. "And three casts be hanged — one shall decide."

The red automaton opposite lapsed into silence, nodded, and followed his example. Wildeve rattled the box, and threw a pair of sixes and five points. He clapped his hands; "I have done it this time — hurrah!"

"There are two playing, and only one has thrown," said the reddleman, quietly bringing down the box. The eyes of each were then so intently converged upon the stone that one could fancy their beams were visible, like rays in a fog.

Venn lifted the box, and behold a triplet of sixes was disclosed.

Wildeve was full of fury. While the reddleman was grasping the stakes Wildeve seized the dice and hurled them, box and all, into the darkness, uttering a fearful imprecation. Then he arose and began stamping up and down like a madman.

"It is all over, then?" said Venn.

"No, no!" cried Wildeve. "I mean to have another chance yet. I must!"

"But, my good man, what have you done with the dice?"

"I threw them away — it was a momentary irritation. What a fool I am! Here — come and help me to look for them — we must find them again."

Wildeve snatched up the lantern and began anxiously prowling among the furze and fern.

"You are not likely to find them there," said Venn, following. "What did you do such a crazy thing as that for? Here's the box. The dice can't be far off."

Wildeve turned the light eagerly upon the spot where Venn had found the box, and mauled the herbage right and left. In the course of a few minutes one of the dice was found. They searched on for some time, but no other was to be seen.

"Never mind," said Wildeve; "let's play with one."

"Agreed," said Venn.

Down they sat again, and recommenced with single guinea stakes; and the play went on smartly. But Fortune had unmistakably fallen in love with the reddleman tonight. He won steadily, till he was the owner of fourteen more of the gold pieces. Seventy-nine of the hundred guineas were his, Wildeve possessing only twenty-one. The aspect of the two opponents was now singular. Apart from motions, a complete diorama of the fluctuations of the game went on in their eyes. A diminutive candle-flame was mirrored in each pupil, and it would have been possible to distinguish therein between the moods of hope and the moods of abandonment, even as regards the reddleman, though his facial muscles betrayed nothing at all. Wildeve played on with the recklessness of despair.

"What's that?" he suddenly exclaimed, hearing a rustle; and they both looked up.

They were surrounded by dusky forms about four feet high, standing a few paces beyond the rays of the lantern. A moment's inspection revealed that the encircling figures were heath-croppers, their heads being all towards the players, at whom they gazed intently.

"Hoosh!" said Wildeve; and the whole forty or fifty animals at once turned and galloped away. Play was again resumed.

Ten minutes passed away. Then a large death's-head moth advanced from the obscure outer air, wheeled twice round the lantern, flew straight at the candle, and extinguished it by the force of the blow. Wildeve had just thrown, but had not lifted the box to see what he had cast; and now it was impossible.

"What the infernal!" he shrieked. "Now, what shall we do? Perhaps I have thrown six — have you any matches?"

"None," said Venn.

"Christian had some — I wonder where he is. Christian!"

But there was no reply to Wildeve's shout, save a mournful whining from the herons which were nesting lower down the vale. Both men looked blankly round without rising. As their eyes grew accustomed to the darkness they perceived faint greenish points of light among the grass and fern. These lights dotted the hillside like stars of a low magnitude.

"Ah — glowworms," said Wildeve. "Wait a minute. We can continue the game."

Venn sat still, and his companion went hither and thither till he had gathered thirteen glowworms — as many as he could find in a space of four or five minutes — upon a foxglove leaf which he pulled for the purpose. The reddleman vented a low humorous laugh when he saw his adversary return with these. "Determined to go on, then?" he said drily.

"I always am!" said Wildeve angrily. And shaking the glowworms from the leaf he ranged them with a trembling hand in a circle on the stone, leaving a space in the middle for the descent of the dice-box, over which the thirteen tiny lamps threw a pale phosphoric shine. The game was again renewed. It happened to be that season of the year at which glowworms put forth their greatest brilliancy, and the light they yielded was more than ample for the purpose, since it is possible on such nights to read the handwriting of a letter by the light of two or three.

The incongruity between the men's deeds and their environment was great. Amid the soft juicy vegetation of the hollow in which they sat, the motionless and the uninhabited solitude, intruded the chink of guineas, the rattle of dice, the exclamations of the reckless players.

Wildeve had lifted the box as soon as the lights were obtained, and the solitary die proclaimed that the game was still against him.

"I won't play any more: you've been tampering with the dice," he shouted.

"How — when they were your own?" said the reddleman.

"We'll change the fame: the lowest point shall win the stake — it may cut off my ill luck. Do you refuse?"

"No — go on," said Venn.

"O, there they are again — damn them!" cried Wildeve, looking up. The heath-croppers had returned noiselessly, and were looking on with erect heads just as before, their timid eyes fixed upon the scene, as if they were wondering what mankind and candle-light could have to do in these haunts at this untoward hour.

"What a plague those creatures are — staring so!" he said, and flung a stone, which scattered them; when the game was continued as before.

Wildeve had now ten guineas left; and each laid five. Wildeve threw three points; Venn two, and raked in the coins. The other seized the die, and clenched his teeth upon it in sheer rage, as if he would bite it in pieces. "Never give in — here are my last five!" he cried, throwing them down. "Hang the glowworms — they are going out. Why don't you burn, you little fools? Stir them up with a thorn."

He probed the glowworms with a bit of stick, and rolled them over, till the bright side of their tails was upwards.

"There's light enough. Throw on," said Venn.

Wildeve brought down the box within the shining circle and looked eagerly. He had thrown ace. "Well done! — I said it would turn, and it has turned." Venn said nothing; but his hand shook slightly.

He threw ace also.

"O!" said Wildeve. "Curse me!"

The die smacked the stone a second time. It was ace again. Venn looked gloomy, threw: the die was seen to be lying in two pieces, the cleft sides uppermost.

"I've thrown nothing at all," he said.

"Serves me right — I split the die with my teeth. Here — take your money. Blank is less than one."

"I don't wish it."

"Take it, I say — you've won it!" And Wildeve threw the stakes against the reddleman's chest. Venn gathered them up, arose, and withdrew from the hollow, Wildeve sitting stupefied.

When he had come to himself he also arose, and, with the extinguished lantern in his hand, went towards the high-road. On reaching it he stood still.

The silence of night pervaded the whole heath except in one direction; and that was towards Mistover. There he could hear the noise of light wheels, and presently saw two carriage-lamps descending the hill. Wildeve screened himself under a bush and waited.

The vehicle came on and passed before him. It was a hired carriage, and behind the coachman were two persons whom he knew well. There sat Eustacia and Yeobright, the arm of the latter being round her waist. They turned the sharp corner at the bottom towards the temporary home which Clym had hired and furnished, about three miles to the eastward.

Wildeve forgot the loss of the money at the sight of his lost love, whose preciousness in his eyes was increasing in geometrical progression with each new incident that reminded him of their hopeless division. Brimming with the subtilized misery that he was capable of feeling, he followed the opposite way towards the inn.

About the same moment that Wildeve stepped into the highway Venn also had reached it at a point a hundred yards further on; and he, hearing the same wheels, likewise waited till the carriage should come up. When he saw who sat therein he seemed to be disappointed. Reflecting a minute or two, during which interval the carriage rolled on, he crossed the road, and took a short cut through the furze and heath to a point where the turnpike-road bent round in ascending a hill. He was now again in front of the carriage, which presently came up at a walking pace. Venn stepped forward and showed himself.

Eustacia started when the lamp shone upon him, and Clym's arm was involuntarily withdrawn from her waist. He said, "What, Diggory? You are having a lonely walk."

"Yes — I beg your pardon for stopping you," said Venn. "But I am waiting about for Mrs. Wildeve: I have something to give her from Mrs. Yeobright. Can you tell me if she's gone home from the party yet?"

"No. But she will be leaving soon. You may possibly meet her at the corner."

Venn made a farewell obeisance, and walked back to his former position, where the by-road from Mistover joined the highway. Here he remained fixed for nearly half an hour; and then another pair of lights came down the hill. It was the old-fashioned wheeled nondescript belonging to the captain, and Thomasin sat in it alone, driven by Charley.

The reddleman came up as they slowly turned the corner. "I beg pardon for stopping you, Mrs. Wildeve," he said. "But I have something to give you privately from Mrs. Yeobright." He handed a small parcel; it consisted of the hundred guineas he had just won, roughly twisted up in a piece of paper.

Thomasin recovered from her surprise, and took the packet. "That's all, ma'am — I wish you good night," he said, and vanished from her view.

Thus Venn, in his anxiety to rectify matters, had placed in Thomasin's hands not only the fifty guineas which rightly belonged to her, but also the fifty intended for her cousin Clym. His mistake had been based upon Wildeve's words at the opening of the game, when he indignantly denied that the guinea was not his own. It had not been comprehended by the reddleman that at half-way through the performance the game was continued with the money of another person; and it was an error which afterwards helped to cause more misfortune than treble the loss in money value could have done.

The night was now somewhat advanced; and Venn plunged deeper into the heath, till he came to a ravine where his van was standing — a spot not more than two hundred yards from the site of the gambling bout. He entered this movable home of his, lit his lantern, and, before closing his door for the night, stood reflecting on the circumstances of the preceding hours. While he stood the dawn grew visible in the northeast quarter of the heavens, which, the clouds having cleared off, was bright with a soft sheen at this midsummer time, though it was only between one and two o'clock. Venn, thoroughly weary, then shut his door and flung himself down to sleep.

Book Fourth: The Closed Door

I

THE RENCOUNTER BY THE POOL

The July sun shone over Egdon and fired its crimson heather to scarlet. It was the one season of the year, and the one weather of the season, in which the heath was gorgeous. This flowering period represented the second or noontide division in the cycle of those superficial changes which alone were possible here; it followed the green or young-fern period, representing the morn, and preceded the brown period, when the heath-bells and ferns would wear the russet tinges of evening; to be in turn displaced by the dark hue of the winter period, representing night.

Clym and Eustacia, in their little house at Alderworth, were living on with a monotony which was delightful to them. The heath and changes of weather were quite blotted out from their eyes for the present. They were enclosed in a sort of luminous mist, which hid from them surroundings of any inharmonious colour, and gave to all things the character of light. When it rained they were charmed, because they could remain indoors together all day with such a show of reason; when it was fine they were charmed, because they could sit together on the hills. They were like those double stars which revolve round and round each other, and from a distance appear to be one. The absolute solitude in which they lived intensified their reciprocal thoughts; yet some might have said that it had the disadvantage of consuming their mutual affections at a fearfully prodigal rate. Yeobright did not fear for his own part; but recollection of Eustacia's old speech about the evanescence of love, now apparently forgotten by her, sometimes caused him to ask himself a question; and he recoiled at the thought that the quality of finiteness was not foreign to Eden.

When three or four weeks had been passed thus, Yeobright resumed his reading in earnest. To make up for lost time he studied indefatigably, for he wished to enter his new profession with the least possible delay.

Now, Eustacia's dream had always been that, once married to Clym, she would have the power of inducing him to return to Paris. He had carefully withheld all promise to do so; but would he be proof against her coaxing and argument? She had calculated to such a degree on the probability of success that she had represented Paris, and not Budmouth, to her grandfather as in all likelihood their future home. Her hopes were bound up in this dream. In the quiet days since their marriage, when Yeobright had been poring over her lips, her eyes, and the lines of her face, she had mused and mused on the subject, even while in the act of returning his gaze; and now the sight of the books, indicating a future which was antagonistic to her dream, struck her with a positively painful jar. She was hoping for the time when, as the mistress of some pretty establishment, however small, near a Parisian Boulevard, she would be passing her days on the skirts at least of the gay world, and catching stray wafts from those town pleasures she was so well fitted to enjoy. Yet Yeobright was as firm in the contrary intention as if the tendency of marriage were rather to develop the fantasies of young philanthropy than to sweep them away.

Her anxiety reached a high pitch; but there was something in Clym's undeviating manner which made her hesitate before sounding him on the subject. At this point in their experience, however, an incident helped her. It occurred one evening about six weeks after their union, and arose entirely out of the unconscious misapplication by Venn of the fifty guineas intended for Yeobright.

A day or two after the receipt of the money Thomasin had sent a note to her aunt to thank her. She had been surprised at the largeness of the amount; but as no sum had ever been mentioned she set that down to her late uncle's generosity. She had been strictly charged by her aunt to say nothing to her husband of this gift; and Wildeve, as was natural enough, had not brought himself to mention to his wife a single particular of the midnight scene in the heath. Christian's terror, in like manner, had tied his tongue on the share he took in that proceeding; and hoping that by some means or other the money had gone to its proper destination, he simply asserted as much, without giving details.

Therefore, when a week or two had passed away, Mrs. Yeobright began to wonder why she never heard from her son of the receipt of the present; and to add gloom to her perplexity came the possibility that resentment might be the cause of his silence. She could hardly believe as much, but why did he not write? She questioned Christian, and the confusion in his answers would at once have led her to believe that something was wrong, had not one-half of his story been corroborated by Thomasin's note.

Mrs. Yeobright was in this state of uncertainty when she was informed one morning that her son's wife was visiting her grandfather at Mistover. She determined to walk up the hill, see Eustacia, and ascertain from her daughter-in-law's lips whether the family guineas, which were to Mrs. Yeobright what family jewels are to wealthier dowagers, had miscarried or not.

When Christian learnt where she was going his concern reached its height. At the moment of her departure he could prevaricate no longer, and, confessing to the gambling, told her the truth as far as he knew it — that the guineas had been won by Wildeve.

"What, is he going to keep them?" Mrs. Yeobright cried.

"I hope and trust not!" moaned Christian. "He's a good man, and perhaps will do right things. He said you ought to have gied Mr. Clym's share to Eustacia, and that's perhaps what he'll do himself."

To Mrs. Yeobright, as soon as she could calmly reflect, there was much likelihood in this, for she could hardly believe that Wildeve would really appropriate money belonging to her son. The intermediate course of giving it to Eustacia was the sort of thing to please Wildeve's fancy. But it filled the mother with anger none the less. That Wildeve should have got command of the guineas after all, and should rearrange the disposal of them, placing Clym's share in Clym's wife's hands, because she had been his own sweetheart, and might be so still, was as irritating a pain as any that Mrs. Yeobright had ever borne.

She instantly dismissed the wretched Christian from her employ for his conduct in the affair; but, feeling quite helpless and unable to do without him, told him afterwards that he might stay a little longer if he chose. Then she hastened off to Eustacia, moved by a much less promising emotion towards her daughter-in-law than she had felt half an hour earlier, when planning her journey. At that time it was to inquire in a friendly spirit if there had been any accidental loss; now it was to ask plainly if Wildeve had privately given her money which had been intended as a sacred gift to Clym.

She started at two o'clock, and her meeting with Eustacia was hastened by the appearance of the young lady beside the pool and bank which bordered her grandfather's premises, where she stood surveying the scene, and perhaps thinking of the romantic enactments it had witnessed in past days. When Mrs. Yeobright approached, Eustacia surveyed her with the calm stare of a stranger.

The mother-in-law was the first to speak. "I was coming to see you," she said.

"Indeed!" said Eustacia with surprise, for Mrs. Yeobright, much to the girl's mortification, had refused to be present at the wedding. "I did not at all expect you."

"I was coming on business only," said the visitor, more coldly than at first. "Will you excuse my asking this — Have you received a gift from Thomasin's husband?"

"A gift?"

"I mean money!"

"What — I myself?"

"Well, I meant yourself, privately — though I was not going to put it in that way."

"Money from Mr. Wildeve? No — never! Madam, what do you mean by that?" Eustacia fired up all too quickly, for her own consciousness of the old attachment between herself and Wildeve led her to jump to the conclusion that Mrs. Yeobright also knew of it, and might have come to accuse her of receiving dishonourable presents from him now.

"I simply ask the question," said Mrs. Yeobright. "I have been ——"

"You ought to have better opinions of me — I feared you were against me from the first!" exclaimed Eustacia.

"No. I was simply for Clym," replied Mrs. Yeobright, with too much emphasis in her earnestness. "It is the instinct of every one to look after their own."

"How can you imply that he required guarding against me?" cried Eustacia, passionate tears in her eyes. "I have not injured him by marrying him! What sin have I done that you should think so ill of me? You had no right to speak against me to him when I have never wronged you."

"I only did what was fair under the circumstances," said Mrs. Yeobright more softly. "I would rather not have gone into this question at present, but you compel me. I am not ashamed to tell you the honest truth. I was firmly convinced that he ought not to marry you — therefore I tried to dissuade him by all the means in my power. But it is done now, and I have no idea of complaining any more. I am ready to welcome you."

"Ah, yes, it is very well to see things in that business point of view," murmured Eustacia with a smothered fire of feeling. "But why should you think there is anything between me and Mr. Wildeve? I have a spirit as well as you. I am indignant; and so would any woman be. It was a condescension in me to be Clym's wife, and not a manœuvre, let me remind you; and therefore I will not be treated as a schemer whom it becomes necessary to bear with because she has crept into the family."

"Oh!" said Mrs. Yeobright, vainly endeavouring to control her anger. "I have never heard anything to show that my son's lineage is not as good as the Vyes' — perhaps better. It is amusing to hear you talk of condescension."

"It was condescension, nevertheless," said Eustacia, vehemently. "And if I had known then what I know now, that I should be living in this wild heath a month after my marriage I — should have thought twice before agreeing."

"It would be better not to say that; it might not sound truthful. I am not aware that any deception was used on his part — I know there was not — whatever might have been the case on the other side."

"This is too exasperating!" answered the younger woman huskily, her face crimsoning, and her eyes darting light. "How can you dare to speak to me like that? I insist upon repeating to you that had I known that my life would from my marriage up to this time have been as it is, I should have said No. I don't complain. I have never uttered a sound of such a thing to him; but it is true. I hope therefore that in the future you will be silent on my eagerness. If you injure me now you injure yourself."

"Injure you? Do you think I am an evil-disposed person?"

"You injured me before my marriage, and you have now suspected me of secretly favouring another man for money!"

"I could not help what I thought. But I have never spoken of you outside my house."

"You spoke of me within it, to Clym, and you could not do worse."

"I did my duty."

"And I'll do mine."

"A part of which will possibly be to set him against his mother. It is always so. But why should I not bear it as others have borne it before me?"

"I understand you," said Eustacia, breathless with emotion. "You think me capable of every bad thing. Who can be worse than a wife who encourages a lover, and poisons her husband's mind against his relative? Yet that is now the character given to me. Will you not come and drag him out of my hands?"

Mrs. Yeobright gave back heat for heat.

"Don't rage at me, madam! It ill becomes your beauty, and I am not worth the injury you may do it on my account, I assure you. I am only a poor old woman who has lost a son."

"If you had treated me honourably you would have had him still," Eustacia said, while scalding tears trickled from her eyes. "You have brought yourself to folly; you have caused a division which can never be healed!"

"I have done nothing. This audacity from a young woman is more than I can bear."

"It was asked for; you have suspected me, and you have made me speak of my husband in a way I would not have done. You will let him know that I have spoken thus, and it will cause misery between us. Will you go away from me? You are no friend!"

"I will go when I have spoken a word. If any one says I have come here to question you without good grounds for it, that person speaks untruly. If any one says that I attempted to stop your marriage by any but honest means, that person, too, does not speak the truth. I have fallen on an evil time; God has been unjust to me in letting you insult me! Probably my son's happiness does not lie on this side of the grave, for he is a foolish man who neglects the advice of his parent. You, Eustacia, stand on the edge of the precipice without knowing it. Only show my son one-half the temper you have shown me today — and you may before long — and you will find that though he is as gentle as a child with you now, he can be as hard as steel!"

The excited mother then withdrew, and Eustacia, panting, stood looking into the pool.

II

HE IS SET UPON BY ADVERSITIES BUT HE SINGS A SONG

THE result of that unpropitious interview was that Eustacia, instead of passing the afternoon with her grandfather, hastily returned home to Clym, where she arrived three hours earlier than she had been expected.

She came indoors with her face flushed, and her eyes still showing traces of her recent excitement. Yeobright looked up astonished; he had never seen her in any way approaching to that state before. She passed him by, and would have gone upstairs unnoticed, but Clym was so concerned that he immediately followed her.

"What is the matter, Eustacia?" he said. She was standing on the hearth-rug in the bedroom, looking upon the floor, her hands clasped in front of her, her bonnet yet unremoved. For a moment she did not answer; and then she replied in a low voice——

"I have seen your mother; and I will never see her again!"

A weight fell like a stone upon Clym. That same morning, when Eustacia had arranged to go and see her grandfather, Clym had expressed a wish that she would drive down to Blooms-End and inquire for her mother-in-law, or adopt any other means she might think fit to bring about a reconciliation. She had set out gaily; and he had hoped for much.

"Why is this?" he asked.

"I cannot tell — I cannot remember. I met your mother. And I will never meet her again."

"Why?"

"What do I know about Mr. Wildeve now? I won't have wicked opinions passed on me by anybody. Oh! it was too humiliating to be asked if I had received any money from him, or encouraged him, or something of the sort — I don't exactly know what!"

"How could she have asked you that?"

"She did."

"Then there must have been some meaning in it. What did my mother say besides?"

"I don't know what she said, except in so far as this, that we both said words which can never be forgiven!"

"O, there must be some misapprehension. Whose fault was it that her meaning was not made clear?"

"I would rather not say. It may have been the fault of the circumstances, which were awkward at the very least. O Clym — I cannot help expressing it — this is an unpleasant position that you have placed me in. But you must improve it — yes, say you will — for I hate it all now! Yes, take me to Paris, and go on with your old occupation, Clym! I don't mind how humbly we live there at first, if it can only be Paris, and not Egdon Heath."

"But I have quite given up that idea," said Yeobright, with surprise. "Surely I never led you to expect such a thing?"

"I own it. Yet there are thoughts which cannot be kept out of mind, and that one was mine. Must I not have a voice in the matter, now I am your wife and the sharer of your doom?"

"Well, there are things which are placed beyond the pale of discussion; and I thought this was specially so, and by mutual agreement."

"Clym, I am unhappy at what I hear," she said in a low voice; and her eyes drooped, and she turned away.

This indication of an unexpected mine of hope in Eustacia's bosom disconcerted her husband. It was the first time that he had confronted the fact of the indirectness of a woman's movement towards her desire. But his intention was unshaken, though he loved Eustacia well. All the effect that her remark had upon him was a resolve to chain himself more closely than ever to his books, so as to be the sooner enabled to appeal to substantial results from another course in arguing against her whim.

Next day the mystery of the guineas was explained. Thomasin paid them a hurried visit, and Clym's share was delivered up to him by her own hands. Eustacia was not present at the time.

"Then this is what my mother meant," exclaimed Clym. "Thomasin, do you know that they have had a bitter quarrel?"

There was a little more reticence now than formerly in Thomasin's manner towards her cousin. It is the effect of marriage to engender in several directions some of the reserve it annihilates in one. "Your mother told me," she said quietly. "She came back to my house."

"The worst thing I dreaded has come to pass. Was mother much disturbed when she came to you, Thomasin?"

"Yes."

"Very much indeed?"

"Yes."

Clym leant his elbow upon the post of the garden gate, and covered his eyes with his hand.

"Don't trouble about it, Clym. They may get to be friends."

He shook his head. "Not two people with inflammable natures like theirs. Well, what must be will be."

"One thing is cheerful in it — the guineas are not lost."

"I would rather have lost them twice over than have had this happen."

Amid these jarring events Yeobright felt one thing to be indispensable — that he should speedily make some show of progress in his scholastic plans. With this view he read far into the small hours during many nights.

One morning, after a severer strain than usual, he awoke with a strange sensation in his eyes. The sun was shining directly upon the window-blind, and at his first glance thitherward a sharp pain obliged him to close his eyelids quickly. At every new attempt to look about him the same morbid sensibility to light was manifested, and excoriating tears ran down his cheeks. He was obliged to tie a bandage over his brow while dressing; and during the day it could not be abandoned. Eustacia was thoroughly alarmed. On finding that the case was no better the next morning they decided to send to Anglebury for a surgeon.

Towards evening he arrived, and pronounced the disease to be acute inflammation induced by Clym's night studies, continued in spite of a cold previously caught, which had weakened his eyes for the time.

Fretting with impatience at this interruption to a task he was so anxious to hasten, Clym was transformed into an invalid. He was shut up in a room from which all light was excluded, and his condition would have been one of absolute misery had not Eustacia read to him by the glimmer of a shaded lamp. He hoped that the worst would soon be over; but at the surgeon's third visit he learnt to his dismay that although he might venture out of doors with shaded eyes in the course of a month, all thought of pursuing his work, or of reading print of any description, would have to be given up for a long time to come.

One week and another week wore on, and nothing seemed to lighten the gloom of the young couple. Dreadful imaginings occurred to Eustacia, but she carefully refrained from uttering them to her husband. Suppose he should become blind, or, at all events, never recover sufficient strength of sight to engage in an occupation which would be congenial to her feelings, and conduce to her removal from this lonely dwelling among the hills? That dream of beautiful Paris was not likely to cohere into substance in the presence of this misfortune. As day after day passed by, and he got no better, her mind ran more and more in this mournful groove, and she would go away from him into the garden and weep despairing tears.

Yeobright thought he would send for his mother; and then he thought he would not. Knowledge of his state could only make her the more unhappy; and the seclusion of their life was such that she would hardly be likely to learn the news except through a special messenger. Endeavouring to take the trouble as philosophically as possible, he waited on till the third week had arrived, when he went into the open air for the first time since the attack. The surgeon visited him again at this stage, and Clym urged him to express a distinct opinion. The young man learnt with added surprise that the date at which he might expect to resume his labours was as uncertain as ever, his eyes being in that peculiar state which, though affording him sight enough for walking about, would not admit of their being strained upon any definite object without incurring the risk of reproducing ophthalmia in its acute form.

Clym was very grave at the intelligence, but not despairing. A quiet firmness, and even cheerfulness, took possession of him. He was not to be blind; that was enough. To be doomed to behold the world through smoked glass for an indefinite period was bad enough, and fatal to any kind of advance; but Yeobright was an absolute stoic in the face of mishaps which only affected his social standing; and, apart from Eustacia, the humblest walk of life would satisfy him if it could be made to work in with some form of his culture scheme. To keep a cottage night-school was one such form; and his affliction did not master his spirit as it might otherwise have done.

He walked through the warm sun westward into those tracts of Egdon with which he was best acquainted, being those lying nearer to his old home. He saw before him in one of the valleys the gleaming of whetted iron, and advancing, dimly perceived that the shine came from the tool of a man who was cutting furze. The worker recognized Clym, and Yeobright learnt from the voice that the speaker was Humphrey.

Humphrey expressed his sorrow at Clym's condition: and added, "Now, if yours was low-class work like mine, you could go on with it just the same."

"Yes; I could," said Yeobright musingly. "How much do you get for cutting these faggots?"

"Half-a-crown a hundred, and in these long days I can live very well on the wages."

During the whole of Yeobright's walk home to Alderworth he was lost in reflections which were not of an unpleasant kind. On his coming up to the house Eustacia spoke to him from the open window, and he went across to her.

"Darling," he said, "I am much happier. And if my mother were reconciled to me and to you I should, I think, be quite happy."

"I fear that will never be," she said, looking afar with her beautiful stormy eyes. "How *can* you say 'I am happier,' and nothing changed?"

"It arises from my having at last discovered something I can do, and get a living at, in this time of misfortune."

"Yes?"

"I am going to be a furze and turf-cutter."

"No, Clym!" she said, the slight hopefulness previously apparent in her face going off again, and leaving her worse than before.

"Surely I shall. Is it not very unwise in us to go on spending the little money we've got when I can keep down expenditure by an honest occupation? The outdoor exercise will do me good, and who knows but that in a few months I shall be able to go on with my reading again?"

"But my grandfather offers to assist us, if we require assistance."

"We don't require it. If I go furze-cutting we shall be fairly well off."

"In comparison with slaves, and the Israelites in Egypt, and such people!" A bitter tear rolled down Eustacia's face, which he did not see. There had been *nonchalance* in his tone, showing her that he felt no absolute grief at a consummation which to her was a positive horror.

The very next day Yeobright went to Humphrey's cottage, and borrowed of him leggings, gloves, a whetstone, and a hook, to use till he should be able to purchase some for himself. Then he sallied forth with his new fellow-labourer and old acquaintance, and selecting a spot where the furze grew thickest he struck the first blow in his adopted calling. His sight, like the wings in *Rasselas*, though useless to him for his grand purpose, sufficed for this strait, and he found that when a little practise should have hardened his palms against blistering he would be able to work with ease.

Day after day he rose with the sun, buckled on his leggings, and went off to the rendezvous with Humphrey. His custom was to work from four o'clock in the morning till noon; then, when the heat of the day was at its highest, to go home and sleep for an hour or two; afterwards coming out again and working till dusk at nine.

This man from Paris was now so disguised by his leather accoutrements, and by the goggles he was obliged to wear over his eyes, that his closest friend might have passed by without recognizing him. He was a brown spot in the midst of an expanse of olive-green gorse, and nothing more. Though frequently depressed in spirit when not actually at work, owing to thoughts of Eustacia's position and his mother's estrangement, when in the full swing of labour he was cheerfully disposed and calm.

His daily life was of a curious microscopic sort, his whole world being limited to a circuit of a few feet from his person. His familiars were creeping and winged things, and they seemed to enroll him in their band. Bees hummed around his ears with an intimate air, and tugged at the heath and furze-flowers at his side in such numbers as to weigh them down to the sod. The strange amber-coloured butterflies which Egdon produced, and which were never seen elsewhere, quivered in the breath of his lips, alighted upon his bowed back, and sported with the glittering point of his hook as he flourished it up and down. Tribes of emerald-green grasshoppers leaped over his feet, falling awkwardly on their backs, heads, or hips, like unskilful acrobats, as chance might rule; or engaged themselves in noisy flirtations under the fern-fronds with silent ones of homely hue. Huge flies, ignorant of larders and wire-netting, and quite in a savage state, buzzed about him without knowing that he was a man. In and out of the fern-brakes snakes glided in their most brilliant blue and yellow guise, it being the season immediately following the shedding of their old skins, when their colours are brightest. Litters of young rabbits came out from their forms to sun themselves upon hillocks, the hot beams blazing through the delicate tissue of each thin-fleshed ear, and firing it to a blood-red transparency in which the veins could be seen.

The monotony of his occupation soothed him, and was in itself a pleasure. A forced limitation of effort offered a justification of homely courses to an unambitious man, whose conscience would hardly have allowed him to remain in such obscurity while his powers were unimpeded. Hence Yeobright sometimes sang to himself, and when obliged to accompany Humphrey in search of brambles for faggot-bonds he would amuse his companion with sketches of Parisian life and character, and so while away the time.

On one of these warm afternoons Eustacia walked out alone in the direction of Yeobright's place of work. He was busily chopping away at the furze, a long row of faggots which stretched downward from his position representing the labour of the day. He did not observe her approach, and she stood close to him, and heard his undercurrent of song. It shocked her. To see him there, a poor afflicted man, earning money by the sweat of his brow, had at first moved her to tears; but to hear him sing and not at all rebel against an occupation which, however satisfactory to himself, was degrading to her, as an educated lady-wife, wounded her through. Unconscious of her presence, he still went on singing: —

> 'Le point du jour
> A nos bosquets rend toute leur parure;
> Flore est plus belle à son retour;
> L'oiseau reprend doux chant d'amour:
> Tout célèbre dans la nature
> Le point du jour.

> 'Le point du jour
> Cause parfois, cause douleur extrême
> Que l'espace des nuits est court
> Pour le berger brûlant d'amour,
> Forcé de quitter ce qu'il aime
> Au point du jour.'

It was bitterly plain to Eustacia that he did not care much about social failure; and the proud fair woman bowed her head and wept in sick despair at thought of the blasting effect upon her own life of that mood and condition in him. Then she came forward.

"I would starve rather than do it!" she exclaimed vehemently. "And you can sing! I will go and live with my grandfather again!"

"Eustacia! I did not see you, though I noticed something moving," he said gently. He came forward, pulled off his huge leather glove, and took her hand. "Why do you speak in such a strange way? It is only a little old song which struck my fancy when I was in Paris, and now just applies to my life with you. Has your love for me all died, then, because my appearance is no longer that of a fine gentleman?"

"Dearest, you must not question me unpleasantly, or it may make me not love you."

"Do you believe it possible that I would run the risk of doing that?"

"Well, you follow out your own ideas, and won't give in to mine when I wish you to leave off this shameful labour. Is there anything you dislike in me that you act so contrarily to my wishes? I am your wife, and why will you not listen? Yes, I am your wife indeed!"

"I know what that tone means."

"What tone?"

"The tone in which you said, 'Your wife indeed.' It meant, 'Your wife, worse luck.'"

"It is hard in you to probe me with that remark. A woman may have reason, though she is not without heart, and if I felt 'worse luck,' it was no ignoble feeling — it was only too natural. There, you see that at any rate I do not attempt untruths. Do you remember how, before we were married, I warned you that I had not good wifely qualities?"

"You mock me to say that now. On that point at least the only noble course would be to hold your tongue, for you are still queen of me, Eustacia, though I may no longer be king of you."

"You are my husband. Does not that content you?"

"Not unless you are my wife without regret."

"I cannot answer you. I remember saying that I should be a serious matter on your hands."

"Yes, I saw that."

"Then you were too quick to see! No true lover would have seen any such thing; you are too severe upon me. Clym — I don't like your speaking so at all."

"Well, I married you in spite of it, and don't regret doing so. How cold you seem this afternoon! And yet I used to think there never was a warmer heart than yours."

"Yes, I fear we are cooling — I see it as well as you," she sighed mournfully. "And how madly we loved two months ago! You were never tired of contemplating me, nor I of contemplating you. Who could have thought then that by this time my eyes would not seem so very bright to yours, nor your lips so very sweet to mine? Two months — is it possible? Yes, 'tis too true!"

"You sigh, dear, as if you were sorry for it; and that's a hopeful sign."

"No. I don't sigh for that. There are other things for me to sigh for, or any other woman in my place."

"That your chances in life are ruined by marrying in haste an unfortunate man?"

"Why will you force me, Clym, to say bitter things? I deserve pity as much as you. As much? — I think I deserve it more. For you can sing! It would be a strange hour which should catch me singing under such a cloud as this! Believe me, sweet, I could weep to a degree that would astonish and confound such an elastic mind as yours. Even had you felt careless about your own affliction, you might have refrained from singing out of sheer pity for mine. God! if I were a man in such a position I would curse rather than sing."

Yeobright placed his hand upon her arm. "Now, don't you suppose, my inexperienced girl, that I cannot rebel, in high Promethean fashion, against the gods and fate as well as you. I have felt more steam and smoke of that sort than you have ever heard of. But the more I see of life the more do I perceive that there is nothing particularly great in its greatest walks, and therefore nothing particularly small in mine of furze-cutting. If I feel that the greatest blessings vouchsafed to us are not very valuable, how can I feel it to be any great hardship when they are taken away? So I sing to pass the time. Have you indeed lost all tenderness for me, that you begrudge me a few cheerful moments?"

"I have still some tenderness left for you."

"Your words have no longer their old flavour. And so love dies with good fortune!"

"I cannot listen to this, Clym — it will end bitterly," she said in a broken voice. "I will go home."

III

SHE GOES OUT TO BATTLE AGAINST DEPRESSION

A FEW days later, before the month of August had expired, Eustacia and Yeobright sat together at their early dinner.

Eustacia's manner had become of late almost apathetic. There was a forlorn look about her beautiful eyes which, whether she deserved it or not, would have excited pity in the breast of anyone who had known her during the full flush of her love for Clym. The feelings of husband and wife varied, in some measure, inversely with their positions. Clym, the afflicted man, was cheerful; and he even tried to comfort her, who had never felt a moment of physical suffering in her whole life.

"Come, brighten up, dearest; we shall be all right again. Some day perhaps I shall see as well as ever. And I solemnly promise that I'll leave off cutting furze as soon as I have the power to do anything better. You cannot seriously wish me to stay idling at home all day?"

"But it is so dreadful — a furze-cutter! and you a man who have lived about the world, and speak French, and German, and who are fit for what is so much better than this."

"I suppose when you first saw me and heard about me I was wrapped in a sort of golden halo to your eyes — a man who knew glorious things, and had mixed in brilliant scenes — in short, an adorable, delightful, distracting hero?"

"Yes," she said, sobbing.

"And now I am a poor fellow in brown leather."

"Don't taunt me. But enough of this. I will not be depressed any more. I am going from home this afternoon, unless you greatly object. There is to be a village picnic — a gipsying, they call it — at East Egdon, and I shall go."

"To dance?"

"Why not? You can sing."

"Well, well, as you will. Must I come to fetch you?"

"If you return soon enough from your work. But do not inconvenience yourself about it. I know the way home, and the heath has no terror for me."

"And can you cling to gaiety so eagerly as to walk all the way to a village festival in search of it?"

"Now, you don't like my going alone! Clym, you are not jealous?"

"No. But I would come with you if it could give you any pleasure; though, as things stand, perhaps you have too much of me already. Still, I somehow wish that you did not want to go. Yes, perhaps I am jealous; and who could be jealous with more reason than I, a half-blind man, over such a woman as you?"

"Don't think like it. Let me go, and don't take all my spirits away!"

"I would rather lose all my own, my sweet wife. Go and do whatever you like. Who can forbid your indulgence in any whim? You have all my heart yet, I believe; and because you bear with me, who am in truth a drag upon you, I owe you thanks. Yes, go alone and shine. As for me, I will stick to my doom. At that kind of meeting people would shun me. My hook and gloves are like the St. Lazarus rattle of the leper, warning the world to get out of the way of a sight that would sadden them." He kissed her, put on his leggings, and went out.

When he was gone she rested her head upon her hands and said to herself, "Two wasted lives — his and mine. And I am come to this! Will it drive me out of my mind?"

She cast about for any possible course which offered the least improvement on the existing state of things, and could find none. She imagined how all those Budmouth ones who should learn what had become of her would say, "Look at the girl for whom nobody was good enough!" To Eustacia the situation seemed such a mockery of her hopes that death appeared the only door of relief if the satire of Heaven should go much further.

Suddenly she aroused herself and exclaimed, "But I'll shake it off. Yes, I will shake it off! No one shall know my suffering. I'll be bitterly merry, and ironically gay, and I'll laugh in derision! And I'll begin by going to this dance on the green."

She ascended to her bedroom and dressed herself with scrupulous care. To an onlooker her beauty would have made her feelings almost seem reasonable. The gloomy corner into which accident as much as indiscretion had

brought this woman might have led even a moderate partisan to feel that she
had cogent reasons for asking the Supreme Power by what right a being of
such exquisite finish had been placed in circumstances calculated to make of
her charms a curse rather than a blessing.

It was five in the afternoon when she came out from the house ready for
her walk. There was material enough in the picture for twenty new con-
quests. The rebellious sadness that was rather too apparent when she sat
indoors without a bonnet was cloaked and softened by her outdoor attire,
which always had a sort of nebulousness about it, devoid of harsh edges anywhere; so that her face looked from its environment as from a cloud, with no
noticeable lines of demarcation between flesh and clothes. The heat of the
day had scarcely declined as yet, and she went along the sunny hills at leisurely pace, there being ample time for her idle expedition. Tall ferns buried
her in their leafage whenever her path lay through them, which now formed
miniature forests, though not one stem of them would remain to bud the
next year.

The site chosen for the village festivity was one of the lawn-like oases
which were occasionally, yet not often, met with on the plateaux of the heath
district. The brakes of furze and fern terminated abruptly round the margin, and the grass was unbroken. A green cattle-track skirted the spot,
without, however, emerging from the screen of fern, and this path Eustacia
followed, in order to reconnoitre the group before joining it. The dusty
notes of the East Egdon band had directed her unerringly, and she now beheld the musicians themselves, sitting in a blue waggon with red wheels
scrubbed as bright as new, and arched with sticks, to which boughs and
flowers were tied. In front of this was the grand central dance of fifteen or
twenty couples, flanked by minor dances of inferior individuals whose gyra-
tions were not always in strict keeping with the tune.

The young men wore blue and white rosettes, and with a flush on their
faces footed it to the girls, who, with the excitement and the exercise, blushed
deeper than the pink of their numerous ribbons. Fair ones with long curls,
fair ones with short curls, fair ones with love-locks, fair ones with braids,
flew round and round; and a beholder might well have wondered how such a
prepossessing set of young women of like size, age, and disposition, could
have been collected together where there were only one or two villages to
choose from. In the background was one happy man dancing by himself,
with closed eyes, totally oblivious of all the rest. A fire was burning under a
pollard thorn a few paces off, over which three kettles hung in a row. Hard
by was a table where elderly dames prepared tea, but Eustacia looked among
them in vain for the cattle-dealer's wife who had suggested that she should
come, and had promised to obtain a courteous welcome for her.

This unexpected absence of the only local resident whom Eustacia knew
considerably damaged her scheme for an afternoon of reckless gaiety. Joining in became a matter of difficulty, notwithstanding that, were she to advance, cheerful dames would come forward with cups of tea and make much
of her as a stranger of superior grace and knowledge to themselves. Having
watched the company through the figures of two dances, she decided to walk

a little further, to a cottage where she might get some refreshment, and then return homeward in the shady time of evening.

This she did; and by the time that she retraced her steps towards the scene of the gipsying, which it was necessary to repass on her way to Alderworth, the sun was going down. The air was now so still that she could hear the band afar off, and it seemed to be playing with more spirit, if that were possible, than when she had come away. On reaching the hill the sun had quite disappeared; but this made little difference either to Eustacia or to the revellers, for a round yellow moon was rising behind her, though its rays had not yet outmastered those from the west. The dance was going on just the same, but strangers had arrived and formed a ring around the figure, so that Eustacia could stand among these without a chance of being recognized.

A whole village-full of sensuous emotion, scattered abroad all the year long, surged here in a focus for an hour. The forty hearts of those waving couples were beating as they had not done since, twelve months before, they had come together in similar jollity. For the time Paganism was revived in their hearts, the pride of life was all in all, and they adored none other than themselves.

How many of those impassioned but temporary embraces were destined to become perpetual was possibly the wonder of some of those who indulged in them, as well as of Eustacia who looked on. She began to envy those pirouetters, to hunger for the hope and happiness which the fascination of the dance seemed to engender within them. Desperately fond of dancing herself, one of Eustacia's expectations of Paris had been the opportunity it might afford her of indulgence in this favourite pastime. Unhappily, that expectation was now extinct within her for ever.

Whilst she abstractedly watched them spinning and fluctuating in the increasing moonlight she suddenly heard her name whispered by a voice over her shoulder. Turning in surprise, she beheld at her elbow one whose presence instantly caused her to flush to the temples.

It was Wildeve. Till this moment he had not met her eye since the morning of his marriage, when she had been loitering in the church, and had startled him by lifting her veil and coming forward to sign the register as witness. Yet why the sight of him should have instigated that sudden rush of blood she could not tell.

Before she could speak he whispered. "Do you like dancing as much as ever?"

"I think I do," she replied in a low voice.

"Will you dance with me?"

"It would be a great change for me; but will it not seem strange?"

"What strangeness can there be in relations dancing together?"

"Ah — yes, relations. Perhaps none."

"Still, if you don't like to be seen, pull down your veil; though there is not much risk of being known by this light. Lots of strangers are here."

She did as he suggested; and the act was a tacit acknowledgment that she accepted his offer.

Wildeve gave her his arm and took her down on the outside of the ring to the bottom of the dance, which they entered.   In two minutes more they were involved in the figure and began working their way upwards to the top. Till they had advanced halfway thither Eustacia wished more than once that she had not yielded to his request; from the middle to the top she felt that, since she had come out to seek pleasure, she was only doing a natural thing to obtain it.   Fairly launched into the ceaseless glides and whirls which their new position as top couple opened up to them, Eustacia's pulses began to move too quickly for longer rumination of any kind.

Through the length of five and twenty couples they threaded their giddy way, and a new vitality entered her form.   The pale ray of evening lent a fascination to the experience.   There is a certain degree and tone of light which tends to disturb the equilibrium of the senses, and to promote dangerously the tenderer moods; added to movement, it drives the emotions to rankness, the reason becoming sleepy and unperceiving in inverse proportion; and this light fell now upon these two from the disc of the moon.   All the dancing girls felt the symptoms, but Eustacia most of all.   The grass under their feet became trodden away, and the hard, beaten surface of the sod, when viewed aslant towards the moonlight, shone like a polished table.   The air became quite still; the flag above the waggon which held the musicians clung to the pole, and the players appeared only in outline against the sky; except when the circular mouths of the trombone, ophicleide, and French horn gleamed out like huge eyes from the shade of their figures.   The pretty dresses of the maids lost their subtler day colours and showed more or less of a misty white.   Eustacia floated round and round on Wildeve's arm, her face rapt and statuesque; her soul had passed away from and forgotten her features, which were left empty and quiescent, as they always are when feeling goes beyond their register.

How near she was to Wildeve! it was terrible to think of.   She could feel his breathing, and he, of course, could feel hers.   How badly she had treated him! yet, here they were treading one measure.   The enchantment of the dance surprised her.   A clear line of difference divided like a tangible fence her experience within this maze of motion from her experience without it. Her beginning to dance had been like a change of atmosphere; outside, she had been steeped in arctic frigidity by comparison with the tropical sensations here.   She had entered the dance from the troubled hours of her late life as one might enter a brilliant chamber after a night walk in a wood.   Wildeve by himself would have been merely an agitation; Wildeve added to the dance, and the moonlight, and the secrecy, began to be a delight.   Whether his personality supplied the greater part of this sweetly compounded feeling, or whether the dance and the scene weighed the more therein, was a nice point upon which Eustacia herself was entirely in a cloud.

People began to say "Who are they?" but no invidious inquiries were made.   Had Eustacia mingled with the other girls in their ordinary daily walks the case would have been different: here she was not inconvenienced by excessive inspection, for all were wrought to their brightest grace by the occasion.   Like the planet Mercury surrounded by the lustre of sunset, her permanent brilliancy passed without much notice in the temporary glory of the situation.

As for Wildeve, his feelings are easy to guess. Obstacles were a ripening sun to his love, and he was at this moment in a delirium of exquisite misery. To clasp as his for five minutes what was another man's through all the rest of the year was a kind of thing he of all men could appreciate. He had long since begun to sigh again for Eustacia; indeed, it may be asserted that signing the marriage register with Thomasin was the natural signal to his heart to return to its first quarters, and that the extra complication of Eustacia's marriage was the one addition required to make that return compulsory.

Thus, for different reasons, what was to the rest an exhilarating movement was to these two a riding upon the whirlwind. The dance had come like an irresistible attack upon whatever sense of social order there was in their minds, to drive them back into old paths which were now doubly irregular. Through three dances in succession they spun their way; and then, fatigued with the incessant motion, Eustacia turned to quit the circle in which she had already remained too long. Wildeve led her to a grassy mound a few yards distant, where she sat down, her partner standing beside her. From the time that he addressed her at the beginning of the dance till now they had not exchanged a word.

"The dance and the walking have tired you?" he said tenderly.

"No; not greatly."

"It is strange that we should have met here of all places, after missing each other so long."

"We have missed because we tried to miss, I suppose."

"Yes. But you began that proceeding — by breaking a promise."

"It is scarcely worth while to talk of that now. We have formed other ties since then — you no less than I."

"I am sorry to hear that your husband is ill."

"He is not ill — only incapacitated."

"Yes: that is what I mean. I sincerely sympathize with you in your trouble. Fate has treated you cruelly."

She was silent awhile. "Have you heard that he has chosen to work as a furze-cutter?" she said in a low, mournful voice.

"It has been mentioned to me," answered Wildeve hesitatingly. "But I hardly believed it."

"It is true. What do you think of me as a furze-cutter's wife?"

"I think the same as ever of you, Eustacia. Nothing of that sort can degrade you: you ennoble the occupation of your husband."

"I wish I could feel it."

"Is there any chance of Mr. Yeobright getting better?"

"He thinks so. I doubt it."

"I was quite surprised to hear that he had taken a cottage. I thought, in common with other people, that he would have taken you off to a home in Paris immediately after you had married him. 'What a gay, bright future she had before her!' I thought. He will, I suppose, return there with you, if his sight gets strong again?"

Observing that she did not reply he regarded her more closely. She was almost weeping. Images of a future never to be enjoyed, the revived sense of her bitter disappointment, the picture of the neighbours' suspended ridicule which was raised by Wildeve's words, had been too much for proud Eustacia's equanimity.

Wildeve could hardly control his own too forward feelings when he saw her silent perturbation. But he affected not to notice this, and she soon recovered her calmness.

"You did not intend to walk home by yourself?" he asked.

"O yes," said Eustacia. "What could hurt me on this heath, who have nothing?"

"The first half of my way home is the same as yours. I shall be glad to keep you company as far as Throope Corner." Seeing that Eustacia sat on in hesitation he added, "Perhaps you think it unwise to be seen in the same road with me after the events of last summer?"

"Indeed I think no such thing," she said haughtily. "I shall accept whose company I choose, for all that may be said by the miserable inhabitants of Egdon."

"Then let us walk on — if you are ready. Our nearest way is towards that holly-bush with the dark shadow that you see down there."

Eustacia arose, and walked beside him in the direction signified, brushing her way over the damping heath and fern, and followed by the strains of the merrymakers, who still kept up the dance. The moon had now waxed bright and silvery, but the heath was proof against such illumination, and there was to be observed the striking scene of a dark, rayless tract of country, under an atmosphere charged from its zenith to its extremities with whitest light. To an eye above them their two faces would have appeared amid the expanse like two pearls on a table of ebony.

On this account the irregularities of the path were not visible, and Wildeve occasionally stumbled; whilst Eustacia found it necessary to perform some graceful feats of balancing whenever a small tuft of heather or root of furze protruded itself through the grass of the narrow track and entangled her feet. At these junctures in her progress a hand was invariably stretched forward to steady her, holding her firmly until smooth ground was again reached, when the hand was again withdrawn to a respectful distance.

They performed the journey for the most part in silence, and drew near to Throope Corner, a few hundred yards from which a short path branched away to Eustacia's house. By degrees they discerned coming towards them a pair of human figures, apparently of the male sex.

When they came a little nearer Eustacia broke the silence by saying, "One of those men is my husband. He promised to come to meet me."

"And the other is my greatest enemy," said Wildeve.

"It looks like Diggory Venn."

"That is the man."

"It is an awkward meeting," said she; "but such is my fortune. He knows too much about me, unless he could know more, and so prove to himself that what he now knows counts for nothing. Well, let it be: you must deliver me up to them."

"You will think twice before you direct me to do that. Here is a man who has not forgotten an item in our meetings at Rainbarrow: he is in company with your husband. Which of them, seeing us together here, will believe that our meeting and dancing at the gipsy-party was by chance?"

"Very well," she whispered gloomily. "Leave me before they come up."

Wildeve bade her a tender farewell, and plunged across the fern and furze, Eustacia slowly walking on. In two or three minutes she met her husband and his companion.

"My journey ends here for tonight, reddleman," said Yeobright as soon as he perceived her. "I turn back with this lady. Good night."

"Good night, Mr. Yeobright," said Venn. "I hope to see you better soon."

The moonlight shone directly upon Venn's face as he spoke, and revealed all its lines to Eustacia. He was looking suspiciously at her. That Venn's keen eye had discerned what Yeobright's feeble vision had not — a man in the act of withdrawing from Eustacia's side — was within the limits of the probable.

If Eustacia had been able to follow the reddleman she would soon have found striking confirmation of her thought. No sooner had Clym given her his arm and led her off the scene than the reddleman turned back from the beaten track towards East Egdon, whither he had been strolling merely to accompany Clym in his walk, Diggory's van being again in the neighbourhood. Stretching out his long legs he crossed the pathless portion of the heath somewhat in the direction which Wildeve had taken. Only a man accustomed to nocturnal ramble could at this hour have descended those shaggy slopes with Venn's velocity without falling headlong into a pit, or snapping off his leg by jamming his foot into some rabbit-burrow. But Venn went on without much inconvenience to himself, and the course of his scamper was towards the Quiet Woman Inn. This place he reached in about half an hour, and he was well aware that no person who had been near Throope Corner when he started could have got down here before him.

The lonely inn was not yet closed, though scarcely an individual was there, the business done being chiefly with travellers who passed the inn on long journeys, and these had now gone on their way. Venn went to the public room, called for a mug of ale, and inquired of the maid in an indifferent tone if Mr. Wildeve was at home.

Thomasin sat in an inner room and heard Venn's voice. When customers were present she seldom showed herself, owing to her inherent dislike for the business; but perceiving that no one else was there tonight she came out.

"He is not at home yet, Diggory," she said pleasantly. "But I expected him sooner. He has been to East Egdon to buy a horse."

"Did he wear a white wideawake?"

"Yes."

"Then I saw him at Throope Corner, leading one home," said Venn drily. "A beauty, with a white face and a mane as black as night. He will soon be here, no doubt." Rising and looking for a moment at the pure, sweet face of Thomasin, over which a shadow of sadness had passed since the time when he had last seen her, he ventured to add, "Mr. Wildeve seems to be often away at this time."

"O yes," cried Thomasin in what was intended to be a tone of gaiety. "Husbands will play the truant, you know. I wish you could tell me of some secret plan that would help me to keep him home at my will in the evenings."

"I will consider if I know of one," replied Venn in that same light tone which meant no lightness. And then he bowed in a manner of his own invention and moved to go. Thomasin offered him her hand; and without a sigh, though with food for many, the reddleman went out.

When Wildeve returned, a quarter of an hour later, Thomasin said simply, and in the abashed manner usual with her now, "Where is the horse, Damon?"

"O, I have not bought it, after all. The man asks too much."

"But somebody saw you at Throope Corner leading it home — a beauty, with a white face and a mane as black as night."

"Ah!" said Wildeve, fixing his eyes upon her; "who told you that?"

"Venn the reddleman."

The expression of Wildeve's face became curiously condensed. "That is a mistake — it must have been someone else," he said slowly and testily, for he perceived that Venn's counter-moves had begun again.

IV

ROUGH COERCION IS EMPLOYED

THOSE words of Thomasin, which seemed so little, but meant so much, remained in the ears of Diggory Venn: "Help me to keep him home in the evenings."

On this occasion Venn had arrived on Egdon Heath only to cross to the other side: he had no further connection with the interests of the Yeobright family, and he had a business of his own to attend to. Yet he suddenly began to feel himself drifting into the old track of manœuvring on Thomasin's account.

He sat in his van and considered. From Thomasin's words and manner he had plainly gathered that Wildeve neglected her. For whom could he neglect her if not for Eustacia? Yet it was scarcely credible that things had come to such a head as to indicate that Eustacia systematically encouraged him. Venn resolved to reconnoitre somewhat carefully the lonely path which led across the hills from Wildeve's dwelling to Clym's house at Alderworth.

At this time, as has been seen, Wildeve was quite innocent of any predetermined act of intrigue, and except at the dance on the green he had not once met Eustacia since her marriage. But that the spirit of intrigue was in him had been shown by a recent romantic habit of his: a habit of going out after dark and strolling towards Alderworth, there looking at the moon and stars, looking at Eustacia's house, and walking back at leisure.

Accordingly, when watching on the night after the festival, the reddleman saw him ascend by the little path, lean over the front gate of Clym's garden, sigh, and turn to go back again. It was plain that Wildeve's intrigue was rather ideal than real. Venn retreated before him down the hill to a place where the path was merely a deep groove between the heather; here he mysteriously bent over the ground for a few minutes, and retired. When Wildeve came on to that spot his ankle was caught by something, and he fell headlong.

As soon as he had recovered the power of respiration he sat up and listened. There was not a sound in the gloom beyond the spiritless stir of the summer wind. Feeling about for the obstacle which had flung him down, he discovered that two tufts of heath had been tied together across the path, forming a loop, which to a traveller was certain overthrow. Wildeve pulled off the string that bound them, and went on with tolerable quickness. On reaching home he found the cord to be of a reddish colour. It was just what he had expected.

Although his weaknesses were not specially those akin to physical fear, this species of *coup-de-Jarnac* from one he knew too well troubled the mind of Wildeve. But his movements were unaltered thereby. A night or two later he again went up the hill to Alderworth, taking the precaution of keeping out of the path. The sense that he was watched, that craft was employed to circumvent his errant tastes, added piquancy to a journey so entirely sentimental, so long as the danger was of no fearful sort. He imagined that Venn and Mrs. Yeobright were in league, and felt that there was a certain legitimacy in combating such a coalition.

The heath tonight appeared to be totally deserted; and Wildeve, after looking over Eustacia's garden gate for some little time, with a cigar in his mouth, was tempted by the fascination that emotional smuggling had for his nature to advance towards the window, which was not quite closed, the blind being only partly drawn down. He could see into the room, and Eustacia was sitting there alone. Wildeve contemplated her for a minute, and then retreating into the heath beat the ferns lightly, whereupon moths flew out alarmed. Securing one, he returned to the window, and holding the moth to the chink, opened his hand. The moth made towards the candle upon Eustacia's table, hovered round it two or three times, and flew into the flame.

Eustacia started up. This had been a well-known signal in old times when Wildeve had used to come secretly wooing to Mistover. She at once knew that Wildeve was outside, but before she could consider what to do her husband came in from upstairs. Eustacia's face burnt crimson at the unexpected collision of incidents, and filled it with an animation that it too frequently lacked.

"You have a very high colour, dearest," said Yeobright, when he came close enough to see it. "Your appearance would be no worse if it were always so."

"I am warm," said Eustacia. "I think I will go into the air for a few minutes."

"Shall I go with you?"

"O no. I am only going to the gate."

She arose, but before she had time to get out of the room a loud rapping began upon the front door.

"I'll go — I'll go," said Eustacia in an unusually quick tone for her; and she glanced eagerly towards the window whence the moth had flown; but nothing appeared there.

"You had better not at this time of the evening," he said. Clym stepped before her into the passage, and Eustacia waited, her somnolent manner covering her inner heat and agitation.

She listened, and Clym opened the door. No words were uttered outside, and presently he closed it and came back, saying, "Nobody was there. I wonder what that could have meant?"

He was left to wonder during the rest of the evening, for no explanation offered itself, and Eustacia said nothing, the additional fact that she knew of only adding more mystery to the performance.

Meanwhile a little drama had been acted outside which saved Eustacia from all possibility of compromising herself that evening at least. Whilst he had been preparing his moth-signal another person had come behind him up to the gate. This man, who carried a gun in his hand, looked on for a moment at the other's operation by the window, walked up to the house, knocked at the door, and then vanished round the corner and over the hedge.

"Damn him!" said Wildeve. "He has been watching me again."

As his signal had been rendered futile by this uproarious rapping Wildeve withdrew, passed out at the gate, and walked quickly down the path without thinking of anything except getting away unnoticed. Half-way down the hill, the path ran near a knot of stunted hollies, which in the general darkness of the scene stood as the pupil in a black eye. When Wildeve reached this point a report startled his ear, and a few spent gunshots fell among the leaves around him.

There was no doubt that he himself was the cause of that gun's discharge; and he rushed into the clump of hollies, beating the bushes furiously with his stick; but nobody was there. This attack was a more serious matter than the last, and it was some time before Wildeve recovered his equanimity. A new and most unpleasant system of menace had begun, and the intent appeared to be to do him grievous bodily harm. Wildeve had looked upon Venn's first attempt as a species of horse-play, which the reddleman had indulged in for want of knowing better; but now the boundary-line was passed which divides the annoying from the perilous.

Had Wildeve known how thoroughly in earnest Venn had become he might have been still more alarmed. The reddleman had been almost exasperated by the sight of Wildeve outside Clym's house, and he was prepared to go to any lengths short of absolutely shooting him, to terrify the young innkeeper out of his recalcitrant impulses. The doubtful legitimacy of such rough coercion did not disturb the mind of Venn. It troubles few such minds in such cases, and sometimes this is not to be regretted. From the impeachment of Strafford to Farmer Lynch's short way with the scamps of Virginia there have been many triumphs of justice which are mockeries of law.

About half a mile below Clym's secluded dwelling lay a hamlet where lived one of the two constables who preserved the peace in the parish of Alderworth, and Wildeve went straight to the constable's cottage. Almost the first thing that he saw on opening the door was the constable's truncheon hanging to a nail, as if to assure him that here were the means to his purpose. On inquiry, however, of the constable's wife he learnt that the constable was not at home. Wildeve said he would wait.

The minutes ticked on, and the constable did not arrive. Wildeve cooled down from his state of high indignation to a restless dissatisfaction with himself, the scene, the constable's wife, and the whole set of circumstances. He arose and left the house. Altogether, the experience of that evening had had a cooling, not to say a chilling, effect on misdirected tenderness, and Wildeve was in no mood to ascend again to Alderworth after nightfall in hope of a stray glance from Eustacia.

Thus far the reddleman had been tolerably successful in his rude contrivances for keeping down Wildeve's inclination to rove in the evening. He had nipped in the bud the possible meeting between Eustacia and her old lover this very night. But he had not anticipated that the tendency of his action would be to divert Wildeve's movement rather than to stop it. The gambling with the guineas had not conduced to make him a welcome guest to Clym; but to call upon his wife's relative was natural, and he was determined to see Eustacia. It was necessary to choose some less untoward hour than ten o'clock at night. "Since it is unsafe to go in the evening," he said, "I'll go by day."

Meanwhile Venn had left the heath and gone to call upon Mrs. Yeobright, with whom he had been on friendly terms since she had learnt what a providential counter-move he had made towards the restitution of the family guineas. She wondered at the lateness of his call, but had no objection to see him.

He gave her a full account of Clym's affliction, and of the state in which he was living; then, referring to Thomasin, touched gently upon the apparent sadness of her days. "Now, ma'am, depend upon it," he said, "you couldn't do a better thing for either of 'em than to make yourself at home in their houses, even if there should be a little rebuff at first."

"Both she and my son disobeyed me in marrying; therefore I have no interest in their households. Their troubles are of their own making." Mrs. Yeobright tried to speak severely; but the account of her son's state had moved her more than she cared to show.

"Your visits would make Wildeve walk straighter than he is inclined to do, and might prevent unhappiness up the hill."

"What do you mean?"

"I saw something tonight up there which I didn't like at all. I wish your son's house and Mr. Wildeve's were a hundred miles apart instead of two or three."

"Then there *was* an understanding between him and Clym's wife when he made a fool of Thomasin!"

"We'll hope there's no understanding now."

"And our hope will probably be very vain. O Clym! O Thomasin!"

"There's no harm done yet. In fact, I've persuaded Wildeve to mind his own business."

"How?"

"O, not by talking — by a plan of mine called the silent system."

"I hope you'll succeed."

"I shall if you help me by calling and making friends with your son. You'll have a chance then of using your eyes."

"Well, since it has come to this," said Mrs. Yeobright sadly, "I will own to you, reddleman, that I thought of going. I should be much happier if we were reconciled. The marriage is unalterable, my life may be cut short, and I should wish to die in peace. He is my only son; and since sons are made of such stuff I am not sorry I have no other. As for Thomasin, I never expected much from her; and she has not disappointed me. But I forgave her long ago; and I forgive him now. I'll go."

At this very time of the reddleman's conversation with Mrs. Yeobright at Blooms-End another conversation on the same subject was languidly proceeding at Alderworth.

All the day Clym had borne himself as if his mind were too full of its own matter to allow him to care about outward things, and his words now showed what had occupied his thoughts. It was just after the mysterious knocking that he began the theme. "Since I have been away today, Eustacia, I have considered that something must be done to heal up this ghastly breach between my dear mother and myself. It troubles me."

"What do you propose to do?" said Eustacia abstractedly, for she could not clear away from her the excitement caused by Wildeve's recent manœuvre for an interview.

"You seem to take a very mild interest in what I propose, little or much," said Clym, with tolerable warmth.

"You mistake me," she answered, reviving at his reproach. "I am only thinking."

"What of?"

"Partly of that moth whose skeleton is getting burnt up in the wick of the candle," she said slowly. "But you know I always take an interest in what you say."

"Very well, dear. Then I think I must go and call upon her." ... He went on with tender feeling: "It is a thing I am not at all too proud to do, and only a fear that I might irritate her has kept me away so long. But I must do something. It is wrong in me to allow this sort of thing to go on."

"What have you to blame yourself about?"

"She is getting old, and her life is lonely, and I am her only son."

"She has Thomasin."

"Thomasin is not her daughter; and if she were that would not excuse me. But this is beside the point. I have made up my mind to go to her, and all I wish to ask you is whether you will do your best to help me — that is, forget the past; and if she shows her willingness to be reconciled, meet her half-way by welcoming her to our house, or by accepting a welcome to hers?"

At first Eustacia closed her lips as if she would rather do anything on the whole globe than what he suggested. But the lines of her mouth softened with thought, though not so far as they might have softened; and she said, "I will put nothing in your way; but after what has passed it is asking too much that I go and make advances."

"You never distinctly told me what did pass between you."

"I could not do it then, nor can I now. Sometimes more bitterness is sown in five minutes than can be got rid of in a whole life; and that may be the case here." She paused a few moments, and added, "If you had never returned to your native place, Clym, what a blessing it would have been for you!... It has altered the destinies of ——"

"Three people."

"Five," Eustacia thought; but she kept that in.

V

THE JOURNEY ACROSS THE HEATH

THURSDAY, the thirty-first of August, was one of a series of days during which snug houses were stifling, and when cool draughts were treats; when cracks appeared in clayey gardens, and were called "earthquakes" by apprehensive children; when loose spokes were discovered in the wheels of carts and carriages; and when stinging insects haunted the air, the earth, and every drop of water that was to be found.

In Mrs. Yeobright's garden large-leaved plants of a tender kind flagged by ten o'clock in the morning; rhubarb bent downward at eleven; and even stiff cabbages were limp by noon.

It was about eleven o'clock on this day that Mrs. Yeobright started across the heath towards her son's house, to do her best in getting reconciled with him and Eustacia, in conformity with her words to the reddleman. She had hoped to be well advanced in her walk before the heat of the day was at its highest, but after setting out she found that this was not to be done. The sun had branded the whole heath with his mark, even the purple heath-flowers having put on a brownness under the dry blazes of the few preceding days. Every valley was filled with air like that of a kiln, and the clean quartz sand of the winter water-courses, which formed summer paths, had undergone a species of incineration since the drought had set in.

In cool, fresh weather Mrs. Yeobright would have found no inconvenience in walking to Alderworth; but the present torrid attack made the journey a heavy undertaking for a woman past middle age; and at the end of the third mile she wished that she had hired Fairway to drive her a portion at least of the distance. But from the point at which she had arrived it was as easy to reach Clym's house as to get home again. So she went on, the air around her pulsating silently, and oppressing the earth with lassitude. She looked at the sky overhead, and saw that the sapphirine hue of the zenith in spring and early summer had been replaced by a metallic violet.

Occasionally she came to a spot where independent worlds of ephemerons were passing their time in mad carousal, some in the air, some on the hot ground and vegetation, some in the tepid and stringy water of a nearly dried pool. All the shallower ponds had decreased to a vaporous mud amid which the maggoty shapes of innumerable obscene creatures could be indistinctly seen, heaving and wallowing with enjoyment. Being a woman not disinclined to philosophize she sometimes sat down under her umbrella to rest and to watch their happiness, for a certain hopefulness as to the result of her visit gave ease to her mind, and between important thoughts left it free to dwell on any infinitesimal matter which caught her eyes.

Mrs. Yeobright had never before been to her son's house, and its exact position was unknown to her. She tried one ascending path and another, and found that they led her astray. Retracing her steps she came again to an open level, where she perceived at a distance a man at work. She went towards him and inquired the way.

The labourer pointed out the direction, and added, "Do you see that furze-cutter, ma'am, going up that footpath yond?"

Mrs. Yeobright strained her eyes, and at last said that she did perceive him.

"Well, if you follow him you can make no mistake. He's going to the same place, ma'am."

She followed the figure indicated. He appeared of a russet hue, not more distinguishable from the scene around him than the green caterpillar from the leaf it feeds on. His progress when actually walking was more rapid than Mrs. Yeobright's; but she was enabled to keep at an equable distance from him by his habit of stopping whenever he came to a brake of brambles, where he paused awhile. On coming in her turn to each of these spots she found half a dozen long limp brambles which he had cut from the bush during his halt and laid out straight beside the path. They were evidently intended for furze-faggot bonds which he meant to collect on his return.

The silent being who thus occupied himself seemed to be of no more account in life than an insect. He appeared as a mere parasite of the heath, fretting its surface in his daily labour as a moth frets a garment, entirely engrossed with its products, having no knowledge of anything in the world but fern, furze, heath, lichens, and moss.

The furze-cutter was so absorbed in the business of his journey that he never turned his head; and his leather-legged and gauntleted form at length became to her as nothing more than a moving handpost to show her the way. Suddenly she was attracted to his individuality by observing peculiarities in his walk. It was a gait she had seen somewhere before; and the gait revealed the man to her, as the gait of Ahimaaz in the distant plain made him known to the watchman of the king. "His walk is exactly as my husband's used to be," she said; and then the thought burst upon her that the furze-cutter was her son.

She was scarcely able to familiarize herself with this strange reality. She had been told that Clym was in the habit of cutting furze, but she had supposed that he occupied himself with the labour only at odd times, by way of useful pastime; yet she now beheld him as a furze-cutter and nothing more — wearing the regulation dress of the craft, and thinking the regulation thoughts, to judge by his motions. Planning a dozen hasty schemes for at once preserving him and Eustacia from this mode of life she throbbingly followed the way, and saw him enter his own door.

At one side of Clym's house was a knoll, and on the top of the knoll a clump of fir trees so highly thrust up into the sky that their foliage from a distance appeared as a black spot in the air above the crown of the hill. On reaching this place Mrs. Yeobright felt distressingly agitated, weary, and unwell. She ascended, and sat down under their shade to recover herself, and to consider how best to break the ground with Eustacia, so as not to irritate a woman underneath whose apparent indolence lurked passions even stronger and more active than her own.

The trees beneath which she sat were singularly battered, rude, and wild, and for a few minutes Mrs. Yeobright dismissed thoughts of her own storm-broken and exhausted state to contemplate theirs. Not a bough in the nine trees which composed the group but was splintered, lopped, and distorted by the fierce weather that there held them at its mercy whenever it prevailed. Some were blasted and split as if by lightning, black stains as from fire marking their sides, while the ground at their feet was strewn with dead fir-needles and heaps of cones blown down in the gales of past years. The place was called the Devil's Bellows, and it was only necessary to come there on a March or November night to discover the forcible reasons for that name. On the present heated afternoon, when no perceptible wind was blowing, the trees kept up a perpetual moan which one could hardly believe to be caused by the air.

Here she sat for twenty minutes or more ere she could summon resolution to go down to the door, her courage being lowered to zero by her physical lassitude. To any other person than a mother it might have seemed a little humiliating that she, the elder of the two women, should be the first to make advances. But Mrs. Yeobright had well considered all that, and she only thought how best to make her visit appear to Eustacia not abject but wise.

From her elevated position the exhausted woman could perceive the back roof of the house below, and the garden and the whole enclosure of the little domicile. And now, at the moment of rising, she saw a second man approaching the gate. His manner was peculiar, hesitating, and not that of a person come on business or by invitation. He surveyed the house with interest, and then walked round and scanned the outer boundary of the garden, as one might have done had it been the birthplace of Shakespeare, the prison of Mary Stuart, or the Château of Hougomont. After passing round and again reaching the gate he went in. Mrs. Yeobright was vexed at this, having reckoned on finding her son and his wife by themselves; but a moment's thought showed her that the presence of an acquaintance would take off the awkwardness of her first appearance in the house, by confining the talk to general matters until she had begun to feel comfortable with them. She came down the hill to the gate, and looked into the hot garden.

There lay the cat asleep on the bare gravel of the path, as if beds, rugs, and carpets were unendurable. The leaves of the hollyhocks hung like half-closed umbrellas, the sap almost simmered in the stems, and foliage with a smooth surface glared like metallic mirrors. A small apple tree, of the sort called Ratheripe, grew just inside the gate, the only one which thrived in the garden, by reason of the lightness of the soil; and among the fallen apples on the ground beneath were wasps rolling drunk with the juice, or creeping about the little caves in each fruit which they had eaten out before stupefied by its sweetness. By the door lay Clym's furze-hook and the last handful of faggot-bonds she had seen him gather; they had plainly been thrown down there as he entered the house.

VI

A CONJUNCTURE, AND ITS RESULT UPON THE PEDESTRIAN

WILDEVE, as has been stated, was determined to visit Eustacia boldly, by day, and on the easy terms of a relation, since the reddleman had spied out and spoilt his walks to her by night. The spell that she had thrown over him in the moonlight dance made it impossible for a man having no strong puritan force within him to keep away altogether. He merely calculated on meeting her and her husband in an ordinary manner, chatting a little while, and leaving again. Every outward sign was to be conventional; but the one great fact would be there to satisfy him: he would see her. He did not even desire Clym's absence, since it was just possible that Eustacia might resent any situation which could compromise her dignity as a wife, whatever the state of her heart towards him. Women were often so.

He went accordingly; and it happened that the time of his arrival coincided with that of Mrs. Yeobright's pause on the hill near the house. When he had looked round the premises in the manner she had noticed he went and knocked at the door. There was a few minutes' interval, and then the key turned in the lock, the door opened, and Eustacia herself confronted him.

Nobody could have imagined from her bearing now that here stood the woman who had joined with him in the impassioned dance of the week before, unless indeed he could have penetrated below the surface and gauged the real depth of that still stream.

"I hope you reached home safely?" said Wildeve.

"O yes," she carelessly returned.

"And were you not tired the next day? I feared you might be."

"I was rather. You need not speak low — nobody will overhear us. My small servant is gone on an errand to the village."

"Then Clym is not at home?"

"Yes, he is."

"O! I thought that perhaps you had locked the door because you were alone and were afraid of tramps."

"No — here is my husband."

They had been standing in the entry. Closing the front door and turning the key, as before, she threw open the door of the adjoining room and asked him to walk in. Wildeve entered, the room appearing to be empty; but as soon as he had advanced a few steps he started. On the hearthrug lay Clym asleep. Beside him were the leggings, thick boots, leather gloves, and sleeve-waistcoat in which he worked.

"You may go in; you will not disturb him," she said, following behind. "My reason for fastening the door is that he may not be intruded upon by any chance comer while lying here, if I should be in the garden or upstairs."

"Why is he sleeping there?" said Wildeve in low tones.

"He is very weary. He went out at half-past four this morning, and has been working ever since. He cuts furze because it is the only thing he can do that does not put any strain upon his poor eyes." The contrast between the sleeper's appearance and Wildeve's at this moment was painfully apparent to Eustacia, Wildeve being elegantly dressed in a new summer suit and light hat; and she continued: "Ah! you don't know how differently he appeared when I first met him, though it is such a little while ago. His hands were as white and soft as mine; and look at them now, how rough and brown they are! His complexion is by nature fair, and that rusty look he has now, all of a colour with his leather clothes, is caused by the burning of the sun."

"Why does he go out at all?" Wildeve whispered.

"Because he hates to be idle; though what he earns doesn't add much to our exchequer. However, he says that when people are living upon their capital they must keep down current expenses by turning a penny where they can."

"The fates have not been kind to you, Eustacia Yeobright."

"I have nothing to thank them for."

"Nor has he — except for their one great gift to him."

"What's that?"

Wildeve looked her in the eyes.

Eustacia blushed for the first time that day. "Well, I am a questionable gift," she said quietly. "I thought you meant the gift of content — which he has, and I have not."

"I can understand content in such a case — though how the outward situation can attract him puzzles me."

"That's because you don't know him. He's an enthusiast about ideas, and careless about outward things. He often reminds me of the Apostle Paul."

"I am glad to hear that he's so grand in character as that."

"Yes; but the worst of it is that though Paul was excellent as a man in the Bible he would hardly have done in real life."

Their voices had instinctively dropped lower, though at first they had taken no particular care to avoid awakening Clym. "Well, if that means that your marriage is a misfortune to you, you know who is to blame," said Wildeve.

"The marriage is no misfortune," she said, showing more emotion than had as yet appeared in her. "It is simply the accident which has happened since that has been the cause of my ruin. I have certainly got thistles for figs in a worldly sense, but how could I tell what time would bring forth?"

"Sometimes, Eustacia, I think it is a judgment upon you. You rightly belonged to me, you know; and I had no idea of losing you."

"No, it was not my fault. Two could not belong to you; and remember that, before I was aware, you turned aside to another woman. It was cruel levity in you to do that. I never dreamt of playing such a game on my side till you began it on yours."

"I meant nothing by it," replied Wildeve. "It was a mere interlude. Men are given to the trick of having a passing fancy for somebody else in the midst of a permanent love, which reasserts itself afterwards just as before. On account of your rebellious manner to me I was tempted to go further than I should have done; and when you still would keep playing the same tantalizing part I went further still, and married her." Turning and looking again at the unconscious form of Clym, he murmured, "I am afraid that you don't value your prize, Clym.... He ought to be happier than I in one thing at least. He may know what it is to come down in the world, and to be afflicted with a great personal calamity; but he probably doesn't know what it is to lose the woman he loved."

"He is not ungrateful for winning her," whispered Eustacia, "and in that respect he is a good man. Many women would go far for such a husband. But do I desire unreasonably much in wanting what is called life — music, poetry, passion, war, and all the beating and pulsing that is going on in the great arteries of the world? That was the shape of my youthful dream; but I did not get it. Yet I thought I saw the way to it in my Clym."

"And you only married him on that account?"

"There you mistake me. I married him because I loved him, but I won't say that I didn't love him partly because I thought I saw a promise of that life in him."

"You have dropped into your old mournful key."

"But I am not going to be depressed," she cried excitedly. "I began a new system by going to that dance, and I mean to stick to it. Clym can sing merrily; why should not I?"

Wildeve looked thoughtfully at her. "It is easier to say you will sing than to do it; though if I could I would encourage you in your attempt. But as life means nothing to me, without one thing which is now impossible, you will forgive me for not being able to encourage you."

"Damon, what is the matter with you, that you speak like that?" she asked, raising her deep shady eyes to his.

"That's a thing I shall never tell plainly; and perhaps if I try to tell you in riddles you will not care to guess them."

Eustacia remained silent for a minute, and she said, "We are in a strange relationship today. You mince matters to an uncommon nicety. You mean, Damon, that you still love me. Well, that gives me sorrow, for I am not made so entirely happy by my marriage that I am willing to spurn you for the information, as I ought to do. But we have said too much about this. Do you mean to wait until my husband is awake?"

"I thought to speak to him; but it is unnecessary. Eustacia, if I offend you by not forgetting you, you are right to mention it; but do not talk of spurning."

She did not reply, and they stood looking musingly at Clym as he slept on in that profound sleep which is the result of physical labour carried on in circumstances that wake no nervous fear.

"God, how I envy him that sweet sleep!" said Wildeve. "I have not slept like that since I was a boy — years and years ago."

While they thus watched him a click at the gate was audible, and a knock came to the door. Eustacia went to a window and looked out.

Her countenance changed. First she became crimson, and then the red subsided till it even partially left her lips.

"Shall I go away?" said Wildeve, standing up.

"I hardly know."

"Who is it?"

"Mrs. Yeobright. O, what she said to me that day! I cannot understand this visit — what does she mean? And she suspects that past time of ours."

"I am in your hands. If you think she had better not see me here I'll go into the next room."

"Well, yes: go."

Wildeve at once withdrew; but before he had been half a minute in the adjoining apartment Eustacia came after him.

"No," she said, "we won't have any of this. If she comes in she must see you — I have done no wrong. But how can I open the door to her, when she dislikes me — wishes to see not me, but her son? I won't open the door!"

Mrs. Yeobright knocked again more loudly.

"Her knocking will, in all likelihood, awaken him," continued Eustacia; "and then he will let her in himself. Ah — listen."

They could hear Clym moving in the other room, as if disturbed by the knocking, and he uttered the word "Mother."

"Yes — he is awake — he will go to the door," she said, with a breath of relief. "Come this way. I have a bad name with her, and you must not be seen. Thus I am obliged to act by stealth, not because I do ill, but because others are pleased to say so."

By this time she had taken him to the back door which was open, disclosing a path leading down the garden. "Now, one word, Damon," she remarked as he stepped forth. "This is your first visit here: let it be your last. We have been hot lovers in our time, but it won't do now. Good-bye."

"Good-bye," said Wildeve. "I have had all I came for, and I am satisfied."

"What was it?"

"A sight of you. Upon my eternal honour I came for no more."

Wildeve kissed his hand to the beautiful girl he addressed, and passed into the garden, where she watched him down the path, over the stile at the end, and into the ferns outside, which brushed his hips as he went along, and became lost in their thickets. When he had quite gone she slowly turned, and directed her attention to the interior of the house.

But it was possible that her presence might not be desired by Clym and his mother at this moment of their first meeting, or that it would be superfluous. At all events, she was in no hurry to meet Mrs. Yeobright. She resolved to wait till Clym came to look for her, and glided back into the garden. Here she idly occupied herself for a few minutes, till finding no notice was taken of her she again retraced her steps, advancing to the front entrance, where she listened for voices in the parlour. But hearing none she opened the door and went in. To her astonishment Clym lay precisely as Wildeve and herself had left him, his sleep apparently unbroken. He had been disturbed and made to dream and murmur by the knocking, but he had not awakened. Eustacia hastened to the door, and in spite of her reluctance to open it to a woman who had spoken of her so bitterly, she unfastened it and looked out. Nobody was to be seen. There, by the scraper, lay Clym's hook and the handful of faggot-bonds he had brought home; in front of her were the empty path, the garden gate standing slightly ajar; and, beyond, the great valley of purple heath thrilling silently in the sun. Mrs. Yeobright was gone.

Clym's mother was at this time following a path which lay hidden from Eustacia by a shoulder of the hill. Her walk thither from the garden gate had been hasty and determined, as of a woman who was now no less anxious to escape from the scene than she had previously been to enter it. Her eyes were fixed on the ground; within her two sights were graven — that of Clym's hook and brambles at the door, and that of a woman's face at a window. Her lips trembled, becoming unnaturally thin, as she murmured, "'Tis too much — Clym, how can he bear to do it! He is at home; and yet he lets her shut the door against me!"

In her anxiety to get out of the direct view of the house she had diverged from the straightest path homeward, and while looking about to regain it she came upon a little boy gathering whortleberries in a hollow. The boy was Johnny Nunsuch, who had been Eustacia's stoker at the bonfire, and, with the tendency of a minute body to gravitate towards a greater, he began hovering round Mrs. Yeobright as soon as she appeared, and trotted on beside her without perceptible consciousness of his act.

Mrs. Yeobright spoke to him as one in a mesmeric sleep. "'Tis a long way home, my child, and we shall not get there till evening."

"I shall," said her small companion. "I am going to play marnels afore supper, and we go to supper at six o'clock, because father comes home. Does your father come home at six, too?"

"No: he never comes; nor my son either, nor anybody."

"What have made you so down? Have you seen a ooser?"

"I have seen what's worse — a woman's face looking at me through a window-pane."

"Is that a bad sight?"

"Yes. It is always a bad sight to see a woman looking out at a weary wayfarer and not letting her in."

"Once when I went to Throope Great Pond to catch effets I seed myself looking up at myself, and I was frightened and jumped back like anything."

... "If they had only shown signs of meeting my advances half-way how well it might have been done! But there is no chance. Shut out! She must have set him against me. Can there be beautiful bodies without hearts inside? I think so. I would not have done it against a neighbour's cat on such a fiery day as this!"

"What is it you say?"

"Never again — never! Not even if they send for me!"

"You must be a very curious woman to talk like that."

"O no, not at all," she said, returning to the boy's prattle. "Most people who grow up and have children talk as I do. When you grow up your mother will talk as I do too."

"I hope she won't; because 'tis very bad to talk nonsense."

"Yes, child; it is nonsense, I suppose. Are you not nearly spent with the heat?"

"Yes. But not so much as you be."

"How do you know?"

"Your face is white and wet, and your head is hanging-down-like."

"Ah, I am exhausted from inside."

"Why do you, every time you take a step, go like this?" The child in speaking gave to his motion the jerk and limp of an invalid.

"Because I have a burden which is more than I can bear."

The little boy remained silently pondering, and they tottered on side by side until more than a quarter of an hour had elapsed, when Mrs. Yeobright, whose weakness plainly increased, said to him, "I must sit down here to rest."

When she had seated herself he looked long in her face and said, "How funny you draw your breath — like a lamb when you drive him till he's nearly done for. Do you always draw your breath like that?"

"Not always." Her voice was now so low as to be scarcely above a whisper.

"You will go to sleep there, I suppose, won't you? You have shut your eyes already."

"No. I shall not sleep much till — another day, and then I hope to have a long, long one — very long. Now can you tell me if Bottom Pond is dry this summer?"

"Bottom Pond is, but Moreford Pool isn't, because he is deep, and is never dry — 'tis just over there."

"Is the water clear?"

"Yes, middling — except where the heath-croppers walk into it."

"Then, take this, and go as fast as you can, and dip me up the clearest you can find. I am very faint."

She drew from the small willow reticule that she carried in her hand an old-fashioned china teacup without a handle; it was one of half a dozen of the same sort lying in the reticule, which she had preserved ever since her childhood, and had brought with her today as a small present for Clym and Eustacia.

The boy started on his errand, and soon came back with the water, such as it was. Mrs. Yeobright attempted to drink, but it was so warm as to give her nausea, and she threw it away. Afterwards she still remained sitting, with her eyes closed.

The boy waited, played near her, caught several of the little brown butterflies which abounded, and then said as he waited again, "I like going on better than biding still. Will you soon start again?"

"I don't know."

"I wish I might go on by myself," he resumed, fearing, apparently, that he was to be pressed into some unpleasant service. "Do you want me any more, please?"

Mrs. Yeobright made no reply.

"What shall I tell mother?" the boy continued.

"Tell her you have seen a broken-hearted woman cast off by her son."

Before quite leaving her he threw upon her face a wistful glance, as if he had misgivings on the generosity of forsaking her thus. He gazed into her face in a vague, wondering manner, like that of one examining some strange old manuscript the key to whose characters is undiscoverable. He was not so young as to be absolutely without a sense that sympathy was demanded, he was not old enough to be free from the terror felt in childhood at beholding misery in adult quarters hitherto deemed impregnable; and whether she were in a position to cause trouble or to suffer from it, whether she and her affliction were something to pity or something to fear, it was beyond him to decide. He lowered his eyes and went on without another word. Before he had gone half a mile he had forgotten all about her, except that she was a woman who had sat down to rest.

Mrs. Yeobright's exertions, physical and emotional, had well-nigh prostrated her; but she continued to creep along in short stages with long breaks between. The sun had now got far to the west of south and stood directly in her face, like some merciless incendiary, brand in hand, waiting to consume her. With the departure of the boy all visible animation disappeared from the landscape, though the intermittent husky notes of the male grasshoppers from every tuft of furze were enough to show that amid the prostration of the larger animal species an unseen insect world was busy in all the fulness of life.

At length she reached a slope about two-thirds of the whole distance from Alderworth to her own home, where a little patch of shepherd's-thyme intruded upon the path; and she sat down upon the perfumed mat it formed there. In front of her a colony of ants had established a thoroughfare across the way, where they toiled a never-ending and heavy-laden throng. To look down upon them was like observing a city street from the top of a tower. She remembered that this bustle of ants had been in progress for years at the same spot — doubtless those of the old times were the ancestors of these which walked there now. She leant back to obtain more thorough rest, and the soft eastern portion of the sky was as great a relief to her eyes as the thyme was to her head. While she looked a heron arose on that side of the sky and flew on with his face towards the sun. He had come dripping wet from some pool in the valleys, and as he flew the edges and lining of his wings, his thighs, and his breast were so caught by the bright sunbeams that he appeared as if formed of burnished silver. Up in the zenith where he was seemed a free and happy place, away from all contact with the earthly ball to which she was pinioned; and she wished that she could arise uncrushed from its surface and fly as he flew then.

But, being a mother, it was inevitable that she should soon cease to ruminate upon her own condition. Had the track of her next thought been marked by a streak in the air, like the path of a meteor, it would have shown a direction contrary to the heron's, and have descended to the eastward upon the roof of Clym's house.

VII

THE TRAGIC MEETING OF TWO OLD FRIENDS

HE IN the meantime had aroused himself from sleep, sat up, and looked around. Eustacia was sitting in a chair hard by him, and though she held a book in her hand she had not looked into it for some time.

"Well, indeed!" said Clym, brushing his eyes with his hands. "How soundly I have slept! I have had such a tremendous dream, too: one I shall never forget."

"I thought you had been dreaming," said she.

"Yes. It was about my mother. I dreamt that I took you to her house to make up differences, and when we got there we couldn't get in, though she kept on crying to us for help. However, dreams are dreams. What o'clock is it, Eustacia?"

"Half-past two."

"So late, is it? I didn't mean to stay so long. By the time I have had something to eat it will be after three."

"Ann is not come back from the village, and I thought I would let you sleep on till she returned."

Clym went to the window and looked out. Presently he said, musingly, "Week after week passes, and yet mother does not come. I thought I should have heard something from her long before this."

Misgiving, regret, fear, resolution, ran their swift course of expression in Eustacia's dark eyes. She was face to face with a monstrous difficulty, and she resolved to get free of it by postponement.

"I must certainly go to Blooms-End soon," he continued, "and I think I had better go alone." He picked up his leggings and gloves, threw them down again, and added, "As dinner will be so late today I will not go back to the heath, but work in the garden till the evening, and then, when it will be cooler, I will walk to Blooms-End. I am quite sure that if I make a little advance mother will be willing to forget all. It will be rather late before I can get home, as I shall not be able to do the distance either way in less than an hour and a half. But you will not mind for one evening, dear? What are you thinking of to make you look so abstracted?"

"I cannot tell you," she said heavily. "I wish we didn't live here, Clym. The world seems all wrong in this place."

"Well — if we make it so. I wonder if Thomasin has been to Blooms-End lately. I hope so. But probably not, as she is, I believe, expecting to be confined in a month or so. I wish I had thought of that before. Poor mother must indeed be very lonely."

"I don't like you going tonight."

"Why not tonight?"

"Something may be said which will terribly injure me."

"My mother is not vindictive," said Clym, his colour faintly rising.

"But I wish you would not go," Eustacia repeated in a low tone. "If you agree not to go tonight I promise to go by myself to her house tomorrow, and make it up with her, and wait till you fetch me."

"Why do you want to do that at this particular time, when at every previous time that I have proposed it you have refused?"

"I cannot explain further than that I should like to see her alone before you go," she answered, with an impatient move of her head, and looking at him with an anxiety more frequently seen upon those of a sanguine temperament than upon such as herself.

"Well, it is very odd that just when I had decided to go myself you should want to do what I proposed long ago. If I wait for you to go tomorrow another day will be lost; and I know I shall be unable to rest another night without having been. I want to get this settled, and will. You must visit her afterwards: it will be all the same."

"I could even go with you now?"

"You could scarcely walk there and back without a longer rest than I shall take. No, not tonight, Eustacia."

"Let it be as you say, then," she replied in the quiet way of one who, though willing to ward off evil consequences by a mild effort, would let events fall out as they might sooner than wrestle hard to direct them.

Clym then went into the garden; and a thoughtful languor stole over Eustacia for the remainder of the afternoon, which her husband attributed to the heat of the weather.

In the evening he set out on the journey. Although the heat of summer was yet intense the days had considerably shortened, and before he had advanced a mile on his way all the heath purples, browns, and greens had merged in a uniform dress without airiness or gradation, and broken only by touches of white where the little heaps of clean quartz sand showed the entrance to a rabbit-burrow, or where the white flints of a footpath lay like a thread over the slopes. In almost every one of the isolated and stunted thorns which grew here and there a night-hawk revealed his presence by whirring like the clack of a mill as long as he could hold his breath, then stopping, flapping his wings, wheeling round the bush, alighting, and after a silent interval of listening beginning to whirr again. At each brushing of Clym's feet white miller-moths flew into the air just high enough to catch upon their dusty wings the mellowed light from the west, which now shone across the depressions and levels of the ground without falling thereon to light them up.

Yeobright walked on amid this quiet scene with a hope that all would soon be well. At length he came to a spot where a soft perfume was wafted across his path, and he stood still for a moment to inhale the familiar scent. It was the place at which, four hours earlier, his mother had sat down exhausted on the knoll covered with shepherd's-thyme. While he stood a sound between a breathing and a moan suddenly reached his ears.

He looked to where the sound came from; but nothing appeared there save the verge of the hillock stretching against the sky in an unbroken line. He moved a few steps in that direction, and now he perceived a recumbent figure almost close at his feet.

Among the different possibilities as to the person's individuality there did not for a moment occur to Yeobright that it might be one of his own family. Sometimes furze-cutters had been known to sleep out of doors at these times, to save a long journey homeward and back again: but Clym remembered the moan and looked closer, and saw that the form was feminine: and a distress came over him like cold air from a cave. But he was not absolutely certain that the woman was his mother till he stopped and beheld her face, pallid, and with closed eyes.

His breath went, as it were, out of his body, and the cry of anguish which would have escaped him died upon his lips. During the momentary interval that elapsed before he became conscious that something must be done all sense of time and place left him, and it seemed as if he and his mother were as when he was a child with her many years ago on this heath at hours similar to the present. Then he awoke to activity; and bending yet lower he found that she still breathed, and that her breath though feeble was regular, except when disturbed by an occasional gasp.

"O, what is it! Mother, are you very ill — you are not dying?" he cried, pressing his lips to her face. "I am your Clym. How did you come here? What does it all mean?"

At that moment the chasm in their lives which his love for Eustacia had caused was not remembered by Yeobright, and to him the present joined continuously with that friendly past that had been their experience before the division.

She moved her lips, appeared to know him, but could not speak; and then Clym strove to consider how best to move her, as it would be necessary to get her away from the spot before the dews were intense. He was able-bodied, and his mother was thin. He clasped his arms round her, lifted her a little, and said, "Does that hurt you?"

She shook her head, and he lifted her up; then, at a slow pace, went onward with his load. The air was now completely cool; but whenever he passed over a sandy patch of ground uncarpeted with vegetation there was reflected from its surface into his face the heat which it had imbibed during the day. At the beginning of his undertaking he had thought but little of the distance which yet would have to be traversed before Blooms-End could be reached; but though he had slept that afternoon he soon began to feel the weight of his burden. Thus he proceeded, like Æneas with his father; the bats circling round his head, nightjars flapping their wings within a yard of his face, and not a human being within call.

While he was yet nearly a mile from the house his mother exhibited signs of restlessness under the constraint of being borne along, as if his arms were irksome to her. He lowered her upon his knees and looked around. The point they had now reached, though far from any road, was not more than a mile from the Blooms-End cottages occupied by Fairway, Sam, Humphrey, and the Cantles. Moreover, fifty yards off stood a hut, built of clods and covered with thin turves, but now entirely disused. The simple outline of the lonely shed was visible, and thither he determined to direct his steps. As soon as he arrived he laid her down carefully by the entrance, and then ran and cut with his pocket-knife an armful of the driest fern. Spreading this within the shed, which was entirely open on one side, he placed his mother thereon: then he ran with all his might towards the dwelling of Fairway.

Nearly a quarter of an hour had passed, disturbed only by the broken breathing of the sufferer, when moving figures began to animate the line between heath and sky. In a few moments Clym arrived with Fairway, Humphrey, and Susan Nunsuch; Olly Dowden, who had chanced to be at Fairway's, Christian and Grandfer Cantle following helter-skelter behind. They had brought a lantern and matches, water, a pillow, and a few other articles which had occurred to their minds in the hurry of the moment. Sam had been despatched back again for brandy, and a boy brought Fairway's pony, upon which he rode off to the nearest medical man, with directions to call at Wildeve's on his way, and inform Thomasin that her aunt was unwell.

Sam and the brandy soon arrived, and it was administered by the light of the lantern; after which she became sufficiently conscious to signify by signs that something was wrong with her foot. Olly Dowden at length understood her meaning, and examined the foot indicated. It was swollen and red. Even as they watched the red began to assume a more livid colour, in the midst of which appeared a scarlet speck, smaller than a pea, and it was found to consist of a drop of blood, which rose above the smooth flesh of her ankle in a hemisphere.

"I know what it is," cried Sam. "She has been stung by an adder!"

"Yes," said Clym instantly. "I remember when I was a child seeing just such a bite. O, my poor mother!"

"It was my father who was bit," said Sam. "And there's only one way to cure it. You must rub the place with the fat of other adders, and the only way to get that is by frying them. That's what they did for him."

"'Tis an old remedy," said Clym distractedly, "and I have doubts about it. But we can do nothing else till the doctor comes."

"'Tis a sure cure," said Olly Dowden, with emphasis. "I've used it when I used to go out nursing."

"Then we must pray for daylight, to catch them," said Clym gloomily.

"I will see what I can do," said Sam.

He took a green hazel which he had used as a walking-stick, split it at the end, inserted a small pebble, and with the lantern in his hand went out into the heath. Clym had by this time lit a small fire, and despatched Susan Nunsuch for a frying-pan. Before she had returned Sam came in with three adders, one briskly coiling and uncoiling in the cleft of the stick, and the other two hanging dead across it.

"I have only been able to get one alive and fresh as he ought to be," said Sam. "These limp ones are two I killed today at work; but as they don't die till the sun goes down they can't be very stale meat."

The live adder regarded the assembled group with a sinister look in its small

black eye, and the beautiful brown and jet pattern on its back seemed to intensify with indignation. Mrs. Yeobright saw the creature, and the creature
saw her: she quivered throughout, and averted her eyes.

"Look at that," murmured Christian Cantle. "Neighbours, how do we
know but that something of the old serpent in God's garden, that gied the
apple to the young woman with no clothes, lives on in adders and snakes still?
Look at his eye — for all the world like a villainous sort of black currant.
'Tis to be hoped he can't ill-wish us! There's folks in heath who've been
overlooked already. I will never kill another adder as long as I live."

"Well, 'tis right to be afeard of things, if folks can't help it," said Grandfer
Cantle. "'Twould have saved me many a brave danger in my time."

"I fancy I heard something outside the shed," said Christian. "I wish
troubles would come in the daytime, for then a man could show his courage,
and hardly beg for mercy of the most broomstick old woman he should see,
if he was a brave man, and able to run out of her sight!"

"Even such an ignorant fellow as I should know better than do that," said
Sam.

"Well, there's calamities where we least expect it, whether or no. Neighbours, if Mrs. Yeobright were to die, d'ye think we should be took up and
tried for the manslaughter of a woman?"

"No, they couldn't bring it in that," said Sam, "unless they could prove
we had been poachers at some time of our lives. But she'll fetch round."

"Now, if I had been stung by ten adders I should hardly have lost a day's
work for't," said Grandfer Cantle. "Such is my spirit when I am on my
mettle. But perhaps 'tis natural in a man trained for war. Yes, I've gone
through a good deal; but nothing ever came amiss to me after I joined the
Locals in four." He shook his head and smiled at a mental picture of himself
in uniform. "I was always first in the most galliantest scrapes in my younger
days!"

"I suppose that was because they always used to put the biggest fool
afore," said Fairway from the fire, beside which he knelt, blowing it with his
breath.

"D'ye think so, Timothy?" said Grandfer Cantle, coming forward to Fairway's side, with sudden depression in his face. "Then a man may feel for
years that he is good solid company, and be wrong about himself after all?"

"Never mind that question, Grandfer. Stir your stumps and get some
more sticks. 'Tis very nonsense of an old man to prattle so when life and
death's in mangling."

"Yes, yes," said Grandfer Cantle, with melancholy conviction. "Well,
this is a bad night altogether for them that have done well in their time; and
if I were ever such a dab at the hautboy or tenor-viol, I shouldn't have the
heart to play tunes upon 'em now."

Susan now arrived with the frying-pan, when the live adder was killed and
the heads of the three taken off. The remainders, being cut into lengths and
split open, were tossed into the pan, which began hissing and crackling over
the fire. Soon a rill of clear oil trickled from the carcases, whereupon Clym
dipped the corner of his handkerchief into the liquid and anointed the wound.

VIII

EUSTACIA HEARS OF GOOD FORTUNE AND BEHOLDS EVIL

IN THE meantime Eustacia, left alone in her cottage at Alderworth, had become considerably depressed by the posture of affairs. The consequences which might result from Clym's discovery that his mother had been turned from his door that day were likely to be disagreeable, and this was a quality in events which she hated as much as the dreadful.

To be left to pass the evening by herself was irksome to her at any time, and this evening it was more irksome than usual by reason of the excitements of the past hours. The two visits had stirred her into restlessness. She was not wrought to any great pitch of uneasiness by the probability of appearing in an ill light in the discussion between Clym and his mother, but she was wrought to vexation; and her slumbering activities were quickened to the extent of wishing that she had opened the door. She had certainly believed that Clym was awake, and the excuse would be an honest one as far as it went; but nothing could save her from censure in refusing to answer at the first knock. Yet, instead of blaming herself for the issue she laid the fault upon the shoulders of some indistinct, colossal Prince of the World, who had framed her situation and ruled her lot.

At this time of the year it was pleasanter to walk by night than by day, and when Clym had been absent about an hour she suddenly resolved to go out in the direction of Blooms-End, on the chance of meeting him on his return. When she reached the garden gate she heard wheels approaching, and looking round beheld her grandfather coming up in his car.

"I can't stay a minute, thank ye," he answered to her greeting. "I am driving to East Egdon; but I came round here just to tell you the news. Perhaps you have heard — about Mr. Wildeve's fortune?"

"No," said Eustacia blankly.

"Well, he has come into a fortune of eleven thousand pounds — uncle died in Canada, just after hearing that all his family, whom he was sending home, had gone to the bottom in the *Cassiopeia*; so Wildeve has come into everything, without in the least expecting it."

Eustacia stood motionless awhile. "How long has he known of this?" she asked.

"Well, it was known to him this morning early, for I knew it at ten o'clock, when Charley came back. Now, he is what I call a lucky man. What a fool you were, Eustacia!"

"In what way?" she said, lifting her eyes in apparent calmness.

"Why, in not sticking to him when you had him."

"Had him, indeed!"

"I did not know there had ever been anything between you till lately; and, faith, I should have been hot and strong against it if I had known; but since it seems that there was some sniffing between ye, why the deuce didn't you stick to him?"

Eustacia made no reply, but she looked as if she could say as much upon that subject as he if she chose.

"And how is your poor purblind husband?" continued the old man. "Not a bad fellow either, as far as he goes."

"He is quite well."

"It is a good thing for his cousin what-d'ye-call-her? By George, you ought to have been in that galley, my girl! Now I must drive on. Do you want any assistance? What's mine is yours, you know."

"Thank you, grandfather, we are not in want at present," she said coldly. "Clym cuts furze, but he does it mostly as a useful pastime, because he can do nothing else."

"He is paid for his pastime, isn't he? Three shillings a hundred, I heard."

"Clym has money," she said, colouring: "but he likes to earn a little."

"Very well; good night." And the captain drove on.

When her grandfather was gone Eustacia went on her way mechanically; but her thoughts were no longer concerning her mother-in-law and Clym. Wildeve, notwithstanding his complaints against his fate, had been seized upon by destiny and placed in the sunshine once more. Eleven thousand pounds! From every Egdon point of view he was a rich man. In Eustacia's eyes, too, it was ample sum — one sufficient to supply those wants of hers which had been stigmatized by Clym in his more austere moods as vain and luxurious. Though she was no lover of money she loved what money could bring; and the new accessories she imagined around him clothed Wildeve with a great deal of interest. She recollected now how quietly well-dressed he had been that morning: he had probably put on his newest suit, regardless of damage by briars and thorns. And then she thought of his manner towards herself.

"O I see it, I see it," she said. "How much he wishes he had me now, that he might give me all I desire!"

In recalling the details of his glances and words — at the time scarcely regarded — it became plain to her how greatly they had been dictated by his knowledge of this new event. "Had he been a man to bear a jilt ill-will he would have told me of his good fortune in crowing tones; instead of doing that he mentioned not a word, in deference to my misfortunes, and merely implied that he loved me still, as one superior to him."

Wildeve's silence that day on what had happened to him was just the kind of behavior calculated to make an impression on such a woman. Those delicate touches of good taste were, in fact, one of the strong points in his demeanour towards the other sex. The peculiarity of Wildeve was that, while at one time passionate, upbraiding, and resentful towards a woman, at another he would treat her with such unparalleled grace as to make previous neglect appear as no discourtesy, injury as no insult, interference as a delicate attention, and the ruin of her honour as excess of chivalry. This man, whose admiration today Eustacia had disregarded, whose good wishes she had scarcely taken the trouble to accept, whom she had shown out of the house by the back door, was the possessor of eleven thousand pounds — a man of fair professional education, and one who had served his articles with a civil engineer.

So intent was Eustacia upon Wildeve's fortunes that she forgot how much closer to her own course were those of Clym; and instead of walking on to meet him at once she sat down upon a stone. She was disturbed in her reverie by a voice behind, and turning her head beheld the old lover and fortunate inheritor of wealth immediately beside her.

She remained sitting, though the fluctuation in her look might have told any man who knew her so well as Wildeve that she was thinking of him.

"How did you come here?" she said in her clear, low tone. "I thought you were at home."

"I went on to the village after leaving your garden; and now I have come back again: that's all. Which way are you walking, may I ask?"

She waved her hand in the direction of Blooms-End. "I am going to meet my husband. I think I may possibly have got into trouble whilst you were with me today."

"How could that be?"

"By not letting in Mrs. Yeobright."

"I hope that visit of mine did you no harm."

"None. It was not your fault," she said quietly.

By this time she had risen; and they involuntarily sauntered on together, without speaking, for two or three minutes; when Eustacia broke silence by saying, "I assume I must congratulate you."

"On what? O yes; on my eleven thousand pounds, you mean. Well, since I didn't get something else, I must be content with getting that."

"You seem very indifferent about it. Why didn't you tell me today when you came?" she said in the tone of a neglected person. "I heard of it quite by accident."

"I did mean to tell you," said Wildeve. "But I — well, I will speak frankly — I did not like to mention it when I saw, Eustacia, that your star was not high. The sight of a man lying wearied out with hard work, as your husband lay, made me feel that to brag of my own fortune to you would be greatly out of place. Yet, as you stood there beside him, I could not help feeling too that in many respects he was a richer man than I."

At this Eustacia said, with slumbering mischievousness, "What would you exchange with him — your fortune for me?"

"I certainly would," said Wildeve.

"As we are imagining what is impossible and absurd, suppose we change the subject?"

"Very well; and I will tell you of my plans for the future, if you care to hear them. I shall permanently invest nine thousand pounds, keep one thousand as ready money, and with the remaining thousand travel for a year or so."

"Travel? What a bright idea! Where will you go to?"

"From here to Paris, where I shall pass the winter and spring. Then I shall go to Italy, Greece, Egypt, and Palestine, before the hot weather comes on. In the summer I shall go to America; and then, by a plan not yet settled, I shall go to Australia and round to India. By that time I shall have begun to have had enough of it. Then I shall probably come back to Paris again, and there I shall stay as long as I can afford to."

"Back to Paris again," she murmured in a voice that was nearly a sigh. She had never once told Wildeve of the Parisian desires which Clym's description had sown in her; yet here was he involuntarily in a position to gratify them. "You think a good deal of Paris?" she added.

"Yes. In my opinion it is the central beauty-spot of the world."

"And in mine! And Thomasin will go with you?"

"Yes, if she cares to. She may prefer to stay at home."

"So you will be going about, and I shall be staying here!"

"I suppose you will. But we know whose fault that is."

"I am not blaming you," she said quickly.

"Oh, I thought you were. If ever you *should* be inclined to blame me, think of a certain evening by Rainbarrow, when you promised to meet me and did not. You sent me a letter; and my heart ached to read that as I hope yours never will. That was one point of divergence. I then did something in haste.... But she is a good woman, and I will say no more."

"I know that the blame was on my side that time," said Eustacia. "But it had not always been so. However, it is my misfortune to be too sudden in feeling. O Damon, don't reproach me any more — I can't bear that."

They went on silently for a distance of a mile and more, when Eustacia said suddenly, "Haven't you come out of your way, Mr. Wildeve?"

"My way is anywhere tonight. I will go with you as far as the hill on which we can see Blooms-End, as it is getting late for you to be alone."

"Don't trouble. I am not obliged to be out at all. I think I would rather you did not accompany me further. This sort of thing would have an odd look if known."

"Very well, I will leave you." He took her hand unexpectedly, and kissed it — for the first time since her marriage. "What light is that on the hill?" he added, as it were to hide the caress.

She looked, and saw a flickering firelight proceeding from the open side of a hovel a little way before them. The hovel, which she had hitherto always found empty, seemed to be inhabited now.

"Since you have come so far," said Eustacia, "will you see me safely past that hut? I thought I should have met Clym somewhere about here, but as he doesn't appear I will hasten on and get to Blooms-End before he leaves."

They advanced to the turf-shed, and when they got near it the firelight and the lantern inside showed distinctly enough the form of a woman reclining on a bed of fern, a group of heath men and women standing around her. Eustacia did not recognize Mrs. Yeobright in the reclining figure, nor Clym as one of the standers-by till she came close. Then she quickly pressed her hand upon Wildeve's arm and signified to him to come back from the open side of the shed into the shadow.

"It is my husband and his mother," she whispered in an agitated voice. "What can it mean? Will you step forward and tell me?"

Wildeve left her side and went to the back wall of the hut. Presently Eustacia perceived that he was beckoning to her, and she advanced and joined him.

"It is a serious case," said Wildeve.

From their position they could hear what was proceeding inside.

"I cannot think where she could have been going," said Clym to someone. "She had evidently walked a long way, but even when she was able to speak just now she would not tell me where. What do you really think of her?"

"There is a great deal to fear," was gravely answered, in a voice which Eustacia recognized as that of the only surgeon in the district. "She has suffered somewhat from the bite of the adder; but it is exhaustion which has overpowered her. My impression is that her walk must have been exceptionally long."

"I used to tell her not to overwork herself this weather," said Clym, with distress. "Do you think we did well in using the adder's fat?"

"Well, it is a very ancient remedy — the old remedy of the viper-catchers, I believe," replied the doctor. "It is mentioned as an infallible ointment by Hoffman, Mead, and I think the Abbé Fontana. Undoubtedly it was as good a thing as you could do; though I question if some other oils would not have been equally efficacious."

"Come here, come here!" was then rapidly said in soft female tones; and Clym and the doctor could be heard rushing forward from the back part of the shed, where they had been standing.

"O, what is it?" whispered Eustacia.

"'Twas Thomasin who spoke," said Wildeve. "Then they have fetched her. I wonder if I had better go in — yet it might do harm."

For a long time there was utter silence among the group within; and it was broken at last by Clym saying, in an agonized voice, "O doctor, what does it mean?"

The doctor did not reply at once; ultimately he said, "She is sinking fast. Her heart was previously affected, and physical exhaustion has dealt the finishing blow."

Then there was a weeping of women, then waiting, then hushed exclamations, then a strange gasping sound, then a painful stillness.

"It is all over," said the doctor.

Further back in the hut the cotters whispered, "Mrs. Yeobright is dead."

Almost at the same moment the two watchers observed the form of a small old-fashioned child entering at the open side of the shed. Susan Nunsuch, whose boy it was, went forward to the opening and silently beckoned him to go back.

"I've got something to tell 'ee, mother," he cried in a shrill tone. "That woman asleep there walked along with me today; and she said I was to say that I had seed her, and she was a broken-hearted woman and cast off by her son, and then I came on home."

A confused sob as from a man was heard within, upon which Eustacia gasped faintly, "That's Clym — I must go to him — yet dare I do it? No: come away!"

When they had withdrawn from the neighbourhood of the shed she said huskily, "I am to blame for this. There is evil in store for me."

"Was she not admitted to your house after all?" Wildeve inquired.

"No; and that's where it all lies! O, what shall I do! I shall not intrude upon them: I shall go straight home.   Damon, good-bye!   I cannot speak to you any more now."

They parted company; and when Eustacia had reached the next hill she looked back.   A melancholy procession was wending its way by the light of the lantern from the hut towards Blooms-End.   Wildeve was nowhere to be seen.

BOOK FIFTH: THE DISCOVERY

I

"WHEREFORE IS LIGHT GIVEN TO HIM THAT IS IN MISERY?"

ONE evening, about three weeks after the funeral of Mrs. Yeobright, when the silver face of the moon sent a bundle of beams directly upon the floor of Clym's house at Alderworth, a woman came forth from within.   She reclined over the garden gate as if to refresh herself awhile.   The pale lunar touches which make beauties of hags lent divinity to this face, already beautiful.

She had not long been there when a man came up the road and with some hesitation said to her, "How is he tonight, ma'am, if you please?"

"He is better, though still very unwell, Humphrey," replied Eustacia.

"Is he light-headed ma'am?"

"No.   He is quite sensible now."

"Do he rave about his mother just the same, poor fellow?" continued Humphrey.

"Just as much, though not quite so wildly," she said in a low voice.

"It was very unfortunate, ma'am, that the boy Johnny should ever ha' told his mother's dying words, about her being broken-hearted and cast off by her son.   'Twas enough to upset any man alive."

Eustacia made no reply beyond that of a slight catch in her breath, as of one who fain would speak but could not; and Humphrey, finding that she was disinclined to say more, went home again.

Eustacia turned, entered the house, and ascended to the front bedroom, where a shaded light was burning.   In the bed lay Clym, pale, haggard, wide awake, tossing to one side and to the other, his eyes lit by a hot light, as if the fire in their pupils were burning up their substance.

"Is it you, Eustacia?" he said as she sat down.

"Yes, Clym.   I have been down to the gate.   The moon is shining beautifully, and there is not a leaf stirring."

"Shining, is it?   What's the moon to a man like me?   Let it shine — let anything be, so that I never see another day!... Eustacia, I don't know where to look: my thoughts go through me like swords.   O, if any man wants to make himself immortal by painting a picture of wretchedness, let him come here!"

"Why do you say so?"

"I cannot help feeling that I did my best to kill her."

"No, Clym."

"Yes, it was so; it is useless to excuse me! My conduct to her was too hideous — I made no advances; and she could not bring herself to forgive me. Now she is dead! If I had only shown myself willing to make it up with her sooner, and we had been friends, and then she had died, it wouldn't be so hard to bear. But I never went near her house, so she never came near mine, and didn't know how welcome she would have been — that's what troubles me. She did not know I was going to her house that very night, for she was too insensible to understand me. If she had only come to see me! I longed that she would. But it was not to be."

There escaped from Eustacia one of those shivering sighs which used to shake her like a pestilent blast. She had not yet told.

But Yeobright was too deeply absorbed in the ramblings incidental to his remorseful state to notice her. During his illness he had been continually talking thus. Despair had been added to his original grief by the unfortunate disclosure of the boy who had received the last words of Mrs. Yeobright — words too bitterly uttered in an hour of misapprehension. Then his distress had overwhelmed him, and he longed for death as a field labourer longs for the shade. It was the pitiful sight of a man standing in the very focus of sorrow. He continually bewailed his tardy journey to his mother's house, because it was an error which could never be rectified, and insisted that he must have been horribly perverted by some fiend not to have thought before that it was his duty to go to her, since she did not come to him. He would ask Eustacia to agree with him in his self-condemnation; and when she, seared inwardly by a secret she dared not tell, declared that she could not give an opinion, he would say, "That's because you didn't know my mother's nature. She was always ready to forgive if asked to do so; but I seemed to her to be as an obstinate child, and that made her unyielding. Yet not unyielding: she was proud, and reserved, no more.... Yes, I can understand why she held out against me so long. She was waiting for me. I dare say she said a hundred times in her sorrow, 'What a return he makes for all the sacrifices I have made for him!' I never went to her! When I set out to visit her it was too late. To think of that is nearly intolerable!"

Sometimes his condition had been one of utter remorse, unsoftened by a single tear of pure sorrow: and then he writhed as he lay, fevered far more by thought than by physical ills. "If I could only get one assurance that she did not die in a belief that I was resentful," he said one day when in this mood, "it would be better to think of than a hope of heaven. But that I cannot do."

"You give yourself up too much to this wearying despair," said Eustacia. "Other men's mothers have died."

"That doesn't make the loss of mine less. Yet it is less the loss than the circumstances of the loss. I sinned against her, and on that account there is no light for me."

"She sinned against you, I think."

"No: she did not. I committed the guilt; and may the whole burden be upon my head!"

"I think you might consider twice before you say that," Eustacia replied. "Single men have, no doubt, a right to curse themselves as much as they please; but men with wives involve two in the doom they pray down."

"I am in too sorry a state to understand what you are refining on," said the wretched man. "Day and night shout at me, 'You have helped to kill her.' But in loathing myself I may, I own, be unjust to you, my poor wife. Forgive me for it, Eustacia, for I scarcely know what I do."

Eustacia was always anxious to avoid the sight of her husband in such a state as this, which had become as dreadful to her as the trial scene was to Judas Iscariot. It brought before her eyes the spectre of a worn-out woman knocking at a door which she would not open; and she shrank from contemplating it. Yet it was better for Yeobright himself when he spoke openly of his sharp regret, for in silence he endured infinitely more, and would sometimes remain so long in a tense, brooding mood, consuming himself by the gnawing of his thought, that it was imperatively necessary to make him talk aloud, that his grief might in some degree expend itself in the effort.

Eustacia had not been long indoors after her look at the moonlight when a soft footstep came up to the house, and Thomasin was announced by the woman downstairs.

"Ah, Thomasin! Thank you for coming tonight," said Clym when she entered the room. "Here am I, you see. Such a wretched spectacle am I, that I shrink from being seen by a single friend, and almost from you."

"You must not shrink from me, dear Clym," said Thomasin earnestly, in that sweet voice of hers which came to a sufferer like fresh air into a Black Hole. "Nothing in you can ever shock me or drive me away. I have been here before, but you don't remember it."

"Yes, I do; I am not delirious, Thomasin, nor have I been so at all. Don't you believe that if they say so. I am only in great misery at what I have done: and that, with the weakness, makes me seem mad. But it has not upset my reason. Do you think I should remember all about my mother's death if I were out of my mind? No such good luck. Two months and a half, Thomasin, the last of her life, did my poor mother live alone, distracted and mourning because of me; yet she was unvisited by me, though I was living only five miles off. Two months and a half — seventy-five days did the sun rise and set upon her in that deserted state which a dog didn't deserve! Poor people who had nothing in common with her would have cared for her, and visited her had they known her sickness and loneliness; but I, who should have been all to her, stayed away like a cur. If there is any justice in God let Him kill me now. He has nearly blinded me, but that is not enough. If He would only strike me with more pain I would believe in Him for ever!"

"Hush, hush! O, pray, Clym, don't, don't say it!" implored Thomasin, affrighted into sobs and tears; while Eustacia, at the other side of the room, though her pale face remained calm, writhed in her chair. Clym went on without heeding his cousin.

"But I am not worth receiving further proof even of Heaven's reprobation.

Do you think, Thomasin, that she knew me — that she did not die in that horrid mistaken notion about my not forgiving her, which I can't tell you how she acquired? If you could only assure me of that! Do you think so, Eustacia? Do speak to me."

"I think I can assure you that she knew better at last," said Thomasin. The pallid Eustacia said nothing.

"Why didn't she come to my house? I would have taken her in and showed her how I loved her in spite of all. But she never came; and I didn't go to her, and she died on the heath like an animal kicked out, nobody to help her till it was too late. If you could have seen her, Thomasin, as I saw her — a poor dying woman, lying in the dark upon the bare ground, moaning, no-body near, believing she was utterly deserted by all the world, it would have moved you to anguish, it would have moved a brute. And this poor woman my mother! No wonder she said to the child, 'You have seen a broken-hearted woman.' What a state she must have been brought to, to say that! and who can have done it but I? It is too dreadful to think of, and I wish I could be punished more heavily than I am. How long was I what they called out of my senses?"

"A week, I think."

"And then I became calm."

"Yes, for four days."

"And now I have left off being calm."

"But try to be quiet: please do, and you will soon be strong. If you could remove that impression from your mind ——"

"Yes, yes," he said impatiently. "But I don't want to get strong. What's the use of getting well? It would be better for me if I die, and it would certainly be better for Eustacia. Is Eustacia there?"

"Yes."

"It would be better for you, Eustacia, if I were to die?"

"Don't press such a question, dear Clym."

"Well, it really is but a shadowy supposition; for unfortunately I am going to live. I feel myself getting better. Thomasin, how long are you going to stay at the inn, now that all this money has come to your husband?"

"Another month or two, probably; until my illness is over. We cannot get off till then. I think it will be a month or more."

"Yes, yes. Of course. Ah, Cousin Tamsie, you will get over your trouble — one little month will take you through it, and bring something to console you; but I shall never get over mine, and no consolation will come!"

"Clym, you are unjust to yourself. Depend upon it, aunt thought kindly of you. I know that, if she had lived, you would have been reconciled with her."

"But she didn't come to see me, though I asked her, before I married, if she would come. Had she come, or had I gone there, she would never have died saying, 'I am a broken-hearted woman, cast off by my son.' My door has always been open to her — a welcome here has always awaited her. But that she never came to see."

"You had better not talk any more now, Clym," said Eustacia faintly, from the other part of the room, for the scene was growing intolerable to her.

"Let me talk to you instead for the little time I shall be here," Thomasin said soothingly. "Consider what a one-sided way you have of looking at the matter, Clym. When she said that to the little boy you had not found her and taken her into your arms; and it might have been uttered in a moment of bitterness. It was rather like aunt to say things in haste. She sometimes used to speak so to me. Though she did not come I am convinced that she thought of coming to see you. Do you suppose a man's mother could live two or three months without one forgiving thought? She forgave me; and why should she not have forgiven you?"

"You laboured to win her round; I did nothing. I, who was going to teach people the higher secrets of happiness, did not know how to keep out of that gross misery which the most untaught are wise enough to avoid."

"How did you get here tonight, Thomasin?" said Eustacia.

"Damon set me down at the end of the lane. He has driven into the village on business, and he will come and pick me up by-and-by."

Accordingly they soon after heard the noise of wheels. Wildeve had come, and was waiting outside with his horse and gig.

"Send out and tell him I will be down in two minutes," said Thomasin.

"I will run down myself," said Eustacia.

She went down. Wildeve had alighted, and was standing before the horse's head when Eustacia opened the door. He did not turn for a moment, thinking the comer Thomasin. Then he looked, started ever so little, and said one word: "Well?"

"I have not yet told him," she replied in a whisper.

"Then don't do so till he is well — it will be fatal. You are ill yourself."

"I am wretched.... O Damon," she said, bursting into tears, "I — I can't tell you how unhappy I am! I can hardly bear this. I can tell nobody of my trouble — nobody knows of it but you."

"Poor girl!" said Wildeve, visibly affected at her distress, and at last led on so far as to take her hand. "It is hard, when you have done nothing to deserve it, that you should have got involved in such a web as this. You were not made for these sad scenes. I am to blame most. If I could only have saved you from it all!"

"But, Damon, please pray tell me what I must do? To sit by him hour after hour, and hear him reproach himself as being the cause of her death, and to know that I am the sinner, if any human being is at all, drives me into cold despair. I don't know what to do. Should I tell him or should I not tell him? I always am asking myself that. O, I want to tell him; and yet I am afraid. If he finds it out he must surely kill me, for nothing else will be in proportion to his feelings now. 'Beware the fury of a patient man' sounds day by day in my ears as I watch him."

"Well, wait till he is better, and trust to chance. And when you tell, you must only tell part — for his own sake."

"Which part should I keep back?"

Wildeve paused. "That I was in the house at the time," he said in a low tone.

"Yes; it must be concealed, seeing what has been whispered. How much easier are hasty actions than speeches that will excuse them!"

"If he were only to die ——" Wildeve murmured.

"Do not think of it! I would not buy hope of immunity by so cowardly a desire even if I hated him. Now I am going up to him again. Thomasin bade me tell you she would be down in a few minutes. Good-bye."

She returned, and Thomasin soon appeared. When she was seated in the gig with her husband, and the horse was turning to go off, Wildeve lifted his eyes to the bedroom windows. Looking from one of them he could discern a pale, tragic face watching him drive away. It was Eustacia's.

II

A LURID LIGHT BREAKS IN UPON A DARKENED UNDERSTANDING

CLYM's grief became mitigated by wearing itself out. His strength returned, and a month after the visit of Thomasin he might have been seen walking about the garden. Endurance and despair, equanimity and gloom, the tints of health and the pallor of death, mingled weirdly in his face. He was not unnaturally silent upon all of the past that related to his mother; and though Eustacia knew that he was thinking of it none the less, she was only too glad to escape the topic ever to bring it up anew. When his mind had been weaker his heart had led him to speak out; but reason having now somewhat recovered itself he sank into taciturnity.

One evening when he was thus standing in the garden, abstractedly spudding up a weed with his stick, a bony figure turned the corner of the house and came up to him.

"Christian, isn't it?" said Clym. "I am glad you have found me out. I shall soon want you to go to Blooms-End and assist me in putting the house in order. I suppose it is all locked up as I left it?"

"Yes, Mister Clym."

"Have you dug up the potatoes and other roots?"

"Yes, without a drop o' rain, thank God. But I was coming to tell 'ee of something else which is quite different from what we have lately had in the family. I be sent by the rich gentleman at the Woman, that we used to call the landlord, to tell 'ee that Mrs. Wildeve is doing well of a girl, which was born punctually at one o'clock at noon, or a few minutes more or less; and 'tis said that expecting of this increase is what have kept 'em there since they came into their money."

"And she is getting on well, you say?"

"Yes, sir. Only Mr. Wildeve is twanky because 'tisn't a boy — that's what they say in the kitchen, but I was not supposed to notice that."

"Christian, now listen to me."

"Yes, sure, Mr. Yeobright."

"Did you see my mother the day before she died?"

"No, I did not."

Yeobright's face expressed disappointment.

"But I zeed her the morning of the same day she died."

Clym's look lighted up. "That's nearer still to my meaning," he said.

"Yes, I know 'twas the same day; for she said, 'I be going to see him, Christian; so I shall not want any vegetables brought in for dinner.'"

"See whom?"

"See you. She was going to your house, you understand."

Yeobright regarded Christian with intense surprise. "Why did you never mention this?" he said. "Are you sure it was my house she was coming to?"

"O yes. I didn't mention it because I've never zeed you lately. And as she didn't get there it was all nought, and nothing to tell."

"And I have been wondering why she should have walked in the heath on that hot day! Well, did she say what she was coming for? It is a thing, Christian, I am very anxious to know."

"Yes, Mister Clym. She didn't say it to me, though I think she did to one here and there."

"Do you know one person to whom she spoke of it?"

"There is one man, please, sir, but I hope you won't mention my name to him, as I have seen him in strange places, particular in dreams. One night last summer he glared at me like Famine and Sword, and it made me feel so low that I didn't comb out my few hairs for two days. He was standing, as it might be, Mister Yeobright, in the middle of the path to Mistover, and your mother came up, looking as pale ——"

"Yes, when was that?"

"Last summer, in my dream."

"Pooh! Who's the man?"

"Diggory, the reddleman. He called upon her and sat with her the evening before she set out to see you. I hadn't gone home from work when he came up to the gate."

"I must see Venn — I wish I had known it before," said Clym anxiously. "I wonder why he has not come to tell me?"

"He went out of Egdon Heath the next day, so would not be likely to know you wanted him."

"Christian," said Clym, "you must go and find Venn. I am otherwise engaged, or I would go myself. Find him at once, and tell him I want to speak to him."

"I am a good hand at hunting up folk by day," said Christian, looking dubiously round at the declining light; "but as to night-time, never is such a bad hand as I, Mister Yeobright."

"Search the heath when you will, so that you bring him soon. Bring him tomorrow, if you can."

Christian then departed. The morrow came, but no Venn. In the evening Christian arrived, looking very weary. He had been searching all day, and had heard nothing of the reddleman.

"Inquire as much as you can tomorrow without neglecting your work," said Yeobright. "Don't come again till you have found him."

The next day Yeobright set out for the old house at Blooms-End, which, with the garden, was now his own. His severe illness had hindered all preparations for his removal thither; but it had become necessary that he should go and overlook its contents, as administrator to his mother's little property; for which purpose he decided to pass the next night on the premises.

He journeyed onward, not quickly or decisively, but in the slow walk of one who has been awakened from a stupefying sleep. It was early afternoon when he reached the valley. The expression of the place, the tone of the hour, were precisely those of many such occasions in days gone by; and these antecedent similarities fostered the illusion that she, who was there no longer, would come out to welcome him. The garden gate was locked and the shutters were closed, just as he himself had left them on the evening after the funeral. He unlocked the gate, and found that a spider had already constructed a large web, tying the door to the lintel, on the supposition that it was never to be opened again. When he had entered the house and flung back the shutters he set about his task of overhauling the cupboards and closets, burning papers, and considering how best to arrange the place for Eustacia's reception, until such time as he might be in a position to carry out his long-delayed scheme, should that time ever arrive.

As he surveyed the rooms he felt strongly disinclined for the alterations which would have to be made in the time-honoured furnishing of his parents and grandparents, to suit Eustacia's modern ideas. The gaunt oak-cased clock, with the picture of the Ascension on the door-panel and the Miraculous Draught of Fishes on the base; his grandmother's corner cupboard with the glass door, through which the spotted china was visible; the dumb-waiter; the wooden tea-trays; the hanging fountain with the brass tap — whither would these venerable articles have to be banished?

He noticed that the flowers in the window had died for want of water, and he placed them out upon the ledge, that they might be taken away. While thus engaged he heard footsteps on the gravel without, and somebody knocked at the door.

Yeobright opened it, and Venn was standing before him.

"Good morning," said the reddleman. "Is Mrs. Yeobright at home?"

Yeobright looked upon the ground. "Then you have not seen Christian or any of the Egdon folks?" he said.

"No. I have only just returned after a long stay away. I called here the day before I left."

"And you have heard nothing?"

"Nothing."

"My mother is — dead."

"Dead!" said Venn mechanically.

"Her home now is where I shouldn't mind having mine."

Venn regarded him, and then said, "If I didn't see your face I could never believe your words. Have you been ill?"

"I had an illness."

"Well, the change! When I parted from her a month ago everything seemed to say that she was going to begin a new life."

"And what seemed came true."

"You say right, no doubt. Trouble has taught you a deeper vein of talk than mine. All I meant was regarding her life here. She has died too soon."

"Perhaps through my living too long. I have had a bitter experience on that score this last month, Diggory. But come in; I have been wanting to see you."

He conducted the reddleman into the large room where the dancing had taken place the previous Christmas; and they sat down in the settle together. "There's the cold fireplace, you see," said Clym. "When that half-burnt log and those cinders were alight she was alive! Little has been changed here yet. I can do nothing. My life creeps like a snail."

"How came she to die?" said Venn.

Yeobright gave him some particulars of her illness and death, and continued: "After this no kind of pain will ever seem more than an indisposition to me. — I began saying that I wanted to ask you something, but I stray from subjects like a drunken man. I am anxious to know what my mother said to you when she last saw you. You talked with her a long time, I think?"

"I talked with her more than half an hour."

"About me?"

"Yes. And it must have been on account of what we said that she was on the heath. Without question she was coming to see you."

"But why should she come to see me if she felt so bitterly against me? There's the mystery."

"Yet I know she quite forgave 'ee."

"But, Diggory — would a woman, who had quite forgiven her son, say, when she felt herself ill on the way to the house, that she was broken-hearted because of his ill-usage? Never!"

"What I know is, that she didn't blame you at all. She blamed herself for what had happened, and only herself. I had it from her own lips."

"You had it from her lips that I had *not* ill-treated her; and at the same time another had it from her lips that I *had* ill-treated her? My mother was no impulsive woman who changed her opinion every hour without reason. How can it be, Venn, that she should have told such different stories in close succession?"

"I cannot say. It is certainly odd, when she had forgiven you, and forgiven your wife, and was going to see ye on purpose to make friends."

"If there was one thing wanting to bewilder me it was this incomprehensible thing!... Diggory, if we, who remain alive, were only allowed to hold conversation with the dead — just once, a bare minute, even through a screen of iron bars, as with persons in prison — what we might learn! How many who now ride smiling would hide their heads! And this mystery — I should then be at the bottom of it at once. But the grave has for ever shut her in; and how shall it be found out now?"

No reply was returned by his companion, since none could be given; and when Venn left, a few minutes later, Clym had passed from the dulness of sorrow to the fluctuation of carking incertitude.

He continued in the same state all the afternoon. A bed was made up for him in the same house by a neighbour, that he might not have to return again the next day; and when he retired to rest in the deserted place it was only to remain awake hour after hour thinking the same thoughts. How to discover a solution to this riddle of death seemed a query of more importance than highest problems of the living. There was housed in his memory a vivid picture of the face of a little boy as he entered the hovel where Clym's mother lay. The round eyes, eager gaze, the piping voice which enunciated the words, had operated like stilettos on his brain.

A visit to the boy suggested itself as a means of gleaning new particulars; though it might be quite unproductive. To probe a child's mind after the lapse of six weeks, not for facts which the child had seen and understood, but to get at those which were in their nature beyond him, did not promise much; yet when every obvious channel is blocked we grope towards the small and obscure. There was nothing else left to do; after that he would allow the enigma to drop into the abyss of undiscoverable things.

It was about daybreak when he had reached this decision, and he at once arose. He locked up the house and went out in the green patch which merged in heather further on. In front of the white garden-palings the path branched into three like a broad-arrow. The road to the right led to the Quiet Woman and its neighbourhood; the middle track led to Mistover Knap; the left-hand track led over the hill to another part of Mistover, where the child lived. On inclining into the latter path Yeobright felt a creeping chilliness, familiar enough to most people, and probably caused by the unsunned morning air. In after days he thought of it as a thing of singular significance.

When Yeobright reached the cottage of Susan Nunsuch, the mother of the boy he sought, he found that the inmates were not yet astir. But in upland hamlets the transition from a-bed to abroad is surprisingly swift and easy. There no dense partition of yawns and toilets divides humanity by night from humanity by day. Yeobright tapped at the upper window-sill, which he could reach with his walking-stick; and in three or four minutes the woman came down.

It was not till this moment that Clym recollected her to be the person who had behaved so barbarously to Eustacia. It partly explained the insuavity with which the woman greeted him. Moreover, the boy had been ailing again; and Susan now, as ever since the night when he had been pressed into Eustacia's service at the bonfire, attributed his indispositions to Eustacia's influence as a witch. It was one of those sentiments which lurk like moles underneath the visible surface of manners, and may have been kept alive by Eustacia's entreaty to the captain, at the time that he had intended to prosecute Susan for the pricking in church, to let the matter drop; which he accordingly had done.

Yeobright overcame his repugnance, for Susan had at least borne his mother no ill-will. He asked kindly for the boy; but her manner did not improve.

"I wish to see him," continued Yeobright, with some hesitation; "to ask him if he remembers anything more of his walk with my mother than what he has previously told."

She regarded him in a peculiar and criticizing manner. To anybody but a half-blind man it would have said, "You want another of the knocks which have already laid you so low."

She called the boy downstairs, asked Clym to sit down on a stool, and continued, "Now, Johnny, tell Mr. Yeobright anything you can call to mind."

"You have not forgotten how you walked with the poor lady on that hot day?" said Clym.

"No," said the boy.

"And what she said to you?"

The boy repeated the exact words he had used on entering the hut. Yeobright rested his elbow on the table and shaded his face with his hand; and the mother looked as if she wondered how a man could want more of what had stung him so deeply.

"She was going to Alderworth when you first met her?"

"No; she was coming away."

"That can't be."

"Yes; she walked along with me. I was coming away too."

"Then where did you first see her?"

"At your house."

"Attend, and speak the truth!" said Clym sternly.

"Yes, sir; at your house was where I seed her first."

Clym started up, and Susan smiled in an expectant way, which did not embellish her face; it seemed to mean, "Something sinister is coming!"

"What did she do at my house?"

"She went and sat under the trees at the Devil's Bellows."

"Good God! this is all news to me!"

"You never told me this before?" said Susan.

"No, mother; because I didn't like to tell 'ee I had been so far. I was picking black-hearts, and they don't grow nearer."

"What did she do then?" said Yeobright.

"Looked at a man who came up and went into your house."

"That was myself — a furze-cutter, with brambles in his hand."

"No; 'twas not you. 'Twas a gentleman. You had gone in afore."

"Who was he?"

"I don't know."

"Now tell me what happened next."

"The poor lady went and knocked at your door, and the lady with black hair looked out of the side-window at her."

The boy's mother turned to Clym and said, "This is something you didn't expect?"

Yeobright took no more notice of her than if he had been of stone. "Go on, go on," he said hoarsely to the boy.

"And when she saw the young lady look out of the window the old lady knocked again; and when nobody came she took up the furze-hook and looked at it, and put it down again, and then she looked at the faggot-bonds; and then she went away, and walked across to me, and blowed her breath very hard, like this. We walked on together, she and I, and I talked to her and she talked to me a bit, but not much, because she couldn't blow her breath."

"Oh!" murmured Clym, in a low tone, and bowed his head. "Let's have more," he said.

"She couldn't talk much, and she couldn't walk; and her face was, O so queer!"

"How was her face?"

"Like yours is now."

The woman looked at Yeobright, and beheld him colourless, in a cold sweat. "Isn't there meaning in it?" she said stealthily. "What do you think of her now?"

"Silence!" said Clym fiercely. And, turning to the boy, "And then you left her to die?"

"No," said the woman, quickly and angrily. "He did not leave her to die! She sent him away. Whoever says he forsook her says what's not true."

"Trouble no more about that," answered Clym, with a quivering mouth. "What he did is a trifle in comparison with what he saw. Door kept shut, did you say? Kept shut, she looking out of window? Good heart of God! — what does it mean?"

The child shrank away from the gaze of his questioner.

"He said so," answered the mother, "and Johnny's a God-fearing boy and tells no lies."

"'Cast off by my son!' No, by my best life, dear mother, it is not so! But by your son's, your son's —— May all murderesses get the torment they deserve!"

With these words Yeobright went forth from the little dwelling. The pupils of his eyes, fixed steadfastly on blankness, were vaguely lit with an icy shine; his mouth had passed into the phase more or less imaginatively rendered in studies of Oedipus. The strangest deeds were possible to his mood. But they were not possible to his situation. Instead of there being before him the pale face of Eustacia, and a masculine shape unknown, there was only the imperturbable countenance of the heath, which, having defied the cataclysmal onsets of centuries, reduced to insignificance by its seamed and antique features the wildest turmoil of a single man.

III

EUSTACIA DRESSES HERSELF ON A BLACK MORNING

A CONSCIOUSNESS of a vast impassivity in all which lay around him took possession even of Yeobright in his wild walk towards Alderworth. He had once before felt in his own person this overpowering of the fervid by the inanimate; but then it had tended to enervate a passion far sweeter than that which at present pervaded him. It was once when he stood parting from Eustacia in the moist still levels beyond the hills.

But dismissing all this he went onward again, and came to the front of his house. The blinds of Eustacia's bedroom were still closely drawn, for she was no early riser. All the life visible was in the shape of a solitary thrush cracking a small snail upon the door-stone for his breakfast, and his tapping seemed a loud noise in the general silence which prevailed; but on going to the door Clym found it unfastened, the young girl who attended upon Eustacia being astir in the back part of the premises. Yeobright entered and went straight to his wife's room.

The noise of his arrival must have aroused her, for when he opened the door she was standing before the looking-glass in her night-dress, the ends of her hair gathered into one hand, with which she was coiling the whole mass round her head, previous to beginning toilette operations. She was not a woman given to speaking first at a meeting, and she allowed Clym to walk across in silence, without turning her head. He came behind her, and she saw his face in the glass. It was ashy, haggard, and terrible. Instead of starting towards him in sorrowful surprise, as even Eustacia, undemonstrative wife as she was, would have done in days before she burdened herself with a secret, she remained motionless, looking at him in the glass. And while she looked, the carmine flush with which warmth and sound sleep had suffused her cheeks and neck, dissolved from view, and the death-like pallor in his face flew across into hers. He was close enough to see this, and the sight instigated his tongue.

"You know what is the matter," he said huskily. "I see it in your face."

Her hand relinquished the rope of hair and dropped to her side, and the pile of tresses, no longer supported, fell from the crown of her head about her shoulders and over the white night-gown. She made no reply.

"Speak to me," said Yeobright peremptorily.

The blanching process did not cease in her, and her lips now became as white as her face. She turned to him and said, "Yes, Clym, I'll speak to you. Why do you return so early? Can I do anything for you?"

"Yes, you can listen to me. It seems that my wife is not very well?"

"Why?"

"Your face, my dear; your face. Or perhaps it is the pale morning light which takes your colour away? Now I am going to reveal a secret to you. Ha-ha!"

"O, that is ghastly!"

"What?"

"Your laugh."

"There's reason for ghastliness. Eustacia; you have held my happiness in the hollow of your hand, and like a devil you have dashed it down!"

She started back from the dressing-table, retreated a few steps from him, and looked him in the face. "Ah! you think to frighten me," she said, with a slight laugh. "Is it worth while? I am undefended, and alone."

"How extraordinary!"

"What do you mean?"

"As there is ample time I will tell you, though you know well enough. I mean that it is extraordinary that you should be alone in my absence. Tell me, now, where is he who was with you on the afternoon of the thirty-first of August? Under the bed? Up the chimney?"

A shudder overcame her and shook the light fabric of her night-dress throughout. "I do not remember dates so exactly," she said. "I cannot recollect that anybody was with me besides yourself."

"The day I mean," said Yeobright, his voice growing louder and harsher, "was the day you shut the door against my mother and killed her. O, it is too much — too bad!" He leant over the footpiece of the bedstead for a few moments, with his back towards her; then rising again: "Tell me, tell me! tell me — do you hear?" he cried, rushing up to her and seizing her by the loose folds of her sleeve.

The superstratum of timidity which often overlies those who are daring and defiant at heart had been passed through, and the mettlesome substance of the woman was reached. The red blood inundated her face, previously so pale.

"What are you going to do?" she said in a low voice, regarding him with a proud smile. "You will not alarm me by holding on so; but it would be a pity to tear my sleeve."

Instead of letting go he drew her closer to him. "Tell me the particulars of — my mother's death," he said in a hard, panting whisper; "or — I'll — I'll —"

"Clym," she answered slowly, "do you think you dare do anything to me that I dare not bear? But before you strike me listen. You will get nothing from me by a blow, even though it should kill me, as it probably will. But perhaps you do not wish me to speak — killing may be all you mean?"

"Kill you! Do you expect it?"

"I do."

"Why?"

"No less degree of rage against me will match your previous grief for her."

"Phew — I shall not kill you," he said contemptuously, as if under a sudden change of purpose. "I did think of it; but — I shall not. That would be making a martyr of you, and sending you to where she is; and I would keep you away from her till the universe come to an end, if I could."

"I almost wish you would kill me," said she with gloomy bitterness. "It is with no strong desire, I assure you, that I play the part I have lately played on earth. You are no blessing, my husband."

"You shut the door — you looked out of the window upon her — you had a man in the house with you — you sent her away to die. The inhumanity — the treachery — I will not touch you — stand away from me — and confess every word!"

"Never! I'll hold my tongue like the very death that I don't mind meeting, even though I can clear myself of half you believe by speaking. Yes, I will! Who of any dignity would take the trouble to clear cobwebs from a wild man's mind after such language as this? No; let him go on, and think his narrow thoughts, and run his head into the mire. I have other cares."

"'Tis too much — but I must spare you."

"Poor charity."

"By my wretched soul you sting me, Eustacia! I can keep it up, and hotly too. Now, then, madam, tell me his name!"

"Never, I am resolved."

"How often does he write to you? Where does he put his letters — when does he meet you? Ah, his letters! Do you tell me his name?"

"I do not."

"Then I'll find it myself." His eye had fallen upon a small desk that stood near, on which she was accustomed to write her letters. He went to it. It was locked.

"Unlock this!"

"You have no right to say it. That's mine."

Without another word he seized the desk and dashed it to the floor. The hinge burst open, and a number of letters tumbled out.

"Stay!" said Eustacia, stepping before him with more excitement than she had hitherto shown.

"Come, come! stand away! I must see them."

She looked at the letters as they lay, checked her feeling, and moved indifferently aside; when he gathered them up, and examined them.

By no stretch of meaning could any but a harmless construction be placed upon a single one of the letters themselves. The solitary exception was an empty envelope directed to her, and the handwriting was Wildeve's. Yeobright held it up. Eustacia was doggedly silent.

"Can you read, madam? Look at this envelope. Doubtless we shall find more soon, and what was inside them. I shall no doubt be gratified by learning in good time what a well-finished and full-blown adept in a certain trade my lady is."

"Do you say it to me — do you?" she gasped.

He searched further, but found nothing more. "What was in this letter?" he said.

"Ask the writer. Am I your hound that you should talk to me in this way?"

"Do you brave me? do you stand me out, mistress? Answer. Don't look at me with those eyes as if you would bewitch me again! Sooner than that I die. You refuse to answer?"

"I wouldn't tell you after this, if I were as innocent as the sweetest babe in heaven!"

"Which you are not."

"Certainly I am not absolutely," she replied. "I have not done what you suppose; but if to have done no harm at all is the only innocence recognized, I am beyond forgiveness. But I require no help from your conscience."

"You can resist, and resist again! Instead of hating you I could, I think, mourn for and pity you, if you were contrite, and would confess all. Forgive you I never can. I don't speak of your lover — I will give you the benefit of the doubt in that matter, for it only affects me personally. But the other: had you half-killed *me*, had it been that you wilfully took the sight away from these feeble eyes of mine, I could have forgiven you. But *that's* too much for nature!"

"Say no more. I will do without your pity. But I would have saved you from uttering what you will regret."

"I am going away now. I shall leave you."

"You need not go, as I am going myself. You will keep just as far away from me by staying here."

"Call her to mind —— think of her — what goodness there was in her: it showed in every line of her face! Most women, even when but slightly annoyed, show a flicker of evil in some curl of the mouth or some corner of the cheek; but as for her, never in her angriest moments was there anything malicious in her look. She was angered quickly, but she forgave just as readily, and underneath her pride there was the meekness of a child. What came of it? — what cared you? You hated her just as she was learning to love you. O! couldn't you see what was best for you, but must bring a curse upon me, and agony and death upon her, by doing that cruel deed! What was the devil's name who was keeping you company and causing you to add cruelty to her to your wrong to me? Was it Wildeve? Was it poor Thomasin's husband? Heaven, what wickedness! Lost your voice, have you? It is natural after detection of that most noble trick.... Eustacia, didn't any tender thought of your own mother lead you to think of being gentle to mine at such a time of weariness? Did not one grain of pity enter your heart as she turned away? Think what a vast opportunity was then lost of beginning a forgiving and honest course. Why did not you kick him out, and let her in, and say, I'll be an honest wife and a noble woman from this hour? Had I told you to go and quench eternally our last flickering chance of happiness here you could have done no worse. Well, she's asleep now; and have you a hundred gallants, neither they nor you can insult her any more."

"You exaggerate fearfully," she said in a faint, weary voice; "but I cannot enter into my defence — it is not worth doing. You are nothing to me in future, and the past side of the story may as well remain untold. I have lost all through you, but I have not complained. Your blunders and misfortunes may have been a sorrow to you, but they have been a wrong to me. All persons of refinement have been scared away from me since I sank into the mire of marriage. Is this your cherishing — to put me into a hut like this, and keep me like the wife of a hind? You deceived me — not by words, but by appearances, which are less seen through than words. But the place will serve as well as any other — as somewhere to pass from — into my grave." Her words were smothered in her throat, and her head drooped down.

"I don't know what you mean by that. Am I the cause of your sin?" (Eustacia made a trembling motion towards him.) "What, can you begin to shed tears and offer me your hand? Good God! can you? No, not I. I'll not commit the fault of taking that." (The hand she had offered dropped nervelessly, but the tears continued flowing.) "Well, yes, I'll take it, if only for the sake of my own foolish kisses that were wasted there before I knew what I cherished. How bewitched I was! How could there be any good in a woman that everybody spoke ill of?"

"O, O, O!" she cried, breaking down at last; and, shaking with sobs which choked her, she sank upon her knees. "O, will you have done! O, you are too relentless — there's a limit to the cruelty of savages! I have held out long — but you crush me down. I beg for mercy — I cannot bear this any longer — it is inhuman to go further with this! If I had — killed your — mother with my own hand — I should not deserve such a scourging to the bone as this. O, O! God have mercy upon a miserable woman!... You have beaten me in this game — I beg you to stay your hand in pity!... I confess that I — wilfully did not undo the door the first time she knocked — but — I — should have unfastened it the second — if I had not thought you had gone to do it yourself. When I found you had not I opened it, but she was gone. That's the extent of my crime — towards *her*. Best natures commit bad faults sometimes, don't they? — I think they do. Now I will leave you — for ever and ever!"

"Tell all, and I *will* pity you. Was the man in the house with you Wildeve?"

"I cannot tell," she said desperately through her sobbing. "Don't insist further — I cannot tell. I am going from this house. We cannot both stay here."

"You need not go: I will go. You can stay here."

"No, I will dress, and then I will go."

"Where?"

"Where I came from, or *else*where."

She hastily dressed herself, Yeobright moodily walking up and down the room the whole of the time. At last all her things were on. Her little hands quivered so violently as she held them to her chin to fasten her bonnet that she could not tie the strings, and after a few moments she relinquished the attempt. Seeing this he moved forward and said, "Let me tie them."

She assented in silence, and lifted her chin. For once at least in her life she was totally oblivious of the charm of her attitude. But he was not, and he turned his eyes aside, that he might not be tempted to softness.

The strings were tied; she turned from him. "Do you still prefer going away yourself to my leaving you?" he inquired again.

"I do."

"Very well — let it be. And when you will confess to the man I may pity you."

She flung her shawl about her and went downstairs, leaving him standing in the room.

Eustacia had not long been gone when there came a knock at the door of the bedroom; and Yeobright said, "Well?"

It was the servant; and she replied, "Somebody from Mrs. Wildeve's have called to tell 'ee that the mis'ess and the baby are getting on wonderful well; and the baby's name is to be Eustacia Clementine." And the girl retired.

"What a mockery!" said Clym. "This unhappy marriage of mine to be perpetuated in that child's name!"

IV

THE MINISTRATIONS OF A HALF-FORGOTTEN ONE

EUSTACIA'S journey was at first as vague in direction as that of thistledown in the wind. She did not know what to do. She wished it had been night instead of morning, that she might at least have borne her misery without the possibility of being seen. Going listlessly along between the dying ferns and the wet white spiders' webs, she at length turned her steps towards her grandfather's house. On reaching it she found the front door closed and locked. Mechanically she went round to the end where the stable was, and on looking in at the stable-door she saw Charley standing within.

"Captain Vye is not at home?" she said.

"No, ma'am," said the lad in a flutter of feeling; "he's gone to Weatherbury, and won't be home till night. And the servant is gone home for a holiday. So the house is locked up."

Eustacia's face was not visible to Charley as she stood at the doorway, her back being to the sky, and the stable but indifferently lighted; but the wildness of her manner arrested his attention. She turned and walked away across the enclosure to the gate, and was hidden by the bank.

When she had disappeared Charley, with misgiving in his eyes, slowly came from the stable-door, and going to another point in the bank he looked over. Eustacia was leaning against it on the outside, her face covered with her hands, and her head pressing the dewy heather which bearded the bank's outer side. She appeared to be utterly indifferent to the circumstance that her bonnet, hair, and garments were becoming wet and disarranged by the moisture of her cold, harsh pillow. Clearly something was wrong.

Charley had always regarded Eustacia as Eustacia had regarded Clym when she first beheld him — as a romantic and sweet vision, scarcely incarnate. He had been so shut off from her by the dignity of her look and the pride of her speech, except at that one blissful interval when he was allowed to hold her hand, that he had hardly deemed her a woman, wingless and earthly, subject to household conditions and domestic jars. The inner details of her life he had only conjectured. She had been a lovely wonder, predestined to an orbit in which the whole of his own was but a point; and this sight of her leaning like a helpless, despairing creature against a wild wet bank, filled him with an amazed horror. He could no longer remain where he was. Leaping over, he came up, touched her with his finger, and said tenderly, "You are poorly, ma'am. What can I do?"

Eustacia started up, and said, "Ah, Charley — you have followed me. You did not think when I left home in the summer that I should come back like this!"

"I did not, dear ma'am. Can I help you now?"

"I am afraid not. I wish I could get into the house. I feel giddy — that's all."

"Lean on my arm, ma'am, till we get to the porch; and I will try to open the door."

He supported her to the porch, and there depositing her on a seat hastened to the back, climbed to a window by the help of a ladder, and descending inside opened the door. Next he assisted her into the room, where there was an old-fashioned horsehair settee as large as a donkey-waggon. She lay down here, and Charley covered her with a cloak he found in the hall.

"Shall I get you something to eat and drink?" he said.

"If you please, Charley. But I suppose there is no fire?"

"I can light it, ma'am."

He vanished, and she heard a splitting of wood and a blowing of bellows; and presently he returned, saying, "I have lighted a fire in the kitchen, and now I'll light one here."

He lit the fire, Eustacia dreamily observing him from her couch. When it was blazing up he said, "Shall I wheel you round in front of it, ma'am, as the morning is chilly?"

"Yes, if you like."

"Shall I go and bring your breakfast now?"

"Yes, do," she murmured languidly.

When he had gone, and the dull sounds occasionally reached her ears of his movements in the kitchen, she forgot where she was, and had for a moment to consider by an effort what the sounds meant. After an interval which seemed short to her whose thoughts were elsewhere, he came in with a tray on which steamed tea and toast.

"Place it on the table," she said. "I shall be ready soon."

He did so, and retired to the door: when, however, he perceived that she did not move he came back a few steps.

"Let me hold it to you, if you don't wish to get up," said Charley. He brought the tray to the front of the couch, where he knelt down, adding, "I will hold it for you."

Eustacia sat up and poured out a cup of tea. "You are very kind to me, Charley," she murmured as she sipped.

"Well, I ought to be," said he diffidently, taking great trouble not to rest his eyes upon her, though this was their only natural position, Eustacia being immediately before him. "You have been kind to me."

"How have I?" said Eustacia.

"You let me hold your hand when you were a maiden at home."

"Ah, so I did. Why did I do that? My mind is lost — it had to do with the mumming, had it not?"

"Yes, you wanted to go in my place."

"I remember. I do indeed remember — too well!"

She again became utterly downcast; and Charley, seeing that she was not going to eat or drink any more, took away the tray.

Afterwards he occasionally came in to see if the fire was burning, to ask her if she wanted anything, to tell her that the wind had shifted from south to west, to ask her if she would like him to gather her some blackberries; to all which inquiries she replied in the negative or with indifference.

She remained on the settee some time longer, when she aroused herself and went upstairs. The room in which she had formerly slept still remained much as she had left it, and the recollection that this forced upon her of her own greatly changed and infinitely worsened situation again set on her face the undetermined and formless misery which it had worn on her first arrival. She peeped into her grandfather's room, through which the fresh autumn air was blowing from the open windows. Her eye was arrested by what was a familiar sight enough, though it broke upon her now with a new significance.

It was a brace of pistols, hanging near the head of her grandfather's bed, which he always kept there loaded, as a precaution against possible burglars, the house being very lonely. Eustacia regarded them long, as if they were the page of a book in which she read a new and a strange matter. Quickly, like one afraid of herself, she returned downstairs and stood in deep thought.

"If I could only do it!" she said. "It would be doing much good to myself and all connected with me, and no harm to a single one."

The idea seemed to gather force within her, and she remained in a fixed attitude nearly ten minutes, when a certain finality was expressed in her gaze, and no longer the blankness of indecision.

She turned and went up the second time — softly and stealthily now — and entered her grandfather's room, her eyes at once seeking the head of the bed. The pistols were gone.

The instant quashing of her purpose by their absence affected her brain as a sudden vacuum affects the body: she nearly fainted. Who had done this? There was only one person on the premises besides herself. Eustacia involuntarily turned to the open window which overlooked the garden as far as the bank that bounded it. On the summit of the latter stood Charley, sufficiently elevated by its height to see into the room. His gaze was directed eagerly and solicitously upon her.

She went downstairs to the door and beckoned to him.

"You have taken them away?"

"Yes, ma'am."

"Why did you do it?"

"I saw you looking at them too long."

"What has that to do with it?"

"You have been heart-broken all the morning, as if you did not want to live."

"Well?"

"And I could not bear to leave them in your way. There was meaning in your look at them."

"Where are they now?"

"Locked up."

"Where?"

"In the stable."

"Give them to me."

"No, ma'am."

"You refuse?"

"I do. I care too much for you to give 'em up."

She turned aside, her face for the first time softening from the stony immobility of the earlier day, and the corners of her mouth resuming something of that delicacy of cut which was always lost in her moments of despair. At last she confronted him again.

"Why should I not die if I wish?" she said tremulously. "I have made a bad bargain with life, and I am weary of it — weary. And now you have hindered my escape. O, why did you, Charley! What makes death painful except the thought of others' grief? — and that is absent in my case, for not a sigh would follow me!"

"Ah, it is trouble that has done this! I wish in my very soul that he who brought it about might die and rot, even if 'tis transportation to say it!"

"Charley, no more of that. What do you mean to do about this you have seen?"

"Keep it close as night, if you promise not to think of it again."

"You need not fear. The moment has passed. I promise." She then went away, entered the house, and lay down.

Later in the afternoon her grandfather returned. He was about to question her categorically; but on looking at her he withheld his words.

"Yes, it is too bad to talk of," she slowly returned in answer to his glance. "Can my old room be got ready for me tonight, grandfather? I shall want to occupy it again."

He did not ask what it all meant, or why she had left her husband, but ordered the room to be prepared.

V

AN OLD MOVE INADVERTENTLY REPEATED

CHARLEY's attentions to his former mistress were unbounded. The only solace to his own trouble lay in his attempts to relieve hers. Hour after hour he considered her wants: he thought of her presence there with a sort of gratitude, and, while uttering imprecations on the cause of her unhappiness, in some measure blessed the result. Perhaps she would always remain there, he thought, and then he would be as happy as he had been before. His dread was lest she should think fit to return to Alderworth, and in that dread his eyes, with all the inquisitiveness of affection, frequently sought her face when she was not observing him, as he would have watched the head of a stockdove to learn if it contemplated flight. Having once really succoured her, and possibly preserved her from the rashest of acts, he mentally assumed in addition a guardian's responsibility for her welfare.

For this reason he busily endeavoured to provide her with pleasant distractions, bringing home curious objects which he found in the heath, such as white trumpet-shaped mosses, red-headed lichens, stone arrow-heads used by the old tribes on Egdon, and faceted crystals from the hollows of flints. These he deposited on the premises in such positions that she should see them as if by accident.

A week passed, Eustacia never going out of the house. Then she walked into the enclosed plot and looked through her grandfather's spy-glass, as she had been in the habit of doing before her marriage. One day she saw, at a place where the high-road crossed the distant valley, a heavily laden waggon passing along. It was piled with household furniture. She looked again and again, and recognized it to be her own. In the evening her grandfather came indoors with a rumour that Yeobright had removed that day from Alderworth to the old house at Blooms-End.

On another occasion when reconnoitring thus she beheld two female figures walking in the vale. The day was fine and clear; and the persons not being more than half a mile off she could see their every detail with the telescope. The woman walking in front carried a white bundle in her arms, from one end of which hung a long appendage of drapery; and when the walkers turned, so that the sun fell more directly upon them, Eustacia could see that the object was a baby. She called Charley, and asked him if he knew who they were, though she well guessed.

"Mrs. Wildeve and the nurse-girl," said Charley.

"The nurse is carrying the baby?" said Eustacia.

"No, 'tis Mrs. Wildeve carrying that," he answered, "and the nurse walks behind carrying nothing."

The lad was in good spirits that day, for the fifth of November had again come round, and he was planning yet another scheme to divert her from her too absorbing thoughts. For two successive years his mistress had seemed to take pleasure in lighting a bonfire on the bank overlooking the valley; but this year she had apparently quite forgotten the day and the customary deed. He was careful not to remind her, and went on with his secret preparations for a cheerful surprise, the more zealously that he had been absent last time and unable to assist. At every vacant minute he hastened to gather furze-stumps, thorn-tree roots, and other solid materials from the adjacent slopes, hiding them from cursory view.

The evening came, and Eustacia was still seemingly unconscious of the anniversary. She had gone indoors after her survey through the glass, and had not been visible since. As soon as it was quite dark Charley began to build a bonfire, choosing precisely that spot on the bank which Eustacia had chosen at previous times.

When all the surrounding bonfires had burst into existence Charley kindled his, and arranged its fuel so that it should not require tending for some time. He then went back to the house, and lingered round the door and windows till she should by some means or other learn of his achievement and come out to witness it. But the shutters were closed, the door remained shut, and no heed whatever seemed to be taken of his performance. Not liking to call her he went back and replenished the fire, continuing to do this for more than half an hour. It was not till his stock of fuel had greatly diminished that he went to the back door and sent in to beg that Mrs. Yeobright would open the window-shutters and see the sight outside.

Eustacia, who had been sitting listlessly in the parlour, started up at the intelligence and flung open the shutters. Facing her on the bank blazed the fire, which at once sent a ruddy glare into the room where she was, and over-powered the candles.

"Well done, Charley!" said Captain Vye from the chimney-corner. "But

I hope it is not my wood that he's burning.... Ah, it was this time last year that I met with that man Venn, bringing home Thomasin Yeobright — to be sure it was! Well, who would have thought that girl's troubles would have ended so well? What a snipe you were in that matter, Eustacia! Has your husband written to you yet?"

"No," said Eustacia, looking vaguely through the window at the fire, which just then so much engaged her mind that she did not resent her grandfather's blunt opinion. She could see Charley's form on the bank, shovelling and stirring the fire; and there flashed upon her imagination some other form which that fire might call up.

She left the room, put on her garden-bonnet and cloak, and went out. Reaching the bank she looked over with a wild curiosity and misgiving, when Charley said to her, with a pleased sense to himself, "I made it o' purpose for you, ma'am."

"Thank you," she said hastily. "But I wish you to put it out now."

"It will soon burn down," said Charley, rather disappointed. "Is it not a pity to knock it out?"

"I don't know," she musingly answered.

They stood in silence, broken only by the crackling of the flames, till Charley, perceiving that she did not want to talk to him, moved reluctantly away.

Eustacia remained within the bank looking at the fire, intending to go indoors, yet lingering still. Had she not by her situation been inclined to hold in indifference all things honoured of the gods and of men she would probably have gone away. But her state was so hopeless that she could play with it. To have lost is less disturbing than to wonder if we may possibly have won: and Eustacia could now, like other people at such a stage, taking a standing-point outside herself, observe herself as a disinterested spectator, and think what a sport for Heaven this woman Eustacia was.

While she stood she heard a sound. It was the splash of a stone in the pond.

Had Eustacia received the stone full in the bosom her heart could not have given a more decided thump. She had thought of the possibility of such a signal in answer to that which had been unwittingly given by Charley; but she had not expected it yet. How prompt Wildeve was! Yet how could he think her capable of deliberately wishing to renew their assignations now? An impulse to leave the spot, a desire to stay, struggled within her; and the desire held its own. More than that it did not do, for she refrained even from ascending the bank and looking over. She remained motionless, not disturbing a muscle of her face or raising her eyes; for were she to turn up her face the fire on the bank would shine upon it, and Wildeve might be looking down.

There was a second splash into the pond.

Why did he stay so long without advancing and looking over? Curiosity had its way: she ascended one or two of the earth-steps in the bank and glanced out.

Wildeve was before her. He had come forward after throwing the last pebble, and the fire now shone into each of their faces from the bank stretching breast-high between them.

"I did not light it!" cried Eustacia quickly. "It was lit without my knowledge. Don't, don't come over to me!"

"Why have you been living here all these days without telling me? You have left your home. I fear I am something to blame in this?"

"I did not let in his mother; that's how it is!"

"You do not deserve what you have got, Eustacia; you are in great misery; I see it in your eyes, your mouth, and all over you. My poor, poor girl!" He stepped over the bank. "You are beyond everything unhappy!"

"No, no; not exactly ——"

"It has been pushed too far — it is killing you: I do think it!"

Her usually quiet breathing had grown quicker with his words. "I — I ——" she began, and then burst into quivering sobs, shaken to the very heart by the unexpected voice of pity — a sentiment whose existence in relation to herself she had almost forgotten.

This outbreak of weeping took Eustacia herself so much by surprise that she could not leave off, and she turned aside from him in some shame, though turning hid nothing from him. She sobbed on desperately; then the outpour lessened, and she became quieter. Wildeve had resisted the impulse to clasp her, and stood without speaking.

"Are you not ashamed of me, who used never to be a crying animal?" she asked in a weak whisper as she wiped her eyes. "Why didn't you go away? I wish you had not seen quite all that; it reveals too much by half."

"You might have wished it, because it makes me as sad as you," he said with emotion and deference. "As for revealing — the word is impossible between us two."

"I did not send for you — don't forget it, Damon; I am in pain, but I did not send for you! As a wife, at least, I've been straight."

"Never mind — I came. O, Eustacia, forgive me for the harm I have done you in these two past years! I see more and more that I have been your ruin."

"Not you. This place I live in."

"Ah, your generosity may naturally make you say that. But I am the culprit. I should either have done more or nothing at all."

"In what way?"

"I ought never to have hunted you out; or, having done it, I ought to have persisted in retaining you. But of course I have no right to talk of that now. I will only ask this: can I do anything for you? Is there anything on the face of the earth that a man can do to make you happier than you are at present? If there is, I will do it. You may command me, Eustacia, to the limit of my influence; and don't forget that I am richer now. Surely something can be done to save you from this! Such a rare plant in such a wild place it grieves me to see. Do you want anything bought? Do you want to go anywhere? Do you want to escape the place altogether? Only say it, and I'll do anything to put an end to those tears, which but for me would never have been at all."

"We are each married to another person," she said faintly; "and assistance from you would have an evil sound — after — after ——"

"Well, there's no preventing slanderers from having their fill at any time; but you need not be afraid. Whatever I may feel I promise you on my word of honour never to speak to you about — or act upon — until you say I may. I know my duty to Thomasin quite as well as I know my duty to you as a woman unfairly treated. What shall I assist you in?"

"In getting away from here."

"Where do you wish to go to?"

"I have a place in my mind. If you could help me as far as Budmouth I can do all the rest. Steamers sail from there across the Channel, and so I can get to Paris, where I want to be. Yes," she pleaded earnestly, "help me to get to Budmouth harbour without my grandfather's or my husband's knowledge, and I can do all the rest."

"Will it be safe to leave you there alone?"

"Yes, yes. I know Budmouth well."

"Shall I go with you? I am rich now."

She was silent.

"Say yes, sweet!"

She was silent still.

"Well, let me know when you wish to go. We shall be at our present house till December; after that we remove to Casterbridge. Command me in anything till that time."

"I will think of this," she said hurriedly. "Whether I can honestly make use of you as a friend, or must close with you as a lover — that is what I must ask myself. If I wish to go and decide to accept your company I will signal to you some evening at eight o'clock punctually, and this will mean that you are to be ready with a horse and trap at twelve o'clock the same night to drive me to Budmouth harbour in time for the morning boat."

"I will look out every night at eight, and no signal shall escape me."

"Now please go away. If I decide on this escape I can only meet you once more unless — I cannot go without you. Go — I cannot bear it longer. Go — go!"

Wildeve slowly went up the steps and descended into the darkness on the other side; and as he walked he glanced back, till the bank blotted out her form from his further view.

VI

THOMASIN ARGUES WITH HER COUSIN, AND HE WRITES A LETTER

YEOBRIGHT was at this time at Blooms-End, hoping that Eustacia would return to him. The removal of furniture had been accomplished only that day, though Clym had lived in the old house for more than a week. He had spent the time in working about the premises, sweeping leaves from the garden-paths, cutting dead stalks from the flower-beds, and nailing up creepers which had been displaced by the autumn winds. He took no particular pleasure in these deeds, but they formed a screen between himself and despair. Moreover, it had become a religion with him to preserve in good condition all that had lapsed from his mother's hands to his own.

During these operations he was constantly on the watch for Eustacia. That there should be no mistake about her knowing where to find him he had ordered a notice-board to be affixed to the garden gate at Alderworth, signifying in white letters whither he had removed. When a leaf floated to the earth he turned his head, thinking it might be her footfall. A bird searching for worms in the mould of the flower-beds sounded like her hand on the latch of the gate; and at dusk, when soft, strange ventriloquisms came from holes in the ground, hollow stalks, curled dead leaves, and other crannies wherein breezes, worms, and insects can work their will, he fancied that they were Eustacia, standing without and breathing wishes of reconciliation.

Up to this time he had persevered in his resolve not to invite her back. At the same time the severity with which he had treated her lulled the sharpness of his regret for his mother, and awoke some of his old solicitude for his mother's supplanter. Harsh feelings produce harsh usage, and this by reaction quenches the sentiments that gave it birth. The more he reflected the more he softened. But to look upon his wife as innocence in distress was impossible, though he could ask himself whether he had given her quite time enough — if he had not come a little too suddenly upon her on that sombre morning.

Now that the first flush of his anger had paled he was disinclined to ascribe to her more than an indiscreet friendship with Wildeve, for there had not appeared in her manner the signs of dishonour. And this once admitted, an absolutely dark interpretation of her act towards his mother was no longer forced upon him.

On the evening of the fifth of November his thoughts of Eustacia were intense. Echoes from those past times when they had exchanged tender words all the day long came like the diffused murmur of a seashore left miles behind. "Surely," he said, "she might have brought herself to communicate with me before now, and confess honestly what Wildeve was to her."

Instead of remaining at home that night he determined to go and see Thomasin and her husband. If he found opportunity he would allude to the cause of the separation between Eustacia and himself, keeping silence, however, on the fact that there was a third person in his house when his mother was turned away. If it proved that Wildeve was innocently there he would doubtless openly mention it. If he were there with unjust intentions Wildeve, being a man of quick feeling, might possibly say something to reveal the extent to which Eustacia was compromised.

But on reaching his cousin's house he found that only Thomasin was at home, Wildeve being at that time on his way towards the bonfire innocently lit by Charley at Mistover. Thomasin then, as always, was glad to see Clym, and took him to inspect the sleeping baby, carefully screening the candlelight from the infant's eyes with her hand.

"Tamsin, have you heard that Eustacia is not with me now?" he said when they had sat down again.

"No," said Thomasin, alarmed.

"And not that I have left Alderworth?"

"No. I never hear tidings from Alderworth unless you bring them. What is the matter?"

Clym in a disturbed voice related to her his visit to Susan Nunsuch's boy, the revelation he had made, and what had resulted from his charging Eustacia with having wilfully and heartlessly done the deed. He suppressed all mention of Wildeve's presence with her.

"All this, and I not knowing it!" murmured Thomasin in an awestruck tone. "Terrible! What could have made her —— O, Eustacia! And when you found it out you went in hot haste to her? Were you too cruel? — or is she really so wicked as she seems?"

"Can a man be too cruel to his mother's enemy?"

"I can fancy so."

"Very well, then — I'll admit that he can. But now what is to be done?"

"Make it up again — if a quarrel so deadly can ever be made up. I almost wish you had not told me. But do try to be reconciled. There are ways, after all, if you both wish to."

"I don't know that we do both wish to make it up," said Clym. "If she had wished it, would she not have sent to me by this time?"

"You seem to wish to, and yet you have not sent to her."

"True; but I have been tossed to and fro in doubt if I ought, after such strong provocation. To see me now, Thomasin, gives you no idea of what I have been; of what depths I have descended to in these few last days. O, it was a bitter shame to shut out my mother like that! Can I ever forget it, or even agree to see her again?"

"She might not have known that anything serious would come of it, and perhaps she did not mean to keep aunt out altogether."

"She says herself that she did not. But the fact remains that keep her out she did."

"Believe her sorry, and send for her."

"How if she will not come?"

"It will prove her guilty, by showing that it is her habit to nourish enmity. But I do not think that for a moment."

"I will do this. I will wait for a day or two longer — not longer than two days certainly; and if she does not send to me in that time I will indeed send to her. I thought to have seen Wildeve here tonight. Is he from home?"

Thomasin blushed a little. "No," she said. "He is merely gone out for a walk."

"Why didn't he take you with him? The evening is fine. You want fresh air as well as he."

"O, I don't care for going anywhere; besides, there is baby."

"Yes, yes. Well, I have been thinking whether I should not consult your husband about this as well as you," said Clym steadily.

"I fancy I would not," she quickly answered. "It can do no good."

Her cousin looked her in the face. No doubt Thomasin was ignorant that her husband had any share in the events of that tragic afternoon; but her countenance seemed to signify that she concealed some suspicion or thought of the reputed tender relations between Wildeve and Eustacia in days gone by.

Clym, however, could make nothing of it, and he rose to depart, more in doubt than when he came.

"You will write to her in a day or two?" said the young woman earnestly. "I do so hope the wretched separation may come to an end."

"I will," said Clym; "I don't rejoice in my present state at all."

And he left her and climbed the hills to Blooms-End. Before going to bed he sat down and wrote the following letter:

My Dear Eustacia — I must obey my heart without consulting my reason too closely. Will you come back to me? Do so, and the past shall never be mentioned. I was too severe; but O, Eustacia, the provocation! You don't know, you never will know, what those words of anger cost me which you drew down upon yourself. All that an honest man can promise you I promise now, which is that from me you shall never suffer anything on this score again. After all the vows we have made, Eustacia, I think we had better pass the remainder of our lives in trying to keep them. Come to me, then, even if you reproach me. I have thought of your sufferings that morning on which I parted from you; I know they were genuine, and they are as much as you ought to bear. Our love must still continue. Such hearts as ours would never have been given us but to be concerned with each other. I could not ask you back at first, Eustacia, for I was unable to persuade myself that he who was with you was not there as a lover. But if you will come and explain distracting appearances I do not question that you can show your honesty to me. Why have you not come before? Do you think I will not listen to you? Surely not, when you remember the kisses and vows we exchanged under the summer moon. Return then, and you shall be warmly welcomed. I can no longer think of you to your prejudice — I am but too much absorbed in justifying you. — Your husband as ever,

CLYM

"There," he said, as he laid it in his desk, "that's a good thing done. If she does not come before tomorrow night I will send it to her."

Meanwhile, at the house he had just left Thomasin sat sighing uneasily. Fidelity to her husband had that evening induced her to conceal all suspicion that Wildeve's interest in Eustacia had not ended with his marriage. But she knew nothing positive; and though Clym was her well-beloved cousin there was one nearer to her still.

When, a little later, Wildeve returned from his walk to Mistover, Thomasin said, "Damon, where have you been? I was getting quite frightened, and thought you had fallen into the river. I dislike being in the house by myself."

"Frightened?" he said, touching her cheek as if she were some domestic animal. "Why, I thought nothing could frighten you. It is that you are getting proud, I am sure, and don't like living here since we have risen above our business. Well, it is a tedious matter, this getting a new house; but

I couldn't have set about it sooner, unless our ten thousand pounds had been a hundred thousand, when we could have afforded to despise caution."

"No — I don't mind waiting — I would rather stay here twelve months longer than run any risk with baby. But I don't like your vanishing so in the evenings. There's something on your mind — I know there is, Damon. You go about so gloomily, and look at the heath as if it were somebody's gaol instead of a nice wild place to walk in."

He looked towards her with pitying surprise. "What, do you like Egdon Heath?" he said.

"I like what I was born near to; I admire its grim old face."

"Pooh, my dear. You don't know what you like."

"I am sure I do. There's only one thing unpleasant about Egdon."

"What's that?"

"You never take me with you when you walk there. Why do you wander so much in it yourself if you so dislike it?"

The inquiry, though a simple one, was plainly disconcerting, and he sat down before replying. "I don't think you often see me there. Give an instance."

"I will," she answered triumphantly. "When you went out this evening I thought that as baby was asleep I would see where you were going to so mysteriously without telling me. So I ran out and followed behind you. You stopped at the place where the road forks, looked round at the bonfires, and then said, 'Damn it, I'll go!' And you went quickly up the left-hand road. Then I stood and watched you."

Wildeve frowned, afterwards saying, with a forced smile, "Well, what wonderful discovery did you make?"

"There — now you are angry, and we won't talk of this any more." She went across to him, sat on a footstool, and looked up in his face.

"Nonsense!" he said; "that's how you always back out. We will go on with it now we have begun. What did you next see? I particularly want to know."

"Don't be like that, Damon!" she murmured. "I didn't see anything. You vanished out of sight, and then I looked round at the bonfires and came in."

"Perhaps this is not the only time you have dogged my steps. Are you trying to find out something bad about me?"

"Not at all! I have never done such a thing before, and I shouldn't have done it now if words had not sometimes been dropped about you."

"What do you mean?" he impatiently asked.

"They say — they say you used to go to Alderworth in the evenings, and it puts into my mind what I have heard about ——"

Wildeve turned angrily and stood up in front of her. "Now," he said, flourishing his hand in the air, "just out with it, madam! I demand to know what remarks you have heard."

"Well, I heard that you used to be very fond of Eustacia — nothing more than that, though told more in a bit-by-bit way. You ought not to be angry!"

He observed that her eyes were brimming with tears. "Well," he said, "there is nothing new in that, and of course I don't mean to be rough towards you, so you need not cry. Now, don't let's speak of the subject any more."

And no more was said, Thomasin being glad enough of a reason for not mentioning Clym's visit to her that evening, and his story.

VII

THE NIGHT OF THE SIXTH OF NOVEMBER

HAVING resolved on flight Eustacia at times seemed anxious that something should happen to thwart her own intention. The only event that could really change her position was the appearance of Clym. The glory which had encircled him as her lover was departed now; yet some good simple quality of his would occasionally return to her memory and stir a momentary throb of hope that he would again present himself before her. But calmly considered it was not likely that such a severance as now existed would ever close up: she would have to live on as a painful object, isolated, and out of place. She had used to think of the heath alone as an uncongenial spot to be in; she felt it now of the whole world.

Towards evening on the sixth her determination to go away again revived. About four o'clock she packed up anew the few small articles she had brought in her flight from Alderworth, and also some belonging to her which had been left here: the whole formed a bundle not too large to be carried in her hand for a distance of a mile or two. The scene without grew darker; mud-coloured clouds bellied downwards from the sky like vast hammocks slung across it, and with the increase of night a stormy wind arose; but as yet there was no rain.

Eustacia could not rest indoors, having nothing more to do, and she wandered to and fro on the hill, not far from the house she was soon to leave. In these desultory ramblings she passed the cottage of Susan Nunsuch, a little lower down than her grandfather's. The door was ajar, and a riband of bright firelight fell over the ground without. As Eustacia crossed the firebeams she appeared for an instant as distinct as a figure in a phantasmagoria — a creature of light surrounded by an area of darkness; the moment passed, and she was absorbed in night again.

A woman who was sitting inside the cottage had seen and recognized her in that momentary irradiation. This was Susan herself, occupied in preparing a posset for her little boy, who, often ailing, was now seriously unwell. Susan dropped the spoon, shook her fist at the vanished figure, and then proceeded with her work in a musing, absent way.

At eight o'clock, the hour at which Eustacia had promised to signal to Wildeve if ever she signalled at all, she looked around the premises to learn if the coast was clear, went to the furze-rick, and pulled thence a long-stemmed bough of that fuel. This she carried to the corner of the bank, and, glancing behind to see if the shutters were all closed, she struck a light, and kindled the furze. When it was thoroughly ablaze Eustacia took it by the stem and waved it in the air above her head till it had burned itself out.

She was gratified, if gratification were possible to such a mood, by seeing a similar light in the vicinity of Wildeve's residence a minute or two later. Having agreed to keep watch at this hour every night, in case she should require assistance, this promptness proved how strictly he had held to his word. Four hours after the present time, that is, at midnight, he was to be ready to drive her to Budmouth, as prearranged.

Eustacia returned to the house. Supper having been got over she retired early, and sat in her bedroom waiting for the time to go by. The night being dark and threatening Captain Vye had not strolled out to gossip in any cottage or to call at the inn, as was sometimes his custom on these long autumn nights; and he sat sipping grog alone downstairs. About ten o'clock there was a knock at the door. When the servant opened it the rays of the candle fell upon the form of Fairway.

"I was a-forced to go to Lower Mistover tonight," he said; "and Mr. Yeobright asked me to leave this here on my way; but, faith, I put it in the lining of my hat, and thought no more about it till I got back and was hasping my gate before going to bed. So I have run back with it at once."

He handed in a letter and went his way. The girl brought it to the captain, who found that it was directed to Eustacia. He turned it over and over, and fancied that the writing was her husband's, though he could not be sure. However, he decided to let her have it at once if possible, and took it upstairs for that purpose; but on reaching the door of her room and looking in at the keyhole he found there was no light within, the fact being that Eustacia, without undressing, had flung herself upon the bed, to rest and gather a little strength for her coming journey. Her grandfather concluded from what he saw that he ought not to disturb her; and descending again to the parlour, he placed the letter on the mantlepiece to give it to her in the morning.

At eleven o'clock he went to bed himself, smoked for some time in his bedroom, put out his light at half-past eleven, and then, as was his invariable custom, pulled up the blind before getting into bed, that he might see which way the wind blew on opening his eyes in the morning, his bedroom window commanding a view of the flagstaff and vane. Just as he had lain down he was surprised to observe the white pole of the staff flash into existence like a streak of phosphorus drawn downwards across the shade of night without. Only one explanation met this — a light had been suddenly thrown upon the pole from the direction of the house. As everybody had retired to rest the old man felt it necessary to get out of bed, open the window softly, and look to the right and left. Eustacia's bedroom was lighted up, and it was the shine from her window which had lighted the pole. Wondering what had aroused her he remained undecided at the window, and was thinking of fetching the letter to slip it under her door, when he heard a slight brushing of garments on the partition dividing his room from the passage.

The captain concluded that Eustacia, feeling wakeful, had gone for a book, and would have dismissed the matter as unimportant if he had not also heard her distinctly weeping.

"She is thinking of that husband of hers," he said to himself. "Ah, the silly goose! she had no business to marry him. I wonder if that letter is really his?"

He arose, threw his boat-cloak round him, opened the door, and said, "Eustacia!" There was no answer. "Eustacia!" he repeated louder, "there is a letter on the mantelpiece for you."

But no response was made to this statement save an imaginary one from the wind, which seemed to gnaw at the corners of the house, and the stroke of a few drops of rain upon the windows.

He went on to the landing, and stood waiting nearly five minutes. Still she did not return. He went back for a light, and prepared to follow her; but first he looked into her bedroom. There, on the outside of the quilt, was the impression of her form, showing that the bed had not been opened; and, what was more significant, she had not taken her candlestick downstairs. He was now thoroughly alarmed; and hastily putting on his clothes he descended to the front door, which he himself had bolted and locked. It was now unfastened. There was no longer any doubt that Eustacia had left the house at this midnight hour; and whither could she have gone? To follow her was almost impossible. Had the dwelling stood in an ordinary road, two persons setting out, one in each direction, might have made sure of overtaking her; but it was a hopeless task to seek for anybody on a heath in the dark, the practicable directions for flight across it from any point being as numerous as the meridians radiating from the pole. Perplexed what to do he looked into the parlour, and was vexed to find that the letter still lay there untouched.

At half-past eleven, finding that the house was silent, Eustacia had lighted her candle, put on some warm outer wrappings, taken her bag in her hand, and, extinguishing the light again, descended the staircase. When she got into the outer air she found that it had begun to rain, and as she stood pausing at the door it increased, threatening to come on heavily. But having committed herself to this line of action there was no retreating for bad weather, since Wildeve had been communicated with, and was probably even then waiting for her. The gloom of the night was funereal; all nature seemed clothed in crape. The spiky points of the fir trees behind the house rose into the sky like the turrets and pinnacles of an abbey. Nothing below the horizon was visible save a light which was still burning in the cottage of Susan Nunsuch.

Eustacia opened her umbrella and went out from the enclosure by the steps over the bank, after which she was beyond all danger of being perceived. Skirting the pool she followed the path towards Rainbarrow, occasionally stumbling over twisted furze-roots, tufts of rushes, or oozing lumps of fleshy fungi, which at this season lay scattered about the heath like the rotten liver and lungs of some colossal animal. The moon and stars were closed up by cloud and rain to the degree of extinction. It was a night which led the traveller's thoughts instinctively to dwell on nocturnal scenes of disaster in the chronicles of the world, on all that is terrible and dark in history and legend — the last plague of Egypt, the destruction of Sennacherib's host, the agony in Gethsemane.

Eustacia at length reached Rainbarrow, and stood still there to think. Never was harmony more perfect than that between the chaos of her mind and the chaos of the world without. A sudden recollection had flashed on her this moment: she had not money enough for undertaking a long journey. Amid the fluctuating sentiments of the day her unpractical mind had not dwelt on the necessity of being well-provided, and now that she thoroughly realized the conditions she sighed bitterly and ceased to stand erect, gradually crouching down under the umbrella as if she were drawn into the Barrow by a hand from beneath. Could it be that she was to remain a captive still? Money: she had never felt its value before. Even to efface herself from the country means were required. To ask Wildeve for pecuniary aid without allowing him to accompany her was impossible to a woman with the shadow of pride left in her: to fly as his mistress — and she knew that he loved her — was of the nature of humiliation.

Anyone who had stood by now would have pitied her, not so much on account of her exposure to weather, and isolation from all of humanity except the mouldered remains inside the Barrow; but for that other form of misery which was denoted by the slightly rocking movement that her feelings imparted to her person. Extreme unhappiness weighed visibly upon her. Between the drippings of the rain from her umbrella to her mantle, from her mantle to the heather, from the heather to the earth, very similar sounds could be heard coming from her lips; and the tearfulness of the outer scene was repeated upon her face. The wings of her soul were broken by the cruel obstructiveness of all about her; and even had she seen herself in a promising way of getting to Budmouth, entering a steamer, and sailing to some opposite port, she would have been but little more buoyant, so fearfully malignant were other things. She uttered words aloud. When a woman in such a situation, neither old, deaf, crazed, nor whimsical, takes upon herself to sob and soliloquize aloud there is something grievous the matter.

"Can I go, can I go?" she moaned. "He's not *great* enough for me to give myself to — he does not suffice for my desire!... If he had been a Saul or a Bonaparte — ah! But to break my marriage vow for him — it is too poor a luxury!... And I have no money to go alone! And if I could, what comfort to me? I must drag on next year, as I have dragged on this year, and the year after that as before. How I have tried and tried to be a splendid woman, and how destiny has been against me!... I do not deserve my lot!" she cried in a frenzy of bitter revolt. "O, the cruelty of putting me into this ill-conceived world! I was capable of much; but I have been injured and blighted and crushed by things beyond my control! O, how hard it is of Heaven to devise such tortures for me, who have done no harm to Heaven at all!"

The distant light which Eustacia had cursorily observed in leaving the house came, as she had divined, from the cottage-window of Susan Nunsuch. What Eustacia did not divine was the occupation of the woman within at that moment. Susan's sight of her passing figure earlier in the evening, not five minutes after the sick boy's exclamation, "Mother, I do feel so bad!" persuaded the matron that an evil influence was certainly exercised by Eustacia's propinquity.

On this account Susan did not go to bed as soon as the evening's work was over, as she would have done at ordinary times. To counteract the malign spell which she imagined poor Eustacia to be working, the boy's mother busied herself with a ghastly invention of superstition, calculated to bring powerlessness, atrophy, and annihilation on any human being against whom it was directed. It was a practice well known on Egdon at that date, and one that is not quite extinct at the present day.

She passed with her candle into an inner room, where, among other utensils, were two large brown pans, containing together perhaps a hundred-weight of liquid honey, the produce of the bees during the foregoing summer. On a shelf over the pans was a smooth and solid yellow mass of a hemispherical form, consisting of beeswax from the same take of honey. Susan took down the lump, and, cutting off several thin slices, heaped them in an iron ladle, with which she returned to the living-room, and placed the vessel in the hot ashes of the fireplace. As soon as the wax had softened to the plasticity of dough she kneaded the pieces together. And now her face became more intent. She began moulding the wax; and it was evident from her manner of manipulation that she was endeavouring to give it some preconceived form. The form was human.

By warming and kneading, cutting and twisting, dismembering and re-joining the incipient image she had in about a quarter of an hour produced a shape which tolerably well resembled a woman, and was about six inches high. She laid it on the table to get cold and hard. Meanwhile she took the candle and went upstairs to where the little boy was lying.

"Did you notice, my dear, what Mrs. Eustacia wore this afternoon be-sides the dark dress?"

"A red ribbon round her neck."

"Anything else?"

"No — except sandal-shoes."

"A red ribbon and sandal-shoes," she said to herself.

Mrs. Nunsuch went and searched till she found a fragment of the narrowest red ribbon, which she took downstairs and tied round the neck of the image. Then fetching ink and a quill from the rickety bureau by the window, she blackened the feet of the image to the extent presumably covered by shoes; and on the instep of each foot marked cross-lines in the shape taken by the sandal-strings of those days. Finally she tied a bit of black thread round the upper part of the head, in faint resemblance to a fillet worn for confining the hair.

Susan held the object at arm's length and contemplated it with a satis-faction in which there was no smile. To anybody acquainted with the inhabitants of Egdon Heath the image would have suggested Eustacia Yeobright.

From her work-basket in the window-seat the woman took a paper of pins, of the old long and yellow sort, whose heads were disposed to come off at their first usage. These she began to thrust into the image in all directions, with apparently excruciating energy. Probably as many as fifty were thus inserted, some into the head of the wax model, some into the shoulders, some into the trunk, some upwards through the soles of the feet, till the figure was completely permeated with pins.

She turned to the fire. It had been of turf; and though the high heap of ashes which turf fires produce was somewhat dark and dead on the outside, upon raking it abroad with the shovel the inside of the mass showed a glow of red heat. She took a few pieces of fresh turf from the chimney-corner and built them together over the glow, upon which the fire brightened. Seizing with the tongs the image that she had made of Eustacia, she held it in the heat, and watched it as it began to waste slowly away. And while she stood thus engaged there came from between her lips a murmur of words.

It was a strange jargon — the Lord's Prayer repeated backwards — the incantation usual in proceedings for obtaining unhallowed assistance against an enemy. Susan uttered the lugubrious discourse three times slowly, and when it was completed the image had considerably diminished. As the wax dropped into the fire a long flame arose from the spot, and curling its tongue round the figure ate still further into its substance. A pin occasionally dropped with the wax, and the embers heated it red as it lay.

VIII

RAIN, DARKNESS, AND ANXIOUS WANDERERS

WHILE the effigy of Eustacia was melting to nothing, and the fair woman herself was standing on Rainbarrow, her soul in an abyss of desolation seldom plumbed by one so young, Yeobright sat lonely at Blooms-End. He had fulfilled his word to Thomasin by sending off Fairway with the letter to his wife, and now waited with increased impatience for some sound or signal of her return. Were Eustacia still at Mistover the very least to be expected was that she would send him back a reply tonight by the same hand; though, to leave all to her inclination, he had cautioned Fairway not to ask for an answer. If one were told or handed to him he was to bring it immediately; if not, he was to go straight home without troubling to come round to Blooms-End again that night.

But secretly Clym had a more pleasing hope. Eustacia might possibly decline to use her pen — it was rather her way to work silently — and surprise him by appearing at his door.

To Clym's regret it began to rain and blow hard as the evening advanced. The wind rasped and scraped at the corners of the house, and filliped the eavesdroppings like peas against the panes. He walked restlessly about the untenanted rooms, stopping strange noises in windows and doors by jamming splinters of wood into the casements and crevices, and pressing together the lead-work of the quarries where it had become loosened from the glass. It was one of those nights when cracks in the walls of old churches widen, when ancient stains on the ceilings of decayed manor-houses are renewed and enlarged from the size of a man's hand to an area of many feet. The little gate in the palings before his dwelling continually opened and clicked together again, but when he looked out eagerly nobody was there; it was as if invisible shapes of the dead were passing in on their way to visit him.

Between ten and eleven o'clock, finding that neither Fairway nor anybody else came to him, he retired to rest, and despite his anxieties soon fell asleep. His sleep, however, was not very sound, by reason of the expectancy he had given way to, and he was easily awakened by a knocking which began at the door about an hour after. Clym arose and looked out of the window. Rain was still falling heavily, the whole expanse of heath before him emitting a subdued hiss under the downpour. It was too dark to see anything at all.

"Who's there?" he cried.

Light footsteps shifted their position in the porch, and he could just distinguish in a plaintive female voice the words, "O Clym, come down and let me in!"

He flushed hot with agitation. "Surely it is Eustacia!" he murmured. If so, she had indeed come to him unawares.

He hastily got a light, dressed himself, and went down. On his flinging open the door the rays of the candle fell upon a woman closely wrapped up, who at once came forward.

"Thomasin!" he exclaimed in an indescribable tone of disappointment. "It is Thomasin, and on such a night as this! O, where is Eustacia?"

Thomasin it was, wet, frightened, and panting.

"Eustacia? I don't know, Clym; but I can think," she said with much perturbation. "Let me come in and rest — I will explain this. There is a great trouble brewing — my husband and Eustacia!"

"What, what?"

"I think my husband is going to leave me or do something dreadful — I don't know what — Clym, will you go and see? I have nobody to help me but you! Eustacia has not come home?"

"No."

She went on breathlessly: "Then they are going to run off together! He came indoors tonight about eight o'clock and said in an off-hand way, 'Tamsie, I have just found that I must go a journey.' 'When?' I said. 'Tonight,' he said. 'Where?' I asked him. 'I cannot tell you at present,' he said; 'I shall be back again tomorrow.' He then went and busied himself in looking up his things, and took no notice of me at all. I expected to see him start, but he did not, and then it came to be ten o'clock, when he said, 'You had better go to bed.' I didn't know what to do, and I went to bed. I believe he thought I fell asleep, for half an hour after that he came up and unlocked the oak chest we keep money in when we have much in the house and took out a roll of something which I believe was bank-notes, though I was not aware that he had 'em there. These he must have got from the bank when he went there the other day. What does he want bank-notes for, if he is only going off for a day? When he had gone down I thought of Eustacia, and how he had met her the night before — I know he did meet her, Clym, for I followed him part of the way; but I did not like to tell you when you called, and so make you think ill of him, as I did not think it was so serious. Then I could not stay in bed: I got up and dressed myself, and when I heard him out in the stable I thought I would come and tell you. So I came downstairs without any noise and slipped out."

"Then he was not absolutely gone when you left?"

"No. Will you, dear Cousin Clym, go and try to persuade him not to go? He takes no notice of what I say, and puts me off with the story of his going on a journey, and will be home tomorrow, and all that; but I don't believe it. I think you could influence him."

"I'll go," said Clym, "O, Eustacia!"

Thomasin carried in her arms a large bundle; and having by this time seated herself she began to unroll it, when a baby appeared as the kernel to the husks — dry, warm, and unconscious of travel or rough weather. Thomasin briefly kissed the baby, and then found time to begin crying as she said, "I brought baby, for I was afraid what might happen to her. I suppose it will be her death, but I couldn't leave her with Rachel!"

Clym hastily put together the logs on the hearth, raked abroad the embers, which were scarcely yet extinct, and blew up a flame with the bellows.

"Dry yourself," he said. "I'll go and get some more wood."

"No, no — don't stay for that. I'll make up the fire. Will you go at once — please will you?"

Yeobright ran upstairs to finish dressing himself. While he was gone another rapping came to the door. This time there was no delusion that it might be Eustacia's: the footsteps just preceding it had been heavy and slow. Yeobright, thinking it might possibly be Fairway with a note in answer, descended again and opened the door.

"Captain Vye?" he said to a dripping figure.

"Is my grand-daughter here?" said the captain.

"No."

"Then where is she?"

"I don't know."

"But you ought to know — you are her husband."

"Only in name apparently," said Clym with rising excitement. "I believe she means to elope tonight with Wildeve. I am just going to look to it."

"Well, she has left my house; she left about half an hour ago. Who's sitting there?"

"My cousin Thomasin."

The captain bowed in a preoccupied way to her. "I only hope it is no worse than an elopement," he said.

"Worse? What's worse than the worst a wife can do?"

"Well, I have been told a strange tale. Before starting in search of her I called up Charley, my stablelad. I missed my pistols the other day."

"Pistols?"

"He said at the time that he took them down to clean. He has now owned that he took them because he saw Eustacia looking curiously at them; and she afterwards owned to him that she was thinking of taking her life, but bound him to secrecy, and promised never to think of such a thing again. I hardly suppose she will ever have bravado enough to use one of them; but it shows what has been lurking in her mind; and people who think of that sort of thing once think of it again."

"Where are the pistols?"

"Safely locked up. O no, she won't touch them again. But there are more ways of letting out life than through a bullet-hole. What did you quarrel about so bitterly with her to drive her to all this? You must have treated her badly indeed. Well, I was always against the marriage, and I was right."

"Are you going with me?" said Yeobright, paying no attention to the captain's latter remark. "If so I can tell you what we quarrelled about as we walk along."

"Where to?"

"To Wildeve's — that was her destination, depend upon it."

Thomasin here broke in, still weeping: "He said he was only going on a sudden short journey; but if so why did he want so much money? O, Clym, what do you think will happen? I am afraid that you, my poor baby, will soon have no father left to you!"

"I am off now," said Yeobright, stepping into the porch.

"I would fain go with ye," said the old man doubtfully. "But I begin to be afraid that my legs will hardly carry me there such a night as this. I am not so young as I was. If they are interrupted in their flight she will be sure to come back to me, and I ought to be at the house to receive her. But be it as 'twill I can't walk to the Quiet Woman, and that's an end on't. I'll go straight home."

"It will perhaps be best," said Clym. "Thomasin, dry yourself, and be as comfortable as you can."

With this he closed the door upon her, and left the house in company with Captain Vye, who parted from him outside the gate, taking the middle path, which led to Mistover. Clym crossed by the right-hand track towards the inn.

Thomasin, being left alone, took off some of her wet garments, carried the baby upstairs to Clym's bed, and then came down to the sitting-room again, where she made a larger fire, and began drying herself. The fire soon flared up the chimney, giving the room an appearance of comfort that was doubled by contrast with the drumming of the storm without, which snapped at the window-panes and breathed into the chimney strange low utterances that seemed to be the prologue to some tragedy.

But the least part of Thomasin was in the house, for her heart being at ease about the little girl upstairs she was mentally following Clym on his journey. Having indulged in this imaginary peregrination for some considerable interval, she became impressed with a sense of the intolerable slowness of time. But she sat on. The moment then came when she could scarcely sit longer; and it was like a satire on her patience to remember that Clym could hardly have reached the inn as yet. At last she went to the baby's bedside. The child was sleeping soundly; but her imagination of possibly disastrous events at her home, the predominance within her of the unseen over the seen, agitated her beyond endurance. She could not refrain from going down and opening the door. The rain still continued, the candlelight falling upon the nearest drops and making glistening darts of them as they descended across the throng of invisible ones behind. To plunge into that medium was to plunge into water slightly diluted with air. But the difficulty of returning to her house at this moment made her all the more desirous of doing so: anything was better than suspense. "I have come here well enough," she said, "and why shouldn't I go back again? It is a mistake for me to be away."

She hastily fetched the infant, wrapped it up, cloaked herself as before, and shovelling the ashes over the fire, to prevent accidents, went into the open air. Pausing first to put the door-key in its old place behind the shutter, she resolutely turned her face to the confronting pile of firmamental darkness beyond the palings, and stepped into its midst. But Thomasin's imagination being so actively engaged elsewhere, the night and the weather had for her no terror beyond that of their actual discomfort and difficulty.

She was soon ascending Blooms-End valley and traversing the undulations on the side of the hill. The noise of the wind over the heath was shrill, and as if it whistled for joy at finding a night so congenial as this. Sometimes the path led her to hollows between thickets of tall and dripping bracken, dead, though not yet prostrate, which enclosed her like a pool. When they were more than usually tall she lifted the baby to the top of her head, that it might be out of the reach of their drenching fronds. On higher ground, where the wind was brisk and sustained, the rain flew in a level flight without sensible descent, so that it was beyond all power to imagine the remoteness of the point at which it left the bosoms of the clouds. Here self-defence was impossible, and individual drops stuck into her like the arrows into Saint Sebastian. She was enabled to avoid puddles by the nebulous paleness which signified their presence, though beside anything less dark than the heath they themselves would have appeared as blackness.

Yet in spite of all this Thomasin was not sorry that she had started. To her there were not, as to Eustacia, demons in the air, and malice in every bush and bough. The drops which lashed her face were not scorpions, but prosy rain; Egdon in the mass was no monster whatever, but impersonal open ground. Her fears of the place were rational, her dislikes of its worst moods reasonable. At this time it was in her view a windy, wet place, in which a person might experience much discomfort, lose the path without care, and possibly catch cold.

If the path is well known the difficulty at such times of keeping therein is not altogether great, from its familiar feel to the feet; but once lost it is irrecoverable. Owing to her baby, who somewhat impeded Thomasin's view forward and distracted her mind, she did at last lose the track. This mishap occurred when she was descending an open slope about two-thirds home. Instead of attempting, by wandering hither and thither, the hopeless task of finding such a mere thread, she went straight on, trusting for guidance to her general knowledge of the district, which was scarcely surpassed by Clym's or by that of the heath-croppers themselves.

At length Thomasin reached a hollow and began to discern through the rain a faint blotted radiance, which presently assumed the oblong form of an open door. She knew that no house stood hereabouts, and was soon aware of the nature of the door by its height above the ground.

"Why, it is Diggory Venn's van, surely!" she said.

A certain secluded spot near Rainbarrow was, she knew, often Venn's chosen centre when staying in this neighbourhood; and she guessed at once that she had stumbled upon this mysterious retreat. The question arose in her mind whether or not she should ask him to guide her into the path. In her anxiety to reach home she decided that she would appeal to him, notwithstanding the strangeness of appearing before his eyes at this place and season. But when, in pursuance of this resolve, Thomasin reached the van and looked in she found it to be untenanted; though there was no doubt that it was the reddleman's. The fire was burning in the stove, the lantern hung from the nail. Round the doorway the floor was merely sprinkled with rain, and not saturated, which told her that the door had not long been opened.

While she stood uncertainly looking in Thomasin heard a footstep advancing from the darkness behind her; and turning, beheld the well-known form in corduroy, lurid from head to foot, the lantern beams falling upon him through an intervening gauze of raindrops.

"I thought you went down the slope," he said, without noticing her face. "How do you come back here again?"

"Diggory?" said Thomasin faintly.

"Who are you?" said Venn, still unperceiving. "And why were you crying so just now?"

"O, Diggory! don't you know me?" said she. "But of course you don't, wrapped up like this. What do you mean? I have not been crying here, and I have not been here before."

Venn then came nearer till he could see the illuminated side of her form.

"Mrs. Wildeve!" he exclaimed starting. "What a time for us to meet! And the baby too! What dreadful thing can have brought you out on such a night as this?"

She could not immediately answer; and without asking her permission he hopped into his van, took her by the arm, and drew her up after him.

"What is it?" he continued when they stood within.

"I have lost my way coming from Blooms-End, and I am in a great hurry to get home. Please show me as quickly as you can! It is so silly of me not to know Egdon better, and I cannot think how I came to lose the path. Show me quickly, Diggory, please."

"Yes, of course. I will go with ye. But you came to me before this, Mrs. Wildeve?"

"I only came this minute."

"That's strange. I was lying down here asleep about five minutes ago, with the door shut to keep out the weather, when the brushing of a woman's clothes over the heath-bushes just outside woke me up (for I don't sleep heavy), and at the same time I heard a sobbing or crying from the same woman. I opened my door and held out my lantern, and just as far as the light would reach I saw a woman: she turned her head when the light sheened on her, and then hurried on downhill. I hung up the lantern, and was curious enough to pull on my things and dog her a few steps, but I could see nothing of her any more. That was where I had been when you came up; and when I saw you I thought you were the same one."

"Perhaps it was one of the heath-folk going home?"

"No, it couldn't. 'Tis too late. The noise of her gown over the he'th was of a whistling sort that nothing but silk will make."

"It wasn't I, then. My dress is not silk, you see.... Are we anywhere in a line between Mistover and the inn?"

"Well, yes; not far out."

"Ah, I wonder if it was she! Diggory, I must go at once!"

She jumped down from the van before he was aware, when Venn unhooked the lantern and leaped down after her. "I'll take the baby, ma'am," he said. "You must be tired out by the weight."

Thomasin hesitated a moment, and then delivered the baby into Venn's hands. "Don't squeeze her, Diggory," she said, "or hurt her little arm; and keep the cloak close over her like this, so that the rain may not drop in her face."

"I will," said Venn earnestly. "As if I could hurt anything belonging to you!"

"I only meant accidentally," said Thomasin.

"The baby is dry enough, but you are pretty wet," said the reddleman when, in closing the door of his cart to padlock it, he noticed on the floor a ring of water-drops where her cloak had hung from her.

Thomasin followed him as he wound right and left to avoid the larger bushes, stopping occasionally and covering the lantern, while he looked over his shoulder to gain some idea of the position of Rainbarrow above them, which it was necessary to keep directly behind their backs to preserve a proper course.

"You are sure the rain does not fall upon baby?"

"Quite sure. May I ask how old he is, ma'am?"

"He!" said Thomasin reproachfully. "Anybody can see better than that in a moment. She is nearly two months old. How far is it now to the inn?"

"A little over a quarter of a mile."

"Will you walk a little faster?"

"I was afraid you could not keep up."

"I am very anxious to get there. Ah, there is a light from the window!"

"'Tis not from the window. That's a gig-lamp, to the best of my belief."

"O!" said Thomasin in despair. "I wish I had been there sooner — give me the baby, Diggory — you can go back now."

"I must go all the way," said Venn. "There is a quag between us and that light, and you will walk into it up to your neck unless I take you round."

"But the light is at the inn, and there is no quag in front of that."

"No, the light is below the inn some two or three hundred yards."

"Never mind," said Thomasin hurriedly. "Go towards the light, and not towards the inn."

"Yes," answered Venn, swerving round in obedience; and, after a pause,

"I wish you would tell me what this great trouble is. I think you have proved that I can be trusted."

"There are some things that cannot be — cannot be told to ——" And then her heart rose into her throat, and she could say no more.

IX

SIGHTS AND SOUNDS DRAW THE WANDERERS TOGETHER

Having seen Eustacia's signal from the hill at eight o'clock, Wildeve immediately prepared to assist her in her flight, and, as he hoped, accompany her. He was somewhat perturbed, and his manner of informing Thomasin that he was going on a journey was in itself sufficient to rouse her suspicions. When she had gone to bed he collected the few articles he would require, and went upstairs to the money-chest, whence he took a tolerably bountiful sum in notes, which had been advanced to him on the property he was so soon to have in possession, to defray expenses incidental to the removal.

He then went to the stable and coach-house to assure himself that the horse, gig, and harness were in a fit condition for a long drive. Nearly half an hour was spent thus, and on returning to the house Wildeve had no thought of Thomasin being anywhere but in bed. He had told the stablelad not to stay up, leading the boy to understand that his departure would be at three or four in the morning; for this, though an exceptional hour, was less strange than midnight, the time actually agreed on, the packet from Budmouth sailing between one and two.

At last all was quiet, and he had nothing to do but to wait. By no effort could he shake off the oppression of spirits which he had experienced ever since his last meeting with Eustacia, but he hoped there was that in his situation which money could cure. He had persuaded himself that to act not ungenerously towards his gentle wife by settling on her the half of his property, and with chivalrous devotion towards another and greater woman by sharing her fate, was possible. And though he meant to adhere to Eustacia's instructions to the letter, to deposit her where she wished and to leave her, should that be her will, the spell that she had cast over him intensified, and his heart was beating fast in the anticipated futility of such commands in the face of a mutual wish that they should depart together.

He would not allow himself to dwell long upon these conjectures, maxims, and hopes, and at twenty minutes to twelve he again went softly to the stable, harnessed the horse, and lit the lamps; whence, taking the horse by the head, he led him with the covered car out of the yard to a spot by the roadside some quarter of a mile below the inn.

Here Wildeve waited, slightly sheltered from the driving rain by a high bank that had been cast up at this place. Along the surface of the road where lit by the lamps the loosened gravel and small stones scudded and clicked together before the wind, which, leaving them in heaps, plunged into the heath and boomed across the bushes into darkness. Only one sound rose above this din of weather, and that was the roaring of a ten-hatch weir a few yards further on, where the road approached the river which formed the boundary of the heath in this direction.

He lingered on in perfect stillness till he began to fancy that the midnight hour must have struck. A very strong doubt had arisen in his mind if Eustacia would venture down the hill in such weather; yet knowing her nature he felt that she might. "Poor thing! 'tis like her ill-luck," he murmured.

At length he turned to the lamp and looked at his watch. To his surprise it was nearly a quarter past midnight. He now wished that he had driven up the circuitous road to Mistover, a plan not adopted because of the enormous length of the route in proportion to that of the pedestrian's path down the open hillside, and the consequent increase of labour for the horse.

At this moment a footstep approached; but the light of the lamps being in a different direction the comer was not visible. The step paused, then came on again.

"Eustacia?" said Wildeve.

The person came forward, and the light fell upon the form of Clym, glistening with wet, whom Wildeve immediately recognized; but Wildeve, who stood behind the lamp, was not at once recognized by Yeobright.

He stopped as if in doubt whether this waiting vehicle could have anything to do with the flight of his wife or not. The sight of Yeobright at once banished Wildeve's sober feelings, who saw him again as the deadly rival from whom Eustacia was to be kept at all hazards. Hence Wildeve did not speak, in the hope that Clym would pass by without particular inquiry.

While they both hung thus in hesitation a dull sound became audible above the storm and wind. Its origin was unmistakable — it was the fall of a body into the stream adjoining, apparently at a point near the weir.

Both started. "Good God! can it be she?" said Clym.

"Why should it be she?" said Wildeve, in his alarm forgetting that he had hitherto screened himself.

"Ah! — that's you, you traitor, is it?" cried Yeobright. "Why should it be she? Because last week she would have put an end to her life if she had been able. She ought to have been watched! Take one of the lamps and come with me."

Yeobright seized the one on his side and hastened on; Wildeve did not wait to unfasten the other, but followed at once along the meadow-track to the weir, a little in the rear of Clym.

Shadwater Weir had at its foot a large circular pool, fifty feet in diameter, into which the water flowed through ten huge hatches, raised and lowered by a winch and cogs in the ordinary manner. The sides of the pool were of masonry, to prevent the water from washing away the bank; but the force of the stream in winter was sometimes such as to undermine the retaining wall and precipitate it into the hole. Clym reached the hatches, the framework of which was shaken to its foundations by the velocity of the current. Nothing but the froth of the waves could be discerned in the pool below. He got upon the plank bridge over the race, and holding to the rail, that the wind might not blow him off, crossed to the other side of the river. There he leant over the wall and lowered the lamp, only to behold the vortex formed at the curl of the returning current.

Wildeve meanwhile had arrived on the former side, and the light from Yeobright's lamp shed a flecked and agitated radiance across the weir-pool, revealing to the ex-engineer the tumbling courses of the currents from the hatches above. Across this gashed and puckered mirror a dark body was slowly borne by one of the backward currents.

"O, my darling!" exclaimed Wildeve in an agonized voice; and, without showing sufficient presence of mind even to throw off his great-coat, he leapt into the boiling hole.

Yeobright could now also discern the floating body, though but indistinctly; and imagining from Wildeve's plunge that there was life to be saved he was about to leap after. Bethinking himself of a wiser plan he placed the lamp against a post to make it stand upright, and running round to the lower part of the pool, where there was no wall, he sprang in and boldly waded upwards towards the deeper portion. Here he was taken off his legs, and in swimming was carried round into the centre of the basin, where he perceived Wildeve struggling.

While these hasty actions were in progress here, Venn and Thomasin had been toiling through the lower corner of the heath in the direction of the light. They had not been near enough to the river to hear the plunge, but they saw the removal of the carriage-lamp, and watched its motion into the mead. As soon as they reached the car and horse Venn guessed that something new was amiss, and hastened to follow in the course of the moving light. Venn walked faster than Thomasin, and came to the weir alone.

The lamp placed against the post by Clym still shone across the water, and the reddleman observed something floating motionless. Being encumbered with the infant he ran back to meet Thomasin.

"Take the baby, please, Mrs. Wildeve," he said hastily. "Run home with her, call the stable-lad, and make him send down to me any men who may be living near. Somebody has fallen into the weir."

Thomasin took the child and ran. When she came to the covered car the horse, though fresh from the stable, was standing perfectly still, as if conscious of misfortune. She saw for the first time whose it was. She nearly fainted, and would have been unable to proceed another step but that the necessity of preserving the little girl from harm nerved her to an amazing self-control. In this agony of suspense she entered the house, put the baby in a place of safety, woke the lad and the female domestic, and ran out to give the alarm at the nearest cottage.

Diggory, having returned to the brink of the pool, observed that the small upper hatches or floats were withdrawn. He found one of these lying upon the grass, and taking it under one arm, and with his lantern in his hand, entered at the bottom of the pool as Clym had done. As soon as he began to be in deep water he flung himself across the hatch; thus supported he was able to keep afloat as long as he chose, holding the lantern aloft with his disengaged hand. Propelled by his feet he steered round and round the pool, ascending each time by one of the back streams and descending in the middle of the current.

At first he could see nothing. Then amidst the glistening of the whirlpools and the white clots of foam he distinguished a woman's bonnet floating alone. His search was now under the left wall, when something came to the surface almost close beside him. It was not, as he had expected, a woman, but a man. The reddleman put the ring of the lantern between his teeth, seized the floating man by the collar, and, holding on to the hatch with his remaining arm, struck out into the strongest race, by which the unconscious man, the hatch, and himself were carried down the stream. As soon as Venn found his feet dragging over the pebbles of the shallower part below he secured his footing and waded towards the brink. There, where the water stood at about the height of his waist, he flung away the hatch, and attempted to drag forth the man. This was a matter of great difficulty, and he found as the reason that the legs of the unfortunate stranger were tightly embraced by the arms of another man, who had hitherto been entirely beneath the surface.

At this moment his heart bounded to hear footsteps running towards him, and two men, roused by Thomasin, appeared at the brink above. They ran to where Venn was, and helped him in lifting out the apparently drowned persons, separating them, and laying them out upon the grass. Venn turned the light upon their faces. The one who had been uppermost was Yeobright; he who had been completely submerged was Wildeve.

"Now we must search the hole again," said Venn. "A woman is in there somewhere. Get a pole."

One of the men went to the foot-bridge and tore off the handrail. The reddleman and the two others then entered the water together from below as before, and with their united force probed the pool forwards to where it sloped down to its central depth. Venn was not mistaken in supposing that any person who had sunk for the last time would be washed down to this point, for when they had examined to about half-way across something impeded their thrust.

"Pull it forward," said Venn, and they raked it in with the pole till it was close to their feet.

Venn vanished under the stream, and came up with an armful of wet drapery enclosing a woman's cold form, which was all that remained of the desperate Eustacia.

When they reached the bank there stood Thomasin, in a stress of grief, bending over the two unconscious ones who already lay there. The horse and car were brought to the nearest point in the road, and it was the work of a few minutes only to place the three in the vehicle. Venn led on the horse, supporting Thomasin upon his arm, and the two men followed, till they reached the inn.

The woman who had been shaken out of her sleep by Thomasin had hastily dressed herself and lighted a fire, the other servant being left to snore on in peace at the back of the house. The insensible forms of Eustacia, Clym, and Wildeve were then brought in and laid on the carpet, with their feet to the fire, when such restorative processes as could be thought of were adopted at once the stableman being in the meantime sent for a doctor. But there seemed to be not a whiff of life left in either of the bodies. Then Thomasin, whose stupor of grief had been thrust off awhile by frantic action, applied a bottle of hartshorn to Clym's nostrils, having tried in vain upon the other two. He sighed.

"Clym's alive!" she exclaimed.

He soon breathed distinctly, and again and again did she attempt to revive her husband by the same means; but Wildeve gave no sign. There was too much reason to think that he and Eustacia both were for ever beyond the reach of stimulating perfumes. Their exertions did not relax till the doctor arrived, when, one by one, the senseless three were taken upstairs and put into warm beds.

Venn soon felt himself relieved from further attendance, and went to the door, scarcely able yet to realize the strange catastrophe that had befallen the family in which he took so great an interest. Thomasin surely would be broken down by the sudden and overwhelming nature of this event. No firm and sensible Mrs. Yeobright lived now to support the gentle girl through the ordeal; and, whatever an unimpassioned spectator might think of her loss of such a husband as Wildeve, there could be no doubt that for the moment she was distracted and horrified by the blow. As for himself, not being privileged to go to her and comfort her, he saw no reason for waiting longer in a house where he remained only as a stranger.

He returned across the heath to his van. The fire was not yet out, and everything remained as he had left it. Venn now bethought himself of his clothes, which were saturated with water to the weight of lead. He changed them, spread them before the fire, and lay down to sleep. But it was more than he could do to rest here while excited by a vivid imagination of the turmoil they were in at the house he had quitted, and, blaming himself for coming away, he dressed in another suit, locked up the door, and again hastened across to the inn. Rain was still falling heavily when he entered the kitchen. A bright fire was shining from the hearth, and two women were bustling about, one of whom was Olly Dowden.

"Well, how is it going on now?" said Venn in a whisper.

"Mr. Yeobright is better; but Mrs. Yeobright and Mr. Wildeve are dead and cold. The doctor says they were quite gone before they were out of the water."

"Ah! I thought as much when I hauled 'em up. And Mrs. Wildeve?"

"She is as well as can be expected. The doctor had her put between blankets, for she was almost as wet as they that had been in the river, poor young thing. You don't seem very dry, reddleman."

"O, 'tis not much. I have changed my things. This is only a little dampness I've got coming through the rain again."

"Stand by the fire. Mis'ess says you be to have whatever you want, and she was sorry when she was told that you'd gone away."

Venn drew near to the fireplace, and looked into the flames in an absent mood. The steam came from his leggings and ascended the chimney with the smoke, while he thought of those who were upstairs. Two were corpses, one had barely escaped the jaws of death, another was sick and a widow. The last occasion on which he had lingered by that fireplace was when the raffle was in progress; when Wildeve was alive and well; Thomasin active and smiling in the next room; Yeobright and Eustacia just made husband and wife, and Mrs. Yeobright living at Blooms-End. It had seemed at that time that the then position of affairs was good for at least twenty years to come. Yet, of all the circle, he himself was the only one whose situation had not materially changed.

While he ruminated a footstep descended the stairs. It was the nurse, who brought in her hand a rolled mass of wet paper. The woman was so engrossed with her occupation that she hardly saw Venn. She took from the cupboard some pieces of twine, which she strained across the fireplace, tying the end of each piece to the firedog, previously pulled forward for the purpose, and, unrolling the wet papers, she began pinning them one by one to the strings in a manner of clothes on a line.

"What be they?" said Venn.

"Poor master's bank-notes," she answered. "They were found in his pocket when they undressed him."

"Then he was not coming back again for some time?" said Venn.

"That we shall never know," said she.

Venn was loth to depart, for all on earth that interested him lay under this roof. As nobody in the house had any more sleep that night, except the two who slept for ever, there was no reason why he should not remain. So he retired into the niche of the fireplace where he had used to sit, and there he continued, watching the steam from the double row of bank-notes as they waved backwards and forwards in the draught of the chimney till their flaccidity was changed to dry crispness throughout. Then the woman came and unpinned them, and, folding them together, carried the handful upstairs. Presently the doctor appeared from above with the look of a man who could do no more, and, pulling on his gloves, went out of the house, the trotting of his horse soon dying away upon the road.

At four o'clock there was a gentle knock at the door. It was from Charley, who had been sent by Captain Vye to inquire if anything had been heard of Eustacia. The girl who admitted him looked in his face as if she did not know what answer to return, and showed him in to where Venn was seated, saying to the reddleman, "Will you tell him, please?"

Venn told. Charley's only utterance was a feeble, indistinct sound. He stood quite still; then he burst out spasmodically, "I shall see her once more?"

"I dare say you may see her," said Diggory gravely. "But hadn't you better run and tell Captain Vye?"

"Yes, yes. Only I do hope I shall see her just once again."

"You shall," said a low voice behind; and starting round they beheld by the dim light a thin, pallid, almost spectral form, wrapped in a blanket, and looking like Lazarus coming from the tomb.

It was Yeobright. Neither Venn nor Charley spoke, and Clym continued: "You shall see her. There will be time enough to tell the captain when it gets daylight. You would like to see her too — would you not, Diggory? She looks very beautiful now."

Venn assented by rising to his feet, and with Charley he followed Clym to the foot of the staircase, where he took off his boots; Charley did the same.

They followed Yeobright upstairs to the landing, where there was a candle burning, which Yeobright took in his hand, and with it led the way into an adjoining room.   Here he went to the bedside and folded back the sheet.

They stood silently looking upon Eustacia, who, as she lay there still in death, eclipsed all her living phases.   Pallor did not include all the quality of her complexion, which seemed more than whiteness; it was almost light. The expression of her finely carved mouth was pleasant, as if a sense of dignity had just compelled her to leave off speaking.   Eternal rigidity had seized upon it in a momentary transition between fervour and resignation. Her black hair was looser now than either of them had ever seen it before, and surrounded her brow like a forest.   The stateliness of look which had been almost too marked for a dweller in a country domicile had at last found an artistically happy background.

Nobody spoke, till at length Clym covered her and turned aside.   "Now come here," he said.

They went to a recess in the same room, and there, on a smaller bed, lay another figure — Wildeve.   Less repose was visible in his face than in Eustacia's, but the same luminous youthfulness overspread it, and the least sympathetic observer would have felt at sight of him now that he was born for a higher destiny than this.   The only sign upon him of his recent struggle for life was in his finger-tips, which were worn and scarified in his dying endeavours to obtain a hold on the face of the weir-wall.

Yeobright's manner had been so quiet, he had uttered so few syllables since his reappearance, that Venn imagined him resigned.   It was only when they had left the room and stood upon the landing that the true state of his mind was apparent.   Here he said, with a wild smile, inclining his head towards the chamber in which Eustacia lay, "She is the second woman I have killed this year.   I was a great cause of my mother's death; and I am the chief cause of hers."

"How?" said Venn.

"I spoke cruel words to her, and she left my house.   I did not invite her back till it was too late.   It is I who ought to have drowned myself.   It would have been a charity to the living had the river overwhelmed me and borne her up.   But I cannot die.   Those who ought to have lived lie dead; and here am I alive!"

"But you can't charge yourself with crimes in that way," said Venn.   "You may as well say that the parents be the cause of a murder by the child, for without the parents the child would never have been begot."

"Yes, Venn, that is very true; but you don't know all the circumstances. If it had pleased God to put an end to me it would have been a good thing for all.   But I am getting used to the horror of my existence.   They say that a time comes when men laugh at misery through long acquaintance with it. Surely that time will soon come to me!"

"Your aim has always been good," said Venn.   "Why should you say such desperate things?"

"No, they are not desperate.   They are only hopeless; and my great regret is that for what I have done no man or law can punish me!"

Book Sixth: Aftercourses

I

THE INEVITABLE MOVEMENT ONWARD

The story of the deaths of Eustacia and Wildeve was told throughout Egdon, and far beyond, for many weeks and months. All the known incidents of their love were enlarged, distorted, touched up, and modified, till the original reality bore but a slight resemblance to the counterfeit presentation by surrounding tongues. Yet, upon the whole, neither the man nor the woman lost dignity by sudden death. Misfortune had struck them gracefully, cutting off their erratic histories with a catastrophic dash, instead of, as with many, attenuating each life to an uninteresting meagreness, through long years of wrinkles, neglect, and decay.

On those most nearly concerned the effect was somewhat different. Strangers who had heard of many such cases now merely heard of one more; but immediately where a blow falls no previous imaginings amount to appreciable preparation for it. The very suddenness of her bereavement dulled, to some extent, Thomasin's feelings; yet, irrationally enough, a consciousness that the husband she had lost ought to have been a better man did not lessen her mourning at all. On the contrary, this fact seemed at first to set off the dead husband in his young wife's eyes, and to be the necessary cloud to the rainbow.

But the horrors of the unknown had passed. Vague misgivings about her future as a deserted wife were at an end. The worst had once been matter of trembling conjecture; it was now matter of reason only, a limited badness. Her chief interest, the little Eustacia, still remained. There was humility in her grief, no defiance in her attitude; and when this is the case a shaken spirit is apt to be stilled.

Could Thomasin's mournfulness now and Eustacia's serenity during life have been reduced to common measure, they would have touched the same mark nearly. But Thomasin's former brightness made shadow of that which in a sombre atmosphere was light itself.

The spring came and calmed her; the summer came and soothed her; the autumn arrived, and she began to be comforted, for her little girl was strong and happy, growing in size and knowledge every day. Outward events flattered Thomasin not a little. Wildeve had died intestate, and she and the child were his only relatives. When administration had been granted, all the debts paid, and the residue of her husband's uncle's property had come into her hands, it was found that the sum waiting to be invested for her own and the child's benefit was little less than ten thousand pounds.

Where should she live? The obvious place was Blooms-End. The old rooms, it is true, were not much higher than the between-decks of a frigate, necessitating a sinking in the floor under the new clock-case she brought from the inn, and the removal of the handsome brass knobs on its head, before there was height for it to stand; but, such as the rooms were, there were plenty of them, and the place was endeared to her by every early recollection.

Clym very gladly admitted her as a tenant, confining his own existence to two rooms at the top of the back staircase, where he lived on quietly, shut off from Thomasin and the three servants she had thought fit to indulge in now that she was a mistress of money, going his own ways, and thinking his own thoughts.

His sorrows had made some change in his outward appearance; and yet the alteration was chiefly within. It might have been said that he had a wrinkled mind. He had no enemies, and he could get nobody to reproach him, which was why he so bitterly reproached himself.

He did sometimes think he had been ill-used by fortune, so far as to say that to be born is a palpable dilemma, and that instead of men aiming to advance in life with glory they should calculate how to retreat out of it without shame. But that he and his had been sarcastically and pitilessly handled in having such irons thrust into their souls he did not maintain long. It is usually so, except with the sternest of men. Human beings, in their generous endeavour to construct a hypothesis that shall not degrade a First Cause, have always hesitated to conceive a dominant power of lower moral quality than their own; and, even while they sit down and weep by the waters of Babylon, invent excuses for the oppression which prompts their tears.

Thus, though words of solace were vainly uttered in his presence, he found relief in a direction of his own choosing when left to himself. For a man of his habits the house and the hundred and twenty pounds a year which he had inherited from his mother were enough to supply all worldly needs. Resources do not depend upon gross amounts, but upon the proportion of givings to takings.

He frequently walked the heath alone, when the past seized upon him with its shadowy hand, and held him there to listen to its tale. His imagination would then people the spot with its ancient inhabitants: forgotten Celtic tribes trod their tracks about him, and he could almost live among them, look in their faces, and see them standing beside the barrows which swelled around, untouched and perfect as at the time of their erection. Those of the dyed barbarians who had chosen the cultivable tracts were, in comparison with those who had left their marks here, as writers on paper beside writers on parchment. Their records had perished long ago by the plough, while the works of these remained. Yet they all had lived and died unconscious of the different fates awaiting their works. It reminded him that unforeseen factors operate in the production of immortality.

Winter again came round, with its winds, frosts, tame robins, and sparkling starlight. The year previous Thomasin had hardly been conscious of the season's advance; this year she laid her heart open to external influences of every kind. The life of this sweet cousin, her baby, and her servants, came to Clym's senses only in the form of sounds through a wood partition as he sat over books of exceptionally large type; but his ear became at last so accustomed to these slight noises from the other part of the house that he almost could witness the scenes they signified. A faint beat of half-seconds conjured up Thomasin rocking the cradle, a wavering hum meant that she was singing the baby to sleep, a crunching of sand as between millstones raised the picture of Humphrey's, Fairway's, or Sam's heavy feet crossing the stone floor of the kitchen; a light boyish step, and a gay tune in a high key, betokened a visit from Grandfer Cantle; a sudden break-off in the Grandfer's utterances implied the application to his lips of a mug of small beer; a bustling and slamming of doors meant starting to go to market; for Thomasin, in spite of her added scope for gentility, led a ludicrously narrow life, to the end that she might save every possible pound for her little daughter.

One summer day Clym was in the garden, immediately outside the parlour-window, which was as usual open. He was looking at the pot-flowers on the sill; they had been revived and restored by Thomasin to the state in which his mother had left them. He heard a slight scream from Thomasin, who was sitting inside the room.

"O, how you frightened me!" she said to someone who had entered. "I thought you were the ghost of yourself."

Clym was curious enough to advance a little further and look in at the window. To his astonishment there stood within the room Diggory Venn, no longer a reddleman, but exhibiting the strangely altered hues of an ordinary Christian countenance, white shirt-front, light flowered waistcoat, blue-spotted neckerchief, and bottle-green coat. Nothing in this appearance was at all singular but the fact of its great difference from what he had formerly been. Red, and all approach to red, was carefully excluded from every article of clothes upon him; for what is there that persons just out of harness dread so much as reminders of the trade which has enriched them?

Yeobright went round to the door and entered.

"I was so alarmed!" said Thomasin, smiling from one to the other. "I couldn't believe that he had got white of his own accord! It seemed supernatural."

"I gave up dealing in reddle last Christmas," said Venn. "It was a profitable trade, and I found that by that time I had made enough to take the dairy of fifty cows that my father had in his lifetime. I always thought of getting to that place again if I changed at all; and now I am there."

"How did you manage to become white, Diggory?" Thomasin asked.

"I turned so by degrees, ma'am."

"You look much better than ever you did before."

Venn appeared confused; and Thomasin, seeing how inadvertently she had spoken to a man who might possibly have tender feelings for her still, blushed a little. Clym saw nothing of this, and added good-humouredly —

"What shall we have to frighten Thomasin's baby with, now you have become a human being again?"

"Sit down, Diggory," said Thomasin, "and stay to tea."

Venn moved as if he would retire to the kitchen, when Thomasin said with pleasant pertness as she went on with some sewing, "Of course you must sit down here. And where does your fifty-cow dairy lie, Mr. Venn?"

"At Stickleford — about two miles to the right of Alderworth, ma'am, where the meads begin. I have thought that if Mr. Yeobright would like to pay me a visit sometimes he shouldn't stay away for want of asking. I'll not bide to tea this afternoon, thank'ee, for I've got something on hand that must be settled. 'Tis Maypole-day tomorrow, and the Shadwater folk have clubbed with a few of your neighbours here to have a pole just outside your palings in the heath, as it is a nice green place." Venn waved his elbow towards the patch in front of the house. "I have been talking to Fairway about it," he continued, "and I said to him that before we put up the pole it would be well to ask Mrs. Wildeve."

"I can say nothing against it," she answered. "Our property does not reach an inch further than the white palings."

"But you might not like to see a lot of folk going crazy round a stick, under your very nose?"

"I shall have no objection at all."

Venn soon after went away, and in the evening Yeobright strolled as far as Fairway's cottage. It was a lovely May sunset, and the birch trees which grew on this margin of the vast Egdon wilderness had put on their new leaves, delicate as butterflies' wings, and diaphanous as amber. Beside Fairway's dwelling was an open space recessed from the road, and here were now collected all the young people from within a radius of a couple of miles. The pole lay with one end supported on a trestle, and women were engaged in wreathing it from the top downwards with wild-flowers. The instincts of merry England lingered on here with exceptional vitality, and the symbolic customs which tradition has attached to each season of the year were yet a reality on Egdon. Indeed, the impulses of all such outlandish hamlets are pagan still: in these spots homage to nature, self-adoration, frantic gaieties, fragments of Teutonic rites to divinities whose names are forgotten, seem in some way or other to have survived mediæval doctrine.

Yeobright did not interrupt the preparations, and went home again. The next morning, when Thomasin withdrew the curtains of her bedroom window, there stood the Maypole in the middle of the green, its top cutting into the sky. It had sprung up in the night, or rather early morning, like Jack's bean-stalk. She opened the casement to get a better view of the garlands and posies that adorned it. The sweet perfume of the flowers had already spread into the surrounding air, which, being free from every taint, conducted to her lips a full measure of the fragrance received from the spire of blossom in its midst. At the top of the pole were crossed hoops decked with small flowers; beneath these came a milk-white zone of Maybloom; then a zone of bluebells, then of cowslips, then of lilacs, then of ragged-robins, daffodils, and so on, till the lowest stage was reached. Thomasin noticed all these, and was delighted that the May-revel was to be so near.

When afternoon came people began to gather on the green, and Yeobright was interested enough to look out upon them from the open window of his room. Soon after this Thomasin walked out from the door immediately below and turned her eyes up to her cousin's face. She was dressed more gaily than Yeobright had ever seen her dress since the time of Wildeve's death, eighteen months before; since the day of her marriage even she had not exhibited herself to such advantage.

"How pretty you look today, Thomasin!" he said. "Is it because of the Maypole?"

"Not altogether." And then she blushed and dropped her eyes, which he did not specially observe, though her manner seemed to him to be rather peculiar, considering that she was only addressing himself. Could it be possible that she had put on her summer clothes to please him?

He recalled her conduct towards him throughout the last few weeks, when they had often been working together in the garden, just as they had formerly done when they were boy and girl under his mother's eye. What if her interest in him were not so entirely that of a relative as it had formerly been? To Yeobright any possibility of this sort was a serious matter; and he almost felt troubled at the thought of it. Every pulse of loverlike feeling which had not been stilled during Eustacia's lifetime had gone into the grave with her. His passion for her had occurred too far on in his manhood to leave fuel enough on hand for another fire of that sort, as may happen with more boyish loves. Even supposing him capable of loving again, that love would be a plant of slow and laboured growth, and in the end only small and sickly, like an autumn-hatched bird.

He was so distressed by this new complexity that when the enthusiastic brass band arrived and struck up, which it did about five o'clock, with apparently wind enough among its members to blow down his house, he withdrew from his rooms by the back door, went down the garden, through the gate in the hedge, and away out of sight. He could not bear to remain in the presence of enjoyment today, though he had tried hard.

Nothing was seen of him for four hours. When he came back by the same path it was dusk, and the dews were coating every green thing. The boisterous music had ceased; but, entering the premises as he did from behind, he could not see if the May party had all gone till he had passed through Thomasin's division of the house to the front door. Thomasin was standing within the porch alone.

She looked at him reproachfully. "You went away just when it began, Clym," she said.

"Yes. I felt I could not join in. You went out with them, of course?"

"No, I did not."

"You appeared to be dressed on purpose."

"Yes, but I could not go out alone; so many people were there. One is there now."

Yeobright strained his eyes across the dark-green patch beyond the paling, and near the black form of the Maypole he discerned a shadowy figure, sauntering idly up and down. "Who is it?" he said.

"Mr. Venn," said Thomasin.

"You might have asked him to come in, I think, Tamsie. He has been very kind to you first and last."

"I will now," she said; and, acting on the impulse, went through the wicket to where Venn stood under the Maypole.

"It is Mr. Venn, I think?" she inquired.

Venn started as if he had not seen her — artful man that he was — and said, "Yes."

"Will you come in?"

"I am afraid that I ——"

"I have seen you dancing this evening, and you had the very best of the girls for your partners. Is it that you won't come in because you wish to stand here, and think over the past hours of enjoyment?"

"Well, that's partly it," said Mr. Venn, with ostentatious sentiment. "But the main reason why I am biding here like this is that I want to wait till the moon rises."

"To see how pretty the Maypole looks in the moonlight?"

"No. To look for a glove that was dropped by one of the maidens."

Thomasin was speechless with surprise. That a man who had to walk some four or five miles to his home should wait here for such a reason pointed to only one conclusion: the man must be amazingly interested in that glove's owner.

"Were you dancing with her, Diggory?" she asked, in a voice which revealed that he had made himself considerably more interesting to her by this disclosure.

"No," he sighed.

"And you will not come in, then?"

"Not tonight, thank you, ma'am."

"Shall I lend you a lantern to look for the young person's glove, Mr. Venn?"

"O no; it is not necessary, Mrs. Wildeve, thank you. The moon will rise in a few minutes."

Thomasin went back to the porch. "Is he coming in?" said Clym, who had been waiting where she had left him.

"He would rather not tonight," she said, and then passed by him into the house; whereupon Clym too retired to his own rooms.

When Clym was gone Thomasin crept upstairs in the dark, and, just listening by the cot, to assure herself that the child was asleep, she went to the window, gently lifted the corner of the white curtain, and looked out. Venn was still there. She watched the growth of the faint radiance appearing in the sky by the eastern hill, till presently the edge of the moon burst upwards and flooded the valley with light. Diggory's form was now distinct on the green; he was moving about in a bowed attitude, evidently scanning the grass for the precious missing article, walking in zigzags right and left till he should have passed over every foot of the ground.

"How very ridiculous!" Thomasin murmured to herself, in a tone which was intended to be satirical. "To think that a man should be so silly as to go mooning about like that for a girl's glove! A respectable dairyman, too, and a man of money as he is now. What a pity!"

At last Venn appeared to find it; whereupon he stood up and raised it to his lips. Then placing it in his breast-pocket — the nearest receptacle to a man's heart permitted by modern raiment — he ascended the valley in a mathematically direct line towards his distant home in the meadows.

II

THOMASIN WALKS IN A GREEN PLACE BY THE ROMAN ROAD

CLYM saw little of Thomasin for several days after this; and when they met she was more silent than usual. At length he asked her what she was thinking of so intently.

"I am thoroughly perplexed," she said candidly. "I cannot for my life think who it is that Diggory Venn is so much in love with. None of the girls at the Maypole were good enough for him, and yet she must have been there."

Clym tried to imagine Venn's choice for a moment; but ceasing to be interested in the question, he went on again with his gardening.

No clearing up of the mystery was granted her for some time. But one afternoon Thomasin was upstairs getting ready for a walk, when she had occasion to come to the landing and call "Rachel." Rachel was a girl about thirteen, who carried the baby out for airings; and she came upstairs at the call.

"Have you seen one of my last new gloves about the house, Rachel?" inquired Thomasin. "It is the fellow to this one."

Rachel did not reply.

"Why don't you answer?" said her mistress.

"I think it is lost, ma'am."

"Lost? Who lost it? I have never worn them but once."

Rachel appeared as one dreadfully troubled, and at last began to cry. "Please, ma'am, on the day of the Maypole I had none to wear, and I seed yours on the table, and I thought I would borrow 'em. I did not mean to hurt 'em at all, but one of them got lost. Somebody gave me some money to buy another pair for you, but I have not been able to go anywhere to get 'em."

"Who's somebody?"

"Mr. Venn."

"Did he know it was my glove?"

"Yes. I told him."

Thomasin was so surprised by the explanation that she quite forgot to lecture the girl, who glided silently away. Thomasin did not move further than to turn her eyes upon the grass-plat where the Maypole had stood. She remained thinking, then said to herself that she would not go out that afternoon, but would work hard at the baby's unfinished lovely plaid frock, cut on the cross in the newest fashion. How she managed to work hard, and yet do no more than she had done at the end of two hours, would have been a mystery to anyone not aware that the recent incident was of a kind likely to divert her industry from a manual to a mental channel.

Next day she went her ways as usual, and continued her custom of walking in the heath with no other companion than little Eustacia, now of the age when it is a matter of doubt with such characters whether they are intended to walk through the world on their hands or on their feet; so that they get into painful complications by trying both. It was very pleasant to Thomasin, when she had carried the child to some lonely place, to give her a little private practice on the green turf and shepherd's-thyme, which formed a soft mat to fall headlong upon when equilibrium was lost.

Once, when engaged in this system of training, and stooping to remove bits of stick, fern-stalks, and other such fragments from the child's path, that the journey might not be brought to an untimely end by some insuperable barrier a quarter of an inch high, she was alarmed by discovering that a man on horseback was almost close beside her, the soft natural carpet having muffled the horse's tread. The rider, who was Venn, waved his hat in the air and bowed gallantly.

"Diggory, give me my glove," said Thomasin, whose manner it was under any circumstances to plunge into the midst of a subject which engrossed her.

Venn immediately dismounted, put his hand in his breast-pocket, and handed the glove.

"Thank you. It was very good of you to take care of it."

"It is very good of you to say so."

"O no. I was quite glad to find you had it. Everybody gets so indifferent that I was surprised to know you thought of me."

"If you had remembered what I was once you wouldn't have been surprised."

"Ah, no," she said quickly. "But men of your character are mostly so independent."

"What is my character?" he asked.

"I don't exactly know," said Thomasin simply, "except it is to cover up your feelings under a practical manner, and only to show them when you are alone."

"Ah, how do you know that?" said Venn strategically.

"Because," said she, stopping to put the little girl, who had managed to get herself upside down, right end up again, "because I do."

"You mustn't judge by folks in general," said Venn. "Still I don't know much what feelings are now-a-days. I have got so mixed up with business of one sort and t'other that my soft sentiments are gone off in vapour like. Yes, I am given up body and soul to the making of money. Money is all my dream."

"O Diggory, how wicked!" said Thomasin reproachfully, and looking at him in exact balance between taking his words seriously and judging them as said to tease her.

"Yes, 'tis rather a rum course," said Venn, in the bland tone of one comfortably resigned to sins he could no longer overcome.

"You, who used to be so nice!"

"Well, that's an argument I rather like, because what a man has once been he may be again." Thomasin blushed. "Except that it is rather harder now," Venn continued.

"Why?" she asked.

"Because you be richer than you were at that time."

"O no — not much. I have made it nearly all over to the baby, as it was my duty to do, except just enough to live on."

"I am rather glad of that," said Venn softly, and regarding her from the corner of his eye, "for it makes it easier for us to be friendly."

Thomasin blushed again, and, when a few more words had been said of a not unpleasing kind, Venn mounted his horse and rode on.

This conversation had passed in a hollow of the heath near the old Roman road, a place much frequented by Thomasin. And it might have been observed that she did not in the future walk that way less often from having met Venn there now. Whether or not Venn abstained from riding thither because he had met Thomasin in the same place might easily have been guessed from her proceedings about two months later in the same year.

III

THE SERIOUS DISCOURSE OF CLYM WITH HIS COUSIN

THROUGHOUT this period Yeobright had more or less pondered on his duty to his cousin Thomasin. He could not help feeling that it would be a pitiful waste of sweet material if the tender-natured thing should be doomed from this early stage of her life onwards to dribble away her winsome qualities on lonely gorse and fern. But he felt this as an economist merely, and not as a lover. His passion for Eustacia had been a sort of conserve of his whole life, and he had nothing more of that supreme quality left to bestow. So far the obvious thing was not to entertain any idea of marriage with Thomasin, even to oblige her.

But this was not all. Years ago there had been in his mother's mind a great fancy about Thomasin and himself. It had not positively amounted to a desire, but it had always been a favourite dream. That they should be man and wife in good time, if the happiness of neither were endangered thereby, was the fancy in question. So that what course save one was there now left for any son who reverenced his mother's memory as Yeobright did? It is an unfortunate fact that any particular whim of parents, which might have been dispersed by half an hour's conversation during their lives, becomes sublimated by their deaths into a fiat the most absolute, with such results to conscientious children as those parents, had they lived, would have been the first to decry.

Had only Yeobright's own future been involved he would have proposed to Thomasin with a ready heart. He had nothing to lose by carrying out a dead mother's hope. But he dreaded to contemplate Thomasin wedded to the mere corpse of a lover that he now felt himself to be. He had but three activities alive in him. One was his almost daily walk to the little graveyard wherein his mother lay; another, his just as frequent visits by night to the more distant enclosure which numbered his Eustacia among its dead; the third was self preparation for a vocation which alone seemed likely to satisfy his cravings — that of an itinerant preacher of the eleventh commandment. It was difficult to believe that Thomasin would be cheered by a husband with such tendencies as these.

Yet he resolved to ask her, and let her decide for herself. It was even with a pleasant sense of doing his duty that he went downstairs to her one evening for this purpose, when the sun was sending up the valley the same long shadow of the housetop that he had seen lying there times out of number while his mother lived.

Thomasin was not in her room, and he found her in the front garden. "I have long been wanting, Thomasin," he began, "to say something about a matter that concerns both our futures."

"And you are going to say it now?" she remarked quickly, colouring as she met his gaze. "Do stop a minute, Clym, and let me speak first, for, oddly enough, I have been wanting to say something to you."

"By all means say on, Tamsie."

"I suppose nobody can overhear us?" she went on, casting her eyes around and lowering her voice. "Well, first you will promise me this — that you won't be angry and call me anything harsh if you disagree with what I propose?"

Yeobright promised, and she continued: "What I want is your advice, for you are my relation — I mean, a sort of guardian to me — aren't you, Clym?"

"Well, yes, I suppose I am; a sort of guardian. In fact, I am, of course," he said, altogether perplexed as to her drift.

"I am thinking of marrying," she then observed blandly. "But I shall not marry unless you assure me that you approve of such a step. Why don't you speak?"

"I was taken rather by surprise. But, nevertheless, I am very glad to hear such news. I shall approve, of course, dear Tamsie. Who can it be? I am quite at a loss to guess. No, I am not — 'tis the old doctor! — not that I mean to call him old, for he is not very old after all. Ah — I noticed when he attended you last time!"

"No, no," she said hastily. "'Tis Mr. Venn."

Clym's face suddenly became grave.

"There, now, you don't like him, and I wish I hadn't mentioned him!" she exclaimed almost petulantly. "And I shouldn't have done it, either, only he keeps bothering me so till I don't know what to do!"

Clym looked out of the window. "I like Venn well enough," he answered at last. "He is a very honest and at the same time astute man. He is clever too, as is proved by his having got you to favour him. But really, Thomasin, he is not quite ——"

"Gentleman enough for me? That is just what I feel. I am sorry now that I asked you, and I won't think any more of him. At the same time I must marry him if I marry anybody — that I *will* say!"

"I don't see that," said Clym, carefully concealing every clue to his own interrupted intention, which she plainly had not guessed. "You might marry a professional man, or somebody of that sort, by going into the town to live and forming acquaintances there."

"I am not fit for town life — so very rural and silly as I always have been. Do not you yourself notice my countrified ways?"

"Well, when I came home from Paris I did, a little; but I don't now."

"That's because you have got countrified too. O, I couldn't live in a street for the world! Egdon is a ridiculous old place; but I have got used to it, and I couldn't be happy anywhere else at all."

"Neither could I," said Clym.

"Then how could you say that I should marry some town man? I am sure, say what you will, that I must marry Diggory, if I marry at all. He has been kinder to me than anybody else, and has helped me in many ways that I don't know of!" Thomasin almost pouted now.

"Yes, he has," said Clym in a neutral tone. "Well, I wish with all my heart that I could say, marry him. But I cannot forget what my mother thought on that matter, and it goes rather against me not to respect her opinion. There is too much reason why we should do the little we can to respect it now."

"Very well, then," sighed Thomasin. "I will say no more."

"But you are not bound to obey my wishes. I merely say what I think."

"O no — I don't want to be rebellious in that way," she said sadly. "I had no business to think of him — I ought to have thought of my family. What dreadfully bad impulses there are in me!" Her lip trembled, and she turned away to hide a tear.

Clym, though vexed at what seemed her unaccountable taste, was in a measure relieved to find that at any rate the marriage question in relation to himself was shelved. Through several succeeding days he saw her at different times from the window of his room moping disconsolately about the garden. He was half angry with her for choosing Venn; then he was grieved at having put himself in the way of Venn's happiness, who was, after all, as honest and persevering a young fellow as any on Egdon, since he had turned over a new leaf. In short, Clym did not know what to do.

When next they met she said abruptly, "He is much more respectable now than he was then!"

"Who? O yes — Diggory Venn."

"Aunt only objected because he was a reddleman."

"Well, Thomasin, perhaps I don't know all the particulars of my mother's wish. So you had better use your own discretion."

"You will always feel that I slighted your mother's memory."

"No, I will not. I shall think you are convinced that, had she seen Diggory in his present position, she would have considered him a fitting husband for you. Now, that's my real feeling. Don't consult me any more, but do as you like, Thomasin. I shall be content."

It is to be supposed that Thomasin was convinced; for a few days after this, when Clym strayed into a part of the heath that he had not lately visited, Humphrey, who was at work there, said to him, "I am glad to see that Mrs. Wildeve and Venn have made it up again, seemingly."

"Have they?" said Clym abstractedly.

"Yes; and he do contrive to stumble upon her whenever she walks out on fine days with the chiel. But, Mr. Yeobright, I can't help feeling that your cousin ought to have married you. 'Tis a pity to make two chimley-corners where there need be only one. You could get her away from him now, 'tis my belief, if you were only to set about it."

"How can I have the conscience to marry after having driven two women to their deaths? Don't think such a thing, Humphrey. After my experience I should consider it too much of a burlesque to go to church and take a wife. In the words of Job, 'I have made a covenant with mine eyes; why then should I think upon a maid?'"

"No, Mr. Clym, don't fancy that about driving two women to their deaths. You shouldn't say it."

"Well, we'll leave that out," said Yeobright. "But anyhow the times have set a mark upon me which wouldn't look well in a love-making scene. I have two ideas in my head, and no others. I am going to keep a night-school; and I am going to turn preacher. What have you got to say to that, Humphrey?"

"I'll come and hear ye with all my heart."

"Thanks. 'Tis all I wish."

As Clym descended into the valley Thomasin came down by the other path, and met him at the gate. "What do you think I have to tell you, Clym?" she said, looking archly over her shoulder at him.

"I can guess," he replied.

She scrutinized his face. "Yes, you guess right. It is going to be after all. He thinks I may as well make up my mind, and I have got to think so too. It is to be on the twenty-fifth of next month, if you don't object."

"Do what you think right, dear. I am only too glad that you see your way clear to happiness again. My sex owes you every amends for the treatment you received in days gone by."

IV

CHEERFULNESS AGAIN ASSERTS ITSELF AT BLOOMS-END, AND CLYM FINDS HIS VOCATION

ANYBODY who had passed through Blooms-End about eleven o'clock on the morning fixed for the wedding would have found that, while Yeobright's house was comparatively quiet, sounds denoting great activity came from the dwelling of his nearest neighbour, Timothy Fairway. It was chiefly a noise of feet, briskly crunching hither and thither over the sanded floor within. One man only was visible outside, and he seemed to be later at an appointment than he had intended to be, for he hastened up to the door, lifted the latch, and walked in without ceremony.

The scene within was not quite the customary one. Standing about the room was the little knot of men who formed the chief part of the Egdon coterie, there being present Fairway himself, Grandfer Cantle, Humphrey, Christian, and one or two turf-cutters. It was a warm day, and the men were as a matter of course in their shirt-sleeves, except Christian, who had always a nervous fear of parting with a scrap of his clothing when in anybody's house but his own. Across the stout oak table in the middle of the room was thrown a mass of striped linen, which Grandfer Cantle held down on one side, and Humphrey on the other, while Fairway rubbed its surface with a yellow lump, his face being damp and creased with the effort of the labour.

"Waxing a bed-tick, souls?" said the new-comer.

"Yes, Sam," said Grandfer Cantle, as a man too busy to waste words. "Shall I stretch this corner a shade tighter, Timothy?"

Fairway replied, and the waxing went on with unabated vigour. "'Tis going to be a good bed, by the look o't," continued Sam, after an interval of silence. "Who may it be for?"

"'Tis a present for the new folks that's going to set up housekeeping," said Christian, who stood helpless and overcome by the majesty of the proceedings.

"Ah, to be sure; and a valuable one, 'a b'lieve."

"Beds be dear to fokes that don't keep geese, bain't they, Mister Fairway?" said Christian, as to an omniscient being.

"Yes," said the furze-dealer, standing up, giving his forehead a thorough mopping, and handing the beeswax to Humphrey, who succeeded at the rubbing forthwith. "Not that this couple be in want of one, but 'twas well to show 'em a bit of friendliness at this great racketing vagary of their lives. I set up both my own daughters in one when they was married, and there have been feathers enough for another in the house the last twelve months. Now then, neighbours, I think we have laid on enough wax. Grandfer Cantle, you turn the tick the right way outwards, and then I'll begin to shake in the feathers."

When the bed was in proper trim Fairway and Christian brought forward vast paper bags, stuffed to the full, but light as balloons, and began to turn the contents of each into the receptacle just prepared. As bag after bag was emptied, airy tufts of down and feathers floated about the room in increasing quantity till, through a mishap of Christian's, who shook the contents of one bag outside the tick, the atmosphere of the room became dense with gigantic flakes, which descended upon the workers like a windless snowstorm.

"I never saw such a clumsy chap as you, Christian," said Grandfer Cantle severely. "You might have been the son of a man that's never been outside Blooms-End in his life for all the wit you have. Really all the soldiering and smartness in the world in the father seems to count for nothing in forming the nater of the son. As far as that chiel Christian is concerned I might as well have stayed at home and seed nothing, like all the rest of ye here. Though, as far as myself is concerned, a dashing spirit has counted for sommat, to be sure!"

"Don't ye let me down so, father; I feel no bigger than a ninepin after it. I've made but a bruckle hit, I'm afeard."

"Come, come. Never pitch yerself in such a low key as that, Christian; you should try more," said Fairway.

"Yes, you should try more," echoed the Grandfer with insistence, as if he had been the first to make the suggestion. "In common conscience every man ought either to marry or go for a soldier. 'Tis a scandal to the nation to do neither one nor t'other. I did both, thank God! Neither to raise men nor to lay 'em low — that shows a poor do-nothing spirit indeed."

"I never had the nerve to stand fire," faltered Christian. "But as to marrying, I own I've asked here and there, though without much fruit from it. Yes, there's some house or other that might have had a man for a master — such as he is — that's now ruled by a woman alone. Still it might have been awkward if I had found her; for, d'ye see, neighbours, there'd have been nobody left at home to keep down father's spirits to the decent pitch that becomes a old man."

"And you've your work cut out to do that, my son," said Grandfer Cantle smartly. "I wish that the dread of infirmities was not so strong in me! — I'd start the very first thing tomorrow to see the world over again! But seventy-one, though nothing at home, is a high figure for a rover.... Ay, seventy-one last Candlemas-day. Gad, I'd sooner have it in guineas than in years!" And the old man sighed.

"Don't you be mournful, Grandfer," said Fairway. "Empt some more feathers into the bed-tick, and keep up yer heart. Though rather lean in the stalks you be a green-leaved old man still. There's time enough left to ye to fill whole chronicles."

"Begad, I'll go to 'em, Timothy — to the married pair!" said Grandfer Cantle in an encouraged voice, and starting round briskly. "I'll go to 'em tonight and sing a wedding song, hey? 'Tis like me to do so, you know; and they'd see it as such. My 'Down in Cupid's Gardens' was well liked in four; still, I've got others as good, and even better. What do you say to my

> 'She cal'-led to' her love'
> From the lat'-tice a-bove,
> "O, come in' from the fog'-gy fog'-gy dew'."'

'Twould please 'em well at such a time! Really, now I come to think of it, I haven't turned my tongue in my head to the shape of a real good song since Old Midsummer night, when we had the 'Barley Mow' at the Woman; and 'tis a pity to neglect your strong point where there's few that have the compass for such things!"

"So 'tis, so 'tis," said Fairway. "Now gie the bed a shake down. We've put in seventy pound of best feathers, and I think that's as many as the tick will fairly hold. A bit and a drap wouldn't be amiss now, I reckon. Christian, maul down the victuals from corner cupboard if canst reach, man, and I'll draw a drap o' sommat to wet it with."

They sat down to a lunch in the midst of their work, feathers around, above, and below them; the original owners of which occasionally came to the open door and cackled begrudgingly at sight of such a quantity of their old clothes.

"Upon my soul I shall be chokt," said Fairway when, having extracted a feather from his mouth, he found several others floating on the mug as it was handed round.

"I've swallered several; and one had a tolerable quill," said Sam placidly from the corner.

"Hullo — what's that — wheels I hear coming?" Grandfer Cantle exclaimed, jumping up and hastening to the door. "Why, 'tis they back again:

I didn't expect 'em yet this half-hour. To be sure, how quick marrying can
be done when you are in the mind for't!"

"O yes, it can soon be *done*," said Fairway, as if something should be added
to make the statement complete.

He arose and followed the Grandfer, and the rest also went to the door.
In a moment an open fly was driven past, in which sat Venn and Mrs. Venn,
Yeobright, and a grand relative of Venn's who had come from Budmouth
for the occasion. The fly had been hired at the nearest town, regardless of
distance and cost, there being nothing on Egdon Heath, in Venn's opinion,
dignified enough for such an event when such a woman as Thomasin was the
bride; and the church was too remote for a walking bridal-party.

As the fly passed the group which had run out from the homestead they
shouted "Hurrah!" and waved their hands; feathers and down floating from
their hair, their sleeves, and the folds of their garments at every motion,
and Grandfer Cantle's seals dancing merrily in the sunlight as he twirled himself
about. The driver of the fly turned a supercilious gaze upon them; he even
treated the wedded pair themselves with something of condescension; for in
what other state than heathen could people, rich or poor, exist who were
doomed to abide in such a world's end as Egdon? Thomasin showed no
such superiority to the group at the door, fluttering her hand as quickly as
a bird's wing towards them, and asking Diggory, with tears in her eyes, if
they ought not to alight and speak to these kind neighbours. Venn, however,
suggested that, as they were all coming to the house in the evening, this was
hardly necessary.

After this excitement the saluting party returned to their occupation, and
the stuffing and sewing was soon afterwards finished, when Fairway harnessed
a horse, wrapped up the cumbrous present, and drove off with it in the cart
to Venn's house at Stickleford.

Yeobright, having filled the office at the wedding-service which naturally
fell to his hands, and afterwards returned to the house with the husband and
wife, was indisposed to take part in the feasting and dancing that wound up
the evening. Thomasin was disappointed.

"I wish I could be there without dashing your spirits," he said. "But I
might be too much like the skull at the banquet."

"No, no."

"Well, dear, apart from that, if you would excuse me, I should be glad. I
know it seems unkind; but, dear Thomasin, I fear I should not be happy in
the company — there, that's the truth of it. I shall always be coming to
see you at your new home, you know, so that my absence now will not much
matter."

"Then I give in. Do whatever will be most comfortable to yourself."

Clym retired to his lodging at the housetop much relieved, and occupied
himself during the afternoon in noting down the heads of a sermon, with
which he intended to initiate all that really seemed practicable of the scheme
that had originally brought him hither, and that he had so long kept in view
under various modifications, and through evil and good report. He had

tested and weighed his convictions again and again, and saw no reason to alter them, though he had considerably lessened his plan. His eyesight, by long humouring in his native air, had grown stronger, but not sufficiently strong to warrant his attempting his extensive educational project. Yet he did not repine: there was still more than enough of an unambitious sort to tax all his energies and occupy all his hours.

Evening drew on, and sounds of life and movement in the lower part of the domicile became more pronounced, the gate in the palings clicking incessantly. The party was to be an early one, and all the guests were assembled long before it was dark. Yeobright went down the back staircase and into the heath by another path than that in front, intending to walk in the open air till the party was over, when he would return to wish Thomasin and her husband good-bye as they departed. His steps were insensibly bent towards Mistover by the path that he had followed on that terrible morning when he learnt the strange news from Susan's boy.

He did not turn aside to the cottage, but pushed on to an eminence, whence he could see over the whole quarter that had once been Eustacia's home. While he stood observing the darkening scene somebody came up. Clym, seeing him but dimly, would have let him pass by silently, had not the pedestrian, who was Charley, recognized the young man and spoken to him.

"Charley, I have not seen you for a length of time," said Yeobright. "Do you often walk this way?"

"No," the lad replied. "I don't often come outside the bank."

"You were not at the Maypole."

"No," said Charley, in the same listless tone. "I don't care for that sort of thing now."

"You rather liked Miss Eustacia, didn't you?" Yeobright gently asked. Eustacia had frequently told him of Charley's romantic attachment.

"Yes, very much. Ah, I wish ——"

"Yes?"

"I wish, Mr. Yeobright, you could give me something to keep that once belonged to her — if you don't mind."

"I shall be very happy to. It will give me very great pleasure, Charley. Let me think what I have of hers that you would like. But come with me to the house, and I'll see."

They walked towards Blooms-End together. When they reached the front it was dark, and the shutters were closed, so that nothing of the interior could be seen.

"Come round this way," said Clym. "My entrance is at the back for the present."

The two went round and ascended the crooked stair in darkness till Clym's sitting-room on the upper floor was reached, where he lit a candle, Charley entering gently behind. Yeobright searched his desk, and taking out a sheet of tissue-paper unfolded from it two or three undulating locks of raven hair, which fell over the paper like black streams. From these he selected one, wrapped it up, and gave it to the lad, whose eyes had filled with tears.

He kissed the packet, put it in his pocket, and said in a voice of emotion, "O, Mr. Clym, how good you are to me!"

"I will go a little way with you," said Clym. And amid the noise of merriment from below they descended. Their path to the front led them close to a little side-window, whence the rays of candles streamed across the shrubs. The window, being screened from general observation by the bushes, had been left unblinded, so that a person in this private nook could see all that was going on within the room which contained the wedding-guests, except in so far as vision was hindered by the green antiquity of the panes.

"Charley, what are they doing?" said Clym. "My sight is weaker again tonight, and the glass of this window is not good."

Charley wiped his own eyes, which were rather blurred with moisture, and stepped closer to the casement. "Mr. Venn is asking Christian Cantle to sing," he replied; "and Christian is moving about in his chair as if he were much frightened at the question, and his father has struck up a stave instead of him."

"Yes, I can hear the old man's voice," said Clym. "So there's to be no dancing, I suppose. And is Thomasin in the room? I see something moving in front of the candles that resembles her shape, I think."

"Yes. She do seem happy. She is red in the face, and laughing at something Fairway has said to her. O my!"

"What noise was that?" said Clym.

"Mr. Venn is so tall that he has knocked his head against the beam in gieing a skip as he passed under. Mrs. Venn hev run up quite frightened and now she's put her hand to his head to feel if there's a lump. And now they be all laughing again as if nothing had happened."

"Do any of them seem to care about my not being there?" Clym asked.

"No, not a bit in the world. Now they are all holding up their glasses and drinking somebody's health."

"I wonder if it is mine?"

"No, 'tis Mr. and Mrs. Venn's, because he is making a hearty sort of speech. There — now Mrs. Venn has got up, and is going away to put on her things, I think."

"Well, they haven't concerned themselves about me, and it is quite right they should not. It is all as it should be, and Thomasin at least is happy. We will not stay any longer now, as they will soon be coming out to go home."

He accompanied the lad into the heath on his way home, and, returning alone to the house a quarter of an hour later, found Venn and Thomasin ready to start, all the guests having departed in his absence. The wedded pair took their seats in the four-wheeled dog-cart which Venn's head milker and handy man had driven from Stickleford to fetch them in; little Eustacia and the nurse were packed securely upon the open flap behind; and the milker, on an ancient overstepping pony, whose shoes clashed like cymbals at every tread, rode in the rear, in the manner of a body-servant of the last century.

"Now we leave you in absolute possession of your own house again," said

Thomasin as she bent down to wish her cousin good-night. "It will be rather lonely for you, Clym, after the hubbub we have been making."

"O, that's no inconvenience," said Clym, smiling rather sadly. And then the party drove off and vanished in the night-shades, and Yeobright entered the house. The ticking of the clock was the only sound that greeted him, for not a soul remained; Christian, who acted as cook, valet, and gardener to Clym, sleeping at his father's house. Yeobright sat down in one of the vacant chairs, and remained in thought a long time. His mother's old chair was opposite; it had been sat in that evening by those who had scarcely remembered that it ever was hers. But to Clym she was almost a presence there, now as always. Whatever she was in other people's memories, in his she was the sublime saint whose radiance even his tenderness for Eustacia could not obscure. But his heart was heavy; that mother had *not* crowned him in the day of his espousals and in the day of the gladness of his heart. And events had borne out the accuracy of her judgment, and proved the devotedness of her care. He should have heeded her for Eustacia's sake even more than for his own. "It was all my fault," he whispered. "O, my mother, my mother! would to God that I could live my life again, and endure for you what you endured for me!"

On the Sunday after this wedding an unusual sight was to be seen on Rainbarrow. From a distance there simply appeared to be a motionless figure standing on the top of the tumulus, just as Eustacia had stood on that lonely summit some two years and a half before. But now it was fine warm weather, with only a summer breeze blowing, and early afternoon instead of dull twilight. Those who ascended to the immediate neighbourhood of the Barrow perceived that the erect form in the centre, piercing the sky, was not really alone. Round him upon the slopes of the Barrow a number of heathmen and women were reclining or sitting at their ease. They listened to the words of the man in their midst, who was preaching, while they abstractedly pulled heather, stripped ferns, or tossed pebbles down the slope. This was the first of a series of moral lectures or Sermons on the Mount, which were to be delivered from the same place every Sunday afternoon as long as the fine weather lasted.

The commanding elevation of Rainbarrow had been chosen for two reasons: first, that it occupied a central position among the remote cottages around; secondly, that the preacher thereon could be seen from all adjacent points as soon as he arrived at his post, the view of him being thus a convenient signal to those stragglers who wished to draw near. The speaker was bareheaded, and the breeze at each waft gently lifted and lowered his hair, somewhat too thin for a man of his years, these still numbering less than thirty-three. He wore a shade over his eyes, and his face was pensive and lined; but, though these bodily features were marked with decay there was no defect in the tones of his voice, which were rich, musical, and stirring. He stated that his discourses to people were to be sometimes secular, and sometimes religious, but never dogmatic; and that his texts would be taken from all kinds of books. This afternoon the words were as follows:

"'And the king rose up to meet her, and bowed himself unto her, and sat down on his throne, and caused a seat to be set for the king's mother; and she sat on his right hand. Then she said, I desire one small petition of thee; I pray thee say me not nay. And the king said unto her, Ask on, my mother: for I will not say thee nay.'"

Yeobright had, in fact, found his vocation in the career of an itinerant open-air preacher and lecturer on morally unimpeachable subjects; and from this day he laboured incessantly in that office, speaking not only in simple language on Rainbarrow and in the hamlets round, but in a more cultivated strain elsewhere — from the steps and porticoes of town-halls, from market-crosses, from conduits, on esplanades and on wharves, from the parapets of bridges, in barns and outhouses, and all other such places in the neighbouring Wessex towns and villages. He left alone creeds and systems of philosophy, finding enough and more than enough to occupy his tongue in the opinions and actions common to all good men. Some believed him, and some believed not; some said that his words were commonplace, others complained of his want of theological doctrine; while others again remarked that it was well enough for a man to take to preaching who could not see to do anything else. But everywhere he was kindly received, for the story of his life had become generally known.

POETRY

PART FOUR

POETRY

FOREWORD

POETRY, among the varieties of literature, has always put forth the highest claims, not only on the respect of its readers, but on their understanding. And in spite of the supposed indifference or hostility of readers, poets in all ages have succeeded in making the deepest impression upon man, arousing his profoundest passion and sympathies, or stimulating his highest thought. In doing either of these things they have added to man's pleasure, for "if the prospect of delight be wanting, which alone justifies the perusal of poetry," the work of the poet is vain.

"Poetry is the most philosophic of all writing.... Poetry is the image of man and nature.... Poetry is the breath and finer spirit of all knowledge.... The Poet binds together by passion and knowledge the vast empire of human society, as it is spread over the whole earth, and over all time." These statements by Wordsworth are no doubt extravagant, but they are characteristic of what poets in all ages have asserted. The age-long attempt to make a fixed and universal definition of poetry usually ends in assertions of this kind, and whatever their broadness or pretension, it is difficult to refute them. But not all apologists have tried, like Wordsworth, to express the poet's mission in the world in terms of his responsibility toward common humanity: The Poet, he said, "is a man speaking to men.... The Poet writes under one restriction only, namely, the necessity of giving immediate pleasure to a human Being possessed of that information which may be expected from him, not as a lawyer, a physician, an astronomer, or a natural philosopher, but as a Man." It is to poets therefore that men have gone in all ages to hear those truths and prophecies that concern their common destiny — their most fundamental needs of mind and spirit, the hopes, purposes, sorrows, braveries, and despairs that lie at the center of existence and demand a hearing there.

Men have never been essentially troubled — in the way the modern reader often feels obliged to be troubled — in recognizing true poetry for what it is, in spite of the prejudices and suspicions that have often hindered that recognition. For just as poetry has always served an irresistible human need, so it has always used a language whose power, richness, and appeal cannot be denied. "Poetry is a language that tells us, through a more or less emotional reaction, something that cannot be said," said one of the foremost modern American poets, Edwin Arlington Robinson, "and it seems to me that poetry has two outstanding characteristics: One is that it is, after all, undefinable. The other is that it is unmistakable."

Poetry's meaning may be undefinable, but that will never discourage poets and readers from attempting to define it according to their personal lights or natures. Poetry's uses may be equally elusive, but that will never curtail the countless employments to which it is put — from expressing a nation's heroic ideals in an epic or battle-song to riming the rules of spelling; from celebrating the wars of Troy or the death of Cleopatra to hymning the murder of a field-mouse or the withering of a hedge-rose; from building a philosophic system to dramatizing the humblest human occupations and ordeals. "Poets are the trumpets that sing to battle; poets are the unacknowledged legislators of the world," said Shelley, describing the poet in his highest and most exalted position among men. But Shakespeare was thinking of the poet in his more impractical and generally condemned character when he assigned him a subtler but perhaps an even greater duty:

> The poet's eye, in a fine frenzy rolling,
> Doth glance from heaven to earth, from earth to heaven;
> And, as imagination bodies forth
> The forms of things unknown, the poet's pen
> Turns them to shapes, and gives to airy nothing
> A local habitation and a name.

The four divisions into which the following anthology of poems is divided show the different uses that poetry serves. The first section of *Poems of Narrative and Situation* begins with primitive folk-ballads, and continues, in the tradition of those ballads, down to narrative and dramatic poems of our own day, thus representing the continuity and popularity of one of the simplest and most candid types of literary art. The second section, *Poems of Human Character*, shows the poet defining the traits of his fellow-men, celebrating their virtues, analyzing their defects and failings, throwing into dramatic relief their acts, sorrows, and achievements. The third section, *Lyrics of Emotion and Experience*, shows poetry growing out of the contacts and ordeals of life, marking its delights or signalizing its griefs, perpetuating in the language of song the pathos or the triumph of human destinies. The fourth section, *Lyrics of Reflection*, finds the poet escaping from the limiting and conditioning facts of experience into the spacious liberties of high thought or imagination. Here poetry ceases to be "the opening and closing of a door," which one American poet, Carl Sandburg, has called it, "leaving those who look through to guess about what is seen during a moment." It becomes, in another of his definitions, "a series of explanations of life, fading off into horizons too swift for explanations."

POEMS OF NARRATIVE AND SITUATION

SIR PATRICK SPENS *

The king sits in Dumferling toun,
  Drinking the blude-reid wine:
"O whar will I get a guid sailor,
  To sail this ship of mine?"

Up and spak an eldern knicht,   5
  Sat at the king's richt knee:
"Sir Patrick Spens is the best sailor
  That sails upon the sea."

The king has written a braid letter,
  And signed it with his hand,   10
And sent it to Sir Patrick Spens,
  Was walking on the sand.

The first line that Sir Patrick read,
  A loud laugh laughed he;
The next line that Sir Patrick read,
  The teir blinded his ee.   15

"O wha is this has done this deed,
  This ill deed don to me,
To send me out this time o' the year,
  To sail upon the sea! "   20

"Mak haste, mak haste, my mirry
    men all,
  Our good ship sails the morne":
"O say not sae, my master deir,
  For I feir a deadlie storm.

"Late late yestreen I saw the new
    moon,   25
  Wi the auld moon in her arm,
And I feir, I feir, my deir master,
  That we will come to harm."

9 braid: broad.   29 laith: loath.

* See p. 1059 for discussion.

O our Scots nobles wer richt laith
  To weet their cork-heild schoon; 30
But lang owre a' the play were
    played,
  Their hats they swam aboone.

O lang, lang may their ladies sit,
  Wi their fans into their hand,
Or e'er they see Sir Patrick Spens 35
  Come sailing to the land.

O lang, lang may the ladies stand,
  Wi their gold kems in their hair,
Waiting for their ain deir lords,
  For they'll see them na mair.   40

Half owre, half owre to Aberdour,
  It's fifty fathom deip,
And there lies guid Sir Patrick Spens,
  Wi the Scots lords at his feet.

ANNAN WATER †

"Annan Water's wading deep,
  And my love Annie's wondrous
    bonny;
And I am loath she shall wet her feet,
  Because I love her best of ony."

He's loupen on his bonny gray,   5
  He rode the right gate and the
    ready;
For all the storm he wadna stay,
  For seeking of his bonny lady.

And he has ridden o'er field and fell,
  Through moor, and moss, and
    many a mire;   10

31 owre: before.   38 kems: combs.

† See p. 1059 for discussion.

His spurs of steel were sair to bide,
And from her four feet flew the
fire.

"My bonny gray, now play your
part!
If ye be the steed that wins my
dearie,   14
With corn and hay ye'll feed for aye,
And never spur shall make you
wearie!"

The gray was a mare, and a right
gude mare;
But when she wan the Annan
Water,
She could not have ridden the ford
that night
Had a thousand merks been
wadded at her.   20

"O boatman, boatman, put off your
boat,
Put off your boat for golden
money!"
But for all the gold in fair Scotland,
He dared not take him through to
Annie.

"O I was sworn so late yestreen,   25
Not by a single oath, but mony!
I'll cross the drumly stream tonight,
Or never could I face my honey!"

The side was stey, and the bottom
deep,
From bank to brae the water
pouring;   30
The bonny gray mare she swat for
fear,
For she heard the water-kelpy
roaring.

He spurr'd her forth into the flood,
I wot she swam both strong and
steady;

²⁰ wadded: wagered.   ²⁷ drumly: turbid.

But the stream was broad, and her
strength did fail,   35
And he never saw his bonny lady!

JOCK OF HAZELDEAN

SIR WALTER SCOTT *

"Why weep ye by the tide, ladie?
Why weep ye by the tide?
I'll wed ye to my youngest son,
And ye sall be his bride:
And ye sall be his bride, ladie,   5
Sae comely to be seen" —
But aye she loot the tears down fa'
For Jock of Hazeldean.

"Now let this wilfu' grief be done,
And dry that cheek so pale;   10
Young Frank is chief of Errington,
And lord of Langley-dale;
His step is first in peaceful ha',
His sword in battle keen" —
But aye she loot the tears down fa' 15
For Jock of Hazeldean.

"A chain of gold ye sall not lack,
Nor braid to bind your hair;
Nor mettled hound, nor managed
hawk,
Nor palfrey fresh and fair;   20
And you, the foremost o' them a',
Shall ride our forest queen" —
But aye she loot the tears down fa'
For Jock of Hazeldean.

The kirk was deck'd at morning-tide,
The tapers glimmer'd fair;   26
The priest and bridegroom wait the
bride,
And dame and knight were there.
They sought her baith by bower and
ha';
The ladie was not seen!   30
She's o'er the Border, and awa'
Wi' Jock of Hazeldean.

¹⁹ managed: trained.   ²⁹ ha': hall.
* See p. 1059 for discussion.

KUBLA KHAN*

SAMUEL TAYLOR COLERIDGE

In Xanadu did Kubla Khan
A stately pleasure-dome decree:
Where Alph, the sacred river, ran
Through caverns measureless to man
  Down to a sunless sea.   5
So twice five miles of fertile ground
With walls and towers were girdled round:
And here were gardens bright with sinuous rills,
Where blossomed many an incense-bearing tree;
And here were forests ancient as the hills,   10
Enfolding sunny spots of greenery.

But oh! that deep, romantic chasm which slanted
Down the green hill athwart a cedarn cover!
A savage place! as holy and enchanted
As e'er beneath a waning moon was haunted   15
By woman wailing for her demon-lover!
And from this chasm, with ceaseless turmoil seething,
As if this earth in fast thick pants were breathing,
A mighty fountain momently was forced:
Amid whose swift half-intermitted burst   20
Huge fragments vaulted like rebounding hail,
Or chaffy grain beneath the thresher's flail:
And 'mid these dancing rocks at once and ever
It flung up momently the sacred river.
Five miles meandering with a mazy motion   25
Through wood and dale the sacred river ran,
Then reached the caverns measureless to man,
And sank in tumult to a lifeless ocean:
And 'mid this tumult Kubla heard from far
Ancestral voices prophesying war!   30

The shadow of the dome of pleasure
Floated midway on the waves;
Where was heard the mingled measure
From the fountain and the caves.
It was a miracle of rare device,   35
A sunny pleasure-dome with caves of ice!

A damsel with a dulcimer
In a vision once I saw:
It was an Abyssinian maid,
And on her dulcimer she played,   40

* See p. 1059 for discussion.

Singing of Mount Abora.
Could I revive with me
Her symphony and song,
To such a deep delight 'twould win me,
That with music loud and long,   45
I would build that dome in air,
That sunny dome! those caves of ice!
And all who heard should see them there.
And all should cry, Beware! Beware!
His flashing eyes, his floating hair!   50
Weave a circle round him thrice,
And close your eyes with holy dread,
For he on honey-dew hath fed,
And drunk the milk of Paradise.

LA BELLE DAME SANS MERCI

JOHN KEATS *

I

Ah, what can ail thee, wretched
    wight,
    Alone and palely loitering?
The sedge is wither'd from the lake,
    And no birds sing.

II

Ah, what can ail thee, wretched
    wight,   5
    So haggard and so woe-begone?
The squirrel's granary is full,
    And the harvest's done.

III

I see a lily on thy brow,
    With anguish moist and fever
    dew;   10
And on thy cheek a fading rose
    Fast withereth too.

IV

I met a lady in the meads,
    Full beautiful — a faery's child;

Her hair was long, her foot was light,
    And her eyes were wild.   16

V

I made a garland for her head,
    And bracelets too, and fragrant
    zone;
She look'd at me as she did love,
    And made sweet moan.   20

VI

I set her on my pacing steed,
    And nothing else saw all day long,
For sideways would she lean, and sing
    A faery's song.

VII

She found me roots of relish sweet, 25
    And honey wild, and manna dew;
And sure in language strange she
    said —
    "I love thee true."

VIII

She took me to her elfin grot,
    And there she gazed, and sighed
    full sore,   30
And there I shut her wild wild eyes
    With kisses four.

* See p. 1060 for discussion.

IX

And there she lullèd me asleep,
  And there I dream'd — Ah! woe
    betide!
The latest dream I ever dream'd 35
  On the cold hill's side.

X

I saw pale kings, and princes too,
  Pale warriors, death-pale were
    they all;
They cried — "La Belle Dame sans
    Merci
  Hath thee in thrall!" 40

XI

I saw their starved lips in the gloam,
  With horrid warning gapèd wide,
And I awoke, and found me here
  On the cold hill's side.

XII

And this is why I sojourn here, 45
  Alone and palely loitering,
Though the sedge is wither'd from
    the lake,
  And no birds sing.

THE PATRIOT
AN OLD STORY

ROBERT BROWNING *

I

It was roses, roses, all the way,
  With myrtle mixed in my path
    like mad:
The house-roofs seemed to heave and
    sway,
  The church-spires flamed, such
    flags they had,
A year ago on this very day!

II

The air broke into a mist with bells,
  The old walls rocked with the
    crowd and cries.

* See p. 1061 for discussion.

Had I said, "Good folk, mere noise
    repels —
  But give me your sun from yonder
    skies!"
They had answered, "And afterward,
    what else?" 10

III

Alack, it was I who leaped at the sun
  To give it my loving friends to
    keep!
Nought man could do, have I left un-
    done:
  And you see my harvest, what I
    reap
This very day, now a year is run. 15

IV

There's nobody on the house-tops
    now —
  Just a palsied few at the windows
    set;
For the best of the sight is, all allow,
  At the Shambles' Gate — or, bet-
    ter yet,
By the very scaffold's foot, I trow. 20

V

I go in the rain, and, more than needs,
  A rope cuts both my wrists behind;
And I think, by the feel, my forehead
    bleeds,
  For they fling, whoever has a
    mind, 24
Stones at me for my year's misdeeds.

VI

Thus I entered, and thus I go!
  In triumphs, people have dropped
    down dead.
"Paid by the World — what dost
    thou owe
  Me?" God might question: now
    instead,
'Tis God shall repay! I am safer
    so. 30

"CHILDE ROLAND TO THE DARK TOWER CAME"

ROBERT BROWNING *

My first thought was, he lied in
    every word,
    That hoary cripple, with malicious
      eye
    Askance to watch the working of
      his lie
On mine, and mouth scarce able to
    afford
Suppression of the glee that pursed
    and scored   5
    Its edge, at one more victim
      gained thereby.

What else should he be set for, with
    his staff?
    What, save to waylay with his lies,
      ensnare
    All travellers who might find him
      posted there,
And ask the road? I guessed what
    skull-like laugh   10
Would break, what crutch 'gin write
    my epitaph
    For pastime in the dusty thorough-
      fare,

If at his counsel I should turn aside
    Into that ominous tract which, all
      agree,
    Hides the Dark Tower. Yet ac-
      quiescingly   15
I did turn as he pointed: neither
    pride
    Nor hope rekindling at the end
      descried,
    So much as gladness that some end
      might be.

For, what with my whole world-wide
    wandering,
    What with my search drawn out
      through years, my hope   20

* See p. 1061 for discussion.

Dwindled into a ghost not fit to
    cope
With that obstreperous joy success
    would bring —
I hardly tried now to rebuke the
    spring
    My heart made, finding failure in
      its scope.

As when a sick man very near to
    death   25
    Seems dead indeed, and feels begin
      and end
The tears, and takes the farewell of
    each friend,
And hears one bid the other go, draw
    breath
Freelier outside ("since all is o'er,"
    he saith,
    "And the blow fallen no grieving
      can amend");   30

While some discuss if near the other
    graves
    Be room enough for this, and when
      a day
    Suits best for carrying the corpse
      away,
With care about the banners, scarves
    and staves:
And still the man hears all, and only
    craves   35
    He may not shame such tender
      love and stay.

Thus, I had so long suffered in this
    quest,
    Heard failure prophesied so oft,
      been writ
    So many times among "The Band"
      — to wit,
The knights who to the Dark Tower's
    search addressed   40
Their steps — that just to fail as
    they, seemed best,
    And all the doubt was now —
      should I be fit?

So, quiet in despair, I turned from
    him,
  That hateful cripple, out of his
    highway
  Into the path he pointed. All the
    day   45
Had been a dreary one at best, and
    dim
Was settling to its close, yet shot one
    grim
  Red leer to see the plain catch its
    estray.

For mark! no sooner was I fairly
    found
  Pledged to the plain, after a pace
    or two,   50
  Than, pausing to throw backward
    a last view
O'er the safe road, 'twas gone; gray
    plain all round:
Nothing but plain to the horizon's
    bound.
  I might go on; naught else re-
    mained to do.

So, on I went. I think I never
    saw   55
  Such starved ignoble nature; noth-
    ing throve:
For flowers — as well expect a
    cedar grove!
But cockle, spurge, according to their
    law
  Might propagate their kind, with
    none to awe,
  You'd think: a burr had been a
    treasure trove.   60

No! penury, inertness and grimace,
  In some strange sort, were the
    land's portion. "See
  Or shut your eyes," said Nature
    peevishly,
"It nothing skills: I cannot help my
    case:

'Tis the Last Judgment's fire must
    cure this place,   65
Calcine its clods and set my prisoners
    free."

If there pushed any ragged thistle-
    stalk
  Above its mates, the head was
    chopped; the bents
  Were jealous else. What made
    those holes and rents
In the dock's harsh swarth leaves,
    bruised as to balk   70
All hope of greenness? 'tis a brute
    must walk
  Pashing their life out, with a
    brute's intents.

As for the grass, it grew as scant as
    hair
  In leprosy; thin dry blades pricked
    the mud
  Which underneath looked kneaded
    up with blood.   75
One stiff blind horse, his every bone
    a-stare,
Stood stupefied, however he came
    there:
  Thrust out past service from the
    devil's stud!

Alive? he might be dead for aught I
    know,
  With that red gaunt and colloped
    neck a-strain,   80
  And shut eyes underneath the
    rusty mane;
Seldom went such grotesqueness with
    such woe;
I never saw a brute I hated so;
  He must be wicked to deserve such
    pain.

I shut my eyes and turned them on
    my heart.   85
  As a man calls for wine before he
    fights,

I asked one draught of earlier,
   happier sights,
Ere fitly I could hope to play my part.
Think first, fight afterwards — the
   soldier's art:
   One taste of the old time sets all to
     rights.   90

Not it! I fancied Cuthbert's redden-
   ing face
   Beneath its garniture of curly gold,
   Dear fellow, till I almost felt him
     fold
An arm in mine to fix me to the place,
That way he used.   Alas, one night's
   disgrace.   95
   Out went my heart's new fire and
     left it cold.

Giles then, the soul of honor — there
   he stands
   Frank as ten years ago when
     knighted first.
   What honest man should dare (he
     said) he durst.
Good — but the scene shifts —
   faugh! what hangman hands
Pin to his breast a parchment? His
   own bands   101
   Read it.   Poor traitor, spit upon
     and curst!

Better this present than a past like
   that;
   Back therefore to my darkening
     path again!
   No sound, no sight as far as eye
     could strain.   105
Will the night send a howlet or a bat?
I asked: when something on the dis-
   mal flat
   Came to arrest my thoughts and
     change their train.

A sudden little river crossed my path
   As unexpected as a serpent comes.
   No sluggish tide congenial to the
     glooms;   111

This, as it frothed by, might have
   been a bath
For the fiend's glowing hoof — to see
   the wrath
   Of its black eddy bespate with
     flakes and spumes.

So petty yet so spiteful! All along,
   Low scrubby alders kneeled down
     over it;   116
   Drenched willows flung them head-
     long in a fit
Of mute despair, a suicidal throng:
The river which had done them all
   the wrong,
   Whate'er that was, rolled by, de-
     terred no whit.   120

Which, while I forded — good saints,
   how I feared
   To set my foot upon a dead man's
     cheek,
   Each step, or feel the spear I thrust
     to seek
For hollows, tangled in his hair or
   beard!
— It may have been a water-rat I
   speared,   125
   But, ugh! it sounded like a baby's
     shriek.

Glad was I when I reached the other
   bank.
   Now for a better country. Vain
     presage!
   Who were the strugglers, what war
     did they wage,
Whose savage trample thus could pad
   the dank   130
Soil to a plash? Toads in a poisoned
   tank,
   Or wild cats in a red-hot iron cage —

The fight must so have seemed in
   that fell cirque.
What penned them there, with all
   the plain to choose?

No footprint leading to that horrid
    mews,   135
None out of it. Mad brewage set to
    work
Their brains, no doubt, like galley-
    slaves the Turk
    Pits for his pastime, Christians
    against Jews.

And more than that — a furlong on
    — why, there!
    What bad use was that engine for,
    that wheel,   140
    Or brake, not wheel — that har-
    row fit to reel
Men's bodies out like silk? with all
    the air
Of Tophet's tool, on earth left un-
    aware,
    Or brought to sharpen its rusty
    teeth of steel.

Then came a bit of stubbed ground,
    once a wood,   145
Next a marsh, it would seem, and
    now mere earth
    Desperate and done with: (so a
    fool finds mirth,
Makes a thing and then mars it, till
    his mood
Changes and off he goes!) within a
    rood —
    Bog, clay and rubble, sand and
    stark black dearth.   150

Now blotches rankling, colored gay
    and grim,
    Now patches where some leanness
    of the soil's
    Broke into moss or substances like
    boils;
Then came some palsied oak, a cleft
    in him
Like a distorted mouth that splits its
    rim   155
    Gaping at death, and dies while it
    recoils.

And just as far as ever from the
    end!
Naught in the distance but the
    evening, naught
To point my footstep further! At
    the thought,
A great black bird, Apollyon's bosom-
    friend,   160
Sailed past, nor beat his wide wing
    dragon-penned
That brushed my cap — perchance
    the guide I sought.

For, looking up, aware I somehow
    grew,
    'Spite of the dusk, the plain had
    given place
    All round to mountains — with
    such name to grace   165
Mere ugly heights and heaps now
    stolen in view.
How thus they had surprised me —
    solve it, you!
    How to get from them was no
    clearer case.

Yet half I seemed to recognize some
    trick
Of mischief happened to me, God
    knows when —   170
In a bad dream perhaps. Here
    ended, then,
Progress this way. When, in the
    very nick
Of giving up, one time more, came a
    click
    As when a trap shuts — you're in-
    side the den!

Burningly it came on me all at
    once,   175
    This was the place! those two hills
    on the right,
    Crouched like two bulls locked
    horn in horn in fight;
While to the left, a tall scalped moun-
    tain... Dunce,

Dotard, a-dozing at the very nonce,
  After a life spent training for the
    sight!   180

What in the midst lay but the Tower
    itself?
  The round squat turret, blind as
    the fool's heart,
  Built of brown stone, without a
    counterpart
In the whole world.   The tempest's
    mocking elf
Points to the shipman thus the un-
    seen shelf   185
  He strikes on, only when the tim-
    bers start.

Not see? because of night perhaps? —
    why, day
  Came back again for that! before it
    left,
  The dying sunset kindled through
    a cleft:
The hills, like giants at a hunting,
    lay   190
Chin upon hand, to see the game at
    bay, —
  "Now stab and end the creature —
    to the heft!"

Not hear? when noise was every-
    where! it tolled
  Increasing like a bell. Names in
    my ears,
  Of all the lost adventurers my
    peers —   195
How such a one was strong, and such
    was bold,
And such was fortunate, yet each of
    old
  Lost, lost! one moment knelled the
    woe of years.

There they stood, ranged along the
    hillsides, met
  To view the last of me, a living
    frame   200

For one more picture! in a sheet of
    flame
I saw them and I knew them all.
    And yet
Dauntless the slug-horn to my lips I
    set,
And blew.   *Childe Roland to the
    Dark Tower came.*"

MY SISTER'S SLEEP

DANTE GABRIEL ROSSETTI [*]

She fell asleep on Christmas Eve:
  At length the long-ungranted shade
  Of weary eyelids overweigh'd
The pain nought else might yet re-
    lieve.

Our mother, who had leaned all day
  Over the bed from chime to chime,
  Then raised herself for the first
    time,   7
And as she sat her down, did pray.

Her little work-table was spread
  With work to finish.   For the
    glare   10
  Made by her candle, she had care
To work some distance from the bed.

Without there was a cold moon up,
  Of winter radiance sheer and thin;
  The hollow halo it was in   15
Was like an icy crystal cup.

Through the small room, with subtle
    sound
  Of flame, by vents the fireshine
    drove
  And reddened.   In its dim alcove
The mirror shed a clearness round. 20

I had been sitting up some nights,
  And my tired mind felt weak and
    blank;

* See p. 1061 for discussion.

Like a sharp strengthening wine it
    drank
The stillness and the broken lights.

Twelve struck.   That sound, by
    dwindling years   25
    Heard in each hour, crept off; and
        then
    The ruffled silence spread again,
Like water that a pebble stirs.

Our mother rose from where she sat:
    Her needles, as she laid them down,
    Met lightly, and her silken gown
Settled, no other noise than that.   32

"Glory unto the Newly Born!"
    So, as said angels, she did say;
    Because we were in Christmas Day,
Though it would still be long till morn.

Just then in the room over us   37
    There was a pushing back of
        chairs,
    As some who had sat unawares
So late, now heard the hour, and rose.

With anxious softly-stepping haste 41
    Our mother went where Margaret
        lay,
    Fearing the sounds o'er head —
        should they
Have broken her long watched-for
    rest!

She stooped an instant, calm, and
    turned   45
    But suddenly turned back again;
    And all her features seemed in pain
With woe, and her eyes gazed and
    yearned.

For my part, I but hid my face,
    And held my breath, and spoke no
        word: 50
    There was none spoken; but I heard
The silence for a little space.

Our mother bowed herself and wept:
    And both my arms fell, and I said,
    "God knows I knew that she was
        dead."   55
And there, all white, my sister slept.

Then kneeling upon Christmas morn
    A little after twelve o'clock
    We said, ere the first quarter
        struck,
"Christ's blessing on the newly
    born!"   60

THE MAN HE KILLED *

THOMAS HARDY †

"Had he and I but met
    By some old ancient inn,
We should have sat us down to wet
    Right many a nipperkin!

"But ranged as infantry,   5
    And staring face to face,
I shot at him as he at me,
    And killed him in his place.

"I shot him dead because —
    Because he was my foe,   10
Just so: my foe of course he was;
    That's clear enough; although

"He thought he'd 'list, perhaps,
    Off-hand like — just as I —
Was out of work — had sold his
    traps —   15
    No other reason why.

"Yes; quaint and curious war is!
    You shoot a fellow down
You'd treat if met where any bar
    is,
    Or help to half-a-crown."   20

* From *Collected Poems of Thomas Hardy*.
By permission of The Macmillan Company,
publishers.

† See p. 1062 for discussion.

THE BALLAD OF READING GAOL

MDCCCXCVIII

OSCAR WILDE *

In Memoriam

C. T. W.

Sometime Trooper of the Royal Horse
Guards.

Obiit H. M. Prison, Reading, Berkshire,
July 7, 1896

I

He did not wear his scarlet coat,
  For blood and wine are red,
And blood and wine were on his
    hands
  When they found him with the
    dead,
The poor dead woman whom he
    loved,   5
  And murdered in her bed.

He walked amongst the Trial Men
  In a suit of shabby grey;
A cricket cap was on his head,
  And his step seemed light and
    gay;   10
But I never saw a man who looked
  So wistfully at the day.

I never saw a man who looked
  With such a wistful eye
Upon that little tent of blue   15
  Which prisoners call the sky,
And at every drifting cloud that went
  With sails of silver by.

I walked, with other souls in pain,
  Within another ring,   20
And was wondering if the man had
    done
  A great or little thing,
When a voice behind me whispered
    low,
  "That fellow's got to swing."

* See p. 1062 for discussion.

Dear Christ! the very prison walls 25
  Suddenly seemed to reel,
And the sky above my head became
  Like a casque of scorching steel;
And, though I was a soul in pain,
  My pain I did not feel.   30

I only knew what hunted thought
  Quickened his step, and why
He looked upon the garish day
  With such a wistful eye;
The man had killed the thing he
    loved,   35
  And so he had to die.

   .   .   .   .   .   .

Yet each man kills the thing he loves,
  By each let this be heard,
Some do it with a bitter look,
  Some with a flattering word,   40
The coward does it with a kiss,
  The brave man with a sword!

Some kill their love when they are
    young,
  And some when they are old;
Some strangle with the hands of Lust,
  Some with the hands of Gold;   46
The kindest use a knife, because
  The dead so soon grow cold.

Some love too little, some too long,
  Some sell, and others buy;   50
Some do the deed with many tears,
  And some without a sigh:
For each man kills the thing he loves,
  Yet each man does not die.

   .   .   .   .   .   .

He does not die a death of shame 55
  On a day of dark disgrace,
Nor have a noose about his neck,
  Nor a cloth upon his face,
Nor drop feet foremost through the
    floor
  Into an empty space.   60

He does not sit with silent men
  Who watch him night and day;

Who watch him when he tries to
    weep,
And when he tries to pray;
Who watch him lest himself should
    rob   65
    The prison of its prey.

He does not wake at dawn to see
    Dread figures throng his room,
The shivering Chaplain robed in
    white,
    The Sheriff stern with gloom,   70
And the Governor all in shiny black,
    With the yellow face of Doom.

He does not rise in piteous haste
    To put on convict-clothes,
While some coarse-mouthed Doctor
    gloats, and notes   75
    Each new and nerve-twitched
    pose,
Fingering a watch whose little ticks
    Are like horrible hammer-blows.

He does not know that sickening
    thirst
    That sands one's throat, before 80
The hangman with his gardener's
    gloves
    Slips through the padded door,
And binds one with three leathern
    thongs,
    That the throat may thirst no more.

He does not bend his head to hear 85
    The Burial Office read,
Nor while the terror of his soul
    Tells him he is not dead,
Cross his own coffin, as he moves
    Into the hideous shed.   90

He does not stare upon the air
    Through a little roof of glass:
He does not pray with lips of clay
    For his agony to pass;
Nor feel upon his shuddering cheek
    The kiss of Caiaphas.   96

11

Six weeks our guardsman walked the
    yard,
    In the suit of shabby grey:
His cricket cap was on his head, 99
    And his step seemed light and gay,
But I never saw a man who looked
    So wistfully at the day.

I never saw a man who looked
    With such a wistful eye
Upon that little tent of blue   105
    Which prisoners call the sky,
And at every wandering cloud that
    trailed
    Its ravelled fleeces by.

He did not wring his hands, as do
    Those witless men who dare 110
To try to rear the changeling Hope
    In the cave of black Despair:
He only looked upon the sun,
    And drank the morning air.

He did not wring his hands nor weep,
    Nor did he peek or pine, 116
But he drank the air as though it held
    Some healthful anodyne;
With open mouth he drank the sun
    As though it had been wine! 120

And I and all the souls in pain,
    Who tramped the other ring,
Forgot if we ourselves had done
    A great or little thing,
And watched with gaze of dull amaze
    The man who had to swing. 126

And strange it was to see him pass
    With a step so light and gay,
And strange it was to see him look
    So wistfully at the day,   130
And strange it was to think that he
    Had such a debt to pay.

For oak and elm have pleasant
    leaves

That in the spring-time shoot:
But grim to see is the gallows-tree,
    With its adder-bitten root,   136
And, green or dry, a man must die
    Before it bears its fruit!

The loftiest place is that seat of grace
    For which all worldlings try: 140
But who would stand in hempen band
    Upon a scaffold high,
And through a murderer's collar take
    His last look at the sky?

It is sweet to dance to violins   145
    When Love and Life are fair:
To dance to flutes, to dance to lutes
    Is delicate and rare:
But it is not sweet with nimble feet
    To dance upon the air!   150

So with curious eyes and sick sur-
        mise
    We watched him day by day,
And wondered if each one of us
    Would end the self-same way,
For none can tell to what red Hell   155
    His sightless soul may stray.

At last the dead man walked no
        more
    Amongst the Trial Men,
And I knew that he was standing
        up   159
    In the black dock's dreadful pen,
And that never would I see his face
    In God's sweet world again.

Like two doomed ships that pass in
        storm
    We had crossed each other's way:
But we made no sign, we said no
        word,   165
    We had no word to say;
For we did not meet in the holy
        night,
    But in the shameful day.

A prison wall was round us both,
    Two outcast men we were: 170
The world had thrust us from its
        heart,
    And God from out His care:
And the iron gin that waits for Sin
    Had caught us in its snare.

III

In Debtors' Yard the stones are
        hard,   175
    And the dripping wall is high,
So it was there he took the air
    Beneath the leaden sky,
And by each side a Warder walked,
    For fear the man might die.   180

Or else he sat with those who watched
    His anguish night and day;
Who watched him when he rose to
        weep,
    And when he crouched to pray;
Who watched him lest himself should
        rob   185
    Their scaffold of its prey.

The Governor was strong upon
    The Regulations Act:
The Doctor said that Death was but
    A scientific fact: 190
And twice a day the Chaplain called,
    And left a little tract.

And twice a day he smoked his
        pipe,
    And drank his quart of beer:
His soul was resolute, and held   195
    No hiding-place for fear;
He often said that he was glad
    The hangman's hands were near.

But why he said so strange a thing
    No Warder dared to ask: 200
For he to whom a watcher's doom
    Is given as his task,
Must set a lock upon his lips,
    And make his face a mask.

Or else he might be moved, and try
  To comfort or console: 206
And what should Human Pity do
  Pent up in Murderers' Hole?
What word of grace in such a place
  Could help a brother's soul?   210

. . . .

With slouch and swing around the ring
  We trod the Fools' Parade!
We did not care: we knew we were
  The Devil's Own Brigade:
And shaven head and feet of lead 215
  Make a merry masquerade.

We tore the tarry rope to shreds
  With blunt and bleeding nails;
We rubbed the doors, and scrubbed
    the floors,
  And cleaned the shining rails: 220
And, rank by rank, we soaped the
    plank,
  And clattered with the pails.

We sewed the sacks, we broke the
    stones,
  We turned the dusty drill:
We banged the tins, and bawled the
    hymns,   225
  And sweated on the mill:
But in the heart of every man
  Terror was lying still.

So still it lay that every day
  Crawled like a weed-clogged wave:
And we forgot the bitter lot   231
  That waits for fool and knave,
Till once, as we tramped in from
    work,
  We passed an open grave.

With yawning mouth the yellow hole
  Gaped for a living thing;   236
The very mud cried out for blood
  To the thirsty asphalte ring:
And we knew that ere one dawn grew
    fair
  Some prisoner had to swing.   240

Right in we went, with soul intent
  On Death and Dread and Doom:
The hangman, with his little bag,
  Went shuffling through the gloom:
And each man trembled as he crept
  Into his numbered tomb.   246

. . . .

That night the empty corridors
  Were full of forms of Fear,
And up and down the iron town
  Stole feet we could not hear, 250
And through the bars that hide the
    stars
  White faces seemed to peer.

He lay as one who lies and dreams
  In a pleasant meadow-land,
The watches watched him as he
    slept,
  And could not understand   255
How one could sleep so sweet a
    sleep
  With a hangman close at hand.

But there is no sleep when men must
    weep
  Who never yet have wept: 260
So we — the fool, the fraud, the
    knave —
  That endless vigil kept,
And through each brain on hands of
    pain
  Another's terror crept.

. . . .

Alas! it is a fearful thing   265
  To feel another's guilt!
For, right within, the sword of Sin
  Pierced to its poisoned hilt,
And as molten lead were the tears we
    shed
  For the blood we had not spilt. 270

The Warders with their shoes of felt
  Crept by each padlocked door,
And peeped and saw, with eyes of
    awe,
  Grey figures on the floor,

And wondered why men knelt to
    pray   275
  Who never prayed before.

All through the night we knelt and
    prayed,
  Mad mourners of a corse!
The troubled plumes of midnight
    were
The plumes upon a hearse: 280
And bitter wine upon a sponge
  Was the savour of Remorse.

.   .   .   .   .   .

The grey cock crew, the red cock
    crew,
  But never came the day:
And crooked shapes of Terror
    crouched,   285
  In the corners where we lay:
And each evil sprite that walks by
    night
  Before us seemed to play.

They glided past, they glided fast,
  Like travellers through a mist: 290
They mocked the moon in a rigadoon
  Of delicate turn and twist,
And with formal pace and loathsome
    grace
  The phantoms kept their tryst.

With mop and mow, we saw them go,
  Slim shadows hand in hand: 296
About, about, in ghostly rout
  They trod a saraband:
And the damned grotesques made
    arabesques,
  Like the wind upon the sand!   300

With the pirouettes of marionettes,
  They tripped on pointed tread:
But with flutes of Fear they filled the
    ear,
  As their grisly masque they led,
And loud they sang, and long they
    sang,   305
  For they sang to wake the dead.

"Oho!" they cried, "The world is wide,
  But fettered limbs go lame!
And once, or twice, to throw the dice
  Is a gentlemanly game,   310
But he does not win who plays with Sin
  In the secret House of Shame."

.   .   .   .   .   .

No things of air these antics were,
  That frolicked with such glee:
To men whose lives were held in
    gyves,   315
  And whose feet might not go free,
Ah! wounds of Christ! they were
    living things,
  Most terrible to see.

Around, around, they waltzed and
    wound;   319
  Some wheeled in smirking pairs;
With the mincing step of a demirep
  Some sidled up the stairs:
And with subtle sneer, and fawning
    leer,
  Each helped us at our prayers.

The morning wind began to moan,
  But still the night went on: 326
Through its giant loom the web of
    gloom
  Crept till each thread was spun:
And, as we prayed, we grew afraid
  Of the Justice of the Sun.   330

The moaning wind went wandering
    round
  The weeping prison-wall:
Till like a wheel of turning steel
  We felt the minutes crawl:
O moaning wind! what had we done
  To have such a seneschal?   336

At last I saw the shadowed bars,
  Like a lattice wrought in lead,
Move right across the whitewashed
    wall
  That faced my three-planked
    bed,   340

And I knew that somewhere in the
    world
God's awful dawn was red.

  .   .   .   .   .

At six o'clock we cleaned our cells,
    At seven all was still,
But the sough and swing of a mighty
    wing   345
    The prison seemed to fill,
For the Lord of Death with icy
    breath
    Had entered in to kill.

He did not pass in purple pomp,
    Nor ride a moon-white steed.   350
Three yards of cord and a sliding
    board
    Are all the gallows' need:
So with rope of shame the Herald
    came
    To do the secret deed.

  .   .   .   .   .

We were as men who through a fen
    Of filthy darkness grope: 356
We did not dare to breathe a prayer,
    Or to give our anguish scope:
Something was dead in each of us,
    And what was dead was Hope. 360

For Man's grim Justice goes its way,
    And will not swerve aside:
It slays the weak, it slays the strong,
    It has a deadly stride:
With iron heel it slays the strong,
    The monstrous parricide!   366

We waited for the stroke of eight:
    Each tongue was thick with thirst:
For the stroke of eight is the stroke
    of Fate
    That makes a man accursed,   370
And Fate will use a running noose
    For the best man and the worst.

We had no other thing to do,
    Save to wait for the sign to come:
So, like things of stone in a valley
    lone,   375

Quiet we sat and dumb:
But each man's heart beat thick and
    quick,
    Like a madman on a drum!

With sudden shock the prison-clock
    Smote on the shivering air,   380
And from all the gaol rose up a
    wail
    Of impotent despair,
Like the sound that frightened
    marshes hear
    From some leper in his lair.

And as one sees most fearful things
    In the crystal of a dream,   386
We saw the greasy hempen rope
    Hooked to the blackened beam,
And heard the prayer the hangman's
    snare
    Strangled into a scream.   390

And all the woe that moved him so
    That he gave that bitter cry,
And the wild regrets, and the bloody
    sweats,
    None knew so well as I:
For he who lives more lives than
    one   395
    More deaths than one must die.

IV

There is no chapel on the day
    On which they hang a man:
The Chaplain's heart is far too sick,
    Or his face is far too wan,   400
Or there is that written in his eyes
    Which none should look upon.

So they kept us close till nigh on
    noon,
    And then they rang the bell,
And the Warders with their jingling
    keys   405
    Opened each listening cell,
And down the iron stair we tramped,
    Each from his separate Hell.

Out into God's sweet air we went,
  But not in wonted way,   410
For this man's face was white with
    fear,
  And that man's face was grey,
And I never saw sad men who looked
  So wistfully at the day.

I never saw sad men who looked   415
  With such a wistful eye
Upon that little tent of blue
  We prisoners called the sky,
And at every careless cloud that
    passed
  In happy freedom by.   420

But there were those amongst us all
  Who walked with downcast head,
And knew that, had each got his due,
  They should have died instead:
He had but killed a thing that lived,
  Whilst they had killed the dead. 426

For he who sins a second time
  Wakes a dead soul to pain,
And draws it from its spotted shroud,
  And makes it bleed again,   430
And makes it bleed great gouts of
    blood,
  And makes it bleed in vain!

. . . .

Like ape or clown, in monstrous garb
  With crooked arrows starred,
Silently we went round and round 435
  The slippery asphalte yard;
Silently we went round and round,
  And no man spoke a word.

Silently we went round and round,
  And through each hollow mind 440
The Memory of dreadful things
  Rushed like a dreadful wind,
And Horror stalked before each man,
  And Terror crept behind.

The Warders strutted up and down,
  And kept their herd of brutes, 446

Their uniforms were spick and span,
  And they wore their Sunday suits,
But we knew the work they had been
    at,
  By the quicklime on their boots. 450

For where a grave had opened wide,
  There was no grave at all:
Only a stretch of mud and sand
  By the hideous prison-wall,
And a little heap of burning lime, 455
  That the man should have his pall.

For he has a pall, this wretched man,
  Such as few men can claim:
Deep down below a prison-yard,
  Naked for greater shame,   460
He lies, with fetters on each foot,
  Wrapt in a sheet of flame!

And all the while the burning lime
  Eats flesh and bone away,
It eats the brittle bone by night, 465
  And the soft flesh by day,
It eats the flesh and bone by turns,
  But it eats the heart alway.

For three long years they will not
    sow
  Or root or seedling there: 470
For three long years the unblessed
    spot
  Will sterile be and bare,
And look upon the wondering sky
  With unreproachful stare.

They think a murderer's heart would
    taint   475
  Each simple seed they sow.
It is not true! God's kindly earth
  Is kindlier than men know,
And the red rose would but blow
    more red,
  The white rose whiter blow.   480

Out of his mouth a red, red rose!
  Out of his heart a white!

For who can say by what strange
    way,
  Christ brings His will to light,
Since the barren staff the pilgrim
    bore   485
  Bloomed in the great Pope's sight?

. . . .

But neither milk-white rose nor red
  May bloom in prison air;
The shard, the pebble, and the flint,
  Are what they give us there: 490
For flowers have been known to heal
  A common man's despair.

So never will wine-red rose or white,
  Petal by petal, fall
On that stretch of mud and sand that
    lies   495
  By the hideous prison-wall,
To tell the men who tramp the yard
  That God's Son died for all.

. . . .

Yet though the hideous prison-wall
  Still hems him round and round, 500
And a spirit may not walk by night
  That is with fetters bound,
And a spirit may but weep that lies
  In such unholy ground,

He is at peace—this wretched man—
  At peace, or will be soon: 506
There is no thing to make him man,
  Nor does Terror walk at noon,
For the lampless Earth in which he
    lies
  Has neither Sun nor Moon.   510

They hanged him as a beast is hanged:
  They did not even toll
A requiem that might have brought
  Rest to his startled soul,
But hurriedly they took him out, 515
  And hid him in a hole.

They stripped him of his canvas
    clothes,
  And gave him to the flies:

They mocked the swollen purple
    throat,
  And the stark and staring eyes: 520
And with laughter loud they heaped
    the shroud
  In which their convict lies.

The Chaplain would not kneel to
    pray
  By his dishonored grave:
Nor mark it with that blessed Cross
  That Christ for sinners gave, 526
Because the man was one of those
  Whom Christ came down to save.

Yet all is well; he has but passed
  To Life's appointed bourne: 530
And alien tears will fill for him
  Pity's long-broken urn,
For his mourners will be outcast
    men,
  And outcasts always mourn.

V

I know not whether Laws be right,
  Or whether Laws be wrong;   536
All that we know who lie in gaol
  Is that the wall is strong;
And that each day is like a year,
  A year whose days are long.   540

But this I know, that every Law
  That men have made for Man,
Since first Man took his brother's
    life,
  And the sad world began,
But straws the wheat and saves the
    chaff   545
  With a most evil fan.

This too I know—and wise it were
  If each could know the same—
That every prison that men build
  Is built with bricks of shame, 550
And bound with bars lest Christ
    should see
  How men their brothers maim.

With bars they blur the gracious
    moon,
And blind the goodly sun:
And they do well to hide their Hell,
    For in it things are done   556
That Son of God nor son of Man
    Ever should look upon!

The vilest deeds like poison weeds
    Bloom well in prison-air: 560
It is only what is good in Man
    That wastes and withers there:
Pale Anguish keeps the heavy gate,
    And the Warder is Despair.

For they starve the little frightened
    child   565
    Till it weeps both night and day:
And they scourge the weak, and flog
    the fool,
    And gibe the old and gray,
And some grow mad, and all grow
    bad,
    And none a word may say.   570

Each narrow cell in which we dwell
    Is a foul and dark latrine,
And the fetid breath of living Death
    Chokes up each grated screen,
And all, but Lust, is turned to dust
    In Humanity's machine.   576

The brackish water that we drink
    Creeps with a loathsome slime,
And the bitter bread they weigh in
    scales
    Is full of chalk and lime,   580
And Sleep will not lie down, but walks
    Wild-eyed, and cries to Time.

But though lean Hunger and green
    Thirst
    Like asp with adder fight,
We have little care of prison fare,   585
    For what chills and kills outright
Is that every stone one lifts by day
    Becomes one's heart by night.

With midnight always in one's heart,
    And twilight in one's cell,   590
We turn the crank, or tear the rope,
    Each in his separate Hell,
And the silence is more awful far
    Than the sound of a brazen bell.

And never a human voice comes near
    To speak a gentle word: 596
And the eye that watches through the
    door
    Is pitiless and hard:
And by all forgot, we rot and rot,
    With soul and body marred.   600

And thus we rust Life's iron chain
    Degraded and alone:
And some men curse, and some men
    weep,
    And some men make no moan:
But God's eternal Laws are kind 605
    And break the heart of stone.

And every human heart that breaks,
    In prison-cell or yard,
Is as that broken box that gave
    Its treasure to the Lord,   610
And filled the unclean leper's house
    With the scent of costliest nard.

Ah! happy they whose hearts can
    break
    And peace of pardon win!
How else may man make straight his
    plan   615
    And cleanse his soul from Sin?
How else but through a broken
    heart
    May Lord Christ enter in?

And he of the swollen purple throat,
    And the stark and staring eyes, 620
Waits for the holy hands that
    took
    The Thief to Paradise;
And a broken and a contrite heart
    The Lord will not despise.

The man in red who reads the Law
  Gave him three weeks of life, 626
Three little weeks in which to heal
  His soul of his soul's strife,
And cleanse from every blot of blood
  The hand that held the knife. 630

And with tears of blood he cleansed
    the hand,
  The hand that held the steel:
For only blood can wipe out blood,
  And only tears can heal:
And the crimson stain that was of
    Cain 635
  Became Christ's snow-white seal.

VI

In Reading gaol by Reading town
  There is a pit of shame,
And in it lies a wretched man
  Eaten by teeth of flame, 640
In a burning winding-sheet he lies,
  And his grave has got no name.

And there, till Christ call forth the
    dead,
  In silence let him lie:
No need to waste the foolish tear, 645
  Or heave the windy sigh:
The man had killed the thing he
    loved,
  And so he had to die.

And all men kill the thing they love,
  By all let this be heard, 650
Some do it with a bitter look,
  Some with a flattering word,
The coward does it with a kiss,
  The brave man with a sword!

BREDON ¹ HILL

A. E. HOUSMAN *

In summertime on Bredon
  The bells they sound so clear;

¹ Pronounced Breedon.
* See p. 1063 for discussion.

Round both the shires they ring them
  In steeples far and near,
A happy noise to hear. 5

Here of a Sunday morning
  My love and I would lie,
And see the coloured counties,
  And hear the larks so high
About us in the sky. 10

The bells would ring to call her
  In valleys miles away:
"Come all to church, good people;
  Good people, come and pray."
But here my love would stay. 15

And I would turn and answer
  Among the springing thyme,
"Oh, peal upon our wedding,
  And we will hear the chime,
And come to church in time." 20

But when the snows at Christmas
  On Bredon top were strown,
My love rose up so early
  And stole out unbeknown
And went to church alone. 25

They tolled the one bell only,
  Groom there was none to see,
The mourners followed after,
  And so to church went she,
And would not wait for me. 30

The bells they sound on Bredon,
  And still the steeples hum.
"Come all to church, good people"—
  Oh, noisy bells, be dumb;
I hear you, I will come. 35

"THE STREET SOUNDS"

A. E. HOUSMAN

The street sounds to the soldiers'
    tread,
  And out we troop to see:
A single redcoat turns his head,
  He turns and looks at me.

My man, from sky to sky's so far, 5
  We never crossed before;
Such leagues apart the world's ends
    are,
    We're like to meet no more;

What thoughts at heart have you
    and I
  We cannot stop to tell; 10
But dead or living, drunk or dry,
  Soldier, I wish you well.

DANNY DEEVER

RUDYARD KIPLING *

"What are the bugles blowin' for?" said Files-on-Parade.
"To turn you out, to turn you out," the Color-Sergeant said.
"What makes you look so white, so white?" said Files-on-Parade.
"I'm dreadin' what I've got to watch," the Color-Sergeant said.
  For they're hangin' Danny Deever, you can 'ear the Dead March play, 5
  The regiment's in 'ollow square — they're hangin' him today;
  They've taken of his buttons off an' cut his stripes away,
  An' they're hangin' Danny Deever in the mornin'.

"What makes the rear-rank breathe so 'ard?" said Files-on-Parade.
"It's bitter cold, it's bitter cold," the Color-Sergeant said. 10
"What makes that front-rank man fall down?" says Files-on-Parade.
"A touch of sun, a touch of sun," the Color-Sergeant said.
  They are hangin' Danny Deever, they are marchin' of 'im round.
  They 'ave 'alted Danny Deever by 'is coffin on the ground;
  An' 'e'll swing in 'arf a minute for a sneakin' shootin' hound — 15
  O they're hangin' Danny Deever in the mornin'!

"'Is cot was right-'and cot to mine," said Files-on-Parade.
"'E's sleepin' out an' far tonight," the Color-Sergeant said.
"I've drunk 'is beer a score o' times," said Files-on-Parade.
"'E's drinkin' bitter beer alone," the Color-Sergeant said. 20
  They are hangin' Danny Deever, you must mark 'im to 'is place,
  For 'e shot a comrade sleepin' — you must look 'im in the face;
  Nine 'undred of 'is country an' the regiment's disgrace,
  While they're hangin' Danny Deever in the mornin'.

"What's that so black agin the sun?" said Files-on-Parade. 25
"It's Danny fightin' 'ard for life," the Color-Sergeant said.
"What's that that whimpers over'ead?" said Files-on-Parade.
"It's Danny's soul that's passin' now," the Color-Sergeant said.
  For they're done with Danny Deever, you can 'ear the quickstep play,
  The regiment's in column, an' they're marchin' us away; 30
  Ho! the young recruits are shakin', an' they'll want their beer today,
  After hangin' Danny Deever in the mornin'.

* See p. 1063 for discussion.

THE MILL *

EDWIN ARLINGTON ROBINSON †

The miller's wife had waited long,
The tea was cold, the fire was dead;
And there might yet be nothing
wrong
In how he went and what he said:
"There are no millers any more," 5
Was all that she had heard him
say;
And he had lingered at the door
So long that it seemed yesterday.

Sick with a fear that had no form
She knew that she was there at last;
And in the mill there was a warm 11
And mealy fragrance of the past.
What else there was would only seem
To say again what he had meant;
And what was hanging from a beam
Would not have heeded where she
went. 16

And if she thought it followed her,
She may have reasoned in the dark
That one way of the few there were
Would hide her and would leave no
mark: 20
Black water, smooth above the weir
Like starry velvet in the night,
Though ruffled once, would soon ap-
pear
The same as ever to the sight.

THE LISTENERS ‡

WALTER DE LA MARE §

"Is there anybody there?" said the
Traveller,
Knocking on the moonlit door;

And his horse in the silence champed
the grasses
Of the forest's ferny floor:
And a bird flew up out of the turret,
Above the Traveller's head: 6
And he smote upon the door again a
second time;
"Is there anybody there?" he said.
But no one descended to the Travel-
ler;
No head from the leaf-fringed sill
Leaned over and looked into his grey
eyes, 11
Where he stood perplexed and still.
But only a host of phantom listeners
That dwelt in the lone house then
Stood listening in the quiet of the
moonlight 15
To that voice from the world of
men:
Stood thronging the faint moon-
beams on the dark stair,
That goes down to the empty hall,
Hearkening in an air stirred and
shaken
By the lonely Traveller's call. 20
And he felt in his heart their strange-
ness,
Their stillness answering his cry,
While his horse moved, cropping the
dark turf,
'Neath the starred and leafy sky;
For he suddenly smote on the door,
even 25
Louder, and lifted his head: —
"Tell them I came, and no one
answered,
That I kept my word," he said.
Never the least stir made the listeners,
Though every word he spake 30
Fell echoing through the shadowiness
of the still house
From the one man left awake:

---

* From *Collected Poems of Edwin Arlington Robinson*. By permission of The Macmillan Company, publishers.

† See p. 1063 for discussion.

‡ From *The Listeners and Other Poems*. By Walter de la Mare, published by Henry Holt and Company.

§ See p. 1064 for discussion.

| Ay, they heard his foot upon the stirrup,
And the sound of iron on stone, | And how the silence surged softly backward, 35
When the plunging hoofs were gone. |

LEPANTO*

GILBERT KEITH CHESTERTON†

White founts falling in the Courts of the sun,
And the Soldan of Byzantium is smiling as they run;
There is laughter like the fountains in that face of all men feared,
It stirs the forest darkness, the darkness of his beard;
It curls the blood-red crescent, the crescent of his lips;　　5
For the inmost sea of all the earth is shaken with his ships.
They have dared the white republics up the capes of Italy,
They have dashed the Adriatic round the Lion of the Sea,
And the Pope has cast his arms abroad for agony and loss,
And called the kings of Christendom for swords about the Cross.　　10
The cold queen of England is looking in the glass;
The shadow of the Valois is yawning at the Mass;
From evening isles fantastical rings faint the Spanish gun,
And the Lord upon the Golden Horn is laughing in the sun.

Dim drums throbbing, in the hills half heard,　　15
Where only on a nameless throne a crownless prince has stirred,
Where, risen from a doubtful seat and half-attainted stall,
The last knight of Europe takes weapons from the wall,
The last and lingering troubadour to whom the bird has sung,
That once went singing southward when all the world was young.　　20
In that enormous silence, tiny and unafraid,
Comes up along a winding road the noise of the Crusade.
Strong gongs groaning as the guns boom far,
Don John of Austria is going to the war,
Stiff flags straining in the night-blasts cold　　25
In the gloom black-purple, in the glint old-gold,
Torchlight crimson on the copper kettle-drums,
Then the tuckets, then the trumpets, then the cannon, and he comes.
Don John laughing in the brave beard curled,
Spurning of his stirrups like the thrones of all the world,　　30
Holding his head up for a flag of all the free.
Love-light of Spain — hurrah!
Death-light of Africa!
Don John of Austria
Is riding to the sea.　　35

* From *Collected Poems of G. K. Chesterton*. By permission of the publishers, Dodd, Mead & Company, Inc.
† See p. 1064 for discussion.

Mahound is in his paradise above the evening star,
(*Don John of Austria is going to the war.*)
He moves a mighty turban on the timeless houri's knees,
His turban that is woven of the sunsets and the seas.
He shakes the peacock gardens as he rises from his ease, 40
And he strides among the tree-tops and is taller than the trees;
And his voice through all the garden is a thunder sent to bring
Black Azrael and Ariel and Ammon on the wing.
Giants and the Genii,
Multiplex of wing and eye, 45
Whose strong obedience broke the sky
When Solomon was king.

They rush in red and purple from the red clouds of the morn,
From the temples where the yellow gods shut up their eyes in scorn;
They rise in green robes roaring from the green hells of the sea 50
Where fallen skies and evil hues and eyeless creatures be,
On them the sea-valves cluster and the gray sea-forests curl,
Splashed with a splendid sickness, the sickness of the pearl;
They swell in sapphire smoke out of the blue cracks of the ground —
They gather and they wonder and give worship to Mahound. 55
And he saith, "Break up the mountains where the hermit-folk can hide,
And sift the red and silver sands lest bone of saint abide,
And chase the Giaours flying night and day, not giving rest,
For that which was our trouble comes again out of the west.
We have set the seal of Solomon on all things under sun, 60
Of knowledge and of sorrow and endurance of things done.
But a noise is in the mountains, in the mountains; and I know
The voice that shook our palaces — four hundred years ago:
It is he that saith not 'Kismet'; it is he that knows not Fate;
It is Richard, it is Raymond, it is Godfrey at the gate! 65
It is he whose loss is laughter when he counts the wager worth,
Put down your feet upon him, that our peace be on the earth."
For he heard drums groaning and he heard guns jar,
(*Don John of Austria is going to the war.*)
Sudden and still — hurrah! 70
Bolt from Iberia!
Don John of Austria
Is gone by Alcalar.

St. Michael's on his Mountain in the sea-roads of the north
(*Don John of Austria is girt and going forth.*) 75
Where the gray seas glitter and the sharp tides shift
And the sea-folk labor and the red sails lift.
He shakes his lance of iron and he claps his wings of stone;
The noise is gone through Normandy; the noise is gone alone;
The North is full of tangled things and texts and aching eyes, 80
And dead is all the innocence of anger and surprise,

And Christian killeth Christian in a narrow dusty room,
And Christian dreadeth Christ that hath a newer face of doom,
And Christian hateth Mary that God kissed in Galilee —
But Don John of Austria is riding to the sea.   85
Don John calling through the blast and the eclipse
Crying with the trumpet, with the trumpet to his lips,
Trumpet that sayeth *ha!*
Domino gloria!
Don John of Austria   90
Is shouting to the ships.

King Philip's in his closet with the Fleece about his neck
(*Don John of Austria is armed upon the deck.*)
The walls are hung with velvet that is black and soft as sin,
And little dwarfs creep out of it and little dwarfs creep in.   95
He holds a crystal phial that has colors like the moon,
He touches, and it tingles, and he trembles very soon,
And his face is as a fungus of a leprous white and gray
Like plants in the high houses that are shuttered from the day,
And death is in the phial and the end of noble work,   100
But Don John of Austria has fired upon the Turk.
Don John's hunting, and his hounds have bayed —
Booms away past Italy the rumor of his raid.
Gun upon gun, ha! ha!
Gun upon gun, hurrah!   105
Don John of Austria
Has loosed the cannonade.

The Pope was in his chapel before day or battle broke,
(*Don John of Austria is hidden in the smoke.*)
The hidden room in man's house where God sits all the year,   110
The secret window whence the world looks small and very dear.
He sees as in a mirror on the monstrous twilight sea
The crescent of his cruel ships whose name is mystery;
They fling great shadows foe-wards, making Cross and Castle dark,
They veil the plumèd lions on the galleys of St. Mark;   115
And above the ships are palaces of brown, black-bearded chiefs,
And below the ships are prisons, where with multitudinous griefs,
Christian captives, sick and sunless, all a laboring race repines
Like a race in sunken cities, like a nation in the mines.
They are lost like slaves that swat, and in the skies of morning hung 120
The stair-ways of the tallest gods when tyranny was young.
They are countless, voiceless, hopeless as those fallen or fleeing on
Before the high Kings' horses in the granite of Babylon.
And many a one grows witless in his quiet room in hell
Where a yellow face looks inward through the lattice of his cell,   125
And he finds his God forgotten, and he seeks no more a sign —

(But Don John of Austria has burst the battle-line!)
Don John pounding from the slaughter-painted poop,
Purpling all the ocean like a bloody pirate's sloop,
Scarlet running over on the silvers and the golds,   130
Breaking of the hatches up and bursting of the holds,
Thronging of the thousands up that labor under sea
White for bliss and blind for sun and stunned for liberty.
Vivat Hispania!
Domino Gloria!   135
Don John of Austria
Has set his people free!

Cervantes on his galley sets the sword back in the sheath
(Don John of Austria rides homeward with a wreath.)
And he sees across a weary land a straggling road in Spain,   140
Up which a lean and foolish knight for ever rides in vain,
And he smiles, but not as Sultans smile, and settles back the blade...
(But Don John of Austria rides home from the Crusade.)

PATTERNS*

AMY LOWELL†

I walk down the garden paths,
And all the daffodils
Are blowing, and the bright blue
    squills.
I walk down the patterned garden
    paths
In my stiff brocaded gown.   5
With my powdered hair and jewelled
    fan,
I too am a rare
Pattern, as I wander down
The garden paths.
My dress is richly figured,   10
And the train
Makes a pink and silver stain
On the gravel, and the thrift
Of the borders.
Just a plate of current fashion,   15
Tripping by in high-heeled, ribboned
    shoes.

Not a softness anywhere about me,
Only whale-bone and brocade.
And I sink on a seat in the shade
Of a lime tree. For my passion   20
Wars against the stiff brocade.
The daffodils and squills
Flutter in the breeze
As they please.
And I weep;   25
For the lime tree is in blossom
And one small flower has dropped
    upon my bosom.

And the plashing of waterdrops
In the marble fountain
Comes down the garden paths.   30
The dripping never stops.
Underneath my stiffened gown
Is the softness of a woman bathing in
    a marble basin,
A basin in the midst of hedges grown
So thick, she cannot see her lover
    hiding.   35
But she guesses he is near,
And the sliding of the water
Seems the stroking of a dear
Hand upon her.

* From *Sword Blades and Poppy Seed*, by
Amy Lowell. By permission of Houghton
Mifflin Company.

† See p. 1064 for discussion.

What is summer in a fine brocaded
    gown!   40
I should like to see it lying in a heap
    upon the ground.
All the pink and silver crumpled up
    on the ground.

I would be the pink and silver as I
    ran along the paths,
And he would stumble after,
Bewildered by my laughter.   45
I should see the sun flashing from his
    sword hilt and the buckles on
    his shoes.
I would choose
To lead him in a maze along the pat-
    terned paths,
A bright and laughing maze for my
    heavy-booted lover,
Till he caught me in the shade,   50
And the buttons of his waistcoat
    bruised my body as he clasped
    me,
Aching, melting, unafraid.
With the shadows of the leaves and
    the sundrops,
And the plopping of the water-
    drops,
All about us in the open afternoon —
I am very like to swoon   56
With the weight of this brocade,
For the sun sifts through the shade.

Underneath the fallen blossom
In my bosom   60
Is a letter I have hid.
It was brought to me this morning by
    a rider from the Duke.
"Madam, we regret to inform you
    that Lord Hartwell
Died in action Thursday se'nnight."
As I read it in the white morning sun-
    light,   65
The letters squirmed like snakes.
"Any answer, Madam?" said my
    footman.
"No," I told him.

"See that the messenger takes some
    refreshment.
No, no answer."   70
And I walked into the garden,
Up and down the patterned paths,
In my stiff, correct brocade.
The blue and yellow flowers stood up
    proudly in the sun,
Each one.   75
I stood upright too,
Held rigid to the pattern
By the stiffness of my gown.
Up and down I walked,
Up and down.   80

In a month he would have been my
    husband.
In a month, here, underneath this
    lime,
We would have broke the pattern;
He for me, and I for him,
He as Colonel, I as Lady,   85
On this shady seat.
He had a whim
That sunlight carried blessing.
And I answered, "It shall be as you
    have said."
Now he is dead.   90

In summer and in winter I shall
    walk
Up and down
The patterned garden paths
In my stiff brocaded gown.
The squills and daffodils   95
Will give place to pillared roses, and
    to asters, and to snow.
I shall go
Up and down,
In my gown,
Gorgeously arrayed,   100
Boned and stayed.
And the softness of my body will be
    guarded from embrace
By each button, hook, and lace.
For the man who should loose me is
    dead,

Fighting with the Duke in Flanders,
In a pattern called a war. 106
Christ! What are patterns for?

CHRISTMAS EVE AT SEA *

JOHN MASEFIELD †

A wind is rustling "south and soft,"
Cooing a quiet country tune,
The calm sea sighs, and far aloft
The sails are ghostly in the moon.

Unquiet ripples lisp and purr, 5
A block there pipes and chirps i'
the sheave,
The wheel-ropes jar, the reef-points
stir
Faintly — and it is Christmas Eve.

The hushed sea seems to hold her
breath,
And o'er the giddy, swaying spars,
Silent and excellent as Death, 11
The dim blue skies are bright with
stars.

Dear God — they shone in Palestine
Like this, and yon pale moon serene
Looked down among the lowing kine
On Mary and the Nazarene. 16

The angels called from deep to deep,
The burning heavens felt the thrill,
Startling the flocks of silly sheep 19
And lonely shepherds on the hill.

Tonight beneath the dripping bows
Where flashing bubbles burst and
throng,
The bow-wash murmurs and sighs
and soughs
A message from the angels' song.
The moon goes nodding down the
west, 25

The drowsy helmsman strikes the
bell;
Rex Judaeorum natus est,
I charge you, brothers, sing *Nowell,
Nowell,*
Rex Judaeorum natus est.

JOHN BROWN ‡

VACHEL LINDSAY §

*(To be sung by a leader and chorus, the
leader singing the body of the poem while
the chorus interrupts with the question.)*

I've been to Palestine.
 What did you see in Palestine?
I saw the Ark of Noah —
It was made of pitch and pine;
I saw old Father Noah 5
Asleep beneath his vine;
I saw Shem, Ham and Japhet
Standing in a line;
I saw the tower of Babel
In a gorgeous sunrise shine — 10
By a weeping-willow tree
Beside the Dead Sea.

I've been to Palestine.
 What did you see in Palestine?
I saw abominations 15
And Gadarene swine;
I saw the sinful Canaanites
Upon the shewbread dine,
And spoil the temple vessels
And drink the temple wine; 20
I saw Lot's wife, a pillar of salt
Standing in the brine —
By a weeping-willow tree
Beside the Dead Sea.

I've been to Palestine. 25
 What did you see in Palestine?
Cedars on Mount Lebanon,
Gold in Ophir's mine,
And a wicked generation

* From *Poems of John Masefield.* By permission of The Macmillan Company, publishers.

† See p. 1065 for discussion.

‡ From *Collected Poems of Vachel Lindsay.*
By permission of The Macmillan Company,
publishers.

§ See p. 1065 for discussion.

Seeking for a sign;   30
And Baal's howling worshippers
Their god with leaves entwine.
And...
I SAW THE WAR-HORSE RAMPING
AND SHAKE HIS FORELOCK FINE — 35
By a weeping-willow tree
Beside the Dead Sea.

I've been to Palestine.
  What did you see in Palestine?
Old John Brown,   40
Old John Brown.
I saw his gracious wife
Dressed in a homespun gown.
I saw his seven sons
Before his feet bow down.   45
And he marched with his seven sons,
His wagons and goods and guns,
To his campfire by the sea,
By the waves of Galilee.

I've been to Palestine.   50
  What did you see in Palestine?
I saw the harp and psaltery
Played for Old John Brown.
I heard the Ram's horn blow,
Blow for Old John Brown.   55
I saw the Bulls of Bashan —
They cheered for Old John Brown.
I saw the big Behemoth —
He cheered for Old John Brown.
I saw the big Leviathan,   60
He cheered for Old John Brown.
I saw the Angel Gabriel
Great power to him assign.
I saw him fight the Canaanites
And set God's Israel free.   65
I saw him when the war was done
In his rustic chair recline —
By his camp-fire by the sea,
By the waves of Galilee.

I've been to Palestine.   70
  What did you see in Palestine?
Old John Brown,
Old John Brown.
And there he sits

To judge the world.   75
His hunting-dogs
At his feet are curled.
His eyes half-closed,
But John Brown sees
The ends of the earth,   80
The Day of Doom.
AND HIS SHOT-GUN LIES
ACROSS HIS KNEES —
Old John Brown,
Old John Brown.   85

BLOOD FEUD*

ELINOR WYLIE†

Once, when my husband was a child,
    there came
To his father's table, one who called
    him kin,
In sunbleached corduroys paler than
    his skin.

His look was grave and kind; he bore
    the name
Of the dead singer of Senlac, and his
    smile.   5
Shyly and courteously he smiled and
    spoke;]
"I've been in the laurel since the
    winter broke;
Four months, I reckon; yes, sir, quite
    a while."

He'd killed a score of foemen in the
    past,
In some blood-feud, a dark and
    monstrous thing;   10
To him it seemed his duty.   At the last
His enemies found him by a forest
    spring,
Which, as he died, lay bright beneath
    his head,
A silver shield that slowly turned to
    red.

* From *Collected Poems*, by Elinor Wylie.
By permission of and special arrangement with
Alfred A. Knopf, Inc., authorized publishers.
† See p. 1066 for discussion.

SWEENEY AMONG THE NIGHTINGALES *

T. S. ELIOT†

Apeneck Sweeney spreads his knees
Letting his arms hang down to laugh,
The zebra stripes along his jaw
Swelling to maculate giraffe.

The circles of the stormy moon   5
Slide westward toward the River
    Plate,
Death and the Raven drift above
And Sweeney guards the horned gate.

Gloomy Orion and the Dog
Are veiled; and hushed the shrunken
    seas;   10
The person in the Spanish cape
Tries to sit on Sweeney's knees

Slips and pulls the table-cloth,
Overturns a coffee-cup,
Reorganized upon the floor,   15
She yawns and draws a stocking up;

The silent man in mocha brown
Sprawls at the window-sill, and
    gapes;
The waiter brings in oranges
Bananas, figs, and hot-house grapes;

The silent vertebrate in brown   21
Contracts and concentrates, with-
    draws;
Rachel *née* Rabinovitch
Tears at the grapes with murderous
    paws;

She and the lady in the cape   25
Are suspect, thought to be in league;
Therefore the man with heavy eyes
Declines the gambit, shows fatigue,

Leaves the room and reappears
Outside the window, leaning in,   30

* From *Poems 1909–1925*, by T. S. Eliot.
By permission of Harcourt Brace and Company, Inc.

† See p. 1066 for discussion.

Branches of wistaria
Circumscribe a golden grin;

The host with someone indistinct
Converses at the door apart,
The nightingales are singing near   35
The Convent of the Sacred Heart,

And sang within the bloody wood
When Agamemnon cried aloud,
And let their liquid droppings fall 39
To stain the stiff dishonored shroud.

THE END OF THE WORLD ‡

ARCHIBALD MacLEISH §

Quite unexpectedly as Vasserot
The armless ambidextrian was light-
    ing
A match between his great and
    second toe,
And Ralph the lion was engaged in
    biting
The neck of Madame Sossman while
    the drum   5
Pointed, and Teeny was about to
    cough
In waltz-time swinging Jocko by the
    thumb —
Quite unexpectedly the top blew off:

And there, there overhead, there,
    there, hung over
Those thousands of white faces, those
    dazed eyes,   10
There in the starless dark the poise,
    the hover,
There with vast wings across the
    cancelled skies,
There in the sudden blackness the
    black pall
Of nothing, nothing, nothing — noth-
    ing at all.

‡ From *Poems, 1924–1933*, by Archibald
MacLeish. By permission of Houghton
Mifflin Company.

§ See p. 1066 for discussion.

GROUP TWO

POEMS OF HUMAN CHARACTER

CHARACTER OF A HAPPY LIFE

HENRY WOTTON*

How happy is he born and taught
That serveth not another's will;
Whose armour is his honest thought
And simple truth his utmost skill! 4

Whose passions not his masters are,
Whose soul is still prepared for death,
Not tied unto the world with care
Of public fame, or private breath;

Who envies none that chance doth
      raise
Or vice; who never understood   10
How deepest wounds are given by
      praise;
Nor rules of state, but rules of good:

Who hath his life from rumours
      freed,
Whose conscience is his strong re-
      treat;
Whose state can neither flatterers
      feed,   15
Nor ruin make oppressors great;

Who God doth late and early pray
More of his grace than gifts to lend;
And entertains the harmless day
With a well-chosen book or friend; 20

—This man is freed from servile bands
Of hope to rise, or fear to fall;
Lord of himself, though not of lands;
And having nothing, yet hath all.

*See p. 1068 for discussion.

TO HIS COY MISTRESS

ANDREW MARVELL †

Had we but world enough, and time,
This coyness, Lady, were no crime
We would sit down and think which
      way
To walk and pass our long love's day.
Thou by the Indian Ganges' side 5
Shouldst rubies find: I by the tide
Of Humber would complain.   I
      would
Love you ten years before the Flood,
And you should, if you please, refuse
Till the conversion of the Jews.   10
My vegetable love should grow
Vaster than empires, and more slow;
An hundred years should go to praise
Thine eyes and on thy forehead gaze;
Two hundred to adore each breast,
But thirty thousand to the rest;   16
An age at least to every part,
And the last age should show your
      heart.
For, Lady, you deserve this state,
Nor would I love at lower rate.   20
   But at my back I always hear
Time's wingèd chariot hurrying near;
And yonder all before us lie
Deserts of vast eternity.   24
Thy beauty shall no more be found,
Nor, in thy marble vault, shall
      sound
My echoing song: then worms shall
      try
That long preserved virginity,
And your quaint honour turn to dust,
And into ashes all my lust: 30

† See p. 1068 for discussion.

The grave's a fine and private place,
But none, I think, do there embrace.
  Now therefore, while the youthful
      hue
Sits on thy skin like morning dew,
And while thy willing soul trans-
      pires 35
At every pore with instant fires,
Now let us sport us while we may,
And now, like amorous birds of prey,
Rather at once our time devour
Than languish in his slow-chapt
      power. 40
Let us roll all our strength and all
Our sweetness up into one ball,
And tear our pleasures with rough
      strife
Thorough the iron gates of life:
Thus, though we cannot make our
      sun 45
Stand still, yet we will make him run.

SHE WAS A PHANTOM OF DELIGHT

WILLIAM WORDSWORTH *

She was a Phantom of delight
When first she gleamed upon my
      sight;
A lovely Apparition, sent
To be a moment's ornament;
Her eyes as stars of Twilight fair; 5
Like Twilight's, too, her dusky hair;
But all things else about her drawn
From May-time and the cheerful
      Dawn;
A dancing Shape, an Image gay,
To haunt, to startle, and way-lay. 10

I saw her upon nearer view,
A Spirit, yet a Woman too!
Her household motions light and free,
And steps of virgin-liberty;
A countenance in which did meet 15
Sweet records, promises as sweet;

A Creature not too bright or good
For human nature's daily food;
For transient sorrows, simple wiles,
Praise, blame, love, kisses, tears, and
      smiles. 20

And now I see with eye serene
The very pulse of the machine;
A Being breathing thoughtful breath,
A Traveller between life and death;
The reason firm, the temperate will,
Endurance, foresight, strength, and
      skill; 26
A perfect Woman, nobly planned,
To warn, to comfort, and command;
And yet a Spirit still, and bright
With something of angelic light. 30

CHARACTER OF THE HAPPY WARRIOR

WILLIAM WORDSWORTH †

Who is the happy warrior? Who is
      he
That every man in arms should wish
      to be?
— It is the generous spirit, who, when
      brought
Among the tasks of real life, hath
      wrought
Upon the plan that pleased his boyish
      thought: 5
Whose high endeavors are an inward
      light
That makes the path before him al-
      ways bright:
Who, with a natural instinct to dis-
      cern
What knowledge can perform, is
      diligent to learn;
Abides by this resolve, and stops not
      there, 10
But makes his moral being his prime
      care;

* See p. 1068 for discussion.

† See p. 1068 for discussion.

Who, doomed to go in company with
    Pain,
And Fear, and Bloodshed, miserable
    train!
Turns his necessity to glorious gain;
In face of these doth exercise a power
Which is our human nature's highest
    dower;   16
Controls them and subdues, trans-
    mutes, bereaves
Of their bad influence, and their good
    receives:
By objects, which might force the
    soul to abate
Her feeling, rendered more com-
    passionate;   20
Is placable — because occasions rise
So often that demand such sacrifice;
More skilful in self-knowledge, even
    more pure,
As tempted more; more able to en-
    dure,
As more exposed to suffering and
    distress;   25
Thence, also, more alive to tender-
    ness.
— 'Tis he whose law is reason; who
    depends
Upon that law as on the best of
    friends;
Whence, in a state where men are
    tempted still
To evil for a guard against worse
    ill,   30
And what in quality or act is best
Doth seldom on a right foundation
    rest,
He labors good on good to fix, and
    owes
To virtue every triumph that he
    knows:
— Who, if he rise to station of com-
    mand,   35
Rises by open means; and there will
    stand
On honorable terms, or else retire,
And in himself possess his own desire;

Who comprehends his trust, and to
    the same
Keeps faithful with a singleness of
    aim;   40
And therefore does not stoop, nor lie
    in wait
For wealth, or honors, or for worldly
    state;
Whom they must follow; on whose
    head must fall,
Like showers of manna, if they come
    at all:
Whose powers shed round him in the
    common strife,   45
Or mild concerns of ordinary life,
A constant influence, a peculiar grace;
But who, if he be called upon to face
Some awful moment to which Heaven
    has joined
Great issues, good or bad for human
    kind,   50
Is happy as a lover; and attired
With sudden brightness, like a man
    inspired;
And, through the heat of conflict,
    keeps the law
In calmness made, and sees what he
    foresaw;
Or if an unexpected call succeed, 55
Come when it will, is equal to the
    need:
— He who, though thus endued as
    with a sense
And faculty for storm and turbulence,
Is yet a soul whose master-bias leans
To homefelt pleasures and to gentle
    scenes;   60
Sweet images! which, whereso'er he
    be,
Are at his heart; and such fidelity
It is his darling passion to approve;
More brave for this, that he hath
    much to love: —
'Tis, finally, the man, who, lifted
    high,   65
Conspicuous object in a nation's eye,
Or left unthought-of in obscurity —

Who, with a toward or untoward lot,
Prosperous or adverse, to his wish or
   not —
Plays, in the many games of life, that
   one   70
Where what he most doth value must
   be won:
Whom neither shape of danger can
   dismay,
Nor thought of tender happiness be-
   tray;
Who, not content that former worth
   stand fast,
Looks forward, persevering to the
   last,   75
From well to better, daily self-surpast:
Who, whether praise of him must
   walk the earth
For ever, and to noble deeds give
   birth,
Or he must fall, to sleep without his
   fame,   79
And leave a dead unprofitable name —
Finds comfort in himself and in his
   cause;
And, while the mortal mist is gather-
   ing, draws
His breath in confidence of Heaven's
   applause:
This is the happy warrior; this is he
That every man in arms should wish
   to be.   85

ULYSSES

ALFRED TENNYSON *

It little profits that an idle king,
By this still hearth, among these bar-
   ren crags,
Matched with an agèd wife, I mete
   and dole
Unequal laws unto a savage race,
That hoard, and sleep, and feed, and
   know not me.   5
I cannot rest from travel; I will
   drink

* See p. 1069 for discussion.

Life to the lees. All times I have en-
   joyed
Greatly, have suffered greatly, both
   with those
That loved me, and alone; on shore,
   and when
Thro' scudding drifts the rainy
   Hyades   10
Vext the dim sea. I am become a
   name;
For always roaming with a hungry
   heart
Much have I seen and known — cities
   of men
And manners, climates, councils,
   governments,
Myself not least, but honored of
   them all —   15
And drunk delight of battle with my
   peers,
Far on the ringing plains of windy
   Troy.
I am a part of all that I have met;
Yet all experience is an arch where-
   thro'
Gleams that untravelled world, whose
   margin fades   20
For ever and for ever when I move.
How dull it is to pause, to make an
   end,
To rust unburnished, not to shine in
   use!
As tho' to breathe were life! Life
   piled on life
Were all too little, and of one to me
Little remains; but every hour is
   saved   26
From that eternal silence, something
   more,
A bringer of new things; and vile it
   were
For some three suns to store and
   hoard myself,
And this gray spirit yearning in de-
   sire   30
To follow knowledge, like a sinking
   star,

Beyond the utmost bound of human
thought.
This is my son, mine own Tele-
machus,
To whom I leave the sceptre and the
isle —
Well-loved of me, discerning to fulfil
This labor, by slow prudence to make
mild   36
A rugged people, and thro' soft
degrees
Subdue them to the useful and the
good.
Most blameless is he, centred in the
sphere
Of common duties, decent not to fail
In offices of tenderness, and pay   41
Meet adoration to my household
gods,
When I am gone. He works his work,
I mine.
There lies the port; the vessel puffs
her sail;
There gloom the dark, broad seas.
My mariners,   45
Souls that have toiled, and wrought,
and thought with me —
That ever with a frolic welcome took
The thunder and the sunshine, and
opposed
Free hearts, free foreheads — you
and I are old;
Old age hath yet his honor and his
toil.   50
Death closes all; but something ere
the end,
Some work of noble note, may yet be
done,
Not unbecoming men that strove
with Gods.
The lights begin to twinkle from the
rocks;
The long day wanes; the slow moon
climbs; the deep   55
Moans round with many voices.
Come, my friends,
'Tis not too late to seek a newer world

Push off, and sitting well in order
smite
The sounding furrows; for my pur-
pose holds
To sail beyond the sunset, and the
baths   60
Of all the western stars, until I die.
It may be that the gulfs will wash us
down;
It may be we shall touch the Happy
Isles,
And see the great Achilles, whom we
knew.
Tho' much is taken, much abides; and
tho'   65
We are not now that strength which
in old days
Moved earth and heaven, that which
we are, we are —
One equal temper of heroic hearts,
Made weak by time and fate, but
strong in will
To strive, to seek, to find, and not to
yield.   70

A GRAMMARIAN'S FUNERAL

SHORTLY AFTER THE REVIVAL OF
LEARNING IN EUROPE

ROBERT BROWNING *

Let us begin and carry up this corpse,
Singing together.
Leave we the common crofts, the vul-
gar thorpes
Each in its tether
Sleeping safe on the bosom of the
plain,   5
Cared-for till cock-crow:
Look out if yonder be not day again
Rimming the rock-row!
That's the appropriate country; there,
man's thought,
Rarer, intenser,   10
Self-gathered for an outbreak, as it
ought,
Chafes in the censer.

* See p. 1069 for discussion.

Leave we the unlettered plain its herd
    and crop;
  Seek we sepulture
On a tall mountain, citied to the top,
  Crowded with culture!   16
All the peaks soar, but one the rest
    excels;
  Clouds overcome it;
No! yonder sparkle is the citadel's
  Circling its summit.   20
Thither our path lies; wind we up the
    heights;
  Wait ye the warning?
Our low life was the level's and the
    night's;
  He's for the morning.
Step to a tune, square chests, erect
    each head,   25
  'Ware the beholders!
This is our master, famous, calm and
    dead,
  Borne on our shoulders.

Sleep, crop and herd! sleep, darling
    thorpe and croft,
  Safe from the weather!   30
He, whom we convoy to his grave
    aloft,
  Singing together,
He was a man born with thy face and
    throat,
  Lyric Apollo!
Long he lived nameless: how should
  Spring take note   35
  Winter would follow?
Till lo, the little touch, and youth was
    gone!
  Cramped and diminished,
Moaned he, "New measures, other
    feet anon!
  My dance is finished"?   40
No, that's the world's way: (keep the
    mountain-side,
  Make for the city!)
He knew the signal, and stepped on
    with pride
  Over men's pity;

Left play for work, and grappled with
    the world   45
  Bent on escaping:
"What's in the scroll," quoth he,
  "thou keepest furled?
  Show me their shaping,
Theirs who most studied man, the
    bard and sage —
  Give!" — So, he gowned him, 50
Straight got by heart that book to its
    last page:
  Learned, we found him.
Yea, but we found him bald too, eyes
    like lead,
  Accents uncertain:
"Time to taste life," another would
    have said,   55
  "Up with the curtain!"
This man said rather, "Actual life
    comes next?
  Patience a moment!
Grant I have mastered learning's
    crabbed text,
  Still there's the comment.   60
Let me know all! Prate not of most
    or least,
  Painful or easy!
Even to the crumbs I'd fain eat up
    the feast,
  Ay, nor feel queasy."
Oh, such a life as he resolved to live,
  When he had learned it,   66
When he had gathered all books had
    to give!
  Sooner, he spurned it.
Image the whole, then execute the
    parts —
  Fancy the fabric   70
Quite, ere you build, ere steel strike
    fire from quartz,
  Ere mortar dab brick!

(Here's the town-gate reached: there's
    the market-place
  Gaping before us.)
Yea, this in him was the peculiar grace
  (Hearten our chorus!)   76

That before living he'd learn how to
  live —
  No end to learning:
Earn the means first — God surely
  will contrive
  Use for our earning.   80
Others mistrust and say, "But time
  escapes:
  Live now or never!"
He said, "What's time? Leave Now
  for dogs and apes!
  Man has Forever."
Back to his book then: deeper
  drooped his head: 85
  Calculus racked him:
Leaden before, his eyes grew dross of
  lead:
  Tussis attacked him.
"Now, master, take a little rest!" —
  not he!
  (Caution redoubled,   90
Step two abreast, the way winds nar-
  rowly!)
  Not a whit troubled,
Back to his studies, fresher than at
  first,
  Fierce as a dragon
He (soul-hydroptic with a sacred
  thirst)   95
  Sucked at the flagon.
Oh, if we draw a circle premature,
  Heedless of far gain,
Greedy for quick returns of profit,
  sure
  Bad is our bargain!   100
Was it not great? did he not throw on
  God
  (He loves the burthen) —
God's task to make the heavenly
  period
  Perfect the earthen?
Did he not magnify the mind, show
  clear   105
  Just what it all meant?
He would not discount life, as fools
  do here,
  Paid by instalment.

He ventured neck or nothing —
  heaven's success
  Found, or earth's failure: 110
"Wilt thou trust death or not?"
  He answered "Yes!
  Hence with life's pale lure!"
That low man seeks a little thing to
  do,
  Sees it and does it:
This high man, with a great thing to
  pursue,   115
  Dies ere he knows it.
That low man goes on adding one to
  one,
  His hundred's soon hit:
This high man, aiming at a million,
  Misses an unit.   120
That, has the world here — should he
  need the next,
  Let the world mind him!
This, throws himself on God, and un-
  perplexed
  Seeking shall find him.
So, with the throttling hands of
  death at strife,   125
  Ground he at grammar;
Still, through the rattle, parts of
  speech were rife:
  While he could stammer
He settled *Hoti's* business — let it
  be! —
  Properly based *Oun* —   130
Gave us the doctrine of the enclitic
  De,
  Dead from the waist down.
Well, here's the platform, here's the
  proper place:
  Hail to your purlieus,
All ye highfliers of the feathered race,
  Swallows and curlews!   136
Here's the top-peak; the multitude
  below
  Live, for they can, there:
This man decided not to Live but
  Know —
  Bury this man there?   140

Here — here's his place, where me-
   teors shoot, clouds form,
  Lightnings are loosened,
Stars come and go! Let joy break
   with the storm,
  Peace let the dew send!

Lofty designs must close in like
   effects: 145
Loftily lying,
Leave him — still loftier than the
   world suspects,
Living and dying.

O PIONEERS!

WALT WHITMAN *

    Come my tan-faced children,
Follow well in order, get your weapons ready,
Have you your pistols? have you your sharp-edged axes?
    Pioneers! O pioneers!

    For we cannot tarry here,   5
We must march my darlings, we must bear the brunt of danger,
We the youthful sinewy races, all the rest on us depend,
    Pioneers! O pioneers!

    O you youths, Western youths,
So impatient, full of action, full of manly pride and friendship,   10
Plain I see you Western youths, see you tramping with the foremost,
    Pioneers! O pioneers!

    Have the elder races halted?
Do they droop and end their lesson, wearied over there beyond the seas?
We take up the task eternal, and the burden and the lesson,   15
    Pioneers! O pioneers!

    All the past we leave behind,
We debouch upon a newer mightier world, varied world,
Fresh and strong the world we seize, world of labor and the march,
    Pioneers! O pioneers!   20

    We detachments steady throwing,
Down the edges, through the passes, up the mountains steep,
Conquering, holding, daring, venturing as we go the unknown ways,
    Pioneers! O pioneers!

    We primeval forests felling,   25
We the rivers stemming, vexing we and piercing deep the mines within,
We the surface broad surveying, we the virgin soil upheaving,
    Pioneers! O pioneers!

* See p. 1069 for discussion.

        Colorado men are we,
From the peaks gigantic, from the great sierras and the high plateaus,   30
From the mine and from the gully, from the hunting trail we come,
        Pioneers!　O pioneers!

        From Nebraska, from Arkansas,
Central inland race are we, from Missouri, with the continental blood inter-
    vein'd,
All the hands of comrades clasping, all the Southern, all the Northern,   35
        Pioneers!　O pioneers!

        O resistless restless race!
O beloved race in all!　O my breast aches with tender love for all!
O I mourn and yet exult, I am rapt with love for all,
        Pioneers!　O pioneers!   40

        Raise the mighty mother mistress,
Waving high the delicate mistress, over all the starry mistress (bend your
    heads all),
Raise the fang'd and warlike mistress, stern, impassive, weapon'd mistress,
        Pioneers!　O pioneers!

        See my children, resolute children,   45
By those swarms upon our rear we must never yield or falter,
Ages back in ghostly millions frowning there behind us urging,
        Pioneers!　O pioneers!

        On and on the compact ranks,
With accessions ever waiting, with the places of the dead quickly fill'd,   50
Through the battle, through defeat, moving yet and never stopping,
        Pioneers!　O pioneers!

        O to die advancing on!
Are there some of us to droop and die? has the hour come?
Then upon the march we fittest die, soon and sure the gap is fill'd,   55
        Pioneers!　O pioneers!

        All the pulses of the world,
Falling in they beat for us, with the Western movement beat,
Holding single or together, steady moving to the front, all for us,
        Pioneers!　O pioneers!   60

        Life's involv'd and varied pageants,
All the forms and shows, all the workmen at their work,
All the seamen and the landsmen, all the masters with their slaves,
        Pioneers!　O pioneers!

All the hapless silent lovers, 65
All the prisoners in the prisons, all the righteous and the wicked,
All the joyous, all the sorrowing, all the living, all the dying,
    Pioneers! O pioneers!

I too with my soul and body,
We, a curious trio, picking, wandering on our way, 70
Through these shores amid the shadows, with the apparitions pressing,
    Pioneers! O pioneers!

Lo, the darting bowling orb!
Lo, the brother orbs around, all the clustering suns and planets,
All the dazzling days, all the mystic nights with dreams, 75
    Pioneers! O pioneers!

These are of us, they are with us,
All for primal needed work, while the followers there in embryo wait behind,
We today's procession heading, we the route for travel clearing,
    Pioneers! O pioneers! 80

O you daughters of the West!
O you young and elder daughters! O you mothers and you wives!
Never must you be divided, in our ranks you move united,
    Pioneers! O pioneers!

Minstrels latent on the prairies! 85
(Shrouded bards of other lands, you may rest, you have done your work),
Soon I hear you coming warbling, soon you rise and tramp amid us,
    Pioneers! O pioneers!

Not for delectations sweet,
Not the cushion and the slipper, not the peaceful and the studious,
Not the riches safe and palling, not for us the tame enjoyment, 90
    Pioneers! O pioneers!

Do the feasters gluttonous feast?
Do the corpulent sleepers sleep? Have they lock'd and bolted doors?
Still be ours the diet hard, and the blanket on the ground, 95
    Pioneers! O pioneers!

Has the night descended?
Was the road of late so toilsome? did we stop discouraged nodding on our way?
Yet a passing hour I yield you in your tracks to pause oblivious,
    Pioneers! O pioneers! 100

Till with sound of trumpet,
Far, far off the daybreak call — hark! how loud and clear I hear it wind,
Swift! to the head of the army! — swift! spring to your places,
    Pioneers! O pioneers!

O CAPTAIN! MY CAPTAIN!

WALT WHITMAN *

O Captain! my Captain! our fearful trip is done,
The ship has weather'd every rack, the prize we sought is won,
The port is near, the bells I hear, the people all exulting,
While follow eyes the steady keel, the vessel grim and daring;
    But O heart! heart! heart!   5
      O the bleeding drops of red,
         Where on the deck my Captain lies,
            Fallen cold and dead.

O Captain! my Captain! rise up and hear the bells;
Rise up — for you the flag is flung — for you the bugle trills,   10
For you bouquets and ribbon'd wreaths — for you the shores a-crowding,
For you they call, the swaying mass, their eager faces turning;
      Here Captain! dear father!
       This arm beneath your head!
         It is some dream that on the deck,   15
          You've fallen cold and dead.

My Captain does not answer, his lips are pale and still,
My father does not feel my arm, he has no pulse nor will,
The ship is anchor'd safe and sound, its voyage closed and done,
From fearful trip the victor ship comes in with object won;   20
      Exult O shores, and ring O bells!
       But I with mournful tread,
         Walk the deck my Captain lies,
           Fallen cold and dead.

* See p. 1069 for discussion.

THE FIDDLER OF DOONEY *

WILLIAM BUTLER YEATS †

When I play on my fiddle in Dooney,
Folk dance like a wave of the sea;
My cousin is priest in Kilvarnet,
My brother in Mocharabuiee.

I passed my brother and cousin: 5
They read in their books of prayer;

* From Collected Poems of W. B. Yeats. By permission of The Macmillan Company, publishers.

† See p. 1070 for discussion.

I read in my books of songs
I bought at the Sligo fair.

When we come at the end of time
To Peter sitting in state,   10
He will smile on the three old spirits,
But call me first through the gate;

For the good are always the merry,
Save by an evil chance,
And the merry love the fiddle,   15
And the merry love to dance:

And when the folk there spy me,
They will all come up to me,
With "Here is the fiddler of Dooney!"
And dance like a wave of the sea. 20

MINIVER CHEEVY *

EDWIN ARLINGTON
ROBINSON †

Miniver Cheevy, child of scorn,
  Grew lean while he assailed the
    seasons;
He wept that he was ever born,
  And he had reasons.

Miniver loved the days of old   5
  When swords were bright and steeds
    were prancing;
The vision of a warrior bold
  Would set him dancing.

Miniver sighed for what was not,
  And dreamed, and rested from his
    labors;   10
He dreamed of Thebes and Camelot,
  And Priam's neighbors.

Miniver mourned the ripe renown
  That made so many a name so
    fragrant:
He mourned Romance, now on the
    town,   15
  And Art, a vagrant.

Miniver loved the Medici,
  Albeit he had never seen one;
He would have sinned incessantly
  Could he have been one.   20

Miniver cursed the commonplace
  And eyed a khaki suit with loath-
    ing;

He missed the mediaeval grace
  Of iron clothing.

Miniver scorned the gold he
    sought,   25
But sore annoyed was he without
    it;
Miniver thought, and thought, and
    thought,
  And thought about it.

Miniver Cheevy, born too late,
  Scratched his head and kept on
    thinking: 30
Miniver coughed, and called it
    fate,
  And kept on drinking.

A LADY ‡

AMY LOWELL §

You are beautiful and faded,
Like an old opera tune
Played upon a harpsichord;
Or like the sun-flooded silks
Of an eighteenth-century boudoir. 5
In your eyes
Smoulder the fallen roses of outlived
    minutes,
And the perfume of your soul
Is vague and suffusing,
With the pungence of sealed spice
    jars.   10
Your half-tones delight me,
And I grow mad with gazing
At your blent colors.

My vigor is a new-minted penny,
Which I cast at your feet.   15
Gather it up from the dust,
That its sparkle may amuse you.

* From *The Town Down the River*, by Edwin Arlington Robinson. By permission of
Charles Scribner's Sons.

† See p. 1071 for discussion.

‡ From *Sword Blades and Poppy Seed*, by
Amy Lowell. By permission of Houghton
Mifflin Company.

§ See p. 1071 for discussion.

ACQUAINTED WITH THE NIGHT*

ROBERT FROST †

I have been one acquainted with the
    night.
I have walked out in rain — and back
    in rain.
I have outwalked the furthest city
    light.

I have looked down the saddest city
    lane.
I have passed by the watchman on
    his beat   5

  * From *West-Running Brook*, by Robert
Frost, copyright, 1928. By permission of
Henry Holt and Company.

  † See p. 1071 for discussion.

And dropped my eyes, unwilling to
    explain.

I have stood still and stopped the
    sound of feet
When far away an interrupted cry
Came over houses from another
    street,

But not to call me back or say good-
    bye;   10
And further still at an unearthly
    height,
One luminary clock against the sky

Proclaimed the time was neither
    wrong nor right.
I have been one acquainted with the
    night.

COOL TOMBS ‡

CARL SANDBURG §

When Abraham Lincoln was shoveled into the tombs, he forgot the copperheads and the assassin... in the dust, in the cool tombs.

And Ulysses Grant lost all thought of con men and Wall Street, cash and collateral turned ashes... in the dust, in the cool tombs.

Pocahontas' body, lovely as a poplar, sweet as a red haw in November or a
pawpaw in May — did she wonder? does she remember?... in the dust, in
the cool tombs?

Take any streetful of people buying clothes and groceries, cheering a hero or
throwing confetti and blowing tin horns... tell me if the lovers are losers...
tell me if any get more than the lovers... in the dust... in the cool tombs.

  ‡ From *Cornhuskers*, by Carl Sandburg, copyright, 1918. By permission of Henry Holt and
Company.

  § See p. 1071 for discussion.

ABRAHAM LINCOLN WALKS AT MIDNIGHT ¶

IN SPRINGFIELD, ILLINOIS

VACHEL LINDSAY ‖

It is portentous, and a thing of state
That here at midnight in our little
    town,

A mourning figure walks, and will
    not rest,
Near the old court-house pacing up
    and down.

  ¶ From *Collected Poems of Vachel Lindsay*.
By permission of The Macmillan Company,
publishers.

  ‖ See p. 1072 for discussion.

Or by his homestead, or in shadowed
  yards, 5
He lingers where his children used to
  play;
Or through the market, on the well-
  worn stones,
He stalks until the dawn-stars burn
  away.

A bronzed lank man! His suit of
  ancient black,
A famous high top-hat and plain
  worn shawl, 10
Make his the quaint great figure that
  men love,
The prairie lawyer, master of us all.

He cannot sleep upon his hillside now.
He is among us — as in times before!
And we who toss and lie awake for
  long 15
Breathe deep, and start, to see him
  pass the door.

His head is bowed. He thinks on
  men and kings.
Yea, when the sick world cries, how
  can he sleep?
Too many peasants fight, they know
  not why;
Too many homesteads in black terror
  weep. 20

The sins of all the war-lords burn his
  heart.
He sees the dreadnaughts scouring
  every main.
He carries on his shawl-wrapped
  shoulders now
The bitterness, the folly and the pain.

He cannot rest until a spirit-dawn 25
Shall come — the shining hope of
  Europe free:
The league of sober folk, the Workers'
  Earth,
Bringing long peace to Cornland,
  Alp and Sea.

It breaks his heart that kings must
  murder still,
That all his hours of travail here for
  men 30
Seem yet in vain. And who will
  bring white peace
That he may sleep upon his hill again?

A DROVER *

PADRAIC COLUM †

To Meath of the pastures,
  From wet hills by the sea,
Through Leitrim and Longford,
  Go my cattle and me.

I hear in the darkness 5
  Their slipping and breathing —
I name them the byways
  They're to pass without heeding;

Then the wet winding roads,
  Brown bogs with black water; 10
And my thoughts on white ships,
  And the King o' Spain's daughter.

O farmer, strong farmer! —
  You can spend at the fair;
But your face you must turn 15
  To your crops and your care.

And soldiers, red soldiers! —
  You've seen many lands;
But you walk two by two,
  And by captain's commands. 20

Oh, the smell of the beasts,
  The wet wind in the morn;
And the proud and hard earth
  Never broken for corn!

And the crowds at the fair, 25
  The herds loosened and blind,

* From *Poems of Padraic Colum*. By permission of The Macmillan Company, publishers.

† See p. 1072 for discussion.

Loud words and dark faces
  And the wild blood behind!

(O strong men, with your best
  I would strive breast to breast —
I could quiet your herds   31
  With my words, with my words.)

I will bring you, my kine,
  Where there's grass to the
    knee;
But you'll think of scant crop-
    pings   35
  Harsh with salt of the sea.

TUMBLING MUSTARD *

TO H. A. L.

MALCOLM COWLEY †

Born in a fence-corner,
  raised in a coulee,
  married in Nebraska,
  parted on the Sound:
They call me Tumbling Mustard, "Hey, Tumbling Mustard, what's your
  business, listen Buddy, where are you bound?"   5

  Monday in Omaha,
  Tuesday in Dakota,
  one day in Memphis,
  three in Allentown:
Mud roads and stony roads, concrete and macadam; she would never leave
  me if I would settle down.   10

  Columbine and larkspur,
  peony and dahlia,
  cornflower, mayflower,
  each has a place:
I am the tumble-weed that rolls across the prairies, winds at the back of it,
  mountains in its face.   15

  Tumble-weed, tumble-weed,
  riding his velocipede
  east side, west side,
  all around the moon:
Denver, San Francisco, Winnipeg and Dallas, maybe if the gas holds out we'll
  get there soon.   20

* From *Blue Juniata*, by Malcolm Cowley.   By permission of the author.
† See p. 1072 for discussion.

LYRICS OF EMOTION AND EXPERIENCE

HARK! HARK! THE LARK

WILLIAM SHAKESPEARE *

Hark! hark! the lark at heaven's gate
   sings,
  And Phoebus 'gins arise,
His steeds to water at those springs
  On chaliced flowers that lies;
And winking Mary-buds begin   5
  To ope their golden eyes;
With every thing that pretty is,
   My lady sweet, arise;
     Arise, arise!

TAKE, O TAKE

WILLIAM SHAKESPEARE

Take, O take those lips away
That so sweetly were forsworn,
And those eyes, the break of day,
Lights that do mislead the morn.
But my kisses bring again,   5
  Bring again —
Seals of love, but seal'd in vain,
  Seal'd in vain!

THE PASSIONATE SHEPHERD TO HIS LOVE

CHRISTOPHER MARLOWE †

Come live with me and be my
   Love,
And we will all the pleasures prove
That hills and valleys, dales and
   fields,
Or woods or steepy mountain yields.

* See p. 1074 for discussion.
† See p. 1074 for discussion.
‡ See p. 1074 for discussion.

And we will sit upon the rocks,   5
And see the shepherds feed their
   flocks
By shallow rivers, to whose falls
Melodious birds sing madrigals.

And I will make thee beds of roses
And a thousand fragrant posies;   10
A cap of flowers, and a kirtle
Embroider'd all with leaves of myrtle.

A gown made of the finest wool
Which from our pretty lambs we
   pull;
Fair-linèd slippers for the cold,   15
With buckles of the purest gold.

A belt of straw and ivy-buds
With coral clasps and amber studs:
And if these pleasures may thee move,
Come live with me and be my Love.

The shepherd swains shall dance and
   sing   21
For they delight each May morning:
If these delights thy mind may
   move,
Then live with me and be my Love.

UPON JULIA'S CLOTHES

ROBERT HERRICK‡

Whenas in silks my Julia goes,
Then, then, methinks, how sweetly
   flows
The liquefaction of her clothes!

Next, when I cast mine eyes and see
That brave vibration each way free
— O how that glittering taketh me! 6

TO THE VIRGINS, TO MAKE MUCH OF TIME

ROBERT HERRICK *

Gather ye rosebuds while ye may,
  Old Time is still a-flying:
And this same flower that smiles
    today
Tomorrow will be dying.

The glorious lamp of heaven, the sun,
  The higher he's a-getting,   6
The sooner will his race be run,
  And nearer he's to setting.

That age is best which is the first, 9
  When youth and blood are warmer;
But being spent, the worse, and worst
  Time still succeed the former.

Then be not coy, but use your time,
  And while ye may, go marry:
For having lost but once your prime,
  You may for ever tarry.   16

TO LUCASTA, ON GOING TO THE WARS

RICHARD LOVELACE †

Tell me not, Sweet, I am unkind,
  That from the nunnery
Of thy chaste breast and quiet mind
  To war and arms I fly.

True, a new mistress now I chase, 5
  The first foe in the field;
And with a stronger faith embrace
  A sword, a horse, a shield.

Yet this inconstancy is such
  As thou too shalt adore;   10
I could not love thee, Dear, so much,
  Loved I not Honour more.

  * See p. 1074 for discussion.
  † See p. 1075 for discussion.

AH, HOW SWEET IT IS TO LOVE!

JOHN DRYDEN ‡

Ah, how sweet it is to love!
  Ah, how gay in young Desire!
And what pleasing pains we prove
  When we first approach Love's
    fire!
Pains of love be sweeter far   5
Than all other pleasures are.

Sighs which are from lovers blown
  Do but gently heave the heart:
Ev'n the tears they shed alone
  Cure, like trickling balm, their
    smart: 10
Lovers, when they lose their breath,
Bleed away in easy death.

Love and Time with reverence use,
  Treat them like a parting friend;
Nor the golden gifts refuse   15
  Which in youth sincere they send:
For each year their price is more,
And they less simple than before.

Love, like spring-tides full and high,
  Swells in every youthful vein; 20
But each tide does less supply,
  Till they quite shrink in again:
If a flow in age appear,
'Tis but rain, and runs not clear.

SONG

MATTHEW PRIOR §

The merchant, to secure his treasure,
  Conveys it in a borrow'd name:
Euphelia serves to grace my measure;
  But Chloe is my real flame.

My softest verse, my darling lyre, 5
  Upon Euphelia's toilet lay;

  ‡ See p. 1075 for discussion.
  § See p. 1075 for discussion.

When Chloe noted her desire
  That I should sing, that I should
    play.

My lyre I tune, my voice I raise; 9
  But with my numbers mix my sighs:
And while I sing Euphelia's praise,
  I fix my soul on Chloe's eyes.

Fair Chloe blush'd: Euphelia
  frown'd:
I sung, and gazed: I play'd, and
  trembled:
And Venus to the Loves around 15
  Remark'd, how ill we all dissembled.

SWEET AFTON

ROBERT BURNS *

Flow gently, sweet Afton! among thy green braes,
Flow gently, I'll sing thee a song in thy praise;
My Mary's asleep by thy murmuring stream,
Flow gently, sweet Afton, disturb not her dream.

Thou stock dove whose echo resounds thro' the glen,   5
Ye wild whistling blackbirds in yon thorny den,
Thou green crested lapwing, thy screaming forbear,
I charge you, disturb not my slumbering Fair.

How lofty, sweet Afton, thy neighbouring hills,
Far mark'd with the courses of clear, winding rills;   10
There daily I wander as noon rises high,
My flocks and my Mary's sweet cot in my eye.

How pleasant thy banks and green valleys below,
Where, wild in the woodlands, the primroses blow;
There oft, as mild Ev'ning weeps over the lea,   15
The sweet-scented birk shades my Mary and me.

Thy crystal stream, Afton, how lovely it glides,
And winds by the cot where my Mary resides;
How wanton thy waters her snowy feet lave,
As, gathering sweet flowerets, she stems thy clear wave.   20

Flow gently, sweet Afton, among thy green braes,
Flow gently, sweet river, the theme of my lays;
My Mary's asleep by thy murmuring stream,
Flow gently, sweet Afton, disturb not her dream.

* See p. 1075 for discussion.

SHE DWELT AMONG THE UNTRODDEN WAYS

WILLIAM WORDSWORTH *

She dwelt among the untrodden ways
  Beside the springs of Dove,
A Maid whom there were none to
    praise
And very few to love:

A violet by a mossy stone   5
  Half hidden from the eye!
— Fair as a star, when only one
  Is shining in the sky.

She lived unknown, and few could
    know
  When Lucy ceased to be;   10
But she is in her grave, and, oh,
  The difference to me!

A SLUMBER DID MY SPIRIT SEAL

WILLIAM WORDSWORTH

A slumber did my spirit seal;
  I had no human fears:
She seemed a thing that could not feel
  The touch of earthly years.

No motion has she now, no force;   5
  She neither hears nor sees;
Rolled in round earth's diurnal
    course,
  With rocks, and stones, and trees.

ROSE AYLMER

WALTER SAVAGE LANDOR †

Ah, what avails the sceptred race!
  Ah, what the form divine!
What every virtue, every grace!
  Rose Aylmer, all were thine.

* See p. 1076 for discussion.
† See p. 1076 for discussion.

Rose Aylmer, whom these wakeful
    eyes   5
  May weep, but never see,
A night of memories and sighs
  I consecrate to thee.

ON HIS OWN DEATH

WALTER SAVAGE LANDOR

Death stands above me, whispering
    low
  I know not what into my ear:
Of his strange language all I know
  Is, there is not a word of fear.

FINIS

WALTER SAVAGE LANDOR

I strove with none, for none was
    worth my strife.
Nature I loved, and, next to Na-
    ture, Art:
I warm'd both hands before the fire
    of life;
It sinks, and I am ready to depart.

THERE BE NONE OF BEAUTY'S DAUGHTERS

LORD BYRON‡

There be none of Beauty's daughters
  With a magic like thee;
And like music on the waters
  Is thy sweet voice to me:
When, as if its sound were causing 5
  The charmed ocean's pausing,
The waves lie still and gleaming,
And the lull'd winds seem dreaming:

And the midnight moon is weaving
  Her bright chain o'er the deep;   10
Whose breast is gently heaving,
  As an infant's asleep:

‡ See p. 1076 for discussion.

So the spirit bows before thee,
To listen and adore thee,
With a full but soft emotion,   15
Like the swell of Summer's ocean.

THE INDIAN SERENADE

PERCY BYSSHE SHELLEY *

I

I arise from dreams of thee
In the first sweet sleep of night,
When the winds are breathing low,
And the stars are shining bright:
I arise from dreams of thee,   5
And a spirit in my feet
Hath led me — who knows how?
To thy chamber window, Sweet!

II

The wandering airs they faint
On the dark, the silent stream —   10
The Champak odours fail
Like sweet thoughts in a dream;
The nightingale's complaint,
It dies upon her heart; —
As I must on thine,   15
Oh, belovèd as thou art!

III

Oh lift me from the grass!
I die! I faint! I fail!
Let thy love in kisses rain
On my lips and eyelids pale.   20
My cheek is cold and white, alas!
My heart beats loud and fast; —
Oh! press it to thine own again,
Where it will break at last.

IN THE VALLEY OF CAUTERETZ

LORD TENNYSON †

All along the valley, stream that
    flashest white,
Deepening thy voice with the deep-
    ening of the night,

* See p. 1077 for discussion.
† See p. 1077 for discussion.

All along the valley, where thy waters
    flow,
I walk'd with one I loved two and
    thirty years ago.
All along the valley while I walk'd
    today,   5
The two and thirty years were a mist
    that rolls away;
For all along the valley, down thy
    rocky bed
Thy living voice to me was as the
    voice of the dead,
And all along the valley, by rock and
    cave and tree,
The voice of the dead was a living
    voice to me.   10

ULALUME

EDGAR ALLAN POE ‡

The skies they were ashen and sober;
    The leaves they were crispèd and
        sere —
    The leaves they were withering and
        sere;
It was night in the lonesome October
    Of my most immemorial year;   5
It was hard by the dim lake of Auber,
    In the misty mid region of Weir —
It was down by the dank tarn of
    Auber,
    In the ghoul-haunted woodland of
    Weir.

Here once, through an alley Titanic,
    Of cypress, I roamed with my
    Soul —   11
    Of cypress, with Psyche, my Soul.
These were days when my heart was
    volcanic
    As the scoriac rivers that roll —
    As the lavas that restlessly roll   15
Their sulphurous currents down
    Yaanek
    In the ultimate climes of the Pole—

‡ See p. 1078 for discussion.

That groan as they roll down Mount
    Yaanek
  In the realms of the boreal pole.

Our talk had been serious and sober,
  But our thoughts they were palsied
    and sere —   21
  Our memories were treacherous
    and sere —
For we knew not the month was
    October,
  And we marked not the night of
    the year —   24
  (Ah, night of all nights in the year!)
We noted not the dim lake of Auber —
  (Though once we had journeyed
    down here) —
Remembered not the dank tarn of
    Auber,
  Nor the ghoul-haunted woodland
    of Weir.   29

And now, as the night was senescent
  And star-dials pointed to morn —
  As the star-dials hinted of morn —
At the end of our path a liquescent
  And nebulous lustre was born,
Out of which a miraculous crescent
  Arose with a duplicate horn — 36
Astarte's bediamonded crescent
  Distinct with its duplicate horn.

And I said — "She is warmer than
    Dian:
  She rolls through an ether of sighs —
  She revels in a region of sighs: 41
She has seen that the tears are not
    dry on
    These cheeks, where the worm
    never dies,
And has come past the stars of the
    Lion   44
    To point us the path to the skies —
    To the Lethean peace of the skies —
Come up, in despite of the Lion,
    To shine on us with her bright
    eyes —

    Come up through the lair of the Lion,
    With love in her luminous eyes." 50

But Psyche, uplifting her finger,
  Said — "Sadly this star I mis-
    trust —
  Her pallor I strangely mistrust: —
Oh, hasten! — oh, let us not linger!
  Oh, fly! — let us fly! — for we
    must."   55
In terror she spoke, letting sink her
  Wings till they trailed in the dust —
In agony sobbed, letting sink her
  Plumes till they trailed in the
    dust —
  Till they sorrowfully trailed in the
    dust.   60

I replied — "This is nothing but
    dreaming:
  Let us on by this tremulous light!
  Let us bathe in this crystalline
    light!
Its Sibylic splendor is beaming
  With Hope and in Beauty to-
    night: —   65
  See! — it flickers up the sky through
    the night!
Ah, we safely may trust to its gleam-
    ing,
  And be sure it will lead us aright —
We safely may trust to a gleaming
  That cannot but guide us aright,
  Since it flickers up to Heaven
    through the night."   71

Thus I pacified Psyche and kissed
    her,
  And tempted her out of her
    gloom —
  And conquered her scruples and
    gloom;
And we passed to the end of the
    vista,   75
  But were stopped by the door of a
    tomb —
  By the door of a legended tomb;

And I said — "What is written, sweet sister,
  On the door of this legended tomb?"
She replied — "Ulalume — Ula-
  lume —   80
'Tis the vault of thy lost Ulalume!"

Then my heart it grew ashen and sober
  As the leaves that were crispèd and sere —
  As the leaves that were withering and sere,
And I cried — "It was surely October
  On *this* very night of last year 86
  That I journeyed — I journeyed down here —
  That I brought a dread burden down here —
  On this night of all nights in the year,
  Ah, what demon has tempted me here? 90
Well I know, now, this dim lake of Auber —
  This misty mid region of Weir —
Well I know, now, this dank tarn of Auber,
  This ghoul-haunted woodland of Weir."

UPHILL

CHRISTINA GEORGINA ROSSETTI *

Does the road wind uphill all the way?
  Yes, to the very end.
Will the day's journey take the whole long day?
  From morn to night, my friend.

But is there for the night a resting-place? 5
  A roof for when the slow, dark hours begin.

* See p. 1078 for discussion.

May not the darkness hide it from my face?
  You cannot miss that inn.

Shall I meet other wayfarers at night?
  Those who have gone before. 10
Then must I knock, or call when just in sight?
  They will not keep you waiting at that door.

Shall I find comfort, travel-sore and weak?
  Of labour you shall find the sum.
Will there be beds for me and all who seek? 15
  Yea, beds for all who come.

REST

CHRISTINA GEORGINA ROSSETTI

O earth, lie heavily upon her eyes;
  Seal her sweet eyes weary of watching, Earth;
  Lie close around her; leave no room for mirth
With its harsh laughter, nor for sound of sighs.
She hath no questions, she hath no replies, 5
  Hush'd in and curtain'd with a blessèd dearth
  Of all that irk'd her from the hour of birth;
With stillness that is almost Paradise.
Darkness more clear than noonday holdeth her,
  Silence more musical than any song; 10
Even her very heart has ceased to stir:
Until the morning of Eternity
Her rest shall not begin nor end, but be;
  And when she wakes she will not think it long.

WHEN THE HOUNDS OF SPRING

ALGERNON CHARLES SWINBURNE *

When the hounds of spring are on winter's traces,
   The mother of months in meadow or plain
Fills the shadows and windy places
   With lisp of leaves and ripple of rain:
And the brown bright nightingale amorous   5
Is half assuaged for Itylus,
For the Thracian ships and the foreign faces,
   The tongueless vigil, and all the pain.

Come with bows bent and with emptying of quivers,
   Maiden most perfect, lady of light,   10
With a noise of winds and many rivers,
   With a clamor of waters, and with might;
Bind on thy sandals, O thou most fleet,
Over the splendor and speed of thy feet;
For the faint east quickens, the wan west shivers,   15
   Round the feet of the day and the feet of the night.

Where shall we find her, how shall we sing to her,
   Fold our hands round her knees, and cling?
O that man's heart were as fire and could spring to her,
   Fire, or the strength of the streams that spring!   20
For the stars and the winds are unto her
As raiment, as songs of the harp-player;
For the risen stars and the fallen cling to her,
   And the southwest-wind and the west-wind sing.

For winter's rains and ruins are over,   25
   And all the season of snows and sins;
The days dividing lover and lover,
   The light that loses, the night that wins;
And time remembered is grief forgotten,
And frosts are slain and flowers begotten,   30
And in green underwood and cover
   Blossom by blossom the spring begins.

The full streams feed on flower of rushes,
   Ripe grasses trammel a traveling foot,
The faint fresh flame of the young year flushes   35
   From leaf to flower and flower to fruit;

* See p. 1078 for discussion.

And fruit and leaf are as gold and fire,
And the oat is heard above the lyre,
And the hoofèd heel of a satyr crushes
    The chestnut-husk at the chestnut-root. 40

And Pan by noon and Bacchus by night,
    Fleeter of foot than the fleet-foot kid,
Follows with dancing and fills with delight
    The Maenad and the Bassarid;
And soft as lips that laugh and hide 45
The laughing leaves of the trees divide,
And screen from seeing and leave in sight
    The god pursuing, the maiden hid.

The ivy falls from the Bacchanal's hair
    Over her eyebrows hiding her eyes; 50
The wild vine slipping down leaves bare
    Her bright breast shortening into sighs;
The wild vine slips with the weight of its leaves,
But the berried ivy catches and cleaves
To the limbs that glitter, the feet that scare, 55
    The wolf that follows, the fawn that flies.

PIED BEAUTY *

GERARD MANLEY HOPKINS†

Glory be to God for dappled things —
    For skies of couple-colour as a brinded cow;
      For rose-moles all in stipple upon trout that swim;
Fresh-firecoal chestnut-falls; finches' wings;
    Landscape plotted and pieced — fold, fallow, and plough; 5
      And all trades, their gear and tackle and trim.

All things counter, original, spare, strange;
    Whatever is fickle, freckled (who knows how?)
      With swift, slow; sweet, sour; adazzle, dim;
He fathers-forth whose beauty is past change:
    Praise him. 10

* From *The Poems of Gerard Manley Hopkins*, by Gerard Hopkins. By permission of Oxford University Press, London.
† See p. 1079 for discussion.

THE WINDHOVER: *

TO CHRIST OUR LORD

GERARD MANLEY HOPKINS†

I caught this morning morning's minion, king-
      dom of daylight's dauphin, dapple-dawn-drawn Fal-
      con, in his riding
      Of the rolling level underneath him steady air, and
      striding
High there, how he rung upon the rein of a wimpling wing
In his ecstasy! then off, off forth on swing,   5
      As a skate's heel sweeps smooth on a bow-bend: the
      hurl and gliding
      Rebuffed the big wind.   My heart in hiding
Stirred for a bird — the achieve of, the mastery of the
      thing!

Brute beauty and valour and act, oh, air, pride, plume, here
      Buckle!   And the fire that breaks from thee then, a
      billion   10
Times lovelier, more dangerous, O my chevalier!

      No wonder of it: shéer plód makes plough down
      sillion
Shine, and blue-bleak embers, ah my dear,
      Fall, gall themselves, and gash gold-vermilion.

* From *The Poems of Gerard Manley Hopkins*. By permission of Oxford University Press, London.

† See p. 1079 for discussion.

WHEN YOU ARE OLD‡

WILLIAM BUTLER YEATS §

When you are old and grey and full of
    sleep,
And nodding by the fire, take down
    this book,
And slowly read, and dream of the
    soft look
Your eyes had once, and of their
    shadows deep;

‡ From *Collected Poems of W. B. Yeats*. By permission of The Macmillan Company, publishers.

§ See p. 1079 for discussion.

How many loved your moments of
    glad grace,   5
And loved your beauty with love
    false or true,
But one man loved the pilgrim soul
    in you,
And loved the sorrows of your
    changing face;

And bending down beside the glowing
    bars,
Murmur, a little sadly, how Love fled
And paced upon the mountains over-
    head   11
And hid his face amid a crowd of stars.

"BE STILL. THE HANGING GARDENS WERE A DREAM"

TRUMBULL STICKNEY[*][†]

Be still. The hanging gardens were
    a dream
That over Persian roses flew to
    kiss
The curlèd lashes of Semiramis.
Troy never was nor green Skamander
    stream.
Provence and Troubadour are merest
    lies,   5
The glorious hair of Venice was a
    beam
Made within Titian's eye. The sun-
    sets seem,
The world is very old and nothing
    is.
Be still. Thou foolish thing, thou
    canst not wake,
Nor thy tears wedge thy soldered
    lips apart,   10
But patter in the darkness of thy
    heart.
Thy brain is plagued. Thou art a
    frighted owl
Blind with the light of life thou'dst
    not forsake,
And error loves and nourishes thy
    soul.

PLOUGHING ON SUNDAY[‡]

WALLACE STEVENS[§]

    The white cock's tail
    Tosses in the wind.
    The turkey-cock's tail
    Glitters in the sun.

    Water in the fields.   5
    The wind pours down.
    The feathers flare
    And bluster in the wind.

    Remus, blow your horn!
    I'm ploughing on Sunday,   10
    Ploughing North America.
    Blow your horn!

    Tum-ti-tum,
    Ti-tum-tum-tum!
    The turkey-cock's tail   15
    Spreads to the sun.

    The white cock's tail
    Streams to the moon.
    Water in the fields.
    The wind pours down.   20

SHE WEEPS OVER RAHOON

JAMES JOYCE[‖]

Rain on Rahoon falls softly, softly
    falling
Where my dark lover lies.
Sad is his voice that calls me, sadly
    calling
At grey moonrise.

Love, hear thou   5
How desolate the heart is, ever
    calling,
Ever unanswered — and the dark
    rain falling
Then as now.

Dark too our hearts, O love, shall lie,
    and cold
As his sad heart has lain   10
Under the moon-grey nettles, the
    black mold
And muttering rain.

---

* By permission of Henry A. Stickney.

† See p. 1079 for discussion.

‡ From *Harmonium*, by Wallace Stevens.
By permission of and special arrangement with
Alfred A. Knopf, Inc., authorized publishers.

§ See p. 1080 for discussion.

‖ See p. 1080 for discussion.

SIMPLES

JAMES JOYCE

O bella, bionda
sei come l'onda

Of cool sweet dew and radiance mild
The moon a web of silence weaves
In the still garden where a child
Gathers the simple salad leaves.

A moon-dew stars her hanging hair, 5
And moonlight touches her young
    brow;
And, gathering, she sings an air:
"Fair as the wave is, fair art thou."

Be mine, I pray, a waxen ear
To shield me from her childish croon;
And mine a shielded heart to her 11
Who gathers simples of the moon.

A VIRGINAL*

EZRA POUND †

No, no! Go from me. I have left
    her lately.
I will not spoil my sheath with lesser
    brightness,
For my surrounding air hath a new
    lightness;
Slight are her arms, yet they have
    bound me straitly
And left me cloaked as with a gauze
    of aether;   5
As with sweet leaves; as with a subtle
    clearness.
Oh, I have picked up magic in her
    nearness
To sheathe me half in half the things
    that sheathe her.

No, no! Go from me. I have still
    the flavour,
Soft as spring wind that's come from
    birchen bowers.   10
Green come the shoots, aye April in
    the branches,
As winter's wound with her sleight
    hand she staunches,
Hath of the trees a likeness of the
    savour:
As white their bark, so white this
    lady's hours.

* From *Personae*, by Ezra Pound, copyright,
1926. By permission of Liveright Publishing
Corporation.

† See p. 1080 for discussion.

DIRGE WITHOUT MUSIC‡

EDNA ST. VINCENT MILLAY§

I am not resigned to the shutting away of loving hearts in the hard ground.
So it is, and so it will be, for so it has been, time out of mind:
Into the darkness they go, the wise and the lovely. Crowned
With lilies and with laurel they go; but I am not resigned.

Lovers and thinkers, into the earth with you.   5
Be one with the dull, the indiscriminate dust.
A fragment of what you felt, of what you knew,
A formula, a phrase remains — but the best is lost.

‡ From *Buck in the Snow*, Harper & Brothers. Copyright, 1928, by Edna St. Vincent Millay.
By permission of the author.

§ See p. 1081 for discussion.

The answers quick and keen, the honest look, the laughter, the love —
They are gone. They are gone to feed the roses. Elegant and curled   10
Is the blossom. Fragrant is the blossom. I know. But I do not approve.
More precious was the light in your eyes than all the roses of the world.

Down, down, down into the darkness of the grave
Gently they go, the beautiful, the tender, the kind;
Quietly they go, the intelligent, the witty, the brave.   15
I know. But I do not approve. And I am not resigned.

CHANSON INNOCENTE *

E. E. CUMMINGS †

in just —
Spring   when the world is mud —
luscious, the little
lame balloon-man

whistles   far   and wee.   5

And eddieandbill come
running from marbles and
piracies and it's
spring,

when the world is puddle-wonderful

the queer   11
old balloon-man whistles
far   and   wee.
And bettyandisbel come dancing
from hop-scotch and jump-rope, and

it's   16
spring,
and
   the
      goat-footed   20
balloon-man whistles
far
and
wee.

* From *Tulips and Chimneys*, by E. E. Cummings. By permission of The Dial Press, Inc.

† See p. 1081 for discussion.

THE RIVER IN THE MEADOWS ‡

LÉONIE ADAMS §

Crystal parting the meads,
A boat drifted up it like a swan.
Tranquil, lovely, its bright front to
   the waters,
A slow swan is gone.

Full waters, O flowing silver,   5
Pure, level with the clover,
It will stain drowning a star,
With the moon it will brim over.

Running through lands dewy **and**
   shorn,
Cattle stoop at its brink,   10
And every fawny-colored throat
Will sway its bells and drink.

I saw a boat sailing the river
With a tranced gait.   It seemed
Loosed by a spell from its moor-
   ings,   15
Or a thing the helmsman dreamed.

They said it would carry no traveller,
But the vessel would go down,
If a heart were heavy-winged,
Or the bosom it dwelt in stone.   20

‡ From *High Falcon*, by Léonie Adams. By permission of The John Day Company, Inc., publishers.

§ See p. 1082 for discussion.

MEMORY OF LAKE SUPERIOR *

GEORGE DILLON †

I know a country of bright anony-
    mous beaches
Where the sand may sleep unprinted
    till it is stone.
Granite grows loud among the hills
    and ditches
Of the blown water when the water is
    blown.

Up on the mountain the sky is every-
    where,   5
The lake fallen hugely underfoot
    as if
Into the bottom of a well of air,
The island upon it little as a leaf.

* From *The Flowering Stone*, by George
Dillon, copyright, 1931. By permission of
The Viking Press, Inc., New York, publishers.

† See p. 1082 for discussion.

The woods are dark with the rank
    lace of hemlock and pine,
Beech, birch, and balsam, and the
    shadow of these.   10
There are mushrooms, and thimble-
    berries sweeter than wine,
And a far noise of wind in the tops of
    the trees.

That country was all the knowledge
    I shall ever learn;
It was all the wisdom I shall ever have.
It was there I looked for the drift-
    wood boughs that burn   15
In colors like a memory of the wave.

It was there I looked along the forest
    floor
For the gray feather of the grouse's
    wing.
It was there I learned to look for
    nothing more,
Looking into the sea-blue eyes of
    spring.   20

LYRICS OF REFLECTION

SONNET XXX

WILLIAM SHAKESPEARE *

When to the sessions of sweet silent
    thought
I summon up remembrance of things
    past,
I sigh the lack of many a thing I
    sought,
And with old woes new wail my dear
    time's waste:
Then can I drown an eye, unus'd to
    flow,   5
For precious friends hid in death's
    dateless night,
And weep afresh love's long-since
    cancell'd woe,
And moan the expense of many a
    vanish'd sight.
Then can I grieve at grievances fore-
    gone,   9
And heavily from woe to woe tell o'er
The sad account of fore-bemoanèd
    moan,
Which I new pay as if not paid be-
    fore:
  But if the while I think on thee,
    dear friend,
  All losses are restor'd, and sorrows
    end.

SONNET CXXIX

WILLIAM SHAKESPEARE *

The expense of spirit in a waste of
    shame
Is lust in action; and till action, lust
Is perjur'd, murderous, bloody, full
    of blame,

* See p. 1083 for discussion.

Savage, extreme, rude, cruel, not to
    trust;
Enjoy'd no sooner but despised
    straight;   5
Past reason hunted; and no sooner
    had,
Past reason hated, as a swallow'd
    bait,
On purpose laid to make the taker
    mad:
Mad in pursuit, and in possession so;
Had, having, and in quest to have,
    extreme;   10
A bliss in proof — and prov'd, a very
    woe;
Before, a joy propos'd; behind, a
    dream.
  All this the world well knows; yet
    none knows well
  To shun the heaven that leads men
    to this hell.

SONNET XXIX

WILLIAM SHAKESPEARE †

When in disgrace with fortune and
    men's eyes
I all alone beweep my outcast state,
And trouble deaf heaven with my
    bootless cries,
And look upon myself, and curse my
    fate;
Wishing me like to one more rich in
    hope,   5
Featured like him, like him with
    friends possest,
Desiring this man's art, and that
    man's scope,

† See p. 1083 for discussion.

With what I most enjoy contented
    least;
Yet in these thoughts myself almost
    despising,
Haply I think on thee — and then
    my state,   10
Like to the lark at break of day aris-
    ing,
From sullen earth, sings hymns at
    heaven's gate;
For thy sweet love remember'd, such
    wealth brings
That then I scorn to change my state
    with kings.

INTEGER VITAE

THOMAS CAMPION *

The man of life upright,
  Whose guiltless heart is free
From all dishonest deeds,
  Or thought of vanity;

The man whose silent days   5
  In harmless joys are spent,
Whom hopes cannot delude,
  Nor sorrow discontent;

That man needs neither towers
  Nor armour for defence,   10
Nor secret vaults to fly
  From thunder's violence:

He only can behold
  With unaffrighted eyes
The horrors of the deep   15
  And terrors of the skies.

Thus, scorning all the cares
  That fate or fortune brings,
He makes the heaven his book,
  His wisdom heavenly things;   20

Good thoughts his only friends,
  His wealth a well-spent age,

* See p. 1083 for discussion.

The earth his sober inn
  And quiet pilgrimage.

DEATH

JOHN DONNE †

I

Death, be not proud, though some
    have callèd thee
Mighty and dreadful, for thou art
    not so,
For those, whom thou think'st thou
    dost overthrow,
Die not, poor death, nor yet canst
    thou kill me.
From rest and sleep, which but thy
    pictures be,   5
Much pleasure, then from thee much
    more, must flow,
And soonest our best men with thee
    do go,
Rest of their bones, and souls' de-
    livery.
Thou art slave to fate, chance, kings,
    and desperate men,
And dost with poison, war, and sick-
    ness dwell,   10
And poppy, or charms, can make us
    sleep as well,
And better than thy stroke; Why
    swell'st thou then?
One short sleep past, we wake
    eternally,
And death shall be no more; death,
    thou shalt die.

II

At the round earth's imagined cor-
    ners, blow
Your trumpets, angels, and arise,
    arise
From death, you numberless in-
    finities
Of souls, and to your scattered bodies
    go,

† See p. 1083 for discussion.

All whom the flood did, and fire shall
 o'erthrow, 5
All whom war, dearth, age, agues,
 tyrannies,
Despair, law, chance, hath slain, and
 you whose eyes
Shall behold God, and never taste
 death's woe.
But let them sleep, Lord, and me
 mourn a space,
For, if above all these, my sins
 abound, 10
'Tis late to ask abundance of thy
 grace,
When we are there; here on this lowly
 ground,
Teach me how to repent; for that's as
 good
As if thou had'st sealed my pardon
 with thy blood.

ON HIS BLINDNESS

JOHN MILTON*

When I consider how my light is
 spent
 Ere half my days in this dark world
  and wide,
 And that one Talent which is
  death to hide
Lodged with me useless, though my
  soul more bent
To serve therewith my Maker, and
 present 5
 My true account, lest He returning
  chide;
 "Doth God exact day-labor, light
  denied?"
I fondly ask. But Patience, to
 prevent
That murmur, soon replies, "God
 doth not need
 Either man's work or his own gifts.
  Who best 10

* See p. 1084 for discussion.

Bear his mild yoke, they serve him
 best. His state
Is kingly: thousands at his bidding
 speed,
 And post o'er land and ocean without rest;
They also serve who only stand
 and wait."

SONG

EDMUND WALLER†

Go, lovely Rose!
Tell her, that wastes her time and me,
 That now she knows,
 When I resemble her to thee, 4
How sweet and fair she seems to be.

 Tell her that's young
And shuns to have her graces spied,
 That hadst thou sprung
 In deserts, where no men abide, 9
Thou must have uncommended died.

 Small is the worth
Of beauty from the light retired:
 Bid her come forth,
 Suffer herself to be desired,
 And not blush so to be admired. 15

 Then die! that she
The common fate of all things rare
 May read in thee: 18
How small a part of time they share
That are so wondrous sweet and fair!

ODE TO SOLITUDE

ALEXANDER POPE‡

Happy the man whose wish and care
 A few paternal acres bound,
Content to breathe his native air,
 In his own ground.

† See p. 1084 for discussion.
‡ See p. 1085 for discussion.

Whose herds with milk, whose fields
    with bread,   5
  Whose flocks supply him with
      attire,
Whose trees in summer yield him
    shade,
    In winter fire.

Blest, who can unconcernedly find
  Hours, days, and years slide soft
    away,   10
In health of body, peace of mind,
    Quiet by day.

Sound sleep by night; study and ease,
  Together mixed; sweet recreation;
And innocence, which most does
    please   15
    With meditation.

Thus let me live, unseen, unknown,
  Thus unlamented let me die,
Steal from the world, and not a stone
    Tell where I lie.   20

THE TIGER

WILLIAM BLAKE*

Tiger! Tiger! burning bright
In the forests of the night,
What immortal hand or eye
Could frame thy fearful symmetry?

In what distant deeps or skies   5
Burnt the fire of thine eyes?
On what wings dare he aspire?
What the hand dare seize the fire?

And what shoulder, and what art, 9
Could twist the sinews of thy heart?
And when thy heart began to beat,
What dread hand and what dread
    feet?

What the hammer? what the chain?
In what furnace was thy brain?

* See p. 1085 for discussion.

What the anvil? what dread grasp 15
Dare its deadly terrors clasp?

When the stars threw down their
    spears,
And watered heaven with their tears,
Did he smile his work to see?
Did he who made the Lamb make
    thee?   20

Tiger! Tiger! burning bright
In the forests of the night,
What immortal hand or eye
Dare frame thy fearful symmetry?

SONNET

WILLIAM WORDSWORTH†

The world is too much with us; late
    and soon,
Getting and spending, we lay waste
    our powers:
Little we see in Nature that is ours;
We have given our hearts away, a
    sordid boon!
This Sea that bares her bosom to the
    moon;   5
The winds that will be howling at all
    hours,
And are up-gathered now like sleep-
    ing flowers;
For this, for everything, we are out of
    tune;
It moves us not. — Great God! I'd
    rather be
A Pagan suckled in a creed out-
    worn;   10
So might I, standing on this pleasant
    lea,
Have glimpses that would make me
    less forlorn;
Have sight of Proteus rising from the
    sea;
Or hear old Triton blow his wreathèd
    horn.

† See p. 1085 for discussion.

LINES

COMPOSED A FEW MILES ABOVE TINTERN
ABBEY, ON REVISITING THE BANKS OF
THE WYE DURING A TOUR

JULY 13, 1798

WILLIAM WORDSWORTH *

Five years have past; five summers,
    with the length
Of five long winters! and again I hear
These waters, rolling from their
    mountain-springs
With a soft inland murmur. — Once
    again
Do I behold these steep and lofty
    cliffs,   5
That on a wild, secluded scene im-
    press
Thoughts of more deep seclusion; and
    connect
The landscape with the quiet of the
    sky.
The day is come when I again repose
Here, under this dark sycamore, and
    view   10
These plots of cottage-ground, these
    orchard-tufts,
Which at this season, with their un-
    ripe fruits,
Are clad in one green hue, and lose
    themselves
'Mid groves and copses.   Once again
    I see
These hedge-rows, hardly hedge-
    rows, little lines   15
Of sportive wood run wild: these
    pastoral farms,
Green to the very door; and wreaths
    of smoke
Sent up, in silence, from among the
    trees!
With some uncertain notice, as might
    seem
Of vagrant dwellers in the houseless
    woods,   20

* See p. 1085 for discussion.

Or of some Hermit's cave, where by
    his fire
The Hermit sits alone.
               These beauteous forms,
Through a long absence, have not
    been to me
As is a landscape to a blind man's
    eye:
But oft, in lonely rooms, and 'mid the
    din   25
Of towns and cities, I have owed to
    them,
In hours of weariness, sensations
    sweet,
Felt in the blood, and felt along the
    heart;
And passing even into my purer
    mind,
With tranquil restoration: — feelings
    too   30
Of unremembered pleasure: such,
    perhaps,
As have no slight or trivial influence
On that best portion of a good man's
    life,
His little, nameless, unremembered
    acts
Of kindness and of love.   Nor less, I
    trust,   35
To them I may have owed another
    gift,
Of aspect more sublime; that blessed
    mood
In which the burden of the mystery,
In which the heavy and the weary
    weight
Of all this unintelligible world,   40
Is lightened: — that serene and
    blessed mood,
In which the affections gently lead us
    on —
Until, the breath of this corporeal
    frame
And even the motion of our human
    blood   44
Almost suspended, we are laid asleep
In body, and become a living soul:

While with an eye made quiet by the
  power
Of harmony, and the deep power of
  joy,
We see into the life of things.
                              If this
Be but a vain belief, yet, oh! how oft —
In darkness and amid the many
  shapes   51
Of joyless daylight; when the fretful
  stir
Unprofitable, and the fever of the
  world,
Have hung upon the beatings of my
  heart —
How oft, in spirit, have I turned to
  thee,   55
O sylvan Wye! thou wanderer thro'
  the woods,
How often has my spirit turned to
  thee!
    And now, with gleams of half-ex-
      tinguished thought,
With many recognitions dim and
  faint,
And somewhat of a sad perplexity, 60
The picture of the mind revives
  again:
While here I stand, not only with the
  sense
Of present pleasure, but with pleasing
  thoughts
That in this moment there is life and
  food
For future years. And so I dare to
  hope,   65
Though changed, no doubt, from
  what I was when first
I came among these hills; when like a
  roe
I bounded o'er the mountains, by the
  sides
Of the deep rivers, and the lonely
  streams,
Wherever nature led: more like a man
Flying from something that he
  dreads, than one   71

Who sought the thing he loved. For
  nature then
(The coarser pleasures of my boyish
  days,
And their glad animal movements all
  gone by)
To me was all in all. — I cannot paint
What then I was. The sounding
  cataract   76
Haunted me like a passion: the tall
  rock,
The mountain, and the deep and
  gloomy wood,
Their colors and their forms, were
  then to me
An appetite; a feeling and a love, 80
That had no need of a remoter
  charm,
By thought supplied, nor any interest
Unborrowed from the eye. — That
  time is past,
And all its aching joys are now no
  more,
And all its dizzy raptures. Not for
  this   85
Faint I, nor mourn nor murmur;
  other gifts
Have followed; for such loss, I would
  believe,
Abundant recompence. For I have
  learned
To look on nature, not as in the hour
Of thoughtless youth; but hearing
  oftentimes   90
The still, sad music of humanity,
Nor harsh nor grating, though of
  ample power
To chasten and subdue. And I have
  felt
A presence that disturbs me with the
  joy
Of elevated thoughts; a sense sub-
  lime   95
Of something far more deeply inter-
  fused,
Whose dwelling is the light of setting
  suns,

And the round ocean and the living air,
And the blue sky, and in the mind of man; 99
A motion and a spirit, that impels
All thinking things, all objects of all thought,
And rolls through all things. Therefore am I still
A lover of the meadows and the woods,
And mountains; and of all that we behold
From this green earth; of all the mighty world 105
Of eye, and ear — both what they half create,
And what perceive; well pleased to recognize
In nature and the language of the sense,
The anchor of my purest thoughts, the nurse,
The guide, the guardian of my heart, and soul 110
Of all my moral being.
                           Nor perchance,
If I were not thus taught, should I the more
Suffer my genial spirits to decay:
For thou art with me here upon the banks
Of this fair river; thou my dearest Friend, 115
My dear, dear Friend; and in thy voice I catch
The language of my former heart, and read
My former pleasures in the shooting lights
Of thy wild eyes. Oh! yet a little while
May I behold in thee what I was once,
My dear, dear Sister! and this prayer I make, 121
Knowing that Nature never did betray

The heart that loved her; 'tis her privilege,
Through all the years of this our life, to lead
From joy to joy: for she can so inform 125
The mind that is within us, so impress
With quietness and beauty, and so feed
With lofty thoughts, that neither evil tongues,
Rash judgments, nor the sneers of selfish men,
Nor greetings where no kindness is, nor all 130
The dreary intercourse of daily life,
Shall e'er prevail against us, or disturb
Our cheerful faith, that all which we behold
Is full of blessings. Therefore let the moon 134
Shine on thee in thy solitary walk;
And let the misty mountain-winds be free
To blow against thee: and, in after years,
When these wild ecstasies shall be matured
Into a sober pleasure; when thy mind
Shall be a mansion for all lovely forms, 140
Thy memory be as a dwelling-place
For all sweet sounds and harmonies; oh! then,
If solitude, or fear, or pain, or grief,
Should be thy portion, with what healing thoughts 144
Of tender joy wilt thou remember me,
And these my exhortations! Nor, perchance —
If I should be where I no more can hear
Thy voice, nor catch from thy wild eyes these gleams
Of past existence — wilt thou then forget

That on the banks of this delightful
    stream   150
We stood together; and that I, so long
A worshipper of Nature, hither came
Unwearied in that service: rather say
With warmer love — oh! with far
    deeper zeal
Of holier love. Nor wilt thou then
    forget,   155
That after many wanderings, many
    years
Of absence, these steep woods and
    lofty cliffs,
And this green pastoral landscape,
    were to me
More dear, both for themselves and
    for thy sake!

TO A SKYLARK

PERCY BYSSHE SHELLEY *

Hail to thee, blithe Spirit!
    Bird thou never wert,
That from Heaven, or near it,
    Pourest thy full heart
In profuse strains of unpremeditated
    art.   5

Higher still and higher
    From the earth thou springest
Like a cloud of fire;
    The blue deep thou wingest,
And singing still dost soar, and soar-
    ing ever singest.   10

In the golden lightning
    Of the sunken sun,
O'er which clouds are bright'ning,
    Thou dost float and run;
Like an unbodied joy whose race is
    just begun.   15

The pale purple even
    Melts around thy flight;

* See p. 1086 for discussion.

Like a star of Heaven,
    In the broad daylight
Thou art unseen — but yet I hear
    thy shrill delight,   20

Keen as are the arrows
    Of that silver sphere,
Whose intense lamp narrows
    In the white dawn clear
Until we hardly see — we feel that it
    is there;   25

All the earth and air
    With thy voice is loud,
As, when night is bare,
    From one lonely cloud
The moon rains out her beams, and
    Heaven is overflowed.   30

What thou art we know not;
    What is most like thee?
From rainbow clouds there flow not
    Drops so bright to see
As from thy presence showers a rain
    of melody.   35

Like a Poet hidden
    In the light of thought,
Singing hymns unbidden,
    Till the world is wrought
To sympathy with hopes and fears it
    heeded not: 40

Like a high-born maiden
    In a palace-tower,
Soothing her love-laden
    Soul in secret hour
With music sweet as love — which
    overflows her bower: 45

Like a glowworm golden
    In a dell of dew,
Scattering unbeholden
    Its aerial hue
Among the flowers and grass which
    screen it from the view: 50

Like a rose embowered
  In its own green leaves,
By warm winds deflowered,
  Till the scent it gives
Makes faint with too much sweet
    those heavy wingèd thieves. 55

Sound of vernal showers
  On the twinkling grass,
Rain-awakened flowers,
  All that ever was
Joyous and clear and fresh, thy
    music doth surpass. 60

Teach us, Sprite or Bird,
  What sweet thoughts are thine;
I have never heard
  Praise of love or wine
That panted forth a flood of rapture
    so divine. 65

Chorus Hymeneal,
  Or triumphal chant,
Matched with thine, would be all
  But an empty vaunt,
A thing wherein we feel there is some
    hidden want. 70

What objects are the fountains
  Of thy happy strain?
What fields or waves or mountains?
  What shapes of sky or plain?
What love of thine own kind? what
    ignorance of pain? 75

With thy clear keen joyance
  Languor cannot be;
Shadow of annoyance
  Never came near thee;
Thou lovest — but ne'er knew love's
    sad satiety. 80

Waking or asleep,
  Thou of death must deem
Things more true and deep

Than we mortals dream —
Or how could thy notes flow in such a
    crystal stream? 85

We look before and after,
  And pine for what is not;
Our sincerest laughter
  With some pain is fraught;
Our sweetest songs are those that tell
    of saddest thought. 90

Yet if we could scorn
  Hate, and pride, and fear;
If we were things born
  Not to shed a tear,
I know not how thy joy we ever
    should come near. 95

Better than all measures
  Of delightful sound,
Better than all treasures
  That in books are found,
Thy skill to poet were, thou scorner of
    the ground! 100

Teach me half the gladness
  That thy brain must know,
Such harmonious madness
  From my lips would flow
The world should listen then — as I
    am listening now. 105

ODE TO THE WEST WIND

PERCY BYSSHE SHELLEY *

I

O wild West Wind, thou breath of
  Autumn's being,
Thou, from whose unseen presence
  the leaves dead
Are driven, like ghosts from an en-
  chanter fleeing,

Yellow, and black, and pale, and
  hectic red,

* See p. 1086 for discussion.

Pestilence-stricken multitudes!   O thou   5
Who chariotest to their dark wintry bed

The wingèd seeds, where they lie cold and low,
Each like a corpse within its grave, until
Thine azure sister of the Spring shall blow

Her clarion o'er the dreaming earth, and fill   10
(Driving sweet buds like flocks to feed in air)
With living hues and odors plain and hill:

Wild Spirit, which art moving everywhere;
Destroyer and Preserver; hear, oh hear!

II

Thou on whose stream, 'mid the steep sky's commotion,   15
Loose clouds like earth's decaying leaves are shed,
Shook from the tangled boughs of heaven and ocean,

Angels of rain and lightning! there are spread
On the blue surface of thine airy surge,
Like the bright hair uplifted from the head   20

Of some fierce Maenad, even from the dim verge
Of the horizon to the zenith's height,
The locks of the approaching storm. Thou dirge

Of the dying year, to which this closing night   24

Will be the dome of a vast sepulchre,
Vaulted with all thy congregated might

Of vapors, from whose solid atmosphere
Black rain, and fire, and hail, will burst: Oh hear!

III

Thou who didst waken from his summer-dreams
The blue Mediterranean, where he lay,   30
Lulled by the coil of his crystalline streams,

Beside a pumice isle in Baiae's bay,
And saw in sleep old palaces and towers
Quivering within the wave's intenser day,

All overgrown with azure moss, and flowers   35
So sweet, the sense faints picturing them! Thou
For whose path the Atlantic's level powers

Cleave themselves into chasms, while far below
The sea-blooms and the oozy woods which wear
The sapless foliage of the ocean know   40

Thy voice, and suddenly grow gray with fear
And tremble and despoil themselves: Oh hear!

IV

If I were a dead leaf thou mightest bear;
If I were a swift cloud to fly with thee;

A wave to pant beneath thy power,
and share   45

The impulse of thy strength, only
less free
Than Thou, O uncontrollable!   If
even
I were as in my boyhood, and could
be

The comrade of thy wanderings over
heaven,
As then, when to outstrip thy skyey
speed   50
Scarce seemed a vision; I would ne'er
have striven

As thus with thee in prayer in my
sore need.
Oh! lift me as a wave, a leaf, a cloud!
I fall upon the thorns of life!   I
bleed!

A heavy weight of hours has chained
and bowed   55
One too like thee — tameless, and
swift, and proud.

V

Make me thy lyre, ev'n as the forest
is:
What if my leaves are falling like its
own!
The tumult of thy mighty harmonies

Will take from both a deep, autum-
nal tone,   60
Sweet though in sadness.   Be thou,
Spirit fierce,
My spirit! be thou me, impetuous
one!

Drive my dead thoughts over the
universe,
Like withered leaves, to quicken a
new birth!   64
And, by the incantation of this verse,

Scatter, as from an unextinguished
hearth
Ashes and sparks, my words among
mankind!
Be through my lips to unawakened
earth

The trumpet of a prophecy!   O wind,
If Winter comes, can Spring be far
behind?   70

ODE TO A NIGHTINGALE

JOHN KEATS *

I

My heart aches, and a drowsy numbness pains
My sense, as though of hemlock I
had drunk,
Or emptied some dull opiate to the
drains
One minute past, and Lethe-wards
had sunk:
'Tis not through envy of thy happy
lot,   5
But being too happy in thine happiness —
That thou, light-wingèd Dryad
of the trees,
In some melodious plot
Of beechen green, and shadows
numberless,
Singest of summer in full-
throated ease.   10

II

O for a draught of vintage! that hath
been
Cooled a long age in the deep-
delved earth,
Tasting of Flora and the country
green,
Dance, and Provençal song, and
sun-burnt mirth!

* See p. 1086 for discussion.

O for a beaker full of the warm
   South,   15
Full of the true, the blushful Hip-
   pocrene,
    With beaded bubbles winking at
      the brim,
    And purple-stainèd mouth;
That I might drink, and leave the
   world unseen,
And with thee fade away into
   the forest dim: 20

III

Fade far away, dissolve, and quite
   forget
   What thou among the leaves hast
     never known,
The weariness, the fever, and the
   fret
Here, where men sit and hear each
   other groan;
Where palsy shakes a few, sad, last
   gray hairs,   25
   Where youth grows pale, and
     spectre-thin, and dies;
    Where but to think is to be full of
      sorrow
    And leaden-eyed despairs,
   Where Beauty cannot keep her
     lustrous eyes,
    Or new Love pine at them be-
     yond tomorrow.   30

IV

Away! away! for I will fly to thee,
   Not charioted by Bacchus and his
     pards,
But on the viewless wings of Poesy,
   Though the dull brain perplexes
     and retards:
Already with thee! tender is the
   night,   35
   And haply the Queen-Moon is on
     her throne,
    Clustered around by all her
      starry Fays;
    But here there is no light,

Save what from heaven is with the
   breezes blown
   Through verdurous glooms and
     winding mossy ways.   40

V

I cannot see what flowers are at my
   feet,
   Nor what soft incense hangs upon
     the boughs,
But, in embalmed darkness, guess
   each sweet
   Wherewith the seasonable month
     endows
The grass, the thicket, and the fruit-
   tree wild;   45
   White hawthorn, and the pastoral
     eglantine;
    Fast-fading violets covered up
     in leaves;
    And mid-May's eldest child,
The coming musk-rose, full of
   dewy wine,
    The murmurous haunt of flies on
     summer eves.   50

VI

Darkling I listen; and for many a
   time
I have been half in love with ease-
   ful Death,
Called him soft names in many a
   mused rhyme,
To take into the air my quiet
   breath;
Now more than ever seems it rich to
   die,   55
To cease upon the midnight with
   no pain,
   While thou art pouring forth thy
     soul abroad
    In such an ecstasy!
Still wouldst thou sing, and I have
   ears in vain —
    To thy high requiem become a
     sod.   60

VII

Thou wast not born for death, im-
    mortal Bird!
  No hungry generations tread thee
    down;
The voice I hear this passing night
    was heard
  In ancient days by emperor and
    clown:
Perhaps the self-same song that
    found a path   65
  Through the sad heart of Ruth,
    when, sick for home,
    She stood in tears amid the alien
      corn;
    The same that oft-times hath
Charmed magic casements, open-
    ing on the foam
  Of perilous seas, in faery lands
    forlorn.   70

VIII

Forlorn! the very word is like a bell
  To toll me back from thee to my
    sole self!
Adieu! the fancy cannot cheat so well
  As she is famed to do, deceiving elf.
Adieu! adieu! thy plaintive anthem
    fades   75
  Past the near meadows, over the
    still stream,
    Up the hill-side; and now 'tis
      buried deep
    In the next valley-glades:
Was it a vision, or a waking dream?
  Fled is that music: — Do I wake
    or sleep?   80

SONNET XXII

From *Sonnets from the Portuguese*

ELIZABETH BARRETT
BROWNING *

When our two souls stand up erect
    and strong,

* See p. 1086 for discussion.

Face to face, silent, drawing nigh and
    nigher,
Until the lengthening wings break
    into fire
At either curvèd point — what bit-
    ter wrong
Can the earth do to us, that we
    should not long   5
Be here contented?   Think.   In
    mounting higher,
The angels would press on us, and
    aspire
To drop some golden orb of perfect
    song
Into our deep, dear silence.   Let us
    stay
Rather on earth, Belovèd — where
    the unfit   10
Contrarious moods of men recoil away
And isolate pure spirits, and permit
A place to stand and love in for a day,
With darkness and the death-hour
    rounding it.

LAST LINES

EMILY BRONTË†

No coward soul is mine,
No trembler in the world's storm-
    troubled sphere:
  I see Heaven's glories shine,
And faith shines equal, arming me
    from fear.

O God within my breast,   5
Almighty, ever-present Deity!
  Life — that in me has rest,
As I — undying Life — have power
    in Thee!

Vain are the thousand creeds
That move men's hearts: unutterably
    vain;   10
  Worthless as wither'd weeds,
Or idlest froth amid the boundless
    main,

† See p. 1087 for discussion.

To waken doubt in one
Holding so fast by Thine infinity;
So surely anchor'd on   15
The steadfast rock of immortality.

With wide-embracing love
Thy Spirit animates eternal years,
Pervades and broods above,
Changes, sustains, dissolves, creates,
          and rears.   20

Though earth and man were gone,
And suns and universes cease to be,
And thou were left alone,
Every existence would exist in Thee.

There is not room for Death,   25
Nor atom that his might could render
          void:
Thou — Thou   art   Being   and
          Breath,
And what Thou art may never be
          destroyed.

I DIED FOR BEAUTY *

EMILY DICKINSON †

I died for beauty, but was scarce
Adjusted in the tomb,
When one who died for truth was laid
In an adjoining room.

He questioned softly why I failed? 5
"For beauty," I replied.
"And I for truth — the two are one;
We brethren are," he said.

And so, as kinsmen met a-night,
We talked between the rooms,   10
Until the moss had reached our lips,
And covered up our names.

* From *The Poems of Emily Dickinson*, Centenary Edition, edited by Martha Dickinson Bianchi and Alfred Leete Hampson. By permission of Little, Brown and Company.

† See p. 1087 for discussion.

THE GARDEN OF PROSERPINE

ALGERNON CHARLES SWINBURNE ‡

Here, where the world is quiet,
   Here, where all trouble seems
Dead winds' and spent waves' riot
   In doubtful dreams of dreams;
I watch the green field growing   5
For reaping folk and sowing,
For harvest time and mowing,
   A sleepy world of streams.

I am tired of tears and laughter,
   And men that laugh and weep   10
Of what may come hereafter
   For men that sow to reap:
I am weary of days and hours,
Blown buds of barren flowers,
Desires and dreams and powers   15
   And everything but sleep.

Here life has death for neighbor,
   And far from eye or ear,
Wan waves and wet winds labor,
   Weak ships and spirits steer;   20
They drive adrift, and whither
They wot not who make thither;
But no such winds blow hither,
   And no such things grow here.

No growth of moor or coppice,   25
   No heather-flower or vine,
But bloomless buds of poppies,
   Green grapes of Proserpine,
Pale beds of blowing rushes
Where no leaf blooms or blushes, 30
Save this whereout she crushes
   For dead men deadly wine.

Pale, without name or number,
   In fruitless fields of corn,
They bow themselves and slumber 35

‡ See p. 1087 for discussion.

All night till light is born;
And like a soul belated,
In hell and heaven unmated,
By cloud and mist abated
  Comes out of darkness morn.   40

Though one were strong as seven,
  He too with death shall dwell,
Nor wake with wings in heaven,
  Nor weep for pains in hell;
Though one were fair as roses,   45
His beauty clouds and closes;
And well though love reposes,
  In the end it is not well.

Pale, beyond porch and portal,
  Crowned with calm leaves, she
    stands   50
Who gathers all things mortal
  With cold immortal hands;
Her languid lips are sweeter
Than love's who fears to greet her
To men that mix and meet her   55
  From many times and lands.

She waits for each and other,
  She waits for all men born;
Forgets the earth her mother,
  The life of fruits and corn;   60
And spring and seed and swallow
Take wing for her and follow
Where summer song rings hollow
  And flowers are put to scorn.

There go the loves that wither,   65
  The old loves with wearier wings;
And all dead years draw thither,
  And all disastrous things;
Dead dreams of days forsaken,
Blind buds that snows have shaken,
Wild leaves that winds have taken,
  Red strays of ruined springs.   72

We are not sure of sorrow,
  And joy was never sure;
Today will die tomorrow;   75
  Time stoops to no man's lure;

And love, grown faint and fretful
With lips but half regretful
Sighs, and with eyes forgetful
  Weeps that no loves endure.   80

From too much love of living,
  From hope and fear set free,
We thank with brief thanksgiving
  Whatever gods may be
That no life lives for ever;   85
That dead men rise up never;
That even the weariest river
  Winds somewhere safe to sea.

Then star nor sun shall waken,
  Nor any change of light: 90
Nor sound of waters shaken,
  Nor any sound or sight:
Nor wintry leaves nor vernal,
Nor days nor things diurnal;
Only the sleep eternal   95
  In an eternal night.

THE SHEPHERDESS *

ALICE MEYNELL †

She walks — the lady of my de-
    light —
  A shepherdess of sheep.
Her flocks are thoughts. She keeps
    them white;
  She guards them from the steep.
She feeds them on the fragrant
    height,   5
  And folds them in for sleep.

She roams maternal hills and bright,
  Dark valleys safe and deep.
Her dreams are innocent at night;
  The chastest stars may peep.   10
She walks — the lady of my de-
    light —
  A shepherdess of sheep.

* From *Poems*, by Alice Meynell. By permission of Charles Scribner's Sons.

† See p. 1088 for discussion.

She holds her little thoughts in sight,
    Though gay they run and leap.
She is so circumspect and right;   15
    She has her soul to keep.
She walks — the lady of my de-
    light —
    A shepherdess of sheep.

THE HOUND OF HEAVEN

FRANCIS THOMPSON*

I fled Him, down the nights and
    down the days;
I fled Him down the arches of the
    years;
I fled Him, down the labyrinthine
    ways
Of my own mind; and in the mist
    of tears
I hid from Him, and under running
    laughter.   5
        Up vistaed hopes I sped;
        And shot, precipitated,
Adown Titanic glooms of chasmèd
    fears,
    From those strong Feet that fol-
        lowed, followed after.
        But with unhurrying chase,   10
        And unperturbèd pace,
    Deliberate speed, majestic in-
        stancy,
    They beat — and a Voice beat
    More instant than the Feet —
    "All things betray thee, who
        betrayest Me."   15

    I pleaded, outlaw-wise,
By many a hearted casement, cur-
    tained red,
    Trellised with intertwining chari-
        ties;
(For, though I knew His love Who
    followèd,
        Yet was I sore adread   20

* See p. 1088 for discussion.

Lest, having Him, I must have
    naught beside);
But, if one little casement parted
    wide,
    The gust of His approach would
        clash it to.
Fear wist not to evade, as Love wist
    to pursue.
Across the margent of the world I
    fled,   25
    And troubled the gold gateways of
        the stars,
    Smiting for shelter on their clangèd
        bars;
        Fretted to dulcet jars
And silvern chatter the pale ports o'
    the moon.
I said to dawn, Be sudden; to eve, Be
    soon;   30
    With thy young skiey blossoms
        heap me over
        From this tremendous Lover!
Float thy vague veil about me, lest
    He see!
    I tempted all His servitors, but to
        find
My own betrayal in their constancy,
In faith to Him their fickleness to
    me,   36
    Their traitorous trueness, and
        their loyal deceit.
To all swift things for swiftness did I
    sue;
    Clung to the whistling mane of
        every wind.
        But whether they swept,
            smoothly fleet,   40
    The long savannahs of the blue;
        Or whether, Thunder-
            driven,
    They clanged his chariot
        'thwart a heaven
Plashy with flying lightnings round
    the spurn o' their feet: —
    Fear wist not to evade as Love
        wist to pursue.   45

Still with unhurrying chase,
And unperturbèd pace,
Deliberate speed, majestic instancy,
Came on the following Feet,
And a Voice above their beat — 50
"Naught shelters thee, who wilt not shelter Me."

I sought no more that after which I strayed
    In face of man or maid;
But still within the little children's eyes
    Seems something, something that replies; 55
They at least are for me, surely for me!
I turned me to them very wistfully;
But, just as their young eyes grew sudden fair
    With dawning answers there,
Their angel plucked them from me by the hair. 60
"Come then, ye other children, Nature's — share
With me" (said I) "your delicate fellowship;
    Let me greet you lip to lip,
    Let me twine with you caresses,
    Wantoning 65
    With our Lady-Mother's vagrant tresses,
    Banqueting
With her in her wind-walled palace,
Underneath her azured daïs,
Quaffing, as your taintless way is, 70
    From a chalice
Lucent-weeping out of the dayspring."
    So it was done:
I in their delicate fellowship was one —
Drew the bolt of Nature's secrecies.

I knew all the swift importings 76
    On the willful face of skies;
    I knew how the clouds arise
    Spumèd of the wild sea-snortings;
    All that's born or dies 80
    Rose and drooped with — made them shapers
Of mine own moods, or wailful or divine —
    With them joyed and was bereaven.
    I was heavy with the even,
    When she lit her glimmering tapers 85
    Round the day's dead sanctities.
    I laughed in the morning's eyes.
I triumphed and I saddened with all weather,
    Heaven and I wept together,
And its sweet tears were salt with mortal mine; 90
Against the red throb of its sunset-heart
    I laid my own to beat,
    And share commingling heat;
But not by that, by that, was eased my human smart.
In vain my tears were wet on Heaven's grey cheek. 95
For ah! we know not what each other says,
    These things and I; in sound *I* speak —
Their sound is but their stir, they speak by silences.
Nature, poor stepdame, cannot slake my drouth;
    Let her, if she would owe me, 100
Drop yon blue bosom-veil of sky, and show me
    The breasts o' her tenderness:
Never did any milk of hers once bless
    My thirsting mouth.

Nigh and nigh draws the
  chase,   105
With unperturbèd pace,
Deliberate speed, majestic in-
  stancy;
And past those noisèd Feet
  A voice comes yet more
    fleet —
"Lo! naught contents thee, who con-
  tent'st not Me."   110

Naked I wait Thy love's uplifted
  stroke!
My harness piece by piece Thou hast
  hewn from me,
  And smitten me to my knee;
  I am defenceless utterly.
I slept, methinks, and woke,
And, slowly gazing, find me stripped
  in sleep.   116
In the rash lustihead of my young
  powers,
  I shook the pillaring hours
And pulled my life upon me; grimed
  with smears,
I stand amid the dust o' the mounded
  years —   120
My mangled youth lies dead beneath
  the heap
My days have crackled and gone up
  in smoke,
Have puffed and burst as sun-starts
  on a stream.
  Yea, faileth now even dream
The dreamer, and the lute the lutanist;
Even the linked fantasies, in whose
  blossomy twist   126
I swung the earth a trinket at my
  wrist,
Are yielding; cords of all too weak
  account
For earth with heavy griefs so over-
  plussed.
  Ah! is Thy love indeed   130
A weed, albeit an amaranthine weed,
Suffering no flowers except its own to
  mount?

Ah! must —
  Designer infinite! —
Ah! must Thou char the wood ere
  Thou canst limn with it? 135
My freshness spent its wavering
  shower i' the dust;
And now my heart is as a broken
  fount,
Wherein tear-drippings stagnate,
  spilt down ever
  From the dank thoughts that
    shiver
Upon the sighful branches of my
  mind.   140
  Such is; what is to be?
The pulp so bitter, how shall taste
  the rind?
I dimly guess what Time in mists
  confounds;
Yet ever and anon a trumpet sounds
From the hid battlements of Eter-
  nity;   145
Those shaken mists a space unsettle,
  then
Round the half-glimpsèd turrets
  slowly wash again.
  But not ere him who sum-
    moneth
  I first have seen, enwound
With glooming robes purpureal, cy-
  press-crowned;   150
His name I know, and what his
  trumpet saith.
Whether man's heart or life it be
  which yields
  Thee harvest, must Thy har-
    vest fields
  Be dunged with rotten death?
  Now of that long pursuit 155
  Comes on at hand the bruit;
  That Voice is round me like a
    bursting sea:
  "And is thy earth so marred,
  Shattered in shard on shard?
Lo, all things fly thee, for thou
  fliest Me!   160
Strange, piteous, futile thing,

Wherefore should any set thee love
apart?
Seeing none but I makes much of
naught" (He said),
"And human love needs human mer-
iting:
How hast thou merited — 165
Of all man's clotted clay the dingiest
clot?
Alack, thou knowest not
How little worthy of any love thou
art!
Whom wilt thou find to love ignoble
thee
Save Me, save only Me? 170
All which I took from thee I did but
take,
Not for thy harms,

But just that thou might'st seek it in
My arms.
All which thy child's mistake
Fancies as lost, I have stored for thee
at home: 175
Rise, clasp My hand, and
come!"

Halts by me that footfall:
Is my gloom, after all,
Shade of His hand, out-
stretched caressingly?
"Ah, fondest, blindest,
weakest, 180
I am He Whom thou seek-
est!
Thou dravest love from thee, who
dravest Me.

ON A SOLDIER FALLEN IN THE PHILIPPINES *

WILLIAM VAUGHN MOODY †

Streets of the roaring town,
Hush for him; hush, be still!
He comes, who was stricken down
Doing the word of our will.
Hush! Let him have his state. 5
Give him his soldier's crown,
The grists of trade can wait
Their grinding at the mill

But he cannot wait for his honor, now the trumpet has been blown.
Wreathe pride now for his granite brow, lay love on his breast of stone. 10

Toll! Let the great bells toll
Till the clashing air is dim,
Did we wrong this parted soul?
We will make it up to him.
Toll! Let him never guess 15
What work we sent him to.
Laurel, laurel, yes.
He did what we bade him do.

Praise, and never a whispered hint but the fight he fought was good;
Never a word that the blood on his sword was his country's own heart's-
blood. 20

* From *Selected Poems of William Vaughn Moody*. By permission of Houghton Mifflin
Company. † See p. 1088 for discussion.

A flag for a soldier's bier
Who dies that his land may live;
O banners, banners here,
That he doubt not nor misgive!
That he heed not from the tomb　　　25
The evil days draw near
When the nation robed in gloom
With its faithless past shall strive.

Let him never dream that his bullet's scream went wide of its island
　　mark,
Home to the heart of his darling land where she stumbled and sinned in the
　　dark.　　　30

HURT HAWKS *

ROBINSON JEFFERS †

I

The broken pillar of the wing jags from the clotted shoulder,
The wing trails like a banner in defeat.
No more to use the sky forever, but live with famine
And pain a few days: cat nor coyote
Will shorten the week of waiting for death, there is game without talons.　5
He stands under the oak-bush and waits
The lame feet of salvation; at night he remembers freedom
And flies in a dream, the dawns ruin it.
He is strong, and pain is worse to the strong, incapacity is worse.
The curs of the day come and torment him　　　10
At distance; no one but death the redeemer will humble that head,
The intrepid readiness, the terrible eyes.
The wild God of the world is sometimes merciful to those
That ask mercy, not often to the arrogant.
You do not know him, you communal people, or you have forgotten him.　15
Intemperate and savage, the hawk remembers him;
Beautiful and wild, the hawks, and men that are dying, remember him.

II

I'd sooner, except the penalties, kill a man than a hawk; but the great redtail
Had nothing left but unable misery
From the bone too shattered for mending, the wing that trailed under his
　　talons when he moved.　　　20
We had fed him six weeks, I gave him freedom.
He wandered over the foreland hill and returned in the evening, asking for
　　death —
Not like a beggar, still eyed with the old

* From *Cawdor*, by Robinson Jeffers.　By permission of Random House, New York.
† See p. 1089 for discussion.

Implacable arrogance. I gave him the lead gift in the twilight. What fell
    was relaxed,
Owl-downy, soft feminine feathers. But what   25
Soared: the fierce rush: the night-herons by the flooded river cried fear at its
    rising
Before it was quite unsheathed from reality.

FONTAINEBLEAU *

SARA TEASDALE †

Interminable palaces front on the green parterres,
    And ghosts of ladies lovely and immoral
Glide down the gilded stairs,
    The high cold corridors are clicking with the heel taps
That long ago were theirs.   5

But in the sunshine, in the vague autumn sunshine,
    The geometric gardens are desolately gay;
The crimson and scarlet and rose-red dahlias
    Are painted like the ladies who used to pass this way
With a ringletted monarch, a Henry or a Louis   10
    On a lost October day.

The aisles of the garden lead into the forest,
    The aisles lead into autumn, a damp wind grieves,
Ghostly kings are hunting, the boar breaks cover,
    But the sounds of horse and horn are hushed in falling leaves,   15
    Four centuries of autumns, four centuries of leaves.

A GRAVE ‡

MARIANNE MOORE §

Man, looking into the sea —
taking the view from those who have as much right to it as you have to it
    yourself —
it is human nature to stand in the middle of a thing
but you cannot stand in the middle of this:
the sea has nothing to give but a well excavated grave.   5
The firs stand in a procession, each with an emerald turkey-foot at the top;
reserved as their contours, saying nothing.

* From *Dark of the Moon*, by Sara Teasdale. By permission of The Macmillan Company,
publishers.

† See p. 1089 for discussion.

‡ From *Selected Poems of Marianne Moore*. By permission of The Macmillan Company
publishers.

§ See p. 1089 for discussion.

Repression, however, is not the most obvious characteristic of the sea;
the sea is a collector, quick to return a rapacious look.
There are others beside you who have worn that look,   10
whose expression is no longer a protest.   The fish no longer investigate them,
for their bones have not lasted:
men lower nets, unconscious of the fact that they are desecrating a grave,
and row quickly away; the blades of the oars
moving together like the feet of water-spiders as if there were no such thing
          as death.   15
The wrinkles progress upon themselves in a phalanx, beautiful under networks
          of foam,
and fade breathlessly while the sea rustles in and out of the sea-weed.
The birds swim through the air at top speed, emitting cat-calls as heretofore;
the tortoise-shell scourges about the feet of the cliffs, in motion beneath them;
and the ocean, under the pulsation of light-houses and noise of bell-buoys,
advances as usual, looking as if it were not that ocean in which dropped things
          are bound to sink —   21
in which, if they turn and twist, it is neither with volition or consciousness.

REPOSE OF RIVERS *

HART CRANE †

The willows carried a slow sound,
A sarabande the wind mowed on the mead.
I could never remember
That seething, steady leveling of the marshes
Till age had brought me to the sea.   5

Flags, weeds.   And remembrance of steep alcoves
Where cypresses shared the noon's
Tyranny; they drew me into hades almost.
And mammoth turtles climbing sulphur dreams
Yielded, while sun-silt rippled them   10
Asunder...

How much I would have bartered! the black gorge
And all the singular nestings in the hills
Where beavers learn stitch and tooth.
The pond I entered once and quickly fled —   15
I remember now its singing willow rim.

And finally, in that memory all things nurse;
After the city that I finally passed

† See p. 1090 for discussion.

With scalding unguents spread and smoking darts
The monsoon cut across the delta   20
At gulf gates... There, beyond the dykes

I heard wind flaking sapphire, like this summer,
And willows could not hold more steady sound.

THE SUBWAY *

ALLEN TATE †

Dark accurate plunger down the
    successive knell
Of arch on arch, where ogives burst
    a red
Reverberance of hail upon the
    dead
Thunder, like an exploding crucible!
Harshly articulate, musical steel
    shell   5
Of angry worship, hurled religiously
Upon your business of humility
Into the iron forestries of hell:

Till broken in the shift of quieter
Dense altitudes tangential of your
    steel,   10
I am become geometries — and
    glut
Expansions like a blind astronomer
Dazed, while the worldless heavens
    bulge and reel
In the cold revery of an idiot.

ARS POETICA ‡

ARCHIBALD MacLEISH §

A poem should be palpable and mute
As a globed fruit;

Dumb
As old medallions to the thumb;

Silent as the sleeve-worn stone   5
Of casement ledges where the moss
    has grown —

A poem should be wordless
As the flight of birds.
.   .   .   .

A poem should be motionless in time
As the moon climbs,   10
Leaving, as the moon releases
Twig by twig the night-entangled
    trees,

Leaving, as the moon behind the
    winter leaves,
Memory by memory the mind.

A poem should be motionless in time

As the moon climbs.   16
.   .   .   .

A poem should be equal to:
Not true.

For all the history of grief
An empty doorway and a maple leaf;

For love   21
The leaning grasses and two lights
    above the sea —

A poem should not mean
But be.

* From *Mr. Pope and Other Poems*, by Allen
Tate. By permission of G. P. Putnam's Sons.
† See p. 1090 for discussion.

‡ From *Poems, 1924–1933*, by Archibald
MacLeish. By permission of Houghton
Mifflin Company.
§ See p. 1090 for discussion.

NOTES

NOTES

POEMS OF NARRATIVE AND SITUATION

OLD BALLADS

One of the earliest expressions of man's poetic imagination was rhymed and chanted story-telling, and it is to that "childhood of fiction" which bred the legends, epics, and traditions of European nations that these old English and Scottish ballads belong. They were not written; they were sung, chanted, and freely expanded, from mouth to mouth, from generation to generation. They flourished in Scotland and England from the thirteenth to the early sixteenth century, but it was not until the eighteenth century that modern poets again began to discover the forgotten beauty of the old ballad heritage, and that Bishop Percy (in 1765) issued his famous collection, the *Reliques of Ancient English Poetry.* "When these good old bards wrote," said one of the new enthusiasts, "we had not yet made use of imported trimming upon our clothes, nor of foreign embroidery in our writings. Their poetry is the product of their own country, not pilfered and spoiled in the transportation from abroad. Their images are native, and their landscapes domestic, copied from those fields and meadows we every day behold. The morning rises (in the poet's description) as she does in the Scottish horizon. We are not carried to Greece or Italy for a shade, a stream, or a breeze. The groves rise in our own valleys; the rivers flow from our own fountains; and the winds blow upon our own hills." Thus there was restored to English poetry a tradition which had flourished down to the time of Shakespeare. It came back into modern literature and soon proved one of the most popular and widely imitated of forms, writers of all degrees of skill and sophistication attempting to recapture the simple art of their ancestors.

Poems appear on p. 973.

SIR WALTER SCOTT
(1771–1832)

Sir Walter Scott was born of the old gentry of the Scottish border which he dedicated his life to celebrating in verse and story. His childhood was steeped in the heroic legends and picturesque atmosphere of the countryside to which he later returned, after indifferent success at the University of Edinburgh and at the bar. His success with his retold ballads in *Minstrelsy of the Scottish Border* (1802–03) and with rhymed medieval or modern romances like *The Lay of the Last Minstrel, Marmion,* and *The Lady of the Lake* brought about such an enormous popularity for this new kind of poetry that Scott became the most successful revivalist of narrative poetry. After

Byron's rise to poetic fame with a new type of romantic verse, Scott turned to the writing of novels; in his long succession of tales beginning with *Waverley* in 1814 he created a panorama of historical romances which possesses, down to our own day, a universal popularity, and in which the color and sweep of action learned through his ballads achieved a fuller play.

Poem appears on p. 974.

SAMUEL TAYLOR COLERIDGE
(1772–1834)

Coleridge was, with Blake, the boldest intelligence among the English Romantic poets, expressing his imaginative gifts in several poems of a suggestive power unrivaled in that age, as well as in critical speculations that inaugurated a new era in literary criticism. Born in 1772, educated at Christ's Hospital, London, and at Cambridge, he was by turns an ardent student of the new social and idealistic philosophy and a reckless squanderer of his excited energies. Through friendship with Wordsworth he at length found the creative powers that were to express themselves so brilliantly and fitfully in his verse and prose. He collaborated with Wordsworth in publishing the *Lyrical Ballads* of 1798, the volume which announced the full arrival in England of the new Romantic genius. It contained *The Rime of the Ancient Mariner*, the ballad which, with *Kubla Khan*, *Christabel*, *Frost at Midnight*, *Love*, and the odes on *Dejection* and the *Departing Year*, marks the climax of his lyric genius. *Kubla Khan* shows that genius at its highest musical power. This unfinished poem was written in the summer of 1797, just after Coleridge rose from a sleep into which he had fallen after reading a description of the Khan's palace in *Purchas's Pilgrimage*. "A person on business from Porlock" then called him to the door, and when Coleridge returned to his desk the vision of the poem had left him. But the fifty-four lines he had written remain among the highest achievements of the English language.

Poem appears on p. 975.

JOHN KEATS
(1795–1821)

John Keats was born in London, the son of a livery-stable keeper and an innkeeper's daughter. Orphaned at fifteen, he was apprenticed to a surgeon, but devoted himself passionately to books and writing. He soon won, through contributions to magazines and with his first volume of *Poems* in 1817, the friendship of some of his famous contemporaries — Leigh Hunt, Shelley, Wordsworth, and Hazlitt. But his books were condemned and savagely attacked in the influential literary reviews of the day, and Keats knew little public honor in his brief life. Hereditary consumption, as well as his hopeless love for Fanny Brawne, darkened the last five years of his life. Through the efforts of friends he went to Italy and settled in Rome in the hope of regaining his health. In five months he was dead. Keats's exquisite poems are the fit embodiment of his lifelong search for the beautiful — beauty translated from its sensuous reality to the absolute of a philosophic ideal. His love of old ballads led him to perfect in his own work the spirit of the early English or Renaissance balladists; in "La Belle Dame sans Merci" he gives its most enduring form to the antique legend of man lured from the ways of earthly vigor and achievement by the baleful beauty of the pitiless lady of love and death.

Poem appears on p. 976.

ROBERT BROWNING
(1812–1889)

Robert Browning is perhaps the greatest of those English dramatic poets who never succeeded in transforming their dramatic gift into the practical terms of the theater. But in his brilliant character poems — mostly monologues in type — Browning used this instinct in depicting subtle and elusive enigmas of human nature. In this type of poetry he is unsurpassed among English poets. Many volumes of shorter poems were interspersed with plays and especially with his great poem, *The Ring and the Book*, completed in 1868, a magnificent recital of the destinies drawn together in a famous Florentine murder-trial of the late Renaissance. Browning's dramatic poems may be roughly divided into two groups: those which analyze a character down to the subtlest and most elusive points of its constitution, and those which develop a situation. In the second group stand the simple tragedy of "The Patriot," and the more complex tale of "Childe Roland to the Dark Tower Came," an allegory of the pursuit of the ideal through all the hideous obstacles and tortures of the knightly quest, and among scenes of distorted and terrifying significance.

Poems appear on pp. 977, 978.

DANTE GABRIEL ROSSETTI
(1828–1882)

The Rossetti family was three-fourths Italian, and lived in London as exiles, the father having fled from Naples during the suppression of the revolutionary movement against the Bourbons. They formed in London a circle of friends whose various skills in poetry, conversation, painting, and criticism led to the formation of the Pre-Raphaelite Brotherhood. This Brotherhood sought to revive the arts of painting and poetry in England, by returning for examples and discipline to the Italian painters of the early Renaissance, in the time before Raphael. In the work of Christina Rossetti the Brotherhood found its most exact and sensitive lyric genius. In the poems of Dante Gabriel was expressed the more exotic and pictorial spirit of the movement, many of his best poems being interpretations of his own pictures or those of other painters. In "My Sister's Sleep" he combines his instinct for decorative charm with the pathos of a domestic tragedy far removed from his usually vivid historical or dramatic subjects.

Poem appears on p. 982.

THOMAS HARDY
(1840–1928)

Thomas Hardy (1840–1928) won his first fame as a novelist. In his great romances and tragedies he expressed the indignation and pathos of his philosophic pessimism — the product of his ordeal in the nineteenth century's "iron age of doubts, disputes, distractions, fears." His earlier tales of Wessex — the southern country of England which forms the living background of his stories — are of a more idyllic character: *Under the Greenwood Tree, Far from the Madding Crowd, A Pair of Blue Eyes*; but in the later novels of his greatest strength — *The Return of the Native, The Mayor of Casterbridge, Tess of the d'Urbervilles,* and *Jude the Obscure* — his ironic portrayal of humanity's obscure destiny reached its heights. In the last thirty years of his life he returned to the writing of poetry, publishing many volumes of lyrics as well as a long epic-drama of the Napoleonic Wars, *The Dynasts.* He may turn from humble themes of Wessex life to problems of larger philosophic scope or historical interest. But throughout his verse he retains a quality of verbal oddity and oblique humor which makes his work as a poet unmistakable.

Poem appears on p. 983.

OSCAR WILDE
(1856–1900)

Oscar Wilde was born in Dublin in 1856, but except for inevitable associations of wit and imagination, his career is little connected with Ireland. His literary beginnings start at Oxford; he then advanced rapidly to a position of public notoriety as an exponent of the new esthetic cult of the eighties; both in England and in America he preached the new gospel of art and beauty, usually before ridiculing audiences but often before devout disciples. From this phase he passed into his success as a satirist and witty writer of social plays — *An Ideal Husband, A Woman of No Importance, The Importance of Being Earnest,* and *Lady Windermere's Fan.* In addition to these plays he wrote verse, prose fantasies, and many papers on his creed, which by this time had become a mixture of refined estheticism and social irony. An abrupt reversal of his fortunes came in 1895 when he was tried and imprisoned for a social offense. Out of his tragedy he shaped the simple and enduring ballad of prison-life which is in many respects a reversal of his earlier poetic manner and doctrine, and which now appears to be his one poem, perhaps his one literary achievement, that will endure beyond the literary fashions of his period. The ballad tells, in a style of eloquent realism, of the execution of one of Wilde's prison mates at Reading Gaol, near London, during his incarceration there in the years 1895–97.

Poem appears on p. 984.

A. E. HOUSMAN
(1859–   )

Alfred Edward Housman, born in 1859, has spent his life at civil and academic occupations, first as a Higher Division Clerk in the British Patent Office, then as a distinguished professor of Latin at the universities of London and Cambridge. Although he has shared little of the public fame of his literary contemporaries, he has had one of the most brilliant reputations. Written in memory of his youth in western England, *The Shropshire Lad*, published in 1896, has become one of the most cherished of modern books of verse. In 1922 he issued, after a quarter-century, another small sheaf of lyrics, *Last Poems*, and announced his withdrawal from poetic labors. Housman has perfected in English the short lyric form whose greatest European master was Heinrich Heine. His exquisite lyrics are perhaps the finest part of his work, but these two poems, "Bredon Hill" and "The Street Sounds" from *The Shropshire Lad*, show how intense he can make a dramatic moment within the narrow confines of his stanzas.

Poems appear on p. 993.

RUDYARD KIPLING
(1865–1936)

Rudyard Kipling's success in two kinds of writing — verse and short story — has been among the greatest popular achievements of the past fifty years. With his first collection of short stories, *Soldiers Three*, in 1888, his fame among the far-flung readers of the British Empire was assured. Born in India and trained at the United Services College in England, he was able to use with hitherto unequaled authority the romantic adventures of British soldiers following the fortunes of imperial armies in India, Egypt, and South Africa. His long succession of tales and novels — including the excellent animal stories of the two *Jungle Books* — brought him a position of astonishing fame in the English-reading world, and the Nobel Prize in 1907. His poetry began to appear in the *Barrack-Room Ballads* of 1892; in its celebration of the rough emotions of plodding soldiers or zealous patriots it struck an inevitable response in the heartily nationalistic public of the day. His colloquial language and swinging rhythms had an invigorating influence. When the particular values they capitalized began to wane, their value began to lessen, but in a number of his most characteristic songs — of which "Danny Deever" is one — Kipling's merit as a poet is unquestionable. He died in January, 1936.

Poem appears on p. 994.

EDWIN ARLINGTON ROBINSON
(1869–1935)

Edwin Arlington Robinson was born in Maine in 1869, and spent almost all of his life there or in New York City, where he died in April, 1935. For two years (1891–93) he attended Harvard College; for five (1905–10) he served as a clerk in the New York Custom House. Robinson's poems appeared in many volumes between his first book, *The Children of the Night* (1897), and his death, but his greatest fame was won by the volumes in which he gave his record of Gardiner, the Maine village of his youth ("Tilbury Town" in his books). Robinson's irony, his eccentric humor, and his austerely stoic conception of man derive, it is not too much to claim, from the taciturn New England background of his youth. In "The Mill" he shows his art in reducing a tragedy to the briefest terms of indirect suggestion.

Poem appears on p. 995.

WALTER DE LA MARE
(1873–   )

Walter de la Mare is chiefly known for his skill at creating a kind of supernatural fantasy which seems at first glance strangely out of place in modern literature. But De la Mare has succeeded in modernizing his elves and spirits, his moon-haunted glens and enchanted country-folk. In novels like *Henry Brocken* (1904), and *Memoirs of a Midget* (1912), this fantasy is usually associated with eccentric psychology or dream-worldliness; in his poems he will employ similar odd types of humanity or he will step boldly and without apology into the moonlit realm of the unreal, its first authentic explorer, perhaps, since Blake and Coleridge. "The Listeners," from the volume to which it gives its title, is his finest poem, an evocation of that haunted world of sacred dreams and idealisms at whose door the reckless spirit of material or physical courage knocks in vain.

Poem appears on p. 995.

G. K. CHESTERTON
(1874–   )

Gilbert Keith Chesterton is primarily a journalist — a writer on an almost endless variety of subjects, literary and social, and a propagandist in several causes, religious and economic. His cause is always on the side of affirmation and tradition, and against the irony and skepticism of the modern spirit. In "Lepanto" he celebrates, in a strident rhythm and gorgeous panoply of images, the "last war of Christendom," the battle of Don John of Austria against the Turks at Lepanto, on the Gulf of Corinth, in the sixteenth century. It is his most celebrated poem, and one of the few from his half-dozen books of verse that promise to survive the topical interests to which most of them are devoted.

Poem appears on p. 996.

AMY LOWELL
(1874–1925)

Amy Lowell, descendant of the famous Massachusetts family that included James Russell Lowell, was a poet of prolific output and unabated energy. Her luxuriant imagination lent her poetry a prodigal variety of materials;

she pillaged the legends of China and Italy, the traditions of England and America, the riches of West and East. She finally came to rest in themes of New England life, whose eccentric sincerity and picturesqueness were always an object of her deepest affection. Miss Lowell was not a supreme artist nor an original craftsman, but she inspired innovations and encouraged talents by her unflagging zeal for modern poetry. Her personality — rich, enthusiastic, vain, self-indulgent, generous — was written down in a long succession of poetic books. In "Patterns" she combines a tragedy of love with the vivid decorative detail upon which her care was always lavished.

Poem appears on p. 999.

JOHN MASEFIELD
(1878–   )

Masefield became Poet Laureate of England on the death of Robert Bridges in 1930, an event which recognized in this writer of sea-songs and ballads, English tales and legends, an appropriate literary officer of the British nation. Masefield's life had equipped him well. He spent his youth at sea, working on various ships, and for a period acting as a barkeeper in a New York saloon. He returned to England in 1897, and soon produced the verses of *Salt Water Ballads* (1902) and the stories of *A Mainsail Haul* (1906), but it was not until the so-called "Georgian" poetic revival of 1911 that he won general recognition with his long narrative poem, *The Everlasting Mercy*. This was followed by a succession of similar story-poems which almost succeeded in instigating a general revival of narrative verse — *The Widow in the Bye-Street* (1912), *Dauber* (1912), *The Daffodil Fields* (1913), *Good Friday* (1916), *Reynard the Fox* (1919), *Right Royal* (1920), and others. "Christmas Eve at Sea," from the *Salt Water Ballads*, shows his ability to evoke the spirit and drama of a maritime episode.

Poem appears on p. 1001.

VACHEL LINDSAY
(1879–1932)

Vachel Lindsay's poetry was the product of the conditions that shaped his life and personality — the frontier optimism and excitement of the Middle West, the visionary enchantment of "the American dream," the fantastic legends and popular superstitions of a small-town boy of the eighties. To this inheritance Lindsay joined the resonant language of the American pulpit and political platform, the swashbuckling rhythms of common speech and song, and the crude impulses of negroid "jazz." The combination gave him a distinctive place in the American poetic revival between 1912 and 1930. Born in Springfield, Illinois, in 1879, he stepped into fame when *Poetry: A Magazine of Verse* published "General William Booth Enters into Heaven" in 1912. In "The Congo" he described a vision of African tribal life conjured up by the negro quarter of an American town. "The Chinese Nightingale" in 1917 showed him at his best in a similar fantasy evoked by the Oriental mysteries of San Francisco's Chinatown. Lindsay's work was a combination of ecstatic brilliance, of almost pyrotechnical originality in rhythm and imagery, with a crude facility which ultimately undermined his talent. He lives chiefly in his contributions to American folklore and balladry. In "John Brown" he converts the legend of the Civil War martyr into the exalted pathos of a Negro sermon.

Poem appears on p. 1001.

ELINOR WYLIE
(1887–1928)

Elinor Wylie's first volume, *Nets to Catch the Wind*, appeared in 1921, when she was thirty-four years old, and was followed, in the seven remaining years of her life, by three others — *Black Armour* (1923), *Trivial Breath* (1928), and *Angels and Earthly Creatures* (1928). The exquisite, dazzling, and sometimes over-precocious artistry of these volumes was spent on themes of tenuous delicacy, sometimes of an exaggerated fragility, but at best invigorated by human sympathies and toward the end by moving personal experiences. One of the strengthening factors in Elinor Wylie's work was her love of American and other historical legends. In "Blood Feud" she recalls a memory of frontier days in the West.

Poem appears on p. 1002.

T. S. ELIOT
(1888–)

T. S. Eliot, an American by birth but a British subject by choice, will probably remain an outstanding poet of the early twentieth century for his presentation of one theme that prevails throughout his work — the spiritual poverty of modern man in a world from which all external manifestations of permanent value, religious, heroic, and artistic, have fled. This theme he developed in many short poems — "The Love Song of J. Alfred Prufrock," "The Portrait of a Lady," and the satires on *Sweeney*, his character of the absurd average man — before he presented it at full length in one of the most brilliant poems of recent times, *The Waste Land*, in 1922. In "Sweeney Among the Nightingales" he shows the crude and sterile horrors of man's physical life, from which the memory of the heroic days of Agamemnon and the Greeks has all but wholly vanished. His work as a poet and critic has won him a wide reputation and one of the most remarkable positions of influence among the writers of our time.

Poem appears on p. 1003.

ARCHIBALD MacLEISH
(1892–)

Archibald MacLeish is an American poet, born in 1892, who has from his earliest work been engrossed with the heroic destiny of the American continent. This idea has been particularly attractive to him because he approached it through the ironic disillusionment of the post-War decade. In *Streets of the Moon* (1926) he passed from his attitude of elegiac regret to a mood of satiric irony, and thus toward his serious handling of American subjects. This continued in his spiritual autobiography, *The Hamlet of A. MacLeish* (1928) and particularly in *New Found Land* (1930), reaching its fullest development in his epic of the Spanish conquest of Mexico, *Conquistador*. "The End of the World" represents Mr. MacLeish's ironic phase; he translates the mood of spiritual and intellectual deflation into a comic allegory whose setting is a stormy night in a circus-tent.

Poem appears on p. 1003.

POEMS OF HUMAN CHARACTER

SIR HENRY WOTTON
(1568–1639)

To define the ideal human character has been the aim of saints, philosophers, and poets in every age — the saint by example, the philosopher by definition, the poet by portraiture and dramatic suggestion. The poet, unlike the didactic philosopher, often finds his greatest pleasure in handling personality in its given state, flawed by imperfections or weaknesses, as well as ennobled by pure motives and happy fortunes. The stuff of character has lent itself to poems of many purposes and styles: to pictures of the complete and perfect man, as well as to drawings of eccentric and distorted natures in which some salient property of mortal life is thrown into relief.

Sir Henry Wotton was a contemporary of Shakespeare and a friend of Donne. His experiences at Oxford, in Italy, as a friend and secretary to the tragic Earl of Essex, as a confidant of Donne, as a friend of the family of James I, and as ambassador in Venice brought him into touch with a great range of human types. From these experiences he extracted the rule of happy living expressed in this poem. Instead of endorsing the political ambitions and struggles for greatness that swayed so many of his contemporaries, he prescribed a course of simple duties and quiet rewards.

Poem appears on p. 1004.

ANDREW MARVELL
(1621–1678)

Although Andrew Marvell was a poet of English Puritanism, a friend of the Commonwealth leaders and Milton's associate in the Latin secretaryship under Cromwell, the poetry by which he is best known is far from puritanical in character. In this famous address "To His Coy Mistress," he pleads with his lady to make the most of the brief hours granted to man for life and love. By borrowing the device of fanciful exaggeration developed by his poetic contemporaries, the "Metaphysicals" of the seventeenth century, Marvell succeeded in giving to the pathos of man's brief existence and quickly snuffed passions a subtle and memorable interpretation.

Poem appears on p. 1004.

WILLIAM WORDSWORTH
(1770–1850)

Wordsworth is the central and typical poet of English Romanticism; his romanticism is typically English in its moderation, its quiet stoicism, its love of familiar nature, and its reverence for humble men. His doctrines of duty, honor, and love found their center in his definition of the good man — that man of "plain living and high thinking" which he himself strove to be. In these two poems Wordsworth gives the ideal characters of woman and man as he saw them from the vantage-point of his sober and intensely human reflection.

Poems appear on p. 1005.

ALFRED LORD TENNYSON
(1809–1892)

Tennyson's long life encompassed the entire nineteenth century — its changes, havoc, hardships, and its English triumphs under Queen Victoria. To the celebration of those triumphs, and of the English spirit which made them possible, Tennyson devoted his facile and expert lyric genius. *In Memoriam* sums up the spiritual ordeal of his generation and of all serious men who were struck by the meaning and force of incalculable changes. In 1850 he received the Laureateship on the death of Wordsworth. More seriously than any other poet of modern times, he set to work to fulfill the duties of that post. He wrote the *Idylls of the King*, the most popular and complete modern version of the Arthurian legends, and his later age was filled with many honors. The pretension and facility in Tennyson's work introduce flaws of conception and craftsmanship even into his most serious projects, but it is in certain soberer poems like "Ulysses" that one finds his finer qualities. In "Ulysses" Tennyson represents the hero of Homer's *Odyssey*, not as a retired home-biding man returned to his native Ithaca, but as the searcher described in Dante's *Inferno*, urged even to his destruction in a whirlpool beyond the straits of Gibraltar by "an ardor to gain experience of the world."

Poem appears on p. 1007.

ROBERT BROWNING
(1812–1889)

Browning here devotes himself to subjects of character, leaving aside for a moment the dramatic circumstances which are usually his favorite conditions for reading the secrets of men's souls. In contrast to highly stirring poems like "The Laboratory" and "Childe Roland," this elegy on the death of a great teacher of the Renaissance is both exalted and reflective, the fulfilment of a long life's meditation on the nature of man and his problems. Perhaps nowhere does Browning's optimism and faith in life arrive at a more stirring expression.

Poem appears on p. 1008.

WALT WHITMAN
(1819–1892)

Whitman was born of mingled Dutch and English ancestry on Long Island, in 1819. From his father's farm he went to school in Brooklyn; then to various jobs in Brooklyn and New York; again to the country where he worked as a school-teacher and printer. In all these tasks he showed in himself a distaste for success and ambition; he was already formulating in his mind that return of mankind to the truth of nature which he was soon to preach in his poems as against the progressive spirit, the "mania of owning things," in the hustling nineteenth-century world around him. At intervals in the following years he wrote the poems which in 1855 appeared in *Leaves of Grass*. With this book a new and startling genius, typically American in style and purposes, was announced. Whitman's reputation as the poet of democracy and "the American dream" began to grow. The Civil War was a severe challenge to his faith in the hopes of democracy; he worked in the ranks as a wound-dresser and hospital attendant, and after the war he continued to live in Washington, devoting himself to the care of soldiers and supporting himself with a government clerkship. His thought, centering in his messianic hope of a reborn humanity, expressed in a freely cadenced poetic style, eventually made him one of the greatest influences in American literature. In "O Pioneers!" he presented his heroic vision of the men who settled the western territories of the North American continent. In "O Captain, My Captain!" he wrote his tribute to Abraham Lincoln on hearing of his tragic assassination at the close of the Civil War.

Poems appear on pp. 1011, 1014.

WILLIAM BUTLER YEATS
(1865–)

In the eighteen-eighties Irish literature was aroused from its long-standing and inveterate indifference to racial and local traditions by the movement for national liberty. A new generation of poets appeared, ready to declare themselves the inheritors of Celtic antiquity and the heralds of a new age of Irish achievement in art. The leaders of this brilliant generation were William Butler Yeats, George Russell ("AE"), Lady Augusta Gregory, George Moore, and John M. Synge. Yeats's activities in the Irish revival have been varied, picturesque, and brilliant. He retold old legends; he was one of the founders of an Irish National Theatre; he has participated in political and patriotic movements; he has applied himself relentlessly to a lifelong discipline of poetic craftsmanship. He won the Nobel Prize in 1923, and his high position among his countrymen won him one of the first seats in the senate of the new Irish Free State when it was founded in 1922. His poetry has explored many mythologies and philosophies in its search for symbols and allegories, but it has never lost touch with Irish character and tradition. In this poem that contact is exhibited in an early ballad. He is perhaps at present the greatest living poet of the English language.

Poem appears on p. 1014.

EDWIN ARLINGTON ROBINSON
(1869–1935)

"Miniver Cheevy" is one of Robinson's typical poems of character. It defines one of the American types that appear throughout his work as embodiments of his thought or examples of his reading of human nature. Among these men Cheevy is treated with the taciturn humor of Robinson's intense compassion for his fellow-creatures. As an example of the social and spiritual misfit, he has already gained his fame among American literary characters.

Poem appears on p. 1015.

AMY LOWELL
(1874–1925)

Miss Lowell's affection for New England life and its traditions recurs throughout her work, but another side of her nature was exotic; it sought expression in themes of fantastic extravagance, of baroque elegance, or of fragile decorative charm as in "A Lady." This poem shows an exactness and aristocracy of imagery that contrasts sharply with the cruder or more realistic spirit of Miss Lowell's narrative and historical poems.

Poem appears on p. 1015.

ROBERT FROST
(1875–   )

Robert Frost brought to the writing of verse an ear subtly attuned to the cadences and inflections of the New England voice. He was born in California in 1875, but he soon returned to the Vermont and Massachusetts homes of his family and there grew up. He stayed only a few months at Dartmouth College, going to work instead in a mill at Lawrence; he later attended Harvard for two years, but abandoned that course also, driven to school-teaching, shoe-making, journalism, and even farming to earn a living for himself and his family. In 1912 he went to England, determined to achieve his ambition as a writer; soon thereafter he was recognized in America as a sensitive and original pastoral poet. *A Boy's Will*, *North of Boston*, *Mountain Interval*, and *New Hampshire* were the four books that brought him, in ten years, to a position of rank and honor in American literature. In "Acquainted with the Night" the serious personal temper of his best verse is felt.

Poem appears on p. 1016.

CARL SANDBURG
(1878–   )

Sandburg is known throughout America as the poet of the city. His city is Chicago, and his poems made a notable contribution to the American poetic revival of 1912–20 by putting into the language of verse the language of its streets and slums, its factories and workshops. Sandburg made no compromise with polite conventions. His *Chicago Poems* of 1916 are full of grim realism, touched, however, with a quality of pathos or humor that lifts it into the higher eloquence of humanitarian idealism. In volumes like *Cornhuskers*, *Smoke and Steel*, *Slabs of the Sunburnt West*, and *Good Morning, America*, he exhibits his affection for the farm-laborers, the factory workers, the harvest-hands, and the hardy pioneers of early America, whose spirit he still sees as dominating the ugly cruelty and inhumanity of industrial life. In "Cool Tombs" Sandburg's talent for a rough kind of pathos, grounded in American life, is expressed.

Poem appears on p. 1016.

VACHEL LINDSAY
(1879–1932)

Lindsay on occasion turned from chanting and fantasy to sober speech and realism. During the dark days of the World War, he imagined Lincoln walking in the night watches through the streets of his and Lindsay's home city, Springfield, Illinois, haunted by the specters of desolation and ruin, and of man's insatiable lust for conquest and revenge. This grave interlude to Lindsay's more jubilant verse shows him in a quieter but stronger manifestation of his talent.

Poem appears on p. 1016.

PADRAIC COLUM
(1881–   )

The Irish literary revival of the nineties aroused many talents among Irishmen, and in the wake of such pioneers as Yeats, Synge, and Lady Gregory came men of a younger generation, like James Stephens, Padraic Colum, and James Joyce, who did their first important writing during the nineteen-hundreds. Colum made his first success as a youthful member of the Irish National Theatre (The Abbey Theatre), with plays like *Broken Soil*, *The Land*, and *Thomas Muskerry*. He is also a practiced story-teller and adapter of old legends, and a chronicler of Irish peasant life and of Irish literary history; out of his intimate knowledge of his native backgrounds come characterizations rich in the feeling and music of Irish character, like "A Drover" and "An Old Woman of the Roads," the first of which is printed here.

Poem appears on p. 1017.

MALCOLM COWLEY
(1898–   )

Malcolm Cowley first came into literary prominence as an experimental poet among the post-war exile group in Paris, but he was born in the hill country of western Pennsylvania, and from that background come some of his most genuine poems, among them this folktune-style chant celebrating the immortal hobo spirit of the American plains and towns.   The decay of the pioneer spirit and of the mountain farms of the Appalachian states may have been a force in directing Cowley's later thought toward social reform and communistic idealism.

Poem appears on p. 1018.

LYRICS OF EMOTION AND EXPERIENCE

WILLIAM SHAKESPEARE
(1564–1616)

In the Elizabethan age music was one of the most popular arts. Taverns, households, courts, and roadsides had their singers; the entire nation agreed in its love of madrigals, serenades, snatches, rounds, and hymns. The dramatists interspersed their comedies and tragedies with exquisite examples of this craft, some of the most brilliant songs of the English Renaissance being embedded in plays by Shakespeare, Marlowe, Jonson, and their contemporaries. Shakespeare's songs are particularly a striking evidence of his lyrical genius — a genius that underlies and strengthens even his most massive dramatic concepts. These two songs are from *Cymbeline* and *Measure for Measure.*

Poems appear on p. 1019.

CHRISTOPHER MARLOWE
(1564–1593)

Marlowe, like Shakespeare, combined dramatic genius with lyrical. In longer poems like *Hero and Leander* he furnished his contemporaries with a model of the long poem of romantic or mythological subject-matter; in "The Passionate Shepherd to His Love" he wrote one of the first and most popular of English love poems. In it the pastoral artificiality of Renaissance amatory verse is converted into an imagery and music that foreshadow the art of the seventeenth-century lyric. Marlowe is here revealed as an ancestor of the long line of cavalier singers that extends from Jonson and Shakespeare to Cowley and Marvell.

Poem appears on p. 1019.

ROBERT HERRICK
(1591–1674)

Herrick is the greatest of the cavalier song-writers of the age of Charles I, but his real schooling came under the later Elizabethans, notably Ben Jonson. As one of "Ben's men" Herrick made his early fame in London as the singer of love-songs, serenades, and exquisite descriptive verses. Later in life he turned away from the pleasures of London taverns and courts, and became an Anglican clergyman, writing devotional poetry and hymns. But he never forgot the gay days that inspired him to write the immortal lyrics of love and pleasure which have insured him his particular immortality.

Poems appear on pp. 1019, 1020.

RICHARD LOVELACE
(1618–1658)

Lovelace shares with Herrick and Suckling the highest mastery of the cavalier lyric. Among English poets his fame rests on perhaps the smallest number of poems. They are songs that combine the elegance of courtly homage and passion with the ideals of military honor that dominated the age of Royalist and Puritan warfare.

Poem appears on p. 1020.

JOHN DRYDEN
(1631–1700)

Dryden is the great poet of the English Restoration (1660–1700), the first master of the neo-classic heroic couplet, and the literary arbiter of his day. His prodigiously active life included the writing of many political satires and philosophical poems, of which *MacFlecknoe, Absolom and Achitophel*, and *The Hind and the Panther* are the finest; of many plays — both comedies and tragedies — for the Restoration playhouses. Occasionally, as in his "Song for St. Cecelia's Day" and his great ode, "Alexander's Feast, or the Power of Music," he showed his rarer ability as a lyric poet. That minor phase of his talent is also shown in this song.

Poem appears on p. 1020.

MATTHEW PRIOR
(1664–1721)

Prior's life, like Marvell's, was one of brilliant successes in public and literary work. He rose from a childhood of humble working-class surroundings and apprenticeship in a tavern, to distinction at the University of Cambridge and high honors in the political world. His most serious literary projects were in the form of satires, epistles, and epigrams favored by the neo-classic age of Dryden and Pope; but Prior's most lasting success was achieved in the graceful verses on personal and informal subjects which make him one of the greatest English masters of *vers de société*. In this poem the delicate charm of his personal sentiment is interwoven with the worldly man's knowledge of life.

Poem appears on p. 1020.

ROBERT BURNS
(1759–1796)

Robert Burns was perhaps the first poet to live up to the fullest expectations of the early Romantic movement that a poet of humble birth, rural training, and unspoiled natural genius would once more be possible in the modern world. Born near Ayr in southwestern Scotland, he based all his poetry on the earthy experiences, the common labors, the simple human devotions and contacts, of his peasant background. By using the language of simple speech, even in its roughest dialect forms, he invigorated the lyric poetry of England at a moment when artificial traditions and conventional usages threatened to stultify it. After brilliant early success, he died in disappointment and obscurity at the age of thirty-six, but left behind him his ballads, love-songs, patriotic poems, and swinging narratives that have, in the following hundred and fifty years, made him not only the great national poet of Scotland, but one of the universally praised lyric poets of modern times. Burns's lyrics are often written around themes of the simplest human affections. This lyric combines his tender conception of human love with his unquenchable devotion to the scenes of his native countryside.

Poem appears on p. 1021.

WILLIAM WORDSWORTH
(1770–1850)

Among Wordsworth's early poems is a series of exquisite elegies on the death of a young girl, Lucy, whom he knew and loved as a child. Her identity has never been revealed, but she was the inspiration of a few of the finest love-songs which English Romanticism was to produce. Here are two of the most finished and moving of them.

Poems appear on p. 1022.

WALTER SAVAGE LANDOR
(1775–1864)

Landor is the classicist of the English Romantic movement. His poems contrast with Shelley's and Keats's in the chaste restraint of their style, in the Latin elegance of their form. His lyric ancestors are Catullus, Martial, and Propertius. Landor's literary career, like his life, was a long one. It began with *Gebir*, a poetic tale, in 1798, and continued through many volumes of prose and verse — notably his brilliant *Imaginary Conversations* — until his death in Florence, Italy, the scene of his fondest associations and experiences, in 1864. These delicate poems offer an immediate contrast to the belligerence of Landor's character; while he kept himself, his family, and his associates in quarrels and temperamental hot water, he produced some of the coolest and most lucid pages of English prose and verse in his century, bearing the stamp of the finest Latin epigrams or of the epitaphs of the Greek Anthology.

Poems appear on p. 1022.

LORD BYRON
(1788–1824)

Byron shares with Shelley a fame characteristic of the later and younger Romantic poets of the early nineteenth century. He proclaimed in his verse the insurgent protest of his generation against English conventions in life and thought. This he expressed in two ways: in vigorous satires like *English Bards and Scotch Reviewers*, *The Vision of Judgment*, and *Don Juan*, or in dramas and narratives of restless spiritual conquest, like *Childe Harold's Pilgrimage*, *Manfred*, and *Cain*. During a career of agitated purposes and restlessness, which included his notable friendship with men like Shelley and Leigh Hunt, he succeeded in writing great quantities of satiric and descriptive verse, much of it hollow in sentiment and pretension, but the best of it typical of the most urgent romantic idealism. His lyrics show a minor aspect of his talent, but one in which his better and more sensitive qualities are expressed.

Poem appears on p. 1022.

PERCY BYSSHE SHELLEY
(1792–1822)

In Shelley the ardent intensity and passion of the Romantic spirit reached its height; he is the most passionate and ecstatic of those poets in whom the ideal of human insurgence against tyranny and oppression was a vital instinct. He rebelled against the conservative conventions among which he was born as the son of a bluff Tory squire in Sussex, and that rebellion drove him later from Oxford University when he issued a pamphlet on *The Necessity of Atheism*. Later still, he became a disciple of the radical reformer, William Godwin, whose daughter Mary became Shelley's second wife. Shelley's defiance of English custom and authority finally led him to leave England altogether; it was on his wanderings in Switzerland and Italy that he planned and wrote in rapid succession the great poems upon which his fame is based: *Prometheus Unbound*, *The Cenci*, *Adonais*, *Epipsychidion*, *The Revolt of Islam*, and the magnificent lyrics and odes. In this lyric his less prophetic but more purely musical genius is seen.

Poem appears on p. 1023.

ALFRED LORD TENNYSON
(1809–1892)

Tennyson's lyrics sometimes stand alone, sometimes they are found within longer poems like *The Princess* and *Maud*. Usually they show his sensitive ear for musical cadence and sound to far better advantage than his more deliberately sonorous blank verse or dramatic poetry. "In the Valley of Cauteretz" is a brief memorial to Arthur Henry Hallam, the youthful friend to whom he dedicated *In Memoriam*; here he recalls him when revisiting, after many years, a scene in Spain which they had traveled together in a walking tour during youthful holidays.

Poem appears on p. 1023.

EDGAR ALLAN POE
(1809–1849)

Poe's poems almost invariably celebrate their crises of human passion against a vivid dramatic background; he instinctively employed his gift for startling circumstance when he wrote elegies or meditations such as "Annabelle Lee," "The Raven" and "The Bells." This is to be expected from the author of such unforgettably arresting stories as "The Masque of the Red Death," "The Pit and the Pendulum," and "The Fall of the House of Usher." In "Ulalume" these properties are present. As a lyric freighted with atmospheric effects and violent symbolism, "Ulalume" becomes a poetic equivalent of the "arabesque and grotesque" allegories that fill Poe's books of tales.

Poem appears on p. 1023.

CHRISTINA ROSSETTI
(1830–1894)

Christina Rossetti was the sister of Dante Gabriel Rossetti, and a member of the Pre-Raphaelite company of poets and painters. She sat as model for several of her brother's most popular paintings, and she supplemented the reformist ardor of her friends with a genius quietly contemplative and deeply religious. Her poems are almost altogether devotional or mystical in theme. Occasionally she wrote a more imaginative poem like the brilliant allegory, *Goblin Market*, or the tragic drama, *The Prince's Progress*. Her best work is in lyrics of religious contemplation like the two quoted here. With Mrs. Browning, Emily Brontë, and Alice Meynell she contributes the special graces of feminine genius to the Victorian achievement in English poetry.

Poems appear on p. 1025.

ALGERNON CHARLES SWINBURNE
(1837–1909)

Swinburne made his first appearance in 1860 with two poetic dramas, *The Queen Mother* and *Rosamund*, but his public fame was gained with his *Poems and Ballads* of 1866, which caused an enormous sensation through their frankly pagan treatment of richly sensuous subject-matter. Swinburne had already passed through his unsuccessful years at Oxford, and had published his beautiful classic play, *Atalanta in Calydon*. He associated himself with the Pre-Raphaelites, and derived also from contemporary French poetry, notably that of Baudelaire. With later volumes like the *Song of Italy* (1867) and *Songs Before Sunrise* (1871) he turned to the problems of political reform and liberty whose cause was being fought in France and Italy. He continued to write poetic dramas, critical essays, and poems until the end of his life, but his real strength is revealed in the chastely paced meters of *Atalanta*, and in the intricately rhythmical *Poems and*

Ballads in which, before he erred by excess and repetition, he virtually created a new manner of lyric poetry in England.

Poem appears on p. 1026.

GERARD MANLEY HOPKINS
(1844–1889)

Gerard Hopkins was beyond doubt one of the most original English poets of his century. He wrote out of an intense feeling for the imagery of nature, for the sounds, sights, and even the tastes of the brilliant world he saw about him; and in order to express this extreme perception in poetry, he invented a language whose word-forms, cadences, and rich patterns of phraseology form a vehicle for his heightened knowledge of his surroundings. He attended Oxford University in the later days of the great religious revival which had been active there in the days of Newman and the Tractarians. He became a convert to Catholicism, and later a Jesuit priest. Many of his poems are on themes of spiritual devotion. During his lifetime little of his verse was printed or known. On his death in 1889 he confided it to his lifelong friend, Robert Bridges, who did not publish it in book form until 1918. At once Hopkins was recognized as a poetic innovator of extraordinary originality. In "Pied Beauty" may be found a typical example of Hopkins's descriptive method in translating the miraculous colors and forms of nature into verse; in his sonnet "The Windhover" he uses the soaring flight of birds to embody his exaltation before the manifestations of God in nature.

Poems appear on pp. 1027, 1028.

WILLIAM BUTLER YEATS
(1865–   )

The early songs of Yeats are among the most popular modern poems. Their faintly Celtic quality appears in certain phrases and in the imagery of their settings, but the nostalgia or "ache of love" expressed in them is confined to no national boundaries. Yeats's later poems grew into a much tougher and firmer style, but these early poems nevertheless remain among the finest products of that lyric revival which, by opposing the didactic solemnity of late Victorian poetry, brought into existence a new style of lyric art in England. "When you are old" is his free redaction of Ronsard's famous sixteenth-century sonnet, "*Quand vous serez bien vieille, au soir, à la chandelle*," a classic of French literature.

Poem appears on p. 1028.

(JOSEPH) TRUMBULL STICKNEY
(1874–1904)

The brilliant promise of Stickney's youthful work as a poet and scholar was never fulfilled, for he died at the age of thirty. He was an honors student at Harvard and at the Sorbonne, and returned to teach Greek at Harvard shortly before his death. His friends William Vaughn Moody, George Cabot Lodge, and E. A. Robinson were among the few who knew the qualities of his style. His *Dramatic Verses* of 1902 and his posthumous *Poems* of 1905 contain all that is left of his unknown but often admirable poetry.

Poem appears on p. 1029.

WALLACE STEVENS

Wallace Stevens is a poet of exact and fastidious style, of elegant mannerism, and of a refined precision of thought. He is the author of only one book, *Harmonium* (1923), but in it some of the most distinguished symbolic poetry of recent times may be found. He combines, with his cavalier exquisiteness, an oblique humor which often intensifies the pathos of his sympathies; but at other times it serves to set off an invention of particular fragility or oddity. In "Ploughing on Sunday" he conjures up a picture of pioneer America, and succeeds in making it a legend worthy of perpetuation in folklore.

Poem appears on p. 1029.

JAMES JOYCE
(1882–   )

James Joyce's lyrics stand in startling contrast to his famous novels, *A Portrait of the Artist as a Young Man* and *Ulysses* — those remarkable narratives in which experimentalism of style joins hands with a tragic interpretation of twentieth-century spiritual ordeal. But Joyce is an heir to various complex literary traditions; he may derive in one place from the monumental satiric art of Rabelais, Sterne, and Swift, and in another from the most delicate lyric styles of Catullus and Horace, or his favorite Elizabethans. The brief lyrics in his two books of verse, *Chamber Music* and *Pomes Penyeach*, descend from the song art of the Elizabethan and Caroline poets, crossed with a strain of Celtic poignance.

Poems appear on pp. 1029, 1030.

EZRA POUND
(1885–   )

In this exquisite sonnet, "A Virginal," Pound is found writing in the vein of courtly and amatory verse which he derives from the medieval poetry of Provence and Italy. His tribute to a lady combines metaphorical elegance with a flawlessly cadenced music similar in tone to that which he has always admired in Cavalcanti, Pierre Vidal, and Dante. He has thus written a modern poem which openly acknowledges its model in a tradition of the remote past — a past which Pound has done much to bring into intimate contact with modern art.

Poem appears on p. 1030.

EDNA ST. VINCENT MILLAY
(1892–   )

In the early poetry of Edna St. Vincent Millay was expressed, at its best, the eager enthusiasm of twentieth-century youth for the life from which it had stripped the encumbering conventions of the Victorian Age, and which it could now invest with a romantic color of its own. Her first success was made in 1912 when her long poem "Renascence" failed to win a prize in a competition conducted by *The Lyric Year*. Among those manuscripts it was easily the most distinguished. Five years later she graduated from Vassar, and in her following volumes she achieved the wide popularity due to a lyrist of her open and human qualities. These qualities often descend to the facile inconsequence of her more pagan and narcissistic humors, but they can rise to the pathos of her finest ballads or of her sonnets. The informing passion of Miss Millay's best work, escaping naïve trivialities as well as literary mannerism, will be the basis of her future fame among poets of this century.

Poem appears on p. 1030.

E. E. CUMMINGS
(1896–   )

Edward Estlin Cummings became famous in the post-War decade as one of the most daring inventors of eccentric expression and personal mannerism that America had yet produced. His novelties — which then seemed more startling than they do now — included uncapitalized proper names and nouns, broken rhythms, and poetic forms dictated solely by the wandering or fitful vagaries of the writer's consciousness. He created, at his best, a poetic form equal to the obscure processes of his impulses and feelings. In collections of verse like *Tulips and Chimneys* and *XLI Poems* he made his extremely personal contribution to the literary innovation of the nineteen-twenties. In "Chanson Innocente" he uses the innocence of childhood as a means toward expressing, with candid lucidity, a conventional kind of delight in the spring of the year.

Poem appears on p. 1031.

LÉONIE ADAMS
(1899–   )

Miss Adams is a poet of exact and delicate mystical intuitions, expressed in a verse of almost crystalline fragility but of remarkable firmness of phrase and form. While at Barnard College she began to publish poems in magazines like *The New Republic*, and issued her first book, *Those Not Elect*, in 1925. This was followed by several years abroad on a Guggenheim Fellowship, and by a second volume, *High Falcon*, in 1929.

Poem appears on p. 1031.

GEORGE DILLON
(1906–   )

George Dillon began writing verse in early youth, and published his first poems while still a student at the University of Chicago, where he received recognition not only through student prizes, but also through his highly popular lyrics in magazines and in his first volume, *Boy in the Wind*, of 1927. His second volume, *The Flowering Stone*, achieved the Pulitzer Prize for poetry in 1931.

Poem appears on p. 1032.

GROUP FOUR

LYRICS OF REFLECTION

WILLIAM SHAKESPEARE
(1564–1616)

Shakespeare followed an Elizabethan vogue for love-poems and sonnet-sequences when he wrote his cycle of one hundred and fifty-four sonnets during the early years of his career as a dramatist in London. He made use of the taste for metrical invention among his contemporaries by varying the classic Italian sonnet form of octave and sestet, producing his English type composed of three quatrains and a final couplet. Into this form he cast thoughts both conventional and personal, transmuting them by his familiar touches of imaginative splendor or unexpected realism, and making, of such standard themes as love, friendship, loyalty, fame, and honor, poems which stand among the highest reflective poetry in English. These three examples show characteristic aspects of the sonnets — their courtly gaiety, their severe moral introspection, and their moments of tranquillity and fortitude.

Poems appear on p. 1033.

THOMAS CAMPION
(1567–1619)

With Byrd, Dowland, Breton, and Jonson, Thomas Campion made much of the finest music in Elizabethan poetry. He was an inventor of new measures and he revived meters modeled on antique types, attacking the facile rhymed verse of his period because of its tendency toward crude and conventional harmonies. In his four *Books of Airs*, published between 1601 and 1613, he combined simplicity with novelty, verbal and figurative richness with homely or rustic grace. Some of his most exquisite songs are to be found in his masques. His greatest contribution to literature in his age lay in his attempt to wed words closely with music. In doing this he not only strengthened the lyrics of his fellow Elizabethans, but prepared the day of the Cavalier song-writers who were shortly to appear on the scene with their gay and elegant measures.

Poem appears on p. 1034.

JOHN DONNE
(1573–1631)

Donne is mentor and master of "metaphysical" poetry in the early seventeenth century. He combined in a verse of subtle angularity and intense symbolism his own life's divided motives and events. He began his career as one of the most elegant of Elizabethan cavaliers, follower of the court and friend of the Earl of Essex on his voyage to the Western Isles. But with the maturity of his thought, and with the desperately changing conditions of his age, he turned from the world toward religion, finally taking orders in the English church and becoming Dean of St. Paul's. These conflicting experiences of flesh and spirit, world and soul, found their issue in a poetry of rare intellectual penetration, clothing its ideas with metaphors more complex than any previously known in English verse, and called by Dr. Johnson "metaphysical." By this style he influenced a new generation of poets, and was destined to become a notable force in twentieth-century poetry. These sonnets on "Death" are from the "divine poems" of his later years, when he was making his deanship of St. Paul's famous through mighty sermons and equally splendid poems on death and eternity.

Poem appears on p. 1034.

JOHN MILTON
(1608–1674)

Milton, the greatest poet of English Puritanism, lives chiefly in his early lyrics ("L'Allegro," "Il Penseroso," "Comus," and "Lycidas") and in the three great epics ("Paradise Lost," "Paradise Regained," "Samson Agonistes") divided from them by his intervening service in the Commonwealth established for twelve years by Cromwell's revolution. He also left a record of his inmost thoughts and observations in the form of a sequence of sonnets. Of these, some of which are on historical events in the stirring years through which he lived, the noblest are those on personal themes — the death of his wife, the loss of friends, and the blindness which overtook him as a result of his immense labors of state. The sonnet on his blindness is the most intimate revelation he ever gave of his own suffering and faith.

Poem appears on p. 1035.

EDMUND WALLER
(1606–1687)

Waller, like Dryden, tacked fitfully between the opposed forces of Puritanism and Royalism during the stormy middle years of the seventeenth century, making, in the midst of a life of arduous political affiliations, his reputation as a wit and song-writer. He wrote only occasional verse, but in that he achieved two noteworthy things: he used the closed heroic couplet, just then beginning to gain ground as the ideal verse-form of the rising poetic classicism, and he perfected in several songs a pure flute-like music which places him, with Nashe, Herrick, Jonson, and Marvell, among the finest singers of the courtly art in his century. "Go, Lovely Rose" is one of the highest achievements in English verse of this vein.

Poem appears on p. 1035.

ALEXANDER POPE
(1688–1744)

Pope, like Milton, is chiefly known for long poems of narrative, philosophical, or satirical content, in only a few works expressing the unobstrusive lyrical phase of his talent. In his brief "Ode to Solitude" he showed that it was possible for the supreme master of English verse-satire to recognize the gentler satisfactions of simple living, and to extoll those virtues of country life which were never far from the urban ideals of literature in the age of Queen Anne. This poem shows in small compass some of Pope's unsurpassed genius for the precise word and exact cadence required by the classical laws of verse in his day; of those laws he was the universally acknowledged master.

Poem appears on p. 1035.

WILLIAM BLAKE
(1757–1827)

Blake contributed to the English Romantic movement a poetry of defiant, revolutionary spirit — the expression of his own candid, vivid, half-mystical nature. An innovator both in poetry and in the arts of painting and drawing, he wrought of his philosophy (an extraordinary fusion of pantheism with Christian beliefs) a large number of poems populated with the elaborate symbols and characters which he invented as an allegory of his ideas. His more purely lyric genius — one of the keenest and most individual among English poets — found outlet in two early books, *Songs of Innocence* and *Songs of Experience* (1789 and 1794), which still stand largely unsurpassed in originality among modern poems of childhood and its afterlife. In "The Tiger" Blake used his gifts for allegory with their sharpest and most intense effect, producing a picture of evil that lives in the imagination far beyond the didactic exhortations of conventional moral verse. This poem is typical of his highest powers.

Poem appears on p. 1036.

WILLIAM WORDSWORTH
(1770–1850)

Wordsworth has already been seen in his lyrics; here are two of his reflective poems, a sonnet and a blank-verse meditation, both among that group of poems which was written at the height of his powers, between 1797 and 1810. In "The world is too much with us" he gives his most classic expression to that love of nature out of which he shaped his practical doctrine of life. In the lines written at the ruins of Tintern Abbey, on revisiting this scene in western England after an absence of five years, the same conception is given fuller form. "Tintern Abbey" ranks with the five or six poems that mark the height of Wordsworth's powers; it was his most distinguished contribution to that small volume of *Lyrical Ballads* with which he and Coleridge, jointly, in 1798, signalized the maturity of the Romantic spirit in English literature.

Poems appear on pp. 1036, 1037.

PERCY BYSSHE SHELLEY
(1792–1822)

Shelley's odes allow the characteristic exaltation of his style its fullest play, usually among themes best suited to express his gift for joining music with prophecy. In the two brilliant odes here printed, those to the Skylark and to the West Wind, he voices his idea of the poet — the "trumpet that sings to battle, the unacknowledged legislator of the world" — but not in the Promethean spirit of his philosophical poems; rather he employs the familiar inspiration of romantic nature to supply him with symbols of that restless search for spiritual power over his fellow-men and for triumph over doubt and negation. Both poems carry the unmistakable character of Shelley's personality, and may perhaps be counted as his lyric masterpieces.

Poems appear on pp. 1040, 1041.

JOHN KEATS
(1795–1821)

Keats's odes share with Shelley's the purpose of finding a means toward asserting the transcendental impulse of the poet to triumph over the material world, but where Shelley expressed that impulse in terms of an almost sublime defiance of human limitations, Keats viewed with greater realism the pathos and tragedy of the human spirit in the face of its ideal ends. Thus his odes carry a greater tone of melancholy and pathos. They also reveal Keats's greater care for verbal felicities, and the most exacting tests which he applied to conventional meters and images. The "Ode to a Nightingale" is a focus for the romantic vision of better and happier worlds, certain of its lines conveying with unmatched beauty the dream that haunted the mind of Keats's generation.

Poem appears on p. 1043.

ELIZABETH BARRETT BROWNING
(1806–1861)

Since Mrs. Browning's fame in English poetry derives largely from her romantic marriage with Robert Browning, it is natural that such fame should rest largely on the love poems which she dedicated to him, the "Sonnets from the Portuguese," first published anonymously under this misleading title. It happens that these sonnets are also her best work as a poet, a saving remnant of a prodigious but extremely uneven output. The single sonnet here printed is among the sincerest in that sequence, carrying with its unforced phrases an eloquence close to the impassioned spirit of Mrs. Browning's Elizabethan ancestors.

Poem appears on p. 1045.

EMILY BRONTË
(1818–1848)

One of the three Brontë sisters who made lasting contributions to the Victorian novel, Emily Brontë was the only member of the family to achieve greatness as a poet. Her verse shows a spirit of militant fortitude and heroic strength similar to that suggested by her great novel, *Wuthering Heights*. "Last Lines" is her finest poem, standing as it does among the noblest poems on death written in the past hundred years. It shares little but verbal and metrical sobriety with the customary poems on this difficult theme written by her nineteenth-century contemporaries.

Poem appears on p. 1045.

EMILY DICKINSON
(1830–1886)

Nineteenth-century America did not boast of many poets of marked original genius, but no one today who knows the finest values of poetry would deny that endowment to Emily Dickinson. Born in Amherst, Massachusetts, she lived out her life in the narrow confines of a strict New England household, a spinster of elusive temperament but an explorer of the world of imagination who must rank among the boldest. Her poetic style combines the eccentric humors of an old poetic tradition with verbal originality and metrical freshness as modern as anything written in her century or in ours. Her verse was not widely recognized for its true qualities until thirty years after her death. Now it is counted with that of Whitman and Hopkins as one of the most important anticipations of the poetic experimentation of our own age. The pathos of "I died for Beauty" shows Emily Dickinson in her fullest powers of word and thought.

Poem appears on p. 1046.

ALGERNON CHARLES SWINBURNE
(1837–1909)

Perhaps it is neither in the measured classical stanzas of *Atalanta in Calydon* nor in his ambitious political poems of later years that Swinburne will be longest remembered. His most popular contributions to Victorian poetry are those lyrics in which he expressed the world-weariness and disillusionment of the age, its skepticism and its search for spiritual and bodily release from mortal oppressions. These sentiments he translated into a poetry of fluent musical splendor, "The Garden of Proserpine" being his finest lyric in this highly personal and unmistakable style. It presents, in terms which proved irresistible to the more discouraged minds of his time, the fatal beauty of nineteenth-century disbelief and doubt.

Poem appears on p. 1046.

ALICE MEYNELL
(1850–1923)

The few and severely disciplined poems of Alice Meynell stand in the tradition of seventeenth-century devotional verse. In this tradition Mrs. Meynell's Catholicism schooled her, while her own austerity of craft and character lent the rigor appropriate to so intense an art. Among her late Victorian contemporaries she was a figure apart, but she never lost touch with the surrounding public and literary world, in which she and her husband Wilfrid Meynell — notably through their discovery and protection of Francis Thompson — held a distinguished place. Among her more intellectual poems and essays may be found several lyrics of gay or ironic temper, of which this one, "The Shepherdess," has won a deserved popularity.

Poem appears on p. 1047.

FRANCIS THOMPSON
(1859–1907)

Francis Thompson, who began life as a medical student but soon drifted into dissolute habits and obscurity, was rescued to English poetry by Wilfrid and Alice Meynell. In a short literary career of less than twenty years he achieved a widespread fame, chiefly through reviving — among the conventions and realities of modern poetry — the intense imaginative obliquity and impassioned style of the seventeenth-century mystics. In "The Hound of Heaven" and other religious poems (he was a Catholic), he wrote some of the most brilliant devotional verse of his century. In "Sister Songs," "The Poppy," and "Daisy," he spoke in more personal terms of human character and its loyalties. In his odes he celebrated the splendors of nature in a style of dazzling richness. His best poems show him restraining his imaginative boldness with the pathos and humility of an intensely human compassion. These qualities are combined in "The Hound of Heaven," his most brilliant achievement.

Poem appears on p. 1048.

WILLIAM VAUGHN MOODY
(1869–1910)

In that uneventful interval of American poetry that lies between the day of Whitman or Emily Dickinson and the remarkable revival of 1912, the verse of Moody carries a special distinction. He seized on themes of serious importance to himself and his contemporaries — their search for moral and personal certainties in a time of instability and doubt, their attitude toward the rising imperialistic spirit in America, their belief in their country and its traditions. These questions concerned him in his best poems, as well as in his plays, *The Great Divide* and *The Faith Healer*. In his lines on a fallen soldier of the Spanish-American War, this sober attitude that dignifies Moody's best verse receives its clearest expression.

Poem appears on p. 1051.

ROBINSON JEFFERS
(1887–)

Jeffers, unknown as a poet to his contemporaries until 1925, is the somber voice of prophecy and scorn in modern American verse. In a succession of violent but often majestic narrative poems, he expresses his aloofness to the frenzy and hypocrisy by which he sees modern lives wasted. He has translated this oracular indictment of his times into poems of rich descriptive background but of invariably terrifying plots, sometimes drawn from the Greek legends that fascinate him with their morality of implacable destinies, but more often from the stark lives of native Californians, among whom, at Carmel, he lives. *Tamar* (1925), *Roan Stallion* (1926), *The Women at Point Sur* (1927), *Cawdor* (1928), *Dear Judas* (1929), *Thurso's Landing* (1932), and *Solstice* (1935) have been among the volumes developing this isolated poetic character; but although his work is usually in lengthier forms, "Hurt Hawks" shows him in a characteristic vein and on a smaller scale.

Poem appears on p. 1052.

SARA TEASDALE
(1882–1933)

Sara Teasdale's verse was always unapologetically feminine in spirit. She wrote without the alert sophistication or the dispassionate intellectuality of many of her feminine contemporaries. She continued, instead, the art of spiritual candor and tenderness typical of her Victorian predecessors. In *Rivers to the Sea* (1915), *Love Songs* (1917), *Flame and Shadow* (1920), and *Dark of the Moon* (1926), this directly personal emotion was developed toward a firmer and clearer integrity of expression. "Fontainebleau" is typical of Miss Teasdale's lyrics in its simplicity of style and intimacy of manner.

Poem appears on p. 1053.

MARIANNE MOORE
(1887–)

Among the sharply individual experimentalists of recent poetry, Marianne Moore is notable. She has converted the subject-matter — and even the intellectual habits — of a prosaic world into a poetry whose cadence and diction themselves derive from the prose tradition. Yet into this unconventional form she has projected the modulations and cadences, the nerve and energy, of an extreme poetic sensibility. Her poems must be read and studied as fusions of two complex forces — an exterior observation with an interior perception and inference. "A Grave" is one of the most beautiful poems in which this extraordinary combination of forces plays its part. Others will be found in her two books, *Observations* (1924), and *Selected Poems* (1935).

Poem appears on p. 1053.

HART CRANE
(1899–1932)

Hart Crane is remarkable in contemporary American poetry for having attempted to revive, in a language of vivid symbolism and metaphor, the pioneer hope in American life as it was once expressed in the work of Whitman and Melville. In his fragmentary epic poem *The Bridge* (1930), he expressed this hope in terms of an allegory drawn from Brooklyn Bridge, which he converted into a symbol of transition from old worlds to new, and from the disorder of the present to the unrealized beauty of a heroic future. Such a concept had been foreshadowed in Crane's briefer and earlier poems collected in 1926 under the title *White Buildings*. This poem, "Repose of Rivers," is a monologue spoken by a great stream, flowing from its source, past the filth and pollution of great cities, toward the sea. In some respects it suggests the river-theme in *The Bridge* — the idealism of search and fulfillment central to Crane's thought. Crane's poetry contains some of the most vigorous lines and images in American verse of this century.

Poem appears on p. 1054.

ALLEN TATE
(1899–   )

Allen Tate is a member of the Southern — or regional — group of writers who first became known through their work in *The Fugitive*, a verse journal of Nashville, Tennessee. His finest work, both as poet and historian, has developed around themes of Southern life and history — notably in his "Ode to the Confederate Dead." He has also written some of the most distinguished poetic criticism of recent years. His verse is severe and intellectual in style, making little compromise with popular sentiment or music. The best of it finds its center in intellectual concepts of a sharp and penetrating austerity. In this sonnet, "The Subway," he depicts the agony of modern civilization in terms of the Inferno of the New York underground, and of the moral resistance by which man's spirit is to be rescued.

Poem appears on p. 1055.

ARCHIBALD MacLEISH
(1892–   )

A vein of classic austerity divides MacLeish's satirical verse from the elegiac romanticism of his historical and personal poems. In this brief sug-

INDEX

INDEX